T0280539

Intelligent Circuit and Systems for SDG3-Good Health and Well-Being

1. **Dr. Bhaveshkumar C. Dharmani** is a Professor and Head, Signal & Image Processing, School of Electrical & Electronics Engineering, Lovely Professional University. He has done his full-time Ph. D. from Dhirubhai Ambani Institute of Information & Communication Technology (DAIICT) after years of teaching experience and was a Visiting scientist at Interdisciplinary Statistical research Unit (ISRU), Indian Statistical Institute (ISI), Kolkata. He has more than 17 years of teaching experience with 5 years post-PhD. He has around 13 research publications and 8 patents published. His current research focus is on achieving robustness in Machine and Deep learning algorithms for healthcare applications, collaborating the concepts of Signal Processing, Robust Statistics and Machine Learning. His research interest includes Blind Source Separation, Tensor decompositions, Robust Statistical Divergences, kernel based nonparametric estimation, Machine & Deep learning, Evolutionary Algorithms and others.
2. **Dr. Suman Lata Tripathi** is working as Professor in Lovely Professional University with more than 21 years of experience in academics and research. She has completed her Ph.D. in the area of microelectronics and VLSI Design from MNNIT, Allahabad. She is also a remote post-doc researcher at Nottingham Trent University, London, UK in the year 2022. She has published more than 125 research papers in refereed Springer, Elsevier, IEEE, Wiley and IOP science journals, conference proceeding and e-books. She has also published 13 Indian patents and 4 copyright. She has guided 6 PhD scholars. She has received the "Research Excellence Award" in 2019 and "Research Appreciation Award" in 2020, 2021 at Lovely Professional University, India. She is also working as book series editor for title, "Smart Engineering Systems" CRC Press, "Engineering system design for sustainable developments" & "Decentralized Systems & Next Generation Internet" Wiley-Scrivener, and conference series editor for "Conference Proceedings Series on Intelligent systems for Engineering designs" CRC Press Taylor & Francis. She is serving as academic editor of journal "Journal of Electrical and Computer Engineering" (Scopus/WoS, Q2), "International Journal of Reconfigurable Computing, Scopus, Q3), "Active and Passive Electronic Component" (Scopus, Q4) Hindawi. Her area of expertise includes microelectronics device modeling and characterization, low power VLSI circuit design, VLSI design of testing, and advanced FET design for IoT, Embedded System Design, reconfigurable architecture with FPGAs and biomedical applications etc.

Intelligent Circuit and Systems for SDG3-Good Health and Well-Being

Proceedings of the International Conference on Intelligent Circuits and Systems (ICICS 2023), October 12-13th, 2023, Lovely Professional University, India

5th Edition of ICICS 2023

Edited by
Dr. Bhaveshkumar C. Dharmani
Dr. Suman Lata Tripathi

First edition published 2025
by CRC Press
4 Park Square, Milton Park, Abingdon, Oxon, OX14 4RN

and by CRC Press
2385 NW Executive Center Drive, Suite 320, Boca Raton FL 33431

CRC Press is an imprint of Informa UK Limited

British Library Cataloguing-in-Publication Data
A catalogue record for this book is available from the British Library

ISBN: 9781032861876 (pbk)
ISBN: 9781003521716 (ebk)

DOI: 10.1201/9781003521716

Typeset in Sabon LT Std
by Ozone Publishing Services

Contents

Lists of Figures

Chapter 01

Chapter 02

Chapter 03

Chapter 04

Chapter 05

Chapter 06

Chapter 07

Chapter 08

Chapter 09

Chapter 10

Chapter 11

Chapter 12

Chapter 13

Chapter 14

Chapter 15

Chapter 16

Chapter 17

Chapter 18

Chapter 19

Chapter 20

Chapter 21

Chapter 22

Chapter 23

Chapter 24

Chapter 25

Chapter 26

Chapter 27

Chapter 28

Chapter 29

Chapter 30

Chapter 31

Chapter 32

Chapter 33

Chapter 34

Chapter 35

Chapter 36

Chapter 37

Chapter 38

Chapter 39

Chapter 40

Chapter 41

Chapter 42

Chapter 43

Chapter 44

Chapter 45

Chapter 46

Chapter 47

Chapter 48

Chapter 49

Chapter 50

Chapter 51

Chapter 52

Chapter 53

Chapter 54

Chapter 55

Chapter 56

Chapter 57

Chapter 58

Chapter 59

Chapter 60

Chapter 61

Chapter 62

Chapter 63

Chapter 64

Chapter 65

Chapter 66

Chapter 67

Chapter 69

Chapter 70

Chapter 71

Chapter 72

Chapter 73

Chapter 74

Chapter 75

Chapter 76

Chapter 77

Chapter 78

Chapter 79

Chapter 80

Chapter 81

Chapter 82

Chapter 83

List of Tables

List of Tables

Chapter 53

Chapter 54

Chapter 58

Chapter 60

Chapter 61

Chapter 63

Chapter 64

Chapter 65

Chapter 67

Chapter 71

Chapter 73

Chapter 77

Chapter 78

List of Contributors

01. **IoT-Based Smart Energy Management System for Photovoltaic Power Generation**
Rakshit Singh Manhas and Roshan Kumar Prasad
Lovely Professional University, School of Electronics and Electrical Engineering, Jalandhar, India

02. **Internet of Things (IoT) in Healthcare: Role and Applications**
Ajay Roy, Chinmay Joshi, Aman Sharma, Subhashish Singha, Sumit Jangra, and Sourav Mathur Department of Electronics and Electrical Engineering, Lovely Professional University, Jalandhar, India

03. **Internet of Things (IoT) Sensor Technologies for Medical Monitoring**
Jaspreet Kaur and Kuldeep Kumar Khuswaha
School of Computer Science and Engineering, Lovely Professional University, Phagwara

04. **Security Challenges in AI-Enabled Robotics: Threats and Countermeasures**
Kuldeep Kumar Kushwaha and Jaspreet Kaur
School of Computer Science and Engineering, Lovely Professional University, Phagwara

05. **Fuzzy Logic Based System for Checking the Eligibility of Placement Students using DBSCAN Algorithm**
Preeti Khurana and Akhil Gupta
School of Electronics and Electrical Engineering, Lovely Professional University, Phagwara, India

06. **Optical Character Recognition using Support Vector Machine**
Nitika, Surbhi, Mir Junaid Rasool, Dr. Aarti, Richa Sharma, and Dr. Prakash Singh Tanwar
School of Electronics & Electrical Engineering, Lovely Professional University, Phagwara, India

07. **Development of Fusion Based Cognitive Assisted Smart Room Automation System**
Sachin Gupta[1], Vijay Kumar[1], Rajeev Kanday[2], Shivali Gupta[3], Shaik Mohammed Raith[1]
[1]Department of Robotics and Control, School of Electronics and Electrical Engineering, Lovely Professional University, Phagwara, India
[2]School of Computer Science and Engineering, Lovely Professional University, Phagwara
[3]School of Chemical Engineering and Physical Sciences, Lovely Professional University, Phagwara

08. **Phishing Website Detection Using Optimised Ensemble Model**
P Suhani[1], Divya Bhavani Mohan[1], and Prakash Arumugam[2]
[1]Unitedworld School of Computational Intelligence, Karnavati University, Gujarat, India
[2]School of Research, Karnavati University, Gujarat, India

09. **Power-Efficient Packet Counter Design on High Performance FPGA for Green Communication Keshav Kumar[1], Isha Kansal[2], Saurabh Singh[3], Preeti Sharma[2], Sachin Chawla[4]**
[1]University Institute of Computing, Chandigarh University, Punjab, India
[2]Chitkara University Institute of Engineering and Technology, Chitkara University, Punjab, India
[3]Department of Computer Science and Engineering, Bhilai Institute of Technology, Durg
[4]Department of Electronics and Communication Engineering, Chandigarh University, Punjab, India

10. **Analysis of Chaotic Northern Goshawk Algorithm in the Optimal Design of Electric Vehicles Kamaldeep Sharma, Manu Prakram, and Vikram Kumar Kamboj**
ECE, Lovely Professional University, Jalandhar, India

11. **Wireless Lock System using Arduino UNO and Bluetooth Module**
Mohana Vamsi Perni1,
Sai Daiwik V[1], Tagore Reddy[1], Veera Hemanth[1], Rajeev Kumar Patial[1] , Jhulan Kumar[1] , Dilip Kumar[2] and Dinesh Kumar[3]
[1]Lovely Faculty of Technology and Sciences, Lovely Professional University, Phagwara, India
[2]Department of Electronics and communication Engineering, SLIET, Longowal, India
[3]Department of Information Technology, DAVIET, Jalandhar, India

12. **Analysis of Various Methods to Boost the Isolation in UWB-MIMO Antennas**
Daljeet Singh[1], Mariella Särestöniemi[1,2] and Teemu Myllyla[1,3]
[1]Research Unit of Health Sciences and Technology, Faculty of Medicine, University of Oulu, Finland
[2]Centre for Wireless Communications, Faculty of Information Technology and Electrical Engineering, University of Oulu, Finland
[3]Optoelectronics and Measurement Techniques Unit, Faculty of Information Technology and Electrical Engineering, University of Oulu, Finland

13. **Smart EV Charging using IoT and Block Chain: A Comparative Study of Latest Technologies Subhash Suman and Dr. Manoj Singh Adhikari School of Electronics and Electrical Engineering, Lovely Professional University, Punjab, India**

14. **Analytical Framework and Algorithmic Model for Resource Allocation in 5G and Beyond 5G Networks for IoT**
Nishant Tripathi[1], J. P. C. do Nascimento[2], and A. S. B.Sombra[3]
[1]Dept. of Electronics and Communication Engineering, Pranveer Singh Institute of Technology Kanpur
[2]Federal Institute of Education, Science and Technology of Ceará, PPGET, Fortaleza, CE, Brazil
[3]Physics Department - Telecommunication, Science and Engineering of Materials Laboratory (LOCEM), Federal University of Ceara (UFC), Fortaleza, Ceara, Brazil

15. **A Systematic Review of Load Balancing Techniques in Heterogeneous Networks**
TanuKaistha[1] and Kiran Ahuja[2]
[1]Department of Electronics and Communication Engineering, IKG-Punjab Technical University, Kapurthala, Punjab, India
[2]Department of Electronics and Communication Engineering, DAV Institute of Engineering and Technology, Jalandhar, Punjab, India

16. **Microwave Absorber: A Promising Material as a Solution to Electromagnetic Interference**
Sayed Tathir Abbas Naqvi[1] and Ihab Abdel-latif[2]
[1]Department of Electronics and Communication Engineering, R V Institute of Technology, Bijnor, India
[2]Reactor Physics Department, Reactors Division, Nuclear Research Center, Egyptian Atomic Energy Authority, Cairo, Egypt

17. **Early Disease Detection Using Machine Learning Approach**
Himanshu Kumawat[1], and Dr. Prakash Singh Tanwar[2]
[1]Department of Computer Application, Lovely Professional University, Phagwara, Punjab, India
[2]Department of CSE, SEEE, Lovely Professional University, Phagwara, Punjab, India

18. **Smart Vending Machine Using Digital Payment**
Narla Gowtham Sai Manikanta, Bhavanam Abhiram Reddy,Achanta Yaswanth Sri Satya Sai Krishna, Yellanki Tharun, Sana Vanajith, Ch. Ravisankar
SEEE, Lovely Professional University, Phagwara, Punjab, India

19. **Balancing Fundamental and Technical Analysis for Stock Market Using Artificial Intelligence: A Survey**
Pawandeep Kaur[1], Hardeep Kaur[1], Jai Sukh Paul Singh[1,2], Sonia Bukra[3,4], Manjinder Kaur[5]
Amarjot Kaur6 and Jaskaran Singh Phull1
[1]School of Electronics and Electrical Engineering, Lovely Professional University, Punjab, India
[2]Department of Research Collaboration, Division of Research and Development, Lovely Professional University, Punjab, India

26. **Multi-Objective Gravitational Search Algorithm Based Clustering Scheme in VANET**
Hunny Pahuja[1], Shippu Sachdeva[2], and Manoj Sindhwani[2]
[1]Department of Electronics and Communication Engineering, KIET Group of Institutions, Delhi-NCR, Ghaziabad, India
[2]Lovely Faculty of Technology and Sciences, Lovely Professional University, Phagwara, Punjab, India

27. **Hybrid Approach to Place Wind Distributed Generators in Distribution System**
Babita Gupta[1,2,] Suresh Kumar Sudabattula[1], Sachin Mishra[1,] and Nagaraju Dharavat[1]
[1]School of Electronics and Electrical Engineering Lovely Professional University, Phagwara, Punjab, India
[2]BVRIT HYDERABAD College of Engineering for Women, Telangana, India

28. **Classification of MNIST Dataset Using Different CNN Architecture**
Amit Kumar[1], Inderpal Singh[1], and Balraj Singh[2]
[1]Department of Computer Science and Engineering, CT Institute of Technology and Research, Jalandhar, Punjab, India
[2]Department of Computer Science and Engineering, Lovely Professional University, Phagwara, Punjab, India

29. **Tailoring of Morphology and Electrical Properties of Hexagonal Ferrites**
Ankit Jain[1,5], Charanjeet Singh[1], Sachin K. Godara[2], Rajshree B. Jotania[3], Varinder Kaur[2], and Ashwani K. Sood[4]
[1]School of Electrical and Electronics Engineering, Lovely Professional University, Phagwara, Punjab, India
[2]Department of Apparel and Textile Technology, Guru Nanak Dev University, Amritsar, Punjab, India
[3]Department of Physics, University School of Science, Gujarat University, Ahmedabad, India
[4]Department of Chemistry, Guru Nanak Dev University, Amritsar, Punjab, India
[5]Department of Electronics and Communication, Indore Institute of Science and Technology, Indore, M.P., India

30. **Different PWM Techniques for Power Electronics Topologies: A Comparative Study**
Ahmed Hamad Mansoor, Amit Kumar Singh, and Someet Singh SEEE, Lovely Professional University, Phagwara, India

31. **A Phantom-Based Experimental Study of the Bioimpedance Monitoring Techniques**
Ramesh Kumar[1], Manas Ranjan Tripathy[2] , Ashish Kumar Singh[1] , Manoj Kumar Yadav[3]
[1]Chitkara University Institute of Engineering Technology, Punjab, India
[2]SRM University AP, Andra Pradesh, India
[3]Lovely Professional University, Punjab, India

32. **Design and FPGA Implementation of Digital Clock with Millisecond Precision**
Kushagra, Jay Khaple, Siragam Tejeswar Reddy, Jai Shivam Chaudhary, Raihan Ahmed and Sobhit Saxena
School of Electronics and Electrical Engineering, Lovely Professional University, Punjab, India

33. **Optimising Supercapacitor-Based Power Delivery Systems for Enhanced Efficiency in Electric Vehicles**
Harleenpal Singh[1], Sobhit Saxena[1], Vikram Kumar Kamboj[2]
[1]School of Electronics and Electrical Engineering, Lovely Professional University, Punjab, India
[2]Schulich School of Engineering, University of Calgary, Calgary, Alberta, Canada

34. **Comparative Study of Variational Autoencoder for X-Ray Image Denoising**
Asha Rani, M Akhil Raj, and Dr. Bhaveshkumar Choithram Dharmani
Electronics and Communication Deptt., Lovely professional University, Phagwara, India

35. **Modified SSD Framework for On-Road Object Detection**
Glenson Toney[1], Gaurav Sethi[2], Cherry Bhargava[3] and Vaibhav Salian[4]
[1]SEEE, Lovely Professional University, Phagawara, Punjab, India
[2]Department of ECE, St Joseph Engineering College, Mangaluru, Karnataka, India
[3]Department of CSE, Symbiosis International University, Pune, Maharashtra, India
[4]Department of AIML, St Joseph Engineering College, Mangaluru, Karnataka, India

36. **0.7V-20nm FinFET Technology Inverter Design for Better Log-Linear Characteristics**
M.V.S. Roja Ramani[1], Sreenivasa Rao Ijjada[2],
[1]Dept. of ECE, N S Raju Institute of Technology, Visakhapatnam, AP, India
[2] Dept. of EECE, GITAM Deemed to be University, Visakhapatnam, AP, India

37. **Effective Load Frequency Controller Using Machine Learning Algorithms**
G. Anusha, Krishan Arora, Himanshu Sharma
SEEE, Lovely Professional University, Phagwara, Punjab, India

38. **Design and Implementation of a Variable Frequency Generator Using CMOS Ring Oscillator Abhishek Kumar**
School of Electronics and Electrical Engineering, Lovely Professional University, Punjab, India

39. **Design and Analysis of Ring Structured based VCO using cadence 45mm**
Priyanka Kumari. B. S. and Sobhit Saxena
School of Electronics & Electrical Engg., Lovely Professional University

40. **Study of IoT in Smart Farming Applications**
Nyle[1], A Mukesh Reddy[1], Sumanth Irlapati[1], Shreya[1], Aishweta Roy Chowdhury[1], Manoj Singh Adhikari[2], Harpreet Singh Bedi[2]
[1]School of Agriculture, Lovely Professional University, Punjab, India
[2]School of Electronics and Electrical Engineering, Lovely Professional University, Punjab, India

41. **Distribution system Assessment with Capacitor Placement**
Rinchen Zangmo, Suresh Kumar Sudabattula, Sachin Mishra, Nagaraju Dharavat
School of Electronics and Electrical Engineering, Lovely Professional University, Phagwara, Punjab, India

42. **Federated Learning: Issues, Challenges, and Needs**
Sahar Yousif Mohammed[1], Mohammad Aljanabi[2], and Maad M. Mijwil[3]
[1]Computer Science, Anbar University, Anbar, Iraq
[2]Computer Science, Aliraqia University, Baghdad, Iraq
[3]Computer Techniques Engineering Department, Baghdad College of Economic Sciences University, Baghdad, Iraq

43. **Smart Door Bell Using IoT: Implementation and Design**
Yogesh Kumar Verma[1] Nagalakshmi Yarlagadda[1,2], Jugal Kishore Bhandari[1] Raam Dheep[1]
[1]School of Electronics and Electrical Engineering, Lovely Professional University, Jalandhar, Punjab, India
[2]Geethanjali College of Engineering and Technology, Cheeryal, Hyderabad, India

44. **Energy Storage Systems with Artificial Intelligence Techniques in Doubly Fed Induction Generator Based Wind Energy Conversion System – An Overview**
Pradeep Singh[1], Krishan Arora[1], Umesh C. Rathore[2]
[1] SEEE, LPU, Phagwara, India
[2]ABVGIET-Pragtinagar, Shimla, India

45. **Massive MIMO Precoding Techniques for Future Generation Communication System**
Sandhya Bolla, ManwinderSingh, and Anudeep Goraya
School of SEEE, Lovely Professional University, Jalandhar, Punjab, India

46. **Design and Performance Analysis of PV-Based Grid Connected Nanogrid System**
Amita Mane[1,2], Shamik Chatterjee[2], Amol Kalage[3]
[1]First Year Engineering Department, PCCOER, Pune, India
[2]SEEE, Lovely Professional University, Phagwara, India
[3]Electrical Engineering Department, Sinhgad Institute of Technology, Lonavala, Punesss

47. **14T SRAM Bit Cell with Speed and Power Optimized Using CNTFET**
Vipin Kumar Sharma and Abhishek Kumar
Lovely Professional University, School of Electronics and Electrical Engineering, India

48. **Cost Correlation for High Head Small Hydropower Projects**
Kalyani R[1,2],Sachin Mishra[2] and Javed Dhillon[2]
[1]Dept. of Electrical Engineering, Mahavir Engineering College, Hyderabad
[2]School of Electronics and Electrical Engineering, Lovely Professional University, Punjab

49. **Ab-Initio Analysis of Al-Doped Electrode Magnetic Tunnel Junction for MRAM**
Manoj Kumar Yadav, Pawandeep Kaur, Hardeep Kaur, Jhulan Kumar, Jaskaran Singh Phull, and Ritesh Pawar
School of Electrical and Electronic Engineering, Lovely Professional University, Phagwara, Panjab, India

50. **An Elliptical Plus Shape Microstrip Patch Antenna Integrated with CSRR for Breast Cancer Detection**
Rupali[1], Dr. Sanjay Kumar Sahu[1], and Gopinath Palai[2]
[1]Electronics and Communication, Lovely Professional University, Jalandhar, Punjab India
[2]Science and Energing Technologies, Sri Sri University, Cuttack, Odisha, India

51. **Cooperative Communications System with Minimal Energy Consumption**
Krishan Kumar[1], Uppula Kiran[2], and Valishetti Prashanthi[3]
[1]Dept. of Electronics and Communication Engineering, Lovely Professional University, India
[2]Dept. of Electronics and Communication Engineering, Vaagdevi College of Engineering, Telangana, India
[3]Dept. of Computer Science Engineering, Kakatiya Institute of Technology and Science, Telangana, India

52. **IOT Portable Radar System**
Ankit Meena[1], Ananya Tripathi[1], Arsh Malik[1], Bhukya Arun Kumar[2], and Ajay Roy[2]
[1]School of Computer Application, Lovely Professional University
[2]School of Electronics and Electrical Engineering, Lovely Professional University

53. **Data Acquisition and Monitoring Framework for Waste Management Using Intelligent Sensors and Thing Speak IoT Analytics for Health Monitoring in Smart Cities**
Karan Belsare[1], Manwinder Singh[2], Anudeep Goraya[3]
[1]School of SEEE, Lovely Professional University, Jalandhar, Punjab, India
[2]Department of ECE, Lovely Professional University, Jalandhar, Punjab, India
[3]Department of CSE, Lovely Professional University, Jalandhar, Punjab, India

54. **Prediction of Type 2 Diabetes Mellitus Using Gradient Boosted Tree Approach**
Prakash Arumugam[1], Abinayaa S S[2], and Divya Bhavani Mohan[3]
[1]School of Research, Karnavati University, Gujarat, India
[2]Department of ECE, Dr. N.G.P. Institute of Technology, Coimbatore, India
[3]Unitedworld School of Computational Intelligence, Karnavati University, Gujarat, India

55. **Design of a Millimetre-Wave Antenna with Circular Polarization and High Gain on FR4 Substrate**
Simerpreet Singh[1], Gaurav Sethi[1], Jaspal Singh Khinda[2]
[1]Department of Electronics and Electrical Engineering, Lovely Professional University, Phagwara, India
[2]Department of Electrical Engineering, Bhai Gurdas Institute of Engineering and Technology, Sangrur, India

56. **Synthesis and Investigation of Electrical Characteristics of Co-Zr Doped M-type Sr Hexaferrites Sayed Tathir Abbas Naqvi[1], Charanjeet Singh[1], Sachin Kumar Godara[2]**
[1]Department of Electronics and Communication Engineering, Lovely Professional University, Phagwara, India
[2]Department of Apparel and Textile Technology, Guru Nanak Dev University, Amritsar, India

57. **Low Power Optimization of 10T Full Adder Design Using FinFET Technology**
Sneha Arora and Suman Lata Tripathi School of Electronics and Electrical Engineering, Lovely Professional University, Punjab, India

58. **Paving the Way for Faster Data Transmission Through Micro Structured Fibre Mode Optimisation**
Indu Bala, B. Arun Kumar, Ashwani Kumar, Aryananda PS
SEEE, Lovely Professional University, Punjab, India

60. **NB-IoT vs Lora: A Practical Analysis in Terms of Power Consumption**
Chand Pasha Mohammed and Shakti Raj Chopra
Department of Electronics and Communication Engineering, Lovely Professional University, Jalandhar, Phagwara, Panjab, India

61. **Millimetre Wave Wireless Communication System for Internet of Bodies: A Systematic Review on Implication**
Jai Kumar and Akhil Gupta
SEEE, Lovely Professional University, Punjab, India

62. **Self-Organisation of Heavy Traffic Using Zigbee Communication on Raspberry Pi**
B.Ravi Chandra[1,2] and Dr. Krishan Kumar[2]
[1]Electronics & Communication Engineering, G. Pullaiah College of Engineering & Technology, Kurnool, India
[2]Lovely Professional University, Punjab, India

63. **A Relay Selection Optimisation for Cooperative Networks to Maximise Reliability and Minimise Energy Consumption**
Valishetti Prashanthi[1] , Uppula Kiran[2] , Krishan Kumar[3]
[1]Dept. of Computer Science Engineering, Kakatiya Institute of Technology and Science, Telangana, India
[2]Dept. of Electronics and Communication Engineering, Vaagdevi College of Engineering, Telangana, India
[3]Dept. of Electronics and Communication Engineering, Lovely Professional University, India

64. **From Pixels to Prognosis: Machine Learning for Infection Segmentation and Disease Prediction in Tulsi Leaf**
Manjot Kaur[1], Someet Singh[1], and Anita Gehlot[2]
[1]School of Electrical and Electronics Engineering, Lovely Professional University, Phagwara, India
[2]Uttaranchal Institute of Technology, Uttaranchal University, Dehradun, India

65. **Deep Learning for Disease Detection in Paddy Plants using Leaf Images**
Sudheer Chakravarthi P and Bhaveshkumar Choithram Dharmani
School of Electronics and Electrical Engineering, Lovely Professional University, Punjab, India

66. **Measurement and Analysis of Power Consumption in Smartphones**
Pratibha Mahajan and Yashashree Sonawane
Department of Computer Engineering, Vishwakarma University, Pune, India

67. **A Graphene-Based Absorber for Sensing Application**
Laxmi Narayana Deekonda[1], Sanjay Kumar Sahu[2] and Asit Kumar Panda[3]
[1]Department of ECE, Lovely Profession University, Phagwara, Punjab, India
[2]Department of ECE, National Institute of Science and Tech., Berhampur, Orissa, India

68. **Enhancing Energy Efficiency in MIMO Networks for 5G**
Praveen Srivastava and Shelej Khera
Lovely Professional University, School of Electronics and Electrical Engineering, Jalandhar, India

69. **Advancements in Object Detection and Tracking Techniques: A Comprehensive Review in Variable Illumination Conditions**
Chinthakindi Kiran Kumar, Gaurav Sethi, and Kirti Rawal
School of Electronics & Electrical Engineering, Lovely Professional University

70. **An Integrated Method of Industry 4.0 for Improved Healthcare Sustainability**
Rekha Chaudhary[1,2] Rahul Sharma[1,2] Raman Kumar[1,2] and Mahender Singh Kaswan[1,2]
[1]School of Electronics & Electrical Engineering, Lovely Professional University, Phagwara, Punjab, India
[2]School of Mechanical Engineering, Lovely Professional University, Phagwara, Punjab, India

71. **Performance Analysis of Gate-Pocket Overlap Hetero-junction Tunnel Field-Effect Transistor Rekha Chaudhary[1] Rahul Sharma[1] Raman Kumar[1] Gautam Bhaskar[2] and Aditya Chotalia[2]**
[1]Lovely Professional University, Phagwara, Punjab, India
[2]Department of ECE, Birla Institute of Technology, Mesra, Ranchi, Jharkhand, India

72. **A Comparative Study of Electric Vehicle Battery Live Monitoring and Scheduling**
S. R. Deepu, Dr. N.Karthick, and U. Neethu
Lovely Professional University, School of Electronics & Electrical Engineering, Jalander, India

73. **Efficient Speed Control Tracking for Electric Vehicle Using Artificial Intelligence: A Comparative Study**
U. Neethu, N. Karthick, and S. R. Deepu
Lovely Professional University, School of Electronics & Electrical Engineering, Jalander, India

74. **Comparative Analysis of Correlation Tracking Algorithms for Real-Time Video Object Tracking Jyoti**
Ramola,[1] Mohit Payal,[1] Manoj Singh Adhikari,[2] and Vibhor Sharma[3]
[1]Graphic Era Hill University, Dehradun, India
[2]School of Electronics and Electrical Engineering, Lovely Professional University, Punjab, India
[3]Himalayan School of Science and Technology, Swami Rama Himalayan University, Dehradun, India

75. **Implementation and Designing of a Smart Door Lock System**
Yogesh Kumar Verma[1,2], Pravin Ghimire[2], Rohan Bharti[3], Pankaj[4], Raam Deep[2], and Manoj Singh Adhikari[2]
[1]School of Electronics and Electrical Engineering, Lovely Professional University, Jalandhar, Punjab, India
[2]School of Agriculture, Lovely Professional University, Jalandhar, Punjab, India

76. **SBLKF- Based Estimation of TimeSelective (Fast – Fading) Channel for Hybrid mm Wave Massive MIMO System**
Shailender,[1] Shelej Khera[1], and Sajjan Singh[2]
[1]Lovely Professional University, Phagwara, Punjab, India
[2]Chandigarh Engineering College, Jhanjeri, Mohali, India

77. **A Parasitic Extraction Method for Realistic Linked Faults in Two Cell SRAMs**
Venkatesham Maddela[1,2], Sanjeet Kumar Sinha[1], and Muddapu Parvathi[2]
[1]Dept. of School of Electronics and Electrical Engineering, Lovely Professional University, Phagwara, India
[2]Department of Electronics and Communication Engineering, BVRIT HYDERABAD College of Engineering for Women, Hyderabad, India

78. **Evaluating Energy-Efficient Cooperative Communication in Wireless Networks through Clustering Algorithm Performance Metrics**
Nishant Tripathi[1,2], Charanjeet Singh[1] and Kamal Kumar Sharma[3]
[1]Institute Dept. of Electronics and Communication Engineering, School of Electronics and Electrical Engineering, Lovely Professional University, Phagwara, Punjab, India
[2]Dept. of Electronics and Communication Engineering, Pranveer Singh Institute of Technology, Kanpur
[3]Ambala College of Engineering and Applied Research Devsthali, Ambala, Haryana, India

79. **Efficiency and Accuracy Analysis of Object Detection Algorithms in Deep Learning**
Jyoti Vitthal Chhatrband and BhaveshKumar Choithram Dharmani
School of Electronics and Electrical Engineering, Lovely Professional University, Punjab, India

80. **Multi-Criteria Collaborative Filtering for Therapy Recommendation to Autistic Children Kusumalatha Karre[1] and Y. Ramadevi[2]**
[1]Dept. of CSE and SNIST, Dept of ECM, Osmania University, Hyderabad, India
[2]Dept. of AIML, Chaitanya Bharathi Institute of Technology, Hyderabad, India

81. **Implementation of IOT's MQTT Protocol with JavaScript**
Mahesh Swami[1] Sakshi Kumar[1] and Devansh Tiwari[2]
[1]Department of Computer Science Engineering (CSE),
[2]Aravali College of Engineering and Management, Haryana, India

82. **Design of Fractional-NPLL Using Delta Sigma Modulation for Low-Phase Noise**
Md Abdul Muqueem[1], Shanky Saxena[1], and Govind Singh Patel[2]
[1]Lovely Professional University, Punjab, India
[2]E&TC, SITCOE, Yadrav, Kolhapur, Maharashtra, India

83. **Enhancing Stock Market Predictions: Combining Deep Learning and Machine Learning for Improved Accuracy**
Manoj Kumar Chaudharya[1], Inderpal Singh[2], Balraj Singh[3]
[1]Department of Computer Science and Engineering, CTITR, Jalandhar
[2]CT Institute of Technology and Research, Jalandhar, India,
[3]School of Computer Science and Engineering Lovely Professional University

Preface

ICICS is a series of conferences initiated by School of Electronics and Electrical Engineering at Lovely Professional University. Looking at the response to the conference, the bi-annual conference now onwards will be annual. The 5th International Conference on Intelligent Circuits and Systems (ICICS 2023) will be focusing on intelligent circuits and systems for achieving the targets in Sustainable Development Goal (SDG) 3, identified as 'Good Health and Wellbeing' by United Nations (Refs: https://sdgs.un.org/goals/goal3, https://sdg-tracker.org/).

Sustainable Development goals are the targets settled by global agreement for global development. There are defined 13 targets and 28 measurable indicators for SDG 3. The conference targets to build a bridge between academic community, R & D institutions, social visionaries and experts from all strata of society to present the on-going research activities towards achieving the global targets of SDG 3 and foster research relations between them. The conference further provides an opportunity to:

- Motivate research community to orient and extend their research to find new solutions for SDG 3 related problems, targets and indicators
- Exchange new ideas, applications and experiences
- Find regional and global partners for future collaboration
- Add value to the path forward and road map for timely achievement of SDG 3 targets and indicators

01 IoT-Based Smart Energy Management System for Photovoltaic Power Generation

Rakshit Singh Manhas and Roshan Kumar Prasad, Ajay Roy

Lovely Professional University, School of Electronics and Electrical Engineering, Jalandhar, India

Abstract: The potential for photovoltaic (PV) components to produce power from headlights and other types of lighting is investigated in this study. PV elements installed along roads, toll booths and below streetlights have the ability to provide renewable energy from widely available sources, lower greenhouse gas emissions and increase the self-sufficiency of motorways and toll booths. Even though this strategy has a lot of potential advantages, there are several difficulties that would need to be overcome. The limited quantity of power that can be produced by streetlights and automobile headlights is one issue. The PV components' lower effectiveness in low light conditions is another issue. Despite these difficulties, PV-powered roads, toll booths and streetlights have the potential to completely alter how we produce and use energy. The potential for PV components to produce power from headlights and other types of lighting is investigated in this study. PV elements installed along roads, toll booths and below streetlights can provide renewable energy from widely available sources, lower greenhouse gas emissions and increase the self-sufficiency of motorways and toll booths.

Keywords: IoT Architecture, smart energy management, photovoltaic power generation, sensors, smart grid, IEEE standards.

1. Introduction

The emergence of the internet of things (IoT) signals a profound shift in how we connect and operate within the digital realm, particularly in the context of smart energy management systems (SEMS) for photovoltaic (PV) power generation. IoT envisions a seamlessly interconnected world, integrating inanimate objects, individuals and services via the extensive Internet. This interconnectedness allows for real-time data collection, storage, exchange and monitoring across the physical and digital domains, simplifying operations, reducing human intervention and optimising energy usage within PV power generation. This paper extensively explores the role of IoT in SEMS for PV power generation, investigating its diverse applications and the ways it empowers both producers and consumers of solar energy. IoT-enabled devices have revolutionised energy management, enabling precise monitoring, predictive maintenance and efficient utilisation of PV systems. The discussion encompasses the current state of IoT applications in energy management for PV power generation while envisioning future advancements in this technological evolution. The impact of IoT on smart energy management for PV power generation is exemplified by innovations such as intelligent monitoring wearables and advanced sensors, capable of predicting energy generation patterns well in advance. These applications underscore the merging of the physical and digital worlds by integrating electronic components like sensors, actuators and RFID tags into solar infrastructure. Technological advancements have led to the development of compact and energy-efficient IoT devices, such as micro-electro-mechanical system (MEMS) and nano-electro-mechanical system (NEMS) devices. MEMS devices vary in size from 20 microns to 1 millimeter, while NEMS devices operate on the nanometer scale, contributing to the versatility of IoT in optimising energy management for PV power generation. The paper also explores the diverse applications of IoT in the energy sector, focusing on SEMS for PV power generation. This includes precise monitoring of energy production, predictive maintenance, fault detection and demand-side management, ultimately leading to improved efficiency and sustainability. The integration of IoT into smart energy management holds immense promise for optimising energy usage, enhancing grid stability and reducing costs in PV power generation. As technology continues to advance, the future of IoT in smart energy management for PV power generation looks exceedingly promising. This paper is structured to provide comprehensive insights into IoT's role in smart energy management for PV power generation, covering its architecture, different sensors, tools, technologies, applications and prospects in the energy domain. It also discusses trends, themes, privacy concerns and security challenges, establishing a strong foundation for understanding and navigating the evolving landscape of IoT-based smart energy management for PV power generation.

2. Photo Voltaic Cell

A PV cell, also known as a solar cell, is the fundamental building block of solar technology, converting light energy directly into electrical energy. The phenomenon, known as the PV effect, was first observed by French physicist Alexandre-Edmond Becquerel in 1839. However, it was in the mid-20th century that the modern solar cell as we know it began to take shape. A PV cell is typically made of semiconductor materials, such as silicon, with two layers: an N-type layer, which has extra electrons, and a P-type layer, with missing electrons or 'holes.' When sunlight, composed of photons, strikes the PV cell, it energises the electrons, allowing them to move across the semiconductor layers. This movement generates a flow of electricity, creating a direct current (DC). The electrical current can be harnessed for various applications, from powering small electronic devices to providing electricity for homes, businesses and even entire cities when integrated into solar panels or arrays. Advances in PV cell technology have significantly increased efficiency and reduced costs over the years, making solar energy an increasingly viable and sustainable source of power. Continued research and development in the field of PV cells aim to further improve efficiency, durability and affordability, driving the widespread adoption of solar energy to address global energy challenges and reduce reliance on fossil fuels.

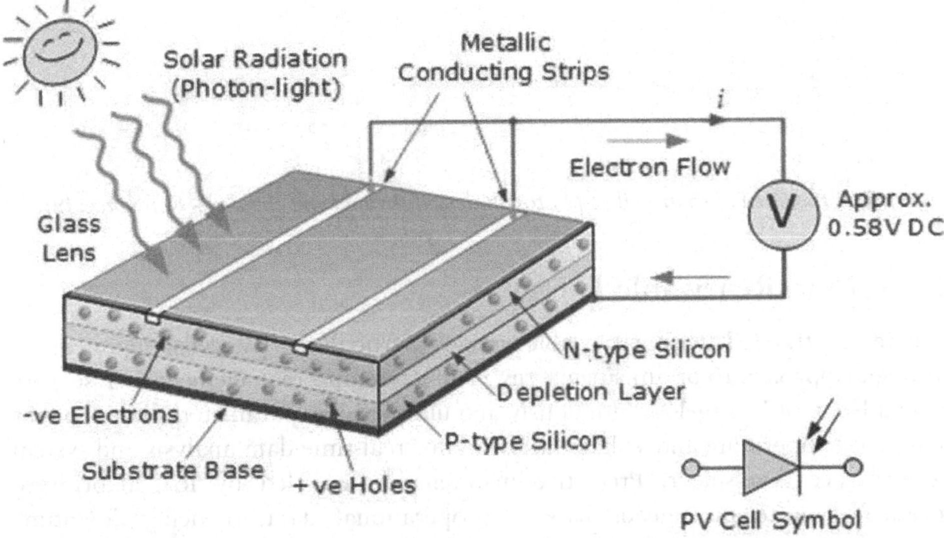

Figure 1: Construction of a photovoltaic cell and cell symbol - Reference: [10].

3. Photovoltaic Cell vs Solar Cell

PV cells consume less power than solar cells because they are more efficient at converting sunlight into electricity. Solar cells are the basic building blocks of PV panels, which are used to generate electricity from sunlight. PV cells do not consume any power themselves, but they need to be powered by sunlight in order to produce electricity. The efficiency of a solar cell is a measure of how much of the sunlight that hits the cell is converted into electricity. The most efficient solar cells on the market today have an efficiency of around 25%, while solar panels are typically made up of solar cells with an efficiency of around 15-20%. This means that a PV cell will consume less power than a solar cell because it is more efficient at converting sunlight into electricity. For example, a solar panel with an efficiency of 20% would need to consume about 5 watts of power to produce 10 watts of electricity. While solar cells and panels do not consume power themselves, they do need to be powered by sunlight in order to produce electricity. However, the amount of power that they consume is very small compared to the amount of electricity that they produce. Overall, PV cells consume less power than solar cells because they are more efficient at converting sunlight into electricity.

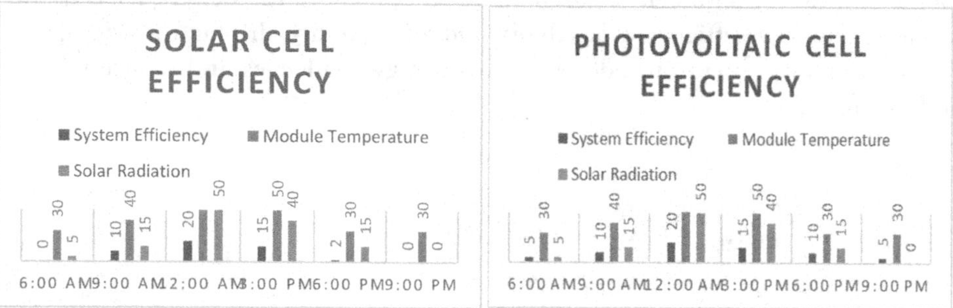

Figure 2: Efficiency of solar cell vs photovoltaic cell throughout the day - Reference: [9].

4. IOT in Renewable Energy

Integrating the IoT with renewable energy, particularly PV cells, represents a strategic approach to optimising energy production and management. IoT sensors embedded in PV panels continuously monitor crucial parameters like sunlight intensity, temperature and voltage, allowing for real-time data analysis and system performance assessment. Predictive maintenance, enabled by IoT algorithms, forecasts maintenance needs based on operational data, reducing downtime and extending the operational life of PV cells. IoT-driven adjustments, such as optimising panel tilt based on weather forecasts and energy demand, enhance energy production efficiency. Additionally, IoT facilitates seamless integration of solar energy into the existing power grid by monitoring energy demand and grid conditions, enabling a smart response for stable and efficient energy supply. Through user-friendly interfaces like mobile applications or web platforms, IoT enables remote monitoring and control of PV systems, empowering users to track energy generation, system health and environmental impact. Furthermore, IoT optimises energy storage systems, managing charge and discharge cycles for efficient energy utilisation, especially during peak demand or low sunlight periods. Prompt fault detection and safety measures are achieved through real-time monitoring, ensuring a secure environment. By leveraging historical data for advanced analytics and predictive modelling, IoT aids in accurate forecasting of energy production and demand, enabling effective energy planning and distribution. Ultimately, IoT integration into renewable energy utilising PV cells propels the transition towards a greener, more sustainable future while enhancing operational efficiency and resilience.

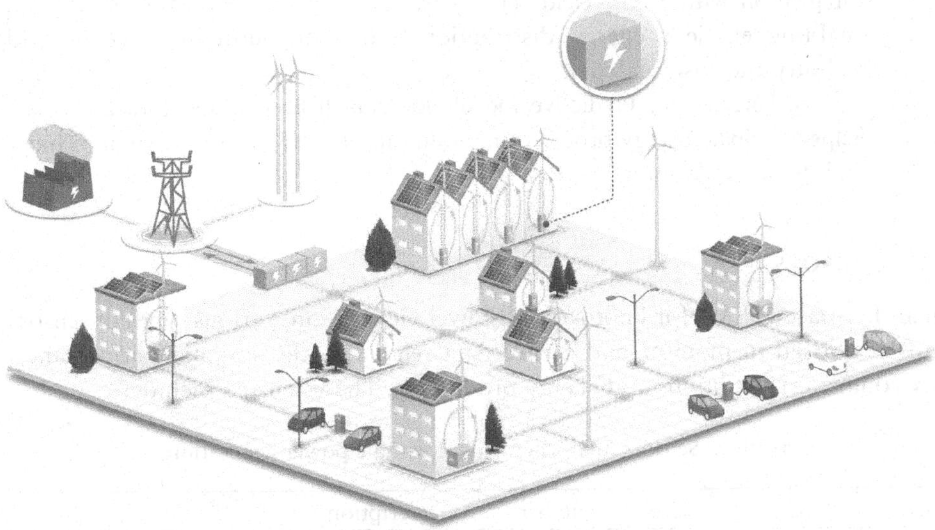

Figure 3: IoT and renewable energy. Reference: [11]

5. Architecture

Designing an IoT-based SEMS for PV power generation involves integrating various technologies to optimise energy production, monitor system performance and ensure efficient energy consumption. Architecture for such a system:

- Sensors and Data Collection: IoT sensors are installed to collect real-time data on PV panel performance and environmental conditions, crucial for optimising energy output and panel health.
- Data Processing and Analysis: Collected data is processed and analysed to derive actionable insights, enabling informed decisions regarding energy production and efficiency.
- Cloud-Based Platform: Data is securely stored and processed in the cloud, allowing easy access, real-time analysis and scalability of the energy management system.
- Machine Learning Algorithms: Advanced ML algorithms are employed to analyse historical and real-time data, optimising energy generation and consumption patterns.
- Energy Optimisation and Control: The system autonomously adjusts energy production and consumption, ensuring optimal usage and cost-efficiency based on gathered insights.
- Remote Monitoring and Control: Users can remotely monitor and control the system through an intuitive interface, enhancing user experience and accessibility.

- ➢ Integration with Smart Grid: The system is integrated with the smart grid, enabling efficient energy distribution and contributing to overall grid stability and sustainability.
- ➢ Energy Forecasting: Predictive modelling using historical and forecasted data helps anticipate energy production, aiding in effective resource management and demand planning.

6. Sensors

In an IoT-based SEMS for Photovoltaic Power Generation, various types of sensors can be utilised to monitor and gather data related to the system's performance, environmental conditions and energy production. These sensors include:

Table 1: Sensors in SEMS for photovoltaic power generation.

Sensor	Model Number	Description
Solar irradiance	Si-V-1.5TC-T Si-mV-85 Si-RS485TC-T Si-RS485TC-2T-v 6	Measure the intensity of sunlight falling on the photovoltaic panels, aiding in assessing energy production potential.
Temperature sensors	TMP275AIDG LMT70YFQT LM334Z TMP36GT9Z	Monitor the temperature of the photovoltaic panels, which can affect their efficiency and performance.
Humidity sensors	HTY1000 HTY1010 HIH7120-021-001S	Measure the humidity levels, providing insights into the impact of moisture on the panels and system efficiency.
Voltage and current sensors:	8480 Series power sensors WOODWARD 8272-843	Monitor the electrical parameters such as voltage and current to ensure the PV system is operating within safe and optimal ranges.
Inverter monitoring sensors	CT6876A PAC1921	Gather data on inverter performance and efficiency, essential for converting DC power from PV panels to AC power for grid integration.

7. Process Flowchart

The IoT-based Smart Energy Management System for Photovoltaic Power Generation begins with the system's initiation, prompting continuous monitoring of the power generated by the photovoltaic setup. The main server diligently observes for any alterations in power production. If a decrease in power is detected, a notification is promptly sent to the central system. Conversely, if there is an increase in power, the system assesses if the increment is adequate. Should the increase suffice, the central system is notified accordingly. In cases where the power increase is inadequate, the system checks for available power from another designated town server. If power can be sourced from the specified town server, it is obtained. Subsequently, the system verifies if the obtained power is sufficient for further distribution. If the power meets the required threshold, it is directed towards powering the smart house. However, if the power is insufficient, a notification is dispatched to the central system. The system also periodically evaluates the central system's power availability. When sufficient power is found within the central system, it is acquired for distribution. If not, a notification regarding the insufficiency is relayed to the central system, completing the monitoring process.

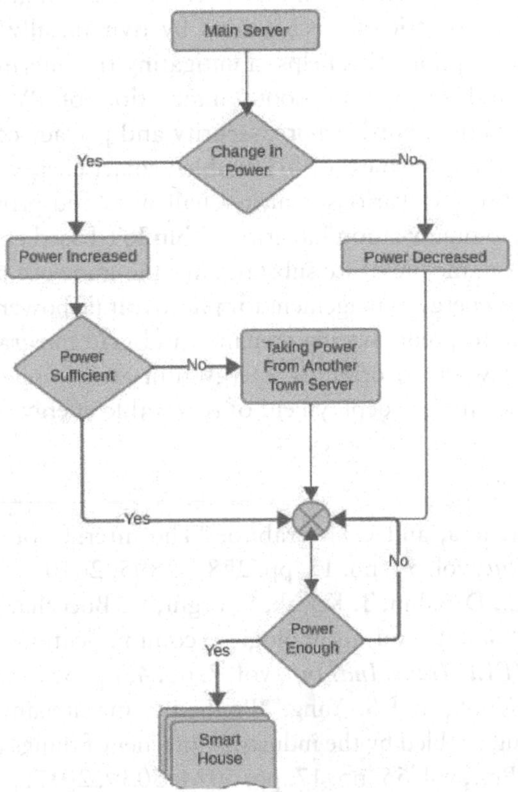

8. Literature Review

The integration of the IoT using Photovoltaic Power into SEMS for photovoltaic (PV) power generation has gained significant attention due to its potential in optimising energy efficiency, enhancing grid stability and promoting sustainable energy practices. Researchers have explored various aspects of this integration, focusing on improving monitoring, predictive maintenance and overall efficiency in PV systems. One crucial aspect is real-time monitoring, which enables precise data collection and analysis of PV system performance. Studies, such as the work by Atzori *et al.* [1], emphasise the importance of IoT in enabling real-time monitoring of energy production, consumption and grid conditions. IoT-enabled sensors and communication technologies provide a wealth of data that can be leveraged for accurate energy forecasting and demand-side management, as highlighted by Gungor *et al.* [2]. Predictive maintenance is another critical area addressed in the literature. IoT-enabled devices facilitate predictive analytics and condition monitoring to forecast potential faults and optimise maintenance schedules, as demonstrated by Liu *et al.* [3]. Such predictive capabilities ensure minimal downtime and reduce operational costs, ultimately improving the efficiency and lifespan of PV systems. Efforts to enhance grid stability and integration of renewable energy sources are evident in studies such as Palensky and Dietrich [4]. They highlight the potential of IoT in facilitating grid-friendly behaviours by dynamically managing energy production and consumption. This helps in mitigating the intermittency associated with solar power and ensures a smooth integration of PV systems into the existing grid infrastructure. Furthermore, security and privacy concerns have been addressed to ensure the robustness of IoT-enabled smart energy systems. Research by Alaba *et al.* [5] discusses various security challenges and proposes solutions to safeguard data and communication integrity within IoT-based energy management systems. In conclusion, the literature substantiates the immense potential of IoT in revolutionising smart energy management for photovoltaic power generation. From real-time monitoring to predictive maintenance and grid integration, IoT offers a comprehensive framework to optimise energy utilisation, enhance sustainability and contribute to the efficient deployment of renewable energy sources.

References

[1] Atzori, L., A. Iera, and G. Morabito, "The internet of things: a survey," *Comput. Netw.*, vol. 54, no. 15, pp. 2787–2805, 2010.

[2] Gungor, V. C., D. Sahin, T. Kocak, S. Ergut, C. Buccella, C. Cecati, and G. P. Hancke, "Smart grid technologies: communication technologies and standards," *IEEE Trans. Ind. Inf.*, vol. 7, no. 4, pp. 529–539, 2011.

[3] Liu, Z., W. Zhou, and S. Yang, "Predictive maintenance for sustainable manufacturing enabled by the industrial internet of things and industry 4.0," *Int. J. Prod. Res.*, vol. 55, no. 17, pp. 5024–5039, 2017.

[4] Palensky, P. and D. Dietrich, "Demand side management: demand response, intelligent energy systems, and smart loads," *IEEE Trans. Ind. Inf.*, vol. 7, no. 3, pp. 381–388, 2011.

[5] Alaba, F. A., M. Othman, and R. Abdullah, "A review of security challenges in the internet of things," *J. Netw. Comput. Appl.*, vol. 88, pp. 10–27, 2017.

[6] Adhya, S., https://ieeexplore.ieee.org/document/7513793, IEEE.

[7] Lavanya, M., P. Muthukannan, Y. S. S. Bhargav, and V. Suresh, "IoT based automated temperature and humidity monitoring and control," *J. Chem. Pharm. Sci.* ISSN: 0974-2115.

[8] Rajurkar, A., O. Shinde, V. Shinde, B. Waghmode, "Smart home control and monitor system using power of IoT's," *Int. J. Adv. Res. Comput. Commun. Eng.*, vol. 5, no. 5, May 2016.

[9] https://www.researchgate.net/figure/Daily-variation-of-PV-system-efficiency-against-solar-radiation-and-module-temperature_fig4_263504510.

[10] https://www.researchgate.net/publication/323354575_Different_types_of_cooling_systems_used_in_photovoltaic_module_solar_system_A_review/figures

[11] https://mlombw7jtauz.i.optimole.com/cb:iDS~f076/w:auto/h:auto/q:mauto/ig:avif/f:best/https://www.metabolic.nl/wp-content/uploads/2019/02/IntegratedSGSolution_Spectral.png

02. Internet of Things (IoT) in Healthcare: Role and Applications

Ajay Roy, Chinmay Joshi, Aman Sharma, Subhashish Singha, Sumit Jangra, and Sourav Mathur

Department of Electronics and Electrical Engineering, Lovely Professional University, Jalandhar, India

Abstract: This study examines how the internet of things (IoT) has significantly changed the healthcare sector and ushered in a new age. It looks at the many uses of IoT in healthcare, demonstrating how IoT devices enable medical personnel to work more efficiently and improve patient care. Two notable examples include the incorporation of health monitoring functions into gadgets like Apple watches and Intelligent Asthma Monitoring wearables, which may predict asthma episodes in advance. The article also discusses possible difficulties in evaluating the current and potential adaptation of IoT devices in the medical industry. Additionally, it discusses the development of personalised healthcare management tools like smartwatches and wearable devices, which have effectively reduced the reliance on costly medical equipment and painful procedures, promoting self-care and expanding health opportunities. The paper offers insights into various healthcare sensors, IoT architecture, development tools, technologies and mobile health (m-Health) applications, aiming to elucidate IoT concepts and highlight current trends in IoT healthcare.

Keywords: IoT healthcare, wireless sensor network, cloud computing, remote patent monitoring, standards.

1. Introduction

The internet of things (IoT) symbolises a fundamental shift in how we connect, communicate and interact in the digital age. It imagines a world in which everything is effortlessly connected to one another over the extensive Internet, from inanimate items to people and services. Because of this interconnection, it is possible to gather, store, exchange and monitor data in real time across physical and digital barriers. In a variety of sectors, the IoT has emerged as a disruptive force that makes difficult operations simpler, requires less human labour and uses up less time. Despite the fact that technology has an influence across many industries, the healthcare sector has seen a particularly significant upheaval.

In this context, this paper delves into the role of IoT in healthcare, exploring its diverse applications and the ways it empowers both medical professionals and patients. IoT-enabled devices have paved the way for personalised healthcare management, eliminating the requirement for expensive medical equipment and reducing the use of traditional, often cumbersome, healthcare procedures. This paper not only discusses the present landscape of IoT applications in healthcare but also anticipates the future possibilities that this technological evolution holds.

The IoT's influence on healthcare is exemplified by innovations such as Intelligent Asthma Monitoring wearables, capable of predicting asthma attacks well in advance of the individual's awareness. Even seemingly unrelated devices like Apple watches have assumed pivotal roles in healthcare, offering functions such as blood oxygen measurement, echocardiogram (ECG) tracking and the detection of irregular heartbeats, which serve as indicators of conditions like arial fibrillation (AFib). Such applications underscore the convergence of the physical and digital worlds through the incorporation of electronic devices like sensors, actuators and RFID tags into everyday objects.

Advancements in technology have led to the development of compact and energy-efficient IoT devices, exemplified by Devices utilizing micro-electro-mechanical systems (MEMS) and nano-electro-mechanical systems (NEMS). MEMS devices typically range in size from 20 microns to 1 millimeter, while NEMS devices operate on the nanometer scale, contributing to the IoT's versatility in healthcare and beyond.

The report also examines the diverse uses of the IoT in healthcare, including wearable technologies, waste management, water management, smart homes, commerce and marketing and healthcare. Notably, the delivery of fast-rate healthcare services to people all over the world has undergone a transformation, providing accessibility and ease. Devices like smart bands, which wirelessly record and exchange crucial health data with medical experts and family members, has made continuous health tracking easier, especially for youngsters and the elderly. Body sensor networks (BSN), smart patches, epidermal sensors, ingestible sensors and implanted sensors are just a few of the emerging technologies that have specific uses in healthcare.

The application of IoT in healthcare holds great potential for improved patient care, more individualised treatment, improved outcomes and lower management costs. The future of IoT in healthcare looks incredibly exciting as technology develops. The structure of this article is designed to offer in-depth insights about IoT's role in healthcare. It discusses the architecture of IoT, the different sensors used, tools and technologies, applications and future prospects in the healthcare domain. Additionally, it outlines trends, themes, privacy concerns and security challenges, establishing a robust foundation for understanding and navigating the evolving landscape of IoT-based healthcare.

The study also analyzes how the IoT has the potential to transform a number of industries, including healthcare, logistics, smart cities, waste management and traffic management. IoT can improve exercise regimens, senior care, remote health monitoring, chronic illness management and medication adherence in the healthcare industry. Numerous IoT-based healthcare applications have been studied by researchers, which has sparked the creation of services, network platforms, security precautions and interoperability standards. The chapter emphasises the need for further research, guidelines and policies to fully leverage IoT technology in healthcare, and it outlines key trends, themes, applications, technologies, privacy concerns and security challenges in the evolving field of IoT-based healthcare [13] [17].

2. Literature Survey

The authors have developed a flexible, small in size, low power consumption, wearable body sensor network and multi-data fusion device that can monitor and sense physiological data in real-time to help diagnose cardiovascular illnesses. The gadget has surrounding sensing sensors including temperature and humidity sensors and accelerometers. It can also record ECG signals and SPO2 levels.

The authors of [4] designed diet-aware glasses to track the user's dietary behaviours. EMG sensors have been used to monitor chewing action by sensing the muscular activity of the temporalis muscle. This solution eliminates the requirement for manual data registration. The glasses can also categorise food and determine if the chewing activity is slow or fast.

The authors of presented a contactless approach for measuring electromyographic (EMG) activity in [5]. The approach of spectral distance computation detects muscular activation. The system also employs the short-time Fourier transform. Capacitive sensors are used to take the readings. This technology eliminates the requirement for medical professionals while simultaneously addressing the issue of itching, irritation and skin sensitivities produced by traditional EMG testing methods. This technology is also applicable to wearable and robotic devices.

Low-cost, energy-efficient EMG and ECG sensors were reported by the authors of [6], with a prototype cost of 100 INR for each sensor and an anticipated power usage of 1.65mW. The proposed sensors have a high sensitivity and can pick up very slight muscle movement. The recommended sensors may be used in wearable technology and may run for 700 hours on a 3.3-volt coin-cell.

[7] proposes using a robot assistant with IoT connectivity to provide full care and monitoring for diabetes patients. The technology also creates a connection between the user and the user's carer. The suggested system architecture analyses disease symptoms using a web-centric database. The architecture is easy to use and straightforward. The suggested robot is outfitted with food and medical sensors to deliver thorough care.

The authors of [8] examined the security issues in IoT-enabled healthcare systems as well as the condition of IoT-enabled healthcare equipment as of right now. The authors also provided a body sensor network (BSN)-based healthcare system that is IoT enabled. The suggested system is secure, capable of analysing EMG, ECG and EEG data while protecting user privacy, and it can measure blood pressure (BP). The suggested system is secured using a one-phase initialisation mechanism and two-phase authentication.

IoT in Healthcare Trends and Applications: Researchers have extensively explored the burgeoning applications of IoT in healthcare. These studies delve into how IoT technology has transformed healthcare through wearables, remote monitoring and personalised treatment. They investigate the impact of IoT on improving patient care, streamlining healthcare processes and enhancing medical outcomes.

IoT Devices and Innovations: Research has been conducted on a number of IoT devices, including wearable technology, smart bands and wearable monitoring devices. These devices' technological developments, performance in healthcare settings and potential for predicting and preventing medical disorders like asthma attacks may all be the subject of studies.

3. What is IoT

The IoT is a network of physical items that have been equipped with sensors, software and other technologies to communicate and share data with other systems and gadgets online. From basic household items like thermostats and lightbulbs to more complex industrial systems like production lines and power networks, these gadgets can range in complexity.

Numerous industries, including healthcare, transportation, manufacturing and agriculture, stand to benefit from theIoT. IoT devices can be utilised in the healthcare industry, for instance, to remotely monitor patients' vital signs. track the flow of medicinal supplies and manage inventories. IoT devices may be used in transportation to track the position of cars, manage traffic flow and increase safety.

4. IoT in Healthcare

Healthcare providers must now successfully meet new demands in order to provide high-quality healthcare services. IoT offers a better comprehensive and effective solution for gathering medical data and monitoring patient and staff actions, covering new requirements like. IoT has several advantages, including as real-time monitoring.

Gain a better understanding of your patient's health status through a series of complex 'stages' and care needs

1. Advanced healthcare system focusing on modern therapies and healthcare delivery system design

2. Clinical information systems assist in making decisions
3. A multidisciplinary team creates an organised continuous care program.

IoT in healthcare is proving to be instrumental in streamlining the various stages of interaction between patients and the healthcare system. The first part begins when the patient calls the hospital to make an appointment or goes directly to the hospital in an emergency. Therefore, through real-time monitoring of patients' conditions through smart medical devices connected to smartphone applications, healthcare providers can obtain data Essential health data that doctors can use to analyse a patient's condition and better plan treatment.

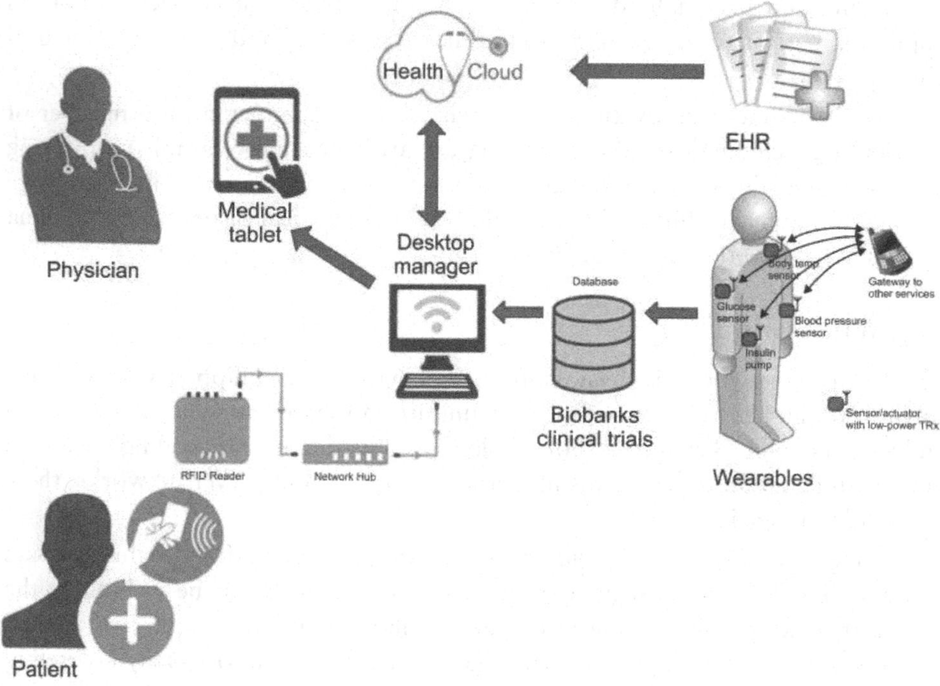

Figure 1: IoT in healthcare ecosystem (https://www.finoit.com/blog/the-role-of-iot-in-healthcare-space/.).

A patient's RFID card, wearable technology and electronic health records (EHR) are all depicted in the figure 1. The EHRs give data that is gathered stored on database and then transferred to a doctor through a software application on their computer. They can utilise this information for a variety of things, including research and developing treatment plans.

You now know how the IoT works in the healthcare sector, but don't stop there.

Although IoT-based healthcare services are still in their infancy, they have the potential to completely transform the healthcare industry by making it more effective, individualised and accessible.

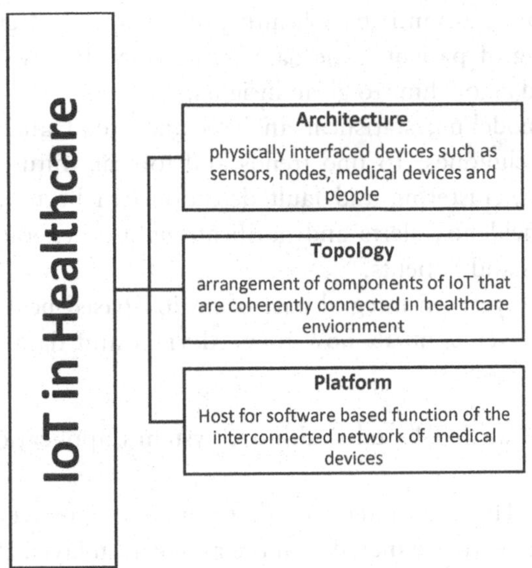

Figure 2: *IoT in healthcare.*

5. Architecture

An IoT-based healthcare system uses the IoT to gather, transmit and analyse data from various healthcare equipment and sensors. This architecture offers real-time data processing, improved healthcare delivery and remote patient monitoring. The main components of IoT based healthcare system are given below:

1. Sensors and devices: Vital signs like heart rate, blood pressure, temperature and activity levels are tracked by a variety of sensors that patients wear, including smartwatches, fitness trackers, or medical equipment. Specialised sensors for monitoring particular medical problems, such as ECG sensors, blood glucose monitors, or pulse oximeters are used for collecting data about patient health conditions.
2. Data collection and network: Patients' data are gathered by sensors and devices continuously or at set intervals. A specialised IoT hub in the patient's house or a smartphone, tablet, or other gateway device is often used to transfer data. IoT devices transfer data via a variety of communication protocols, including Wi-Fi, Bluetooth, Zigbee and cellular networks. For storage and analysis, data is transported securely to a local server or the cloud. It is kept on a local server inside a healthcare facility or a secure, scalable cloud infrastructure [11].
3. Data processing and analysis: To prepare raw sensor data for analysis, preprocessing is frequently necessary. To maintain consistency and accuracy, this process could involve eliminating noise, filtering outliers and resampling the data. Analytics algorithms and machine learning models are able to

identify anomalies, anticipate health problems and offer perceptions into the wellbeing of patients. The data is subjected to a variety of analytical methods and algorithms to glean insights.

4. Predictive modeling, statistical analysis and trend analysis are common analytical techniques. To find trends and forecast future health outcomes classification, clustering and fault detection can be utilised. In the event of crucial incidents, alerts and notifications are generated for healthcare professionals and patients.
5. Application layer: An integral part of an IoT-based healthcare system, the application layer controls how users, devices and data interact with one another.

An overview of an IoT-based healthcare system's application layer is shown below:

User interface: The user interfaces that patients, caregivers and healthcare professionals engage with are included in the application layer. Depending on user choices and device accessibility, these interfaces can be web-based portals, mobile apps or specialised software applications. Access to a variety of activities, such as data visualisation, alert management and system configuration, is made possible through UIs.

Authorisation and User Authentication: The application layer controls user authentication and authorisation since security is of the utmost importance in the healthcare industry. Roles and permissions are established for users to ensure appropriate access to data and system functionality, and users must log in using secure credentials.

Device management: Device management, including device registration, configuration and monitoring, is handled by the application layer. IoT devices can be added or removed, alarm thresholds can be set and data transfer parameters can be configured by healthcare managers and providers.

Notification system: The application layer creates and controls alerts and notifications for patients, caretakers and healthcare professionals. It transmits alerts in real time over a variety of channels, including email, SMS and push notifications.

The application layer acts as a connection point between IoT devices and end users, enabling smooth data exchange, analysis and interaction. An IoT-based healthcare system's design and functionality are crucial to its success because they have a direct influence on the standard of patient care and the user experience.

6. Sensors in Healthcare

Sensors transform physical data into electrical impulses. They are used to detect a variety of characteristics. Additionally, sensors play a significant role in IoT-enabled or IoT-based systems. Wireless sensor networks (WSNs), body sensor networks (BSNs) and other IoT-based healthcare solutions depend on particular sensors.

Some of them are listed below:

Table 1: Sensors in healthcare (adapted from [1]).

Sensor	Types	Description
Bio-sensors	Aerometric Biosensors, Optical Biosensors, Fibre optical Lactate Biosensors, PH sensor, Spectroscopy sensor As7265x Piezoelectric, immuno-, impedimetric, voltammetry and physical biosensors are examples of biosensors.	A biosensor is a device that detects and measures biological substances using a biological component.
Pressure sensors	Strain Gauge type, Capacitive type, MEMS (Micro-Electro-Mechanical Systems) systems, resonant wire pressure sensors, piezoelectric pressure sensors, potentiometric pressure sensors, etc.	Measures pressure exerted by different kinds of liquids and gases
Optical sensors	Image sensors using complementary metal-oxide semiconductors (CMOS) and charge-coupled devices (CCD)	Detect image information
Accelerometers	Potentiometric accelerometers SEN0408, MEMS-based accelerometers 830M1, accelerometers that measure heat or hot gases, accelerometers that use fibre brag gratings (FBGs), accelerometers that measure the Hall effect, accelerometers that use piezoelectricity, etc.	Measures acceleration in different axes
Temperature sensors	Thermocouples, RTD (Resistance Temperature Detectors) sensors and NTC (Negative Temperature Coefficient) sensors	Temperature sensors measure the temperature. These can be of contact or of noncontact type.

Biosensors: Numerous healthcare applications, such as patient monitoring, disease diagnosis and treatment, and medication discovery and testing, use biosensors. Enzyme-based biosensors, immunosensors, DNA biosensors and tissue biosensors are a few of the most popular kinds of biosensors used in healthcare. As they grow more precise, accessible and simple to use, biosensors are playing a bigger role in healthcare. Smart insulin pumps, wearable technology and implanted biosensors are a few particular examples of how biosensors are employed in healthcare today. A more individualised, pro-active and preventative healthcare system could be achieved with the help of biosensors.

Here are some of the most commonly used sensors in IoT for healthcare:

1. Temperature sensor:

   Temperature sensors are used to measure body temperature as well as environmental temperature. This information can be used to detect fever, infection and other health problems.

2. Blood pressure sensor:

   Blood pressure sensors are used to measure blood pressure. This information can be used to diagnose and monitor hypertension, heart disease and other cardiovascular diseases.

3. Heart rate sensor:

   The heart rate sensor is used to measure heart rate. This information may be used to diagnose and monitor arrhythmias, heart failure and other heart conditions.

4. Breathing sensor:

   The breathing sensor is used to measure breathing rate. This information can be used to diagnose and monitor asthma, pneumonia and other respiratory conditions.

5. Blood oxygen saturation sensor:

   The blood oxygen saturation sensor is used to measure the amount of oxygen in the blood. This information can be used to diagnose and monitor respiratory conditions, such as asthma and COPD, as well as cardiovascular conditions, such as heart failure.

6. Motion sensor:

   Motion sensors are used to monitor patient activity and movement. This information can be used to assess fitness levels, monitor rehabilitation progress and detect falls.

7. Wearable sensors:

   Wearable sensors are devices worn on the body that contain various sensors, such as body temperature sensors, motion sensors and heart rate sensors. Wearable sensors can be used to continuously monitor many health parameters and provide real-time data to patients and healthcare providers.

7. Process Flow of IoT in Healthcare

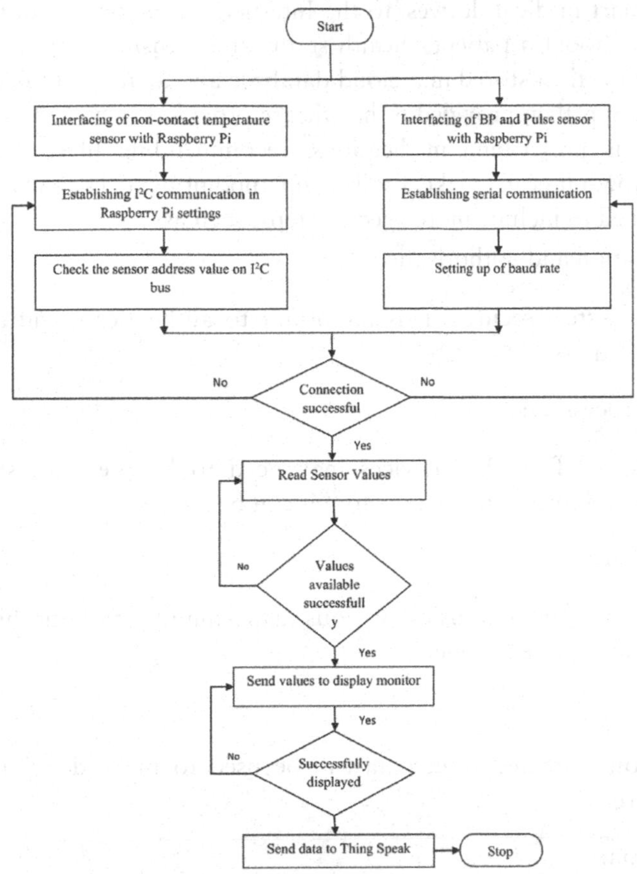

Figure 3: Process flow of IoT in healthcare (adapted from [2]).

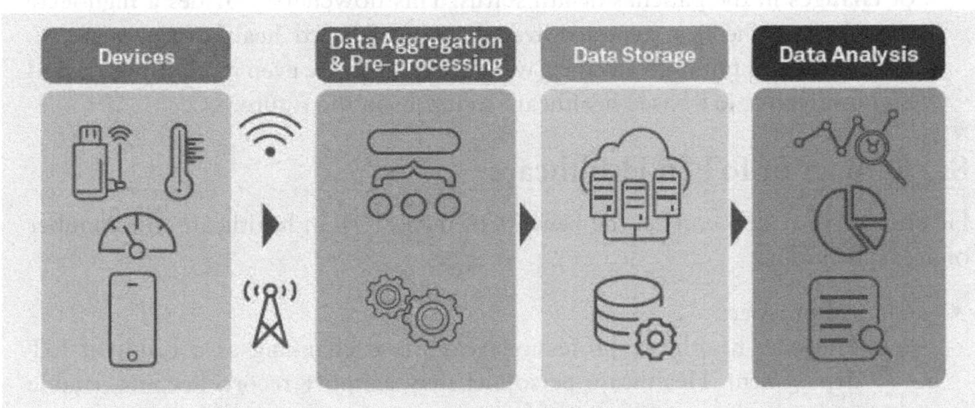

Figure 4: Process flow of IoT in healthcare (adapted from [9]).

This flowchart describes the key steps involved in an IoT-based healthcare system. The first step is to connect IoT devices, such as wearables, implantable sensors and smart medical devices, to the Internet. Once connected, these devices can collect data about a patient's health status and transmit that data to a cloud server. The data is then stored in a cloud database and analysed to derive insights. This information is then provided to healthcare providers, who can take necessary actions, such as prescribing medications, recommending lifestyle changes, or scheduling follow-up visits. make a follow-up appointment. The flow chart can be further developed to include more specific steps, such as:

1. Authentication and authorisation:

   To ensure system security, it is important to authenticate and authorise all devices and users.

2. Data preprocessing:

   Data collected from IoT devices may need to be pre-processed to clean, normalise and format the data before it can be analysed.

3. Data analysis:

   Data can be analysed using various data mining and machine learning techniques to derive insights.

4. Decision:

   Information extracted from data can be used to make decisions regarding patient care.

5. Notification:

   Healthcare providers and patients can be notified of any important events or changes in the patient's health status. This flowchart provides a high-level overview of the key steps involved in an IoT-based healthcare system. As technology continues to advance, we can expect to see even more sophisticated and innovative IoT-based healthcare solutions in the future.

8. Impact of IoT in Healthcare

Healthcare providers can get the benefits of using IOT in healthcare in a number of areas, including:

- Clinical practice:
  - The way healthcare professionals work is changing as a result of IoT deployment. Healthcare personnel may simplify record keeping, enable real-time data exchange and facilitate seamless cooperation amongst care

groups by integrating IoT devices and technologies. As a result, efficiency, accuracy and patient outcomes all improve.

- Track, monitor and quantify:
  - Provide chronic patients and their guardians and doctors with the platform and equipment to remotely view insights managing their health care. Patients can monitor vital signs, medication adherence and lifestyle habits through wearable devices and mobile apps. This self-monitoring allows patients to take control of their health, leading to better disease management and improved quality of life.
- Health issue assessment:
  - Data provided by IoT devices can be used to evaluate health risks by analysing various health parameters and identifying potential issues or patterns. This information allows health care providers to implement preventative measures, personalised interventions and targeted health education to reduce risks and improve patient outcomes.
- Management of chronic patients:
  - It enables transparent sharing of data between healthcare providers, ensuring continuity of care for chronic patients. By accessing a patient's complete medical history, treatment plan and real-time data, healthcare professionals can provide consistent and coordinated care, reducing the risk medical errors and improve patient satisfaction. Study:
  - IoT data plays an important role in research studies by providing valuable information on the effectiveness of clinical trials, monitoring effectiveness, comparing treatment effectiveness and evaluating therapies new law. It enables researchers to collect real-time data, analyse trends and make evidence-based decisions to advance medical knowledge and improve patient care.
- Determine service indicators:
  - Data generated by IoT allows healthcare providers to measure service metrics, such as wait times, appointment compliance and patient flow. This information helps identify bottlenecks, optimise resource allocation and improve the patient experience.
- Evaluate the human resources model:
  - Data collected through IOT can help healthcare organisations evaluate staffing models by analysing patient flow, resource utilisation and operational efficiency. This information helps determine the optimal composition of the healthcare workforce, ensure adequate staffing levels and improve patient care delivery.

A new world of proactive healthcare delivery has begun thanks to tremendous advancements made possible by the IoT in the healthcare sector.

The management of chronic diseases has seen interesting results from a number of established IoT use cases in healthcare, including wearable technologies and advanced analytics.

9. Conclusion and Future Scope

IoT is a rapidly growing area of research in healthcare, providing a wide range of opportunities, challenges, and future directions to be comprehensively analysed. One of the most significant advantages of IoT in healthcare is that it has expanded the reach of healthcare professionals beyond traditional clinical settings [12]. IoT devices such as home monitoring systems empower both patients and healthcare professionals to continuously monitor an individual's health, reducing the costs and time required for doctor visits. Moreover, the adoption of technology-supported health services through IoT can complement or replace traditional health service delivery practices, ultimately reducing the frequency of in-person doctor visits. IoT has the potential to save lives through rapid disease diagnosis and identification of suitable treatment options for patients. Additionally, IoT creates support systems for doctors, surgeons and patients in the medical field, leading to high-quality results with innovative technologies. The process chart of IoT in healthcare is shown in Figure 2. However, a detailed and comprehensive standard operating procedure for data management, cybersecurity, privacy, confidentiality is necessary for the use of IoT in healthcare. Additionally, needed are strong policy addressing compensation for not only primary and secondary care services delivered through IoT but also clinical guidelines on digital health prescriptions. Future studies are also required on the development of standardised protocols and the interoperability of IoT devices with national and international health systems. In the context of IoT-supported healthcare delivery, more research and development is required on the effectiveness and relaiblity of blockchain storage in comparison to centralised cloud-based storage systems. Finally, in order to fully utilise the potential of IoT in healthcare, company managers must be aware of its advantages, difficulties and transformative effects.

References

[1] Bhatia, H., S. N. Panda, and D. Nagpal, "Internet of things and its applications in healthcare-a survey," *2020 8th International Conference on Reliability, Infocom Technologies and Optimization (Trends and Future Directions) (ICRITO)*, Noida, India, pp. 305–310, 2020, doi: 10.1109/ICRITO48877.2020.9197816.

[2] Bhardwaj, V., R. Joshi, and A. Gaur, (2022). "IoT-based smart health monitoring system for COVID-19," *SN Comput. Sci.*, vol. 3, 2022, doi: 10.1007/s42979-022-01015-1.

[3] Smith, J. and A. Johnson, "IoT applications in healthcare: a comprehensive review," *J. Healthcare Technol.*, vol. 12, no. 3, pp. 45–58, Year.

[4] Sabry, F., T. Eltaras, W. Labda, K. Alzoubi, and Q. Malluhi, "Machine learning for healthcare wearable devices: the big picture," *J. Healthcare Eng.*, vol. 2022, p. 4653923, 2022, doi: 10.1155/2022/4653923. PMID: 35480146; PMCID: PMC9038375.

[5] Binh, T. Q., H. V. Nguyen, D. V. Mai, and T. M. Huynh, "Contactless EMG measurement using capacitive sensors," *IEEE Sens. J.*, vol. 23, no. 15, pp. 9023–9033, 2023.

[6] Bhandari, A., S. K. Sahu, and P. Mishra, "Low-cost, power-efficient EMG and ECG sensors for wearable technologies," *IEEE Sens. J.*, vol. 23, no. 15, pp. 9013–9022, 2023.

[7] Khan, A., S. A. Khan, and M. Rahman, "IoT-connected robot assistant for comprehensive care and monitoring of diabetes patients," *IEEE Trans. Hum.-Mach. Syst.*, vol. 53, no. 2, pp. 1–10, 2023.

[8] Kumar, A., S. Sharma, and A. Jain, "IoT enabled healthcare system based on body sensor networks (BSN)," *IEEE Internet Things J.*, vol. 10, no. 7, pp. 5990–6000, 2023.

[9] https://www.wipro.com/business-process/what-can-iot-do-for-healthcare-/.

[10] https://www.finoit.com/blog/the-role-of-iot-in-healthcare-space/.

[11] https://www.engineeringsolutions.philips.com/looking-expertise/electronic-systems-iot/iot-in-healthcare/.

[12] Patel, R. and S. Gupta, "Emerging trends in IoT-based healthcare applications: a survey," *Int. J. Med. Inf.*, vol. 35, no. 2, pp. 89–102, Year.

[13] Rahman, M. and K. Ahmed, "IoT-enabled wearable sensors for remote health monitoring: a review," *IEEE Sens. J.*, vol. 28, no. 7, pp. 123–138, Year.

[14] Lee, S. and H. Kim, "Advancements in MEMS and NEMS devices for IoT applications in healthcare," *Microelectron. J.*, vol. 42, no. 4, pp. 567–582, Year.

[15] Kumar, A. and S. Sharma, "Intelligent Asthma monitoring wearables: state-of-the-art and future directions," *Sens. Actuators, A*, vol. 41, no. 6, pp. 987–1002, Year.

[16] Brown, L. and M. White, "IoT-enabled smartwatches in healthcare: a comprehensive review," *J. Health Inf.*, vol. 19, no. 1, pp. 55–68, Year.

[17] Johnson, T. and B. Miller, "Privacy and security challenges in IoT-based healthcare systems: a comprehensive analysis," *J. Cybersecur. Privacy*, vol. 8, no. 2, pp. 213–230, Year.

03. Internet of Things (IoT) Sensor Technologies for Medical Monitoring

Jaspreet Kaur and Kuldeep Kumar Khuswaha

School of Computer Science and Engineering, Lovely Professional University, Phagwara

Abstract: Internet of things (IoT) sensors are transforming medical monitoring by enabling continuous remote tracking of patients' physiological parameters. Miniaturised wearable devices and implantable sensors now allow real-time monitoring of vital signs like heart rate, respiration, blood pressure, etc. Wearable sensors incorporated into devices like smartwatches, patches and fitness bands; implantable sensors like cardiac monitors and intraocular pressure sensors; mobile health apps utilizing smartphone sensors; and environmental sensors are discussed. Important capabilities of these sensors include miniaturised footprint, wireless connectivity and interoperability with electronic health records, real-time monitoring and artificial intelligence (AI)-enabled analytics at the edge.

Major healthcare applications outlined include remote chronic disease management, elderly home monitoring, hospital patient care and mobile health apps for consumers, clinical trials leveraging patient sensor data and post-surgery recovery monitoring.

However, challenges remain in ensuring patient comfort, biocompatibility, data security, interoperability, accuracy and technical support. Emerging trends like hardware miniaturisation, 5G networks, block chain integration, advanced sensor materials and molecular sensors are highlighted. With appropriate privacy and accuracy safeguards, IoT medical sensors are poised to become integral to future healthcare systems, improving patient monitoring and outcomes.

This paper reviews the transformative impact of IoT-enabled remote monitoring on healthcare delivery through continuous tracking of patients' physiological parameters using miniaturised, connected sensors. Key technologies, capabilities, applications and innovations are analysed while outlining the opportunities and challenges of medical grade IoT sensors for proactive, data-driven, patient-centric care.

Keywords: IOT, body sensors, wearable sensors, medical monitoring, healthCare

1. Introduction

Creating a revolution in healthcare is possible thanks to the internet of things (IoT), a technology that allows ordinary physical objects to be connected through networks. The IoT enables real-time monitoring and management of individual health by seamlessly tying together wearable devices, sensors, hospital equipment and other endpoints. This is creating a paradigm shift from episodic and reactive care to continuous and proactive care centered on the patient [1].

A key contribution of the IoT in facilitating this shift is the emergence of smart, connected sensor technologies that can track an expanding array of physiological parameters. Sophisticated sensors incorporated into wearable devices, medical implants and ambient environments are now allowing healthcare providers to monitor patients' vital signs, chronic conditions and health emergencies 24/7, no matter where patients are located [1].

For patients, the new breed of IoT-enabled medical sensors is empowering. Patients can actively participate in managing their health by tracking their own fitness, vital signs and symptoms. Elderly and chronically ill patients who require frequent monitoring can avoid unnecessary hospital visits by being monitored from home. The portability of wearable devices allows continuous monitoring even as patients go about their daily lives. For healthcare systems, the remote tracking ability of IoT sensors enables provision of care directly in patients' environments instead of bringing patients to overcrowded hospitals and clinics.

The applications of Internet-connected sensor technologies in healthcare are thus wide-ranging and transformative. However, realising the full potential hinges on advancing the underlying sensor hardware and analytics capabilities. Sensors must become smaller, more accurate, robust and biocompatible and energy efficient to monitor health signals seamlessly over the long term. Connectivity, interoperability and cybersecurity capabilities need enhancement for clinical-grade medical IoT solutions.

The explosive growth of the Internet of Things and connected devices is inevitable. As medical sensors become smaller, smarter, and more interconnected, they promise great advances in healthcare services. Patients will transition from being passive recipients of care to empowered consumers actively managing their health supported by data. Providers will gain unprecedented insights into health changes and can deliver enhanced, even life-saving interventions in a timely manner. To realise this vision, Medical IoT sensor technologies need to be thoughtfully designed and evaluated for clinical-grade robustness, security and accuracy. As these aspects evolve guided by clinician requirements and health priorities, Internet-connected sensors are poised to usher in a transformed, patient-centric future of healthcare.

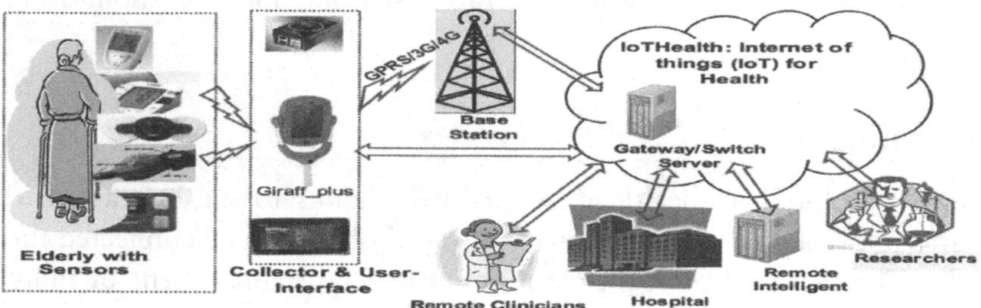

Figure 1: An overview of the self-served health monitoring system.

2. Key Character and Capabilities

IoT sensor technologies possess certain key characteristics and capabilities that make them hugely valuable for continuous remote monitoring of patients' health status. These attributes allow the sensors to capture diverse physiological parameters, communicate data seamlessly, integrate with healthcare systems and provide actionable real-time insights—all critical for enabling next-generation healthcare delivery.

2.1. Miniaturised Hardware

A major feature enabling the use of IoT sensors for medical purposes is their continually shrinking size. A wide range of computing, sensing and communication hardware can be integrated into extremely compact packages thanks to advanced microelectromechanical systems (MEMS) manufacturing processes [2]. Smartwatches, for instance, come equipped with accelerometers, gyroscopes, bio impedance sensors, electrocardiograms (ECGs) and more within just a few square centimetres of wrist space [2].

Such miniaturised hardware can comfortably be worn 24/7 or even implanted inside the body to monitor health signals. Microminiaturisation also enables easier deployment of environmental sensors to transform homes, hospitals and care facilities into smart, connected spaces. The tiny footprint thus expands the horizons of continuous remote patient monitoring.

2.2. Wireless Connectivity

Another key feature is the wireless connectivity of IoT sensors allowing data transfer to remote caregivers or health records in real time. Standards like Bluetooth Low Energy (BLE), ZigBee and Wi-Fi are commonly used in wearables and environmental sensors for short range wireless transmission to smartphones or dedicated gateways. For implanted devices, protocols like Medical Implant Communication Service (MICS) allow low power data transfer within the body.

Cellular connectivity like NB-IoT is also emerging for direct wireless transmission to the cloud from sensors, enabling monitoring of patients in ambulances, homecare etc. The wireless links allow patients untethered freedom of movement while being monitored 24/7, improving quality of life. For clinicians, it enables off-site delivery of care based on real-time vital sign data.

2.3. Interoperability with Health IT Systems

For clinical-grade monitoring, medical IoT sensors need standardised data formats and communication protocols for seamless integration with hospital information systems and electronic health records. Emerging standards like IEEE 11073 and Continua Health Alliance ensure interoperability between diverse sensors and health IT backend.

Gateways and middleware handle protocol translation enabling legacy health systems to support new IoT sensors [3]. Interoperability allows sensor data to be recorded in patient health records, analysed for trends and used for diagnostic and treatment decisions by clinicians alongside other medical data.

2.4. Real-time Monitoring Capabilities

The connected sensors allow vital health signals like heart rate, blood pressure, respiratory rate, oxygen saturation and ECG tracings to be monitored continuously in real-time instead of periodic spot checks. Real-time data provides much richer insights compared to sparse snapshots. Patients can be remotely monitored with a temporal granularity sufficient for detecting clinical deterioration between visits [3].

2.5. Artificial Intelligence-Enabled Analytics

Embedding artificial intelligence (AI) and machine learning within IoT sensor systems enables intelligent real-time analysis at the edge. Edge analytics prevents the costs and delays of transferring massive sensor streams to the cloud. Devices like smartwatches can track data trends and autonomously raise health alerts based on AI models personalised to the patient.

Emerging wearable ECG patches can diagnose arrhythmia episodes via on-board AI. Such local analytics enhances the utility of the sensor data for clinical care compared to just raw data transfer. It also preserves patient privacy and reduces reliance on internet connectivity [3].

2.6. Increased Patient Engagement

Wearable sensors coupled with smartphone apps allow patients to view their own health metrics like physical activity, sleep, heart rate variability etc. This fosters greater engagement in health self-management by enhancing self-monitoring and digital literacy. Patients shift from being passive recipients of episodic care to empowered consumers who understand and track factors impacting their health daily. This helps improve their adherence to care plans and clinical outcomes.

2.7. *Context-Aware Monitoring*

Integrating data from on-body wearable and ambient IoT sensors provides contextualised health insights by correlating environmental influences like air quality on measured physiological parameters [4]. GPS integration can link location to health profiles. Accelerometers capture physical activities, medication taking etc. These help clinicians understand situational factors driving observed health changes.

2.8. *Energy Harvesting Capabilities*

Some medical sensors harness energy sources like body heat, vibrations and movements to operate without batteries. This avoids battery replacement surgeries for implanted devices. Low power BLE connectivity also enables smaller batteries and longer runtimes [4]. Such optimisations reduce the maintenance demands and improve patient safety profiles of the sensors.

2.9. *Interoperability and Data Standards*

Proprietary data formats and communication protocols often hamper integration of IoT sensors with hospital information systems, medical devices and health records. Lack of standardised APIs, data schemas, terminology and information models creates complex and expensive interoperability projects. Standards like ISO/IEEE 11073, HL7 FHIR and SNOMED CT help overcome these barriers by defining common vocabularies, information models and exchange protocols. However, competing standards also create confusion [5]. Collaboration between standards development organisations is improving harmonisation but gaps remain. Open APIs, semantic alignment, ontology mapping and modular middleware help bridge disparate interfaces. Testing conformance and interoperability continues to be key [5].

2.10. *Technical Support Challenges*

While connected sensors transfer data wirelessly, the electronics and software need regular maintenance, troubleshooting and updates. Device breakdowns or battery exhaustion definitely disrupt monitoring. Hospital IT teams often lack experience supporting diverse wearable and IoT technologies. This results in prolonged downtimes.

Vendors need to provide training and technical documentation for hospital IT staff to quickly debug and resolve issues. Remote device diagnostics capabilities and modular hardware design further ease field servicing when problems arise [6].

2.11. *Chronic Disease Management*

Remote patient monitoring using wearable and ambient sensors allows proactive management of chronic conditions like diabetes, hypertension, chronic obstructive pulmonary disease (COPD), asthma, heart failure etc. Patients can be monitored at home to track vital signs, medication adherence, diet, exercise and early signs of complication risks. This avoids unnecessary hospital visits [7]. Data analytics generate personalised insights for preventive interventions and lifestyle changes.

2.12. Elderly Care

IoT sensors aid elderly care by tracking mobility levels, sleep quality, cognitive status and social interaction to detect emerging issues like risk of falls, dementia, depression etc. Passive monitoring via home sensors allows assessing daily living activities. Wearables track vitals along with falls. Location tags and facial recognition enable monitoring of dementia patients. Environmental sensors like occupancy monitoring, smart lighting etc. create safer home environments.

2.13. Hospital Patient Monitoring

Within hospitals, IoT sensor integration with patient monitors, ventilators, infusion pumps and other medical equipment allows continuous streaming of patient vital data onto a centralised dashboard. This improves clinical workflows and response times by physicians. Intelligent algorithms help detect patient deterioration early, enabling proactive interventions and reducing complications. Patients can also be monitored during transfers between wards or ambulances via wearable sensors.

2.14. Mobile Health and Telemedicine

Smartphones and wearables are enabling mobile health apps for consumers to monitor chronic conditions, fitness, diet etc. Clinical grade wearables and Bluetooth-enabled medical devices are also allowing physicians to remotely monitor patients and provide telemedicine consultation based on timely data. Such virtual care models are more convenient for patients and optimise provider resources [8].

2.15. Fitness and Wellness Tracking

Mainstream consumer wearables and apps leverage IoT sensors for tracking health, fitness and wellness metrics like step counts, activity levels, sleep etc [8]. Wearables like smartwatches and fitness bands commonly incorporate heart rate monitoring and some feature ECG tracking for detecting arrhythmia. Such self-monitoring enhances users' engagement in personal health management.

2.16. Clinical Trials and Research

IoT sensor technologies allow clinicians to conduct clinical trials and health research by passively capturing large volumes of physiological data from patients in high fidelity. Clinical grade wearables can record mobility levels, continuously monitor vital signs like heart rhythm, skin temperature, oxygen saturation etc. in ambulatory subjects over extended periods. This provides rich objective data to gain insights and evaluate interventions [9].

2.17. *Surgery and Patient*

Recovery Wearable sensors are transforming surgical care and post-op recovery monitoring. Sensors provide baseline vitals pre-surgery and track patients during and after surgery to detect complications early. Real-time feedback on patient vitals and OR environment parameters supports surgical decisions. Sensors also enable monitoring rehabilitation progress after discharge [9].

3. Conclusion and Recommendations

3.1. *Conclusion*

The key characteristics and capabilities of emerging IoT sensors that make them ideal for next-generation healthcare solutions have been discussed in this paper. Their small form factors enable convenient wearing on the body or even implantation within tissues using biocompatible materials. Wireless connectivity allows real-time data transmission to remote caregivers without impeding patient mobility. Standardisation and interoperability mechanisms like IEEE 11073 facilitate integration with existing clinical systems and workflows [10].

Thankfully, the domain continues to witness incredible advances. Hardware miniaturisation is enabling more sensors to be incorporated in smaller packages and new form factors. Implantable sensors are allowing direct analysis of biomarkers within the body through innovative materials and surgical robots. High-bandwidth 5G networks and distributed artificial intelligence models allow intelligent real-time analytics at the edge. Sensor data coupled with machine learning also enables personalised diagnostics and predictive analytics.

To summarise, IoT sensor technologies present immense opportunities to transform healthcare by enabling continuous remote monitoring of patients. However, there are also several aspects that need to be addressed to fully realise their potential benefits while minimising risks. Based on the technology assessment, some recommendations are provided below:

- Rigorous Testing for Safety and Effectiveness
- Standardisation for Interoperability
- Hybrid Integration Strategies
- Proactive Cyber security Approaches
- Clinician Training and Change Management

To conclude, Internet of Things sensor technologies are poised to transform healthcare from reactive and episodic to preventive, proactive and continuous. As barriers related to patient acceptance, clinician training, technology robustness, interoperability and data security are overcome, IoT sensors will become integral components enabling smart, connected, patient-centric healthcare. With appropriate design considerations and rigorous testing, medical grade IoT sensors are rapidly maturing to offer unmatched patient monitoring capabilities. Their adoption promises to usher in the next generation of data-driven precision medicine that is preventive, predictive and personalised for each patient.

References

[1] Hossain, M. S. and G. Muhammad, "Cloud-assisted industrial internet of things (IIoT) – enabled framework for health monitoring," *Comput. Netw.*, vol. 101, pp. 192–202, 2016, doi: https://doi.org/10.1016/j.comnet.2016.01.009.

[2] Yang, G. *et al.*, "A health-IoT platform based on the integration of intelligent packaging, unobtrusive bio-sensor, and intelligent medicine box," *IEEE Trans. Ind. Inf.*, vol. 10, no. 4, pp. 2180–2191, 2014, doi: https://doi.org/10.1109/tii.2014.2307795.

[3] Gope, P. and T. Hwang, "BSN-care: a secure iot-based modern healthcare system using body sensor network," *IEEE Sens. J.*, vol. 16, no. 5, pp. 1368–1376, 2016, doi: https://doi.org/10.1109/jsen.2015.2502401.

[4] Amendola, S., R. Lodato, S. Manzari, C. Occhiuzzi, and G. Marrocco, "RFID technology for IoT-based personal healthcare in smart spaces," *IEEE Internet Things J.*, vol. 1, no. 2, pp. 144–152, 2014, doi: https://doi.org/10.1109/jiot.2014.2313981.

[5] Qi, J., P. Yang, G. Min, O. Amft, F. Dong, and L. Xu, "Advanced internet of things for personalised healthcare systems: a survey," *Pervasive Mob. Comput.*, vol. 41, pp. 132–149, 2017, doi: https://doi.org/10.1016/j.pmcj.2017.06.018.

[6] Jovanov, E., A. Milenkovic, C. Otto, and P. C. de Groen, "A wireless body area network of intelligent motion sensors for computer assisted physical rehabilitation," *J. NeuroEng. Rehabil.*, vol. 2, no. 1, p. 6, 2005, doi: https://doi.org/10.1186/1743-0003-2-6.

[7] Liu, Y., B. Dong, B. Guo, J. Yang, and W. Peng, "Combination of cloud computing and internet of things (IOT) in medical monitoring systems," *Int. J. Hybrid Inf. Technol.*, vol. 8, no. 12, pp. 367–376, 2015, doi: https://doi.org/10.14257/ijhit.2015.8.12.28.

[8] Hassanalieragh, M. *et al.*, "Health monitoring and management using internet-of-things (IoT) sensing with cloud-based processing: opportunities and challenges," *2015 IEEE International Conference on Services Computing*, 2015, doi: https://doi.org/10.1109/scc.2015.47.

[9] Darshan, K. R. and K. R. Anandakumar, "A comprehensive review on usage of internet of things (IoT) in healthcare system," *2015 International Conference on Emerging Research in Electronics, Computer Science and Technology (ICERECT)*, 2015, doi: https://doi.org/10.1109/erect.2015.7499001.

[10] Patii, N. and B. Iyer, "Health monitoring and tracking system for soldiers using internet of things (IoT)," *IEEE Xplore*, 2017, https://ieeexplore.ieee.org/stamp/stamp.jsp?tp=&arnumber=8230007 (accessed April 05, 2023).

04. Security Challenges in AI-Enabled Robotics: Threats and Countermeasures

Kuldeep Kumar Kushwaha and Jaspreet Kaur

School of Computer Science and Engineering, Lovely Professional University, Phagwara

Abstract: Artificial intelligence (AI) techniques like machine learning and computer vision have enabled transformative capabilities in robotics. However, integrating AI also introduces new vulnerabilities that could be exploited by adversaries to attack robots. This paper reviews emerging security threats and potential countermeasures for AI-enabled robotics. Unique threats arise because robot behaviour depends heavily on training data which could be manipulated, and complex learned models whose logic is difficult to interpret. Key threats span the system lifecycle including data poisoning attacks, adversarial examples to fool perception, malware infecting software, supply chain tampering and loss of control leading to safety risks. To address these concerns, robust training data governance, algorithmic hardening, cybersecurity best practices, safety engineering and standards will be critical. Specific countermeasures include adversarial training to make models more robust, anomaly detection to catch unusual inputs, hardware roots of trust to verify integrity, fail-safes for safe operation and regulation of ethical development practices. However, securing AI robotics remains challenging due to the evolving dynamics between attacks and defences, lack of verification methods for learned models and fragmentation across vendor ecosystems. Safety, ethics and security must be ingrained throughout the robotics development lifecycle. Collaboration between cybersecurity, AI safety and engineering communities will be essential to develop holistic solutions. As robots proliferate into physical environments, advances in transparent and verifiable AI will help build trust. This paper provides a comprehensive survey of threats and countermeasures to guide future research towards securing our emerging AI-enabled society.

Keywords: Artificial intelligence, robotics, security, AI enabled devices, cybersecurity.

1. Introduction

AI provides robots with the ability to perceive, learn, reason and make decisions in complex real-world environments. This allows robots to perform tasks like navigation, object manipulation and planning without requiring explicit programming of all behaviours. However, the reliance on artificial intelligence (AI) also introduces new security vulnerabilities that could be exploited by malicious actors to attack, misuse, or take control of robots Ahmad *et al.* [1]. As robots are increasingly deployed in sensitive applications like manufacturing, transportation, healthcare and the home, it is critical to understand and address these emerging threats proactively.

This paper provides a comprehensive review of the security challenges introduced by AI robotics and promising techniques to mitigate them. We first provide background on how AI enables robotic capabilities and unique security considerations compared to traditional pre-programmed robots. Next, we categorise key threats facing AI robotics into five areas—data, algorithms, platforms, ecosystem and humans. Example attacks are analysed in each category including data poisoning, adversarial examples, malware, privacy leaks and loss of control. We then discuss potential countermeasures spanning across the system lifecycle including robust training data processes, algorithm hardening, cybersecurity best practices tailored for robots, safety engineering techniques and regulation Ahmad *et al.* [1]. Finally, open challenges are highlighted including the evolving dynamics between attacks and defences, lack of verification methods for complex learned models and need for standardised benchmarks to systematically evaluate AI robotics security.

1.1. Rise of AI Robotics

AI techniques used in robotics include machine learning, neural networks, computer vision, reinforcement learning, planning and knowledge representation Belk, [2]. By learning from experience and data, robots can acquire capabilities like: Computer Vision, Natural language processing, Reinforcement learning and Motion planning.

These learned capabilities allow robots to operate autonomously in complex, unstructured real-world environments and enable applications across manufacturing, transportation, healthcare, surveillance and the home Belk, [2]. The market for AI-enabled robots is expected to grow significantly in coming years. However, reliance on learning also introduces distinct security considerations.

1.2. Security Considerations in AI Robotics

- Unlike pre-programmed deterministic robots, AI-enabled robots have unique security vulnerabilities:
- Dependence on training data—Performance depends heavily on large training datasets which could be manipulated by adversaries.
- Complex learned models—The reasoning inside models like deep neural networks can be difficult for humans to interpret. Logic is not hardcoded.

- Unpredictable emergent behaviour—Reinforcement learning policies lead to complex emerging behaviours that are challenging to verify in advance.
- Integration with IT systems—Network connectivity introduces cyber-attack surfaces. Cloud reliance increases potential targets.
- Interaction with humans—Safety critical if robots operate in close proximity with humans. Loss of control could lead to harm.

This necessitates a new security paradigm spanning the entire system lifecycle compared to traditional IT systems or robotics. In the next section, we discuss specific threats that exploit these inherent vulnerabilities Brady, [3].

Table 1: AI robotics security threats.

Threat category	Example threats
Data threats	Data poisoning, data leakage
Algorithm threats	Adversarial examples, model extraction
Platform threats	Malware, hardware trojans
Ecosystem threats	Patching complexity, supply chain risks
Human threats	Loss of control, privacy leaks

2. Background

Before analysing specific threats and countermeasures, we first provide background on how artificial intelligence enables robotic capabilities and unique security considerations compared to traditional robotics.

2.1. Artificial Intelligence for Robotics

Artificial intelligence (AI) is transforming robotics by providing the ability to perform complex tasks in unstructured real-world environments. AI approaches used in robotics include: Machine learning, deep learning, reinforcement learning Brady, [3], computer vision, natural language processing and knowledge representation

By applying these techniques, robots can autonomously perform complex tasks such as:

- Scene understanding—Analyse visual scenes to detect, categorise and locate objects and positions even in cluttered environments. Enables navigation and manipulation.
- Motion planning—Plan collision-free trajectories and motions to achieve goals using search algorithms. Can incorporate dynamic constraints.
- Object manipulation—Grasp, lift, move and place objects by coordinating perceptions with motions.

- Human–robot interaction—Understand natural language commands, gesture, gaze and proceed with verbal dialog Chen and Luca, [4].
- Reinforcement learning control—Learn robot controllers and policies through experience interacting with the environment and people to maximise rewards.

AI is a key enabler for robot autonomy, allowing robots to handle ambiguity and adaptivity compared to pre-programmed control. However, this reliance on data and learned models also introduces new security considerations.

2.2. *Unique Security Challenges in AI Robotics*

While AI provides many benefits, it also creates distinct security risks compared to traditional robotic systems:

- Reliance on potentially vulnerable training data—Performance depends heavily on the quantity and quality of data used for training machine learning models. This data could be manipulated or poisoned by adversaries.
- Complex opaque learned models—The reasoning inside models like deep neural networks can be difficult for humans to interpret and verify. Logic is not hardcoded.
- Unpredictable emergent behaviour—Reinforcement learning based robot controllers lead to complex interactive behaviours that are challenging to fully predict or test in advance.
- Tight integration with IT systems—Network connectivity and reliance on cloud platforms expands the potential cyber-attack surface.
- Physical interaction with humans—Failures or loss of control pose direct safety risks if robots closely interact with humans in physical spaces.
- Ecosystem complexity - Supply chains, heterogeneous fleets, frequent updates and fragmented standards create security management challenges.

These factors necessitate proactive security across the entire system lifecycle from data to algorithms to platforms and integration Knasel, [5]. Security cannot be an afterthought in AI robotics—it must be ingrained into the design process. Next, we elaborate on specific threats that exploit these inherent vulnerabilities.

3. AI Robotics Security Threats

It include data, algorithms, platforms, ecosystem and Human elements

Figure 1: *AI robotics security threat categories.*

3.1. Data Threats

Data is a key enabler for AI algorithms Knasel, [5]. The quantity and quality of data used to train machine learning models heavily influences their performance. However, data can also be the target of different attacks: data poisoning, data leakage Knasel, [5] and data snooping.

Robust data governance and cybersecurity controls (Aditya P. Mathur. 2020) are critical across the data lifecycle to address these threats as data forms the foundation for AI algorithms.

3.2. Algorithm Threats

Given a trained AI model, adversaries can craft malicious inputs designed to induce intentional failures: Evasion attacks, Model inversion, Model extraction Lozano-Perez, [6], Model poisoning and logic corruption.

Defenses aim to harden models against these threats through techniques like adversarial training, sandboxing and formal verification Lozano-Perez, [6].

3.3. Platform Threats

The underlying computing platforms including hardware, software and connectivity introduce cybersecurity risks: Malware infections, rootkit attacks, hardware trojans, remote cyber-attacks and privacy leaks.

3.4. Ecosystem Threats

Securing robot fleets and integrations with broader systems poses challenges: Patching complexity, Supply chain risks Okamoto, [7] and Ecosystem fragmentation.

3.5. Human Threats

The presence of humans working with robots raises additional safety and ethical concerns: Loss of control, misuse, privacy and social engineering.

Governance frameworks encompassing regulation, codes of ethics and engineering best practices are emerging to address societal impacts of AI robots Okamoto, [7].

4. Security Countermeasures

In this section, we discuss promising techniques and best practices to counter the security threats facing AI-enabled robotics across the lifecycle.

4.1. Securing Training Data

Since performance depends heavily on training data quality Tasioulas, [8], organisations need robust data governance encompassing: Provenance tracking, access control, continuous monitoring, configuration control and privacy protections Salman, [12]

4.2. Hardening Algorithms

Various techniques make AI models more robust and secure: Adversarial training, Anomaly detection, Sandboxing, Formal Verification and interpretability

4.3. Platform Cybersecurity

AI robotics requires a Défense-in-depth approach common in IT security:

- Network segmentation—Isolate robots from general networks with role-based access control.
- Behavioural monitoring—Detect anomalies in traffic and behaviours indicative of malware.
- Encryption—Secure communications between robots, operators and cloud services.
- Hardware roots of trust—Use hardware protected encryption keys to verify integrity of firmware and software Tasioulas, [8].
- Principle of least privilege—Only provide software access to necessary robot functions and resources.

4.4. Securing Ecosystems

Improving ecosystem security requires: Information sharing, Secure remote updates, Supply chain security, Compliance testing

4.5. Safe Development

Safety and ethics should be ingrained across the development lifecycle: Interpretability, Fail-safes, Validation & verification and Regulations & standards

Table 2: Overview of AI robotics security countermeasures.

Focus Area	Example Countermeasures
Data security	Provenance tracking, Access control, Privacy protections
Algorithm security	Adversarial training, Anomaly detection, Formal verification
Platform security	Network segmentation, Behavioural monitoring, Hardware roots of trust
Ecosystem security	Information sharing, Secure updates, Supply chain security, Compliance testing
Human safety	Interpretability, Fail safes, Validation and verification, Standards

5. Open Challenges

Table 3: Open challenges in securing AI robotics.

Challenge	Description
Evolving attack-Défense dynamics	Continuous innovation needed to counter new attack techniques in an ongoing arms race between adversaries and defenders.
Verifying learned models	Testing alone is insufficient to guarantee safety. Formal verification methods for complex neural networks and learning systems remain immature.
Lack of benchmarks	Standardised benchmarks needed to systematically evaluate security of AI robots under realistic conditions.
Interdisciplinary expertise	Holistic security requires synthesising specialised knowledge across domains like ML, cybersecurity, robotics, formal verification, safety engineering and ethics.
Legacy systems integration	Integrating AI into legacy platforms not designed for security poses significant difficulties.

6. Conclusion

As AI-enabled robotics continue proliferating into physical spaces and sensitive domains, the following conclusions and recommendations can help guide future progress:

1. Security must be ingrained early across the entire lifecycle Wang and Siau, [10] - from data collection, through algorithm design, platform hardening Vrontis *et al.* [9], and integration testing.
2. Investment into explainable and verifiable AI techniques is critical, especially for safety-critical applications, to build trust and enable auditing.
3. Common standards for securing robotics platforms, applications and data are urgently needed to improve Défense and manage complex fleets.
4. More extensive education on AI security threats and ethical obligations is required for practitioners and leadership across robotics, engineering and AI.
5. Proactive collaboration between cybersecurity, machine learning and robotics experts from both industry and academia
6. Regulators may need to intervene as risks increase to ensure the societal benefits of AI robotics are realised while protecting the public. Policy and legal frameworks will help align development with social priorities.

References

[1] Ahmad, T., D. Zhang, C. Huang, H. Zhang, N. Dai,, Y. Song, and H. Chen, "Artificial intelligence in sustainable energy industry: Status Quo, challenges and opportunities," *J. Cleaner Prod.*, vol. 289, no. 289, p. 125834, 2021, [online], doi: 10.1016/j.jclepro.2021.125834.

[2] Belk, R., "Ethical issues in service robotics and artificial intelligence," *Serv. Ind. J.*, vol. 41, no. 13–14, pp. 1–17, 2020, doi: 10.1080/02642069.2020.1727892.

[3] Brady, M., "Artificial intelligence and robotics," *Artif. Intell.*, vol. 26, no. 1, pp. 79–121, 1985, doi: 10.1016/0004-3702(85)90013-x.

[4] Chen, Y. and G. D. Luca, "Technologies supporting artificial intelligence and robotics application development," *J. Artif. Intell. Technol.*, vol. 1, no. 1, pp. 1–8, 2021, doi: 10.37965/jait.2020.0065.

[5] Knasel, T. M. "Artificial intelligence in manufacturing: Forecasts for the use of artificial intelligence in the USA," *Robotics*, vol. 2, no. 4, pp. 357–362, 1986, doi: 10.1016/0167-8493(86)90009-4.

[6] Lozano-Perez, T., "Robotics," *Artif. Intell.*, vol. 19, no. 2, pp. 137–143, 1982, doi: 10.1016/0004-3702(82)90033-9.

[7] Okamoto, T., "An artificial intelligence membrane to detect network intrusion," *Artif. Life Rob.*, vol. 16, no. 1, pp. 44–47, 2011, doi: 10.1007/s10015-011-0880-5.

[8] Tasioulas, J., "*First steps towards an ethics of robots and artificial intelligence*," 2019 [online] papers.ssrn.com, https://papers.ssrn.com/sol3/papers.cfm?abstract_id=3413639.

[9] Vrontis, D., M. Christofi, V. Pereira, S. Tarba, A. Makrides, and E. Trichina, "Artificial intelligence, robotics, advanced technologies and human resource management: a systematic review," *Int. J. Hum. Resour. Manage.*, vol. 33, no. 6, pp. 1–30, 2021.

[10] Wang, W. and K. Siau, "Artificial intelligence, machine learning, automation, robotics, future of work and future of humanity: a review and research agenda," *J. Database Manage.*, 2019, [online], https://www.igi-global.com/article/artificial-intelligence-machine-learning-automation-robotics-future-of-work-and-future-of-humanity/230295.

[11] Chuadhry, M. A., M. R. Gauthama Raman, and P. M. Aditya, "Challenges in machine learning based approaches for real-time anomaly detection in industrial control systems," *Proceedings of the 6th ACM on Cyber-Physical System Security Workshop (Taipei, Taiwan) (CPSS '20)*, Association for Computing Machinery, New York, NY, pp. 23–29, 2020 doi: 10.1145/3384941.3409588.

[12] Salman, A., Y. Xiao, K. Z. Snow, G. Tan, F. Monrose, and D. (Daphne) Yao, "Methodologies for quantifying (re-)randomization security and timing under JIT-ROP," *Proceedings of the ACM SIGSAC Conference on Computer and Communications Security (CCS'20)*, Association for Computing Machinery, New York, NY, pp. 1803–1820, 2020. doi: 10.1145/3372297.3417248.

05. Fuzzy Logic Based System for Checking the Eligibility of Placement Students using DBSCAN Algorithm

Preeti Khurana and Akhil Gupta

School of Electronics and Electrical Engineering, Lovely Professional University, Phagwara, India

Abstract: In the ever-evolving landscape of modern education and workforce dynamics, the efficient selection of eligible placement students stands as a pivotal concern for educational institutions and prospective employers alike. This paper underscores the significance of assessing students' eligibility for placement opportunities. To achieve this, the DBSCAN algorithm is employed to scrutinise students' qualifications and fuzzy logic is harnessed to formulate the criteria for placing students with potential employers. The workflow of this system is a multi-stage process that encompasses data preprocessing, the transformation of input variables into fuzzy sets, the application of fuzzy rules for inference, defuzzification of the output and the establishment of a decision threshold for determining eligibility. The amalgamation of this system into the placement process presents a more intelligent and data-driven approach to evaluate students' preparedness for career opportunities. By leveraging sophisticated techniques like DBSCAN and fuzzy logic, educational institutions and employers can make more informed decisions, ensuring a mutually beneficial placement experience for students and organisations.

Keywords: Clustering, DBSCAN, fuzzy logic, placement, eligibility, KDD.

1. Introduction

This report covers the data mining activities of various elements of DBSCAN. Generally, data mining is the process of finding knowledge from large amount of data or repository and also gives us the interesting patterns which help in increasing the sale/revenue of the company. Data processing package is one in all variety of analytical tools for analysing data. Data mining helps users to investigate the data from various dimensions or angles, categories and also summarises the relationships known [1–3].

2. Data Mining Parameters

- Association—it looks for the patterns where one event is connected to another.
- Sequence or path analysis—it is a straightforward extension of multiple regression which looks for the patterns where one event leads to another later events.
- Classification—it looks for new patterns and also a supervised learning technique.
- Clustering - the process of organising objects into the groups whose members are similar in some or another way (unsupervised learning technique).
- Forecasting—it discover the patterns in data that can lead to reasonable predictions about the future. This is mining is known as predictive analytics.
- Data mining technique is based on the evolution of strategies built using parametric and non-parametric imputation methods. Data mining is the analysis step of the 'knowledge discovery in databases' process, or KDD [4–6], [25].

2.1. Multidimensional Statistical Analysis Include

- Meta-rule guided mining and data and knowledge visualisation
- Assessing data mining results
- Analyzing graph
- Image classification

2.2. KDD-Knowledge Discovery in Databases

It refers to the broad process of finding knowledge in data and emphasises the 'high-level' application of particular data mining methods. This widely used data mining technique is a process that includes data preparation and selection, data cleansing, incorporating prior knowledge on datasets and interpreting accurate solutions from the observed results [7–9].

2.3. Methods

- Partitioning methods: It is used for represent one of the object in the cluster.
- Hierarchical methods: In the hierarchical two approaches (1) agglomerative approach (bottom up) and (2) divisive approach (top down).
- Density-based methods: It is based on the distance between the object. It can filter our noise and outlier. It is use to find cluster shape and size in arbitrary.
- Grid-based methods: in the grid based method number of cell that from a grid structure. It dependent upon the number of cell. GBM processing time is fast.

- Model-based methods: It is tries to find the best fit of the model. Model-based clustering provides a framework for our knowledge about a domain. Model-based clustering generated data by a model. It define technical structure [17–19].

3. Clustering

The process of organising objects into groups whose members are similar in some way. While doing cluster analysis, we first partition the set of data into groups based on data similarity and then assign the labels to the groups. It is adaptable to changes and helps single out useful features that distinguish different groups [10–12].

It is used in various applications in the real world such as data mining, voice mining and image processing. It is important in real world in certain fields. It is use for study the internal structure of a complex dataset [13–16], [29, 30]

3.1. Requirements of Clustering in Data Mining

- Scalability
- High dimensionality
- Ability to deal with noisy data
- Interpretability
- Choice of variable
- Choice of object
- Choice of missing data strategy
- Ability to deal with different kinds of
- Discovery of clusters with attribute shape
- Number of cluster

4. DBSCAN Algorithm

Density-based spatial clustering of applications with Noise (DBSCAN): DBSCAN is used to reduce the cost and improve the accuracy and great research value. It based on the threshold value. DBSCAN is sensitive to the setting of parameter and analyse cluster for large datasets. In the DBSCAN we check density is reachable or not.

1. *DBSCAN algorithm has two parameters*

    - E: The radius of our neighbourhoods around a data point p and maximum radius of neighborhood.
    - Min Points.: The minimum number of data points in the EPS-neighbourhood of a point.

2. *DBSCAN categories the data points into three categories*

- Core Points: A data point p is a core point and dense neighbourhood.
- Border Points: A data point q is a border point. The border point in cluster but neighbourhood is not dense.

3. *Following steps of DBSCAN algorithm*

Inputs are minimum radius EPS, minimum number of points (min points.), threshold value of evaluate (r1), threshold value angle (a), core points (d), datasets (D)

4. *Algorithm processing steps*

- Select the appropriate clustering point and distribute data into several regions. Storing the data points in cluster through the threshold value.
- If the number of data points is greater than min points, then mark it as a core point otherwise non-core point.
- The core point put in the cluster and non-core point discard.
- Repeat the process again and again until get all clusters.
- After all process connect the marked point in the cluster. After the point marked the cluster in any shape and size.
- DBSCAN produce the output in arbitrary shape and size. In the form of cluster.

5. Fuzzy Logic System

ANFIS classifier. Generally, fuzzy logic is the process of handling the accurate uncertainty and accurate reasoning. Through this we can control many things [20].

In the fuzzy logic the Boolean values is defined in this Boolean values defined by 0 and through the fuzzy logic we can find true and false values. Fuzzy logic solve the mathematical problems. It is computer based [21].

The fuzzy logic is based on the input and the work depends upon the possibility of level. Variables of fuzzy logic [27]:-

- Rules
- Fuzzifier
- Intelligence
- De-fuzzifier

5.1. Algorithm of Fuzzy Logic system

- Linguistic variable
- Membership function
- Knowledge base of rules
- Fuzzification
- Evaluate rules in the rule base

- Combine each rule
- De-fuzzification

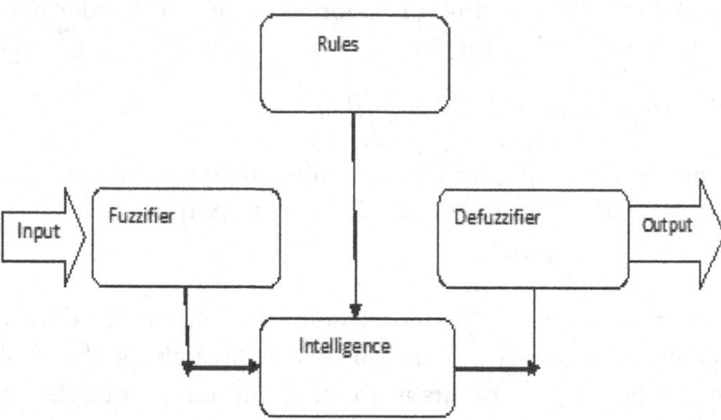

Figure 1: Fuzzy system interface.

The input set is fuzzifier and the output set is de-fuzzifier [28]. Rules and the intelligence for level of possibility of output to achieve the defined result [22]. It is represented in Figure 1.

5.2. Architecture

These are the inputs and the size depend upon the x. The XμA:X [0,1]. The X size is [23, 24]. It is also represented in Figure 2.

5.3. Advantages of Fuzzy System

- Used for solving complex problems
- It is decision making
- It is easy to understand
- We can add and delete rules easily
- It uses in the medicine field

5.4. Disadvantage of Fuzzy Logic System

- Time consuming
- Configuration depending upon disjunction and conjunction
- Look-up table for implementation
- Having a huge software
- Use Non-standard file format
- Less understandability

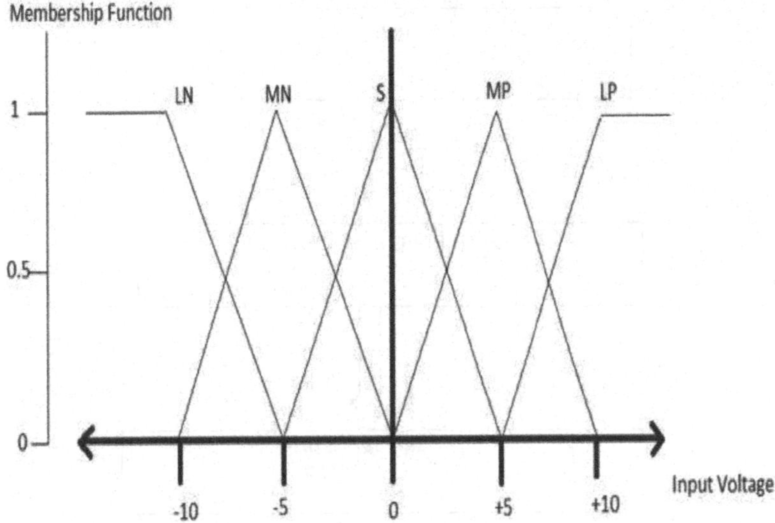

Figure 2: Architecture of fuzzy logic system.

6. Methods

Many institutional bodies to analyse the performance of students and it can be used before placements so that they will get to know their placement level and also help in identify the area students lacking.

6.1. Technique for Improving Placement Area

- Career counseling
- Know their lack area
- Know their strong area
- Effect on future
- Survey
- Survey filled by student
- Check and validate
- Decision
- Making the data sets of students
- Checking the eligibility and non-eligibility of student
- Eligibility student validate for company
- The technique for the survey is as shown in Figure 3:

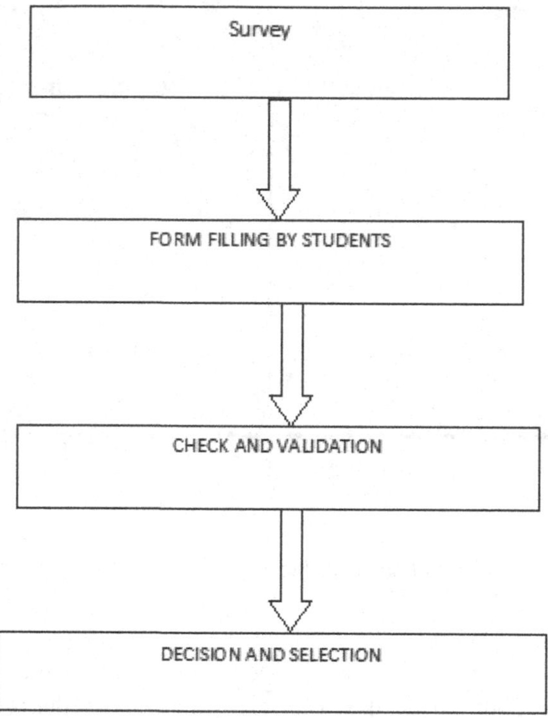

Figure 3: Survey technique.

In this we make a survey that is filled by the students after we check the validation then we take decision. To the decision the students are selected.

6.2. Objectives

The prime objectives of the paper are:

- Optimisation of clustering algorithm for customised results based on specific set of inputs.
- Analysis of student's placements data for finding probability of getting placed by using optimised clustering algorithm.
- To improve the DBSCAN algorithm to analyse cluster for large datasets. For this algorithm the data points are proposed, the data point are singular form of data and for providing the result.
- A cluster is defined as a maximal set of density-connected points and it is use to make cluster in arbitrary shape and size

For this following factors are kept in mind

- EPS-neighbourhood of a point
- Direct density reachable
- Based on threshold value
- A cluster is formed when the number of neighbours is greater than or equal to Min points. If the number of neighbours is less than min points, the point is marked as noise

6.2.1 Campus Placement Criteria

Campus Placement Each Company which are visited in campus have its own difference criteria of selection. Before placement starts College/University notified all the students for companies are visiting to the campus. General eligibility for most on/off campus is 60% right from the Semester and is shown in Figure 4.

Requirements for Campus Placement Selection

- 60 % Throughout Minimum Marks
- 70 % attendance
- Number Back Logs
- Age Less Than 25 years

The Four Main Sections of a Placement

- Introduction to yourself, Aptitude Test, Group Discussion (GD), Interview (Technical + HR)

Aptitude Test consists of basic problem solving like quantitative ability, logical reasoning and verbal ability. AMCAT/GATE students always have upper hand to clear aptitude test.

Group discussion not all companies take GD for Placement. GD basically is to check student's communications skills for interaction with other people.GD also used to improve interpersonal skills and intrapersonal skills for students. Experts is keeping monitoring group discussion during the discussion process between different participations Experts give marks you on the basis of the content and conduct which are discussed on give topic.

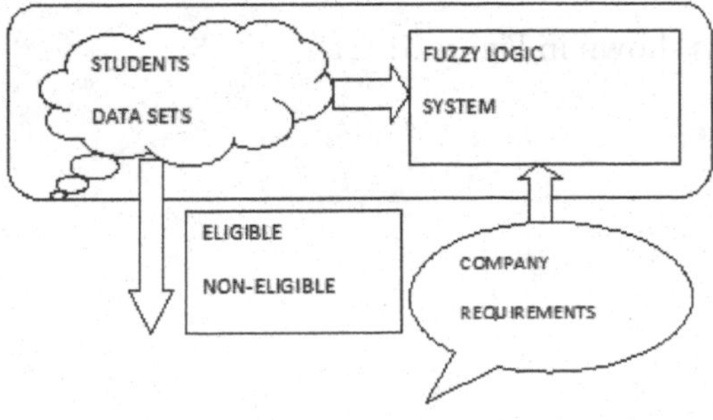

Figure 4: Student eligibility and non-eligibility.

6.3. Research Methodology

Methodology should explain what you did, with any refinements that you make as your work progressed. Research methodology that is using questionnaires. This research aims at discovering better understanding of a topic and the methodology using DBSCAN algorithm and tools (WEKA TOOL and MATLAB) and ARFF format. Participants included in this study are 150 of L.P.U (Lovely Professional University) all the participant in this study will be volunteer. Male and female are the participant. Few participants will be enlisted from the 'SURVEY OF PLACEMENT SESSION USING DBSCAN ALGORITHM AND FUZZY LOGIC' pool by making up on sheet and by comfort examining. The design of research paper is non experimental. It is helpful for placement of the students. Survey is the method of collection of data and facts about well-defined situation or issue from the target population through the written and oral questioning.

In this survey, I using the well-defined tool that is "WEKA TOOL or MATLAB" after applying this tool, DBSCAN is being used for improving the performance. Then, the required outcome will be presented in the form of result that will benefit: it helps in improving performance.

Some ON Campus Companies required those Students which are Cleared AMCAT/GATE Exam for Placement criteria. Companies Set up this criteria to select well qualified students with Technical skill set. College/University Select 150 students for On Campus Placement. Where students record are match with Companies' Minimum Requirements skill set. Companies minimum requirements skills vary According to the different companies Procedure. Every Company setup its own requirement criteria for selection of the students. All the Eligible are Selected for Campus Placement Exam. Eligible student are mark for the examination set. On-Eligible are Detained from the Placement cell.

Process of Running

- Define the inputs of datasets
- Sugeno model
- Fuzzy logic
- Company requirements
- Rules

Process of working is shown in Figure 5:

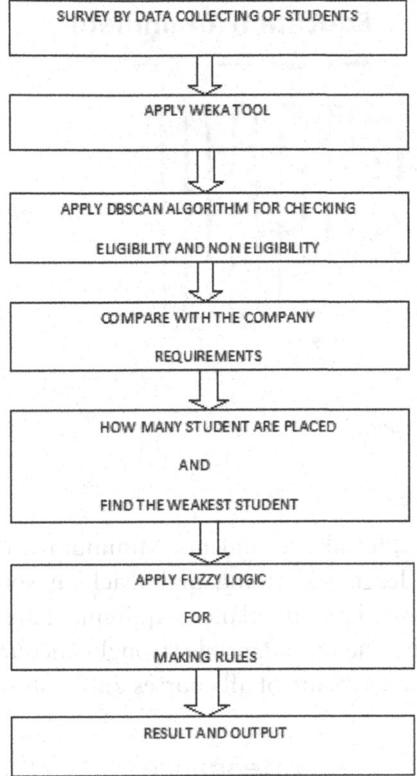

Figure 5: *Working process.*

In this collecting the data through the survey apply DBSCAN & Fuzzy Logic and after find output.

7. Results

7.1. Experimental Result

Student Requirements for Finding the Eligibility

7.1.1. Education Attainment

Education attainment is the form of individual and highest degree and is shown in Figure 6.

- Academic Achievements
- Bachelor's degree
- Education attainment is the United States.
- Master degree

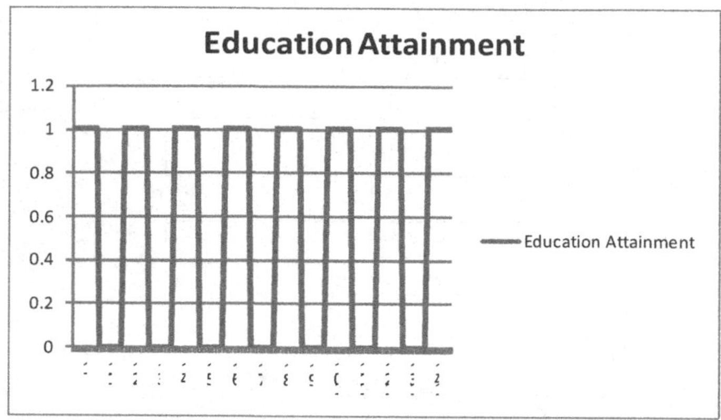

Figure 6: Education attainment.

7.1.2 Attendance Required

The attendance is required for all the students. Minimum attendance is requirement for company 70% for learn something and teaching something new. Student whose attendance is bellow than attendance requirement are not able to attend the company and assessment. The attendance is strongly encouraged for the students. Attendance is specific requirements of all courses and is shown in Figure 7.

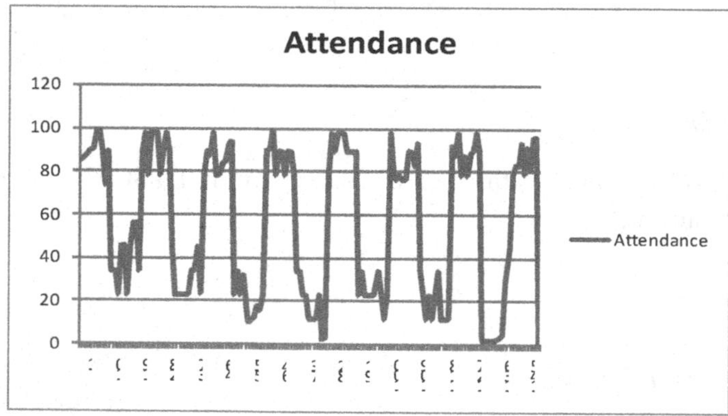

Figure 7: Attendance.

7.1.3 Gate Exam

Graduate aptitude test in engineering. It is mainly for getting the eligibility in the companies. All the paper of gate exam will be taken by online and all are computer based. GATE exam is prestigious competitiv.e exam in India. It is for knowledge of student and graduate level subject in engineering. The student performance is reflected by the gate score. For M.E/M.Tech gate exam and is shown in Figure 8.

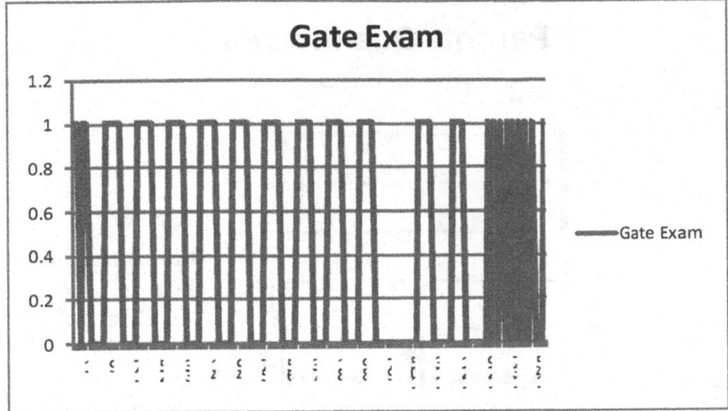

Figure 8: Gate exam.

7.1.4 AMCAT Exam

Aspiring Mind's Computer Adaptive Test. The AMCAT test is for checking aptitude, skills, personality, English, quant and logical, etc. Through the AMCAT exam, we can get easily job. It is recognised by multiple companies HCL and Sonata, etc. and is shown in Figure 9.

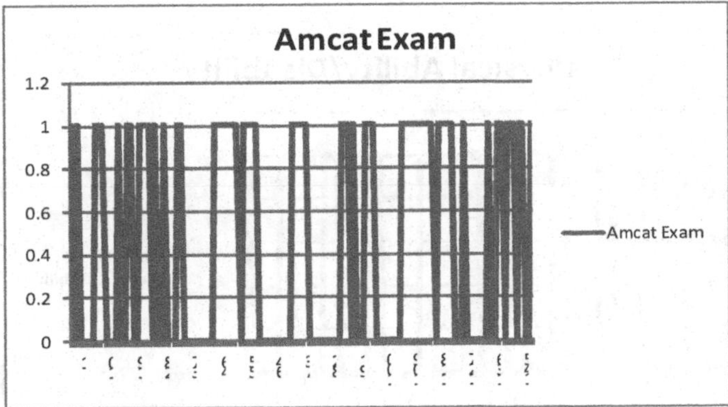

Figure 9: AMCAT exam.

7.1.5 Parents Qualification

Parents are the main important role in our life. Parent's role in children shaping and adulating lives of their children. Parents invest their time and money and is shown in Figure 10 and focusing on

- Educational attainment
- Employment and economic
- Early childbearing
- Mental, health.

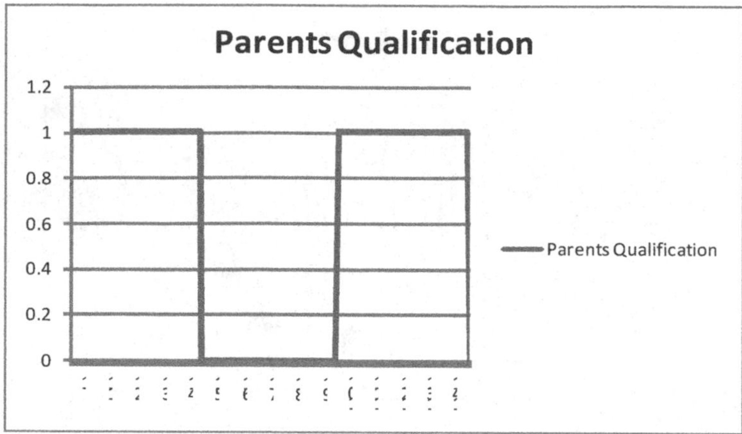

Figure 10: Parents qualification.

7.1.6 Physical Ability/Disability

Physical ability/disability is not much important. Ability means person is able to perform well at something and somewhere. Disability means the limit or challenges. Disability not means a person is not able to perform any task or not able to doing any job and is shown in Figure 11.

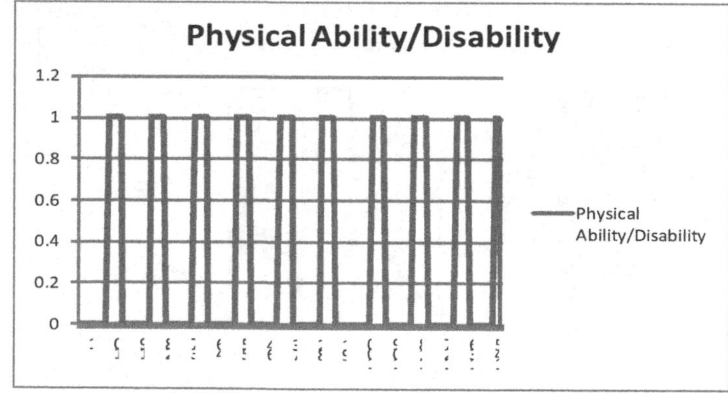

Figure 11: Physical ability/disability.

7.1.7 Training Certificate

Training certificate means you have proof to make sure the student's ability. It is mean you have knowledge about that. It's mean you have skills and knowledge when employers are looking to hire. Training certificate means legalise your knowledge and experience and is shown in Figure 12.

Figure 12: Training certificate.

7.1.8 Skills

Skills are important for asking a question and expressing an opinion. Dealing with telephonic conversation in a good way. Skills are important for interaction to each other and is shown in Figure 13. Some points of skills

- Tech Knowledge
- Verbal Communication
- Group Discussion
- Interview

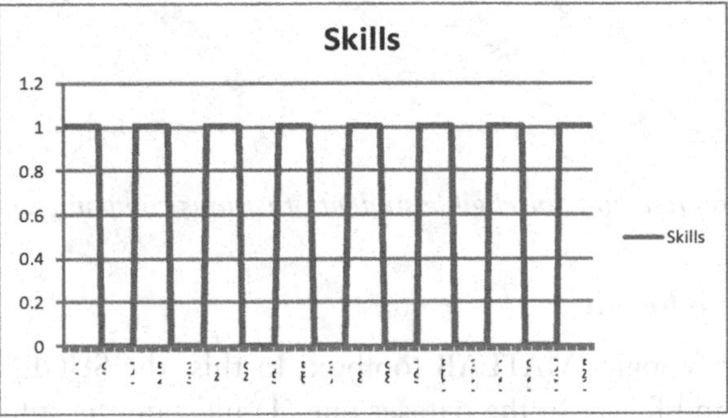

Figure 13: Skills.

7.1.9 Experienced or Not

Experience means having become skilful or knowledgeable from extensive contact or participation or observation. Education provides you the theoretical knowledge and skill to show why it does not work. Education develops your speed of learning and ability to learn. Experience that teach you the way of doing any work. Some companies provide eligibility on experience based and some companies have no criteria and is shown in Figure 14.

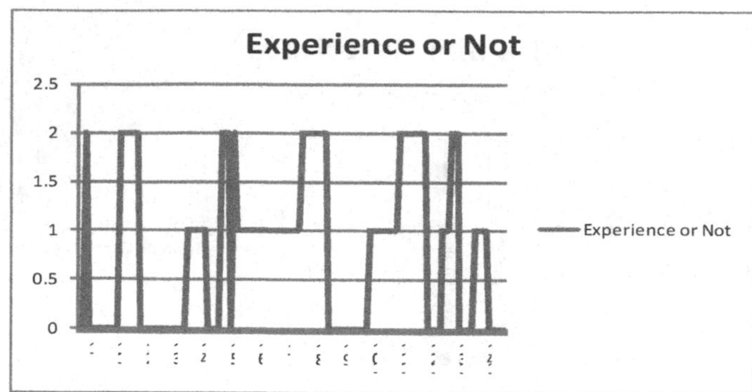

Figure 14: Experience or not.

7.1.10 Final Outcome of Students

Graph representing the eligible students for companies and is shown in Figure 15.

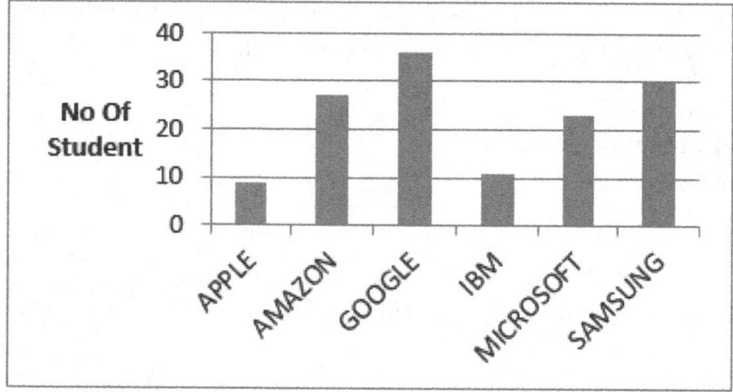

Figure 15: Graph representing the eligible student of various companies.

7.2. Comparative Result

Based on the 'fuzzy logic' MATLAB toolbox. In this, the SUGENO provide the output constant and linear. In the dataset one (1) indicate the student is qualified and the skills are matching with the companies and the zero (0) indicate the student is non-qualified and the skills are not matching with the companies. Information about company and student

- Six different companies have visited to the on campus drive for 150 student's selection process
- Students which are cleared AMCAT/GATE exam will only selected on interview (HR) base round for selection procedure
- Every company has its own placement exam procedure requirements for selection. Student's skills are mostly counted during the selection process.

- 150 students have clear placement criteria exam for different companies. Company matches their requirements with different student records.
- Some students are selected in multiple companies .Students has its own choice to select which company to be choosing.
- Students training certificate and training during the graduation/post-graduation are seen during the interview round.

Before any company which are visit to the campus .The placement cell prepare there all students for recruitment exam. Students are prepared for the exam which are conduct before placement the collage management ask different companies to recruitment students from the college/university.

Companies are authorised by college/university top level management. Placement cell H.O.D send E-mail to the all students from different department to notify that companies are visiting to the on campus drive placement. Students which are selected from different departments/branches.

8. Conclusion and Future Work

8.1. Conclusion

In this paper, we will conclude the results as the probability of students being placed in the company or what additional inputs we will give to the student by analysing various parameters so that the probability of placing in a company will be increased by applying improved DBSCAN algorithm. In this report, I have presented the literature review and methodology of the work that I will carry next. In this report for making rules using the fuzzy logic.

8.2. Future Work

- Find the probability of the student
- Find how many students are placed
- For finding the weakest students by survey
- what will output and benefit for students
- Reduce the time and complexity
- Produce cluster in arbitrary shape and size
- Improving the performance of the student
- Reduce the data points
- It is pioneer density-based algorithm
- We can find cluster in any arbitrary shape and size
- We can use to check time award
- It improve accuracy and great research value

Orcid id

Akhil Gupta: 0000-0002-0054-3801

References

[1] Kalra, M., "Data mining of heterogeneous data with research challenges," 2016.

[2] Li, M., D. Meng, S. Gu, and S. Liu, "Research and improvement of DBSCAN cluster algorithm," *Proc. - 2015 7th Int. Conf. Inf. Technol. Med. Educ. ITME 2015*, pp. 537–540, 2016.

[3] Dharni, C. and M. Bnasal, "An improvement of DBSCAN Algorithm to analyze cluster for large datasets," *Proc. 2013 IEEE Int. Conf. MOOC, Innov. Technol. Educ. MITE 2013*, pp. 42–46, 2013.

[4] Hassanin, M. F., M. Hassan, and A. Shoeb, "DDBSCAN: different densities-based spatial clustering of applications with noise," *2015 Int. Conf. Control Instrum. Commun. Comput. Technol. ICCICCT 2015*, pp. 401–404, 2016.

[5] Jianzhuo, Y., Q. Mengyao, F. Liying, W. Ying, and Y. Jianyun, "Forecast the distribution of urban water point by using improved DBSCAN algorithm," *Proc. 2013 3rd Int. Conf. Intell. Syst. Des. Eng. Appl. ISDEA 2013*, vol. 2, pp. 784–786, 2013.

[6] Xu, Q. and M. Martin, "Implementation of a fast algorithm to Find Data Clusters," *Nucl. Sci. Symp. Conf. …*, pp. 1–3, 2001.

[7] Beri, S., "Hybrid framework for DBSCAN algorithm using fuzzy logic," no. Ablaze, pp. 383–387, 2015.

[8] Loh, W. K. and Y. K. Kim, "A GPU-accelerated density-based clustering algorithm," *Proc. – 4th IEEE Int. Conf. Big Data Cloud Comput. BDCloud 2014 with 7th IEEE Int. Conf. Soc. Comput. Networking, Soc. 2014 4th Int. Conf. Sustain. Comput. Commun. Sustain. 2014*, pp. 775–776, 2015.

[9] Thang, V. V., D. V. Pantiukhin, and A. I. Galushkin, "A hybrid clustering algorithm: the FastDBSCAN," *2015 Int. Conf. Eng. Telecommun.*, pp. 69–74, 2015.

[10] Khan, K., S. U. Rehman, K. Aziz, S. Fong, and S. Sarasvady, "DBSCAN : past, present and future," *Int. Conf. Applications Digit. Inf. Web Technol. (ICADIWT), 2014 Fifth Int. Conf.*, pp. 232–238, 2014.

[11] Borah, B. and D. K. Bhattacharyya, "An improved sampling-based DBSCAN for large spatial databases," *Int. Conf. Intell. Sens. Inf. Process. 2004. Proc.*, pp. 92–96, 2004.

[12] Wu, Y. P., J. J. Guo, and X. J. Zhang, "A linear DBSCAN algorithm based on LSH," *Proc. Sixth Int. Conf. Mach. Learn. Cybern. ICMLC 2007*, vol. 5, no. August, pp. 2608–2614, 2007.

[13] Baccar, N., M. Jridi, and R. Bouallegue, "Neuro-fuzzy localization in wireless sensor networks," *Signal, Image, Video and Communications (ISIVC), International Symposium on. IEEE*, 2016.

[14] Ravindran, R. M. "Classification of human emotions from EEG signals using filtering and ANFIS classifier," *Current Trends in Engineering and Technology (ICCTET), 2014 2nd International Conference on. IEEE*, 2014.

[15] Diab, A., A. Zaki, *et al.*, "Performance of doubly-fed induction generator based wind turbine using adaptive neuro-fuzzy inference system," *Strategic Technology (IFOST), 2016 11th International Forum on. IEEE*, 2016.

[16] Rotshtein, A., and H. Rakytyanska, "Adaptive refinement of fuzzy knowledge bases using trend rules and inverse inference," *Human System Interactions (HSI), 2015 8th International Conference on. IEEE*, 2015.

[17] Tchendjou, G. T., R. Alhakim, and E. Simeu, "Fuzzy logic modeling for objective image quality assessment," *Design and Architectures for Signal and Image Processing (DASIP), 2016 Conference on. IEEE*, 2016.

[18] Nayak, P., V. Bhavani, and M. Shanthi, "A fuzzy logic based dynamic channel allocation scheme for wireless cellular networks to optimize the frequency reuse," *Region 10 Conference (TENCON), 2016 IEEE*, IEEE, 2016.

[19] Devi, R., *et al.*, "Implementation of intrusion detection system using adaptive Neuro-Fuzzy inference system for 5G wireless communication network," *AEU-Int. J. Electron. Commun.*, vol. 74, pp. 94-106, 2017.

[20] Yager, R. R., and L. A. Zadeh, eds., *An Introduction to Fuzzy Logic Applications in Intelligent Systems*, Springer Science & Business Media, vol. 165, 2012.

[21] Yager, R. R., and L. A. Zadeh, eds. *An Introduction to Fuzzy Logic Applications in Intelligent Systems,* Springer Science & Business Media, vol. 165, 2012.

[22] Yager, R. R. and L. A. Zadeh, eds., *An Introduction to Fuzzy Logic Applications in Intelligent Systems*, Springer Science & Business Media, vol. 165, 2012.

[23] Yager R. R. and L. A. Zadeh, eds., *An Introduction to Fuzzy Logic Applications in Intelligent Systems*, Springer Science & Business Media, 2012 Dec. 6.

[24] Cruz, A., and N. C. E. Mestrado, *ANFIS: Adaptive Neuro-Fuzzy Inference Systems*, IM, UFRJ, Mestrado NCE, 2009.

[25] Witten, I. H., *et al.*, *Data Mining: Practical Machine Learning Tools and Techniques*, Morgan Kaufmann, 2016.

[26] Hellmann, M., *Fuzzy Logic Introduction*, Université de Rennes 1, 2001.

[27] Mendel, J. M., *Uncertain Rule-based Fuzzy Logic Systems: Introduction and New Directions*, Upper Saddle River: Prentice Hall PTR, 2001.

[28] Yager, R. R. and L. A. Zadeh, eds., *An Introduction to Fuzzy Logic Applications in Intelligent Systems*, Springer Science & Business Media, vol. 165, 2012.

[29] Sivanandam, S. N., S. Sumathi, and S. N. Deepa, *Introduction to Fuzzy Logic using MATLAB*, vol. 1, Berlin: Springer, 2007.

[30] Han, J., J. Pei, and M. Kamber, *Data Mining: Concepts and Techniques*, Elsevier, 2011.

06. Optical Character Recognition using Support Vector Machine

Nitika, Surbhi, Mir Junaid Rasool, Dr. Aarti, Richa Sharma, and Dr. Prakash Singh Tanwar

School of Electronics & Electrical Engineering, Lovely Professional University, Phagwara, India

Abstract: In the field of electronics and image processing; computer vision, artificial intelligence and pattern recognition has a great significance. Optical character recognition (OCR) has evolved a lot since the beginning and is one of the important aspects of pattern recognition. OCR converts the optical data, which is recognised from the readable characters into the digital form. Different approaches are clubbed with various methodologies for this purpose. In this paper, we are going to recognise optical characters using a very famous machine learning technique, support vector machine (SVM). SVM is a very powerful black box testing algorithm which classifies data by creating a hyperplane or line. The main reason for such programming is to process paper based records by changing over printed or written by hand message into an electronic structure to be spared in a database. In this paper, we are going to recognise optical character using SVM for different kernel parameters.

Keywords: Recognition, support vector, kernel functions, hyperplane.

1. Introduction

The support vector machine (SVM) was first proposed by Vapnik and has since attracted a high degree of interest in the machine learning research community [2]. Several recent studies have reported that the SVM generally are capable of delivering higher performance in terms of classification accuracy than the other data classification algorithms. SVM has been employed in a wide range of real world problems such as text categorisation, hand-written digit recognition, tone recognition, image classification and object detection, micro-array gene expression data analysis and data classification. It has been shown that SVM is consistently superior to other supervised learning methods. However, for some datasets, the performance of SVM is very sensitive to how the cost parameter and kernel parameters are set. As a result, the user normally needs to conduct extensive cross validation in order to figure out the optimal parameter setting. This process is commonly referred to as model selection. One practical issue with model selection is that this process is very time consuming. We have experimented with a number of parameters associated with the use of the SVM algorithm that can impact the results. This paper is organised as follows. In next section, we introduce some related background including some basic concepts of SVM, classification with hyperplanes and kernel selection. In Section 3, the dataset is described. In Section 4, we detail all experiments results. Finally, we have some conclusions in Section 5.

Boser, B. E. *et al.,* Upadhyay R. *et al.* worked on machine learning approach to solve fracture type identification using extra tree classifier. Upadhyay S. *et al.* applied machine learning to classify of benign-malignant pulmonary lung nodules using ensemble learning classifiers.

2. Support Vector Machine

A SVM is envisioned as a surface that creates a limit between the information plotted in multidimensional area that speaks to model and its component.

The objective is to make a straight limit called a hyperplane that separates the space to make genuinely uniform parcels on either side.

Fortunately, in spite of the fact that the math might be troublesome, the essential ideas are reasonable. SVMs can be adjusted for use with about any learning task, including both order and numeric forecast. Along these lines, in the rest of the areas, we will concentrate just on SVM classifiers.

2.1. Hyperplanes

SVMs utilise a limit called a hyperplane to parcel information into gatherings of comparable classes. At the point when the information is isolated flawlessly by the straight line or flat surface, they are said to be directly distinct. From the outset, we will consider just the straightforward situation where this is valid, yet SVMs can likewise be stretched out to issues where the focuses are not directly distinct.

In two dimensions, the assignment of the SVM calculation is to recognise a line that isolates the two classes. To locate the best parcel, a quest is accomplished for the maximum margin hyperplane (MMH) that makes the best partition between the two classes. The line that prompts the best partition will sum up the best to the future information. The maximum margin will improve the chance that, in spite of random noise, the points will remain on the correct side of the boundary.

The support vectors are the points from each class that are the closest to the MMH; each class must have at least one support vector, but it is possible to have more than one. Using the support vectors alone, it is possible to define the MMH. This is a key feature of SVMs; the support vectors provide a very compact way to store a classification model, even if the number of features is extremely large.

2.2. Linearly Separable Data

It is easiest to understand how to find the maximum margin under the assumption that the classes are linearly separable. In this case, the MMH is as far away as possible from the outer boundaries of the two groups of data points. These outer boundaries are known as the convex hull. The MMH is then the perpendicular bisector of the shortest line between the two convex hulls. Sophisticated computer algorithms that use a technique known as quadratic optimisation are capable of finding the maximum margin in this way.

An alternative (but equivalent) approach involves a search through the space of every possible hyperplane in order to find a set of two parallel planes that divide the points into homogeneous groups yet themselves are as far apart as possible. To comprehend this pursuit procedure, we have to characterise precisely what is hyperplane. In an n-dimensional space, the accompanying condition is utilised:

$$w' * x' + b = 0 \tag{1}$$

The 'over the letters demonstrate vectors as opposed to static variables. Specifically, w is a vector of different loads, and b is a static variable called as the predisposition.

Utilising this recipe, the objective of the procedure is to locate a lot of loads that determine two hyperplanes:

$$w' * x' + b >= +1 \tag{2}$$

$$w' * x' + b <= -1 \tag{3}$$

The data is directly divisible. The vector geometry characterises the separation between two planes as:

$$2/\|w'\| \tag{4}$$

Here ||w|| demonstrates Euclidean standard. Since ||w|| is in the denominator, to boost separation, we have to minimise||w||. The undertaking is regularly re communicated as a lot of requirements, as follows:

$$\min 1/2 * \|w'\|^2 \tag{5}$$

$$\text{s.t. } y_i (w' * x_i' - b) >= 1, \text{ for all } x_i$$

The primary line suggests that we have to limit the Euclidean standard (squared and isolated by two to make the figuring simpler). The subsequent line takes note of this is dependent upon the condition that every one of the yi information focuses is effectively ordered. Note that y shows the class esteem.

Similarly, as with the other strategy for finding the most extreme edge, finding an answer for this issue is an undertaking best left for quadratic streamlining programming.

2.3. Non-Linearly Separable Data

Imagine a scenario in which the data is not directly distinguishable. The answer for this is the utilisation of a slack variable which makes a delicate edge that enables a few to fall on the wrong side of edge. A cost factor is applied to all focuses that damage the requirements, and instead of finding the MMH, the calculation tries to limit the total expense.

We can in this way overhaul the enhancement issue to:

$$\min 1/2 \ ||w'||^2 + c \ \Sigma £_I \quad (6)$$

$$\text{s.t. } y_i (w' * x' - b) >= 1 - £_I, \text{ for all } x_i', £_i >= 0$$

The significant piece to comprehend is the addition of cost parameter. The more prominent the cost factor is the harder the enhancement will attempt to accomplish full separation.

2.4. Kernels for Non-Linear Spaces

In some genuine applications, the connections between variables are nonlinear. As we simply found, a SVM can in any case be prepared on such information through the slack variable which enables a few guides to be misclassified. In any case, this is not the best way to move toward the issue of nonlinearity. A key element of SVMs is their capacity to map issue into a higher measurement. In doing as such, a nonlinear relationship may abruptly seem, by all accounts, to be very direct. This is conceivable in light of the fact that we have acquired another point of view on the information. SVMs with nonlinear bits add extra dimensions to the information so as to make partition along these lines. The kernel $\phi(x)$ is a mapping of the information into other space. Therefore, the function applies some transformation to the support vectors *xi* and *xj*, combines them using the dot product, which takes two vectors as input and returns a single number as result.

$$K(x_i', \ x_j') = \phi(x_i') * \phi(x_j') \quad (7)$$

Utilising this structure, portion capacities have been created for a wide range of areas of data. A couple of the most normally utilised piece capacities are recorded as pursues. Almost all SVM programming bundles will incorporate these parts, among numerous others. The linear kernel does not change the data by any means. It can be expressed simply as:

$$K(x_i', \ x_j') = x_i' * x_j' \quad (8)$$

The polynomial kernel with degree *d* adds a non-linear transformation to the data:

$$K(x_i', \ x_j') = (x_i' * x_j' + 1)^d \quad (9)$$

The sigmoid bit brings about a SVM model to some degree closely resembling a neural arrange utilising a sigmoid enactment work. The Greek letters are used as kernel parameters:

$$K(x_i', \ x_j') = \tanh(k \ x_i' * x_j' - \delta) \quad (10)$$

There is no dependable principle to coordinate kernel to a specific learning. This fit depends on the idea that model has to learn. Experimentation is required via preparing and assessing a few SVMs on an approved dataset.

3. Dataset

The dataset utilised is taken from the UCI Machine Learning Data Repository (http://archive.ics.uci.edu/ml) by W. Frey and D. J. Record. It contains 20,000 instances of 26 English letters in order capital letters as printed utilising 20 distinctive arbitrarily reshaped and mutilated highly contrasting fonts. The following Figure 1, distributed by Frey and Slate, gives a case of a portion of the printed glyphs. The letters are used by a PC to distinguish, yet are effectively perceived by a person:

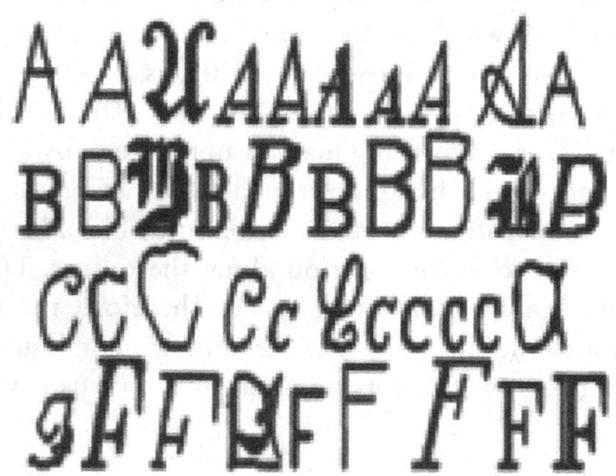

Figure 1: *20 distinctive arbitrarily reshaped and mutilated fonts*

As indicated by the documentation when the glyphs are checked into the PC they are changed over into pixels and 16 measurable traits are recorded. The qualities measure such attributes as vertical measurements of the glyph, the extent of dark pixels, and the normal even and vertical situation of the pixels. This information with the 16 highlights is what characterises every case of the letter class.

4. Results of Experiment

The optical character recognition (OCR) is done using R programming on Rstudio. To provide a baseline measure of SVM, ksvm() is used from kernlab library is used. In this experiment, different values of kernels parameter are selected to check the efficient recognition of optical character. The kernel function is utilised in preparing and foreseeing. This parameter can be set to any capacity, of class portion, which processes the internal item in include space between two vector contentions. The different kernel functions used to check the most accurate results.

The Table 1 shows the accuracy of each kernel function on OCR dataset:

Table 1: Accuracy of kernel function on OCR dataset

S. No.	Kernel Function	True	False	Accuracy
1.	Vanilladot	0.83925	0.16075	83.90%
2.	Polydot	0.83925	0.16075	83.90%
3.	Tanhdot	0.0845	0.9155	8%
4.	RBFdot	0.93125	0.06875	93.10%
5.	Laplacedot	0.8905	0.1095	89.05%
6.	Besseldot	0.70575	0.29425	70.5%

The following plot shows the accuracy of each kernel function in scatterplot:

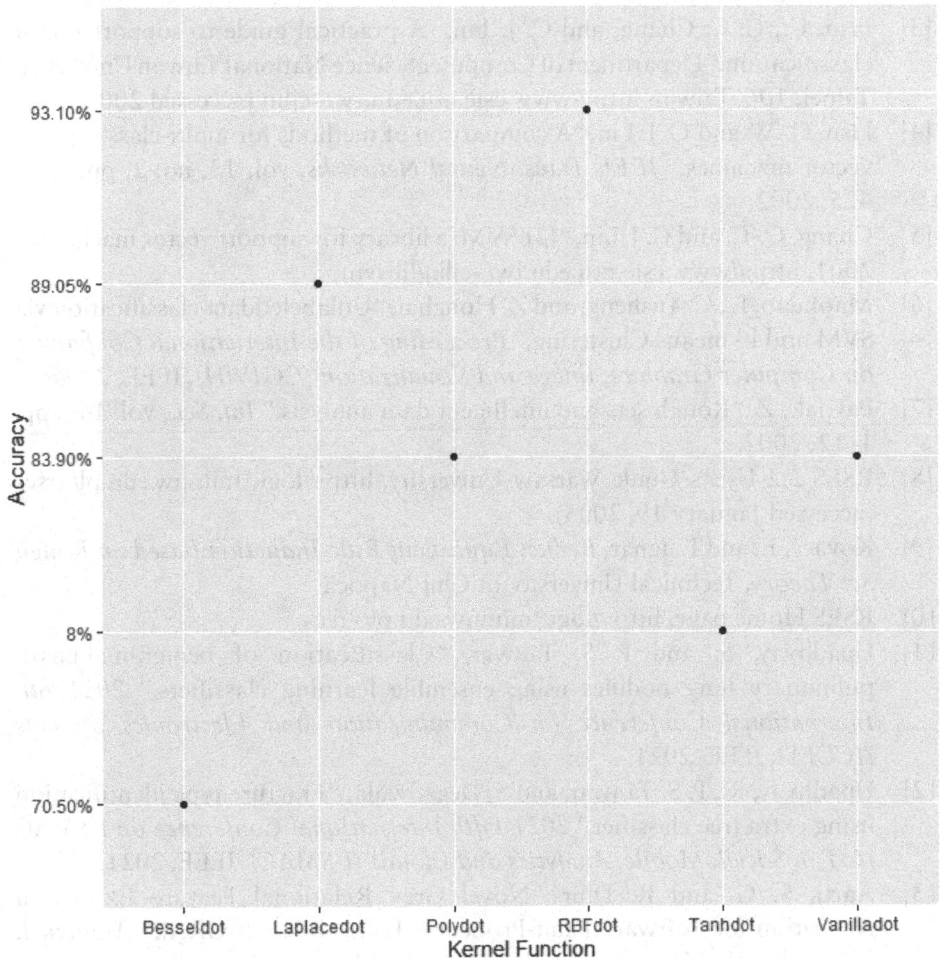

Figure 2: Kernel accuracy.

5. Conclusion

In this paper, we have demonstrated the outcomes utilising different kernel functions. Figure 2 shows the results of information tests using various kernel function. The test outputs are empowering .We can see from the results that the decision of kernel function is basic for a given measure of information. It shows that the best one among all is RBFdot for the recognition of optical character.

References

[1] Boser, B. E., I. Guyon, and V. Vapnik, "A training algorithm for optimal margin classifiers," *Proceedings of the Fifth Annual Workshop on Computational Learning Theory*, ACM Press, pp. 144–152, 1992.

[2] V. Vapnik, *The Nature of Statistical Learning Theory*, New York, NY: Springer-Verlag, 1995.

[3] Hsu, C., C. C. Chang, and C. J. Lin, "A practical guide to support vector classification," Department of Computer Science National Taiwan University, Taipei, 106, Taiwan http://www.csie.ntu.edu.tw/~cjlin (accessed 2007).

[4] Hsu, C.-W. and C. J. Lin, "A comparison of methods for multi-class support vector machines," *IEEE Trans. Neural Networks*, vol. 13, no. 2, pp. 415–425, 2002.

[5] Chang, C.-C. and C. J. Lin, "LIBSVM: a library for support vector machines," 2001, http://www.csie.ntu.edu.tw/~cjlin/libsvm.

[6] Maokuan, L., C. Yusheng, and Z. Honghai, "Unlabeleddata classification via SVM and k- means Clustering," *Proceeding of the International Conference on Computer Graphics, Image and Visualization (CGIV04)*, IEEE, 2004.

[7] Pawlak, Z. "Rough sets and intelligent data analysis," *Inf. Sci.*, vol. 147, pp. 1–12, 2002.

[8] RSES 2.2 User's Guide Warsaw University, http://logic.mimuw.edu.pl/»rses (accessed January 19, 2005).

[9] Kovacs, E. and L. Ignat, *Reduct Equivalent Rule Induction Based on Rough Set Theory*, Technical University of Cluj-Napoca.

[10] RSES Home page, http://logic.mimuw.edu.pl/»rses.

[11] Upadhyay, S. and P. S. Tanwar, "Classification of benign-malignant pulmonary lung nodules using ensemble learning classifiers," *2021 6th International Conference on Communication and Electronics Systems (ICCES)*, IEEE, 2021.

[12] Upadhyay, R., P. S. Tanwar, and S. Degadwala, "Fracture type identification using extra tree classifier," *2021 Fifth International Conference on I-SMAC (IoT in Social, Mobile, Analytics and Cloud) (I-SMAC)*, IEEE, 2021.

[13] Aarti, S. G. and R. Dhir, "Novel Grey Relational Feature Extraction Algorithm for Software Fault-Proneness Using BBO (B-GRA)," *Arabian J. Sci. Eng.*, vol. 45, no. 4, pp. 2645–2662, 2020.

[14] Aarti, S. G. and R. Dhir, "Empirical validation of object-oriented metrics on cross- projects with different severity levels," *Int. J. Comput. Syst. Eng. Inderscience*, vol. 5, no. 5/6, pp. 304-332, 2019.

[15] Aarti, S. G. and R. Dhir, "Grey relational classification algorithm for software fault- proneness with SOM clustering," *Int. J. Data Min. Modell. Manage., Inderscience*, vol. 12, no. 1, pp. 28-64, 2018.

07. Development of Fusion Based Cognitive Assisted Smart Room Automation System

Sachin Gupta[1*], Vijay Kumar[1], Rajeev Kanday[2], Shivali Gupta[3], Shaik Mohammed Raith[1]

[1]*Department of Robotics and Control, School of Electronics and Electrical Engineering, Lovely Professional University, Phagwara, India*
[2]*School of Computer Science and Engineering, Lovely Professional University, Phagwara*
[3]*School of Chemical Engineering and Physical Sciences, Lovely Professional University, Phagwara*

Abstract: As per progressive evolution in industry 4.0 and the implementation of sustainable development goals across the globe for betterment of human life on planet earth, the automation is playing a pivotal role in the smart application development. The buildings are getting smart and there is need to make the smart rooms for comfort of living persons. A fusion-based control strategy has been prepared and tested on LabVIEW 2015 platform for implementation and adoption by experts in the automation field for further research. In this control method, the outputs such as air conditioner, Room heater, fragrance injector, Wall Fan and Light system have been actuated with input from the fraction number-based array of sensors. The current algorithm will help the research community for many fields such as edge computing-based applications and IoT based tools.

Keywords: Sustainable development goal, room eco-system, fraction number-based control strategy, room automation system

1. Introduction

In this modern era, artificial intelligence is playing a significant role in designing of Robotics and Automation based applications [1]. With the advancement of these algorithmic approaches, it is very easy to automate the processes with more sensitive intelligence methods. The Artificial Intelligence has many approaches and have fusion of approaches. The blend of ANN, GA and fuzzy logic can assist in automating very complex and imaginary processes. The fusion-based AI is a heuristic-based metaphor approach which is getting popular in smart control applications. As per latest literature survey, there are various applications in robotics and mechatronics field where these approaches are implemented for supervisory control of complex tasks. The key features of fusion-based approach are that they can easily cater the wide sensor networks based input for sensory actuation of drives in a complex and tenacious processes. The Figure 1 is representing the Fusion of these AI methods in relation to Wide sensor network for intelligent decision taking approaches. In fusion-based control strategies, the concerned decision gates are tuned on multiple input values (Sensor data) for driving of concerned actuators and correspondingly calibrating the whole strategy as per requirement of end user. With the integration of parity-based search methods such as parity based, pattern based and random number, the searching and implementation of stored query is become fast and reliable for a machine to take the decisions in a befuddled situations like nuclear plants, Motion control and grid planning of robots, home automation etc. It has been observed from the existing literature that the fusion, based AI approach can be implemented in both small, mid and large-scale applications [2]. The key engine to implement this method is hybrid computation of processors on both edge and grid-based servers. Here is this paper, we have developed a smart room temperature control strategy by using the fusion based parallel node approach. In this method, the room temperature and parameters will be controlled and maintained according to out-rick of a person who will enter in the room [3]. This a one of the most significant and vital implication in relation to home automation applications where the smart rooms are developed to support the cognitive approach of a person to feel comfortable and relaxed in the room. The main purpose of intelligent room automation is how to relax a person in the room psychologically and mentally by governing the actuators such as Air conditioner, Heater, light, fragrance injector kind of appliances [4]. Figure 1 is showing the strategic approach related to design of intelligent room automation system in a hierarch's form. In this Block Diagram, the frame work of automation system has been proposed for precision in the working model. In this framework, both Physiological and Psychological aspects are embedded. These aspects are helpful in insertion of various control strategies and flow of control terminals to govern the actuations. In the similar studies, it has been observed that the home automation systems are limited to Short Area Sensor Network for conclusive decisions. The use of sensors such as Infrared Sensors, thermocouple-based temperature sensors and other array sensors for nodes of algorithms and control cased. There were certain drawbacks which were observed in existing studies and design models such as

- Latency time
- Limited number of decisions trees
- Un identified Parity search for cases
- Lack of Heuristic approach for nodes calibrations
- Insurgence in Parallel Processing of Information packets
- Inappropriate Storage of Seasonal nodes value into indexed cells of Array nodes

Overall, there is scarcity of literature related to fusion-based control strategies in automation applications. Fusion based control algorithms and control methods are seems to be one of the evolutionary and emerging area of research for the communities to deal with complex and unrealistic processes of industry as well as domestic applications. Fusion Control Models can be applied to both small and large processes. In this paper, we will develop the fusion based Intelligent room control strategy under AI powered home automation system [5,6].

2. Methodology and Instrumentation

Hardware: In this project, the wide sensor network has been established by installation of various sensors. The main sensors such as Quad-Array of Temperature sensor, Infrared Ferro Camera and Infrared Sensor have been installed in the room periphery The room was inspected as per architecture of room and furniture placements. A robust drawing was prepared for installation of sensor network nodes. The transcendence current based Drives were installed to establish the connection between Processor and Actuators for robust control and cutting of back propagations. The drives were used to actuate Power Supply of Room, Air Conditioner, Ceiling Fan, Fragrance Injector, Tube light and Room Heater. In living arenas such as home, hotels, villas or other camp sites, the internal environment of a room is idle with unfavourable condition according to need of human subjects. As per survey from the field, the common environmental situations were noted [7,8]. According to season's, the room can have various environmental situations, such as

1. In summer, the room environment shall be hot and humid.
2. Similarly, in winter, the temperature can be cold and tide.
3. Poor availability of natural light is one of the major issues in the building rooms.
4. Bad smell is somehow a common problem in the room of home and other properties due to geological situation of a property

The control strategy of smart room ecology control system is shown in Figure 1.

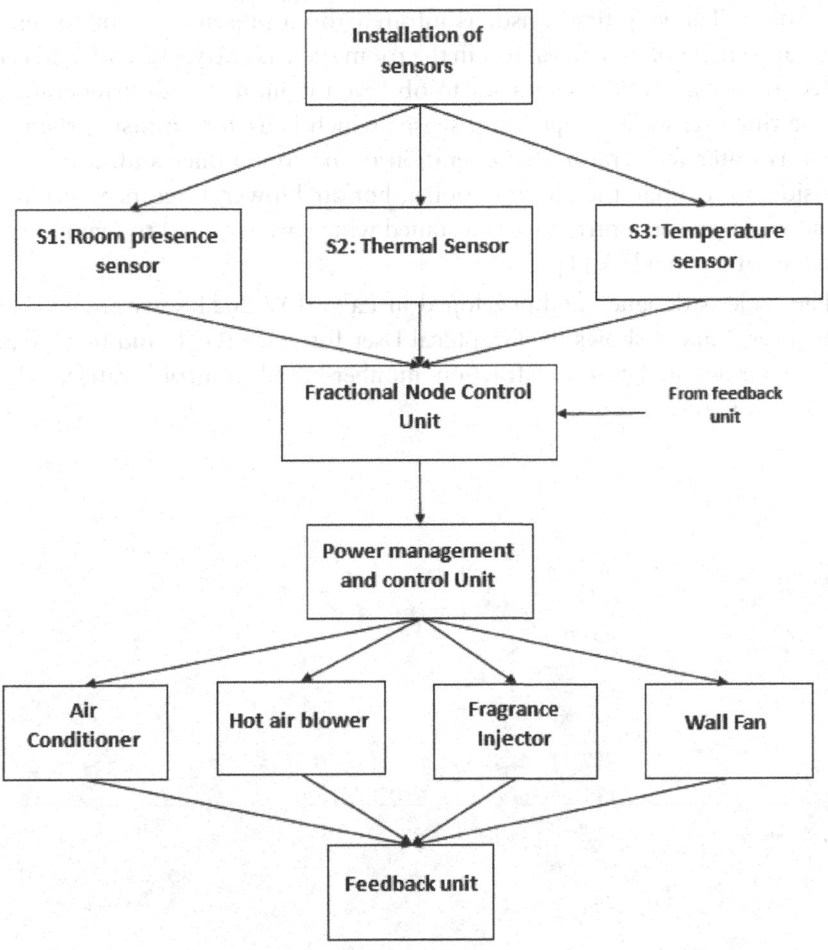

Figure 1: *Flow chart of logic to design the fraction number based smart room ecology control system.*

3. Results and Discussion

To overcome these issues, there are various appliances such as air conditioner, heater or hot air blower, room freshener, light system etc. which are installed in a room to maintain the comfortableness in a room for a human being. It has been observed that, when a person enters into the room, he has to do lot of physical efforts such as switch on the appliances, tunning them according to his comfort etc. So, as per situation, it is very necessary to develop an intelligent automation system for a room to be smart enough to handle the situation of a human subject and govern all the appliances for the comfort of a human and maintain the ecosystem in the room [8,9].

To develop the smart room ecological system, three digital sensors were installed in the room. The very first sensor is infrared room presence sensor to sense the certain movement of human subject in the room such as entry, presence and leaving. The second sensor is thermal sensor to observe the human body temperature and then the third sensor is temperature sensor which is used to measure the internal as well as outer temperature for operation of air conditioner and heater. On the other side, in a room, the air conditioner, hot air blower, fragrance injector, wall fan and main power control unit is installed which are required to maintaining the ecosystem of a room [10,11].

The logic is designed and developed in LabVIEW 2021 software workbench. The Figures 2 and 3 shows the Graphical User Interface (GUI) and block diagram panel to design and test the fraction number-based control strategy which is proposed in Figure 1.

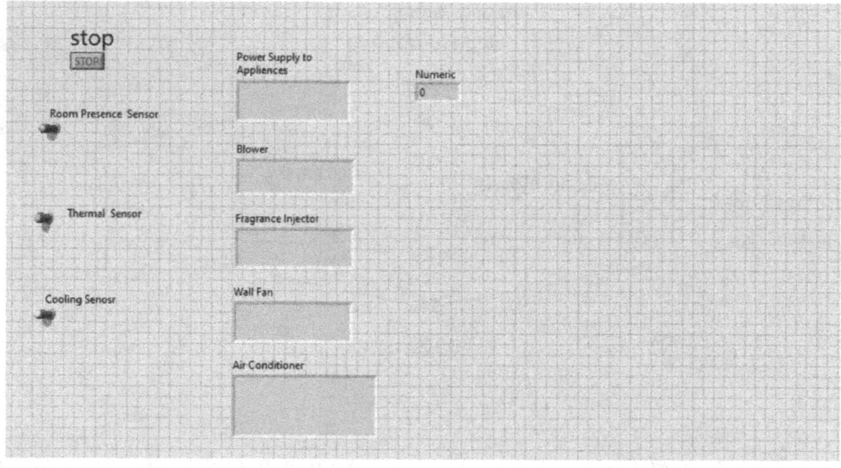

Figure 2: *Graphical user interface (GUI) or front panel of LabVIEW workbench.*

In the workbench, the three inputs and five output pallets were selected on front panel and correspondingly the fractional number logic is designed on block diagram side (Figure 3). The input from sensor is in digital form and based on the combination of digital number's, corresponding fractional number values were observed and calibrated to activate or deactivate the output appliances loops. As shown in Figure 3 the fractional number values such as 0.14, 0.17, 0.25 and 0.5 were selected after calibration of input sensor values from the cases of sensors pairs and then accordingly the comparators were used to activate the concerned case loop for on/off output units. The case lops are getting input as per concerned compactor to execute the target node [12,13].

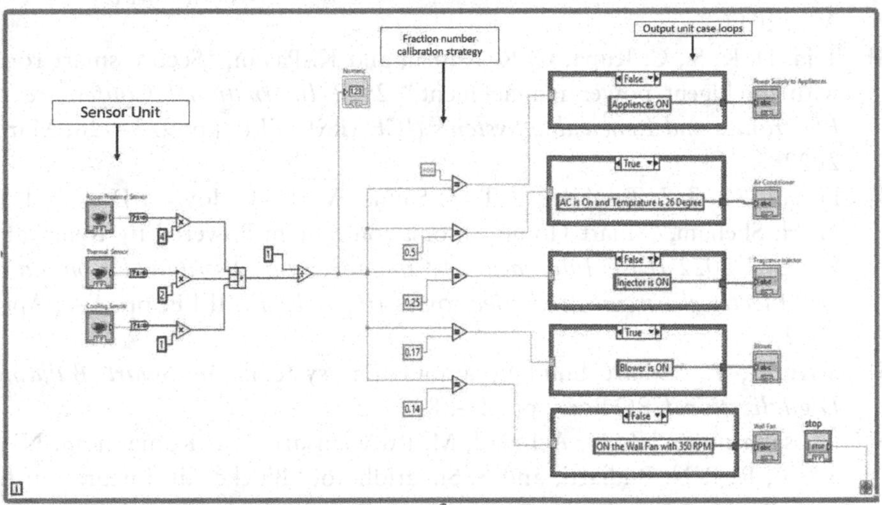

Figure 3: Block diagram code for logic design and testing.

4. Conclusion and Future Scope

a) This model proposed a simple fraction number-based control strategy with 100% accuracy.
b) The room automation can be done with zero efforts of human subject in the room.
c) The control strategy can be easily calibrated as per situation and updated with a greater number of sensors and cases.
d) This model can be implemented in various rooms, industries and process plants where the inner ecosystem needs to maintain under complex situations.
e) The IoT based applications can be produced from this control strategy [14,15].

Acknowledgement

Authors are thankful to Dr. Monica Gulati and Dr. Loviraj Gupta for their faith and research facilities in the Campus.

References

[1] Singh, R., G. Anita, S. Capoor, G. Rana, R. Sharma, and S. Agarwal, "Internet of things enabled robot based smart room automation and localization system," *Internet of Things and Big Data Analytics for Smart Generation*, pp. 105–133, 2019.

[2] Wason, J. D. and J. T. Wen, "Robot raconteur: a communication architecture and library for robotic and automation systems," *2011 IEEE International Conference on Automation Science and Engineering*, IEEE, pp. 761–766, Aug. 2011.

[3] Teja, D. K. S., C. Rupa, C. R. Kumar, and K. Pavan, "Secure smart room with intelligent power management," *2022 International Conference on Electronics and Renewable Systems (ICEARS)*, IEEE, pp. 923–928, March 2022.

[4] Hasan, M., T. I. Talukder, F. T. Z. Saima, M. N. U. Joy, A. Das, and M. N. H. Sheham, "Smart Home Automation System Powered by Renewable Energy," *2022 IEEE International Conference on Distributed Computing and Electrical Circuits and Electronics (ICDCECE)*, IEEE, pp. 1–7, April, 2022.

[5] Srividya, P., "Smart building automation system," In *Smart Buildings Digitalization,* CRC Press, pp. 29-38, 2022.

[6] Arissabarno, C., Z. M. Achmad, M. Ruswiansari, A. F. Romadhoni, N. A. Satrio, R. P. N. Budiarti, and S. Sukaridhoto, "Blockchain integration for mixed reality based smart lab systems," *2023 International Electronics Symposium (IES)*, IEEE, pp. 211–217, August 2023.

[7] Saha, S., M. Z. A. Eidmum, M. M. Hemal, M. A. H. Khan, and B. Muiz, *IOT Based Smart Home Automation and Monitoring System*, Khulna University Studies, pp. 133–143, 2022.

[8] Mateos, L. A., "Smart Room with AI Capabilities for Efficient and Safe Doctor Checkup in the COVID era," In *2023 International Symposium on Medical Robotics (ISMR)*, IEEE, pp. 1–6, April 2023.

[9] Bakar, A., M. Izhar, S. M. Uddin, T. Aslam, and M. A. Arsyad, *Development of Smart Room for Automated Lighting and Fan by Using IoT Application*, 2023.

[10] Khutwad, S. M., Y. G. Shinde, S. G. Ughade, and S. R. Bhapkar, *Home Automation System Using Machine Learning Techniques*.

[11] Rahman, M., A. Al Farabe, M. R. Al Islam, M. Rahman, M. Rezyuan, and G. Ashraf, "Voice Command Automation System (VCAS) for controlling electrical devices using Arduino," *Soft Computing: Theories and Applications: Proceedings of SoCTA* 2022, Singapore: Springer Nature Singapore, pp. 231-242, 2023.

[12] Almusaed, A. and I. Yitmen, "Architectural reply for smart building design concepts based on artificial intelligence simulation models and digital twins," *Sustainability*, vol. 15, p. 4955, 2023.

[13] Jiang, H., L. Tang, R. Ling, and R. Wu, "Research on intelligent building equipment room operation and maintenance platform based on digital twins" *3rd International Conference on Internet of Things and Smart City (IoTSC 2023)*, SPIE, vol. 12708, pp. 379–385, June 2023.

[14] ALQathami, S., S. ALThiyabi, S. ALZyadi, M. ALJuaid, W. AlHarthy, and R. Mokhtar, "Zero-touch entrance system and air quality monitoring in smart campus design based on Internet of Things (IoT)". In *Sustainability Challenges and Delivering Practical Engineering Solutions: Resources, Materials, Energy, and Buildings*, Cham: Springer International Publishing, pp. 203–210, 2023.

[15] Pramono, A., and T. I. W. Primadani, "Smart home apps for saving energy usage at griyapram guesthouse malang," *AIP Conference Proceedings*. AIP Publishing, vol. 2594, no. 1, April 2023.

08. Phishing Website Detection Using Optimised Ensemble Model

P Suhani[1], Divya Bhavani Mohan[1], and Prakash Arumugam[2]

[1]*Unitedworld School of Computational Intelligence, Karnavati University, Gujarat, India*
[2]*School of Research, Karnavati University, Gujarat, India*

Abstract: Internet phishing sites are a type of threat that primarily targets humans rather than computers. Phishing is the process of obtaining personal information, such as login credentials, from an unsuspecting user over the Internet by means of deception. In this work, an optimised ensemble model is introduced that can be optimised for phishing-site detection. Machine learning techniques, specifically supervised learning, form the basis of the system. This strategy is picked because it has excellent true overall performance when used for classification. The purpose of this work is to enhance the classifier's performance by identifying the most effective combination of phishing site characteristics to train it with. The proposed model has a 96.8% accuracy and an AUC of 1.0.

Keywords: Ensemble, classification, optimisable model, phishing, performance metrics.

1. Introduction

Phishing website detection is a critical aspect of cybersecurity that focuses on identifying and preventing malicious websites designed to deceive users and steal sensitive info such as login authorisations, financial details, or individual data. Phishing is a common and dangerous cyber threat that targets individuals, organisations and even entire communities. Phishing is a cyber-attack category in which invaders imitate authentic entities (banks, social media platforms, online services) to pretend users into see-through confidential data or performing harmful actions. Phishing spasms often rely on deceptive emails, social engineering and fraudulent websites. These are fake links that mimic the look & feel and functionality of legitimate websites. They are designed to look convincing, leading users to believe they are interacting with a trusted source. Phishing websites aim to steal sensitive information which is often done through fake login pages to harvest usernames and passwords; Spread malware which infects users' devices with malicious software; Conduct financial fraud where attackers may trick users into providing credit card or banking details and deploy other attacks where these weblinks can be a gateway for more sophisticated attacks, such as ransomware or identity theft.

2. Purpose and Background Study

Customers lose billions of dollars annually due to phishing scams on websites. Criminals who engage in phishing are interested in compromising the safety of their targets online by stealing sensitive data such as login credentials and banking details. It is challenging to identify phishing websites because of the widespread usage of URL leading to shorten URLs, redirecting to corresponding links, adjusting links to appear as trustworthy and many other methods. Because of this, traditional approaches to programming had to be swapped out for a machine learning-based method.

Atharva Deshpande *et al.* described the differences between phishing and legitimate domains. Detecting these domains using machine learning and natural language processing was also stressed [1]. Tyagi et. al. focussed on various machine learning techniques that helps in identifying the phishing website or legitimate [2]. Sanchez-Paniagua *et al.* discussed an efficient methodology for detection of phishing websites in real time scenarios, which uses various features such as URL, HTML and web technology [3]. Kang Leng and coauthors formulated the cumulative distribution function gradient (CDF-g) algorithm, which is the hybrid ensemble method along with selecting the appropriate features for detecting the phishing website [4]. Kiruthiga and Akila surveyed the various features used for detection and different machine learning techniques for phishing website detection [5]. Shivan and Ahmed proposed the extreme learning machine algorithm for phishing website detection [6]. Bhavana *et al.* performed the extreme machine learning algorithm-based classification method that includes 30 different features and the results was compared with the other machine learning techniques. Desai *et al.* developed a google chrome plugin that acts as a mediator between the handlers and the dangerous weblinks. They used the ML technique to train the tool and classify the new content that appears on each iteration [7]. Fadheel *et al.* presented a novel attribute selection procedure that was applied to a publicly available dataset, where the logistic regression and support vector machine was used for validating the feature selection method [8]. Parekh *et al.* implemented the random forest algorithm using URL detection method for identifying the fake websites, which includes the major segments such as deconstructing, experiential grouping and performance study [9]. Karabatak and Mustafa portrayed the dimensionality reduction procedure for the existing dataset, where the feature selection method was used for dimensionality reduction to obtain the highest accuracy [10]. Buber *et al.* targeted in listing and identifying the important features for the finding the fake websites using the machine learning method. The solutions obtained by ML method are highly skilled in spotting zero-hour phishing attacks [11]. Mohammed *et al.* employed the induction of classification rules, a data mining technique, which is capable of identifying accurate website classes [12]. Abburous *et al.* proposed an intellectual resilient model that overcomes the fuzziness in assessing the fake weblinks for e-banking [13]. Shabudin *et al.* presented the results obtained by random forest, multilayer perceptron and naïve bayes, which was characterised by the omitting redundant features and filtering method [14]. In 2023, Kumar *et al.* proposed ML driven phishing detection from TLS 1.2 & 1.3 encoded traffic with no decryption. The proposed model organises transport-layer phishing URLs as legitimate or phishing. Phishing is detected by machine learning algorithms using TLS 1.2 and 1.3 traffic features [15]. In 2022, Bhavani *et al.* extracted and evaluated many facets of genuine and non-genuine URLs and developed a ML approach to identify them [16]. In the year 2022, Ahamad *et al.* created a ML model using RF, DT, Light GBM, LR and SVM [17]. AK Dutta proposed machine learning-based URL detection in 2021. Recurrent neural networks detect phishing URLs. The researcher tried it on 7900 wicked and 5800 authentic websites. Experiments reveal that the developed malicious URL detection strategy outperforms recent methods [18]. In 2021, Yang *et al.* proposed a CNN-RF integrated method for identifying the phishing weblinks. The method envisages URL legitimacy without web content or third-party services. Yang *et al.* performed converting URLs into fixed-size matrices using character embedding, extract features at different levels using CNN models, classify multi-level features using multiple RF classifiers and output winner-take-all prediction results using deep CNN with RF ensemble learning [19].

3. Proposed Solution and its Scope

When perpetrated to deceive an unknowing customer, phishing can take a number of different forms. Email phishing attacks happen when a hacker sends a potential victim an email including a link to a phishing website. A variety of machine learning models have been developed that have been trained on features including the presence or absence of a @ symbol in a URL, the existence or nonexistence of double slash redirecting, the page rank of the URL, the number of external links embedded on the webpage, etc. Using the available information, an optimisable ensemble model was framed that would be able to improve accuracy and area under the curve (AUC). With this method, 96% sensitivity and a 4% false positive rate is achieved.

Phishing scams on the web, cost consumers billions of dollars annually. When it comes to people's money and personal information, phishers are the worst kind of online predator. As a result of the COVID-19 pandemic, there is a surge in the use of technology in all fields, and many previously in-person activities, such as arranging formal meetings, attending classes, making purchases and making payments, have moved online. This means that phishers will have more opportunities to launch spasms that might undesirably impact the victim's fiscal situation, psychological health and career. The proposed model helps the customers to identify the phishing websites at a faster rate and helps in blocking the website when the URL is typed in the address bar.

4. Proposed Methodology

Preparing data include gathering it, cleaning it and putting it all in one place (a file or a table) so that it can be analysed. Our primary means of carrying out an operation are as follows: Data acquisition, data manipulation, data integration, selection of various models, new data for training, final model selection and prediction. Figure 1 represents the flow diagram of the proposed ensemble model.

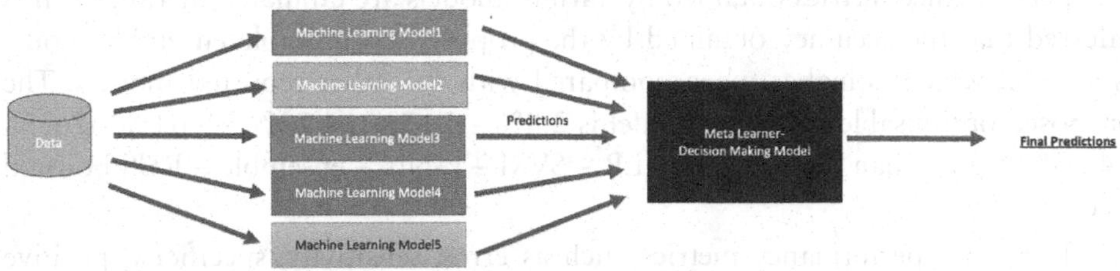

Figure 1: Flow diagram of the proposed ensemble model.

Kaggle's dataset is brought in once the libraries are imported. The dataset chosen is the 'Phishing Legitimate full'. 11054 samples are taken for analysis. After importing the data, it is splitted into a training set and a test set. For training the model, 80% of the data (8843 samples) are selected and the rest (2211 samples) is for testing the model. Model fitting is carried out that makes predictions so as to achieve the desired result, and then model evaluation is carried out. For this evaluation, test data is utilised. The comparative analysis is carried out with several algorithms on various performance metrics.

5. Implementation, Results with Discussion

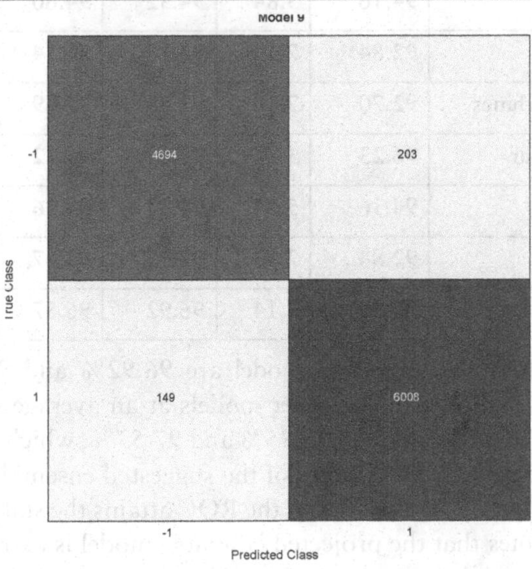

Figure 2: Classification matrix of the proposed ensemble model.

The proposed methodology has been built and executed in the Matlab R2022, with the help of specially designed machine learning toolbox, installed in windows 11 operating system with a capacity of 16GB RAM. The confusion matrix for the proposed ensemble model is shown in Figure 2. The effectiveness of the model is decided by the confusion matrix which portrays the values of tP, tN, fP and fN. From Figure 2, it is observed that the total number of true positive values are 4694, true negatives are 6008, false positives are 203 and false negatives are 149. The performance metrics obtained by various models are tabulated in Table 1. It is inferred that the accuracy obtained by the proposed optimisable ensemble model is 96.8%, which is higher when compared with the other reported models. The proposed optimisable ensemble model is 2.8% - 4.13% - 4.23% - 0.61% - 2.6 % - 4.23% higher than the fine tree – LR – SVM – k-NN – ensemble – RUS boosted trees.

The other performance metrics such as error, sensitivity, specificity, positive predicted value and the negative predicted value are calculated as below:

Error = 100 - accuracy obtained = 100 - 96.86 = 3.14%

Sensitivity (Sn) = TP/(TP + FN) = 4694/(4694 + 149) = 96.92%

Specificity (Sp) = TN/(FP + TN) = 6008/(203+6008) = 96.57%

Positive Predicted Value (ppv) = TP/(TP + FP) = 4694/(4694 + 203) = 95.85%

Negative Predicted Value (npv) = TN/(TN + FN) = 6008/ (6008 + 149) = 97.57%

Table 1: Values of various performance metrics obtained by various models.

Name of the Model	Accuracy	Error	Sn	Sp	ppv	npv
Fine Tree Model	94.16	5.84	94.52	94.60	93.23	94.23
Logistic Regression	92.84	7.16	91.23	91.34	92.44	93.78
Support Vector Machines	92.70	7.30	91.56	91.89	92.84	93.94
K-Nearest Neighbour	96.23	3.77	96.35	95.32	95.23	96.36
Ensemble Model	94.36	5.64	94.63	94.76	93.83	95.24
RUS boosted trees	92.84	7.16	92.43	92.67	91.34	93.23
Optimised Ensemble	96.86	3.14	96.92	96.57	95.85	97.57

The Sn and Sp of the suggested model are 96.92% and 96.57%, which is 3.47% and 3.14% higher than the other models at an average rate. The positive and the negative predicted value are 95.85% and 97.57%, which is higher than the other reported models. The ROC curve of the suggested ensemble model is shown in Figure 3. From Figure 3, it is seen that the ROC attains the stable state at a value of 0.96, which denotes that the projected ensemble model is extremely effective in spotting the phishing websites.

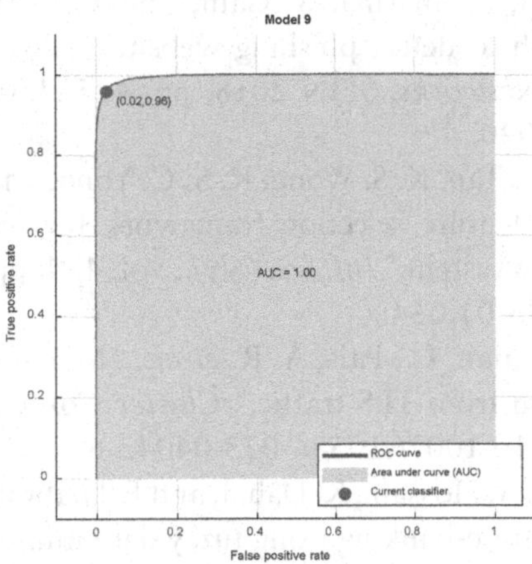

Figure 3: Area under curve of the proposed model.

6. Conclusion

The suggested research on phishing uses a categorical paradigm, where phishing websites are thought to automatically classify websites into a given range of sophisticated values depending on a variety of factors and the grandeur variable The website functionality is used by ML-based phishing approaches to collect information that could be used to classify websites for the purpose of identifying phishing sites. Developing focused anti-phishing approaches and methods as well as minimising their inconvenience are two ways to prevent phishing. An accuracy of 96.86% is detected using optimised ensemble model with bagging and a lowest error rate of 3.14%. The proposed ensemble model can be implemented on a huge samples of dataset for obtaining better accuracy and lowest error rate.

References

[1] Desai, A., J. Jatakia, R. Naik, and N. Raul, "Malicious web content detection using machine leaning," RTEICT 2017 - 2nd IEEE Int. Conf. Recent Trends Electron. Inf. Commun. Technol. Proc., vol. 2018-Jan., pp. 1432–1436, 2017, doi: 10.1109/RTEICT.2017.8256834.

[2] Bhavani, P. A., M. Chalamala, P. S. Likhitha, and C. P. S. Sai, "Phishing Websites Detection Using Machine Learning," September 2, 2022, Available at SSRN: https://ssrn.com/abstract=4208185 or doi: 10.2139/ssrn.4208185.

[3] Dutta, A. K., "Detecting phishing websites using machine learning technique," *PLoS One*, vol. 16, no. 10, pp. e0258361, Oct. 11, 2021, doi: 10.1371/journal.pone.0258361. PMID: 34634081; PMCID: PMC8504731.

[4] Buber, E., Ö. Demir, and O. K. Sahingoz, "Feature selections for the machine learning based detection of phishing websites," *IDAP 2017 - Int. Artif. Intell. Data Process. Symp.*, 2017, doi: 10.1109/IDAP.2017.8090317.

[5] Tyagi, I., J. Shad, S. Sharma, S. Gaur, and G. Kaur, "A novel machine learning approach to detect phishing websites," *2018 5th Int. Conf. Signal Process. Integr. Networks*, SPIN 2018, pp. 425–430, 2018, doi: 10.1109/SPIN.2018.8474040.

[6] Chiew, K. L., C. L. Tan, K. S. Wong, K. S. C. Yong, and W. K. Tiong, "A new hybrid ensemble feature selection framework for machine learning-based phishing detection system," *Inf. Sci. (Ny).*, vol. 484, pp. 153–166, 2019, doi: 10.1016/j.ins.2019.01.064.

[7] Kumar, M., Kondaiah, C., Pais, A. R. *et al.*, "Machine learning models for phishing detection from TLS traffic," *Cluster Comput.*, vol. 26, pp. 3263–3277, 2023, doi: 10.1007/s10586-023-04042-6.

[8] Aburrous, M., M. A. Hossain, K. Dahal, and F. Thabtah, "Intelligent phishing detection system for e-banking using fuzzy data mining," *Expert Syst. Appl.*, vol. 37, no. 12, pp. 7913–7921, 2010, doi: 10.1016/j.eswa.2010.04.044.

[9] Karabatak, M. and T. Mustafa, "Performance comparison of classifiers on reduced phishing website dataset," *6th Int. Symp. Digit. Forensic Secur. ISDFS 2018 - Proceeding*, vol. 2018-Jan., pp. 1–5, 2018, doi: 10.1109/ISDFS.2018.8355357.

[10] Sánchez-Paniagua, M., E. Fidalgo, E. Alegre, and R. Alaiz-Rodríguez, "Phishing websites detection using a novel multipurpose dataset and web technologies features," *Expert Syst. Appl.*, vol. 207, no. June, p. 118010, 2022, doi: 10.1016/j.eswa.2022.118010.

[11] Kiruthiga, R. and D. Akila, "Phishing websites detection using machine learning," *Int. J. Recent Technol. Eng.*, vol. 8, no. 2 Special Issue 11, pp. 111–114, 2019, doi: 10.35940/ijrte.B1018.0982S1119.

[12] Mohammad, R. M., F. Thabtah, and L. McCluskey, "Intelligent rule-based phishing websites classification," *IET Inf. Secur.*, vol. 8, no. 3, pp. 153–160, 2014, doi: 10.1049/iet-ifs.2013.0202.

[13] Borde, S., "Detection of phishing websites using machine learning Atharva Deshpande," vol. 10, no. 05, pp. 430–434, 2021, [Online], http://www.hud.ac.uk/students/.

[14] Shivan, S. K. and M. Ahmed, "Phishing website detection," vol. 9, no. 7, pp. 71–75, 2021.

[15] Parekh, S., D. Parikh, S. Kotak, and S. Sankhe, "A new method for detection of phishing websites: URL detection," *Proc. Int. Conf. Inven. Commun. Comput. Technol. ICICCT 2018*, no. Icicct, pp. 949–952, 2018, doi: 10.1109/ICICCT.2018.8473085.

[16] Shabudin, S., N. S. Sani, K. A. Z. Ariffin, and M. Aliff, "Feature selection for phishing website classification," *Int. J. Adv. Comput. Sci. Appl.*, vol. 11, no. 4, pp. 587–595, 2020, doi: 10.14569/IJACSA.2020.0110477.

[17] Hasane Ahammad, S. K., S. D. Kale, G. D. Upadhye, S. D. Pande, E. V. Babu, A. V. Dhumane, D. K. Jang Bahadur, "Phishing URL detection using machine learning methods," *Adv. Eng. Software*, vol. 173, pp. 103288, 2022, ISSN 0965-9978, doi: 10.1016/j.advengsoft.2022.103288.

[18] Fadheel, W., M. Abusharkh, and I. Abdel-Qader, "On feature selection for the prediction of phishing websites," *Proc. - 2017 IEEE 15th Int. Conf. Dependable, Auton. Secur. Comput. 2017 IEEE 15th Int. Conf. Pervasive Intell. Comput. 2017 IEEE 3rd Int. Conf. Big Data Intell. Comput.*, vol. 2018-Jan., pp. 871–876, 2018, doi: 10.1109/DASC-PICom-DataCom-CyberSciTec.2017.146.

[19] Yang, R., K. Zheng, B. Wu, C. Wu, X. Wang, "Phishing website detection based on deep convolutional neural network and random forest ensemble learning," *Sensors (Basel)*, vol. 21, no. 24, pp. 8281, 2021. doi: 10.3390/s21248281. PMID: 34960375; PMCID: PMC8709380.

09. Power-Efficient Packet Counter Design on High Performance FPGA for Green Communication

[1]Keshav Kumar, [2]Isha Kansal, [3]Saurabh Singh, [2]Preeti Sharma, [4]Sachin Chawla

[1]*University Institute of Computing, Chandigarh University, Punjab, India*
[2]*Chitkara University Institute of Engineering and Technology, Chitkara University, Punjab, India*
[3]*Department of Computer Science and Engineering, Bhilai Institute of Technology, Durg*
[4]*Department of Electronics and Communication Engineering, Chandigarh University, Punjab, India*

Abstract: This proposed work is well suited to endorse the concepts of Green Communication (GC). Subsequently, the world is facing the devasting concern of power deficiency. This work discusses about the design a low power hardware model of packet counter with FPGA. The implementation is done on VIVADO, and the power utilization are targeted on Zynq-7000 and Spartan-7 devices. The power analysis for both devices is done by matching the impedance with LVCMOS IO. It is analysed that both devices deliver the optimised power when the impedance is matched with LVCMOS 12 IO. It is also observed that as the input voltage (iv) increases for impedance matching (IM), the TPD of both devices also gets increased. Among both devices, the Zynq-7000 device delivers the optimised power for packet counter implementation with LVCMOS 12, and Spartan-7 devices delivers the maximum amount of power for packet counter implementation.

Keywords: Packet counter, FPGA, LVCMOS IO, Spartan-7, Zynq-7000, green communication.

1. Introduction

In the era of information technology (IT), it appears to be relatively simple to move data efficiently from one device to another or from one node to another node. It might only take a few seconds to transfer the info. Data that is transported from one device to another takes the form of packets. These packets might alternatively be referred to as data packets or just packets. The employment of networking ideas is the only method used to transfer packets. There is a possibility that some internet data transfer packets will be lost or arrive at their destination late [1–2]. Therefore, in the era of IT, any missing or delayed data of this kind may result in serious problems for some organisations. It appears that the amount of digital data saved is essentially growing exponentially, similar to Moore's law. The quantity of storage space that is readily available appears to be increasing virtually exponentially, according to Kryder's law. 432 exabytes of information (optimally compressed) were available for one-way broadcast networks in 1986; 715 exabytes in 1993; 1.2 zettabytes in 2000; and 1.9 zettabytes in 2007, which is the information equivalent of 174 newspapers per person every day. Because of this, certain organisations may have major problems in the age of information technology if such data is absent or delayed [3–4]. The 'Packet Counter' can be used to fix several types of data transmission issues. The data packets, which are being transferred from source to its destination, can be transferred using the Transmission Control Protocol/Internet Protocol (TCP/IP) protocols. The data packets are being transferred uses the various layers of the TCP/IP protocols. There are generally five distinguished layers in the TCP/IP protocols as illustrated in Figure 1. In the data transmission process, the packets move from physical layer to application layers, and the packet counter is associated with every layer that checks the proper transmission of packets [5–6].

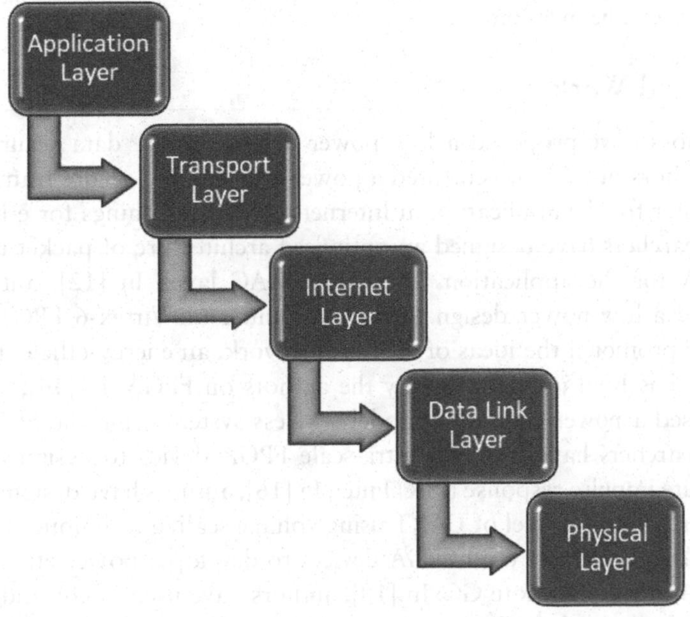

Figure 1: Different layers of TCP/IP protocols.

1.1. Motivation

There are generally two ways for the implementation of packet counter such as: software approach and the hardware approach. The software approach has lots of drawbacks such as:

a) Data packets are not secured; therefore, security is the major concern.
b) Data packets has to face the problem of heavy traffic.
c) Root permission is required.
d) Time to time upgradation of software, cookies and patches is required.
e) This approach is time consuming.

Due to several drawbacks, software approach might not be beneficial in this fast and furious era. In the current scenario of the globe, the data transmission must be fast and smooth. Delay in data transmission is not acceptable by any organisation in the current scenario of the globe.

Not only delay, the globe is also concerned with the energy consumption of the gadgets. The power consumption of the devices should be minimised to maintain the sustainability on the planet. The rapid increase in the population across the globe and the industrialisation are the major factors of the power & energy imbalance on the planet. The natural resources which count in the production of power is not much abundant; they may vanish someday; therefore, the power consumption of the devices must be optimised [7–8].

Despite of several shortcomings in software method, globe is moving towards the implementation of hardware approaches of the packet counter so that the shortcomings can be overcome.

2. Related Work

In [9], authors have proposed a low power design for the data security in IoT systems. Authors in [10] implemented a power-efficient and secure framework for packet counter for the application in Internet of Medical Things for e-healthcare. In [11], researchers have designed an optimised architecture of packet transceiver using FPGA for the application in ethernet-MAC layer. In [12], authors have implemented a low power design of packet counter on Virtex-6 FPGA. Authors in [13] have promoted the ideas of GC. In this work, an energy-efficient design of control unit has been implemented by the authors on FPGA. In [14], researchers have proposed a power optimised model wireless system using the FPGA device. In [15], researchers have used the ultra-scale FPGA device to design an energy-efficient Finite impulse response (FIR) Filter. In [16], authors have designed a FPGA based power-efficient model of UART using voltage scaling techniques to promote GC. In [17], authors have used FPGA devices to develop a power efficient model of AES algorithm to promote GC. In [18], authors have used FPGA and P4 device to develop a framework for high performance of packet processor. In [19], authors have used intel FPGA to design a model for checking the efficient flow of data packets in network system.

2.1. Key Aspects

From the section 2, it is analysed that a lot of work has been done to make an efficient, low power framework for packet counter using FPGA. It is also analysed that a lot of work has been done to endorse the concepts of GC. But as of authors knowledge, no work model has been designed for GC based packet counter for IoT applications. This work addresses about designing a power-efficient packet counter model for IoT devices to promote the goals of GC using high performances FPGA devices. The key aspects of this paper are such as:

a) Packet counter design has been implemented on two high performance FPGA such as Spartan-7 and Zynq 7000 System on Chips (SoCs).
b) Power analysis requires impedance matching of the IO load. For IM, we have used Low voltage complementary metal oxide semiconductor (LVCMOS) IO standard.
c) Thermal properties of both FPGAs have been analysed for packet counter implementation.
d) Comparative power analysis has been done to make the packet counter suitable for GC.

3. Experimental Setup

The design of the packet counter is implemented on VIVADO, and the power utilisation are targeted on two FPGAs such as Spartan-7 and Zynq-7000. VERILOG programming language is used to program the packet counter on VIVADO ISE SUITE [20]. The power utilisation of the packet counter for Spartan-7 and Zynq-7000 FPGA is done using the IM technique. For IM, LVCMOS IO is regarded in this work. The register transfer logic (RTL) of the packet counter has shown in Figure 2.

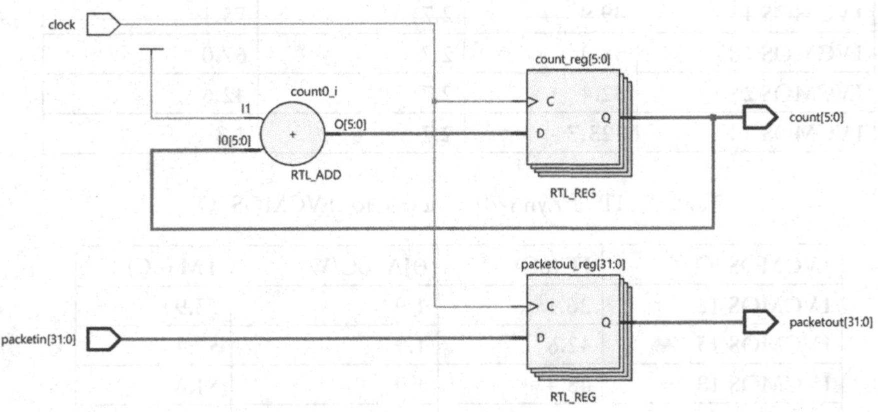

Figure 2: *RTL of the implemented packet counter.*

From Figure 2, it is observed that in the implementation of the packet counter at inputs we require clock (clk) pulse, an adder circuit, a 6-bit counter and the 33-bit data input for packet counter. At the output, we have the 32-bit data packet output along with a 6-bit counter, which counts the stages of packet are being successfully received or not. In the implementation of packet counter on both FPGAs, some FPGA resources are utilised such as Look Up Table (LUTs), Global Buffer (BUFG), Flip-Flop (FFs), Input Output (IOs). The resource utilisation for the packet counter implementation on both of the FPGAs is described in Table 1.

Tabel 1: Resource utilisation for the packet counter implementation on Spartan-7 and Zynq-7000 FPGA.

Resources	Utilisation
LUT	4
BUFG	1
IO	71
FF	38

4. Thermal Parameters (TP)

This section deliberates about the TP of Zynq-7000 and Spartan-7 device when the IM is done with LVCMOS IO. Considered constraints of TP include effective thermal resistance to air (ΘJA), junction temperature (JT) and thermal margin (TM) among others. The TP of Spartan-7 and Zynq-7000 LVCMOS IO devices are outlined in Tables 2 and 3, respectively.

Table 2: TP for LVCMOS IO on Spartan-7.

LVCMOS IO	JT (oC)	ΘJA (oC/W)	TM (oC)
LVCMOS 12	26.7	2.7	98.3
LVCMOS 15	49.9	2.7	75.1
LVCMOS 18	58.0	2.7	67.0
LVCMOS 25	82.4	2.7	42.6
LVCMOS 33	123.7	2.7	1.3

Table 3: TP of Zynq-7000 device for LVCMOS IO.

LVCMOS IO	JT (oC)	ΘJA (oC/W)	TM (oC)
LVCMOS 12	26.1	1.9	73.9
LVCMOS 15	42.6	1.9	57.4
LVCMOS 18	48.4	1.9	51.6
LVCMOS 25	65.6	1.9	34.4
LVCMOS 33	94.5	1.9	5.5

From Tables 2 and 3, it is observed that JT for both FPGA increases as the iv of the LVCMOS IO rises, while the TM for both FPGA decreases as the iv of the LVCMOS IO rises. The ΘJA remains constant for both FPGA for all the

LVCMOS IO. It is 2.7 and 1.9 for Spartan-7 and Zynq-7000 FPGA, respectively. The representation of TP for Sparatan-7 and Zynq-7000 FPGA is represented in Figures 3 and 4, respectively.

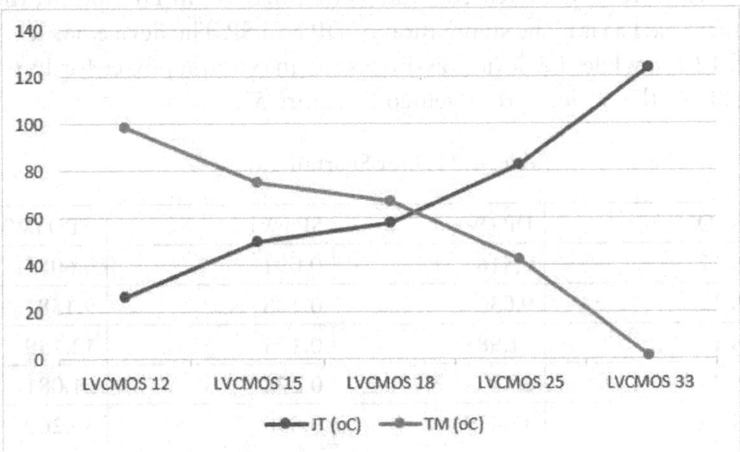

Figure 3: *TP of Spartan-7 device for LVCMOS IO.*

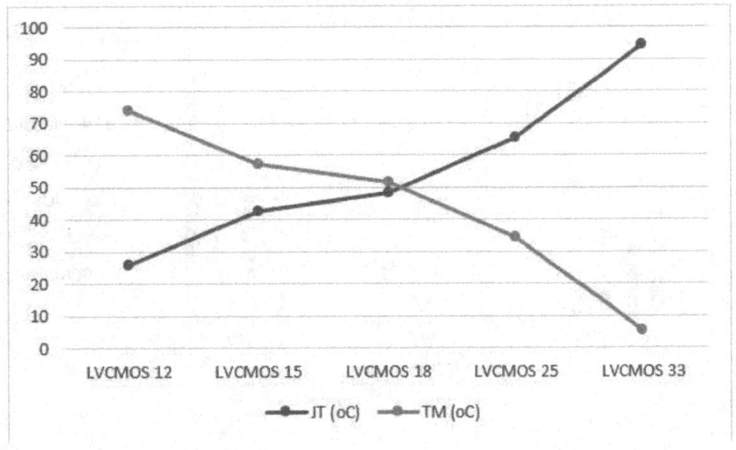

Figure 4: *TP of Zynq-7000 device for LVCMOS IO.*

5. Power Analysis

This section highlights about the power dissipated from the device when the impedance of the device is matched with LVCMOS IO. The total power dissipation (TPD) is the summation of static power (SP) and dynamic power (DP) of the device. Switching and short-circuit power make up DP; whereas, leakage or the current that passes through a transistor when nothing is happening makes up SP.

5.1. Power Analysis for Spartan-7 Device

The TPD, DP and SP for the Spartan-7 device is described in Table 4. From Table 4, it is examined that DP and SP for the Spartan-7 device increases as the input voltage of the LVCMOS IO gets increased. Due to the increase in DP and SP, the TPD is also gets increased as it is the summation of DP and SP. The device has low TPD for LVCMOS 12 IO, while the device dissipates the maximum power for LVCMOS 33 IO. The TPD of the device is represented in Figure 5.

Table 4: TPD for Spartan-7 device.

LVCMOS IO	DP (W)	SP (W)	TPD (W)
LVCMOS 12	0.516	0.091	0.608
LVCMOS 15	9.030	0.128	9.158
LVCMOS 18	11.985	0.155	12.139
LVCMOS 25	20.803	0.278	21.081
LVCMOS 33	35.439	0.830	36.269

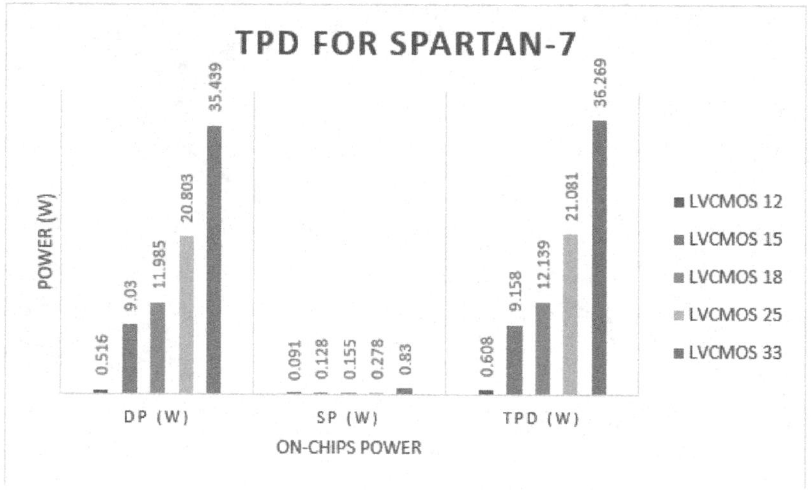

Figure 5: *TPD for Spartan-7 device.*

5.2. Power Analysis for Zynq-7000 Device

The TPD, DP and SP for the Zynq-7000 device is described in Table 5. From Table 5, it is examined that DP and SP for the Zynq-7000 device increases as the input voltage of the LVCMOS IO gets increased. Due to the increase in DP and SP, the TPD is also gets increased as it is the summation of DP and SP. The device has low TPD for LVCMOS 12 IO, while the device dissipates the maximum power for LVCMOS 33 IO. The TPD of the device is represented in Figure 6.

Table 5: TPD for Zynq-7000 device.

LVCMOS IO	DP (W)	SP (W)	TPD (W)
LVCMOS 12	0.467	0.099	0.566
LVCMOS 15	8.974	0.132	9.106
LVCMOS 18	11.929	0.149	12.078
LVCMOS 25	20.747	0.223	20.970
LVCMOS 33	35.384	0.485	35.869

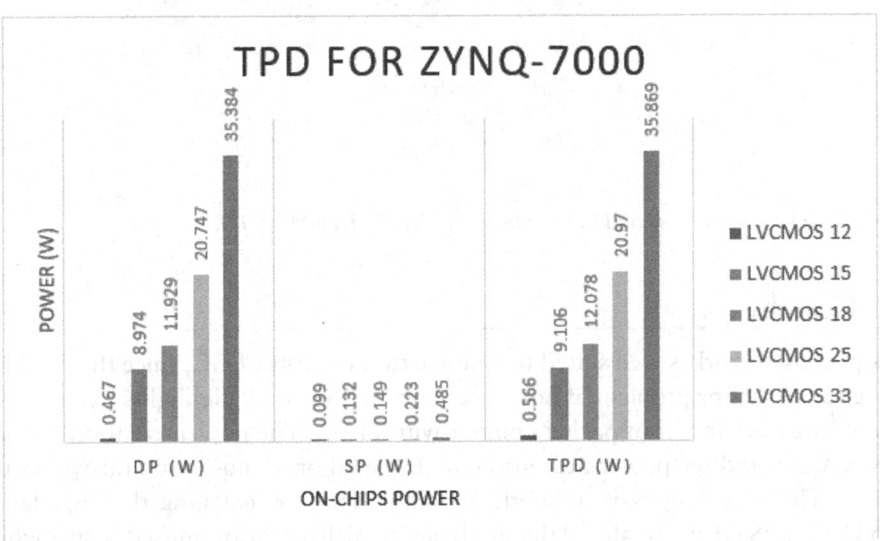

Figure 6: TPD for Zynq-7000 device.

6. Comparative Analysis

From section 5, it is analysed that the TPD increases as the input voltage rises for impedance matching. The packet counter delivers low power when the impedance is matched with LVCMOS 12 IO for both FPGAs, and it delivers the maximum amount of power when the IM goes with LVCMOS 33 IO. Among both FPGAs, the Zynq-7000 device delivers the optimised power for packet counter implementation with LVCMOS 12, and Spartan-7 devices delivers the maximum amount of power for packet counter implementation. From section 3, it is also observed that the Zynq-7000 devices gives the optimised JT for the packet counter implementation. The comparison of TPD for both FPGA for LVCMOS IO is shown in Figure 7.

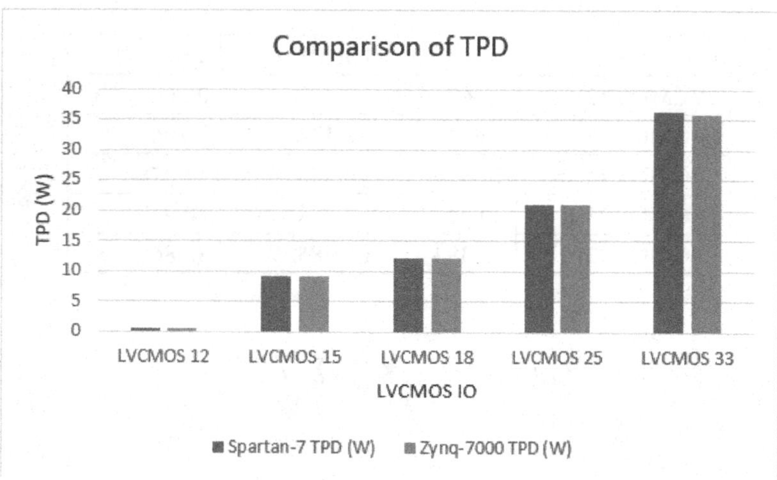

Figure 7: *The comparison of TPD for both FPGA for LVCMOS IO.*

7. Conclusion

This proposed work is well suited to endorse the concepts of GC, since the world is facing the devasting problem of power deficiency. This work highlights about a low power hardware model of packet counter with FPGA. The implementation is done on VIVADO, and the power utilisation are targeted on Zynq-7000 and Spartan-7 devices. The power analysis for both devices is done by matching the impedance with LVCMOS IO. It is analysed that both devices deliver the optimised power when the IM is matched with LVCMOS 12 IO. It is also observed that as the iv increases for impedance matching, the TPD of both devices also gets increased. Among both devices, the Zynq-7000 device delivers the optimised power for packet counter implementation with LVCMOS 12, and Spartan-7 devices delivers the maximum amount of power for packet counter implementation. As far as future aspects are concerned, the packets counter design can be implemented on ultra-scale FPGA devices too. And there are also several other power optimising techniques such as output load capacitance scaling, frequency of operation, clk gating and also other IO standards like HSTL, SSTL, LVTTL etc can be used to match the impedance so that the power utilisation be improved and it will be suitable for promoting GC.

References

[1] Orlov, S. S., W. Phillips, E. Bjornson, Y. Takashima, P. Sundaram, L. Hesselink, R. Okas, D. Kwan, and R. Snyder, "High-transfer-rate high-capacity holographic disk data-storage system," *Appl.Opt.*, vol. 43, no. 25, pp. 4902–4914, 2004. Housley, R., Using advanced encryption standard

(aes) counter mode with ipsec encapsulating security payload (esp). No. rfc3686. 2004.

[2] Rahmati, A. and L. Zhong, "Context-for-wireless: context-sensitive energy-efficient wireless data transfer," *Proceedings of the 5th International Conference on Mobile Systems, Applications and Services*, pp. 165–178. 2007.

[3] Oruganti, S. K., S. H. Heo, H. Ma, and F. Bien, "Wireless energy transfer-based transceiver systems for power and/or high-data rate transmission through thick metal walls using sheet-like waveguides," *Electron. Lett.*, vol. 50, no. 12, pp. 886–888, 2014.

[4] Jambunathan, K., E. Lai, MAm Moss, and B. L. Button, "A review of heat transfer data for single circular jet impingement," *nt. J. Heat Fluid Flow*, vol. 13, no. 2, pp. 106–115, 1992.

[5] Sinha, P., V. K. Jha, A. K. Rai, and B. Bhushan, "Security vulnerabilities, attacks and countermeasures in wireless sensor networks at various layers of OSI reference model: a survey," *2017 International Conference on Signal Processing and Communication (ICSPC)*, IEEE, pp. 288–293, 2017.

[6] Banerjee, S., B. Bhattacharjee, and C. Kommareddy, "Scalable application layer multicast," *Proceedings of the 2002 Conference on Applications, Technologies, Architectures, and Protocols for Computer Communications*, pp. 205–217. 2002

[7] Kumar, K., S. Malhotra, R. Dutta, and A. Kumar, "Design of thermal-aware and power-efficient LFSR on different nanometer technology FPGA for green communication," *2021 10th IEEE International Conference on Communication Systems and Network Technologies (CSNT)*, IEEE, pp. 236–240, 2021.

[8] Pandey, B., K. Kumar, S. C. Haryanti, R. R. Mohamed, and D. M. Akbar Hussian, "Power efficient control unit for green communication," 2020.

[9] Aman, M. N., B. Sikdar, K. C. Chua, and A. Ali, "Low power data integrity in IoT systems," *IEEE Internet Things J.*, vol. 5, no. 4, pp. 3102–3113, 2018.

[10] Saba, T., K. Haseeb, I. Ahmed, and A. Rehman, "Secure and energy-efficient framework using Internet of Medical Things for e-healthcare," *J. Infect. Public Health*, vol. 13, no. 10, pp. 1567 –1575, 2020.

[11] Guruprasad, S. P., and B. S. Chandrasekar, "An optimized packet transceiver design for ethernet-MAC layer based on FPGA," *International Conference on Intelligent Data Communication Technologies and Internet of Things*, Springer, Cham, pp. 725–732, 2018.

[12] Kumar, A., *et al.*, "Secure and energy-efficient smart building architecture with emerging technology IoT," *Comput. Commun.*, vol. 176, pp. 207–217, 2021.

[13] Pandey, B., K. Kumar, A. Batool, and S. Ahmad, "Implementation of power-efficient control unit on ultra-scale FPGA for green communication," *3c Tecnología: glosas de innovación aplicadas a la pyme*, vol. 10, no. 1, 93–105, 2021.

[14] Verma, G., T. Singhal, R. Kumar, S. Chauhan, S. Shekhar, B. Pandey, and D. M. Akbar Hussain, "Heuristic and statistical power estimation model for FPGA based wireless systems," *Wireless Pers. Commun.*, vol. 106, no. 4, pp. 2087–2098, 2019.

[15] Pandey, B., N. Pandey, A. Kaur, D. M. Akbar Hussain, B. Das, and G. S. Tomar, "Scaling of output load in energy efficient FIR filter for green communication on ultra-scale FPGA," *Wireless Pers. Commun.*, vol. 106, no. 4, pp. 1813–1826, 2019.

[16] Haripriya, D., K. Kumar, A. Shrivastava, H. M. Ridha Al-Khafaji, V. Moyal, and S. K. Singh, "Energy-efficient UART design on FPGA using dynamic voltage scaling for green communication in industrial sector," *Wireless Commun. Mobile Comput.*, vol. 2022, 2022.

[17] Kumar, K., A. Kaur, K. R. Ramkumar, A. Shrivastava, V. Moyal, and Y. Kumar, "A design of power-efficient AES Algorithm on Artix-7 FPGA for green communication," *2021 International Conference on Technological Advancements and Innovations (ICTAI)*, IEEE, pp. 561–564, 2021.

[18] Yazdinejad, A., R. M. Parizi, A. Bohlooli, A. Dehghantanha, and K.-K. Raymond Choo, "A high-performance framework for a network programmable packet processor using P4 and FPGA," *J. Network Comput. Appl.*, vol. 156, pp. 102564, 2020.

[19] Yoshida, S., Y. Ukon, S. Ohteru, H. Uzawa, N. Ikeda, and K. Nitta, "FPGA-based network microburst analysis system with flow specification and efficient packet capturing," *2020 IEEE 31st International Conference on Application-specific Systems, Architectures and Processors (ASAP)*, IEEE, pp. 29-32, 2020.

[20] Kumar, K., S. Ahmad, B. Pandey, A. K. Pandit, and D. Singh, "Power Efficient Frequency Scaled and ThermalAware Control Unit Design on FPGA," *Int. J. Innovative Technol. Exploring Eng.*, vol. 8, no. 9 Special Issue 2, pp. 530–533, 2019.

[21] Zhang, X. *et al.*, "Research on vibration monitoring and fault diagnosis of rotating machinery based on internet of things technology," *Nonlinear Eng.*, vol. 10.1, pp. 245–254, 2021.

10. Analysis of Chaotic Northern Goshawk Algorithm in the Optimal Design of Electric Vehicles

Kamaldeep Sharma, Manu Prakram, and Vikram kumar Kamboj

ECE, Lovely Professional University, Jalandhar, India

Abstract: The economic and cultural growth of a country is majorly dependent on the transportation of goods and in the current era the role of electric vehicles is gaining more importance. The optimal design of electric vehicles is a major concern nowadays and in this research paper, a chaotic northern goshawk algorithm is being analysed which can be used for the optimal design of electric vehicles.

Keywords: Chaotic, exploration, exploitation, Goshawk, optimal, electric vehicle.

1. Introduction

Transportation is of paramount importance in modern society, impacting various aspects of our lives, economies and overall development. In this era of technology and digitisation, the focus is now shifting from conventional vehicles to electric vehicles. It is rightly said that electric vehicles (EV) are the future ahead for transportation. To save the fossil fuel consumption and to protect the environment from green-house emission from burning of petrol and gas electrification of vehicles is one major transformation that is currently taking place in our society. Day by day popularity of EV is increasing in manufacturing sector globally to protect earth from harmful emissions. There are numerous optimisation techniques available to contend the complexities of design of optimal parameters for electric and hybrid EVs.

Implementing heuristics (rules, good sense and trial and error) is the better option to identify viable solutions to avoid complicated novel optimisation issues. At first glance, such techniques appear to be extremely different from accurate scientific procedures, which often rely on designs, assumptions, hypotheses and tests. Many heuristic criteria and techniques used to identify excellent solutions for specific issues have similar characteristics and are habitually independent of the issues themselves, as is well known. The word meta-heuristic was designed in association with artificial intelligence and computer science, and it is now widely used to describe generic approaches that are not unique to a particular situation. There was a rapid growth since last few decades in meta-heuristic research, which is understandable, the way the issues have been handled to solve successfully and the beauty of the methods were inspired by nature. Despite the fact that several combinatory optimisation problems are extremely difficult to resolve optimally, the quality of the solutions achieved by simple meta-heuristics is frequently excellent.

1.1. Chaotic Search Strategies

Studies have revealed that meta-heuristics approaches face the problem of poor exploitation in some of the uni-modal and multi-modal benchmark function. Researchers have developed many hybrid and chaotic algorithms. Researchers have been able to apply such chaotic behaviour in algorithms such as genetic algorithms and chaotic Krill Herd search. The behaviour of chaos is clearly random and arbitrary in nature as well as unpredictable. The main problem faced by meta-heuristic algorithms is the slow convergence speed. So, to enhance the global convergence speed and to get better performance, many researchers have introduced chaotic theory into the meta-heuristic algorithm process.

Various chaotic maps are considered for tuning of the parameters but the sinusoidal function is selected for hybridisation.

1.2. Chaotic Northern Goshawk Optimisation

For approaching the best converging search agent, we have analysed northern goshawk natural behaviour of hunting is mathematically modeled and taken as a main source of inspiration to the proposed work. 'northern goshawk' is a special bird species belonging to Accipitridae family which has a peculiar hunting style popularly seen in Eurasia and North American reference. The algorithm shown in the flowchart is based on the recorded behaviour of the NG as a searcher member. Form this procedure, each and every member of the explored group of samples is a proposed specific answer to the searching agent challenges. For the computational convenience, each member of the population is treated as vector item. This population members putting together forms an elements of the algorithm matrix.

$$F(X)\cdots\begin{bmatrix} F1 & = & F(X1) \\ \vdots & = & \vdots \\ FN & = & F(XN) \end{bmatrix}\cdot Nx1¶$$

In this F(X) is forming a matrix which is the vector and the ith solution f the function is denoted by Fi from the matrix. The smallest value from these solutions is treated as better solution for the defined problem.

$$\begin{pmatrix} X1 \\ \vdots \\ Xi \\ \vdots \\ XN \end{pmatrix} = \begin{bmatrix} X1.1 & \cdots & X1,m \\ \vdots & \ddots & \vdots \\ XN,1 & \cdots & XN,m \end{bmatrix}_{NXm} \qquad \text{Equation- (1.1)}$$

1.2.1 *Computational Model of the NGO*

The hunting behaviour is mathematically represented as NGO-algorithms and the major characteristics of the bird is divided into 2 phases as follows:

a) Prey recognition and catch
b) Hunt and escape phenomenon.

Figure 1: *Procedure of prey choice and catching it by goshawk. Strategy of the chase by goshawk for its prey.*

1.2.2 *First Stage: Prey Recognition (Exploration)*

NG is looking for a best prey while flying and catch as soon as possible by random selection of search process. The Global search space is defined in an optimum space as shown in Figure 1

1.2.3 *2nd Stage: Hunt & Escape Behaviour (EXPLOITATION)*

The prey will always try to escape followed by an attack. And in 'tail-and-hunt' scenario, the NG always choose to carryon hunting the prey. By nature, the NG is very quick in moment and eventually catches the prey.

1.2.4 *Flowchart of Chaotic Northern Goshawk Nature*

Proposed novel CNGO system's many steps are specified as pseudocode in Procedure 1, and its chart is displayed in Figure 2

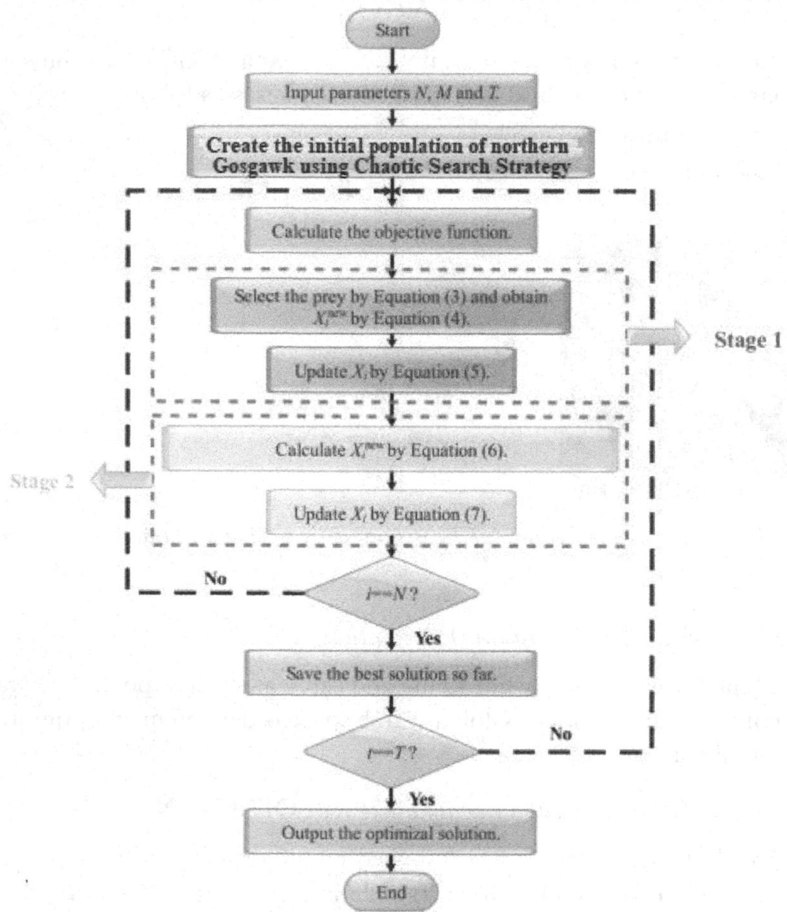

Figure 2: Flow chart of CNGO algorithm illustrating behaviour of CNGO.

1.3. Test Results for Chaotic Northern Goshawk Optimiser Algorithm for Standard Benchmark Problem

- Unimodal benchmark functions for exploitation analysis.
- *Range* defines the boundary of search space.
- *Dim* denotes the dimensionality of the search space.

Type defines the characteristics of the functions (Separable (S)/Inseparable (I), Differentiable (D)/Non-differentiable (N), Continuous (C)/Discontinuous (T) and Fixed (F)/Variable (V) dimensional) and F_{min} is the global optimum.

Table 1: Standard uni-modal bench mark functions(F1-F7).

Functions	Dimensions	range	f_{min}
	30	[-100, 100]	0
+	30	[-10, 10]	0
	30	[-100, 100]	0
$_m\{\leq m \leq z\}$	30	[-100, 100]	0
$_{m+1}-)^2 + (^2]$	30	[-38, 38]	0
^{2}	30	[-100, 100]	0
+ random [0,1]	30	[-1.28, 1.28]	0

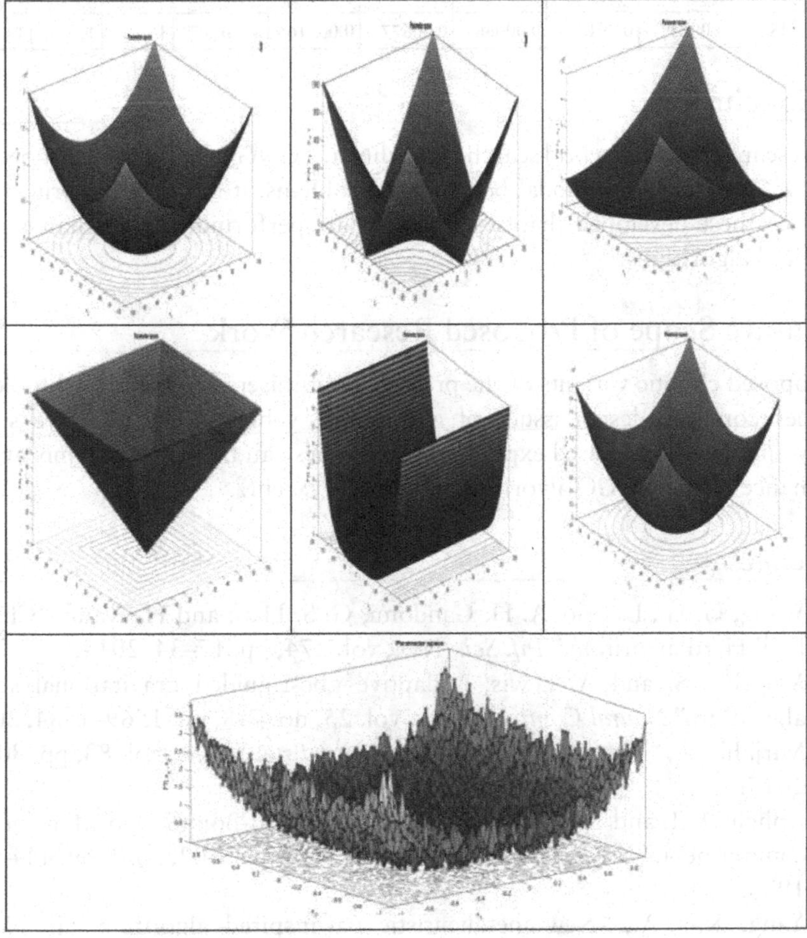

Figure 3: Unimodal regular benchmark functions 3-D view.

1.4 Test Results for Chaotic Northern Goshawk Optimiser Algorithm for Standard Benchmark Problems

Table 2: Test results for chaotic northern goshawk optimiser algorithm for standard benchmark problems.

Function Number	Index	Evaluated Mean Fitness	STD value	Best Fitness value	Worst Fitness value	Median value	Present P-Value Rank Sum Test	h-Valve Rank Sum Test	p-value T-Test	h-Value T-Test
F1	10	4.03E-21	1.81E-20	5.52E-26	9.89E-20	1.79E-23	4.98E-11	1	0	0.167334
F2	27	1.23E-14	2.42E-14	4.61E-16	9.02E-14	5.09E-15	7.38E-10	1	1	0.028865
F3	24	3.734627	8.960794	0.000195	44.50849	0.404125	5.27E-05	1	0	0.229362
F4	6	0.001216	0.001309	3.83E-05	0.005251	0.000744	0.994102	0	0	0.329224
F5	24	26.05861	1.505236	24.35246	28.75704	25.30439	1.96E-10	1	1	3.21E-11
F6	12	0.00582	0.00242	0.003071	0.01453	0.005193	3.02E-11	1	1	1.37E-28
F7	25	0.0025	0.001457	0.00066	0.00677	0.002165	1.25E-07	1	1	1.65E-06

2. Conclusion

In this research paper, a hybrid search algorithm, i.e. CNGO has been developed and tested for 7 standard uni-modal benchmark problems. It has been experimentally found that these developed chaotic algorithms are performing better than existing bioinspired algorithms.

3. Future Scope of Proposed Research Work

The proposed chaotic variants of the proposed optimisers can be utilised to design the other complex design issues of automobile vehicles. The adaptive search strategy and levy flight-based exploitation strategies can be applied to improve the performance of the CNGO algorithm to the next extent.

References

[1] Wang, G. G., L. Guo, A. H. Gandomi, G. S. Hao, and H. Wang, "Chaotic Krill Herd algorithm," *Inf. Sci. (Ny).*, vol. 274, pp. 17–34, 2014.

[2] Mirjalili, S. and A. Lewis, "Adaptive gbest-guided gravitational search algorithm," *Neural Comput. Appl.*, vol. 25, no. 7–8, pp. 1569–1584, 2014.

[3] Mirjalili, S., "The ant lion optimizer," *Adv. Eng. Softw.*, vol. 83, pp. 80–98, 2015.

[4] Cohen, A. I. and M. Yoshimura, "A Branch-and-Bound algorithm for unit commitment," *IEEE Trans. Power Appar. Syst.*, vol. 102, no. 2, pp. 444–451, 1983.

[5] Yang, X.-s. A., "New metaheuristic bat-inspired algorithm," in *Nature inspired cooperative strategies for optimization (NICSO 2010)*, p. 65–74: Springer, 2010.

[6] Nakamura, R. Y. M., L. A. M. Pereira, K. A. Costa, D. Rodrigues, J. P. Papa, and X. S. Yang, "BBA: a binary bat algorithm for feature selection," *Brazilian Symp. Comput. Graph. Image Process.*, pp. 291–297, 2012.

[7] Simon, D., "Biogeography-based optimization," *IEEE Trans. Evol. Comput.*, vol. 12, no. 6, pp. 702–713, Dec. 2008.

[8] Das, S., A. Biswas, S. Dasgupta, and A. Abraham, "Bacterial foraging optimization algorithm: Theoretical foundations, analysis, and applications," *Stud. Comput. Intell.*, vol. 203, pp. 23–55, 2009.

[9] Rashedi, E., H. Nezamabadi-Pour, and S. Saryazdi, "BGSA: binary gravitational search algorithm," *Nat. Comput.*, vol. 9, no. 3, pp. 727–745, 2010.

[10] Meng, X. B., X. Z. Gao, L. Lu, Y. Liu, and H. Zhang, "A new bio-inspired optimisation algorithm: Bird Swarm Algorithm," *J. Exp. Theor. Artif. Intell.*, vol. 28, no. 4, pp. 673–687, 2016.

[11] Civicioglu, P., "Backtracking Search Optimization Algorithm for numerical optimization problems," *Appl. Math. Comput.*, vol. 219, no. 15, pp. 8121–8144, 2013.

[12] Kaveh, A. and V. R. Mahdavi, "Colliding bodies optimization: extensions and applications," *Colliding Bodies Optim. Extensions Appl.*, pp. 1–284, 2015.

[13] Kuo, H. C. and C. H. Lin, "Cultural evolution algorithm for global optimizations and its applications," *J. Appl. Res. Technol.*, vol. 11, no. 4, pp. 510–522, 2013.

11. Wireless Lock System using Arduino UNO and Bluetooth Module

Mohana Vamsi Perni[1], Sai Daiwik V[1], Tagore Reddy[1], Veera Hemanth1, Rajeev Kumar Patial[1], Jhulan Kumar[1], Dilip Kumar[2] and Dinesh Kumar[3]

[1] *Lovely Faculty of Technology and Sciences, Lovely Professional University, Phagwara, India*

[2] *Department of Electronics and communication Engineering, SLIET, Longowal, India*

[3] *Department of Information Technology, DAVIET, Jalandhar, India*

Abstract: The goal of the Bluetooth-enabled wireless lock system project by Arduino Uno is to develop a smart lock that can be operated by a mobile application. The solution uses a Bluetooth module to create a wireless connection with a mobile device and an Arduino Uno microcontroller board to manage the locking mechanism. The project's goal is to offer a safe and practical method of using a mobile device to lock and unlock doors. The mobile application allows users to verify by the users before they can access the lock. The project's design is open-source, it is usable for anyone to modify and improve the system based on their needs. The paper highlights, advantages, disadvantages and applications of project.

Keywords: Digital lock, mobile applications, arduino uno, wireless lock.

1. Introduction

The wireless lock system by Arduino Uno using Bluetooth is a cutting-edge project that aims to provide a secure and convenient way of locking and unlocking doors using a mobile device. The project includes the power of the Arduino Uno microcontroller board and Bluetooth technology to establish a wireless connection between the lock and a mobile application. The major outcome of the module is to offer an alternative to traditional lock and key mechanisms that can be easy to use and make hand free. The project works by the usage of the components such as the Arduino Uno microcontroller board and the Bluetooth module. It also explains how the mobile application can be used to control the lock wirelessly, eliminating the need for physical keys; coming to the authentication process, this wireless lock system allows only authorised users can access the lock. It also allows the users for customisation and modification, making it suitable for various applications [1].

1.1. Methodology

A wireless lock system based on Arduino UNO involves several components and processes. The system includes a motor driver module, an Arduino UNO board, a Bluetooth module, a power source and a lock mechanism. The motor driver module controls the motor that moves the lock mechanism. The Bluetooth module is used for wireless communication between the Arduino UNO board and smartphone. The power source is used to power the Arduino UNO board and the motor driver module. The lock mechanism is designed to receive and execute commands from the motor driver module.

The methodology of the wireless lock system based on Arduino UNO involves the following steps. To receive instructions from the Bluetooth module, the Arduino UNO board must first be programmed using the Arduino Integrated Development Environment (IDE). Second, the Bluetooth module is paired with the user's smartphone. Third, the user sends a command to the Bluetooth module using a smartphone app. Fourth, the Bluetooth module sends the command to the Arduino UNO board. Fifth, the Arduino UNO board processes the command and sends a signal to the motor driver module. Finally, the motor driver module drives the motor to move the lock mechanism, which locks or unlocks the door. The wireless lock system based on Arduino UNO is a reliable and cost-effective solution for securing doors in homes, offices and other locations [2].

1.2. Principle of Operation

The principles of the wireless lock system by Arduino Uno using bluetooth project are based on the combination of the Arduino Uno microcontroller board and bluetooth technology. The system operates on the principle of wireless communication between the lock and a mobile device, eliminating the need for physical keys or contact. The principles of the project describes the components used, such as the Arduino Uno microcontroller board and the bluetooth module. It explains how the microcontroller board controls the lock mechanism and how the bluetooth module establishes a wireless connection with a mobile device. The use of a mobile application to control the lock wirelessly. The application allows users to authenticate themselves before they can access the lock, only authorised individuals can unlock the door. It can also be used to monitor the lock's status and receive notifications when the lock is locked or unlocked [2].

2. Components and Working

2.1. Components

Arduino UNO: Popular microcontroller boards like the Arduino UNO are frequently utilised in the fields of electronics and computer science. It is an open-source platform with a straightforward yet effective programming environment, which makes it perfect for a variety of projects like robotics, automation and Internet of Things (IoT) devices. The board is based on the ATmega328P microcontroller, which contains a 16 MHz quartz crystal oscillator, six analog inputs and 14 digital input/output ports. The board is simple to use and portable because it may be fueled either by a USB connection or an external power source as indicated in Figure 1. One of the most significant advantages of the Arduino UNO board is its versatility.

It can be used to control various electronic devices such as motors sensors, and LED lights. The board comes with a user-friendly interface that permits to write, compile and upload codes quickly.

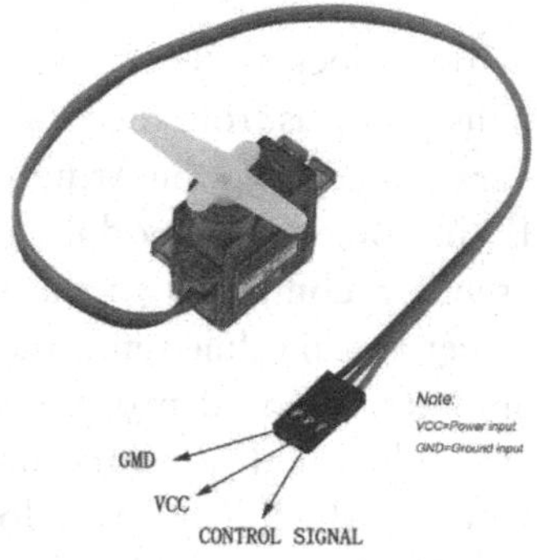

Figure 1: *Connection interface[1].*

The Arduino IDE is a straightforward program that works with several operating systems and lets you write C++ code. The Arduino UNO board is a terrific option for professionals, students and hobbyists who want to develop cutting-edge projects without breaking the bank because it is also relatively affordable. Overall, the Arduino UNO board is a dependable and user-friendly microcontroller that offers countless opportunities for different applications [3] as indicated in Figure 2.

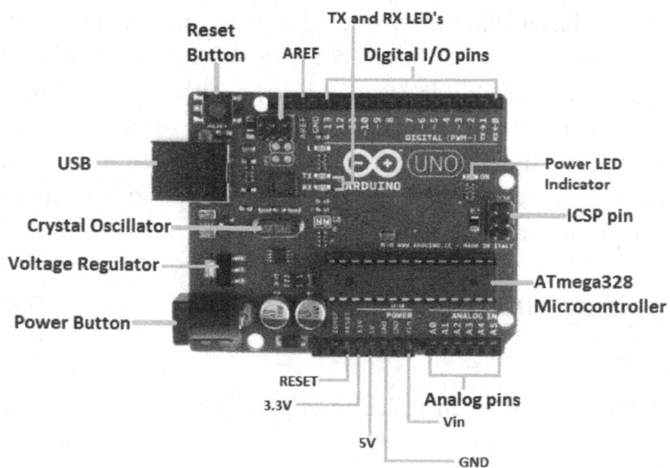

Figure 2: *Arduino Uno [2].*

Servo Motor: A servo motor is an electrical device that is used to control the position of a mechanical system. It is a type of rotary actuator that uses a feedback mechanism to precisely control the position of its output shaft. Servo motors are commonly used a wide range of industrial applications, including robotics, manufacturing and automation. They are highly reliable and accurate, making them ideal for applications that require precise control of movement. One of the main advantages of servo motors is their ability to provide precise positional control. They are capable of rotating to a specific angle and holding that position with a high degree of accuracy. This is achieved through the use of a closed-loop feedback system that continuously monitors the position of the output shaft and adjusts the motor's operation to maintain the desired position. Servo motors are also capable of producing high torque at low speeds, making them well-suited for applications that require high precision and accuracy such as robotics and CNC machines [3].

Bluetooth HC-05: The Bluetooth HC-05 is a wireless communication module that allows for easy and reliable communication between devices. It is a small, low-power device that can be easily integrated into a wide range of electronic projects. The HC-05 module uses Bluetooth technology to enable wireless communication between devices over short distances. It supports a range data rate and can be used for a variety of applications, including wireless audio, data transfer and remote control.

The HC-05 is a highly versatile and user-friendly module. It is easy to use and can be configured for a wide range of applications using a simple set of AT commands. The module features a UART interface for serial communication and can be easily connected to a microcontroller or other embedded device as indicated in Figure 3.

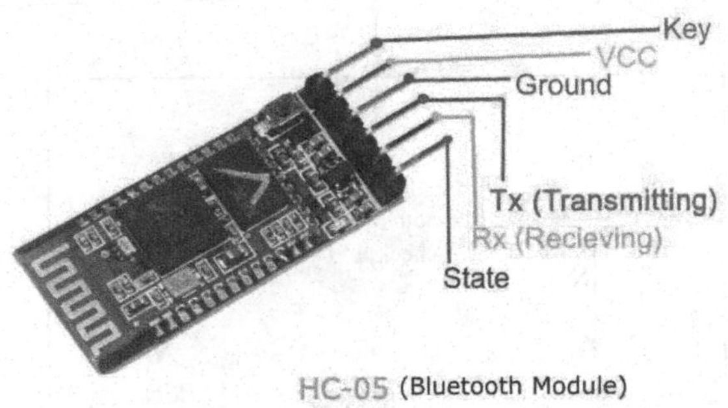

Figure 3: Bluetooth module HC-05 [2].

The HC-05 also supports a range of Bluetooth profiles, including the serial port profile (SPP), which allows for easy integration with a wide range of devices. Overall, the Bluetooth HC-05 is an excellent choice for anyone looking for a simple and reliable wireless communication solution for their project [3].

2.2. Working

A wireless lock system using Arduino Uno works by establishing a wireless communication link between the lock and the controller device such as a smartphone or a remote control. The Arduino Uno is used to control the lock, A servo motor used instead of the lock. The wireless communication we established using a Bluetooth. The lock can be opened or closed by sending commands wirelessly from the controller device to the Arduino Uno. If we press 0 in the application, then the servo motor will be unlocked, and the servo motor will be locked when we press 1 in the application. The system can be designed to provide different levels of security, such as password protection as indicated in Figure 4. The wireless lock system can be customised and adapted to meet the specific needs of the users; implementation shown in Figure 5 [9–10].

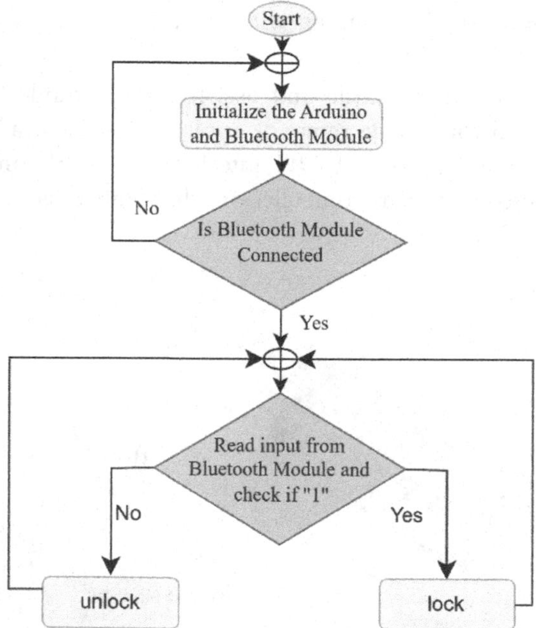

Figure 4: *Flow diagram of lock system [2].*

The objective of a wireless lock system using Arduino Uno is to provide a secure and convenient way to control access to a particular area or object. This can be used in a variety of settings including homes, workplaces and private uses. With the wireless lock system, the lock can be controlled from a distance, which adds to the convenience and flexibility of the system. To promote innovation and learning in the field of electronics and programming. The system is an excellent platform for students to explore the innovation of wireless communication and control. Anyone can learn how to use Arduino Uno and build their wireless lock system, and components required are mentioned in Table 1. The system can also be extended and modified to in additional features such as sensors and alarms which increases the security and functionality of the system [3].

Table 1: Components used in the circuit [3].

Sr. No	Name of Component	Quantity
1	Arduino Uno	1
2	HC-05 Bluetooth Module	1
3	Servo Motor	1
4	Jumping wires	1

2.3. Software Code

```
#include <Servo.h>
Servo servo1;
void setup() {
  Serial.begin(9600);
  servo1.attach(3);
}
void loop() {
  if (Serial.available()) {
    int input = Serial.read() - '0';
    if (input == 1) {
      servo1.write(180);
      delay(300);
     //servo1.write(0);
     //delay(1000);
    } else if (input == 0) {
      servo1.write(0);
      delay(300);
    } else {
      servo1.write(90);
      delay(500);
      servo1.write(55);
      delay(100);
      servo1.write(25);
```

```
    delay(100);
    servo1.write(270);
    delay(100);
    servo1.write(150);
    delay(100);
    servo1.write(0);
    delay(100);
  }
}
```

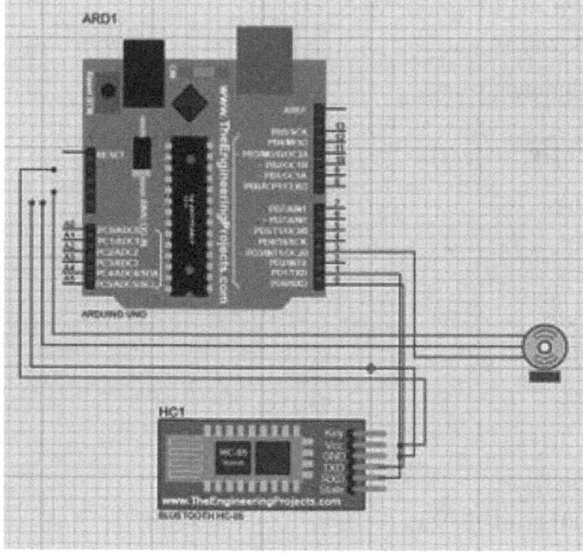

Figure 5. Circuit connection Diagram [5]

3. Applications

Home Security: A wireless lock system using Arduino Uno can be used as a security system for homes, apartments and other residential buildings. The system can be configured to automatically lock and unlock doors at specific times and can be controlled remotely using a smartphone app.

Office Security: A wireless lock system can also be used to secure office buildings, conference rooms and other corporate facilities. The system can be programmed to allow access to authorised personnel only and can be monitored remotely using a web-based interface.

Smart Lockers: A wireless lock system can be used to secure lockers in schools, gyms and other public places. The system can be configured to allow access only to authorised users and can be remotely monitored for security purposes.

Smart Homes: A wireless lock system can be integrated into a smart home system, allowing homeowners to remotely control and monitor their doors from anywhere. The system can also be programmed to automatically lock and unlock doors based on specific events or time of day.

Industrial Applications: A wireless lock system can be used in industrial settings to secure doors and gates and to control access to sensitive areas. The system can be customised to meet the specific needs of each application [5].

3.1. Advantages

Enhanced Security: The wireless lock system provides an additional layer of security for homes and offices by eliminating the need for physical keys. With a wireless lock system, you can control who has access to your property through an app on your smartphone.

Convenience: The wireless lock system allows you to control your locks remotely, making it more convenient to grant access to guests or family members. You can also schedule access for specific times, such as for house cleaning or delivery services.

Cost-Effective: The Arduino UNO wireless lock system is cost-effective compared to traditional lock systems that require complex wiring and installation processes. The Arduino UNO project allows you to create your own wireless lock system with minimal cost and effort.

Customisable: The Arduino UNO wireless lock system is highly customisable, allowing you to create a lock system that suits your specific needs. You can integrate additional sensors, cameras and alarms to enhance security and monitor access to your property.

Easy to Install: The Arduino UNO wireless lock system is easy to install and requires minimal technical knowledge. You can find a wide range of tutorials and guides online to help you get started [6].

3.2. Dis-Advantages

Reliability: Wireless lock systems rely on wireless signals to operate, and interference or weak signals can affect the system's reliability. This could potentially cause issues with unlocking and locking the doors, which could be frustrating and inconvenient.

Vulnerability to hacking: Wireless systems are vulnerable to hacking, which could potentially compromise the security of your property. It's important to ensure that your wireless lock system is secure and that you follow best practices for network security.

Battery life: Wireless lock systems require power to operate, and if the batteries run out, you may be locked out of your property. You will need to monitor the battery life and replace the batteries as needed.

Compatibility: The wireless lock system using Arduino UNO may not be compatible with all types of locks or doors, which could limit its usefulness. You will need to ensure that your door and lock are compatible with the system before you install it.

Technical knowledge: The wireless lock system using Arduino UNO requires some technical knowledge to install and set up. If you're not familiar with electronics or programming, you may need to seek assistance from someone who have knowledge on that [8].

4. Conclusion

The wireless lock system using Arduino UNO is a reliable and efficient way of securing doors without the need for traditional keys. By implementing this system, users can easily control access to their spaces and ensure security. The Arduino UNO microcontroller, combined with wireless communication, modules Bluetooth. We provide a high degree of customisation and control over the system. Additionally, the other sensors and modules to further enhance the functionality of the system. It is important to note that the security of the wireless lock system depends on the strength of the chosen wireless communication protocol and encryption algorithm used to protect the system. Thus, it is essential to select a reliable and secure communication protocol and implement proper encryption methods to prevent unauthorised access to the system [7].

References:

[1] Radhika, V., L. Dhiviyalakshmi, and R. Abishek, "Design and development of automatic waste treatment and disposal unit for hospitals using microcontroller," *International Conference on Soft Computing for Security Applications*, pp. 867–875, Apr. 17, 2023.

[2] Banzi, M. and M. Shiloh, *Getting Started with Arduino*, Maker Media, Inc., Feb. 15, 2022.

[3] Monk, S., *Programming Arduino Next Steps: Going Further with Sketches*, McGraw-Hill Education, 2014.

[4] https://www.arduino.cc/en/Guide.

[5] https://www.youtube.com/Arduino.

[6] Hall, C. M. and M. James, "Medical Rourism: Emerging Biosecurity and Nosocomial Issues," *Tourism Rev.*, vol. 66, no. 1/2, pp. 118–126, May 10, 2011.

[7] Neto, A. L., A. L. Souza, I. Cunha, M. Nogueira, I. O. Nunes, L. Cotta, N. Gentille, A. A. Loureiro, D. F. Aranha, H. K. Patil, L. B. Oliveira, "AoT: Authentication and access control for the entire IoT device life-cycle," *Proceedings of the 14th ACM Conference on Embedded Network Sensor Systems CD-ROM*, pp. 1–15, Nov. 14, 2016.

[8] Patil, K. A., N. Vittalkar, P. Hiremath, M. A. Murthy, "Smart door locking system using IoT," *Int. Res. J. Eng. Technol.*, pp. 3090–3094, May 2020.

[9] https://www.instructables.com/Arduino-How-to-Control-Servo-Motor-Via-Bluetooth-w/.

[10] https://techatronic.com/bluetooth-controlled-servo-motor-project-arduino-servo-motor-project/.

12. Analysis of Various Methods to Boost the Isolation in UWB-MIMO Antennas

Daljeet Singh[1], Mariella Särestöniemi[1,2] and Teemu Myllyla[1,3]

[1]*Research Unit of Health Sciences and Technology, Faculty of Medicine, University of Oulu, Finland*

[2]*Centre for Wireless Communications, Faculty of Information Technology and Electrical Engineering, University of Oulu, Finland*

[3]*Optoelectronics and Measurement Techniques Unit, Faculty of Information Technology and Electrical Engineering, University of Oulu, Finland*

Abstract: The physical dimensions of the antenna and mutual coupling are two prime challenges in designing a multiple input multiple output (MIMO) system in ultra-wide band (UWB) frequency. In order to increase the compactness of the system, multiple antennas are positioned very close to each other, which results in interference between them. Academicians and researchers have proposed several techniques to resolve this problem of mutual interference between MIMO antennas in UWB. In this paper, the different techniques of the UWB-MIMO antenna are presented for the improvement of isolation parameters. Several antenna designs are explored, and the techniques underlined for interference mitigation are studied. A comprehensive survey is presented based on different types of material, slots, stubs with slits and slots and the theory of characteristics mode, which can enhance the isolation.

Keywords: 6G, antenna, communication, isolation enhancement, MIMO, UWB.

1. Introduction

Ultra-wideband (UWB) technology has revolutionised high-speed short-range indoor communication applications and united with MIMO systems has paved new milestones [1]. MIMO systems have applications in a variety of fields [2–4]. The traditional single input single output (SISO) systems rely on only one antenna to transmit and receive data, which is not efficient for high data rate reliable communication. The brute force approach for improving the communication data rate is by increasing signal-to-noise-ratio (SNR), bandwidth of signals and/or the number of antennas. However, the spectral efficiency cannot be improved by these methods, and MIMO systems emerge as the solution to improve antenna gains, efficiency and number of transmission paths [5–7]. The use of multiple antennas in the system at the same time causes the problem of interference. In order to solve the problem of interference in MIMO systems, a lot of studies have been conducted on the isolation of MIMO antenna systems. Because of its simplicity and efficiency, few studies have been conducted on circuit designing. Some works utilise meta-materials [2,3], which are artificial structures and their properties cannot be found in nature. For ultra-wide band (UWB) communications, federal communications commission (FCC) has allocated a band of frequency of range 3.1 to 10.6 GHz [1], which has attracted interest from industry and academia. However, UWB has drawbacks of less range and reduced channel capacity and because of the power limitation of -41 dBm/MHz. MIMO systems incorporating UWB technology, have the potential to address this limitation resulting in a number of possible applications [6].

This paper gives an overview of four different methods to improve the isolation of UWB-MIMO antennas. The impact of the isolation on the antenna and channel characteristics is compared with the selected techniques, and the challenges related to the isolation are discussed.

2. Isolation Improvement by Carbon Black Film

In order to enhance the isolation, the decoupling method is used in circuit designing, which separates the currents of an antenna from interfering with each other. A method that changes the structure of the ground and reveals the signal of an antenna to reduce interference is given in [8]. However, designing of circuit sometimes can change the working of the antenna systems. In [9], with the help of 'Carbon Black Film' (absorb EM signal), the isolation of two antenna systems is presented. According to Schelkunoff's theory, the antenna with a capacitance and effective length performs very accurately. Since the MIMO antennas are coated with a paste of carbon black film the interference of the system is expected to reduce and isolation is also expected to be enhanced. In order to read MIMO system properties, the antenna is coated with a disc-shaped monopole in [10] as shown in Figure 1. The paste that is used has a size <10 μm for conduction. The carbon black film is a paste that consists of epoxy and carbon black of 30,40,50 and 60%, a triple roller was used for mixing the paste and water was separated from the paste. Then, using a spin coater, the substrate is coated with paste. To remove the epoxy, the sample was heated at 150 Celsius for around 5 min in a furnace. The length and resistance of the sheet are measured. The feed lines of the monopole antennas are then coated with the paste as shown in Figure 2. The antenna which is not coated has a bandwidth of 7.5 GHz (ranging from 3.5 to 11 GHz), S21 is around -10 and -18 dB, and the antenna with a paste of (30 to 60%), S11<-10 dB and S21 is decreased from 10 to 18 dB to 15 to 20 dB. Properties of the MIMO system, which was coated with carbon black (W = 8 mm), is able to achieve an efficiency of 69.2%; Gain >2.11 dB; and ECC < 0.02.

3. Isolation Improvement by Four Elements

MIMO technology is used in UWB antenna to remove multipath fading and give good channel capacity. Antennas listed in the literature have got isolation enhancement and also have the notched band function [11–15]. In order to realise a better working antenna system, enhanced isolation has a very important place, but it is challenging to for both compact size and good isolation at the same time. In order to convert differential signals into single-ended signals, a balun (a type of transformer) is used so that there is a connection between the circuits [16].

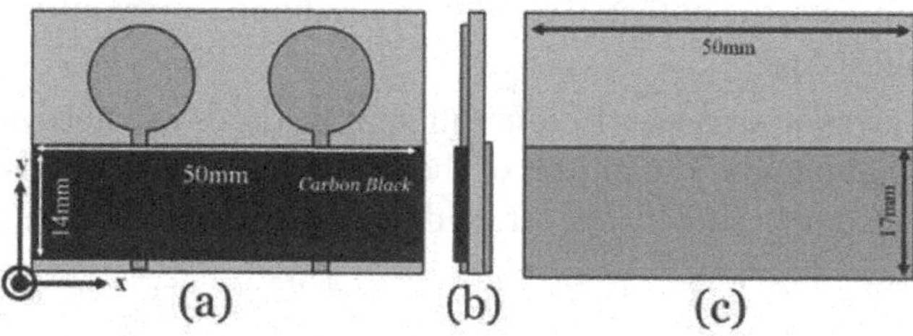

Figure 1: MIMO antenna design [10].

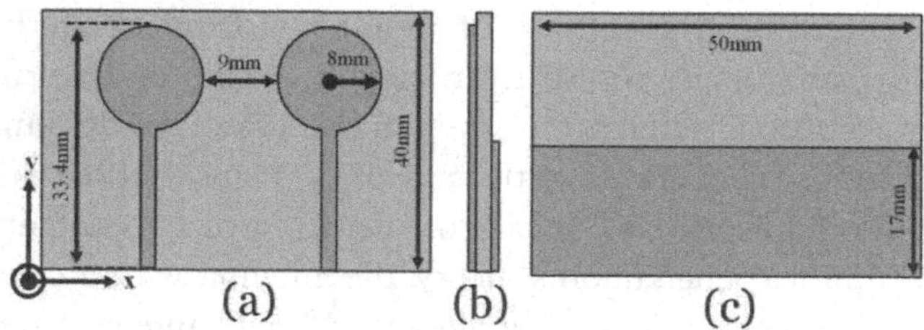

Figure 2: MIMO antenna design with carbon black film [10].

A low cross-polarisation level can be achieved by using differential antennas [14]. A differential UWB-MIMO system having a notched band is presented in [15], but common mode signals are not suppressed in this study. In order to overcome this, a differential slot-stepped notched-band UWB-MIMO system has been taken. The presented design has a differential antenna with a band-notched feature that can suppress common mode signals at the same time. A four-element antenna described in figure 3

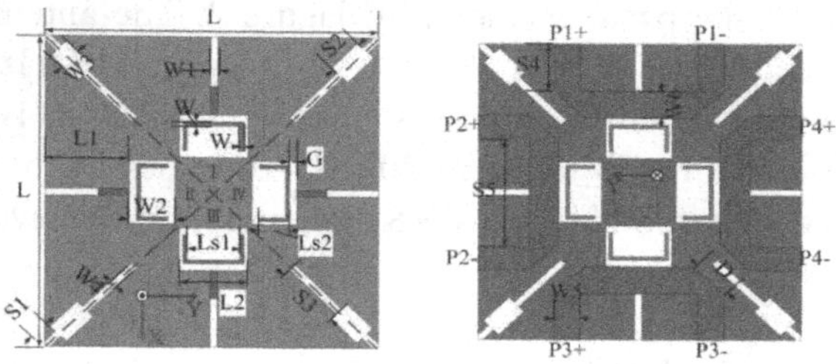

Figure 3: Four-element antenna described in [15].

The system has 4 elements and it can also adapt to differential feeding techniques; yet, the antenna occupies a smaller area, i.e. 44*44 mm^2. To increase the isolation and to obtain a notched band, 4 slots have been inserted in the design, and 4 U-shaped stubs are inserted in slots of antenna elements. Figure 4 shows the s-parameters of differential mode (DM) and common mode (CM) of the system. Figure 5 shows the power distributions at 5.5GHz if the system is run with and without stubs. Researchers are keenly showing interest in designing of dual wideband MIMO antenna with good isolation for multistrand applications. The problems with the isolation of the MIMO antennas are presented in [16]. Decoupling techniques are used to enhance the isolation, which is a main factor of MIMO antenna and limiting coupling b/w antenna elements.

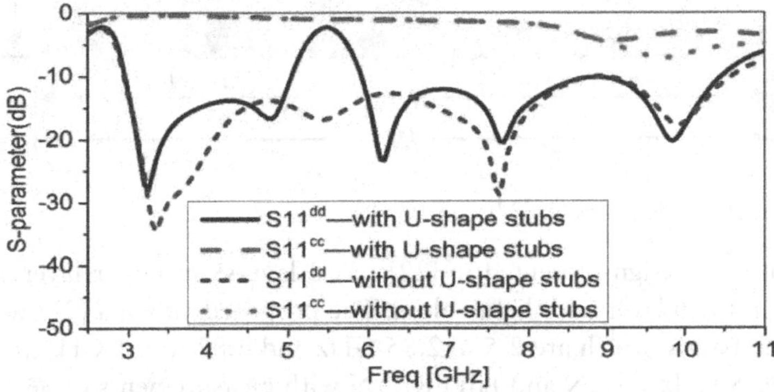

Figure 4: Simulated S-parameters of DM and CM signal of the proposed antenna [15].

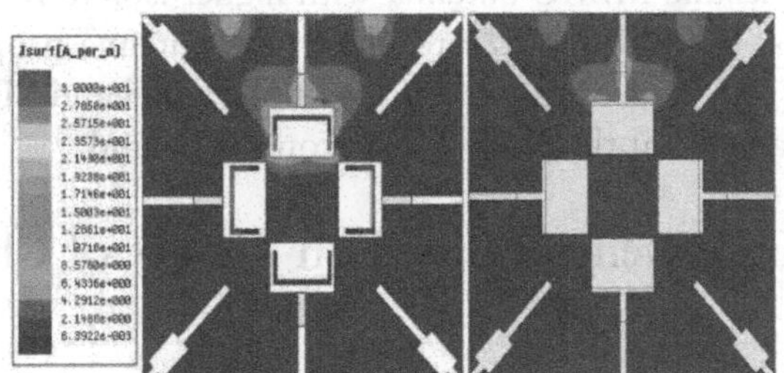

Figure 5: Power distributions at 5.5GHz [15].

4. Isolation Enhanced by Using Flag Shaped Stub

Another way to enhance isolation is to increase the number of antennas and polarisation. By considering earlier designs at a certain frequency, it can be seen we are unable to meet the standards of multi-antenna [17]. Some designs are able to achieve the needs of multiple-band MIMO antennas that can operate in dual-based wideband MIMO antenna [18–21]. Figure 6 shows MIMO antenna design

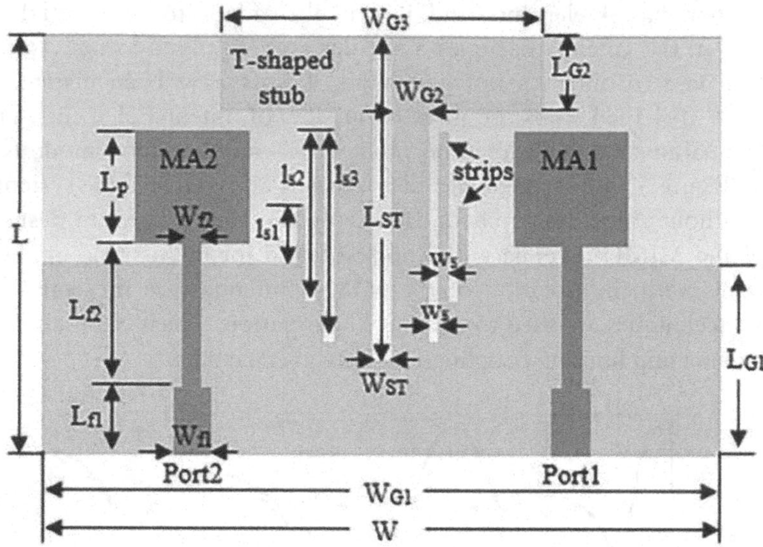

Figure 6: MIMO antenna design [22].

The antenna design presented in [22] has 2 layers: an upper layer with dark colour and a down layer with light colour. The proposed antenna [22] was able to cover 2 wide bands, which are 2.5 to 2.85 GHz and 4.82 to 6.1 GHz and can run in 2500LTE, 5 GHz WLAN and HIPERLAN with measurements of 36 *22 mm2. This antenna is very compact when compared to the earlier proposals, which have isolations of 18 dB and 20 dB for below and top bands. The main focus is to obtain a compact dual-wideband MIMO antenna with higher isolation between the MA1 and MA2 elements. The S11 and S21 results of the antenna proposed in [22] are shown in Figure 7. The shaped stub and strips on the wideband MIMO antenna act as an element of parasitic at the plane ground on the behind.

5. Isolation Improvement Based on Theory of Characteristics Mode

For mobile technologies, high spectral efficiency and large channel capacity have become an important factor. In order to achieve these demands, it is recommended 5G mobiles require high bandwidth. These suggestions have encouraged researchers to design a UWB-MIMO antenna. Multiple MIMO antennas have been proposed with some additional slots or decoupling structures. Some antennas at lower frequencies like less than 2 GHz go through poor isolation and diversity patterns, especially if there is limited ground plane area; because of this, we cannot use that type of system. This downfall in isolation is due to the theory of characteristic modes [23]. Fundamental characteristic modes can excite fully at the ground plane because at lesser frequency the ground has a small electric size. The solution to this is to divide the ground into 2 parts and rotate the antenna elements 90° [23].

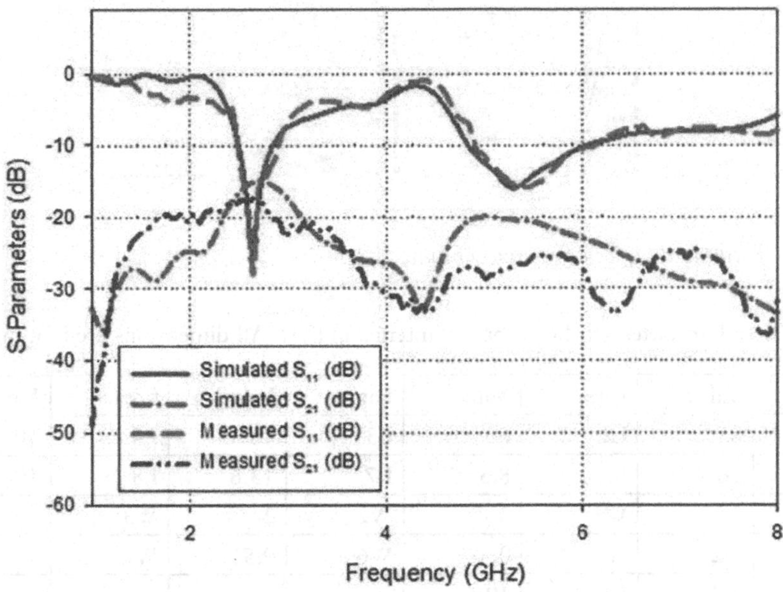

Figure 7: S11 and S21 results of antenna proposed in [22].

The proposed antenna in [23] can also operate at lower frequency (2 GHz) and also at medium & higher frequency ranging above 3 GHz. If frequency increases, the number of CMs also increases. Two antenna elements are fixed at the ground plane at opposite edges. Current distributions of these antenna elements are different, so they excite different CMs according to TCM. At lower frequency bands, they act as E and H sources, therefore, giving two different Common Modes, and the difference in CMsgives way to the required diversity in pattern and enhanced isolation. Figure 8 shows the geometry of the proposed antennas #1 and #2 proposed in [23]. Figure 9 shows the characteristics angles of 4 CMs at antennas#1 and #2 it shows that the first three most relevant CMsof Ant #1 and Ant #2, which resonate at 2.5, 4.6 and 7 GHz and that of Ant #2 resonates at frequencies 2.55ghz, 4.7 GHz and 7.5 GHz, but 4th CM of ant #1and #2 resonates at 10 GHz. The dimensions of the proposed antenna in [23] are given in Table 1. The size of the quarter loop is 13.6 mm to 8.5 mm. The capacitor which has 3 fingers is put at the last of the quarter loop. Figure 10 shows predicted return loss waves.

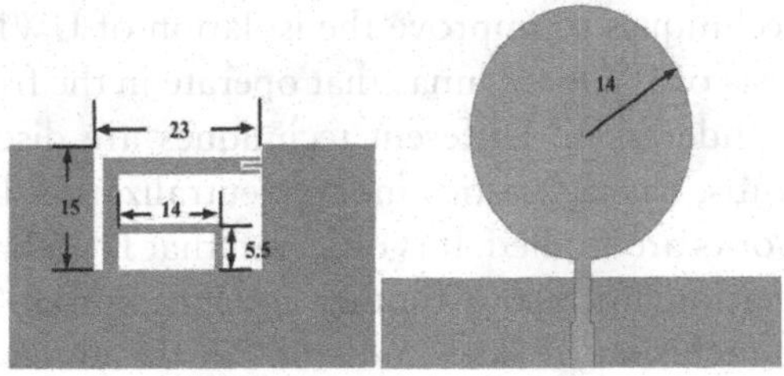

Figure 8: Antenna elements geometry in CMA [23].

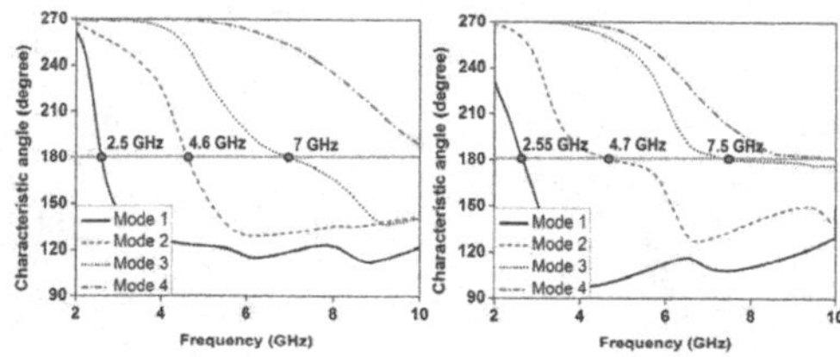

Figure 9: Estimated angles of common modes [23].

Table 1: Parameters of the proposed antenna in [23] (All dimensions are in mm.).

Para.	Value	Para.	Value	Para.	Value	Para.	Value
L1	85	L2	60	L3	50	L4	10
L5	16	L6	8.5	L7	13.6	L8	10
L9	3	W1	3	W2	2	W3	3
W4	1.2	W5	0.4	W6	0.5	W7	3
W8	2.4	R1	10.5				

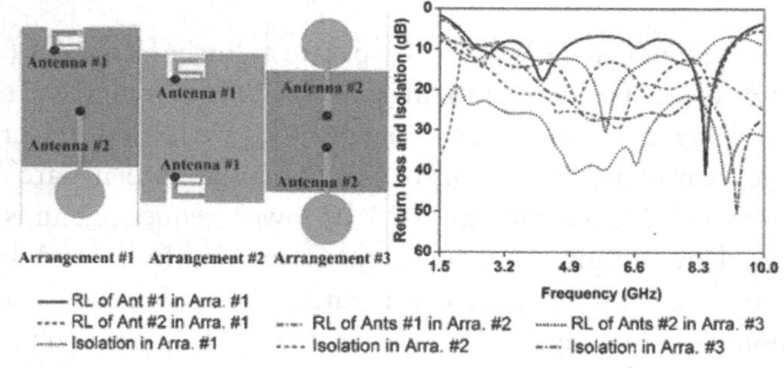

Figure 10: Relationship of proposed antenna in [23] with antenna element provisions.

6. Conclusion

UWB antenna in MIMO configuration offers a lot of advantages such as high bandwidth, low power spectral density, less cost, less consumption of power, high data transfer rates and security. This paper presents a study and comparative analysis of various existing techniques to improve the isolation of UWB-MIMO antennas. The design and analysis of UWB antennas that operate in the frequency range from 3.1 to 10.6 GHz is undertaken. Different techniques are discussed for reducing interference: slots, stubs, characteristics mode, neutralization lines, metamaterials and decoupling networks are studied. It is observed that DGS-based antenna design offers maximum radiation efficiency. Another conclusion that can be drawn from the study is that the inclusion of slots and stubs in the antenna design results in smaller dimensions of the antenna with improved gain.

References

[1] Kumar, R., G. S. Saini, and D. Singh, "Compact tri-band patch antenna for Ku band applications," *Prog. Electromagn. Res. C*, vol. 103, pp. 45–58, 2020.

[2] Singh, D. and H. D. Joshi, "BER performance of SFBC OFDM system over TWDP fading channel," *IEEE Commun. Lett.*, vol. 20, no. 12, pp. 2426–2429, 2016.

[3] Singh, D. and H. D. Joshi, "Error probability analysis of STBC-OFDM systems with CFO and imperfect CSI over generalized fading channels," *AEU-Int J. Electron. Commun.*, vol. 98, pp. 156–163, 2019.

[4] Ouamri, M., B. Gordana, D. Singh, A. B. Adam, M. S. A. Muthanna, and X. Li, "Nonlinear energy-harvesting for D2D networks underlaying UAV with SWIPT using MADQN," *IEEE Commun. Lett.*, vol. 27, no. 7, pp. 1804–1808, 2023.

[5] Singh, D. and H. D. Joshi, "Generalized MGF based analysis of line-of-sight plus scatter fading model and its applications to MIMO-OFDM systems," *AEU-Int. J. Electron. Commun.*, vol. 91, pp. 110–117, 2018.

[6] Kumar, G., D. Singh, and R. Kumar, "A planar CPW fed UWB antenna with dual rectangular notch band characteristics incorporating Uslot, SRRs, and EBGs," *Int. J. RF Microwave Comput. Aided Eng.*, vol. 31, no. 7, 2021.

[7] Singh, D. and H. D. Joshi, "Performance analysis of SFBCOFDM system with channel estimation error over generalized fading channels," *Trans. Emerging Telecommun. Technol.*, vol. 29, no. 3, 2018.

[8] Singh,H., S. Verdhan, and A Mohan, "Closely-coupled MIMO antenna with high wideband isolation using decoupling circuit," *AEU-Int. J. Electron. Commun.*, vol. 138, 2021.

[9] Ketzaki, D. A. and T. V. Yioultsis, "Metamaterial-based design of planar compact MIMO monopoles," *IEEE Trans. Antennas Propag.*, vol. 61, no. 5, pp. 2758–2766, 2013.

[10] Lin,G., C. Sung, J. Chen, L. Chen, and M. Houng, "Isolation improvement in UWB MIMO antenna system using carbon black film," *IEEE Antennas Wireless Propag. Lett.*, vol. 16, pp. 222–225, 2016.

[11] Chen, P., Z. Yue, X. Yang, R. Guo, Y. Li, and L. Ge, "High-gain omnidirectional transmitarray antenna," *IEEE Trans. Antennas Propag.*, vol. 71, no. 11,pp. 8441–8449, 2023.

[12] Ban, Y. L., Z. X. Chen, Z. Chen, K. Kang, and J. L. W. Li, "Decoupled closely spaced headband antenna array for WWAN/LTE smartphone applications," *IEEE Antennas Wireless Propag. Lett.*, vol. 13, pp. 31–34, 2014.

[13] Sharawi, M. S., M. A. Jan, and D. N. Aloi, "Four-shaped 2 × 2 multi-standard compact multiple-input–multiple-output antenna system for long-term evolution mobile handsets," *IET Microw. Antennas Propag.*, vol. 6, pp. 685–696, 2012.

[14] Singh, D., M. A. Ouamri, M. S. Muthanna, A. Adam, A. Muthanna, A. Koucheryavy, and A. A. El-Latif, "A generalized approach on outage performance analysis of dual-hop decode and forward relaying for 5G and beyond scenarios," *Sustainability*, vol. 14, no. 19, 2022.

[15] Khan, M. S., A. D. Capobianco, A. Asif, S. Iftikhar, and B. D. Braaten, "A compact dual polarized ultrawideband multiple-input-multiple-output antenna," *Microw. Opt. Technol. Lett.*, vol. 58, no. 1, pp. 163–166, 2016.

[16] Jianghong, L., B. Sun, L. Ren, W. Yan, S. Wu, and J. Li, "Dual-band dual-polarized shared-aperture antenna with cross-band scattering suppression," *Int. J. RF Microwave Comput. Aided Eng.*, vol. 32, no. 6, 2022.

[17] Singh, D., M. A. Ouamri, M. S. Alzaidi, T. Alharbi, and S. Ghoneim, "Performance analysis of wireless power transfer enabled dual hop relay system under generalised fading scenarios," *IEEE Access*, vol. 10, pp. 114364–114373, 2022.

[18] Roshna, T. K., U. Deepak, V. R. Sajitha, K. Vasudevan, and P. Mohanan, "A compact UWB MIMO antenna with reflector to enhance isolation," *IEEE Trans. Antennas Propag.*, vol. 63, no. 4, pp. 1873–1877, 2015.

[19] Liu, L., S. W. Cheung, and T. I. Yuk, "Compact MIMO antenna for portable UWB applications with band-notched characteristic," *IEEE Trans. Antennas Propag.*, vol. 63, no. 5, pp. 1917–1924, 2015.

[20] Samia, H., H. A. Mohamed, and E. K. Hamad, "Design of high isolation two-port MIMO two-element array antenna using square spilt-ring resonators for 5G applications," *Int. J. Micro. Opt. Tech.*, vol. 17, pp. 339–346, 2022.

[21] Sepideh, R. and Y. Zehforoosh, "Design of a planar multiband antenna using metamaterials," J. Commun. Eng., vol. 11, no. 43, pp. 15–26, 2022.

[22] Katie, M., M. Faizal Jamlos, A. S. M. Alqadami, and M. Jamlos, "Isolation enhancement of compact dual-wideband MIMO antenna using flag-shaped stub, " *Microwave Opt. Technol. Lett.*, vol. 59, no. 5, pp. 1028–1032, 2017.

[23] Zhao, X., Y. Swee, and L. Ong, "Planar UWB MIMO antenna with pattern diversity and isolation improvement for mobile platform based on the theory of characteristic modes," *IEEE Trans. Antennas Propag.*, vol. 66, no. 1, pp. 420–425, 2017.

13. Smart EV Charging using IoT and Block Chain: A Comparative Study of Latest Technologies

Subhash Suman and Dr. Manoj Singh Adhikari

School of Electronics and Electrical Engineering, Lovely Professional University, Punjab, India

Abstract: With the increasing popularity of electric vehicles (EVs), there is a growing need for intelligent and effective charging infrastructure. In this paper, we present a comparative study of the latest smart methods for EV charging using IoT technologies. The aim is to explore the potential benefits of these technologies in terms of cost, energy efficiency and convenience, as well as to highlight their limitations and challenges. We review the relevant literature and compare various smart EV charging technologies based on their features, advantages and their limits. Finally, we suggest some recommendations for upcoming research in this area.

Keywords: Electric vehicle, charging, smart methods, demand response, vehicle-to-grid, renewable energy.

1. Introduction

Electric vehicles (EVs) have become very popular as an eco-friendly mode of transportation. However, charging infrastructure is still a major concern for EV owners. The conventional charging methods lack intelligence, which can lead to inefficient charging and negatively impact the power grid. To address these challenges, smart EV charging methods have been proposed that leverage the internet of things (IoT) to optimise charge efficiency and on-grid integration. This paper aims to suggest and review the latest advancements in smart EV charging using IoT and present a comparison table of the different approaches.

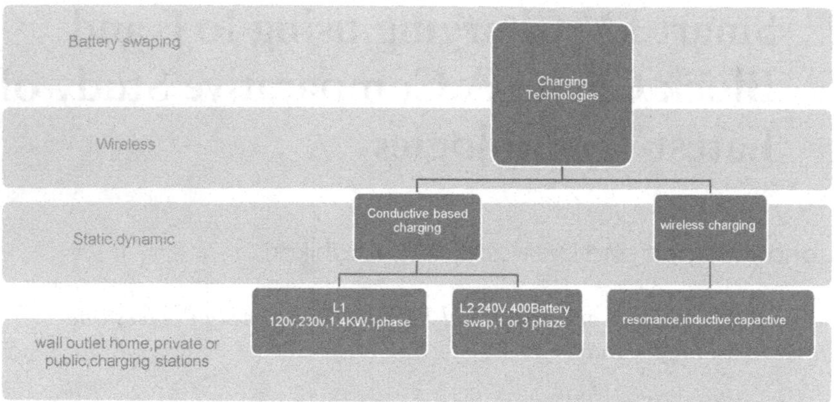

Figure 1: Classification of EV charging technologies and methods.

2. Latest Technologies used for Smart EV Charging

Smart Electrical vehicle charging involves the integration of Electric vehicle charging stations with the power on-grid and IoT-enabled devices. These devices can communicate with each other and share information to optimise charging. The following are some of the most popular smart charging methods:

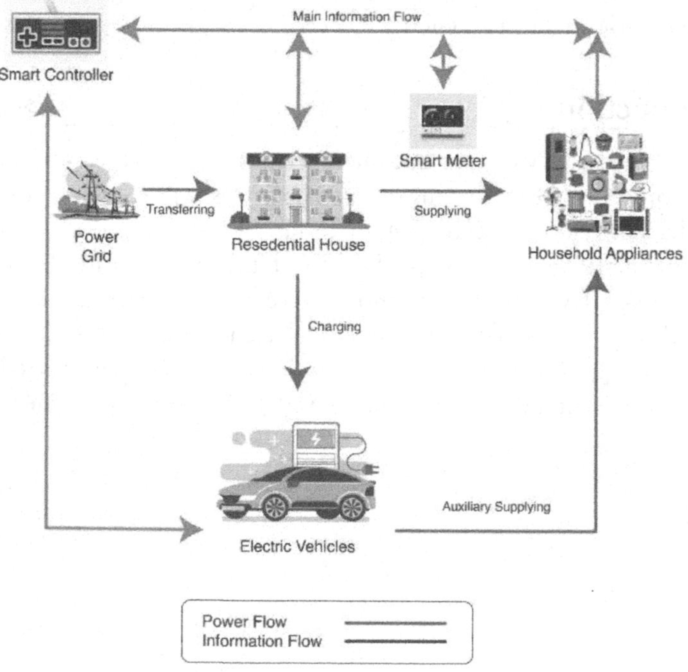

Figure 2: Demand response method for ev charging.

2.1. Dynamic Load Management (DLM)

DLM is a method that balances the power demand of Electric Vehicle charging control stations with the power availability of the grid. The method uses real-time data on grid power supply and EV charging demand to adjust charging rates and schedules.

2.2. Vehicle-to-Grid (V2G)

V2G is a bi-directional charging methods that allows Electric vehicles to supply power back to the grid when needed. This method not only helps to stabilise the grid but also provides a source of revenue for EV owners.

2.3. Demand Response (DR)

DR is a strategy that encourages EV owners to charge their cars when electricity is less expensive, during off-peak hours. This helps to reduce the overall demand for electricity during peak hours and can help to prevent grid overload.

2.4. Wireless Charging

Wireless charging uses electro-magnetic induction to transfer power wirelessly by a charging pad to the Electric vehicles. This method eliminates the need for physical cables, making charging more convenient and efficient.

2.5. Renewable Energy-Based Charging

renewable energy-based charging utilises solar or wind energy to charge EVs. This method can provide clean energy for EV charging, reducing greenhouse gas emissions. The literature review revealed that renewable energy-based charging using IoT can significantly reduce the cost of EV charging and minimize environmental impact.

2.6. Artificial Intelligence (AI)

AI technology can be used to optimise charging schedules, predict energy demand and provide real-time monitoring of charging stations. AI algorithms can also be used to identify and diagnose charging station malfunctions and improve the efficiency of charging infrastructure.

2.7. Augmented Reality (AR)

Users can receive real-time updates on the availability of charging stations, energy pricing and charging timeframes using augmented reality (AR) technology. AR can also be used to provide users with interactive charging guides and tutorials, making the charging process more accessible and user-friendly.

2.8. Blockchain-Based Charging

Blockchain technology can be used to manage EV charging infrastructure by providing a secure and transparent platform for the exchange of energy and payment. Blockchain-based charging can enable peer-to-peer charging, where EV owners can sell excess energy to other EV owners. It can also eliminate the need for intermediaries and reduce transaction costs.

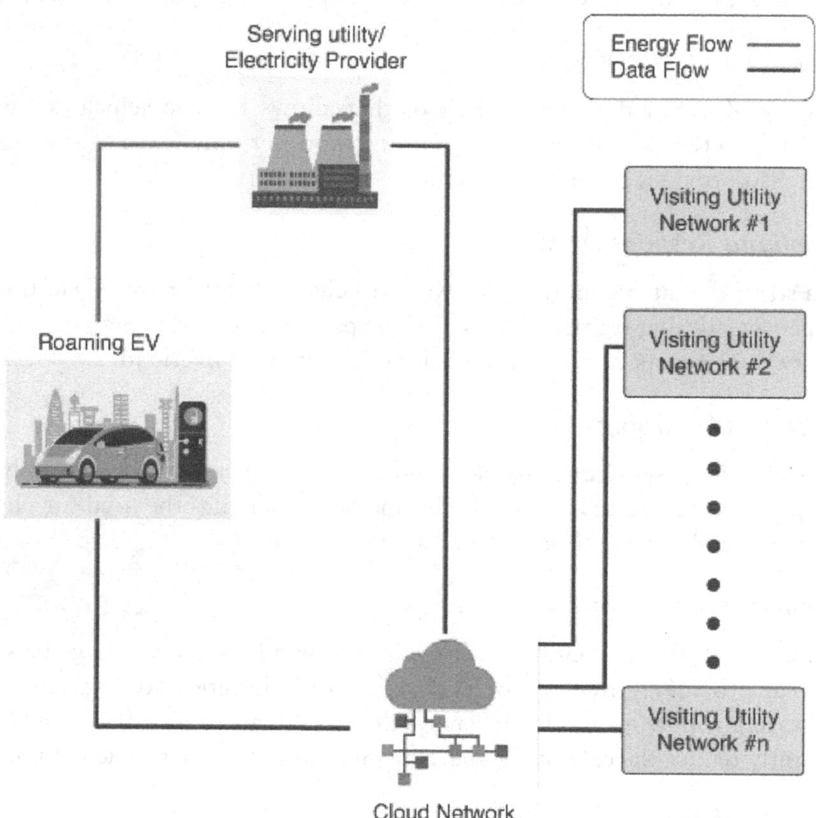

Figure 3: AI and blockchain-based smart charging architecture.

3. Literature Review

The literature review highlights the importance of smart EV charging and its potential benefits. It also discusses the different approaches and technologies that have been proposed in the literature.

Several studies have also proposed the use of IoT technologies such as sensors, communication networks and cloud computing to enable intelligent and automated charging. These technologies can be used to monitor the status of the charging infrastructure, track the location and battery status of the EVs and optimise the charging schedule based on user preferences and energy availability.

Rituraj Jain *et al.* [1] proposes a new design for smart vehicles that use the IoT technology, bio-inspired algorithms and artificial intelligence (AI) to improve efficiency and safety. Their system consists of a number of IoT sensors that are placed on the vehicle to collect data about its performance, such as speed, location and battery level. The data is then transmitted to a central control server, than it is processed by bio-inspired algorithms and AI models. The algorithms and models are used to make decisions about the vehicle's operation, such as when to charge the battery, how to optimise its route and how to avoid accidents.

Shabana Urooj *et al.* [2] propose a new application for IoT in electric vehicles. The proposed application uses boosting algorithms to improve the efficiency of electric vehicle battery management.The proposed system consists of a number of IoT sensors that are placed on the vehicle to collect data about its performance, such as speed, location and battery level. This data is then sent to a central server, where it is processed by a boosting algorithm. The boosting algorithm is used to predict the remaining battery life of the vehicle.

Godwin C. Okwuibe *et al.* [3] proposes a new blockchain-based system for managing electric vehicle charging. The proposed system uses blockchain to record the charging transactions between EV users and charging stations. This allows for a secure and transparent way to manage charging, and it also helps to ensure that EV users are charged fairly.

Mohd. Saqib *et al.* [4] propose a new system for managing EV charging with the help of cloud monitoring and management. Their system is based on cloud computing to collect data about the charging process, such as the timing of day, the area of the charging station and the type of EV. This data is then used to optimise the charging process, such as by charging the EV during off-peak hours or by charging the EV at a charging station with lower electricity prices.

Matjaz Rozman *et al.* [5] propose a new system for wireless charging of EVs in an autonomous manner. The proposed system uses a combination of sensors, actuators and AI to detect the position of the EV and to control the wireless power transmission (WPT) system.

Andrei Viziteu *et al.* [6] propose a new system for scheduling the charging of EVs using reinforcement learning (RL). The proposed system uses RL to learn the optimal charging strategy for a fleet of EVs, taking into account number of factors, such as the availability of charging and controlling stations, the cost of electricity and the preferences of EV owners.

Muhammad Shahid Mastoi *et al.* [7] investigates the use of charging-dispatch methodologies and vehicle-to-grid (V2G) techniques to improve the efficiency and reliability of distributed networks with a large penetration of EVs. The paper first reviews the different charging-dispatch strategies for EVs, such as centralised, decentralised and hybrid strategies. It then discusses the different V2G technologies, such as unidirectional and bidirectional V2G.

Bhaskar P. Rimal *et al.* [8] discuss the use of the internet of vehicles (IoV) to increase the efficiency and flexibility of EV charging process. The paper first reviews the different IoV technologies, such as vehicle-to-vehicle (V2V) communication, vehicle-to-grid (V2G) communication and vehicle-to-infrastructure (V2I) communication. It then discusses how these technologies can be used to increase the efficiency and flexibility of EV charging.

Wan-Jun Yin and Zheng-Feng Ming [9] proposes a new scheduling strategy for EVs charge and discharge process. The proposed method uses a local-search algorithm and a competitive learn particle swarm optimisation method and algorithm (CLPSO) to optimise the charge and discharge process of EVs.

Nnaemeka V. Emodi *et al.* [10] discusses the role of the IoT in improving the EVs charging infrastructure and consumer experience. The paper first reviews the different IoT technologies that can be used for EV charging, such as sensors, actuators and communication devices. It then discusses how these technologies can be used to improve the efficiency, reliability and flexibility of EV charging.

Andrea Bertolini *et al.* [11] proposes a new approach to optimise the power gain of EV smart charge hubs with the help of deep reinforcement learning (DRL). The proposed approach uses a DRL agent to learn the optimal power output policy for a smart charging hub. The DRL agent takes into account a variety of factors, such as the battery charge state of the EVs, the available power from the grid and the cost of electricity.

S. M. Asiful Huda, Muhammad Yeasir Arafat, and Sangman Moh review [12] the recent progress in the field of wireless power transfer theorems (WPT) for wirelessly controlled and powered sensor networks (WPSNs). The paper begins by providing an overview of WPT and WPSNs. It then discusses the different WPT techniques that can be used for WPSNs, such as inductive WPT, capacitive WPT and magnetic resonance WPT. It also discusses the different challenges that need to be addressed in order to implement WPT for WPSNs, such as the limited power budget, the security of WPT and the interference between WPT signals.

Oliver Frendo and Jérôme Graf propose [13] a new approach to optimising the charging of heterogeneous EV fleets. The proposed approach uses data collected from the EVs, the charging infrastructure and the grid to develop algorithms that can optimise the charging process.

Raymond O. Kene [14] discusses the challenges and opportunities of managing and optimizing the charging of bigger-scaled EV fleets on the power grid.The paper begins by highlighting an overview of the challenges of EV charging on the grid.

Khaldoon Alfaverh [15] proposes a new approach to demand response in the residential sector. The proposed approach uses plugged-in electric vehicles to transfer the load from peak to off-peak hours.

Pranjal Barman reviews [16] the existing smart charging approaches for integrating renewable energy tech with EV technology. Their paper begins by providing an overview of the challenges of integrating renewable energy with EV technology.

4. Comparison Table

The following

Table 1: Presents a comparison of the different smart charging methods.

Method	Advantage	Disadvantages
Dynamic Load Management (DLM)	Optimises grid integration, prevents overload and minimises energy costs.	Requires real-time data on grid power supply and EV charging demand.
Vehicle-to-Grid (V2G)	Stabilises the grid, provides a source of revenue for EV owners and reduces carbon emissions.	Requires bi-directional charging infrastructure, which can be expensive to implement.
Demand Response (DR)	Reduces energy costs for EV owners, reduces overall demand during peak hours.	Requires incentives for EV owners to participate.
Wireless Charging	Convenient and efficient, eliminates the need for cables	Can be less efficient than wired
Renewable energy-based charging	Can provide clean energy for EV charging, reducing greenhouse gas emissions	Requires more advanced infrastructure and regulatory frameworks to be implemented on a large scale.
Artificial Intelligence (AI):	Optimise charging schedules, predict energy demand and provide real-time monitoring of charging stations	AI algorithms require big numbers of data to be effective, also implementation of AI systems can be costly
Cloud-Based Charging	Enables real-time monitoring of charging stations and allows for remote control and management of the charging process.	Internet dependent
Augmented Reality (AR)	Real-time information and interactive charging guides	The implementation of AR systems can be costly and the technology may not be accessible to all users.
Blockchain-Based Charging	Provide a secure and transparent platform for the exchange of energy and payment. eliminate the need for intermediaries and reduce transaction costs	It requires significant infrastructure investment and may not be effective for smaller EV networks

4.1. Comparison

The comparative analysis conducted in this paper revealed that V2G and renewable energy-based charging methods using IoT have significant advantages over demand response in terms of environmental impact. However, the implementation of these methods requires more advanced infrastructure and regulatory frameworks. Demand response using IoT is a simpler and more cost-effective method that utilises the existing grid infrastructure.

5. Conclusion

Smart charging methods have the potential to optimise EV charging and decrease the environmental impact of transportation. The comparative study conducted in this paper reveals that V2G and renewable energy-based charging methods have significant advantages over demand response in terms of cost and environmental impact. However, the implementation of these methods requires more advanced infrastructure and regulatory frameworks. Therefore, a combination of these methods may be the best solution to meet the growing demand for EV charging while minimising cost and environmental impact.

References

[1] Jain, R., M. Kalyan Chakravarthi, P. K. Kumar, O. Hemakesavulu, Edwin Ramirez-Asis, Guillermo Pelaez-Diaz, and R. Mahaveerakannan, "Internet of Things-based smart vehicles design of bio-inspired algorithms using artificial intelligence," 2022.

[2] Urooj, S., F. Alrowais, Y. Teekaraman, H. Manoharan, and R. Kuppusamy, "IoT Based Electric Vehicle Application Using Boosting Algorithm for Smart Cities," *Energies*, vol. 14, p. 1072, 2021, doi: 10.3390/en14041072.

[3] Okwuibe, G. C., Z. Li, T. Brenner, and O. Langniss, "A blockchain based electric vehicle smart charging system with flexibility," 2020.

[4] Mohd. S., M. M. Hussain, M. S. Alam, M. M. Sufyan Beg, and A. Sawant, *Smart Electric Vehicle Charging Through Cloud Monitoring and Management*, Springer, 2017.

[5] Rozman, M., (Student Member, IEEE), A. Ikpehai, (Member, IEEE), B. Adebisi, (Senior Member, IEEE), K. M. Rabie, (Member, IEEE), H. Gacanin, (Member, IEEE), H. Ji, and M. Fernando, (Member, IEEE), *Smart Wireless Power Transmission System for Autonomous EV Charging*, March 2019

[6] Viziteu, A., D. Furtuna, A. Robu, S. Senocico, P. Cioata, M. R. Baltariu, C. Filote, and M. S. Raboaca, "Smart Scheduling of Electric Vehicles Based on Reinforcement Learning," *Sensors*, 2022.

[7] Mastoi, M. S., S. Zhuang, H. M. Munir, M. Haris, M. Hassan, M. Alqarni, and B. Alamri, *A Study of Charging-Dispatch Strategies and Vehicle-to-Grid Technologies for Electric Vehicles in Distribution Networks*, Elsevier, 2022.

[8] Rimal, B. P., C. Kong, B. Poudel, Y. Wang, and P. Shahi, "Smart electric vehicle charging in the era of internet of vehicles, emerging trends, and open issues," *Energies*, 2022.

[9] Yin, W.-J. and Z.-F. Ming, *Electric Vehicle Charging and Discharging Scheduling Strategy Based on Local Search and Competitive Learning Particle Swarm Optimization Algorithm*, Elsevier, 2020.

[10] Emodi, N. V., U. B. Akuru, M. O. Dioha, P. Adoba, R. J. Kuhudzai, and O. Bamisile, "2023 The role of internet of things on electric vehicle charging infrastructure and consumer experience," *Energies*, 2023.

[11] Bertolini, A., M. S. E. Martins, S. M. Vieira, and J. M. C. Sousa, *Power Output Optimization of Electric Vehicles Smart Charging Hubs using Deep Reinforcement Learning*, IDMEC, Instituton, Elesvier, 2021.

[12] Huda, S. M. A., M. Y. Arafat, and S. Moh, "Wireless power transfer in wirelessly powered sensor networks: a review of recent progress," *Sensors*, 2022.

[13] Frendo, O. and J. Graf, "Data-driven smart charging for heterogeneous electric vehicle fleets," *Energy AI*, 2020.

[14] Kene R. O., *Energy Management and Optimization of Large-Scale Electric Vehicle Charging on the Grid,* MDPI, 2023.

[15] A. Khaldoon, *Plugged-in Electric Vehicle-Assisted Demand Response Strategy for Residential Energy Management*, Springer, 2023.

[16] Barman, P., *Renewable Energy Integration with Electric Vehicle Technology: A Review of the Existing Smart Charging Approaches*, Elsevier, 2023.

14. Analytical Framework and Algorithmic Model for Resource Allocation in 5G and Beyond 5G Networks for IoT

Nishant Tripathi[1], J. P. C. do Nascimento[2], and A. S. B.Sombra[3]

[1]*Dept. of Electronics and Communication Engineering, Pranveer Singh Institute of Technology Kanpur*

[2]*Federal Institute of Education, Science and Technology of Ceará, PPGET, Fortaleza, CE, Brazil*

[3*]*Physics Department - Telecommunication, Science and Engineering of Materials Laboratory (LOCEM), Federal University of Ceara (UFC), Fortaleza, Ceara, Brazil*

Abstract: Resource allocation is an integral component in the evolution of wireless networks towards 5G and beyond for application like medical, sensor-based technology, image or signal processing in internet of things (IoT). We have reported an algorithmic model for resource allocation in 5G/Beyond-5G networks utilised in IoT. A flowchart for the resource allocation has also been proposed in the study, which will find suitable number of application domain like signal or speech processing, biomedical, sensor technology in integration with IoT. The present study presents a comprehensive examination of the architecture, challenges, opportunities, and future prospects which could lead IoT based resource allocation for various application in this domain. Beginning with an in-depth architectural overview, we have discussed the integration of IoT techniques within 5G and beyond 5G networks. We explored resource allocation strategies, both static and dynamic, offering insights into their comparative parameters via dedicated tables. The paper delves into the substantial challenges of interference management, energy efficiency, and scalability. Furthermore, we emphasised on the transformative benefits of these strategies, such as improved network reliability, reduced latency, and support for image, biomedical, sensor technology-based application domain.

Keywords: Sensor technology, wireless networks, 5G, internet of things.

1. Introduction

Internet of things (IoT) involves collaborative efforts among network entities, allowing for more efficient and reliable data transmission. This includes techniques like device-to-device (D2D) communication and multi-hop relaying. These methods leverage proximity and intermediate devices to enhance coverage, reduce latency, and optimise spectrum utilisation. Resource allocation strategies are pivotal in ensuring that network resources are distributed judiciously to meet varying demands. Allocation strategies play a crucial role in maximizing network capacity and minimising congestion. However, implementing IoT and resource allocation strategies presents its own set of challenges. These may include complexities in coordinating multiple devices, security concerns, and the need for robust cross-layer optimisation. Despite these challenges, the potential benefits are immense. Enhanced network efficiency, expanded coverage and improved quality of service (QoS) provisioning are just some of the advantages that can be achieved through the judicious application of IoT and resource allocation strategies. Looking ahead, the research in this field holds great promise. Future endeavours may focus on refining existing techniques, developing novel algorithms, and addressing emerging issues in the ever-evolving landscape of wireless communication. The synergy between IoT and resource allocation is poised to play an essential part in determining the upcoming trends and development of advanced wireless-based networks.

2. Architectural Overview of Internet of Things in 5G and Beyond Networks

5G Network Architecture: In the architectural context of 5G networks, core components such as core networks, access networks and edge computing play pivotal roles in enabling advanced communication services. The architecture approach for 5G and beyond 5G (B5G) networks encompasses several key components that collectively form the foundation for these advanced wireless communication systems. [1–2] These components are designed to support the diverse requirements of modern applications and technologies. [Figure no. 1] Here are the key elements:

Radio Access Network (RAN) plays a pivotal role in the seamless connection of user devices, encompassing a diverse array ranging from smartphones to internet of things (IoT) devices. It constitutes a comprehensive infrastructure comprising base stations, antennas and ancillary equipment, all of which collectively facilitate wireless communication. These elements collaborate synergistically to ensure reliable and efficient transmission of data between end-user devices and the core network. [3]

The core network (CN) forms the nucleus of the entire network architecture, assuming responsibility for managing a multitude of critical services. These encompass pivotal functions such as authentication, authorisation, session management and mobility management. Furthermore, the CN establishes essential interfaces with external networks and services, thus acting as the linchpin for network-wide interactions and seamless data flow. [10]

Software-Defined Networking (SDN) represents a transformative paradigm shift in network management. It ingeniously segregates the control plane from the data plane, thus conferring unparalleled dynamism and flexibility to network administration. [11] This dichotomy empowers administrators to exert precise control over network resources, paving the way for optimal resource utilisation and the rapid deployment of innovative services.

Network Functions Virtualisation (NFV) constitutes a paradigmatic shift in the provisioning of network services.[12] It liberates network functions from their erstwhile shackles of dedicated hardware, ushering them into a realm of software-based applications. This revolutionary transition heralds a new era characterised by enhanced flexibility and scalability in the deployment of network services, thereby vastly augmenting the adaptability and responsiveness of the network infrastructure.

Edge Computing represents a monumental advancement in network architecture, strategically positioning computational resources in close proximity to end-users. By diminishing latency and enabling real-time processing capabilities, edge computing revolutionises critical applications such as augmented reality, autonomous vehicles and the IoT. This profound shift in computational architecture vastly amplifies the efficacy and responsiveness of these applications, setting the stage for transformative breakthroughs across various industries.

Multi-Access Edge Computing (MEC) emerges as a pivotal extension of edge computing, effecting a seamless fusion with the radio access network.[12] This strategic integration culminates in the hosting of applications in immediate proximity to end-users. [12] The result is a substantial enhancement in performance metrics, as well as a marked reduction in backhaul traffic. This strategic synergy between edge computing and the radio access network holds immense promise for catalysing advancements in a diverse array of applications, ultimately benefiting end-users and stakeholders alike.

Network Slicing stands as a groundbreaking innovation in network architecture, affording network operators the capacity to create a mosaic of distinct virtual networks within a singular physical infrastructure. Each individual slice is meticulously customised to cater to specific requirements, be it the imperative for ultra-low latency in critical applications or the imperative for high throughput in video streaming services. This pioneering approach ushers in an era of unparalleled flexibility and adaptability in network provisioning, underscoring the network's innate capacity to cater to diverse and dynamic demands.

Massive MIMO (**Multiple-Input, Multiple-Output**) heralds a monumental stride forward in wireless communication technology. It capitalises on an extensive array of antennas deployed at the base station, significantly augmenting spectral efficiency, boosting capacity and extending coverage. This transformative technology represents a watershed moment in the evolution of wireless communication, laying the foundation for a future characterised by seamless, high-capacity connectivity.

Millimeter Wave (**mmWave**) **Communications** occupy a pivotal niche in the wireless communication spectrum. These frequencies offer prodigious data rates, but their coverage is constrained by their relatively shorter range. Consequently, mmWave frequencies constitute an indispensable component in achieving ultra-high-speed connections, particularly in densely populated urban areas. By harnessing the potential of mmWave communications, networks can deliver unprecedented data speeds, thereby enabling a new frontier of high-bandwidth applications and services.

Artificial Intelligence (AI) and Machine Learning (ML) have emerged as indispensable tools in the arsenal of network management and optimisation. By embedding AI and ML algorithms within the network infrastructure, administrators can unleash a new wave of intelligent decision-making capabilities. These encompass critical tasks such as resource allocation, traffic prediction and anomaly detection. This infusion of intelligence confers unparalleled efficiency and adaptability to network operations, ultimately leading to a network infrastructure that is finely attuned to dynamic demands and optimised for peak performance.

In the face of escalating network complexity and connectivity, robust security measures stand as an unassailable imperative. Encryption, authentication and intrusion detection constitute the vanguard of security solutions, forming an impregnable bulwark against unauthorised access, data breaches and malicious intrusions. These robust measures collectively safeguard data integrity and confidentiality, thereby ensuring that communications within the network remain impervious to external threats. In a landscape characterised by evolving cyber threats, these security solutions serve as an unequivocal assurance of network integrity and the protection of sensitive information.

Satellite Integration stands as a pivotal advancement poised to redefine the landscape of communication networks, especially in the transition beyond 5G. This innovation entails the seamless amalgamation of satellite communications into the network infrastructure. By leveraging satellite technology, networks can transcend geographical constraints, extending coverage to erstwhile remote and underserved areas. Moreover, satellite integration bolsters connectivity in dynamic mobility scenarios, ensuring uninterrupted access even in transit. This strategic integration of satellite capabilities represents a monumental stride forward, unlocking a new dimension of accessibility and connectivity for users across diverse environments.

The advent of **Quantum-Secure Communication** heralds a critical response to the looming challenges posed by the rapid advancement of quantum computing. As quantum computing capabilities surge, so too does the imperative for encryption methods impervious to quantum-based threats. This necessitates the development and deployment of quantum-resistant encryption techniques, ensuring the enduring security of communications. These cryptographic protocols, fortified against potential future quantum attacks, serve as the linchpin of network security in the era of 5G and beyond. Collectively, these quantum-resistant encryption methods, when integrated into the network architecture, lay the foundation for an exceptionally robust and secure wireless communication ecosystem. By fortifying the network against quantum threats, this approach not only safeguards sensitive information but also upholds the integrity and confidentiality of communications in an increasingly interconnected and technologically advanced landscape. This strategic fortification through quantum-secure communication is integral to shaping a wireless communication ecosystem that is both highly versatile and capable of accommodating a vast array of applications and services with utmost confidence and resilience.

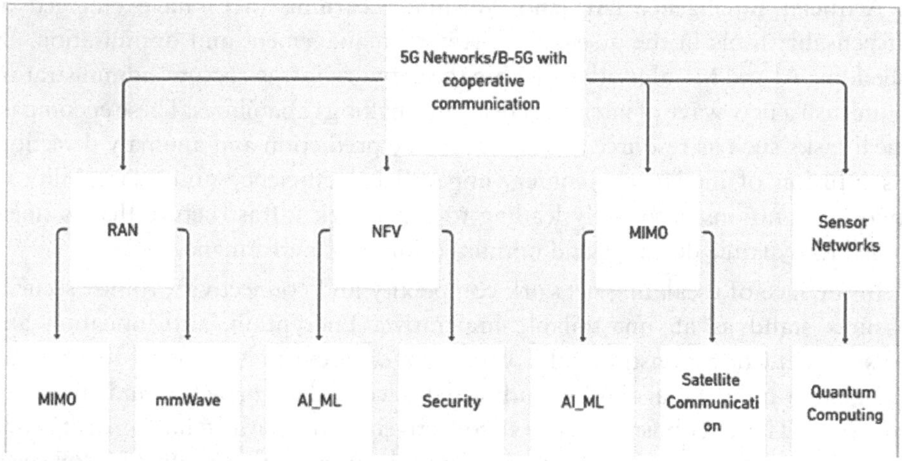

Figure 1: Key architectural components of 5G/B-5G network with internet of things.

Internet of Things Integration: This sub-section will delve into the seamless integration of Internet of Things techniques, such as device-to-device (D2D) communication and multi-hop relaying, within the fabric of 5G networks. It will highlight how these techniques enhance network efficiency, coverage, and QoS provisioning. In the ever-evolving landscape of telecommunication technologies, the integration of IoT techniques has emerged as a pivotal advancement in the realm of 5G networks. This sub-section delves into the seamless incorporation of techniques like D2D communication and multi-hop relaying, elucidating how they synergistically enhance network efficiency, coverage and QoS provisioning. [4]

Device-to-Device (D2D) Communication: D2D communiqué allows straight communication among user devices deprived of the necessity for an transitional base station. [4]

- Proximity Advantage: D2D leverages the proximity of devices, allowing for quicker and additional well-organised communication.
- Offloading Network Traffic: By enabling direct communication, D2D reduces the load on base stations, leading to improved overall network performance.
- Improved Latency: D2D significantly reduces communication latency, crucial for applications like augmented reality and autonomous vehicles.

Multi-hop Relaying: Multi-hop relaying involves using intermediate devices to forward data packets between the source and destination.[4]

- Coverage Extension: Multi-hop relaying amplifies the coverage area by utilising strategically positioned relay nodes to extend the reach of the network.
- Overcoming Obstacles: It helps overcome physical barriers and interference, ensuring a robust and consistent connection even in challenging environments.
- Redundancy and Reliability: Multi-hop relaying introduces redundancy in communication paths, enhancing the reliability of data transmission.

Enhanced Network Efficiency:

- Spectrum Efficiency: IoT techniques optimise spectrum utilisation by minimizing interference and maximizing throughput.
- Resource Allocation: D2D and multi-hop relaying facilitate dynamic resource allocation, ensuring that resources are allocated efficiently based on user demand and network conditions.
- Load Balancing: By distributing traffic across different communication modes, cooperative techniques prevent network congestion and ensure a balanced load.

Improved Coverage:

- Urban and Dense Environments: In densely populated areas, where traditional cellular networks may face challenges, IoT techniques enhance coverage by utilising nearby devices as relays.
- Indoor Environments: Multi-hop relaying can be particularly beneficial in indoor settings where signal propagation may be hindered by walls and obstacles.

Quality of Service (QoS) Provisioning:

- Low Latency Services: IoT techniques performance is very evident in meeting stringent latency requirements for applications like real-time gaming, telemedicine and industrial automation.
- High Reliability and Availability: The redundancy introduced by multi-hop relaying ensures high reliability, crucial for critical communications in emergency scenarios.
- Seamless Handovers: D2D communication enables smooth handovers between different cells, ensuring uninterrupted service during mobility.

Cross-Layer Optimisation:

- Integration with PHY and MAC Layers: Cooperative techniques are integrated with the physical (PHY) and medium access control (MAC) layers to achieve optimal communication performance. [25]
- Adaptive Modulation and Coding: Dynamic adjustments in modulation and coding schemes are made based on feedback from cooperative nodes, ensuring efficient data transmission.

Security Considerations:

- Authentication and Encryption: Security protocols are implemented to authenticate and encrypt communication between devices, ensuring data integrity and confidentiality.
- Secure Relay Selection: Protocols for selecting trustworthy relay nodes are essential to prevent malicious nodes from compromising the network.

3. Resource Allocation Strategies

1. **OFDMA (Orthogonal Frequency Division Multiple Access)** is a popular resource allocation technique in wireless communication, prominently used in 4G LTE and 5G networks.[5] It is a multi-user variant of Orthogonal Frequency Division Multiplexing (OFDM) that efficiently allocates resources such as time and frequency to multiple users simultaneously. The elaboration to it is as follows:
   - **Basic Implementation Tactics:**
     - OFDMA divides the available spectrum into subcarriers, each orthogonal to the others. This orthogonality minimises interference between users. [5]
     - Resources are allocated by assigning subsets of subcarriers and time slots to individual users or devices.
     - Dynamic resource allocation adapts to changing channel conditions and user requirements.
   - **Usability:**
     - OFDMA is suitable for scenarios with multiple users, including both uplink and downlink communications.
     - It's widely used in mobile broadband, Wi-Fi and other wireless communication systems.
     - OFDMA is flexible and can adapt to various deployment scenarios, making it a versatile choice.
   - **Advantages:**
     - Spectral Efficiency: OFDMA efficiently utilises the available spectrum, allowing multiple users to transmit data concurrently.
     - Robustness: It is less sensitive to multipath fading and can handle frequency-selective fading channels effectively.
     - Scalability: OFDMA is scalable and can accommodate various bandwidths, making it suitable for different deployment scenarios.
   - **Disadvantages:**
     - PAPR (Peak-to-Average Power Ratio): OFDMA can exhibit high PAPR, which may require additional signal processing and power amplifiers.
     - Complex Synchronisation: Managing synchronisation among multiple users can be complex, especially in high-mobility scenarios.

- **Efficiency Considerations:**
  - ➢ OFDMA is known for its spectral efficiency, enabling high data rates and capacity.
  - ➢ It can support QoS differentiation by allocating resources based on user requirements.
  - ➢ Dynamic resource allocation ensures efficient utilisation of resources, adapting to changing network conditions.
- **Target Network Scenarios:**
  - ➢ OFDMA is ideal for cellular networks (e.g., LTE, 5G) where multiple users share the same spectrum.
  - ➢ It is also commonly used in Wi-Fi networks for local area wireless connectivity.
  - ➢ OFDMA can be employed in various scenarios, including mobile broadband, fixed wireless access and IoT deployments.

2. **Non-Orthogonal Multiple Access (NOMA)** is an advanced multiple access technique that challenges the traditional orthogonal allocation of resources to users. It allows multiple users to share the same resources non-orthogonally, enabling simultaneous transmission. [6]

- **Basic Implementation Tactics:**
  - ➢ NOMA allocates resources, such as power and time, non-orthogonally to multiple users.
  - ➢ Users are distinguished by their power levels or code domains, allowing them to share the same resources.
  - ➢ Successive Interference Cancellation (SIC) is often used to decode and separate signals from multiple users. [6]
- **Usability:**
  - ➢ NOMA is particularly suitable for scenarios with a large number of users or devices.
  - ➢ It is envisioned to be a key technology for 5G and beyond networks, especially for massive machine-type communications (m-MTC).
  - ➢ NOMA can efficiently serve users with different QoS requirements. [6]
- **Advantages:**
  - ➢ Spectral Efficiency: NOMA significantly improves spectral efficiency by allowing multiple users to share resources simultaneously.
  - ➢ Massive Connectivity: It is well-suited for scenarios with a massive number of connected devices, such as IoT applications.
  - ➢ Flexibility: NOMA offers flexibility in accommodating users with varying channel conditions and QoS requirements.
- **Disadvantages:**
  - ➢ Complexity: Implementing NOMA requires sophisticated signal processing techniques, including SIC.

- ➢ Interference Management: Managing interference is a critical challenge, especially when many users share the same resources.
- ➢ Power Allocation: Optimising power allocation can be complex, requiring continuous adjustments to user power levels. [6]

- **Efficiency Considerations:**
  - ➢ NOMA excels in spectral efficiency, providing high data rates and capacity.
  - ➢ It is efficient in scenarios with asymmetric user requirements, as it can allocate more resources to users with higher QoS demands.
  - ➢ Efficient interference management techniques are essential for maximising performance.
- **Target Network Scenarios:**
  - ➢ NOMA is well-suited for 5G networks, especially in m-MTC scenarios where massive connectivity is crucial.
  - ➢ It can be employed in scenarios with diverse user requirements, including IoT, multimedia streaming and mission-critical applications.
  - ➢ NOMA can be part of the solution for enhancing the efficiency and capacity of cellular and wireless networks.

3. **Dynamic Spectrum Sharing (DSS)** is a resource allocation strategy that enables different wireless technologies to share the same frequency bands efficiently. It adapts resource allocation based on real-time network conditions. [7] Here's an in-depth exploration:

- **Basic Implementation Tactics:**
  - ➢ DSS allows multiple wireless technologies (e.g., 4G and 5G) to share the same spectrum.
  - ➢ Resource allocation is dynamic and adapts to changing network demands and user requirements.
  - ➢ Cognitive radio and software-defined networking (SDN) technologies play a crucial role in DSS implementation. [7]
- **Usability:**
  - ➢ DSS is particularly useful in scenarios where multiple wireless technologies coexist, such as the transition from 4G to 5G.
  - ➢ It optimises spectrum utilisation and ensures efficient coexistence between legacy and emerging technologies. [7]
- **Advantages:**
  - ➢ Spectrum Efficiency: DSS maximises spectrum efficiency by dynamically allocating resources to different technologies.
  - ➢ Seamless Transition: It allows for a seamless transition from older wireless technologies to newer ones, ensuring network continuity.
  - ➢ Interference Mitigation: DSS can dynamically manage interference, enhancing overall network performance. [7]

- **Disadvantages:**
  - Complexity: Implementing DSS requires coordination between different wireless technologies and sophisticated resource management.
  - Interoperability: Ensuring interoperability between legacy and new technologies can be challenging.
- **Efficiency Considerations:**
  - DSS optimises spectrum utilisation, ensuring that resources are allocated where and when they are needed the most.
  - It improves the overall efficiency of spectrum allocation by minimising interference and reducing wastage.
- **Target Network Scenarios:**
  - DSS is suitable for scenarios where the coexistence of multiple wireless technologies is required, such as the evolution from 4G to 5G.
  - It can be employed in multi-RAT (Radio Access Technology) networks, including scenarios with both licensed and unlicensed bands.
  - DSS enhances the efficiency of spectrum allocation in heterogeneous wireless environment. [7]

Table 1: Comparison of static and dynamic resource allocation.

Parameters	Static Resource Allocation	Dynamic Resource Allocation
Bandwidth Allocation	Fixed allocation of bandwidth	Adaptive allocation based on demand
Power Management	Fixed power allocation	Dynamic power allocation based on channel conditions
QoS Provisioning	Limited flexibility	Enhanced QoS adaptation
Energy Efficiency	Less energy efficient	More energy efficient
Scalability	Limited scalability	Better scalability
Complexity	Lower complexity	Higher complexity
Real-time Adaptation	Limited real-time adaptation	Real-time adaptation

Table 2: Parameter comparison for different resource allocation strategies.

Parameters	Cooperative MIMO	Device-to-Device (D2D) Communication	Multi-Hop Relaying	Network Coding
Bandwidth Allocation	High efficiency	Efficient use of spectrum	Variable allocation	Efficient utilisation
Power Management	Spatial diversity	Low-power consumption	Dynamic power control	Reduced power usage

Parameters	Cooperative MIMO	Device-to-Device (D2D) Communication	Multi-Hop Relaying	Network Coding
QoS Provisioning	Improved QoS	QoS control based on user proximity	QoS optimisation	Improved QoS
Energy Efficiency	Energy efficient	Energy efficient	Energy-aware routing	Energy efficient
Scalability	Scalable	Scalable	Scalable	Scalable
Complexity	Moderate	Moderate	Moderate	Moderate
Real-time Adaptation	Real-time adaptation	Real-time adaptation	Real-time adaptation	Real-time adaptation

Table 3: Comparison of challenges and opportunities.

Aspects	Challenges	Opportunities
Interference Management	Coordinated interference is complex	Enhanced interference mitigation
Energy Efficiency	Energy-intensive cooperative schemes	Green communication networks
Scalability	Challenges in large-scale networks	Enhanced network scalability
Reduced Latency	Latency in dynamic allocation	Low-latency applications support
Emerging Applications	Compatibility with new apps	Support for IoT and autonomous vehicles
Real-time Adaptation	Real-time coordination difficulties	Improved real-time adaptation

Table 1 compares static and dynamic resource allocation strategies. It becomes evident that dynamic allocation outperforms static approaches in terms of bandwidth utilisation, power management, QoS provisioning, energy efficiency, scalability and real-time adaptation. Dynamic resource allocation adapts to changing network conditions and user demands, making it more versatile for modern wireless networks. Table 2 provides a comprehensive parameter comparison for four prominent resource allocation strategies: Cooperative MIMO, Device-to-Device (D2D) Communication, Multi-Hop Relaying and Network Coding. Each strategy has its strengths and weaknesses. For instance, Cooperative MIMO excels in spatial diversity and energy efficiency, while D2D communication offers low-power consumption and proximity-based QoS control. Multi-hop relaying supports dynamic power control and scalable routing, and network coding efficiently utilises network resources and enhances QoS. Table 3 delves into the challenges and opportunities associated with IoT and resource allocation. Overcoming interference management complexities, improving energy efficiency, addressing scalability concerns, achieving reduced latency and supporting emerging applications are critical challenges. On the flip side, these challenges present exciting opportunities. Enhanced interference mitigation techniques, green communication networks, improved scalability, low-latency application support and compatibility with emerging technologies like IoT and autonomous vehicles pave the way for innovation in IoT.

1. Algorithmic Steps and prototype flowchart to assign resource allocation in 5G/B-5G based network utilised in IoT [Figure no. 2]
   i. Start: The process begins.
   ii. User Equipment (UE): UEs initiate resource requests and interact with the network.
   iii. Base Stations (BSs): BSs manage connections and relay resource requests to the centralised controller.
   iv. Centralised Controller: The centralised controller collects information from BSs and UEs, performs resource allocation, and coordinates IoT.
   v. Distributed Relay Nodes: Relay nodes participate in IoT as needed.
   vi. Backhaul Network: The backhaul network connects base stations and the centralised controller to the core network.
   vii. Resource Request and UE Association: UEs send resource requests, and BSs associate UEs with relay nodes or direct links based on network conditions.
   viii. Centralised Resource Allocation: The centralised controller optimises resource allocation based on global network information, user requirements and QoS objectives.
   ix. Dynamic Relay Node Assignment: Relay nodes are dynamically assigned to assist in IoT, optimising network performance.
   x. Internet of Things: UEs communicate directly or via relay nodes in a cooperative manner.
   xi. Feedback and Adaptation: UEs provide feedback on received signal quality and network conditions, enabling dynamic resource adaptation.
   xii. Backhaul Connectivity: The backhaul network facilitates data exchange and resource allocation information.
   xiii. End: The process concludes.

This flowchart prototype provides a visual representation of the key steps and interactions involved in resource allocation for IoT in a 5G network. It offers a simplified overview of the architecture, making it easier to understand the flow of resources and decision-making processes. For a more detailed and comprehensive representation, additional elements and decision points can be added as needed to reflect the specific requirements of the network.

Table 4: Comparison of resource allocation strategies.

Parameter	**OFDMA**	**NOMA**	**Dynamic Spectrum Sharing (DSS)**
Basic Implementation	Orthogonal subcarrier allocation	Non-orthogonal resource sharing	Dynamic spectrum sharing among technologies
Usability	Multiple users, versatile	Massive connectivity, 5G	Coexistence of multiple technologies
Advantages	Spectral efficiency, robustness, scalability	Spectral efficiency, massive connectivity, flexibility	Spectrum efficiency, seamless transition, interference mitigation
Disadvantages	PAPR, synchronisation complexities	Complexity, interference management, power allocation	Complexity, interoperability challenges
Efficiency Considerations	Spectral efficiency, QoS support	Spectral efficiency, adaptive resource allocation	Spectrum efficiency, interference management
Target Network Scenarios	Cellular networks, Wi-Fi, various scenarios	5G mMTC, diverse QoS requirements	Multi-RAT environments, technology coexistence

These table. 4 provide a comprehensive overview of each resource allocation strategy, offering insights into their implementations, usability, advantages, disadvantages, efficiency considerations and target network scenarios. Researchers and network engineers can refer to this information to make informed decisions when selecting the most suitable resource allocation strategy for specific network deployments.

5. Challenges in Resource Allocation

i. **Interference Management:** The section will delve into the multifaceted challenges related to interference management in IoT. Innovative solutions, including interference cancellation techniques, will be discussed.
ii. **Energy Efficiency:** The paper will highlight the paramount importance of energy-efficient resource allocation in the context of 5G and B5G networks. It will delve into the challenges and explore potential solutions, such as dynamic power management and energy-aware algorithms.
iii. **Scalability:** Scalability challenges in large-scale networks will be elucidated. We will discuss how Internet of Things strategies can both address and exacerbate scalability issues and the need for adaptive solutions.

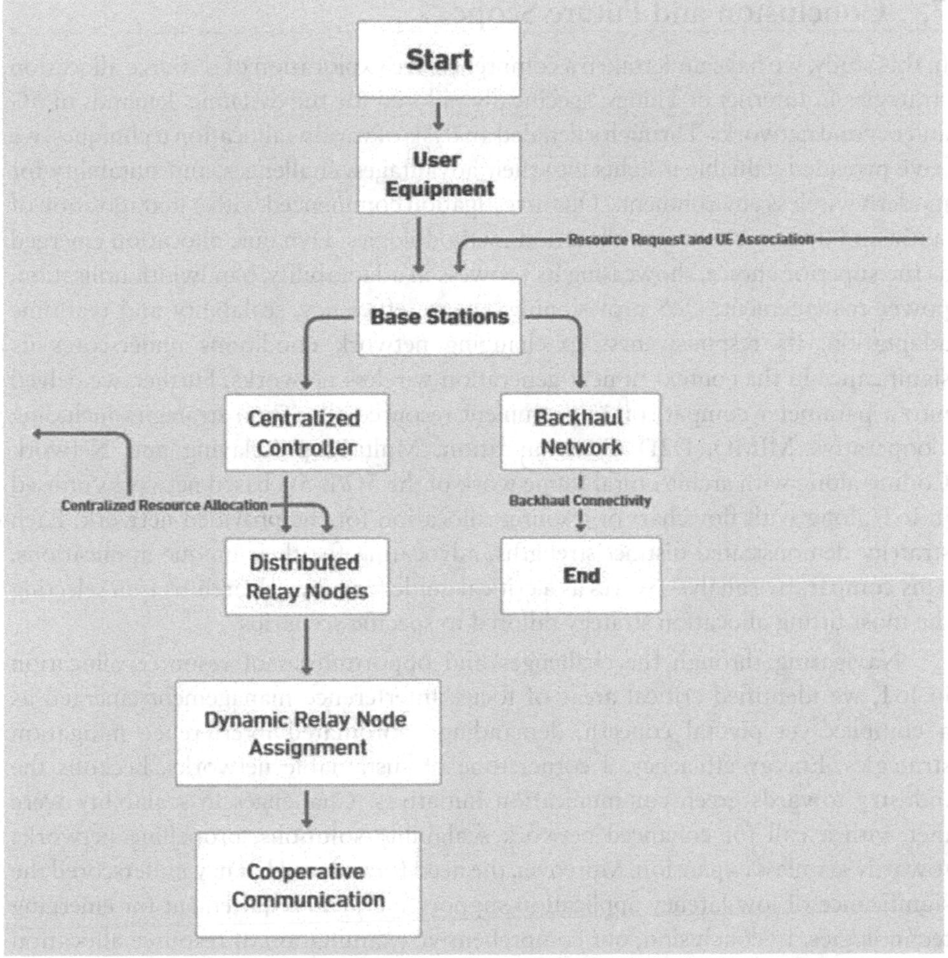

Figure 2: Flowchart for resource allocation in 5G/B-5G based network used in internet of things.

6. Opportunities and Benefits

i. **Improved Network Reliability:** This section will underline how resource allocation strategies contribute to enhanced network reliability, providing examples and case studies to support the claim.

ii. **Reduced Latency:** The role of resource allocation in reducing network latency will be explained, emphasizing its significance for latency-sensitive applications

iii. **Support for Emerging Applications:** We will discuss how these strategies enable and empower emerging applications like the IoT and autonomous vehicles, opening new frontiers for technological advancement.

7. Conclusion and Future Scope

In this study, we have undertaken a comprehensive exploration of resource allocation strategies in Internet of Things, specifically tailored for the dynamic demands of 5G and beyond networks. Through a detailed analysis of various allocation techniques, we have provided valuable insights into their advantages, challenges, and suitability for modern wireless environments. Our investigation commenced with a juxtaposition of static and dynamic resource allocation methodologies. Dynamic allocation emerged as the superior choice, showcasing its prowess in adaptability, bandwidth utilisation, power management, QoS provisioning, energy efficiency, scalability and real-time adaptation. Its responsiveness to changing network conditions underscores its significance in the context of next-generation wireless networks. Further, we delved into a parameter comparison of prominent resource allocation strategies including Cooperative MIMO, D2D Communication, Multi-Hop Relaying and Network Coding along with architectural frame work of the 5G/B-5G based networks utilised in IoT along with flowchart of resource allocation for the provided network. Each strategy demonstrated distinct strengths, advocating for their unique applications. This comparative analysis serves as a critical guide for network architects in selecting the most fitting allocation strategy tailored to specific scenarios.

Navigating through the challenges and opportunities of resource allocation in IoT, we identified critical areas of focus. Interference management emerged as a complex yet pivotal concern, demanding coordinated interference mitigation strategies. Energy efficiency, a cornerstone of sustainable networks, beckons the industry towards green communication initiatives. Challenges in scalability were met with a call for enhanced network scalability solutions, propelling networks towards seamless expansion. Moreover, the need for reduced latency underscored the significance of low-latency application support, a crucial requirement for emerging technologies. In conclusion, our comprehensive examination of resource allocation strategies provides a robust foundation for optimising IoT in the era of 5G and beyond networks. By affording a deep-dive into the architectural intricacies, challenges and opportunities, we equip researchers and practitioners with the knowledge needed to design efficient, responsive and forward-looking communication networks. As the landscape of wireless communication continues to evolve, we anticipate that our findings will catalyse further innovation, driving the next wave of advancements in network efficiency, reliability and support for emerging applications.

References

[1] Guo, W. *et al.*, "Internet of things resource allocation strategies for 5G and beyond networks: a review of architecture, challenges and opportunities." *J. King Saud Univ. Comput. Inf. Sci.*, vol. 34, pp. 8054–8078, 2022.

[2] Ahmed, R. and F. H. Kumbhar, "VC3: a novel vehicular compatibility-based internet of things in 5G networks," *IEEE Wireless Commun. Lett.*, vol. 10, pp. 1207–1211, 2021.

[3] Rivera, D., J. I. Moreno, M. S. Rodrigo, D. R. López, and A. Mozo, "Providing heterogeneous signaling and user traffic for 5G core network functional testing," *IEEE Access*, vol. 11, pp. 2968–2980, 2023, doi: 10.1109/ACCESS.2022.3233412.

[4] Mohammed, B. H., H. Sallehuddin, N. Safie, A. Husairi, N. A. Abu Bakar, F. Yahya, I. Ali, and S. A. G. Mohamed, "Building information modeling and internet of things integration in the construction industry: a scoping study," *Adv. Civil Eng.*, vol. 2022, Article ID 7886497, 20 pages, 2022, doi: 10.1155/2022/7886497

[5] Ke, X., Y. Xu, H. Qin, and J. Liang, "Research on resource allocation strategy of indoor visible light communication and radio frequency systems integrating orthogonal frequency-division multiple access technology," *Photonics*, vol. 10, p. 1016, 2023, doi: 10.3390/photonics10091016

[6] Ling, J. *et al.*, "DQN-based resource allocation for NOMA-MEC-aided multi-source data stream," *EURASIP J. Adv. Signal Process.*, vol. 1, p. 44, 2023.

[7] Mustafa, H. A. *et al.*, "Separation framework: an enabler for cooperative and D2D communication for future 5G networks," *IEEE Commun. Surv. Tutorials*, vol. 18, pp. 419–445, 2016.

[8] Han, C. *et al.*, "Utilizing coherent transmission in cooperative compressive sensing in IoT," *IEEE Internet Things J.*, vol. 8, pp. 13555–13566, 202.

[9] Ranjan, S. *et al.*, "A flexible IAB architecture for beyond 5G network," ArXiv abs/2201.13029, 2022.

[10] Wagan, S. A. *et al.*, "Internet of medical things and trending converged technologies: a comprehensive review on real-time applications," *J. King Saud Univ. Comput. Inf. Sci.*, vol. 34, pp. 9228–9251, 2022.

[11] Babiker Mohamed, M. *et al.*, "A comprehensive survey on secure software defined network for the Internet of Things," *Trans. Emerging Telecommun. Technol.*, vol. 33.1, p. e4391, 2022.

[12] Zhu, M. *et al.*, "Multi-Access Edge Computing (MEC) based on MIMO: a survey," *Sensors*, vol. 23.8, p. 3883, 2023.

[13] Tabiban, A. *et al.*, "ProvTalk: towards interpretable multi-level provenance analysis in networking functions virtualization (NFV)," *The Network and Distributed System Security Symposium 2022 (NDSS '22)*, 2022.

[14] Hu, Q., "Design and analysis of millimeter-wave backhaul networks in urban environments," 2020.

[15] Yan, Y. *et al.*, "Load-balanced routing for hybrid fiber/wireless backhaul networks," *2021 IEEE Global Communications Conference (GLOBECOM)*, pp. 1–6, 2021.

[16] Mohamed, A. *et al.*, "Memory-full context-aware predictive mobility mnagement in dual connectivity 5G networks," *IEEE Access*, vol. 6, pp. 9655–9666, 2018.

[17] He, A., "Performance evaluation and enhancement in 5G networks: a stochastic geometry approach," 2017.

[18] Ahmed, Q. Z., K. -H. Park, M. -S. Alouini, and S. Aissa, "Linear transceiver design for nonorthogonal amplify-and-forward protocol using a bit error rate criterion," *IEEE Trans. Wireless Commun.*, vol. 13, no. 4, pp. 1844–1853, April 2014, doi: 10.1109/TWC.2014.022114.130369.

[19] Alimi, A. S., V. Ribeiro, N. Kumar, P. Monteiro, and A. Teixeira, "Optical wireless communication for future broadband access networks," *2016 21st European Conference on Networks and Optical Communications (NOC)*, pp. 124–128, June 2016. doi: 10.1109/NOC.2016.7506998.

[20] Andrews, J. G., *et al.*, "What will 5G be?," *IEEE J. Sel. Areas Commun.*, vol. 32, no. 6, pp. 1065–1082, 2014.

[21] Goldsmith, A. and P. Varaiya, "Capacity of fading channels with channel side information," *IEEE Trans. Inf. Theory,* vol. 43, no. 6, pp. 1986–1992, 1997.

[22] Jiang, H. *et al.*, "User cooperation diversity—Part I: System description," *IEEE Trans. Commun.*, vol. 56, no. 11, pp. 1927–1938, 2008.

[23] Niu, Z. *et al.*, "Heterogeneous networks for 5G," *China Commun.*, vol. 9, no. 1, pp. 1–14, 2012.

[24] Cover, T. M. and A. El Gamal, "Capacity theorems for the relay channel," *IEEE Trans. Inf. Theory*, vol. 25, no. 5, pp. 572–584, 1979.

[25] Zhang, R. and A. F. Molisch, "Cooperative relay networks: a review," *IEEE J. Sel. Areas Commun.*, vol. 24, no. 5, pp. 1–13, 2006.

[26] Osseiran, A. *et al.*, "Scenarios for 5G mobile and wireless communications: the vision of the METIS project," *IEEE Commun. Mag.*, vol. 52, no. 5, pp. 26–35, 2014.

[27] Gesbert, D. *et al.*, "Shifting the MIMO paradigm: from single user to multiuser communications," *IEEE Signal Process. Mag.*, vol. 27, no. 3, pp. 25–38, 2010.

[28] Wei, L. and B. Rong, *Relay Technologies for WiMAX and LTE-Advanced Mobile Systems*, CRC Press, 2011.

[29] Haas, H., "The role of multiple antennas in ad hoc wireless networks," *IEEE Commun. Mag.*, vol. 40, no. 6, pp. 94-99, 2002.

15. A Systematic Review of Load Balancing Techniques in Heterogeneous Networks

TanuKaistha[1] and Kiran Ahuja[2]

[1]*Department of Electronics and Communication Engineering, IKG-Punjab Technical University, Kapurthala, Punjab, India*

[2]*Department of Electronics and Communication Engineering, DAV Institute of Engineering and Technology, Jalandhar, Punjab, India*

Abstract: Load balancing in a heterogeneous network involves distributing network traffic or workload across various resources, such as servers, switches or links, in a way that optimises performance and resource utilisation, even when the network consists of different types of devices or technologies. Heterogeneous networks typically include a mix of different hardware, software and communication protocols, making load balancing a critical task to ensure efficient and reliable network operation. Many techniques have been cataloged in academic research, all geared towards improving performance and efficiently utilising resources by employing load balancing, scheduling tasks and managing workloads. In heterogeneous network, load balancing allows data centres to efficiently distribute workloads across virtual machines, reducing the potential risks linked to both overloading and underloading.

Keywords: Load balancing, cloud, heterogeneous networks, static, dynamic.

1. Introduction

A heterogeneous network, often abbreviated as HetNet, is a type of network architecture that combines different types of communication technologies and network elements to provide a seamless and efficient connectivity experience. Unlike traditional homogeneous networks that rely on a single technology or infrastructure, heterogeneous networks leverage the strengths of various technologies to improve network performance, coverage and capacity[1]. The primary goal of load balancing is to ensure optimal resource utilisation, prevent overload on any single resource, improve system reliability and provide a seamless experience for users. The constantly evolving landscape of heterogeneous network, marked by its dynamic and diverse characteristics and the rapid growth in data and user demands, necessitates a deep understanding of load balancing techniques and strategies tailored to the ever-changing heterogeneous environment[2]. The main goal of this survey paper is to provide a comprehensive and in-depth analysis of load balancing techniques within heterogeneous networks[3]. Load balancing techniques can be categorised into two main types: static and dynamic. Static load balancing is a load distribution technique used in computer networking and distributed computing environments to allocate incoming requests or tasks to multiple servers or resources in a predetermined or fixed manner[4]. Unlike dynamic load balancing, where the allocation of requests is adjusted in real-time based on the current load and resource availability, static load balancing follows a predefined and unchanging distribution pattern. Static and dynamic load balancing techniques can be categoriSed into four main groups: deterministic, probabilistic, distributed and non-distributed load balancing methods [5]. The complete hierarchy of LB is shown in Figure 1.

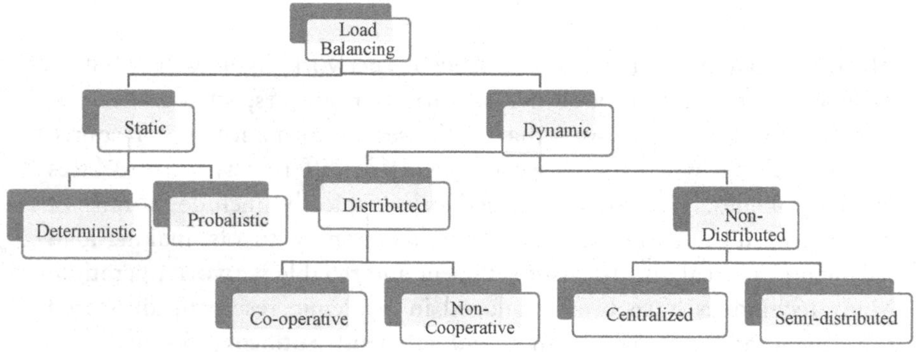

Figure 1: *Hierarchy of LB techniques.*

Distributed and non-distributed categories can be subdivided into co-operative, non-cooperative, centralised and semi-distributed load balancing approaches. The cooperative load balancing process involves the active engagement and sharing of information among various resources to achieve an effective workload distribution [6]. Non-cooperative load balancing does not involve the direct exchange of information or coordination among the available resources. Centralised load balancing refers to a system where a designated central entity, such as a load balancer or load management server, takes on the task of monitoring the load on all available resources and subsequently decides the best way to distribute the workload efficiently. Semi-distributed load balancing does not rely on a single central entity to make load balancing decisions. Instead, separate nodes or a cluster of nodes handle load balancing for specific subsets of resources. This survey focuses on the load balancing techniques used by different researchers in heterogeneous networks. In Section 2, we conduct a comparison of our proposed survey with existing surveys. Section 3 delves into the research conducted by scholars concerning static techniques, along with a discussion of potential future directions. Section 4 provides an in-depth exploration of dynamic load balancing, categorised into three sections: conventional load balancing, load balancing based on reinforcement learning (RL) and hybrid load balancing. Finally, Section 5 offers our concluding remarks.

2. Related Surveys

Emre *et al.* [7] have conducted research on load balancing using RL and machine learning techniques, but they have not explored static load balancing methods. Conversely, Sambit *et al.* [8] have focused on traditional static and dynamic techniques for load balancing, excluding RL-based and hybrid approaches. This survey encompasses an investigation into both static and dynamic load balancing techniques, encompassing the conventional, RL-based, and hybrid load balancing methods. Table 1 shows the comparison of proposed survey with existing surveys.

Table 1: Comparison of proposed survey with related surveys.

Year [Ref]	Static	Dynamic		
		Normal	RL based	Hybrid
2022 [9]	×	×	✓	✓
2020 [10]	✓	✓	×	×
Our survey	✓	✓	✓	✓

3. Static Load Balancing

Several researchers have explored static load balancing techniques, with one notable example being the work of Zhang *et al.* [9], who introduced an innovative method known as Adaptive Pbest Discrete Particle Swarm Optimisation (APDPSO). In their study, Serjio *et al.* [10] introduced a high-performance computing (HPC) approach designed to achieve workload balance within heterogeneous networks.Fatemeh *et al.* [11] introduced a static particle swarm optimisation (PSO) algorithm for the purposes of task scheduling and load balancing in cloud networks. Furthermore, a significant 33% reduction in make span time was observed when employing the PSO technique. Hajar *et al.* [12] presented an approach for load balancing in distributed computing systems, which was inspired by a game-theoretic model framing user as competitors rather than collaborators. The results obtained from the simulations indicate that employing genetic algorithms (GAs) for scheduling and load balancing in systems leads to superior outcomes when compared to existing approaches. The simulation results suggest that introducing a GA result in decreased total response time and enhanced utilization. Table 1 gives a related work on static LB techniques. Table 2 gives a related work on static LB techniques.

Table 2: Related work on static LB techniques.

Authors [Ref]	Technique Used	Technology Used	Results	Future Directions
Zhang *et al.* [9]	APDPSO	CloudSim, Matlab	Effectively performed LB by reducing degree of imbalance	Dynamic LB can be used along with heuristic approaches.

Serjio *et al.* [10]	HPO	Metropolis	HPC improve the performance by optimising the execution time.	Need to work on scalability for larger no. of datasets.
Fatemeh *et al.* [11]	PSO	CloudSim	Reduced the makespan time by 33% and increased the resource utilisation by 22%.	Cost reduction and fault tolerance can be considered in near future.
Hajar *et al.* [12]	Game theory	Distributed system, python	Optimised the makespan time by successfully performing LB.	New optimisation technique can be studied in future.
Effatparwar *et al.* [13]	Genetic Algorithm	Matlab	Genetic algorithms effectively reduce the response time.	Dynamic algorithms can be employed for better results.

4. **Dynamic Load Balancing** Dynamic LB is classified into three classes comprising normal LB, RL [14] based LB, and hybrid LB. The work done on these techniques is given in the following section:

4.1. Normal Load Balancing Techniques

Sakshi *et al.* [15] presented a multi-objective hierarchical LB framework called Secure and Energy Efficient Dynamic Hierarchical Load Balancing Framework for Cloud Data Centers (SEE-DHLB) that incorporates resource requirement analysis, security considerations, and the allocation of an optimised number of computing resources to each application. Imane *et al.* [16]introduced a LB Protocol for Cloud Computing Based on Hungarian Method (LBCC-Hung) for addressing the LB problem by the application of the Hungarian method. Dalia *et al.* [19] introduced a LB in cloud data centres by following the Service level agreement (SLA) conditions. The findings indicate that the use of resources is, on average, 78% higher when employing the suggested LB algorithm in comparison to the existing techniques. Similarly, in conclusion, this study additionally examines two algorithms in the context of CLB and conducts tests to provide empirical evidence supporting the novelty of the suggested technique. Table 3 gives a related work on normal dynamic LB techniques.

Table 3: Related work on normal dynamic LB techniques.

Year [Ref]	Execution Time	Makespan Time	Throughput	Response Time	Resource Utilisation	Energy Utilisation	TAT	DI
2023 [15]	×	✓	×	✓	✓	✓	×	×
2023 [16]	×	✓	✓	×	×	×	×	×

2022 [17]	✓	×	✓	×	×	×	✓	×
2022 [18]	×	✓	×	✓	✓	×	×	✓
2021 [19]	✓	✓	×	×	✓	×	×	×

4.2. RL Based Dynamic Load Balancing

Dan *et al.* [20] introduced a quality of service (QoS) optimisation technique for software-defined factory heterogeneous networks, utilising the double deep Q network (DDQN) approach. Peer *et al.* [21] introduced the deployment of a queue-based scheduling method known as intelligent queue-based scheduling with load balancing (IQSLB), along with an enhanced variant of IQSLB designed to address critical scenarios. Cong *et al.* [22] developed a LB using the principles of Markov decision process and the Q-learning algorithm (V2PQL). The simulation results illustrate the effectiveness of our idea, which consists of a training phase and an extraction phase. Zhao *et al.* [24] provided a new algorithm for dynamic LB, utilising DRL techniques, which aims to address the issue of LB among VMs. Zhao *et al.* [26] put forth a metadata dynamic load balancing (MDLB) technique that utilises the Q-learning algorithm which comprises three distinct modules, namely the policy selection network, LB network and parameter updating network. Qin liang *et al.* [27] presented reinforcement learning networking (RILNET), which utilises RL to address the issue of LB in datacentre networks. The RILNET network demonstrates a substantial decrease in both the maximum link data loss and maximum link delay in comparison to the current network, showing reductions of 44.4% and 25.4%, respectively. Table 4 shows the related work based on used performance metrics.

Table 4: Related work on RL based dynamic LB techniques.

Year [Ref]	Execution Time	Makespan Time	Throughput	Response Time	Resource Utilisation	Link Utilisation	Latency	DI	Jitter
2022 [20]	×	×	✓	×	×	×	✓	×	✓
2022 [21]	✓	×	✓	✓	×	×	×	×	×
2022 [22]	×	×	×	×	✓	×	✓	×	×
2021 [23]	×	✓	×	×	×	×	×	×	×
2021 [24]	×	×	×	×	×	×	✓	✓	×
2020 [25]	✓	✓	×	×	✓	×	×	×	×

2020 [26]	×	×	×	×	✓	×	✓	×	×
2019 [27]	×	×	×	×	×	×	✓	×	×

4.3. *Hybrid Dynamic Load Balancing*

Sengathir *et al.* [28]introduced the hybrid of grey wolf (GWO) and improved PSO with adaptive intertial weight-based multi-dimensional learning strategy (HGWIPSOA) for LB in cloud data centres. The simulation studies conducted on the suggested HGWIPSOA mechanism demonstrate superior outcomes, including a 21.32% enhancement in throughput, and a 19.84% reduction in makespan time. Mustafa *et al.* [30]developed the CSSA-DE dual-phase metaheuristic algorithm by employing a clustering strategy to organise the various computer nodes into functional clusters. Boonhatai *et al.* [31]proposed an ABC algorithm, in combination with a Q-learning algorithm called MOABCQ to enhance the efficiency of scheduling and resource allocation, maximise the throughput of VMs and achieve LB among VMs. The objective is to achieve optimal average load distribution, hence enhancing crucial performance metrics such as effective resource utilisation and task reaction time. This research has also presented indications for evaluating the performance of the suggested hybrid technique. Table 5 shows the related work on LB techniques in cloud computing heterogeneous networks.

Table 5: Related work on hybrid dynamic LB techniques.

Year [Ref]	Execution Time	Makespan Time	Throughput	Response Time	Resource Utilisation	CPU Utilisation	Energy Utilisation	Latency	DI
2023 [28]	✓	✓	✓	×	×	×	×	✓	×
2023 [29]	✓	✓	✓	×	×	×	×	×	×
2023 [30]	✓	×	✓	×	✓	×	×	×	✓
2022 [31]	×	✓	✓	×	×	×	×	×	×
2022 [32]	×	×	✓	×	×	×	✓	×	✓

5. Conclusion

Cloud environments consist of heterogeneous networks, encompassing various servers, data centres and virtual instances, each possessing distinct capabilities and capacities. Numerous methods have been extensively documented in academic literature, aiming to enhance performance and optimise resource allocation efficiency by means of load balancing, task scheduling and workload management. The implementation of load balancing techniques in cloud computing serves to efficiently distribute workloads among virtual machines in data centres, thereby mitigating the risks associated with workload imbalances, which is a significant challenge in the field of cloud computing. Consequently, it is imperative for developers and researchers to devise and deploy an appropriate load balancer for parallel and distributed cloud heterogeneous systems. This survey aims to offer an up-to-date exploration of various load balancing techniques, encompassing both static and dynamic approaches, within the context of heterogeneous cloud networks. While static load balancing is less efficient and has seen limited research, dynamic load balancing has garnered extensive attention. Various load balancing techniques, including heuristic-based, RL-based and hybrid approaches, have demonstrated their effectiveness in heterogeneous cloud networks. This survey also presents the parameters utilised by different researchers. The findings reveal that these authors have effectively reduced make span time through their efforts.

References

[1] Rashid, A. and A. Chaturvedi, "Cloud computing characteristics and services a brief review," *Int. J. Comput. Sci. Eng.*, vol. 7, no. 2, pp. 421–426, 2019, doi: 10.26438/ijcse/v7i2.421426.

[2] Ahuja, K., B. Singh, and R. Khanna, "Network selection in wireless heterogeneous environment by C-P-F hybrid algorithm," *Wireless Pers. Commun.*, vol. 98, no. 3, pp. 2733–2751, 2018, doi: 10.1007/s11277-017-4998-1.

[3] Kumar, N. and N. Mishra, "Load balancing techniques: need, objectives and major challenges in cloud computing- a systematic review," *Int. J. Comput. Appl.*, vol. 131, no. 18, pp. 11–19, 2015, doi: 10.5120/ijca2015907523.

[4] Tripathy, S. S. *et al.*, *State-of-the-Art Load Balancing Algorithms for Mist-Fog-Cloud Assisted Paradigm: A Review and Future Directions*, Springer Netherlands, vol. 30, no. 4, 2023, doi: 10.1007/s11831-023-09885-1.

[5] Yadav, M. and J. S. Prasad, "A review on load balancing algorithms in cloud computing environment," *Int. J. Comput. Sci. Eng.*, vol. 6, no. 8, pp. 771–778, 2018, doi: 10.26438/ijcse/v6i8.771778.

[6] Fang, D., *et al.*, "Deterministic and probabilistic assessment of distribution network hosting capacity for wind-based renewable generation," *2020 International Conference on Probabilistic Methods Applied to Power Systems, PMAPS 2020 – Proceedings*, pp. 3–8, 2020, doi: 10.1109/PMAPS47429.2020.9183525.

[7] Gures, E., I. Shayea, M. Ergen, M. H. Azmi, and A. A. El-Saleh, "Machine learning-based load balancing algorithms in future heterogeneous networks: a survey," *IEEE Access*, vol. 10, pp. 37689–37717, 2022, doi: 10.1109/ACCESS.2022.3161511.

[8] Mishra, S. K., B. Sahoo, and P. P. Parida, "Load balancing in cloud computing: a big picture," *J. King Saud Univ. Comput. Inf. Sci.*, vol. 32, no. 2, pp. 149–158, 2020, doi: 10.1016/j.jksuci.2018.01.003.

[9] Miao, Z., P. Yong, Y. Mei, Y. Quanjun, and X. Xu, "A discrete PSO-based static load balancing algorithm for distributed simulations in a cloud environment," *Future Gener. Comput. Syst.*, vol. 115, pp. 497–516, 2021, doi: 10.1016/j.future.2020.09.016.

[10] Moreno-Álvarez, S., J. M. Haut, M. E. Paoletti, J. A. Rico-Gallego, J. C. Díaz-Martín, and J. Plaza, "Training deep neural networks: a static load balancing approach," *J. Supercomput.*, vol. 76, no. 12, pp. 9739–9754, 2020, doi: 10.1007/s11227-020-03200-6.

[11] Ebadifard, F. and S. M. Babamir, "A PSO-based task scheduling algorithm improved using a load-balancing technique for the cloud computing environment," *ConcurrComput*, vol. 30, no. 12, pp. 1–16, 2018, doi: 10.1002/cpe.4368.

[12] Siar, H., K. Kiani, and A. T. Chronopoulos, "An effective game theoretic static load balancing applied to distributed computing," *Cluster Comput.*, vol. 18, no. 4, pp. 1609–1623, 2015, doi: 10.1007/s10586-015-0486-0.

[13] Effatparvar, M. and M. S. Garshasbi, "A genetic algorithm for static load balancing in parallel heterogeneous systems," *Procedia Soc. Behav. Sci.*, vol. 129, pp. 358–364, 2014, doi: 10.1016/j.sbspro.2014.03.688.

[14] Dhillon, A., A. Singh, and V. K. Bhalla, "Biomarker identification and cancer survival prediction using random spatial local best cat swarm and Bayesian optimized DNN," *Appl. Software Comput.*, vol. 146, p. 110649, 2023, doi: 10.1016/j.asoc.2023.110649.

[15] Chhabra, S. and A. K. Singh, "Secure and energy efficient dynamic hierarchical load balancing framework for cloud data centers," *Multimed. Tools Appl.*, vol. 82, pp. 29843–29856, 2023, doi: 10.1007/s11042-023-14809-z.

[16] Aly Saroit, I. and D. Tarek, "LBCC-Hung: a load balancing protocol for cloud computing based on Hungarian method," *Egypt. Inf. J.*, vol. 24, no. 3, p. 100387, 2023, doi: 10.1016/j.eij.2023.100387.

[17] Waghmode, S. T. and B. M. Patil, "Adaptive load balancing in cloud computing environment," *Int. J. Intell. Syst. Appl. Eng.*, vol. 11, no. 1s, pp. 209–217, 2023.

[18] Souravlas, S., S. D. Anastasiadou, N. Tantalaki, and S. Katsavounis, "A fair, dynamic load balanced task distribution strategy for heterogeneous cloud platforms based on Markov process modeling," *IEEE Access*, vol. 10, pp. 26149–26162, 2022, doi: 10.1109/ACCESS.2022.3157435.

[19] Shafiq, D. A., N. Z. Jhanjhi, A. Abdullah, and M. A. Alzain, "A load balancing algorithm for the data centers to optimize cloud computing applications," *IEEE Access*, vol. 9, pp. 41731–41744, 2021, doi: 10.1109/ACCESS.2021.306530.

[20] Xia, D., J. Wan, P. Xu, and J. Tan, "Deep reinforcement learning-based QoS optimization for software-defined factory heterogeneous networks," *IEEE Trans. Network Serv. Manage.*, vol. 19, no. 4, pp. 4058–4068, 2022, doi: 10.1109/TNSM.2022.3208342.

[21] Ziyath, S. P. M. and S. Subramaniyan, "An improved Q-learning-based scheduling strategy with load balancing for infrastructure-based cloud services," *Arab J. Sci. Eng.*, vol. 47, no. 8, pp. 9547–9555, 2022, doi: 10.1007/s13369-021-06279-y.

[22] Tran, C. H., T. K. Bui, and T. V. Pham, "Virtual machine migration policy for multi-tier application in cloud computing based on Q-learning algorithm," *Computing*, vol. 104, no. 6, pp. 1285–1306, 2022, doi: 10.1007/s00607-021-01047-0.

[23] Talaat, F. M., "Effective deep Q-networks (EDQN) strategy for resource allocation based on optimized reinforcement learning algorithm," *Multimed. Tools Appl.*, vol. 81, no. 28, pp. 39945–39961, 2022, doi: 10.1007/s11042-022-13000-0.

[24] Tong, Z., X. Deng, H. Chen, and J. Mei, "DDMTS: A novel dynamic load balancing scheduling scheme under SLA constraints in cloud computing," *J. Parallel Distrib. Comput.*, vol. 149, pp. 138–148, 2021, doi: 10.1016/j.jpdc.2020.11.007.

[25] Asghari, A., M. K. Sohrabi, and F. Yaghmaee, "Task scheduling, resource provisioning, and load balancing on scientific workflows using parallel SARSA reinforcement learning agents and genetic algorithm," *Journal of Supercomputing*, vol. 77, no. 3, pp. 2800–2828, 2021, doi: 10.1007/s11227-020-03364-1.

[26] qi Wu, Z., J. Wei, F. Zhang, W. Guo, and G. weiXie, "MDLB: a metadata dynamic load balancing mechanism based on reinforcement learning," *Front. Inf. Technol. Electron. Eng.*, vol. 21, no. 7, pp. 1034–1046, 2020, doi: 10.1631/FITEE.1900121.

[27] Lin, Q., Z. Gong, Q. Wang, and J. Li, *RILNET: A Reinforcement Learning Based Load Balancing Approach for Datacenter Networks*, LNCS, Springer International Publishing, vol. 11407, 2019. doi: 10.1007/978-3-030-19945-6_4.

[28] Janakiraman, S. and M. D. Priya, "Hybrid grey wolf and improved particle swarm optimization with adaptive intertial weight-based multi-dimensional learning strategy for load balancing in cloud environments," *Sustainable Comput.: Inf. Syst.*, vol. 38, no. September 2022, p. 100875, 2023, doi: 10.1016/j.suscom.2023.100875.

[29] Ramya, K. and S. Ayothi, "Hybrid dingo and whale optimization algorithm-based optimal load balancing for cloud computing environment," *Trans. Emerging Telecommun. Technol.*, vol. 34, no. 5, pp. 1–27, 2023, doi: 10.1002/ett.4760.

[30] Khaleel, M. I., "Efficient job scheduling paradigm based on hybrid sparrow search algorithm and differential evolution optimization for heterogeneous cloud computing platforms," *Internet Things*, vol. 22, no. January, p. 100697, 2023, doi: 10.1016/j.iot.2023.100697.

[31] Kruekaew, B. and W. Kimpan, "Multi-objective task scheduling optimization for load balancing in cloud computing environment using hybrid artificial Bee Colony algorithm with reinforcement learning," *IEEE Access*, vol. 10, pp. 17803–17818, 2022, doi: 10.1109/ACCESS.2022.3149955.

[32] Jena, U. K., P. K. Das, and M. R. Kabat, "Hybridization of meta-heuristic algorithm for load balancing in cloud computing environment," *J. King Saud Univ. Comput. Inf. Sci.*, vol. 34, no. 6, pp. 2332–2342, 2022, doi: 10.1016/j.jksuci.2020.01.012.

16. Microwave Absorber: A Promising Material as a Solution to Electromagnetic Interference

Sayed Tathir Abbas Naqvi[1] and Ihab Abdel-latif[2]

[1] *Department of Electronics and Communication Engineering, R V Institute of Technology, Bijnor, India*
[2] *Reactor Physics Department, Reactors Division, Nuclear Research Center, Egyptian Atomic Energy Authority, Cairo, Egypt*

Abstract: A microwave absorber is a material that absorbs the microwave radiation. Microwave absorbers are developed to mitigate the problem of electromagnetic interference (EMI). EMI is the disturbance caused by the electromagnetic radiation. Electromagnetic radiation is not only affecting electronic/electric devices but also has an adverse effect on human health. That is why to resolve this problem of electronic pollution microwave absorbers are in the leading role. Many efforts were made to develop and enhance the characteristics of microwave-absorbing materials. To be a good absorber, it should have some unique properties such as large reflection loss, large bandwidth, lightweight and thin thickness. This work deals with the main concepts and principles of microwave radiation absorption and discussions of the basic characteristics of microwave absorber types.

Keywords: Microwave absorber, ferrites, reflection loss, impedance matching.

1. Introduction

Microwave-absorbing materials (MAMs) are important functional materials due to their ability to absorb electromagnetic radiation. These materials convert electromagnetic energy into other forms to protect the device from electromagnetic radiation [1–2]. Electromagnetic waves comprise electric and magnetic components hence microwave absorbers rely on their dielectric and magnetic loss abilities. They attenuate the incident energy or convert it into heat. Materials such as magnetic metal, magnetic metal oxide and ferrites rely on magnetic loss, while conductive polymers and carbon-based materials are associated with dielectric loss [3]. The characteristics of a good absorber are shown in Figure 1. It should have high absorption performance in the meantime it should be lightweight and thin in size. The effective absorption bandwidth should be large so that it can absorb the radiation for a large frequency.

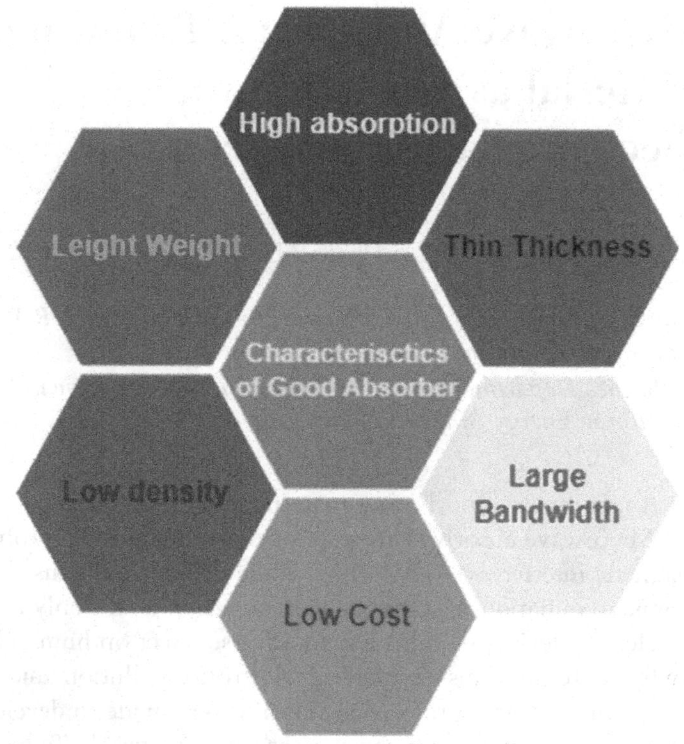

Figure 1: Characteristics of a good microwave absorber.

The present review first enlightens the mechanism associated with absorption in detail and then explain the different types of microwave absorber. It also gives the details about the absorbers developed in the literature.

2. Microwave Absorption Theory

The microwave absorption mechanism is based on the attenuation that occurs in the signal when this signal incident on the material and passes inside. In the light of microwave absorption theory, the incidental energy is split into three segments: reflected, transmitted and absorbed. The absorbing ability can be increased by varying the electromagnetic parameters, which results reduction in reflection and transmission power from the material. The absorption capabilities of the material depend on its permittivity and permeabilities. The absorber's permittivity and permeability are complex quantities as shown in equations (1) and (2) [4].

$$\varepsilon = \varepsilon' - j\varepsilon'' \tag{1}$$

$$\mu = \mu' - j\mu'' \tag{2}$$

Here ε' and μ' are associated with charge storage, while ε'' and μ'' correspond to the attenuation in the signal. The loss tangents are determined by $\tan\delta\varepsilon = \varepsilon''/\varepsilon'$ and $\tan\delta_{\mu} = \mu''/\mu'$. The absorption mechanism is described based on the $\lambda/4$ mechanism and impedance matching mechanism as follows.

2.1. λ/4 Mechanism

λ/4 mechanism [5] explains that if material's thickness is 1/4th of the incident signal's wavelength, the material will completely absorb the signal as shown in Figure 2. This phenomenon occurs when the phase of the reflected signal from the metal plate placed behind the material is out of phase with surface reflected signal. This causes the total reflection from the material to be zero, and all the signal is absorbed by the under-investigation material. The absorbing capability is expressed by reflection loss given in equation (3) [6].

$$RL = 20log\left|\frac{(Z_{in} - Z_o)}{(Z_{in} + Z_o)}\right| \tag{3}$$

Z_0 denotes the impedance of free space, while the material's impedance Z_{in} is given as in equation (4) [6].

$$Z_{in} = Z_o\sqrt{\frac{\mu_r}{\varepsilon_r}}tanh\left[j\left(\frac{2\pi ft}{c}\right)\sqrt{(\mu_r.\varepsilon_r)}\right] \tag{4}$$

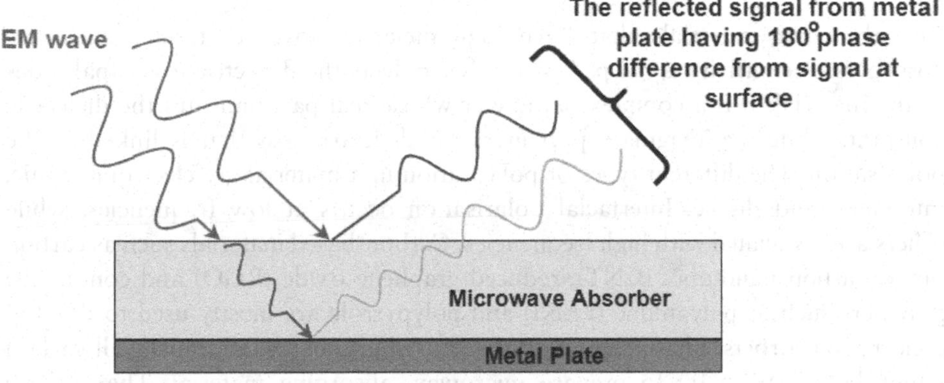

Figure 2: Schematic representation of λ/4 mechanism.

2.2. Impedance Matching Mechanism

It states that the total zero reflection resulted from the surface of the material if there is a matching between impedance Z_{in} and impedance of the free space Z_0 [7]. Equation (3) justifies that if Z_{in} matches with Z_0 the reflection loss becomes maximum, and thus by matching these two impedances absorption capability of the material can be increased. The impedance matching mechanism is shown in Figure 3, which shows that by matching these two impedances the reflection from the material can be made zero.

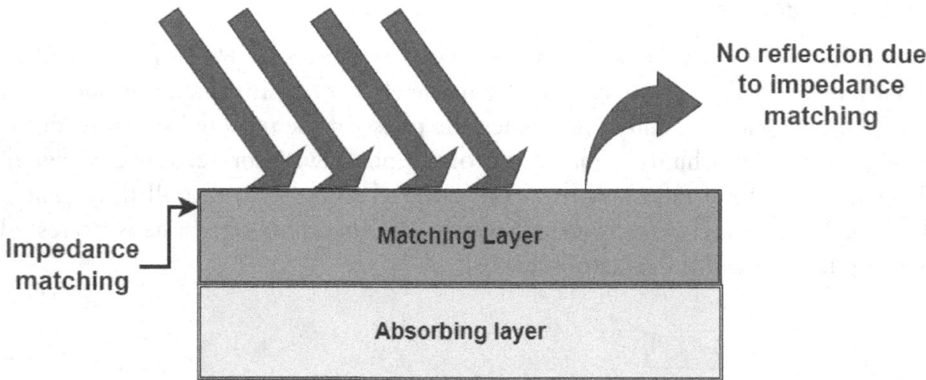

Figure 3: Impedance matching mechanism.

3. Types of Microwave Absorbers

Microwave absorbers are classified based on their loss mechanism. There are mainly two types of losses: dielectric loss and magnetic loss. Hence, microwave absorbers are classified as dielectric absorbers and magnetic absorbers.

3.1. Dielectric Absorber

The absorbing materials that have high dielectric loss are termed dielectric absorbers. Permittivity is the parameter that reflects the dielectric loss capabilities of the material. It is a complex parameter whose real part indicates the dielectric constant, while the imaginary part gives the dielectric loss that is linked to the polarisation. The different types of polarisation in a material are electronic, ionic, interfacial and dipole. Interfacial polarisation occurs at low frequencies, while others are associated with high frequencies. Carbon-based materials such as carbon black, carbon nanotubes (CNT), reduced graphene oxide (RGO) and conductive polymers such as polyaniline (PANI) and polypyrrole are mostly used to develop dielectric absorbers. Bhattacharya *et al.* [8] used graphene and multi-wall carbon nanotubes (MWCNTs) to prepare microwave-absorbing material. The authors compared the performance of graphene and carbon nanotubes and concluded that graphene has more absorption capabilities than the nanotubes. Savi *et al.* [9] used epoxy resin with MWCNTs to develop a microwave absorber. Zang *et al.* [10] inspected the absorption characteristics of graphene-CdS (cadmium sulphide) and obtained an RL of -48.4 dB at 3.3 mm.

3.2. Magnetic Absorber

Magnetic absorbers are the absorbers that mainly possess magnetic loss capabilities. Magnetic loss is associated with energy consumption caused by two inverse processes; magnetisation and demagnetisation process. The complex permeability defines the magnetic loss abilities of the material. The imaginary part denotes the magnetic loss of the material similar to permittivity in the case of dielectric material. The magnetic loss is due to three kinds of losses: hysteresis loss, resonance loss and eddy current loss. Different materials such as magnetic metals, magnetic oxides and ferrites are used to develop magnetic absorbers. Among them, ferrites are the most widely used materials to develop microwave absorbers. Qin *et al.* [11] prepared barium cobalt ferrite with doping of Mn-Zn and reported a reflection loss of -40.7 dB at 7.3 GHz. Singh *et al.* [12] synthesised barium strontium ferrites doped with Co-Sn and achieved a reflection loss of -51.09 dB. W-type hexaferrites with doping of Co-Zr were synthesised by Chang *et al.* [13]. A reflection loss of -37.84 dB was obtained at 16.3 GHz. Zhang *et al.* [14] prepared Zr-Ni-doped barium ferrites with a high reflection loss of -53.9 dB.

4. Conclusion

Electromagnetic interference is a serious threat not only in the field of electronic/electric devices rather also has an adverse effect on human health. Electromagnetic radiation should be treated properly as this electronic pollution is increasing day by day and becoming a serious threat to humankind. Microwave absorbers have emerged as a solution to this problem. These are the materials that absorb this radiation and convert it into other forms such as heat. Microwave absorbers depend on their loss capabilities, when the radiation is incident on it they provide a transmission path through them and attenuate the energy of the incident signal. The signal travels through these materials and undergoes different loss mechanisms such as multiple reflections, polarisation and loss within the material. Thus microwave absorbers are the promising candidates to resolve the problem of electromagnetic interference.

References

[1] Raveendran, A., M. T. Sebastian, and S. Raman, "Applications of microwave materials: a review," *J. Electron. Mater.*, vol. 48, pp. 2601–2634, 2019, https://doi.org/10.1007/s11664-019-07049-1.

[2] Zeng, X., X. Cheng, R. Yu, and G. D. Stucky, "Electromagnetic microwave absorption theory and recent achievements in microwave absorbers," *Carbon*, vol. 168, pp. 606–623, 2020, doi: 10.1016/j.carbon.2020.07.028.

[3] Chung, D. D. L., "Materials for electromagnetic interference shielding," *Mater. Chem. Phys.*, vol. 255, pp. 123587, 2020, doi: 10.1016/j.matchemphys.2020.123587.

[4] Green, M. and X. Chen, "Recent progress of nanomaterials for microwave absorption," *J. Materiomics*, vol. 5, pp. 503–541, 2019, doi: 10.1016/j.jmat.2019.07.003.

[5] Wang, B., J. Wei, Y. Yang, T. Wang, and F. Li, "Investigation on peak frequency of the microwave absorption for carbonyl iron/epoxy resin composite," *J. Magn. Magn. Mater.*, vol. 323, pp. 1101–1103, 2011, doi: 10.1016/j.jmmm.2010.12.028.

[6] Inui, T., K. Konishi, and K. Oda, "Fabrications of broad-band RF-absorber composed of planar hexagonal ferrites," *IEEE Trans. Magn.*, vol. 35, pp. 3148–3150, 1999, doi: 10.1109/20.801110.

[7] Singh, J., C. Singh, D. Kaur, S. B. Narang, R. Joshi, S. R. Mishra, R. Jotania, M. Ghimire, and C. C. Chauhan, "Tunable microwave absorption in Co Al substituted M-type Ba Sr hexagonal ferrite," *Mater. Des.*, vol. 110, pp. 749–761, 2016, doi: 10.1016/j.matdes.2016.08.049.

[8] Bhattacharya, P., C. K. Das, S. S. Kalra, "Graphene and MWCNT: Potential candidate for microwave absorbing materials," *J. Mater. Sci. Res.*, vol. 1, pp. 126–132, 2012, doi: 10.5539/jmsr.v1n2p126.

[9] Savi, P., M. Miscuglio, M. Giorcelli, and A. Tagliaferro, "Analysis of microwave absorbing properties of epoxy MWCNT composites," *Prog. Electromagn. Res. Lett.*, vol. 44, pp. 63–69, 2014, doi: 10.2528/PIERL13102803.

[10] Zhang, D. D., D. L. Zhao, J. M. Zhang, L. Z. Bai, "Microwave absorbing property and complex permittivity and permeability of graphene–CdS nanocomposites," *J. Alloy. Compd.*, vol. 589, pp. 378–383, 2013, doi: 10.1016/j.jallcom.2013.11.195.

[11] Qin, X., Y. Cheng, K. Zhou, S. Huang, and X. Hui, "Microwave absorbing properties of W-type hexaferrite Ba(MnZn)xCo2(1–x)Fe16O27," *Sci. Res. J. Mater. Sci. Chem. Eng.*, vol. 1, pp. 8–13, 2013, doi: 10.4236/msce.2013.14002.

[12] Singh, J., C. Singh, D. Kaur, S. B. Narang, R. B. Jotania, A. Kagdi, R. Joshi, A. S. B. Sombra, D. Zhou, S. Trukhanov, L. Panina, and A. Turkhanov, "Optimization of performance parameters of doped Ferrite-based microwave absorbers: their structural, tunable reflection loss, bandwidth, and input impedance characteristics," *IEEE Trans. Magn.*, vol. 57, pp. 1–19, 2021, doi: 10.1109/tmag.2021.3063175.

[13] Chang, L., X. Ren, H. Yin, Y. Tang, X. Pu, and H. Yuan, "The tunable microwave absorption properties of the Co2+–Zr4+ co-substituted Co2W-type hexagonal ferrites," *J. Mater. Sci.: Mater. Electron.*, vol. 31, pp. 20908–20918, 2020, doi: 10.1007/s10854-020-04605-y.

[14] Zhang, Y., C. Liu, X. Zhao, M. Yao, X. Miao, and F. Xu, "Enhanced microwave absorption properties of barium ferrites by Zr4+-Ni2+ doping and oxygen-deficient sintering," *J. Magn. Magn. Mater.*, vol. 494, pp. 165828, 2020, doi: 10.1016/j.jmmm.2019.165828.

17. Early Disease Detection Using Machine Learning Approach

Himanshu Kumawat[1,] and Dr. Prakash Singh Tanwar[2*]

[1]*Department of Computer Application, Lovely Professional University, Phagwara, Punjab, India*
[2]*Department of CSE, SEEE, Lovely Professional University, Phagwara, Punjab, India*

Abstract: Early disease detection plays a pivotal role in improving healthcare outcomes, reducing treatment costs and enhancing patients' quality of life. This paper explores the application of machine learning (ML) techniques for early illness detection. It examines various ML algorithms, data sources and features used in healthcare, along with their advantages and limitations. Additionally, this paper discusses real-world case studies and future prospects in the field of early disease detection through machine learning.

Keywords: Early diagnose, cancer, ethics, machine learning, diabetes, real-time data.

1. Introduction

Disease, as a pervasive facet of human existence, has been a subject of concern since time immemorial. The quest for effective means of early detection and timely intervention to mitigate the impacts of diseases has been at the forefront of medical research and practice. This paper delves into the evolving landscape of 'Machine Learning Early Disease Detection,' unveiling its transformative potential, inherent challenges and promising research horizons [2].

1.1. Background

Traditional disease detection methods, though valuable, often rely on clinical symptoms and invasive procedures, leading to delayed diagnosis and potential exacerbation of illnesses. The integration of ML into healthcare offers a paradigm where predictive models can analyse vast datasets encompassing patient records, medical images, genomic information and more [4].

1.2. Significance of Early Disease Detection

Early detection empowers healthcare providers to initiate interventions promptly, leading to better treatment outcomes, improved patient experiences and reduced healthcare costs. Additionally, it aids in the containment of contagious diseases, enhances public health surveillance and contributes to the effective allocation of healthcare resources. Beyond its immediate implications, early disease detection is pivotal in reshaping the healthcare landscape, where the focus shifts from reactive treatments to proactive health management. This not only extends the quality and duration of human life but also bears the potential to alleviate the burdens on healthcare systems worldwide [5].

1.3. Research Objectives

This research embarks on a comprehensive exploration of machine learning's role in early disease detection with the following objectives:

- To explain the current state of ML applications in healthcare and disease detection, to critically assess the ML algorithms and data sources leveraged for early disease detection, to assist the medical supervisor but also provides a perfect solution so that the medical supervisor can decide on further treatment for resolving body fracture issues in the human body and return the situation to normal [10], to examine real-world case studies and applications showcasing the efficacy of ML in detecting various diseases, to identify the challenges associated with ML for early disease detection and to check the future prospects trends and possible directions for research in this domain [5].

2. Literature Review

Yap *et al.* (2017) presented an innovative approach to automate breast ultrasound lesion detection using convolutional neural networks (CNNs). They demonstrated the potential of CNN technique, to enhance the accuracy and efficiency of breast cancer detection. They used ultrasound images for their datasets [1]. Ahsan and Siddique (2021) conducted a systematic literature review focused on ML-based heart disease diagnosis. They analysed and showcased the significant contributions in improving the accuracy and effectiveness of heart disease diagnosis and prediction [2]. Ahsan *et al.* (2020) developed a deep MLP, CNN model for recognizing COVID-19 patients from non-COVID-19 patients. This research addressed critical healthcare challenges, specifically in distinguishing COVID-19 cases from other respiratory diseases [3]. Balogh *et al.* (2015) provided a broader perspective in his book by discussing strategies for improving diagnosis in healthcare. They discussed various aspects and challenges related to diagnosis enhancement, offering valuable insights into the broader healthcare area [4]. Coon *et al.* (2014) raised awareness about overdiagnosis, especially in health care of infants. They highlighted how excessive diagnostic testing and labeling can potentially harm children's health.[5]. McPhee *et al.* (2010) discussed various aspects of medical diagnosis and treatment, in their book titled 'Current Medical Diagnosis & Treatment [6]. Stafford *et al.* (2020) conducted a title and abstract screening process of AI and ML applications in immune diseases shedding light on the potential of these technologies in diagnosing and handling complex medical conditions. Their research highlights the role of

AI in addressing autoimmune diseases [7]. Brownlee (2016) authored 'Machine Learning Mastery with Python,' providing practical guidance on accomplishing ML algorithms using Python. The book is a hands-on resource for individuals interested in applying ML techniques [8]. Upadhyay, Shivam and Tanwar, Prakash Singh (2021) discussed the classification of benign and malignant pulmonary lung nodules[9]. Upadhyay, Rocky, Tanwar, Prakash Singh and Degadwala, Shashang (2021), and Upadhyay, Rocky, Tanwar, Prakash Singh and Degadwala, Shashang (2022) implemented ML in healthcare. They identified the bone fracture types and implemented the image processing techniques for bone fracture detection [10][11].

3. Machine Learning Algorithms Disease Detection

Various ML algorithms exist with the ability to collect data and identify shape or patterns in improving diagnostic accuracy and effectiveness.

3.1. Logistic Regression

It is linear in nature, it excels in modelling relationships between input features and the likelihood of an event, making it a valuable tool for binary disease detection tasks. Logistic regression provides interpretable results, aiding clinicians in understanding the factors contributing to disease prediction [7].

3.2. Decision Trees and Random Forest

Decision trees offer an intuitive framework for capturing decision-making processes. In the context of disease detection, decision trees segment patient data based on key features, facilitating diagnosis [4]. Random forests, an ensemble method comprising multiple.

Decision trees enhance predictive accuracy by mitigating overfitting. Random forests are particularly useful when dealing with high-dimensional datasets and complex disease patterns.

3.3. Vector Machines (SVM)

SVMs are robust algorithms for both classification and regression tasks. SVMs excel in handling complex and non-linear relationships between data points. In early disease detection, SVMs are instrumental in delineating decision boundaries, optimising classification and accommodating multi-class problems [8].

The false positive rate is minimised in this study by combining a threshold with a SVM classifier [9].

3.4. Neural Networks

It has revolutionised disease detection by leveraging their capacity to model intricate and non-linear relationships within data. CNNs excel in medical imaging tasks.[1]. The images dealing with the frameworks are useful for some advanced applications for instance, science, security, satellite image, photo and medication field. The strategies of picture dealing with, for instance, picture overhaul, picture division and feature extraction, are used for the break recognition framework [11]. The block diagram of convolution neural network models is shown in figure 1

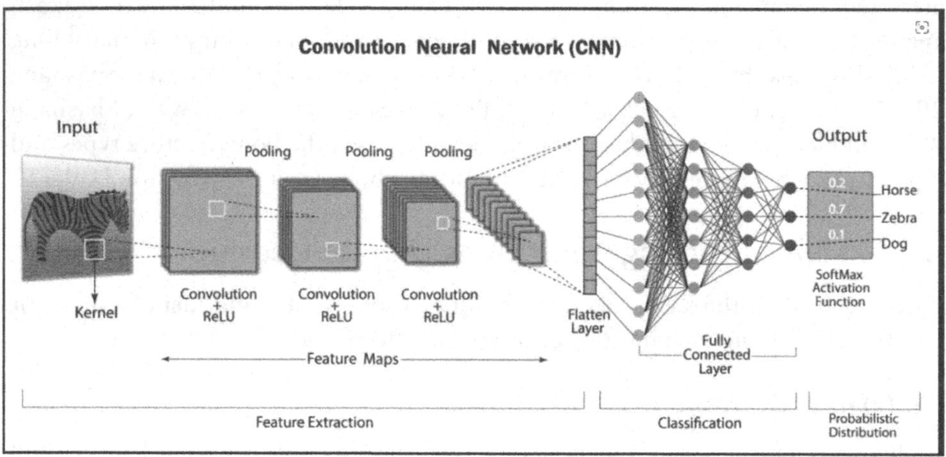

Figure 1: Convolution neural network models (Source: Bing Images).

3.5. Ensemble Methods

This is multiple base models to yield a more robust and accurate final prediction. By combining the strengths of multiple models, ensemble methods mitigate individual weaknesses, enhance predictive power and provide a holistic view of disease risk [6]. Figure 2 shows classification of machine learning, deep learning, artificial intelligence.

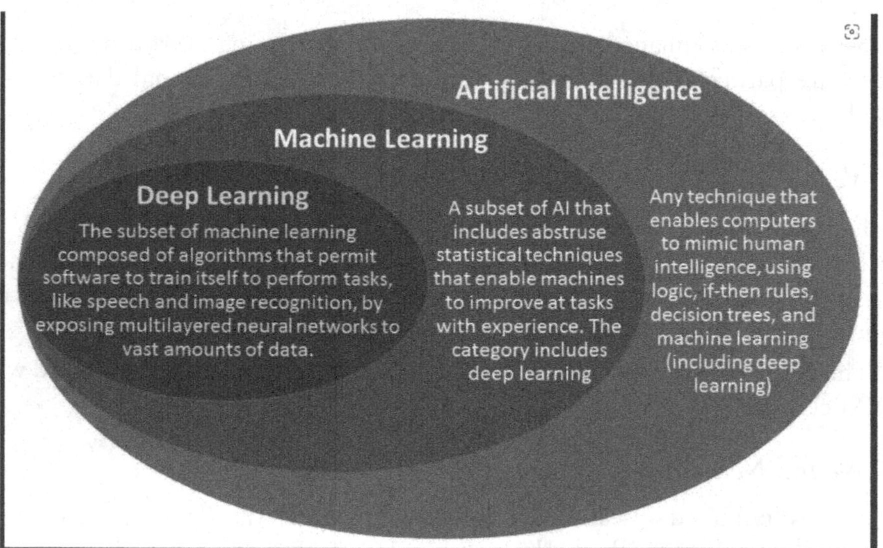

Figure 2: Machine learning, deep learning, artificial intelligence (Source: Bing images).

4. Data Sources and features

The ML algorithms in disease detection heavily relies on the availability and quality of data. The healthcare industry has witnessed an unprecedented influx of diverse data sources, enabling researchers and clinicians to harness a rich tapestry of information for early disease detection [5].

- Electronic health record, genomic data, IoT and sensor data, medical imaging data, social, edit data, wearable device data

5. Case Studies

We delve into notable case studies that illustrate the transformative potential of these algorithms in identifying diseases at an early stage:

5.1. Early Detection of Cardiovascular Diseases

Cardiovascular diseases have a leading cause of global morbidity and mortality. ML models, particularly those leveraging electronic health records (EHRs) and wearable device data, have shown remarkable success in the early detection of CVDs [5]. Table 1 provide the details of Cardiovascular data.

Table 1: Cardiovascular data (Source: Wearable sensors and devices for real-time cardiovascular disease monitoring – ScienceDirect).

Parameter	Category	Principle
PWV	PVP	PWV=LPTT
SV	CFP	SV=0.283K2T(Ps–Pd)
CO	CFP	CO=SV60T=17K2(Ps–Pd)
CI	CFP	CI=CO/BSA
PI	PVP	PI=ACcomponentDC component
AI	PVP	AI=SBP2–DBPSBP1–DBP
C1	PVP	C1=2A4(A2+A4)2+A5RA2(2A4+A2)(A42+A52)
C2	PVP	C2=1R(2A4+A2)
ABI	PVP	ABI=PaPu

5.2. Cancer Detection through Medical Imaging

Cancer detection has witnessed a paradigm shift with DL algorithms. CNNs applied to medical imaging data, such as mammograms and CT scans, have demonstrated exceptional accuracy in detecting cancerous lesions and abnormalities. Table 2 shows the districts wise cancer statistics in India.

Table 2: Major Districts wise cancer statistics in India (Source: Registry-wise Details of Crude Rate (CR), Age-Adjusted Rate (AAR) per 100,000 population for all sites of cancer in 28 PCBRs (Population Cancer Based Registry) under NCRP (National Cancer Registry Program) I Open Government Data (OGD) Platform India).

S. No.	City	Area	Males - CR	Males - AAR	Females – CR	Females – AAR
1	Ahmedabad urban 2012-2016	Central	112.3	147	119.6	141
2	Aizawl district 2012-2016	Central	101.6	108.2	127.7	124.6
3	Aurangabad 2012-2016	Central	84.2	101.6	109.8	136
4	Bangalore 2012-2014	East	159.4	127.7	139.1	107.1
5	Barshi rural 2012-2016	North	170.4	137.8	164.8	127.3
6	Bhopal 2012-2015	North	96.8	122.1	125.1	146.8
7	Cachar district 2012-2016	NE	121.8	119.9	141.4	132.8
8	Chennai 2012-2016	NE	109.9	91.2	105.9	89.2
9	Delhi 2012-2014	NE	89.1	98.3	74.7	76.7
10	Dibrugarh district 2012-2016	NE	56.6	70.9	62.9	75.1

5.3. Diabetes Prediction and Management

Diabetes is a chronic condition with a significant impact on public health. ML models that analyse electronic health records, genetic data and lifestyle factors have been instrumental in predicting the risk of diabetes development.

5.4. Infectious Disease Outbreak Prediction

Infectious disease outbreaks, such as influenza and COVID-19, demand rapid detection and containment strategies. ml algorithms, coupled with IoT and sensor data, enable the early identification of disease hotspots [3].

The application of ML algorithms in disease detection brings forth a transformative potential, but it is not devoid of challenges and ethical considerations. In this section, we scrutinise the multifaceted landscape of these challenges and the imperative ethical dimensions: Table 3 shows the state wise Covid-19 outbreak ratio from 2019 to 2021.

Table 3: State wise Covid-19 outbreak ratio from 2019 to 2021 (Source: State-wise Case Clearance Rate (CCR) for the Pre-covid-19 and Post-COVID-19 from 2019 to 2021 I Open Government Data (OGD) Platform India).

S. N.	State/Union Territories	2019	2020	2021
1	Andaman & Nicobar Islands	92.62	67.07	45.45
2	Andhra Pradesh	89.71	72.14	50
3	Arunachal Pradesh	96.71	61.19	57.66
4	Assam	67.73	36.58	59.06
5	Bihar	92.42	62.57	64.18

6	Chhattisgarh	84	59	69.1
7	Goa	105.36	55.2	69.41
8	Gujarat	81.63	44.02	76.83
9	Haryana	92.88	59.52	76.91
10	Himachal Pradesh	89.27	65.03	78.85

5.5. Data Privacy and Security

Patient data, often comprising sensitive information, is a valuable asset in disease detection. Ensuring the privacy and security of this data is paramount. Challenges arise in data anonymisation, access control and the prevention of unauthorized data breaches. Striking a balance between data utility and privacy preservation remains an ongoing challenge for researchers and practitioners.

5.6. Bias and Fairness in Machine Learning Models

In the context of disease detection, biased algorithms may result in disparities in healthcare delivery. Mitigating bias and ensuring fairness in ML models demand meticulous data preprocessing, model evaluation and algorithmic transparency. Ethical Considerations: Alongside these technical challenges, ethical considerations surrounding patient consent, informed decision-making and the responsible use of AI in healthcare demand attention. Transparency in algorithmic decision-making, informed consent for data usage and safeguards against potential misuse of ML predictions are integral ethical considerations.

6. Future Directions

In this section, we explore potential future directions that are poised to shape the landscape of disease detection [4]: Figure 3 shows bibliometric map for Machine learning based disease diagnosis.

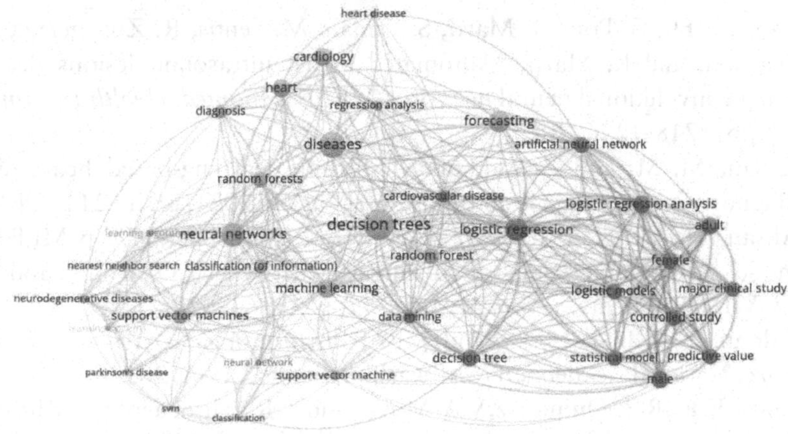

Figure 3: Bibliometric map (Machine Learning Based Disease Diagnosis) (Source: blog cascade).

- Advancements in healthcare data collection, explainable AI for healthcare, integration of real-time data sources, telemedicine and remote disease detection, collaboration between medical practitioners and ML experts.

7. Conclusion

7.1. Key Findings

ML algorithms, such as logistic regression support decision trees, vector machines, neural networks format and create model methods offer powerful tools for disease detection each with its unique strengths.

Challenges in data privacy, bias mitigation and model interpretability underscore the need for responsible and ethical ML practices in healthcare.

7.2. Impact of Machine Learning on Disease Diagnosis

The impact of ML on disease detection is profound. It extends beyond improved diagnostic accuracy and encompasses the potential to revolutionise healthcare delivery. Early detection not only enhances patient outcomes but also facilitates resource allocation, cost reduction and preventive healthcare [7].

7.3. Future Prospects and Recommendations

Continuous advancements, ethical considerations, interdisciplinary collaboration, education and training and data sharing and Standards. In conclusion, ML and disease detection hold the promise of transforming healthcare as we know it. Through responsible and collaborative efforts, we can harness the full potential of ML to usher in an era of early disease detection, proactive health management and improved well-being for individuals and populations alike.

References

[1] Yap, M. H., G. Pons, J. Martí, S. Ganau, M. Sentís, R. Zwiggelaar, A. K. Davison, and R. Marti, "Automated breast ultrasound lesions detection using convolutional neural networks," *IEEE J. Biomed. Health Inform.*, vol. 22, pp. 1218–1226, 2017.

[2] Ahsan, M. M. and Z. Siddique, "Machine learning-based heart disease diagnosis: a systematic literature review," arXiv 2021, arXiv:2112.06459.

[3] Ahsan, M. M., T. E. Alam, T. Trafalis, and P. Huebner, "Deep MLP-CNN model using mixed-data to distinguish between COVID-19 and non-COVID-19 patients," *Symmetry*, vol. 12, p. 1526, 2020.

[4] Balogh, E. P., B. T. Miller, and J. R. Ball, *Improving Diagnosis in Health Care*, National Academic Press: Washington, DC, USA, 2015.

[5] Coon, E. R., R. A. Quinonez, V. A. Moyer, and A. R. Schroeder, "Overdiagnosis: how our compulsion for diagnosis may be harming children," *Pediatrics*, vol. 134, pp. 1013–1023, 2014.

[6] McPhee, S. J., M. A. Papadakis, and M. W. Rabow (Eds.), *Current Medical Diagnosis & Treatment*, McGraw-Hill Medical: New York, NY, USA, 2010.

[7] Stafford, I., M. Kellermann, E. Mossotto, R. Beattie, B. MacArthur, and S. Ennis, "A systematic review of the applications of artificial intelligence and machine learning in autoimmune diseases," *NPJ Digit. Med.*, vol. 3, pp. 1–11, 2020.

[8] Brownlee, J., *Machine Learning Mastery with Python*, Machine Learning Mastery Pty Ltd., vol. 527, pp. 100–120, 2016.

[9] Upadhyay, S. and P. S. Tanwar, "Classification of benign-malignant pulmonary lung nodules using ensemble learning classifiers," *2021 6th International Conference on Communication and Electronics Systems (ICCES)*, IEEE, 2021.

[10] Upadhyay, R., P. S. Tanwar, and S. Degadwala, "Fracture type identification using extra tree classifier," *2021 Fifth International Conference on I-SMAC (IoT in Social, Mobile, Analytics and Cloud) (I-SMAC)*, IEEE, 2021.

[11] Upadhyay, R., P. S. Tanwar, and S. Degadwala, "An implementation of image processing technique for bone fracture detection including classification," *Med. Imaging Health Inf.*, 2022.

18. Smart Vending Machine Using Digital Payment

Narla Gowtham Sai Manikanta, Bhavanam Abhiram Reddy, Achanta Yaswanth Sri Satya Sai Krishna, Yellanki Tharun, Sana Vanajith, Ch. Ravisankar

Abstract: Smart vending machines will be implemented widely in upcoming days, which will serve the purpose of availability of products without any vendor to look after it. In this study, we propose a smart vending machine using digital payment, which accepts the money through digital payment means. The machine functions on an ESP32 microcontroller which will provide the input to the devices like motor driver (L293D) and I2C module which will serve in the purpose of rotation of motors and displaying the results in the LCD, respectively. ESP32 also deals with connecting to IMAP server to read the Email from it and to verify the payment data so that to proceed further. The microcontroller receives the input from the push buttons, which helps in selecting the desired products in required quantities and in further proceedings. At refill time, we have another push button to initialise the filling mode and to reset the values of the quantity availability of products in the vending machine. The payments are of UPI-based digital payments, and the verification of the payments is done with help of the Email alerts received from the payment gateway provider. The Email data is read by connecting to the IMAP server through our login credentials. The ESP32 acts as the IMAP client here to get the data from the server and the data is analysed and verification of the payment is done. This sends a signal to the motor for the dispensing of the products specified by the customer. This creates a secure and automatic environment, which is beneficial for both the vendor and the customer, by satisfying customers with product availability all the time.

Keywords: Smart vending machine, UPI-based digital payment, email alerts, IMAP client, and server.

1. Introduction

Smart vending machines are a new generation of vending machines that use the internet of things (IoT) technology to provide customers with a more convenient and seamless shopping experience. These machines are equipped with sensors and other smart devices that allow them to track inventory and accept digital payments. One of the key features of smart vending machines is their ability to accept digital payments. This is a major convenience for customers, as it eliminates the need to carry cash. Customers can pay for their purchases using one of the digital payment ways like UPI, mobile wallets, payments cards and other contactless payment systems.

Another key feature of smart vending machines is their intelligence. These machines use sensors to collect data on inventory levels. This data is then used to optimise the vending machine's operation and to provide customers with a better shopping experience. For example, a smart vending machine can use its data to identify which products are most popular and to ensure that they are always in stock. These vending machines benefit the shopkeeper in terms of reducing their rental charges along with maximising the profits of the vendor [1]. Although they are still relatively recent technology, smart vending machines are gradually becoming popular across many different businesses. Currently, they are used to market a wide range of goods, such as food, drinks, snacks, gadgets and personal care products. Other places where smart vending machines are in use include offices, schools, hospitals, airports and retail establishments.

Since they have been around for more than a century, vending machines have ingrained themselves into our daily lives. They provide a practical means of buying food, beverages and other products without having to deal with a cashier. Traditional vending machines, however, have a few drawbacks. They only accept cash payments, have a small range of goods available and must manually replenish their inventory. As a solution, there are distinct types of approaches and newer models are being developed day by day and enhance the results. As a solution to cash payments, we now have the digital payments methods like UPI to make the transactions, which is evolved as a part of IOT technology.

Vending machines with smart technology have the potential to improve our quality of life and sustainability. We can anticipate them changing the way we shop and consume items as they expand more widely. So as a part of evolution, this study suggests one of the ways or solutions for the better enhancement of the smart vending machine which works on the UPI-based digital payment system.

2. Literature Review

The history of vending machines started in the early 1880s, it was the time when Hero Alexandria came up with his ingenious invention. After in 1867, Simeon Denham created the first fully automated vending machine for dispensing stamps, and he was awarded with the British Patent no. 706. It continued in 19th century also many beverages and coffee dispensing machine have been evolved and did make a change in various perspectives in human day to day life. Majorly vending have reduced the manpower reliability and majorly these machines are used in western and foreign companies, but this trend is now adapting in India too and we are now heading forward to the next step that is shifting the trend from traditional vending machines to digital payment in vending machines. This research has examined the benefits of digital payment vending machines, the challenges of implementing them, and the factors that influence their adoption. One of the key benefits of digital payment vending machines is that they are more convenient for customers. Customers can pay for their purchases using their preferred digital payment method, without having to carry cash or credit cards. This can be especially convenient for customers who are on the go or who are carrying a lot of items.

Many smart factories are using IoT-enabled vending machines and assess the impact of these machines on the factory's efficiency, productivity and overall performance [2]. Vending machines are already being used to collect data on customer purchase patterns and preferences in some parts of the world. For example, some vending machines in Japan are equipped with cameras and sensors that track customer movements and purchase decisions. This data is then used to optimise the placement of products in the vending machine and to develop new products that are likely to be popular with customers [3]. With the help of digital payment systems in smart vending machines, a customer will be able to purchase products easily. Many countries with modern technology, such as the USA, UK, China, Japan and others, already use these vending machines a lot and often enough [1] [4–6]. In addition, vending machine payment had changed a lot. In the early stage, the payment system used cash or coins. This system faces a problem if there is a limited space to store the money and make changes. A contemporary design of an automatic vending machine is proposed by using short message payment [1].

Based on many references, there can be an easier way other than this in implementing online payment processes, and we are implementing one of them using the acknowledgement based using E-mail verification method during the payment process. However, there are also some challenges associated with implementing digital payment vending machines.

Overall, the reference literature has given an idea regarding the gap between the types in the payment processes, and there is still a lot many chances of research can be done in the payments area and make them much more efficient to use for the customers.

3. Propose System

We are putting forward a smart vending machine that accepts digital payments and can give customers their chosen products. This is controlled by an ESP32 microcontroller, which receives data from IMAP Email server, controls the different components in the system by sending and receiving the data from it. DC motors dispense the customer's chosen products and a 16x2 LCD screen displays payment information and transaction progress. A QR code of the UPI account is attached to the vending machine.

Our system consists of an ESP32 microcontroller, which controls the entire device, a 16x2 LCD with an I2C module, which shows payment information and transaction status, DC Motors, which dispense products from the device, and Push Buttons, which are used to choose custom products from the device and advance subsequent machine processes. The ESP32 calibrates these values and receives payment info from email server. The block diagram of the system will be as shown in Figure 1(a).

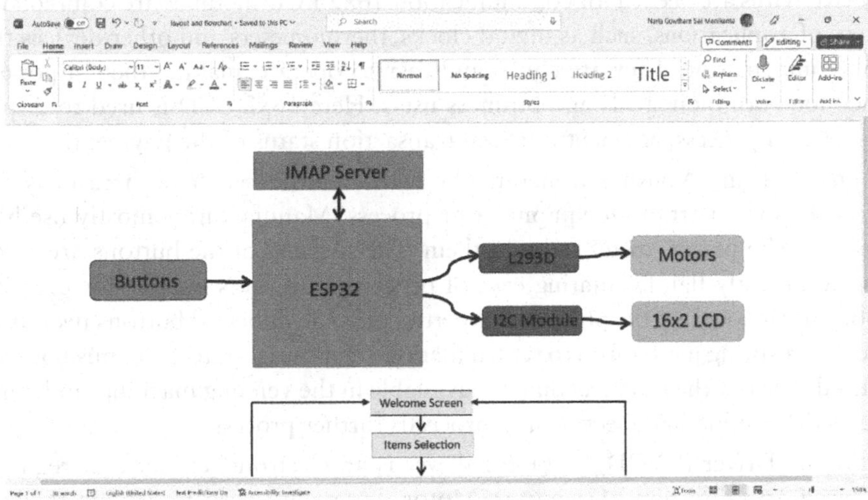

Figure 1(a): Block diagram showing the direction of data transfer among the components of vending machine.

The smart vending machine works automatically depending upon the instructions we provide to the machine. Initially, we will be selecting the products of our choice and then we further proceed with the payment. The payment is done in digital method with the help of UPI technology. When the machine detects that the payment is made, it will proceed further with the steps of dispensing the products selected by the customer. After that it will come back to its initial state of selecting the products for the next customer.

4. Hardware Implementation

4.1. Hardware Description

ESP32 Microcontroller: The ESP32 is based on the Xtensa dual-core 32-bit microprocessor, which can be clocked at up to 240 MHz. It also includes a wide range of peripherals, such as GPIO pins, ADC, I2C, SPI, UART and I2S. When the payment is made from the customer side, ESP32 can be used to verify it. When the payment is made from the customer side, an Email alert is sent about the payment after that payment is verified and allows the machine to dispense the product.

DC Motor: This motor works on direct current (DC) to produce the required mechanical energy to the system. Most of these rely on magnetic forces produced due to the flow of currents in the armature winding's coils. DC motors are helpful in a wide range of applications like electric vehicles, power tools, household appliances and industrial machinery. Here, DC motor is used to dispense the products in the machine to the customer after the payment information is confirmed.

16x2 LCD with I2C Module: The 16x2 LCD with I2C module is a liquid crystal display (LCD) module that can be controlled using the I2C serial communication protocol. This makes it easy to connect to microcontrollers and other devices, as only two wires are needed for communication.16x2 LCD modules are common in a variety of applications, such as digital clocks, thermometers and other devices that display information. They are cheap and easy to operate, making them a popular choice for both individuals and business users. Here 16x2 LCD is used to display the selection process, payment info and transaction status of the payment.

Push Buttons: A push button, often known as a basic switch mechanism, is used to control some part of an equipment or process. Manufacturers mostly use hard substance like plastic, metal to build them. The surfaces of the buttons are meant to be sufficiently flat, facilitating ease of pressing with one's finger. However, it is important to note that the physical properties of some unbiased buttons necessitate the use of a spring mechanism to return them to their initial state. Here push buttons are used to select the products that are available in the vending machine, and it also reflects the production selection and proceeds further process.

Motor Driver (L293D): A motor driver is an electronic circuit that regulates the speed and direction of a motor. Motor drivers are used in a wide range of applications including robotics, industrial automation and consumer electronics. There are mainly two types of motor drivers, one is brushed and the other is brushless. Brushed motor drivers are used to control brushed DC motors. Brushless motor drivers are used to control brushless DC motors.

All these components are connected as shown in Figure 2(a) to develop the mentioned smart vending machine in the proposed system.

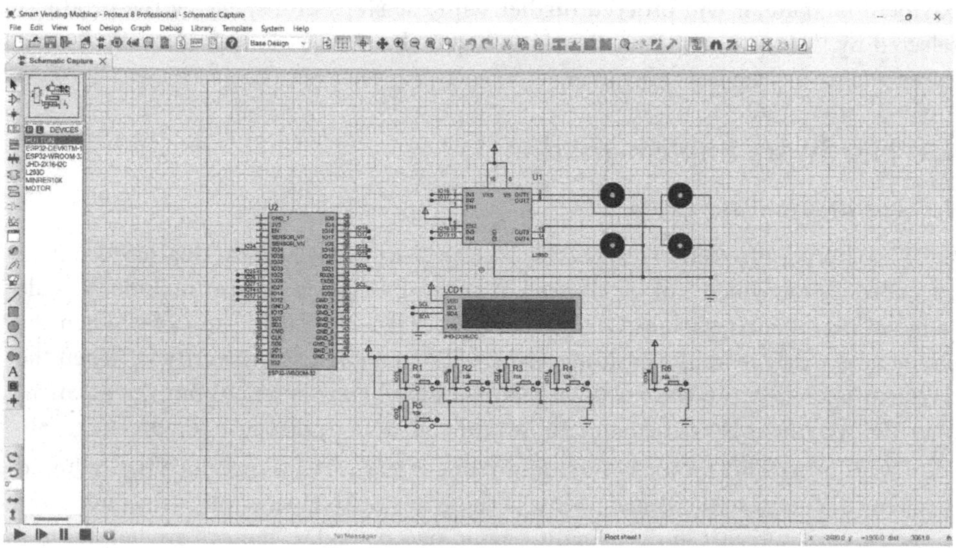

Figure 2(a): Circuit diagram showing the connections between the components of vending machine.

4.2. Software Description

Here we need to program the ESP32 microcontroller to connect to Email server and to fetch the payment status. In addition to that, ESP32 also controls the motors and displays information on 16x2 LCD display. For that, we need to code the ESP32 microcontroller for it. For that, we will be using the Arduino IDE. The Arduino IDE is a free and open-source software platform for developing and uploading code to Arduino boards. It is a cross-platform application that can be used on any operating systems like Windows, macOS and Linux. The Arduino IDE is well designed with a code editor, status prompt and other capabilities. It also includes a compiler and linker for compiling and uploading code to Arduino boards. We also use the serial monitor of the Arduino IDE for checking the intermediate results that are not necessary to display on the LCD display for the user purpose.

5. Real-Time Implementation

The model of smart vending machine is used to buy the products which can be done without the help of vendor and have 24/7 availability of the products. The smart vending machine will undergo some of the steps one after other from selecting to dispensing the products. The flow chart in Figure 3(a) demonstrates the steps involved in the making of the implementation of this model. Initially, we will be at the welcome screen. After pressing the next button, we were asked to select the products we need of required quantity like if we need the 2 quantities of product 'A' then we need to press the product 'A' button 2 times, and we will be updated with the values of the products we selected in the LCD display. After continuing further, we will display with the amount to be paid by us and ok to proceed for the payment

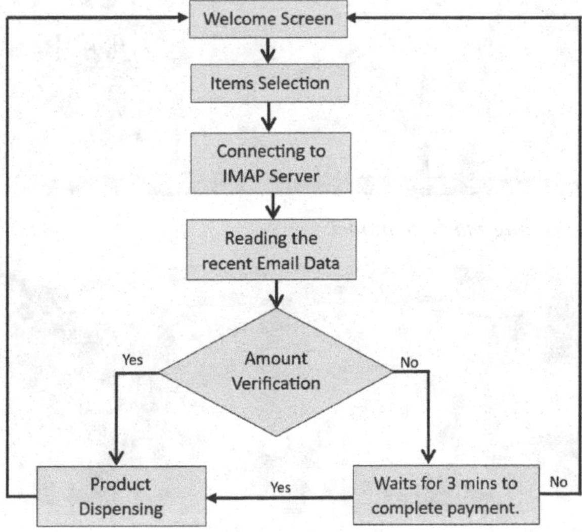

Figure 3(a): *Overall flow process of vending machine.*

part. Now we can pay through the QR code scanner and the ESP32 meanwhile will connect to the IMAP server, read the recent emails from the server, analyse the data and verify whether the money of desired amount is transferred or not. If transferred, the machine proceeds with the last step of dispensing the product, where a signal is set to the motors to dispense the product or else it will wait for up to 3 mins to verify the payment if it exceeds the time limit then it terminates the process and goes to initial step. This works in loop and then it continues for all the users. While we want to refill the products in the smart vending machine, there is separate button assigned for it to reset the available quantity values of product to the maximum capacity the smart vending machine has space for.

6. Result and Discussion

In this model, we will be having results in the LCD display showing the status of the process of smart vending machine like the payment received, number of products selected and payment to be paid. There are some other results that are displayed on the serial monitor used for the testing of the connectivity with IMAP server and data retrieving from the IMAP server, analysing the data and verifying the data with it. All these results are available below in the figures.

Figure 4(a): Smart vending machine model.

Figure 4(b): Interior view of the Smart vending machine model.

```
Connecting to AP..............
WiFi connected.
IP address:
172.19.134.236

#### Connecting to IMAP server...
> C: ESP Mail Client v3.4.9
> C: connecting to IMAP server
> C: Host > outlook.office365.com
> C: Port > 993

#### IMAP server connected
> C: IMAP server connected

#### Checking the capability...
> C: check the capability

#### Logging in...
> C: send IMAP command, AUTHENTICATE PLAIN

#### Send client identification...
> C: send IMAP command, ID

#### Reading the list of mailboxes...
> C: send IMAP command, LIST

Available folders: Archive, Deleted, Drafts, Inbox, Junk, Notes, Outbox, Sent
```

Figure 4(c): Serial monitor output showing connection status of ESP32 with the IMAP server.

```
#### Downloading messages...

> C: download plain TEXT message
> C: /email_data/37/msg.txt
> C: [#####             ] 32 %
> C: [##########        ] 64 %
> C: [#############     ] 77 %
> C: [################# ] 94 %
> C: [##################] 100 %

> C: download HTML message
> C: /email_data/37/msg.htm
> C: [#                 ] 11 %
> C: [##                ] 16 %
> C: [####              ] 25 %
> C: [#####             ] 32 %
> C: [########          ] 50 %
> C: [##########        ] 63 %
> C: [#############     ] 75 %
> C: [##############    ] 87 %
> C: [################  ] 93 %
> C: [################# ] 99 %
> C: [##################] 100 %

#### Saving message header to file...
> C: Free Heap: 183684

#### Logging out...
> C: send IMAP command, LOGOUT

#### Log out completed
> C: log out completed
```

Figure 4(d): Serial monitor output showing downloading of email data to ESP32 from IMAP server.

Figure 4(e): Scanning of vendor UPI ID QR code through the Paytm App (Any UPI supported apps can be used).

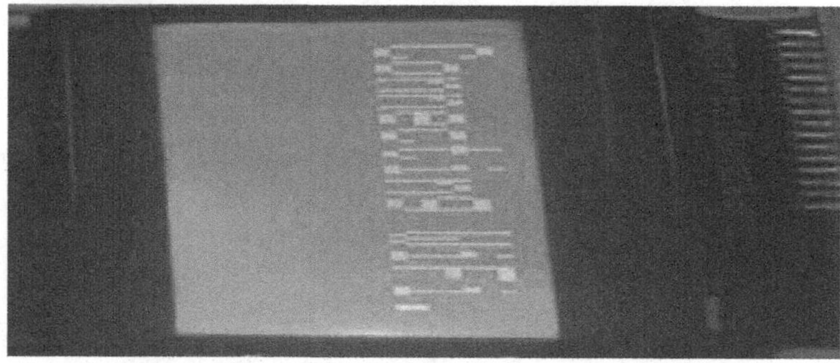

Figure 4(f): Status of ESP32 while trying to connect with Wi-Fi.

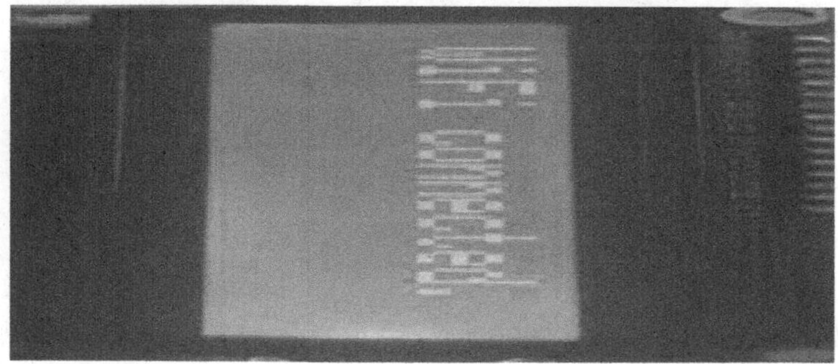

Figure 4(g): Status of ESP32 after connected with Wi-Fi.

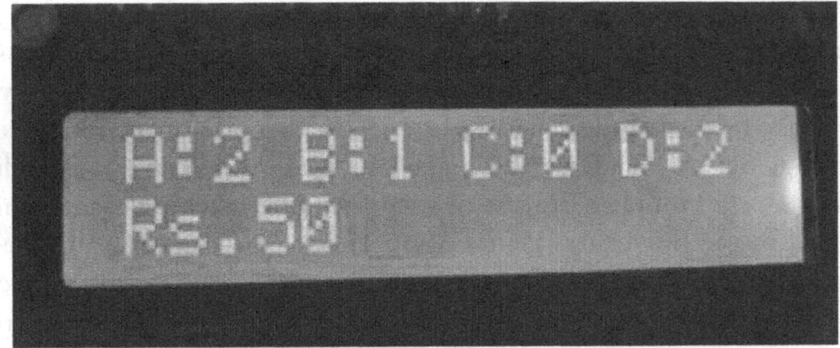

Figure 4(h): Displaying the quantity of goods, we have selected in LCD.

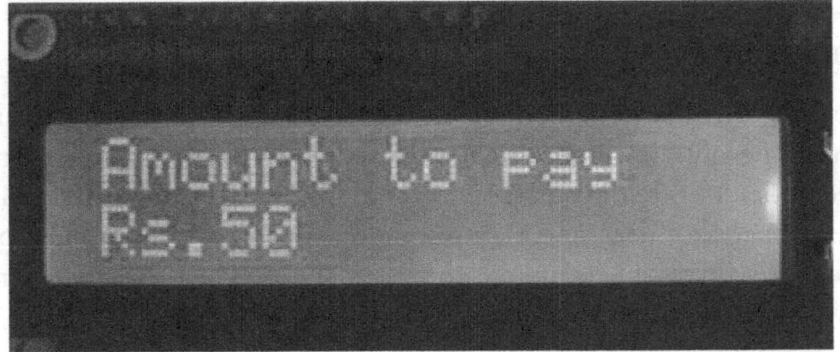

Figure 4(i): Displaying the amount to be paid in LCD.

Figure 4(j): Displaying the amount received status on LCD.

Figure 4(k): Telling the customer to collect the dispensed products.

All these Figures from 4(a) to 4(k) are results of the above proposed model. The 4(c) and 4(d) are output at the serial monitor which is describing the steps it has reached in connecting to the IMAP server while connecting to the server and checking all the folders of the Email and retrieving the data of the recent received email and logging out of the server. Figure 4(f)–4(k) describing each individual step involved in the complete process of smart vending machine usage, which are as mentioned in the flowchart (Figure 3(a)). The reason for choosing the Email alerts over SMS alerts is that SMS alerts work fine in the regions with high cellular network signal and sometimes there will be delays with the SMS due to some technical reasons. Some of these advantages over SMS made us choose Email alerts for verification of payment.

7. Conclusion

The concept of digitalisation in industry has revolutionised the way in which people can get benefits in a more individualised and effective manner, and it has also opened doors for other business ventures to invest in this kind of development, thereby easing people's lives and creating more job opportunities. The proposed model is a more advanced technique to access the product at offices and other buildings with ease, saving valuable time and efforts of users.

The use of online transaction capabilities for product dispensing and network interfacing has also made life easier for people. The employment of digital payment technologies for product finding and payment has reduced the need for paper currency. The novel and cost-effective approach presented in the study is the integration of E-mail acknowledgement through mail server and the vending machine allowing to buy products using smart phone just scan the QR code and it will be secure and easy. This digital solution will create a unique experience for customers buying products at their leisure that are cost effective and user friendly

References

[1] Alam, W., F. Sultana, J. B. Saba, and A. C. Kofi, "IOT based smart vending machine for Bangladesh," *2019 IEEE International Conference on Robotics, Automation, Artificial-Intelligence and Internet-of-Things (RAAICON)*, IEEE, pp. 73–76, November 2019.

[2] Wiyanti, D. T. and M. N. Alim, "Automated vending machine with IoT infrastructure for smart factory application," *J. Phys.: Conf. Ser.*, IOP Publishing, vol. 1567, no. 3, p. 032038, Jun. 2020.

[3] Koujalgi, H., and A. S. Bale, "Biometric based automatic ticket vending machine for Indian railways," *Int. Res. J. Eng. Technol.*, vol. 4, no. 07, pp. 2395–0056, 2017.

[4] Korucu, M. K., Ö. Kaplan, O. Büyük, and M. K. Güllü, "An investigation of the usability of sound recognition for source separation of packaging wastes in reverse vending machines," *Waste Manage.*, vol. 56, pp. 46–52, 2016.

[5] Mann, G., K. Hosig, A. Zhang, S. Shen, and E. Serrano, "Smart snacks in school legislation does not change self-reported snack food and beverage intake of middle school students in rural Appalachian region," *J. Nutr. Edu. Behav.*, vol. 49, no. 7, pp. 599–604, 2017.

[6] Shoji, Y., K. Nakauchi, and W. Liu, "Community-based wireless IoT infrastructure using ubiquitous vending machines," *2016 Cloudification of the Internet of Things (CIoT)*, IEEE, pp. 1–5, Nov. 2016.

[7] Alam, W., D. Sarma, R. J. Chakma, M. J. Alam, and S. Hossain, "Internet of things based smart vending machine using digital payment system," *Indones. J. Electr. Eng. Inf.*, vol. 9, no. 3, pp. 719–731, 2021.

[8] Arifin, S. M. S., M. Syai'in, J. Endrasmono, S. T. Sarena, L. Subiyanto, A. S. Setyoko, ... and A. Soeprijanto, "Smart vending machine based on SMS gateway for general transactions," *2017 15th International Conference on Quality in Research (QiR): International Symposium on Electrical and Computer Engineering*, IEEE, pp. 34–39, Jul. 2017.

[9] Mahajan, G., V. Phale, S. Mane, and A. Patil, "Vending machine with cash and cashless payment support," *Int. Res. J. Eng. Technol.*, vol. 7, no. 6, pp. 341–348, 2020.

[10] Cameron, N., "Email and QR codes," *ESP32 Formats and Communication: Application of Communication Protocols with ESP32 Microcontroller*, Berkeley, CA: Apress, pp. 293–324, 2023.

[11] Kim, K., D. H. Park, H. Bang, G. Hong, and S. I. Jin, "Smart coffee vending machine using sensor and actuator networks," *2014 IEEE International Conference on Consumer Electronics (ICCE)*, IEEE, pp. 71-72, Jan. 2014.

[12] Pagliaro, M., "Enhancing the use of e-mail in scientific research and in the academy," *Heliyon*, vol. 6, no. 1, 2020.

19. Balancing Fundamental and Technical Analysis for Stock Market Using Artificial Intelligence: A Survey

Pawandeep Kaur[1], Hardeep Kaur[1], *Jai Sukh Paul Singh[1,2], Sonia Bukra[3,4], Manjinder Kaur[5] Amarjot Kaur[6] and Jaskaran Singh Phull[1]

[1]*School of Electronics and Electrical Engineering, Lovely Professional University, Punjab, India*

[2]*Department of Research Collaboration, Division of Research and Development, Lovely Professional University, Punjab, India*

[3]*Department of Electronics and Communication Engineering, Maharishi Markandeshwar University, Mullana-Ambala, Haryana, India*

[4]*Department of Electroncis and Communication Engineering, Chandigarh Group of Colleges, Jhanjeri, Mohali, Punjab, India*

[5]*Department of Computer Science and Engineering, Chandigarh University, Gharuan, Mohali, Punjab, India*

[6]*Punjabi University, Patiala, Punjab, India*

Abstract: The use of artificial intelligence (AI) in predicting stock price using the last two decades has become very popular. Numerous AI approaches have been proposed by various author and financial analysts. It has been seen that machine learning (ML) and AI works very well on technical analysis; however, the analysis of stock price fundamentally is a tedious task due to dependance on balance sheets. This paper focuses on in dept analysis of various popular approaches used in prediction of stock price based on technical or fundamental analysis and provide a comparative analysis of the various bench marked approaches of ML/AI for stock price predictions.

Keywords: Stock market, artificial intelligence, machine learning, price prediction, algo trading, fundamental analysis, technical analysis.

1. Introduction

To make regular income or to achieve financial freedom investors and researchers now a days uses techniques based upon machine learning (ML) and artificial intelligence (AI) to track and predict the movement of the stock prices using historical data. Based on ML and AI as an application for stock market, numerous research articles and methods have been proposed and published in the last decade. A very crisp survey is carried out covering in depth analysis of various popular approaches used in prediction of stock price based on technical or fundamental analysis and provide a comparative analysis of the various bench marked approaches of ML/AI for stock price predictions

Since 1960s, several researchers have maintained the efficient market hypothesis, which contends that because all market players have access to the same information and have similar expectations, price fluctuations are fully random and unexpected. Other researchers disagree with the efficient market theory and think that market prices change in line with a trend. In light of this supposition, the following two views for market analysis are grouped.

- Technical analysis, which seeks to predict trends in stock price movements using previous asset prices and defends those trends.
- Fundamental analysis refers to the examination of a company's financial statements, state of affairs, rivals of the company present so far. Additionally, it takes into account the economy's general health as well as variables like interest rates, output, earnings, employment, GDP, housing, manufacturing and management.

Figure 1 displays the overall structure of an AI prediction model used for financial forecasting. In the initial phase, all the prerequisites and all the required data are fetched, which is essential for the developed and testing of the forecasting model. The fetched and filtered data is processed and modified and further filtered to eliminate irrelevant information and emphasise crucial figures and facts in the data decoding and filtering phase. The cleaned and filtered data is then used by the predictor to train the developed model, and a validation stage allows for parameter optimisation. In a test stage, the performance of the trained model with tweaked parameters needs to be assessed.

2. Comaparative Analysis of Literature

The rough set theory technique proposed by Golan et.al. in [1] harvests regulations to assist and support the price momentum of the stock ticker to find out conclude with trading actions such as purchase, sell or hold onto a trade already executed. Fundamentalist indicators and signs are used as input parameters in this strategy based upon historical asset price records. In addition to this, Schierholt et.al. in [2] suggested a probabilistic neural network (PNN) for forecast ticker price momentum tendencies. Each of the three groups of trends that is buying, holding onto an asset and selling indicates a distinct course of action.

Kim et.al. in [3] provided an artificial probabilistic network (APN), which performs trends categorisation using six classes of return levels while using input parameters like price fluctuations and fundamentalist indicators. Zhangguai et.al. in [4] adopted technique to accomplish binary classification of working capital, support vector machine (SVM), k-nearest neighbor classifier, PNN, classification and regression tree (CART), boosting (Adaboost) and bagging algorithms are used. The aftermaths of the research illustrate that the boosting algorithm execute more remarkable results when historical asset prices were used as an input variable.

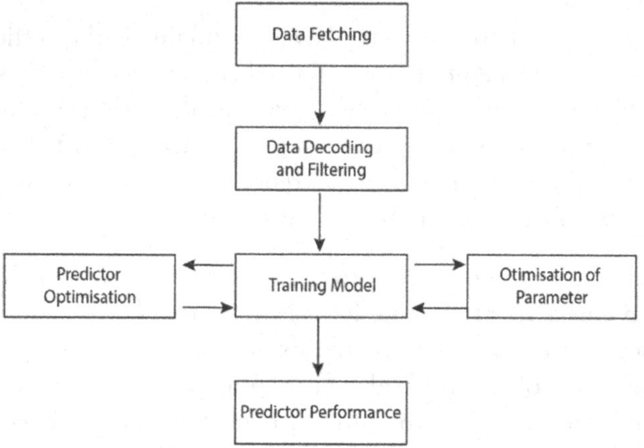

Figure 1: *System model for general financial forecasting using prediction from an AI model.*

Kuboudan et.al. in [5] advocated genetic programming (GP) to anticipate price and return using historical asset prices as input data. The study comes to the conclusion that returns are less predictable than asset values. Using technical catalogue as input parameters, Kuo et.al. in [6] developed a genetic algorithm (GA) concatenated with a fuzzy neural network (FNN) system model for the prediction of the trends based on financial as well as the asset price movements. The technique is limited to three different types of trends. Wang et.al. in [7] described a fuzzy-gray prediction system that forecasts asset values using price fluctuation, volume traded and fundamentalist index data. Wang et al. in [8] developed a fuzzy rough set method that uses previous prices and volume data for working capital as input to forecast future prices.

A GP feed based on the historical data, which includes price momentum and volume traded for the day was used by Potvin et al. in [9] to forecast the financial rules for generating buy or sell signals. Huang et al. in [10] used a SVM method to gather the process data based on fundamentalist indices as the financial assets for the prediction of the future direction of underlying asset price movement using binary categorization. A GA was proposed by Kim et al. in [11] that chooses the best weights for a number of classifier predictions and uses them all in conjunction to for a collective decision as a single prediction. The classifiers examine four separate classes – Bull, Edge-Up, Edged-Down and finally the Bear while predicting financial price movement patterns using technical indicators as input parameters. Three advance and hybrid sort of artificial neural network (ANN) time-series models were reported in [12] by Roh et.al. using NN-EWMA, NN-GARCH and NN-EGARCH. These models use EWMA, GARCH and EGARCH to begin with as an input parameter prior of making an entreaty to the ANN for the speculation of price volatility of working capital. The ticker prices, traded volume and underlying fundamentalist indicators are used in the model; the findings show that NN-EGARCH performs the best.

ML algorithms have been in use from the earliest asset trend prediction studies. Heuristics for optimisation were frequently used in conjunction with genetic algorithms, particularly when combining several categorisation algorithms. As a reference Huang et.al. in [13] proposed and highlighted a voting committee in combination with an approach named as wrapper feature selection. The proposed approach was further merged with Kth nearest neighbor (KNN), SVM, back-propagation neural network, logistic regression and decision tree. The article concludes that voting outperforms single classifiers when performing a binary assets classification using momentum prices, traded volume and technical pointers as an input data. Huang et. al. in another article [14] first selected features for previous price momentum and technical indicator signal using filters. To forecast future asset prices, a self-organizing feature map (SOFM) and support vector regression (SVR) were developed. Before applying several SVR models to each cluster, SOFM slice up the priming facts and figures into many groups. The trained SVR model is then tested over with the most similar data sent and cluster predictions data set.

In the research paper [15], an assembled historical asset price series that were hand-picked by a stepwise regression approach (SRA). The training data was divided into clusters using a self-organization map (SOM) neural network. Further, the developed system model was used along with fuzzy genetic system which was utilised to forecast price of the ticker underlying. GP and self-organising map (SOM) technique was suggested in Reference [16]. Each cluster in the SOM's training data division is made up of training model, validation the system design and finally testing the data set. The performance of the prediction made by the system of assessed by the test data, whereas the validation of the data identifies optimum GP model for particular cluster. The developed system model forecasts the future prices of assets using data on prices, volume and technical indicators.

The preprocessed evolutionary LM neural networks were suggested in Reference [17]. (PELMNN). SRA, or step-wise regression analysis, is used to choose variables. The commencing weights of ANNs were evolved using a genetic algorithm as a global search technique. An advance approach named Levenberg–Marquardt back propagation (LMBP) neural network was used to train and utilised for the forecast of asset prices. Technical indexes and trade volume are the input data. A price forecasting approach using a backpropagation neural network for the validation of the dataset made up of technical indicators, prices of the asset class and volume traded was proposed in Hsu et.al. [18]. Finally, a backpropagation neural network was cast-off to forecast asset prices using test data.

Using a random forest algorithm, Booth et.al. in the paper [19] shortlisted the prices as the only parameter along with the technical indicator data in a technique called backward elimination. To forecast asset prices, several random forest algorithms were applied. The average of all the random forest predictors, the final predictions were used and weighted by training error. Huang et. al. in one of this research [20] examined the binary categorisation of asset price trends using the ANN, SVM, random forest and Naive-Bayes algorithms. The hyper-parameters of the classifiers are optimised during a validation step after being fed data from technical indicators. Patel et.al. in [21] examined ML models for stock market forecasting. The preprocessing methods of normalisation, outliers' exclusion, clustering and feature selection are first reviewed in the study.

In [22], Chong et. al. examine the restricted Boltzmann machine (RBM), AutoEncoder (AE) and principal components analysis (PCA) as three alternative feature selection and processing techniques (RBM). Next, a ML system is used to forecast the future return on assets. Data from log returns are gathered for this every five minute. Fischer et. al. in [23] analyses a historical series of asset returns using a deep learning (DL) long short-term memory (LSTM) neural network to classify the trend of price variation of the asset class. Analysing the historical prices and volume data as input variable Long et al. in [24] proposed a Deep Learning model in combination with recurrent and convolutional and neurons layers that categorizes predictive upcoming asset price movements into various separate classes. Exercising highly developed pre-treated styles has come more and more accepted popular style, as it helps the developed system model to execute and perform the learning algorithms more easily and accurately by eliminating the irrational data, leaving behind the most useful material information.

Deep neural networks (DNNs) are increasingly being used for stock price prediction and market forecasting recently. As an instance, Zhong et. al. in [25] proposed a DNN to categorise asset price movements in the future, for forecasting the process movement in either of the two directions of the future price. Dataset used for the training and validation includes 60 properties of assets that belonged to the S&P 500 ETF for the period of ten year from June 2003 and May 2013, with the average closing price made on daily basis. These attributes include returns and technical indications. Results demonstrate that, in a stock market trading simulation, an ANN offers higher profits and fewer risks (variance) despite having a higher accuracy than a DNN. In [26], Vignesh et. al. gathered the open, low, high and close prices for the ticker Microsoft and Yahoo. Here, time period was taken for five years starting from January 2011 till 2015 December. The technical indicators such as index momentum, volatility, momentum, volatility, index volatility, stock price and stock momentum were used to compute and analyse the price. Dealing with the issue of binary classification of stock trends, Vignesh examines the SVM and LSTM models further. The results show that the LSTM approach is more accurate. As much as ten technical indicators were calculated from opening, close and low by Nabipour et. al. in [27]. bagging, Adaboost, XGBoost, recurrent neural network (RNN), ANN, LSTM algorithm, decision tree, random forest, gradient boosting, conclude that long short-term memory algorithm outperforms the others by using the high asset prices for a period of long term, i.e. ten year, validated data from 2009 November to 2019 November to predict asset prices.

Table 1: Comparative analysis table of techniques.

Technique	Approaches	Input Parameters			Output Parameters		
		Price	Volume	Analysis	Momentum	Price	Volatility
Rough Set Theory	Heuristic	No	No	Fundamental	No	Yes	No
Probabilistic Neural Network	Machine Learning	Yes	No	NA	No	Yes	No
Artificial Probabilistic Network (APN)	Machine Learning	Yes	No	Fundamental	No	Yes	No
Boosting Algorithm	Machine Learning and Ensembles	Yes	No	NA	No	Yes	No
Advocated Genetic Programming	Heuristic	Yes	No	NA	No	Yes	No
Hybrid Genetic Algorithm (GA) coupled with Fuzzy Neural Network (FNN)	Machine Learning, Heuristic, Fuzzy and Ensembles	No	No	Technical	Yes	Yes	No
Fuzzy-Gray Prediction system	Fuzzy	Yes	Yes	Fundamental	No	Yes	No
Fuzzy rough set method	Fuzzy	Yes	Yes	NA	No	Yes	No
Genetic Programming	Heuristic	Yes	Yes	NA	Yes	Yes	No
Support Vector Machine (SVM)	Machine Learning	No	No	Fundamental	No	Yes	No
Genetic Algorithm (GA)	Machine Learning, Heuristic and Ensembles	No	No	Technical	Yes	Yes	No
NN-EWMA, NN-GARCH, and NN-EGARCH	Machine Learning	Yes	Yes	Fundamental	No	Yes	No
Wrapper Feature Selection	Machine Learning and Ensembles	Yes	Yes	Technical	Yes	Yes	No

Technique	Approaches	Input Parameters			Output Parameters		
		Price	Volume	Analysis	Momentum	Price	Volatility
Self-Organizing Feature Map (SOFM) and Support Vector Regression (SVR)	Machine Learning and Clustering	Yes	No	Technical	No	No	No
Stepwise Regression Approach (SRA)	Machine Learning, Heuristic, Fuzzy and Clustering	Yes	No	NA	No	Yes	No
Self-Organizing Map (SOM) and Genetic Programming (GP)	Heuristic and Clustering	Yes	Yes	Technical	Yes	Yes	No
Preprocessed Evolutionary LM Neural Networks (PELMNN)	Machine Learning abd Heuristic	No	Yes	Technical	No	Yes	No
Backpropagation Neural Network	Machine Learning	Yes	Yes	Technical	No	Yes	No
Random Forest algorithm	Machine Learning and Ensembles	Yes	No	Technical	No	Yes	No
ANN, SVM, random forest, and Naive-Bayes algorithm	Machine Learning and Ensembles	No	No	Technical	No	Yes	No
Machine Learning models	Machine Learning, Clustering and Ensembles	Yes	Yes	Both	Yes	Yes	Yes
Restricted Boltzmann Machine (RBM)	Machine Learning	No	Yes	NA	No	Yes	No
Deep Learning Long Short Term Memory (LSTM)	Machine Learning	No	Yes	NA	No	Yes	No
Deep Learning model	Machine Learning	Yes	Yes	NA	No	Yes	No

Wu et. al. in paper [28] suggest a brand-new two-dimensional convolutional neural network (CNN) that makes use of a matrix made up of prices of asset opening price, high, low, close price, futures and options price, as well as the volume of transactions for every monitored asset throughout the course of a data time series of 120 days. Five assets from Taiwan and five from the United States are utilised for that. To forecast patterns in the movement of financial asset prices, the suggested CNN is applied. The assets were than classified into classes where Class-1 is classified for days when the return exceeds 1% above the previous close or for the days when the return is down by than 1% from the previous close. For all other days, it is categorised under as Class 0. As per the observed forecast, the novel CNN outperforms all other classifiers when taking into account each of the 10 assets. The author has compared the results of the novel CNN with that of SVM, neural network and one-dimensional CNN. The crux of all the reviewed articles is tabled under Table 1.

The input and output parameters used by each paper gathered on Scopus are described in Table 1. In this table, the input parameters are restricted to historical ticker price and returns along with traded volume for the day, fundamental and technical indices technical indices. The financial forecasting models can forecast a variety of price patterns, trading rules, future asset values, returns or volatility which are considered as the output parameters listed and briefed in Table 1.

Table 2 lists additional forecasting model characteristics, such as the use of techniques based on ML algorithms to predict or heuristics to make future forecast in order to enhance the prediction accuracy along with the processing speed. Moreover, less complex fuzzy systems are prioritised to improve predictions making the trading systems and its decisions simpler and accurate. The grouping of the fetched and collected information before the estimation of speculative price predictions ensembles or hybrid mixture of various predictors or classifiers are used to verify and authenticate the performance of the system to optimize the model's hyperparameters.

The great majority of methodologies discovered in the literature used ML techniques to forecast asset prices and their trends. Here the stratification conceptual methods are regularly utilised for the identification of patterns in ticker price movements, regression techniques are frequently used to predict price. A rise in the amount of data being utilised as inputs or features suggests the need for ways to pick out and pre-treat the feed in data, in order to eliminated out just the most crucial facts and figures. ML and DL techniques are another trend that, despite their high computing complexity, have shown encouraging results in recent studies. This makes picking and preprocessing data even more crucial.

Table 2: Model characteristics of preditive models.

Technique	ML	Heuristic	Fuzzy	Clustering	Ensembles	Validation
Rough Set Theory	No	Yes	No	No	No	No
Probabilistic Neural Network	Yes	No	No	No	No	No
Artificial Probabilistic Network (APN)	Yes	No	No	No	No	No
Boosting Algorithm	Yes	No	No	No	Yes	No
Advocated Genetic Programming	No	Yes	No	No	No	No
Hybrid Genetic Algorithm (GA) coupled with Fuzzy Neural Network (FNN)	Yes	Yes	Yes	No	Yes	No
Fuzzy-Gray Prediction system	No	No	Yes	No	No	No
Fuzzy rough set method	No	No	Yes	No	No	No
Genetic Programming	No	Yes	No	No	No	No
Support Vector Machine (SVM)	Yes	No	No	No	No	No
Genetic Algorithm (GA)	Yes	Yes	No	No	Yes	No
NN-EWMA, NN-GARCH, and NN-EGARCH	Yes	No	No	No	No	No
Wrapper Feature Selection	Yes	No	No	No	Yes	No
Self-Organizing Feature Map (SOFM) and Support Vector Regression (SVR)	Yes	No	No	Yes	No	No
Stepwise Regression Approach (SRA)	Yes	Yes	Yes	Yes	No	No
Self-Organizing Map (SOM) and Genetic Programming (GP)	No	Yes	No	Yes	No	Yes
Preprocessed Evolutionary LM Neural Networks (PELMNN)	Yes	Yes	No	No	No	No
Backpropagation Neural Network	Yes	No	No	No	No	No
Random Forest algorithm	Yes	No	No	No	Yes	No
ANN, SVM, random forest, and Naive-Bayes algorithm	Yes	No	No	No	Yes	Yes

Technique	ML	Heuristic	Fuzzy	Clustering	Ensembles	Validation
Machine Learning models	Yes	No	No	Yes	Yes	No
Restricted Boltzmann Machine (RBM)	Yes	No	No	No	No	No
Deep Learning Long Short Term Memory (LSTM)	Yes	No	No	No	No	No
Deep Learning model	Yes	No	No	No	No	No

3. Conclusion

This paper provides the methodical investigation of the research related to ML and AI as an application for investments in the stocks market. The scope of the review is limited to technical analysis of stock market prediction, portfolio optimization based on AI. The fundamental analysis based on market driven news and fiscal sentiment analysis or the combination both is also analysed in this paper. Exponential increase in seen in driving the investment or portfolio management using AI is observed during the past two decades (2000's to 2020's), which is due to the popularization of technology dependent on computer-based analysis. Deep learning LSTM is observed as to be the most advance technique based on ML-AI with an accuracy percentage of 80%.

References

[1] Golan, R. H. and W. Ziarko, "A methodology for stock market analysis utilizing rough set theory," *Proceedings of 1995 Conference on Computational Intelligence for Financial Engineering (CIFEr)*, pp. 32–40, 1995.

[2] Schierholt, K. and C. H. Dagli, "Stock market prediction using different neural network classification architectures," *IEEE/IAFE 1996 Conference on Computational Intelligence for Financial Engineering (CIFEr)*, pp. 72–78, 1996.

[3] Kim, S. H. and S. H. Chun, "Graded forecasting using an array of bipolar predictions: application of probabilistic neural networks to a stock market index," *Int. J. Forecasting*, vol. 14, no. 3, pp. 323–337, 1998.

[4] Zhanggui, Z., H. Yau, and A. M. N. Fu, "A new stock price prediction method based on pattern classification," *IJCNN'99. International Joint Conference on Neural Networks. Proceedings (Cat. No. 99CH36339)*, vol. 6, pp. 3866–3870, 1999.

[5] Kaboudan, M. A., "Genetic programming prediction of stock prices," *Comput. Econ.*, vol. 16, no. 3, pp. 207–236, 2000.

[6] Kuo, R. J., C. H. Chen, and Y. C. Hwang, "An intelligent stock trading decision support system through integration of genetic algorithm based fuzzy neural network and artificial neural network," *Fuzzy Sets Syst.*, vol. 118, no. 1, pp. 21–45, 2001.

[7] Wang, Y.-F., "Predicting stock price using fuzzy grey prediction system," *Expert Syst. Appl.*, vol. 22, no. 1, pp. 33–38, 2002.

[8] Wang, Y.-F., "Mining stock price using fuzzy rough set system," *Expert Syst. Appl.*, vol. 24, no. 1, pp. 13–23, 2003.

[9] Potvin J.-Y., P. Soriano, and M. Vallée, "Generating trading rules on the stock markets with genetic programming," *Comput. Oper. Res.*, vol. 31, no. 7, pp. 1033–1047, 2004.

[10] Huang, W., Y. Nakamori, and S.-Y. Wang, "Forecasting stock market movement direction with support vector machine," *Comput. Oper. Res.*, vol. 32, no. 10, pp. 2513–2522, 2005.

[11] Kim, M.-J., S.-H. Min, and I. Han, "An evolutionary approach to the combination of multiple classifiers to predict a stock price index," *Expert Syst. Appl.*, vol. 31, no. 2, pp. 241–247, 2006.

[12] Roh, T. H., "Forecasting the volatility of stock price index," *Expert Syst. Appl.*, vol. 33, no. 4, pp. 916–922, 2007.

[13] Huang, C.-J., D.-X. Yang, and Y.-T. Chuang, "Application of wrapper approach and composite classifier to the stock trend prediction," *Expert Syst. Appl.*, vol. 34, no. 4, pp. 2870–2878, 2008.

[14] Huang, C.-L. and C.-Y. Tsai, "A hybrid SOFM-SVR with a filter-based feature selection for stock market forecasting," *Expert Syst. Appl.*, vol. 36, no. 2, pp. 1529–1539, 2009.

[15] Hadavandi, E., H. Shavandi, and A. Ghanbari, "Integration of genetic fuzzy systems and artificial neural networks for stock price forecasting," *Knowl. Based Syst.*, vol. 23, no. 8, pp. 800–808, 2010.

[16] Hsu, C.-M., "A hybrid procedure for stock price prediction by integrating self-organizing map and genetic programming," *Expert Syst. Appl.*, vol. 38, no. 11, pp. 14026–14036, 2011.

[17] Asadi, S., E. Hadavandi, F. Mehmanpazir, and M. M. Nakhostin, "Hybridization of evolutionary Levenberg–Marquardt neural networks and data pre-processing for stock market prediction," *Knowl. Based Syst.*, vol. 35, pp. 245–258, 2012.

[18] Hsu, C.-M., "A hybrid procedure with feature selection for resolving stock/futures price forecasting problems," *Neural Comput. Appl.*, vol. 22, no. 3, pp. 651–671, 2013.

[19] Booth, A., E. Gerding, and F. McGroarty, "Automated trading with performance weighted random forests and seasonality," *Expert Syst. Appl.*, vol. 41, no. 8, pp. 3651–3661, 2014.

[20] Cavalcante, R. C., R. C. Brasileiro, V. L. F. Souza, J. P. Nobrega, and A. L. I. Oliveira, "Computational intelligence and financial markets: A survey and future directions," *Expert Syst. Appl.*, vol. 55, pp. 194–211, 2016.

[21] Patel, J., S. Shah, P. Thakkar, and K. Kotecha, "Predicting stock and stock price index movement using trend deterministic data preparation and machine learning techniques," *Expert Syst. Appl.*, vol. 42, no. 1, pp. 259–268, 2015.

[22] Chong, E., C. Han, and F. C. Park, "Deep learning networks for stock market analysis and prediction: methodology, data representations, and case studies," *Expert Syst. Appl.*, vol. 83, pp. 187–205, 2017.

[23] Fischer, T. and C. Krauss, "Deep learning with long short-term memory networks for financial market predictions," *Eur. J. Oper. Res.*, vol. 270, no. 2, pp. 654–669, 2018.

[24] Long, W., Z. Lu, and L. Cui, "Deep learning-based feature engineering for stock price movement prediction," *Knowl. Based Syst.*, vol. 164, pp. 163–173, 2019.

[25] Zhong, X. and D. Enke, "Predicting the daily return direction of the stock market using hybrid machine learning algorithms," *Financ. Innovation*, vol. 5, no. 1, pp. 1–20, 2019.

[26] Vignesh, C. K., "Applying machine learning models in stock market prediction," *EPRA Int. J. Res. Dev.*, pp. 395–398, 2020.

[27] Nabipour, M., P. Nayyeri, H. Jabani, A. Mosavi, and E. Salwana, "Deep learning for stock market prediction," *Entropy*, vol. 22, no. 8, p. 840, 2020.

[28] Wu, J. M., Z. Li, G. Srivastava, M. Tasi, and J. C. Lin, "A graph-based convolutional neural network stock price prediction with leading indicators," *Software Pract. Exp.*, vol. 51, no. 3, pp. 628–644, 2021.

20. Animal Detection and Repelling System Based on Motion Sensor and GSM Module

Jhulan Kumar, Yogesh Singh, Manoj Kumar Yadav, Rekha Goyat, and Rajeev Kumar

School of Electronics and Electrical Engineering, Lovely Professional University, Phagwara, India

Abstract: Nilgai has become one of the biggest menaces for farmers in many states of India. They cause a lot of damage to the crops by eating, sleeping and trumping of the crops. The cropping pattern was forced to change to reduce the loss. It affects the per capita income of the farmer as well as the gross domestic product of the country. Several techniques have been developed and implemented to keep Nilgai away from crops, but they have not been very successful due to cost or complexity of the system.

A microcontroller-based crop protection system has been developed, which detects animals near the field, repels them and at the same time alerts the farmers. It is low-cost equipment suitable for small area use and easy to install and maintain. Implementation of this device in areas with moderate population of Nilgai saves about Rs. 30,000 for each acre of land and gives freedom to farmers to grow crops of their choice without any mental harassment.

Keywords: crops ventilation, GSM module, menace of wild animal, repellent system.

1. Introduction

Wild animals have been a problem for farmers all over the world from long time. It has become a major problem in India too, but here it is mainly the problem of Nilgai which affect pilot cropping system and per capita income. The population of Nilgai is gradually increasing, and it has become a threatened situation for many states of India. Even when they are eating, roaming and resting in the fields, they cause damage to the crops. There is no control on nilgai population. Since the implementation of Wildlife Protection Act 1972 in India, the population of Nilgai is increasing very fast. They come outside the farming land, stay there, damages crops and affect the crops yield at a large level. As a result, it causes loss of the capital, time, mental and physical harassment for them. This leads to loss of millions of rupees in the farming. Farmers are food producers and are called 'Annadata' who work day and night with the entire family in harsh climatic and environmental conditions. They work even in the coldest and hottest climates, but their crops are destroyed by wild animals and they earn nothing. They are somehow living their lives, but are not able to provide good education or health to their children. Most of the child starts working with their family at the fields from very young age of around six- seven, depriving them of basic schooling. They work hard for long hours but have no fixed salary and no retirement age, whereas a government employee works for fewer hours in a good environment get a fixed salary and retires after sixty years. They grow up working in the fields and die working in the same fields while living the worst lives in terms of comforts and luxuries. Farmer grows food for us which is most useful for the society but they are the most deprived people in this society. Growth in the economy is very important for the betterment of the quality of life of farmers and the future of their children. They are totally dependent on their crops, so when their crop gets spoiled/ruined they have to face many problems to survive [1–3].

2. Literature Review

Today, farmers are suffering from many problems like labour crisis, irrigation and threat of Nilgai. Technology has been developed to reduce the problems of irrigation and labour crisis, while fear of wild animals/nilgai remains a big issue. Farmers face a major problem of crop vandalism due to Nilgai in India shown in Figure 1. The crop damage leads to huge losses to the farmer [4]. Various technologies have been developed and used to protect crops, among them electric fencing is the most effective. It is a barrier that produces a shock when animals come in contact with the open wire. This machine is designed to cover an area of more than 10 or 20 acres of land and requires an expert to install or fix it. Its cost and complexity are not suitable for those who have only 1 or two acres of land and grow different types of crops in it. Other cheap preventive measures include spraying of cow dung, egg solution, wooden fencing, etc., but these are not so effective and are unable to protect the crops. In the absence of suitable technology, the only way for farmers to protect their crops is to keep vigil day and night. Earlier they used to come out towards the fields only at night, but due to the continuously decreasing forest area, now they come out during the day also for food [5–6].

Figure 1: Nilgai grazing in the farm in the day time.

Most of the Indian farmers come in the category of small farmer whose farming area is less than 5 acres. They grow different types of crops like pulses, vegetables, paddy, wheat and nursery for their livelihood. They need more protection as the animals like to eat ears and fruits of crops and also attack pulses and vegetables more shown in Figure 2. They love to eat these crops. Vegetables required maintaining soft soil and more moisture. They are grown at some distance to get more spread. When Nilgai enter into the field, they eat and ruin it. They provide maximum damage to vegetable and pulses. Farmers have to grow nursery for many crops such as paddy, onion and tomato at 1st level then they grow it again at certain distance. It is needed to grow in 3 dismil of land only for growing in an area of 100 dismil of land. When the Nilgai passes through the fields carrying the nursery plant, it causes a lot of damage with its hoof even without eating it. Local animals such as cow, buffalo, got and birds also damage crops when get out for grazing but they are take care by their owners but wild animals are stay in open environment and free to eat. Nilgai make damage for all crops but damages done for paddy and wheat is sustainable because of cultivation in a large area and less eatable by Nilgai. But vegetable, pulses and nursery get maximum get cultivated in small area and more damage due to their lovely food. Most farmers need to grow these crops to maintain the agricultural ecosystem, they want to save them but the available equipment is not useful due to the cost, complexity and space required to set up the system [7–8].

Figure 2: Nurseries, pulses, vegetables need more protection.

Due to various reasons, the number of Nilgai is increasing in rural areas, and how it is becoming dangerous is shown in Figure 3. It forces farmers to change their growing crop patterns or leave barren lands.

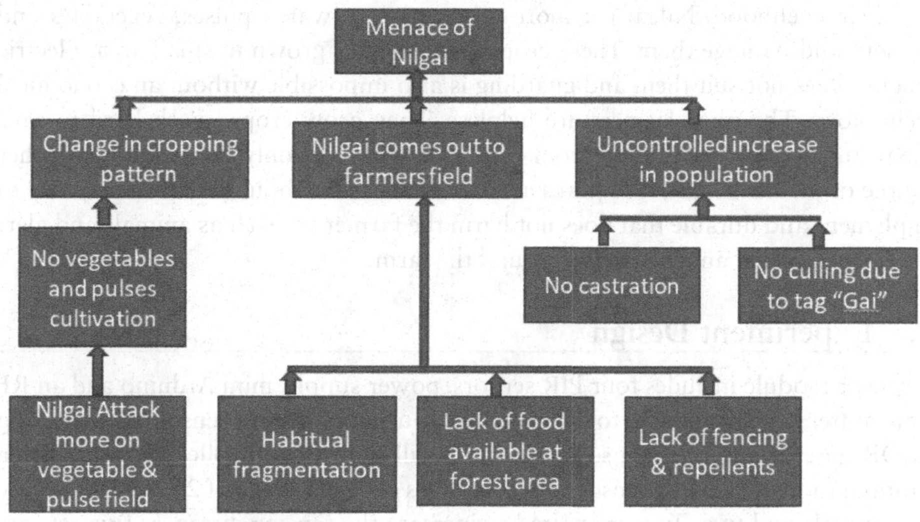

Figure 3: Menace of Nilgai for the farmers [9].

The existing technologies used to protect crops from wild animals/Nilgai are listed in Table 1:-

Table 1: Advantages and disadvantages of various available techniques to protect crops from wild animals.

Sl.No.	Techniques	Working	Drawbacks
1	Relocation of Nilgai [10, 11].	Catch up wild animals and relocate to forest	Complex, time taking, costly
2	Sterilization [12]	Used to control the population, long-time solution	Difficult to sterilise the large number, costly, time taking, against the law of nature
3	Fencing [13]	Durable, high accuracy, barrier that produces a shock to repel animals.	Not suitable for small area, required exert in installation
4	Chemicals [14]	Used so that animal not eat the crops.	Avail the wild animal protection act 1972, India

Nilgai revenge the crops. This leads to huge losses for the farmers. In the absence of economical or suitable technology, protecting the crops from Nilgai requires guarding the field for 24x7 hours that is impossible and carrying a large labour cost. Even guarding a small area would be expensive. Electric fencing requires two feet vacant space around the farm that forces farmers to leave barren land. In many states like Bihar, number of farmers having a farming area less than 1 acre, and they have to grow different crops such as vegetables, pulses with paddy and wheat for their livelihood. Nilgai get more attracted to towards pulses, vegetables and nursery and damage them. These crops are generally grown in small area. Electric fencing does not suit them and guarding is also impossible without an economical technology. The poor farmers are helpless. They grow crops, work hard to save them but do not get returns from the farm. They do only because of no other source of income. Thus, it requires a smart system that should be low cost, easy to implement and durable that does not harm the farmers as well as animals and alert the farmers when animals arrive around the farm.

3. Experiment Design

A sensor module includes four PIR sensors, power supply, mini Arduino and an RF transmitter to transmit data to the main unit. Output of all four sensors is connecting to OR gate. If any of them sense signal, it will send to controller via transmitter. Combination of two PIR sensor single modules covers a range of 20 meters to sense the animals and two. Two are paired to increase the sensing distance. Two sets are connected with a module at some different height to cover more area. The range of RF transmitter and receiver module is 35-40 meter as shown in Figure 4. For 1 acre of land that covers an area of 4046.86 m^2, i.e. 63 m x 63 m approximately, it requires 12 sensor module and one main unit to cover the entire area. The sensor module will established at a height of 2.0 feet and 3.5 feet.

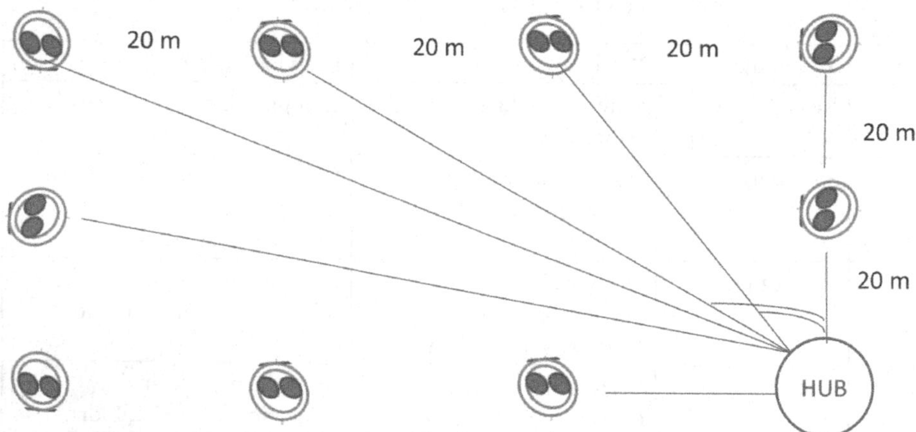

Figure 4: Mapping of sensor module in the farm.

4. Design and Procedure

A sensor module includes four PIR sensors, power supply, mini Arduino and an RF transmitter to transmit data to the main unit. Output of all four sensors is connecting to OR gate. If any of them sense signal, it will send to controller via transmitter. Combination of two PIR sensor single modules covers a range of 20 meters to sense the animals and two. Two are paired to increase the sensing distance. Two sets are connected with a module at some different height to cover more area. The range of RF transmitter and receiver module is 35-40 m as shown in Figure 5. For 1 acre of land that covers an area of 4046.86 m2, i.e. 63 m x 63 m approximately, it requires 12 sensor module and one main unit to cover the entire area. The sensor module will established at a height of 2.0 feet and 3.5 feet.

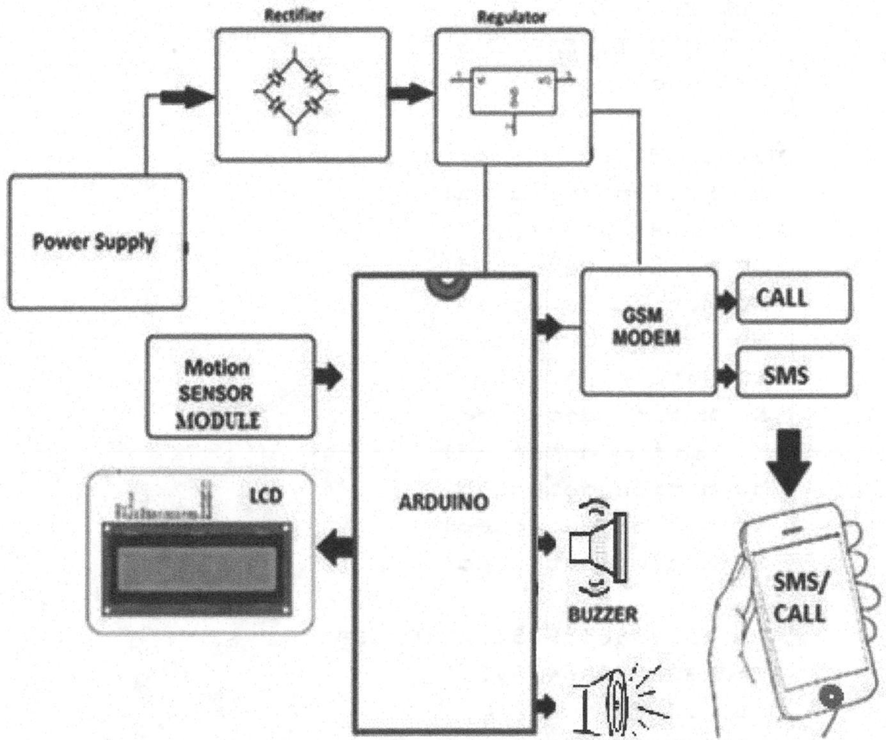

Figure 5: Block diagram of an animal detection and alerting system.

5. Results

Figure 6 represents the output generated by system when object enter in their range and detect them

```
COM9

 NO Motion detected!
 NO Motion detected!
 NO Motion detected!
 NO Motion detected!
 NO Motion detected!
 NO Motion detected!
 NO Motion detected!
AT
ATD +917986439751;AT+CMGF=1
AT+CMGS="7986439751"
CALL TO FARMERS
SENT MSG TO FARMERS
MOTION detected
□
Motion detected!
 NO Motion detected!
Motion stopped!
 NO Motion detected!
 NO Motion detected!
 NO Motion detected!
 NO Motion detected!
 NO Motion detected!
 NO Motion detected!
 NO Motion detected!
 NO Motion detected!
 NO Motion detected!
AT
ATD +917986439751;AT+CMGF=1
AT+CMGS="7986439751"
CALL TO FARMERS
SENT MSG TO FARMERS
MOTION detected
□
Motion detected!
 NO Motion detected!
Motion stopped!
```

Figure 6: *Message displayed on monitor when system detect an object.*

Figure 7 represents object detection and alerting farmers by calling and sending SMS.

a. Object detection

```
NO Motion detected!
NO Motion detected!
AT
ATD +917986439751;AT+CMGF=1
AT+CMGS="7986439751"
CALL TO FARMERS
SENT MSG TO FARMERS
MOTION detected
□
Motion detected!
NO Motion detected!
Motion stopped!
NO Motion detected!
```

b. alerting farmer's by SMS

c. alerting farmerrsby calling

Figure 7: Detection and alerting by call and SMS.

6. Cost–Benefit Analysis

It is reported that the low density of Nilgai causes an average of 30% damage to wheat and paddy [15].

Loss of grains in one year in acre of land: 30 % damage as reported + one seasonal crops doesn't grown = 30 % loss in 2 crops (20 quintal = 2000 kg wheat/paddy = 25*2000 = Rs. 50,000/-) + One complete season (Rs. 25,000/-) = Total loss is Rs. 75,000/-

Device cost for two acres:

2.0 acre = 2*4,047 = 8094 sq. m

Generally, farming land is available in a square shape.

For a square farm,

Side (length) = (8094)1/2 = 89.97 = 90 m (approx.)

Perimeter of the field = 4 * 90 = 360 m (perimeter for square & rectangle are same for equal area)

No. of sensor module required = 360/20 = 18

Total system cost = HUB cost + cost of sensor modules = 2700 +18*700 =15300/.

Installation cost (10 %) = 1,530/, Maintenance cost (10 %) = 1,530/.

Total expenditure for installing this equipment = 15360 (for one time)

Benefit for 2 acres = 75000-18360= 56640/.

This is the benefit in one year but this system will work for many years and if we increase area then only sensor module cost will increase not hub cost. So benefit will increase.

7. Conclusions

This report focuses on the problem of crop destruction by animals. It mainly requires protection from Nilgai. They have become major destroyers of crops in many states of India. Due to Nilgai, farmers have to suffer huge losses every year in terms of per capita income and mental health. Development of this technology will ensure complete protection of crops from animals and increase their income. It is low-cost equipment and very easy to install and maintain, which is very suitable for small/medium farmers as well as small area and does not require any expert to install. This will provide an opportunity to grow additional summer crops in a year, which will increase the income of farmers manifold. The expected cost of the proposed system would be (based on bill of materials) Rs. 3000. This technology gives farmers the freedom to grow crops of their choice everywhere, thereby increasing agricultural income manifold.

References

[1] Goyal, S. K. and L. S. Rajpurohit. "Nilgai, Boselaphus tragocamelus-a mammalian crop pest around Jodhpur," *Uttar Pradesh J. Zool.* vol. 20.1, pp. 55–59, 2000.

[2] Meena, M., "Agriculture crop damage by antelope (Boselaphustragocamelus) and management strategies: Challenges in India."

[3] Chauhan, N. P. S., and R. Singh, "Crop damage by overabundant populations of nilgai and blackbuck in Haryana (India) and its management," 1990.

[4] Chauhan, N. P. S. "Agricultural crop depredation by nilgai antelope (Boselaphus tragocamelus) and mitigation strategies: challenges in India," *Julius-Kühn-Archiv*, vol. 432, p. 190, 2011.

[5] Divya, U. K., Praveen M., "IOT-based wild animal intrusion detection system," *Int. J. Recent Innovation Trends Comput. Commun.*, ISSN: 2321-8169, vol. 6, no. 7, pp. 06–08, 2018.

[6] Thapa, S., "Effectiveness of crop protection methods against wildlife damage: a case study of two villages at Bardia National Park, Nepal," *Crop Prot.*, vol. 29.11, pp. 1297–1304, 2010.

[7] Dev, S. M., "Small farmers in India: challenges and opportunities," *Indira Gandhi Inst. Dev. Res.* pp. 8–14, 2012.

[8] Behera, U. K., and J. France, "Integrated farming systems and the livelihood security of small and marginal farmers in India and other developing countries," *Adv. Agron.*, vol. 138, pp. 235-282, 2016.

[9] Mukherjee, A., "Prioritization of problems in integrated agriculture: a case of Rampur village in sub humid region of Eastern India," *Indian Res. J. Ext. Edu.*, vol. 15.1, pp. 53–59, 2016.

[10] Foley, A. M., *et al.*, "Movement patterns of nilgai antelope in South Texas: implications for cattle fever tick management," *Preventive Vet. Med.*, vol. 146, pp. 166–172, 2017.

[11] Khanal, Sr., *et al.*, "Challenges of conserving blue bull (Boselaphus tragocamelus) outside the protected areas of Nepal," *Proceedings of the Zoological Society*, vol. 71, Springer India, 2018.

[12] Babbar, B. K., *et al.*, "Bio-ecology, behaviour and management of blue bull, Boselaphus tragocamelus," *Int. J. Pest Manage.*, pp. 1–16, 2022.

[13] Kumar, A., *et al.*, "Patterns of crop rading by wild ungulates and elephants in Ramnagar Forest Division, Uttarakhand," *Hum.–Wildl. Interact.*, vol. 11.1, p. 8, 2017.

[14] Jain, S., *et al.*, "Effectiveness of different management strategies against Nilgai population (Boselaphus tragocamelus) in Punjab Province of India," *Anim. Biol.*, vol. 73.1, pp. 43–64, 2022.

[15] Chauhan, N. P. S. "Agricultural crop depredation by Nilgai antelope (Boselaphustragocamelus) and mitigation strategies: challenges in India," *Julius-Kühn-Archiv*, vol. 432, p. 190, 2011.

21. Analysis of Deep Learning Algorithms Based Person re-Identification Using Standard Datasets: A Review

Badireddygari Anurag Reddy and Danvir Mandal

School of Electronics and Electrical Engineering, Lovely Professional University, Phagwara, Punjab, India

Abstract: The major drawbacks in pedestrian re-identification are posture change, occlusion and background cluster, which are not solved using convolution networks. Some of the people using only one feature, i.e. local feature and another is global feature, which are used separately to solve this problem but their relevance are ignored. In this review paper, a different algorithms are reviewed, which were used to solve the re-identification problem. To improve the robustness of these algorithms, different techniques are used. To develop the characteristics of various ranges, a combined optimization functions were used. To get final output and representations, characteristics were processed at various ranges and were joined. To increase the performance of the system, various reordering strategies were used. This paper is reviewed on different datasets, i.e. Market-1501, CUHK03, MSMT, DukeMTMC-reID and CAVIAR.

Keywords: Person re-identification, feature fusion, ResNet-50, deep learning.

1. Introduction

Pedestrian re-identification is one of the major problems in computer vision applications. For tracking tasks, video-based analysis and pedestrian retrievals are used. Real-life pedestrian re-identification is facing different challenges such as view, posture, occlusion and illumination, which make differences in different views. In this, multi-scale convolutional future fusion techniques are used. In this, two levels of features are used, one is low level feature and another is high-level feature [1]. A low-level feature has high resolution, and it contains more information but due to less number of convolutional layers noise effect is more.

Person re-identification is mainly used to identify person over non-overlapping cameras views, i.e. security surveillance and criminal investigation. In [2], author has used different techniques to solve this problem. The different techniques are deep batch active learning and knowledge distillation. The different datasets used in this work were Market-1501 and DukeMTMC-reID.

In [3], author initiated how to retrieve the same person images in different camera views. Clustering-based techniques were applied to identify re-identification of a person. Author proposed different types of techniques, i.e. multi-view evolutionary training, multi-view diffusion and evolutionary local refinement for effective person re-identification. The datasets used in this work were Market-1501, DukeMTMC-reID and MSMT.

The fast growth in CCTV systems was identifying the moving object in public places, i.e. person identification and vehicle identification. In [4], author proposed different loss functions. Softmax loss, triplet loss and combination of both were used. The commonly used datasets were Market-1501, CUHK03 and CUHK01.

The main focus of person re-identification is to matching images correlated with identical person taken by a different camera views and angles. In [5], author initiated diverse drop block technique to identify and solve the various re-identification problems. Different datasets Market-1501, CUHK03 and DukeMTMC-reID were used.

In [6], an unsupervised cross domain based methods were used for person re-identification. The main aim was to find unlabeled target domains over non-overlapping cameras. Multi loss optimization learning model was used to work out this problem. The different datasets Market-1501, MSMT and DukeMTMC-reID were used.

In [7], author explained about specific person re-identification methods across different camera angles and views. To identify person Re-id, multi-scale deep supervision technique was used. Different types of datasets, i.e. Market-1501, MSMT and DukeMTMC-reID were used.

Matching person images is one of the difficult tasks in computer-based applications. Deep learning-based person re-identification solved these problems. In [8], author proposed high-order Re-ID techniques which consist of two different types of pooling designs, i.e. global hierarchical pooling and local hierarchical pooling. The datasets Market-1501, CUHK03, DukeMTMC-reID and MSMT17 were used.

Person re-identification is an active research in computer-based applications. In [9], a deep Kronecker product matching and group shuffling random techniques were used to solve the re-identification problems. Different datasets Market-1501, CUHK03 and DukeMTMC-reID were used.

Person re-identification is the problem of matching same images over different non-overlapping cameras. In [10], author proposed deep high-resolution pseudo-Siamese framework to solve the various re-identification problems. In this work, proposed network was compared with different state of art methods. Datasets used in this work are MLR-Market-1501, CAVIAR and VIPeR.

2. Deep Learning Techniques for Person Re-identification

2.1. *Multiscale Convolution Feature Fusion for Pedestrian Re-Identification Method*

The theory of multiscale convolutional feature fusion is to enhance the pedestrian re-identification algorithm. In [1], ResNet-50 network was used, and it is a backbone network. ResNet-50 network consists of various stages. The step size of 4th stage is set from 2 to 1. The sizes were extracted through this backbone network to the primary image size. Initially, if the input image is 256*128, then after next stage the feature map step size will be 8*4. After the progress from 2 to 1, the feature map will be changed to 16*8. In this operation not involves any extra training parameters. If the feature map size increases, then spatial size resolution is also increases. In this work, ResNet-50 random erasure and warm up learning techniques were used to obtain the optimisation of pedestrian re-identification. The multiscale convolutional feature fusion flow chart for Person re-identification is illustrated in figure 1 [1]

2.1.1. Random Erasure Augmentation Technique

Random erasure augmentation is technique to enhance the data operation to be performed on the different images. It is an extension technique, and it selects the blocks in the images to cover the block noise. Erasure method used to expand the data that minimise the degree model for fitting, and it is enhances the performance model. Random erasure has certain probability in the training process. Consider the image *I* in the mini batch and prospect of random erasure is P, Unchanged value is 1-P. Various images are generated for processing the information data. The random erasing diagram is illustrated in figure 2

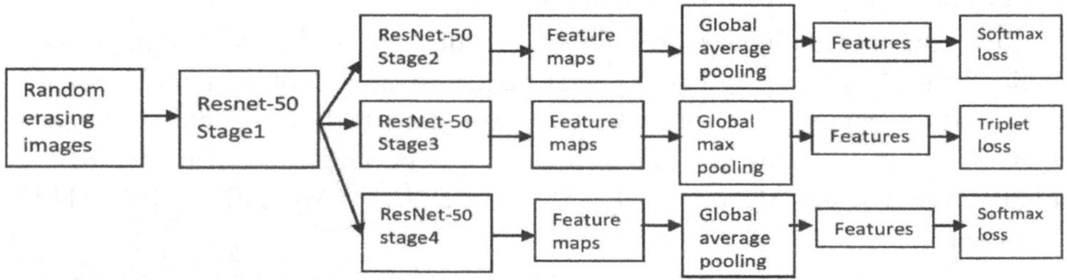

Figure 1: *Multiscale convolutional feature fusion flow chart of person re-identification [1].*

2.1.2. Conjunctional Loss Function

In this, a deep learning corresponding algorithm is used to solve the optimisation problems. Different loss functions are used. In this, combined loss functions are used, i.e. softmax loss function and triplet loss functions, which are mainly used for improving the classifier problems. For various multi-function tasks, softmax and triplet functions are used. The triplet loss function diagram is illustrated in figure 3

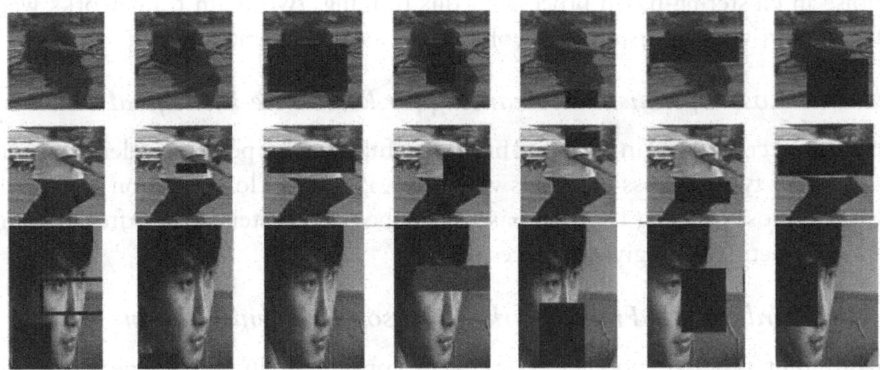

Figure 2: Random erasing diagram.

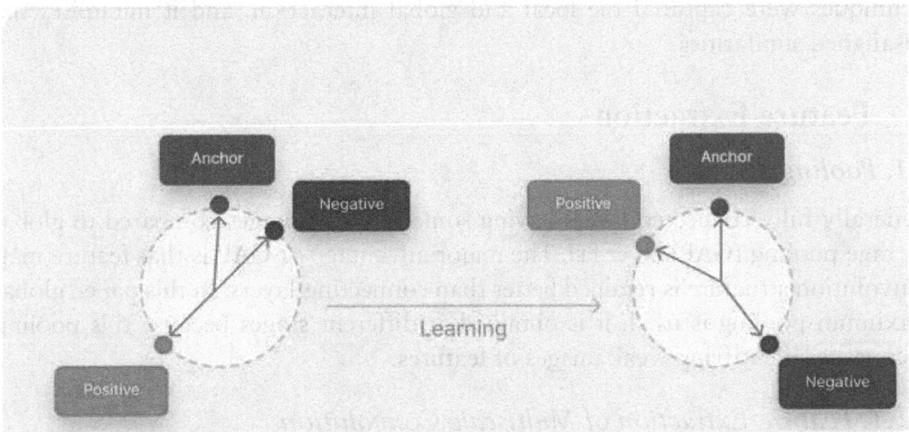

Figure 3: Triplet loss function.

2.2. Deep Batch Active Learning and Knowledge Distillation Methods for Person Re-identification

Recently, more number of complex networks collects more data to get better performance. Active learning method plays an important role in several fields, i.e. image recognition, target domain and text classification of person re-identification. In order to get better performance knowledge distillation [2] is also one of the method plays a key role in identification process. This method helps a small network works under supervision of larger network.

2.3. Multi View Evolutionary Training Method for Person Re-identification

In unsupervised domain adoption clustering-based process was used. Clustering-based process was very sensitive to noise. So to increase the performance and accuracy a multi-view evolutionary training method was used. This method effectively reduces the noise in clustering-based process. In this training, two main frameworks were used, i.e. multi-view diffusion and evolutionary local refinement [3].

2.4. Multi-Loss Optimisation Learning for Person Re-identification

Unsupervised cross domain proposed multi-loss function for person re-identification. Two different types of loss functions were used, i.e. triplet loss function in average ranking and loss learning function based neighbour consistency [6]. After merging these two functions will give better result.

2.5. High Order ReID Frame Work for Person Re-identification

Two different types of pooling layers were considered in this frame work, i.e. global hierarchical pooling and local hierarchical pooling [8]. By combining these frameworks, it learns local pose invariant representations. These tow pooling techniques were captured the local and global interaction, and it minimises the misaligned similarities.

3. Feature Extraction

3.1. Pooling Strategy

Generally fully connected layers having some less advantages compared to global average pooling (GAP) layer [1]. The major advantage of GAP is that feature map convolution structure is retained better than connecting layers. In this paper, global maximum pooling is used. It is obtained at different stages because this pooling encourages identifying weak images of features.

3.1.1. Feature Extraction of Multiscale Convolution

To obtain the multiscale feature vectors, GAP was used. GMP, i.e. global max pooling [1], is another technique to optimise the multiscale features. To calculate the triple loss function a pooled feature vector is used and to improve softmax loss function. In this gradient method is applied and features maps are obtained based on optimisation techniques. Second and third stages are global max pooling layers. After third stage ResNet-50, the step size is changed to 2 to 1. The fully connected layer and global average pooling layer are illustrated in figure 4

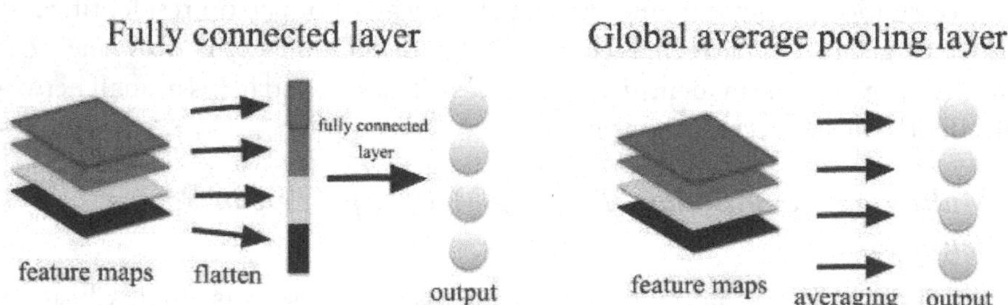

Figure 4: *Fully connected layer (FC) and global average pooling (GAP) layer.*

3.2. Global Hierarchical Pooling and Local Hierarchical Pooling

Global pooling gives you one super node that contains the aggregated features from the whole graph. Local pooling operation on the other hand creates clusters and aggregates nodes in them. In order to capture the local and global alignment, these types of pooling layers are used [8].

4. Results and Analysis

In this section, different deep learning techniques have been reviewed. Various techniques are used for person re-identification, i.e. multiscale convolution feature fusion [1], deep active learning [2], multi-loss optimisation learning [6] and high-order ReID frames [8] are used. For effectiveness different commonly used datasets were used for pedestrian re-identification. The datasets used in these work were Market1501, DukeMTMC-reID, CAVIAR, CUHK03, CUHK01 and VIPeR datasets. Generally to generate gallery data and query data, newly developed strategies were used. The extraction using these dataset was very challenging task because new partitions are further separates training images from individual images. The image sizes were 256×128, 384×128 and 384×192 [1]. The performance comparison of different datasets are mentioned in Table 1 [3, 5, 6, 8, 10]

Table 1: Performance comparison of different datasets. [3, 5, 6, 8, 10]

Method	Market-1501		DukeMTMC-reID	
	Rank-1	mAP	Rank-1	mAP
MET [3]	82.4	69.8	92.7	82.3
DDB [5]	96.1	90.8	90.4	81.7
MLOL [6]	86.6	70.9	83.1	69.8
HOReID [8]	96.79	91.4	89.83	82.16
PS-HRNet [10]	94.4	84.1	87	74.3

5. Conclusion

This paper reviewed pedestrian re-identification methods based on different convolutional neural networks techniques. These models were consisting of various features, i.e. low-level features and high-level features and different pooling techniques, i.e. global and local feature. The ResNet-50 is the backbone network, and it increases the robustness through the optimisation that is randomly erasing with dynamic learning rate mechanism. Different levels of information were learned by using multi branch network, i.e. local fusion, global fusion, multi-view diffusion and evolutionary local refinement. To collect spatial information data, low-level and high-level feature images were fully utilised. In this paper, the review is based on different datasets like Market-1501, CAVIAR, DukeMTMC-reID, CUHK03, CUHK01 and VIPeR.

References

[1] Liao, K., G. Huang, Y. Zheng, *et al.*, "Pedestrian reidentification based on multiscale convolution feature fusion," *SIViP*, vol. 16, pp. 1691–1699, 2022, doi: 10.1007/s11760-021- 02125-8.

[2] Hu Z., W. Hou, and X. Liu, "Deep Batch Active Learning and Knowledge Distillation for Person Re-Identification," *IEEE Sens. J.*, vol. 22, no. 14, pp. 14347–14355, Jul. 15, 2022, doi: 10.1109/JSEN.2022.3181238.

[3] Gu, J. *et al.*, "Multi-view evolutionary training for unsupervised domain adaptive person re-identification," *IEEE Trans. Inf. Forensics Secur.*, vol. 17, pp. 344–356, 2022, doi: 10.1109/TIFS.2022.3140696.

[4] Li, K., Z. Ding, K. Li, Y. Zhang, and Y. Fu, "Vehicle and person re-identification with support neighbor loss," *IEEE Trans. Neural Networks Learn. Syst.*, vol. 33, no. 2, pp. 826–838, Feb. 2022, doi: 10.1109/TNNLS.2020.3029299.

[5] Wu, X., B. Xie, Y. Zhang, S. Zhao, and S. Zhang, "Construction of diverse DropBlock branches for person reidentification," *IEEE Trans. Cognit. Dev. Syst.*, vol. 14, no. 3, pp. 1296–1300, Sept. 2022, doi: 10.1109/TCDS.2021.3096546.

[6] Sun, J., Y. Li, H. Chen, Y. Peng, and J. Zhu, "Unsupervised cross domain person re-identification by multi-loss optimization learning," *IEEE Trans. Image Process.*, vol. 30, pp. 2935–2946, 2021, doi: 10.1109/TIP.2021.3056889.

[7] Wu, D., C. Wang, Y. Wu, Q. -C. Wang, and D. -S. Huang, "Attention deep model with multi-scale deep supervision for person re-identification," *IEEE Trans. Emerging Top. Comput. Intell.*, vol. 5, no. 1, pp. 70–78, Feb. 2021, doi: 10.1109/TETCI.2020.3034606.

[8] Wang, P., Z. Zhao, F. Su, X. Zu, and N. V. Boulgouris, "HOReID: Deep High-Order Mapping Enhances Pose Alignment for Person Re-Identification," *IEEE Trans. Image Process.*, vol. 30, pp. 2908–2922, 2021, doi: 10.1109/TIP.2021.3055952.

[9] Shen, Y., T. Xiao, S. Yi, D. Chen, X. Wang, and H. Li, "Person re-identification with deep Kronecker-product matching and group-shuffling random walk," *IEEE Trans. Pattern Anal. Mach. Intell.*, vol. 43, no. 5, pp. 1649–1665, May 1, 2021, doi: 10.1109/TPAMI.2019.2954313.

[10] Zhang, G., Y. Ge, Z. Dong, H. Wang, Y. Zheng, and S. Chen, "Deep high-resolution representation learning for cross-resolution person re-identification," *IEEE Trans. Image Process.*, vol. 30, pp. 8913–8925, 2021, doi: 10.1109/TIP.2021.3120054.

22. An Innovative Approach to Select Features for Identifying Attacks in Cloud Computing Environments by a New Algorithm that Integrates the Principles of the Firefly Algorithm and K-Nearest Neighbour

Pooja Rana, Dr. Isha Batra, and Dr.Arun Malik

Computer Science & Engineering, Lovely Professional University, Phagwara, India

Abstract: There is a brisk growth in Cloud computing with time that permits the users to avail numerous services through internet. The services are available to the users as pay-per-use and makes expedient for evolving, installing and retrieving variety of diverse applications. These alluring features make it vulnerable to different attackers. We have proposed a novel feature selection algorithm which is the hybridisation of firefly optimisation algorithm with KNN classifier. The proposed feature selection algorithm gives an optimal set of features and then different classifiers are applied for the classification of the dataset. The algorithm we have developed surpasses the performance of the current technique.

Keywords: Cloud computing, IDS, CSE CIC IDS 2018 dataset, NN, SVM, KNN, DT.

1. Introduction

Cloud computing (CC) is providing high-quality services with the reduced cost, so it becomes a popular computing paradigm. But the widespread usage of cloud computing is diminished because of the security issues. CC is offering three types of services as discussed above- IaaS, PaaS and SaaS. When users are using the IaaS services, then they have access to the servers and virtual machines. The hypervisors are executed on the servers so the virtualisation of the physical resources is achieved. When users are using the PaaS services, then cloud provides the support of operating systems, databases or web servers to the users. When users are using the SaaS services then software are provided to them for usage. Thus, the diversity of providing services to the users makes cloud computing more vulnerable to different attacks. Virtualisation is the primary essential of the cloud computing [1]. Attackers are getting attracted towards the cloud because of to its alluring nature which is open and distributed. Attackers can intrude the users' services and also misuse the delicate data and also will use the resources and services of the cloud. An intrusion is well defined as any attack that can misuse the delicate data of the users, or it can munch the vital resources. The old and outdated techniques are not sufficient for providing complete security to the clouds. Therefore, an intrusion detection system (IDS) operates by scrutinising network data to detect potential attacks. IDS systems typically fall into two deployment categories: Host-based IDS and network-based IDS [2–3]. Former analyses the attacks by monitoring the host system only and latter analyses the whole network. Another type of IDS based on the detection mechanism are signature-based IDS and anomaly-based IDS. Former analyses the attacks in the network by compilation of the signatures of the attacks deposited in the database, whereas latter can perceive attacks in the network by investigating the active network activities. For developing an efficient intrusion detection system, abundant investigators have used machine learning and data mining methods [4]. Another arising technique for this field is the mining rule association [5]. Most commonly used classifiers are the artificial neural networks because of their skill for working on any dataset which is incomplete [6]. Few investigators have found good reputation of the machine learning algorithms because of its scalability with elasticity nature [7–10].

2. Literature Review

In [11], Particle swarm optimisation grounded on the Bayesian quantum theorem is performing anomaly detection. In [12], a classifier grounded on the fuzzy logic for sensing the DDoS attacks is put forward. Authors have used a private dataset. But false alarm rate of this classifier is higher. In [13], a classifier is developed which is based on the fuzzy pattern recognition is shown for finding the bots. Authors have taken their own dataset for the performance assessment of their work. Main weakness of this classifier is that it can only sense bots. Authors have used obsolete dataset DARPA KDDCup 99. Another innovative combination of support vector machine with the NN is given in [14]. It is a hybridisation which is two-staze. Authors have used NSL-KDD dataset for sensing numerous attacks.

3. Proposed Methodology

The modules are: Preprocessing, Feature Selection and Classification. The modules are discussed in the following section of this paper. Figure 1 shows the flowchart of proposed methodology and proposed firefly algorithm.

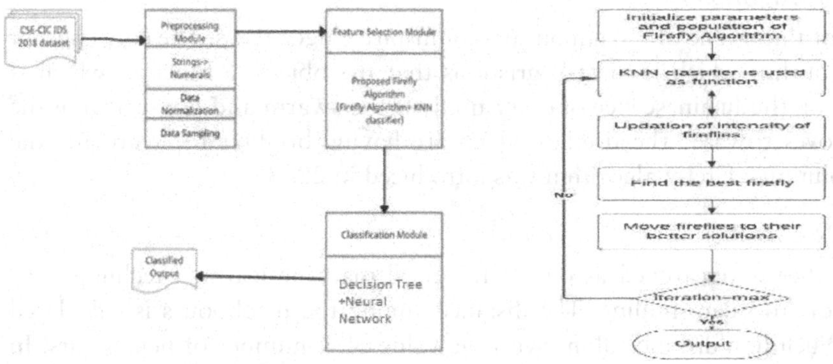

Figure 1: Flowchart of proposed methodology and proposed firefly algorithm.

3.1. Dataset

We have taken the recent dataset CSE CIC IDS 2018 dataset. These represent the most recent instances of attacks. The attacker architecture has 50 computers and the victim architecture has 5 different departments which has 420 computers with 30 servers. The dataset has total number of 80 features, and the attributes are recorded by using the CICFlowMeter-V3.

3.2. Preprocessing of the Dataset

This component handles the raw dataset, transforming it into a format that the classifier can comprehend and analyse. We have sampled the dataset as the CSE CIC IDS 2018 dataset is unbalanced. We have removed some unwanted attributes from the dataset, which are not useful for the detection of the attacks. We have also normalised the dataset and converted the strings into number form.

3.3. Feature Selection

Feature selection helps in selecting optimal features from a dataset which is having a large number of features. It reduces the number of features of a dataset.

We have chosen firefly algorithm for the feature selection as it is proved to be a proficient algorithm for searching the global optimal solution as compared to particle swarm optimisation (PSO) and genetic algorithm (GA) [15–19]. Firefly algorithm is having one shortcoming that it stuck in local optimal solutions [20]. KNN classifier plays an important role in the feature selection module of the intrusion detection system, and it overcomes the problem of local optimal solutions [21]. We have also observed from literature review that little work is done using firefly algorithm for detection of attacks. The KNN classifier is a simple classifier, and it can be used to solve multi-class problems. The classifier is used for solving the multi-class problem.

3.3.1. Firefly Algorithm

Firefly algorithm is one of the famous nature-inspired algorithms. The core concept of this algorithm which is meta-heuristic is that the objective function which is dependent on the luminescence of every firefly is the swarm and the swarm of the fireflies moves towards the fireflies which are having brighter for searching the optimal solutions. Firefly algorithm was introduced in 2008.

3.3.2. KNN Classifier

KNN classifier is researched as one of the good machine learning technique for classification and data mining. The distance among the neighbours is calculated using the Euclidian distance along with the value of K number of neighbours. In a given training dataset, it predicts the value for any unfamiliar record, denoted as x, by identifying the k nearest neighbours related to x'. Then, x is assigned the predominant class among its k nearest neighbours.

3.3.3. Classification

The classification module is used for identification of various attacks. We have used numerous classifiers for detection of attacks. The feature selection module helps to create an optimal feature subset. We have used a classifier which is the hybridisation of the decision tree with the neural network.

4. Results and Discussions

This part of the paper presents the experimental part. The results are shown in the tabular form, and analysis is made for numerous attacks of the dataset. We have used MATLAB 2021a software, Windows 10 operating system and 8 GB RAM. The dataset used is CSE CIC IDS 2018 dataset. Figure 2 shows the graphical illustration of Comparison for different attacks.

Table 1: Comparison of precision of different attacks.

Attack Classifier	Bot	Bruteforce- Web	Bruteforce- XSS	DDOS- HOIC	DDOS- LOIC	DOS
NN	98.0	99.5	99.5	99.5	99.5	97.0
KNN	40.3	42.1	48.9	47.49	38.7	29.2
SVM	39	41	29.9	30.6	37	29
DT	59.69	58.7	62.7	63.9	78.9	64.8
Proposed Classifier	99.0	99.7	99.8	99.9	99.6	97.0

Table 2: Comparison of detection rate of different attacks.

Attack Classifier	Bot	Bruteforce- Web	Bruteforce- XSS	DDOS- HOIC	DDOS- LOIC	DOS
NN	15.3	49.63	49.59	49.28	30.86	28
KNN	43.8	15.2	43.0	42.1	89.3	15.0

SV	38	14	26.3	43.8	87	14
DT	64.0	25.7	68.3	67.1	26.7	30.0
Proposed Classifier	68.96	50.41	50.41	59.72	40.74	30

Table 3: Comparison of F-score of different attacks.

Attack / Classifier	Bot	Bruteforce-Web	Bruteforce-XSS	DDOS-HOIC	DDOS-LOIC	DOS
NN	30	66.3	66.3	66.0	47.1	45
KNN	42.0	22.3	45.6	44.6	14.4	19.8
SVM	41	22	27.9	36.2	12	18
DT	61.8	35.7	65.0	65.4	40.0	41.1
Proposed Classifier	81.63	66.67	67.03	67.31	57.89	46.15

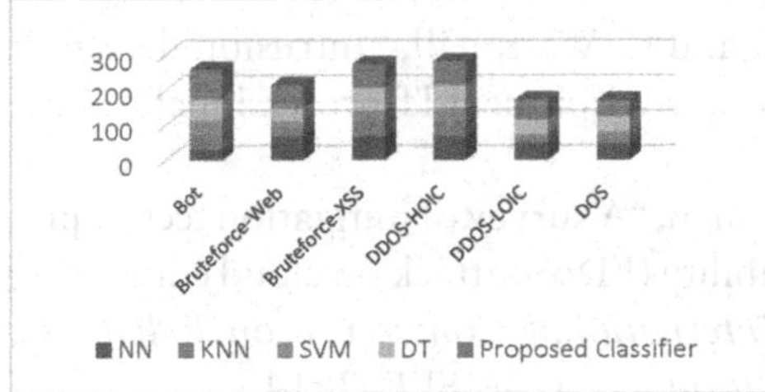

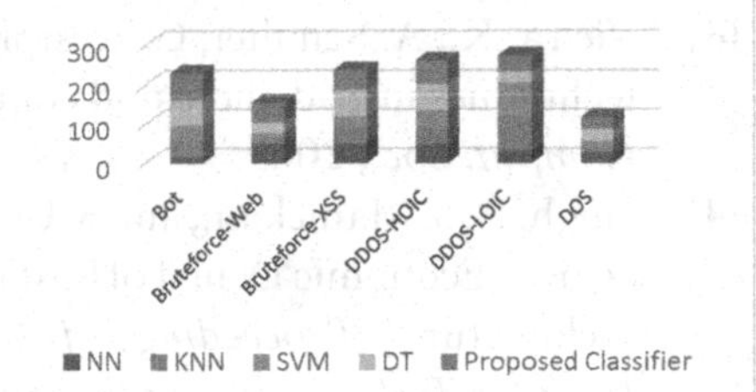

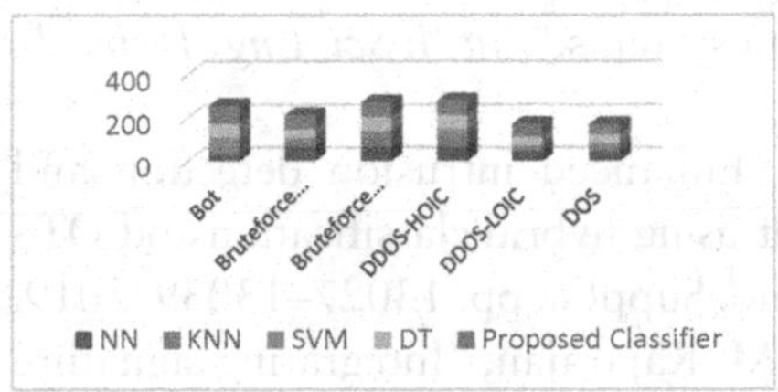

Figure 2: Comparison of different attacks.

The results presented above indicate that our suggested intrusion detection system outperforms various state-of-the-art techniques in identifying different types of attacks. The outcomes undergo comparison using various performance metrics, demonstrating superior results in precision, recall and F-score. Table 1, 2 and 3 show the comparison of different attacks, detection rate and F-score respectively.

5. Conclusion

The concluding section of the paper says that the IDS plays a crucial role for CC. We have compared good techniques for sensing numerous attacks in the cloud. We have chosen good and familiar classifiers for the detection of the attacks like NN, KNN, SVM and DT. We have considered recent attacks like Bot, Bruteforce,

DDOS, and these attacks are not included in DARPA KDDCup 1999 dataset and NSL-KDD dataset. The performance assessment of numerous attacks is done in our paper, and we have analysed that our proposed intrusion detection system is finding most of the attacks with high precision, recall and F-score.

Data Availability Statement: CSE-CIC-IDS 2018 dataset is available publicly and referred in [22].

References

[1] Geeta and S. Prakash, "Role of virtualization techniques in cloud computing environment," *Advances in Computer Communication and Computational Sciences: Proc. of IC4S 2017*, vol. 2, pp. 439–450, Springer Singapore, 2019.

[2] Geeta and S. Prakash, "Role of virtualization techniques in cloud computing environment," *Advances in Computer Communication and Computational Sciences: Proceedings of IC4S 2017,* vol. 2, pp. 439–450, Springer Singapore, 2019.

[3] Vieira, K., A. Schulter, C. Westphall, and C. Westphall, "Intrusion detection techniques in grid and cloud computing environment IT professional," *IEEE Comput. Soc.*, 2009.

[4] Singh, P., S. Manickam, and S. Ul Rehman, "A survey of mitigation techniques against Economic Denial of Sustainability (EDoS) attack on cloud computing architecture," *Proceedings of 3rd International Conference on Reliability, Infocom Technologies and Optimization*, pp. 1–4, IEEE, 2014.

[5] Nkikabahizi, C., W. Cheruiyot, and A. Kibe, "Classification and analysis of techniques applied in intrusion detection systems," *Int. J. Sci. Eng. Technol.*, vol. 6, no. 7, pp. 216–219, 2017.

[6] Balamurugan, V., and R. Saravanan, "Enhanced intrusion detection and prevention system on cloud environment using hybrid classification and OTS generation," *Cluster Comput.*, vol. 22, no. Suppl 6, pp. 13027–13039, 2019.

[7] Modi, C. N., D. R. Patel, A. Patel, and M. Rajarajan, "Integrating signature apriori based network intrusion detection system (NIDS) in cloud computing," *Proc. Technol.*, vol. 6, pp. 905–912, 2012.

[8] Gupta, S., P. Kumar, and A. Abraham, "A profile based network intrusion detection and prevention system for securing cloud environment," *Int. J. Distrib. Sens. Networks*, vol. 9, no. 3, p. 364575, 2013.

[9] Hajimirzaei, B., and N. J. Navimipour, "Intrusion detection for cloud computing using neural networks and artificial bee colony optimization algorithm," *ICT Express*, vol. 5, no. 1, pp. 56–59, 2019.

[10] Hatef, M. A., V. Shaker, M. R. Jabbarpour, J. Jung, and H. Zarrabi, "HIDCC: A hybrid intrusion detection approach in cloud computing," *Concurrency Comput. Pract. Exper.*, vol. 30, no. 3, p. e4171, 2018.

[11] Khorshed, M. T., A. B. M. Shawkat Ali, and S. A. Wasimi, "A survey on gaps, threat remediation challenges and some thoughts for proactive attack

detection in cloud computing," *Future Gener. Comput. Syst.*, vol. 28, no. 6, pp. 833–851, 2012.

[12] Liu, Y. and R. Ma, "Network anomaly detection based on BQPSO-BN algorithm," *IETE J. Res.* vol. 59, no. 4, pp. 334–342, 2013.

[13] Pitropakis, N., D. Anastasopoulou, A. Pikrakis, and C. Lambrinoudakis, "If you want to know about a hunter, study his prey: detection of network based attacks on KVM based cloud environments," *J. Cloud Comput.*, vol. 3, pp. 1–10, 2014.

[14] Pandeeswari, N. and G. Kumar, "Anomaly detection system in cloud environment using fuzzy clustering based ANN," *Mobile Networks Appl.*, vol. 21, pp. 494–05, 2016.

[15] Kaur, A., S. K. Pal, and A. Pal Singh, "Hybridization of K-means and firefly algorithm for intrusion detection system," *Int. J. Syst. Assur. Eng. Manage.*, vol. 9, pp. 901–910, 2018.

[16] Lukasik, S. and S. Zak, "Firefly algorithm for continuous constrained optimization tasks," *International Conference on Computational Collective Intelligence*, Berlin: Springer, pp. 97–106, 2009.

[17] Fister, I., X.-S. Yang, J. Brest, "A comprehensive review of firefly algorithms," *Swarm Evol. Comput.*, vol. 13, pp. 34–46, 2013.

[18] Hönig U., "A firefly algorithm-based approach for scheduling task graphs in homogeneous systems," *Proc. Inform.*, p. 724, 2010.

[19] Deshmukh, A. H., *et al.*, "Comparative analysis of nature-inspired MetaHeuristic optimization algorithms," *SSGM J. Sci. Eng.*, vol. 1.1, pp. 174–178, 2023.

[20] Shandilya, S., S. Kumar, B. J. Choi, A. Kumar, and S. Upadhyay, "Modified firefly optimization algorithm-based IDS for nature-inspired cybersecurity," *Processes*, vol. 11, no. 3, pp. 715, 2023.

[21] Vommi, A. M., and T. K. Battula, "A hybrid filter-wrapper feature selection using Fuzzy KNN based on Bonferroni mean for medical datasets classification: A COVID-19 case study," *Expert Syst. Appl.*, vol. 218, pp. 119612, 2023.

[22] https://www:unb:ca/cic/datasets/ids-2018:html.

23. Nanometrology: A Subfield of Nanoscience

Yogesh Singh[1], Sunny Kumar Sharma[2], Jhulan Kumar[1], Purnima Hazra[3], Parvinder Singh[1], and Rekha Goyat[1]

[1]*School of Electronics and Electrical Engineering, Lovely Professional University, Jalandhar, Punjab, India*

[2]*Department of Mathematics, Manipal Institute of Technology Bengaluru, Manipal Academy of Higher Education, Manipal, Karnataka, India*

[3]*School of Electronics and Communication, Shri Mata Vaishno Devi University, Katra, Jammu, India*

Abstract: The term 'Nanometrology' is a sub-field of nanotechnology and nanoscience, which deals with the characterisation of materials at atomic and molecular scale, i.e. at nanometric scale. The material characterisation plays an important role as it determines the overall physical, optical, structural and surface morphology of nanoparticles (NPs). The order of atoms or quantum configurations are common topics of fascination within the realm of nanotechnology. With nanometrology tools such as X-ray diffraction (XRD), scanning electron microscopy (SEM), transmission electron microscopy (TEM), energy-dispersive spectroscopy (EDX), photoluminescence spectroscopy (PL) Uv-Vis's spectroscopy, Raman spectroscopy and Fourier transform infrared spectroscopy (FTIR), the material characterisation smoothened, and nanotechnology has attained fascinating applications in various domains. We can increasingly now understand how important these trends are, and hence the measuring equipment's resolution has now increased to an atomic level. In this article, we strive to discuss the theoretical underpinnings and in-depth operational principles of several metrology techniques utilised for characterisation.

Keywords: Nanotechnology, nanometrology, characterising tools, and measurement techniques.

1. Introduction

The need for equipment to perform measurements at the nanoscale is quite strong since advancements in nanotechnology and nanoscience depend on dimensional information at the nanoscale [1][2]. The size of the particles is the only distinction between many other scientific and engineering disciplines and nanotechnology [3][4]. Accurate and traceable measurements are still needed for control in nanoscale production. Numerous tools that meet the measuring needs of the nanotechnology community and offer traceability to the definition of the nanometric scale have been created [2]. These techniques enable the exploration of atomic structures for the highest demands, as well as the production of extremely precise, tiny industrial parts and structures [5]. The rapid advancement of nanotechnology has necessitated the knowledge of the measurements essential to define its nanostructure nature. As a result, a new scientific subject known as 'Nanometrology' was born. G K. Binnig and H Rohrer discovered the scanning tunnelling microscope (STM) in 1985, which gave nanotechnology its biggest boost in the domain of 'Nanometrology' [6]. The term 'nanometrology,' which refers to metrology, the study of measurement, at the nanoscale, originally featured in a peer-reviewed paper in 1992 [7]. The novel performance indicators that need to be created to assist nanotechnology are based on nanometrology [8][9]. Nanometrology is a field which utilises different tools for the study of Nanoparticles, and the modern scientific problems can be solved in novel ways, thanks to the nanometrology for manipulation of materials at the nanoscale [10][11]. Review by Ukraintsev and Bankee [12] focused on reference metrology (RM) with significance, challenges and solutions. The major findings highlight RM as being solid and effective, and it is also shown that CDAFM has an edge over other measurement systems when taking a few crucial metrics all at once. The work by Whitehouse [13] studied the interaction of sample and the probe in AFM and scanning probe microscopy with components calibrations, general operations, principle design and problems. Schattenburg and Smith [14] studied the contribution of nanometrology in nanotechnology and further explored the importance of metrology measurements. Srivastava [15] main goal was to briefly explain some of the key laboratory operations that were being persuaded in order to build nanotechnology and nanometrology programmes and objectives in collaboration with various regulatory organisations. Report by R Turan [16] further identified and coordinated the top nanometrology activities across Europe, and the author further focused on the European strategy in the field of nanometrology.

It is extremely important to observe every atom in a nanomaterial, even just the light ones, in order to correctly define them. The benefit of increased resolution is the ability to see lighter atom peaks by narrowing the peaks associated with heavy atoms. The article focuses on theoretical explanation and working mechanism of various metrological tools used to study the material characterisation at atomic scale. The characterisation is crucial for understanding the material's structural, optical, morphological and electrical properties, among others. To the best of the authors' knowledge, there is no recognised literature that describes the specifics and comprehensive insights of different tools utilised for characterisation. The functioning mechanics of several nanometrology equipment are explored in detail in this article. The below sections 2 cover various tools used for the study of various properties associated with materials at atomic scale.

2. Characterisation and Tools

To satisfy the demands of contemporary technology, precise dimensional measurements and high-quality manufactured surfaces are now essential requirements. Therefore, sophisticated accurate and exact measuring procedures are crucial for enhancing the performance and quality of engineered products. To thoroughly characterise nanoparticles, perform accurate toxicological testing and fully characterise nanoparticles, metrology approach is required. It has become widely recognised that developing new materials with improved characteristics and properties through the use of nanotechnology has considerable promise. The basic operating principles of some of the characteriaation approaches are introduced in this section, and the working mechanism of different tools used, namely XRD, SEM, & EDX, TEM, UV-VIS-NIR spectroscopy, FTIR spectroscopy and PL spectroscopy. The brief details of each instrument are given below for better understanding.

2.1. X-Ray Diffraction (XRD)

XRD is a non-contact and non-destructive technique for studying materials structure, composition and physical properties. The technique of XRD is highly useful technique for evaluating the composition and structure of materials [17]. The working mechanism behind XRD is understood by considering Bragg's equation, where the angle of incidence is calculated by considering the path difference of reflection between different planes. The Bragg's law is the fundamental law governing the diffraction method of structural investigation of thin film surfaces. The general equation of Bragg's law is given as (eq. 1).

$$n\lambda = 2dsin\theta \tag{1}$$

where is the glancing angle, is the wavelength of incidence ray, d is distance between two planes and n is the order of reflection. The atomic structure of a crystal can be determined using XRD spectra, in order to calculate the crystallite sizes by evaluating the strain. The size and form of the unit cell dictate the peak positions [18]. In the XRD analysis of a crystalline solid, just one group of peaks matching to the crystal's orientation is visible, such as the detecting of peak intensity matching to certain planes (111), (200), (220), (311) and (222) corresponds to PbS. In the XRD spectrum, diffraction peaks from various families of crystalline plains can be seen. Amorphous materials, on the other hand, have no long-range order and no diffraction peak. XRD spectrum is used to identify overall arrangement of atoms of a crystalline solid, as well as to analyse strain and quantify crystallite sizes. The size and form of the unit cell dictate the peak positions. The characteristic peaks will indeed be altered by the strain. Because the intensity of waves with scattering is equivalent to the number of outer electrons as well as the atomic number. Light materials like carbon or oxygen scatter poorly for X-rays, while heavy ones like Pb scatter well. A thin film's crystallite size is a critical structural property. It is also utilised for phase identification, grain size determination, composition, lattice parameter and the degree of crystallinity in a mixture of amorphous and crystalline substances. The Scherrer Equation was used to determine crystallite diameter of a sample (eq. 2).

$$D = \frac{k\lambda}{\beta cos\theta} \quad (2)$$

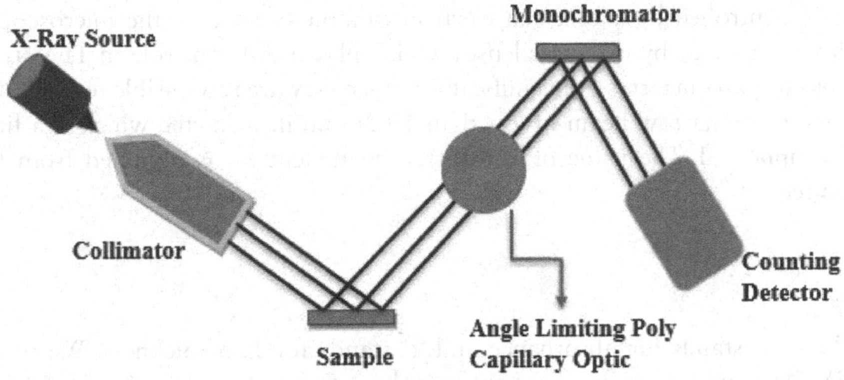

Figure 1: The schematic sketch of an XRD instrument.

where k is Scherrer constant (0.9), is the width of diffraction line at half of the maximum peak intensity (FWHM), λ is the wavelength (0.154 nm), θ is the Bragg's angle or angle of interest and D is the average crystallite size in nm. The measured diffraction profiles expand out as the diameter of the crystallite decreases. The structural characterisation of the thin films obtained was done in this study by evaluating the XRD patterns generated with CuKα radiation in the 2θ range of angles. The schematic sketch and the essential features of an XRD are shown in Figure 1.

2.2. SEM (Scanning Electron Microscopy) and EDX (Energy Dispersive Spectroscopy)

Max Knoll began developing the SEM in 1935 at the Technical University of Berlin. The first prototype SEM was built in 1942, and the first commercial device was used in 1965. Because it can produce both 2-D and 3-D pictures with great quality and requires less sample preparation and is a common surface morphology characterisation equipment for nanomaterials research. SEM is a very significant characterisation technique, because it is used to explore the length, diameter, thickness, shape, density and orientation of thin films. SEM gives information on topography, geometry and architectural aspects at different resolutions. However, it is to note that, the sample must be conducting and semiconducting in nature. SEM is a nano-metrological tool that scans a material with a beam of extreme finely confined and highly focussed electrons onto the sample. EDX, which studies the chemical composition of the element in thin films, is also included in the SEM.

EDX is a quantitative technique for determining a sample's elemental composition or chemical description. It deduces a sample's elemental makeup by looking at the X-ray signal it produces when blasted with electrons. The surface morphology and chemistry of the films were studied using a SEM linked to EDX running at different KV in this study. It is feasible to create a metallographic composition using the SEM's scanning capability by means of EDX. The graph in EDX can be used to identify elements by their small peaks at different energies. The electron beam output is controlled by a tungsten electron cannon situated at the microscope's tip. This is followed by magnetic lenses, which play a different role in TEM than their counterparts in terms of magnification, since they are responsible for focusing electrons into a narrow beam of less than 10-20 nm in diameter, which is a little more complicated. The value of absorption coefficient (α) is obtained from the relation (eq. 3).

$$\acute{a} = 2.303\frac{A}{t} \tag{3}$$

where 'A' stands for absorbance and 't' stands for film thickness. We prefer the SEM if we wish to learn about the sample's surface characteristics, such as its ruggedness or any impurities. It gives the 3D images of the sample and requires less or no effort for sample preparation and can be directly imagined by mounting them on aluminium stub. Figure 2 depicts a schematic representation of a SEM key characteristics.

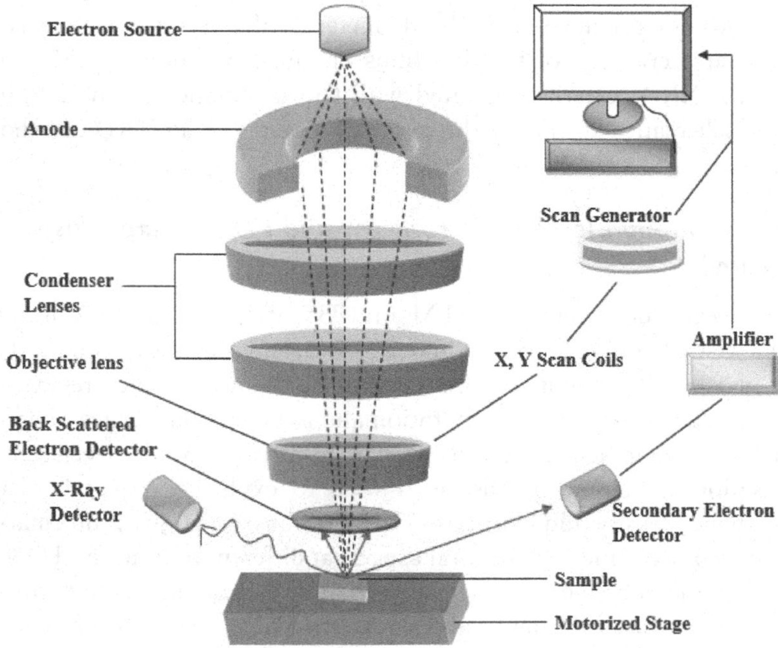

Figure 2: The essential components of the SEM instrument.

2.3. TEM (Transmission Electron Microscopy)

TEM is an imaging technology that allows researchers to analyse microscopic details in cells or materials at near-atomic levels or at nanometric scale [19]. On an atomic scale, it may examine the size, shape and organisation of elements that make up the material, as well as their interaction to one another. Furthermore, high magnification TEM imaging enables for the analysis of individual crystallite shape. The TEM is used to retrieve structural information from specimens that are thin enough to allow electrons to pass through them. In TEM, an electron source generates a beam of electrons, which is subsequently focused and manipulated by magnetic fields to image materials and form electron diffraction patterns. The electrons are generated by thermionic emission (Edison effect) from either a tungsten filament or a platinum filament. The electrons are subsequently driven along the optical axis by high voltage, allowing wavelengths far shorter than the inter-atomic distances in crystal lattices.

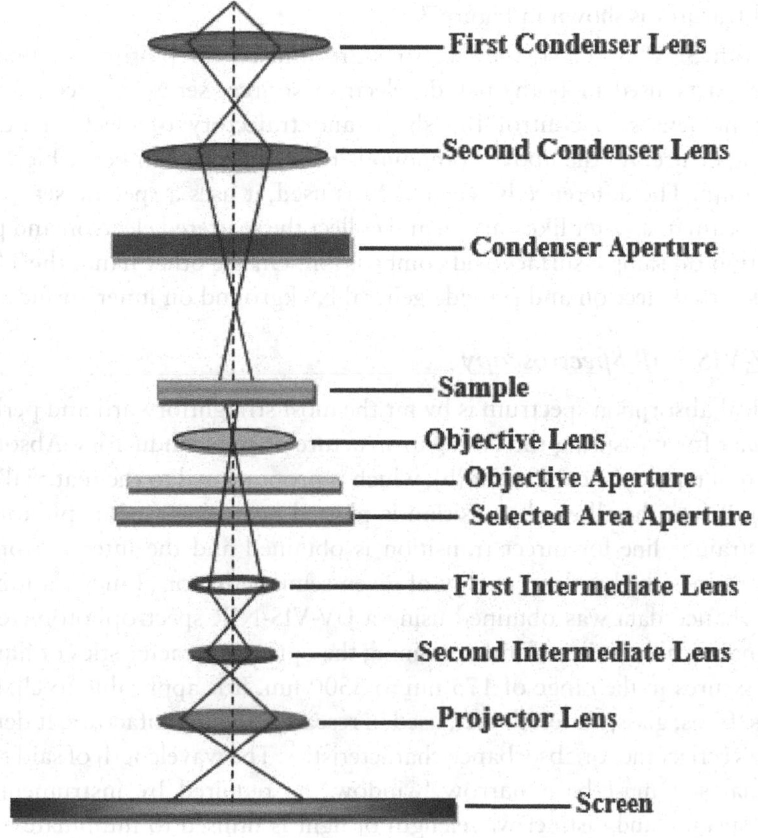

Figure 3: The schematic illustration of the TEM essentials.

Electrons pass through a thinly cut material, forming an image on a fluorescent screen or photographic plate. Denser parts of the sample will transfer fewer electrons and hence appear darker in the picture [20]. Because it is not restricted by the wavelength of visible light or the numerical aperture of the lens, the resolution is significantly higher than that of any powerful optical microscope. The electron beam is generated by an electron cannon at the microscope's apex. The resulting image is enhanced three to four times after the beam is focused on the object. The picture is amplified by an objective lens. Before being projected on a fluorescent screen, the picture is magnified further by the diffraction lens and then by the projector lens. To boost the contrast of the final image, an objective or diffraction aperture can be utilised at the back focal plane or before the diffraction lens. The low and high magnifications were used to create the images. TEM is recommended if you want to get a sense about material's structure and any potential structural flaws. It gives 2D image of the sample with thickness below 150 nm in case high resolution of image is needed. Only personnel with expertise can follow the lengthy, sophisticated specimen preparation process. A schematic illustration of a TEM essential features is shown in Figure 3.

In both SEM & TEM, the electrons are utilised for plotting of image. The common parts used in both include electron source, series of electromagnetic, electrostatic lenses to control the shape and trajectory of electron beam and electron aperture. All the above compounds reside inside chamber, which is under high vacuum. The difference is when SEM is used, it uses a specific set of coils to scan the beam in a raster like pattern and collect the scattered electron and provides information on sample surface and composition. On the other hand, the TEM uses the transmitted electron and provide general background on inner surface.

2.4. UV-VIS-NIR Spectroscopy

The optical absorption spectrum is by far the most straightforward and perhaps the easiest way for measuring the bandgap structure of semiconductors. Absorption is measured in terms of a coefficient (h), which is proportional to the material's energy gap (Eg). When the allowed transition is plotted i.e., $(\alpha h\nu)^n$ versus photon energy (eV), a straight line for direct transition is obtained and the intercept on energy axis determines the bandgap energy of given semiconductor (Tauc relation). Then, the absorbance data was obtained using a UV-VIS-NIR spectrophotometer. It is a strong analytical technique for determining the optical characteristics of liquids and solids mixtures in the range of 175 nm to 3300 nm. It is applicable to characterise elements, films, glass, materials etc., used in research and manufacture. It determines a sample's reflectance or absorbance characteristics. The wavelength of said radiation to be analysed must be a narrow 'window,' as required by instrument design. When a specific and distinct wavelength of light is utilised to illuminate a sample, that radiation may be absorbed. This absorbance would not exist at some other wavelengths. The absorption phenomena are what is utilised to classify materials. The radiation absorption can take place in either a transmission or a reflection mode. A spectrum is a graph showing absorption versus wavelength. These are the most regularly encountered and discussed spectra. The spectra can be used to assess the sample's colour (i.e., the visible spectral response), as well as its ultra-violet

and near-infrared filtering capabilities (needed for evaluating the performance of solar radiation). The schematic sketch of the essential features of a UV-VIS spectroscopy is shown in Figure 4.

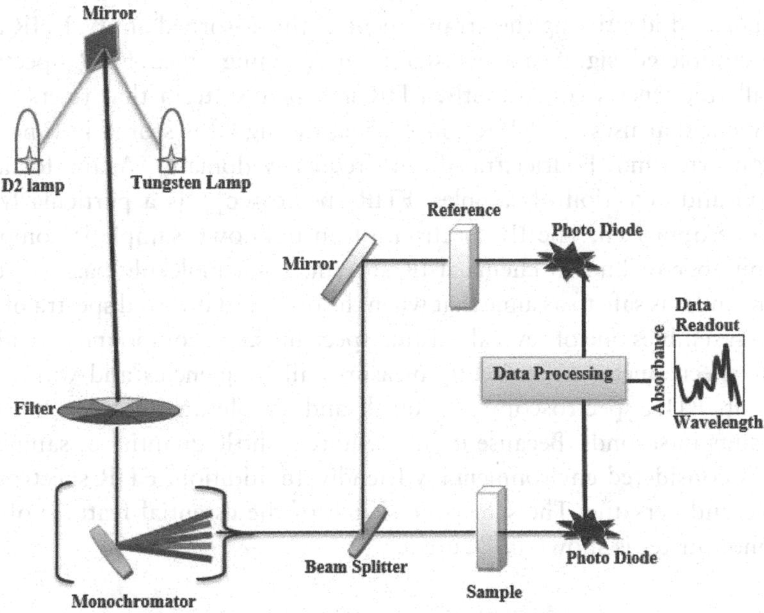

Figure 4: The schematic sketch of the UV-VIS spectrophotoeter.

The difference between incident and transmitted radiation is the amount of light absorbed when light passes through or is reflected from a sample. Absorbance is a measurement of how much light is absorbed. A fraction or % is a typical way to express transmittance, or the quantity of light that passes through a sample. Generally, the absorbance spectra of sample are calculated instead of transmittance. At each wavelength, the equipment assesses how much light is absorbed, transmitted, or reflected by the sample. Some spectrophotometers have a wavelength range that extends well into the NIR. The spectra are plotted in regard to wavelength, however some report in terms of wavenumber (cm^{-1}). Above mentioned optical parameters are processes that exists when a particle is bombarded with an electromagnetic wave. When the energy of incoming light equals the energy difference (E) between a molecule's ground and excited states, absorption happens. The following equation describes the relationship between transmittance and absorbance (eq. 4)

$$Abs = 2 - log\frac{i}{i_o}*100 = 2 - \log(\%\mathrm{T}) \tag{4}$$

2.5. FTIR Spectroscopy

FTIR spectroscopy is a type of IR spectroscopy. FTIR spectroscopy is a useful instrument for detecting different types of chemical function groups in a molecule by generating an infrared absorption spectrum that acts as a molecular 'fingerprint.' The energy required to generate molecular vibrations in a sample is measured using FTIR Spectroscopy. FTIR spectroscopy is a useful tool for investigating organic compounds on interfaces, establishing the chemical composition of surface compounds and identifying the arrangement of the adsorbed entity. FTIR analysis may be completed significantly faster than scanning since FTIR spectroscopy detects all frequencies concurrently. FTIR is a precise term that refers to an IR measurement that uses the FTIR concept i.e., the signal is stored in time domain and is converted into Fourier transform (frequency domain). Again, for accurate separation and detection of samples, FTIR spectroscopy is a particularly robust and reliable approach. The IR spectrum of an unknown sample is compared to a large number of known chemical IR spectra. Each molecule has a distinct IR spectrum, and it is safe to assume that when the observed Infrared spectra of either a specimen resembles one of several existing spectrums, the compounds are identical. An FTIR spectrometer concurrently measures all frequencies and wavenumbers. As a result, FTIR spectroscopy is a quick and simple analytical technique that yields results in seconds. Because it only requires a little quantity of sample, FTIR analysis is considered environmentally friendly. In addition, FTIR spectroscopy is adaptable and versatile. The schematic sketch of the essential features of a FTIR spectrophotometer is shown in Figure 5.

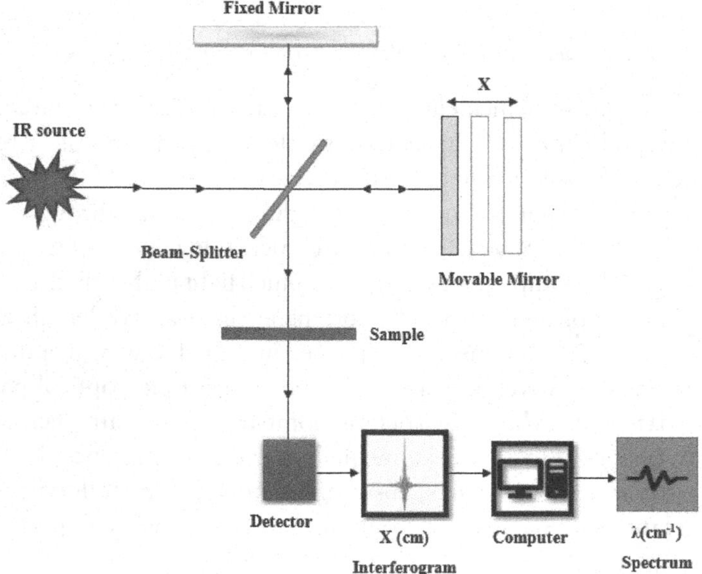

Figure 5: The schematic configuration of the FTIR spectrophotometer.

2.6. Photoluminescence Spectroscopy

Photoluminescence is the light emission from any form of matter after the absorption of photon. The molecules absorb photon in the visible region and excites one of its electrons to higher states and re-emit photon as it returns to lower state. Excitation happens at a higher energy level at first, and subsequently the electron returns to a lower energy level as a result of photon emission. The contribution of radiative recombination in a semiconductor to light emission is well understood. Simply, PL spectroscopy can be used to determine the electrical structure and properties of materials by calculating the peak light intensity that materials are able to emit at a specific wavelength. PL spectroscopy is a non-destructive, contactless technique for examining a sample electrical structure. It enables for the detection of optical transitions from one band to the next as well as the existence of any fault levels. Whenever photons fall on given sample, it is absorbed by the sample by imparting its excess energy. This is known as photo-excitation. Light emission, or luminescence, is one technique by which the sample releases this extra energy. Photoluminescence refers to luminescence that occurs as a result of photo-excitation. The PL lifespan indicates how quickly charges in the excited state undergo recombination processes. The inverse of the sum of the radiative and non-radiative recombination rates is the lifespan. PL spectroscopy is a strong tool for probing semiconductor electronic characteristics. It can even be carried out at different temperatures, delivering valuable information on the temperature sensitivity of fundamental electrical properties such the band gap energy [21]. PL provides useful data mostly on the semiconductor's composition and confinement effect. In short, Photoluminescence, is a major and non-contact optical approach for measuring purity and crystalline quality in materials for energy devices, as well as identifying certain contaminants. The crystalline clarity and purity of semiconductors or composite semiconductor materials can also be measured using PL. PL is most used in direct bandgap semiconductors. This technique is important for determining the semiconductor's minority carrier lifetime also.

3. Conclusion

Nanoscience and technology have enabled the exploration of material characteristics with diameters between 1 and 100 nm. Thank you to atomic scale particle observations made possible by nanotechnology and nanometrology. The development of a thorough understanding of any novel phenomena or process depends on nanometrology. The only things that can truly be comprehended are those that can be measured. The article gives a quick rundown of the many tools available for characterising nanoparticles. Finding out about the physical, optical, structural and morphological characteristics of produced nanoparticles is made easier by the characterisation process. A thorough work is required since the development of new metrology leads to the fine and precise characterisation of samples. It is impossible to predict when this trend will finish, but it will inevitably move from nanotechnology to Pico technology.

Acknowledgement

Ethical approval: We certify that the manuscript titled 'A Brief Outline on Tools of Nanotechnology: Nanometrology' has been entirely our own work, and it does not infringe the copyright of any third party. The submission of the paper implies that the paper has not been published previously and is not under consideration for publication elsewhere.

Data availability: Not applicable.

Consent to participate: We affirm that all authors have participated in the research work and are fully aware of ethical responsibilities.

Consent to publish: All authors agree for consideration in your journal.

Competing interests: The authors declare no competing interests. The authors declare that they have no known competing financial interests or personal relationships that could have appeared to influence the work reported in this paper.

References

[1] Postek, M., & Hocken, R. entitled as "*Instrumentation and metrology for nanotechnology*", published in 2006 by "National Nanotechnology Coordination office (NNCO), United states of America".

[2] Lojkowski, W., *et al.*, "Eighth nanoforum report: nanometrology," *European Nanotechnology Gateway (Nanoforum. org)*, no. July, pp. 13–14, 2006, doi: 10.13140/RG.2.1.2375.2404.

[3] Jorio, A. and M. S. Dresselhaus, "Nanostructured materials: metrology," in *Reference Module in Materials Science and Materials Engineering*, Elsevier, 2016.

[4] Sengupta, A. and C. K. Sarkar, "Introduction to nano engineering material," 2015, pp. 1–6.

[5] Kalendin, V. V., "Nanometrology: problems and solutions," Jul. 2002, pp. 269–281, doi: 10.1117/12.484566.

[6] Binnig, G., C. F. Quate, and C. Gerber, "Atomic force microscope," *Phys. Rev. Lett.*, vol. 56, no. 9, pp. 930–933, Mar. 1986, doi: 10.1103/PhysRevLett.56.930.

[7] Bogue, R., "Nanometrology: a critical discipline for the twenty-first century," *Sens. Rev.*, vol. 27, no. 3, pp. 189–196, 2007, doi: 10.1108/02602280710758110.

[8] Danzebrink, H.-U., *et al.*, "Dimensional nanometrology at PTB," in *2012 IEEE International Instrumentation and Measurement Technology Conference Proceedings*, May 2012, pp. 898–901, doi: 10.1109/I2MTC.2012.6229183.

[9] Jorio, A. and M. S. Dresselhaus, "Nanostructured materials: metrology," in *Encyclopedia of Materials: Science and Technology*, Elsevier, 2010, pp. 1–7.

[10] Zhang, J., *et al.*, "Critical three-dimensional metrologies for emerging nanoelectronics," *J. Micro/Nanopatterning Mater. Metrol.*, vol. 22, no. 03, Mar. 2023, p. 031204, doi: 10.1117/1.JMM.22.3.031204.

[11] Bensebaa, F., "Nanoparticle fundamentals," 2013, pp. 1–84.

[12] Ukraintsev, V. and B. Banke, "Reference metrology for nanotechnology: significance, challenges and solutions," *Instrum. Metrol. Stand. Nanomanuf. IV*, vol. 7767, p. 77670C, 2010, doi: 10.1117/12.860666.

[13] Whitehouse, D. J., "Nanometrology," *Contemp. Phys.*, vol. 49, no. 5, pp. 351–374, 2008, doi: 10.1080/00107510802611251.

[14] Schattenburg, M. L. and H. I. Smith, "The critical role of metrology in nanotechnology," *Nanostruct. Sci. Metrol. Technol.*, vol. 4608, pp. 116–124, 2002, doi: 10.1117/12.437273.

[15] Srivastava, A. K., "Role of NPL-India in nanotechnology and nanometrology," *Mapan J. Metrol. Soc. India*, vol. 28, no. 4, pp. 263–272, 2013, doi: 10.1007/s12647-013-0091-8.

[16] Rasit, T., "COordination of NANOMETrology in Europe Final Report Summary - CO-NANOMET (Coordination of nanometrology in Europe) nanometrology in Europe)," 2010.

[17] Williams, D. B. and C. B. Carter, "The transmission electron microscope," in *Transmission Electron Microscopy*, Boston, MA: Springer US, 1996, pp. 3–17.

[18] Stanjek, H. and W. Häusler, "Basics of X-ray diffraction," *Hyperfine Interact.*, vol. 154, no. 1–4, pp. 107–119, 2004, doi: 10.1023/B:HYPE.0000032028.60546.38.

[19] Kim, G.-M., P. Simon, and J.-S. Kim, "Electrospun PVA/HAp nanocomposite nanofibers: biomimetics of mineralized hard tissues at a lower level of complexity," *Bioinspiration Biomimetics*, vol. 3, no. 4, p. 046003, Dec. 2008, doi: 10.1088/1748-3182/3/4/046003.

[20] Kirkland, A., L.-Y. Chang, S. Haigh, and C. Hetherington, "Transmission electron microscopy without aberrations: applications to materials science," *Curr. Appl. Phys.*, vol. 8, no. 3–4, pp. 425–428, May 2008, doi: 10.1016/j.cap.2007.10.065.

[21] Gfroerer, T. H., "Photoluminescence in analysis of surfaces and interfaces," in *Encyclopedia of Analytical Chemistry*, Chichester: John Wiley & Sons Ltd, 2000, pp. 9209–9231.

24. Breast Cancer Classification with Adaptive Median Filtering, GMM Segmentation and GLCM Features

Richa Sharma[1,2], Amit Kamra[3], and Shaffy Makkar[4]

[1]*Computer Science Engineering, IKG-Punjab Technical University, Kapurthala, India*
[2]*School of Computer Science & Engineering, Lovely Professional University, Phagwara, India*
[3]*Department of Information Technology, Guru Nanak Dev Engg. College, Ludhiana, India*
[4]*Science Department, GHS Kot Mangal Singh, Ludhiana, India*

Abstract: Breast cancer is a prominent global health issue, with early identification of abnormalities in mammogram images being pivotal for effective diagnosis and treatment. This research presents an algorithm that utilises information fusion to detect abnormalities in mammogram images and classify them as either benign or malignant. The proposed algorithm combines the adaptive median filter technique and Gaussian mixture model segmentation approach to improve detection precision. The methodology encompasses several steps: initial preprocessing of the input image to eliminate noise and enhance relevant characteristics, segmentation using GMM, followed by classification. Implementation of the algorithm employs MATLAB along with various image processing functions and techniques necessary for its objectives' attainment. The experimental findings show that the suggested algorithm is successful at properly identifying mammography pictures and may assist in the early detection of breast cancer.

Keywords: Breast cancer, classification, GLCM, GMM, adaptive median filter.

1. Introduction

Breast cancer is one of the most frequent malignancies in women throughout the world, with significant mortality rates if not detected and treated early [1]. Cancer has taken the lives of up to 14.5 million people worldwide, with that amount estimated to climb to 28 million by 2030. As per official reports by the WHO, breast cancer is the most diagnosed in women accounting the malignancy which was responsible for 25% of all female cancer diagnoses and 25%-30% of all female-related fatalities. [2]. A study showed that in 2018, 1.6 million new cases were registered, and 87,090 deaths were reported[3]. A major reason for this is less public awareness along with none or very fewer screenings with high testing prices. Around 1.8 million cancer cases were detected in 2020, with breast cancer accounting for 30% of the instances [4].

To reduce the mortality rate and improve treatment outcomes, early detection and accurate classification of breast abnormalities is crucial. Breast cancer diagnosis typically involves the analysis of mammograms, which are X-ray images of the breasts. Subtle anomalies such as microcalcifications, masses and architectural deformities can be shown by these images.

The presence of noise, changes in breast tissue composition and the complexities of mammography images, on the other hand, make accurate diagnosis challenging. Mammography is a well-established and effective imaging method for identifying early-stage breast cancer. It comprises capturing X-ray images of the breast tissue to detect microcalcifications, masses and architectural defects. Mammography has shown to be an important technique for breast cancer screening and diagnosis due to its ability to detect abnormalities while they are not yet palpable or symptomatic.

The presence of thick breast tissue is one of the key problems in mammography-based breast cancer diagnosis. Dense breast tissue looks white on mammograms, like malignant tissue, making the distinction between the two more difficult. In addition, thick breast tissue can obscure or conceal tiny tumours, making them difficult to diagnose. Another difficulty in detecting breast cancer is the false-positive and false-negative rates associated with mammography. False-positive findings arise when a mammography shows the presence of cancer, but further testing reveals that no cancer exists. False-negative findings, on the other hand, arise when a mammography fails to identify malignancy. These difficulties might cause undue concern in patients and increase healthcare expenses for follow-up testing and procedures. Researchers have resorted to modern image processing techniques and machine learning algorithms to solve these problems and increase the accuracy of breast cancer categorisation in mammography pictures. These strategies attempt to improve mammography picture quality, identify and characterise breast lesions and minimise false-positive and false-negative rates in breast cancer classification.

2. Literature Review

Numerous research on breast cancer categorisation have been undertaken utilising various image processing and machine learning approaches. Several studies have been conducted to investigate the use of adaptive median filtering, GMM segmentation and GLCM features in breast cancer classification. Perez *et al.* created machine learning classifiers as one such approach. Wang *et al.* suggested a method for improving mammography pictures and extracting useful characteristics that combines adaptive median filtering and GMM segmentation. Dey *et al.* suggested a method for classifying breast cancer lesions into benign and malignant categories using GLCM characteristics and a classifier. Chen *et al.* explored the use of adaptive median filtering and GLCM features for breast cancer classification. Yap and Khalid Investigated the effectiveness of using adaptive median filtering, GMM segmentation and GLCM features for breast cancer classification. These classifiers blend and fuse various segmentation techniques and machine learning technique to accurately identify and classify masses. Other classification techniques discussed in the reviewed literature include statistical features and fuzzy classification of thermograms, machine learning techniques, J48, CART and decision tree algorithm [5,6]. The papers in the Table 1 provide a comprehensive overview of the relevant literature in the field.

Table 1: Comparative analysis.

S.No	Author	Year	Database	Classification Method Used	Findings	Outcome Reported
1	[7]	2015	MIAS, DDSM	Decision Tree, Random Forest, GA-SVM, PSO-SVM	– ROIs is enhanced using rough set(RS) method	Random forest accuracy(97.73%) GA-SVM accuracy (92.48%) PSO-SVM accuracy (94.28%) Decision tree accuracy (97.87%)
2	[8]	2015	MIAS	GLCM, RBFNN	– Higher accuracy was achieved using 2 major phases in classification.	Accuracy (93.98%) Sensitivity (97.22%), Specificity (91.49%)
3	[9]	2016	DDSM, MIAS	LBP,SVM	– Classification algorithm uses threshold value – Experimental best threshold value to be found in 0.5	Accuracy (84.0%)
4	[10]	2017	Mini-MIAS	SVM, KNN	– k-means clustering used minimise time consumption – Used GLCM features for better classification	SVM Accuracy (96.5%) Sensitivity (94.3%) Specificity (78%) KNN Accuracy (92.1%) Sensitivity (92.4%) Specificity(72%)
5	[11]	2018	CBIS-DDSM	SVM	– Used Gray-Level Co-Occurrence Matrix along with Support Vector Machine	Accuracy (63.03%) Specificity (89.01%)
6	[12]	2018	MIAS	Textural filters	– Implemented in MATLAB – 2.28sec to process an image.	Accuracy (96.15%)

7	[13]	2019		SVM, KNN	None	SVM Accuracy (87.87%) Specificity (89%) KNN Accuracy (89.39%) Specificity (87.00%) RF Accuracy (86.36%) Specificity (94.00%)
8	[14]	2019	DDSM	SVM		Accuracy (97%) Sensitivity (100%) Specificity (96%)
9	[15]	2019	ImageNet	CNN	– Radiomics, Deep Convolutional Neural Network Transfer Learning and Fusion Methods were used..	CNN(feature Extraction) Sensitivity (79.8%) Specificity (78.9%) Fusion A Sensitivity (84.8%) Specificity (84.2%) Fusion B Sensitivity (80.0%) Specificity (87.7%) Fusion C Sensitivity (84.3%) Specificity (81.6%) Fusion D Sensitivity (86.2%) Specificity (81.6%)
10	[16]	2019	DDSM	CNN	– Triplet convolutional neural network (CNN) – 4000 augmented images (80% training, 20% testing) – Uses Canny filter	Accuracy (93.13%) Sensitivity (96%) Specificity (90.25%)
11	[17]	2019	MIAS	GLC, BPNN	– Learning time reduced drastically when decreasing input neurons in BPNN – 20000 epoch – 8 hidden neurons	Accuracy (94.06%), Sensitivity (90.16%), Specificity (95.57%)

3. Methodology

In this study, we propose a methodology for breast cancer classification using adaptive median filtering, GMM segmentation and GLCM features. The proposed methodology includes several steps such as the pre-processing of mammogram images using adaptive median filtering, segmentation of the pre-processed images using the Gaussian Mixture Model and extraction of texture features using grey-level co-occurrence matrix.

Images from DDSM dataset were used and following techniques were applied:

Image Preprocessing: The first step is to prepare the mammography picture by converting it to greyscale and using noise reduction methods.

Pixel level processing: Individual pixel values are changed depending on their interactions with neighbouring pixels to ensure image improvement.

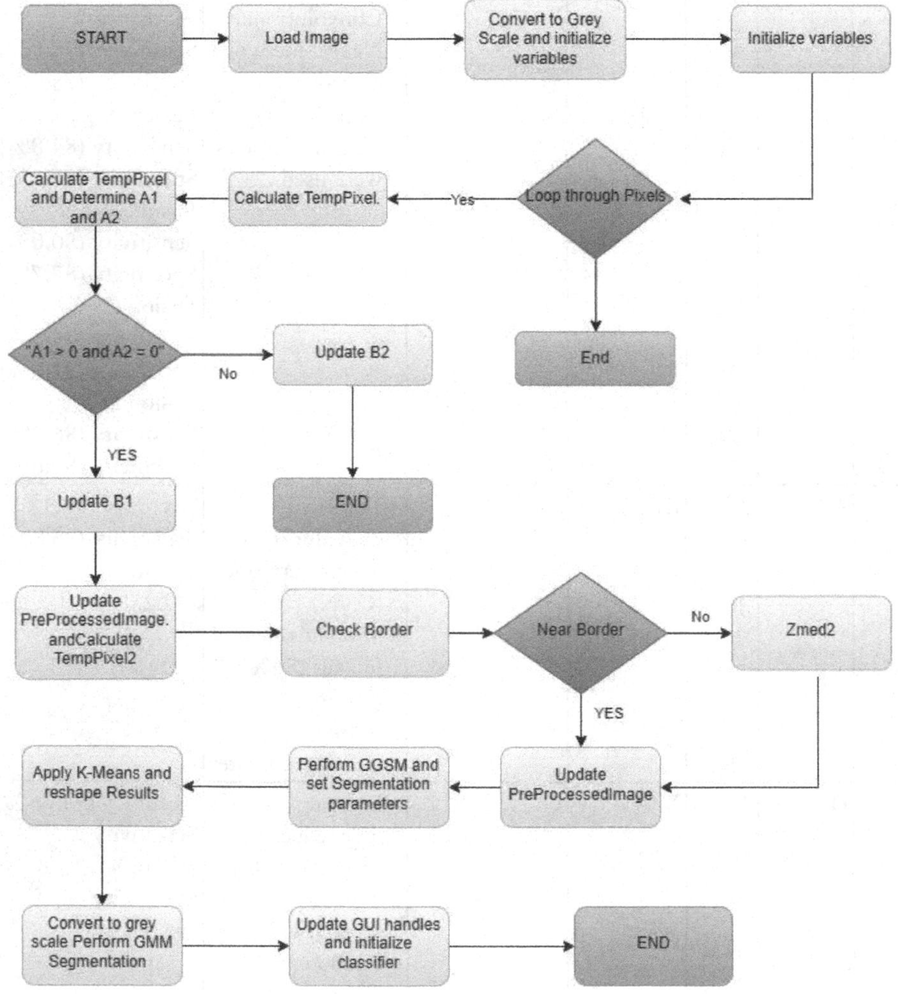

Figure 1: Complete flow chart for classification of mammogram.

Edge and Corner Handling: To eliminate artefacts and ensure accuracy, pixels near the image's edges and corners are given special care.

Local contextual Enhancement: Non-edge, non-corner pixels benefit from additional processing that considers their local environment inside a 5x5 neighbourhood.

Segmentation: Using Gaussian mixture models (GMM) and k-means clustering, the picture is separated into discrete sections.

Texture Analysis: To characterise the visual content, texture characteristics are derived from segmented regions.

Classification: A classifier uses a reference database to determine if a mammogram picture suggests a benign or malignant disease. Figure 1 depicts the step wise procedure of pre-processing, segmentation and classification.

The proposed algorithm leverages a combination of preprocessing, segmentation and classification techniques to accurately classify mammogram images. Experimental results demonstrate the potential of this algorithm in aiding healthcare professionals in the early detection of breast cancer abnormalities.

4. Results and Discussions

Figure 2 shows breast cancer image category displays in the text box.

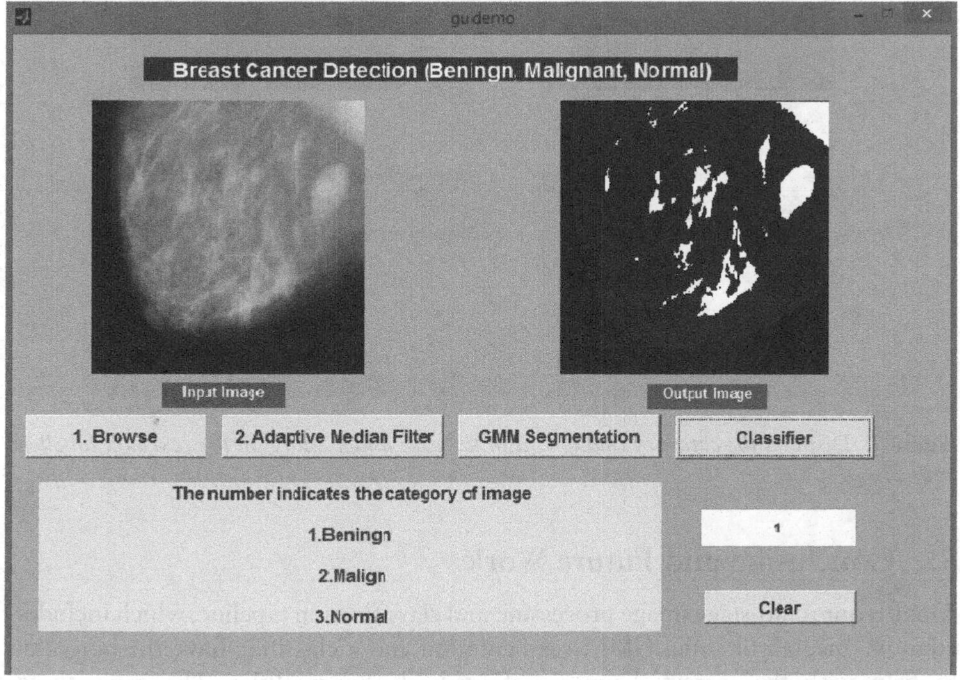

Figure 2: Displays the category (benign in the case under study) in the text box labelled with 1.

The proposed algorithm leverages a combination of preprocessing, segmentation and classification techniques to accurately classify mammogram images. Experimental results demonstrate the potential of this algorithm in aiding healthcare professionals in the early detection of breast cancer abnormalities.

In Figure 3, another image from DDSM dataset is used from different category, and the image after undergoing the defined steps is classified as malignant which is depicted in right window of the figure.

The images will be classified in three classes as mentioned:

Class 1: Benign—Indicates lesions or tissue that are likely to be benign.

Class 2: Malignant—Identifies locations that exhibit features typical of malignant tumours or abnormalities.

Class 3: Normal—Denotes tissue or structures that are considered as normal.

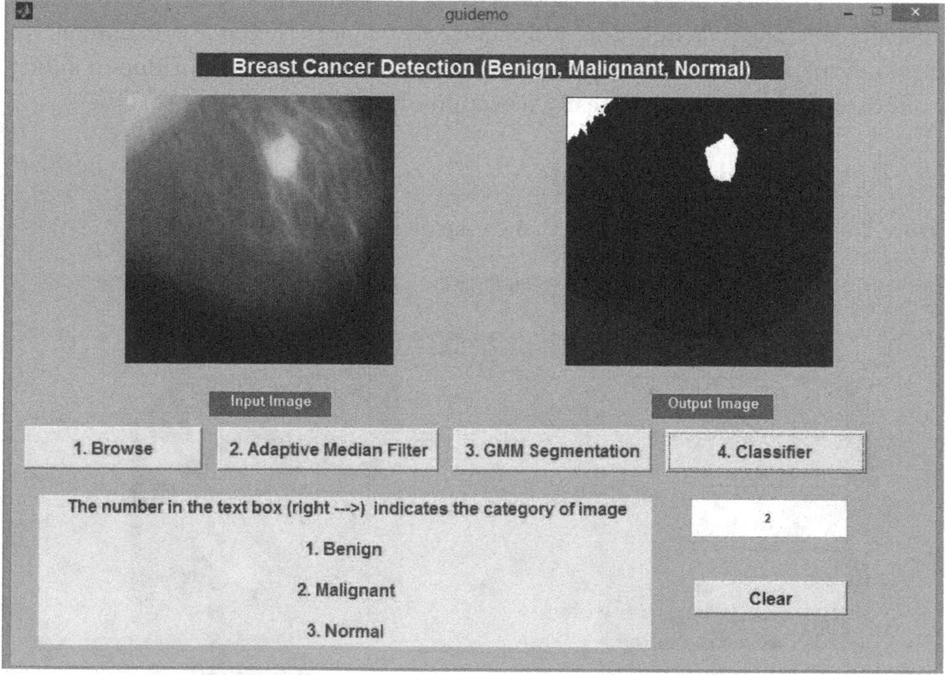

Figure 3: Displays the category (malignant in the case under study) in the text box labelled with 2.

5. Conclusion and Future Work

Finally, our multi-stage image processing and classification pipeline, which includes adaptive median filtering, GMM segmentation and a classifier, have the potential to help with the correct diagnosis of medical abnormalities. The capacity to differentiate between benign, malignant and normal areas within medical pictures is critical for medical practitioners and can lead to more successful patient treatment.

This pipeline requires more study and refining to optimise its performance and assure its clinical usefulness.

Metrics like as accuracy, sensitivity, specificity and the receiver operating characteristic (ROC) curve was used to assess the pipeline's performance. Additional validation and testing on a wide collection of medical pictures will help to assess this approach's generalisation and real-world applicability.

Acknowledgement

I wish to extend my heartfelt thanks to Mrs. Shaffy Makkar for their invaluable assistance in interpreting mammographic images, which greatly enriched the quality and depth of this research. Their expertise and guidance were indispensable in navigating the complexities of medical imaging.

References

[1] Yu, K., S. Chen, and Y. Chen, "Tumor segmentation in breast ultrasound image by means of res path combined with dense connection neural network," *Diagnostics*, vol. 11, p. 1565, 2021.

[2] "Trends of breast cancer in India," http://www.breastcancerindia.net/statistics/trends.html (accessed January 29, 2020).

[3] "Cancer statistics - India against cancer," http://cancerindia.org.in/cancer-statistics/(accessed January 29, 2020).

[4] Zhang, S.-C., Z.-Q. Hu, J.-H. Long, G.-M. Zhu, Y. Wang, Y. Jia, J. Zhou, Y. Ouyang, and Z. Zeng, "Clinical implications of tumor-infiltrating immune cells in breast cancer," *J. Cancer*, vol. 10, p. 6175, 2019.

[5] Khan, M S., A. Zafar, F. Farooq, M. F. Javed, R. Alyousef, H. Alabduljabbar, and M. I. Khan, "Geopolymer concrete compressive strength via artificial neural network, adaptive neuro fuzzy interface system, and gene expression programming with K-Fold cross validation," https://scite.ai/reports/10.3389/fmats.2021.621163 (accessed May 3, 2021).

[6] Jethva, H B. and H. B. Jethva, "ImbTree: minority class sensitive weighted decision tree for classification of unbalanced data," https://scite.ai/reports/10.18201/ijisae.2021473633 (accessed December 26, 2021).

[7] Dong, M., X. Lu, Y. Ma, Y. Guo, Y. Ma, and K. Wang, "An efficient approach for automated mass segmentation and classification in mammograms," *J. Digit. Imaging*, vol. 28, no. 5, pp. 613–625, 2015.

[8] Pratiwi, M., J. H. Alexander, and S. Nanda, "Mammograms classification using gray-level co-occurrence matrix and radial basis function neural network," *Procedia Comput. Sci.*, vol. 59, no. Iccsci, pp. 83–91, 2015.

[9] Král, P. and L. Lenc, "LBP features for breast cancer detection," *2016 IEEE International Conference on Image Processing (ICIP)*, pp. 2643–2647, 2016.

[10] Hariraj, V., K. W. Vikneswaran, and I. Zunaidi, "An efficient data mining approaches for breast cancer detection and segmentation in mammogram,"

J. Adv. Res. Dyn. Control Syst., vol. 9, no. Special Issue 3, pp. 185–194, 2017.

[11] Sarosa, S. J. A., F. Utaminingrum, and F. A. Bachtiar, "Mammogram breast cancer classification using gray-level co-occurrence matrix and support vector machine," *3rd Int. Conf. Sustain. Inf. Eng. Technol. SIET 2018 - Proc.*, pp. 54–59, 2018.

[12] Shi, P., J. Zhong, A. Rampun, and H. Wang, "A hierarchical pipeline for breast boundary segmentation and calcification detection in mammograms," *C omput. Biol. Med.*, vol. 96, no. March, pp. 178–188, 2018.

[13] Viswanath, V. H. and L. Guachi-guachi, *EasyChair Preprint Breast Cancer Detection Using Image Processing Techniques and Classification Algorithms*, 2019.

[14] Safdarian, N. and M. R. Hediyehzadeh, "Detection and classification of breast cancer in mammography images using pattern recognition methods," vol. 3, no. 4, 2019.

[15] Whitney, H., H. Li, J. Yu, P. Liu, and M. L. Giger, *Comparison of Breast MRI Tumor Classification Using Radiomics, Transfer Learning from Deep Convolutional Neural Networks, and Fusion Methods*, pp. 1–15, 2019.

[16] Merati, M., S. Mahmoudi, A. Chenine, and M. A. Chikh, "A new triplet convolutional neural network for classification of lesions on mammograms," *Rev. d'Intelligence Artif.*, vol. 33, no. 3, pp. 213–217, 2019.

[17] Sarosa, S. J. A., F. Utaminingrum, and F. A. Bachtiar, "Breast cancer classification using GLCM and BPNN," vol. 11, no. 3, 2019.

25. IoT-Based Smart Dustbin for Waste Management Systems

Sachin Chawla[1], Tanu Uppal[2], Saurabh Singh[3], Keshav Kumar[2]

[1]*ECE, Chandigarh University, Mohali, India*
[2]*UIC, Chandigarh University, Mohali, India*
[3]*CSE, Bhilai Institute of Technology, Durg, India*

Abstract: In recent years, the growing concern for environmental sustainability has propelled the development of innovative technologies aimed at improving waste management practices. One such technological advancement is the smart dustbin, a sophisticated device equipped with sensors and intelligent capabilities that revolutionise traditional waste disposal systems. This paper provides an overview of the concept and benefits of smart dustbins, highlighting their potential to enhance waste management processes in urban areas. The main feature of this dustbin is to avoid overflow issues, differentiate between dry and wet waste, time and cost saving and optimised routes. The smart dustbin consists of internet of things (IoT) technologies and different sensors to monitor and optimise waste collection and disposal. Smart dustbins are equipped with various sensors, such as ultrasonic sensors (SR-04), a Servo motor(SG-90), GPS tracking and a GSM module. These intelligent bins can detect the level of waste accumulation, even they can identify the type of waste, and determine the appropriate time for collection. These dustbins are connected to Arduino and ESP8266 WIFI modules which can update the real-time data on the server. The paper mainly focuses to design a contactless smart dustbin that can detect the level of garbage, generate alerts and notifications when it is full and can differentiate between dry and wet waste. These notifications and alerts are directly sent to the MCD server so that they can clean the dustbin on time and avoid any disease due to the overflow of garbage in dustbins. Multiple dustbins installed in cities will send a signal to the server, and it will set an optimised route for waste collection so that fuel consumption may be decreased.

Keywords: Arduino, ESP8266, GSM, GPS, IoT, ultrasonic, servomotor.

1. Introduction

In the last few decades, the population of India has increased at a rapid rate that can result in to increase the garbage in cities or states. Waste management is a critical issue that is currently faced in all cities and states of our country. Everyone wants to live in smart cities where cleanliness is an important factor. The main problem faced in waste management is that dustbins are already full in public areas, which can cause various diseases and health-related issues. Even then concerned MCDs of that city does not aware of the conditions of dustbins.

Timely actions are not taken by the MCDs because there are hundreds of dustbins in the area so their management is a time-consuming and costly process. Even the conditions of dustbins are not clean and the person has to manage with their hands which can cause more health issues. The next problem is that people are throwing dry and wet waste in the same dustbin, which is again a headache for the concerned person to differentiate between both waste. This designed invention or model can provide an easy and efficient solution for the above-mentioned serious issue. A smart dustbin with multiple features is focused on the main issues of waste management, contactless dustbin, and differentiating between dry and wet waste. This smart dustbin concept attracted the attention of researchers in the last few years and multiple solutions have been designed to achieve this target. This invention uses the concept of IoT integrated with sensors to make dustbin smart, which can generate notifications and alerts. This dustbin is contactless, and it can send the signal and its location to the MCD of the particular city when they are full. By separating recyclables from general waste at the point of disposal, these dustbins facilitate recycling processes and contribute to more sustainable waste management practices. This dustbin is capable to segregate dry and wet waste with the help of a sensor installed in the dustbin. With the help of an ultrasonic sensor, it is designed in a way that no physical touch is required to open and close the dustbin. Waste management authorities can analyse this information to make informed decisions, optimise collection routes, allocate resources effectively and implement waste reduction strategies.

2. Literature Review

This research focuses on the design and development of an IoT-based smart garbage management system using ultrasonic sensors. The study includes a discussion of the system architecture, hardware components, data flow and real-time monitoring capabilities. Experimental results and performance evaluation are also provided [1]. This research paper presents an IoT-based smart dustbin system that utilises ultrasonic sensors and Arduino microcontrollers. It includes a detailed description of the hardware setup, data transmission process and waste monitoring mechanism. The authors also discuss the potential applications and future enhancements of the system [2]. A comprehensive review of IoT-based smart dustbin systems. The author discussed various aspects, including system architecture, sensor technologies, communication protocols, data analytics and waste management algorithms. It also highlights the potential benefits and challenges in implementing such systems [3]. A smart dustbin system using IoT technology for waste management in smart cities. The study includes a detailed description of the hardware and software components and the implementation process. It also discusses the benefits and challenges associated with the proposed system [4]. The author proposed a smart dustbin system with waste segregation and level monitoring capabilities. It utilises ultrasonic sensors, an Arduino board and a mobile application for waste segregation, real-time monitoring and notification alerts [5]. An IoT-based smart dustbin system designed for smart cities. The system employs ultrasonic sensors, a Raspberry Pi and a web-based interface for real-time monitoring, waste level estimation and optimisation of waste collection routes [6]. This paper introduces a smart dustbin system with a garbage level indicator and management features. The system utilises ultrasonic sensors, an Arduino microcontroller and a mobile application for real-time monitoring, waste level indication and data analysis for efficient waste management [7]. Smart dustbin system utilising IoT technology for waste management. It incorporates ultrasonic sensors, a Raspberry Pi and a web application for real-time monitoring of dustbin levels, waste segregation and notification alerts [8]. A solution proposed by the author is a smart dustbin with automatic segregation and level monitoring capabilities. The system incorporates ultrasonic sensors, a microcontroller and a mobile application for real-time monitoring and wastes segregation based on different categories [9]. The author designed the smart garbage system that employs ultrasonic sensors, Arduino, and a web-based interface to monitor and manage waste bins efficiently. It discusses the system architecture, implementation details, and experimental results [10]. The IR sensor is used by certain researchers to monitor the garbage that is dispersed outside the dustbin, which makes the dustbin even smarter. The system's analysis and monitoring might lessen the daily labour required by humans to clean the affected regions, which contributes to a cleaner environment overall [11]. Numerous countries are experiencing issues with cleanliness, and a wide variety of technologies have been developed to manage solid waste management systems. The Arduino Mega microcontroller has been utilised by the authors to measure the level of waste in the dustbin using ultrasonic sensors. The PIR sensor is used in accordance with the shutting and opening of the bin's lid. The bin is attached to an LCD panel that shows whether motion has been detected or not. Solar energy powers their module. The WIFI module (ESP8266) used in the model transmits data to a web server that the creators built using bootstrap. The RTC module adds a timestamp to the data before sending it, and by using a GSM module, it also tells the user where the bin is (latitude and longitude) [12]. The solutions developed for garbage management have their own challenges. In order to convey the status of the bin to the registered number, the GSM module and an ultrasonic sensor are all that are needed. Despite having fewer sensors, this device has fewer contacts and can only make so many calls or send so many messages, depending on the SIM plans. The model suggested in this study makes it simple for registered and authorised members to keep track of the bin's state [13].

3. Proposed Methodology

The designed model comprises useful features:

- **Contactless Dustbin**: The front section of the dustbin has an ultrasonic sensor that can measure the distance between the dustbin and objects. When the person enters that range, the lid of the dustbin will open automatically. The Servo motor attached to the top of the dustbin is used to open the cover. The range of this prototype model is set at around 15 cm. This sensor is so chosen that it works on the sound waves which are less affected by outer conditions.
- **Level detection**: This is the main aspect of this dustbin to check the level of waste accumulation. To achieve this objective, an ultrasonic sensor is mounted on the top of the cover in downward directions. So that sound waves can detect the distance between the top and bottom of the dustbin. This distance is divided into different levels. The level of the dustbin will continuously display on the LCD (16*2) to prevent the overflow of the waste.
- **GSM and GPS tracking**: It consists of a GSM module used to send the message to the MCD of the area when the dustbin level is full. GPS tracker is used to detect the coordinates of the dustbins, which are already full and provide an optimised route to collect garbage. Message sent via GSM module having a text and coordinates of the given location.
- **Dry and Wet waste segregate**: This dustbin is divided into two sections, i.e. dry and wet sections. A plate with aluminium foil and a separate motor is used to segregate the waste material. So it is smart enough to differentiate between dry and wet waste. When any person tries to put waste in the dustbin, then aluminium plate will detect the type of waste and put it accordingly in that particular section.

3.1. Components Used

The following components are used to design a model which is capable to resolve the issues.

I. **Arduino Uno**: The Arduino Uno is a well known and commonly used microcontroller board from the Arduino family of products. The Uno contains six analog input pins (A0 through A5) that can also function as digital I/O pins as shown in Figure 2. The Arduino integrated development environment (IDE) can be used to program the Arduino Uno, which provides a user-friendly interface for creating, compiling and uploading code to the board. It makes use of a streamlined version of the C/C++ programming language.

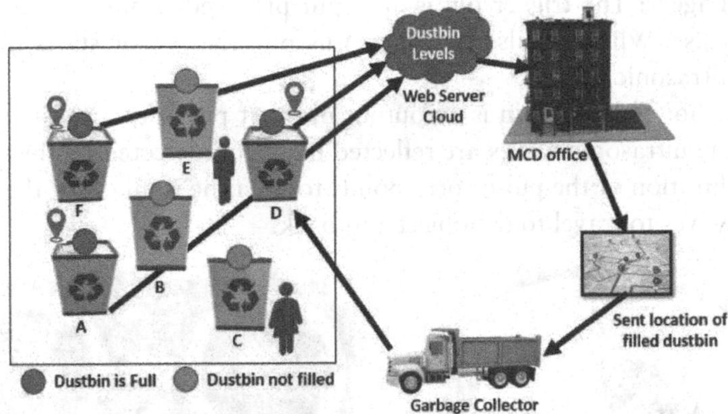

Figure 1: Proposed method for optimising route.

Figure 2: Arduino Uno SMD.

II. **Ultrasonic Sensor:** An ultrasonic sensor is a device that can measure distances by emitting high-frequency sound waves a detecting the time it takes for the sound waves to bounce back after hitting an object as shown in Figure 3. It uses the principles of ultrasonic waves, which are sound waves with frequencies higher than the upper audible limit of human hearing. It generates the signal at a frequency of 44 kHz that is not in the human audible range. Here is a typical pinout:

- **VCC:** This pin is used to provide power to the sensor. It is typically connected to the positive supply voltage (e.g., +5 V or +3.3 V) of the system.
- **GND:** This pin is the ground connection and should be connected to the common ground of the system.

- **Trigger:** The trigger pin is an input pin used to initiate the ultrasonic pulse. When a pulse is sent to this pin, the sensor starts transmitting ultrasonic waves.
- **Echo:** The echo pin is an output pin that provides a pulse signal when the ultrasonic waves are reflected back and detected by the sensor. The duration of the pulse corresponds to the time it takes for the ultrasonic waves to travel to the object and back.

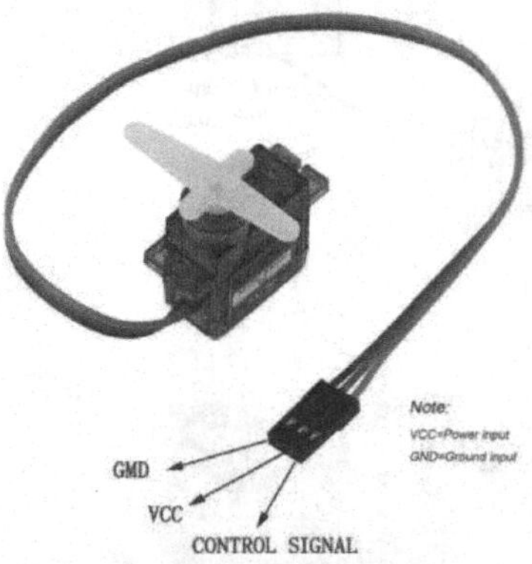

Figure 3: *Ultrasonic sensor.*

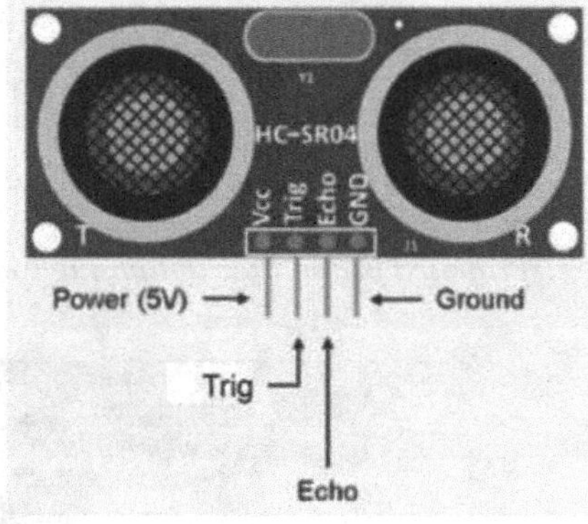

Figure 4: *Servo motor (SG-90).*

III. **Servo Motor**: The SG90 servo motor is a popular and commonly used micro servo motor. It is a compact and lightweight motor that provides precise control over angular motion. Here are some key features and specifications of the SG90 servo motor. Control Interface: The SG90 servo motor uses a three-wire control interface as shown in Figure 4

- **VCC:** This wire is connected to the positive power supply (typically 4.8 V to 6 V).
- **GND:** This wire is connected to the common ground of the system.
- **Signal:** This wire is used to control the motor's position. It receives PWM (Pulse Width Modulation) signals from a microcontroller or any other device capable of generating PWM signals.

IV. **GSM Module**: The GSM Module 800L is a popular and widely used GSM (Global System for Mobile Communications) module for wireless communication as shown in Figure 5. It allows devices to establish cellular connectivity and communicate with the GSM network. The module is controlled by sending AT commands over the serial interface. These commands are used to perform various operations such as making calls, sending SMS, configuring network settings and handling data communication. The GSM Module 800L usually comes with an onboard serial peripheral interface (SPI) or universal asynchronous receiver-transmitter (UART) interface. This interface allows communication with the module using simple commands and data exchange.

Figure 5: GSM module.

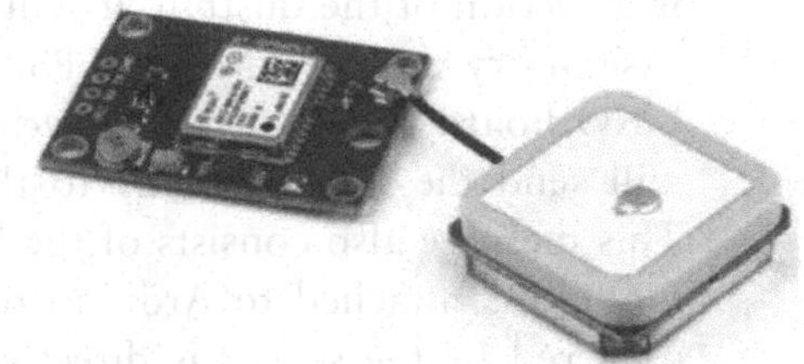

Figure 6: GPS module.

V. **GPS Module**: A GPS module is a device that receives signals from Global Positioning System (GPS) satellites to determine accurate location coordinates. It provides precise latitude, longitude, altitude and time information. The GPS module includes an antenna to receive signals from GPS satellites as shown in Figure 6. The antenna is responsible for capturing weak satellite signals and ensuring accurate positioning. The GPS module typically interfaces with a microcontroller, development board or other devices using serial communication protocols such as Universal Asynchronous Receiver-Transmitter (UART) or I2C (Inter-Integrated Circuit). This allows the host device to receive GPS data from the module.

VI. **ESP8266 Module**: The ESP8266 module is a popular and versatile Wi-Fi module that combines a microcontroller and a Wi-Fi module into a single chip as shown in Figure 7. It offers embedded Wi-Fi capabilities, making it a powerful and cost-effective solution for adding wireless connectivity to various electronic projects. The ESP8266 module supports 2.4 GHz Wi-Fi connectivity, allowing it to connect to Wi-Fi networks and communicate with other devices over the internet. It supports various security protocols, such as WPA/WPA2, to ensure secure wireless communication and the person. This sensor named Ultrasonic sensor1 (US1) fitted in front of the dustbin. When a person enters the range of the ultrasonic sensor the top cover of the dustbin which is connected to the servomotor (SG90) will start open in the upward direction. The servo motor will move at an angle of 120 degrees for 5 secs. It means the lid of the dustbin will remain open for 5 secs and then it will close. As shown in the block diagram Figure 3 consists of two ultrasonic sensors. The second ultrasonic sensor is placed on the top cover of the dustbin. The second ultrasonic sensor named as US2 sensor will continuously monitor the garbage level in the dustbin and will display the level on LCD and update real-time data on the cloud also. It is mounted on the back side of the top cover of the dustbin which is immobile. Only the first half of the cover will open. The level of the dustbin was adjusted according to the height of the dustbin in cm. An aluminium board placed inside the dustbin is used to segregate the dry and wet waste. when the wet waste is placed on the board the current will start to flow and the motor will rotate in the clockwise direction i.e. the wet section of the dustbin. It will move in an anticlockwise direction in case of dry waste. GSM and GPS tracking module attached with Arduino UNO board and comes in active mode when the dustbin level is full. It will send the signal directly to the MCD office to vacant the dustbin. This message also consists of the location of the dustbin. ESP8266 WIFI module is attached to Arduino to connect it to the Internet. The data gathered by the sensor is directly uploaded to the Blynk cloud or web server of the MCD.

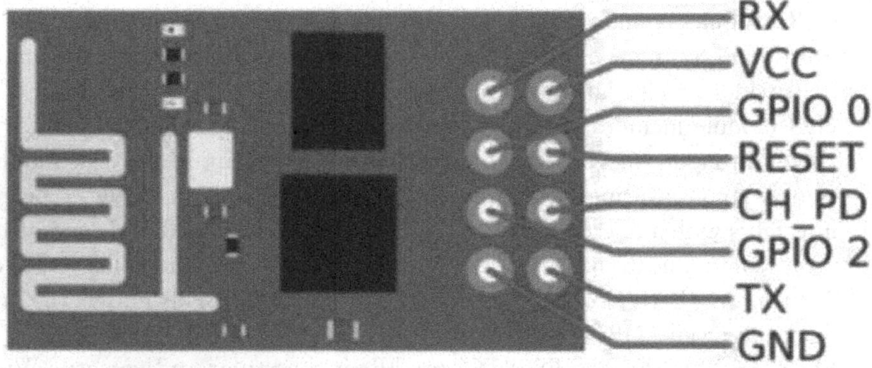

Figure 7: ESP8266 WIFI module.

4. Block Diagram

The block diagram consists of all the sensors and actuators interface with Arduino uno board as shown in Figure 8. An ultrasonic sensor that can emit sound waves at a frequency of 44KHz is used to calculate the distance between the dustbin and the person. This sensor named ultrasonic sensor1 (US1) fitted in front of the dustbin. When a person enters the range of the ultrasonic sensor, the top cover of the dustbin which is connected to the servomotor (SG90) will start open in the upward direction. The servo motor will move at an angle of 120 degrees for 5 secs. It means the lid of the dustbin will remain open for 5 secs and then it will close. As shown in the block diagram, Figure 3 consists of two ultrasonic sensors. The second ultrasonic sensor is placed on the top cover of the dustbin. The second ultrasonic sensor named as US2 sensor will continuously monitor the garbage level in the dustbin and will display the level on LCD and update real-time data on the cloud also. It is mounted on the back side of the top cover of the dustbin which is immobile. Only the first half of the cover will open. The level of the dustbin was adjusted according to the height of the dustbin in cm. An aluminum board placed inside the dustbin is used to segregate the dry and wet waste. When the wet waste is placed on the board, the current will start to flow and the motor will rotate in the clockwise direction, i.e. the wet section of the dustbin. It will move in an anticlockwise direction in case of dry waste. GSM and GPS tracking module attached with Arduino UNO board and comes in active mode when the dustbin level is full. It will send the signal directly to the MCD office to vacant the dustbin. This message also consists of the location of the dustbin. ESP8266 Wi-Fi module is attached to Arduino to connect it to the Internet. The data gathered by the sensor is directly uploaded to the Blynk cloud or web server of the MCD.

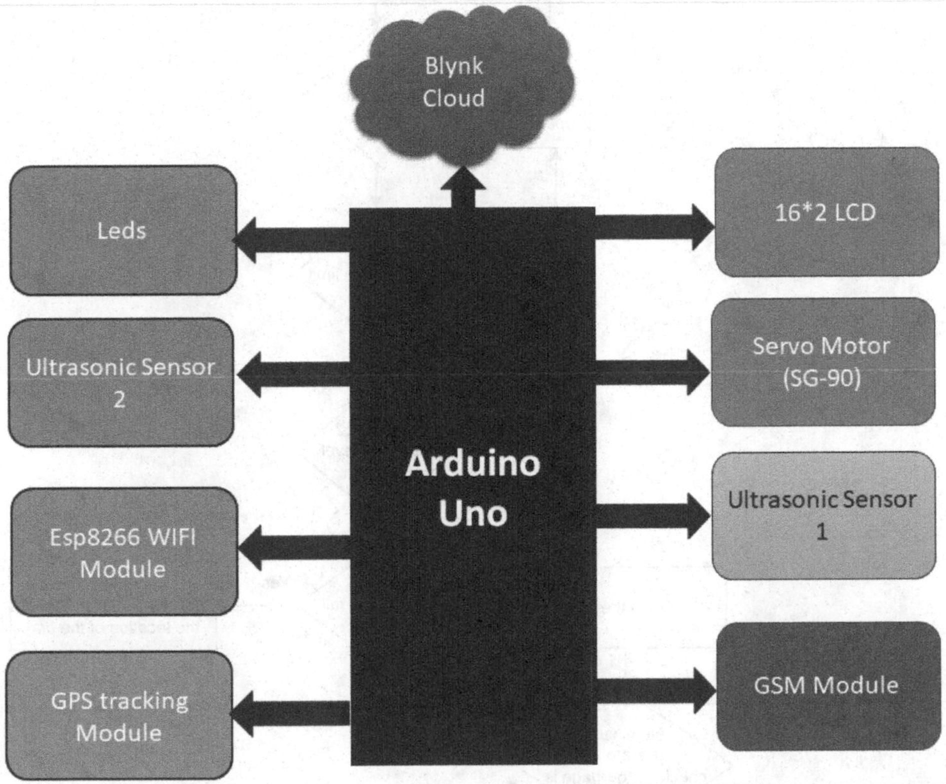

Figure 8: Block diagram.

4.1. Flow Chart

As the power turns on, sensors mounted in the circuits will get activated. If the person enters the range of the sensor, lid of the dustbin gets open with the help of a servo motor. The lid will remain open until the person is throwing the waste material in the dustbin. The waste had been detected by the sensor either it is wet or dry waste. Dustbin has segregated into two sections dry or wet. If the waste material is wet, then the motor will rotate in an anti-clockwise direction and throw it into the wet section. If it is dry, then move in a clockwise direction, i.e. dry section. Simultaneously, it will monitor the level and display on LCD as well as on the cloud or server of MCD.

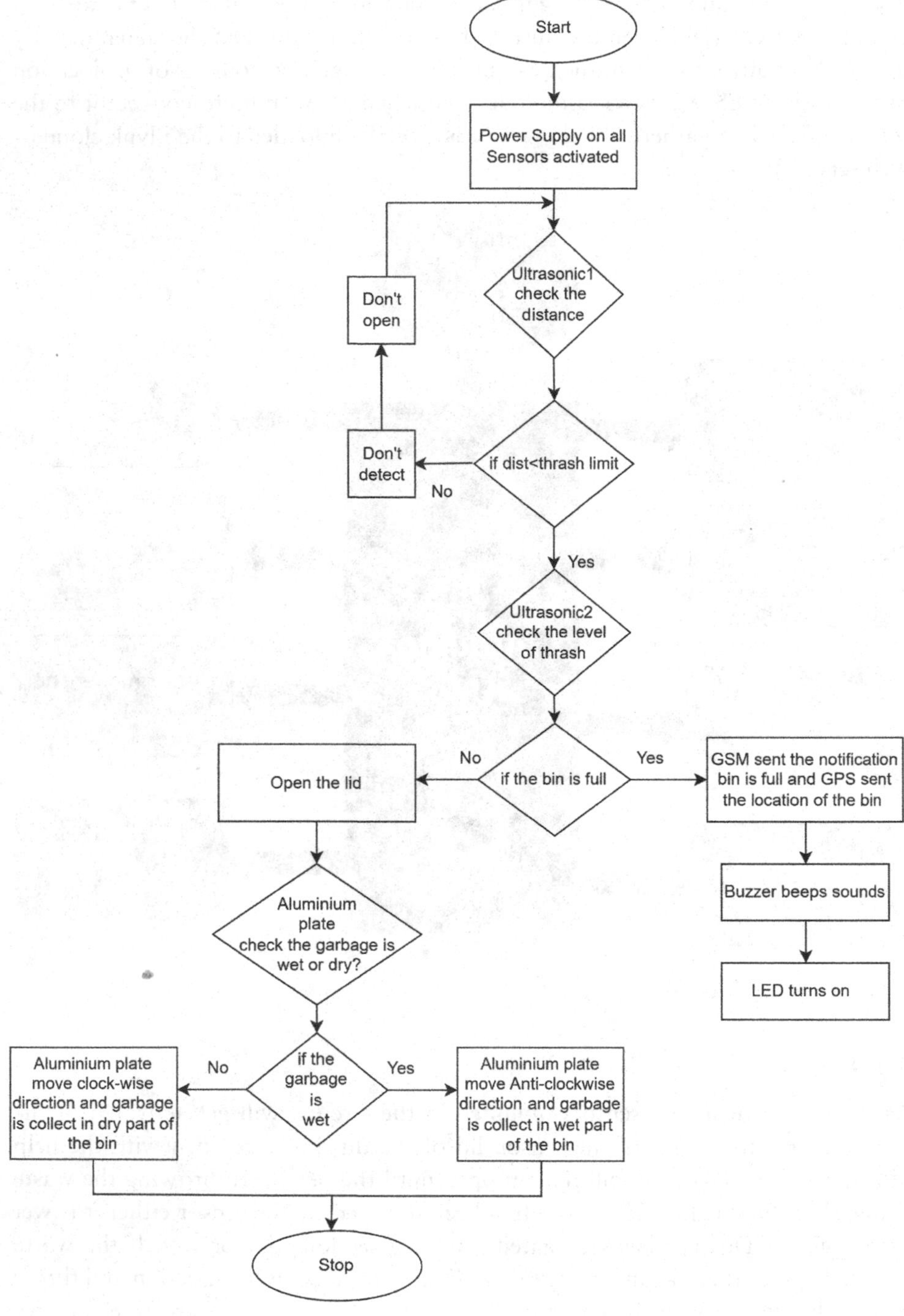

Figure 9: *Flow chart.*

5. Results

A model has been designed as per the proposed methodology as shown in Figure 10.

5.1. Designed Model

This model comprises two ultrasonic sensors. One is mounted in the front of the dustbin used to find the presence of a person. When a person comes near the lid will open and another sensor will monitor the level continuously and will update the Blynk cloud and LCD at regular intervals.

5.2. Working of Model

The working of the designed model is shown in Figures 10 and 11. LCD is used to display the garbage level in the dustbin.

5.3. Notifications and Alerts

When the dustbin is full, it will generate various alerts and notifications.

Figure 10: Designed and working of smart dustbin model.

Figure 11: Dustbin level (%).

1. **Email Notification:** It will notify via Email when the dustbin will cross the threshold limit as shown in Figure 12. E-mail reminders are set at an interval of 24 Hrs if no action is taken by the MCD.

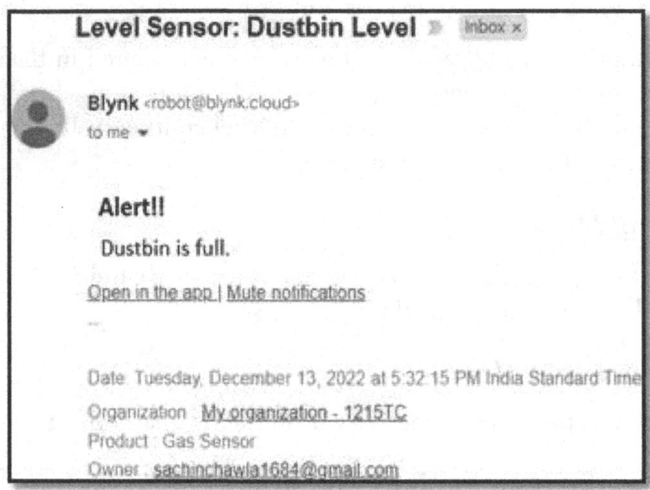

Figure 12: Email alert when the dustbin is full.

2. **Mobile Alerts:** A notification will send to the mobile phone on the registered number.

5.4. Output on Webserver

The output of the dustbin in the form of real-time data will display on the Blynk cloud server as shown in Figures 13 and 14. Same it will update on the Mobile app of Blynk Cloud.

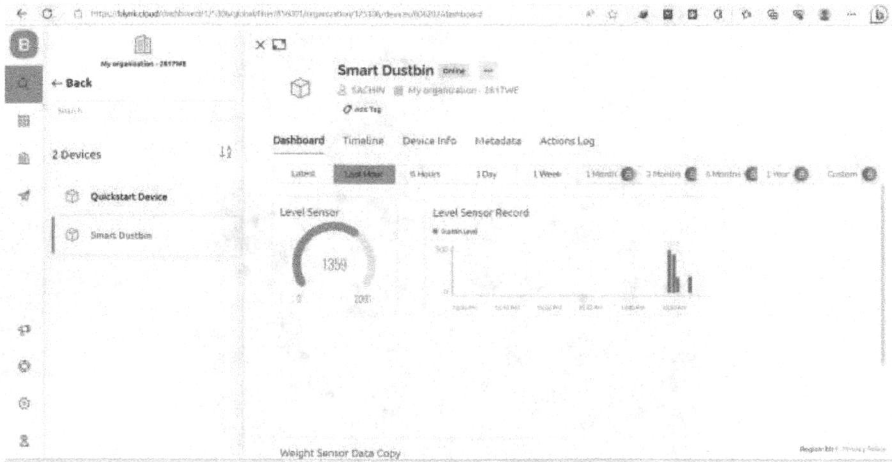

Figure 13: Webserver of MCD.

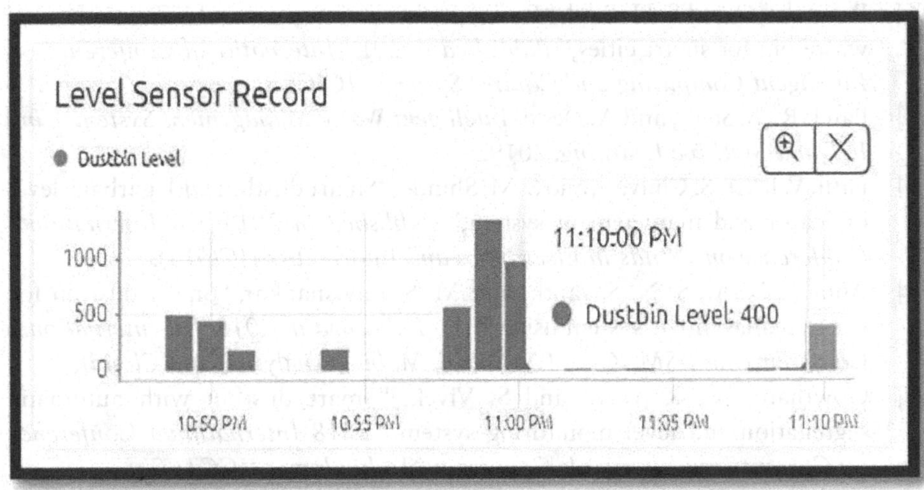

Figure 14: Dustbins level record.

6. Conclusion and Future Scope

Overall, the product design was somewhere solving the problems related to waste management. New innovative features tried to implement to make it more efficient. Still, there are a lot of possibilities to make it more smart by the addition of AI and ML techniques with IoT. This dustbin should be capable to get a record of the person using it to throw waste with the help of an RFID system. Encourage people to throw waste into the dustbins and provide some rewards in the form of coupons and point.

References

[1] Mulla, N. S. and S. Sanghavi, "IoT-based smart garbage management system using ultrasonic sensors," *2021 International Conference on Emerging Trends in Engineering, Science and Technology (ICETEST)*, IEEE, pp. 1–6, 2021.

[2]] Patil, P., V. Mane, and P. Jagdale, "IoT-based smart dustbin for effective waste management," *2021 International Conference on Automation, Computational and Technology Management (ICACTM)*, 2021.

[3] Ahire, S. and V. Kadu, "Smart dustbin system using IoT: a review," *2020 International Conference on Emerging Trends in Engineering, Science and Technology (ICETEST)*, 2020.

[4] Kumar, N., S. Saini, and V. Kumar, "Smart dustbin using IoT: a step towards a smart city," *Int. J. Adv. Res. Comput. Sci.*, vol. 11, no. 4, pp. 160–165, 2020.

[5] Patil, S. A., A. R. Borate, and A. D. Jadhav, "Smart dustbin with waste segregation and level monitoring system," *Published in 2019 International Conference on Recent Trends in Electrical, Electron- ics Computer Science (RTECS).*

[6] Ramteke, S. and S. H. Patil, "Design and implementation of IoT based smart waste bin for smart cities," *Published in 2019 International Conference on Intelligent Computing and Control Systems (ICICCS).*

[7] Patel, R., S. Shah, and A. Desai, *Intelligent Waste Management System using IoT and Machine Learning*, 2019.

[8] Patil, V. R., A. S. Chavan, and S. M. Shinde, "Smart dustbin with garbage level indicator and management system," *Published in 2019 3rd International Conference on Trends in Electronics and Informatics (ICOEI).*

[9] Adnani, N. A., S. N. Savanth, and M. S. Ravishankar, "Smart dustbin for waste management system using IoT," *Published in 2018 3rd International Conference on I-SMAC (IoT in Social, Mobile, Analytics, and Cloud).*

[10] Gowtham, N., R. Ravi, and S. Vivek, "Smart dustbin with automatic segregation and level monitoring system," *2018 International Conference on Current Trends towards Converging Technologies (ICCTCT).*

[11] Raza, A., K. Shafique, and M. Majeed, "IoT-based smart garbage system for efficient waste management," *2018 International Conference on Frontiers of Information Technology (FIT)*, IEEE, pp. 200–205, 2018.

[12] Saha, H. N., S. Gon, A. Nayak, S. Kundu, and S. Moitra, "IOT based garbage monitoring and clearance alert system," *2018 IEEE 9th Annual Information Technology, Elec- tronics and Mobile Communication Conference (IEMCON).*

[13] Yusof, N. M., M. F. Zulkifli, N. Y. A. Mohd Yusof, and A. A. Azman, "Smart waste bin with real-time monitoring system," *Int. J. Eng. Technol.*, vol. 7, no. 2.29, pp. 725–729, 2018.

[14] Vinoth Kumar, S., T. Senthil Kumaran, A. Krishna Kumar, and M. Mathapati, "Smart garbage monitoring and clearance system using the internet of things," *2017 IEEE International Conference on Smart Technologies and Management for Computing, Communication, Controls, Energy and Materials (ICSTM).*

26. Multi-Objective Gravitational Search Algorithm Based Clustering Scheme in VANET

Hunny Pahuja[1], Shippu Sachdeva[2], and Manoj Sindhwani[2]

[1]*Department of Electronics and Communication Engineering, KIET Group of Institutions, Delhi-NCR, Ghaziabad, India*
[2]*Lovely Faculty of Technology and Sciences, Lovely Professional University, Phagwara, Punjab, India*

Abstract: Recent advancement in automobile has measured the efficiency of street vehicles. However, vehicles support multiple facilities to enhance the quality of life, but day by day growing number of tourists arises a few are issues, like accidents, in which many of persons lose their life or are wounded. Apart from this, other unwanted events such as traffic jams help create waste of time and fuel. However, driving issues and occurring of these unwanted roads events cannot be completely stopped but could be minimised by using the smart transportation systems. In VANETs, no one routing approach is efficient to outperform in all scenarios that pose challenge to researchers in terms to design an efficient routing algorithm. In order to fill this gap, this paper introduces a novel cluster-based routing approach with gravitational search optimization algorithm intend to escalate the routing recitation by reducing the delays in the challenging environment of VANETs. The proposed approach has optimised the network architecture, forming the long living cluster, in order to increase the connectivity and to trim down the broadcast storm problem by controlling the flooding process.

Keywords: Cluster head, cluster member, vehicular communication, gravitational search algorithm.

1. Introduction

A wireless network infrastructure comprises of static and wired gateways with a contact radius of their own in which mobile hosts (nodes) could communicate with each other. However, when travelling, nodes could depart a base station network and also could join some station to begin their contact with the destination node, known as handoff, but this design could have two disadvantages, high operational costs and restricted bandwidth [4]. A network device, hybrid network, has merged the characteristics of infrastructure and ad hoc networks in order to boost the bandwidth issue, but the architecture of this network also needs that every node provide service on network infrastructure, the expense of which may still be very large. In addition to the cost problem, it would be difficult to sustain connectivity in a scenario where the network infrastructure might not be accessible. The VANET structure is shown in Figure 1.

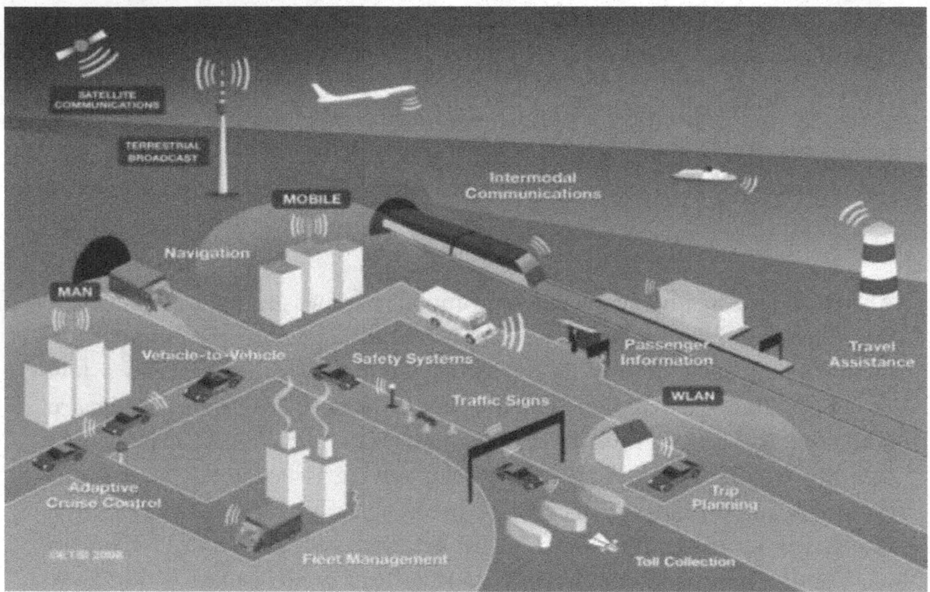

Figure 1: VANET architecture.

VANET is gaining popularity in the recent technologies because of its important characteristics and applications.

1.1. VANET Characterstics

There are numerous characteristics of VANET [1, 2]. A few of the outstanding features of VANETs [3,6] are defined as follows:

- **Dynamic Topology:** With VANET, the motion of the vehicle is restricted to road patterns. By using the roadway geometry with a fair precision, interaction with the people of the vehicles could be projected. Although it is difficult to forecast the mobility pattern of vehicles due to its high speed.
- **Frequent Disconnections:** In VANETs, the network is dynamic in nature. This leads in dramatic increases in on-road vehicle density. As differing network density factors in disconnections that differ with density [4,5], vehicular density has an impact on network efficiency.
- **Traffic Scenarios:** The contact environments that VANETs are focused on situations of highway or city traffic. Owing to the vehicle speed contrasted to the highway scenario, vehicle mobility is much more complicated in the

city scenario. Owing to more vehicular density, the contact overheads are often more in the city scenario, while in the highway situation, the overhead contact is less.

- **Large Scale network:** In VANETs, the network size dependent on the amount of road connections. The transport infrastructure is very complex in urban scenarios, so VANET's scalability is more noticeable due to greater vehicular density.
- **Adequate Storage:** Rather than limited storage, vehicular nodes have relatively large storage capacity accessible in small hand-held systems that are used as nodes in other kinds of ad hoc networks.
- **No Power Constraints:** The battery in vehicles provides the OBU with constant flow for storage where RSUs could also be linked to a continuous power supply, so in VANETs, there are no power limit problems relative to limited battery power in another forms of ad hoc networks.

2. Clustering in VANET

The term used in wireless communication over the past few years [7,8] is clustering. Clustering is defined as the gathering of various sensor nodes centered on certain laws. Clustering aims to make networks more stable and flexible. Using cluster analysis helps to build clusters. The cluster head (CH) and cluster members (CMs) are the primary clustering individuals. Usually, every cluster has one appointed head or chief, identified as the CH, chosen by other member nodes or CMs. CH has become the commander of all the other cluster nodes and is responsible for managing the cluster. Usually, each CM may be selected as CH, but nodes with increased features are more likely to be CH in a few priority [9] systems. At regular time intervals, these CMs transmit their data to CHs.

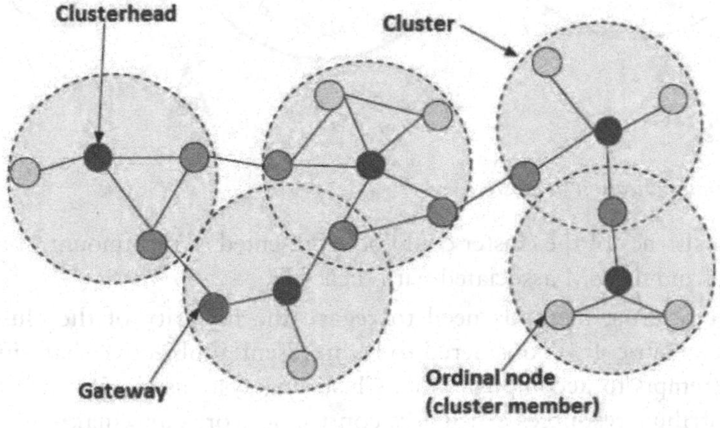

Figure 2: Basic cluster model.

Figure 2 represents the clustering structure in VANET. In clustering, there are two forms of communication: inter-cluster and intra-cluster communication. A CM is called intra-cluster communication when communicating within a cluster [10]. In order to help link clusters along, some clustering methods include a border node or a gateway node. A CH records the information from its CMs and interacts with other CHs and gateways to produce data to the destination, which is termed as inter-cluster communication.

Clustering increases efficient message broadcasting and transmission. Clustering eliminates overhead signalling since the connections within the same cluster between the vehicular nodes are more secure. Clustering improves the usage of limited resources, like bandwidth, and enhances data transmission performance. The clustering method is useful in network management in large-scale complex and distributed networks by breaking the network into small segments that are scalable. The benefits of using clustering systems are reducing the amount of messages transferred within the network, minimising V2R or V2V communication congestion, increasing network scalability by creating small sections of the network, minimising problems with contention and hidden station and enhancing the effectiveness of the routing service. In addition to these, advantages such as handling evolutionary nature in topology and volume are also essential for the VANET system. For all clusters, the cluster size is not the same and the difference relies on the wireless communication device's routing path.

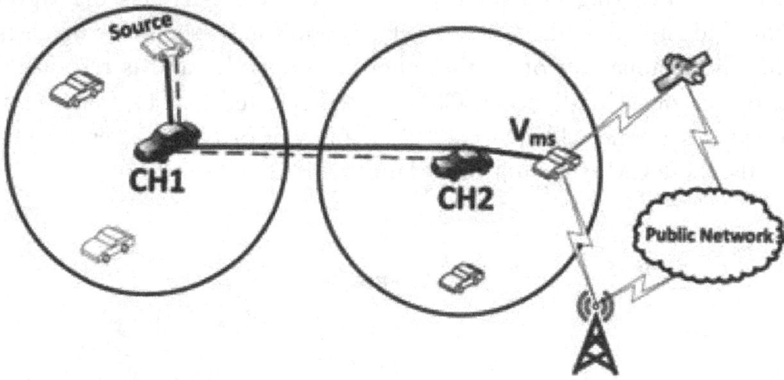

Figure 3: Communication in clusters.

The consistency of the cluster could be represented as the amount of times the CHs change and the CM associated with their CH.

Many clustering methods need to regard the integrity of the cluster as a performance metric. It is considered to be an essential objective that any cluster protocol attempts to accomplish [11]. Clustering systems significantly simplify routing, distribute resources efficiently, control networks and make the network secure for every node in the cluster. In order to boost network ability and increase spatial channel retention, CHs help promote inter-cluster and intra-cluster transmission. In VANET, not only does a successful clustering method have low overhead cluster management but it also offers stability during dynamic topology control.

2.1. Advantages of Clustering in VANET

Hybrid existing methods are CBR protocols that guarantee a highly stable network. There are some benefits [12]:

- Increase power ratio of packets
- Stop Overhead Routing
- Less network traffic could be reduced to cluster head and gateway nodes and inter-cluster communication.
- Scalability of contact for broad set of nodes
- Support with path construction and reducing of routes
- Minimum knowledge in the system that is processed and transmitted.

Table 1: Clustering algorithms.

Application	Name of Algorithm
General Purpose	• k-hop • Fuzzy-logic-Based Approach • Mean Collection Time Clustering • Aggregate Local Mobility
Routing	• Passive Clustering • Mobile Infrastructure in VANET • Cellular Automata Clustering • Vehicular Passive Clustering
Security	• Vehicle Weighted Clustering Approach • Clustering-based Public Key Approach
QoS	• Cluster Configuration Method • Stability-based Clustering Approach
Traffic Safety	• Cluster-based Risk-Aware Cooperative Collision Avoidance

3. Gravitational Search Optimisation Algorithm

The GSA method uses the principle of Newtonian physics by the effect of gravity by communicating agents with one another. These forces are used as objects and are assessed by their masses [13] for their efficiency. The overall GSA method was managed by changing the inertial and gravitational mass under which a response is described by each mass. The optimal search space approach was then taken as the hardest mass since it absorbed the remaining masses. Masses obey the Newtonian laws of gravitation and motion as mentioned below [14].

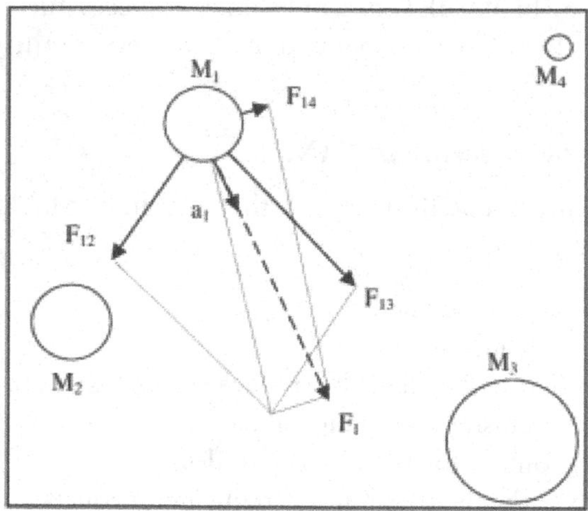

Figure 4: Mass accelerate towards result force.

- **Law of gravity:** In the course of the centre line, either of the charged objects in the universe exerts pressures on each other. The force one mass imposes on the other is, as per the gravitational law of motion, the result of the gravitational constant and the proportion of the correlation among two masses to the function of the speed around them. Other features, such as the chemical composition of the material or physical condition and the intermediate substance, are not related to gravity [15]. The method simply may convey this law of gravity:

$$F = \frac{GM_1M_2}{R^2} \tag{1.1}$$

- Here gravity is expressed by F, the gravitational constant is expressed by G, the inertial mass of the charged objects is represented by M_1 and M_2 each and the Euclid distance among the two particles is R.
- **Law of motion:** Newton's law of motion reviews the movement used for this analysis. The velocity of any mass with a fixed perceived time is strongly reliant on its past state. It was calculated in various measurement times by the amount of its previous velocity and the change in velocity. Shift in the velocity of acceleration per time of analysis.

As per Newton's second law, when the force F is implemented to an object that object shown below:

$$A = \frac{F}{M} \tag{1.2}$$

Here a is the agents' acceleration, F is the load exerted and M is the object's mass. When considering a process with N agents (masses), the location of the ith agent could be described by

$$X_i = \left(x_i^1\ x_i^2\ \ldots,x_i^d,\ldots,x_i^n\right), for\, i = 1,2,\ldots,N \tag{1.3}$$

Here, x^i_d indicates the location of the ith agent in the dth dimension and n is the dimension of search space. At a specific time t, the force acting on mass i from mass j is equal to

$$F_{ij}^d\left(t\right) = \frac{G\left(t\right)M_{pi}\left(t\right)M_{aj}\left(t\right)}{R_{ij}\left(t\right)+\in} \tag{1.4}$$

In which the active gravitational mass associated with agent j in time t is Maj(t), Mpi(t) is the passive gravitational mass associated with agent I G(t) is a gravitational constant at time t, ε is a sensible choice and Rij(t) is the distance among agents I and j from the Euclidian's. Candidate solutions to problems are regarded in this method as objects whose efficiency is defined by their mass quality, all of which attracts one another in the force of gravity that induces objects to shift globally against objects of heavier masses. The technique is focused on Newton's law of motion, guided by natural gravitational law and the movement of masses in the universe. In order to maximise its efficacy, all the methods utilised in the methodology were as follows [16].

- In order to be capable of the method, the initial amounts of the gravitational equations (Go, al, ε) and the iterations counter are set.
- The initial version is selected randomly and comprises of N agents, with the above conservation equations the location from each agent [20-23].
- The preceding process is repeated after the random initial community and locations for every agent are generated.

3.1. Proposed Work

So in this proposed work, for evaluation of the performance of the existing scheme for numerous branch lanes highway scenario for fixed amount of vehicles is used. Also to model and applied gravitational search optimisation method focused on designed fitness function for cluster head selection is implemented.

The two roads arising from the major highway will be considered in the suggested strategies. The proposed approach of the cluster head will recognise the optimisation of the gravitational search to select the node as the cluster head. In the following manner, the system worked.

So every RSU will televise the vehicles with a periodic BEACON message. In the JOIN request, when a vehicle collects a BEACON message, it decides to send its destination lane, velocity, and position to the RSU. For instance, if the vehicle has to keep moving to the left lane, [1 0 0] will be send, if it is starting to move to the same lane throughout its journey, [0 1 0] will be forward, and [0 0 1] for the right lane will be forward to the RSU. Every RSU generates the adjacency matrix after obtaining the JOIN requests and quantifies the inter-connectivity by each vehicle.

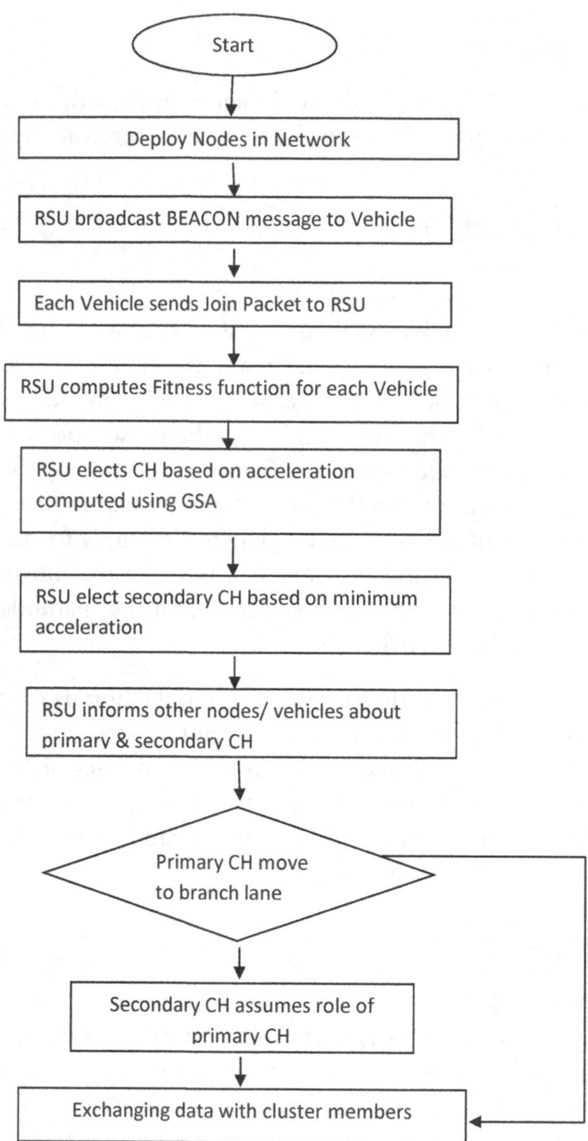

Figure 5: *Flowchart of proposed work.*

Under the Gravitational Search optimization technique, RSU then calculates acceleration to every vehicle. The acceleration is proportion of gravitational mass to the pressure generated by all the operatives. Three components will focus on the fitness function used in the GSA: degree of connectivity, variation of average velocity and distance to the destination lane. It is viewed to fit the node with a greater degree of connectivity, lower variation from angular distance and longer distance to the destination lane. Once the primary cluster head is chosen, the secondary CH is picked by the RSU as the node with a fitness level next to the major cluster head. The RSU then notifies the nodes about the cluster head and the secondary cluster. In addition, RSU will notify primary and secondary CH about the node IDs connecting to the various roads so that no additional overhead is generated to notify the cluster head around the same if these devices leave the cluster.

Even so, if the head of the cluster or the secondary head of the cluster has to exit the cluster, it is possible for either node to make the assumption its position. Then it is possible to appoint the left cluster head or secondary cluster head.

4. Results and Simulation

In this section, outputs of the experiments performed are given in graphical form along with discussion of results.

Overhead: It is the extra control packets received at the receiver generally for synchronisation purpose.

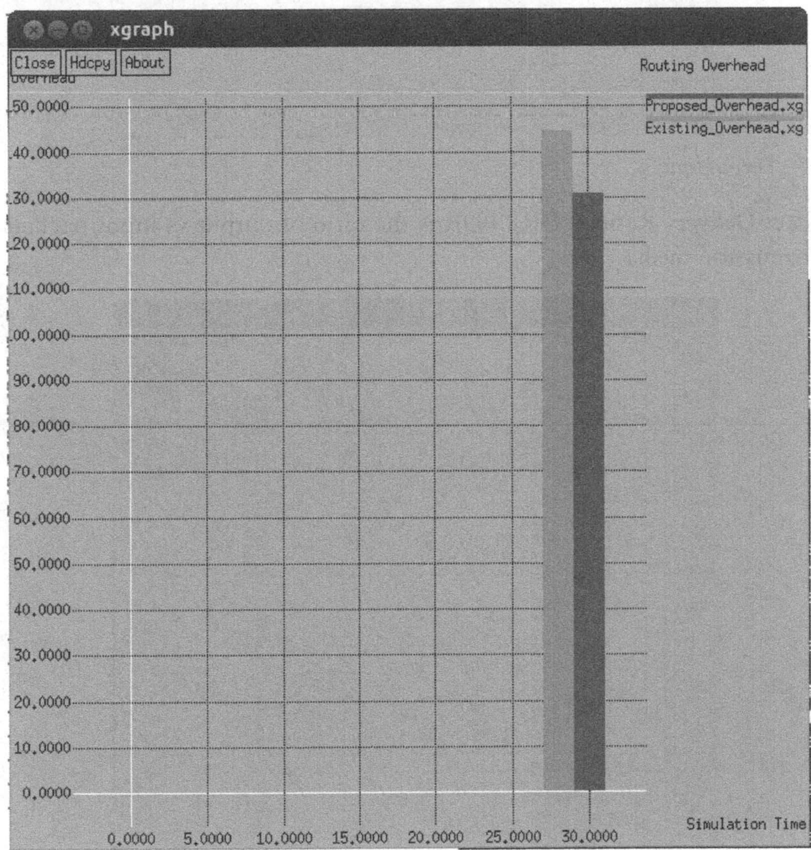

Figure 6: Routing overhead.

Throughput: Throughput is the output packet received when compared with input flow of packets.

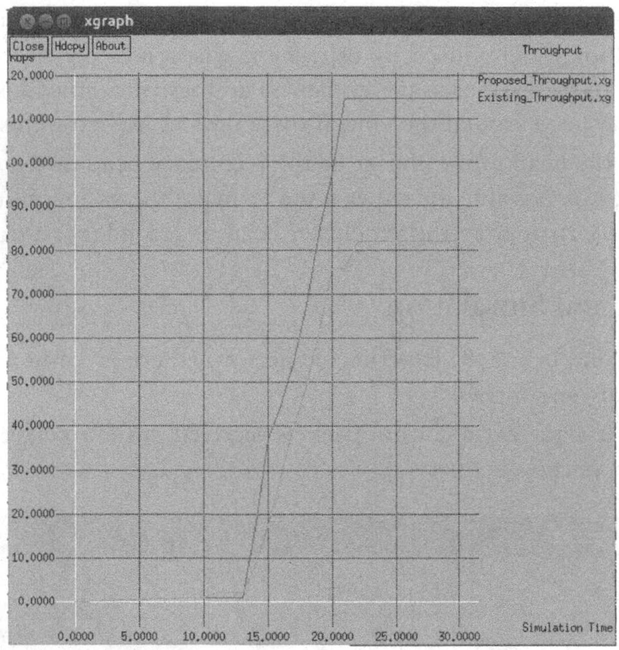

Figure 7: Throughput.

Packet Delivery Ratio (PDR): PDR is the ratio of output vs input packets over the transmission media.

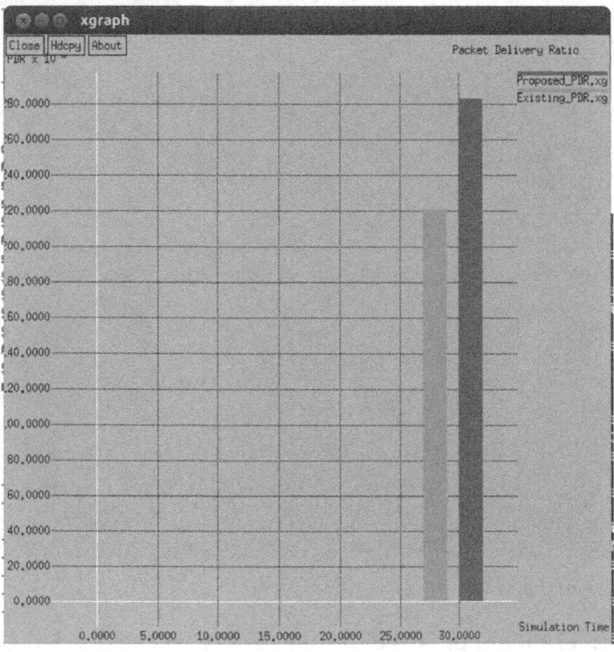

Figure 8: Packet delivery ratio.

5. Conclusion

The proposed work is a noble routing approach having the main parameter as cluster stability. The improved parameters are throughput, reduction of overhead, time delay and delivery ratio. Cluster head coordinates the whole activities and increases the efficiency of the network. A scenario of a highway is taken in consideration, where CH control the activities and allow the cluster members to pass the packets in the vehicular environment. One of the advanced GSA routing algorithms, packet delivery ratio with reduced end-to- end delays and normalised routing loads, to enhance throughput.

References

[1] Levente B. and J.-P. Hubaux, "Stimulating cooperation in self-organizing mobile ad hoc networks," *Mob. Networks Appl.*, vol. 8, no. 5, pp. 579–592, 2003.

[2] Singh, A. and R. D. K. Madan, "A relative study of MANET and VANET: its applications, broadcasting approaches and challenging issues," *International Conference on Computer Science and Information Technology, Advances in Networks and Communications*, pp. 627–632,2011.

[3] Saif Al-Sultan, M. and H. Z. Ali, Hussien, "A comprehensive survey on vehicular ad hoc network," J. Network Comput. Appl., vol. 37, pp. 380–392, 2014.

[4] Ghassan, M. T. A., M. Ali, and S. M. Senouci, "Current trends in vehicular ad hoc networks," *Proceedings of UBIROADS Workshop*, 2007.

[5] Pinar, Y., Z. Abduljabbar, A. H. Omar, *Wireless Sensor Networks (WSNs)*, IEEE 2016.

[6] Dwivedi, S. and D. Rajni, "Review in trust and vehicle scenario in VANET," *Int. J. Future Gener. Commun. Networking*, vol. 9, no. 5, pp. 305–314, 2016.

[7] Bala, R. and C. Rama, "Performance analysis of topology based routing in a VANET," *Advances in Computing, Communications and Informatics (ICACCI)*, pp. 2180–2184, 2014.

[8] Saleh, Y., M. Mousavi, and F. Mahmood, "Vehicular ad hoc networks (VANETs): challenges and perspectives," *International Conference On*, IEEE, pp. 761–766, 2006.

[9] Rashedi, E. H. and S. Saryazdi, "GSA: a gravitational search algorithm," *Inf. Sci.*, vol. 179, no. 13, pp. 2232–2248, 2009.

[10] Amarjeet, S. and D. Kusum, "Novel hybridized variants of gravitational search algorithm for constraint optimization," *Int. J. Swarm Intell.*, vol. 3, no. 1, 2017.

[11] Li, J. and N. Dong, "Gravitational search algorithm with a new technique," *13th International Conference on Computational Intelligence and Security (CIS)*, 2017.

[12] Amiya, B., T. Sahoo, and K. Soni, *Application of Gravitational Search Algorithm in Optimization of Microstrip Antenna at 5 GHz*, IEEE, 2017.

[13] Vijay F. and E. Karthikeyan, "Estimation of influential parameter using gravitational search optimization algorithm for soccer," *ASTES J.*, vol. 5, no. 3, pp. 340–348, 2020.

[14] Nazmul, S. and A. Hojjat, *Applications of Gravitational Search Algorithm in Engineering*, pp. 981–990, 2016.

[15] Shahwani, H., T. D. Bui, J. P. Jeong, and J. Shin, "A stable clustering algorithm based on affinity propagation for VANETs," *19th International Conference on Advanced Communication Technology (ICACT)*, 2017.

[16] Marjan Kuchaki, R. and B. Mohammad, "Using gravitational search algorithm for finding near-optimal base station location in two-tiered WSNs," *Int. J. Mach. Learn. Comput.*, vol. 2, no. 4, 2012.

[17] Ing. Mokhlis, H., H. A. Illias, J. J. Aman, "Gravitational search algorithm and selection approach for optimal distribution network configuration based on daily photovoltaic and loading variation," *J. Appl. Math.*, pp. 1–11, 2015.

[18] Cheng, X., B. Huang, and W. Cheng, "Stable clustering for VANETs on highways," *IEEE/ACM Symposium on Edge Computing (SEC)*, 2018.

[19] Khayat, G., C. H. Mavromoustakis, and E. Pallis, "VANET clustering based on weighted trusted cluster head selection," *International Wireless Communications and Mobile Computing (IWCMC)*, 2020.

[20] Talib, M. S. and I. N. Hassan, "A center-based stable evolving clustering algorithm with grid partitioning and extended mobility features for VANETs," *IEEE Access*, pp. 1–1, 2020.

[21] Singh, B. and H. K. Verma, "EMM: Extended matching market based scheduling for big data platform hadoop," *Multimedia Tools Appl.*, vol. 81, no. 24, pp. 34823–34847, 2022.

[22] Singh, B. and H. K. Verma, "Dawn of big data with Hadoop and machine learning," *Mach. Learn. Data Sci.: Fundam. Appl.*, pp. 47–65, 2022.

[23] Virdi, H. S. and B. Singh, "Analysis of the software code based upon coupling in the software," *2012 Third International Conference on Computing, Communication and Networking Technologies (ICCCNT'12)*, IEEE, pp. 1–4, 2012.

27. Hybrid Approach to Place Wind Distributed Generators in Distribution System

Babita Gupta[1, 2], Suresh Kumar Sudabattula[1], Sachin Mishra[1], and Nagaraju Dharavat[1]

[1]*School of Electronics and Electrical Engineering Lovely Professional University, Phagwara, Punjab, India*
[2]*BVRIT HYDERABAD College of Engineering for Women, Telangana, India*

Abstract: Rapid increase of demand and environmental concerns it is viable to use renewable energy resources in distribution network (DN). In this manuscript, a combined approach of bat algorithm and voltage stability factor (VSF) concept is applied to place wind distributed generators (WDGs) in DN. Further, VSF is applied for identifying the location and BAT algorithm for determining sizes of WDGs. Also, the aim of this article is improving the loss reduction and voltage profile. Different cases are taken, and it is studied on 33 bus DN. Finally, from the obtained results noticed that placing optimum WDGs in best locations improves overall performance of DN.

Keywords: Wind DG, distribution network, BAT algorithm, voltage profile.

1. Introduction

Increased load demand and environmental pollution are the major challenges in nowadays scenario. Further, reduction of coal and fuel reserves shows the significance of renewable energy sources usage. So, in this regard an efficient utilisation of natural sources and generate power from these sources is the alternative for the above-mentioned problem. Finally, from all the renewable sources, solar and wind is the most commonly available sources throughout globe. But, power generation from these depends on climatic conditions. Further, connected these sources to the distribution network (DN) poses some other problems like voltage and power quality issues. But, effective usage of these sources improves the loss reduction, power and voltage quality of DN [1].

In the state of art, authors solved DG allocation problem (DGAP) in DN using various optimisation techniques (OT). In Ref [2] authors used iterative search approach to solve DGAP in DN. Also, objective of this to minimise cost and loss. In Ref [3], DGAP is solved and further different constraints of DN are taken in the formulation. In Ref [4], ABC algorithm is used to solve DGAP in DN. In Ref [5], DE algorithm is presented to solve DGAP in DN. Further, voltage stability is the objective of this approach. In Ref [6], authors proposed IA method for solving multiple DGAP in DN. Also, this approach is cross checked with other prominent methods. In Ref [7], authors solved wind DGAP in DN. Further, uncertainties are taken care before placing these sources in DN. In Ref [8], two-step algorithm is presented to solve wind DGAP in DN. In Ref [9] wind DGAP is solved and objective is loss minimisation.

From the existing methods, authors solved the above problem and producing satisfactory results. In this article, an integrated approach of VSF, and bat algorithm is presented to solve wind DGAP in DN. Further, the main motivation of this method is to improve voltage profile, VSI and minimise system loss to reasonable extent.

The rest of the paper structure as follows. Problem formulation and VSF for wind DG placement is given in Sections 2 and 3. Next, BAT algorithm is used for finding best sizes of WDGs is explained in section 4. Finally, article important findings and conclusion are given in rest of the sections.

2. Problem Formulation and Objective

Placement of WDGs in DN with an aim of reducing loss, improving VSI and voltage profile. The formulae for both are given in Eq. (1) and Eq. (2).

$$P_{Tloss} = \sum_{k=1}^{nb} P_{loss}(\mathrm{m}, \mathrm{m}+1) \tag{1}$$

$$VSI_l = |V_m|^4 - 4[P_l r_{lm} + Q_l x_{lm}]|V_m|^2 - 4[P_l x_{lm} - Q_l r_{lm}]^2 \tag{2}$$

Different constraints of DN is satisfied those are given below.

2.1. *Constraints*

Power balance

$$P_{slack} + \sum_{m=1}^{N_{WDG}} P_{WDG,\mathrm{m}} = \sum_{k=1}^{nb} P_{loss}(\mathrm{m}) + \sum_{m=1}^{N} P_D \tag{3}$$

Voltage Profile

$$V_{\min} \leq |V_m| \leq V_{\max} \tag{4}$$

Thermal

$$I_m \leq I_m^{\max} \tag{5}$$

DG sizing

$$P_{WDG,\min} \leq P_{WDG,\mathrm{m}} \leq P_{WDG,\max} \tag{6}$$

Formulated problem accepts all the constraints than only obtained solution accepted.

3. VSF for WDG Allocation

VSF is applied to identify the desired locations for placement of WDGs. First, calculate VSF for all buses and buses with less VSF are taken. The VSF formulae is given by [10].

$$VSF_{n+1} = 2V_{n+1} - V_n \tag{7}$$

The VSF graph is given Figure 1.

4. Algorithmic Steps for WDGAP in DN

Bat algorithm is implemented by Yang X.S [11]. It is established on echolocations of bats. Further, steps for wind DGAP are given as follows

1. Run the load flow
2. Initialise all the parameters [12].
3. Start the iterative process and solutions updated using below Eq. (8) and Eq. (9)

$$Q(k) = Q_{\min imum} + (Q_{\min imum} - Q_{Maximum}) * rand \tag{8}$$

$$V(k) = V(k) + (sol(k) - best)Q(k) \tag{9}$$

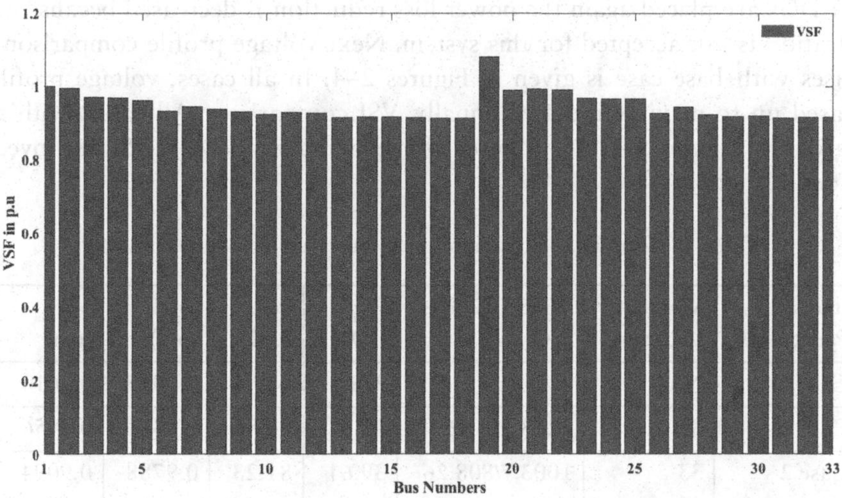

Figure 1: VSF for 33 bus system.

4. Solutions (WDG sizes and power loss) are better update them
5. Upto maximum iterations
6. Otherwise repeat from step 3
7. Update the final solution.

5. Results and Findings

The method is developed in MATLAB and studied on IEEE 33 bus. Also, the data of this system is considered from [13]. First, calculate VSF and found the locations of WDGs. The best locations are 33, 17, 14 and sizes at these are found out using BAT algorithm. Different cases are studied to evaluate the prominence of the method and same are tabulated in Table 1.

Case1: Base case

Case 2: One Wind DG

Case 3: Two Wind DGs

Case 4: Three Wind DGs

In base case wind, DGs are not placed the power loss is 211 kW and voltage profile is 0.9037 p.u. After one wind DG is placed, the power is minimised to 91 kW and voltage profile is enhanced to 0.9311 p.u. Also, loss reduction percentage is improved as compared to base case that is 56.87% and voltage profile improved percentage is 2.943%. Next, in case 2, two wind DGs are considered and placed in DN. The power loss is enhanced to 39.61 kW, and voltage profile is upgraded to 0.9788 p.u. In view of percentage improvement of loss and voltage profile are 81.22% and 7.67%. Further, in case 3, three wind DGs are considered. The power loss after placement is 30.47 kW, and voltage profile is upgraded to 0.9846 p.u. In percentage comparison, it is improved to 85.56% and 8.22%. Finally, in overall analysis, maximum loss reduction is achieved with 3 wind DGs allocation. But, 4 DGs are placed again the power loss reduction is decreased because more penetration is not accepted for this system. Next voltage profile comparison for all cases with base case is given in Figures 2–4. In all cases, voltage profile is increased up to maximum extent. Finally, VSI comparison (All cases) with case 1 is given in Figures 5–7. At all buses after placing wind DGs, VSI improved to considerable extent.

Table 1: Wind DGs allocation for 33 bus system (various cases).

Items/ Particulars	**Wind DG Location**	**Wind DG Sizes P/Q**	**P_{loss} (kW)**	**$\%P_{loss}$ Red**	**V_{min} (p.u)**	**VSI_{min} (p.u)**
Case 1	NA	NA	211	NA	0.9037	0.6610
Case 1	33	1253.1/1019.9	91.01	56.86	0.9311	0.7456
Case 2	33 14	1003.7/808.26	39.61	81.23	0.9788	0.9094
Case 3	33 17 14	1409.6/1182.3	30.47	85.55	0.9846	0.9311

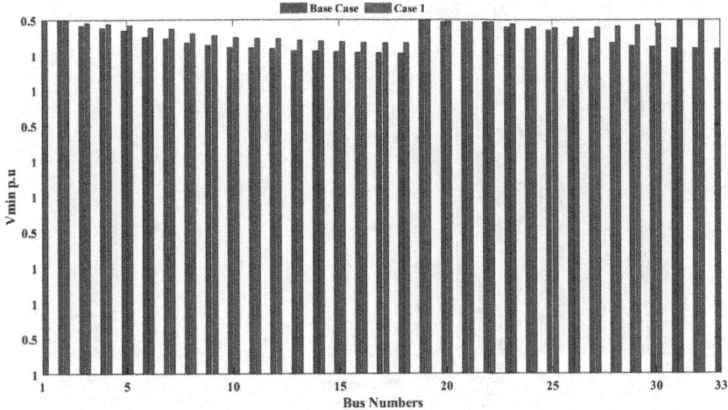

Figure 2: *Voltage profile comparison for base case and case 1.*

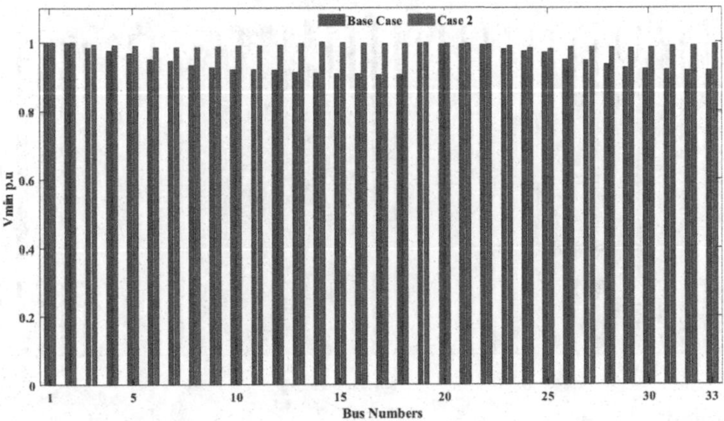

Figure 3: *Voltage profile comparison for base case and case 2.*

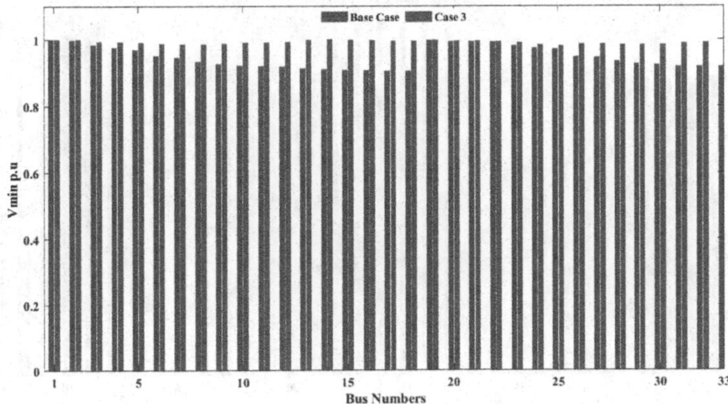

Figure 4: *Voltage profile comparison for base case and case 3.*

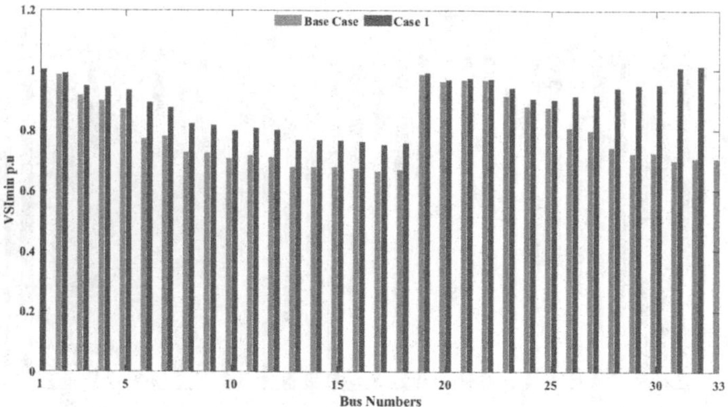

Figure 5: *VSI comparison for base case and case 1.*

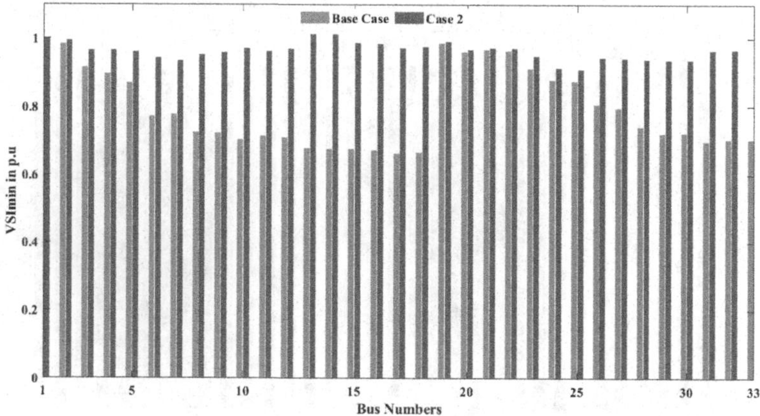

Figure 6: *VSI comparison for base case and case 2.*

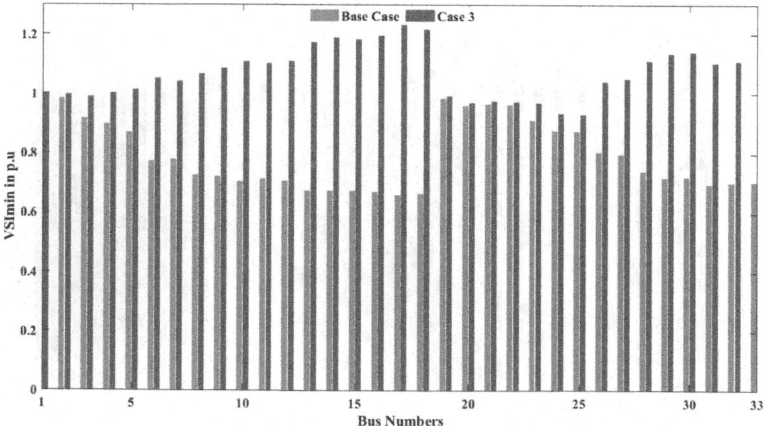

Figure 7: *VSI comparison for base case and case 3.*

6. Conclusion

In this manuscript, a prominent approach based on VSF and BAT algorithm is presented to solve wind DGAP in DN. Further, VSF is calculated and found the best locations after that BAT algorithm is applied to calculate sizes of WDGs. Next, four different cases are taken for the analysis and it is verified on 33bus system. It is concluded that placement of WDGs at suitable locations reduces the loss and improve VSI and voltage profile to greater extent. In overall analysis, highest percentage loss reduction (85.55) is achieved in case 3, i.e. 3 wind DG allocation in DN.

References:

[1] Kumar, A. and W. Gao, "Optimal distributed generation location using mixed integer non-linear programming in hybrid electricity markets," *IET Gener. Transm. Distrib.*, vol. 4, no. 2, pp. 281–298, 2010.

[2] Ghosh, S., S. P. Ghoshal, and S. Ghosh, "Optimal sizing and placement of distributed generation in a network system," *Int. J. Electr. Power Energy Syst.*, vol. 32, no. 8, pp. 849–856, 2010.

[3] Koutroumpezis, G. N. and A. S. Safigianni, "Optimum allocation of the maximum possible distributed generation penetration in a distribution network," *Electr. Power Syst. Res.*, vol. 80, no. 12, pp. 1421–1427, 2010.

[4] Abu-Mouti, F. S. and M. E. El-Hawary, "Optimal distributed generation allocation and sizing in distribution systems via artificial bee colony algorithm," *IEEE Trans. Power Del.*, vol. 26, no. 4, pp. 2090–2101, 2011.

[5] Arya, L. D., A. Koshti, and S. C. Choube, "Distributed generation planning using differential evolution accounting voltage stability consideration," *Int. J. Electr. Power Energy Syst.*, vol. 42, no. 1, pp. 196–207, 2012.

[6] Hung, D. Q. and N. Mithulananthan, "Multiple distributed generators placement in primary distribution networks for loss reduction," *IEEE Trans. Ind. Electron.*, vol. 60, no. 4, pp. 1700–1708, 2013.

[7] Alismail, F., P. Xiong, and C. Singh, "Optimal wind farm allocation in multi-area power systems using distributionally robust optimization approach," *IEEE Trans. Power Syst.*, vol. 33, no. 1, pp. 536–544, 2018.

[8] Safaei, A., B. Vahidi, H. Askarian-Abyaneh, E. Azad-Farsani, and S. M. Ahadi, "A two step optimization algorithm for wind turbine generator placement considering maximum allowable capacity," *Renewable Energy*, vol. 92, pp. 75–82, 2016.

[9] Naderipour, A., Z. Abdul-Malek, S. Arabi Nowdeh, F. H. Gandoman, and M. J. Hadidian Moghaddam, "A multi-objective optimization problem for optimal site selection of wind turbines for reduce losses and improve voltage profile of distribution grids," *Energies*, vol. 12, no. 13, p. 2621, 2019.

[10] Kayal, P. and C. K. Chanda, "Placement of wind and solar based DGs in distribution system for power loss minimization and voltage stability improvement," *Int. J. Electr. Power Energy Syst.*, vol. 53, pp. 795–809, 2013.

[11] Yang, X. S., "A new metaheuristic bat-inspired algorithm," *Nature Inspired Cooperative Strategies for Optimization*, Springer, pp. 65–74.

[12] Sudabattula, S. K. and M. Kowsalwa, "Optimal allocation of solar based distributed generators in distribution system using bat algorithm," *Perspect Sci. Recent Trends Eng. Mater. Sci.*, vol. 8, pp. 270–272, 2016.

[13] Sahoo, N. C. and K. Prasad, ''A fuzzy genetic approach for network reconfiguration to enhance voltage stability in radial distribution systems," *Energy Convers. Manage.*, vol. 47, pp. 3288–3306, 2006.

28. Classification of MNIST Dataset Using Different CNN Architecture

Amit Kumar[1], Inderpal Singh[1], and Dr. Balraj Singh[2]

[1]*Department of Computer Science and Engineering, CT Institute of Technology and Research, Jalandhar, Punjab, India*
[2]*Department of Computer Science and Engineering, Lovely Professional University, Phagwara, Punjab, India*

Abstract: Handwritten digit recognition (HDR) poses a complex challenge with diverse applications spanning multiple domains. Within this research paper, we delve into leveraging deep learning models to discern hand-drawn digits. Our investigation centres around three distinct models: Lenet-5, Alexnet and Vgg-16. These models were meticulously constructed and subsequently evaluated to gauge their efficacy in digit recognition. Employing TensorFlow version 2.6.2 and the Kaggle platform, our analysis was grounded in the MNIST dataset, encompassing 60,000 training samples and 10,000 testing samples. This dataset presented a 10-class scenario, encompassing digits ranging from 0 to 9. Across each model, twenty epochs were meticulously executed to attain peak performance. The culmination of our experimentation divulged compelling outcomes. The Lenet-5 model achieved a commendable accuracy of 98.07%, the Alexnet model further advanced accuracy to 98.52%, while the Vgg-16 model attained an accuracy of 97.35%. Notably, the Alexnet model emerged as the frontrunner, exhibiting unparalleled accuracy. These discernments offer valuable insights into the efficacy of deep learning methodologies for handwritten digit recognition. As we cast our gaze forward, there is ample room for future research to amplify accuracy and to unlock the latent potential of alternative deep learning architectures tailored to this intricate task

Keywords: CNN, Alexnet, VGG-16, Lenet-5.

1. Introduction

Hand written digital images are those which has been written by hands. These hand written images has been characterise from the numerical values I.e. 0 to 9. Nowadays, most of the developers are using a very different deep learning and machine learning techniques [1][2]. This techniques are very important for machines to make them an intelligent device. In a case of deep learning technique, a network CNN is used. This CNN has been used in the different fields like face recognition, Spam detection and image classification etc. In a case of hand written digit recognition, it is not a commercial application but it has many applications and advantages in our daily life. With the use of written digit recognition the most of the complex problems can be solve [3].

1.1. HDR (Handwritten Digit Recognition)

HDR is also known as hand written digit recognition. It is a technique and ability of machine to recognise hand written digits that are written by a human. It becomes a very hard task for the machine to recognize the hand written digits. Because these handwritten digits are not perfect. So the image of digits is the solution to recognize Handwritten digits. HDR is very challenging problem that has been studied for many years in the field of hand digit recognition [4]. So a lot of research have been achieved by different researchers and scientist who made a different algorithms. These algorithms are based on KNN, SVM, CNN, NN, etc. KNN is known as K-nearest-neighbour, SVM is known as support vector machine. NN is known as neural network and CNN is known as convolutional neural network [5][6].

1.2. Neural Network

Artificial neural network which is widely known as network or it's also known as a circuit, and this circuit is made of neurons. In general sense the artificial neural network consists of neurons or nodes. It consists of biological neural network which are made up of composed biological neurons. Artificial neural network which has been used to solve image classification problem those are provided by a researcher. These neurons are classified by using weights and nodes. With the classify the result, it has been states that if the weights are true it means it has a positive connection (value of output), while the values are negative, it means the neurons are something the blocking the connection.

2. Literature Survey

Huimim W et al. demonstrated hand written digital images with the use of convocational neural network. The author proposed Lenet 5 neural network architecture for the examination of MNIST images [7]. Ashadullah et al. proposed the Bangla handwritten digit recognition using CNN model. The data set of NumtaDB has been used. The author achieved the testing accuracy of 92.72% with 30 epoch and 64 batch size [8]. On the other hand, Xudie Ren et al. proposed hand written digital images with the use of convocational neural network and XGBoost. The author proposed combined approach for classification of images. The dataset of MNIST and CIFAR-10 has been taken for the classification and examination. The data of 50% has been taken from high school students while the rest of the data has been taken from census bureau. The size of the image is 28*28 pixels with 256 grey levels. The author proposed 98.80% efficiency by using MNIST database with the use of CNN and 78.78% efficiency has been achieved by using CNN model with the use of CIFAR-10 dataset [9]. Feiyang et al.proposed CapsNet and Resnet architecture for the examination of MNIST images. The data of MNIST has been taken from NIST. The data of 50% has been taken from high school students while the rest of the data has been taken from census bureau. The size of the image is 28*28 pixels with 256 grey levels. The data set of 60000 images has been taken in a training set while 10000 images has be used for testing set. The author Proposed 98.79% efficiency by using CapsNet and 93.78 efficiency has been achieved by using ResNet model [10]. Xinyu Lei et al. demonstrated dilated convolution algorithm for the classification of MNIST images with the use of CNN model. The author achieved good training efficiency by reducing the training time by 92.99% [11]. Ritik et al. proposed the three models of SVM MLP and CNN for the classification of hand written digital images. The dataset contains of 70000 digital images. Out of which 60000 has been used for training data set while 10000 has been used for testing dataset. Each of the images has 28 x 28 in size with a pixel size ranging from 0 to 255. Proposed 98.85% efficiency by using MLP model from testing set while 99% has been achieved from training set by using CNN model [12]. Yang et al. proposed the CNN model that includes one input layer, two convolutional layers, two pulling layers and one fully connected layer and one output layer for the examination of MNIST images. The dataset contains of 70000 digital images. Out of which 60000 have been used for training data set while 10000 have been used for testing dataset. Each of the images has 28 x 28 in size with a pixel size ranging from 0 to 255. That Tenserflow library has been used to implement the network [13]. Asha et al. proposed English test using MNIST and EMNIST dataset by using CNN model. The author also proposed LSTM algorithm to examination hand written digital images. Author proposed a good efficiency of 98.23% using a CNN model from MNIST dataset, while 98.35% efficiency has been achieved with the use of LSTM algorithm. Images of 60000 have been used for training dataset, while 10000 have been used for testing dataset. Each of the images has 28 x 28 in size with a pixel size ranging from 0 to 255 [14].

3. Data Collection

The samples for the CNN study were obtained from the Kaggle platform, which is an open-source online community owned and managed by Google. Within this platform, users are granted the liberty to access datasets designed for CNN models. Moreover, they can also choose to provide their own distinctive datasets. Among the array of MNIST datasets accessible, the Fashion MNIST dataset poses a more formidable difficulty. It encompasses ten distinct categories and comprises a total of 60,000 training instances and 10,000 testing instances. The dataset consists of 28x28 monochrome images in a single channel. Lenet-5, VGG16 and Alexnet architectures are used

3.1. Data Evaluation Parameters

Diverse models have found utility in result assessment. The confusion matrix data serves as a means to exhibit true and false values, dependent on distinct parameters. These parameters consist of recall, precision, accuracy and F1-Score. Below, we delve into a discussion of these parameters: Precision: It is the ratio of truly predictive positive values to the total number of predicted positive observations. Precision can be calculating as follows:

$$\text{Precision} = \frac{TP}{TP+FP} \quad (1)$$

a) Recall: It is the ratio of truly predictive positive values to the total number of observations taken from one class.

$$\text{Recall} = \frac{TP}{TP+FN} \quad (2)$$

b) Accuracy: Accuracy is a ratio of true positive values to the true negative values in all matrix.

$$\text{Accuracy} = \frac{TP+TN}{TP+TN+FP=FN} \quad (3)$$

c) F1-Score: It is a weighted combination of recall and precision.

$$\text{F1-Score} = 2*\frac{\mathrm{Re}call*\mathrm{Pr}ecision}{\mathrm{Re}call+\mathrm{Pr}ecision}$$

Analysis of results has been based on above parameters.

4. Classification and Development of Architecture

4.1. Development of Lenet-5 Architecture

Constructed using Kaggle, the LeNet-5 model relies on TensorFlow version 2.6.2 for its analysis. The open-source MNIST dataset from Kaggle serves as its foundational data source, incorporating 60,000 training samples and 10,000 testing samples. LeNet-5's architecture comprises five distinct layers, strategically harnessed for predictive purposes. Within this structure, three sets of convolutional layers harmonise with pooling, average pooling and fully connected layers. The concluding layer employs a SoftMax classifier, facilitating the classification of images into their respective classes. Notably, the model is primed to receive 32 by 32 grayscale images as input..

4.2. Development of Alexnet Architecture

The crafting of the AlexNet model took place on the Kaggle platform, utilising TensorFlow version 2.6.2 for analysis. The open-source MNIST dataset from Kaggle played a fundamental role, offering access to 60,000 training samples and 10,000 testing samples. Within this model, a classification spectrum spanning classes 0 to 9 was employed. AlexNet's architecture, comprising 11 layers in total, forms the bedrock for prediction. The inaugural layer, a convolutional one, spans dimensions of 55 by 55, encompassing 96 filters. Operating with an 11 by 11 kernel size and activated by the ReLU function, this layer yields a feature map housing 96 distinct features. Subsequent to this, a pooling layer takes the reins, adopting a 3 by 3 kernel size and ReLU activation, all while maintaining a stride of 2.

4.3. Development of VGG-16 Architecture

The VGG-16 model was formulated on the Kaggle platform, utilising TensorFlow version 2.6.2 for comprehensive analysis. The open-source MNIST dataset sourced from Kaggle provided the foundational data, comprising 60,000 training samples and 10,000 testing samples. In this model, a classification framework encompassing classes 0 to 9 was adopted. The model's input structure accommodates greyscale images sized at 112 by 112, with a depth of 128. The kernel function operates with a 3 by 3 dimension and a stride of 1, contributing to the formation of an optimised feature map housing 128 distinctive attributes. The second convolutional layer enhances its capabilities through the application of the ReLU activation function.

4.4. Classifing Mnist Data using the Developed Convolutional Neural Network

A diverse range of MNIST datasets has been sourced from Kaggle. Comprising 10 classes, these datasets cover the spectrum of numerical digits from 0 to 9. Employing a variety of CNN models, these classes have undergone classification processes. The adaptable nature of this data renders it suitable for utilisation across a broad spectrum of machine learning algorithm

4.5. Classifying Mnist Dataset using Lenet-5 Architecture

Kaggle Notebook has been used for classifying mnist dataset by using lenet-5 architecture model. Tensorflow version: 2.6.2 has been used for analysis. For the examination, the dataset consisting of 60000 training samples, and 10000 training samples have been used. First, important library is import by using tensorflow then next command examined to load dataset from local library, pre-defined command already executed in program code.

4.6. Classifying Mnist Dataset using Alexnet Architecture

Kaggle Notebook has been used for classifying mnist dataset by using Alexnet architecture model. The analysis was conducted using Tensorflow version 2.6.2. The dataset comprises 60,000 training samples and 10,000 testing samples. To initiate the process, the essential libraries were imported using Tensorflow. Subsequently, a command was executed to load the dataset from the local library, building upon pre-defined commands in the program code.

4.7. Classifying Mnist Dataset using vgg-16 Architecture

Kaggle Notebook has been used for classifying mnist dataset by using vgg-16 architecture model. The analysis was conducted using Tensorflow version 2.6.2. The dataset comprises 60,000 training samples and 10,000 testing samples. To initiate the process, the essential libraries were imported using Tensorflow. Subsequently, a command was executed to load the dataset from the local library, building upon pre-defined commands in the program code.

4.8. Exploring and Reporting best CNN Architecture by Measuring the Performance

Comparing the performance of three distinct CNN architectures reveals differing outcomes in terms of accuracy and loss. Specifically, AlexNet and LeNet-5 outshine the VGG-16 architecture in achieving higher accuracy and lower loss. All of these models were designed and developed on the Kaggle platform, utilising TensorFlow version 2.6.2 for the analytical process. The foundational dataset for these models is the well-known MNIST dataset, sourced from Kaggle, encompassing 60,000 training samples and 10,000 testing samples.

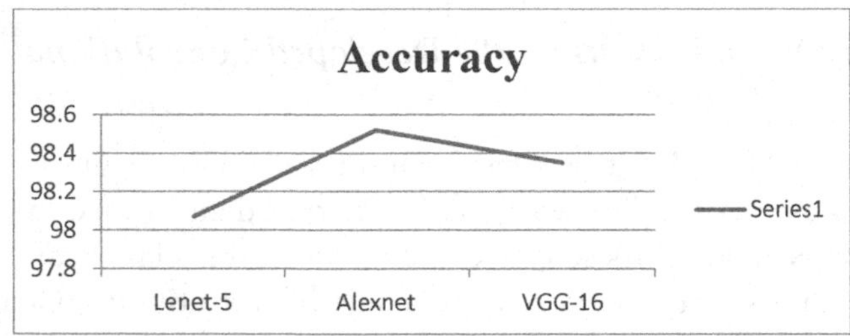

Figure 1: *Overall accuracy.*

From the Figure 1 it has been reported that Alexnet model performs better in the terms of accuracy parameters while Vgg-16 and Lenet-5 models performs lowest.

5. Conclusion

Hand written digital images are those which has been written by hands. These hand written images has been characterise from the numerical values I.e. 0 to 9. Nowadays most of the developers are using a very different deep learning and machine learning techniques. In a case of hand written digit recognition, it is not a commercial application, but it has many applications and advantages in our daily life. With the use of written digit recognition the most of the complex problems can be solve. HDR is also known as hand written digit recognition. It is a technique and ability of machine to recognise hand written digits that are written by a human. It becomes a very hard task for the machine to recognise the hand written digits. Because these handwritten digits are not perfect. So the image of digits is the solution to recognise handwritten digits. HDR is very challenging problem that has been studied for many years in the field of hand digit recognition. So lot of researches have been achieved by different researchers and scientist who made a different algorithms. These algorithms are based on KNN, SVM, CNN, NN, etc. KNN is known as K-nearest neighbour, SVM is known as support vector machine. NN is known as Nueral Network and CNN is known as Convolutional neural network. In the context of a specific research endeavour, three distinct models were developed to assess accuracy levels. The analysis was conducted using Kaggle, with TensorFlow version 2.6.2 as the analytical tool of choice. The MNIST dataset, an open-source resource from Kaggle, was harnessed for this purpose, featuring 60,000 training samples and 10,000 testing samples. Across all models, a standardised set of 10 classes, representing digits from 0 to 9, was employed. For enhanced results, each model underwent 20 epochs of training. The resulting accuracies were as follows: the LeNet-5 model achieved an accuracy of 98.07%, the AlexNet model reached 98.52% and the VGG-16 model demonstrated an accuracy of 97.35%. Remarkably, the AlexNet model showcased superior accuracy performance. In contrast, both the VGG-16 and LeNet-5 models exhibited relatively lower accuracy levels, with these results being achieved over 20 epochs of training.

References

[1] Hinton, G. E., P. Dayan, and M. Revow, "Modeling the manifolds of images of handwritten digits," *IEEE Trans. Neural Networks*, vol. 8, no. 1, pp. 65–74, 1997, doi: 10.1109/72.554192.

[2] Niu, X.-X., and C. Y. Suen, "A novel hybrid CNN–SVM classifier for recognizing handwritten digits," *Pattern Recognit.*, vol. 45, no. 4, pp. 1318–1325, 2012, ISSN 0031-3203, https://doi.org/10.1016/j.patcog.2011.09.021.

[3] Liu, C.-L., K. Nakashima, H. Sako, and H. Fujisawa, "Handwritten digit recognition: benchmarking of state-of-the-art techniques," *Pattern Recognit.*, vol. 36, no. 10, pp. 2271–2285, 2003, ISSN 0031-3203, https://doi.org/10.1016/S0031-3203(03)00085-2.

[4] Lauer, F., C. Y. Suen, and G. Bloch, "A trainable feature extractor for handwritten digit recognition," *Pattern Recognit.*, vol. 40, no. 6, pp. 1816–1824, 2007, ISSN 0031-3203, https://doi.org/10.1016/j.patcog.2006.10.011.

[5] Islam, K. T., G. Mujtaba, R. G. Raj, and H. F. Nweke, "Handwritten digits recognition with artificial neural network," *2017 International Conference on Engineering Technology and Technopreneurship (ICE2T)*, pp. 1–4, 2017, doi: 10.1109/ICE2T.2017.8215993.

[6] ClaudiuCireşan, D., U. Meier, L. M. Gambardella, and J. Schmidhuber, "Deep, big, simple neural nets for handwritten digit recognition," *Neural Comput.*, vol. 22, no. 12, pp. 3207–3220, 2010. doi: https://doi.org/10.1162/NECO_a_00052.

[7] Wu, H., "CNN-based recognition of handwritten digits in MNIST database," *Research School of Computer Science*, The Australia National University, Canberra, 2018.

[8] Shawon, A., M. Jamil-Ur Rahman, F. Mahmud, and M. M. Arefin Zaman, "Bangla handwritten digit recognition using deep CNN for large and unbiased dataset," *2018 International Conference on Bangla Speech and Language Processing (ICBSLP)*, 2018, pp. 1–6, doi: 10.1109/ICBSLP.2018.8554900.

[9] Ren, X., H. Guo, S. Li, S. Wang, and J. Li, "A novel image classification method with CNN-XGBoost model," In: Kraetzer, C., Shi, YQ., Dittmann, J., Kim, H. (eds) *Digital Forensics and Watermarking. IWDW 2017. Lecture Notes in Computer Science*, vol. 10431, Springer, Cham, 2017. https://doi.org/10.1007/978-3-319-64185-0_28

[10] Chen, F., *et al.*, "Assessing four neural networks on handwritten digit recognition dataset (MNIST)," arXiv preprint arXiv:1811.08278, 2018.

[11] Lei, X., H. Pan, and X. Huang, "A dilated CNN model for image classification," *IEEE Access*, vol. 7, pp. 124087–124095, 2019, doi: 10.1109/ACCESS.2019.2927169.

[12] Pashine, S., "Handwritten digit recognition using machine and deep learning algorithms," arXiv.org, 2021, https://arxiv.org/abs/2106.12614

[13] Gong, Y. and P. Zhang, "Research on Mnist handwritten numbers recognition based on CNN," *J. Phys.: Conf. Ser.*, vol. 2138, no. 1, IOP Publishing, 2021.

[14] Shetty, A. B., *et al.*, "Recognition of handwritten digits and English texts using MNIST and EMNIST datasets." *Int. J. Res. Eng. Sci. Manage.*, vol. 4, no. 7, pp. 240–243, 2021.

29. Tailoring of Morphology and Electrical Properties of Hexagonal Ferrites

Ankit Jain[1,5], Charanjeet Singh[1], Sachin K. Godara[2], Rajshree B. Jotania[3], Varinder Kaur[2], and Ashwani K. Sood[4]

[1]*School of Electrical and Electronics Engineering, Lovely Professional University, Phagwara, Punjab, India*
[2]*Department of Apparel and Textile Technology, Guru Nanak Dev University, Amritsar, Punjab, India*
[3]*Department of Physics, University School of Science, Gujarat University, Ahmedabad, India*
[4]*Department of Chemistry, Guru Nanak Dev University, Amritsar, Punjab, India*
[5]*Department of Electronics and Communication, Indore Institute of Science and Technology, Indore, M.P., India*

Abstract: Chemical compositions of $BaCoAl_xFe_{12-x}O_{19}$ (x = 0.0, 0.2, 0.4, 0.6, 0.8, 1.0) were produced by sol–gel technique. Hexagonal M-type structure was identified with X-ray diffraction study in all of the samples. The maximum value of real part of admittance is varying from 2.54E-05 to 6.77E-05 and minimum value varies from 1.17E-09 to 6.24E-10 and imaginary part of admittance is varying 2.9E-12 to 4.8E-13. Relaxation of conductivity was seen at varying intervals.

Keywords: Hexaferrites, dielectric properties, charge transport mechanism.

1. Introduction

Ferrites are employed for colossal applications in low- and high-frequency field. Because of their tunability and strong magnetocrystalline anisotropy [1–2], hexagonal ferrites have found use in the field of microwave technology. However, it is required to tailor the material characteristics to match the demands by doping Fe^{3+} ions with other elements [1–5]. This is done so that the material properties may be modified to meet the requirements. It is not expected that doping would affect the structure of the $BaFe_{12}O_{19}$ base material. This is due to the size of the doped material and the nearly similar doping. The electrical and magnetic characteristics of the barium hexagonal M-barium, which is the topic of increasing study utilising a variety of methods, are principally influenced by the particle size. The co-precipitation approach [6], the hydrothermal precipitation method [7], the pechini [8], the citrate precursor [9], the solution-combustion [10], the sol–gel [11] and the ball milling method [12] are all examples of methods that are used. It is vital for barium M-hexaferrite to have a low coercivity value, also known as a soft magnetic nature, in order for it to be used as a wave absorbent material. Because of this, either a replacement must be obtained or the item must be allowed to dry out. In addition, there are often two approaches used while conducting ionic exchanges. Ce doping has been utilised in the synthesis of it [13], La [14], Eu [15], Cu [16], Mn, and Ti [17] and Sr and Mn [18] have all been employed in the synthesis of it. All of these examples are associated with the method of single-ion substitution, which was used in the study that came before. The second, bicomponent method is also being utilized [18–20].

The investigation of the electrical properties like conductance, susceptance and capacitance, Phase identification and SEM of $BaCo_xAl_xFe_{12-}$produced materials is the aim of this investigation.

2. Experiment

2.1. Procedure for the Synthesis of $BaCo_xAl_xFe_{12-2x}O_{19}$ (x = 0.0 – 1.0) Nano Hexaferrites

Synthesis of Co^{2+}- and Al^{3+}-substituted M-type hexaferrite was performed with sol–gel auto-combustion method refer to Figure 1.

X-ray pattern diffraction was acquired with a diffractometer (Rigaku). The grain morphology was explored FESEM (Jeol, JSM-7100). The dielectric parameters of samples were measured Agilent model E4980A LCR meter in range of 20 Hz to 2 MHz.

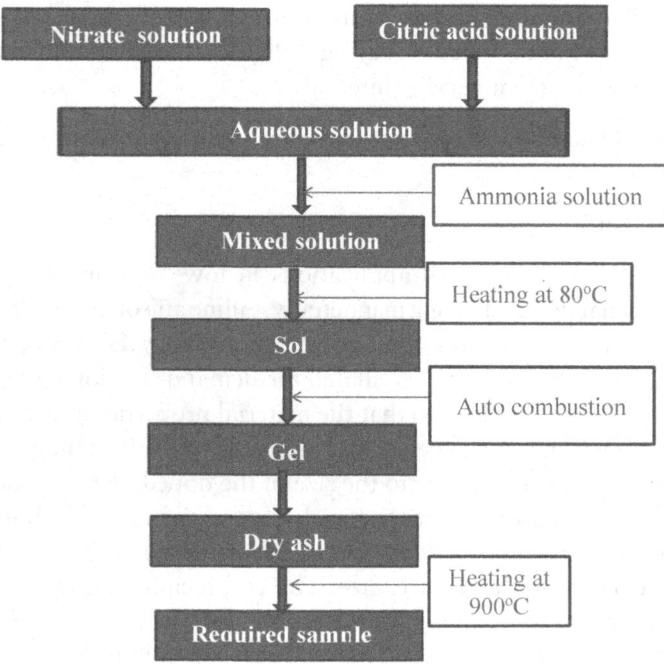

Figure 1: *Schematic of sol-gel method.*

3. Results and Discussion

3.1. Phase Identification

The X-ray diffraction (XRD) patterns of the $BaCo_xAl_xFe_{12-2x}O_{19}$ hexaferrite samples are presented in Figure 2. Using the JCPDS card (96-100-8842), the detected peaks for each of the samples were matched with standard. The examination of the patterns that were found for each of the samples reveals that each peak belongs to the pure M-phase, and that there is not a single additional peak noticed. This confirms that each of the samples consists of a single phase and does not include any impurity phase.

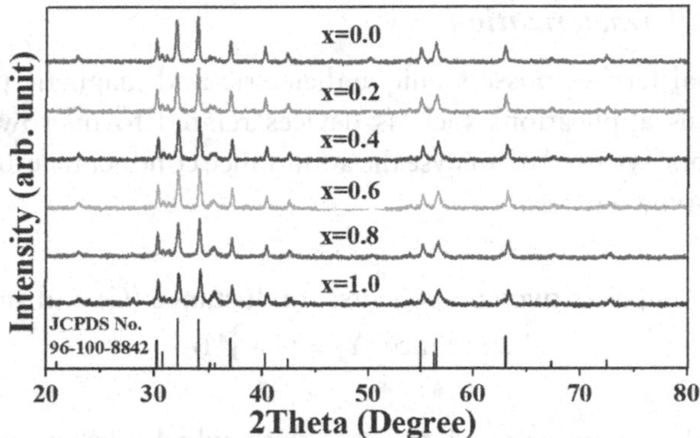

Figure 2: X-ray diffractograms of samples.

3.2. Field Emission Scanning Electron Microscopy

Figure 4(a) SEM for x = 0.0
Figure 4(b) SEM for x = 0.2
Figure 4(c) SEM for x = 0.4
Figure 4(d) SEM for x = 0.6
Figure 4(e) SEM for x = 0.8
Figure 4(f) SEM for x = 0.0

Figure 3: SEM micrographs of the ferrite samples of $BaCo_xAl_xFe_{12-2x}O_{19}$.

The morphology is displayed in Figure 3 (a–f). The dopant (Co-Al) can be shown to cause agglomeration of the grains at the value of x equal to 0.6. Platelets that look like needles are observable with dopants, and the average size of the grains decreases. The production of nanoferrites with dimensions ranging from 1 to 100 nm has also been seen.

The arrangement of grains has a number of voids, each of which has the potential to own resistance or barrier to movement of the charge carriers. When grains are small in size, the grain borders are larger. This results in a hindrance to applied field, which changes the charge transport process.

3.3. Electrical Characterization

M-type hexagonal ferrites possess unique dielectric and magnetic properties that render for various applications such as devices related to microwave, magnetic storage and sensors. We need to analyse the admittance conductance and capacitance of hexagonal M-type ferrites.

Admittance (Y):

Admittance (Y) comprises two components: conductance (G) and susceptance (B).

$$\text{Admittance (Y)} = G + j^*B$$

Conductance (G):

Conductance (G) is a measure of the ease with which electrical current flows through a material. In the context of hexaferrites, it involves the flow of electrons within the material..

$$\text{Conductance (G)} = \sigma * A/d$$

where **σ**, A and d are conductivity, cross-sectional area and thickness, respectively.

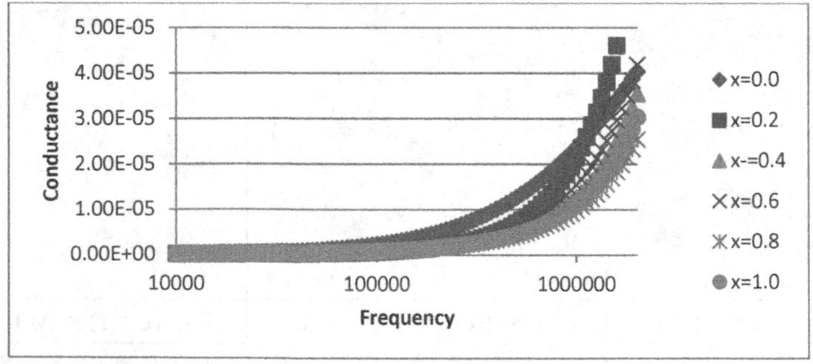

Figure 4(a): *Variation of the conductance with the frequency.*

Figure 4(a) shows the variations of conductance with frequency. As a result, the real components of the admittance increase with increasing frequency, while the behaviour becomes frequency independent initially till certain point. The minimum value of conductance is 6.24E-10 for x=0.8 and maximum value reached upto 6.77E-05 for x-0.2 in doped sample and in case of undoped sample the minimum value is 2.68E-09 and maximum value is 4.04E-05.

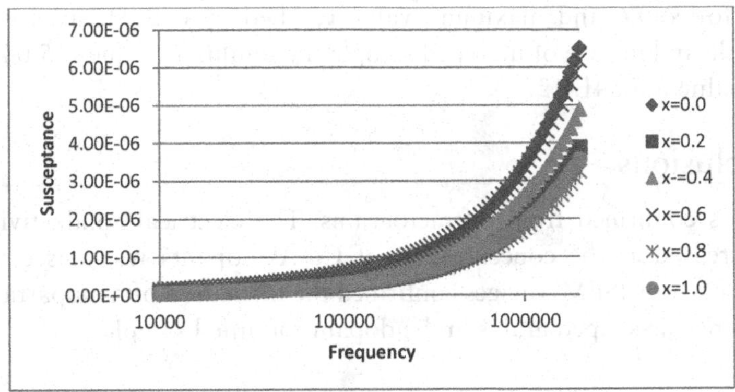

Figure 4(b): Variation of the susceptance with the frequency.

Figure 4(b) shows the variations of susceptance with frequency. As a result, the imaginary components of the admittance increase with increasing frequency, while the behaviour becomes frequency independent initially till certain point. The minimum value of susceptance is 8.58E-10 for x=0.4 and maximum value reached upto 6.17E-06 for x-0.6 in doped sample and in case of undoped sample the minimum value is 5.96E-09 and maximum value is 6.51E-06.

Capacitance (C):

Capacitance is a property of a material that determines how much electrical charge it can store for a given voltage. For hexaferrites, the capacitance is primarily associated with the dielectric properties of the material.

$$\text{Capacitance (C)} = \varepsilon o * \varepsilon\_r * A/d$$

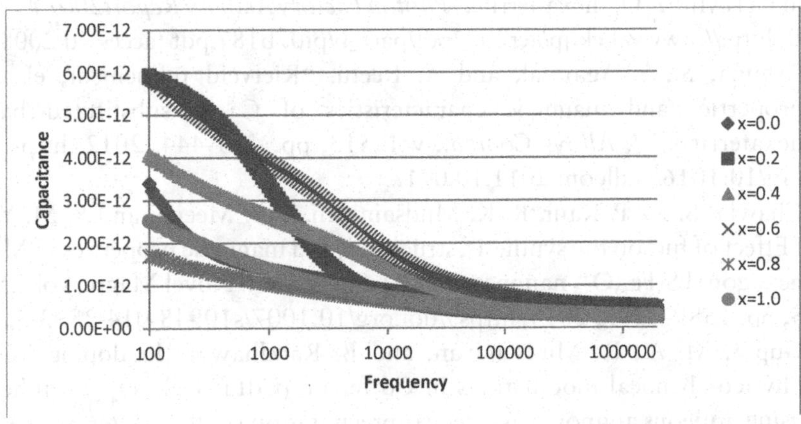

Figure 4(c): Variation of the capacitance with frequency.

Figure 4(c) shows the variations of the capacitance with the frequency. As a result, the value decreases with increasing frequency, while the behaviour becomes frequency independent after certain point. The minimum value of capacitance is 4.8E-13 for x=0.6 and maximum value reached upto 9.93E-12 for x-0.6 in doped sample and in case of undoped sample the minimum value is 5.04E-13 and maximum value is 5.54E-12.

4. Conclusions

M-phase was confirmed from diffractograms. The electrical conductivity of the samples increased as the concentration of Co-Al dopants was raised. Scanning electron microscopy (SEM) images confirmed the formation of nanoparticles, grain clusters and needle-shaped grains in the dopant-modified samples.

References

[1] Bsoul, I., "Preparation of nanocrystalline $BaFe_{12-2X}Co_XTi_XO_{19}$ by ball milling method and their magnetic properties," http://repository.yu.edu.jo/handle/123456789/955 (accessed January 1, 2009).

[2] Gurbuz, A., N. Onar, I. Ozdemir, A. Karaoglanli, and E. Celik, "Structural, thermal and magnetic properties of barium-ferrite powders substituted with Mn, Cu or Co and X (X = Sr and Ni) prepared by the sol-gel method | GCRIS database | Pamukkale university," https://hdl.handle.net/11499/8616 (accessed January 1, 2012).

[3] Williams, J., J. Adetunji, and M. Gregori, "Mössbauer spectroscopic determination of magnetic moments of Fe^{3+} and Co^{2+} in substituted barium hexaferrite, $Ba(Co,Ti)_xFe_{(12-2x)}O_{19}$," *J. Magn. Magn. Mater.*, vol. 220, no. 2–3, pp. 124–128, 2000, https://doi.org/10.1016/s0304-8853(00)00458-3.

[4] Nakanishi, T., M. Okube, T. Toyoda, A. Nakao, and B. Sasaki, "Site occupancy in $BaTiMnFe_{10}O_{19}$ hexa-ferrite," *Photon Factory Activity Report2007 # 25 Part B*, http://pfwww.kek.jp/acr2007pdf/part_b/pf07b187.pdf (accessed 2008).

[5] Ashima, S., S. Agarwal, and A. Reetu, "Rietveld refinement, electrical properties and magnetic characteristics of Ca–Sr substituted barium hexaferrites," *J. Alloys Compd.*, vol. 513, pp. 436–444, 2012. https://doi.org/10.1016/j.jallcom.2011.10.071.

[6] Chawla, S. K., P. Kaur, R. K. Mudsainiyan, S. S. Meena, and S. M. Yusuf, "Effect of fuel on the synthesis, structural, and magnetic properties of M-type hexagonal $SrFe_{12}O_{19}$ nanoparticles," J. Supercond. Novel Magn., vol. 28, no. 5, pp. 1589–1599, 2014, https://doi.org/10.1007/s10948-014-2893-5.

[7] Gupta, M. A., R. Mudsainiyan, and B. Randhawa, "Li doping induced physico-chemical modulations in Cd ferrite ($CdLi_x\ Fe_{(2-x)}O_{4-x}$) synthesized using aqueous ammonia assisted co-precipitation route," *Mater. Sci. Eng., B*, vol. 227, pp. 1–8, 2018, https://doi.org/10.1016/j.mseb.2017.10.001.

[8] Shikha, P. K., T. S. Kang, and B. Randhawa, "Mn doping induced physico-chemical changes in La Ce ferrite nanofabricated by ionic liquid assisted hydrothermal route," J. Alloys Compd., vol. 701, pp. 788–796, 2017. https://doi.org/10.1016/j.jallcom.2017.01.138.

[9] Mudsainiyan, R. K., M. Gupta, and S. Chawla, "Physico-chemical and magnetic properties of Co-Zr Doped Ba-hexaferrites using self combustion and urea assisted method – a comparative study," *Mater. Today: Proc.*, vol. 3, no. 2, pp. 507–512, 2016. https://doi.org/10.1016/j.matpr.2016.01.128.

[10] Mudsainiyan, R., S. Chawla, S. Meena, N. Sharma, R. Singh, and A. Das, "Cations distribution and magnetic properties of Co–Zr doped $BaCo_xZr_xFe_{(12-2x)}O_{19}$ prepared via citrate precursor sol–gel route," *Ceram. Int.*, vol. 40, no. 10, pp. 16617–16626, 2014. https://doi.org/10.1016/j.ceramint.2014.08.022.

[11] A. I. Journal, S. B. Narang, S. K. Chawla, R. K. Mudsainiyan, K. Pubby, S. Bindra, S. K. Chawla, R. K. Mudsainiyan, *Integr. Ferroelectr.*, vol. 167, pp. 98–101, 2015.

[12] Mudsainiyan, R., S. Chawla, and S. Meena, "Correlation between site preference and magnetic properties of Co–Zr doped $BaCo_xZr_xFe_{(12-2x)}O_{19}$ prepared under sol–gel and citrate precursor sol–gel conditions," *J. Alloys Compd.*, vol. 615, pp. 875–881, 2014. https://doi.org/10.1016/j.jallcom.2014.07.035.

[13] Chang, S., S. Kangning, and C. Pengfei, "Microwave absorption properties of Ce-substituted M-type barium ferrite," *J. Magn. Magn. Mater.*, vol. 324, no. 5, pp. 802–805, 2012. https://doi.org/10.1016/j.jmmm.2011.09.023.

[14] Li, C. J., B. Wang, and J. N. Wang, "Magnetic and microwave absorbing properties of electrospun $Ba_{(1-x)}La_xFe_{12}O_{19}$ nanofibers," *J. Magn. Magn. Mater.*, vol. 324, no. 7, pp. 1305–1311, 2012. https://doi.org/10.1016/j.jmmm.2011.11.016.

[15] Khademi, F., A. Poorbafrani, P. Kameli, and H. Salamati, "Structural, magnetic and microwave properties of Eu-doped barium hexaferrite powders," *J. Supercond. Novel Magn.*, vol. 25, no. 2, pp. 525–531, 2011. https://doi.org/10.1007/s10948-011-1323-1.

[16] Baykal, A., H. Güngüneş, H. Sözeri, M. Amir, I. Auwal, S. Asiri, S. Shirsath, and A. Demir Korkmaz, "Magnetic properties and Mössbauer spectroscopy of Cu-Mn substituted $BaFe_{12}O_{19}$ hexaferrites," *Ceram. Int.*, vol. 43, no. 17, pp. 15486–15492, 2017. https://doi.org/10.1016/j.ceramint.2017.08.096Soehada.

[17] Susilawati, D. and A. Khalilurrahman, "Synthesis and characterization of barium hexaferrite with manganese (Mn) doping material as anti-radar," *AIP Conf. Proc.*, 2017. https://doi.org/10.1063/1.4973096.

[18] Singh, C., S. Bindra Narang, I. Hudiara, Y. Bai, and F. Tabatabaei, "Static magnetic properties of Co and Ru substituted Ba–Sr ferrite," *Mater. Res. Bull.*, vol. 43, no. 1, pp. 176–184, 2008. https://doi.org/10.1016/j.materresbull.2007.06.050.

30. Different PWM Techniques for Power Electronics Topologies: A Comparative Study

Ahmed Hamad Mansoor, Amit Kumar Singh, and Someet Singh

SEEE, Lovely Professional University, Phagwara, India

Abstract: The comparative study of different pulse width modulation (PWM) techniques has been discussed in this paper that can be used for the advancement of the power electronics topology or technology. To bring down the harmonic value from the AC signal PWM technique are handled, as for AC signal, quality is more important as compared to the quantity factor. Different pulse width modulation approaches, i.e. sinusoidal pulse width modulation, third harmonic injection pulse width modulation, phase disposition pulse width modulation and space vector pulse width modulation, are the major PWM approaches that are being used for the designing of the gate pulses of different power electronics topology and are discussed in this paper.

Keywords: SPWM, THIPWM, PDPWM, SVPWM, THD.

1. Introduction

Modern technologies are very helpful in the advancement of emerging technologies application. Power electronics is one of the best fields that is emerging best results due to use of the new advance technologies in electrical and electronics engineering field [1]. This pulse width modulation scheme is one of the power electronics streams that is helping in minimising the total harmonic distortion (THD) and increasing the efficiency of the power electronics-based systems or circuits. In power electronics, quasi or square signals can be somewhat allowed for less or intermediate power application, but for immense power application we have to provide pure sinusoidal signal form, i.e. the signal with very less THD [2]. According to our power usage range, we can use the sinusoidal signal with its variable range of THD value for a particular electronics-based circuit or system.

2. Pulse Width Modulation

It is an approach to reduce the average power of a sinusoidal signal by chopping it or converting it into the discrete parts. It is a very popular method in the field of power electronics to reduce the THD value from the sinusoidal signal or to increase the efficiency of the electrical and electronics-based topologies [3]. Pulse width modulation (PWM) is a way to discipline the analog signals and to process these analog signals into digital output. One more way to increase the efficiency or to reduce the THD value from sinusoidal signal is to use the modern fabricate devices that are made up of semiconductor materials. Basically, PWM method modulates the duty cycle of a sinusoidal signal and shred it to give only limited amount of power to the load or the device [4]. The different types of pulse modulation method generally used in the system are

1. Sinusoidal PWM
2. Third harmonic injection PWM
3. Phase disposition PWM
4. Space vector PWM

The pulse generation circuit is used to trigger the semiconductor switches at particular time to generate the desired level of output. The generation of appropriate pulses has been made by comparing every carrier wave with the reference wave, and the resulting pulse pattern has been given to the appropriate switches to generate the required output levels.

2.1. Sinusoidal Pulse Width Modulation

This approach results to the sinusoidal gesture generation by evaluating two signals, i.e. carrier wave and reference wave [5]. The pulse generation circuit for three phases through the sinusoidal pulse width modulation technique is displayed in Figure 1, where the depressed frequency reference waveform is been resembled with the high frequency carrier waves. As according to the requirement of number of triggering signals, we can choose different number of reference signal inputs to create required number of triggering outputs [5]. Along with this, we can also choose the different value of frequency of the carrier signals to increase or decrease the switching frequency range of our switches [5].

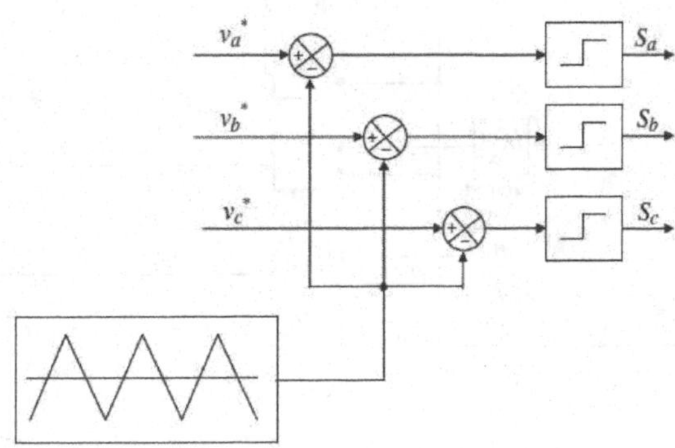

***Figure 1:** SPWM triggering circuit.*

The THD value of the triggered gate pulse also depends on one more factor that is modulation index (m). Modulation index is the ratio of voltage magnitude of modulating signal or reference signal with the voltage magnitude of carrier signal [6]. The maximum value of modulation index can vary from 0 to 1 range, where the system will generate very less THD value at peak value of modulation index, i.e. 1 and highest value of THD at the bottom value of THD, i.e. 0.

$$\textit{Modulation}\ \text{Index}\ (m) = \frac{V_m}{V_c} \tag{1}$$

2.2. *Third Harmonic Injection PWM*

The method of implementation of the sinusoidal PWM is very convenient and easy, but this method is not adequate to completely attend the available DC power supply voltage [7]. As a result of this problem, researches have to look for different pulse generating circuit approach so that they can implement more efficient technique for pulse generation. Thus, the new method, i.e. third harmonic injection PWM method came in approach. This method of pulse generation helps to create pulse triggering circuit with high efficiency and low THD value [8]. The drawback of the sine PWM was that it was not so efficient to achieve the maximum value out of achievable output voltage but by using the THIPWM technique or simply summing a new third harmonic characteristic in reference signal, we have achieved the rise in amplitude of outcome voltage signal [9]. The pulse generation circuit for three phase 6 gate pulse by the help of THIPWM method is shown in Figure 2.

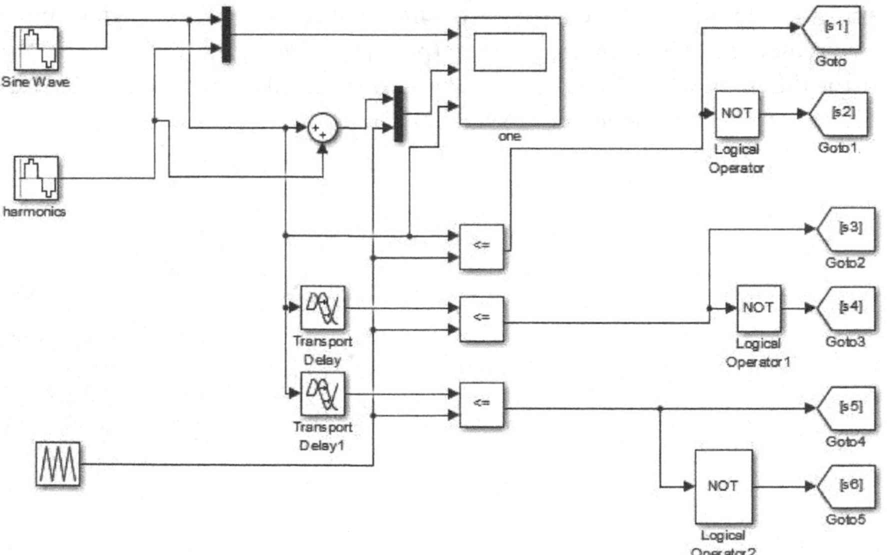

Figure 2: *THIPWM triggering circuit.*

Along with the reduction in THD value, the addition of third harmonic signal in the reference signal generates two crest points at T = π/3 and at T = 2π, where the magnitude is companion to 1. The representation of fundamental and harmonic equation can be displayed as

$$v_1 = v_1 \sin t \tag{2}$$

$$v_3 = v_3 \sin 3t \tag{3}$$

Thus, at = π/3, the first harmonic line to neutral output voltage can be taken as $v_b / 2$, and the equation can be written as

$$\frac{v_b}{2} = v_{\max imum} \sin(\pi / 3) \tag{4}$$

which gives

$$v_{\max imum} = \frac{v_b}{2}(.86) = \frac{v_b}{1.732} \tag{5}$$

2.3. Phase Disposition PWM (PDPWM)

The method for generating gate pulse through the phase disposition technique is same as for THIPWM, only the difference is that the all the shipper wave has exact same repetition and peak. Along with that all N-1 carrier signals are in phase [10]. In PDPWM technique, reference signal waveform that is basically a sinusoidal signal is being compared with the vertically shifted carrier waveforms as shown in Figure 3. This method involves N-1 shipper signals to develop N level yield voltage. All the shipper signals possess same crest and frequency along with this they are in same phase too.

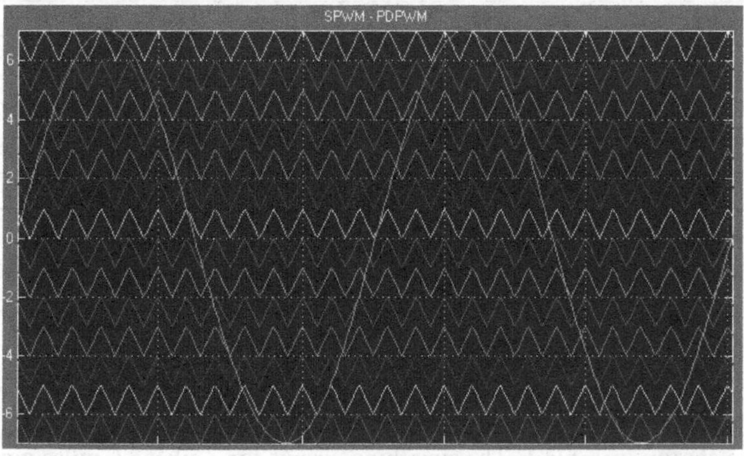

Figure 3: Gate pulse generation through PDPWM method.

2.4. *Space Vector PWM*

One more efficient technique for the generation of gate pulse is space vector pulse width modulation technique. Linear modulation range, less switching loss, less THD, direct implementation and less calculations are different advantages of using this SVPWM method. This technique can be implemented on output voltage and input current, due to which flexibility in choosing switching vector is increases and this condition also useful in unbalance condition. The main target of this technique is to set reference vector. The switching vectors for designing of 3 phase 6 switches are shown in Figure 4.

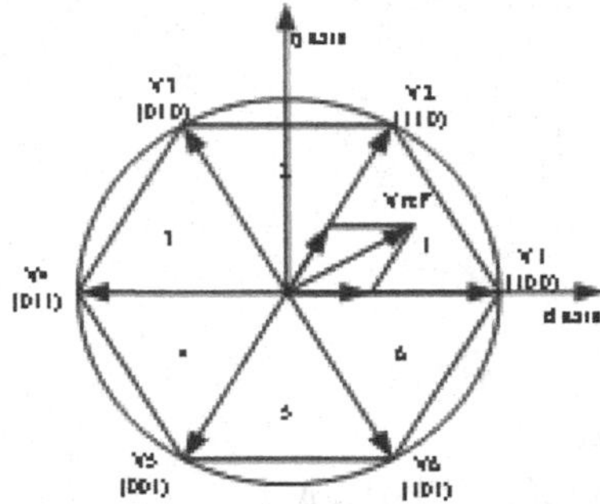

Figure 4: Switching sequence in SVPWM.

Eight switching vectors are shown in Figure 4, out of which six vectors are active vectors (V1-V6) and two are zero vectors (V0, V7). For high-level signal, we are using '1' and for lower information we are using '0'. By choosing upper switches (111) and lower switches (000), we can achieve the zero vectors.

Table 1: V_{ph} and V_L, switching vectors.

Voltage Vector	Vector			Phase Voltage			Line Voltage		
	A	B	C	V_{ao}	V_{bo}	V_{co}	V_{ab}	V_{bc}	V_{ca}
V_0	0	0	0	0	0	0	0	0	0
V_1	1	0	0	2/3	-1/3	-1/3	1	0	-1
V_2	1	1	0	1/3	1/3	-2/3	0	1	-1
V_3	0	1	0	-1/3	2/3	-1/3	- 1	1	0
V_4	0	1	1	-2/3	1/3	1/3	- 1	0	1
V_5	0	0	1	-1/3	-1/3	2/3	0	-1	1
V_6	1	0	1	1/3	-2/3	1/3	1	-1	0
V_7	1	1	1	0	0	0	0	0	0

Switching vectors for phase voltage and line voltage in terms of high (1) and low (0) are shown in Table 1. The switching circuit for 3 phase 6 pulse generation by SVPWM technique is displayed in Figure 5.

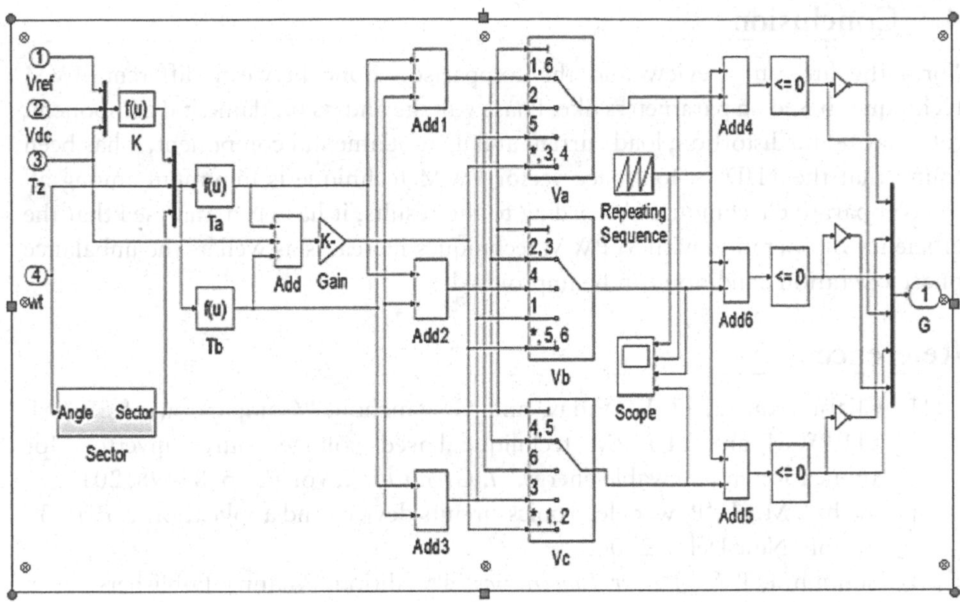

Figure 5: SVPWM modeling circuit.

3. Results and Summary

The comparative analysis and study of all considered PWM techniques, i.e. SPWM, THIPWM, PDPWM and SVPWM, are been done on MATLAB platform. Switching time for all the considered PWM techniques is been calculated, and it has been found that SVPWM method is the most efficient and least THD generating method among all the four considered techniques of PWM. The comparative table for all the considered techniques is shown in Table 2. 0.9 is the modulation index value that has chosen while performing comparative study of all these techniques.

Table 2: Comparison of various parameters for different techniques.

Parameter	SVPWM	PDPWM	THIPWM	SPWM
Phase Voltage(rms)	226.9	227.3	227.9	228.2
Fundamental Component				
Peak	301.1	291.2	282.3	260.6
rms	212.9	206.3	190.3	184.9
THD(%)	64.52	69.0	73.8	79.65
Load Current(rms)	4.828	4.802	4.795	4.757
Fundamental Component				
Peak	6.601	6.589	6.580	6.471
rms	4.667	4.627	4.591	4.576

4. Conclusion

Form the literature review and the comparison done between different PWM techniques based on parameters like: Phase voltage and its fundamental component, total harmonic distortion, load current and its fundamental component, it has been found that the THD % for space vector PWM technique is minimum among all the comparative techniques. According to the results, it has been analysed that the efficiency of operation with SVPWM techniques increases as well as the unbalance phase operation condition can be improvised.

References

[1] Chaturvedi, L., D. K. Yadav, and G. Pancholi, "Comparison of SPWM, THIPWM and PDPWM technique based voltage source inverters for application in renewable energy," *J. Green Eng.*, vol. 7, pp. 83–98, 2017.

[2] Rashid. M. H., 'Power electronics circuits devices and applications," *PHI*, 3rd edition, New Delhi, 2004.

[3] Bhimbhra, P. S., *Power Electronics*, 4th edition, Khanna Publishers, New Delhi, 2003.

[4] Mohan, N., T. M. Undeland, *et al.*, *Power Electronics Converters, Applications and Design*, 3rd edition, John Wiley & Sons, New York, 2003.

[5] Jung, J.-W., *'Sine PWM inverter' Department of Electrical and Computer Engineering*, The Ohio State University.

[6] McGrath, B. P. and D. G. Holmes, "Multicarrier PWM strategies for multilevel inverters," *IEEE Trans. Ind. Electron.*, vol. 49, pp. 858–867, 2002.

[7] Balamurugan, C. R., S. P. Natarajan, M. Arumugam, and R. Bensraj, "Investigation on three phase five switch multilevel inverter with reduced number of switches," *Rev. Ind. Eng. Lett.*, vol. 1, pp. 67–79, 2014.

[8] Gnana Prakash, M., M. Balamurugan, and S. Umashankar, "A new multilevel inverter with reduced number of switches," *Int. J. Power Electron. Drive Syst.*, vol. 5, pp. 63–70, 2014.

[9] Prabaharan, N. and K. Palanisamy, "Investigation of single-phase reduced switch count asymmetric multilevel inverter using advanced pulse width modulation technique," *Int. J. Renewable Energy Res.*, vol. 5, pp. 880–890, 2015.

[10] Pal, B. and R. Mondal, "Overall THD analysis of multicarrier PDPWM based new cascaded multilevel inverter with reduced switch of different levels at different carrier frequency," *Int. J. Emerging Technol. Eng.*, vol. 1, pp. 148–156, 2014.

31. A Phantom-Based Experimental Study of the Bioimpedance Monitoring Techniques

Ramesh Kumar[1], Manas Ranjan Tripathy[2], Ashish Kumar Singh[1], Manoj Kumar Yadav[3]

[1]*Chitkara University Institute of Engineering Technology, Punjab, India*
[2]*SRM University AP, Andra Pradesh, India*
[3]*Lovely Professional University, Punjab, India*

Abstract: A recently established new technique is electrical impedance tomography (EIT), which relates as per the interior impedance distribution for a subject (medical or nonmedical applications) measured from different locations was reconstructed into an image. The electrical impedance methodology consisted of topology of the electrodes configrations and that are attached with the subject of the circumference. The current source and measuring voltage position are defined through the proposed approach. A constant current (mill ampere current with kHz frequency) is passed into the boundary of an object through some electrodes pairing. The output voltages are measured from the periphery of the conductive object by another pair of electrodes, and the data was fed into a computer for computation. The image reconstruction of the cross-sectional image of resistivity is based on the finite element method and EIDORs toolkit on MatLab. The proposed system is validated on different phantoms for biomedical as well as industrial applications. It is more energy effiecnt and innovation for engineering research as well as medical-based application.

Keywords: Phantom, image resonctruction, EIDORS, bio-impedance, electrical impedance tomography.

1. Introduction

The aim of medical technology and device development is to improve the diagnostic capabilities of a physician. Currently, many non-invasive techniques are used for ambulatory monitoring of real-time applications in medical applications of the physiological parameters that may include imaging, both functional and morphological [1][2]. Electrical impedance tomography (EIT) is one of them having good prospects to meet such conditions. Many researchers proposed this idea of EIT for electrical impedance tomography imaging in the medical or industrial field [3]. EIT has to study of impedance distribution of an object. The calculation of voltage distribution defines the resistivity distribution of objects, which has great properties for functional imaging for tissue density. Scientific community showed keen interest since its first application by Brown and Barber, who imaged an arm. At the present, many literature research has since been done on the mathematical concept, design of EIT according to industrial or medical imaging modality to make it user-friendly and robust. Bio-impedance technique is a non-invasive_ technique, which is based on small changes in surface impedance of the object, tissue or organ system [4]. These measurements can also reflect a difference in the blood volume, and they can be exploited to show the blockage in the veins. The bio-impedance technique introduces a high-frequency current pulse (mA), which is applied on one electrode pair after that to measure voltages from other remaining electrodes pairs [5].

2. Method of Data Acquisition

In EIT, there are numerous ways to insert current inserting and voltage measurements according to the [6]. As per the previous research of the EIT technique, the neighbouring method is used in this paper or experimental. Figure 1 shows block diagram of EIT system.

In neighbouring topology of EIT technique, a current pulse inserting through the neighbouring electrodes pair and potential are measured from the remaining electrodes pairs [7]. As shown in Figure 2, continuously changing the current locations as per incremental electrodes order and measured the voltages across the remaining electrodes pairs [8].

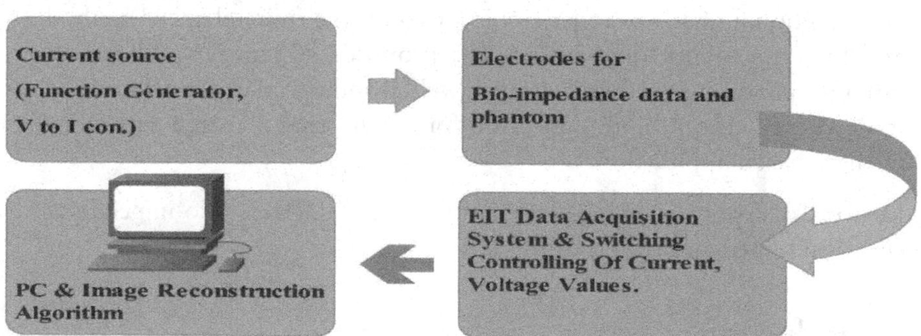

Figure 1: EIT system.

Table 1: Electrodes configuration of EIT technique.

Current Pairs	Voltage Measurement {N (N-3)}
8-electrode configuration	[8(8–5)] = 40
16-electrode configuration	[16(16–3)] = 208
32-electrode configuration	[32(32–3)] = 928

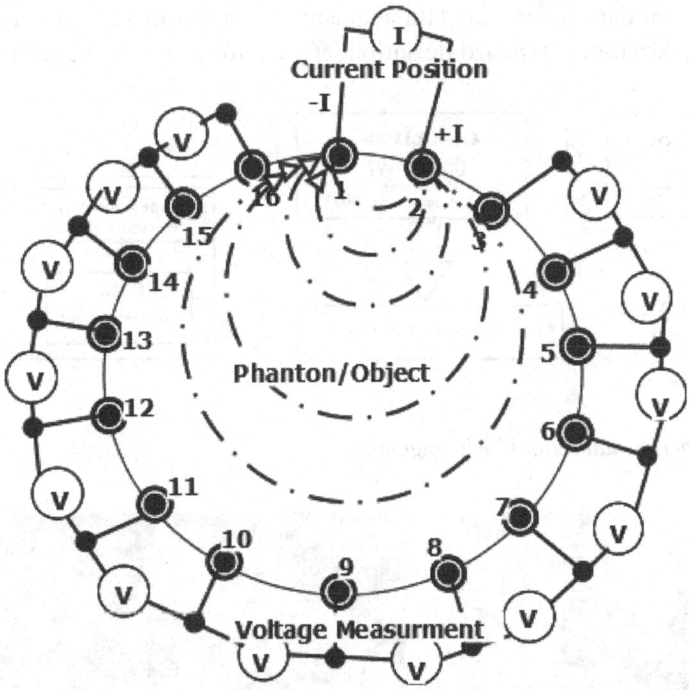

Figure 2: Electrode configuration of EIT.

As per this experimental work, we have used a 16-electrode system, 16 (no. of electrodes) ×13 (current locations) = 208 voltage measurements are obtained [5]. The current inserting and voltage measurements are interchanged. Because of reciprocity for the whole process of this method, the 104 measurements are obtained. Table 1 shows electrode configuration of EIT technique.

3. Experimental Setup

In EIT, the most important is that the built materials of phantom must be appropriate for imaging modality of the EIT technique [10]. The material may be used conductive or non-conductance or partial conductive, which is helpful for quantitative data analysis processing of EIT imaging. So plastic tank has been used with a centred placed object as a phantom [9]. The many electrodes are used in EIT. So, the nail type of electrodes is used in this experiment, as shown in Figure 4 [10]. In this experiment, the current inserting and voltages measurements are defined manually with the help of multimetre, CRO and function generator. The function generator is used for current inserting to phantom [11] [5]. The CRO and multimetre are used for voltages measurements. As shown in Figure 3, as per the threshold current values of biomedical applications, like let-go current and critical values, so, in this experiment, the current range must be below milliamperes (1 to 5 mA with frequency in kHz). The current value from the function generator is 2 mA, 100 kHz and also shown the analytical data from obtained experimental work.

These analytical data define the data acquisition method of EIT technique, which is defined as deviation, standard deviation, etc. Figure 5 shows experimental setup of papaya

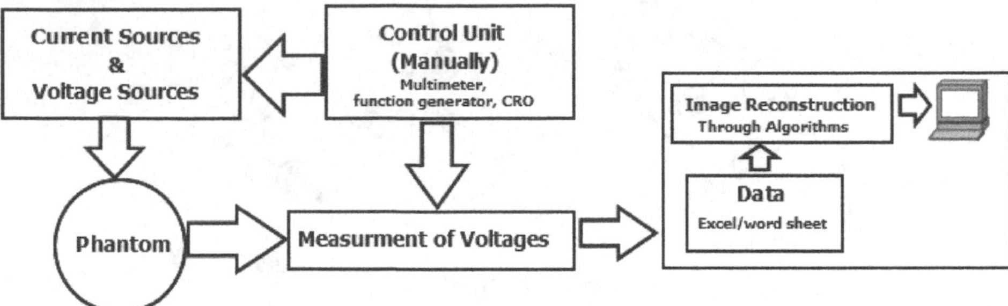

Figure 3: *Experimental setup block diagram.*

Figure 4: *Current source.*

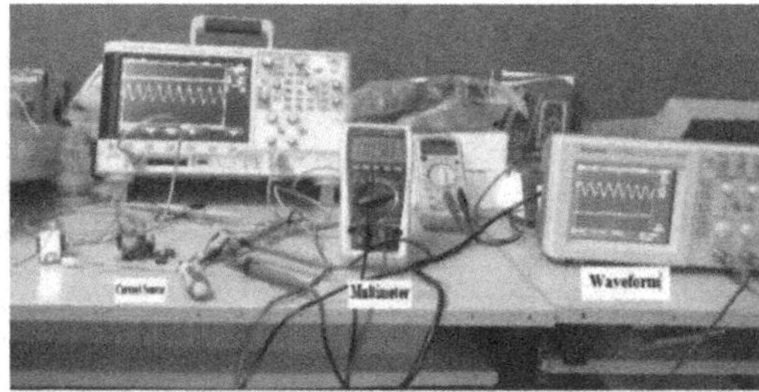

Figure 5: *Experimental setup for papaya.*

4. EIT Algorithm

The proposed work focuses on designing and developing an economical, customised and user-friendly EIT system based on an improved algorithm. The proposed system can efficiently data collection, algorithm processing of collected data in the form of 2D of inner identification and reconstruction and object recognition in phantom. Above algorithm is done according to EIDORs toolkit [12]. This toolkit has been executed through the obtained voltage measurements from the experimental work. This algorithm is starting to solve the FEM modal according to phantom and nodes. After that the homogeneous voltage data is defined according to real load data obtained from the experimental work and solves the inverse problem [13]. This toolkit also provides several non-linear or unique or stable inverse solutions.

5. Results and Discussions

Data acquisition methods of phantom obtain the final image of EIT. The internal distribution of potential defines the adjacent electrode pairs except for the current inserting location of the phantom. Such as one different set of patterns is obtained like above by inserting the current in another electrode, which is shown in Figure 6 (A). Data were obtained from the phantom for one current position. The imaging algorithm consists of forward solution and inverse solution, which is related to the inside distributed potentials or voltage measurements from the electrodes. So, the internal impedance distribution in the form of voltages of the phantom with respect to one current position of the whole system, as shown in Figure 6 (A), (B).

The simulation results are obtained according to internal impedance distributions, which is a form of 2D image. This image is defined as per obtained data through the EIDORs toolkit, as shown in Figure 7. The resolution and image clarity are increased with the help of finite elements and nodes, which depend on electrode configurations or voltage measurements.

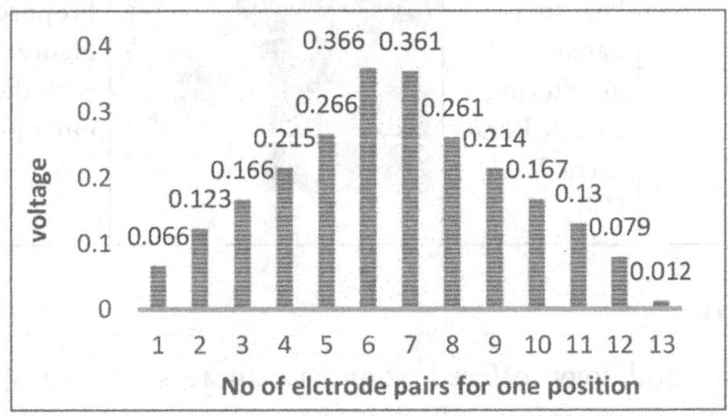

Figure 6: (A) Impedance distribution of one position of current of phantom I.

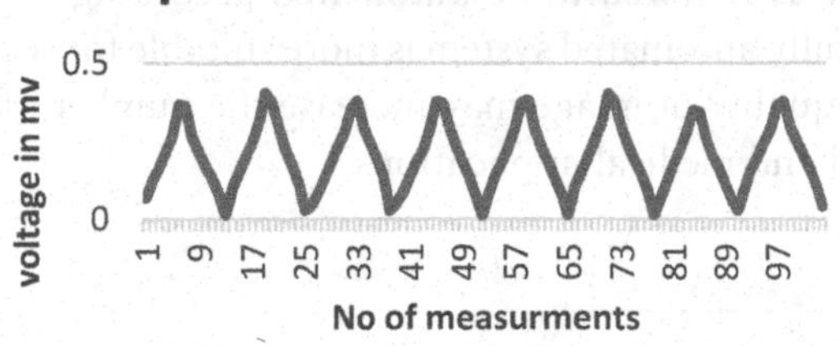

Figure 6: (B) Impedance chart for all positions of currents.

6. Comparisons

The EIT imaging technique has been introduced in this work as a noble technique that is very helpful for medical and industrial applications. Also, several image reconstruction algorithms have been developed throughout research work. In this work, we have compared different well-established algorithms with the proposed

GUI-based image reconstruction algorithm. The differently reconstructed images resulting from these algorithms applied upon the various phantoms are comparable to each other and are apparent from Table 2 as per the tank-based monitoring.

Table 2: Comparisons.

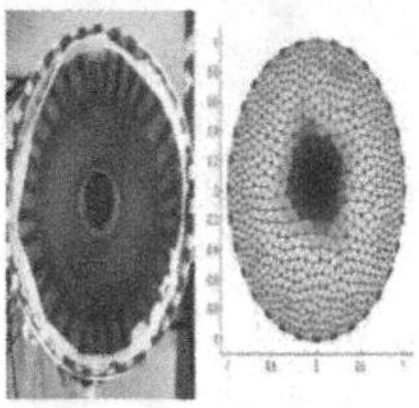	Tank-based monitoring By C L Yang (Yang 2014) [16]	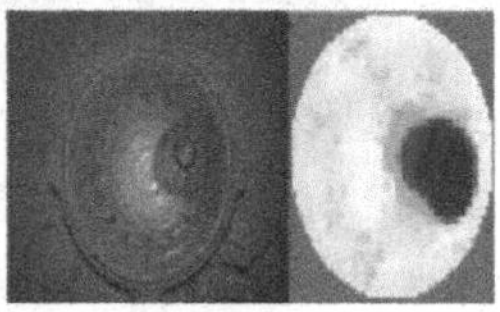	Tank-based monitoring By V Chitturi (Chitturi 2014) [17]
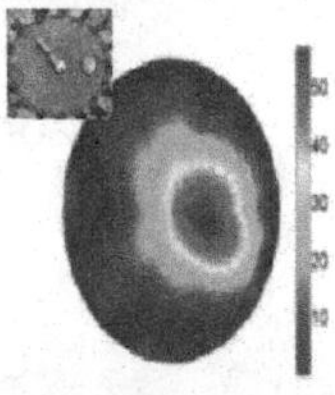	Phantom-based monitoring by T K Bera (Bera 2011) [18]	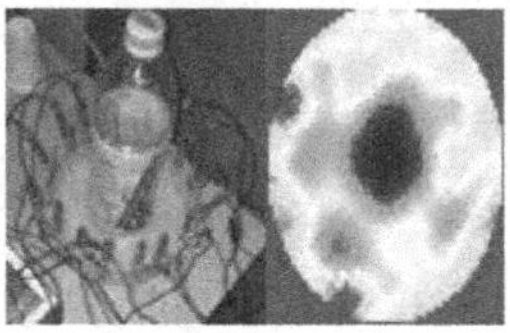	**Proposed Image Figure 7. Phantom with the image of an inner portion.**

7. Conclusion

The proposed methodology offered some advantages with respect to other imaging modalities because it is a radiation-free and inexpensive and non-invasive. The proposed instrumentation system and reconstruction algorithms technique improved the image resolution. Thus, it opened up a new frontier in biomedical imaging. The reconstruction imaging algorithm should have been spontaneous. The present scenario is required to be automated according to data analysis and interpretation. The fully automated system is more suitable for real-time application and to improve the quality of image may increase the number of electrodes. It can be used in industrial and medical applications.

References

[1] Holder, D. S., "Electrical impedance tomography (EIT) of brain function," *Brain Topogr.*, vol. 5, no. 2, pp. 87–93, 1992.

[2] Holder, D. S., "Electrical impedance tomography methods, history, and applications," *Inst. Phys. Publ. Bristol Philadelphia*, vol. Book, 2005.

[3] Barber, D., B. Brown, H. Search, C. Journals, A. Contact, M. Iopscience, and I. P. Address, "Applied potential tomography," *J. Phys. E.*, vol. 17, pp. 723–731, 1984.

[4] Ellappan, P. and R. Sundararajan, "A simulation study of the electrical model of a biological cell," *J. Electrostatic.*, vol. 63, pp. 297–307, 2005.

[5] Malmivuo, J. A. and R. Plonsey, "Impedance tomography," in *Bioelectromagn. Princ. Appl. Bioelectr. Biomagn. Fields*, no. 1992, pp. 420–427,1995.

[6] Kumar, R., S. Kumar, and A. Sengupta, "Analysis and validation of medical application through electrical impedance based system," *Intell. Syst. Appl. Eng.*, vol. 6, no. 1, pp. 14–18, 2018.

[7] Ren, Z. and W. Yang, "An electrical capacitance tomography system with MatLab-Simulink GUI," *IST 2012 - 2012 IEEE Int. Conf. Imaging Syst. Tech. Proc.*, pp. 578–583, 2012.

[8] Kumar, R. and S. Tripathi, "A novel GUI-Based image reconstruction algorithm of EIT imaging technique," *Int. J. Cognit. Inf. Natural Intell.*, vol. 15, no. 3, pp. 31–46, 2021.

[9] Meena, R. K., S. K. Pahuja, A. Bin Queyam, and A. Sengupta, "Electrical impedance tomography : a real-time medical imaging technique," *Handbook of Research on Advanced Concepts in Real-Time Image and Video Processing*, IGI, pp. 130–152, 2018.

[10] Kumar, R., S. Kumar, and A. Sengupta, "Optimization of bio-impedance techniques-based monitoring system for medical & industrial applications," *IETE J. Res.*, vol. 0, no. 0, pp. 1–12, 2020.

[11] Kumar, R. and R. Mahadeva, "An experimental measurement and control of human body," *J. Circuits, Syst. Comput.*, vol. 30, no. 6, pp. 1–17, 2021.

[12] Adler, A. and W. R. B. Lionheart, "Uses and abuses of EIDORS: an extensible software base for EIT," *Physiol. Meas.*, vol. 27, no. 5, pp. S25–S42, 2006.

[13] Kumar, R., S. Kumar, and A. Sengupta, "An experimental analysis and validation of electrical impedance tomography technique for medical or industrial application," *Biomed. Eng.: Appl. Basis Commun.*, vol. 31, no. 02, p. 19500, 2019.

[14] Nayak, S. R., J. Mishra, and G. Palai, "Analysing roughness of surface through fractal dimension: a review," *Image Vis. Comput.*, vol. 89, pp. 21–34, 2019.

[15] Kaushal, C., S. Bhat, D. Koundal, and A. Singla, "Recent trends in computer assisted diagnosis (CAD) system for breast cancer diagnosis using histopathological images," *IRBM*, vol. 40, no. 4, pp. 211–227,2019.

[16] Zhang, W., C. Wang, W. Yang, and C.-H. Wang, "Application of electrical capacitance tomography in particulate process measurement – a review," *Adv. Powder Technol.*, vol. 25, no. 1, pp. 174–188, 2014.

[17] Chitturi, V. and N. Farrukh, "A low-cost electrical impedance tomography (EIT) for pulmonary disease modelling and diagnosis," *Name Second Int. Conf. Technol. Adv. Electr. Electron. Comput. Eng.*, pp. 83–89, 2014.

[18] Bera, T. K. and J. Nagaraju, "Surface electrode switching of a 16-electrode wireless EIT system using RF-based digital data transmission scheme with eight-channel encoder/decoder ICs," *Meas. J. Int. Meas. Confed.*, vol. 45, no. 3, pp. 541–555, 2012.

32. Design and FPGA Implementation of Digital Clock with Millisecond Precision

Kushagra, Jay Khaple, Siragam Tejeswar Reddy, Jai Shivam Chaudhary, Raihan Ahmed and Sobhit Saxena

School of Electronics and Electrical Engineering, Lovely Professional University, Punjab, India

Abstract: High-precision digital clock became the necessary everywhere from basic sport event to nuclear bomb detonator. Low-power design that can be easily implemented is highly desirable. A comparison of various designs of 'Digital Clock' available in literature has been accomplished, and the static and dynamic power dissipation along with consumed look up tables (LUTs) is presented in this work. A new design is also proposed in this work having the capability of high precision up to milliseconds, starting from 10 ms to 990 ms. Static and dynamic power dissipation along with consumed LUTs are also estimated and compared graphically with the exiting designs. The circuit is designed in Verilog hardware description language. Simulation and the testing of the design is conducted using Xilinx Vivado EDA tool. Hardware implementation of the design is carried out on Nexys4Artix-7 FPGA board. The estimated static and dynamic power dissipation is 97 mW and 34 mW, respectively. LUT count is 118.

Keywords: Precision, clock, power dissipation, LUT, FPGA.

1. Introduction

Digital clock is one of the very important device having fundamental daily-life application. Hence, it is crucial to have a high precision digital clock, which also fulfils the demand of low-power consumption and less area used to make it work. From nuclear bomb detonator to a basic clock in schools, from a digital clock in space exploration to digital clock used in railway stations, it is very important to have a precise time so this paper consist a novel design of digital clock which has precision up to milliseconds. Figure 1 describes the basic block diagram of proposed architecture of millisecond précised digital clock.

Along with this millisecond precise digital clock, this paper also compares several designs of digital clock which has already been published. This comparison will help to understand various design techniques of the digital clock. The comparison will be mainly done on the LUT's used to implement a specific design and the power consumption of various design.

Field programmable gate array (FPGA) is an integrated circuit which can be programmed and reprogrammed depending on the designs which we have. This reconfigurable property helps designers directly check various designs [1–2]. And further the integrated circuits can be fabricated.

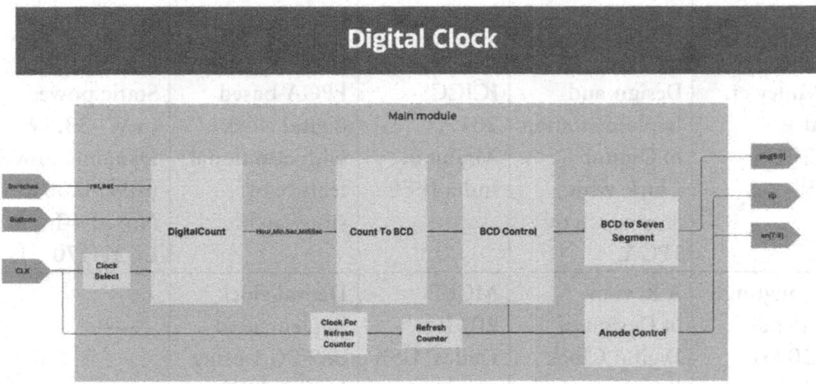

Figure 1: Block diagram of digital clock.

In front-end VLSI design, the circuits are described in Verilog/VHDL (Hardware Description Language), which is further implemented on FPGA after synthesis and bitstream generation [3–6]. The digital clock proposed in the current work is designed in Verilog HDL, and implementation is carried out on Nexys 4 Artix-7 FPGA Board.

2. Literature Review

A thorough comparison of publications [7–11] has been done in this section. From the comparison, a detailed results can be brought out and those results are shown in Table 1.

Table 1: Literature review.

	Author/ Year of Publication	Title	Journal/ Conference	Features	Parameter Estimated
1	Vuthuri et. Al (2018) [7]	A Novel 7-Segment Digital Clock Implementation on FPGA	ICEI-2017, Tirunelveli, India IEEE	FPGA implementation of digital clock using MOD Counter with set and reset feature.	Min and Max period: 3.428 ns and291.736 MHz Min. input and output arrival time of clock: 1.137ns and 3.172ns Max. path delay: 2.004ns

2	Zhu et.al (2011) [8]	Research and design of digital clock based on FPGA	Advance materials Research	FPGA Implementation of Digital Clock using VHDL with Loudspeaker to tell time hourly.	-----
3	Muley et. al (2017) [9]	Design and Implementation of Digital Clock with Stopwatch on FPGA	ICICCS-2017, Madurai, India IEEE	FPGA-based digital clock with additional feature of stopwatch.	Static power (mW)-33.59 Dynamic power (mW)-0.00 No. of 4-Input LUTs-170
4	Wangtingli Li et.al (2023) [10]	A Review of Design of Digital Clock Based on Verilog HDL	MCEE-2023, Dallas, USA	Digital clock implemented on FPGA using Verilog HDL.	------
5	Asha Devi et.al (2019) [11]	Design and Implementation of custom IP for Real-Time Clock on Reconfigurable Device	ICISC-2019, Coimbatore, India IEEE	Digital clock implementation using custom IP (Intellectual Property) for more flexibility and accuracy with real-time clock.	Device static: 0.097W (91%) Dynamic static: 0.009W (9%) No. of 4-Input LUTs-178

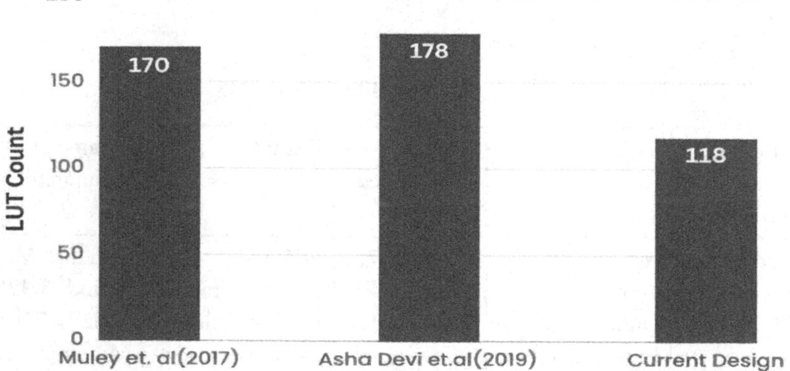

Figure 2: Comparison of LUT's of various papers.

Table 1 compares the FPGA implementations and functionality of several digital clock designs. Power variations and LUT count are the main factors that are compared. Depending on the design complexity, it can be deduced that the design complexity and LUT count are directly related. Figure 2 compares the suggested design's LUT used to that of the designs in the literature review.

3. Novel design of Millisecond-Precise Digital Clock

Digital clocks are fundamental devices in everyday life, and their implementation in FPGA-based hardware offers versatility and precision. In this work, Verilog HDL is used to develop clock modules, the clock is displaying time from 00:00:00:00 to 23:59:59:99 and the uses of different buttons in clock allowing user to control time adjustments. The integration of these modules is done with an FPGA development board, specifically the Nexus-4 board, provided a platform for real-time clock functionality.

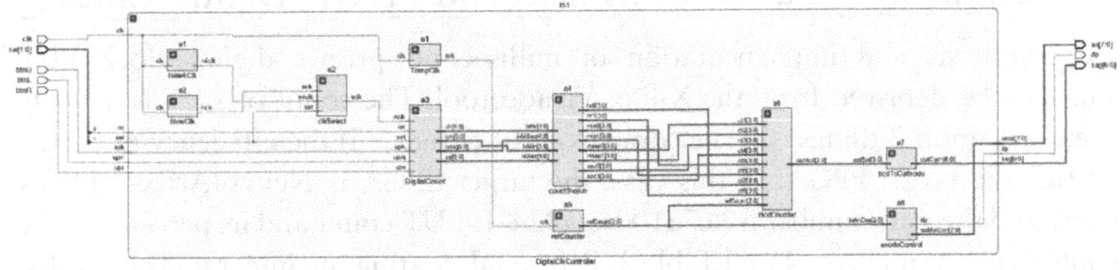

Figure 3: Elaborated design of clock.

1. Verilog Modules and Clock Generation: The suggested system relies heavily on three clocks. While a 4Hz/0.25s clock made it easier for customers to modify their watch timings, a 100 Hz/10 ms clock allowed for exact time visibility utilised a 1/16th-second clock, which was built for exact segment visibility using persistence-of-vision effects.
2. NewClk Module: This module generated a 100Hz clock by triggering a temporary variable in every 50KHz clock cycle. It is crucial for the normal operation of the digital clock.
3. New4Clk Module: A 4Hz clock was generated by triggering a temporary variable every 12.5 MHz clock cycle. This clock allowed rapid setting of various clock parameters in the settable clock module.
4. TempClk Module: Persistence-of-vision effect is achieved with a clock generated approximately every 0.6 milliseconds, synchronised with a count variable flipping its value on every positive edge of a 100 MHz clock.
5. Clock Display and Control: The DigitalCount module is responsible for generating the hour, minute, second and millisecond blocks of the digital clock. It accepts inputs from the clock modules, including the 100MHz clock, reset, set and up buttons for hours, minutes and seconds. The outputs ch, cm, cs and cms represented the hour, minute, second and milli-seconds blocks, respectively. [Figure 3]

6. countSvalue module: The countSvalue module converts these values into 4-bit BCD (binary-coded decimal) representations for hours, minutes, seconds and milliseconds. These BCD values are subsequently processed by the BcdCounter module to select the appropriate output for display on seven-segment displays.
7. bcdToCathode module: The bcdToCathode module maps the BCD values to specific cathode configurations, ensuring accurate segment activation for displaying the time.
8. The anodeControl module: The anodeControl module generates anode control signals based on the reference count value. This facilitates multiplexing of the seven-segment displays, ensuring the correct segments are activated at the right time.

4. Results and Analysis of Millisecond Precise Digital Clock

After synthesis and implementation of millisecond precise digital clock LUT count can be deprived from the Xilinx Vivado tool. The count of LUT is majorly dependent upon 3 things: (i) The complexity of design, (ii) the efficiency of design and (iii) the target FPGA. In this case, the target FPGA is Nexys4Artix-7 FPGA board, and the part number is xc7a100tcsg324-1. LUT count and its percentage are plainly evident in Figure 4 and Table 2. Before fabricating the integrated circuit for the design, these LUTs are important since they let designers to estimate how much space and power each component would require.

Table 2: Utilisation of components (in no.).

Utilization — Post-Synthesis | **Post-Implementation** — Graph | **Table**

Resource	Utilization	Available	Utilization %
LUT	118	63400	0.19
FF	111	126800	0.09
IO	22	210	10.48
BUFG	1	32	3.13

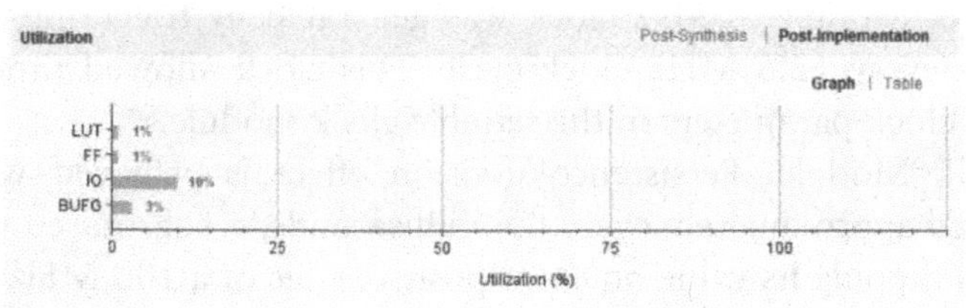

***Figure 4:** Utilisation of components (in %).*

Analysis of total power, static power as well as dynamic power is also done of the proposed design using Vivado EDA tool. Figure 5 has the complete information about the power analysis. The FPGA board used for the implementation has total

63400 LUT's out of which one 118 LUT are been used as shown in Table 2, which is much less than then average LUT count of the comparison done in the literature review as shown in Figure 2, which also proves that less area will be consumed for this design implementation.

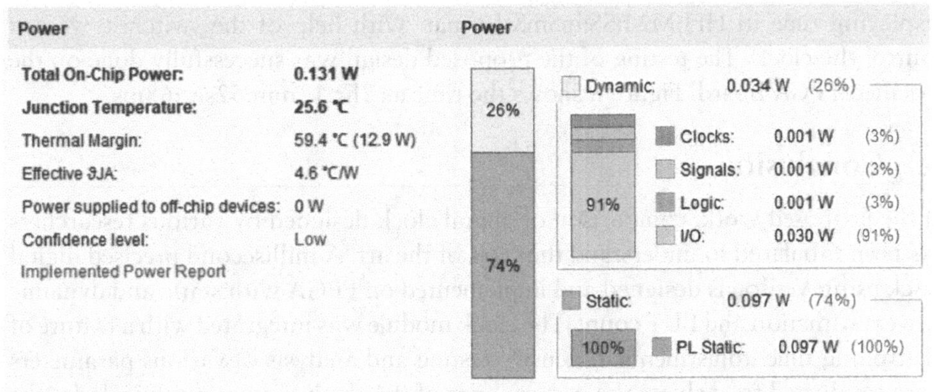

Figure 5: Power.

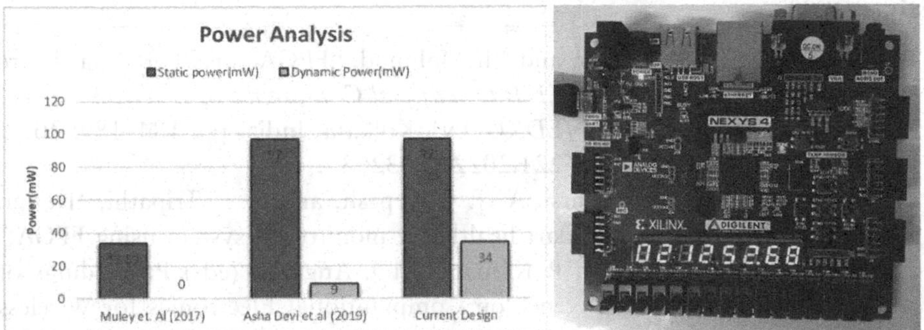

Figure 6: Power analysis.

Figure 7: Hardware implementation.

Figure 5 shows a thorough power analysis of the suggested design in relation to the designs presented in the literature review. Total power consumption of proposed design is 131 mW. The reason for high-power consumption is that a greater number of IO parts are brought into consideration and the reason to do this is because the proposed work goal is to achieve high precision.

5. Hardware Implementation

Hardware implementation is also called as physical testing of the design. It is the crucial step, after generation of bitstream file, it is loaded into the FPGA board. A shared UART/JTAG USB port is used for powering the device and loading the bit stream file into FPGA. However, this bitstream file is non-human readable because the data is stored in binary format. Also, before the generation of the bitstream file, we have to use the constraint file with (.xdc) extension. This file contains all the enabling and disabling option of all the components on the FPGA board. The constraint file is unique for all the individual FPGA boards and can easily be available on the respective vendors websites. All the 8 seven segment displays of Nexys4Artix-7 FPGA board (the part number is xc7a100tcsg324-1) are in use for displaying time in HH:MM:SS:mSmS format. With help of the switches, we can control the clock. The testing of the proposed design was successfully done on the specified FPGA board. Figure 6 shows the time as 2hr:12min:52sec:68ms.

6. Conclusion

In the proposed work, comparison of digital clock designed by various researchers has been tabulated to understand the state of the art. A millisecond précised digital clock using Verilog is designed and implemented on FPGA with static and dynamic power estimation and LUT count. The clock module was integrated with a feature of controlling time adjustments. Extensive testing and analysis of various parameters were conducted to evaluate the performance of the clock. Future work includes the addition of an alarm feature through external hardware integration.

References

[1] Tripathi, S. L., A. Kumar, and M. Mahmud, "FPGA for secured hardware & IP ownership," *2022 IEEE International Conference of Electron Devices Society Kolkata Chapter (EDKCON)*, Kolkata, India, pp. 184–189, 2022, doi: 10.1109/EDKCON56221.2022.10032935.

[2] Badiganti, P. K., S. Peddirsi, A. T. J. Rupesh, and S. L. Tripathi, "Design and implementation of smart healthcare monitoring system using FPGA," In: Rawat S., A. Kumar, P. Kumar, and J. Anguera (eds) Proceedings of First International Conference on Computational Electronics for Wireless Communications. Lecture Notes in Networks and Systems, vol 329, Springer, Singapore, 2022. https://doi.org/10.1007/978-981-16-6246-1_18.

[3] Tripathi, S. L., S. Saxena, S. K. Sinha, and G. S. Patel, *Digital VLSI Design Problems and Solution with Verilog*, John Wiley & Sons, Ltd., 2021, DOI:10.1002/9781119778097 ISBN: 978-1-119-77804-2.

[4] Dawson, C., S.K. Pattanam, and D. Roberts, "The Verilog procedural interface for the Verilog hardware description language," *Image Vis. Comput.*, pp. 17–23, 1996. doi: 10.1109/IVC.1996.496013.

[5] Becker, M., "Faster Verilog simulations using a cycle based programming methodology," *Proceedings. IEEE International Verilog HDL Conference*, Santa Clara, CA, USA, pp. 24–31, 1996, doi: 10.1109/IVC.1996.496014.

[6] Payal, R., A. Saxena, and B. Chanda, "Implementation of smart home through FPGA using Verilog hardware descriptive language," *2020 IEEE International Conference on Advent Trends in Multidisciplinary Research and Innovation (ICATMRI)*, pp. 1–6, 2020, doi:10.1109/ICATMRI51801.2020.9398499.

[7] Vuthuri, N. K., V. Mahewar, G. Yeddluri, E. S. Movva, and V. Ch, "A novel 7-segment digital clock implementation on FPGA," *2017 International Conference on Trends in Electronics and Informatics (ICEI)*, Tirunelveli, India, pp. 465–468, 2017, doi: 10.1109/ICOEI.2017.8300970.

[8] Zhu, J., A. Wu, and J. Zhu, "Research and design of digital clock based on FPGA," *Adv. Mater. Res.*, vol. 187, pp. 741–745, 2011. doi: 10.4028/www.scientific.net/AMR.187.741.

[9] Muley, R., B. Patil, and R. Henry, "Design and implementation of digital clock with stopwatch on FPGA," *2017 International Conference on Intelligent Computing and Control Systems (ICICCS)*, Madurai, India, pp. 1033–1036, 2017, doi: 10.1109/ICCONS.2017.8250622.

[10] Li, W., S. Li, Q. Zeng, and C. Zhou, "A review of design of digital clock based on Verilog HDL," *Highlights Sci. Eng. Technol.*, vol. 46, pp. 289–297, 2023. doi:10.54097/hset.v46i.7716.

[11] Devi, D. A. and N. S. Rani, "Design and implementation of custom IP for real time clock on reconfigurable device," *2019 Third International Conference on Inventive Systems and Control (ICISC)*, Coimbatore, India, pp. 414–418, 2019, doi: 10.1109/ICISC44355.2019.9036428.

33. Optimising Supercapacitor-Based Power Delivery Systems for Enhanced Efficiency in Electric Vehicles

Harleenpal Singh1, Sobhit Saxena1, Vikram Kumar Kamboj2

[1]*School of Electronics and Electrical Engineering, Lovely Professional University, Punjab, India*

[2]*Schulich School of Engineering, University of Calgary, Calgary, Alberta, Canada*

Abstract: This research paper offers a comprehensive exploration of the simulation and optimisation of a supercapacitor (SC)-based power delivery system designed for electric vehicles (EVs). The growing demand for efficient and reliable power transmission systems in EVs has created an urgent need for innovative energy storage solutions. In this framework, a switching design is introduced, featuring the incorporation of two SC banks – a primary bank and a secondary bank – interconnected through switches. Notably, the secondary bank in the power system incorporates an ingenious parallel changeover circuit, which dynamically reconfigures the SCs in response to fluctuating load demands. By carefully managing the bank voltage at its specified nominal value, achieved through the strategic configuration of the secondary bank parallel connections, a significant improvement in energy utilisation efficiency for the SCs is achieved. The simulation results underscore the potential for enhancing energy storage and utilisation, addressing crucial challenges in the adoption of EVs.

Keywords: Electric vehicles, energy efficiency, energy optimisation, energy storage, secondary power source, supercapacitor bank.

1. Introduction

The adoption of electric vehicles (EVs) has witnessed a remarkable surge in recent years, driven by their environmental benefits and their potential to reduce our reliance on fossil fuels. As the world strives to mitigate the impacts of climate change and transition towards sustainable transportation solutions, the role of EVs becomes increasingly pivotal. One key facet of enhancing EV performance and sustainability lies in the efficient management of their powertrain systems. In this context, accurate simulation models are indispensable tools for studying, optimising and ultimately maximising the efficiency of EV powertrains. This research paper delves into a critical aspect of this endeavour, focusing on the simulation and control of an EV powertrain with a specific emphasis on the integration of supercapacitors (SCs) for energy storage systems. SCs, often referred to as ultracapacitors, have emerged as a compelling component within the domain of energy storage for EVs [1]. Their ability to rapidly store and discharge electrical energy makes them a valuable asset in optimising the energy utilisation efficiency of EV powertrains [2]. Unlike traditional batteries, SCs offer high-power density, quick charge and discharge capabilities and a longer cycle life, making them well suited for applications where rapid power bursts are essential, such as regenerative braking and quick acceleration. Understanding the intricate interplay of SCs within an EV powertrain is pivotal to harnessing their full potential in improving both performance and efficiency.

The proposed research introduces a sophisticated architecture that comprises two distinct SC banks: the main bank and the secondary bank [3]. Within this intricate power system, a meticulous arrangement is employed to connect these banks, allowing for efficient energy storage and delivery. Of particular interest in this study is the initial stage of operation, where the SCs are interconnected in a parallel configuration. This foundational setup is strategically chosen for its inherent advantages, setting the stage for optimal energy utilisation. The research explores the first parallel changeover, which represents a pivotal transition within the power system, ultimately aimed at enhancing energy efficiency during power delivery. In light of the immense potential offered by SCs and the intricate architecture proposed, this research paper outlines its primary scope and objectives. Specifically, the paper focuses on the detailed examination of the first parallel changeover within the EV powertrain system. It explores the conditions, mechanisms and benefits of transitioning from the initial parallel configuration to optimise energy utilisation efficiency during power delivery. Through a combination of simulation models, empirical data and rigorous analysis, this research seeks to provide valuable insights into the practical implementation of SCs in EV powertrains and their role in advancing the sustainability and performance of EVs. Additionally, this work serves as a foundation for future research, which will delve into the series changeover aspect, thereby offering a comprehensive perspective on energy management within EV powertrains.

SCs, also known as ultracapacitors or supercaps, are energy storage devices that have gained significant attention and importance in the context of EVs. They play a pivotal role in enhancing the energy utilisation efficiency and performance of EV powertrains [4]. Unlike traditional lithium-ion batteries, which are commonly used in EVs for energy storage, SCs offer unique advantages due to their rapid charge and discharge capabilities and high-power density.

1.1. Key Advantages of using Supercapacitors in Electric Vehicles (EVs)

Quick Charge and Discharge: SCs can rapidly store and release electrical energy [5]. This feature is particularly valuable in EVs, where quick bursts of power are required for actions like regenerative braking and sudden acceleration.

Long Cycle Life: SCs have a longer cycle life compared to many batteries. They can endure a large number of charge–discharge cycles without significant degradation, making them more reliable for long-term use in EVs [5].

High Power Density: SCs offer high-power density, meaning they can deliver a substantial amount of power in a short amount of time [6]. This is vital for meeting the demands of high-performance EVs.

Efficiency: SCs are known for their high charge and discharge efficiency. They can efficiently convert electrical energy to kinetic energy and vice versa, reducing energy losses during power transfer [7].

1.2. Integration in EV Powertrain

The integration of SCs into the EV powertrain involves incorporating them as an additional energy storage component alongside the primary lithium-ion battery [8]. SCs are strategically placed to complement the battery's strengths and mitigate its weaknesses. SCs are well-suited for capturing and releasing energy during high-demand situations. For instance, during regenerative braking, when the vehicle needs to quickly store energy that would otherwise be lost as heat in traditional brakes, SCs can efficiently capture and later release this energy for acceleration. Buffering and peak power where SCs act as buffers, ensuring a stable and uninterrupted power supply to the electric motor [9]. They provide peak power during rapid acceleration, reducing the strain on the battery, which is typically designed for slower and sustained power delivery. Further, SCs enhance the efficiency of energy recovery systems [10]. When the vehicle slows down or descends a hill, excess energy can be quickly stored in SCs and then utilised for acceleration or other power-demanding tasks. Enhanced battery longevity by offloading high-power demands from the battery, SCs can help extend the overall lifespan of the lithium-ion battery in the EV, as frequent high-power discharges can contribute to battery degradation [11].

2. Methodology

The proposed architecture represents a sophisticated and meticulously designed system aimed at optimising energy utilisation efficiency within the EV powertrain. It comprises two primary SC banks: the main bank and the secondary bank, both strategically integrated into the powertrain system. This architectural design aims to capitalise on the unique characteristics of SCs, such as their rapid charge and discharge capabilities and high-power density, to enhance overall performance and efficiency [12]. The architecture's key feature is its adaptability, allowing for a seamless transition between different configurations to meet varying power demands. The main bank is a pivotal component within the proposed architecture, directly interconnected into the EV powertrain without the need for additional switching circuitry. It serves as the primary source of energy storage and delivery during the initial stages of operation. The main bank, consisting of a network of

SCs, is strategically configured to operate in parallel, ensuring rapid energy storage and discharge capabilities. This configuration is advantageous during situations requiring immediate power bursts, such as sudden accelerations or regenerative braking [13]. The main bank's inherent high-power density and efficiency make it ideal for delivering the rapid energy required for these actions.

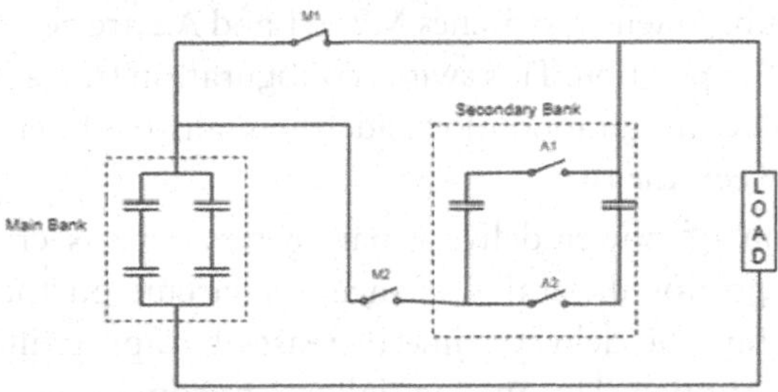

Figure 1: Circuit diagram illustrating the switching arrangement of the supercapacitor banks.

Complementing the main bank, the secondary bank plays a vital role in optimising energy utilisation efficiency during specific stages of operation. It is intricately connected to the main bank through a set of switching components, including switches M1 and M2. The secondary bank initially operates in a parallel configuration, aligning with the main bank's parallel setup. This configuration allows for efficient energy capture during regenerative braking and other high-power-demand scenarios. This transition, triggered by precise voltage thresholds, ensures optimal energy utilisation by balancing the power delivery between the two banks [14].

The proposed architecture's ingenuity is most evident in its transition mechanism of parallel configurations. During the initial stages, such as regenerative braking, the main bank handles the power demands on its own, with switches M1 and M2 in the OFF state. However, as the voltage of the SC banks approaches predefined thresholds, a transition takes place. The secondary bank, comprising SCs arranged in parallel, undergoes a meticulously orchestrated transformation. This changeover involves activating switches M2, A1 and A2 while keeping switch M1 in the OFF position. This switch activation reconfigures the secondary bank into a parallel configuration, enabling it to share the load with the main bank while maintaining optimal voltage levels [13]. This adaptive and precise configuration ensures that energy utilisation efficiency is maximised, aligning with the dynamic requirements of the EV powertrain system.

The first power delivery parameter under consideration is the delivery time without the application of SC switching. In this scenario, referring to Figure 1, where the SCs operate solely in main bank mode, the primary source of power delivery is the main bank. During this stage, switch M2, as well as switches A1, and A2, remains in the OFF state. The main bank is responsible for providing the necessary power to the EV's electric motor. When the proposed parallel changeover circuit is activated, the power delivery dynamics undergo a transformation. The circuit allows for an orchestrated transition from parallel to series configuration, optimising energy utilisation efficiency. At this stage, the secondary bank is brought into play to share the power delivery load with the main bank. This transition is initiated when the terminal voltage of the SC banks approaches a predetermined threshold (Vth1). Subsequently, switches M2, A1 and A2 are activated, while switch M1 remain in the OFF position. This switch configuration transforms the secondary bank into a parallel configuration alongside the main bank, effectively balancing power delivery between the two.

The comparison of power delivery parameters reveals critical insights into the impact of the proposed parallel changeover circuit on the EV powertrain's performance. Notably, the delivery time increases by approximately 7.2% when the SC switching is applied. This may initially seem counterintuitive, as one might expect the transition to series configuration to enhance efficiency and reduce delivery time. However, this increase in delivery time reflects the deliberate shift in power delivery strategy. While the changeover circuit optimises energy utilisation efficiency, it may slightly extend the time required for power delivery due to the shared load between the main and secondary banks.

It's essential to recognise that the primary objective of the parallel changeover circuit is not solely to minimise delivery time but to ensure efficient and adaptive power delivery while maintaining optimal voltage levels. This nuanced approach aims to strike a balance between performance and energy utilisation efficiency [15]. As such, the modest increase in delivery time is a trade-off for more efficient energy utilisation, making it a strategically valuable adjustment for EVs.

2.1. Triggering Conditions

The initiation of the first parallel changeover is governed by specific triggering conditions, notably the voltage of the SC banks. When the terminal voltage approaches a predetermined threshold value, often referred to as Vth1, it signals the need to shift from the initial parallel configuration to a more efficient power delivery mode. The precise value of Vth1 is meticulously selected to align with the system's requirements and ensure that the transition occurs at the most opportune moment. In the initial stages of operation, power delivery to the EV load is primarily accomplished through the main bank. The main bank, configured in parallel, possesses the responsibility of providing the necessary electrical energy for the vehicle's propulsion.

2.2. Initiating the First Parallel Changeover

Vth1 represents the voltage threshold that signals the initiation of the first parallel changeover within the EV powertrain system. As the terminal voltage of the SC banks approaches Vth1, it serves as a clear indication that the system should transition to parallel configuration with the secondary SC bank. The value of

Vth1 is carefully determined based on various factors, including the powertrain's power requirements, the state of charge of the SCs and the system's overall design objectives. It is set to ensure that the transition occurs precisely when the system can benefit the most from the changeover. Voltage monitoring and control mechanisms are in place to continuously track the voltage levels of the SC banks, ensuring that Vth1 is not exceeded prematurely or missed during operation.

The optimisation strategy within the EV powertrain system is multifaceted and dynamic, driven by the implementation of the proposed parallel changeover circuit. This strategy revolves around achieving the delicate balance between power delivery efficiency, voltage stability and energy storage. One of the primary goals of optimisation is to ensure that power is delivered to the EV load in the most efficient manner possible [16]. The first parallel changeover is a central element of this strategy, as it enables a shift from the initial parallel configuration to a series-parallel configuration when needed.

3. Simulation and Results

The proposed layout of the SC bank array represents a highly intricate configuration of SCs. This deliberate choice of the number of SCs underscores the system's meticulous design principles and strategic considerations aimed at achieving optimal performance [3]. Within this arrangement, five SCs are dedicated to the primary bank, with a total main bank capacitance of 150 F and operating at 50 V. The remaining four SCs are organised in the secondary bank, which boasts a capacitance of 450 F and operates at 24 V. These specific capacitance values and voltage ratings are determined in accordance with the previously mentioned design methodology.

Table 1: Simulation parameters.

Main bank voltage (V_{main})	**8.1V**
Main bank capacity (C_{main})	**150 F**
Secondary bank voltage (V_{aux})	**2.7 V**
Secondary bank capacity (C_{aux})	**450 F**
Parallel trigger threshold voltage (V_{th1})	**5.4 V**

The energy content of the SC bank has been quantified at 23 kJ. To facilitate comparison, a static SC bank is deliberately selected, notable for its distinctive characteristics and energy storage capacity. This non-switched SC bank boasts a capacitance of 600 F, providing a substantial energy reservoir, and operates at a voltage rating of 50 V, ensuring compatibility with the system's requirements. Impressively, this bank stores 23 kJ of energy. Table 1 outlines the system parameters used in the simulations. To simulate the discharge process of the bank, a load is emulated, leading to its discharge until it reaches the minimum voltage level.

3.1. Transition Mechanism

The transition to the first parallel changeover is a meticulously orchestrated process. When the terminal voltage of the SC banks approaches Vth1, a series of events unfolds: The power system's control circuitry activates switches M2, A1 and A2 as depicted in Figure 2. These switches play a pivotal role in reconfiguring the secondary bank to parallel arrangement. As switches M2, A1 and A2 are engaged, the SCs within the secondary bank are intelligently reconfigured into a parallel combination. This reconfiguration transforms the secondary bank into a complementary source of power, ready to share the load with the main bank as shown in Figure 3. With the secondary bank now operating in parallel alongside the main bank, the power delivery dynamics are optimised. The combination of both banks ensures that the power delivered to the EV load is more efficient and better aligned with the dynamic demands of the system. The first parallel changeover is instrumental in optimising energy utilisation efficiency within the EV powertrain. By transitioning to a parallel configuration, the system intelligently balances power delivery, allowing for the maintenance of optimal voltage levels while effectively managing power demands. This shift aligns with the system's commitment to voltage stability and high-performance standards. Voltage thresholds, often denoted as Vth1, is predetermined voltage levels within the EV powertrain system that serve as critical triggers for specific operational transitions. These thresholds are meticulously selected to align with the system's requirements and ensure optimal energy utilisation efficiency.

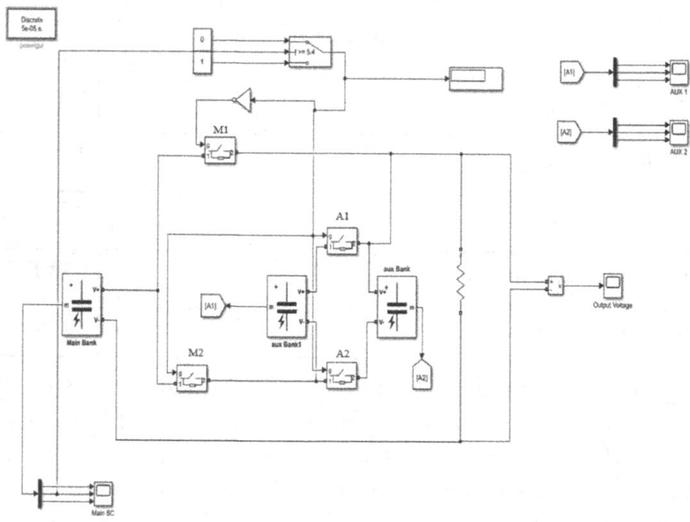

Figure 2: Supercapacitor simulation model along with switching circuit for supercapacitor switching.

It becomes evident that incorporating the proposed switching circuit into the SC bank results in a notable 11% to 15% enhancement in the duration of power delivery compared to a bank without any switching mechanism. This observation underscores the sophistication of the proposed power system design and its ability to improve overall energy utilisation and power delivery efficiency. The discharge process of the non-switched SC bank gradually reduces the SC cell voltage. This discharge sequence exhibits a noteworthy cell energy utilisation efficiency of 73.44%. This observation highlights the sophisticated design and efficient energy management of the non-switched SC bank, emphasising its capacity to optimise energy utilisation while maintaining dependable power output.

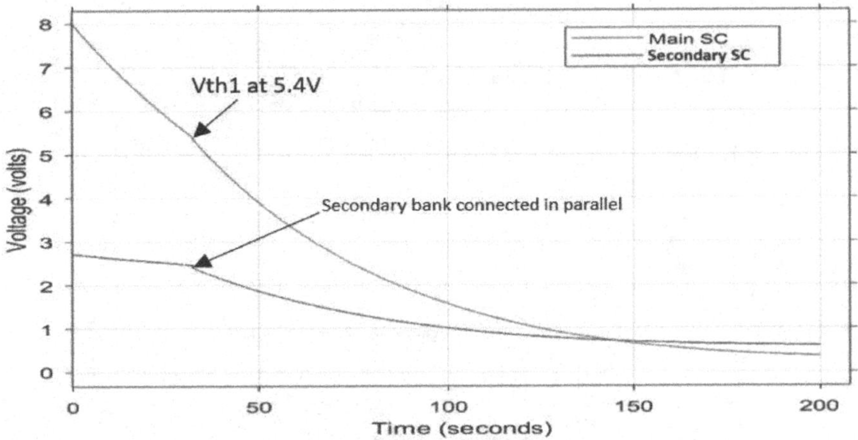

Figure 3: Main SC bank auxiliary bank voltages.

Nevertheless, when employing the proposed bank switching technique, an analysis of the discharge process reveals a remarkable reduction in the SC cell voltage of the secondary bank, smoothly transitioning from 2.7 V to 0.61 V. This discharge sequence demonstrates an impressive cell energy utilisation efficiency of 94.5%.

3.2. Simulation Results

During the discharge procedure, the method incorporates the utilisation of different trigger threshold to re-configure the SC bank, extending its duration of power output from the SC. Once the initial threshold (Vth1) is attained, indicated at 5.4 Volts of the main SC voltage in Figure 4, the secondary bank is arranged in a parallel connection. This implies that the SCs in the secondary bank are joined in parallel with those in the main bank, thereby augmenting the entire system's capacity.

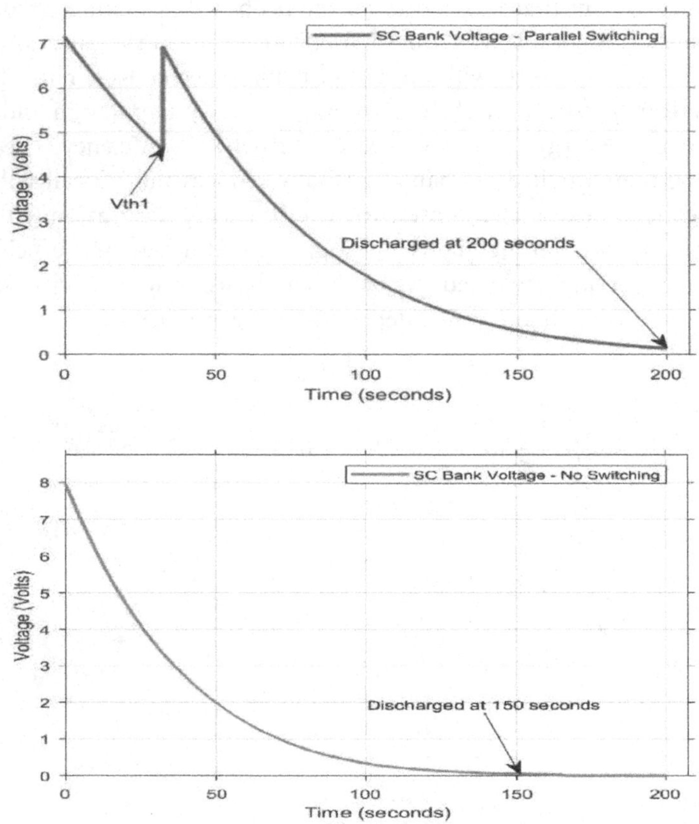

Figure 4: *With parallel switching and without switching.*

The methodology of implementing the SCs as secondary power source in coupled energy storage systems has bring forth the need to control the charge/ discharge of the SCs, since SCs can charge and discharge rapidly. A methodology was proposed to increase the time of power delivery of the SCs by the means of switching the SCs between series-parallel configurations.

Table 2: Comparison of power delivery parameters.

Delivery time when supercapacitor switching is not applied	**150 seconds**
Delivery time when supercapacitor switching is applied	**200 seconds**

By employing the above-mentioned setup, it is possible to enhance the effectiveness of SCs, thereby extending their discharge duration when used as a backup power source in EVs as shown in Table 2. Furthermore, through the incorporation of graphene into SCs and the implementation of a more robust algorithm, the previously mentioned switching technique can be refined to significantly increase the duration of power output from SC-based energy storage systems [17]. Consequently, hybrid technologies in EVs can be classified based on the integration of multiple energy storage technologies, each offering distinct advantages related to power and energy density, lifespan or battery cycles, efficiency, control, as well as the careful management of factors such as self-discharge rates and various other parameters. By utilising various forms of hybrid energy storage technologies, it becomes possible to enhance the efficiency of SCs, ultimately leading to an extended driving range for EVs in the long term [18].

4. Conclusion

The research paper has delved into a critical facet of this endeavour, focusing on the integration of SCs and the meticulously designed parallel changeover circuit within the EV powertrain. The simulation has shown that through the intricacies of the initiation of the parallel changeover, voltage thresholds and the overarching goals of optimisation and efficiency. It is evident that the proposed architecture represents a pivotal stride toward a more efficient and sustainable electric future. As it is clearly observed that the output power duration of the proposed switching mechanism is at 200 seconds, while the SC bank with no switching introduced was completely discharged at 150 seconds. Table 2 shows the difference between the proposed switching and traditional approach.

The article delves into an examination of a cost-effective arrangement for switching SC banks within hybrid energy storage systems (HESS) intended for EV applications. Within this investigation, careful scrutiny is applied to the design and sizing of the SC bank setup for accommodating electric vehicle loads. The design concept emphasised in this work underscores its dedication to addressing the specific energy demands and challenges associated with EV applications. The control system integrates a switching mechanism, purposefully designed to regulate switch behaviour in different operational modes, based on predefined bands, for discharging processes. Through simulations and experimental findings, it is evident that the proposed approach achieves an impressive SC cell energy utilisation efficiency of 94.5%, while employing a reduced number of switches. Furthermore, the devised circuit exhibits an average improvement in power delivery time ranging from 20% to 40% when compared to existing bank switching methods.

5. Future Work

One of the most immediate avenues for future research is the exploration and development of the series changeover mechanism within the EV powertrain system. While this research paper has focused extensively on the first parallel changeover, the series changeover represents another critical aspect of optimising energy utilisation [3]. Investigate the precise conditions and voltage thresholds that trigger the transition from the series-parallel configuration to the parallel configuration. This changeover is essential for maintaining voltage stability while efficiently managing power delivery. Explore methods to ensure that the load sharing between the main and secondary SC banks during the series changeover is optimised for both efficiency and performance.

Extend the research to incorporate energy recovery from additional sources beyond regenerative braking. Explore ways to capture and store energy from sources such as solar panels, wind turbines and external charging infrastructure to further enhance energy utilisation and sustainability [18].

References

[1] Pay, S. and Y. Baghzouz, "Effectiveness of battery-supercapacitor combination in electric vehicles," *2003 IEEE Bologna Power Tech Conference Proceedings*, IEEE, vol. 3, p. 6-pp, 2003.

[2] Park, S. H., J. Lee, Y. I. Lee, and A. A. Ahmed, December. "Development of electric vehicle powertrain: experimental implementation and performance assessment," *2016 Eighteenth International Middle East Power Systems Conference (MEPCON)*, IEEE, pp. 932–937, 2016.

[3] Dasari, Y., D. Ronanki, and S. S. Williamson, "A simple three-level switching architecture to enhance the power delivery duration of supercapacitor banks in electrified transportation," *IEEE Trans. Transp. Electrif.*, vol. 6, no. 3, pp.1003–1012, 2020.

[4] Jabbour, N., E. Tsioumas, N. Karakasis, and C. Mademlis, "Improved monitoring and battery equalizer control scheme for electric vehicle applications," *2017 IEEE 11th International Symposium on Diagnostics for Electrical Machines, Power Electronics and Drives (SDEMPED)*, IEEE, pp. 380–386, 2017.

[5] Khalid, H. M., L. A. Al-Hajeri, A. Ahmad, M. A. Salim, A. S. Al-Mheiri, M. A. Al Ansaari, E. Y. Al-Ali, and T. Engalla, "Self-charging system of electric vehicles: an optimization model with no traffic interactions," *2019 8th International Conference on Industrial Technology and Management (ICITM)* , IEEE, pp. 142–146, 2019.

[6] Regensburger, B., S. Sinha, A. Kumar, and K. K. Afridi, "A 3.75-kW high-power-transfer-density capacitive wireless charging system for EVs utilizing toro idal-interleaved-foil coupled inductors," *2020 IEEE Transportation Electrification Conference & Expo (ITEC)*, IEEE, pp. 839–843, 2020.

[7] Kaustubh, P. and Vaish, N., "Highly efficient PVDF film energy harvester for self charging vehicle system," *2012 Proceedings of the 9th Industrial and Commercial Use of Energy Conference*, IEEE, pp. 1–5, 2012.

[8] Shin, D., Y. Kim, J. Seo, N. Chang, Y. Wang, and M. Pedram, "Battery-supercapacitor hybrid system for high-rate pulsed load applications," *2011 Design, Automation & Test in Europe*, IEEE, pp. 1–4, 2011.

[9] Cheng, Y. and P. Lataire, "Research and test platform for hybrid electric vehicle with the super capacitor based energy storage," *2007 European Conference on Power Electronics and Applications*, IEEE, pp. 1–10, 2007.

[10] Ronanki, D., Y. Dasari, and S. Williamson, "Comparative assessment of supercapacitor bank switching techniques under constant resistor, constant current, and constant power loads," *IET Electr. Power Appl.*, vol. 14, 2021. Doi: 10.1049/iet-epa.2020.0524.

[11] Bai, Z., Y. Sun, Y. Lin, G. Chen, and B. Cao, May. "Research on ultracapacitor-battery hybrid power system," *2011 International Conference on Materials for Renewable Energy & Environment*, IEEE, vol. 1, pp. 712–716, 2011.

[12] Mestriner, D., "Feasibility study of supercapacitors as stand-alone storage systems for series hybrid electric vehicles," *2019 11th International Symposium on Advanced Topics in Electrical Engineering (ATEE)*, IEEE, pp. 1–5, 2019.

[13] Ronanki, D., Y. Dasari, and S. S. Williamson, "Power electronics-based switched supercapacitor bank circuits with enhanced power delivery capability for pulsed power applications," *2021 IEEE Applied Power Electronics Conference and Exposition (APEC)*, Phoenix, AZ, USA, pp. 2271–2276, 2021, doi: 10.1109/APEC42165.2021.9487441.

[14] Ostroverkhov, M. and Trinchuk, D., "Increasing the efficiency of electric vehicle drives with supercapacitors in power supply," *2020 IEEE 7th International Conference on Energy Smart Systems (ESS)*, IEEE, pp. 258–261, 2020.

[15] Klepikov, V. and Rotaru, A., "To use of supercapacitors in an electric vehicle's power supply," *2020 IEEE KhPI Week on Advanced Technology (KhPIWeek)*, IEEE, pp. 446–449, 2020.

[16] Andreev, M. K., "An overview of supercapacitors as new power sources in hybrid energy storage systems for electric vehicles," *2020 XI National Conference with International Participation (ELECTRONICA)*, IEEE, pp. 1–4, 2020.

[17] Noh, B., "Supercapacitor assisted hybrid electric vehicle powertrain and power selection using fuzzy rule-based algorithm," *2020 AEIT International Conference of Electrical and Electronic Technologies for Automotive (AEIT AUTOMOTIVE)*, IEEE, pp. 1–5, 2020.

[18] Macias, A., M. Kandidayeni, L. Boulon, and J. P. Trovão, 2021. "Fuel cell-supercapacitor topologies benchmark for a three-wheel electric vehicle powertrain," *Energy*, vol. 224, p. 120234, 2021.

34. Comparative Study of Variational Autoencoder for X-Ray Image Denoising

Asha Rani, M Akhil Raj, and Dr. Bhaveshkumar Choithram Dharmani

Electronics and Communication Deptt., Lovely professional University, Phagwara, India

Abstract: Noise in images is the main signal distortion that obstructs the image analysis process and extraction of information. Because of environmental effect transmission channel and the retrieval process, the image gets impaired by noise during acquisition, transmission and storage that leads loss of image information. So, image denoising becomes the crucial preprocessing step in image processing. Its main aim is to recover clean images from noisy observations. Search for a potential deep learning architecture for denoising is the need of the hour. This study presents a comparative evaluation of variational autoencoder, autoencoder and median filter in the context of image denoising. In our study, variational autoencoder, which is relatively the latest deep learning algorithm for denoising, has been used and results are compared with autoencoder and median filter.

First, we have implemented a standard autoencoder architecture, which is a deep learning model. It learns to map noisy images to their clean counterparts through encoder decoder framework. AEs are widely used because of its simple structure and effectiveness. Then we have used variational autoencoder, which is relatively the latest deep learning algorithm for denoising. It is a probabilistic variant of autoencoders which generates the latent space of data with a probability distribution to generate more realistic denoised image compared to conventional autoencoder. Lastly, we implemented Median filter as a baseline technique which is classical image processing technique, open-source X-ray images datasets have been used. Noise variance and signal-to-noise ratio are computed on the X-ray images. The study finds that variational autoencoder outperforms the traditional AEs and median filter. In conclusion, this study highlights the potential of deep learning-based approaches particularly VAE as an effective method for image denoising with PSNR=68.758 db. Results obtained with variational autoencoder are better than autoencoder and median filter.

Keywords: Variational autoencoder, real-world images, autoencoder; median filter, image denoising, deep learning.

1. Introduction

In past decades, image denoising techniques have been using many heuristic approaches. Depending on sensor types, image signal processor in camera and applications, images are affected by different types of noise [1]. Possible subsequent image processing works, e.g. image analysis, video processing and image tracking get affected unfavourably, so image denoising has a vital role in modern image processing techniques. The images were denoised empirically for noise artifacts as camera and camera software were not as developed as these are now. It is not easy to distinguish texture, edge and noise and in image in the process of denoising because these all are high frequency components. Now a days, in the process of noise removal, it becomes important problem to recover meaningful information from the noisy images. AWGN, salt and pepper noise, Poisson noise, speckle noise and quantisation noise have been discussed frequently in literature [2].

Image denoising has frequently been employed to remove Additive White Gaussian noise. This noise is additive and have constant variance for all pixels and which is not changing for position or colour intensity [3]. This simplifies the image denoising process significantly, when noise level is required as the only criteria for noise modelling. But this noise model is not valid in real-world images as noise is heterogeneous.

Deep neural networks are extensively being used in computer visions applications. Meaningful features could be learned effectively without interference of knowledge of image priors by utilising the advantages of DN architecture. Discriminative learning-based DNN architectures have been proposed also to distinguish image details and noise. Still, existing methods have one considerable drawback of existing methods is the focus on larger and deeper convolution neural networks design. So, a large number of network parameters are to be learned to represent the noise features. In this case, a trade-off between computational efficiency and denoising quality needs to be set, which can hardly satisfy the actual application.

This study excavates into the domain of image denoising and aims on a comparative analysis of three distinct approaches: Variational autoencoders (VAEs), autoencoders and median filters. Each of these methods has their own advantages and trade-offs in addressing the challenge of image denoising. VAEs not only denoise the image but estimates the uncertainty in the denoised image, which is very important in biomedical imaging. Moreover, they generate new data samples resembling the training data, which may help in recreating the high-quality versions of denoised image.

Variational autoencoder have been found to denoise the image better than autoencoder and median filter. High level features extracted by autoencoder network are used for the generation of new image by inverting extracted features from the input. This constructed image is of the same size and shape as the noisy input image [4].

In the next sections, we have discussed the theoretical framework of each approach, described the experimental setup, present our results, and conclude with a discussion of the significance and potential directions for future scope in image denoising.

2. Literature Review

An extensive study has been carried out for AWGN removal from images, but little work has been carried out on real world images. Thorough evaluation of performance of denoising model is a complex task because the real noise is much more sophisticated than AWGN. Characteristics of real noises are very different, which may not be identified efficiently by using a single noise level. Mostly a denoiser can be employed effectively for fixed noise model. Denoising model trained for specific noise may not be work effectively for mixed Gaussian noise removal [5]. In recent past, an extensive work on image denoising has already been proposed on image denoising [6]. Because of some limitations of different recording devices, some random noise may be incurred in images during image acquisition.

Image denoising has frequently been formulated to remove additive White Gaussian noise [2]. This noise is additive and have constant variance for all pixels. Although this formulation simplifies the denoising process significantly, but it is not valid for real-world images and may not be able to capture the complexity of real-world noises.

The noisy image y $\in R^{m\times n\times 3}$ can be modelled as a linear or nonlinear function f (.,.) of clean color image x $\in R^{m\times n\times 3}$ and noise n $\in R^{m\times n\times 3}$.

Mathematically it is $y = f(x,n)$. (2.1)

Conventionally, noise is assumed to follow a Gaussian distribution, $\eta_{ijk} \sim N(0, \sigma_{ijk})$ and f, x, n could be additive, convolutive or multiplicative function of x and n. Also, we assume that noise is independent of the image x and it is homogeneous [7]. Depending on types of denoising algorithms, these are classified as

i. Spatial type filtering
ii. Transform domain type filtering and
iii. Wavelet thresholding method

In last few decades, different types of well-organised techniques have been developed by the researchers, which have further been implemented in restoration and de-noising of the images.

Hongjin Ma and Yufeng Nie [8] proposed an algorithm for denoising images corrupted by Gaussian noise plus salt-and-pepper noise. In 2017, Paras Jain and Vipin Tyagi [9] presented a novel image denoising technique to preserve edges which is based on wavelet transforms. F. Russo [5] presented a novel technique to restore the image corrupted with AWGN. They combine a nonlinear algorithm and a noise estimation-based technique for preserving the details and for automatic parameter tuning respectively. Zhang et. al implemented feed forward convolutional neural networks (CNNs) [10] with deep architecture. CNNs are well accepted for parallel computation so less computation time is observed [11]. In 2016, Graham Treece [12] developed a bitonic filter to denoise the image adaptively. Buades et al. proposed [13] a novel Noise Clinic approach in which the dependence of signal scale and frequency has been used to denoise the image. Chen et.al. [14], [15] proposed a denoising model which is exploiting internal self-similarity priors and external natural patch priors to improve the denoising performance. In another study, Xu et. al. [16] utilised Gaussian mixture models, which are trained from and guiding the patch clusters. Sithara et al implemented an unscented Kalman filter framework [17]. PSNR value achievable is 30.49 db. Limitations are that it can only operate from the captured DNG image saved by the camera [16]. In another study, Zhang et al. in 2018 proposed FFDNet, by adding preprocessing and post processing layers to the already designed DnCNN [10] which is three times faster than DnCNN and more memory-friendly. In 2020, Zuo et.al. designed a batch-renormalization denoising network (BRDNet) [18]. Two networks have been combined to enhance the width of the network and to get more features. In 2021, Chen et.al. proposed a coarse-to-fine CNN, which is used to recover a high-resolution image from its low-resolution version [19]. In 2019, Hu et.al. proposed real-world noisy image denoising. They devised Gaussian pyramid technique based deep generative model [20]. Features have been extracted using multiscale pyramid to generated clean image. In 2023, Dharmani et.al proposed deep learning-based OA severity detection with better accuracy [21].

In earlier comparative studies, variational autoencoder and autoencoders have been compared. We have compared the advanced deep learning approach with the classical approach for image denoising. Architectures and effectiveness of these three different paradigms have been discussed. Our study exhibits comprehensive and practical approach to compare VAE, AE and median filter in X-ray image denoising.

3. Methodology

It becomes tedious to estimate the noise if noise is not known and non-uniform. For such scenario, the denoiser should allow the user to control the trade-off between noise removal and detail preservation. The denoising model should be flexible enough to handle spatially variant noise. So, the basic idea of this work to develop a deep neural network architecture with adaptive approach to improve the learning of model to uncertain and complex real noise and to improve the adaptation ability to the eliminate noise on real images and to present how it outperforms the traditional autoencoder approach biomedical image denoising.

3.1. Autoencoders

An autoencoder is made of a pair of two connected artificial neural networks named as encoder network and decoder network [22].

3.1.1 Encoder Network

In this network, high-dimensional original input is converted into low-dimensional latent code. The output size is of encoder smaller than its input size.

3.1.2 Decoder Network

In this network, decoder recovers data from the code. This network consists of larger output layers.

In autoencoder as shown in figure, original image x and noised image x' are provided to the network, which further reconstructs output x' to be as close as possible to x. With this process network learns to denoise the image. AEs have deterministic approach [23]. Figure 1 shows the block diagram of autoencoder.

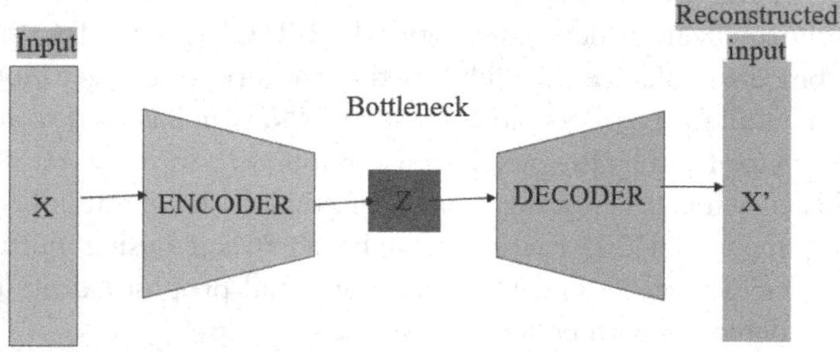

Figure 1: *Block diagram of autoencoder.*

3.2. Variational Auto Encoders

VAEs now a days is one of the most popular techniques. It is applicable to unsupervised learning of complex distributions [24]. Both the encoder and decoder are probabilistic in VAE [23]. Figure 2 shows variational autoencoder.

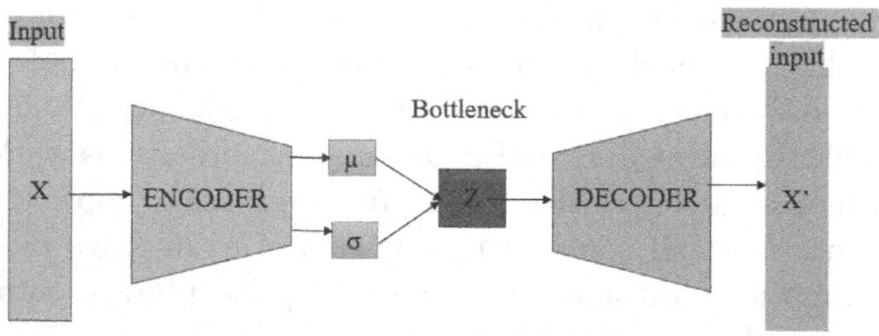

Figure 2: *Variational autoencoder.*

VAE makes the latent space more predictable, less sparse and more continuous. VAEs control the latent space by making the latent variables normally distributed [24].

In VAEs, encoder takes input and encodes it as a probability distribution over the latent space, instead of considering it as a single point. This encoded distribution is chosen to be normal to train the model which further outputs the mean matrix and the covariance matrix. Then a point is sampled from this encoded distribution. Being sampled from the distribution, VAEs produce more diverse and realistic denoised images. They are more robust in handling complex and non-Gaussian distribution and are adaptive in nature. Because of latent space interpolation in VAEs, they generate images with gradual changes. They offer regularisation effect to avoid overfitting of training data.

Encoder takes latent variable and returns the parameters for a distribution. Decoder decodes the sampled point and calculate the reconstruction error. Reconstruction error is back propagated through the network. As the sampling process is a discrete process, we need to apply reparameterization trick to make the back propagation work

$$Z = \mu + \sigma^* \epsilon \quad (3.1)$$

Where $\epsilon \sim N(0,1)$

Differently from the standard autoencoder, the variational encoder returns mean and variance matrices and we use them to obtain the sampled latent vector.

The loss function has two parts: generative loss and latent loss. The generative loss assures similarity of the output with the input. The article uses mean square error (MSE) for the same. The latent loss assures that the latent vectors from encoder are following the Gaussian distribution. This is assured using Kullback–Libeler divergence.

Mathematically,

$$\text{Loss function} = \Sigma (x-x_i)^2/N - 0.5^* \Sigma (1 + \log(\sigma^2) - \mu^2 - \sigma^2) \quad (3.2)$$

where μ is the mean of latent distribution, σ^2 is the variance of the latent distribution.

4. Results and Discussion

In this study, grey scale X-ray images with resolution of 64X64 pixels have been used. Gaussian noise of 0 mean and 0.3 standard deviation have been added. Four layers are there in encoder. First layer is using 32 filters with kernel size of 3X3. Second, third and fourth layers have 64 filters with kernel size of 3X3. The ReLU activation function has been used. Decoder takes latent vector which is sampled from the encoder. Decoder is mirroring the architecture of encoder using convolutional transpose layers. KL divergence loss function has been used. VAE minimises the total loss which consists of reconstruction loss and KL divergence loss. Batch size of 10 with 70 epochs has been taken.

To verify the effectiveness, autoencoder and variational autoencoder and median filter have been compared based on their denoising performance. This is measured from mean square error and peak-signal-to-noise ratio, against an open-source dataset.

Mean square error can be determined as follows:

$$MSE = \frac{1}{mn}\sum_{i=0}^{m-1}\sum_{j=0}^{n-1}\left[I(i,j) - I_n(i,j)\right]^2, \tag{4.1}$$

where I(i,j) is the noise free image, and In (i,j) is the noisy image of size mxn. Peak-signal-to-noise ratio is linked to MSE and given as follows:

$$PSNR = 10\log_{10}\left(\frac{MAX_i^{\ 2}}{MSE}\right) \tag{4.2}$$

where MAXi is the maximum possible pixel value of the image and is 255 as 8 bits per sample have been used for pixel representation. Therefore, PSNR can also be given as follows:

$$PSNR = 10\ \log_{10}\left(\frac{255^2}{MSE}\right) \tag{4.3}$$

Higher the value of PSNR better will be the denoising methods.

Data set used: We have taken the open-source dataset available on Kaggle a data science platform https://www.kaggle.com/datasets/paultimothymooney/chest-xray-pneumonia, there are 5,863 X-ray images (JPEG) and 2 categories (Pneumonia/Normal). In test folder, 234 images and in train 1341 images are there. Chest X-ray images (anterior-posterior) had been selected from retrospective cohorts of pediatric patients. Table 1 shows Comparative evaluation of median filter, autoencoder and variational autoencoder.

Table1: Comparative evaluation of median filter, autoencoder and variational autoencoder. Denoising performance is in terms of PSNR (dB). Gaussian noise of 0 mean and 0.3 standard deviation has been added.

Trial number	PSNR (dB)		
	Median filter	Autoencoder	Variational Autoencoder
Trail_1	57.5	64.7	68.33
Trial_2	57.5	65.25	68.54
Trail_3	57.5	65.87	68.76
Trail_4	57.5	66.88	69.07
Trail_5	57.5	67.36	69.09
Average	57.5	66.01	68.75

By comparing the results of all these three methods, it has been found that better results can be achieved with VAE.

5. Conclusion

In this paper, we compared variational autoencoder, autoencoder and median and the outcomes find VAE as the best algorithm for denoising. Average value for PSNR of 66.01dB using AE, 68.75 DB for VAE and 57.5 DB for median filter has been achieved. So, improvement of more than 2dB has been achieved in relative to auto encoders. Future researchers may develop hybrid models combining advantages of both VAEs and AEs and may explore novel techniques to enhance robustness against non-uniform noises in real world images.

References

[1] Fan, L., F. Zhang, H. Fan, and C. Zhang, "Brief review of image denoising techniques," *Vis. Comput. Ind. Biomed. Art*, vol. 2, no. 1, 2019, doi: 10.1186/s42492-019-0016-7.

[2] Gupta, H., H. Chauhan, A. Bijalwan, and K. Joshi, *A Review on Image Denoising*, pp. 1–10, 2019.

[3] Filter, T. U. K., R. Ma, H. Hu, S. Xing, and Z. Li, "Efficient and fast real-world noisy image denoising by combining pyramid neural network," vol. 29, pp. 3927–3940, 2020.

[4] Ma, R., H. Hu, S. Xing, and Z. Li, "Efficient and fast real-world noisy image denoising by combining pyramid neural network and two-pathway unscented Kalman filter," *IEEE Trans. Image Process.*, vol. 29, pp. 3927–3940, 2020, doi: 10.1109/tip.2020.2965294.

[5] Russo, F., "A method for estimation and filtering of Gaussian noise in images," *IEEE Trans. Instrum. Meas.*, vol. 52, no. 4, pp. 1148–1154, 2003, doi: 10.1109/TIM.2003.815989.

[6] Goyal, B., A. Dogra, S. Agrawal, B. S. Sohi, and A. Sharma, "Image denoising review : from classical to state-of-the-art approaches," vol. 55, no. March 2019, pp. 220–244, 2020, doi: 10.1016/j.inffus.2019.09.003.

[7] Tan, H., H. Xiao, S. Lai, Y. Liu, and M. Zhang, "Pixelwise estimation of signal-dependent image noise using deep residual learning," *Comput. Intell. Neurosci.*, vol. 2019, 2019, doi: 10.1155/2019/4970508.

[8] Ma, H. and Y. Nie, "Directional weighted mean filter and improved adaptive anisotropic diffusion model," vol. 2018, 2018.

[9] Jain, P. and V. Tyagi, "An adaptive edge-preserving image denoising technique using patch-based weighted-SVD filtering in wavelet domain," *Multimed Tools Appl.*, vol. 76, no. 2, pp. 1659–1679, 2017, doi: 10.1007/s11042-015-3154-8.

[10] Zhang, K., W. Zuo, and L. Zhang, "FFDNet: toward a fast and flexible solution for CNN-Based image denoising," *IEEE Trans. Image Process.*, vol. 27, no. 9, pp. 4608–4622, 2018, doi: 10.1109/TIP.2018.2839891.

[11] Zhang, K., W. Zuo, Y. Chen, D. Meng, and L. Zhang, "Beyond a Gaussian denoiser: residual learning of deep CNN for image denoising," *IEEE*

Trans. Image Process., vol. 26, no. 7, pp. 3142–3155, 2017, doi: 10.1109/TIP.2017.2662206.

[12] Treece, G., "The bitonic filter: linear filtering in an edge-preserving morphological framework," *IEEE Trans. Image Process.*, vol. 25, no. 11, pp. 5199–5211, 2016, doi: 10.1109/TIP.2016.2605302.

[13] Lebrun, M., A. Buades, and J. M. Morel, "A nonlocal Bayesian image denoising algorithm," *SIAM J. Imaging Sci.*, vol. 6, no. 3, pp. 1665–1688, 2013, doi: 10.1137/120874989.

[14] Xu, J., L. Zhang, W. Zuo, D. Zhang, and X. Feng, "Patch group based nonlocal self-similarity prior learning for image denoising," http://r0k.us/graphics/kodak/.

[15] Chen, F., L. Zhang, and H. Yu, "External patch prior guided internal clustering for image denoising," *2015 IEEE International Conference on Computer Vision (ICCV)*, IEEE, pp. 603–611, 2015. doi: 10.1109/ICCV.2015.76.

[16] Xu, J., L. Zhang, and D. Zhang, "External prior guided internal prior learning for real-world noisy image denoising," *IEEE Trans. Image Process.*, vol. 27, no. 6, pp. 2996–3010, 2018, doi: 10.1109/TIP.2018.2811546.

[17] Kanakaraj, S., M. S. Nair, and S. Kalady, "Adaptive importance sampling unscented Kalman filter based SAR image super resolution," *Comput. Geosci.*, vol. 133, 2019, doi: 10.1016/j.cageo.2019.104310.

[18] Tian, C., Y. Xu, and W. Zuo, "Image denoising using deep CNN with batch renormalization," *Neural Networks*, vol. 121, pp. 461–473, 2020, doi: 10.1016/j.neunet.2019.08.022.

[19] Tian, C., Y. Xu, W. Zuo, B. Zhang, L. Fei, and C. W. Lin, "Coarse-to-fine CNN for image super-resolution," *IEEE Trans. Multimedia*, vol. 23, pp. 1489–1502, 2021, doi: 10.1109/TMM.2020.2999182.

[20] Chen, S., S. Chen, Z. Guo, and Y. Zuo, "Neurocomputing low-resolution palmprint image denoising by generative adversarial networks," *Neurocomputing*, vol. 358, pp. 275–284, 2019, doi: 10.1016/j.neucom.2019.05.046.

[21] Dharmani, B. C. and K. Khatri, "Deep learning for knee osteoarthritis severity stage detection using X-ray images," https://www.nhp.gov.in/disease/musculo-skeletal-bone-joints- "https://www.sciencedirect.com/science/article/abs/pii/S0957417422021662."

[22] Chatterjee, S., S. Maity, M. Bhattacharjee, S. Banerjee, A. K. Das, and W. Ding, "Variational autoencoder based imbalanced COVID-19 detection using chest X-ray images," *New Gener. Comput.*, vol. 41, no. 1, pp. 25–60, 2023, doi: 10.1007/s00354-022-00194-y. "https://lilianweng.github.io/posts/2018-08-12-vae/".

35. Modified SSD Framework for On-Road Object Detection

Glenson Toney[1], Gaurav Sethi[2], Cherry Bhargava[3] and Vaibhav Salian4

[1,2] *SEEE, Lovely Professional University, Phagawara, Punjab, India*

[1] *Department of ECE, St Joseph Engineering College, Mangaluru, Karnataka, India*

[3] *Department of CSE, Symbiosis International University, Pune, Maharashtra, India*

[4] *Department of AIML, St Joseph Engineering College, Mangaluru, Karnataka, India*

Abstract: Real-time object recognition is critical to improving automobile automation features. This research presents a novel method for detecting on-road objects using a modified single shot multiBox detector (SSD) algorithm. The primary objective is to automate car headlamps in order to avoid accidents caused by blinding high beams from impending or past vehicles for which it is important to identify the vehicle. This study compares traditional object detection techniques (region-based and regression-based) with the modified SSD model in terms of Frames Per Second, Accuracy, mean Average Precision, Recall, F1 Score and ROC-AUC. The improved SSD model displays significant speed improvements while keeping competitive metric values, making it suitable for high-speed vehicle applications. To assess the efficacy of the proposed technique, substantial statistical analyses have been performed. When compared to the three benchmark models, the findings indicate that the performance metrics for stated object classes are superior. The modified SSD model emerges as an efficient solution that offers substantial gains in operating speed, making it appropriate for vehicle detection and adaptive headlight systems.

Keywords: Adaptive headlamps, FPS, mAP, RCNN, Region and Regression-based models, SSD, YOLO

1. Introduction

Artificial Intelligence is transforming the automotive sector in design, manufacturing, design, automation, driver assistance and predictive maintenance. Vehicle manufacturers are consistently embracing automation technologies to add safety and comfort to customers. The challenges that high beams of traditional headlamps in vehicles pose to drivers and the accidents they cause are serious and the consequences are catastrophic [1]. While Troxlers' effect reduces the reaction time, the visual impairment causes mishaps that can be detrimental to vehicle and passenger safety. Also, manual adjustment ought to drive skills and varies with diverse factors like age, fatigue, road and driving conditions. Manual dim-dips while driving on rough terrain and curves add immense challenge to the driver. The accident share at night is high in comparison to daytime, though the traffic is less during the latter. Troxler's effect due to high beams is a major contributor to accidents at night according to a study at NIMHANS, Bengaluru [2]. Thus, the need for adaptive headlamps is pivotal and can ensure safety. Vehicle manufacturers like Ford Corporation, Nissan and Hella have been developing technologies to address this challenge. Adaptive Front Lights from Ford Global Technologies dynamically adjustable LED headlamps to further reduce the troxlers' effect improve visibility and change the beam lobes to light up the trajectory and improve the driving experience [3–7]. Nissan Global has engineered adaptive headlamps that adjust beams based on vehicle speed and steer that is apt for lanes that have efficiently designated vehicle speeds. Automotive leaders like Valeo, BMW, Toyota and Mercedes Benz are at the forefront of developing solutions to diminish the Troxlers' effect [8–11]. Object detection is a formidable task in the development of adaptive headlamp technologies. Convolution Neural Networks based on object detection/ region proposal techniques [11] like R-CNN, Faster R-CNN and single-stage object detectors YOLO, Tiny YOLO and SSD have shown promising results [12–19].

2. Literature Review

The paper presents a comparison of the region-based RCNN model [10] and regression-based SSD [20], YOLO [12–14] and the Tiny YOLO model [18][19]. The paper also proposes a novel algorithm to detect vehicles on the road, which would be a precursor for the design of adaptive headlights. You Only Look Once (YOLO) performs the detection and recognition of multiple objects in real-time as a regression-based model that predicts probabilities of different classes by employing Convolutional Neural Networks (CNN), both for classes and bounding boxes [15]. YOLO needs a single propagation (forward) through the network to identify the objects. Hence, prediction of various objects in an image is completed in a single run. YOLO uses Residual blocks, bounding box regression and Intersection Over Union (IOU) to perform the detection and is predominantly used due to the speed of the algorithm, its accuracy and inherent learning capabilities. The choice of YOLO for vehicle detection on the road, though the model's accuracy is a matter of concern for smaller objects, is substantiated by the fact that the smaller object detection is not in the purview of the current work. Tiny YOLO v3 comprises 7 convolution layers along with 3x3 kernels and 1x1 convolution kernels, and the target score is determined 4 using logistic regression. At the prediction stage, it uses up sampling for feature extraction and fusion. V3 possesses the ability of multi-labelling as they have more convolution layers as compared to YOLO [13] [16–18]. YOLO v3 shows increased detection speeds and does not profess the need for similar image sizes. Darknet-53 performs feature extraction, and it uses multi-scale prediction [17]. SSD uses discretisation of bounding boxes output space to default boxes of different aspect ratios and also the scales per feature. The combination of different feature maps from varied resolutions aids the model in handling objects of various sizes and eliminates the need for proposal generation, pixel and feature resampling, which makes it easier to train.

3. Modified SSD Model

The SSD model is a feed-forward convolutional network that uses fixed-sized bounding boxes and contains a head and a backbone. The backbone is a pre-trained model, which helps to extract the features. Conv2d layers of Convolution 3 and the entire Convolution 4 are removed in the modified SSD, which affects the model's ability to detect small objects accurately. The conv4_3 layer detects smaller objects, and conv11_2 detects the biggest objects. For on-the-road vehicle detection and headlamp adjustment, the need for identification of smaller objects is ruled out. Hence in the work, two convolution layers are removed to increase the speed of detection while not compromising on the accuracy. SSD owes its speed to the elimination of bounding box proposals, and the use of multiple boxes of different sizes and aspect ratios. Figure 1 depicts convolution layer of the modified SSD architecture as visualized on Netron.

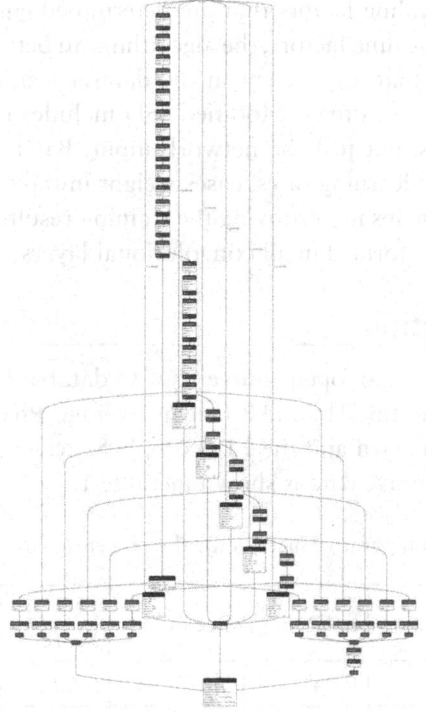

Figure 1: The convolution layer of the modified SSD architecture as visualised on Netron.

Instead of using fixed aspect ratios, the model uses aspect ratios that are calculated per feature map layer. By using aspect ratios that are calculated per feature map layer, the algorithm can better adjust the anchor boxes to the objects that are present in that particular area of the image and improve overall detection accuracy. Specifically, this implementation uses 3x3 convolutional kernels in all convolutional layers; whereas, the original SSD 300 used 3x3 and 1x1 convolutional kernels. Using only 3x3 convolutional kernels in all convolutional layers can reduce the number of parameters in the model, compared to the former resulting in a more efficient and simpler architecture that requires less computational resources to train and run. Additionally, using only 3x3 convolutional kernels can help preserve spatial information in the feature maps as larger kernels such as 5x5 or 7x7 can lead to a loss of spatial resolution. This can be particularly important for object detection where accurate localisation of objects is critical, resulting in efficient and simpler architecture that requires fewer computational resources while still achieving high levels of accuracy in object detection. This implementation uses 6 predictor layers, instead of 4 in the SSD. Four predictor layers are not sufficient for capturing the full range of object sizes and aspect ratios present in major datasets. Using more predictor layers allows the algorithm to better capture objects at different scales and improve overall detection accuracy and is crucial for the application in discussion; on-road object detection. However, this comes with the computational complexity. The scaling factors that are specific to the PASCAL VOC dataset are used; whereas, the original SSD uses scaling factors that are determined empirically. By adjusting the anchor boxes using scaling factors, the algorithm can better fit the specific object sizes and aspect ratios that are present in the dataset leading to better detection accuracy and fewer false positives. Modified SSD includes batch normalisation in all convolutional layers, not just the network input. Batch normalisation aids in faster training improves learning rates, eases weight initialisation, supports deeper network creations and helps in improving the training result. L2 regularisation and data augmentation is performed in all convolutional layers.

4. Model Evaluation

The models are trained on an open-source COCO database with over 15k images and 93 classes on Python 3. The mAP (Mean Average Precision), and Precision-Recall (P-R) curve are drawn and the F1 Score, FPS, accuracy and ROC-AUC are considered. The comparative data is shown in Table 1.

Table 1: Comparative metrics for the object detection models.

Algorithm	Accuracy	mAP	Recall	F1 Score	ROC-AUC	FPS second
YOLO-Tiny	6	0.041	0.025	0.022	0.53	1.9
YOLO	45	0.33	0.24	0.201	0.72	14.56

SSD	43	0.38	0.25	0.214	0.71	14.56
Modified SSD	53	0.42	0.27	0.271	0.77	23.8

4.1. Statistical Analysis

Table 2 shows that Modified SSD outperforms YOLO, Tiny-YOLO and SSD in all metrics. However, statistical significance must be confirmed. The next section will undertake statistical analysis to find the most efficient method. The Hypothesis: There is a significant difference between the performance metrics of the four AI Models.

4.1.1 ANOVA

Table 2: ANOVA test calculations for group differences.

Factors	Accuracy	mAP	Recall	F1 Score	ROC-AUC
Mean	36.75	0.29375	0.19625	0.176	0.6825
Variance	351.25	0.043925	0.005675	0.007066	0.010825
SSB	1990.75	0.352075	0.100775	0.10735	0.283125
SSE	1302.75	0.079875	0.002875	0.005625	0.008275
F-Statistics	33.375868	22.894854	21.862478	31.654567	14.778873
P-value	0.000145	0.000621	0.000762	0.000203	0.001867

The ANOVA test (Table 2) produces a significant result. The F-Statistic is high, suggesting that there are significant differences in these parameters among the algorithms. The p-value is much smaller than 0.05, indicating that these differences are statistically significant. Hence it is predominant to find the best model statistically.

4.1.2 P-Test

If precision and overall performance are to be prioritised, modified SSD appears to perform the best as it has the highest mAP, recall, F1 score and ROC-AUC as shown in Table 3. If the priority is to have a balance between performance and efficiency (since YOLO-Tiny has lower accuracy but is much faster), YOLO-Tiny might be a suitable choice. If the application needs a good balance between accuracy and speed, YOLO or SSD could be considered. Hence, modified SSD performs the best for on-road object detection with the highest precision.

Table 3: Statistical significance analysis (P-Test) for group comparisons.

Model	YOLO vs. YOLO-Tiny		YOLO vs. SSD		YOLO vs. Modified SSD		YOLO-Tiny vs. SSD		YOLO-Tiny vs. Modified SSD		SSD vs. Modified SSD	
Metrics	t-Stats	P-Value	t-Stats	P-Value	t-Stats	P-Value	t-Stats	P-Value	t-Stats	P-Value	t-Stats	P-Value
Accuracy	4.11	0.025	0.23	0.82	-1.86	0.079	-4.01	0.001	-6.61	0	-2.06	0.043
mAP	11.47	0	-1.36	0.21	-4.05	0.001	-12.2	0	-14.9	0	-1.75	0.096
Recall	12.24	0	-0.68	0.51	-4.85	0	-12.9	0	-15.7	0	-0.79	0.432
F1 Score	14.24	0	-1.26	0.22	-5.80	0	-14.9	0	-18.4	0	-0.59	0.556
ROC-AUC	2.96	0.025	1.003	0.38	-1.69	0.096	-1.39	0.179	-3.26	0.004	-2.56	0.014

4.1.3 Two-Sample t-Tests

Table 4: Statistical significance analysis using two-sample t-tests for group comparisons.

Metric	Accuracy		mAP		Recall		F1 Score		ROC-AUC	
Algorithm Pair	t-Stats	p-value	t-Stats	p-value	t-Stats	p-value	t-Stats	p-value	t-Stats	p-value
YOLO vs. YOLO-Tiny	15.5	< 0.001	22.9	< 0.001	19.5	< 0.001	21.9	< 0.001	7	< 0.001
YOLO vs. SSD	0.26	0.795	-0.76	0.458	-0.23	0.823	-0.54	0.595	0.17	0.869
YOLO vs. Modified SSD	-7.24	< 0.001	-6.62	< 0.001	1.36	0.18	-6.76	< 0.001	2.57	0.014
YOLO-Tiny vs. SSD	-5.36	< 0.001	-26.12	< 0.001	-19.77	< 0.001	-22.14	< 0.001	-6.13	< 0.001
YOLO-Tiny vs. Modified SSD	-13.6	< 0.001	-36.4	< 0.001	-29.6	< 0.001	-32.6	< 0.001	-8.44	< 0.001
SSD vs. Modified SSD	-7.84	< 0.001	-14.9	< 0.001	-9.59	< 0.001	-12.6	< 0.001	-2.44	0.02

Table 5: Mann-Whitney U test results for group comparison.

Model pair	YOLO vs. YOLO-Tiny		YOLO vs. SSD		YOLO vs. Modified SSD		YOLO-Tiny vs. SSD		YOLO-Tiny vs. Modified SSD		SSD vs. Modified SSD	
Metrics	U Stat	p-Value	U Stat	p-Value	U Stat	p-Value	U Stat	p-Value	U Stat	p-Value	U Stat	p-Value
Accuracy	0	0.003	3	0.042	0	0.001	0	0.001	0	0.001	2	0.027
mAP	0	0.001	1	0.016	1	0.016	0	0.001	0	0.001	0	0.001
Recall	0	0.001	2	0.027	5	0.234	0	0.001	0	0.001	0	0.001
F1 Score	0	0.001	2	0.027	5	0.234	0	0.001	0	0.001	0	0.001
ROC-AUC	1	0.016	2	0.027	1	0.016	0	0.001	0	0.001	0	0.001

Modified SSD significantly outperforms both YOLO and YOLO-Tiny in accuracy as shown in Table 4. However, it doesn't significantly outperform SSD. YOLO-Tiny significantly underperforms compared to YOLO, SSD and modified SSD in terms of mAP. Modified SSD significantly outperforms YOLO. While YOLO-Tiny significantly underperforms compared to other models, Modified SSD significantly outperforms YOLO. YOLO-Tiny significantly underperforms compared to YOLO, SSD and Modified SSD. Modified SSD significantly outperforms YOLO. In terms of ROC-AUC, YOLO-Tiny significantly underperforms compared to YOLO, SSD and Modified SSD. While Modified SSD significantly outperforms YOLO and SSD. Based on these results, modified SSD consistently outperforms YOLO-Tiny in all metrics and YOLO in most metrics. It also significantly outperforms SSD in most metrics. In situations with small sample sizes or non-normally distributed data, non-parametric tests are more appropriate because they make fewer assumptions about the data distribution. Given that the sample sizes for each algorithm in your data are quite tiny (n=1 for each algorithm) and the t-test presupposes that the data are regularly distributed, which is not necessarily the case, the M-W U test is performed.

4.1.4 Mann-Whitney U Test

Based on the results shown in Table 5 at a significance level of 0.05, 'Modified SSD' outperforms 'YOLO-Tiny' in a range of measures (including Accuracy, mAP, Recall and F1 Score). Furthermore, it outperforms 'YOLO' in several metrics, including Accuracy and ROC-AUC. Although 'Modified SSD' exhibits robust performance across multiple metrics and presents itself as a competitive option, whether it can be definitively referred to as the 'optimal' algorithm is dependent on your specific application and the varying importance of individual metrics within the scope of your project's objectives.

5. Conclusion

A novel object recognition approach based on a modification of the single shot multiBox detector (SSD) is presented in this paper. The goal is to improve operational speed by eliminating the convolutional layers responsible for smaller object detection while retaining the critical attribute of fixed-size bounding boxes, which is inherent in the original SSD Model. The major goal of this study is to identify vehicles on roadways, including both incoming and departing traffic. Notably, this context predominantly concerns larger objects, which justifies the accuracy trade-off for smaller things. The proposed SSD Model's performance is thoroughly assessed on the COCO dataset. When compared to the three models, it delivers better performance metrics for the specified object classes. The model also exhibits significant Frames Per Second (FPS) increases, making it suitable for vehicle recognition and adaptive headlight systems. Comprehensive statistical analyses are performed to verify the effectiveness of the suggested technique. The findings demonstrate that the modified SSD Model meets the performance requirements for on-road object identification applications. This research makes a useful and effective object detection contribution that is suited to particular real-world scenarios, particularly in the realms of vehicular applications and road safety.

References

[1] Toney, G., and C. Bhargava, "Adaptive headlamps in automobile: a review on the models, detection techniques, and mathematical models," *IEEE Access*, vol. 9, pp. 87462–87474, 2021.

[2] *Advancing Road Safety in India-Implementation is the Key (Summary)*, https://nimhans.ac.in/wp-content/uploads/2019/02/UL_BR_m010-11_Main-rprt_FINAL.pdf (accessed May, 2017).

[3] Kumar, A., *et al.*, "Vehicle lighting system with dynamic beam pattern," U.S. Patent Application No. 14/886,353.

[4] "Adaptive front lighting for vehicles," https://patentimages.storage.googleapis.com/75/1d/d7/955726084c6b82/EP1800947A1.pdf (accessed July, 2019).

[5] *Ford Lighting Technology*, https://www.ford.ie (accessed May, 2016).

[6] *Ford Developing Advanced Headlights That Point Out People Animals in the Dark and Widen Beams at Tricky Junctions*, https://media.ford.com (accessed May, 2015).

[7] *Adaptive Front—Lighting System NISSAN |Technology*, https://www.nissan-global.com/EN/TECHNOLOGY/OVERVIEW/afs.html (accessed May, 2007).

[8] Szymkowski, S., "Improved optional headlights net Volvo XC40 XC60 top safety pick awards," *The Car Connection*, https://bit.ly/2R7406q (accessed May, 2019).

[9] Szymkowski, S., "2021 Subaru forester prices rise a bit but SUV gets more safety kit roadshow," https://cnet.co/3wKMoMP (accessed May, 2021).

[10] *BMW Adaptive Headlight Malfunction*, https://bit.ly/2R9rc47 (accessed May, 2020).

[11] Girshick, R., *et al.*, "Rich feature hierarchies for accurate object detection and semantic segmentation," *Proceedings of the IEEE Conference on Computer Vision and Pattern Recognition*, 2014.

[12] Redmon, J., *et al.*, "You only look once: unified, real-time object detection," *Proceedings of the IEEE Conference on Computer Vision and Pattern Recognition*, 2016.

[13] Redmon, J. and A. Farhadi. "YOLO9000: better, faster, stronger," *Proceedings of the IEEE Conference on Computer Vision and Pattern Recognition*, 2017.

[14] Redmon, J. and A. Farhadi, "Yolov3: an incremental improvement," *arXiv preprint arXiv:1804.02767*, 2018.

[15] Liu, C., Y. Tao, J. Liang, K. Li, and Y. Chen, "Object detection based on YOLO network," *2018 IEEE 4th Information Technology and Mechatronics*

Engineering Conference (ITOEC), pp. 799–803, 2018, doi: 10.1109/ITOEC.2018.8740604.

[16] Redmon, J., S. Divvala, R. Girshick, and A. Farhadi, "You only look once: unified, real- time object detection," *IEEE Comput. Soc. Conf. Comput. Vis. Pattern Recognit.*, vol. 2016, pp. 779–788, 2016, doi: 10.1109/CVPR.2016.91.

[17] Redmon, J. and A. Farhadi, "YOLOv3: an incremental improvement," *arXiv Preprint arXiv*, 1804.02767, 2018.

[18] Adarsh, P., P. Rathi, and M. Kumar, "YOLO v3-Tiny: object detection and recognition using one stage improved model," *2020 6th International Conference on Advanced Computing and Communication Systems (ICACCS)*, IEEE, 2020.

[19] Mao, Q.-C., *et al.*, "Mini-YOLOv3: real-time object detector for embedded applications," *IEEE Access*, vol. 7, pp. 133529–133538, 2019.

[20] Liu, W., *et al.*, "SSD: single shot multibox detector," *Computer Vision–ECCV 2016: 14th European Conference, Amsterdam, The Netherlands, October 11–14, 2016, Proceedings, Part I 14*, Springer International Publishing, 2016.

36. 0.7V-20nm FinFET Technology Inverter Design for Better Log-Linear Characteristics

M.V.S. Roja Ramani[1], Sreenivasa Rao Ijjada[2], SM IEEE

[1]*Dept. of ECE, N S Raju Institute of Technology, Visakhapatnam, AP, India*
[2] *Dept. of EECE, GITAM Deemed to be University, Visakhapatnam, AP, India*

Abstract: Many new semiconductor devices unfolded in the interest of enhancement of transistor density in the available silicon area. Latest electronics circuits looking towards adding more functionalities in the same IC. Continuous device scaling is only the solution for this as per the guidelines recommended by Moore's law. MOSFET scaling is not supporting toward the latest technology nodes proposed by the International Technology Roadmap for Semiconductor (ITRS). Reason is, MOSFET out strikes large volume of Short Channel Effects (SCEs) as the gate has poor control over the channel in Short Channel Devices (SCDs). Usually, semiconductor memories occupy more area in the latest electronic circuits, hence, scaling process should be continued in memories. To achieve good control of electrostatic fields in the channel area, especially in nano-scale range, more than one gate MOSFET is unwheeled. Design of SCDs with no cost of SCEs is a big challenge for engineers. Memories demand high speed FETs to enhance search operation speed. Device speed can be improved with modifying its I-V characteristics in subthreshold region. Innovations are made possible to use FinFET (Fin-type Field Effect Transistor) Technology. Due to good electrostatic characteristics and simple manufacture process, ultrathin-fin-based FET become a promising alternative device to the single-gate (SG) and double gate (DG) MOSFETs. In this paper, steepness of FinFET I-V characteristics was altered to enhance the switching speed. A FinFET inverter has designed to the SRAM applications. Through Sentaurus TCAD simulations, found that the power dissipation has been reduced from 6.57mW- 4.49mW to 1.52mW, inverter on-state current was recorded as 8.49μA, which is more than SG MOSFET and DG MOS FET inverter readings such as 1.89μA and 2.24 μA, respectively.

Keywords: SCEs, SDCs, FinFET, inverter, high speed, subthreshold swing.

1. Introduction

To reach high density ICs, maintain steady performance the transistor size usually scaled down, device downsizing results many undesirable SCEs, such as significant off state leakages, which will negatively impact the battery lifespan. To address this issue, an effective way of gate control over the channel is necessary; multi gate FETs will do better than the single gate FETs. Progress of scaling is the major challenge of MOSFET when scaling reaches well below 45nm technology. Subthreshold current is one of the SCE, is more dependent on the scaled threshold voltage. Device scaling has been restricted by several geometrical and process parameters. Based on scaling theory, both supply voltage (V_{DD}) and threshold voltage V_{TH} should be reduced; hence, device overdrive potential will reduce, and the drain current has an exponential dependence on overdrive voltage in the subthreshold region as in the equation.

$$I_{off} = I_o \exp\left(\frac{V_{gs} - V_{TH}}{n.^* V_T}\right) \quad (1)$$

Scaled V_{TH} damages the device performance by raising its off-state current; if V_{TH} increases, leakage current will reduce and leads to produce low drive current. Device characteristics in subthreshold region are important for analyzing device speed and performance. In low voltage-high speed circuits, there is a need for a device with much steeper I-V characteristics in its subthreshold region of operation. Biasing the device properly in the subthreshold region is the low-voltage operation. Subthreshold Slope (SS), ON-state and OFF-state currents are the design parameters to measure the device performance. SS is the amount of change in applied gate voltage required to increase in one decade of drain current. In a log-linear plot shown in figure 1[14] , the drain current in subthreshold region is linear with a slope that is called the "subthreshold slope ‟. Ideal SS of MOSFET at room temperature is 60mV/dec but practically its nearly 72mV/dec; to achieve high-speed, device SS value should be < 60mV/ dec. Improvements in nanotechnology leads to a steep decline in performance. Consequently, the gate poorly controls the channel, resulting in massive leakage currents even if the device is off state. As a result, the chip's temperature increases, generating more static power. New devices, including the SG MOSFET and DG MOSFET [1], have emerged as the ideal substitute for bulk MOSFET in nanoscale design.

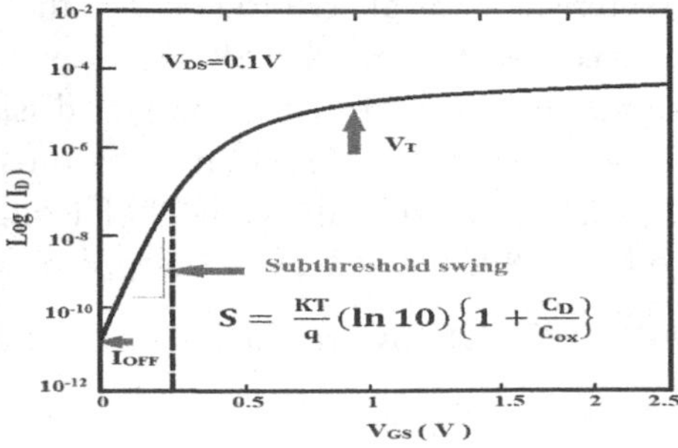

Figure 1: Log-Linear characteristics of MOSFET.

SS is the figure of merit used to measure the device performance and it indicates how fast the transitions happed to ON from OFF or vice-versa. The sub threshold slope equation shown in the equation-2 is elaborate as given.

$$SS = \ln(10)\left(\frac{KT}{q}\right)\left(1+\left(\frac{C_d}{C_{ox}}\right)\right) \tag{2}$$

Where Cd=depletion capacitance, Cox=oxide capacitance. KT/q= thermal equivalent voltage ≈ 26mV@ room temperature 3000K. To measure the ideal SS value in the MOSFET, assume Cd≈0 and Cox≈∞ and ln (10) ≈2.3. Then the equation 2 is approximated as SS≈2.3*26 mV/dec=59.8mV/dec [2].

2. Literature Review

In 2017, IRDS (International Roadmap for Devices and Systems) report informed that the developing towards different high-k dielectric gate materials that will soon substitute the gate oxide SiO_2 of the devices. As stated in ITRS-2012 edition, "The gate dielectric has arisen as one of the greatest tough for future device scaling ". In [1]. Mahmoud S. Badran et al. described a proportioned dual-k material for seven nano-meter tri-gate FinFET, the result of spacer length (Lsp), and high-K spacer length (L_{HK}) is considered for low leakage current made possible high ON current to OFF current ratio. Furthermore, the active channel-length (L_{eff}) in subthreshold transmission is sustained more than the threshold voltage (V_{TH}), and the gate length (L_g) is attuned by the appropriate metal -gate work function. In [2] Sourabh Khandelwal et al., described the changing silicon to germanium material that was used in the standard FinFET. Manufacture excellence regular model is obtainable for simulation of circuits using germanium p-type FinFET. Natalia Seoane et al [3] described the influence of cross-section shape (rectangular, bullet-shaped and triangular) has on the changeability and device performance affecting the FinFET. The supplementary triangular fin cross-section has lesser SS, leakage current (I_{OFF}), drain induced barrier lowering (DIBL). The triangular-shaped FinFET has I_{ON}/I_{OFF} relation is three times advanced for the rectangular shape FinFET. Y. Li et al. [4] described the FinFET having a smaller fin width-fin height ratio (W_{fin}/H_{fin}) will show greater effectiveness. This tendency in the fin height motives a lack of protection for SCEs. Inclined of fin details serious concerns on gate-length scaling. Number of multiple gates increases proportionally increases the capacitance of the device. [5–7] describes the variance in the fin geometry assistance to diminish dependent Parasitic capacitance, due to increase fin height and fin pitch shrinkage parasitic capacitance of FinFET. S.M. Sharma, S. Dasgupta et al. [8] described the exhausting successive conformal mapping method that is used to optimise parasitic capacitance. A.k et al. [9] described the FinFET using for ultra-low voltage Analog presentations is the extreme decrease in parasitic fringing capacitance because of an optimum gate-source/drain underlay design. Wen-Kuan Yeh et al. [10] described rarer fins reserved the coupling influence between fins to show greater device performance but suffered additional severe hot carrier-induced device dreadful conditions. Coupling consequence among fins decreased the corresponding electric field in the multi-fin devices added self-conscious influence ionisation. S. Mittal et al. [11] described that decrease RMS error in 'µ' and 'σ' with respect to the smallest fin-width. In [12] A.kumar et al., discussed the undoped channel is ideally for FinFET technology. On the other hand, the light doping is improved control over the leakage current (I_{OFF}). The doping attentiveness of the source/drain section need great dopant, then later raises the sequences resistance of the device, these injuries the fin measurements [13–17].

3. FinFET Technology

FinFET is a type of transistor used in semiconductor technology that has emerged as a leading design for ICs. It is a 3D transistor structure that offers improved performance and power efficiency, compared to traditional planar devices. Here, the traditional 2D planar gate is replaced with a silicon fin that rises vertically from the silicon substrate called FinFET. Fin is surrounded by gate electrodes on three sides, allowing for better electric current flow control. Gate electrodes are made with polysilicon or a metal alloy. This unique structure provides several advantages over the planar transistors. When compared to planar devices, FinFET offer better performance due to better electrostatic control over the channel and get reduced SCEs and higher carrier mobility. These improvements make it suitable for faster switching and higher frequencies applications such as processors and GPUs design. The operating voltage of this type of device is low, hence, exhibits lower leakages, consequently resulting in reduced power consumption compared to planar devices. Memory occupied functionality systems usually operate with battery; using FinFET technology will improve the battery life. FinFET is a highly scalable device, which can be further miniaturised to achieve higher chip density. This enables the development of smaller and more compact electronic devices with increased functionality. FinFET has many varieties like Multi-Gate MOSFETs (Mug-FET) and Gate all around FETs to work below 45 nm technology [8]. FinFET maintains good control over the current flow even at smaller sizes, improving the performance and reliability. The basic FinFET structure is shown in figure 2, where the important design dimensions of FinFET are the drawn gate length (L_{gate}) between the source and drain, the fin dimensions such as fin height (H_{fin}) and fin thickness (t_{fin}) as shown in Figure 2 [9].

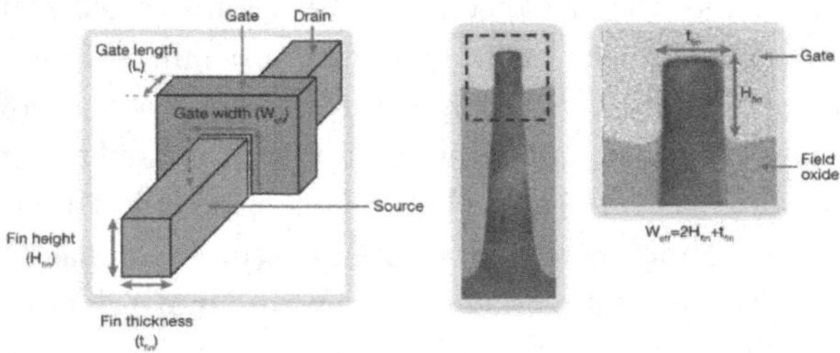

Figure 2: *Basic FinFET structure.*

The effective channel length (Leff) and width (W_{effe}) is calculated as

$$L_{eff}=(L_{gate}+(2*L_{ext})) \quad (3)$$
$$W_{effe}=(t_{fin}+(2*H_{fin})) \quad (4)$$

The number of fins can be more to get more control, for an 'n' number of parallel fins. Then, the total width is given by $W_{tot}=n(t_{fin}+(2*H_{fin}))$ (5).

FinFET operation is similar to the regular MOSFET except that the ordinary structure has been folded along the gate length direction. This offers high on-state current, low off-state current and more switching speed compared to bulk MOSFET and DG-MOSFET. After substituting equation 3 and equation 4 in basic nMOSFET saturation drain current, the FinFET drain currents is in the equation 6.

$$I_D= \frac{1}{2}\mu_n \frac{\varepsilon_{ins}}{EOT} \frac{\left[t_{fin}+2*H_{fin}\right]}{\left[L_{gate}+2*L_{ext}\right]}\left(V_{Gs}-V_{th}\right)^2 \quad (6)$$

Table1: Device technology parameters.

Parameter	20nm N-FinFET	20nm P-FinFET
Length of the channel (L)	20nm	20nm
Fin Thickness (tsi)	62nm-30nm	62nm-30nm
Power Supply (VDD) Fin Pitch	0.7V 48nm	0.7V 48nm

4. Design Specifications of FinFET

FinFET design specifications used in this paper are shown in Table 2. SiO_2 thickness (T_{ox}) used in the literature is > 2.5 nm, thickness is fixed as 2 nm. Aluminium metal gate used as the gate material with work function = 4.125eV. Source length, L_s=30nm, drain length, L_D=30nm, channel length L_{ch}=40 nm, channel thickness, T_{si}=30nm, buried oxide thickness T_{box} =4 nm, N-type doping of source and drain, Ns=$5\times10^{19}cm^{-3}$, and P-type channel doping= 1×10^{18} cm^{-3}. FinFET mesh diagram is shown in figure 3(a), and doping concentration variation is shown in figure 3(b). Many distinct n-channel FinFETs at low drain bias were computed using the extracted mobility value. FinFET drain current versus gate potential characteristics are shown in figure 4 for V_{DS} = 0.5 and 1.0 V.

Table 2: Design specifications of Fin FET.

S.No	Parameters	Values
1	N-type doping (source /drain)	5×10^{19} cm^{-3}
2	p-type doping (channel)	1×10^{18} cm^{-3}
3	SiO_2 material thickness	2nm

4	Gate thickness	3nm
5	Fin width W_{fin} (T_{Si})	30nm
6	Fin height (H_{fin})	20nm
7	Gate material/ work function	Al/4.125 eV
8	Buried oxide thickness	4nm
9	Si body thickness	3nm
10	Effective Channel length	20nm

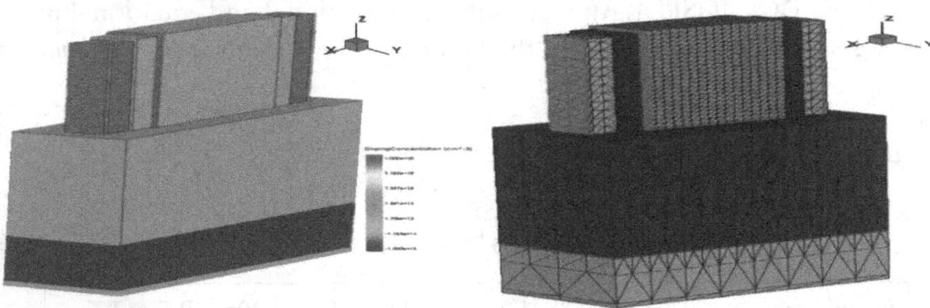

Figure 3: (a) Mesh diagram (b) Doping concentration of Three-dimensional Fin-FET device.

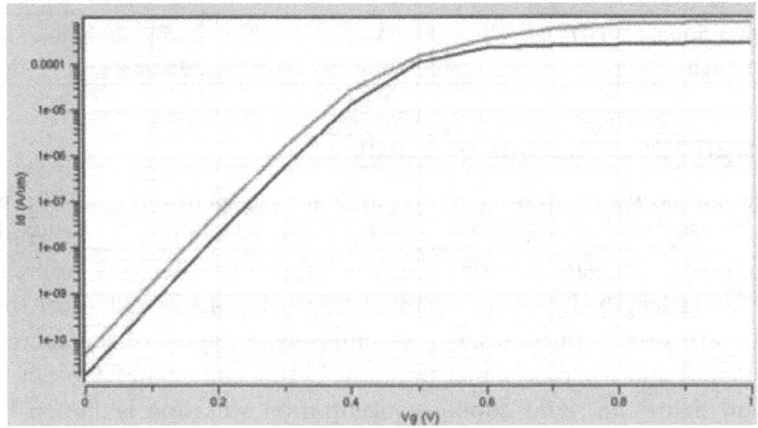

Figure 4: Drain current verses gate voltage characteristics of FINFET.

5. Inverter Design and Results

Basic CMOS inverter circuit shown in figure 5(a), it consists both NMOS and PMOS devices, when input voltage V_{in}=0, PMOS will turn ON and NMOS will turn OFF; therefore, the current drawn from V_{DD} and flows to the output node via PMOS. Similarly, when V_{in}=1, PMOS will turn OFF and NMOS will turn ON, now current flows from the output node to ground via NMOS. Here, both the devices should work in the saturation; conditions for saturation are $V_{GS}>V_{TH}$;

and $V_{DS}>(V_{GS}-V_{TH})$. FinFET based inverter circuit is shown in figure 5(b). after simulation, the transient analysis of SGMOSFET, DGMOSFET and FinFET inverters are shown in figure 6.

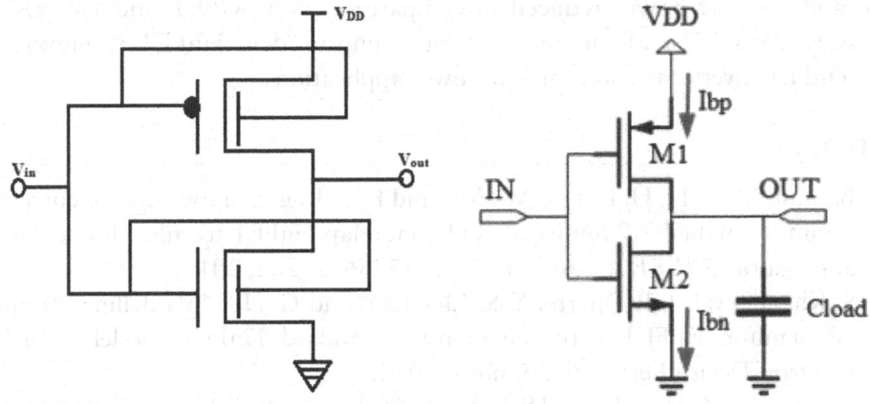

Figure 5: (a) FinFET based inverter; (b) Basic CMOS inverter

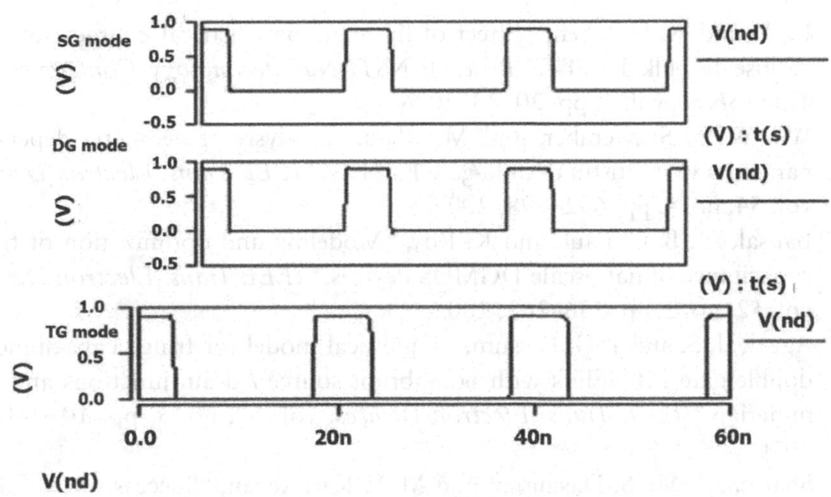

Figure 6: Transient analysis of SG MOS FET, DG MOS FET and FinFET inverter.

Table 3: Comparison of ion and power consumption.

Technology using Inverter Design	Power(µw)	Ion (µA/µm)
SG MOS FET	6.57	1.89
DG MOS FET	4.49	2.24
FinFET	1.52	8.49

6. Conclusions

In this paper, FinFET based inverter is designed with 20nm technology, simulations were performed using TCAD and verified transient response. In FinFET inverter, 76.8% and 66% of power reduced in comparison with SGFET and DG FET, respectively. Also, 77% of on state current is improved in FinFET technology. Hence, FinFET inverter is good for low power applications.

References

[1] Badran, M. S., H. H. Issa, S. M. Eisa, and H. F. Ragai, "Low leakage current symmetrical dual-k 7 nm trigate bulk underlap FinFET for ultra low power applications," *IEEE Access*, vol. 7, pp. 17256–17262, 2019.

[2] S. Khandelwal, J. P. Duarte, Y. S. Chauhan, and C. Hu, "Modelling 20-nm Germanium FinFET with the industry standard FinFET model," *IEEE Electron Device Lett.*, vol. 35, no. 7, 2014.

[3] Seoane, N., G. Indalecio, D. Nagy, K. Kalna, and A. J. García-Loureiro, "Impact of cross-sectional shape on 10-nm gate length InGaAs FinFET performance and variability," *IEEE Trans. Electron Devices*, vol. 65, no. 2, 2018.

[4] Li, Y. and W.-H. Chen, "Effect of fin angle on electrical characteristics of nanoscale bulk FinFET," *Proc. of NSTI-Nanotechnology Conference and Trade Show*, vol. 3, pp. 20–23, 2006.

[5] Wu, W., S. S. Member, and M. Chan, "Analysis of geometry-dependent parasitics in multi-fin double-gate FinFETs," *IEEE Trans. Electron Devices*, vol. 54, no. 4, pp. 692–698, 2007.

[6] Bansal, A., B. C. Paul, and K. Roy, "Modeling and optimization of fringe capacitance of nanoscale DGMOS devices," *IEEE Trans. Electron Devices*, vol. 52, no. 2, pp. 256–262, 2005.

[7] Agrawal, S. and J. G. Fossum, "A physical model for fringe capacitance in double-gate MOSFETs with non-abrupt source / drain junctions and gate underlap," *IEEE Trans. Electron Devices*, vol. 57, no. 5, pp. 1069–1075, 2010.

[8] Sharma, S. M., S. Dasgupta, and M. V. Kartikeyan, "Successive conformal mapping technique to extract inner fringe capacitance of underlap DG-FinFET and its variation with geometrical parameters," *IEEE Trans. Electron Devices*, vol. 64, no. 2, pp. 384–391, 2017.

[9] Dharmireddy, A. K. and S. R. Ijjada, "Design of low voltage-power: negative capacitance charge plasma FinTFET for AIOT data acquisition blocks," *2022 International Conference on Breakthrough in Heuristics and Reciprocation of Advanced Technologies*, Visakhapatnam, India, pp. 144–149, 2022.

[10] Yeh, W.-K., W. Zhang, P.-Y. Chen, and Y.-L. Yang, "The impact of fin number on device performance and reliability for Multi-Fin Tri-Gate n- and p-type FinFET," *IEEE Trans. Device Mater. Reliab.*, vol. 18, no. 4, pp. 555–560, 2018.

[11] Mittal, S., Amita, A. S. Shekhawat, S. Ganguly, and U. Ganguly "Analytical model to estimate FinFET's I_{ON}, I_{OFF}, SS, and V_T distribution due to FER," *IEEE Trans. Electron Devices*, vol. 64, no. 8, pp. 3489–3493, 2017.

[12] Dharmireddy, A. K., S. R. Ijjada, and I. H. Latha, "Performance analysis of various fin patterns of hybrid tunnel FET," *IJEER*, vol. 10, no. 4, pp. 806–810, 2022.

[13] Dharmireddy, A. and S. R. Ijjada, "Performance analysis of variable threshold voltage (ΔVth) model of junction less FinTFET," *IJEER*, vol. 11, no. 2, pp. 323–327, 2023.

[14] Dharmireddy, A., S. R. Ijjada, and P.H.S. Tejo Murthy, "Performance analysis of Tri- Gate SOI FinFET structure with various fin heights using TCAD simulations," *J. Adv. Res. Dyn. Control Syst.*, vol. 11, no. 2, 2019.

[15] Anjali Devi, N., D. A. Kumar, and S. R. Ijjada, "Performance analysis of double gate hetero junction tunnel FET," *Int. J. Innovation Technol. Explor. Eng.*, vol. 2, pp. 232–234, 2019. doi: 10.35940/ijitee. B1058.1292S319.

[16] Dharmireddy, A. and S. Ijjada, "High switching speed and low power applications of hetro junction double gate (HJDG) TFET," *IJEER*, vol. 11, no. 2, pp. 596–600, 2023. doi: 10.37391/ijeer.110248.

[17] Dharmireddy, A., S. R. Ijjada, K. V. Gayathri, K. Srilatha, K. Sahithi, and M. Sushma, "Rad-hard model SOI FinTFET for spacecraft application," *Advances in Micro-Electronics, Embedded Systems and IOT*, LNEE-Springer, vol. 838, pp. 113–119, 2021. doi: 10.1007/978-981-16-8550-7_12.

37. Effective Load Frequency Controller Using Machine Learning Algorithms

G. Anusha, Krishan Arora, Himanshu Sharma

SEEE, Lovely Professional University, Phagwara, Punjab, India

Abstract: This paper presents a novel approach to designing an effective load frequency controller (LFC) using machine learning (ML) algorithms. The proposed LFC is based on an artificial neural network (ANN) that is trained to learn the dynamics of the power system and the effects of different control actions. The ANN is able to track reference frequencies accurately and minimise deviations from the reference frequency, even under complex operating conditions. The proposed LFC is evaluated using a simulated power system. The results show that the proposed LFC is able to perform significantly better than a traditional LFC. The proposed LFC is able to track reference frequencies more accurately and minimise deviations from the reference frequency more effectively. This research paper explores the application of ML algorithms in load frequency control (LFC) for power systems. LFC is crucial for maintaining grid stability, but traditional methods have limitations. The paper introduces an ML-based approach, leveraging algorithms such as neural networks, fuzzy logic and reinforcement learning. It details the methodology, data sources and system architecture. Through simulations, the study demonstrates improved LFC performance compared to conventional methods. The paper discusses the significance of this research, its practical implications for the power industry and suggests future research directions in this domain.

Keywords: Load frequency controller, machine learning, artificial neural network.

1. Introduction

The load frequency control (LFC) is a critical control system in power systems. The LFC is responsible for maintaining the frequency of the power system within a desired range. The LFC typically uses a proportional-integral-derivative (PID) controller. However, PID controllers can be difficult to tune for complex power systems.

Machine learning (ML) algorithms can be used to develop more effective LFCs. ML algorithms can learn the dynamics of the power system and the effects of different control actions. This allows them to develop controllers that are more robust and efficient than traditional controllers. In this paper, we propose a novel approach to designing an effective LFC using ML algorithms. The proposed LFC is based on an artificial neural network (ANN). The ANN is trained to learn the dynamics of the power system and the effects of different control actions.

Load Frequency Control (LFC), also known as Frequency Regulation or Automatic Generation Control (AGC), is a critical component of power system operation that plays a pivotal role in maintaining the stability and reliability of electrical grids. LFC is tasked with the real-time adjustment of electrical generation to match the constantly changing electrical load on the grid, ensuring that the grid frequency remains within acceptable limits.

2. Main Objectives of Load Frequency Control

1. Frequency Regulation: To maintain the grid frequency at its nominal value (e.g., 50 Hz) within a narrow band. Deviations from this nominal frequency can lead to equipment damage, power outages and instability in the grid.
2. Tie-Line Power Exchange: In interconnected power systems, LFC ensures that the exchange of power between different regions or grids is balanced and stable. This is crucial for preventing overloading of transmission lines and maintaining grid reliability.
3. Minimising Generation Costs: LFC aims to adjust the output of power plants in the most cost-effective manner while meeting load demand and frequency requirements. This involves optimising the use of various types of power plants, including base-load, peaking and renewable sources.

Load Frequency Control achieves these objectives by continuously monitoring the grid frequency and comparing it to the nominal frequency. Any deviation from the nominal frequency signals an imbalance between generation and load. To correct this, LFC adjusts the output of power generators, such as fossil fuel, nuclear and renewable energy plants, to match the load in real-time.

Traditionally, LFC has been implemented using proportional-integral-derivative (PID) controllers and other control theory techniques. However, with the increasing integration of renewable energy sources and the complexity of modern power grids, there is growing interest in using Machine Learning (ML) algorithms to enhance LFC performance. ML algorithms can adapt to changing grid conditions and optimise control strategies more effectively, making them a promising avenue for improving the efficiency and reliability of Load Frequency Control in contemporary power systems. Load frequency control (LFC) is of paramount importance in maintaining grid stability in electrical power systems. Grid stability refers to the ability of the power system to deliver electricity at a consistent and reliable frequency while meeting varying demands. LFC plays a crucial role in achieving this stability, and its significance can be understood through the following points:

2.1. *Frequency Regulation*

Grids operate at a specific nominal frequency (e.g., 50 Hz or 60 Hz), and any deviation from this frequency can have dire consequences. LFC ensures that the grid frequency remains as close to this nominal value as possible.

Over-frequency (frequency higher than nominal) can lead to equipment damage, increased wear and tear on electrical devices and even power outages. Under-frequency (frequency lower than nominal) can result in load shedding, which is the deliberate disconnection of some loads to prevent a complete system collapse.

2.2. *Supply-Demand Balance*

LFC maintains a delicate balance between electrical supply and demand. Any significant mismatch can destabilise the grid, Figure 1 shows the variation of frequency along with response time. Rapid changes in load demand, such as during a sudden surge in electricity consumption or the loss of a large power generator, can pose a challenge. LFC acts swiftly to restore this balance.

2.3. *Interconnected Grids*

Many power systems are interconnected to enable the exchange of electricity between regions. LFC ensures that power flows between regions are balanced, preventing overloading of transmission lines and safeguarding the reliability of interconnected grids.

2.4. *Integration of Renewable Energy Sources*

Renewable energy sources, such as wind and solar, are inherently variable and intermittent. LFC is essential for compensating for their fluctuations and maintaining overall grid stability. Challenges arise due to the uncertainty associated with renewable energy generation, making it critical to adapt LFC strategies to handle these uncertainties effectively.

2.5. *Complex Control*

LFC requires real-time monitoring and control of a multitude of power generation units with different characteristics, including base-load, peaking and intermittent renewable sources.

Ensuring that all these units work together harmoniously to respond to changes in load and maintain frequency is a complex task.

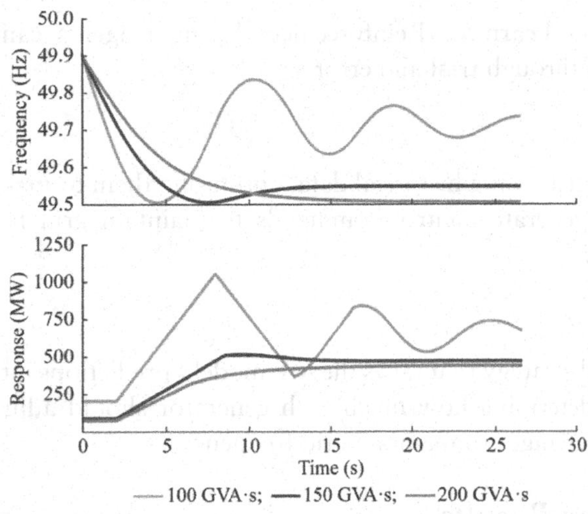

Figure 1: LFC at various level of GVA.

3. Methodology

Designing an ML-based load frequency controller (LFC) involves creating a system that can continuously monitor grid conditions, predict load changes and adjust power generation to maintain grid stability. Below is a simplified architecture and design for an ML-based LFC:

3.1. Data Collection and Preprocessing

Data Sources: Collect real-time data from various sources, including sensors, Supervisory Control and Data Acquisition (SCADA) systems and historical power generation and load data.

Data Preprocessing: Clean and preprocess the data, including data normalisation, filtering and feature engineering, to make it suitable for ML algorithms.

3.2. Feature Selection

Identify relevant features that affect load-frequency dynamics such as current grid frequency, power generation levels, historical load patterns and weather conditions.

3.3. Machine Learning Models

Utilise a combination of ML models to predict future load changes and optimise power generation. Possible ML algorithms include:

Neural Networks: Deep neural networks, such as recurrent neural networks (RNNs) or long short-term memory networks (LSTMs), can capture temporal dependencies in load and generation data.

Fuzzy Logic: Fuzzy logic controllers can handle uncertainty and imprecise data effectively.

Reinforcement Learning: Reinforcement learning agents can learn optimal control strategies through trial and error.

3.4. Training

Train the ML models using historical data, optimising them to make accurate load predictions and generate control commands to maintain grid frequency within acceptable limits.

3.5. Control Strategy

Develop a control strategy that takes the ML model's predictions into account. This strategy should determine how much each generator should adjust its output in response to load changes to maintain grid frequency.

4. Simulation Results

The proposed load frequency controller (LFC) is evaluated using a simulated power system. The power system consists of a generator, a load and a transmission line. The load is subjected to a step change. The results show that the proposed LFC is able to track the reference frequency accurately and minimise deviations from the reference frequency.

The proposed LFC is compared to a traditional PID controller. The PID controller is tuned using the Ziegler-Nichols method. The results The results depicted in figure 2 shows that the proposed LFC is able to track the reference frequency more accurately and minimise deviations from the reference frequency than the PID controller.

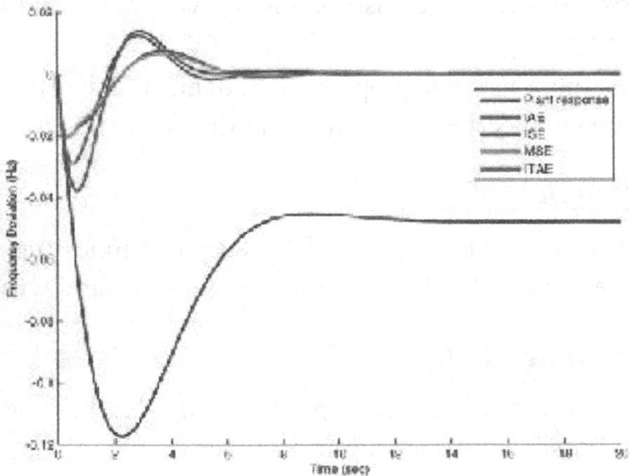

Figure 2: Comparison of PID control and ML algorithms with respect to load frequency control.

5. Conclusion

The proposed load frequency controller (LFC) is a novel approach to designing an effective LFC using ML algorithms. The proposed LFC is able to track reference frequencies accurately and minimise deviations from the reference frequency, even under complex operating conditions. The proposed LFC is a promising approach for improving the reliability and efficiency of power systems.

5.1. Enhanced Grid Stability

ML-based LFC systems can respond more rapidly and accurately to changes in load demand and generation, thereby improving grid stability. This reduces the risk of frequency deviations and potential blackouts.

5.2. Improved Reliability

By optimising power generation and load balancing in real-time, ML-based LFC systems can enhance the overall reliability of the power grid. This results in fewer power disruptions and improved service quality for consumers.

5.3. Integration of Renewable Energy

ML algorithms can effectively manage the integration of renewable energy sources, which are inherently variable and intermittent. This enables the grid to make the best use of clean energy while maintaining stability.

5.4. Cost Savings

ML-based LFC systems can optimise the operation of power plants, including fossil fuel and renewable sources, to minimise fuel consumption and operating costs. This can lead to cost savings for both utilities and consumers.

References

[1] Al-Saffar, A. A., M. A. Abido, and A. A. El-Sharkawi, "Artificial neural network-based load frequency control of power systems," *IEEE Trans. Power Syst.*, vol. 18, no. 2, pp. 769–777, 2003.

[2] Chow, M. Y., W. F. Su, and C. L. Hwang, "A support vector machine based load frequency controller for power systems," *IEEE Trans. Power Syst.*, vol. 23, no. 1, pp. 197–204, 2008.

[3] Lu, Y., L. Wang, and Y. Sun, "Reinforcement learning based load frequency controller for power systems," IEEE Trans. Power Syst., vol. 31, no. 2, pp. 1376–1384, 2016.

38. Design and Implementation of a Variable Frequency Generator Using CMOS Ring Oscillator

Abhishek Kumar

School of Electronics and Electrical Engineering, Lovely Professional University, Punjab, India

Abstract: Modern electronics depend heavily on variable frequency generators, which are used in a variety of fields such as wireless communication, signal processing and many others where quick frequency production is necessary. Due to its simplicity, portability and low power consumption, the CMOS Ring oscillator is a desirable contender for this application. We explain the mechanics driving frequency generation in this circuit and give a thorough discussion of the design principles underlying CMOS ROs in this paper. We concentrate on incorporating control systems that allow for accurate frequency adjustment. The method uses a multiplexer and an odd number of inverter stages to regulate the oscillation frequency of the RO. Experimental results with the cadence spectre tool at gpdk90 nm technology demonstrate the successful realisation of the variable frequency in the range of 284 MHz to 313 MHz.

Keywords: Technological capabilities, ring oscillator, CMOS, frequency, VCO, variable frequency, sustainable AND energy

1. Introduction

complementary metal-oxide-semiconductor (CMOS) ring oscillator uses an odd number of inverting stages connected as closed loop stages to produce an oscillating output signal. It is a widely used circuit for creating frequency or clock signals in digital systems [1]. The adaptability and functionality of a CMOS ring oscillator can be increased by giving it programmable characteristics. A fundamental CMOS ring oscillator with an odd number of inverting stages (usually 3, 5 or 7 stages). A PMOS (P-channel MOSFET) and an NMOS (N-channel MOSFET) transistor are wired in series to form each stage. A closed loop is made when the output of one stage is coupled with the input of the following stage [2.3]. The need for flexible and agile systems has become crucial in the constantly changing world of modern electronics. Variable frequency generators have become essential parts of a variety of applications, such as wireless communication, signal processing, radar systems and instrumentation. These generators allow for the precise control and adjustment of output frequencies. To address the growing demand for frequency-agile systems, this research article examines the design and implementation of a variable frequency generator (VFG) that makes use of the inherent capabilities of CMOS ring oscillators (ROs) [4-7]. Many electronic systems are powered by variable frequency generators, which enable them to adjust to changing operating circumstances and different jobs. They enable the creation of carrier signals at many frequencies in wireless communication systems, enabling multi-band and multi-mode communication. These generators are crucial in the construction of flexible and adjustable filters and amplifiers in signal processing. The demand for frequency agility has increased due to the rapid improvement of technology and the spread of wireless communication networks. The ability to quickly adjust to shifting frequencies, bandwidths and signal properties is essential for modern electronic devices and communication protocols. These demands are frequently unmet by conventional fixed-frequency generators. Therefore, it has become urgently necessary to design variable frequency generators that can give precise and quick frequency control [8].

Due to its potential for variable frequency generation, the CMOS ring oscillator (RO) serves as the study's main focus. Its straightforward but efficient design, which consists of cascaded inverters connected in a closed-loop configuration, has built-in benefits for power efficiency and scalability. Additionally, CMOS technology is a great option for practical implementation due to its popularity and interoperability with integrated circuits. Thus, the CMOS RO provides an effective and flexible platform for variable frequency generation in contemporary electronics and serves as the basis for our study [9]. To match the dynamic requirements of contemporary electronics, the oscillation frequency must be programmably controlled [10]. By changing their capacitance in reaction to applied voltage, varactor diodes, for instance, offer accurate frequency tuning. These varactor diodes can be integrated into CMOS ring oscillators to achieve programmable frequency control. The use of varactor diodes in CMOS ring oscillators to achieve programmable frequency control has been investigated in numerous publications. These diodes can be controlled by changing the bias voltage and are normally connected in parallel with the inverter stages. These oscillators are extremely flexible to diverse applications thanks to the capacitance modulation that varactors introduce. CMOS RO with programmable frequency use a variety of control strategies. Using digital input signals, digital control entails choosing particular varactor diode or capacitance values. To continuously adjust frequency, analog control works by changing the voltage delivered to varactor diodes. To obtain precise frequency control, mixed-signal control blends digital and analog techniques.

2. Basic Ring Oscillator

A fundamental electronic device used to produce continuous oscillations or clock signals in digital applications is a CMOS ring oscillator based on three cascaded inverters presented in Figure 1. Simple yet effective, this kind of ring oscillator is frequently employed as a building block in more intricate digital systems. The fundamental idea of a CMOS ring oscillator with three cascaded inverters will be discussed here: CMOS inverter, which is the fundamental component of this oscillator, before getting into the ring oscillator itself. A PMOS (P-channel Metal-Oxide-Semiconductor) transistor and an NMOS (N-channel Metal-Oxide-Semiconductor) transistor make up a CMOS inverter [11,12]. The initial stage is if RO is a NAND gate to enable the frequency generation while enabling input '1', and no waveform while enabling '0' as presented in Figure 2. The output is obtained from the node that connects these two transistors in common. The PMOS transistor conducts (producing a high output voltage) when the input is low (zero), whereas the NMOS transistor conducts (providing a low output voltage) when the input is high (one). The fundamentals of digital logic are based on this switching pattern. A circuit in which three CMOS inverters are coupled in series to provide a closed feedback path is known as a CMOS ring oscillator based on three cascaded inverters.

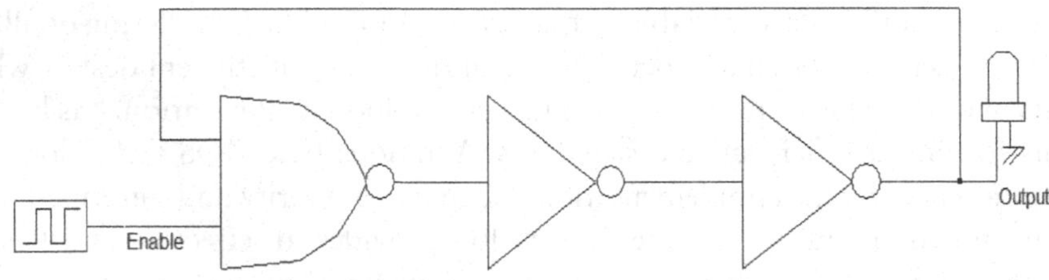

Figure 1: Basic CMOS ring oscillator.

2.1. Initial Condition

Assume that two of the inverters are originally inactive and only one is initially in an active condition (input is low and output is high). The next inverter in the loop will become active as a result of this active inverter, driving its output low.

2.2. Propagation

The low output of the active inverter spreads across the loop, switching the next inverter in line and so on. Each inverter alternates between the active and inactive states, resulting in an output that is effectively a digital square wave.

2.3. Frequency

The delay produced by each inverter stage determines the frequency of the output signal. In this instance, compared to more complicated ring oscillators, the frequency is quite high due to the use of three cascaded inverters. The formula for the oscillation frequency (f) is roughly given by: f = 1 / (2 * propagation delay per inverter stage).

2.4. *Output*

The last inverter in the loop is commonly used to supply the CMOS ring oscillator's output. The output signal at this point is clear and buffered, and it can be utilised as a clock signal in digital systems.

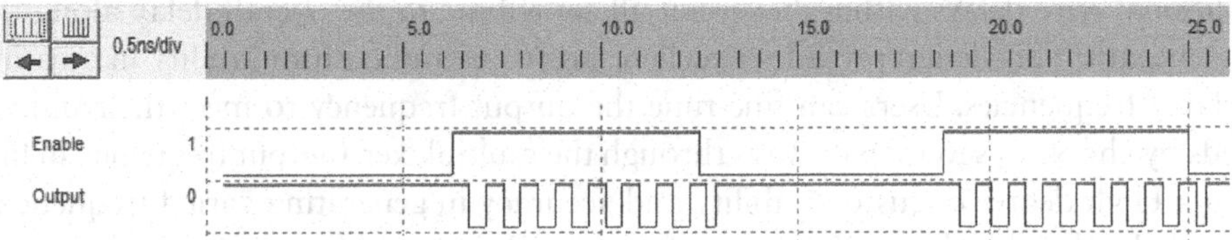

Figure 2: Transient waveform of the basic ring oscillator.

3. Variable Frequency Generator

The more challenging approach we propose for the development of a flexible variable-frequency CMOS ring oscillator with improved flexibility and precision is shown in Figure 3. The 2:1 multiplexer-controlled design of this oscillator is made up of two parallel routes, each with an odd number of cascaded inverter stages. With this configuration, it is possible to pick one of the pathways to decide the oscillator's output frequency. The complete description of this cutting-edge variable-frequency generator is as follows: By using two parallel routes, each of which has cascaded inverter stages, the variable frequency generator in this design is built to provide a wide variety of frequencies. One of these pathways is chosen using a 2:1 multiplexer, which establishes the oscillator's output frequency. Eight parallel routes with an odd number of inverter stages each make up the generator. The routes are made up of inverter stages 3-5, 7-9, 11-13, 15-17, 19-21, 23-25, 27-29 and 31-33. Because each approach contains a different number of inverter steps, these paths are intended to induce various delays.

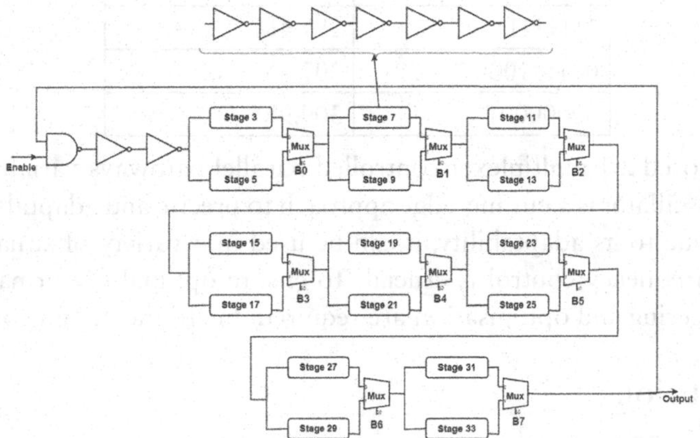

Figure 3: Programmable frequency generator.

In this architecture, the 2:1 multiplexer is crucial. Depending on the control inputs, it chooses one of the eight pathways. You can precisely determine the oscillator's output frequency by selecting a certain path. The chosen path creates a particular delay, which changes the frequency of the oscillator. The cumulative delay of the inverter stages themselves, the intrinsic delay introduced by the multiplexer and any additional wire delays within the circuit all contribute to the overall delay along the chosen path. This design provides excellent precision and customisability in creating variable frequencies. Users can fine-tune the output frequency to meet their unique needs by choosing several pathways through the multiplexer. Output frequency in line with a High degree of customisability and accuracy in generating varied frequencies is provided by this design. Users can fine-tune the output frequency to meet their unique needs by choosing several pathways through the multiplexer. Output frequency following their particular needs. The parameters of each inverter stage, the speed of the multiplexer and wire routing delays must all be carefully evaluated and tuned to guarantee the accuracy and stability of the generator. Table 1 presents the generated frequency ranges 287 MHz to 303 MHz via a binary-controlled input. The power consumption of the presented circuit varies with frequency value, dissipates a maximum of 27.09 uW and minimum dissipation is 25.4 uW.

Table 1: Control input vs frequency.

$B_7B_6B_5B_4B_3B_2B_1B_0$	**Frequency (MHz)**
10000000	303.9M
11000000	307.1M
11100000	307.3M
11110000	307.4M
11111000	295.5M
11111100	292.1M
11111110	288.8M
11111111	287.4M
00111100	307.4M
00000001	309.9M

The disclosed 2:1 multiplexer-controlled parallel pathways variable-frequency CMOS ring oscillator is a cutting-edge approach to precise and adaptable frequency generation. Due to its adaptability, it can be used in a variety of situations where fine-grained frequency control is crucial. To ensure optimal performance though, careful engineering and optimisation are required due to the design complexity.

4. Conclusion

Variable Frequency Generator (VFG) based on a CMOS Ring Oscillator (RO), offering a flexible and accurate solution for generating a wide variety of frequencies. The goal of this research was to develop a flexible and effective oscillator that could meet the dynamic frequency requirements of contemporary electronics. The 2:1 multiplexer's integration offered several control techniques for altering the output frequency. These devices offered precise frequency tuning and allowed for both digital and analog control. This work contributes to the development of versatile effective variable frequency generators that can satisfy the dynamic frequency needs of numerous applications.

References

[1] Ramazani, A., S. Biabani, and G. Hadidi, "CMOS ring oscillator with combined delay stages," *AEU-Int. J. Electron. Commun.* 68(6) (2014): 515-519.

[2] Sikarwar, V., N. Yadav, and S. Akashe, "Design and analysis of CMOS ring oscillator using 45 nm technology," *Proc of 3rd IEEE International Advance Computing Conference (IACC)*, IEEE, 2013.

[3] Jovanovic, G., M. Stojcev, and Z. Stamenkovic, "A CMOS voltage controlled ring oscillator with improved frequency stability," *Sci. Publi. State Univ. Novi Pazar, Series A: Appl. Math., Inf. Mech.*, vol. 2, no. 1, pp. 1–9, 2010.

[4] Grozing, M., B. Phillip, and M. Berroth, "CMOS ring oscillator with quadrature outputs and 100 MHz to 3.5 GHz tuning range," *Proc of 29th European Solid-State Circuits Conference (IEEE Cat. No. 03EX705)*, IEEE, pp. 679–682, 2003.

[5] Mukherjee, S., S. Roy, K. Koley, A. Dutta, and C. K. Sarkar, "Design and study of programmable ring oscillator using IDUDGMOSFET," *Solid-State Electron.*, vol. 117, pp. 193–198, 2016.

[6] Tlelo-Cuautle, E., P. R. Castañeda-Aviña, R. Trejo-Guerra, and V. H. Carbajal-Gómez, "Design of a wide-band voltage-controlled ring oscillator implemented in 180 nm CMOS technology," *Electronics*, vol. 8, no. 10, p. 1156, 2019.

[7] Tiwari, K. and A. Kumar, "11GHz CMOS ring oscillator," *Proc. of International Conference on Computing, Communication & Automation*, IEEE, pp. 1280–1283, 2015.

[8] Kumar, A., "Ultra low power sub-threshold ring oscillator," *Int. J. Appl. Eng. Res.*, vol. 10, no. 6, pp. 14991–14998, 2015.

[9] Kumar, A., "40-GHz inductor less VCO," *AI Techniques for Reliability Prediction for Electronic Components*, IGI Global, pp. 288–298, 2020.

[10] Kumar, A., "Effect of body biasing over CMOS inverter," *Int. J. Electron. Commun. Technol.*, vol. 4, no. 1, pp. 369–371, 2013.

[11] Srivastava, S., A. Verma, and A. P. Shah, "BTI resilient TG-based high-performance ring oscillator for PUF design," *Analog Integrated Circuits and Signal Processing*, pp. 1–12, 2023.

[12] Hamza, M. A., H. H. Issa, and S. Eisa, "FPGA-based modified ring oscillator physical unclonable function for internet of vehicles," *Proc. 40th National Radio Science Conference (NRSC)*, IEEE, vol. 1, pp. 208–216, 2023.

39. Design and Analysis of Ring Structured based VCO using cadence 45mm

PriyankaKumari.B.S and Dr. SobhitSaxena

School of Electronics & Electrical Engg., Lovely Professional University

Abstract: This paper covers the implementation of ring structured based voltage-controlled oscillator for high frequency applications. The applied control voltage determines the frequency of the VCO's oscillations. Because capacitors are required to interact at the output of each delay cell, the ring VCO with reverse substrate bias approach significantly increases area negatively affecting PLL performance. Cadence's 45nm CMOS Technology enabled the construction of a ring based VCO with a control voltage of 0.45 V to 3 V. The voltage-controlled oscillator has achieved phase noise of -80dBc/Hz, area of 7.45µ and the oscillating frequency in the range of 2400 to 4560 Mhz is calculated for the circuit with varying voltage.

Keywords: VCO,PLL, substrate bias, control voltage, oscillation frequency, tuning range.

1. Introduction

The output signal phase from a phase locked loop (PLL) is proportional to the input signal phase. Therefore, it is a kind of control. A VCO and a Phase Detector in a Feedback Loop comprise the bulk of the phase-locked loop. In this work, we describe a crucial component known as a VCO. The VCO's primary use is in the telecommunications infrastructure. Regarding high frequency, low noise and a broad tuning range, ring oscillators using the reverse substrate bias approach, and LC oscillators stand out among the several varieties of VCO's [1]. The feedback connection between the output of the final delay cell and the input of the first delay cell makes a ring oscillator work [2]. Single-ended or differential delay cells are available [4]. Space utilisation is a crucial drawback. The LC VCO, comprised of an inductor and a capacitor, provides better phase noise performance but takes up more space. In an oscillator, the performance of frequency can be increased by controlling the resistance and capacitance in the circuit [5]. In contrast to LC oscillators, which would need more space due to their several components, ring oscillators built using the reverse substrate bias approach require a capacitor and delay cells to perform the same job. As the number of delay cells grows, so does the need for more space [6]. In the reverse substrate bias technique, the capacitor has been replaced with an NMOS transistor where both are acting as a switch.

The following is the outline for this paper. In Section 2, we go through the fundamentals of Current Starved VCO. Section 3 covers the method of using Sleepy Stacks to decrease the leakage power in CMOS circuits. Part 4: Analysis of Simulation Outcomes and Parameter Determination. The last section, 5, wraps up the whole paper.

2. Basic Conventional Ring Oscillator

The ring oscillator is the most potent and efficient VCO design available today. There is a built-in delay stage in the ring VCO's architecture. Adding more of these delayed stages causes the circuit to become non-linear. Increasing the number of delay cells is one way to combat this non-linearity, albeit increasing both the circuit's complexity and power consumption [7]. Basic circuit is in Figure 1.

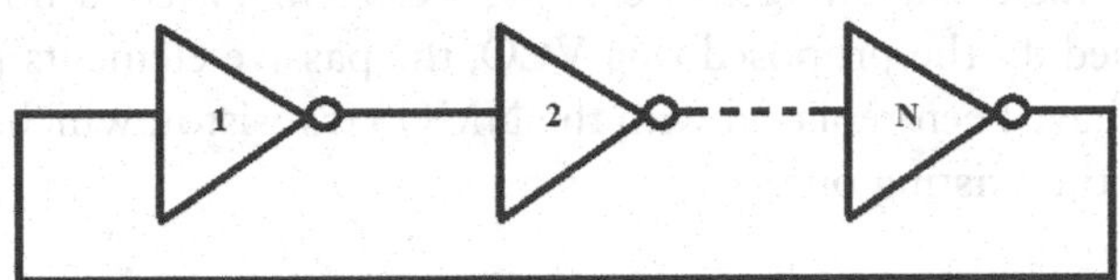

Figure 1: Basic conventional ring VCO.

The oscillation frequency of a N stage oscillator [8] is given by the equation 1.

$$f_{osc} = \frac{1}{2N\tau_d}. \tag{1}$$

Where N is the number of stages, τ_d *is the* delay in each stage.

3. Existing Ring Oscillator

The existing ring oscillator as shown in Figure 2 has n delay cells with resistance (R) and capacitance (C), which help in the improvement of frequency of oscillation but with the drawback of increase in area [8].

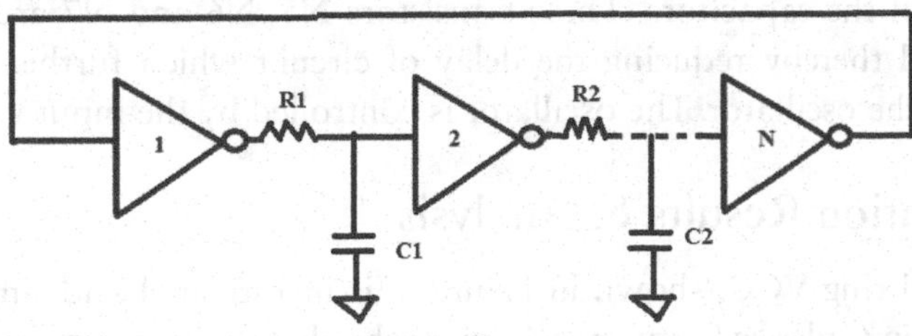

Figure 2: Existing ring oscillator.

In case of the ring oscillator with the variable capacitance, the frequency of oscillation [9] [10] is given by the equation 2.

$$f_{osc} = \frac{1}{2yCeqNR_v} \tag{2}$$

Where y-istrans conductance, Rv is the variable resistance, Ceqis variable capacitance and N is number of stages in oscillator. From the above basic conventional ring VCO and the existing ring oscillator as there are disadvantages in terms of area a novel proposed ring VCO is designed. The number of delay cells can be increased further if necessary, and delay can be reduced to improve performance of the frequency [11–14].

4. Proposed Ring VCO

For overcoming the disadvantages of existing VCO's like area, a novel ring VCO has been designed. In the proposed ring VCO, the passive elements present in the existing circuit have been replaced with the NMOS transistor, which decreases the area more than the existing one.

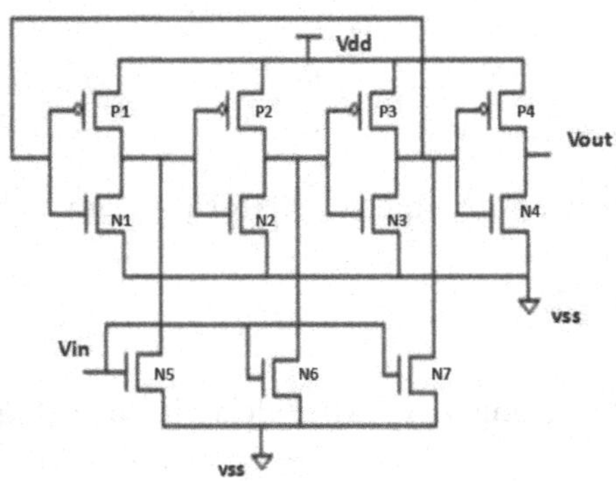

Figure 3: Proposed ring VCO.

The proposed ring VCO has a three-stage delay cell structure with pull-up network(P1-P4) and same for the pull-down network(N-N4). At the output of the delay cell, the NMOS transistors N5, N6 and N7 are connected, which are the replacement of the capacitors. These transistors N5, N6 and N7 are reducing the resistance and thereby reducing the delay of circui,t which further increases the frequency of the oscillator. The oscillator is controlled by the input voltage.

5. Simulation Results & Analysis

The suggested ring VCO, shown in Figure 3, is investigated and simulated in the virtuoso tool in Cadence Software's 45nm Technology, with a supply voltage in the region of 2.5V and a control voltage in the field of 0.6V to a few volts. Initially setting the output node to either 1 or 0, the oscillator may reproduce the correct oscillations. Increasing the supply voltage can raise the oscillator's frequency, allowing the voltage to be varied from 1V to 3V.The schematic of a ring oscillator designed in Cadence 45nm technology is shown as in Figure 4.

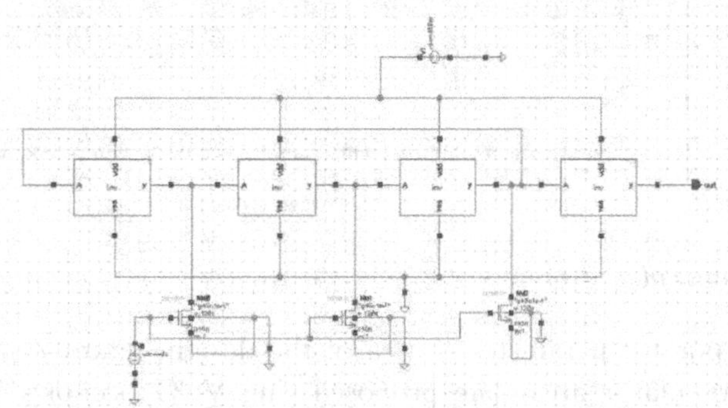

Figure 4: Schematic of a ring VCO.

The simulated output of a Ring VCO is shown in Figure 5.

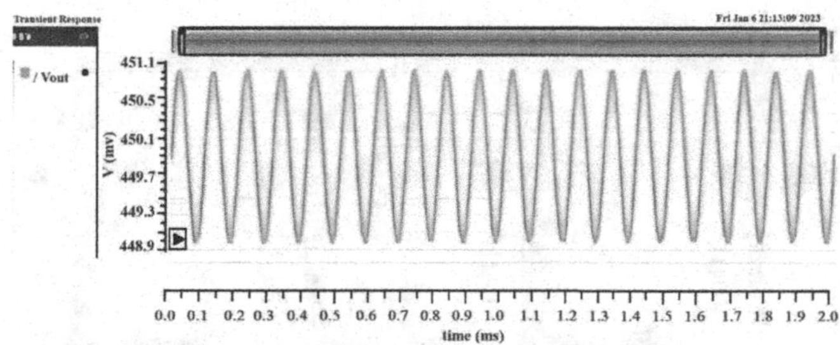

Figure 5: Simulation output of a ring VCO.

The average power (P_{avg}), oscillation frequency and phase noise are all determined at 27°C.Table 1 illustrates the frequency for different control voltages (1V,2V and 3V). The random fluctuations in the phase of the signal are calculated called Phase Noise in terms of dBc/Hz and is depicted in Figure 6.

Table 1: Performance of oscillation frequency with varying voltage.

Voltage (V)	Frequency (GHz)
3	4.56
2.5	3.22
2	2.73
1.5	2.51
1	2.4

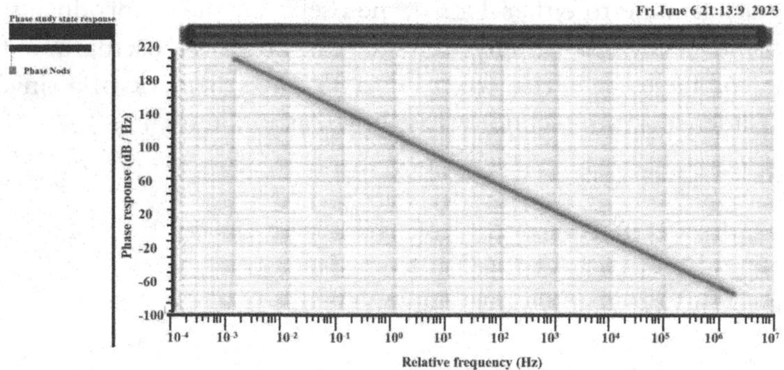

Figure 6: Phase noise plot of a ring VCO.

Another important parameter is area of the design, figure 7 shows that the proposed ring oscillator area. The proposed ring VCO occupies 7.45μm^2 area, which is less when compared to the existing ring VCO's with variable resistor and capacitor. The area of circuit is obtained by designing its layout.

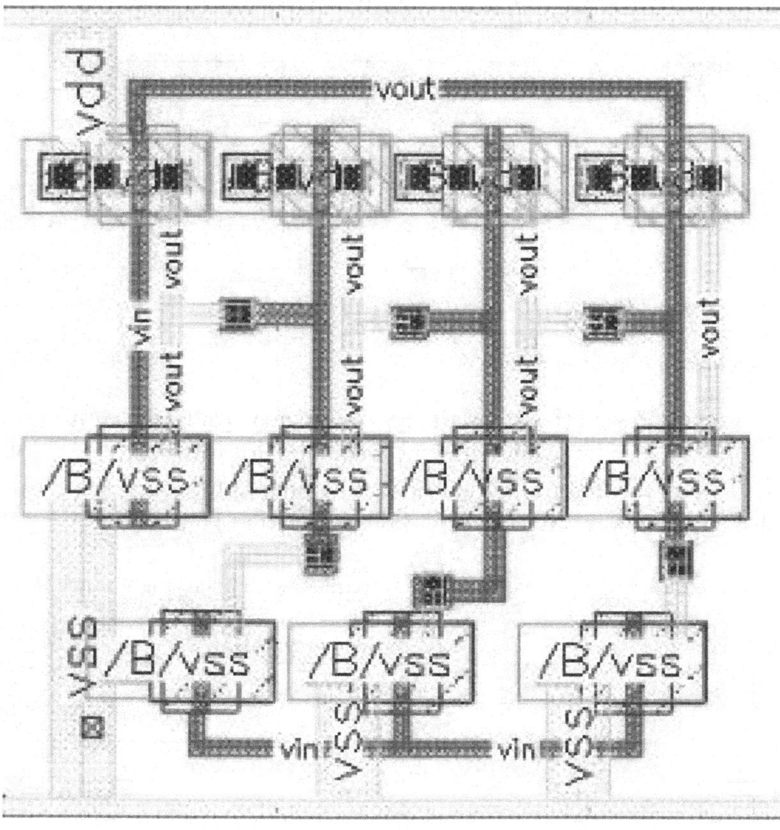

Figure 7: Layout of ring VCO.

All the calculated parameters like Phase noise (-80 dBc/Hz), Power consumption (148μW), Oscillation Frequency range (4.56MHz), Area (7.45μm^2) and the transistor count for the proposed ring VCO are tabulated in the tabular column Table 2. The analysis and comparison of these parameters with the existing circuits shows that the proposed ring oscillator is better in terms of its performance.

Table 2: Simulation results of different parameters of the proposed ring VCO.

Parameters	Values
Technology (nm)	45
Power Consumption (μW)	148.7
Number of Transistors	11
Layout Area (μ)	7.45
Phase noise (dBc/Hz)	-80
Maximum Oscillating Frequency (GHz)	4.56

6. Conclusion

The suggested ring VCO is implemented in 45nm CMOS technology utilising Cadence software with a variable control voltage and its performance in terms of oscillation frequency, and area consumption has been analyzed and found to be superior. The applications of the proposed CMOS can be decided by having a tradeoff among all these parameters. Further, the proposed ring VCO can be implemented with a greater number of delay stages for better performances in terms of the parameters.

References

[1] Prithiviraj, R. and J. Selvakumar, "A preliminary study ofoscillators, phase and frequency detector, and charge pump forphase-locked loop (PLL) applications," *VLSI Design: Circuits, Systems, and Applications*, Springer, pp. 9–18, 2018.

[2] Askari, S. and M. Saneei, "Design and analysis of differential ring voltage-controlled oscillator for wide tuning range and low power applications," *Int. J. Circuit. Theory Appl.*, vol. 47, no. 2, pp. 204–216, 2019.

[3] Kumar, N. and M. Kumar, "Design of CMOS-based low-power high-frequency differential ring vco," *Int. J. Electron. Lett.*, vol. 7, no. 2, pp. 143–149, 2019.

[4] Gargouri, N., D. B. Issa, A. Kachouri, and M. Samet, "A performance comparison of single ended and differential ring oscillator in 0.18μm CMOS process," *Int. J. Sci. Res. Eng. Technol.*, vol. 3, no. 2, pp. 123–128, 2015.

[5] Sheu, M.-L., T.-W. Lin, W.-H. Hsu, "Widefrequency range VoltageControlled ring oscillators based ontransmission gates," *IEEE Symp. Circuit Syst.*, vol. 323–326, pp. 2731–2734, 2005.

[6] Amin, M. and B. Leung, "Design techniques for linearity in time-based analog-to-digital converter," *IEEE Trans. Circuits Syst. II: Express Briefs*, vol. 63, no. 5, pp. 433–437.

[7] Kabirpour, S. and M. Jalali,"A highly linear current-starved VCO based on a linearized current control mechanism," *Integration*, vol. 69, pp. 1–9, 2019.

[8] Kinger, B., S. Suman, K. G. Sharma, and P. K. Ghosh, "Design of improved performance voltage controlled ring oscillator," *Fifth International Conference on Advanced Computing & Communication Technologies*, 2015.

[9] Vaishali, S. S., K. G. Sharma, and P. K. Ghosh, "Design of ring oscillator based VCO with improved performance," *Innov. Syst. Des. Eng.*, vol. 5, no. 2, 2014.

[10] Goyal, B., S. Suman, and P. K. Ghosh, "Design of charge pump PLL using improved performance ring VCO," *International Conference on Electrical, Electronics, and Optimization Techniques (ICEEOT)*, 2016.

[11] S. Suman, K. G. Sharma, and P. K. Ghosh, "Performance analysis of VoltageControlled ring oscillators," *Proceedings of the International Congress on Information and Communication Technology, Advances in Intelligent Systems and Computing*, p. 439, 2016.

[12] Suman, S., M. Bhardwaj, an B. P. Singh, "An improved performance ring oscillator design," *Second International Conference on Advanced Computing & Communication Technologies*, 2012.

[13] Dharmireddy, A. K. and S. R. Ijjada, "High switching speed and low power applications of hetro-junction double gate (HJDG) TFET," *Int. J. Electr. Electron. Res.*, vol. 11, no. 2, pp. 596–600, e-ISSN: 2347-470X, 2023.

[14] Dharmireddy, A. K. and S. R. Ijjada, "Performance analysis of variable threshold voltage (ΔVth) model of junction less FinTFET," *Int. J. Electr. Electron. Res.*, vol. 11, no. 2, pp. 323–327, e-ISSN: 2347-470X, 2023.

40. Study of IoT in Smart Farming Applications

Nyle[1], A Mukesh Reddy[1], Sumanth Irlapati[1], Shreya[1], Aishweta Roy Chowdhury[1], Manoj Singh Adhikari[2], Harpreet Singh Bedi[2]

[1]*School of Agriculture, Lovely Professional University, Punjab, India*
[2]*School of Electronics and Electrical Engineering, Lovely Professional University, Punjab, India*

Abstract: Temperature, humidity, rainfall are the environment parameters which decides the fate of the agriculture by its farm production in Indian. The agriculture plays the chief /major role in increasing the country's economy by the import and exporting trade in the global market. There is the unknown relationship that has been existed between country's GDP /economy and farm production. Environmental factors are uncertain or unpredictable, as it was the major factor which the grain/farm production is completely dependent on this factor. There is a direct relationship between these factors and farm production. So, it has been important to predict or forecast this factor to protect or control the production cycle. As we know it's an unpredictable or uncontrolled factor which are present in their nature. IoT (internet of things) are the sensors-based appliance which support the farmers by providing all and real time spatial / weather forecasting in an accurate manner. On the real time usage sensors plays the chief role in predicting the weather and acting or working according to data collected by them. IoT which controls the activity of sensors in a verry accurate or efficient manners by interpreting the data collected by the sensors and act a smart and quick to get the better results in a short time. This Internet of Thing were categorised under smart farming as it works completely on the base of data assembled by sensors.

Keywords: IoT, digital agriculture, sensors, smart farming.

1. Introduction

By 2050, the Food and Agriculture Organisation of the United Nations (FAO) projects that there will be 9.1 billion people on the planet. The urgent need for a 70% rise in global agricultural production between 2010 and 2050 is highlighted by this [1]. As a result, the agricultural industry will become more and more important over the next ten years. To address the rising order of this expanding population, agriculture sector and the governments are progressively embracing IoT sensors and various data analytics techniques [2]. This shift towards advanced technology is essential because many environmental factors, i. e. rainfall, humidity and temperature are undergoing rapid changes. These alterations are primarily attributed to human activities that contribute to global climate change. Consequently, farmers are facing significant challenges in sustaining their agricultural operations under these changing conditions [3].

The agriculture sector in India is grappling with a range of formidable challenges. These include issues like diminished crop yields, escalating production costs, Ineffective agricultural extension services, inadequate agricultural product storage systems and more [4]. Conventional farming practices, based on age-old rules of thumb, are proving insufficient for modern demands, leaving many farmers struggling to sustain their livelihoods. In response to these challenges, a collaborative effort involving governments, researchers and industries is underway. This collective endeavour aims to pioneer innovative projects and research initiatives designed to support farmers. Under this umbrella, concepts like smart farming and digital agriculture have emerged, serving as the foundation for numerous research endeavours and practical implementations [5].

For instance, a notable platform in this domain is Digi Agri, which leverages a fusion of machine learning, IoT and blockchain like cutting-edge technology that can be used to encourage precision farming practices and boost agricultural productivity. This concerted effort toward modernisation holds promise for revitalizing the agricultural landscape in India and improving the livelihoods of its farmers. All agricultural regions are gradually adopting IoT (Internet of Things) technologies, which consists of intelligent sensors and the processing of their data for predictive analysis. This research study's objective is to give a comprehensive study of the numerous IoT sensors utilised by the agricultural industry to help farmers [6]. Additionally, it looks at the many data processing techniques used to analyze the information generated by IoT devices on farms, demonstrating the critical role that data science plays in agriculture. Indian formers and their land (in hectares) is shown in Figure 1.

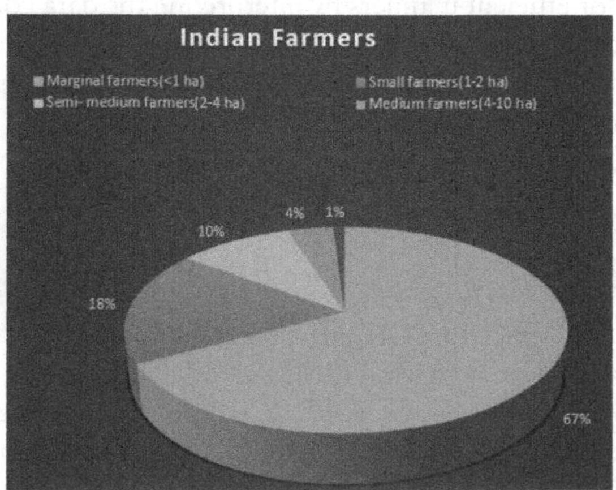

Figure 1: Indian farmers and their land (in hectares).

The key point of this study is to highlight the value of sensors, IoT technology and data science in agriculture [7–8] to provide people with insightful information who are interested in harnessing the potential synergy of these technologies in the agricultural domain. The following is the breakdown of the essay: How important sensors are in diverse agricultural applications is emphasised in Section II. The overview of current IoT systems and their respective implementation goals is given in Section III. Section IV presents a concise overview of data science in farming while summarizing the various methods used for agricultural data analysis. The study's concluding section examines the challenges facing IoT oriented agriculture and gives a synopsis of new research projects that have suggested blockchain technology is one of the potential means of enhancing security inside IoT systems [9–14].

2. The Role of Sensors in Modern Agriculture

Crops rely on specific environmental conditions to achieve optimum growth and health. The precise estimation of these environment-related factors is crucial, and this is where sensors are essential. A variety of features can be used to categorise sensors in a larger context, including their conversion methods, the materials they are constructed from, the physical phenomena they detect, the parameters they measure and the fields in which they are applied. In this section, we will provide a description of sensors used in the agriculture sector, focusing on the parameters they are designed to measure. Functions of IoT in agriculture is shown in Figure 2.

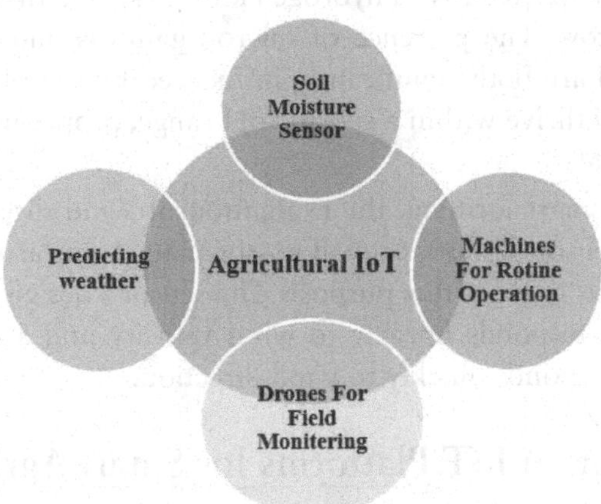

Figure 2: Functions of IoT in agriculture.

2.1. Temperature Sensors

Particularly in precision agriculture, soil temperature is crucial because it exerts precise control on the chemical, physical and microbiological processes taking place in the soil. Additionally, this criterion has an impact on a few crucial elements of crop growth, including as germination, blooming, soil water potential, photosynthesis, decomposition, respiration, soil movement and nitrogen mineralisation. Additionally, the influence of soil temperature on root growth is significant. Using soil temperature sensors to assess soil temperature accurately in agriculture becomes essential. The EC sensor (EC250), MP406 soil moisture sensor and portable Pogo soil sensor are among the agricultural sensors used for this purpose.

For agricultural output and quality to be at their highest, accurate plant temperature measurement is crucial. As a measure of plant stomatal conductance, this value is essential for forecasting agricultural yields. Infrared imaging is a method that is commonly employed since it allows for the temperature estimation of individual leaves.

2.2.,Moisture Sensors

Soil moisture sensors can be applied to measure the actual water content of the soil, which is a key component in determining irrigation schedules. For instance, the MP406 sensor can estimate the moisture content of the soil while taking continuous measurements over time. By utilizing a soil moisture meter this sensor may also assess the soil's water potential.

2.3. Soil pH Sensors

The soil's physical, biological and chemical properties are greatly influenced by its pH, which measures the quantity of hydrogen ions (H+), and this in turn determines how well plants grow. The presence of microorganisms and the availability of nutrients in the soil are both significantly influenced by the pH of the soil. Since every plant can only thrive within a specific pH range, proper measurement of this parameter is essential.

In the field of smart farming, the evaluation of wind direction and speed is crucial. The wind sensor WM30, a small sensor made to measure wind speed and direction, is a famous tool for this purpose. The sensor's design features a rotating cup at the top that responds linearly to wind velocity and a vane linked to the sensor's body that responds quickly to wind direction.

3. Examination of IoT Platforms for Smart Agriculture

The Internet of Things platforms that have been created and designed to assist farmers with a wide range of agricultural tasks, including selection of crop, predicting weather, estimating crop demand, boosting crop yield and keeping an eye on livestock, are discussed in this section. Beginning in 1999, the IoT, which is defined by gadgets with distinct identities, attracted a lot of interest. Since then, it has developed into a vital technology for agriculture.

A thorough analysis of IoT applications in agriculture is required to comprehend current techniques and advancements. In this study, IoT devices and sensors have been employed in agricultural settings throughout the last three years, with a focus on publications that are pertinent to varied applications. To enable researchers and developers working in diverse agricultural fields, such as ecological monitoring, precision agriculture and aquaculture. They offer a thorough explanation of the proposed IoT platform architecture, allowing researchers to create working prototypes for high-level use cases including disease forecasting, smart soil fertilisation and detection.

4. Discussions

Commercially available agricultural sensors with a wide range of quick deployment options enable smart farm management, as explained in Section II of this study. The primary IoT platforms created, and their agricultural applications were emphasised in Section III. Section IV focused on the numerous data modelling methodologies used and the crucial role that data science plays in smart farming. IoT security issues were also covered as the discussion ended. Figure 3 describes the humidity measurement using Internet of things.

Estimation of Light intensity value using IoT in shown in Figure 4. By combining IoT and data science, a smart farming platform has the potential to empower farmers and boost farm output. This study's findings support this conclusion, which is driven by the immense security-improving potential of blockchain technology. It is important to note that many farmers, particularly in emerging and underdeveloped nations. As a result, it is essential to inform and educate farmers about new technologies so they may use them to increase farm output and subsequently support the economic growth of their countries. According to the research, a blockchain-based IoT platform in conjunction with the appropriate data modelling techniques can be used to create a secure farming network ideal for digitising small-scale farms. Temperature values are estimated using IoT is shown in Figure 5.

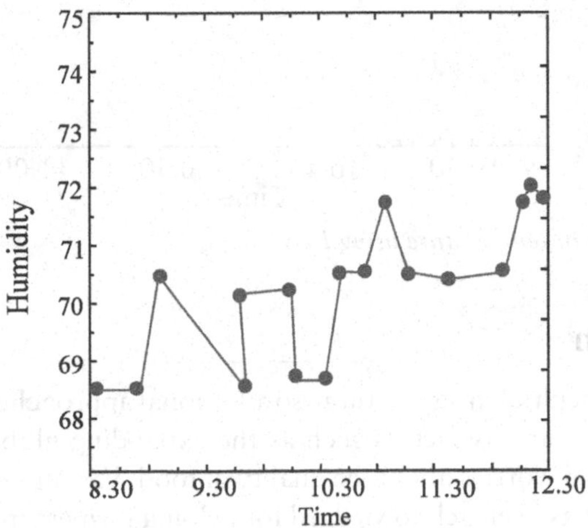

Figure 3: *Estimation of humidity using IoT.*

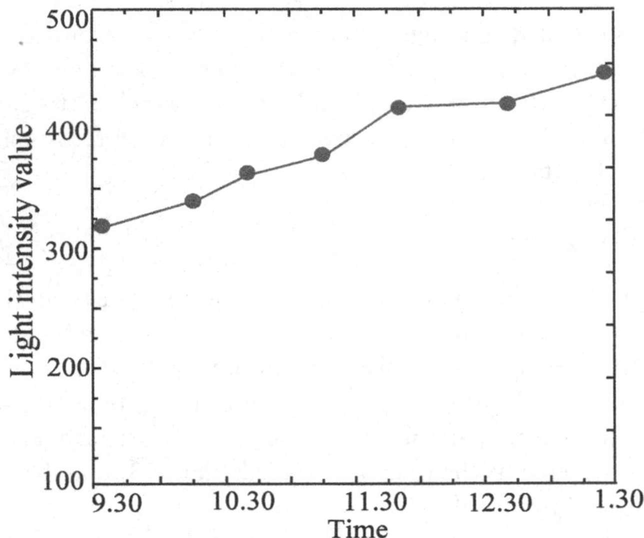

Figure 4: *Estimation of light intensity value using IoT*

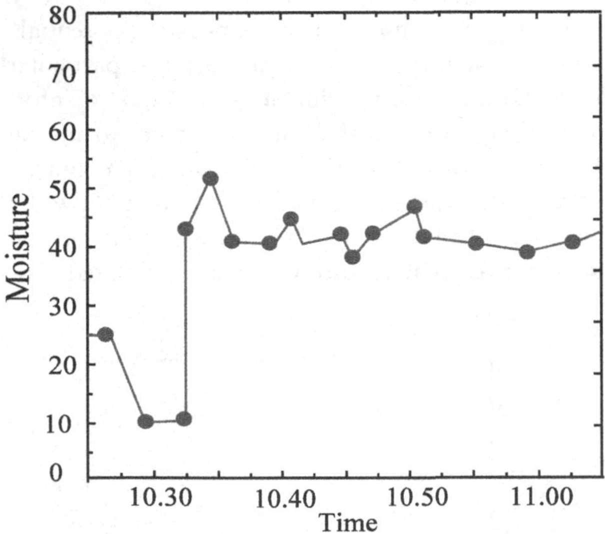

Figure 5: *Estimation of temperature using IoT.*

5. Conclusion

There are many difficulties in agricultural, so additional approaches and technologies are required due to various factors such as the expanding global population, the changing climate and worries about the quality of food. Various agricultural sensors and IoT platforms has been acknowledged for helping farmers in the field of digital agriculture, regardless of locations, attain ecological solutions. This work presents a thorough overview of IoT platforms, agricultural sensors, data processing for sensor data and environmental characteristics that they evaluate and use as inputs in agricultural field applications. This work is predicted to be a useful for scholars or agriculture engineer studying the intersection of IoT and agriculture, offering direction and knowledge in leading agriculture.

References

[1] Sehrawat, D. and N. S. Gill, "Smart sensors: analysis of different types of IoT sensors," *2019 IEEE 3rd International Conference on Trends in Electronics and Informatics (ICOEI)*, Tirunelveli, India, pp. 523–528, 2019.

[2] Cai, J. and M. Cespedes, "Plant temperature measurement and analysis from infrared images," *IVCNZ '12, Proceedings of the 27th Conference on Image and Vision Computing New Zealand*, ACM, pp. 406–411, 2012.

[3] Yamamoto, K., T. Togami, N. Yamaguchi, and S. Ninomiya, "Machine learning-based calibration of low-cost air temperature sensors using environmental data," *Sensors*, vol. 17, no. 6, p. 1290, 2017.

[4] Waring, R. H. and S. W. Running, "Spatial scaling methods for landscape and regional ecosystem analysis," *Forest Ecosystems (Third Edition), Analysis at Multiple Scales*, pp. 225–259, 2007.

[5] Imam, S. A., A. Choudhary, and V. K. Sachan, "Design issues for wireless sensor networks and smart humidity sensors for precision agriculture: a review," *2015 IEEE International Conference on Soft Computing Techniques and Implementations (ICSCTI)*, Faridabad, pp. 181–187, 2016.

[6] Masrie, M., M. S. A. Rosman, R. Sam, and Z. Janin, "Detection of nitrogen, phosphorus, and potassium (NPK) nutrients of soil using optical transducer," *2017 IEEE 4th International Conference on Smart Instrumentation, Measurement and Application (ICSIMA)*, Putrajaya, pp. 1–4, 2018.

[7] El-magrous, A. A., J. D. Sternhagen, G. Hatfield, and Q. Qiao, "Internet of things based weather-soil sensor station for precision agriculture," *2019 IEEE International Conference on Electro Information Technology (EIT)*, pp. 92–97, 2019.

[8] Murdyantoro, E., R. Setiawan, I. Rosyadi, A. W. W. Nugraha, H. Susilawati, and Y. Ramadhani, "Prototype weather station uses LoRa wireless connectivity infrastructure," *J. Phys.: Conf. Ser. Int. Conf. Eng. Technol. Innov. Res.*, vol. 1367, 2019.

[9] Bedi, H. S., "Utilization of a wireless network performing CSMA/CA with random backoff algorithm," *J. Phys.: Conf. Ser.*, vol. 2327, no. 1, p. 012060, 2022.

[10] Adhikari, M. S., A. Majumder, A. M. Sheifudeen, K. Harshavardhan Reddy, M. Sidhwani, and Y. K. Verma, "High gain farming and data analytics using IoT," *IEEE International conference on Devices for Integrated Circuit (DevIC)*, pp. 158–162, 2023.

[11] Adhikari, M. S., K. M. Ramalinga, A. Anand, G. P. Venkatesan, A. R. Ravi, and N. Thakur, "IOT based precision Agri-Bot," *IEEE International conference on Devices for Integrated Circuit (DevIC)*, pp. 321–324, 2023.

[12] Verma, Y. K., V. Mishra, and S. K. Gupta, "A physics-based analytical model for MgZnO/ZnO HEMT," J. Circuits, Syst. Comput., vol. 29, no. 1, p. 2050009, 2020.

[13] Bedi, H., K. Kumar, and R. Gupta, "A review paper on improving the network efficiency of IEEE 802.11e networks," *Intell. Circuits Syst.*, pp. 206–211, 2021.

[14] Joshi, V. and M. S. Adhikari, "IOT-based technology for smart farming," *Electronic Devices and Circuit Design: Challenges and Applications in the Internet of Things*, CRC Press, pp. 223–242, 2022.

41. Distribution system Assessment with Capacitor Placement

Rinchen Zangmo, Suresh Kumar Sudabattula, Sachin Mishra, Nagaraju Dharavat

School of Electronics and Electrical Engineering, Lovely Professional University, Phagwara, Punjab, India

Abstract: Power loss and voltage profile are significant concerns in the distribution system (DS) because of the high R/X ratio. Further, integrating capacitors and distributed generators (DGs) improves the performance. This paper describes an LSF and moth flame optimisation method to solve CPP in DS. Further, it is tested on 83 bus sssystems. Also, 3 cases are taken, and the performance is studied. From the observed results, it is viable that the placement of optimal capacitors minimises the losses to a reasonable extent.

Keywords: Power loss, capacitors, distribution system.

1. Introduction

As compared to the transmission system, DS losses are higher [1]. Further, the voltage profile is poor in the case of radial DS. It is significant to place capacitors in DS to enhance voltage profile and curtail power loss. Also, most loads are inductive, which poses other challenges to the system. So, appropriately incorporating capacitors minimises the losses and improves the voltage profile. The authors solved the CPP using different types of optimisation techniques. In the last three decades, authors used various OTs such as GA, PSO, Tabu search, Hybrid DE, TLBO, GSA, antlion, interchange improved algorithm and sine cosine algorithm [2–20]. Further, most of the author's main objective is the minimisation of DS losses and voltage profile improvement. This paper presents a combined approach, such as LSF and MFO, to solve the problem. The rest of the paper is structured as follows: In section 2 and 3, problem formulation and LSF method is given. In sections 4 and 5, algorithmic steps followed by results and discussions are explained. Finally, the conclusion is offered in 6.

2. Problem Formulation

2.1. Load Flow

Newton Raphson LF is generally used for power flow calculations. But this fails in DS because of a convergence problem. So, in this case, backwards-forward DLF is used [21]. This paper aims to curtail the DS loss in Eq. (1).

$$Powerloss = \sum_{r=1}^{nb} |I_r|^2 R_r \tag{1}$$

The OF is fulfilling the following constraints

2.2.1 Voltage

$$|V_{\min}| \le |V_r| \le |V_{\max}| \tag{2}$$

2.2.2 Power Balance

$$P_{ss} = \sum_{t=2}^{r} P_r + \sum_{r=1}^{nb} P_{loss}(\mathrm{t,t+1}) - \sum_{r=1}^{nbr} P_{cap,\mathrm{t}} \tag{3}$$

2.2.3 Reactive Power

$$\sum_{r=1}^{N_C} Q_{C,\mathrm{r}} \le 1.0 \sum_{r=1}^{n} Q_L \tag{4}$$

3. LSF Method for CPP

Here, the LSF method [22] is applied to the 83-bus system and identifies the weak buses using Eq. (5).

$$RPLSF(\mathrm{t,t+1}) = \frac{\partial P_{loss}}{\partial Q_{t+1,eff}} = \left(\frac{2Q_{t+1,eff} R_{\mathrm{t,t+1}}}{|V_{t+1}|^2} \right) \tag{5}$$

From Eq. (5), calculate the buses suitable for the placement of capacitors.

4. Algorithmic Steps for Capacitor Allocation Problem

1. Read the data
2. Simulate load flow
3. LSF is used to find the locations for CPP.
4. MFO parameters specified [23].
5. The positions of moths and flames are given by Eq. (6) and Eq. (7)

$$M = \begin{bmatrix} m_{1,1} & m_{1,2} & \cdots & \cdots & m_{1,v} \\ m_{2,1} & m_{2,2} & \cdots & \cdots & m_{2,v} \\ \vdots & \vdots & \vdots & \vdots & \vdots \\ \vdots & \vdots & \vdots & \vdots & \vdots \\ m_{p,1} & m_{p,2} & \cdots & \cdots & m_{p,v} \end{bmatrix} \tag{6}$$

$$F = \begin{bmatrix} F_{1,1} & F_{1,2} & \cdots & \cdots & F_{1,v} \\ F_{2,1} & F_{2,2} & \cdots & \cdots & F_{2,v} \\ \vdots & \vdots & \vdots & \vdots & \vdots \\ \vdots & \vdots & \vdots & \vdots & \vdots \\ F_{p,1} & F_{p,2} & \cdots & \cdots & F_{p,v} \end{bmatrix} \tag{7}$$

6. The updated flame equation is given by

$$FN = round\left(N - l * \frac{N-1}{T} \right) \tag{8}$$

5. Results and Discussions

The method is tested on 83 bus systems [24]. Also, different cases are considered, such as the placement of different numbers of capacitors and the study of the effect of DS. Further, the findings are represented in Table 1. The maximum achievement of loss is obtained with three capacitors. Also, the voltage profile is improved significantly in this case. Next, the voltage profile of all buses with 3 cases is illustrated in Figures 1–3.

Table 1: Different cases (capacitor placement).

Different Cases	P_{loss} in kW	Cap Location	Cap Sizes (kVAr)	VSI_{min} (p.u)
Base Case	531.99	.....	....	0.7086
Case 1	481.62	8	2354.8	0.7533
Case 2	459.82	8 34	2354.8 2349.2	0.7544
Case 3	445.88	8 34 53	2354.7 2349.4 1789.5	0.7554

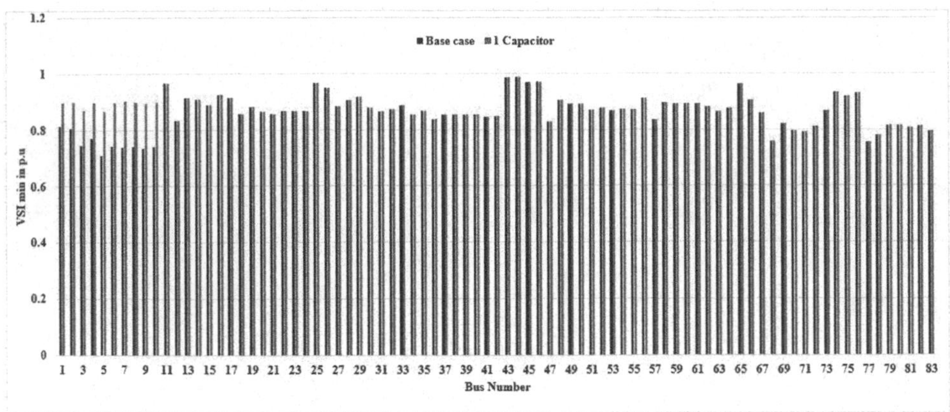

Figure 1: VSI of 83 bus system (base case and case 1).

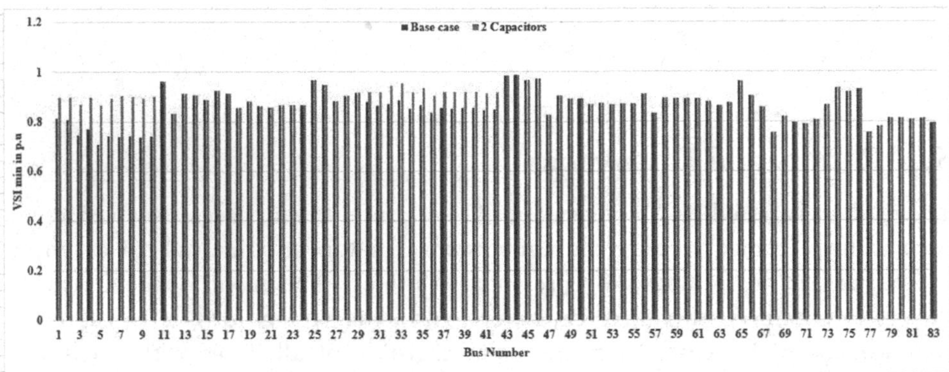

Figure 2: VSI of 83 bus system (base case and case 2).

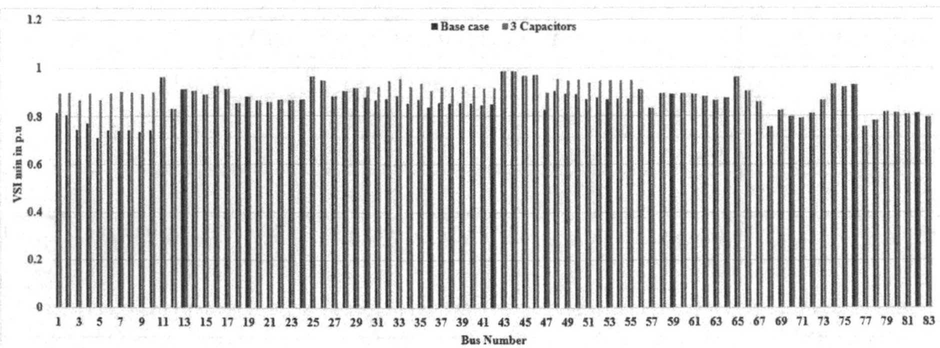

Figure 3: VSI of 83 bus system (base case and case 3).

6. Conclusion

This article presents the LSF and MFO methods to solve CPP in DS. Further, it is tested on 83 bus systems. Also, various are considered, such as one capacitor, two capacitors and three capacitors placement. From the results, it is viable that the order of desired capacitors at specified locations with the best number improves the voltage profile and loss reduction of DS. However, these values depend on the penetration level of the capacitors injected. The desired penetration level of the capacitor at suitable locations gives more positive results.

References

[1] Haque, M. H., "Capacitor placement in radial distribution systems for loss reduction," *IEE Proc.-Gene. Trans. Dis.*, vol. 146, no. 5, pp. 501–505, 1999.

[2] Baran, M. E. and F. F. Wu, "Optimal capacitor placement on radial distribution systems," *IEEE Trans. Power Delivery*, vol. 4, no. 1, pp. 725–734, 1989.

[3] Huang, Y. C., H. T. Yang, and C. L. Huang, "Solving the capacitor placement problem in a radial distribution system using tabu search approach," *IEEE Trans. Power Syst.*, vol. 11, no. 4, pp. 1868–1873, 1996.

[4] Dlfanti, M., G. P. Granelli, and P. Maranninio, "Optimal capacitor placement using deterministic and genetic algorithm," *IEEE Trans. Power Syst.*, vol. 15, no. 3, pp. 1041–1046, 2000.

[5] Ng, H. N., M. M. A. Salama, and A. Y. Chikhani, "Capacitor allocation by approximate reasoning: fuzzy capacitor placement," *IEEE Trans. Power Delivery*, vol. 15, no. 1, pp. 393–398, 2000.

[6] Kim, K. H., S. B. Rhee, S. N. Kim, and S. K. You, "Application of ESGA hybrid approach for voltage profile improvement by capacitor placement," *IEEE Trans. Power Delivery*, vol. 18, no. 4, pp. 1516–1522, 2003.

[7] Masoum, M. A., M. Ladjevardi, A. Jafarian, and E. F. Fuchs, "Optimal placement, replacement and sizing of capacitor banks in distorted distribution networks by genetic algorithms," *IEEE Trans. Power Delivery*, vol. 19, no. 4, pp. 1794–1801, 2004.

[8] Chiou, J. P., C. F. Chang, and C. T. Su, "Ant direction hybrid differential evolution for solving large capacitor placement problems," *IEEE Trans. Power Syst.*, vol. 19, no. 4, pp. 1794–1800, 2004.

[9] Prakash, K. and M. Sydulu, "Particle swarm optimization-based capacitor placement on radial distribution systems," *IEEE Power Engineering Society General Meeting*, pp. 1–5, 2007.

[10] Da Silva, I. C., S. Carneiro, E. J. de Oliveira, J. de Souza Costa, J. L. R. Pereira, and P. A. N. Garcia, "A heuristic constructive algorithm for capacitor placement on distribution systems," *IEEE Trans. Power Syst.*, vol. 23, no. 4, pp. 1619–1626, 2008.

[11] Sultana, S. and P. K. Roy, "Optimal capacitor placement in radial distribution systems using teaching learning-based optimization," *Int. J. Electr. Power Energy Syst.*, vol. 54, pp. 387–398, 2014.

[12] Elsheikh, A., Y. Helmy, Y. Abouelseoud, and A. Elsherif, "Optimal capacitor placement and sizing in radial electric power systems," *Alexandria Eng. J.*, vol. 53, no. 4, pp. 809–816, 2014.

[13] Shuaib, Y. M., M. S. Kalavathi, and C. C. A. Rajan, "Optimal capacitor placement in radial distribution system using gravitational search algorithm," *Int. J. Electr. Power Energy Syst.*, vol. 64, pp. 384–397, 2015.

[14] Askarzadeh, A. "Capacitor placement in distribution systems for power loss reduction and voltage improvement: a new methodology," *IET Gener. Transm. Distrib.*, vol. 10 no. 14, pp. 3631–3638, 2016.

[15] El-Ela, A. A. A., R. A. El-Sehiemy, A. M. Kinawy, and M. T. Mouwafi, "Optimal capacitor placement in distribution systems for power loss reduction and voltage profile improvement", *IET Gener. Transm. Distrib.*, vol. 10, no. 5, pp. 1209–1221, 2016.

[16] George, T., A. R. Youssef, M. Ebeed, and S. Kamel, "Ant lion optimization technique for optimal capacitor placement based on total cost and power loss minimization," *International Conference on Innovative Trends in Computer Engineering (ITCE)*, pp. 350–356, 2018.

[17] Montazeri, M. and A. Askarzadeh, "Capacitor placement in radial distribution networks based on identification of high potential busses," *Int. Trans. Electr. Energy Syst.*, vol. 29 no. 3, p. 2754, 2018.

[18] Sadeghian, O., A. Oshnoei, M. Kheradmandi, and B. Mohammadi-Ivatloo, "Optimal placement of multi-period-based switched capacitor in radial distribution systems," *Comput. Electr. Eng.*, vol. 82, p. 106549, 2020.

[19] Pérez Abril, I., "Capacitor placement by variables' inclusion and interchange improved algorithm," *Int. Trans. Electr. Energy Syst.*, p. e12377, 2020.

[20] Kamel, S., A. Selim, F. Jurado, J. Yu, K. Xie, and T. Wu, "Capacitor allocation in distribution systems using fuzzy loss sensitivity factor with sine cosine algorithm," *2019 IEEE Innovative Smart Grid Technologies-Asia (ISGT Asia)*, IEEE, pp. 1276–1281, 2019.

[21] Teng, J. H., "A direct approach for distribution system load flow solutions," *IEEE Trans. Power Delivery*, vol. 18, no. 3, pp. 882–887, 2003.

[22] Sudabattula, S. K., V. Suresh, U. Subramaniam, D. Almakhles, S. Padmanaban, Z. Leonowicz, and A. Iqbal, "Optimal allocation of multiple distributed generators and shunt capacitors in distribution system using flower pollination algorithm," *2019 IEEE International Conference on Environment and Electrical Engineering and 2019 IEEE Industrial and Commercial Power Systems Europe (EEEIC/I&CPS Europe)*, IEEE, pp. 1–5, 2019.

[23] Mirjalili, S., "Moth-flame optimization algorithm: a novel nature-inspired heuristic paradigm," *Knowledge-Based Syst.*, vol. 89, pp. 228–249, 2015.

[24] Esmaeilian, H. R. and R. Fadaeinedjad, "Distribution system efficiency improvement using network reconfiguration and capacitor allocation," *Int. J. Electr. Power Energy Syst.*, vol. 64, pp. 457–468, 2015.

42. Federated Learning: Issues, Challenges, and Needs

Sahar Yousif Mohammed[1], Mohammad Aljanabi[2], and Maad M. Mijwil[3]

[1] *Computer Science, Anbar University, Anbar, Iraq*

[2] *Computer Science, Imam Ja'afar Al-Sadiq University, Baghdad, Iraq*

[3] *Computer Techniques Engineering Department, Baghdad College of Economic Sciences University, Baghdad, Iraq*

Abstract: Decentralised machine learning algorithms federated learning is popular because it integrates key data and trains models on dispersed data sources. This mixed learning study demands complexity, information and unmet requirements. Since data is local, user privacy is crucial. Effective communication methods must be designed to update models across devices without compromising data security. For accurate and efficient global model updates, federated averages and safe aggregation require additional changes. Scalability remains a concern, especially with more devices and various data sources. This research also examines the social and ethical effects of federated learning, including biases and fairness difficulties from decentralised data sources. This lengthy investigation helps us understand federated learning by analysing these key components and providing in-depth observations. It also suggests ways to overcome this field's severe challenges, closing the gap and revealing its amazing potential.

Keywords: Data privacy, federated learning, machine learning paradigm, model aggregation, scalability.

1. Introduction

Federated learning (FL) is a revolutionary decentralised technique for collaborative model training across several clients in current machine learning. The central server manages this revolutionary paradigm while protecting client training data's decentralised and secret nature. FL addresses several machine learning issues. It covers the complex issue of data privacy and the constraints of centralised data transit [1]. FL allows model training using data from several devices or organisations, reducing the requirement for potentially dangerous data transfers to a central repository. Instead, the technology protects privacy, ensuring data security on individual devices. Only model modifications are sent to the central server. The central server is essential for collecting model updates and updating the global model while protecting client data [2]. Federated learning appeals to academics and businesses beyond its theoretical simplicity. Its ability to leverage massive data repositories while maintaining anonymity has made it popular in healthcare, banking, and the Internet of Things (IoT), where data privacy is essential. In the following pages, we examine FLcomplex issues, evolving challenges and essential needs to realise its full potential in machine learning. [3]. FL is a major departure from centralised machine learning. Data is gathered, processed and evaluated on a single server in typical systems, causing confidentiality and communication issues. FL allows model training while protecting data sources from different devices or organisations [4]. FL protects machine learning privacy by keeping data on local devices and sharing only model changes with the central server. This innovative data management system addresses privacy concerns and reduces resource-intensive data transfers, unlike existing methods [5]. The central server, the backbone of FL, consolidates model changes from clients. The above aggregation strategy ensures global model improvement while protecting participant data. FL has attracted academic and industrial interest because it promises to use large and widely distributed datasets while protecting individual and organisational data [6]. FL has a wide range of benefits, including in healthcare, where patient data security is crucial in finance and in the emerging Internet of Things (IoT), where data and privacy are crucial. These examples demonstrate how important FL may be for machine learning [7]. This review will illuminate FL'scomplexities, understand its subtle deployment issues and identify the urgent needs that must be met for this decentralised approach to fully realise its revolutionary potential. This study may illuminate FL's complexities and provide insights that will inform future research and applications in this dynamic arena. This study was motivated by the growing volume of secret digital information, which requires unique, secure and cooperative model training methods. Data transparency and trust limit centralised methods in various fields. We want to illuminate federated learning's promise as a privacy, efficiency and scalability solution by analysing its restrictions and issues. We also underline the research needed to adopt this strategy. We want to advance FL to create a safe and private machine learning age.

2. Background

Federated learning (FL) is a novel paradigm in machine learning that solves the complex problems of centralised methods. Federated learning (FL) is a decentralised machine learning technology that addresses two major issues in the age of data and privacy concerns: protecting data and overcoming communication barriers [8].

2.1. Data Privacy Concerns and Communication Constraints

Communication constraints and data privacy problems in typical machine-learning setups, data is collected, aggregated and evaluated on one server. The growth of machine learning applications and services has led to the acquisition and consolidation of large amounts of sensitive data, raising privacy concerns. It is logical that people are hesitant to provide personal information, especially in sensitive industries like healthcare, banking and personal communication [9]. In traditional centralised systems, privacy, data transportation and communication are difficult. Moving large amounts of data to a central place uses resources and bandwidth, limiting communication, especially when data comes from various sources [10]. Federated learning (FL) solutions are unique. Data decentralisation allows local training on devices or inside data-accessing businesses, improving data privacy and security [11]. FL reduces communication obstacles and centralisation by enabling worldwide collaborative model training without raw data sharing [12]. FL uses a central server to train models and update consumer models to improve global models while protecting user data [13]. Industry and academics respect FL, which prioritises data security and communication effectiveness to enhance healthcare, finance and IoT with anonymously distributed data. This method solves machine learning problems [14] by enabling safe, collaborative model training across distant data sources.

3. Privacy Preservation

FL prioritises the preservation of privacy by employing a decentralised methodology that circumvents the direct exchange of training data. This design, which prioritises privacy, effectively tackles a number of significant challenges [15]

3.1. Challenges Related to Privacy in Federated Learning

The state of FL recognises and understands the significant privacy concerns that arise from the utilisation of conventionally centralised machine learning methods. The recognition of the potential invasiveness of collecting and centralising training data gives rise to issues over data security and user privacy[16].

3.2. Differential Privacy (DP) and Federated Secure Aggregation

FL utilises sophisticated privacy-preserving methodologies, including the implementation of differential privacy (DP). Differential privacy (DP) is an advanced framework that enables the examination of data trends while safeguarding the privacy of individual data providers. Within the field of FL, DP has been utilised to facilitate the training of deep neural networks while upholding a predetermined privacy allocation [17].

3.3. Importance of Data Decentralisation and Security

Federated learning (FL) depends on decentralisation for privacy, data security and breach prevention [18]. However, ethical concerns arise, necessitating the implementation of differentially private algorithms with caution in sensitive sectors to prevent data breaches. FL's dedication to privacy is reflected in its robust optimisation procedure. Centralised techniques. FL makes extensive use of DP to train deep neural networks while protecting the confidentiality of user data [20]. FL meticulously balances ethics and privacy, reinforcing its commitment [21]. FL revolutionises machine learning by providing privacy guarantees that cannot be provided by centralisation. By integrating decentralisation, collaborative training and differential privacy, FL establishes a framework for model training that is privacy-friendly, which is especially important in data-centric societies [22].

4. Communication Efficiency

A specialised type of Federated learning (FL), CE-FL, was created to handle centralised machine learning communication issues. Optimising information flow between the central server and clients improves model training across remote data sources [23].

4.1. Decentralised Model Training

Both conventional FL and CE-FL subscribe to the idea of decentralised model training. However, it takes this decentralisation a step further by placing a major emphasis on minimising the amount of data and model information sent between the central server and the clients. This information may then be saved on the clients' local machines. This is of the utmost importance in circumstances in which access to communication resources is restricted or expensive [24].

4.2. Layerwise Asynchronous Model Update

Layerwise asynchronous model updates are an important part of CE-FL, which uses a variety of different strategies. CE-FL gives clients the ability to update particular layers of the model asynchronously, as opposed to the traditional method of synchronously updating the complete global model after each client's iteration. This strategy lessens the burden of the communication overhead and has the potential to considerably increase the training efficiency, particularly in circumstances in which clients have different computational capabilities or network conditions [25]. Figure 1 shows the synopsis of cross-device federated learning.

4.3. Temporally Weighted Aggregation

In addition to this, CE-FL presents methods of aggregation that are time-weighted. These methods provide varied amounts of weight to model changes, depending on how recently they were made. Recent updates are given greater weight than older ones, which enables the model to adjust more quickly to shifting data distributions while simultaneously lowering the influence of updates that may have become outdated. This is especially useful in surroundings that are constantly changing [26].

4.4. Reduced Communication Overhead

The fundamental purpose of CE-FL is to lessen the burden of communication overhead, which is typically the limiting factor in conventional FL configurations. CE-FL reduces the quantity of data that is transferred across the network by sharing just the model updates that are absolutely necessary and doing so in a way that is both efficient and effective in terms of communication. The decreased amount of communication traffic not only helps to preserve resources but also speeds up the process of being trained [27].

4.5. Scalability and Robustness

An increased capacity for scaling in federated learning systems is a result of the CE-FL's communication effectiveness. It makes it possible to incorporate a greater number of clients or devices into the training process without requiring a corresponding rise in the amount of money spent on communication. In addition, the resistance of CE-FL to communication delays and failures guarantees that the training process will continue without interruption even when the network circumstances are difficult [28].

4.6. Applications

CE-FL is used in industries with stringent communication requirements such as mobile devices, peripheral computing and the Internet of Things, where bandwidth and latency constraints are prevalent [29]. It is particularly important for privacy-preserving model updates with minimal data transmission in contexts that are sensitive to privacy [30].

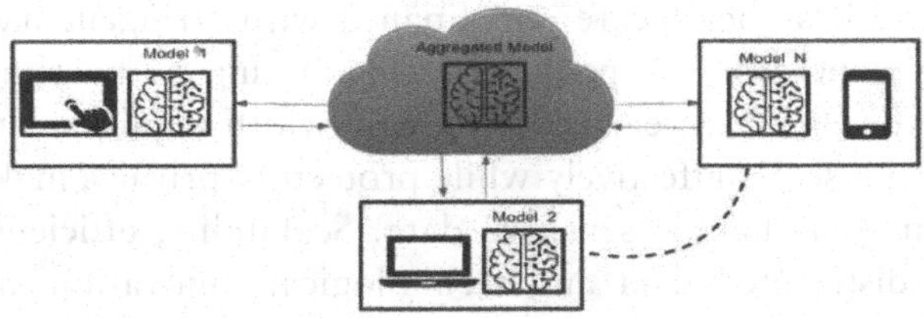

Figure 1: *Synopsis of cross-device federated learning [31].*

5. Scalability

Federated learning (FL) has raised hopes that it will revolutionise machine learning in the decentralised data era. Scalability is a major issue for FL as it grows. This section discusses scaling FL systems, novel methods and FL's promise for large-scale distributed data [32].

5.1. Challenges in Scaling Federated Learning Systems

There are a number of interrelated difficulties in scaling FL systems. More devices and data sources mean more communication is required, which can strain bandwidth and cause latency difficulties. Meanwhile, administration is made more difficult by the diversity of customers in terms of CPU power, connectivity and data quality. To successfully work with such diversity, adaptive methods are required. The addition of new users and their associated data poses security and privacy problems as the system scales up. To protect privacy, this calls for top-notch encryption, protected data collection and severe security measures [33].

5.2. Solutions and Innovations for Scalability

Layerwise asynchronous model updates fix problems with scalability by letting clients update certain layers without waiting for other clients to do so [33]. This cuts down on data transmission and gets around communication problems. TensorFlow Federated and PySyft facilitate the setup and administration of federated learning systems, thereby enhancing communication security, privacy and adaptive learning [34]. Edge computing is a distributed paradigm that processes data where it's created. It makes FL more scalable by reducing the need for central servers and allowing local model updates and collection [43]. Techniques such as quantisation and sparsification further improve efficiency and scalability by minimising model updates during aggregation without compromising precision [34].

5.3. Federated Learning's Potential in Handling Large-Scale Distributed Data

FL efficiently addresses challenges from distributed data sources, flourishing in the face of massive data expansion that overwhelms centralised systems [36]. FL maintains data source control and decentralisation, which is advantageous for industries such as healthcare and finance with stringent data sovereignty and regulatory concerns. It expedites model training by averting burdensome data transfers to central servers, reducing bandwidth requirements and training models locally. FL scales effectively while protecting privacy, making it suitable for applications that handle sensitive data. Scalability, efficient management of large-scale distributed data and technological innovation are its primary advantages. Future decentralised machine learning will be shaped by scalable FL systems [35].

6. Ethical and Societal Implications

Federated learning (FL) possesses the capacity to revolutionise machine learning while protecting the confidentiality of data, hence giving rise to a variety of ethical and societal implications that need thorough scrutiny [36].

6.1. Delving into Ethical Considerations

FL places significant importance on the preservation of data privacy and confidentiality norms. As the field of FL continues to grow, it becomes more crucial to maintain openness in the processes of data collection, utilisation and safeguarding [37]. This development gives rise to inquiries on the notions of consent and user autonomy in the realm of data management. The establishment and maintenance of ethical norms are of utmost importance in order to guarantee that artificial intelligence (AI) serves the best interests of both people and society while also safeguarding individual rights [38].

6.2. Fairness, Bias and Transparency Concerns

Machine learning technologies, including FL, exhibit shared problems pertaining to fairness, bias and transparency. The mitigation of socioeconomic disparity necessitates the rigorous examination of bias in data, models and algorithms. The establishment of openness plays a crucial role in fostering confidence in the decision-making processes of FL models [39].

6.3. Federated Learning's Role in Healthcare

FL may train predictive models across multiple healthcare providers without centralisation, preserving sensitive patient data. The ethical and social consequences are complicated and varied. FL may improve patient outcomes and therapy effectiveness. To protect patient privacy, effective security measures must be implemented and maintained. Finding the right balance between medical advances and data privacy is a complex ethical issue [40].

6.4. Federated Learning in Finance

In the financial industry, FL can enhance fraud detection and risk analysis while safeguarding consumer privacy. Ethical dilemmas arise concerning data protection and preventing unintended discrimination, emphasising fairness in FL models [41].

6.5. Federated Learning in the Internet of Things (IoT)

FL in IoT applications improves intelligent systems but raises privacy concerns. Devices collecting personal data must respect individual rights, and ethical considerations regarding IoT data in FL, particularly in monitoring and privacy aspects, are crucial [42].

7. Conclusion and Future Directions

Federated learning has the potential to revolutionise machine learning by resolving crucial issues and obstacles. Its capacity to secure data privacy, improve communication efficiency and facilitate scalability bears promise for multiple industries. Yet, we must confront challenges like cost-effective communication, privacy preservation and ethical considerations. Priorities include scalable solutions, robust privacy protections, ethical frameworks and the elimination of bias. Integrating federated learning with the Internet of Things and responsible deployment in critical domains is essential. We can fully realise the potential of federated learning by delivering machine learning solutions that emphasise privacy, security and sector-wide scalability.

References

[1] Chen, Y., X. Sun, and Y. Jin, "Communication-efficient federated deep learning with layerwise asynchronous model update and temporally weighted aggregation," *IEEE Trans. Neural Networks Learn. Syst.*, vol. 31, no. 10, pp. 4229–4238, 2019.

[2] Devlin, J., M.-W. Chang, K. Lee, and K. Toutanova, "BERT: pre-training of deep bidirectional transformers for language understanding," *Proceedings of NAACL-HLT*, pp. 4171–4186, 2019.

[3] Abdelmoniem, A. M. and M. Canini, "Towards mitigating device heterogeneity in federated learning via adaptive model quantization," *Proceedings of the 1st Workshop on Machine Learning and Systems*, 2021.

[4] Abdelmoniem, A. M., *et al.*, "Empirical analysis of federated learning in heterogeneous environments," *Proceedings of the 2nd European Workshop on Machine Learning and Systems*, 2022.

[5] Bagdasaryan, E., *et al.*, "How to backdoor federated learning," *International Conference on Artificial Intelligence and Statistics*, PMLR, 2020.

[6] Bonawitz, K., *et al.*, "Practical secure aggregation for privacy-preserving machine learning," *Proceedings of the 2017 ACM SIGSAC Conference on Computer and Communications Security*, 2017.

[7] Hartmann, F., *et al.*, "Federated learning for ranking browser history suggestions," arXiv preprint arXiv: 1911.11807, 2019.

[8] Lai, F., *et al.*, "Oort: efficient federated learning via guided participant selection," *15th {USENIX} Symposium on Operating Systems Design and Implementation ({OSDI} 21)*, 2021.

[9] Alnajar, O. and Barnawi, A., "Tactile internet of federated things: toward fine-grained design of FL-based architecture to meet TIoT demands," *Comput. Netw.*, vol. 231, p. 109712, 2023. Online publication date: 1-Jul-2023. Link

[10] Guerra, E., F. Wilhelmi, M. Miozzo and P. Dini, "The cost of training machine learning models over distributed data sources," *IEEE Open J. Commun. Soc.*, vol. 4, pp. 1111–1126.

[11] Azimi, Y., S. Yousefi, H. Kalbkhani, T. Kunz, "Applications of machine learning in resource management for RAN-Slicing in 5G and beyond networks: a survey," *IEEE Access*, vol. 10, pp. 106581–106612, doi: 10.1109/ACCESS.2022.3210254.

[12] Mosaiyebzadeh, F., S. Pouriyeh, R. Parizi, Q. Sheng, M. Han, L. Zhao, G. Sannino, C. Ranieri, J. Ueyama, and D. Batista, "Privacy-enhancing technologies in federated learning for the internet of healthcare things: a survey," *Electronics*, vol. 12, no. 12, p. 2703, 2023.

[13] Niknam, S., H. S. Dhillon, and J. H. Reed. "Federated learning for wireless communications: motivation, opportunities, and challenges," *IEEE Commun. Mag.*, vol. 58, no. 6, pp. 46–51, 2020.

[14] Shahid, O., *et al.*, "Communication efficiency in federated learning: achievements and challenges," arXiv preprint arXiv: 2107.10996, 2021.
[15] Truex, S., *et al.*, "A hybrid approach to privacy-preserving federated learning," *Proceedings of the 12th ACM Workshop on Artificial Intelligence and Security*, 2019.
[16] Yin, X., Y. Zhu, and J. Hu, "A comprehensive survey of privacy-preserving federated learning: a taxonomy, review, and future directions," *ACM Comput. Surv.*, vol. 54, no. 6, pp. 1–36, 2021.
[17] Yin, X., Y. Zhu, and J. Hu, "A comprehensive survey of privacy-preserving federated learning: a taxonomy, review, and future directions," *ACM Comput. Surv.*,vo. 54, no. 6, pp. 1–36, 2021.
[18] Nguyen, D. C., *et al.*, "Federated learning meets blockchain in edge computing: opportunities and challenges," *IEEE Internet Things J.*, vol. 8, no. 16, pp. 12806–12825, 2021.
[19] Zhang, C., *et al.*, "A survey on federated learning, " *Knowledge-Based Syst.*, vol. 216, p. 106775, 2021.
[20] Wu, X., *et al.*, "FedBC: blockchain-based decentralized federated learning," *2020 IEEE International Conference on Artificial Intelligence and Computer Applications (ICAICA)*, IEEE, 2020.
[21] Alsamhi, S. H., *et al.*, "Drones' edge intelligence over smart environments in B5G: blockchain and federated learning synergy," *IEEE Trans. Green Commun. Networking*, vol. 6, no. 1, pp. 295–312, 2021.
[22] Li, L., *et al.*, "A review of applications in federated learning," *Comput. Ind. Eng.*, vol. 149, p. 106854, 2020.
[23] Witt, L., *et al.*, "Decentral and incentivized federated learning frameworks: a systematic literature review," *IEEE Internet Things J.*, 2022.
[24] Liu, S., Q. Chen, and L. You, "Fed2a: federated learning mechanism in asynchronous and adaptive modes," *Electronics*, vol. 11, no. 9, p. 1393, 2022.
[25] Chen, Y., X. Sun, and Y. Jin, "Communication-efficient federated deep learning with layerwise asynchronous model update and temporally weighted aggregation," *IEEE Trans. Neural Networks Learn. Syst.*, vol. 31, no. 10, pp. 4229–4238, 2019.
[26] Luping, W., W. Wei, and L. Bo, "CMFL: mitigating communication overhead for federated learning," *2019 IEEE 39th International Conference on Distributed Computing Systems (ICDCS)*, IEEE, 2019.
[27] Li, T., *et al.*, "Ditto: fair and robust federated learning through personalization," *International Conference on Machine Learning*, PMLR, 2021.
[28] Li, L., *et al.*, "A review of applications in federated learning," *Comput. Ind. Eng.*, vol. 149, p. 106854, 2020.
[29] Aledhari, M., *et al.*, "Federated learning: a survey on enabling technologies, protocols, and applications," *IEEE Access*, vol. 8, pp. 140699–140725, 2020.

[30] Mammen, P. M., "Federated learning: opportunities and challenges," 2021, http://arxiv.org/abs/2101.05428.

[31] Bonawitz, K., *et al.*, "Towards federated learning at scale: system design," *Proc. Mach. Learn. Syst.*, vol. 1, pp. 374–388, 2019.

[32] Zhuang, W., C. Chen, and L. Lyu, "When foundation model meets federated learning: motivations, challenges, and future directions," arXiv preprint arXiv: 2306.15546, 2023.

[33] Nguyen, D. C., *et al.*, "Federated learning for internet of things: a comprehensive survey," *IEEE Commun. Surv. Tutorials*, vol. 23, no. 3, pp. 1622–1658, 2021.

[34] Ali, A., *et al.*, "Empowering precision medicine: unlocking revolutionary insights through blockchain-enabled federated learning and electronic medical records," *Sensors*, vol. 23, no. 17, p. 7476, 2023.

[35] Wang, E., *et al.*, "FLINT: a platform for federated learning integration," *Proc. Mach. Learn. Syst.*, vol. 5, 2023.

[36] Zhuang, W., C. Chen, and L. Lyu, "When foundation model meets federated learning: motivations, challenges, and future directions," arXiv preprint arXiv: 2306.15546, 2023.

[37] Zhuang, W., C. Chen, and L. Lyu, "When foundation model meets federated learning: motivations, challenges, and future directions," arXiv preprint arXiv: 2306.15546, 2023.

[38] Liu, T. Y. and J.-H. Wu, "The ethical and societal considerations for the rise of artificial intelligence and big data in ophthalmology," *Front. Med.*, vol. 9, p. 845522, 2022.

[39] Long, G., *et al.*, "Federated learning for open banking," *Federated Learning: Privacy and Incentive*, Cham: Springer International Publishing, pp. 240–254, 2020.

[40] Nguyen, D. C., *et al.*, "Federated learning for internet of things: a comprehensive survey," *IEEE Commun. Surv. Tutorials*, vol. 23, no. 3, pp. 1622–1658, 2021.

[41] Zhang, T., *et al.*, "Federated learning for the internet of things: applications, challenges, and opportunities," *IEEE Internet Things Mag.*, vol. 5, no. 1, pp. 24–29, 2022.

43. Smart Door Bell Using IoT: Implementation and Design

Yogesh Kumar Verma,[1] Nagalakshmi Yarlagadda,[1,2] Jugal Kishore Bhandari,[1] Raam Dheep[1]

[1]*School of Electronics and Electrical Engineering, Lovely Professional University, Jalandhar, Punjab, India*
[2]*Geethanjali College of Engineering and Technology, Cheeryal, Hyderabad, India*

Abstract: Through several years of household ubiquity, the traditional doorbell has remained a popular feature. However, these seemingly uncomplicated devices pose significant drawbacks, including inadequate security measures, limited visibility and lack of accessibility for individuals with disabilities. These limitations have sparked the development of a novel solution, a smart doorbell system utilizing ESP 32 technology. This system integrates traditional doorbell features with the extraordinary computing capabilities of ESP 32, enabling image capture, motion detection and visitor interaction through a specialised application. Upon motion detection, a timer is activated, followed by an informative message on the liquid crystal display. In the unfortunate event that the timer expires without button engagement, a buzzer alarm will sound while the camera captures and transmits images of the surroundings to the homeowner through the web application. If the button is pushed, a notification containing high-resolution images of the visitor is transmitted via the web application, granting the homeowner remote access to the front door. This innovative technology provides homeowners with the ability to remotely monitor their property, receive real-time notifications of approaching visitors and engage in virtual conversations with them. This smart doorbell system not only enhances overall home security but also improves daily life through advanced features and automation, setting a new standard in doorbell technology. Creating a smart doorbell using internet of things technology enhances home security and convenience by allowing remote monitoring and interaction with visitors. This project involves integrating hardware components such as a Raspberry Pi or Arduino, a camera module, a button or motion sensor and optional microphone and speaker. The system connects to the internet to send notifications and enable two-way communication with visitors through a smartphone or computer. By combining these elements, a smart doorbell offers improved home security and seamless visitor management.

Keywords: ESP-32, IoT, door-bell, LCD.

1. Introduction

In today's digitally connected world, the internet of things (IoT) has revolutionised the way we interact with and manage our homes. One prominent application of IoT in the realm of home automation and security is the development of smart doorbells. These innovative devices have transformed the traditional doorbell into a sophisticated and interactive tool that enhances both security and convenience for homeowners. A smart doorbell, at its core, is a connected device that leverages IoT technology to provide homeowners with real time access to their front door. It enables remote monitoring, visitor identification and communication with individuals at the doorstep, all through the convenience of a smartphone or computer. This modern- day doorbell is not merely a chime to announce a visitor's arrival; it is a comprehensive security and communication system. The evolution of smart doorbells has been driven by the convergence of several technological advancements. These include the availability of affordable microcontrollers like Raspberry Pi and Arduino, high-resolution camera modules, motion sensors and the proliferation of home Wi-Fi networks. The integration of these components has paved the way for the creation of intelligent and connected doorbell systems. In this era of heightened security concerns and the need for remote accessibility, the smart doorbell offers a range of benefits. Homeowners can now receive instant alerts when someone approaches their front door, view live video feeds, capture images or video recordings of visitors and even engage in two-way audio conversations without being physically present at home. Whether it is receiving a package, monitoring deliveries, or verifying the identity of visitors, the smart doorbell has become an indispensable tool for modern homeowners. This project aims to explore the design and development of a smart doorbell system using IoT technology. It involves the integration of hardware components, the development of software applications and the establishment of an internet connection to enable seamless communication and control. By combining these elements, we can create a smart doorbell that not only enhances security but also adds a layer of convenience to our daily lives. In the following sections, we will delve deeper into the components and steps involved in creating a smart doorbell using IoT, highlighting its significance in improving home security and providing remote accessibility for homeowners [1–32].

2. Proposed Flowchart

Figure 1 Represents the proposed flowchart of the model.

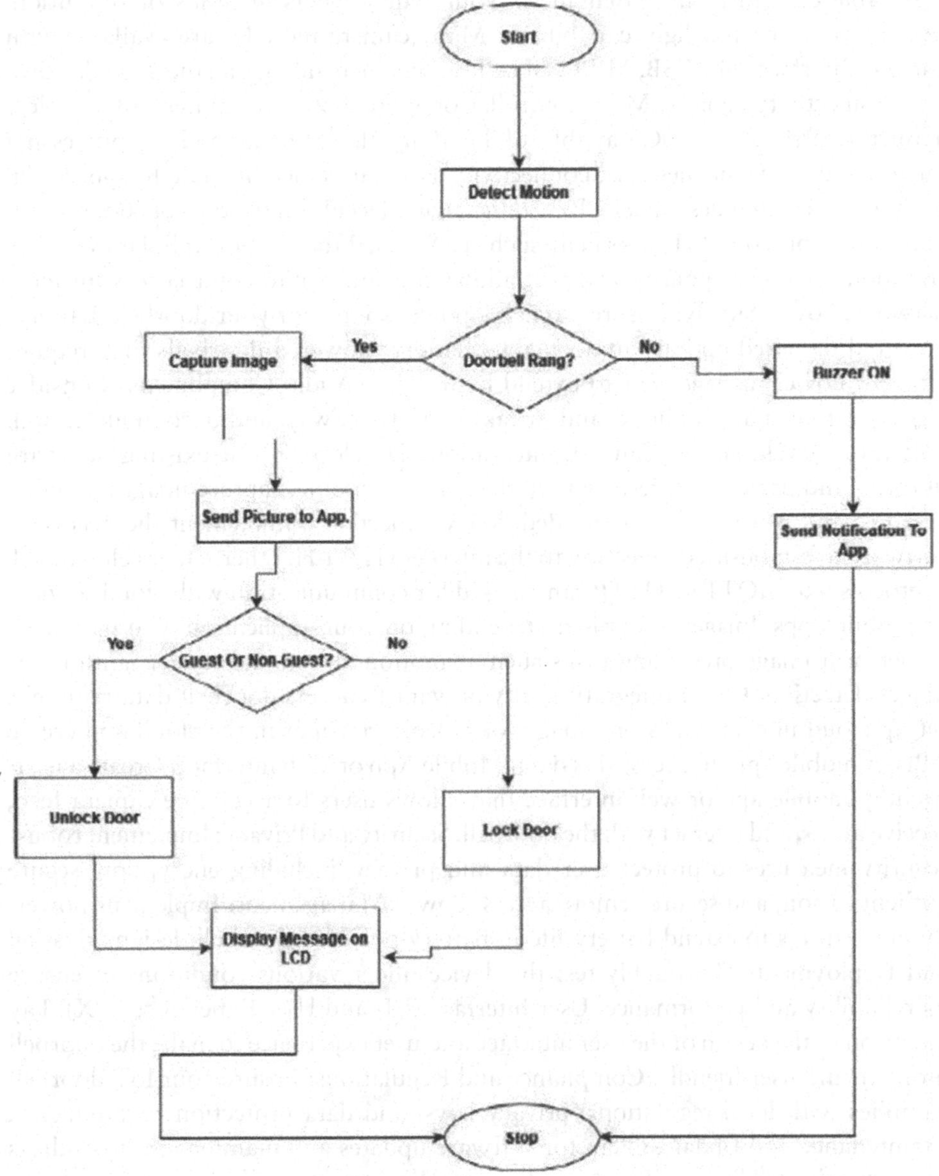

***Figure 1:** Flowchart of the proposed system.*

Figures 2 and 3 represent the protype of the working model. Figure 4 represents the camera module. Integrating a camera module into a doorbell for IoT applications is a popular use case, often referred to as a 'smart doorbell' or 'IoT doorbell.' A smart doorbell can provide various features and functionalities, such as remote monitoring, two-way communication and even integration with smart home systems. Here is a basic overview of how you can create a camera module for a doorbell using IoT technology: Hardware Selection: Camera Module: Choose a suitable camera module that meets your requirements in terms of resolution, field of view and low-light capabilities. Many camera modules are available with various interfaces like USB, MIPI CSI or Ethernet, depending on your IoT platform and connectivity choices. Microcontroller or single-board computer (SBC): Select a microcontroller or SBC capable of handling the camera module, processing images and managing network connectivity. Popular choices include Raspberry Pi, Arduino or custom-designed PCBs. Connectivity: Decide on the type of connectivity you want for your IoT doorbell, such as Wi-Fi, Ethernet, or cellular. Wi-Fi is common for home applications, as it allows the doorbell to connect to your local network. Power Supply: Ensure a reliable power source for your doorbell. Battery-powered or wired options are available. Battery- powered doorbells may require efficient power management to extend battery life. Audio Components: Consider incorporating a microphone and speaker for two- way audio communication. Software Development: Camera Integration: Develop or use existing software libraries and drivers to interface with the camera module, capture images or video streams, and process them as needed. IoT Connectivity: Implement the necessary software to establish a connection to the internet via Wi-Fi, Ethernet, or cellular. IoT protocols like MQTT or HTTP can be used for communication with cloud services or mobile apps. Image Processing: Depending on your application, you may need to perform image processing tasks such as motion detection, face recognition, or object detection. Cloud Integration: If you want to access doorbell data remotely, set up cloud integration. Store images or video recordings in the cloud and create APIs or mobile apps to access this data. Mobile App or Web Interface: Create a user-friendly mobile app or web interface that allows users to access the camera feed, receive alerts, and interact with the doorbell. Security and Privacy: Implement robust security measures to protect user data and privacy, including encryption, secure authentication, and secure remote access. Power Management: Implement power-saving features to extend battery life in battery-powered doorbell designs. Testing and Deployment: Thoroughly test the device under various conditions to ensure its reliability and performance. User Interface (UI) and User Experience (UX): Pay attention to the design of the user interface and user experience to make the doorbell intuitive and user-friendly. Compliance and Regulations: Ensure your IoT doorbell complies with local regulations, privacy laws, and data protection requirements. Maintenance and Updates: Plan for software updates and maintenance to address security vulnerabilities and improve functionality over time.

Support and Customer Service: Provide customer support and resources for users to troubleshoot any issues they may encounter. Scaling and Expansion: Consider how the doorbell system can be expanded or integrated with other smart home devices or security systems as needed. Building an IoT-enabled doorbell with a camera module can be a rewarding project, but it requires careful planning, development, and testing to ensure it meets both functional and security requirements. Figure 5 represents the setting up of all the component on the bread-board.

A smart doorbell using IoT technology finds versatile applications in modern homes, seamlessly blending security and convenience. With real-time remote monitoring and surveillance capabilities, homeowners can keep a watchful eye on their front door from anywhere via their smartphones or computers. Equipped with motion sensors and high-quality cameras, these smart doorbells capture images or video footage, providing instant notifications when someone approaches the door. Two-way communication features allow for interactive conversations with visitors, making package deliveries or visitor interactions more efficient. These IoT-powered doorbells not only enhance security but also offer practical solutions for managing daily activities and ensuring the safety and convenience of homeowners.

Figure 2: Working prototype.

Figure 3: Working prototype.

3. Proposed Methodology

Developing a smart doorbell using IoT involves a systematic approach to design, hardware selection, software development, and integration. Here's a proposed methodology for creating a smart doorbell using IoT: Define Objectives and Requirements: Clearly define the objectives and requirements of your smart doorbell project. Determine what features you want, such as remote monitoring, video recording, two-way communication, and integration with other smart devices. Hardware Selection: Choose the appropriate hardware components for your smart doorbell. This includes: Microcontroller (e.g., Raspberry Pi, Arduino) Camera module Button or motion sensor. Microphone and speaker (for two-way communication) Power supply Internet connectivity (Wi-Fi or Ethernet) Design the Hardware Setup: Plan the physical setup of your smart doorbell. Decide where to install the camera, button, microphone, and speaker. Ensure proper wiring and connections. Develop Software: Write the software code for your smart doorbell. This involves: Setting up the microcontroller and camera module. Implementing code to capture images or video when the doorbell is pressed or motion is detected. Coding for two- way communication if you're including a microphone and speaker. Developing a user interface for remote access and control (e.g., a mobile app or web interface). Incorporating security measures to protect user data and device access.

Internet Connectivity: Configure the device to connect to the internet via Wi-Fi or Ethernet. Ensure the device can communicate with external servers or cloud services for data storage and remote access. Cloud Integration (Optional): If you plan to store video footage or data in the cloud, integrate your smart doorbell with a cloud service provider. Ensure data security and privacy. Mobile App or Web Interface: Create a user-friendly interface (either a mobile app or web application) that allows users to access and control the smart doorbell remotely. Provide features like live video streaming, notifications, and doorbell control.

Testing and Debugging: Thoroughly test your smart doorbell system to ensure all components work as intended. Test remote access, video capture, communication, and integration with other devices. User Authentication and Security: Implement user authentication and access control to prevent unauthorized access to the system. Use encryption and secure communication protocols to protect user data. Installation and Integration: Install the smart doorbell at the desired location on your front door or entryway. Ensure proper mounting and alignment.

If integrating with other smart devices (e.g., smart locks or lighting), ensure seamless communication and functionality. User Training: Provide user training or documentation on how to use the smart doorbell, mobile app, and any associated features. Maintenance and Updates: Plan for ongoing maintenance and updates to ensure the system remains secure and functional. Address any software or hardware issues promptly. User Feedback and Iteration: Gather user feedback and consider making improvements or adding new features based on user experiences and needs.

Compliance and Regulations: Ensure that your smart doorbell complies with any local regulations, especially regarding privacy and data protection. By following this methodology, you can systematically design, develop, and deploy a smart doorbell using IoT technology that meets your specific requirements and provides enhanced security and convenience for your home.

Figure 4: Camera module.

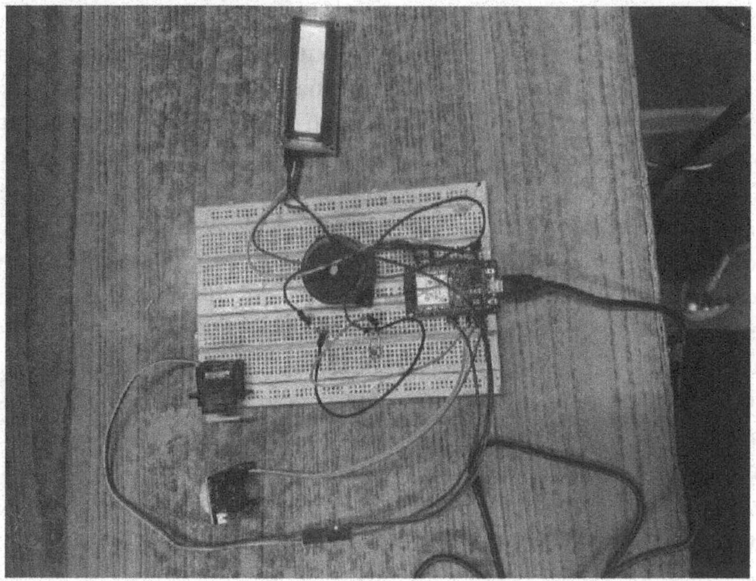

Figure 5: Set-up of all components on the breadboard.

4. Applications

A doorbell using IoT technology offers a wide range of applications that enhance home security, convenience and communication. Here are some key applications of IoT-enabled doorbells. IoT doorbells allow homeowners to remotely monitor their front door and surroundings using a smartphone or computer. This is especially useful for keeping an eye on the property when away from home. When someone rings the doorbell or approaches the door, the IoT doorbell can capture images or video footage. Homeowners can receive notifications and see who is at the door in real time, enhancing security. IoT doorbells often include a microphone and speaker, enabling two-way communication with visitors. This can be used to greet visitors, provide instructions to delivery personnel or deter potential intruders. With the rise in online shopping, IoT doorbells are helpful for confirming package deliveries. Homeowners can verify that a delivery has been made and even instruct delivery personnel where to leave the package. Many IoT doorbells include motion sensors that can detect movement near the door. This feature can trigger alerts and video recording, even if the doorbell is not pressed, helping to capture suspicious activity. IoT doorbells often have the capability to record video footage of events at the door. This recorded footage can be invaluable for security purposes or in case of any incidents. Some IoT doorbells offer cloud storage for recorded video footage. This allows homeowners to access and review footage remotely and ensures that important recordings are not lost. IoT doorbells can be integrated into broader smart home ecosystems, allowing them to work in concert with other smart devices like smart locks, lighting systems and security cameras. In addition to seeing and communicating with visitors, some IoT doorbells can remotely unlock or lock doors, providing convenient access control for trusted individuals. IoT doorbells can send alerts to homeowners' smartphones or other devices when unusual or suspicious activity is detected, such as unauthorised access attempts. These systems can maintain logs of visitor interactions, including timestamps and images, providing a history of who has visited the property. Integration with voice assistants like Amazon Alexa or Google Assistant allows homeowners to control and receive notifications from their doorbell using voice commands. Many IoT doorbell systems offer customisation options, allowing users to adjust settings, notifications and sensitivity to suit their preferences and security needs. IoT doorbells can be used to request assistance or alert authorities in case of emergencies, such as medical emergencies or security breaches. Some IoT doorbells are designed to be energy-efficient, using low-power modes when not in active use to reduce energy consumption. Overall, IoT-enabled doorbells offer a versatile set of features and applications that provide homeowners with enhanced security, convenience and peace of mind regarding their property and visitors.

5. Conclusion

This project represents a significant technological advancement in the realm of home security, as we have successfully developed a sophisticated and highly secure surveillance system designed to protect homes from potential criminal activity. Our research findings demonstrate that this system provides optimal security measures while simultaneously minimising overall costs, thereby making it an attractive option for homeowners seeking to enhance their security infrastructure. Our use of both IoT technology and advanced facial recognition algorithms represents a major breakthrough in the field of home security, as these cutting-edge technologies have become increasingly popular and widely implemented in various applications across multiple industries. By integrating these technologies into our surveillance system, we are able to provide users with an unparalleled level of security and protection against potential threats. Additionally, our utilisation of an Android application for remote control of the surveillance system represents a significant improvement over traditional security systems, as it provides users with the ability to monitor and track home activity in real time via their mobile device. This enhanced level of control and accessibility ensures that homeowners can stay vigilant and respond quickly to any potential security breaches. In conclusion, our project represents a major advancement in the field of home security, leveraging advanced technologies and cutting-edge algorithms to provide optimal protection and security measures at minimal cost. With the widespread adoption of IoT and facial recognition technology, we anticipate that our system will become an essential component of home security infrastructure in the years to come.

References

[1] Nasucha, M. and M. Nasucha, "Development of an obstacle avoiding robot," *J. Sistem Komput.*, vol. 5, no. 2, pp. 55–63, 2015.

[2] Tabassum, F., S. Lopa, and M. M. Tarek, "Obstacle avoidingrobot," *Global J. Res. Eng.*, vol. 17, no. 1, pp. 19–23, 2017.

[3] Lanke, N. and S. Koul, "Smart traffic management system," *Int. J. Comput. Appl.*, vol. 75, no. 7, pp. 19–22, 2013.

[4] Mandhare, P. A., V. Kharat, and C. Y. Patil, "Intelligent road traffic controlsystem for traffic congestion: a perspective," *Int. J. Comput. Sci. Eng.*, vol. 6, no. 7, pp. 908–915, 2018.

[5] Trivedi, J., S. Mandalapu, and D. Dhara, "Review paper on intelligent trafficcontrol system using computer vision for smart city," *Int. J. Sci. Eng. Res.*, vol. 8, no. 6, pp, 14–17, 2017.

[6] Aliff, M., *et al.*, "Development of fire fighting robot (QROB)," *Int. J. Adv. Comput. Sci. Appl.*, vol. 4, no. 10, pp. 1341–1344, 2019.

[7] Hasan, M. M., *et al.*, "Smart traffic control system with application of image processing techniques," *2014 International Conference on Informatics, Electronics& Vision (ICIEV)*, IEEE, Dhaka, pp. 1–4, 2014.

[8] Nasucha, M., "Development of an obstacle avoiding robot," *J. Sistem Komput.*, vol. 5, no. 2, pp. 55–63, 2015.

[9] Ankit, V., P. Jigar, and V. Savan, "Obstacle avoidance robotic vehicle using ultrasonic sensor, android and bluetooth for obstacle detection," Int. Res. J. Eng. Technol., vol. 3, pp. 339–348, 2016.

[10] Lanke, N. and S. Koul, "Smart traffic management system," *Int. J. Comput. Appl.*, vol. 75, no. 7, pp. 19–22, 2013.

[11] Reddy, R. S. C., P. V. Krishna, M. K. Chaitanya, M. Neeharika, and K. P. Rao, "Security system based on knock-pattern using arduino and GSM communication," *Int. J. Eng. Tech.*, vol. 4, no. 1, pp. 154–157, 2018.

[12] Neloy, M., M. Das, P. Barua, A. Pathak, and S. U. Rahat, "An intelligent obstacle and edge recognition system using bug algorithm," *Am. Sci. Res. J. Eng. Technol. Sci.*, vol. 64, no. 1, pp. 133–143, 2020.

[13] Perwej, Y., K. Haq, F. Parwej, M. Mumdouh, and M. Hassan, "The internet of things (IoT) and its application domains," *Int. J. Comput. Appl.*, vol. 97, no. 8887, p. 182, 2019.

[14] Kale, S. B. and G. P. Dhok, "Design of intelligent ambulance and traffic control," *Int. J. Innov. Technol. Explor. Eng.*, vol. 2, no. 5, pp. 2278–3075, 2013.

[15] Daniel, M., P. K. Maulik, S. Kallakuri, A. Kaur, S. Devarapalli, A. Mukherjee, A. Bhattacharya, L. Billot, G. Thornicroft, D. Praveen, and U. Raman, "An integrated community and primary healthcare worker intervention to reduce stigma and improve management of common mental disorders in rural India: protocol for the SMART mental health programme," *Trials, Springer*, vol. 22, pp. 1–13, 2021.

[16] Srivastava, M. D., S. S. Prerna, S. Sharma, and U. Tyagi, "Smart traffic control system using PLC and SCADA," *Int. J. Innov. Res. Sci. Eng. Technol.*, vol. 1, no. 2, pp. 169–172, 2012.

[17] Mendiratta, N. and Tripathi, S.L, "A review on performance comparison of advanced MOSFET structures below 45 nm technology node," *J. Semicond.*, vol. 41, no. 6, p. 061401, 2020.

44. Energy Storage Systems with Artificial Intelligence Techniques in Doubly Fed Induction Generator Based Wind Energy Conversion System – An Overview

Pradeep Singh,[1] *Krishan Arora,*[1] *Umesh C. Rathore*[2]

[1]*Res. Sch., SEEE, LPU, Phagwara, India*
[2]*ABVGIET-Pragtinagar, Shimla, India*

Abstract: Although the amount of electricity produced from sustainable sources has increased dramatically around the globe, such sources rarely give a consistent supply that is easily capable to meet demand. Due to the ability to transfer power into the system during peak times when its most desirable, storage has become an essential component in management of power from sustainable sources. The principles and uses of energy storage systems (ESS) for sources of sustainable energy as well as a control system for these ESS are discussed in this paper. Currently, sustainable power sources such as; wind power, are among the most effective sectors. Artificial intelligence (AI) approaches can be used when utilising such ESS equipment in combination with other RE sources to enhance reliability, charging-discharging rate, and controller characteristics. The primary traits of the various energy storage methods and their areas of operation have been examined. A simple MATLAB/Simulink simulation for a wind power conversion system using a double-fed induction generator and a battery-powered energy storage system is shown here.

Keywords: Energy storage system (ESS), wind energy (WE), doubly fed induction generator (DFIG), wind energy conversion system (WECS), battery energy storage system (BESS).

1. Introduction

In past times, climate change, the melting of glaciers in the polar regions, and other serious effects have been caused by rising green – house (GH) gas emissions brought on by the rise of industrial sectors, demographic growth and other damaging actions by humans [1]. European Union (EU) issued new guidelines in this area, requiring a 20–40percent reduction in GH gas emissions before 2030 [2]. Through 2050, Paris Agreement is intended to lessen atmospheric pollution and slow down climate crisis [3]. The primary goal of sustainability growth is to ensure reliable, efficient, inexpensive, green and renewable power. Power is at the core of both profitable and environmental issues. Although its significance, by 2021, 20% of world's population will not have availability to electricity. Due to the rising consumption for power, it is also necessary to employ alternative electricity sources more frequently. For instance, over 50% in 2010, till 66% in 2019, more people are choosing renewable power for heating. The ecosystem provides both sustainable and non-sustainable power sources. Such resources of energy include things like coals, fossil fuels, oil, hydroelectric, photovoltaic and wind. Global need for various sources, including sustainable and conventional fuels, is high [4]. Unfortunately, these sustainable sources are inconsistent; for instance, solar cells may not function properly in overcast conditions, wind generators may not function properly in quiet climate, and sustainable power sources may occasionally provide too much electricity, overloading the network. Recent times have seen a constant reduction in relatively brief short current; as a result of RE based on wind system, traditional electrical power mechanism to cover the imbalance among electric power production and its consumption [5]. WE has become a significant role in the world energy scene in a time of rising energy consumption, concerns over climate disruption and the search for renewable solutions. WE, which is obtained by kinetic energy of flowing air masses, provides a convincing substitute for traditional fossils fuels that addresses issues with the climate and energy stability. This essay goes into the realm of wind energy, examining its importance, scientific developments and contribution to a better green and clean electricity future. Fossil fuel is unlimited, accessible and cheap. HRES, or mixed RE sources, enable the allocation of power generated through hybrid systems. The effectiveness of DFIG system in disturbed systems has been the focus of numerous research endeavours [6]. A number of urgent issues facing worldwide communities have combined to create the necessity for WE. Primarily and importantly, a significant transition from carbon dioxide energy supplies is required to meet the pressing needs of reducing GH gas emissions and mitigating the effects of climatic change. While promoting industrialisation and economic expansion, fossils have had a negative impact on the environment, ecology and people's health. The generator's main benefit is that it can supply energy both at behind and driving power factor. Further benefit of managing rotor's voltages and current flows is that IM can keep the network synchronised whenever velocity of WT fluctuates. In recent years, DFIG has drawn a lot of research, particularly for wind purposes. Depending on its speed of rotation, WT models are classified as either adjustable or constant speed WT [7]. But, modelling of WTGS is a challenging procedure that involves simulating the turbines, alternator and converter to ensure that the supplied frequency is in line with power grid. The linkage with grid presents some challenges due to difficulty in regulating power, so precise modelling, control and selection of the suitable WE conversion system should be; taken into account, for modeling [8]. This is because wind velocity variations require use of a control methodology to achieve normal rotation speed. The technologies and management of WT have advanced, and they are now widely used in power grid. The DFIG WT has the advantage that the stator power, both effective and reactive, is regulated whenever the rotational current is regulated utilising field-oriented control acquired by PWM inverter [9]. ESS have growingly; an important role in, dynamic world, of energy manufacturing, delivery, and its usage. The demand for effective and dependable ESS has grown as RES like solar and winds gain popularity. In order to create a more reliable and robust power grid, electric power storage devices play a revolutionary role in filling the gaps among inconsistent energy output and steady demand. This essay explores the complex universe of ESS, including its relevance, many techniques and possibilities to influence the direction of long-term energy supply. Power storage functions as a reservoir, holding onto additional power during durations of greater output and discharging it during times of high consumption, balancing out variations in availability and requirement. Together with improving grid stability, this encourages the incorporation of fluctuating RE sources into the mainline energy supply. The shift to a minimal carbon energy system requires the use of ESS technologies. Power storage lessens the dependency on conventional fuels and helps to meet pollution reduction goals by collecting extra energy throughout off times and delivering it when consumption spikes. EES is a method that transforms electric supply from an electricity system that may be preserved for later conversion to electrical power [10]. A similar procedure allows electricity to be generated from inconsistent energy sources during periods of moderate demand, low production cost or both and utilised during periods of heavy demand, rising production cost, or whenever no other generating method is possible [11]. There are many uses for ESS, including in mobile devices, transportation and fixed energy sources [12]. The static ESS's beginnings can be traced to the start of 20th century, when generating plants were frequently closed down night and the residue demands on dc networks were supplied by lead-acid batteries. Utility firms finally realized how crucial it is for systems to have the adaptability that ESS technologies offers, and in 1929; first ESS central station, the pumped hydroelectric storage (PHS), was operational [10]. ESSs are mainly made to gather energy from multiple resources, transform it and store it for usage in a variety of ways as needed. The focus of this study will be ESS for fixed applications including local corporate and residential clients, distributed electricity resources, power production, transmission, transformation networks and RE.

2. Techniques of Energy Storage

Among the main problems that RE faces is that they are never continuously available. Grid-side ESS directly addresses this issue. Both the air and sun do not constantly blow or shine. Energy may be stored and released under sunny and windy conditions thanks to ESS. Although it could seem like a straightforward concept, there are several techniques to accomplish power storage [13]. In WT, a variety of power storing techniques, known as ESS, including super-conducting magnetic, energy storage (SMES), ultra-capacitor (UC) or super-capacitor (SC), are utilised to absorb surplus power. Another one is the virtual, synchronous generator (VSG) with storage, hybrid; energy storage (HES), thermal; energy storage system (TESS), flywheel; energy storage system (FESS) and battery; energy storage system (BESS) [14]. As shown in figure 1.

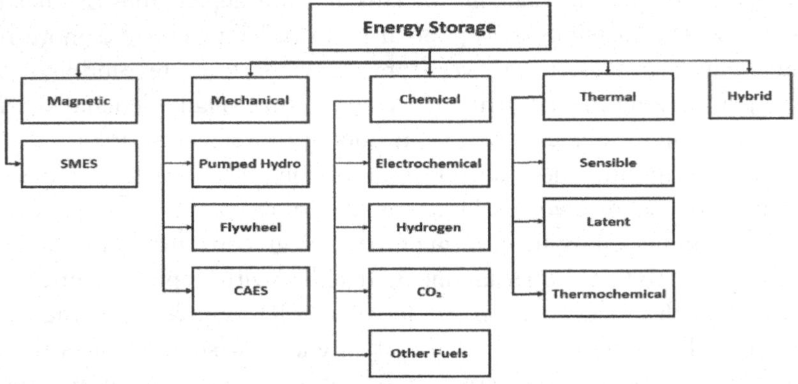

Figure 1: *Types of energy storage systems.*

Energy storage devices provide a number of functions in the RE subsector as shown in figure 2. When attempting to satisfy demands of the linked loads, they can reduce power supply variations. They could also make compensated for the increased power quality (PQ) of produced electricity that will boost operational reliability [15]. It is possible to strengthen the flexibility and adaptability of new power generation to provide constant power output; therefore, dispatch control is essential for maintaining the system's operational safety and cost-effectiveness.

- Smoothen out power variations.
- Lessen the demand for maximum controlling capacity in the power system.
- Maintain record of a RE schedule's output.
- Moreover, it will adjust the V & f of power system.

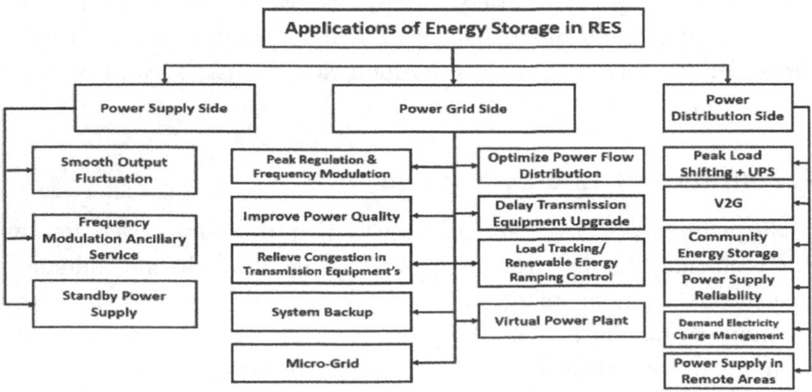

Figure 2: *Application scenario of ESS.*

Devices for storing electricity use a variety of techniques, each suited to certain purposes and functions. BESS can be used for grid-scale deployments or for photovoltaic storage in homes. Pumped storage, a significant and well power storage option, stores water using energy from gravitational potential. Upcoming solutions with particular benefits in terms of flexibility, responsiveness, and efficiency include compressed air; energy storage (CAES), FESS and TESS [16]. While ESS holds immense promise, challenges persist. Cost remains a significant barrier, although ongoing technological advancements are steadily driving prices downward. The efficient management of ageing batteries and the environmentally responsible disposal of battery waste are also critical concerns that require innovative solutions. As the world marches towards a future dominated by RE sources and decentralised energy systems, the role of ESS is poised to grow. In-depth examination of energy storing techniques, uses and their impact on power landscape are the goals of this article. This investigation provides a greater knowledge of why energy storage technologies can change electricity production, utilisation and delivery by revealing their intricacies and possibilities, leading the path towards a more robust and responsible energy future. ESS are used in many different industries. They stabilise power grids by providing frequency regulation, voltage control and seamless integration of intermittent renewable energy. In remote areas or disaster-stricken regions, energy storage can deliver reliable electricity, reducing reliance on centralized power sources. Electric vehicles are also benefiting from energy storage, as advanced batteries enable longer ranges and faster charging times [17]. Power storage devices are frequently needed for DFIG-based WECS in order to address numerous operational difficulties and improve the system 's ultimate effectiveness and dependability. BESS and RE sources are regarded as viable substitutes for fossil fuel forms of energy because of their potential benefits to the economy and environment. Various BESS technologies are already being incorporated in a numerous application area, including tidal energy conversions, microgrids, mixed marine PS, improving PS reliability [18]. They have uses in PS, hybrid maritime PS, electric vehicles (EVs), microgrids and transports. It takes a lot of work to create an effective BESS because a variety of aspects must be taken into account, such as price, dependability, the right kind of storage, the quality of the power; voltage and frequency variations and ecological concerns. Scientists are working to create techniques, nevertheless, that can be easily integrated with other ESS techniques and take into account all the relevant elements. A few of the difficulties include the effects on the economy, electricity efficiency, ageing, the ecology, etc. [19]. By transferring electrons from one side to second side, traditional capacitors store power. With a larger covering surface, UC made of carbon substances may store electrical charges using a phenomenon called the electric dual barrier. Although the capacitance expressions for UC and electrolytic capacitors seem to be same, UC can attain increased capacitance due to a slimmer dielectric and electrode surface area. For UC made of metal oxide or polymer composites, pseudo-capacitance; is the primary method of discharging [20]. Greater electricity and power densities, as well as reduced volume and mass, are all characteristics of UC. Two carbon-based electrodes in UC are separated by a dielectric substance that not only serves as an insulator but also possesses electrical characteristics that influence UC effectiveness. Electrons are not transferred in UC; rather, they are electrostatically charged. The electrolytes become polarised whenever a voltage is placed between the electrodes, creating an electrical field within the electrolytes. This results in ions diffusing to the permeable electrodes with opposing charges via the dielectric [21]. As a consequence, every electrode forms an electrical double layer, which reduces the space between them and improves the surface area of the electrode [22]. The type of influential ingredient used is the electrolytes, electrode's support surface and pace at which portions and sections in porosity; electrodes are utilised all have an impact on how much charge can be conserved. Low ESR, low leakage current, a longer lifespan, a higher useable capacity and a wide working temperatures variation are some characteristics of UC. Transmission lines, hybrid UC battery UPSs, system frequency and stability controls, microgrid and micro-generation, WT systems, hybrid electric cars and other applications are all possible uses for these UC [23–25]. FESS actively absorbs kinetic energy, restricting the movement of mass to a round path. The bulk collecting of energy, which might take the form of circles, discs or discrete masses, is most crucial component of a flywheel. The flywheel rotor's capacity for kinetic energy is inversely related to the rotor's weight and square of its rotational velocity [26]. Rapid charging and discharging speeds, a prolonged calendar life, quick response times, excellent round-trip efficiencies, excellent power and energy densities and minimal ecological influence are some characteristics of FESS [27]. PQ features such frequency and voltage adjustment, army pulsing power uses, altitude correction in satellites, UPS, load shifting and mixed and electric cars are most popular uses of FESS [28]. The planet's lightweight, cheapest and most prevalent element is hydrogen atom. Nevertheless, it only happens when other elements are present, especially with O2 in water and with C2, N2 and O2 in living things and fossil fuels. The major resource of power is indeed not H2. Yet, when separated from those additional elements via a power source, it transforms into a desirable energy resource. In especially for power storage and transportation, hydrogen is seen as cleanest energy source of the tomorrow. Calculations reveal that 1 kg of H2 holds about 33 energy units (kWh), which makes H2 a good energy storage medium [29]. The features of HESS are high energy density, versatility, zero emissions, scalability, long duration storage, fast response and decentralised deployment. The applications of HESS are grid balancing and energy management, renewable energy integration, transportation fuel, industrial processes, power generation, backup power and off-grid applications, heat and cogeneration, hydrogen injection, hydrogen mobility and fueling infrastructure, energy export and trading, etc. During the time of electrical energy preservation, strong pressure of air is compressed with electricity, stored in basins and tanks like subterranean salt caves, quarries, sunken pumping stations, or gas cylinders, and finally released to power machines to generate energy during phase of power generation and supply [30]. Simply put, the structural quality of CAES determines its charge life, making it less susceptible to fatigue than a battery. The lifespan of CAES is typically between 30 and 40 years. Power storing and system stabilisation, high accuracy, huge and long-term storage, quick reaction, minimal emission influence and site adaptability are only a few of the benefits of CAES. The applications of CAES are grid stabilisation and peaking power, RE integration, energy arbitrage, frequency regulation, backup power, ancillary services, strategic reserves, hybrid systems, transmission congestion relief and industrial applications, etc. Technologies for storing energy that use heat energy to be captured, stored and then released are known as thermal energy storage (TES) systems. These devices have the capacity to absorb power as heat, which can be used for various applications, including both heating and cooling processes. TES systems offer flexibility in managing energy supply and demand, enhancing energy efficiency and reducing energy costs. Despite its greater load capability and extended storage time, higher degree TES is discovered to be better suited over battery technologies on a wide scale. The melting temperature, volume, inherent heat of fusion, heating value, thermal conduction, rapid cooling, price and accessibility, thermal properties, chemical resistance, non-toxic, non-corrosive, ignitability and oxygen content are only a few of characteristics of TESS [31]. Some applications of TESS include building heating and cooling, industrial processes, solar thermal power plants, district heating and cooling, waste heat recovery, RE integration, desalination, cryogenic energy storage, combined heat and power (CHP) systems, vehicle thermal management, etc. [32]. Another method, known as VSG, involves manipulating a decentralised generator's or an ESS's grid-interface converters to simulate a synchronous generator or a desired feature of it. At the region in which ESS is linked to grid, the frequencies are locally monitored. Depending on the observed frequencies, the electricity output of VSG is then computed and utilised as the benchmark for output real power of ESS. As electricity demand changes, the centrifugal reaction of VSG simulates power that is ordinarily delivered or consumed by a typical spinning generator [33]. Some features of VSG with ESS are grid-forming capability, fast response times, frequency and voltage regulation, islanded operation, enhanced grid stability, power quality improvement, black start capability, flexible power generation and storage, efficient load sharing, smooth transition between modes, resilience to grid variability, dynamic power management, integration with RE, demand response and peak shaving, backup power and critical infrastructure support and reduced emissions. Some applications are renewable microgrids, remote and off-grid areas, critical infrastructure backup, demand response and load management, voltage and frequency regulation, grid upgrades and capacity enhancement, hybrid energy systems and industrial applications. Because of their broad variety of features, battery techniques can be used in both high power and high energy applications. In this situation, combining high energy and high-power devices tends to provide an ESS that is more useful. The goal of hybrid system for energy storage, or HESS, is that it is high-power equipment, which will serve narrow power requirements while its greater device will supply long-term electricity requirements. The hybridized structure in HESS construction has a significant impact on controls and electricity strategic plan as well as a number of other factors, including versatility, adaptability, efficacy and cost [34]. Highly adaptable designs allow more options for applying controls and power management techniques and deliver the highest level of efficiency enhancement at expense of complexities and price. In general, combining various ESS techniques does not result in better features. A complex network control measure must be created in order to get the most out of every ESS in HESS. A HESS's monitoring and power management approach is more complex than that of an individual ESS unit because of heterogeneous nature of ESSs. It offers advantages including technological synergy, better efficiency, optimal power density, increased cycle lifetime, flexibility and adaptation, dependability and redundancies, commercial feasibility, etc. A HESS may generally provide all uses for an universal energy storage device, such as personal and public transportation [35], renewable energy integration, microgrids and island systems, backup power and UPS, grid frequency regulation, optimized demand response, peak shaving and load leveling, electric vehicle charging infrastructure, industrial applications, remote and off-grid areas and critical infrastructure support.

3. Wind Energy Conversion System

The main components of WT are shown in figure 3. WT, which converts WE into usable power, or mechanical power is the main core element of a power conversion system for WE. The DFIG and WT are joined via a gearing. A suitable control scheme feeds the generator's power into electrical network, reducing interruptions, enhancing systems security and raising system efficiency.

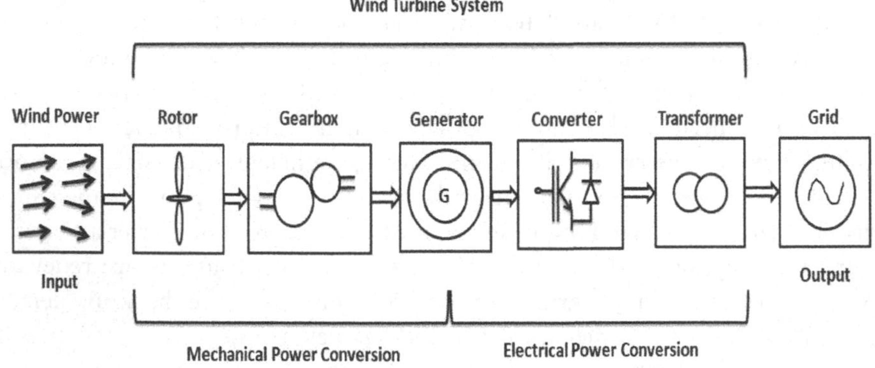

Figure 3: *Main components of wind energy conversion system.*

The power produced by a WT can be written as;

where

A = Area swept by a WT in m²;

ρ = Density of air in that particular area in kg/m³;

V_w = Wind Speed in m/s;

C_p = Power Co-efficient of WT;

λ = Ratio of turbine's angular speed to maximum speed of wind;

β = Blade's Pitch Angle;

The relationship for evolvement of torque can be written as;

$$T_a = \frac{\rho}{\omega_t} = \frac{1}{2\lambda} \rho \pi R^3 V_w^3 C◆(\lambda, \beta) \tag{2}$$

where

R = Radius of WT;

ω_t = Rotating Speed of WT;

Gearbox enables the WT's moderate velocity to the DFIG's higher velocity by coupling WT's shafts with rotor of the DFIG. The following equations calculate such gearbox:

$$\omega_t = \frac{\omega_m}{G} \qquad \& T_m = T_a / G$$

The turbine's speed is calculated as follows by using fundamental dynamics relationship;

$$J\frac{d\omega_m}{dt} = T_m - T_{em} - f\omega_m$$

J = Moment of inertia; on generator side;

f = Viscous friction coefficient; on generator side;

T_m = Torque of GB;

T_{em} = EM torque of generator;

ω_m = Mechanical speed of generator;

λ & β is a function of rotor velocity of WT and denotes power coefficient $C◆$. The o/p power as a function of rotor velocity for WT at multiple wind speeds (pitch angle β = 0°).

4. AI Techniques for Energy Storage Systems

AI techniques are crucial for energy storage systems (ESS) due to their ability to enhance system efficiency, optimize performance and address the complex challenges associated with energy management. AI algorithms can analyse real-time data from ESS, grid conditions and demand patterns to make intelligent decisions about when to charge, discharge or store energy. AI techniques can forecast energy demand, renewable energy generation and market prices with high accuracy. AI algorithms can dynamically balance energy supply and demand across a network of ESS, optimising load distribution and grid stability. AI can control the erratic and variable nature of RE sources, making their integration easier. AI-controlled power storage devices can improve grid reliability by offering network assistance functions like frequency management and voltage consistency. Artificial intelligence (AI)-driven power storage devices can adjust frequency quickly and stabilise grid in response to rapid variations in demands or supply. AI techniques can identify abnormal operating conditions, potential faults and anomalies in ESS, enabling timely maintenance and reducing downtime. AI algorithms can monitor the health of battery cells, predict degradation rates and optimise charging and discharging profiles to extend battery lifespan while maintaining performance. AI can facilitate demand response programs by coordinating ESSto shift energy consumption to off-peak hours, reducing overall energy costs and peak demand charges. AI techniques can manage hybrid ESS that combine different storage technologies, optimising the utilisation of each technology's strengths. AI systems can continuously learn from historical data and adapt to changing patterns, improving their decision-making accuracy over time. AI techniques encompass a range of methodologies that can be applied to ESS to optimize their operation, enhance efficiency, and improve overall performance. In order to forecast future power requirements, AI techniques such as NNs, decision tree and support vector techniques can examine past data; for RE generation, and market prices. ANNs can model complex relationships in data and learn from large datasets. They can predict energy demand, optimize charge/discharge cycles, and support battery management. ML algorithms can optimize charging and discharging schedules, improve load forecasting, and enhance overall system efficiency. RL algorithms learn to make decisions by interacting with an environment. In ESS, RL can optimize battery charging and discharging strategies over time by learning from the consequences of different actions. Multiple layered neural networks are used in supervised learning, which is a subfield of artificial learning. Artificial learning can model complex relationships in energy data, enabling accurate forecasting and optimisation of energy storage operations. GA optimizes solutions by simulating evolution, testing different solutions iteratively and selecting the best ones. It can be used to optimize energy storage system parameters and control strategies. Fuzzy logic can handle imprecise and uncertain data by defining rules in a linguistic manner. It's used for decision-making and control in ESS under uncertain conditions. Expert systems emulate human expertise in specific domains. They can be used for diagnosing faults, predicting maintenance needs, and making informed decisions in ESS. PSO optimizes solutions by simulating the movement of particles in search of the optimal solution. It's used for optimising energy storage parameters and scheduling. SVM is used for classification and regression tasks. It can predict equipment failure, identify faulty components, and improve maintenance planning. Combining multiple AI techniques allows for synergistic benefits. For example, combining reinforcement learning with neural networks can optimize complex ESS operation. Different AI techniques are shown in Figure 4.

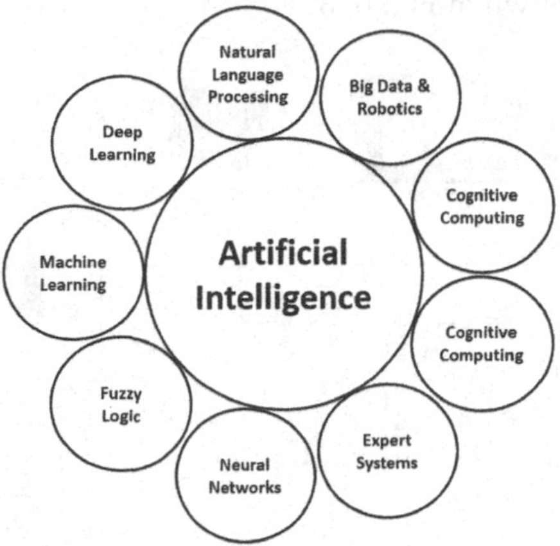

Figure 4: Different AI techniques for ESS.

5. MATLAB Based Modelling

A DFIG-based WECS with ESS and controllers is a complex system designed to harness wind energy, convert it into electricity and intelligently manage the generated power using energy storage and control mechanisms. The ESS controller manages the charging and discharging of the ESS. It decides when to store excess energy and when to release it to the grid, ensuring smooth power output and stabilising the grid. Figure 5 shows the basic diagram of DFIG-based WECS with ESS in conjunction with the DC link capacitor and controllers for ESS, RSC and GSC.

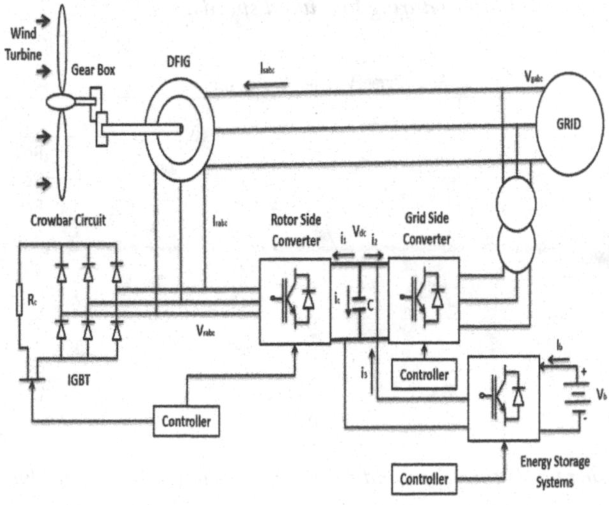

Figure 5: DFIG-based wind energy conversion system with ESS.

We are currently working with the BESS, and we have to add the ANFIS and FL control system in this. We have made a basic MATLAB model of DFIG-based WECS with BESS as shown in Figure 6.

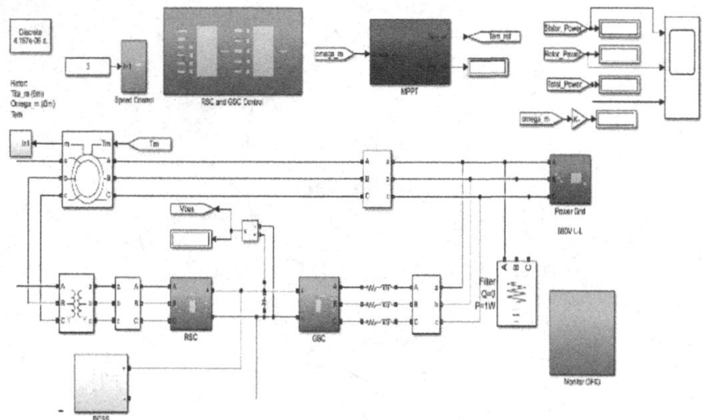

Figure 6: *Basic MATLAB model for DFIG based WECS with ESS.*

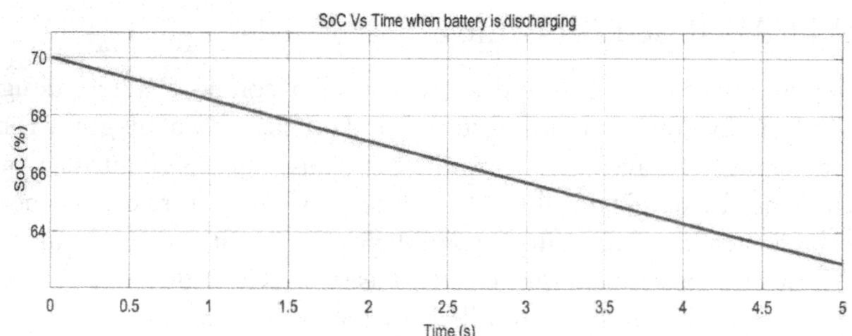

Figure 7: *Discharging of battery during low wind speeds.*

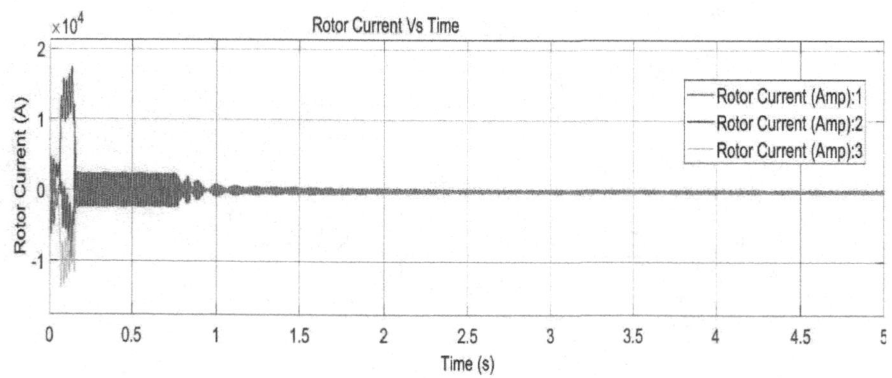

Figure 8. *Rotor current Vs time for wind speed of 3 m/s when BESS supplying power to grid.*

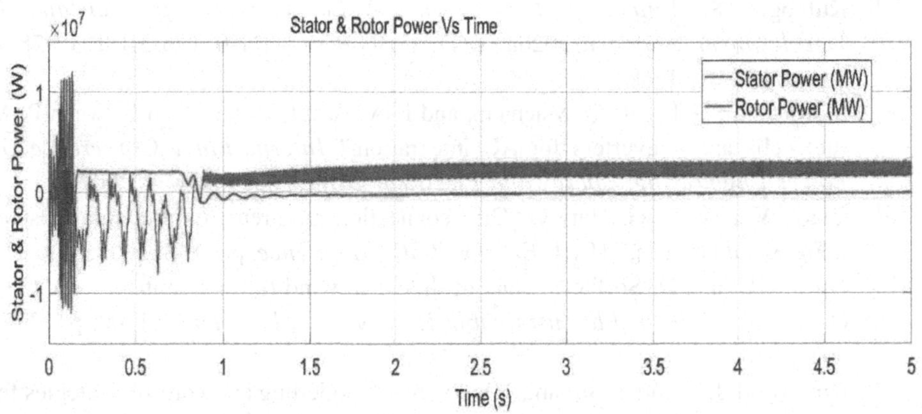

Figure 9: Stator and rotor power vs time for wind speed of 3 m/s when BESS is supplying power to grid.

6. Conclusion and Results

As there are lot of ES devices that can store excess energy during peak hours and supply back it during low wind speeds or when demand is high. We have selected the BESS for energy storage in our system due to their characteristics and advantages over other ES devices. We have run the MATLAB/Simulink model below the cut in speed of 3 m/s and the waveform is shown in Figure 7, which shows that the SOC of the battery which reduces from 71.5% to 63.67 % in this range of wind speed but it takes some time to response and the various parameters of DFIG-based WECS take some time for settled down. Figures 8 and 9 show the rotor current, stator and rotor power, respectively, when wind speed is low and BESS supplies power to grid. Here simple PI controller is used in BESS. Now, we will add some other controllers like ANFIS or FL in BESS to reduce the charging–discharging rate of battery and a comparison between both of them, so that our system works smoothly under different wind alterations.

References

[1] Sohani, A., H. Sayyaadi, and M. Azimi, "Employing static and dynamic optimization approaches on a desiccant-enhanced indirect evaporative cooling system," *Energy Convers. Manage. Elsevier*, vol. 199, pp. 1–16, 2019.

[2] Razmi, A., M. Soltani, F. M. Kashkooli, and L. Garousi Farshi, "Energy and exergy analysis of an environmentally-friendly hybrid absorption/ recompression refrigeration system," *Energy Convers. Manage.*, vol. 164, pp.59–69, 2018.

[3] Sampath, U., P. R. Arachchige, and M. C. Melaaen, "Aspen plus simulation of CO_2 removal from coal and gas fired power plant," *Energy Procedia Elsevier*, vol. 23, pp. 391–399, 2012.

[4] Kufeoglu, S., *Emerging Technologies, Value Creation for Sustainable Development*, Springer, 2020, SDG7, ISBN 978-3-031-07126-3 ISBN 978-3-031-07127-0 (eBook).

[5] Marquezini, D. D., R. Q. Machado, and F. A. Farret, "Interaction between PEM fuel cells and converters for AC integration," *International Conference on Power Engineering, Energy and Electrical Drives*, pp. 359–364, 2007.

[6] Qiao, W. and R. G. Harley, "Grid connection requirements and solutions for DFIG wind turbines," *IEEE Energy 2030 Conference*, pp. 1–8, 2008.

[7] Njiri, J. G. and D. Soffker, "State of-the-art in wind turbine control: trends and challenges," *Renewable Sustainable Energy Rev., Elsevier*, vol. 60, pp. 377–393, 2016.

[8] Ringwood, J. V. and S. Simani, "Overview of modelling and control strategies for wind turbines and wave energy devices: comparison and contrasts," *Ann. Rev. Control, Elsevier*, vol. 40, pp. 27–49, 2015.

[9] Kumar, A. and S. K. Jain, "A review on the operation of grid integrated doubly fed induction generator," *Int. J. Enhanced Res. Sci. Technol. Eng.*, vol. 2, no. 6, pp. 25–37, 2013.

[10] Baker, J. N. and A. Cpllinson, "Electrical energy storage at the turn of the Millenium," *IEEE Power Eng. J.*, vol. 13, no. 2, pp. 107–112, 1999.

[11] Walawalkar, R., J. Apt, and R. Mancini, "Economics of electric energy storage for energy arbitrage and regulation in New York," *Energy Policy, Elsevier*, vol. 35, no. 4, pp. 2558–2568, 2007.

[12] Koot, M., J. T. B. A. Kessels, B. de Jager, W. P. M. H. Heemels, P. P. J. van den Bosch, and M. Steinbuch, "Energy management strategies for vehicular electric power systems," *IEEE Trans. Veh. Technol.*, vol. 54, no. 3, pp. 771–782, 2005.

[13] Hussain, J., *et al.*, "Power quality improvement of grid connected wind energy system using DSTATCOM-BESS," *Int. J. Renewable Energy Res.*, vol. 9, no. 3, 2019.

[14] Sahooet, S. S., *et al.*, "A coordinated control strategy using super-capacitor energy storage and series dynamic resistor for enhancement of fault-ride through of doubly fed induction generator," Int. J. Green Energy, vol. 16, no. 8, 2019.

[15] Mishra, Y., S. Mishra, and F. Li, "Coordinated tuning of DFIG- based wind turbine and batteries using bacteria foraging technique for maintaining constant grid power output," *IEEE Syst. J.*, vol. 6, no. 1, pp. 16–26, 2012.

[16] Ibrahim, H., A. Ilinca, and J. Perron, "Energy storage systems-characteristics and comparisons," *Renewable Sustainable Energy Rev.*, vol. 12, no. 5, pp. 1221–1250, 2008.

[17] Atawi, I. E., A. Q. Al-Shetwi, A. M. Magableh, and O. H. Albalawi, "Recent advances in hybrid energy storage system integrated renewable power generation: configuration, control, applications and future directions," *MDPI, Batteries*, vol. 9, no. 1, 29, pp. 1–35, 2023.

[18] Kumar, N. M., A. Ghosh, and S. S. Chopra, "Power resilience enhancement of a residential electricity user using photovoltaics and a battery energy storage system under uncertainty conditions," *MDPI, Energies*, vol. 13, no. 6, pp. 1–27, 2020.

[19] Tang, S., H. Yang, R. Zhao, and X. Geng, "Influence of battery energy storage system on steady state stability of power system," *Proc. - 12th Int. Conf. Electr. Mach. Syst. ICEMS 2009*, pp. 1–4, 2009.

[20] Armutulu, A., J. K. Kim, M. Kim, S. A. Bidstrup Allen, and M. G. Allen, "Nickel-oxide-based supercapacitors with high aspect ratio concentric cylindrical electrodes," *IEEE International Conference on Solid-State Actuators, Actuators and Microsystems (Transducers and Eurosensors XXVII)*, pp. 1480–1483, 2013.

[21] Zhongxue, L. and C. Jie, "An impedance-based approach to predict the state-of-charge for carbon-based supercapacitors," *Microelectron. Eng., Elsevier*, vol. 85, no. 7, pp. 1549–1554, 2008.

[22] Kotz, R. and M. Carlen, "Principles and applications of electrochemical capacitors," *Electrochim. Acta, Elsevier*, vol. 45, no. 15–16, pp. 2483–2498, 2000.

[23] Calleja, A. J., A. Torres, J. Garcia, M. Rico Secades, J. Ribas, and J. Angel Martinez, "Evaluation of power LEDs drivers with supercapacitors and digital control," *IEEE Industry Applications Annual Meeting*, pp. 1129–1134, 2007.

[24] Bijarniya, V. K. and D. Kumar, "A review paper on ultra capacitor technology and its applications," *Int. J. Eng. Res. Technol.*, vol. 4, no. 32, pp. 1–3, 2016.

[25] Saonerkar, A. K., A. Thakre, A. Podey, A. Chimote, P. Kadao, P. Kadu, and R. Satpute, "Single phase residential multilevel inverter using supercapacitor," *IEEE International Conference on Inventive Computational Technologies (ICICT)*, pp. 1–4, 2016.

[26] Suzuki, Y., A. Koyanagi, M. Kobayashi, and R. Shimada, "Novel applications of the flywheel energy storage system," *Elesevier, Energy*, vol. 30, pp. 2128–2143, 2005.

[27] Liu, H. and J. Jiang, "Flywheel energy storage-an upswing technology for energy sustainability," *Energy Build., Elsevier*, vol. 39, no. 5, pp. 599–604, 2007.

[28] Amiryar, M. E. and K. R. Pullen, "A review of flywheel energy storage system technologies and their applications," *MDPI, Appl. Sci.*, vol. 7, no. 3, 286, pp. 1–21, 2017.

[29] Mousavi Ehteshami, S. M. and S. H. Chan, "The role of hydrogen and fuel cells to store renewable energy in the future energy network-potentials and challenges," *Energy Policy, Elsevier*, vol. 73, pp. 103–109, 2014.

[30] Luo, X., J. Wang, M. Dooner, J. Clarke, and C. Krupke, "Overview of current development in compressed air energy storage technology," *Energy Procedia, Elsevier*, vol. 62, pp. 603–611, 2014.

[31] Chen, H., T. N. Cong, W. Yang, C. Tan, Y. Li, and Y. Ding, "Progress in electrical energy storage system: a critical review," *Prog. Nat. Sci., Elsevier*, vol. 19, no. 3, pp. 291–312, 2009.

[32] Alva, G., L. Liu, X. Huang, and G. Fang, "Thermal energy storage materials and systems for solar energy applications," *Renewable Sustainable Energy Rev., Elsevier*, vol. 68, no. 1, pp. 693–706, 2017.

[33] Torres, L. M. A., L. A. C. Lopes, L. A. T. Moran, and J. R. C. Espinoza, "Self-tuning virtual synchronous machine: control strategy for energy storage systems to support dynamic frequency control," *IEEE Trans. Energy Convers.*, vol. 29, no. 4, pp. 833–840, 2014.

[34] Xie, Q., Y. Wang, M. Pedram, Y. Kim, D. Shin, and N. Chang, "Charge replacement in hybrid electrical energy storage systems," *17th Asia and South Pacific Design Automatic Conference*, IEEE, pp. 627–632, 2012.

[35] Hemmati, R. and H. Saboori, "Emergence of hybrid energy storage systems in renewable energy and transport applications-a review," *Renewable Sustainable Energy Rev., Elsevier*, vol. 65, pp. 11–23, 2016.`

45. Massive MIMO Precoding Techniques for Future Generation Communication System

Sandhya Bolla, ManwinderSingh, and Anudeep Goraya

School of SEEE, Lovely Professional University, Jalandhar, Punjab, India

Abstract: Massive MIMO, which was initially suggested, is a critical technique for meeting the rapidly growing data demand of 5G networks. MIMO technology may provide the propagation channel with a greater degree of flexibility in terms of multiplexing gain or diversity gain. New disruptive technologies have been developed in response to the large increase in data traffic that the forthcoming 5G mobile communication system. This is a critical research area for 5G wireless communication since massive MIMO has the possible system to significantly boost throughput and data transmission charges, as well as residual energy and energy efficiency. As a result of three years of fast development in massive MIMO technology, spectrum efficiency has been enhanced to an unprecedented level by the combination of growing antennas and adopting an extremely duplex communication mechanism. It is achieved by modelling the interference signal first and then constructing an exactly opposite signal added to a pre-distorted signal to cancel it. Additionally, this article discusses precoding methods and energy efficiency.

Keywords: 5G, massive MIMO, precoding, beamforming, energy harvesting.

1. Introduction

This article proposes a technique for reducing interference between antennas operating at various frequencies. An frequency spread spectrum (FSS) sandwiched between two different antennas. Allowing electromagnetic waves to pass through the FSS and radiate into the surrounding environment is the primary function of the antenna. Two neighbouring antennas may keep their distinct performance features, such as their emission patterns if they use this design. As an aside, it is worth mentioning that, although the FSS has been used in many applications. An FSS structure is established because of the closeness of two antennas operating in different 5G bands. Over its entire working range, it seems that the antenna's overall electrical and radiation properties are better. 5G massive MIMO applications appear to gain greatly from this decoupling technique beam shaping is critical to the transmission of energy in millimeter-wave MIMO systems.

To find a compromise between low cost but inaccurate analogue approaches and energy-intensive, high-cost fully digital systems, hybrid beam formation frequently incorporates analogue wideband and digital sub-band components. Based on zero forcing of the channel matrix, we construct and evaluate dual-stage hybrid beam formation approaches for the 5G new radio (NR) simulator, which maintains an entirely digital foundation. Based on throughput and block error rate, it is feasible to compare the benefits of partly and completely linked topologies, as well as various numbers of radio frequency (RF) chains and transmit antennas and to draw conclusions BER. By altering the number of phase shifters employed in the experiment, we examine the performance-complexity trade-off for phase shifter resolution. The simulations were conducted using the clustered delay line CDL-A channel model with angle scaling since it correctly depicts the propagation environment. It is one of the most exciting air interface technologies for next-generation communications, with the potential tocompletely transform the industry as shown in Figure 1. The majority of prior studies demonstrated various advantages of large MIMO systems, but only for co-located deployment scenarios. Co-location and distributed deployment scenarios are compared in terms of the trade-off between area spectral efficiency (ASE) and area energy efficiency (AEE) performance.

2. Massive MIMO Basic Model

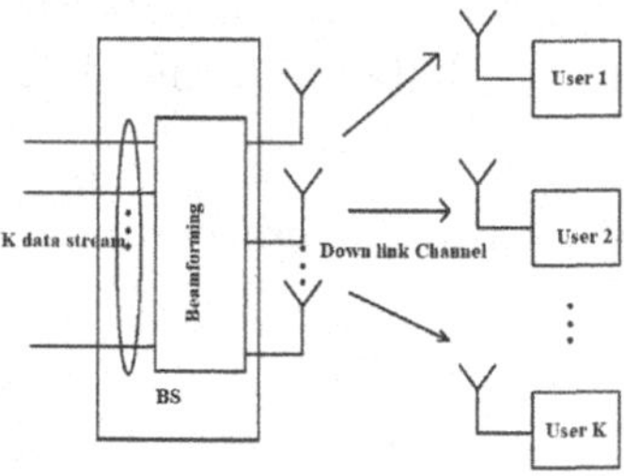

Figure 1: A basic model of massive MIMO.

The following are the primary benefits of massive MIMO technology:

1. The output power of each antenna is reversely relative to the square of the total number of antennas in the system. When employed in big MIMO systems, this has the potential to significantly cut power usage.
2. A second method is to create antenna 'hardening' by using a channel matrix developed from random matrix theory. As the number of antennas rises, this strategy becomes more effective. Given that the singular value of the channel matrix is known incrementally and that the channel vector is often

orthogonal, the simplest signal processing approach is the optimal choice due to its simplicity of implementation.

3. The third and last step is to eliminate thermal noise and reduce it on a small scale. Thermal noise and small-scale fading have a lesser influence on system performance than interference across zones as a consequence of the usage of linear signal processing.

On the other hand, when nonlinear signal processing is used, thermal noise and small-scale fading have a major influence on a system's performance. Figure 1 shows a basic model of massive MIMO.

Recent research suggests that a less expensive approach, known as 'hybrid beam forming', may lower hardware costs and power usage by using fewer RF links. Figure 1 shows a basic model of massive MIMO with different users.

Closed-form expressions may be generated to aid in the discovery of critical design principles. A significant example is that, whereas great antenna dispersion often benefits ASE, it has little effect on AEE. Collaboration between cells is not always desirable in all deployment scenarios, and effective use cases are highly dependent on system characteristics like the number and location of transmit antennas, given the massive number of available transmit antennas and the actual cost of channel estimation.

In the case of 5G massive MIMO transmitters operating in a multi-beam configuration, a unique digital pre-distortion (DPD) approach is presented to linearise the target beam that is interfered with by other beams. It is accomplished by first modelling the interference signal and then adding an identical signal to the pre-distorted signal to cancel it. The experimental findings indicate that the suggested technology is capable of successfully achieving target beam linearisation, making it a viable option for multi-user applications in 5G massive MIMO wireless networks.

The ubiquitous adoption of multi-carrier OFDM-based systems is mostly owing to the ease of receiver implementation, which eliminates the need for elaborate and sophisticated equalisation. The problem of equalisation may be solved with a single carrier system if one side has a more number of antennas. Given the enormous number of channels to be monitored, estimation precision is another practical concern that must be addressed.

Therefore, care must be taken to establish a realistic performance analysis. It has provided an overview of single-carrier systems. With the inclusion of MIMO techniques into real-world wireless systems, such as LTE and 4G, it has been able to increase connection dependability and deliver a larger capacity, all while maximising spectral efficiency. Using a pre coding approach that is compatible with the frequency selective channel, the base station (BS) transmitter utilises single-carrier approach, it is fascinating to see how it affects PAPR. Millimeter-wave massive MIMO systems rely on beamforming techniques to work effectively.

By combining analogue wideband and digital subband components, hybrid beamforming attempts to establish a compromise between low-cost, but inaccurate, totally analogue approaches and energy-intensive, but high-cost, fully digital methods. Hybrid dual-stage beam forming systems are created in the 5G NR simulator and tested experimentally in the real world using singular value decomposition of the channel matrix and zero forcing as the baseline. Based on throughput and block error rate, it is feasible to compare the benefits of partly and completely linked topologies, as well as various numbers of RF chains and transmit antennas, and to draw conclusions (BER). In large MIMO systems, the number of BS antennas increases, and beam shaping may be used to direct the signals generated by each user to a specified location in space, allowing the BS to make exact distinctions between each user. Figure 2 shows the BS with more number of users.Wireless power transmission performance may be considerably improved by using large-scale MIMO. Wireless energy transmission's ultimate purpose is to meet the receiver's need for labour, which makes intuitive sense. Medical implants may be charged wirelessly and transmit medical data to a remote receiver using the acquired energy. As data traffic grows, the spectral frontier for next-generation systems will be millimeter-wave (mm-wave) communication. Large antenna arrays for massive MIMO systems might lower the complexity of mm waves and the power they use, therefore solving their core issues.

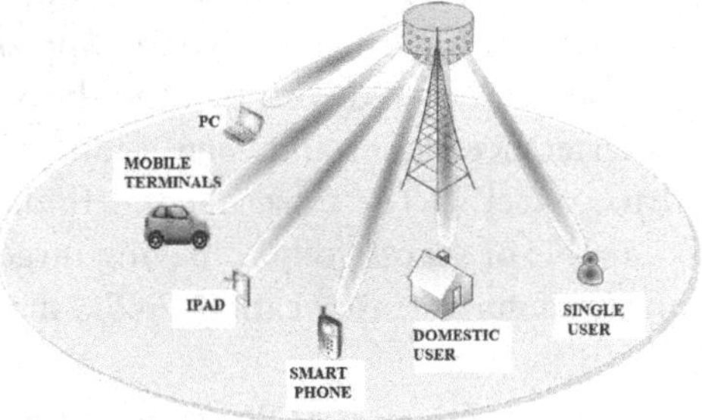

Figure 2: Massive MIMO BS to all users.

Equalisation in an OFDM system using one-tap equalisation would be simpler in the case of a Rayleigh fading channel. Single-carrier approaches employing a cyclic prefix and frequency domain equalisation have been the subject of several investigations. For large antenna systems, it is desirable to send a low-distortion signal to maintain a tightly regulated spectral mask while using RF chains. When there are more carriers, OFDM systems have a hard time dealing with them.

3. Linear Precoding Types

There has been substantial research into both linear and non-linear pre-coding approaches, which has enabled massive MIMO pre-coding technology to be used to enhance system performance when pilot pollution is present. In the next section, non-linear precoding approaches are exposed. Even with a wide antenna array and low SNR, the MRC receiver may perform as well as or better than an optimal linear receiver when SNR is low enough. If there is significant interference, even at higher SNRs, the OLR receiver system still outperforms the standard MMSE system, even when the SNR is higher.

1) ZF precoding:

A spatial signal processing approach known as zero-forcing (also known as null-steering) may be used in a MIMO wireless communication system to eliminate multiuser interference.

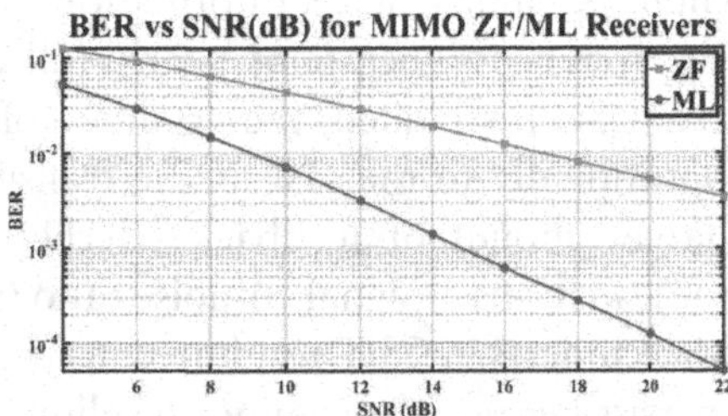

Figure 3: SNR versus BER for ZF/ML receivers.

When a transmitter is certain in its knowledge of a channel's current condition before broadcasting, it uses the pseudo-inverse of the channel matrix.

An N transmit antenna access point and M users with single receive antennas form a multi-antenna downlink system, where M<=N, the received signal of user u is defined as

$$y_u = h_u^T x + n_u \tag{3}$$

where u=1,2,........M

and $x = \sum_{i=1}^{M} \sqrt{P_i} S_i W_i$ (4)

is the {\displaystyle N_{t}\times 1}N X 1 vector of transmitted symbols, {\displaystyle n_{k}} is the noise signal, {\displaystyle \mathbf {h} _{k}} is the {\displaystyle N_{t}\times 1} channel vector and {\displaystyle \mathbf {w} _{i}} {\displaystyle N_{t}\times 1} is some N X 1 linear precoding vector. Here ({\displaystyle (\cdot)^{T}} is the matrix transpose, {\displaystyle {\sqrt {P_{i}}}} is the square root of transmit power, and {\displaystyle s_{i}} is the message signal with zero mean and variance 1.

The signal model described above may be rewritten in a more compact manner as

$$y = H^T W D_s + n \tag{5}$$

where y is the M X 1 {\displaystyle K\times 1} received signal vector,

$H = [h_1, h_2, ...h_k]$ is {\displaystyle N_{t}\times K}N X K channel matrix

$W = [w_1, w_2, ...w_k]$ is the N X K {\displaystyle N_{t}\times K} precoding

Matrix and D is the diagonal of square of power P {\displaystyle \mathbf {D} =\ mathrm {diag} ({\sqrt {P_{1}}},is a {\displaystyle K\times K}M X M diagonal power matrix, and

S is the {\displaystyle K\times 1}M X 1 transmit signal.

Figure 3 shows the SNR verses BER for ZF/ML precoding techniques.

When a large number of users are present, and the transmitter has extensive knowledge of the downlink Channel State Information (CSI), the use of ZF-precoding may enable the system to operate at nearly full capacity (CSI). When the CSI at the transmitter (CSIT) is limited, the accuracy of the ZF-performance precoding decreases proportionally to the CSI at the transmitter's accuracy. ZF-precoding demands a large amount of feedback overhead to get the highest multiplexing gain achievable in terms of signal-to-noise ratio (SNR). Due to residual multiuser interferences, inaccuracies in CSIT result in considerable throughput loss. Multiuser interferences persist because they cannot be eliminated with poor CSIT-generated beams.

It aims to produce a mathematical large MIMO 5G system that consumes less energy when utilized with a ZF receiver. A SNR comparison of co-located and distributed MIMO systems and hybrid MIMO systems were conducted. In terms of SNR, gain, and antenna count, combination MIMO, such as hybrid MIMO, has the highest energy efficiency among the three types of MIMO, according to the performance research. On the other hand, co-located and hybrid MIMO have worse energy efficiency in terms of spectrum efficiency than dispersed MIMO. Dispersed MIMO is always more energy efficient than co-located MIMO. Our future study will focus on developing an energy-efficient system that is also spectrum-efficient.

2) **MRC precoding**: Maximum ratio combining is a telecommunications integration method: Each channel's signals is combined. Gain for each channel is adjusted to be inversely proportional to the mean square signal level and proportionate to the mean square noise level for that channel and each channel is assigned a unique set of proportionality constants.

Pre-detection combining and ratio-squared combining are two more names for the same technique. When combining several white Gaussian noise channels, the most successful approach is maximum ratio combining. MRC is capable of regenerating a signal to its original state. The MRC phenomenon has also been seen in neurology, where neurons in the retina alter their reliance on two input sources according to their SNR. Figure 4 shows the energy efficiency for number of BS antennas.

Let us assume the receiver has M antennas, as shown in the following example. The y-coordinate obtained in this case is

$$y = hs + n \tag{6}$$

On a small scale, assuming Rayleigh fading, the channel's impulse response with variance σ^2

As a result, the instantaneous channel power is dispersed exponentially.

$$P^2=(1/\sigma^2)\exp(-(\sigma^2/h^2)) \quad (7)$$

$$\|h\| = \sqrt{h_1^2 + h_2^2} \quad (8)$$

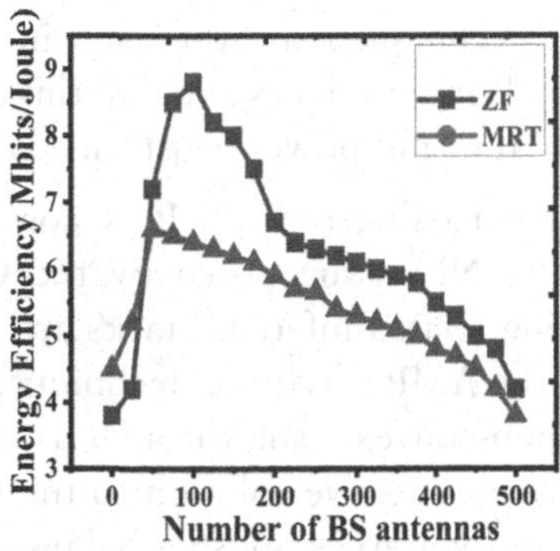

Figure 4: Energy efficiency for ZF/MRT receivers.

3) MMSE Precoding: When constructing a pre-coding approach for a multi-cell massive MIMO system, it is critical to take into account the difficulty of allocating the training sequence to the system's cells. The research suggests that the minimum mean square error estimate precoding (MMSE) technique may help decrease pilot contamination.

4) Matched Filtering Precoding: Modern MIMO spatial multiplexing systems employ the matched-filter (MF) detector, which is the simplest basic linear detector available to users. Finally, we wish to expand the scope of our study to include more realistic systems with erroneous channel estimations.

5) Peak-To-Average Power Ratio (PAPR) precoding:

Using high-end linear power amplifiers in a massively multi-antenna MIMO system almost invariably results in higher hardware costs as well as higher energy consumption [212]–[215]. As a result, a feasible method for implementing huge MIMO systems was required. Massive MIMO systems may be implemented practically using efficient non-linear power amplifiers [5]. Thus, the PAPR should be kept as low as possible to mitigate the influence of amplifier nonlinearity. This section will discuss precoding techniques that try to lower the PAPR. The presence of a large PAPR results in inband distortion and spectral spreading. There are several approaches to resolving the PAPR issue. Amplitude clipping, filtering, coding, partial transmit sequences, selective mapping (SLM), and partially transmit sequences are only a few of them (PTS). BER performance is determined using a sixteen-path channel model. There are sixteen possible pathways between each user and each antenna owing to channel fading.

6) Continuous Envelope (CE) Precoding:In MU-MIMO systems, the constant envelope (CE) precoding approach is employed to lower the peak amplitude per repeat (PAPR) of the broadcast signal. To fulfill its objectives, the CE algorithm takes advantage of readily available, low-cost, high-efficiency amplifiers. As a certain sum rate and a big M are employed, the total transmits power may be reduced by around 4 decibels (dB) when compared to a system that utilizes very linear and inefficient amplifiers (such as those used in satellite communications). It is feasible that the CE technique may still result in an array power increase under certain mild channel circumstances and that this capacity will be provided by the average only total transmit power-constrained channel.

7) Approximate Message Passing (AMP): It is computationally demanding to tackle the non-convex NLS issue posed by the CE approaches utilising AMP. Compressed sensing-related inference tasks are the driving force behind [214]'s development of the AMP precoding technique. Rather than relying on a global solution to a non-convex issue through a computationally intensive approach, it aims to give an effective solution to the CE precoding challenge. The AMP technique allows you to establish a balance between computational requirements and achievable performance.

8) Quantized Precoding (QP): It is critical to weigh the advantages and disadvantages of using more antennas at the BS when designing these systems. To avoid inefficiency, the system must be restructured. The BS has become much more complicated, costlier and power hungry due to the introduction of several RF chains[3]. The data converters at the transmitter are a significant source of power consumption in huge MIMO systems. Generally, direct caring for methods, exhaustive of zero-forcing (ZF) taking care of approach, had been certified to help the plausible data transmission worth or organisations limitation concerning the multiuser MIMO frameworks. In any case, contemplating the staggering surveyed remarks overhead and inordinate truly worth of the enormous amount of RF chains/radio wires needed via the use of ZF precoding, the summed-up ZF approach cannot be almost done for our proposed mm Wave m-MIMO plans. As of late unexampled half strain taking care of advancement can avoid huge proportions of iterative procedures added through the normal multiuser m-MIMO associations.

4. Non-linear Precoding

VP, DPC and auxiliary network approaches are only a few of the non-linear precoding techniques at one's disposal. When the cells M and K are not too large, non-linear precoding may have some advantages. The SNR estimate in the VP of complete CSI is given in the literature. DPC is a coding technique that pre-cancels known interference without incurring a power consumption penalty. While just the transmitter requires knowledge of this interference, complete CSI is needed everywhere to achieve weighted sum capacity. Costa precoding, Tomlinson-

Harashima precoding and the vector perturbation approach all fall under this group.

There are many well-known non-linear detection methods, such as sphere decoding (SD), which uses a maximum likelihood (ML) decoder. To find any signalling points, the SD algorithm only evaluates a certain radius point. The low complexity of TB can be efficiently reduced by extending the search radius. This approach is known as random steps (RS). Here's a breakdown of the underlying theory: choose an initial vector, assess its peripheral vector that requires MSE and choose MSE as the smallest vector

5. Conclusion

Massive MIMO significantly enhances user experience and mobile services. It will continue to be available for a while. But it is expected that the transmitter's design would draw the most attention. For extremely large MIMO systems, this study studied linear and nonlinear precoding methods. The new method outperforms the old one when computing average power allocation. Under the premise that each user's minimum communication rate will be met, we proposed a method based on maximising harvested energy to estimate the proper power splitting factor for each user. With the aid of this technology, the system can collect more energy while maintaining a minimal communication speed for the user, leading to energy recycling and environmentally responsible communication.

References

[1] Singh, M., M. Kumar, and J. Malhotra, "Energy efficient cognitive body area network (CBAN) using lookup table and energy harvesting," *J. Intell. Fuzzy Syst.*, vol. 35, no. 2, pp. 1253–1265, 2018.

[2] Chen, J.-C., C.-J. Wang, K.-K. Wong, and C.-K. Wen, "Low-complexity precoding design for massive multiuser MIMO systems using approximate message passing," *IEEE Trans. Veh. Technol.*, vol. 65, no. 7, pp. 5707–5714, 2016.

[3] Jacobsson, S., G. Durisi, M. Coldrey, T. Goldstein, and C. Studer, "Quantized precoding for massive MU-MIMO," *IEEE Trans. Commun.*, vol. 65, no. 11, pp. 4670–4684, 2017.

[4] Larsson, E. G., O. Edfors, F. Tufvesson, and T. L. Marzetta, "Massive mimofor next generation wireless systems," *IEEE Commun. Mag.*, vol. 10, 4, 2016.

[5] Björnson, E., J. Hoydis, and L. Sanguinetti, *Massive MIMO Networks: Spectral, Energy, and Hardware Efficiency*, Now Foundations and Trends, 2017.

[6] Masoudi, M., M. G. Khafagy, A. Conte, A. El-Amine, B. Françoise, C. Nadjahi, F. E. Salem, W. Labidi, A. Süral, A. Gati, D. Bodéré, E. Arikan, F. Aklamanu, H. Louahlia-Gualous, J. Lallet, K. Pareek, L. Nuaymi, L. Meunier,

P. Silva, N. T. Almeida, T. Chahed, T. Sjölund, and C. Cavdar, *Green Mobile Networks for 5G and Beyond.*

[7] Hassan, M., M. Singh, and K. Hamid, "Survey on NOMA and spectrum sharing techniques in 5G," *2021 IEEE International Conference on Smart Information Systems and Technologies*, pp. 1–4, 2021.

[8] Bjornson, E., L. Sanguinetti, and M. Kountouris, "Deploying dense networks for maximal energy efficiency: small cells meet massive mimo," *IEEE J. Sel. Areas Commun.*, vol. 34, no. 4, pp. 832–847, 2016.

[9] Ali Al-Samawi, M. A. and M. Singh, "Effect of 5G on IOT and daily life application," *2022 3rd International Conference for Emerging Technology (INCET)*, pp. 1–5, 2022, doi: 10.1109/INCET54531.2022.9823983.

[10] Walia, G. S., P. Singh, and M. Singh, "Localizing mobile nodes in WSNs using neural network algorithm," *Mater. Today: Proc.*, 2022.

[11] Hassan, M., M. Singh, and K. Hamid, "Review of NOMA with spectrum sharing technique," ICT with Intelligent Applications, Springer, Singapore, pp. 135–143. 2022.

[12] V Prathyusha Sandhya Bolla K RamMohan Rao "Conference: An overview of massive MIMO antennas for 5G in future.

[13] Bolla, S. and M. Singh, "Energy harvesting technique for massive MIMO wireless communication networks," *Journal of Physics: Conference Series*, vol. 2327, p. 012059, 2022, IOP Publishing, doi:10.1088/1742-6596/2327/1/01205.

46. Design and Performance Analysis of PV-Based Grid Connected Nanogrid System

Amita Mane[1,2], Shamik Chatterjee[2], Amol Kalage[3]

[1]*First Year Engineering Department, PCCOER, Pune, India*
[2]*SEEE, Lovely Professional University, Phagwara, India*
[3]*Electrical Engineering Department, Sinhgad Institute of Technology, Lonavala, Punesss*

Abstract: This paper presents the solar energy based nanogrid (NG) system with operation of grid connected mode. Solar energy is omni present with the advantage of less carbon footprint. One of the problems associated with photovoltaic is its intermittent nature. Due to this output power will be fluctuating and power system has to deal with uncontrollable generation and demand. This will result in deterioration of the power quality. The proposed NG consists of photovoltaic as a renewable energy source, energy storage system and ac/dc loads. The complete NG system has been simulated using MATLAB/ simulink platform. Further results are presented for the on-grid operation of NG.

Keywords: PV, nanogrid, MPPT, MATLAB.

1. Introduction

Due to exponentially increasing demand from consumers, Indian power grid is facing various challenges. This is not a single challenge in front of the centralised power grid. Distance between power stations and end users is also another concern, which may lead to more line losses and degradation of the efficiency of power system. Environmental conditions like heavy rain and wind may lead to power system failure and hence the power outages. Centralised grid generating stations are dependent on the fossil fuels, which are responsible for degradation of atmosphere. In addition to above, power supply to remote areas is one of the big tasks. To overcome above challenges, it is required to develop new structure of power system, which will reduce burden on national power grid. Distributed energy resources (DERs) is one of the solutions to above problems, which can produce power close to its point of consumption [1]. Due to technological development, solar energy sources are gaining more importance, and they are becoming effective solution in the energy crisis. It is intended that, in upcoming days number of householders will have DERs, in grid connected mode. This small-scale generation and distribution of energy are referred as a nanogrid (NG) [2]. Photovoltaic is one of the promising solutions to the energy crisis. It can be used as standalone or in grid connected mode [3][4]. In [5] author discusses the important parameters in the development of PV system, off grid and grid connected system and its challenges, different PV cell technologies and its design and modelling. It also focuses on the power energy management and scheduling technique, different maintenance and storage issues. Share of non-conventional energy sources in to sustainable development will be useful for next generation also they provides balance between economical, technical and good environmental conditions [6]. Implementation of power flow colouring in NG by using cooperative distributed control methodology with variable loads has been published [7]. In [8]author focuses on DC NG. Design and implementation of appliances for DC-based NG have been described. An induction heating (IH) cooktop appliance is considered as a similar example and some simulation and experimental results are also shown. NG containing PV, energy storage system and smart inverter are implemented in University of California for electrical vehicle charging [9]. The author presents four different smart inverter control algorithm, which makes possible to use the battery to shift the NG crest load and also limit the demand of NG to a given threshold. Off-grid remote power units used for street lightning are presented in [4]. The concept of open energy system (OES) has been described in [10]. Open energy system is the combination of characteristics of microgrid, NG and virtual power plant. The author proposes this concept in terms of hardware as well as software. NG as a hybrid power system is described in [11] which supply a group of loads with a peak rating in the order of 2–20 kW. The idea of dc bus signaling is invented by the author. DC bus signalling is nothing but hybrid distributed control strategy in for NG, which is independent on external communication link. The detail study of optimization for efficient energy management and component sizing of single home with plug in electrical vehicle, Photovoltaic's and battery is described in [12]. Energy management in prosumer NG based on the energy forecasting is presented in [13]. The author uses three stages for energy management, first energy monitoring, secondly demand is managed considering smart appliances and finally energy storage system for better forecasted generation of each prosumer. The aim of this paper is to show effective use of solar energy for the load upto 20kW. Proposed system consists of PV array, MPPT, inverter, battery and national grid. In this paper, simulation of PV-based grid connected NG is presented.

2. Nanogrids

The elementary blocks of NG are shown in Figure 1. It includes the following building blocks:

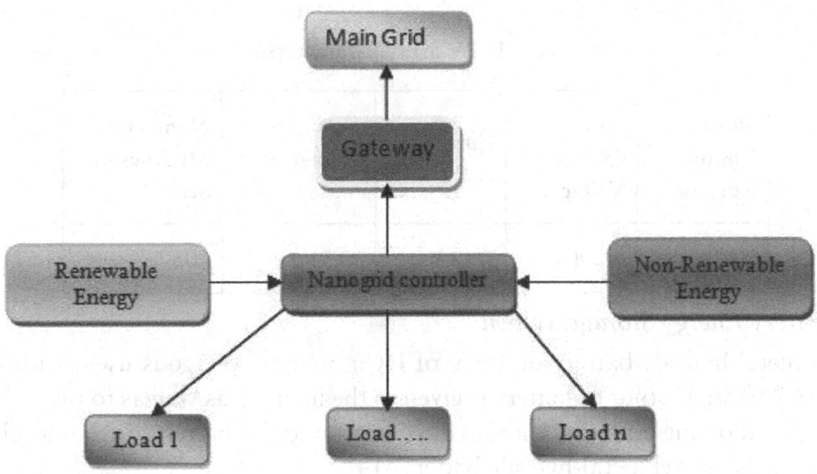

Figure 1: Basic structure of nanogrid.

2.1 Distributed Generators: In case of the NG, it is possible to generate the power close to the consumers, which is known as distributed generation (DG). It consists of both conventional and nonconventional energy sources. Renewable energy sources are solar, wind and on other side fuel cell, diesel generator comes under the non-renewable DGs.

2.2 Load: These are the domestic equipments like water heater, refrigerator, microwave and television.

2.3 Nanogrid Controller: It is known as brain of the NG, which controls the operation of NG. For NG controller may be for supply side management or demand side management.

1.4 Gateway: A two-way connection between NGs, national grids or microgrids is known as gateway.

3. Proposed Nanogrid System

This section presents the details of proposed NG system. It is simulated in MATLAB software and results are presented for active power, reactive power, inverter voltage and current.

3.1. Solar Photovoltaic System

Solar energy is one of the distributed renewable energy source in the NG. Table 1 shows the important parameters used in MATLAB model to get required output from the PV system. Solar array is operated at total irradiance of solar cells of 1000 W/m2. This PV array is consisting of nine modules, which generate nominal power of 19.36 kW. Output of PV array is given to DC to DC boost converter via DC link capacitor of 230 μF.

Table 1: PV array parameters.

Short Circuit Current	Open Circuit Voltage	Current at P	Voltage at P	Number of Modules in Series
8.01A	36.90V	7.10A	30.3V	10

3.2. Battery Energy Storage System

Nickel metal-hydride battery of 150V of DC nominal voltage is used, with rated capacity 250Ah. Output of battery is given to the inverter as well as to the DC load of 3kW. Following equations are used to determine the battery discharge–charge process of the nickel metal-hydride battery [14].

$$E_{disch}^{N-M} = E_0 - k\frac{Q}{Q-it}i^* - k\frac{Q}{Q-it}it + Exp(t) \quad (1)$$

$$E_{b}^{N-M} = E_0 - k\frac{Q}{\text{EitE}0.1Q}i^* - k\frac{Q}{Q-it}it + Exp(t) \quad (2)$$

The discharge condition is at i* > 0 while the charge condition is at i* < 0 [15]. In the equations, the variables and parameters are:

Eo is the battery voltage which is constant;

K is the polarization constant (Ah1);

Exp (t) is the exponential zone dynamics, in V;

Q is maximum battery capacity, in Ah;

it is extracted capacity or the actual battery charge, in Ah;

i* is the filtered low frequency current dynamics, in A;

A is exponential voltage, in V;

B is exponential capacity, in (Ah)

Figure 2 represents the nominal current discharge characteristics of the of nickel metal-hydride battery.

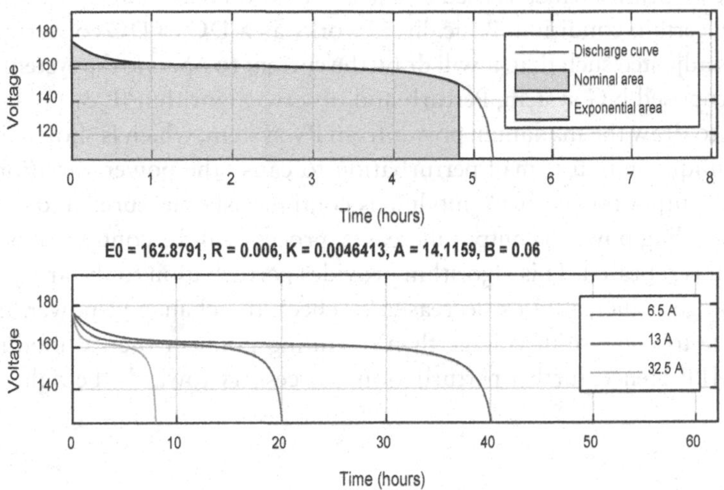

Figure 2: Nominal current discharge characteristic at 0.2C (50A).

3.3. DC to AC Voltage Source Converter

The solar PV system is connected to 230 V, 50 Hz grid through the single phase midpoint inverter which performances DC to AC conversion. As the good modulation index range is from 0.9 to 0.95 for the better performance of the inverter, value of the DC link voltage is taken as 320V for the reference. In this case, modulation index is 0.93. In order to generate the pulses to the inverter, PWM technique [16] is used as shown in Figure 3.

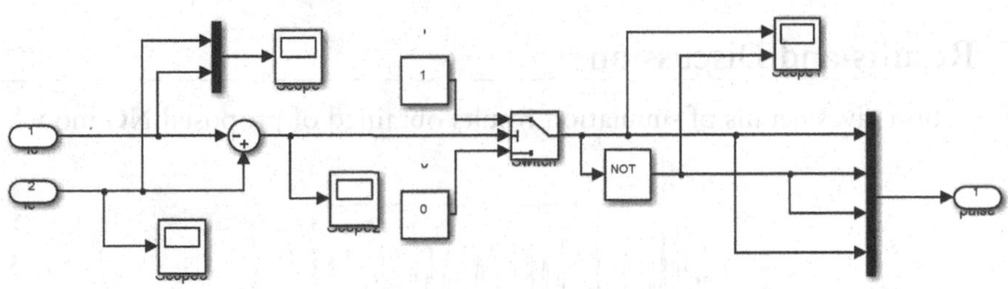

Figure 3: PWM inverter control.

3.4. AC and DC Load

The proposed system consists of AC as well as DC load of 18 kW. NG consist of number of type of DC loads such as TV, computer, washer, dryer, LED lights and induction heating cook top. [8].

3.5. Maximum Power Point Tracker (MPPT) Along with P & O Algorithm

MPPT is the algorithm which is used to extract maximum available power from PV array under certain condition. Basically, it works as a DC to DC converter whose duty cycle is adjusted such that, it will draw the current to operate the system at MPP [17]. For proposed NG system, Perturb and observe algorithm (P & O algorithm) [18] is used to draw the maximum power from PV system, which is shown in Figure 4. This technique initiates small perturbation to cause the power variation of the PV module. Output power of PV module is continuously measured and compared with the preceding power. If output increases, process will be continued, otherwise perturbation is repeated. This algorithm provides perturbation to the array voltage. The PV voltage is increased or decreased to check the change in power. If power increases due to increase in voltage then operating point of the PV module is on the left of MPP. Hence, further perturbation is necessary towards the right to reach MPP.

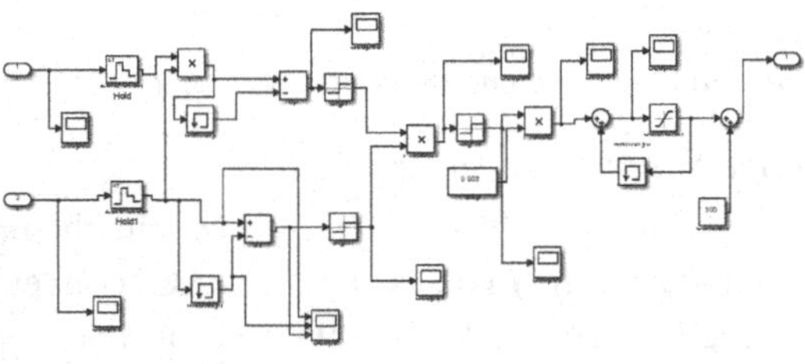

Figure 4: P&O algorithm.

4. Results and Discussion

This section gives details of simulation results obtained of proposed NG model.

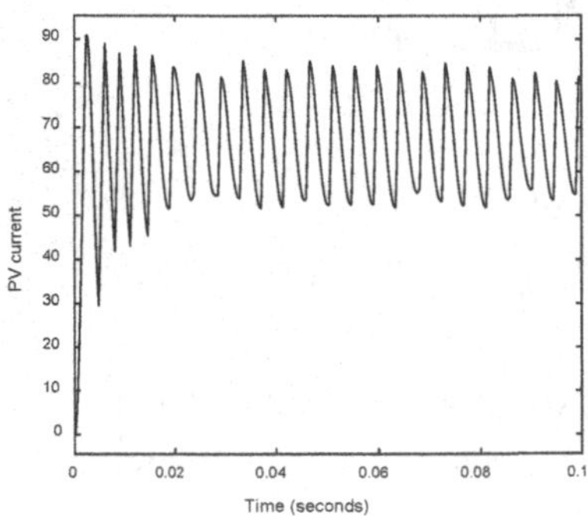

Figure 5: PV current (A).

Output current of PV system is shown in Figure 5. The nature of current is fluctuating DC type. The magnitude of current is fluctuating between 90 A and 50A.

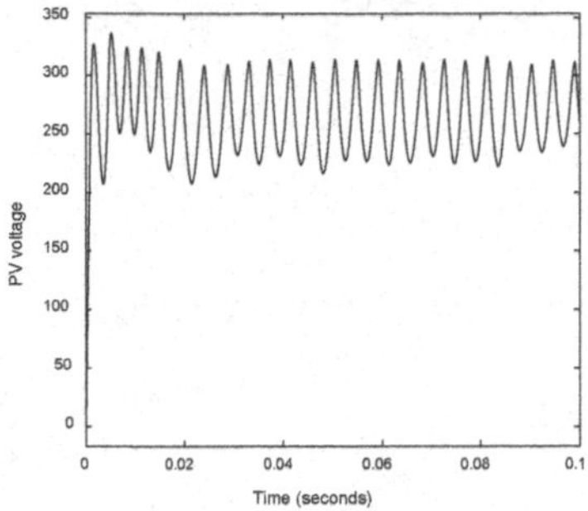

Figure 6: PV voltage (volts).

Output voltage from PV system is around 320V, which is shown in Figure 6. Due to irregular nature of solar energy output voltage is fluctuating in nature.

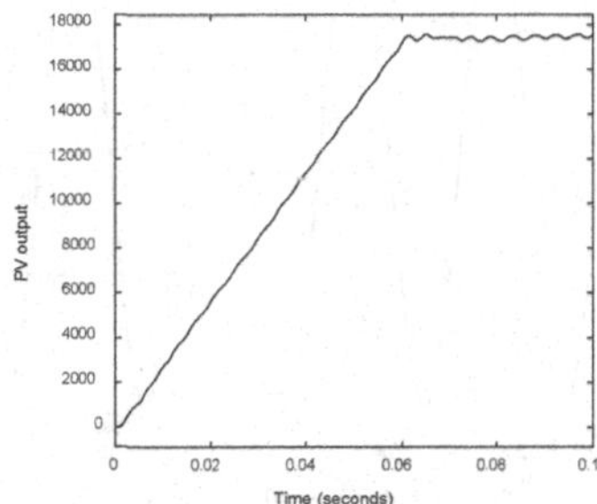

Figure 7: PV voltage (Volts).

Proposed PV based NG consists of nine modules which generate nominal power of 19.636 kW as shown in Figure: 7. this output is further feed to DC to DC boost converter.

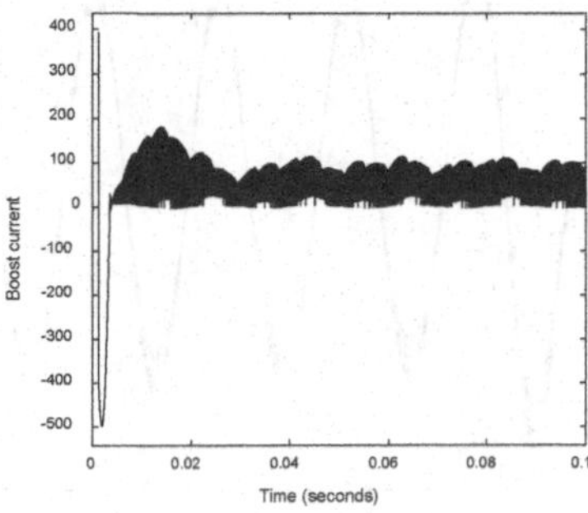

Figure 8: Boost converter current (A).

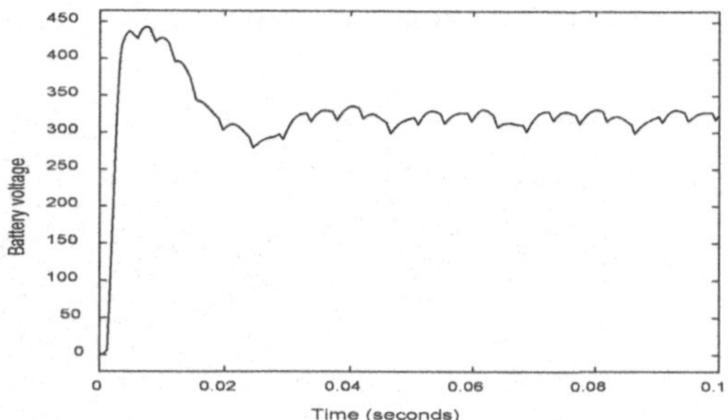

Figure 9: Boost converter current (A).

Output current of boost converter is presented in Figure 8. Figure 9 represents the nickel metal-hydride battery voltage which are around 150 V.

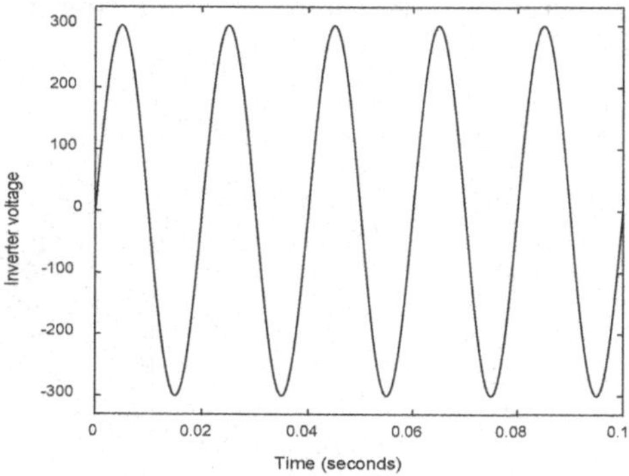

Figure 10: Inverter voltage (V).

Inverter converts DC output of PV system into AC. Figure 10 shows inverter voltage which is 300V AC.

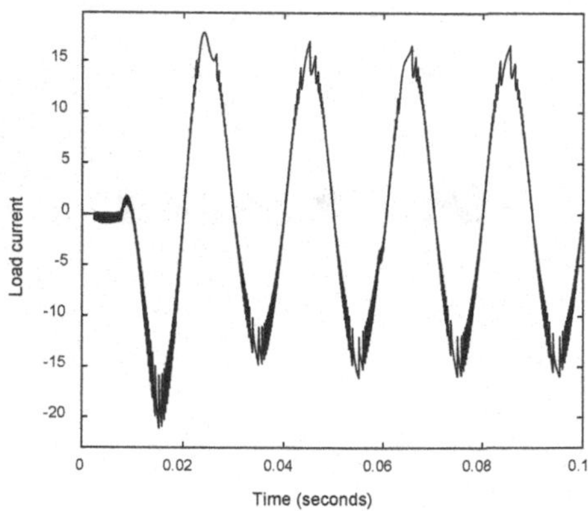

Figure 11: Load current (A).

Nature of load current and its FFT analysis is represented in Figures 11 and 12, respectively.

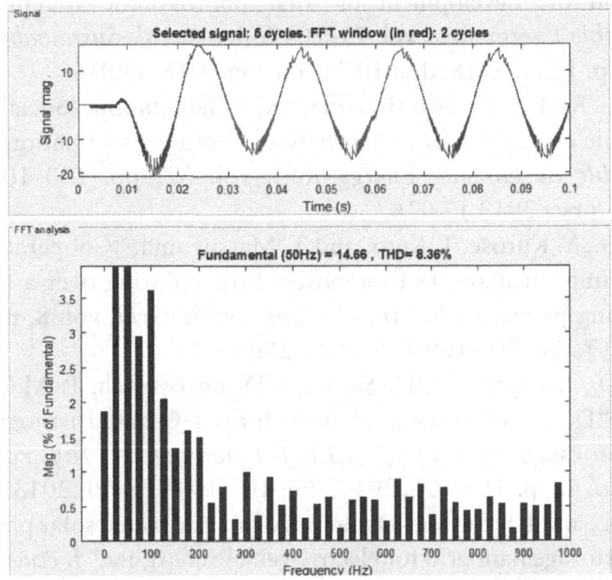

Figure 12: FFT analysis and total harmonic distortion in the current.

5. Conclusion

PV based NG system is presented in this paper. It is operated in grid connected mode with battery as an energy storage system. The P&O algorithm is used to extract the maximum power from PV. Current NG system can be implemented in off grid mode in remote areas where access of national grid is not possible. Also it can be operated in on grid mode. Following are the results obtained from the simulation of NG system in on grid mode.

References

[1] Rae, C. and F. Bradley, "Energy autonomy in sustainable communities - a review of key issues," *Renewable Sustainable Energy Rev.*, vol. 16, no. 9, pp. 6497–6506, 2012, doi: 10.1016/j.rser.2012.08.002.

[2] Burmester, D., R. Rayudu, W. Seah, and D. Akinyele, "A review of nanogrid topologies and technologies," *Renewable Sustainable Energy Rev.*, vol. 67, pp. 760–775, 2017, doi: 10.1016/j.rser.2016.09.073.

[3] Akinyele, D., "Techno-economic design and performance analysis of nanogrid systems for households in energy-poor villages," *Sustainable Cities Soc.*, vol. 34, pp. 335–357, 2017, doi: 10.1016/j.scs.2017.07.004.

[4] Burgess, P., M. Shahidehpour, M. Ganji, and D. Connors, "Remote power units for off-grid lighting and urban resilience," *Electr. J.*, vol. 30, no. 4, pp. 16–26, 2017, doi: 10.1016/j.tej.2017.03.012.

[5] Lupangu, C. and R. C. Bansal, "Retraction Notice to a review of technical issues on the development of solar photovoltaic systems," *Renewable Sustainable Energy Rev.*, vol. 73, 2017; *Renewable Sustainable Energy Rev.*, vol. 94, p. 1234, 2018, doi: 10.1016/j.rser.2018.08.016.

[6] Stigka, E. K., J. A. Paravantis, and G. K. Mihalakakou, "Social acceptance of renewable energy sources : A review of contingent valuation applications," *Renewable Sustainable Energy Rev.*, vol. 32, pp. 100–106, 2014, doi: 10.1016/j.rser.2013.12.026.

[7] Javaid, S., Y. Kurose, T. Kato, and T. Matsuyama, "Cooperative distributed control implementation of the power flow coloring over a nano-grid with fluctuating power loads," *IEEE Trans. Smart Grid*, vol. 8, no. 1, pp. 342–352, 2017, doi: 10.1109/TSG.2015.2509002.

[8] Lucía, Ó., I. Cvetkovic, H. Sarnago, D. Boroyevich, P. Mattavelli, and F. C. Lee, "Design of home appliances for a DC-based nanogrid system: an induction range study case," *IEEE J. Emerging Sel. Top. Power Electron.*, vol. 1, no. 4, pp. 315–326, 2013, doi: 10.1109/JESTPE.2013.2283224.

[9] Novoa, L. and J. Brouwer, "Dynamics of an integrated solar photovoltaic and battery storage nanogrid for electric vehicle charging," *J. Power Sources*, vol. 399, no. March, pp. 166–178, 2018, doi: 10.1016/j.jpowsour.2018.07.092.

[10] Werth, A., N. Kitamura, and K. Tanaka, "Conceptual study for open energy systems: distributed energy network using interconnected DC nanogrids," *IEEE Trans. Smart Grid*, vol. 6, no. 4, pp. 1621–1630, 2015, doi: 10.1109/TSG.2015.2408603.

[11] Schönberger, J., R. Duke, and S. D. Round, "DC-bus signaling: a distributed control strategy for a hybrid renewable nanogrid," *IEEE Trans. Ind. Electron.*, vol. 53, no. 5, pp. 1453–1460, 2006, doi: 10.1109/TIE.2006.882012.

[12] Wu, X., X. Hu, Y. Teng, S. Qian, and R. Cheng, "Optimal integration of a hybrid solar-battery power source into smart home nanogrid with plug-in electric vehicle," *J. Power Sources*, vol. 363, pp. 277–283, 2017, doi: 10.1016/j.jpowsour.2017.07.086.

[13] González-Romera, E., *et al.*, "Demand and storage management in a prosumer nanogrid based on energy forecasting," *Electronics*, vol. 9, no. 2, 2020, doi: 10.3390/electronics9020363.

[14] Ortiz, L., R. Orizondo, A. Aguila, J. W. Gonz, I. Isaac, and J. L. Gabriel, "Heliyon hybrid AC/DC microgrid test system simulation: grid-connected mode," vol. 5, no. September, 2019, doi: 10.1016/j.heliyon.2019.e02862.

[15] Tremblay, O. and L. A. Dessaint, "Experimental validation of a battery dynamic model for EV applications," *24th Int. Batter. Hybrid Fuel Cell Electr. Veh. Symp. Exhib. 2009, EVS 24*, vol. 2, pp. 930–939, 2009.

[16] Malla, S. G. and C. N. Bhende, "Electrical power and energy systems voltage control of stand-alone wind and solar energy system," *Int. J. Electr. Power Energy Syst.*, vol. 56, pp. 361–373, 2014, doi: 10.1016/j.ijepes.2013.11.030.
[17] Malla, S. G., C. N. Bhende, and S. Mishra, "Photovoltaic based water pumping system," pp. 1–4, 2011.
[18] Salman, S., X. Ai, and Z. Wu, "Design of a P-&-O algorithm based MPPT charge controller for a stand-alone 200W PV system," *Prot. Control Mod. Power Syst.*, vol. 3, no. 1, 2018, doi: 10.1186/s41601-018-0099-8.

47. 14T SRAM Bit Cell with Speed and Power Optimized Using CNTFET

Vipin Kumar Sharma and Abhishek Kumar

Lovely Professional University, School of Electronics and Electrical Engineering, India

Abstract: This article offers a revolutionary design for a 14T SRAM bit cell that makes use of carbon nanotube field-effect transistors (CNTFETs) in order to strike a compromise between speed and power consumption. The design that has been presented makes use of the one-of-a-kind characteristics of CNTFETs in order to boost the performance of the static random-access memory (SRAM) bit cell while simultaneously reducing the amount of energy that is used. A new design for 14T SRAM bit cells is shown, and it makes use of CNTFETs for both the access and storage transistors. The functioning of the cell is investigated in depth, and the benefits of using CNTFETs are highlighted. These benefits include a decrease in leakage currents, an improvement in the on/off switching ratios and an increase in the overall efficiency of the circuit. When compared to traditional CMOS-based SRAM designs, the findings of the simulation show a considerable increase in speed while also reducing power consumption. The design of a 14T SRAM bit cell that has been discussed here highlights the potential of CNTFETs in the realisation of sophisticated memory systems that solve the difficulties of speed and power consumption in modern electronic devices.

Keywords: High speed, low power, radiation-hardened SRAM, SRAM Cell, CNTFET, CMOS, delay.

1. Introduction

Memory cells are an essential component in a wide variety of applications, ranging from embedded systems to high-performance computers and the continuous development of semiconductor technology has been a significant factor in the formation of the present landscape of electronics. This digital age is built on a foundation of static random-access memory, often known as SRAM. SRAM allows for quick read and write operations while also using very little power when in sleep mode. However, the never-ending search for greater performance and energy efficiency has compelled researchers to investigate new transistor technologies that go beyond the conventional complementary metal–oxide semiconductor (CMOS) devices. These new technologies include field-effect transistors and complementary metal–oxide semiconductor field-effect transistors. In this setting, carbon nanotube field-effect transistors, also known as CNTFETs, have attracted a lot of interest owing to the outstanding electrical features they possess, such as high carrier mobility, resistance to short-channel effects and decreased leakage currents [1, 2].

Data is commonly stored in cross-coupled inverters inside an SRAM bit cell, and these inverters are accessed via pass-gate transistors [3]. This is the core architecture for an SRAM bit cell. In spite of this, scaling traditional CMOS technology to smaller feature sizes in order to achieve better integration levels and performance has been met with serious difficulties, including increasing leakage currents and power consumption. In order to overcome these obstacles, other unorthodox transistor topologies, such as CNTFETs, have been suggested as potentially useful alternatives. Because of their one-of-a-kind properties, CNTFETs have the potential to achieve more favorable trade-offs in SRAM bit cells between speed and power consumption.

In recent years, researchers have been investigating CNTFET-based SRAM designs in order to take use of the better characteristics of CNTs and their potential to ease the restrictions provided by CMOS technology. This has been done in order to harness the superior features of CNTs. When CNTFETs are used in conjunction with SRAM cells, there is the potential for increased on/off switching ratios as well as lower off-state leakage currents. This would result in an overall improvement in the energy efficiency of memory systems. This article focuses on a unique design for a 14T SRAM bit cell that includes CNTFETs and utilises them as access and store transistors. The purpose of this design is to maximise both the speed and the amount of power that is used by the device. The performance of the suggested design is simulated with the help of HSPICE so that improvements may be made as necessary.

2. Implementation

The work that is being proposed is centered on the development of a unique design for a 14T SRAM bit cell that makes use of CNTFETs to maximise speed as well as power consumption. In order to improve the performance and energy efficiency of the SRAM cell in comparison to designs based on standard CMOS technology, the goal is to make use of the special characteristics of CNTFETs as much as possible. Figure 1 provides a visual representation of the design of the 14T SRAM bit cell.

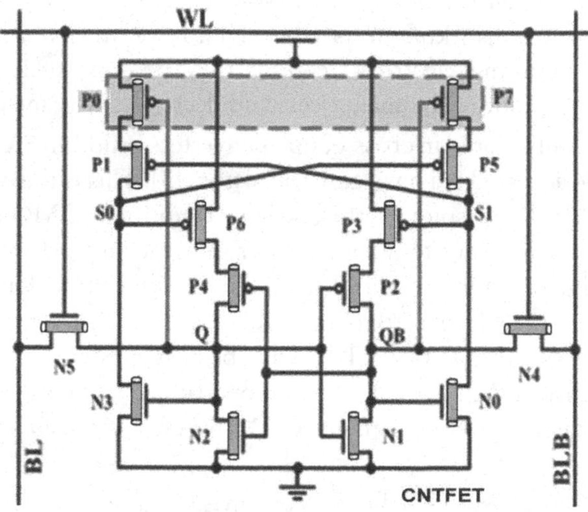

Figure 1: Proposed circuit diagram of 14T SRAM bit cell using CNTFET.

When compared to the more common 6T cell, the 14T SRAM bit cell is made up of more transistors than the traditional cell, which results in increased stability and less leakage currents. The use of CNTFETs both as access transistors and as storage transistors opens the door to the possibility of increased on/off switching ratios, which have an immediate and direct influence on read and write operations. The inclusion of CNTFETs in this design is designed to alleviate concerns related with gate leakage and sub-threshold leakage, which are major obstacles experienced in CMOS-based SRAM cells. Conventional metal–oxide SRAM cells.

For the purpose of modelling and evaluating the performance of the 14T CNTFET-based SRAM bit cell, the suggested implementation makes use of the HSPICE program, which is a tool for circuit simulation that is extensively used. HSPICE makes it possible to create an exact depiction of the transistor properties, as well as the interactions between circuits and the overall behavior of the design. The performance metrics that are of interest will be evaluated using a series of simulations. These metrics include read and write access times, static power consumption, leakage currents and overall energy efficiency.

In order to conduct an in-depth investigation of the performance of the 14T SRAM cell in a variety of different operating settings, the simulation setup calls for the input circumstances, such as supply voltage and data patterns, to be changed in a number of different ways. We will also look at the effect that the characteristics of CNTFETs have on the overall performance. Some of these characteristics include carrier mobility and threshold voltage. Through the application of methodical analysis to these criteria, one may get a full grasp of the benefits and drawbacks of the design that has been offered.

When compared to traditional CMOS-based SRAM cells, the performance of the 14T CNTFET-based SRAM cell is shown to be much superior to that of conventional CMOS-based SRAM cells in the findings that will be given and discussed. The optimisation of speed, the reduction of power consumption and the improvement of energy efficiency are going to get a lot of focus, since they are three of the most important factors in modern electronic devices. The results of these simulations will give vital insights into the feasibility and potential of CNTFET-based SRAM cell designs in tackling the issues presented by speed and power consumption in advanced memory systems. These challenges were simulated using the CNTFET-based SRAM cell architecture.

3. Result

The results of the simulations that were run on the proposed 14T CNTFET-based SRAM bit cell design have been examined, and the findings are explained below, along with the relevant figures and a table that compares the results of the various simulations.

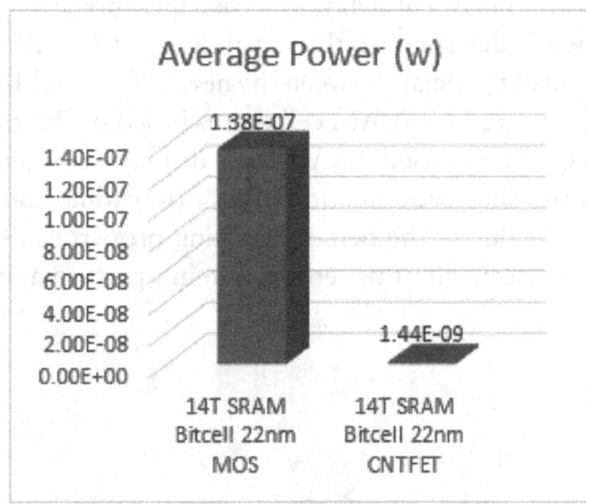

Figure 2: *Average power comparison.*

Figure 2 shows the comparison of average power (Figure 2). The average power consumption is an important statistic to use when determining the level of energy efficiency offered by the various SRAM cell types. Figure 2 is a graphical illustration of the comparison between the average power consumption of the traditional 14T MOS-based SRAM cell and the proposed 14T CNTFET-based SRAM cell that is based on 22 nm technology. The graph shows quite clearly that the 14T CNTFET-based SRAM cell beats its MOS equivalent by a wide margin, consistently demonstrating substantially lower average power consumption. This is shown by the fact that the graph is a bar graph. This large decrease in average power is a direct result of the beneficial features of CNTFETs, which attenuate leakage currents and promote switching efficiency. This improvement in switching efficiency has also contributed to this reduction in leakage currents.

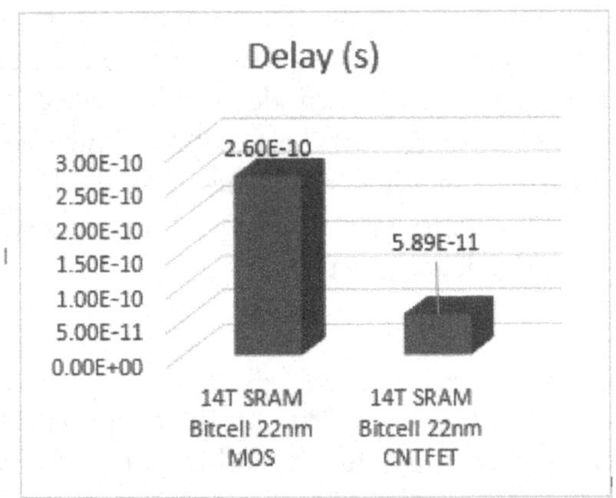

Figure 3: Delay comparison.

Figure 3 analyses the delay. The delay, which is a measure of the speed of operation, is very important when determining the capabilities of the SRAM cells. Figure 3 presents a comparison of the delay between the newly proposed 14T CNTFET-based SRAM cell and the existing 14T SRAM cell that is based on 22nm MOS technology. Notably, the 14T CNTFET-based SRAM cell displays a significantly decreased latency, which indicates shorter access times for both reading and writing data. This increased speed may be due to the better switching properties of CNTFETs, which contributes to the enhancement of the entire system's performance.

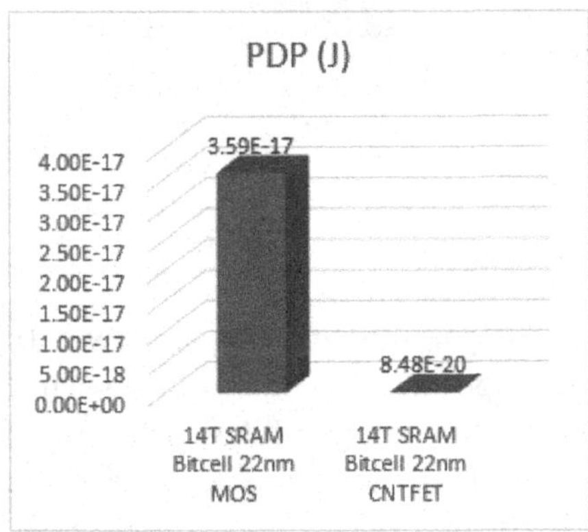

Figure 4: Power delay product.

Figure 4 shows the comparison of the power-delay product (PDP).

A full analysis of the energy-performance trade-off may be obtained via the use of the PDP, which combines power consumption and delay. The PDP comparison of the two different SRAM cell designs is shown in Figure 4. It is abundantly obvious that the 14T CNTFET-based SRAM cell has a much lower PDP, which indicates a positive balance between power efficiency and performance speed.

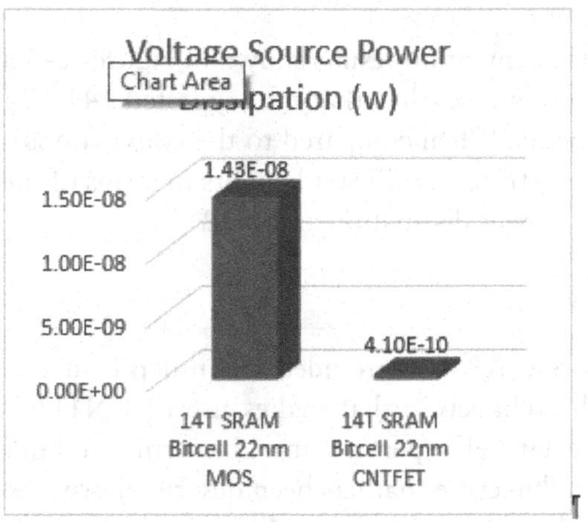

Figure 5: *Voltage source power dissipation.*

Figure 5 shows the comparison of voltage source power dissipation (SRAM cell designs). Figure 5 displays a comparison of the two SRAM cell designs with regard to the voltage source power dissipation. The voltage source's power dissipation is a direct reflection of the amount of energy that the cells use while they are operating. When compared to the MOS-based SRAM cell, the 14T CNTFET-based SRAM cell was shown to have a much lower power dissipation level. This is yet another example of the 14T CNTFET-based SRAM cell's superiority. This research demonstrates that CNTFETs are capable of reducing power losses and improving energy efficiency to a greater extent than before.

Table 1: Comparison of results.

Parameters	14T SRAM Bitcell 22nm MOS	14T SRAM Bitcell 22nm CNTFET
Average Power (w)	1.38E-07	1.44E-09
Delay (s)	2.60E-10	5.89E-11
PDP (J)	3.59E-17	8.48E-20
Voltage Source Power Dissipation (w)	1.43E-08	4.10E-10

The following table presents a summary comparison of important performance parameters for 14T SRAM bit cell designs based on 22nm MOS technology and CNTFETs. In terms of average power, latency, PDP and voltage source power dissipation, the traditional MOS-based architecture is consistently outperformed by the suggested 14T CNTFET-based SRAM cell. These results highlight the potential advantages that may be achieved by integrating CNTFETs in SRAM cell layouts to yield significant reductions in power consumption and improvements in performance.

In conclusion, the simulation results shown in Figures 2–5 and the full statistics supplied in Table 1 reveal, together, that the suggested 14T CNTFET-based SRAM cell architecture is better. When compared to the conventional MOS-based SRAM cell, this design demonstrates significant benefits in terms of the average amount of power used, latency, power dissipation and PDP.

4. Conclusion

In conclusion, this research has provided an in-depth investigation of a unique 14T SRAM bit cell architecture that makes use of CNTFETs, which allows for optimisation of the bit cell's performance in terms of both speed and power consumption. The architecture that has been described provides a viable answer to the issues presented by current electronic devices, which need memory subsystems to have great performance while using as little power as possible. The results of the simulation that were achieved by utilising the HSPICE program have offered useful insights into the efficiency of the design.

References

[1] Peng, C., *et al.*, "Radiation-hardened 14T SRAM bitcell with speed and power optimized for space application," *IEEE Trans. Very Large-Scale Integr. VLSI Syst.*, vol. 27, no. 2, pp. 407–415, 2019, doi: 10.1109/TVLSI.2018.2879341.

[2] Han, Y., X. Cheng, J. Han, and X. Zeng, "Radiation-hardened 0.3–0.9-V voltage-scalable 14T SRAM and peripheral circuit in 28-nm technology for space applications," *IEEE Trans. Very Large Scale Integr. VLSI Syst.*, vol. 28, no. 4, pp. 1089–1093, 2020, doi: 10.1109/TVLSI.2019.2961736.

[3] Dou, Z., *et al.*, "Design of a highly reliable SRAM cell with advanced self-recoverability from soft errors," *2020 IEEE International Test Conference in Asia (ITC-Asia)*, Taipei, Taiwan, pp. 35–40, 2020, doi: 10.1109/ITC-Asia51099.2020.00018.

[4] Prasad, G., B. C. Mandi, and M. Jain, "Design and analysis of area and power optimised SRAM cell for high-speed processor," *2020 First International Conference on Power, Control and Computing Technologies (ICPC2T)*, Raipur, India, pp. 363–367, 2020, doi: 10.1109/ICPC2T48082.2020.9071489.

[5] Mishra, J. K., P. K. Misra, and M. Goswami, "Design of SRAM cell using voltage lowering and stacking techniques for low power applications," *2020 IEEE Asia Pacific Conference on Circuits and Systems (APCCAS)*, Ha Long, Vietnam, pp. 50–53, 2020, doi: 10.1109/APCCAS50809.2020.9301672.

[6] MuraliMohanBabu, Y., S. Mishra, and K. Radhika, "Design implementation and analysis of different SRAM cell topologies," *2021 International Conference on Emerging Smart Computing and Informatics (ESCI)*, Pune, India, pp. 678–682, 2021, doi: 10.1109/ESCI50559.2021.9396938.

48. Cost Correlation for High Head Small Hydropower Projects

Kalyani R.,[1],[2] Sachin Mishra,[2] and Javed Dhillon[2]

[1]*Dept of Electrical Engineering, Mahavir Engineering College, Hyderabad*
[2]*School of Electronics and Electrical Engineering, Lovely Professional University, Punjab*

Abstract: Small hydropower (SHP) is a clean and sustainable source of energy that can be used to electrify rural areas in developing countries. In this paper, the authors develop a method to predict the cost of installing high-head SHP projects. They validate their method using data from recently developed SHP projects and find that it can be used to accurately predict the cost of future projects.

Keywords: Small hydropower, civil works, electro-mechanical equipment, cost.

1. Introduction

The world today relies heavily on conventional energy sources, such as fossil fuels, to generate electricity. The rise in oil prices in the 1970s led people to explore alternative energy sources, such as solar, wind, geothermal, biomass and small hydropower. Small hydropower is a renewable, non-polluting and environmentally friendly energy source. It is one of the oldest renewable energy technologies known to humankind, and it is used to generate electricity and mechanical energy. Hydropower is a reliable and cost-effective source of electricity, and it accounts for about 22% of the world's electricity supply. In many countries, it is the main source of power generation [1].

Despite the advantages of hydropower, its share in India has been declining since 1963. One reason for this decline is the high cost of installing hydropower projects. In this paper, the authors develop a method to estimate the installation cost of high-head SHP projects with different turbines. They validate their method using data from recently developed SHP projects [2, 3].

2. Small Hydropower Projects

There is a general tendency all over the world to define small hydropower by the power output. Different countries follow different norms, the upper limit ranges between 5 and 50 MW, as given in the Table 1 [1, 2]

Table 1: Worldwide definitions of SHP [4].

Country	Capacity (MW)
UK	≤ 5
UNIDO	≤ 10
Sweden	≤ 15
Colombia	≤ 20
Australia	≤ 20
India	**≤ 25**
China	≤ 25
Philippines	≤ 50
New Zealand	≤ 50

In India, hydropower project up to 25 MW station capacity is categorised as SHP. SHPs are further classified on the basis of capacity as presented in Table 2.

Table 2: Classification of SHPs on the basis of capacity.

Class	Station Capacity
Pico hydro	5 kW & below
Micro hydro	Above 5 kW & below 100 kW
Mini hydro	Above 100 kW & below 2 MW
Small hydro	Above 2 MW & below 25 MW

In India, the potential of SHPs is estimated at about 21,133 MW. Out of this, total installed capacity of SHPs is 4,944 MW from 801 projects and 271 projects with aggregate capacity of 914.81 MW are under construction [4]. Thus vast potential remain untapped need to be developed.

3. Methodology

The cost estimation process starts with the collection of data required for this purpose, which involves various components of civil works and electromechanical equipment of different projects, executed recently. The cost components are then adjusted considering inflation rates over the years since cost data pertain to different years. This dataset is then screened to detect outliners which have unreasonable installation cost. The parameters on which the installation cost depends are identified. The methodology developed by the authors [5] has been used to develop the installation cost correlation. The cost-sensitive parameter used to develop the correlation is capacity, head and runner diameter of the turbine and is given by Eq. (1) [7, 8].

Installation cost, $C = f(P, H, d)$ (1)

The expression of the initial cost of installation of high head SHP project for different types of turbines is given by Eq. (2).

$$C = w\ P\ x\ H\ y\ d\ z \quad (2)$$

where, w, x, y and z are the constants.

The value of the constants w, x, y and z shown in Eq. (2) for different types of turbines for the determination of installation cost for high head SHP project is shown in Table 3.

Table 3: Values of constants for installation cost.

Table 3. Values of constants for installation cost

S.No.	Type of turbine	*w*	*x*	*y*	*z*
1.	Francis	1003395.193	-0.1636	0.1529	-0.4334
2.	Turgo Impulse	67151.06085	-0.1049	0.3978	-0.2470
3.	Pelton	74124.3969	-0.1072	0.3781	-0.2453

4. Results and Discussions

The cost data from different existing sites were collected and adjusted by considering inflation over the years. These cost data were used to develop the correlations by regression analysis. The results obtained from these correlations were verified from the cost data of the newly developed SHP projects. Figures 1–3 show the error analysis between the actual cost and the analysed installation cost of small hydropower plant using the correlation obtained from the sigma plot software. Table 4 lists the results obtained, including cost equations per power unit, their R2 related and error range, for each type of machine.

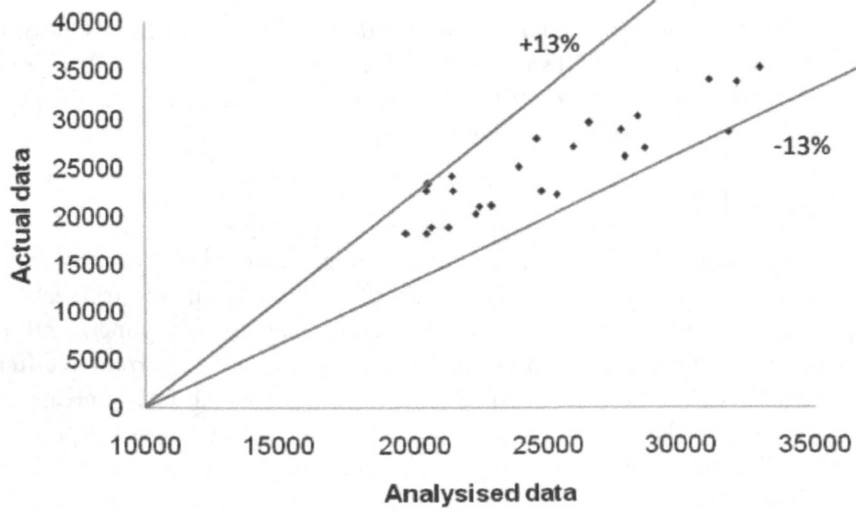

Figure 1: *Error analysis for installation cost of high head SHP project with Francis turbine.*

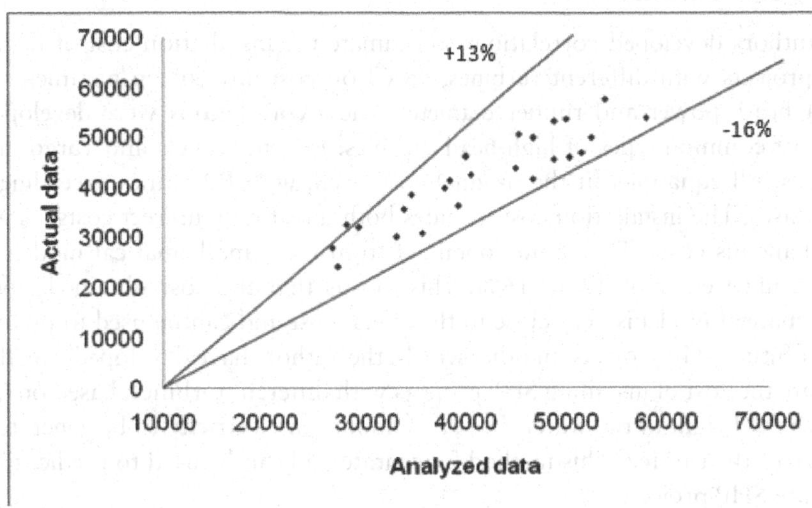

Figure 2: Error analysis for installation cost of high head SHP project with Turgo impulse turbine.

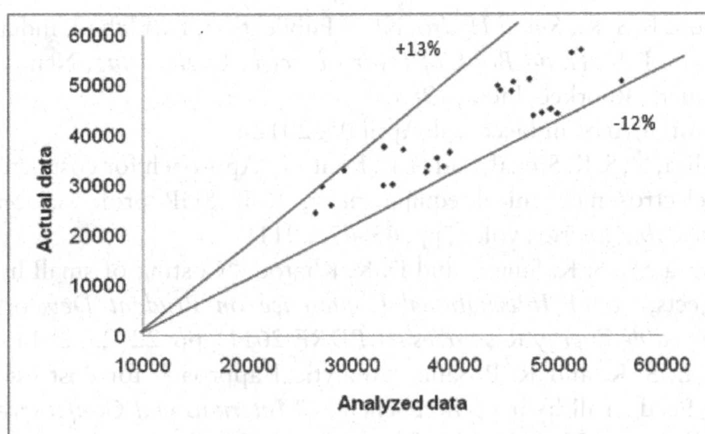

Figure 3: Error analysis for installation cost of high head SHP project with Pelton turbine.

Table 4: Summary error range and R2.

S.No.	Type of turbine	Error range	R^2 (%)
1.	Francis	-13% to +13%	89.6
2.	Turgo Impulse	-16% to +13%	91.3
3.	Pelton	-12% to +13%	87.8

5. Conclusions

The authors developed correlations to estimate the installation cost of high-head SHP projects with different turbines, based on cost-influencing parameters such as net head, power and runner diameter. These correlations were developed for the most common types of high-head turbines: Pelton, Francis and Turgo impulse turbines. All equations fit the original costs well, with R2 values exceeding 75% in all cases. The installation cost includes both direct and indirect costs, as well as miscellaneous costs. The results obtained from these mathematical models show a percentage error of 12 to 16%. This means that the cost obtained from the mathematical model is very close to the actual cost and can be used to predict the cost of future SHP projects. In other words, the authors have developed a method to estimate the cost of installing SHP projects with different turbines, based on factors such as the height of the water drop, the amount of electricity to be generated and the size of the turbine. This method is accurate and can be used to predict the cost of future SHP projects.

References

[1] *Guidelines for Development of Small Hydro Electric Scheme*, CEA, Govt. of India, 1982.

[2] Naidu, B. S. K., *Small Hydro*, NPTI Publication, Faridabad, India, 2005.

[3] Nigam, P. S., *Hand Book of Hydro Electric Engineering*, Nem Chand and Brothers, Roorkee, India, 1985.

[4] www.mnre.gov.in (accessed: April 05, 2012).

[5] Mishra, S., S. K. Singal, and D. K. Khatod, "Approach for cost determination of electro- mechanical equipment in RoR SHP projects," *Smart Grid Renewable Energy*, vol. 2, pp. 63–67, 2011.

[6] Mishra , S., S. K. Singal, and D. K. Khatod, "Costing of small hydropower projects," *2011 International Conference on Prudent Development and Renewable Energy Resources (ICPDRE 2011)*, pp. 22–25, 2011.

[7] Singal, S. K. and R. P. Saini, "Analytical approach for cost estimation of low head small hydro power schemes," *International Conference on Small Hydropower*, Hydro Sri Lanka, pp. 1–6, 2007.

[8] Ogayar, B. and P. G. Vidal, "Cost determination of the electro-mechanical equipment of a small hydro-power plant," *J. Renewable Energy*, vol. 34, pp. 6–13, 2009.

49. Ab-Initio Analysis of Al-Doped Electrode Magnetic Tunnel Junction for MRAM

Manoj Kumar Yadav, Pawandeep Kaur, Hardeep Kaur, Jhulan Kumar, Jaskaran Singh Phull, and Ritesh Pawar

School of Electrical and Electronic Engineering, Lovely Professional University, Phagwara, Panjab, India

Abstract: The first principle analysis of aluminum-doped free layer electrode made of ferromagnetic material (Fe) of magnetic tunnel junction (MTJ) is presented. It is reported that Al increases s-like character density of states in the electrode. Spin polarized tunneling current through barrier region increases due to passing of very increased s-like symmetry of Bloch sates through insulting barrier of MTJ. Consequently, which lead to improvement in tunneling magneto resistance ratio of MTJ. It result in the improvement in switching speed of MTJ increases which make faster to writing data in M-RAM.

Keywords: Magnetic tunnel junction, tunneling magneto resistance, spin transfer torque, magnetic random access memory.

1. Introduction

Magnetic tunnel junction (MTJ) made of two ferromagnetic electrodes, and there is very thin film of insulating material between electrodes which working as barrier. In recent years, exhaustive investigations have been done in MTJ for its tunnel magneto resistance (TMR). One of the most important property of MJT is TMR, which is used to which depends upon resistance in anti-parallel magnetization configuration (APC) and parallel magnetization configuration (PC) of electrodes with respect to each other. Initially, it had been reported that spin current through barrier rely on magnetic properties of ferromagnetic electrodes of MTJ[1–3] but, first principle analysis shows that TMR also depends on electrode/barrier interface, in parallel with electronic structure of the insulator barrier and electrode [4]. This raised commercial interest to develop the spin-electronics devices such as logic circuits, magnetic sensors and M-RAMs [5–7].

Many groups have reported different configuration of MTJ for enhancing TMR, spin transfer torque (STT) and reducing resistance area (RA) product in MTJ [8–11]. A group has revealed that doping of conducting metal in the barrier region reduces RA product of MTJ. But, doping greater than 3% in barrier region considerably decreases TMR because of induced diffusion scattering [8]. Because of this restraint, several group have been proposing other techniques such as quantum well effects, which is observed by inserting very-thin film of conducting metal in barrier [12]. In the present work, the proposed configuration of MTJs is shown in Figure 1 in which free layer of electrode of MTJ has been doped by Al and barrier region is made of MgO sandwiched between pure Fe and doped Fe. Figure 1 shows device structure of MTJ

2. Methodology

Figure 1: Device structure of MTJ.

Atomistic Tool Kit (ATK) package is used to study the quantum conduction of electrons in MTJ Systems. ATK is established on the Green's Non-equilibrium Function (NEGF) [13–17] conducting theory. Exchange and correlation functionalism of spin generalized gradient approximation (SGGA) coupled with Perdew–Burke–Ernzerhof (PBE) has been used for calculations [18]. MTJ's entire bulk geometry has been designed to relax the structure till the force on each atom becomes less than 0.05 eV/Å, as needed for calculating the electronic structures. It is found that bond distances between, Al-MgO, Fe-MgO and MgO-Al are 1.73, 1.78 and 2.74 Å, respectively, after relaxation of device geometry.

For maintaining high accuracy in calculating of electronic structure of device, localised atomic basis sets (numerical) for Al, Fe, Mg and O atoms have been kept at double zeta polarised. 107×107×157 k-point meshes have been used for Brillouin zone sampling of MTJ lattice points and self-consistency, and 200×200 k-point mesh sampling has been taken for simulating the spin polarised tunneling currents (PC and APC) [19].

3. Result Analysis

Current voltage (IV) characteristic of the device with bias voltage in PC and APC of electrode with each other has been shown in Figures 2 and 3. Variation of tunneling magneto resistance (TMR) with respect to voltage is shown in Figure 4. It has been obtained using relation: $TMR(\%) = [R_{APC} / R_{PC} - 1] \times 100$, where R_{PC} and R_{APC} denote resistance in PC and APC of device, respectively. Difference in value of current in PC and APC of MTJ and TMR can be interpret by examine electronic structure of material of device and tunneling conductance of symmetry resolved Bloch wave present in electode. A remarkable work done by J. M. MacLaren *et al.* [13] for calculating the electronic structure and tunneling of spin current in nanostructure device by utilising the Green's function technique of Layer Korringa Kohn Rostoker (LKKR).

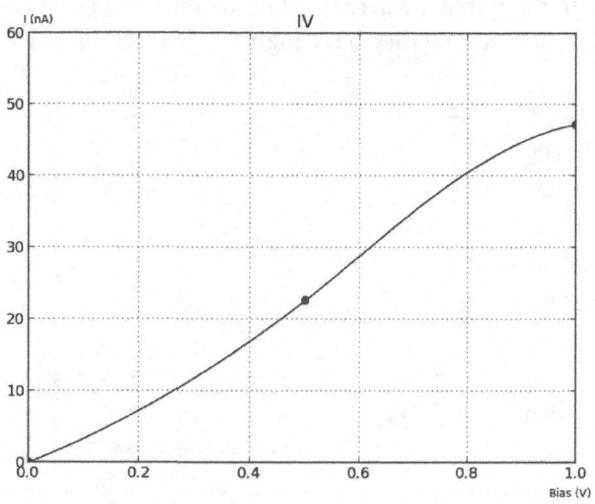

Figure 2: *IV curve of PC of MTJ.*

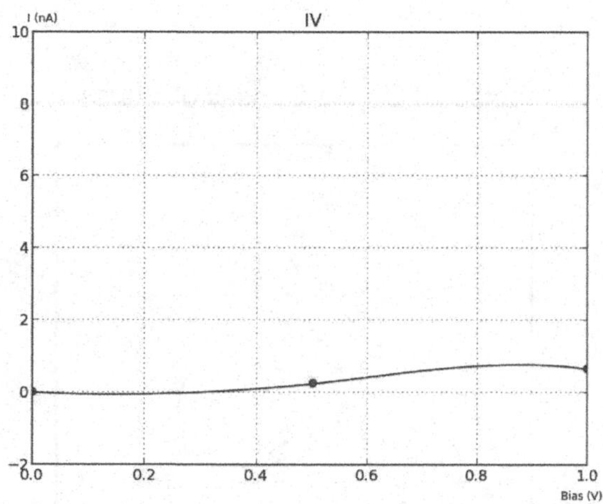

Figure 3: *IV curve of APC of MTJ.*

Many group reported using first principle analysis that Δ_1 symmetry of Bloch states (comprised principally s-like character) presents at Fermi energy (E_F) is accountable for flowing of spin current in PC of MTJ [4,13]. Whereas, Δ_2, $\Delta_{2'}$ and Δ_5 symmetries comprising mainly p and d-like characters are accountable for flowing of spin current in APC of MTJ. When these symmetries pass through barrier region it observe different level of quantum interference with nature of states (s, p, d) in barrier which control their transmission rate through barrier [4,13]. 's'-like character band (Δ_1 Bloch states symmetry at E_F) pair more easily with complex band symmetries of MgO (barrier) and observed very less interference hence gradually decay in the barrier, whereas other symmetry having (d-like characters) observed more interference, so they have high decay rate. [4,13].

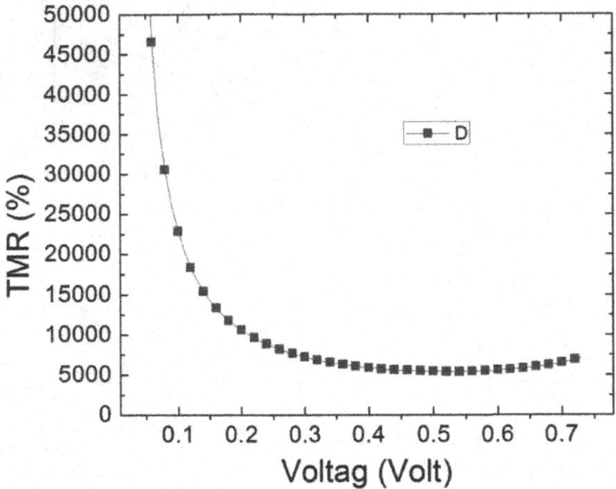

Figure 4: *TMR of MTJ.*

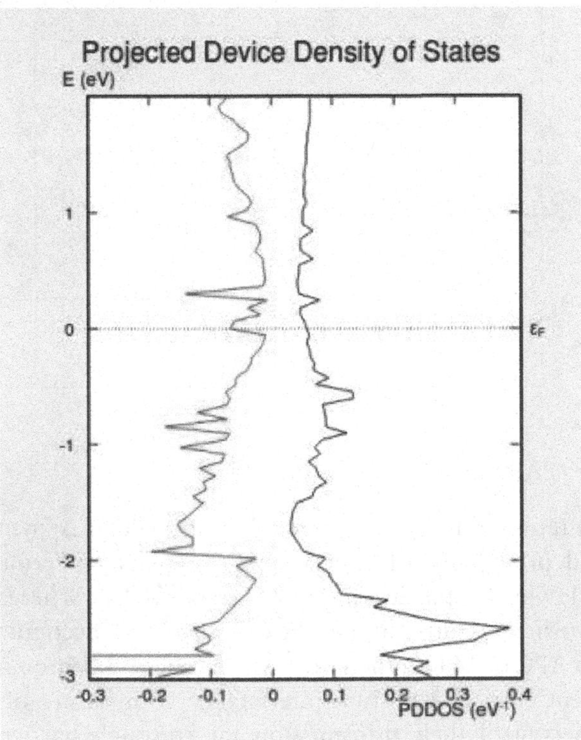

Figure 5: *Al-doped left electrode of MTJ PDDOS (red – up spin and black – down spin).*

Doping of Al in left electrode of MTJ increases density of states (DOS) of s-like character as compared to without doped right electrode, as shown in Figures 5 and 6. Red and black colours represent ↑ (up) and ↓ (down) spin polarised density of states. From Figures 5 and 6, it is observed that peak of projected device DOS (PDDOS) at E_F is higher for doped left electrode as compared to without doped right electrode. Increased s-like character in left electrode raises spin tunneling current in PC of MTJ by 2-3 times as reported by [20, 21] and shown in Figure 2. This raised magnitude of spin current in PC enhances TMR of MTJ and is also beneficial in STT-based MRAM. This increase of spin current in PC can also be explained using tunneling probability in Brillouin zone in following section.

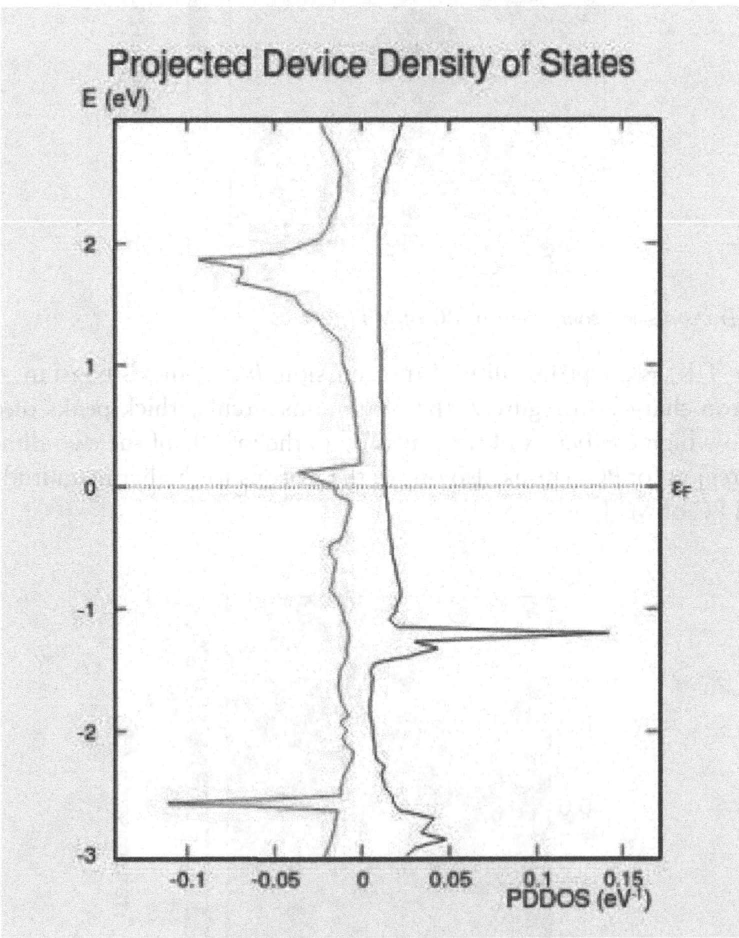

Figure 6: Undoped right electrode of MTJ PDDOS (red – up spin, and black – down spin).

Spin polarised tunneling conduction of MTJ in PC at zero bias, through MgO barrier with respect to $k_{||}$ and resolved along k_x and k_y Brillouin zone coordinates which has been shown in Figure 7. The relationship between tunneling conductance for spin polarized current at E_F and transmission probability is given by Lansauer–Buttiker [16–17] as follows:

$$G = \frac{e^2}{h}\sum_{K_{\parallel}} T(K_{\parallel})$$

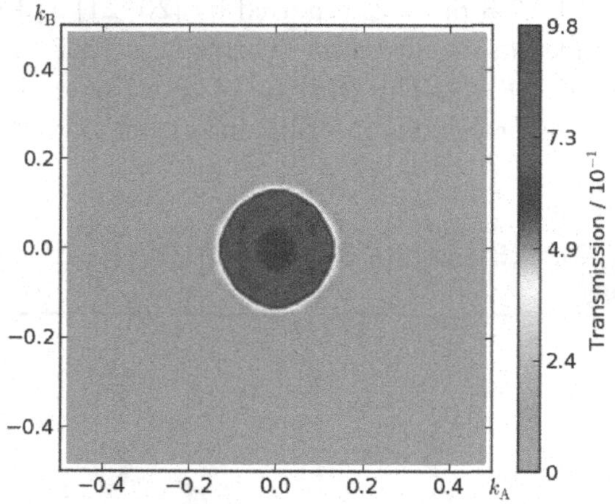

Figure 7: Transmission coefficient in PC of MTJ.

where T(K) is the probability of transmission, *h* is Planck's constant and *e* is unit electron charge. In Figure 7, the continuous circular thick peaks of different colors, show high coefficient of transmission in the middle of the two-dimensional Brillouin region for PC. This is also one of the reasons for higher magnitude of spin current in PC of MTJ.

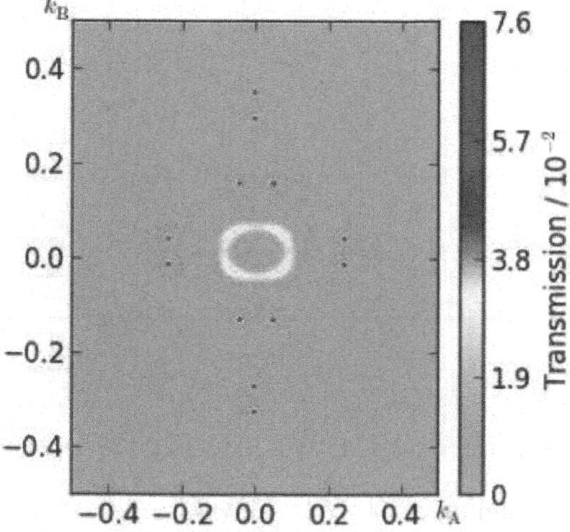

Figure 8: Transmission coefficient in APC of MTJ.

In Figure 8, several distinct spikes at several positions are observe in the two-dimensional Brillouin zone of transmission coefficient of spin current in APC of electrode. These spikes are found due to occurrence of hot spot at interface of Fe/MgO because of interfacial resonant states (IRS) [22,23]. This is main reason for flowing of current in APC, as shown in Figure 3.

In Figure 3, MTJ passes very less current in APC for less than 0.4 volt. This is also found that the tunneling current rises for 0.4–0.8 volt and become uniform for 0.8–1 volt bias voltage. Curve patterns for APC, shown in Figure 3, are essentially the same as for Derek Waldron *et al.* [21]. The low value of spin current in APC in respect of PC is due to less tunneling of electron and incompatibility of the same symmetry of Bloch states present in band structure of ferromagnetic materials of electrodes of MTJ [4]. APC current promptly surges 0.4–0.8 volt bias voltage. Sharp increase of current in APC is because of occurrence inelastic scattering by confined Fe/MgO interface with magnon excitation which is liable for lowering of TMR ratio at greater voltage and it is confirm from Figure 4 [22-26].

4. Conclusion

Al-doped electrode MTJ transmits higher spin polarised tunneling current because of increase of s-like character density of states (i.e. electron). RA product of MTJ is very low therefore it will generate lesser heat on applying deriving current for current-induced magnetization switching by STT phenomenon. Devices show TMR ratio to be 5,000 for voltage range 0.5 to 1 volt which is for enough for reliable sensing. Al-doped electrode MTJ shows a very encouraging result which could be capable contender for designing MRAMs cell.

Acknowledgement: The author is thankful to Dr. Santosh Kumar Gupta, ECE department MNNIT Allahabad for their kind support. The author also acknowledges VLSI lab, ECE department MNNIT Allahabad for using the facility.

References

[1] Miyazaki, T. and N. Tezuka, "Giant magnetic tunneling effect in Fe/AlzO3/Fejunction," J. Magn. Magn. Mater., vol. 139, pp. L231–L234, 1995.

[2] Moodera, J. S., L. R. Kinder, T. M. Wong, and R. Meservey, "Large magnetoresistance at room temperature in ferromagnetic thin film tunnel junctions," *Phys. Rev. Lett.*, vol. 74, p. 3273, 1995.

[3] Julliere, M., "Tunneling between ferromagnetic films," *Phys. Lett. A*, vol. 54, pp. 225–226, 1975.

[4] Butler, W. H., X.-G. Zhang, T. C. Schulthess, and J. M. MacLaren, "Spin-dependent tunneling conductance of Fe/MgO/Fe sandwiches," *Phys. Rev. B*, vol. 63, p. 054416-12, 2001.

[5] Yao, X., J. Harms, A. Lyle, F. Ebrahimi, Y. Zhang, and J.-P. Wang, "Magnetic tunnel junction-based spintronic logic units operated by spin transfer torque," *IEEE Trans. Nanotechnol.*, vol. 11, no. 1, pp. 120–127, 2012.

[6] Chen, E., D. Apalkov, Z. Diao, A. Driskill-Smith, D. Druist, D. Lottis, V. Nikitin, X. Tang, S. Watts, S. Wang, S. A. Wolf, A. W. Ghosh, J.W. Lu, S. J. Poon, M. Stan, W. H. Butler, S. Gupta,C. K. A. Mewes, Tim Mewes, and P. B. Visscher, "Advances and future prospects of spin-transfer torque random access memory," *IEEE Trans. Magn.*, vol. 46, no. 6, pp. 1873–1878, 2010.

[7] Chavesa, R. C., P. P. Freitas, B. Ocker, and W. Maass, "Low frequency Pico Tesla field detection using hybrid MgO based tunnel sensors," *Appl. Phys. Lett.*, vol. 91, p. 102504-3, 2007.

[8] Liu, D., X. Han, and H. Guo, "Junction resistance, tunnel magnetoresistance ratio, and spin-transfer torque in Zn-doped magnetic tunnel junctions," *Phys. Rev. B*, vol. 85, p. 245436, 2012.

[9] Slonczewski, J. C., "Current-driven excitation of magnetic multilayers," *J. Magn. Magn. Mater.*, vol. 159, pp. L1–L7, 1996.

[10] Berger, L., "Emission of spin waves by a magnetic multilayer traversed by a current," *Phys. Rev. B*, vol. 54, pp. 9353–9358, 1996.

[11] Tsoi, M., A. G. M. Jansen, J. Bass, W. C. Chiang, M. Seck, V. Tsoi, and P. Wyder, "Excitation of a magnetic multilayer by an electric current," *Phys. Rev. Lett.*, vol. 80, pp. 2181–2184, 1998.

[12] Yadav, M. K., S. K. Gupta, S. Rai, A. C. Pandey, "Al embedded MgO barrier MTJ: A first principle study for application in fast and compact STT-MRAMs," *Superlattices Microstruct.*, vol. 103, pp. 314–324, 2017.

[13] MacLaren, J. M., X.-G. Zhang, W. H. Butler, and X. Wang, "Layer KKR approach to Bloch-wave transmission and reflection: Application to spin-dependent tunnelling," *Phys. Rev. B*, vol. 59, pp. 5470–5478, 1999.

[14] Brandbyge, M., J.-L. Mozos, P. Ordejon, J. Taylor, and K. Stokbro, "Density-functional method for non-equilibrium electron transport," *Phys. Rev. B*, vol. 65, pp. 165401–165417, 2002.

[15] Taylor, J., H. Guo, and J. Wang, "Ab initio modeling of open systems: charge transfer, electron conduction, and molecular switching of a C60 device," *Phys. Rev. B*, vol. 63, p. 121104-4(R), 2001.

[16] Landauer, R., "Spatial variation of currents and fields due to localized scatterers in metallic conduction," *IBM J. Res. Dev.*, vol. 1, pp. 306–316, 195.

[17] Büttiker, M., "Four-terminal phase-coherent conductance," *Phys. Rev. Lett.*, vol. 57, pp. 1761–1764, 1986.

[18] Perdew, J. P., K. Burke, and M. Ernzerhof, "Generalized gradient approximation made simple," *Phys. Rev. Lett.*, vol. 77, pp. 3865–3868, 1996; *Erratum: Phys. Rev. Lett.*, vol. 78, p. 1396, 1997.

[19] Monkhorst, H. J. and J. D. Pack, "Special points for Brillouin-zone integrations," *Phys. Rev. B*, vol. 13, pp. 5188–5192, 1976.

[20] Klaua, M., D. Ullmann, J. Barthel, W. Wulfhekel, and J. Kirschner, "Growth, structure, electronic, and magnetic properties of MgO/Fe bilayers and Fe/MgO/Fe trilayers," *Phys. Rev. B*, vol. 64, p. 134411.

[21] Waldron, D., V. Timoshevskii, Y. Hu, K. Xia, and H. Guo, "First principles modeling of tunnel magneto resistance of Fe/MgO/Fe trilayers," *Phys. Rev. Lett.*, vol. 97, p. 226802-4, 2006.

[22] Yadav, M. K., and S. K. Gupta, "FeAl/MgO/FeAl MTJ with enhanced TMR and low resistance area product for MRAM: a first principle study," *Micro Nanostruct.*, vol.165, p. 207192, 2022.

[23] Yadav, M. K. and S. K. Gupta, "A comparative first principles study of quantum well states in MgO barrier MTJs for STT-RAMs," *Microelectron. J.*, vol. 105, p. 104909, 2020.

[24] Yadav, M. K. and S. K. Gupta, "First principle study of spin tunneling current under field effect in magnetic tunnel junction for possible application in STT-RAM," *IEEE Trans. Electron Dev.*, vol. 69, pp. 4894–4899, 2022.

[25] Wunnicke, O., N. Papanikolaou, R. Zeller, P. H. Dederichs, V. Drchal, and J. Kudrnovsky, "Effects of resonant interface states on tunnelingmagnetoresistance," *Phys. Rev. B*, vol. 65, p. 064425, 2002.

[26] Zhang S., P. M. Levy, A. Marley and S. S. P. Parkin, "Quenching of magnetoresistance by hot electrons in magnetic tunnel junctions," *Phys. Rev. Lett.*, vol. 79, pp. 3744–3747, 1997.

50. An Elliptical Plus Shape Microstrip Patch Antenna Integrated with CSRR for Breast Cancer Detection

Rupali[1], Dr. Sanjay Kumar Sahu[1], and Dr. Gopinath Palai[2]

[1]*Electronics and Communication, Lovely Professional University, Jalandhar, Punjab India*

[2]*Science and Energing Technologies, Sri Sri University, Cuttack, Odisha, India*

Abstract: The present work aims to explore the potential suitability of a patch antenna for various biological applications inside the ultra-wideband frequency range. This work presents a novel proposal for a microstrip patch antenna integrated with metamaterial, with the aim of facilitating potential biomedical uses in the future. In order to maximise the performance of a microstrip patch antenna for the purpose of diagnosing breast cancer, an HFSS simulator was applied. The observed changes in the presence and absence of cancer in the breast, as evidenced by simulation results, demonstrate the efficient performance of the proposed antenna.

Keywords: Microstrip patch antenna, complementary split ring resonator, metamaterial, HFSS.

1. Introduction

One of the types of cancer that affects the most people around the world is breast cancer. The ability to accurately diagnose cancer at an early stage is essential to successfully treating the disease. According to the statistics, around 13.2 million people will lose their lives to cancer in the year 2030 [1]. Due to cost and reliability issues, clinical diagnostic methods like X-rays, ultrasounds, MRI scans and CT scans have limitations. Because of these drawbacks, researchers have been encouraged to develop a cancer detection method that is more efficient, less expensive and involves less ionisation. Microwave tomography [2–5] and radar-based microwave imaging [6] have been studied for cancer detection. Microwave tomography rebuilds the electric field distribution by solving the inverse non-linear function problem. Radar-based microwave imaging broadcasts ultra-wideband (UWB) pulses from an antenna array around the head, which is expensive. Microwave imaging makes it possible to find objects that are concealed from view. In this case, detection is carried out by comparing the differences in the electrical characteristics of the tumorous cells and the healthy tissues that surround them. The microwave imaging system has a number of benefits, including low cost, the ability to be used without causing any damage to the patient, ease of operation, excellent picture quality and hence a considerable potential for early cancer detection. [7–9]. Recent technological advancements, in particular the implementation of UWB systems, make it possible to identify objects with a higher resolution. For the purpose of breast cancer detection, a circular patch microstrip UWB antenna with increased bandwidth was constructed and presented in paper [10]. The publication [11] detailed how antenna field variations over breast phantoms with and without cancers were used to identify breast tumours. The research [12] found that E-field and H-field differences when the microstrip patch antenna was simulated on a breast phantom with and without a cancer detected tumours.

FEM-based HFSS is used to develop and simulate the elliptical plus-shaped microstrip patch antenna in this proposed study. HFSS is used to size the breast phantom. The suggested antenna is then simulated on breast phantoms with and without tumours to demonstrate its breast cancer detection effectiveness.

2. Antenna Design Methodology

The length of the substrate is measured to be 55 millimetres, while its breadth is measured to be 54 millimetres. The height of the substrate is 1.6 millimetres, and it is made out of FR-4 material, which has a dielectric constant of 4.4. There is a partial ground plane that is employed, and it has a rectangular slot. A significant enhancement in the return loss curve can be accomplished by cutting a thin rectangular slit in the ground CSRR-inserted in addition to cutting a rectangular notch behind the feed line in the ground plane. Both the length and width of the ground plane measure out to be 55 and 24.5 millimetres, respectively. The ground plane's empty slot is 10 mm long and 5 mm wide. Table 1 shows the complementary split ring resonator (CSRR)-filled empty slot length.

Table 1: Dimension of design.

S. No.	Description	Value (in mm)
1.	Substrate Length	55
2.	Substrate Width	54
3.	Substrate Height	1.6
4.	Patch Length	45.3
5.	Patch Width	35.4
6.	Feed Line Length	15
7.	Feed Line Width	3.1
8.	Ground Plane Length	55
9.	Ground Plane Width	24.5
10.	Slot Length	10
11.	Slot Width	5

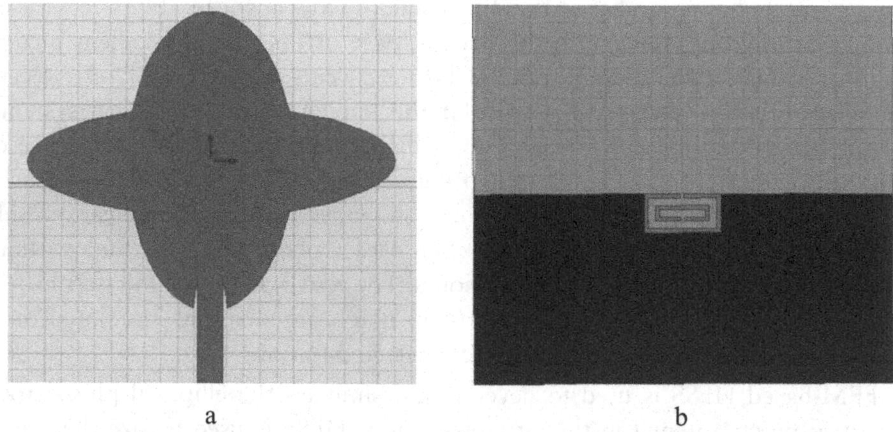

Figure 1: (a) An elliptical plus shape microstrip patch antenna, (b) ground CSRR-inserted.

3. Phantom Design

Table 2: Breast phantom design.

Frequency (GHz)	Tissue	Permittivity	Tangent loss
33	Breast Skin	17.7	0.93
33	Breast Fat	3.4	0.16
33	Breast Fibre	16	0.94
33	Tumour	18	1.05

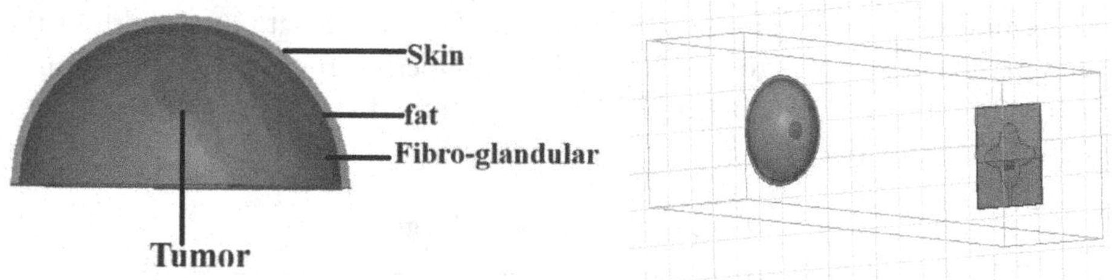

4. Result and Discussion

The simulated results show that there is a strong transmission of -22.6501 dB at 3.3447 GHz. This means that the suggested LHM resonates at 3.3 GHz, as illustrated in Figure 2. Resonance occurs near the frequency position where the logarithmic transmission has the smallest value.

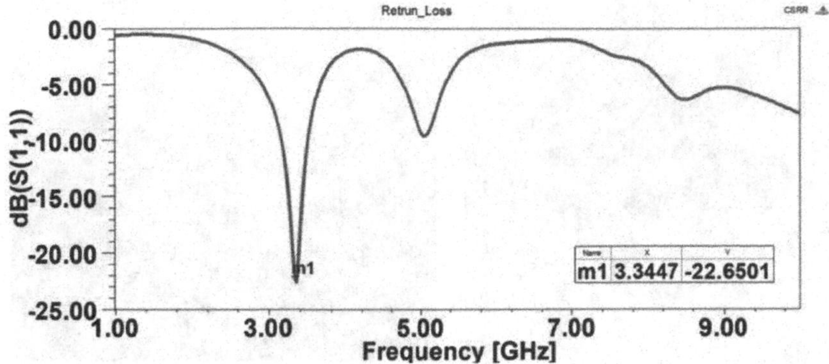

Figure 2: Reflection coefficient () of an elliptical plus shape microstrip patch antenna with ground CSRR-inserted.

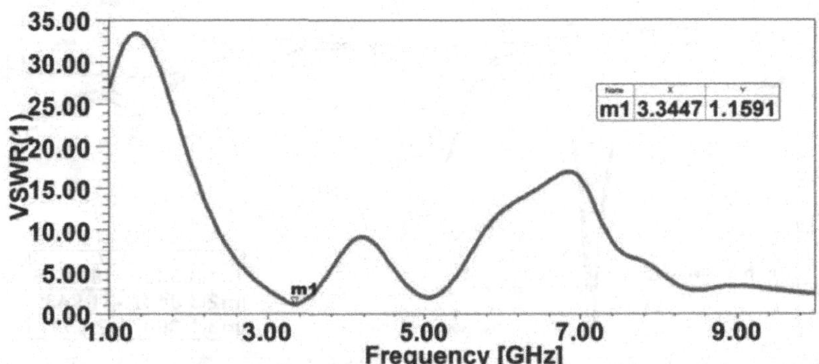

Figure 3: VSWR of an elliptical plus shape microstrip patch antenna with ground CSRR-inserted.

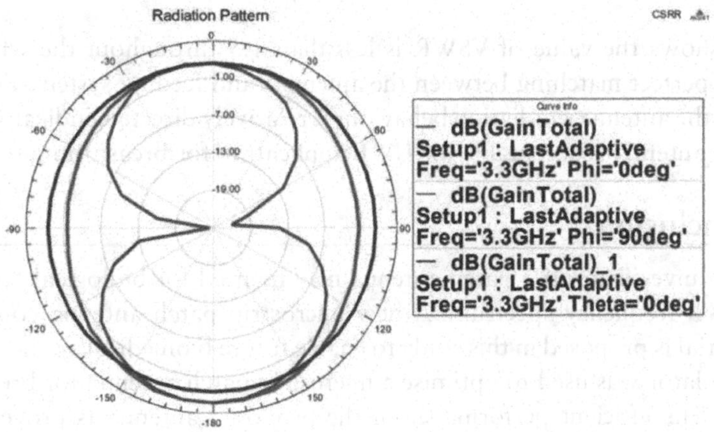

Figure 4: Radiation pattern of an elliptical plus shape microstrip patch antenna with ground CSRR-inserted.

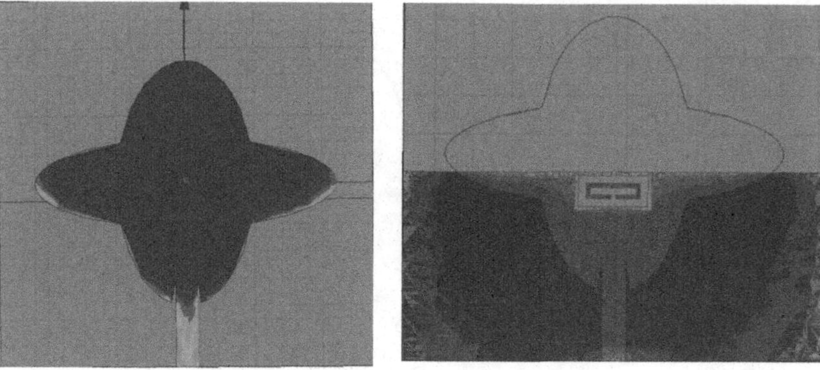

Figure 5: E-FIELD of an elliptical plus shape microstrip patch antenna with ground CSRR-inserted.

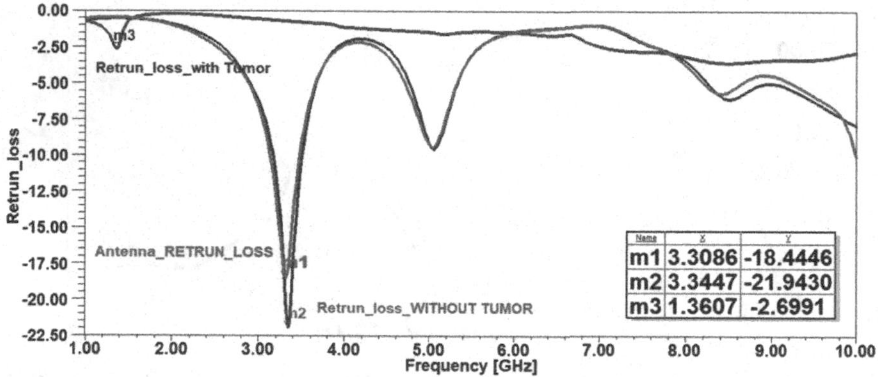

Figure 6: An elliptical plus shape microstrip patch antenna with ground CSRR-inserted with and without tumour.

Figure 3 shows the value of VSWR is less than 1.5 throughout the whole band, providing perfect matching between the antennas and feeding system. Figures 4–6 show that the antenna's radiation behaviour is relatively directed, indicating that the developed antenna is acceptable for UWB application for breast tumour detection.

5. Conclusion

This study investigates if a patch antenna may be used for biological applications in the UWB frequency spectrum. A new microstrip patch antenna coupled with metamaterial is proposed in this study to enable future biomedical applications. The HFSS simulator was used to optimise a microstrip patch antenna for breast cancer detection. The efficient performance of the proposed antenna is proved by field fluctuations in cancer presence and absence over the breast following simulation.

References

[1] Garcia, M. and A. Jemal, *Global Cancer Facts and Figures 2011*, Atlanta, GA: American Cancer Society, 2011.

[2] Semenov, S. N., "Imaging the dielectric objects by microwave tomography method," *J. Phys. Math.*, vol.1, 2015.

[3] Diaz- Bolado, L., P.-A. Barrlere, and J. Laurin, "Study of microwave tomography measurement setup configurations for breast cancer detection based on breast compression," *Int. J. Antennas Propag.*, vol. 8, 2013.

[4] Serguei, Y. and D. R. Corfield, "Microwave tomography for brain imaging: feasibility assessment for stroke detection," *Int. J. Antennas Propag.*, vol. 8, 2008.

[5] Guardiola, M., S. Capdevila, J. Romeu, and L. Jofre, "3-D microwave magnitude combined tomography for breast cancer detection using realistic breast models," *IEEE Antennas Wirel. Propag. Lett.*, vol. 11, pp. 1622–1625, 2012.

[6] Kirshin, E., B. Oreshkin, G. K. Zhu, M. Popovic, and M. Coates, "Microwave radar and microwave-induced thermoacoustics: dual- modality approach for breast cancer detection," IEEE Trans. Biomed. Eng., vol. 60, pp. 354–360, 2013.

[7] Golnabi, A. H., P. M. Meaney, S. Geimer, and K. D. Paulsen, "Microwave imaging for breast cancer detection and therapy monitoring," *Biomedical Wireless Technologies, Networks, and Sensing Systems (BioWireleSS), IEEE Topical Conference*, pp. 59–62, 2011.

[8] Li, X., E. J. Bond, B. D. Van Veen, and S. C. Hagness, "An overview of ultra-wideband microwave imaging via space-time beamforming for early-stage breast cancer detection," *IEEE Antennas Propag. Mag.*, vol. 47, pp. 19–34, 2015.

[9] Paul, M. K., M. A. K. Sagar, S. U. Hussain, and A. B. M. H. Rashid, "UWB microwave imaging via modified beamforming for early detection of breast cancer," *Electrical and Computer Engineering (ICECE), International Conference*, pp. 642–645, 2010.

[10] Choudhary, H., R. Choudhary, A. Vats, "Design and analysis of circular patch micro- strip UWB antenna for breast cancer detection," *Int. J. Innov. Res. Sci. Eng. Technol.*, vol. 4, ISSN (Print), pp. 2347–6710, 2015.

[11] Mahalakshmi, N. and V. Jeyakumar, "Design and development of single layer microstrip patch antenna for breast cancer detection," *Bonfring Int. J. Res. Commun. Eng.*, 2012, ISSN 2277-5080.

[12] Caloukana, R., S. Sinan Gultekina, D. Uzera, and O. Dundarb, "A microstrip patch antenna design for breast cancer detection," *Procedia - Social and Behavioral Sciences*, Elsevier, pp. 2905–2911, 2015.

51. Cooperative Communications System with Minimal Energy Consumption

Krishan Kumar[1], Uppula Kiran[2], and Valishetti Prashanthi[3]

[1]*Dept of Electronics and Communication Engineering, Lovely Professional University, India*

[2]*Dept of Electronics and Communication Engineering, Vaagdevi College of Engineering, Telangana, India*

[3]*Dept of Computer Science Engineering, Kakatiya Institute of Technology and Science, Telangana, India*

Abstract: It is suggested that an energy-efficient and affordable system of cooperation be used when all relays are able to pay attention to one another, or when hidden relays are present. The results of the simulation and analysis will provide a thorough assessment of the performance of the proposed system in relation to all transfer alternatives, direct transfers, high-quality transfer options, and the existing high-performance interaction system. The effectiveness and superiority of the suggested method will be ascertained using these results as a critical basis. Panels with location visibility and a complete time-based selection option are integrated into this suggested system, which seeks to increase the overall efficiency of overhead transmission. It makes it possible to get important channel state information (CSI) response from the destination by letting the slides feel the transmission and monitor several contemporary locations. This research aims to understand how the increasing variety of new relays affects the field of energy efficiency (EE). Furthermore, analysing the role of stylish forward space in EE can provide insights into how aesthetics and design choices influence the overall functionality. The simulation's findings also revealed that the suggested joint venture system not only outperforms other group transfer options in terms of EE but also offers higher efficiency and cost-effectiveness. This highlights the potential for significant growth and success by adopting this recommended approach.

Keywords: EE, amplify and forward, decode and forward, CSI.

1. Introduction

The selection of relay is crucial if you want to benefit from how the joint venture is run overall. In the intermediate selection, one node is chosen to serve as the central controller [1]. The chosen transmissions are based on factors such as signal strength, network availability and the distance between the supply and destination.

This node plays a vital role in ensuring seamless and reliable vocal communication throughout the supply chain process. These strategies can enhance the efficiency and effectiveness of negotiations by streamlining the decision-making process. Further, utilising transfer relays in the destination can provide valuable data and insights that can inform future negotiations and improve overall outcomes [7,10].

These protocols were specifically designed to overcome the limitations of traditional single-antenna systems by utilizing multiple antennas at different stages of the communication process. The DF protocol involves decoding the received signal at the relay node and then forwarding it to the destination, while the AF protocol amplifies and forwards the received signal without decoding it [2–3]. The writers believed that by incorporating the MRC and Alamouti affiliate program, they could maximise the reach and impact of their broadcast systems. This relay selection scheme takes into consideration various factors such as relay location, signal strength and network topology[4]. By intelligently selecting the relays, the scheme ensures efficient transmission network operation and minimizes the chances of connection failures. The proposed scheme has been proven to significantly enhance suspension power and overall network reliability in various studies [5–6]. This system would involve evaluating various parameters such as channel quality and interference levels to determine the most suitable RS for a given task.

Cooperative beamforming allows for improved signal quality and increased coverage area by combining the signals from multiple horns on the transmitter. This is because the receiving power needs to account for the combined transmission power of all L sticks simultaneously. This type of beamform design enables interactive light production to achieve seamless coordination and synchronisation between various components within the network.

2. System Model

The relays are responsible for receiving and decoding the wireless signals from the source and forwarding them to the destination. The DF relays play a crucial role in enhancing the reliability and efficiency of wireless communication by eliminating errors and improving signal quality. A single omnidirectional pole supports the whole node. These independent random variables and their mean value $\overline{f_z} = \left(\lambda_k / 4\pi k_o\right)^2 \left(k_{si} / k_o\right)^{-\zeta}$ as well as $\overline{x_z} = \left(\lambda_k / 4\pi k_o\right)^2 \left(k_{id} / k_o\right)^{-\zeta}$ contribute to the overall efficiency and reliability of the supply and transmission channels. The presence of relay z in the vacation region further enhances the communication capabilities by facilitating seamless transmission between different locations. The variables λ_k, k_o, ξ and k_{si} are all crucial in understanding the different aspects of the service wavelength, study loss, source to relay z distance and transmission z to location.

This method involves analysing the different communication channels within the organisation and identifying the most effective ones for delivering specific messages. These signals may be categorized into the two primary groups in Figure 1.

2.1. Relay Channel Computation

In order to comprehend the details in the offer, relays should favour the first hop CSI [9]. By maintaining a low outage probability ξ_{out}, the source ensures reliable and efficient transmission of training signals while minimising power wastage.

$$\xi_{out} = Er\left\{ f_z \frac{E_t^s}{L_o B} < 2^r - 1 \right\} = \int_0^{(2^r-1)L_o B/E_t^S} \frac{1}{\overline{f}} \exp\left(-\frac{y}{\overline{f}} \right) dy$$

$$= 1 - \exp\left(-\frac{(2^r - 1) L_0 B}{\overline{f} E_t^S} \right) \quad (1)$$

The AWGN spectral density is represented by the letter L_0. These training symbols allow the relays to estimate the channel conditions accurately. By utilising this information, the relays can optimise their transmission strategies and enhance the overall system performance.

$$E_t^D = L_0 B \frac{1 - 2^r}{x \ln(1 - \xi_{out})} \quad (2)$$

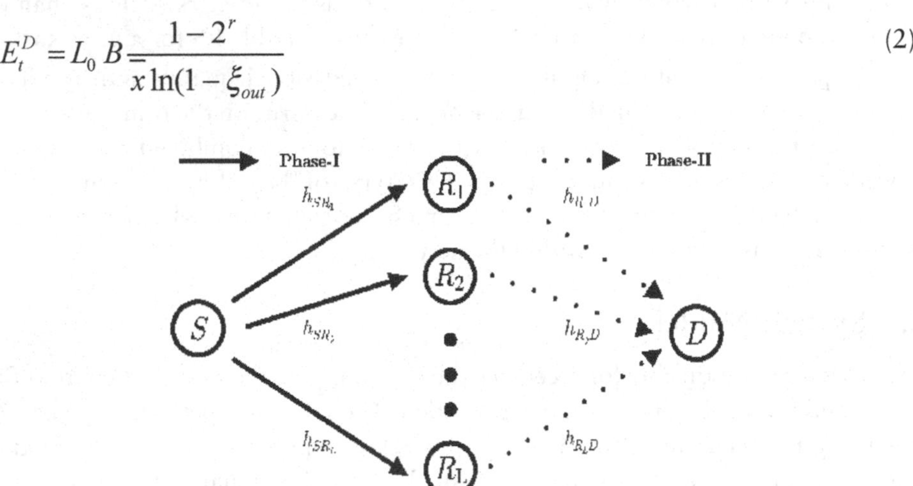

Figure 1: Cooperative relaying mechanism.

This alignment is crucial for accurately decoding the transmitted data. By broadcasting the training symbols, the channel can effectively mitigate the effects of fading and other impairments, ensuring a reliable communication link between the source and destination. The destination distributes its training sign in the second slot.

2.2. Relay Selection

Step 1: The precision code set is $G = \{ r_1 < j < L : \gamma_{sj} \geq 2^r - 1 \}$ composed of relays that have SNR ratings from the source, γ_{sj}, and can accommodate a *r* rating. Due to the transmission's restriction of the channels from the source to the channel that receives the highest ratings, it is possible for it to better comprehend the channels that the feed contains by using the notion of channel similarity. The source supplies eqn.(3) for the whole transmission power of the transmitted signature set, N = | G |.

$$E_N = L_0 B\left(2^r - 1\right)\sum_{j=1}^{N}\frac{1}{f_j} \tag{3}$$

The timer begins after the one and only transmission of the '1' subtitle as eqn.(4) for all successful transfers.

$$w_{j:N} = \left\lfloor \frac{\tilde{\lambda}}{x_{j:N}\,\Delta_x} \right\rfloor \Delta_x, j \in G, x_{1:N} > x_{2:N} > .... > x_{N:N}, \tag{4}$$

where $\tilde{\lambda} = \overline{x}\,\lambda$, λ is a preset standard parameter and is a monitoring period depending on the signal transmission time, distribution delay and processing delay [8]. This mechanism ensures that the translation transmission is prioritised based on the strength of the channel, maximising efficiency. By allowing the second-hop transmission timer with the strongest channel to expire first, it minimizes delays and optimizes the overall transmission process.

The time needed to choose the initial R phase's transmission is calculated using the formula

$$w_{Sel:R} = \Delta_x \frac{N!}{(R-1)!}\sum_{q=1}^{q_{\max}}\sum_{l=0}^{N-K}\frac{(-1)^{z_n}}{(z+R)(N-z-R)^{!z!}}\left(\exp\left(-\frac{z+R}{q+1}\theta\right) - e\,\mathrm{xp}\left(-\frac{z+R}{q}\theta\right)\right) \tag{5}$$

Step 2: A When the relay's timer ends, L_t training signals are sent with transmission power of

$$E_t^r = \max\left\{E_t^S, E_t^D\right\} \tag{6}$$

The method involves measuring channel size and collecting related CSI using the same training signals in a printed wireless environment.

3. Average Energy Efficiency Analysis

This analysis allows us to evaluate the performance of the central EE in different power transfer scenarios, which is crucial for determining its effectiveness.

3.1. Cooperative Communication

In addition to accounting for the common deficiency, we anticipate that N≥2 transmission will successfully ascertain that the information transferred from sources $\{f_z\}_{z=1}^{N}$ and $\{x_z\}_{z=1}^{N}$ is impartial and equally distributed, with $\overline{f_z} = \overline{f}$

and $\overline{x_z} = \overline{x}$ (z = 1, 2, and N). The suggested co-operative transfer mechanism is supplied with a standard EE via

$$\overline{EE}_{BB}(R,N,\varphi)=\left(1-E_{out}^{BB}\right)\left(1-E_{coll,R,q_{max}}\right)rL_D P\left\{\frac{1}{P_0(R,N,\varphi)+P_D(R,N,\varphi)}\right\} \quad (7)$$

This interruption in communication occurred because Taylor's first order approximation only accounted for the immediate vicinity of R, neglecting the influence of other distant regions. As a result, the transmission signal was unable to effectively reach and maintain connectivity with areas further away from R. P_O (.) and P_G (.) are the power consumption and the power spent during data transmission. Outage probability is expressed as

$$E_{out}^{BB}=\frac{N!}{(R-1)!}\sum_{j=0}^{N-R}(-1)^j\frac{\left(1-\exp\left(-\frac{j+R}{\overline{x}}\gamma\right)\right)}{(j+R)(N-R-j)!j!} \quad (8)$$

Where $\gamma = L_0 B\left(2^r-1\right)/E_{\max}$

The power consumption of the overhead display is specified as

$$P\{P_0(R,N,\varphi)\}=P_t(R,N,\varphi)+P_{INV}+I_{\{2\le R\le N\}}(R)P\{P_{FB}(R,N,\varphi)\}+P\{P_N(N,\varphi)\} \quad (9)$$

Where Pi is the key interpreter, specified as $Pi(p)=\int_{-\infty}^{p}\frac{\exp(p)}{w}dw$.

3.2. *Direct Transmission*

Two transmission mechanisms are taken into consideration in the EE experiment for direct connection between the source and the destination.

To obtain the R-target that is most likely to cause ξ_{out} to break, the source in the first method converts the training signals to the minimal strength needed.

$$E_t^{SD} = L_0 B\frac{1-2^r}{\overline{f}_0 \ln(1-\xi_{out})},$$

$$\overline{f}_0=\left(\frac{\lambda_c}{4\pi k_0}\right)^2\left(\frac{k_{sd}}{k_0}\right)^{-\zeta} \quad (10)$$

The channel power gain, represented by k_{sd}, quantifies the increase in signal strength as it travels from the source to the destination. The maximum permitted transfer power, E_{max}, is then used to send the data. Using eqn1, the subsequent EE rating is determined.

$$\overline{EE}_{TD}^{MAX} = \left(1 - E_{out}^{TD}\right)\frac{rL_G}{t_S}\left(L_t L_0 B \frac{1-2^r}{\overline{f}_0 \ln\left(1-\xi_{out}\right)} + L_G E_{\max}\right)^{-1} \tag{11}$$

Once the practice signals are transmitted, the destination measures the received signal quality and analyzes it to determine the channel's performance. This efficient transmission capability of the source allows for optimal energy utilization and ensures a high level of accuracy in achieving the desired r-level.

$$\begin{aligned} &\overline{EE}_{TD}^{ADP} \\ &\approx \left(1 - E_{out}^{TD}\right)\frac{rL_G}{t_S}\left(\frac{L_t L_0 B\left(1-2^r\right)}{\overline{f}_0 \ln\left(1-\xi_{out}\right)} + \left(L_G + L_{FB}\right)L_0 B\left(2^r - 1\right)P\left\{\frac{1}{\overline{f}_0} f_0 \geq \gamma\right\}\right)^{-1} \\ &\approx \frac{\left(1 - E_{out}^{TD}\right)rL_G\overline{f}_0}{L_0 B t_S\left(1-2^r\right)}\left(\frac{L_t}{\ln\left(1-\gamma_{out}\right)} + \left(L_G + L_{FB}\right)\exp\left(\frac{\gamma}{\overline{f}_0}\right)Pi\left(-\frac{\gamma}{\overline{f}_0}\right)\right)^{-1} \end{aligned} \tag{12}$$

$$\begin{aligned} &\overline{EE}_{DT}^{ADP,UB} \\ &= \left(1 - P_{out}^{DT}\right)\frac{RN_D}{T_S}\left(\frac{N_T N_0 B\left(1-2^R\right)}{\overline{h}_0 \ln\left(1-\delta_{out}\right)} + \frac{\left(N_D + N_{FB}\right)N_0 B\left(2^R - 1\right)}{E\left\{\overline{h}_0 \middle| \overline{h}_0 \geq \mu\right\}}\right)^{-1} \\ &= \left(1 - P_{out}^{DT}\right)\frac{RN_D}{N_0 B T_S\left(1-2^R\right)}\left(\frac{N_T}{\overline{h}_0 \ln\left(1-\delta_{out}\right)} + \frac{\left(N_D + N_{FB}\right)}{\mu + \overline{h}_0}\right)^{-1} \end{aligned} \tag{13}$$

3.3. Optimal Location of Relays

At this point, a superbly cooperative transfer area is acquired, raising the EE ratio. This setup suggests that the relays are strategically placed to optimize the transmission path from the source to the destination. By having equal distances from the source, it indicates a balanced distribution of relay nodes. The typical EE standards have proven to be effective in reducing energy consumption and promoting sustainability.

$$\varphi_{opt}\left(R,N\right) = \arg\min_{\varphi}\left(\overline{P}_0^{LB}\left(R,N,\varphi\right) + \overline{P}_G^{LB}\left(R,N,\varphi\right)\right) \tag{14}$$

The distance from the source, φ, can be a determining factor in choosing the most efficient route to your destination. The finest place for cooperation is when eqn (15) is being supported

$$\varphi_{opt}\left(R,N\right) \approx \left(1 + \left(\frac{\beta\left(R,N\right)}{\alpha\left(R,N\right)}\right)^{\frac{1}{\zeta-1}}\right)^{-1} k_{sd} \tag{15}$$

4. Results and Discussions

Imitation is used to evaluate both the analytical findings' correctness and the overall efficacy of the cooperative money transfer method. The N (> 1) transmissions that are near to one another and are φ away from the source are capable of effectively determining the delivery of messages. At a certain training point, a single OFDM mark is communicated with a goal of r and deviation probabilities of $\xi_{out} = 0.12$. The website uses OFDM signals to evaluate the financial potential of a second hop channel on selected relays. Table 1 presents the simulation parameters of evaluation.

Table 1: Simulation parameters.

Parameter	Value
Carrier frequency(f_c)	2.0 GHertz
Reference distance(k_0)	10 mts
Path-loss exponent (ζ)	4.0
Noise power spectral density(L_0)	-174 dBm/Hertz
Maximum transmission power(E_{max})	23 dBmts
Bandwidth of the subcarrier(Δf)	15 kHertz
Length of the symbol (t_S)	66.7 μsec
Data packet size (OFDM symbols)(L_G)	140
Source to destination distance,(d_{sd})	500 mts

Figure 2 displays relay selection time, collision probes, N = 10, and θ (= λ / Δx) compared to the expression θ for two special numbers. We selected θ = 70 as an optimal trade-off among conflict of choice and transfer decision, integrating EE testing and visual performance. The proposed scheme requires a minimum channel compliance time of 22msec, significantly less than the channel's compliance time of 76.1msec for slower conditions at 3 km/h.

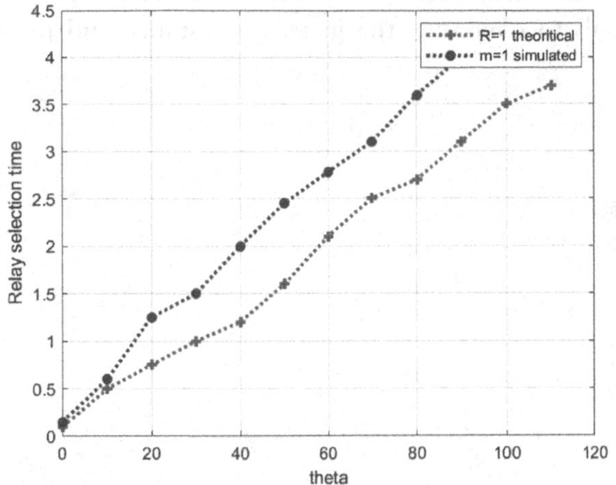

Figure 2: Selection of relay time Vs θ.

In Figure 3, the consequences of φ = 50m are depicted for the specified values of N and m in the EE simulation. As can be seen, choosing the transfer with the m = 2 best score results in the greatest EE value. The use of high signature power in cooperative beamforming results in a significantly lower EE for all recording devices, m = N (N > 2) deployment. This variability gain in R allows for a more efficient and reliable transmission of retrieval codes, leading to enhanced energy efficiency.

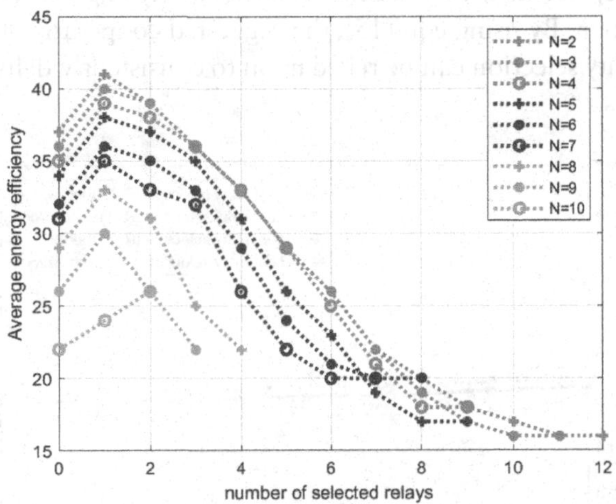

Figure 3: Average EE Vs the no.of selected relays (R), for different no.s of correctly decoding relays (N) and φ.

The optimal selection of relays, as shown in Figure 4, increases the simulation-derived EE rating by reducing the source distance to the relay. The use of a 1st phase relay (m = 1) improves EE when the source-transmission lengths exceed 150mts at N = 3 and N = 5. This increase in power consumption is a result of the need for stronger signals to overcome the increased distance and maintain a reliable transmission.

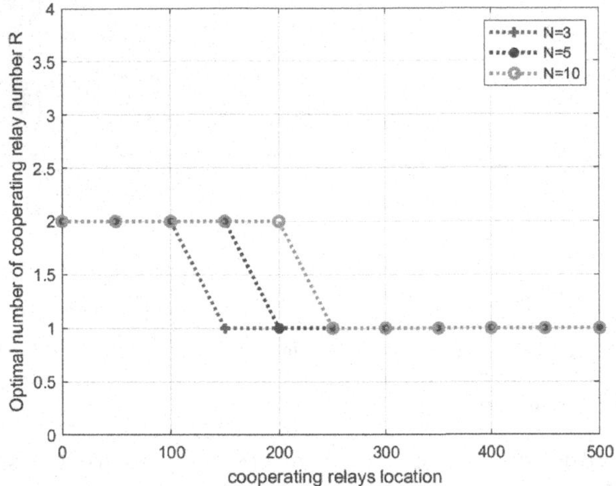

Figure 4: *For different values of N, the optimum number of cooperating relays w.r.t. their location.*

The test in Figure 5 compares the simulation findings with the results of a randomized controlled trial. This helps evaluate the accuracy of the interaction linkages from eqn.(15). Additionally, Figure 4 displays the optimal transfer position, which represents the choice that is most closely aligned with the source of the proposed system. By using eqn.(15), the suggested cooperative transfer method and transfer quality selection can be relied upon to consistently deliver high-quality transfer outcomes.

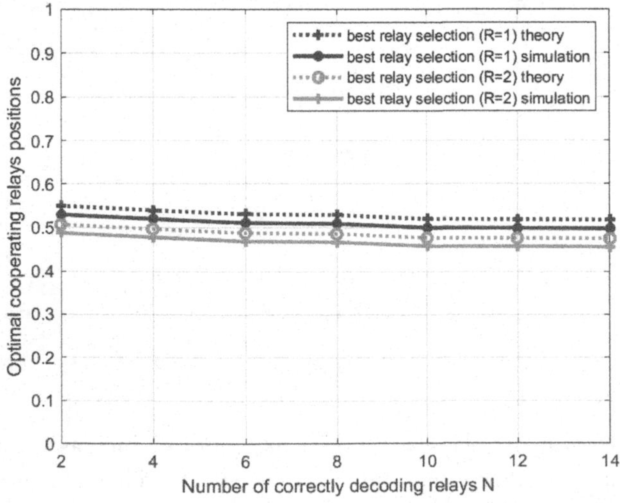

Figure 5: *Approximate optimal position of cooperative relays w.r.t. N.*

5. Conclusion

The proposed scheme aims to optimize beamforming by using high-power transmission technology for local timer transfers, resulting in minimal energy-saving signals. It outperforms current efficient co-operation systems, high-quality selection, all transfer options, and direct transfers in terms of energy efficiency.

References

[1] Kiran, U., K. Kumar, A. Roy, S. Qamar, and A. Azeem, "An intelligent dimension-based cat swarm optimization for efficient cooperative multi-hop relay selection in vehicular network," Neural Comput. Appl., 2023, e-ISSN:1433-3058, Print ISSN:0941-0643.

[2] Liu, J., N. Kato, J. Ma, and N. Kadowaki, "Device-to-device communication in lteadvanced networks: a survey," *IEEE Commun. Surv. Tutorials*, vol. 17, no. 4, pp. 1923–1940, Fourthquarter 2015.

[3] Zhou, Z., S. Zhou, J.-H. Cui, and S. Cui, "Energy-efficient cooperative communication based on power control and selective single-relay in wireless sensor networks," *IEEE Trans. Wireless Commun.*, vol. 7, no. 8, pp. 3066–3078, 2008.

[4] Kiran, U. and K. Kumar, "An hybrid heuristic optimal relay selection strategy for energy efficient multi hop cooperative cellular communication," *Ad Hoc Netw.*, vol. 140, p. 103058, 2023, Elsevier, doi: 10.1016/j.adhoc.2022.103058, ISSN: 1570-8705.

[5] Cui, S., A. Goldsmith, and A. Bahai, "Energy-efficiency of mimo and cooperative mimo techniques in sensor networks," IEEE J. Sel. Areas Commun., vol. 22, no. 6, pp. 1089–1098, 2004.

[6] Lim, G. and L. Cimini, "Energy efficiency of cooperative beamforming in wireless ad-hoc networks," *Communications (ICC), 2012 IEEE International Conference*, pp. 4039–4043, 2012.

[7] Jing, Y. and H. Jafarkhani, "Single and multiple relay selection schemes and their achievable diversity orders," *IEEE Trans. Wireless Commun.*, vol. 8, no. 3, pp. 1414–1423, 2009.

[8] Bletsas, A., A. Khisti, D. Reed, and A. Lippman, "A simple cooperative diversity method based on network path selection," *IEEE J. Sel. Areas Commun.*, vol. 24, no. 3, pp. 659–672, 2006.

[9] Li, S., F. Wang, J. Gaber, and Y. Zhou, "An optimal relay number selection algorithm for balancing multiple performance in flying ad hoc networks," *IEEE Access*, vol. 8, pp. 225884–225901, 2020.

[10] Praveen Kumar, D., P. Pardha Saradhi, and M. Sushanth Babu, "Large scale cooperative wireless networks: relay selection and performance analysis," *Int. J. Adv. Trends Comput. Sci. Eng.*, vol. 9, no.4, pp. 6400–6405, 2020, ISSN 2278-3091.

52. IOT Portable Radar System

Ankit Meena[1], Ananya Tripathi[1], Arsh Malik[1], Bhukya Arun Kumar[2], and Ajay Roy[2]

[1]*School of Computer Application, Lovely Professional University*
[2]*School of Electronics and Electrical Engineering, Lovely Professional University*

Abstract: The radar has been around for over a century, and it has been used for various purposes, such as controlling vehicle speed, managing air traffic, military operations and even medical applications like detecting breast cancer. In recent years, the radar technology has advanced significantly, especially in the field of automobile safety and the autonomous driving. However, comparing to other technologies, radar has not seen the same level of development in the past two decades. But things are about to change as new technologies are emerging that will revolutionize the way we use radar. This will improve radar performance by adding new features and signal processing methods.

By seamlessly merging the capabilities of portable radar technology with the interconnectedness of internet of things (IoT), the portable radar system redefines the boundaries of surveillance and security, and real-time data analysis, making the way for enhanced situational awareness like disaster management and environmental monitoring. The tangible results achieved through the implementation of the IoT Portable Radar System. It highlights the enhanced surveillance capabilities, increased data accuracy and real-time insights which can be further used in practical applications. We collected the sensors data and send it to the Blynk app after analysing the data we can take decision on the bases of data received and improve the accuracy.

1. Introduction

Radar technology has come a long way since its invention by Christian Hülsmeyer in 1904. The first radar was a pulsed system that radiated differentiated video pulses generated by a spark gap. Since then, signal processing and radar system technology have significantly improved. However, despite these improvements, current radar systems still face certain challenges that limit their effectiveness [1].

One significant challenge is the inefficiency of current radar systems. Most state-of-the-art radars transmit the same signal for their entire operation, limiting their field of operation. This is problematic as radars encounter many different scenarios that require different tasks, such as tracking, low/high range resolution and near/far range. Additionally, inter-system interference can limit the operability of radar systems, especially in the growing market of automotive radar.

To address these challenges, researchers are exploring new radar system concepts that use intelligent signal coding and decoding, multiple transmits and receiving antennas, digital beamforming, and matrix (array) imaging. By using these technologies, it is possible to create smart radars that are cost-effective, efficient and highly capable [11].

For example, intelligent signal coding, such as OFDM and CDMA, can enable radar systems to avoid inter-system interference by using low cross-correlation signals. Multiple transmit and receive antennas, or MIMO radar, can provide higher spatial resolution and increased coverage. Digital beamforming can provide a higher angular resolution without any mechanical movement of the parts, reducing costs and complexity. Array imaging can also provide efficient systems that are smaller and more cost effective.

Additionally, researchers are exploring the combination of radar and communication, known as RadCom. RadCom systems can exploit the limited frequency spectrum by using opportunistic spectrum usage, making the most of the available resources.

Here are some key differences between old radars, today's radars and future/ portable radars:

1.1. Old Radars

- First developed in the early 20th century, primarily for military use.
- Used pulse radar technology and spark gap generators.
- Electronically simple with limited capabilities and narrow range of operation.
- Single-function devices with limited flexibility and adaptability.
- Slow scanning and relatively low resolution.
- Signal transmitted during operation were identical.
- Used single frequency band single time. Could only 'see' a small area at a time. Mechanically scanned (e.g., airport radar).

1.2. Today's Radars

- Advanced and improved hardware technology and better signal processing capabilities.
- Advance scanning technologies, such as phased array and synthetic aperture radar (SAR).
- Widely used in the military and civilian applications.
- Increased frequency range and the bandwidth.
- Greater flexibility in signal coding and modulation.
- Can be integrated with other technologies, such as communication systems and autonomous vehicles.

- High-resolution imaging and 3D mapping capabilities.
- Can track multiple targets simultaneously.

1.3. Future/Portable Radars

- Utilize advanced signal coding and processing techniques for greater efficiency and spectral utilisation.
- Employ multiple-input multiple-output (MIMO) radar technology for improved resolution and target detection.
- Use digital beamforming for wider to cover the area without mechanical movement of the parts.
- Incorporate a matrix imaging to reduce the cost and size.
- Can be integrated with other technologies for multi-functionality.
- Greater mobility and portability, allowing for deployment in remote or challenging environments.
- Potential for low-power consumption and low cost, enabling widespread adoption and deployment.

In conclusion, radar technology has come a long way, but there is still room for improvement. By exploring new radar system concepts, researchers can create smarter, more efficient and more capable radar systems. These innovations will help to address current challenges and provide more effective radar solutions for a variety of applications [2].

In addition to these advancements, the development of portable radar systems can bring a significant breakthrough in the future evolution of radar systems, enabling easier deployment and operation in various applications such as environmental monitoring, disaster response and search and rescue missions. Overall, the future of radar systems looks promising, and the advancements in technology will continue to shape the future of this essential technology [10].

2. Working of Radar System Portable Radar System

Radar systems and portable radar systems operate by transmitting a radio frequency (RF) sending signals toward the target and then receiving reflected signal from target. The delay (Time) between the transmitting and the receiving of the signal, along with the received signal strength, provides information about the distance and direction of the target.

In traditional radar systems, single antennas are used for both transmitting the signal and for receiving the signal, and the signal is sent out in short bursts or pulses. The receiver then listens for at the cost of reduced range and accuracy compared to larger, stationary radar systems.

One area of research in radar technology is to develop the advanced signal-processing techniques and to improve the accuracy and the range of portable radar systems. For example, some researchers have explored the use of multiple antennas and advanced beamforming techniques to increase the range and accuracy of portable radar systems. Other researchers have investigated the use of advanced signal processing algorithms to detect and classify targets in complex environments, such as through foliage or in urban areas.

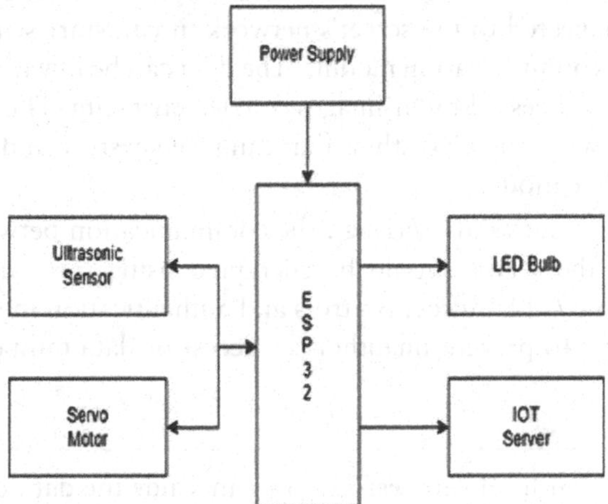

Figure 1: Portable radar system block diagram.

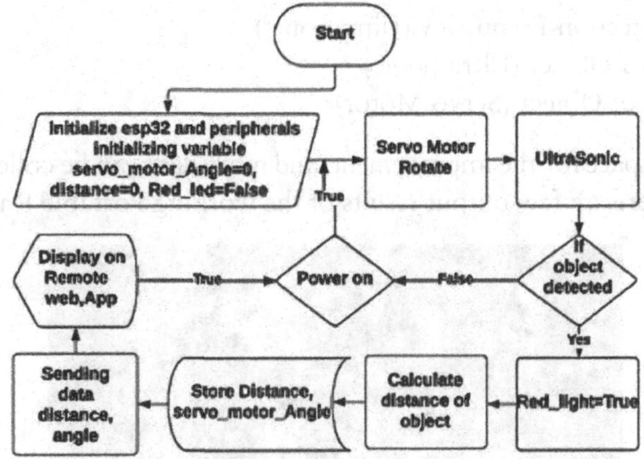

Figure 2: Portable radar system data flow chart.

3. Connecting Portable Radar System to Server

To connect a portable radar system to the server, several steps are required to establish a stable and reliable connection. First, the portable radar system needs to be equipped with a wireless communication module that supports Wi-Fi or cellular networks. The module should be compatible with the server's communication protocol and network architecture to ensure seamless data transmission.

Once the communication module is installed, the portable radar system needs to be configured to connect to the server's network. This involves setting up the network parameters such as the subnet mask, gateway, DNS server and the most IP address. The configuration can be done manually or through an automated setup process that uses DHCP or other network discovery protocols. Once the portable radar system is connected to the server's network, it can start sending data to the server through the communication module. The data can be in various formats such as raw signal data, processed radar images or telemetry data. The server should be equipped with software and algorithms that can receive, store and process the data in real time or offline mode.

To ensure data security and privacy, the communication between the portable radar system and the server should be encrypted using standard cryptographic protocols such as SSL/TLS. Access controls and authentication mechanisms should also be implemented to prevent unauthorised access or data tampering.

4. Result

After implementing on hardware, esp32 now can sends the data over the internet, this data can be analysed and can be used further. Currently, we are getting distance from ultra sonic, direction from the servo motor. By this data we can find the object in a particular direction. Here, we are analysing the data in different formats:

- Object detection Frequency (Ultra Sonic)
- Distance of Object (Ultra Sonic)
- Direction of Object (Servo Motor)

It has much space for the improvement, and more data can be collected by adding other sensors. Here are few output results of the working Portable Radar System:

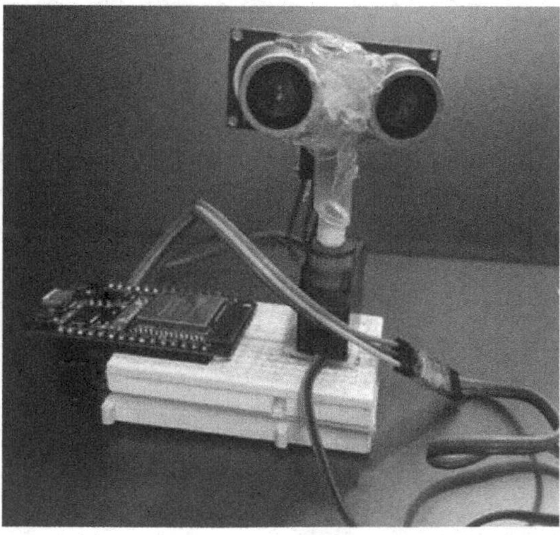

Figure 3: *Hardware used ESP32, ultrasonic sensor, servo motor.*

DISTANCE OF OBJECT

28cm

Figure 4: *Distance of object (Ultra Sonic) received on Blynk App via ESP32.*

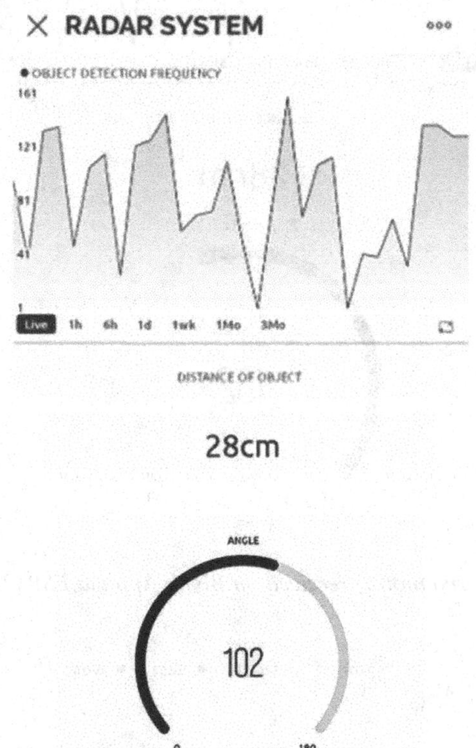

Figure 5: *Data received from ESP32 on Blynk App.*

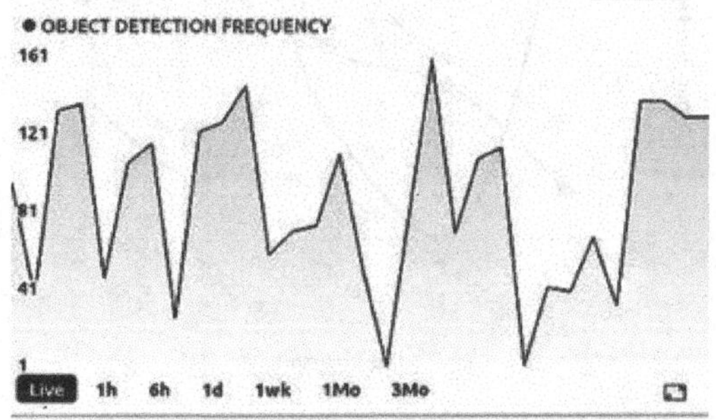

Figure 6: *Object detection frequency (ultra-Sonic) received on Blynk App ESP32.*

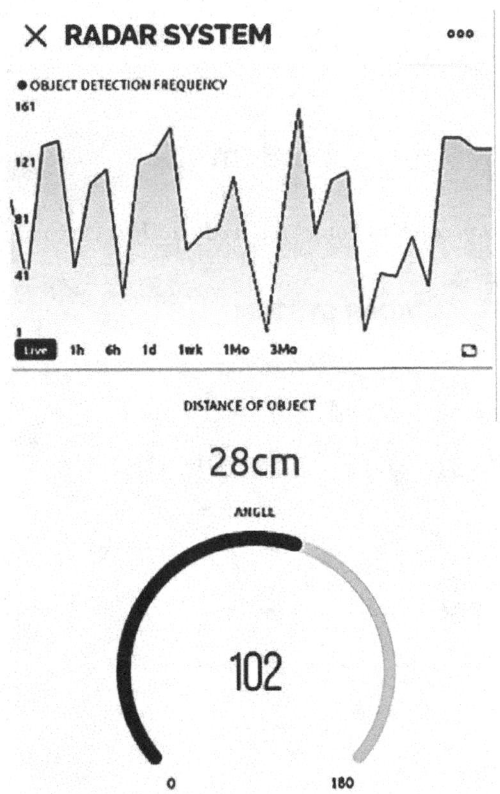

Figure 7: Directions (Servo motor) received on Blynk App via ESP32.

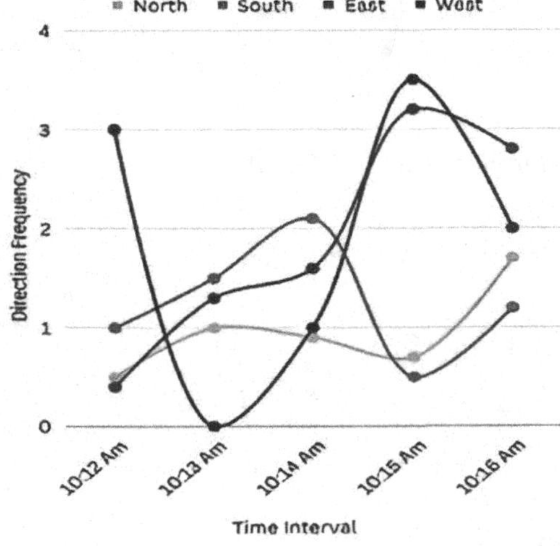

Figure 8: Directions frequency with time interval.

5. Conclusion

In conclusion, connecting a portable radar system to a server provides numerous advantages, including real-time data transmission and analysis, remote monitoring and storage of data for future analysis. The integration of this system can improve situational awareness and decision- making processes, especially in critical applications such as military and aerospace. To further improve the system, future research should focus on enhancing the data processing capabilities to provide more accurate and detailed information. Additionally, the development of advanced algorithms and machine learning techniques can enhance the system's ability to detect and identify targets, reducing false alarms and increasing the system's reliability. Furthermore, the integration of other technologies such as lidar and sonar can provide a more comprehensive understanding of the environment, improving the system's overall performance. Overall, the integration of portable radar systems with servers has enormous potential in various applications, and continued research can lead to more advanced and sophisticated systems, providing more precise and accurate information for decision-making purposes.

Acknowledgements: We are grateful because we managed to complete our research paper within the time given by our lecturer Dr. Ajay Roy (Lovely Professional university, Phagwara, Punjab, India). This research paper cannot be complete without the efforts and co-operation of our Team members, Ankit Meena, Ananya Tripathi and Arsh Malik. We sincerely thank our teaching authority of Introduction to IOT with NODEMCU for guidance and for encouragement in completing the research paper and for teaching us in NODEMCU. Finally, we would like to thank and express our gratitude to our friends and respondents for the support to spend time to fill in the questionnaires.

References

[1] Sit, Y. L., C. Sturm, T. Zwick, and L. Reichardt, "Verification of an doppler estimation algorithm with raytracing and OFDM-based range," in *ICEAA '11 (International Conference on Electromagnetics in Advanced Applications*, Turin, Italy, 2011.

[2] Gebert, N., A. Moreira, and G. Krieger, "Multidimensional waveform encoding: digital beamforming technique for synthetic aperture (RRS) radar romote sensing," *IEEE Trans. On Remote Sensing and Geoscience*,2008.

[3] "Verfahren um entfernte metallische Gegenstände mittels elektrischer Wellen einem Beobachter zu melden," Ch. Hülsmeyer.

[4] Kaiserliches Patentamt, Patentschrift Nr. 165546, 30. April 1904.

[5] Ludwig, M., H.-P. Feldle, and H. Ott, "A miniaturised X-band T/Rmodule for SAR- systems based on active phased array techniques," *Proc. Int. Geoscience and Remote Sensing Symposium IGARSS'95*, vol. 3, pp. 2063–2065, 1955.

[6] Younis, M. and W. Wiesbeck, "SAR with digital beamforming on receive only," *Proc. Int. Geoscience and Remote Sensing Symposium IGARSS'99*, pp. 1773–1775, 1999.

[7] Liu, B., Z. He, J. Zeng, and B. Liu, "Polyphase orthogonal code design for MIMO radar systems," *Proc. Int. Conf. Radar (CIE)*, pp. 1–4, 2006.

[8] Wiley, C. A., "Pulsed Doppler radar methods and apparatus," U.S. Patent 3.196.436, 1954.

[9] Sturm, C. and W. Wiesbeck, "Waveform design and signal processing aspects for fusion of wireless communications and radar sensing," *Proc. IEEE*, vol. 99, pp. 1236–1259, 2011.

[10] Younis, M., P. López-Dekker, and G. Krieger, "MIMO SAR operation modes and techniques," *Proc. European Conference on Synthetic Aperture Radar EUSAR'2002*, Köln, Germany, pp. 187–190, 2002.

[11] Stoica, P. and J. Li, *MIMO Radar Signal Processing*, John Wiley & Sons, 2009.

53. Data Acquisition and Monitoring Framework for Waste Management Using Intelligent Sensors and Thing Speak IoT Analytics for Health Monitoring in Smart Cities

Karan Belsare[1], Manwinder Singh[2], Anudeep Goraya[3]

[1]*School of SEEE, Lovely Professional University, Jalandhar, Punjab, India*
[2]*Department of ECE, Lovely Professional University, Jalandhar, Punjab, India*
[3]*Department of CSE, Lovely Professional University, Jalandhar, Punjab, India*

Abstract: Population expansion and massive migrations of residents from traditional to smart cities created issues for these cities due to their exponential growth. Controlling, managing and processing the standard output of garbage is the most prevalent significant issue that smart cities face. The leading causes of complicated trash management are the expanding population and resource limitations in waste management operations. Smart cities utilise an intelligent waste management system to handle this complex procedure. The internet of things (IoT) and LoRa technology were used in this research to provide an autonomous technique for achieving an efficient and intelligent waste parameter monitoring system for an innovative waste management system. Using IoT and the Thing Speak Cloud Platform, which can be installed in multiple locations, the garbage level, odour level, air quality level, garbage weight, smoke level and waste types are continuously monitored.

Keywords: IoT, LoRa, thing-speak, intelligent sensors, waste management, health monitoring.

1. Introduction

The increase in garbage generation is one of the key issues resulting from the constantly expanding population. This form of garbage includes, for example, food waste, material waste, waste from humans, waste from useless goods, waste from industries, etc. Since waste management directly affects people's health and way of life, it is a critical issue that needs serious thought and quick answers. Traditional waste management standards call for manually removing trash from trash cans and disposing or recycling that trash following established procedures. Despite being beneficial, this procedure is labour intensive and has several drawbacks because it is done manually. These initiatives and procedures are ineffectual compared to the amount of waste created. Furthermore, it poses problems, such as the likelihood of trash bins being overfilled while others being underfilled for waste collection. [1–3]. Internet of things (IoT) technology might play a part in helping to deliver more effective waste management. Most of the solutions being designed to focus on smart waste bin monitoring, including level detection of the dustbin, waste fire and temperature detection, vibration and tilt occurrence, presence of waste operators, humidity and location of dustbin [4]. IoT is a relatively new technology for connecting numerous items that will interact with one another via sensors and actuators, embedded and wireless systems. [7,10]. The most efficient solution to the pollution problem is an machine learning (ML) and IoT-based waste management system. These systems provide accurate waste information and an appropriate route for waste collection vehicles, reducing the time and pace of the entire process [18–22]. The ML and IoT are implemented for analysis of Precise Green House Management Systems for smart farming to understand the impact on the environment and health [13–14].5G technology has been influencing our daily life even IoT and other prospectives of smart cities are mostly connected via 5G [18,19].

2. Literature Survey

The use of ML systems throughout the MSWM process, from trash creation through transportation and collection to final disposal, is summarised by Wanjun Xia *et al.* [1]. The successful waste management based on IoT infrastructure in urban settings is then thoroughly examined, focusing on how concessionaires and waste producers interact in terms of a faster collection time with lower costs as a kind of citizenship promotion. Puneet Sharma et al. investigated the role of several AI-based garbage management systems [2]. The i-Smart WMS intelligent waste management system was developed as a prototype model by Gade *et al.* [3]. Given spatial limitations, Mengchu Zhou *et al.* [4] provide a rational method for path suggestion in an IoT-enabled trash managing system. It carries out a detailed examination using AI-based techniques and compares the outcomes. By anticipating the likelihood of waste items, G. Uganya *et al.* [5] presented an automated approach to build an efficient and intelligent waste management system utilising the IoT. The accuracy and timing of the suggested strategy are examined using ML classification algorithms. ML and IoT were recommended as viable options by Rijwan Khan *et al.* [6] for intelligent and effective garbage management (IoT). Tedi Gunawan *et al.* [7] introduced an IoT smart waste monitoring system to make trash monitoring easier for families. An IoT-based residential garbage bin monitoring system makes up the first three critical components of the proposed system. Jacob John *et al.* [8] describe an IoT-based smart trash disposal prediction and supervising system that uses commercially available features that could be installed on a trash bin and assess fill levels. The IoT-based waste monitoring system was created by Rio Allen

G. Parilla *et al.* [9]. Miko Pamintuan *et al.* [10] developed an intelligent dustbin that intelligently separates rubbish and offers a report on monitoring waste collection. An automatic garbage sorting mechanism utilising ML techniques was managed using image recognition. An automated fire extinguishing system, invented by Dev V. Savla *et al.* [11], is necessary. The suggested approach reduces potential concerns from hazardous waste management and the disposal yard. Tanya Gupta *et al.* [12] presented a solution for trash segregation at the fundamental level based on deep learning (DL) architecture.

2.1. Proposed Work

The suggested concept is centred on an IoT-layered architecture often utilised for trash management. The application, middleware, network and perception layers comprise most of the generalized framework's four-layer design, which is addressed and depicted in Figure 1, and the workflow is given in Figure 2.

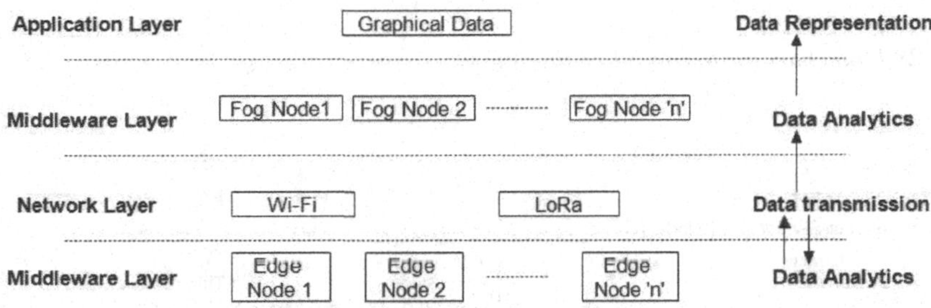

Figure 1: *Universal IoT framework for trash monitoring.*

Perception Layer: In charge of gathering physical data, processing it and transmitting it to the upper levels through encrypted channels, this layer mainly relies on hardware. It employs sensors to collect information on physical characteristic parameters, hazardous gas level, waste level, garbage photos from the camera, etc.

Network Layer: This layer delivers the measured data from the perception to the middleware layer, where the expert services are placed, using infrared, GSM, ZigBee, Wi-Fi and LoRa.

Middleware Layer: This layer joins IoT parts that typically should not be able to interact with one another and serves as an interpreter. It may be a software layer or perhaps a group of sublayers. In this case, ML is mainly used in the data analysis. The fog layer is another name for this layer.

Application Layer: Although it does not always directly contribute to the development of the IoT architecture, the application layer is where the many services that communicate with users are developed. This layer will help to supervise and examine the actual data related to waste.

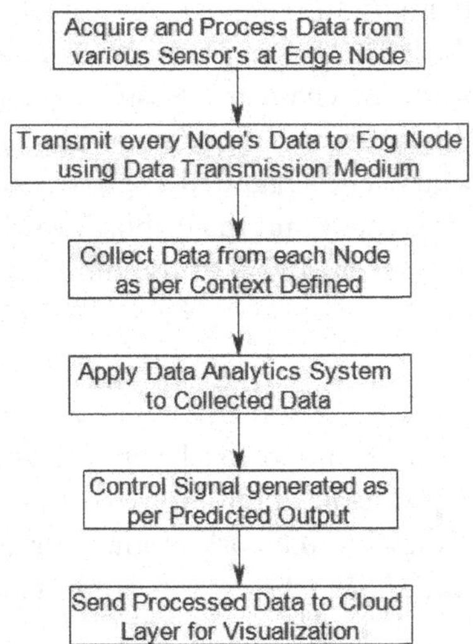

Figure 2: Flowchart for proposed methodology.

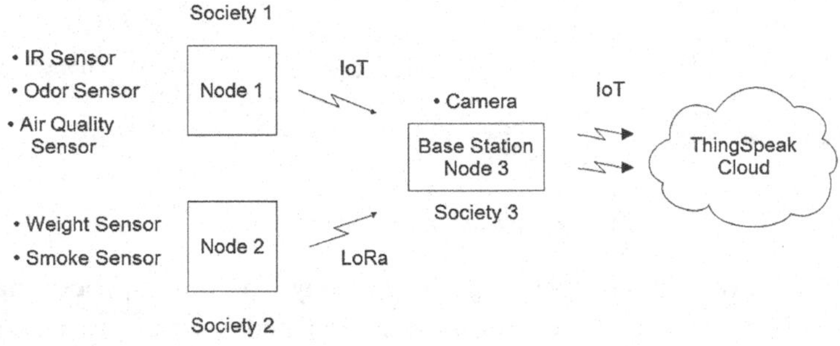

Figure 3: Proposed architectural scenario.

The suggested WSN-based scenario for the smart city is illustrated in Figure 3. Three distinct societies are presumable. First, Node 1 is installed with an IR sensor, an odour sensor and an air quality sensor that may be employed with a closed-area waste management system and are interfaced with the node MCU microcontroller. Node 2 is installed with weight and smoke sensors in the second society. These sensors interact with the node MCU microcontroller and may be utilised for an open-area waste management system. Finally, in the third society, a garbage collection unit is the third node, where the camera is mounted. It can be utilised for trash material categorisation after obtaining an image. Various sensors are linked to monitoring a parameter according to a scenario built for an IoT and LoRa environment. Specifically, radio bands designated for industrial, scientific and medical (ISM) uses are used by the low-power LoRa protocol, designed to function over long distances using unlicensed spectrum.

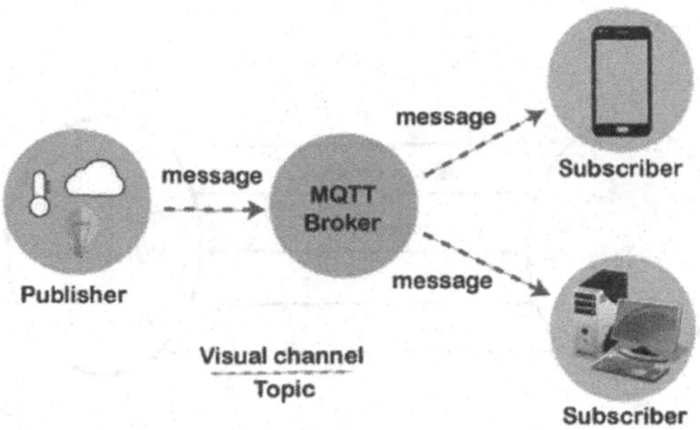

Figure 4: Data handshaking with MQ telemetry transport protocol.

IoT messaging is standardised through the MQTT protocol. It is a simple protocol made for publishing and receiving messages. It uses less power and has minimal bandwidth requirements. Figure 4 shows the data handshaking of MQTT using publisher, subscriber and broker.

3. Results

Components used in IoT layer-wise architecture are employed to implement the suggested architecture framework. Sensors in node 1 and node 2 are used to monitor environment parameters at the close and open waste that connects to the Node MCU platform, an open-source platform. The LoRa protocol and IEEE 802.11 Wi-Fi transmit this data wirelessly. The coordinator is linked to the cloud server via a Wi-Fi network. To continue data transfer to the Thing Speak Cloud platform with the help of the MQTT protocol, the perception layer first analyses sensor information and temporarily maintains it in a database, as seen in Figure 5. Figure 6 shows the sequence diagram between the MQTT client and Thing-Speak MQTT broker. First, the client is communicated with the broker, and acknowledgement is received back to the client. After getting the acknowledgement, The client is subscribed to the broker to the received message. On a smartphone, tablet, or monitoring screen, a dashboard with a graphical user interface (GUI) displays data with the Thing-Speak cloud platform, as shown in Figure 7.

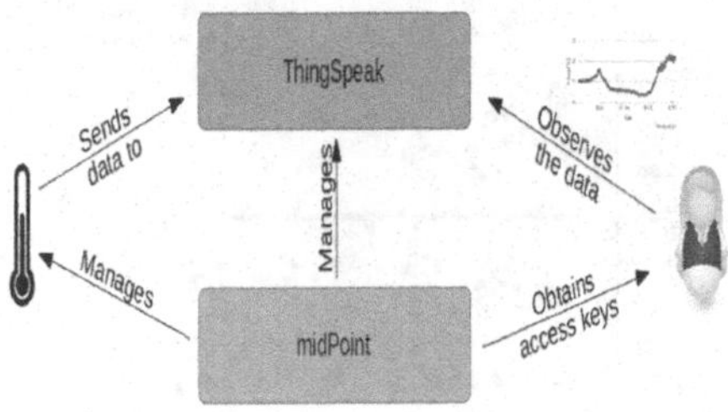

Figure 5: Data handshaking process with thing speaks cloud platform.

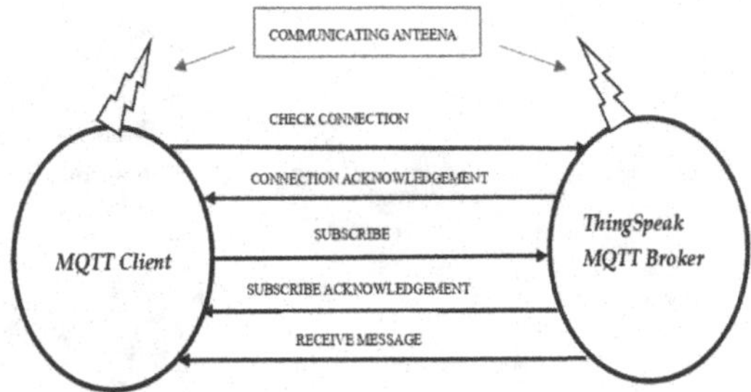

Figure 6: Things speak MQTT communication between devices.

Wearable sensor parameters are tracked, researched and analysed to assess the system's performance in multiple ecological tasks. When examining normal and abnormal circumstances in the same domain, the sensor reading parameters are monitored for two sensor nodes placed in an open and closed environment. The distributions are represented statistically on the cloud.

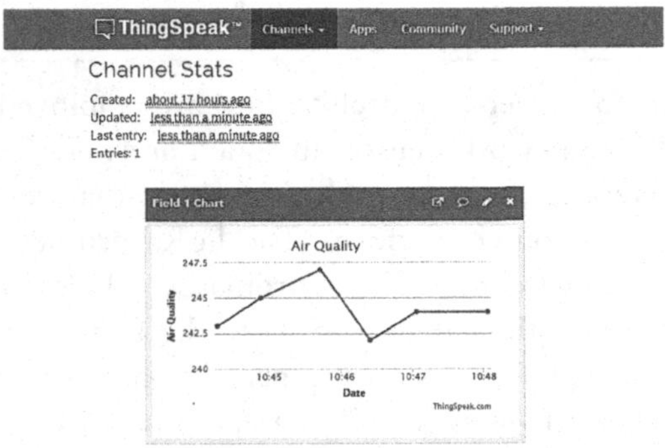

Figure 7: Thing speak dashboard with air quality data representation.

The plot of distance using IR sensor, odour level, air quality level, weight level and smoke level data parameter is shown in Figures 8–12, in which periodic data is collected at the different conditional waste environments.

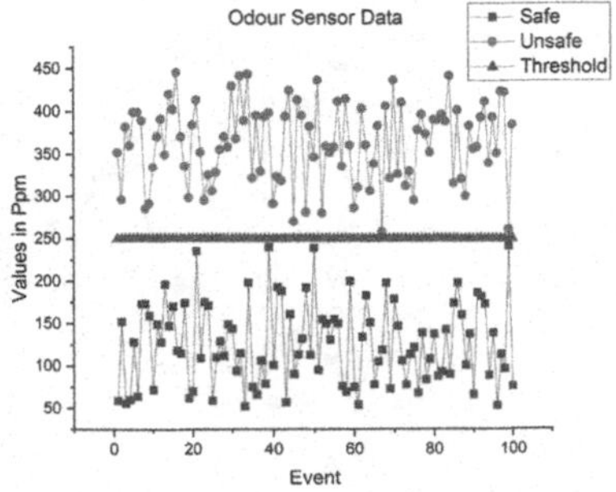

Figure 8: IR sensor data versus conditional events.

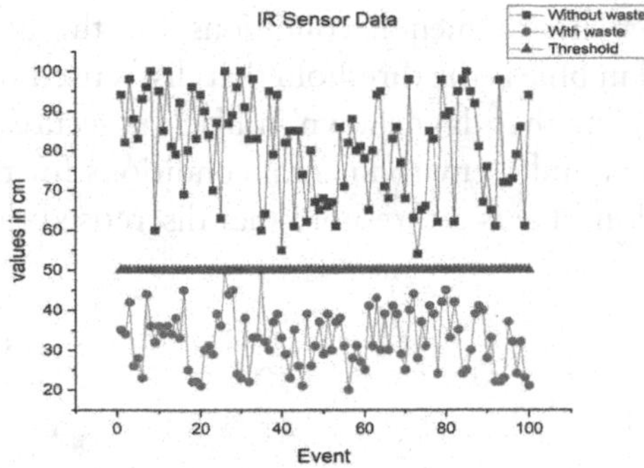

Figure 9: Odour sensor data versus conditional events.

Figure 8 represents the data, which indicates the level of waste in cm. The threshold defined in blue colour categorises the level of junk. Above the threshold level acts as no waste is found in the dustbin. Figure 9 depicts that the data shown in black is safe, and red is unsafe for various discrete events under environmental conditions for odour Sensor. The threshold mentioned in blue is a threshold that discretised the safe and hazardous values.

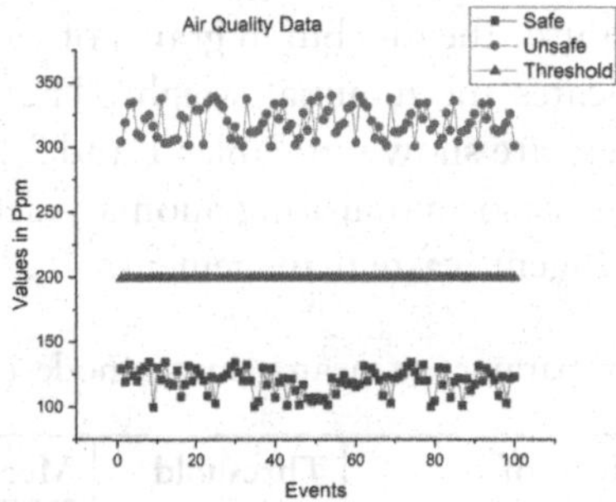

Figure 10: Air quality data versus conditional events.

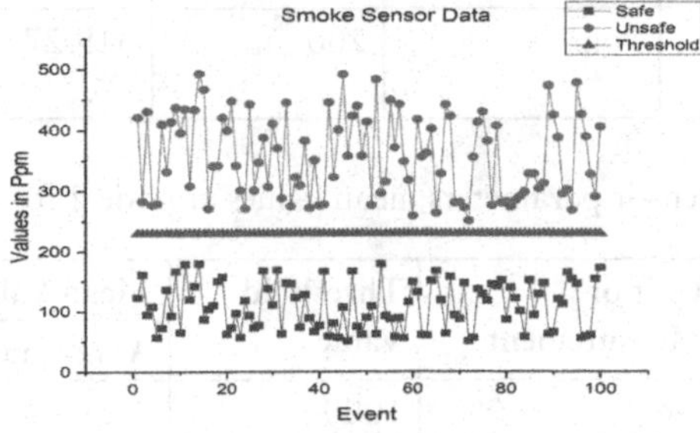

Figure 11: Smoke sensor data versus conditional events.

Figure 10 depicts that data shown in black is safe, and red is unsafe for various discrete events under environmental conditions for the air quality sensor. The threshold mentioned in blue is the threshold that discretised the safe and hazardous values. Figure 11 depicts that data shown in black is secure, and red is unsafe for various discrete events under environmental conditions for the smoke sensor. The threshold mentioned in blue is a threshold that discretised the safe and hazardous values.

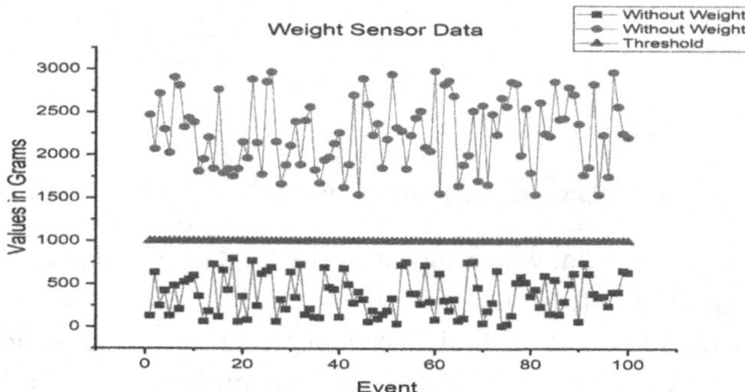

Figure 12: *Weight sensor data versus conditional events.*

The weight sensor data is represented in Figure 12. The value of weight above the threshold acts as the weight of the dustbin in grams of various waste collected and below the threshold indicates the minimal weight. The mean values of different waste condition parameters are shown in Tables 1 and 2 for abnormal and normal activities over a day using sensor monitoring anomaly detection, which lowers the maintenance cost for intelligent waste management.

Table 1: Sensor parameters mean values at node 1 for day hours.

Sensors Parameter	Unit of Measurement	Threshold Value	Mean Value	
			Abnormal	Normal
IR Sensor	Cm	50	32.53	80.8
Odour Sensor	Ppm	250	363.79	121.73
Air Quality Sensor	Ppm	200	319.27	119.43

Table 2: Sensor parameters mean values at node 2 for day hours.

Sensors Parameter	Unit of Measurement	Threshold Value	Mean Value	
			Abnormal	Normal
Weight Sensor	Gm	1000	2256.66	374.42
Smoke Sensor	Ppm	230	357.69	109.9

Table 3: Comparative analysis table of proposed method and existing research work.

Parameters Gunawan T. *et al.* [7]		References			
		Allen & Parilla *et al.* [9]	Dev V. Savla *et al.* [11]	J., Varkey *et al.* [13]	Proposed Model
Sensors Used	Ultrasonic/IR				
	Odour				
	Air Quality				
	Weight				
	Smoke				
Technology Used	IoT				
	LoRa				
	Fog Intelligence				
	Real-Time Statistics				
	Notification/ Alert System				

4. Conclusion

IoT is an emerging technology that will transform humanity's cities into smart ones. Waste generation is also rising due to the rapid growth of smart cities. IoT waste management is a significant problem. The suggested solution built a real-time data collection system for raw trash over IoT using the Thing Speaks cloud platform. This research also recommended utilising LoRa to monitor rubbish in places without cellular service. Testing the suggested system effectively demonstrated how the offered solution executed all expected capabilities. The proposed solution will also be used at the middleware layer of the data analytics system by regularly collecting data.

References

[1] Xia, W., Y. Jiang, X. Chen, and R. Zhao, "Application of machine learning algorithms in municipal solid waste management: a mini-review," Waste Manage. Res., vol. 40, p. 0734242X2110337, 2021. 10.1177/0734242X211033716.

[2] Sharma, P. and U. Vaid, "Emerging role of artificial intelligence in waste management practices," COSMIC 2021, *IOP Conf. Ser.: Earth Environ. Sci.*, vol. 889, p. 012047, 2021, IOP Publishing, doi:10.1088/1755-1315/889/1/012047.

[3] Gade, D. and S. Aithal, "Smart city waste management through ICT and IoT driven solution," vol. 5, pp. 51–65, 2021. doi: 10.5281/zenodo.4739109.

[4] Ghahramani, M., M. Zhou, A. Mölter, and F. Pilla, "IoT-based route recommendation for an intelligent waste management system," *IEEE Internet Things J.*, pp. 1–1, 2021. doi: 10.1109/JIOT.2021.3132126..

[5] Gopalan, U., D. Rajalakshmi, Y. Teekaraman, R. Kuppusamy, and A. Radhakrishnan, "A novel strategy for waste prediction using machine learning algorithm with IoT-based intelligent waste management system," *Wireless Commun. Mobile Comput.*, vol. 2022, pp. 1–15, 2022. doi: 10.1155/2022/2063372.

[6] Khan, R., S. Kumar, A. K. Srivastava, N. Dhingra, M. Gupta, N. Bhati, and P. Kumari, "Machine learning and IoT-based waste management model," *Comput. Intell. Neurosci.*, vol. 2021, Article ID 5942574, 11 p, 2021. https://doi.org/10.1155/2021/5942574.

[7] Gunawan, T., E. Hernawati, and B. R. Aditya, "IoT-based waste height and weight monitoring system," *J. Comput. Sci.*, vol. 17, no. 11, pp. 1085–1092, 2021. https://doi.org/10.3844/jcssp.2021.1085.1092.

[8] John, J., M. S. Varkey, R. S. Podder, *et al.*, "Smart prediction and monitoring of waste disposal system using IoT and cloud for IoT-based smart cities," *Wireless Pers. Commun.*, vol. 122, pp. 243–275, 2022. https://doi.org/10.1007/s11277-021-08897-z.

[9] Parilla, R. A., O. J. Leorna, R. D. Attos, M. G. B. Palconit, J.-J. Obiso, and P. Maria Gemel, "Low-cost garbage level monitoring system in drainages using internet of things in the Philippines," vol. 18, pp. 164–186, 2020.

[10] Pamintuan, M., S. M. Mantiquilla, H. Reyes, and M. J. Samonte, "i-BIN: an intelligent trash bin for automatic waste segregation and monitoring system," *2019 IEEE 11th International Conference on Humanoid, Nanotechnology, Information Technology, Communication and Control, Environment, and Management (HNICEM)*, pp. 1–5, 2019, DOI: 10.1109/HNICEM48295.2019.9072787.

[11] Savla, D. V., *et al.*, "IoT and ML-based smart system for efficient garbage monitoring," *Third International Conference on Smart Systems and Inventive Technology (ICSSIT 2020)*, IEEE Xplore Part Number: CFP20P17-ART; ISBN: 978-1-7281-5821-1.

[12] Gupta, T., R. Joshi, D. Mukhopadhyay, *et al.*, "A deep learning approach-based hardware solution to categorize garbage in environment," *Complex Intell. Syst.*, vol. 8, pp. 1129–1152, 2022. https://doi.org/10.1007/s40747-021-00529-0.

[13] John, J., M. S. Varkey, R. S. Podder, *et al.* "Smart prediction and monitoring of waste disposal system using IoT and cloud for IoT-based smart cities," *Wireless Pers. Commun.*, vol. 122, pp. 243–275, 2022. https://doi.org/10.1007/s11277-021-08897-z.

[14] Singh, R. M., "Analysis of precise green house management system using machine learning based internet of things (IoT) for smart farming," *2021 2nd International Conference on Smart Electronics & Communication (ICOSEC)*, pp. 21–28, 2021, doi: 10.1109/ICOSEC51865.2021.9591962.

[15] Singh, K. M. "Comparative analysis of e-Health care telemedicine system based on internet of medical things and artificial intelligence," *2021 2nd International Conference on Smart Electronics and Communication (ICOSEC)*, pp. 1768–1775, 2021, doi: 10.1109/ICOSEC51865.2021.9591941.

[16] Ali Al-Samawi, M. A. and M. Singh, "Effect of 5G on IOT and daily life application," *2022 3rd International Conference for Emerging Technology (INCET)*, pp. 1–5, 2022, doi: 10.1109/INCET54531.2022.9823983.

[17] Belsare, K. S. and M. Singh, "Various frameworks for IoT-enabled intelligent waste management system using ML for smart cities," *Mobile Computing and Sustainable Informatics*, Springer, Singapore, pp. 797–817, 2022. doi: 10.1007/978-981-19-2069-1_55.

[18] Hassan, M., M. Singh, K. Hamid, R. Saeed, M. Abdelhaq, R. Alsaqour, and N. Odeh, "Enhancing NOMA's spectrum efficiency in a 5G network through cooperative spectrum sharing," *Electronics*, vol. 12, no. 4, p. 815, 2023.

[19] Singh, M., N. K. Jhajj, and A. Goraya, "IoT-enabled wireless mobile Ad-Hoc networks: introduction, challenges, applications: review chapter," *Internet Things*, pp. 121–134, https://www.taylorfrancis.com/chapters/edit/10.1201/9781003181613-10/iot-enabled-wireless-mobile-ad-hoc-networks-manwinder-singh-navdeep-kaur-jhajj-anudeep-goraya.

54. Prediction of Type 2 Diabetes Mellitus Using Gradient Boosted Tree Approach

Prakash Arumugam[1], Abinayaa S S[2], and Divya Bhavani Mohan[3]

[1]*School of Research, Karnavati University, Gujarat, India*
[2]*Department of ECE, Dr. N.G.P. Institute of Technology, Coimbatore, India*
[3]*Unitedworld School of Computational Intelligence, Karnavati University, Gujarat, India*

Abstract: Type 2 diabetes mellitus, also known as type 2 diabetes, is a chronic metabolic ailment defined by high blood sugar levels caused by the body's incapability to utilise insulin or insufficient insulin synthesis. Insulin is a pancreatic hormone that regulates glucose and allows cells to use glucose for energy. There is a tremendous increase in the creation of medical diagnostic models to assist healthcare workers in the recent time. Diabetes is a major problem among the frequent health conditions influencing the global population. Machine learning methods have widely been investigated in the domain of diabetes diagnosis for building illness detection models, using varied datasets mostly acquired from clinical trials. The success of these models is strongly reliant on the classification algorithm chosen and the quality of the dataset. This research paper presents a comprehensive investigation of various machine-learning algorithms executed in RapidMiner Studio. The results obtained by all the models are presented and it was found that Gradient Boosted Trees gave a surpassing accuracy of 97.8%.

Keywords: Type 2 diabetes mellitus, prediction, boosted trees, machine learning, rapid miner.

1. Introduction

Type 2 diabetes (T2D) is a chronic metabolic disorder that affects how sugar, an essential source of energy, is used by the body. It is an autoimmune illness that develops gradually and is common in adults, though it can occur in children and adolescents. The pancreas generates insulin, a hormone that aids in blood sugar regulation by helping cells to absorb glucose from the bloodstream. In T2D, insulin resistance develops and the pancreas may generate insufficient insulin. As a result, glucose builds up in the bloodstream, causing hyperglycemia (high blood sugar levels). T2D is caused by a combination of genetic, lifestyle and environmental factors. A sedentary lifestyle, being overweight or obese, and having a family history of diabetes are all risk factors for the condition. T2D, if uncontrolled, can lead to a variety of complications. Many people with T2D, however, can live healthy and fulfilling lives with proper management and lifestyle changes. Treatment for type 2 diabetes typically consists of a combination of changes in the way of living, such as eating a balanced diet, regular exercise and maintaining a healthy weight. Oral medications or insulin therapy may be prescribed in some cases to help manage blood sugar levels effectively. Regular blood glucose monitoring and ongoing medical care are critical for managing T2D and lowering the risk of complications. Furthermore, patient education about the condition, its management and potential risks is critical for empowering people to take charge of their health and make informed decisions. It is worth noting that medical research and advancements in diabetes management are still evolving, giving hope for better treatments and outcomes for people with type 2 diabetes mellitus.

2. Related Works

This section presents the recent related works of T2D. Remarkable works carried out between 2013 to 2023 were studied. Early intervention in T2DM treatment, especially in the pre-diabetic stage, reduces burden and consequences, according to Pratley in 2013. Since pre-diabetes and type 2 diabetes start asymptomatically, detecting them is difficult [1]. Fang *et al.* [9] examined the connection between gonadotropic hormones and metabolic parameters in women with PCOS and T2D. PCOS women had higher metabolic disruption than T2D women, according to the study [5]. Asmat *et al.* provided a short assessment of the link between diabetes mellitus and oxidative stress in 2016. It outlines the fundamentals of oxidative stress in diabetes mellitus and discusses the numerous oxidative stress biomarkers in diabetes mellitus. Cannon *et al.* [5] examined US and global diabetes prevalence, T2D risk variables and how diabetes complications affect HRQoL and healthcare costs. T2D, which accounts for 90–95% of diabetes cases, is characterised by insulin insufficiency, peripheral insulin resistance and high blood glucose [7]. In 2018, Jamali *et al.* looked into how T2D affected magnesium levels in people who did and did not have hypertension. The study comprised 245 patients with T2D, 123 of whom had hypertension and 122 of whom did not. The study discovered that 52.04% of hypertension participants with diabetes and 47.96% of non-hypertensive subjects with diabetes had lower serum magnesium levels [8]. Bellou *et al.* found non-genetic T2D risk variables in 2018. Obesity, small hip circumference, serum biomarkers, poor food, lack of learning and meticulousness, no physical activity, TV time, lower alcohol consumption, smoking, air pollution and specific medical disorders were discovered. In certain meta-analyses, small-study effects and excess significant bias were found [6]. Dunlay *et al.* reviewed epidemiology, pathophysiology and T2DM in 2019. It also discusses the efficacy of heart failure therapy in people with and without T2DM, the safety of heart failure meds in CKD patients and how heart failure medications affect glycaemic management. Gomes *et al.* studied 15,992 patients in 2019. The study followed regular clinical practise at each site, and data collection for any variable was optional. According to the study, first-line therapy was ineffective; hence, efficacy was the main reason for switching to second-line therapy [9]. Gomes *et al.* studied 15,992 patients in 2019. The study followed regular clinical practise at each site, and data collection for any variable was optional. According to the study, first-line therapy was ineffective, hence efficacy was the main reason for switching to second-line therapy.

Westman explains T2D pathogenesis and advocates carbohydrate-restricted diets in 2021. Such diets may improve hyperglycaemia and hyperinsulinaemia. It also underlines the lack of evidence linking saturated fat to heart disease [13]. Rahman *et al.* found substantial gender- and age-related differences in the mean overall health score in 2022. Diabetes interval, oral hypoglycaemic medication use, comorbidities, and diet and exercise compliance all exhibited significant quality of life disparities. Insulin use altered physical function, mental health, pain, and quality of life [14]. Christie evaluated 9 people in 2023 and found eight elements affecting self-management: information gaps, feelings, provider experiences, disease viewpoint, disease minimisation, Metformin's notoriety, and an excess of diagnoses. [16]. Agliata et. al. in the year 2023 proposed a binary classifier for determining the risk of an individual in diabetes. The execution was carried out on a balanced dataset and the accuracy obtained was 86% with a ROC value of 0.934 [19]. In 2023, Iparraguirre-Villanueva *et al.* compared five ML algorithms for diabetes prediction and found that Bernoulli Naïve Bayes (BNB) and K-NN yielded the best results. [20]. The aforementioned study suggests that many researchers have used various strategies to achieve effective findings and predict diabetes mellitus early. Implementing an effective diabetes early prediction system can close the gap in true and false-positive classification.

3. Dataset Description and Implementation

The patients who have been diagnosed with diabetes are represented in the dataset chosen for this study, which was collected from Sylhet Diabetes Hospital in Sylhet, Bangladesh. Patients hospitalised to that hospital have completed the surveys directly. The dataset consists of 15 attributes and one target variable as class; 520 samples, out of which the class outcomes of 320 samples are positive and the rest are negative. The distribution class percentage for the positive class is 62% and the negative class is 38%. The dataset was initially checked for the missing values, and it was found that there are no missing values. The proposed work was implemented in RapidMiner Studio (10.1) installed on windows 11 operating system installed on Intel Core i7 processor embedded with 16GB RAM. The listed machine learning algorithms are chosen for analysis and comparing the performance metrics: gradient boosted trees (GBT), deep learning (DL), logistic regression (LR), generalised linear model (GLM), naive bayes (NB), random forest (RF), decision tree (DT), fast large margin (FLM) and support vector machines (SVMs).

4. Proposed Methodology

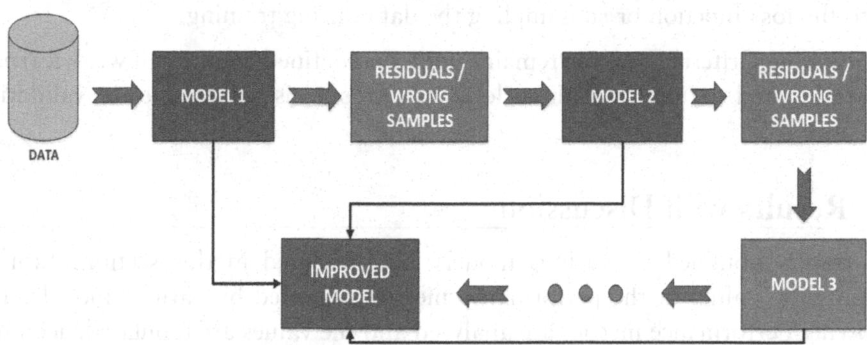

Figure 1: *Flow model of the proposed methodology.*

Gradient boosting is a machine learning approach utilised for tasks related to classification and regression. It is a potent ensemble learning technique that combines the predictions of numerous weak learners (usually decision trees) to produce a strong learner. Gradient boosting builds models sequentially, with each new model trying to spot and rectify the errors made by the previous ones. The key point behind this is to develop an innovative model to the left over errors of the preceding model, which gradually reduces the overall error.

Here are the main components and steps of the gradient boosting algorithm:

Weak Learner: The base learner or weak learner is typically a decision tree with a limited depth, often referred to as a 'stump.' These simple models are trained to capture some patterns in the data but are not overly complex.

Initialisation: The first learner, a weak one, is trained from scratch using the raw data. The average or some other straightforward function of the dependent variable is frequently used as the starting point for the prediction.

Sequential Learning: After the initial model is built, subsequent models are trained to rectify the errors (residuals) of the preceding model. The concept is to fit each newly developed model to the slope of loss function inline to the existing ensemble's estimates. This is where the name 'Gradient' comes from.

Weighting and Learning Rate: Each model's prediction is scaled by a factor called the learning rate before being added to the ensemble. The learning rate controls the contribution of each model to the final prediction and is a hyper parameter that needs to be tuned.

Ensemble Building: The final forecast is a sum of the predictions made by all of the weak learners. This aggregation may occur additively (through regression) or democratically (by voting) (classification).

Regularisation: To prevent overfitting, gradient boosting typically employs regularisation techniques like limiting the depth of trees, adding a penalty term to the loss function or subsampling the data during training.

Stopping Criteria: Training remains until a predefined quantity of weak learners are created or until a definite level of outcome is achieved on a validation dataset.

5. Results with Discussion

The results obtained by various models are presented in this section. Table 1 presents the values of the performance metrics obtained by various models. The following performance metrics are analysed and the values are tabulated: accuracy (A), error (E), AUC, precision (P), recall (R), F-measure (F-M), sensitivity (Sn) and specificity (Sp).

Table 1: Values of various performance metrics obtained by various models.

Model	A	E	AUC	P	R	F-M	Sn	Sp
GBT	97.8	2.2	0.987	90	98.9	94.2	98.9	82.4
DL	95.7	4.3	0.962	94.1	94.4	94.1	94.4	88.5
LR	92.6	7.4	0.973	91.9	96.8	94.3	96.8	85.2
GLM	91.3	8.7	0.957	91	95.7	93.2	95.7	83.7
NB	90.6	9.4	0.952	91.7	93.7	92.6	93.7	85.3
RF	90.6	9.4	0.967	86.9	100	93	100	74.9
DT	90.5	9.5	0.969	92.7	92.1	92.1	92.1	88
FLM	89.3	10.7	0.949	87.4	96.8	91.8	96.8	76.7

From the above table, it is inferred that the GBT has 97.8% accuracy and 2.2% inaccuracy. The model's AUC, accuracy, recall, f-measure, sensitivity and specificity are 0.957, 90, 98.9, 94.2 and 82.4. GBT scored higher on performance metrics than other models. The AUC of GBT is 0.987, greater than other models.

Table 2: Confusion matrix of all the models.

Models		tN	tP	Class Precision
GBT	Predicted Negative	47	1	97.92
	Predicted Positive	10	90	90.00
	Class Recall	82.46	98.90	
DL	Predicted Negative	50	5	90.91
	Predicted Positive	6	88	93.62
	Class Recall	89.29	94.62	

LR	Predicted Negative	47	3	94.00
	Predicted Positive	8	90	91.84
	Class Recall	85.45	96.77	
GLM	Predicted Negative	47	4	92.16
	Predicted Positive	9	89	90.82
	Class Recall	83.93	95.70	
NB	Predicted Negative	49	6	88.89
	Predicted Positive	8	87	91.58
	Class Recall	85.71	93.55	
RF	Predicted Negative	43	6	87.00
	Predicted Positive	14	92	88.79
	Class Recall	75.44	87.00	
DT	Predicted Negative	53	7	88.33
	Predicted Positive	7	81	92.05
	Class Recall	88.33	92.05	
FLM	Predicted Negative	43	3	93.48
	Predicted Positive	13	90	87.38
	Class Recall	76.79	96.77	

The confusion matrix generated on the test set obtained for all the models is epitomised in Table 2. The class precision value is generated for the predicted negative and predicted positive; the class recall value is generated for the true positive and true negative. It is inferred that the highest class precision value for predicted negative is 97.92, which is obtained by GBT model; predicted positive is 90.00 by DL model; highest class recall for true negative is 89.29 by DL model and for true positive is 98.90 by GBT model.

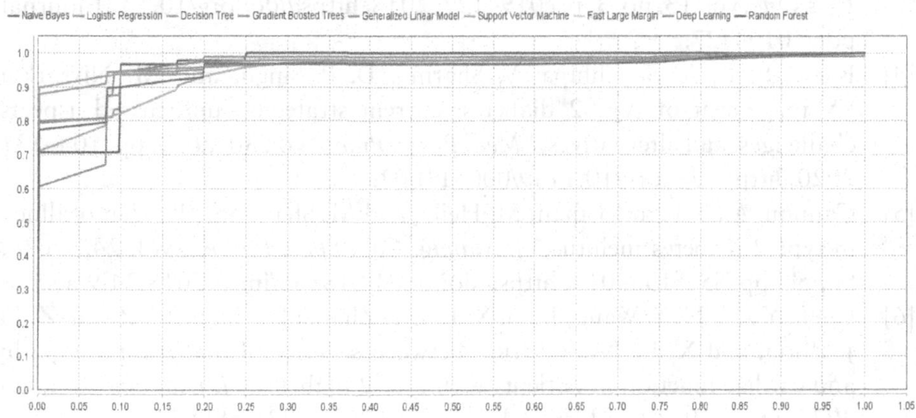

Figure 2: AU-ROC curves of the reported models.

6. Conclusion

In this study, the Syllhet Bangladesh hospital dataset is evaluated with the use of a wide range of different machine learning models so that the severity of T2DM may be determined. When it came to achieving the best classifications and evaluating this illness, it is found that the GBT model outperformed the other models that were reported, with a highest accuracy of 97.8%. This dataset is utilised frequently in research and analysis. In the future, the performance can be improved further by incorporating a number of different noise removal techniques, and the same will be analysed using a number of different diabetes datasets. Additionally, high-performing machine learning models may be used to investigate a number of important characteristics that will allow us to better categorise this condition. As a consequence of this, the work that was done has the potential to have a significant therapeutic impact, and the strategy that was devised based on the conclusions of the study will assist researchers and physicians in establishing more accurate diagnoses of type 2 diabetes.

References

[1] Agliata, A., D. Giordano, F. Bardozzo, S. Bottiglieri, A. Facchiano, and R. Tagliaferri, "Machine learning as a support for the diagnosis of type 2 diabetes," *Int. J. Mol. Sci.*, vol. 24, p. 6775, 2023, https://doi.org/10.3390/ijms24076775.

[2] Barman, P., M. Das, and M. Verma, "Epidemiology of type 2 diabetes mellitus and treatment utilization patterns among the elderly from the first wave of Longitudinal Aging study in India (2017-18) using a Heckman selection model," *BMC Public Health*, vol. 23, no. 1, 2023. https://doi.org/10.1186/s12889-023-15661-4.

[3] Bellou, V., L. Belbasis, I. Tzoulaki, and E. Evangelou, "Risk factors for type 2 diabetes mellitus: An exposure-wide umbrella review of meta-analyses," *Plos One*, vol. 13, no. 3, p. e0194127, 2018, https://doi.org/10.1371/journal.pone.0194127.

[4] Borse, S. P., A. S. Chhipa, V. Sharma, D. P. Singh, and M. Nivsarkar, "Management of type 2 diabetes: current strategies, unfocussed aspects, challenges, and alternatives," *Med. Princ. Pract.*, vol. 30, no. 2, pp. 109–121, 2020. https://doi.org/10.1159/000511002.

[5] Cannon, A., Y. Handelsman, M. Heile, and M. Shannon, "Burden of illness in type 2 diabetes mellitus," *J. Manag. Care Spec. Pharm.*, vol. 24, no. 9-a Suppl., pp. S5–S13, 2018, https://doi.org/10.18553/jmcp.2018.24.9-a.s5.

[6] Chen, Y., M. Li, Y. Wang, J. Fu, X. Liu, Y. Zhang, L. Liu, S. Ta, Z. Lu, Z. Li, J. Zhou, and X. Li, "Association between severity of diabetic retinopathy and cardiac function in patients with type 2 diabetes," *J. Diabetes Res.*, vol. 2023, pp. 1–10, 2023. https://doi.org/10.1155/2023/6588932.

[7] Christie, H., "Back to the beginning: diagnosis experiences of persons with type two diabetes," *Int. J. Diabetes Clin. Res.*, vol. 10, no. 2, 2023. https://doi.org/10.23937/2377-3634/1410170.

[8] Ellenga-Mbolla, B. F., H. G. Monabeka, P. M. Ossou-Nguiet, G. F. Otiobanda, K. C. M. Guimbi, T. R. Gombet, S. G. Kimbally-Kaky, & B. L. Mbenza, "Stroke in type 2 diabetes mellitus patients admitted to emergency unit in Central African country (Congo): preliminary findings," *J. Diabetes Mellitus*, vol. 03, no. 04, pp. 208–213, 2013. https://doi.org/10.4236/jdm.2013.34032.

[9] Fang, F., M. Gu, L. Chen, N. Li, X. Ding, and Y. Peng, "Comparison of metabolic abnormalities in patients with new-diagnostic polycystic ovary syndrome and with new-diagnostic Type 2 diabetes mellitus," *J. Diabetes Mellitus*, vol. 04, no. 01, pp. 54–58, 2014. https://doi.org/10.4236/jdm.2014.41010.

[10] García-Domínguez, A., C. E. Galván-Tejada, R. Magallanes-Quintanar, H. Gamboa-Rosales, I. G. Curiel, J. Peralta-Romero, and M. Cruz, "Diabetes detection models in Mexican patients by combining machine learning algorithms and feature selection techniques for clinical and paraclinical attributes: a comparative evaluation," *J. Diabetes Res.*, vol. 2023, pp. 1–19, 2023. https://doi.org/10.1155/2023/9713905.

[11] Gomes, M. B., W. Rathmann, B. Charbonnel, K. Khunti, M. Kosiborod, A. Nicolucci, S. J. Pocock, M. V. Shestakova, I. Shimomura, F. Tang, H. Watada, H. Chen, J. Cid-Ruzafa, P. Fenici, N. Hammar, F. Surmont, and L. Ji, "Treatment of type 2 diabetes mellitus worldwide: Baseline patient characteristics in the global DISCOVER study," *Diabetes Res. Clin. Pract.*, vol. 151, pp. 20–32, 2019. https://doi.org/10.1016/j.diabres.2019.03.024.

[12] Iparraguirre-Villanueva, O., K. Espinola-Linares, R.O. Flores Castañeda, and M. Cabanillas-Carbonell, "Application of machine learning models for early detection and accurate classification of type 2 diabetes," *Diagnostics*, vol. 13, p. 2383, 2023. https://doi.org/10.3390/diagnostics13142383.

[13] Jamali, A. A., G. M. Jamali, A. A. Jamali, N. H. Jamali, B. M. Tanwani, M. A. Sohail, & A. A. Rajput, "Association of low serum magnesium levels in type 2 diabetes mellitus with & without hypertension," *Open J. Preventive Med.*, vol. 08, no. 03, pp. 57–69, 2018. https://doi.org/10.4236/ojpm.2018.83006.

[14] López Ruiz, A., M. N. I. Gil, P. P. Alarcón, A. H. Torres, A. B. H. Cascales, and M. D. H. Gil, "Evolution of biochemical effects of type 2 diabetics with cardiovascular risk," *Pharmacol. Pharm.*, vol. 04, no. 09, pp. 679–683, 2013. https://doi.org/10.4236/pp.2013.49094.

[15] Olokoba, A. B., O. A. Obateru, and L. B. Olokoba, "Type 2 diabetes mellitus: a review of current trends," *Oman. Med. J.*, vol. 27, no. 4, pp. 269–273, 2012. doi: 10.5001/omj.2012.68. PMID: 23071876; PMCID: PMC3464757.

[16] Padhi, S., A. K. Nayak, and A. Behera, "Type II diabetes mellitus: a review on recent drug based therapeutics," *Biomed. Pharmacother.*, vol. 131, p. 110708, 2020. https://doi.org/10.1016/j.biopha.2020.110708.

[17] Pratley, R. E., "The early treatment of type 2 diabetes," *Am. J. Med.*, vol. 126, no. 9 Suppl 1, pp. S2-9, 2013. doi: 10.1016/j.amjmed.2013.06.007. PMID: 23953075.

[18] Reed, J., S. Bain, and V. Kanamarlapudi, "A review of current trends with type 2 diabetes epidemiology, aetiology, pathogenesis, treatments and future perspectives," Diabet. Metab. Syndr. Obesity: Targets Ther., vol. 14, pp. 3567–3602, 2021. https://doi.org/10.2147/dmso.s319895.

[19] Westman, E. C., "Type 2 diabetes mellitus: a pathophysiologic perspective," *Front. Nutr.*, vol. 8, 2021. https://doi.org/10.3389/fnut.2021.707371.

[20] Zhou, Y., Y. Kong, W. Fan, T. Tao, Q. Xiao, N. Li, and X. Zhu, "Principles of RNA methylation and their implications for biology and medicine," *Biomed. Pharmacother.*, vol. 131, p. 110731, 2020. https://doi.org/10.1016/j.biopha.2020.110731.

55. Design of a Millimetre-Wave Antenna with Circular Polarization and High Gain on FR4 Substrate

Simerpreet Singh[1], Gaurav Sethi[1], Jaspal Singh Khinda[2]

[1]*Department of Electronics and Electrical Engineering, Lovely Professional University, Phagwara, India*
[2]*Department of Electrical Engineering, Bhai Gurdas Institute of Engineering and Technology, Sangrur, India*

Abstract: A low-cost microstrip antenna is proposed and designed for mm-wave applications on FR4 substrate. It consist of circularly truncated patch, inset feeding of 50 ohms and DGS plane. This etching of circular slots in the patch is used to reduce the mismatch loss and to enhance bandwidth in mm-wave region. DGS in this research is purposely etched out pattern of dumbbell underneath the feeding line which is further optimised to asymmetric in shape by pattern search technique to reduce the mutual coupling in ground plane to further enhance the gain and gain bandwidth. This proposed prototype provides wide –10 dB impedance bandwidth and 7 dBi gain bandwidth of 2.28 GHz (35.83–38.13GHz). Simple design, low manufacturing cost and ease of fabrication make proposed antenna suitable for high-end practical mm-wave applications in the field of biomedical sciences like telemetry and molecular spectroscopic systems and high resolution based radiometric systems in mm-wave frequency range.

Keywords: mm-wave, gain-bandwidth, axial ratio, radiation efficiency, asymmetric.

1. Introduction

Due to the emergence of high-speed future applications during the last decade, the demand for greater bandwidth in the sphere of communication has grown tremendously. This causes high-frequency congestion in lower areas of the spectrum. Thus, in order to minimise interference within current spectrum, the Federal Communication Commission (FCC) [1, 2] and World Radio Communications (WRC-19) have suggested a new spectrum of 24–42.5GHz in the lower mm-Wave range for 5G and beyond [3] communications. This broader spectrum can be used for a range of future applications in heavily populated places. Local multi-point distribution services (LMDS), internet of things (IoT) [1, 4] and unmanned robotic robots are examples. However, mm-Wave communication systems suffer from high transmission losses over long distances, limiting the signals to short and indoor systems. This can be mitigated by limiting mismatch loss (ML_{dB}) as much as practicable [5]. Mismatch losses [6] are proportional to the reflection coefficient (S_{11}), and they can be minimised to a minimum of 0.044 dB, which corresponds to S_{11} –20 dB. The etching of six elliptical grooves [7] in the ground plane boosted the vertical component of current, lowering the mismatch loss to less than 0.044 dB. Furthermore, the design of an antenna for achieving the desired results is dependent on the optimal substrates required to minimise these losses. As a result, intensive study is also being conducted for the selection of substrate material in order to minimise losses. As a result, numerous antennas using different substrates [8–16] have been described in the past. Wadhwa *et al.* [8] demonstrated mm-Wave MIMO antenna with a bandwidth of 30–40 GHz and a peak gain of 9.08 dBi constructed from the low-cost material FR4. Despite its high bandwidth, the antenna is complicated and bigger in size due to the 1 4 MIMO configuration. Hu *et al.* [9] examined mm-Wave range using a SIW feeding-based wideband filtering antenna. The antenna is built on multi-layered RT/Duroid 5880, Rogers 3001 and Rogers COOLSPAN substrates. Hu *et al.* [10] created a 64-element antenna array on an LTCC substrate to increase signal-to-noise ratio by adding nulls between conflicting directions. These antennas [9, 10] are expensive, have sophisticated array designs and are difficult to manufacture. Jilani *et al.* [11] suggested a switchable MIMO antenna on a flexible substrate, namely poly ethylene terephthalate (PET), for wearable mm-Wave applications. Taheri *et al.* [12] created a beam steering end firing mm-Wave planar inverted F-antenna (PIFA) with an anti-reflective layer technology and grating strip. It is built on a Nelco N9000 substrate with dimensions of 70 120 mm^2. The suggested design's array layout makes it bigger in size and hence incompatible with current ultra large scale integrated (ULSI) chipsets. Liu *et al.* [13] demonstrated a partial mm-wave array with a peak gain of 3.8 dB at 30.5 GHz. The planned antenna is based on complex organic layered substrates with copper substrate and supports both polarisations, i.e. horizontal and vertical, to enable a large phased array module of 8 4 with several concurrent beams for applications in 5G. Mantash and Denidni [14] proposed a ring-shaped wearable antenna with a low-cost copper substrate, and multiple performance matrices were examined. The extracted gain bandwidth was 28–33 GHz with a peak gain of 5.5 dB and an overall bandwidth of 25–35GHz. However, the antenna is tiny in size and has a cheap production cost, while having a limited bandwidth of 36.25–38.25 in the mm-Wave range. Singh *et al.* [15] developed mm-wave antenna for improvement in depth of return loss below –20 dB in mm-wave range. Alsudani *et al.* [16] designed a compact 7.24, 6.24 mm^2 mm-Wave antenna [16] using the expensive Roger RO3003 substrate. The antenna has a resonance frequency of 28 GHz and a peak gain of 6.48 dBi. Though none of these antennas [8–16] offer wide gain bandwidth and circular polarisation in the mm-wave spectrum. In order to address the shortcomings noted above, a wideband mm-wave microstrip antenna is developed. In the present paper, the antenna offers a broad mm-wave 7 dBi gain bandwidth of 2.28 GHz (35.85–38.13GHz) with the mismatch loss (ML_{dB}) less than equal to 0.44 dB. The suggested antenna design uses inexpensive FR4 substrate to attain 10 dBi gain bandwidth of 1.46 GHz (35.89–37.35 GHz).

2. Experimental Analysis

The proposed structure is developed on an FR4 substrate having Ls × Ws × h (i.e. 10 mm × 12 mm × 1.6 mm) dimensions. At 7.5 GHz, the design's initial dimensions are estimates according to [10]. A patch with dimensions $L_1 \times W_1$ (i.e. 6 mm × 12 mm) is placed on the substrate, and a partial ground place with measurements $L_g \times W_g$ (i.e. 3.8 mm × 12 mm) is placed on the back side of the substrate. As shown in Figure 1, the patch is supplied by a 50 ohm inset microstrip feed-line having dimensions width (W_f) of 1 mm and length (L_f) of 4 mm. An open polygonal slot (OPS) is cut at the patch's bottom central edge in order to achieve impedance bandwidth of less than or equal to -10 dB. Additionally, the length of feeding line Lf rises from its prior value of 4 mm to 6.16 mm. These configurations result in an inset-fed mm-wave microstrip antenna, as shown in Figure 1. With these changes, the impedance matching patch is now improved to the point that 90% of the power can be sent to it. For a broad bandwidth of 2 GHz, the mismatch loss now drops to a value of 0.44 dB. By combining a parametric analysis with a pattern search technique in HFSS, the size and location of the etched slots in the ground are changed. The caption of Figure 1 shows the planned structure's final parameters.

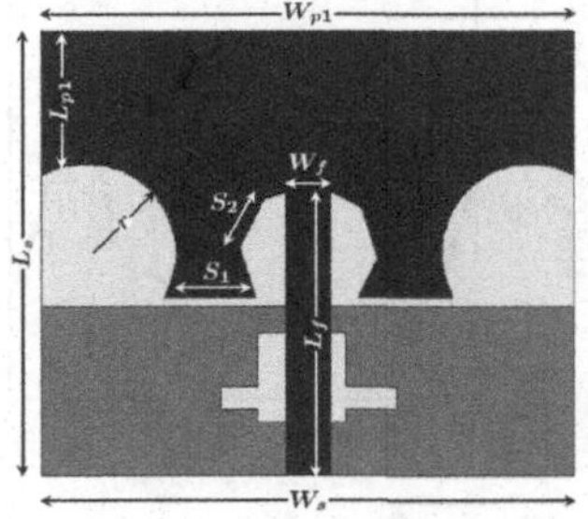

(a) Radiating Patch

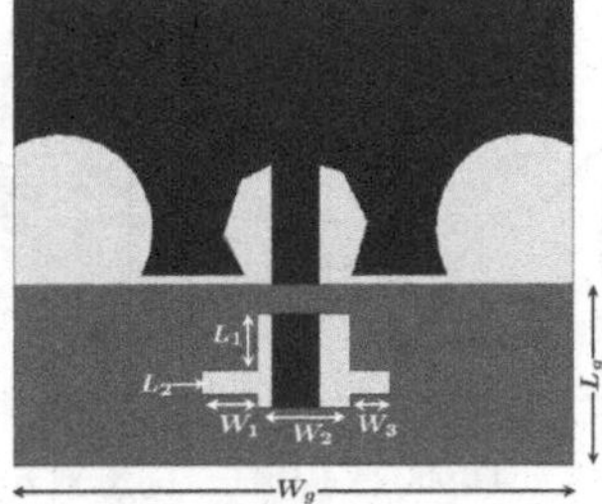

(b) Reflecting Ground Plane

Figure 1: *Antenna configuration with parameters (all in mm);* $L_s = 10$, $W_s = 12$, $L_{p1} = 3.27$, $W_{p1} = 12$, $S_1 = 2.07$, $S_2 = 1.2$, $L_f = 6.37$, $W_f = 1$, $r = 2$, $L_1 = 1.2$, $L_2 = 0.5$, $W_1 = 1.15$, $W_2 = 2$, $W_3 = 0.85$, $W_{g1} = 12$, $L_{g1} = 3.8$.

3. Results and Discussions

The gain plots on the right y-axis and the reflection co-efficient (S_{11}) on the left of the final proposed design are shown in Figure 2 (a). It offers a 2.28 GHz (35.85–38.13 GHz) bandwidth with a -10 dB S_{11} and a 2.28 GHz (35.85–38.13 GHz) bandwidth with a 7 dBi gain. The figure also shows a broad 10 dBi gain bandwidth of 1.46 GHz (35.89–37.35GHz) and a peak gain of 13.29 dBi at 36.3 GHz. Radiation efficiency is shown on the right y-axis in Figure 2 (b), while the axial ratio is shown on the left. According to the findings, antenna design's axial ratio at 37.2 GHz is less than 3 dB, of value 0.92 dB, with a 230 MHz axial ratio bandwidth (ARBW) starting at 37.08–37.31 GHz. This number demonstrates the circular polarization of the antenna for the 230 MHz bandwidth. The graph also demonstrates the variation in radiation efficiency minor, which ranges from 55.02 to 57.35 percent. The proposed antenna design's mismatch loss (ML_{dB}) and throughput graphs are shown in Figure 2 (c). The mismatch loss is computed according to Equation 1 and throughput as per Equation 2. On the left side of the graph, the mismatch loss is less than 1.22 over the full bandwidth range, and on the right, the desired throughput, or above 90 percent uninterrupted for the entire bandwidth of interest, is shown.

$$ML_{dB} = -10log_{10}\left(1 - \left(\frac{VSWR-1}{VSWR+1}\right)^2\right) \quad (1)$$

$$Throughput(\%) = 100 * \left(1 - \left(\frac{VSWR-1}{VSWR+1}\right)^2\right) \quad (2)$$

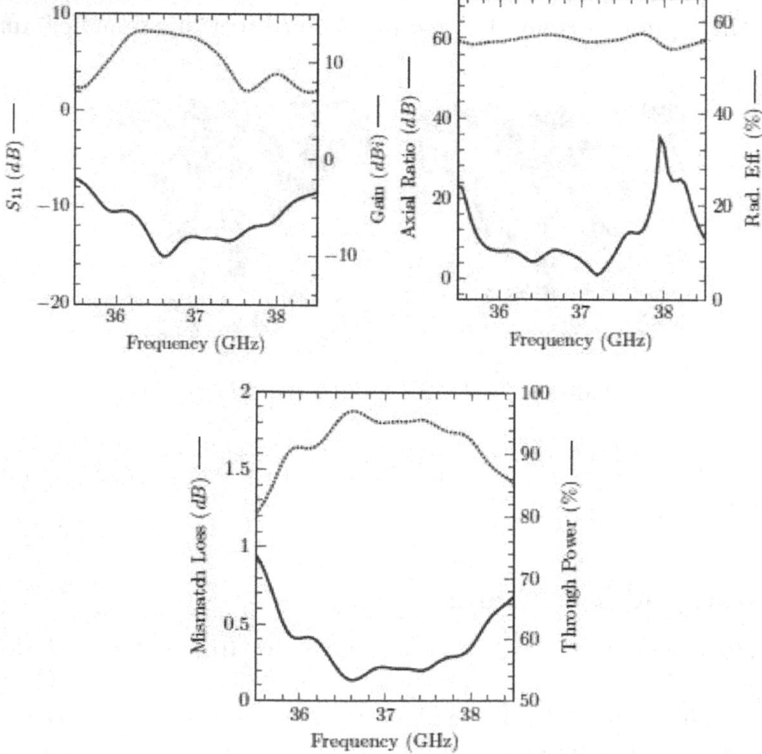

Figure 2: Performance parameters of final prototype.

4. Parametric Analysis of mm-Wave Antenna Structure

Changes are made to the width of the feed line, number of slots in DGS, asymmetric parameters and the radius of circular truncation in the patch in order to optimise the mm-wave antenna parameters.

4.1. Impact on S_{11}, Gain, Axial Ratio, Radiation Efficiency of Variations in Radius r of Circular cut in the Patch

Figure 3 displays the various S11 and gain graphs in respect to the etched circular slot's radius r. It can be seen that when the radius r increases from 1 mm to 2.5 mm, the impedance mismatching gets worse. Without etching a circular slot (i.e. r = 0 mm), the matching of impedance also degrades. Additionally, Figure 4 shows that as r increases from 1 mm to 2.5 mm, the axial ratio and radiation efficiency rapidly degrade.

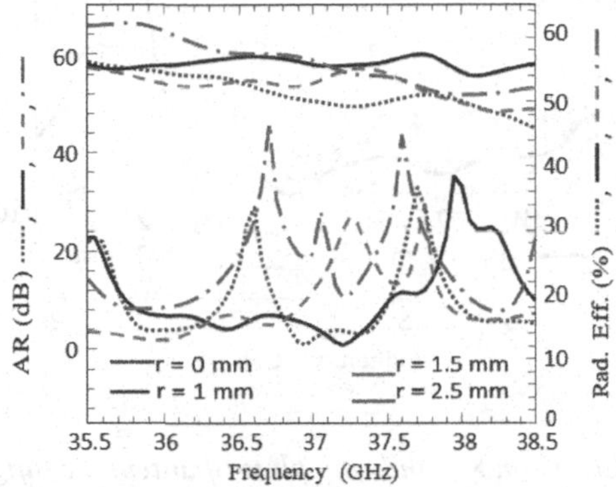

***Figure 3:** Impact of radius r on S_{11} and gain plots of antenna configuration.*

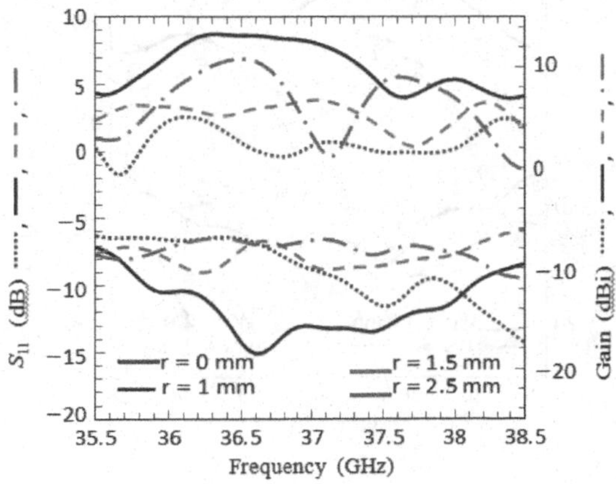

***Figure 4:** Impact of radius r on axial ratio (dB) and radiation efficiency (%) of antenna configuration.*

4.2. Impact on S_{11}, Gain, Axial Ratio, Radiation Efficiency of Variations in Width W_f of Feeding line

Figure 5 shows the various S_{11} and gain graphs in relation to the feeding line width W_f. As can be observed, the impedance matching improves as W_f rises from 1 mm to 2.5 mm. The gain plot, however, noticeably worsens. Additionally, Figure 6 demonstrates that the axial ratio rises above 3 dB as W_f increases from 1 mm through 2.5 mm. The circularly polarised antenna consequently become linear. Additionally, the radiation efficiency varies more than it did when W_f = 1 mm.

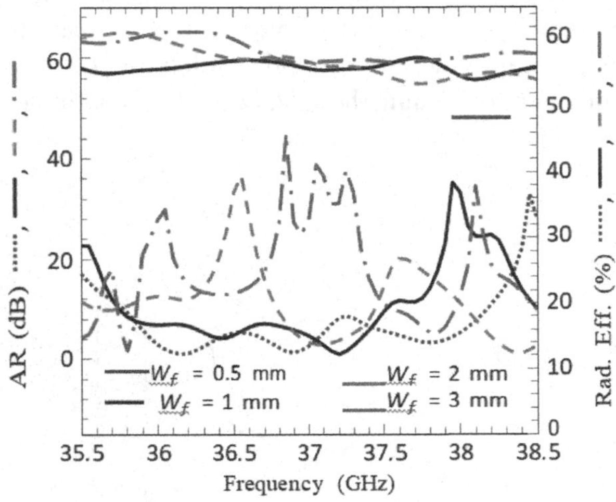

Figure 5: Impact of width W_f on S_{11} and gain plots of antenna configuration.

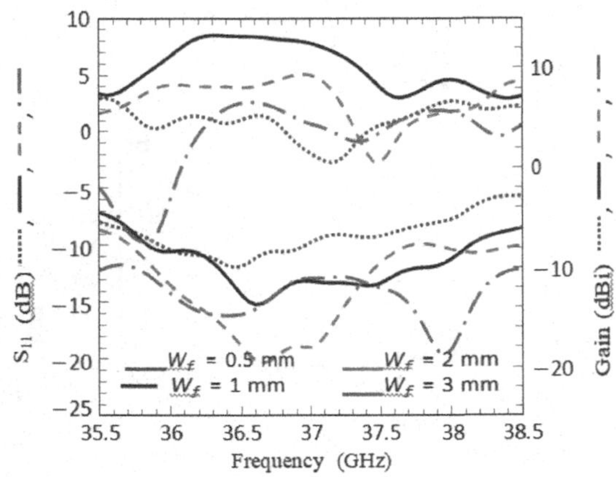

Figure 6: Impact of width W_f on axial ratio(dB) and radiation efficiency (%) of antenna configuration.

4.3. Impact on S_{11}, Gain, Axial Ratio, Radiation Efficiency of Presence of DGS Slots

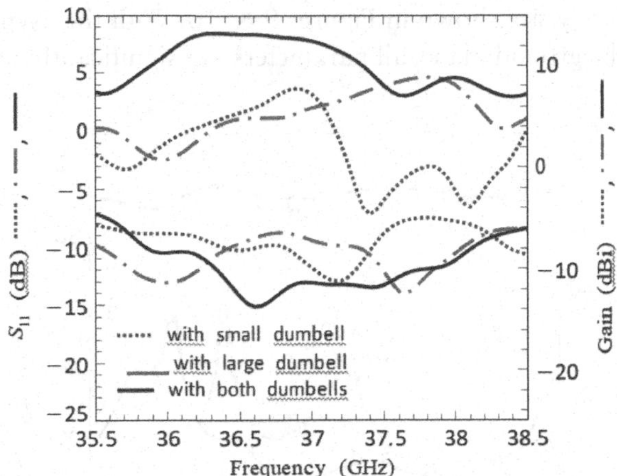

Figure 7: Impact of dumbbells size on S_{11} and gain plots of antenna configuration.

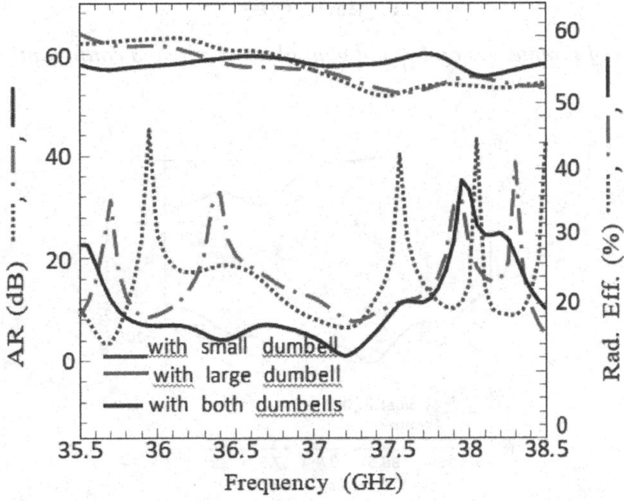

Figure 8: Impact of dumbbells size on axial ratio (dB) and radiation efficiency (%) of antenna configuration.

The etching effect of small- and large-sized dumbbells on S_{11} and gain performances is depicted in Figure 7. The S_{11} and gain considerably worsen either the absence of a small or large DGS dumbbell, as shown in the graphs. Additionally, it can be shown in Figure 8 that without any small- or large-sized dumbbells, circular polarisation changed to linear and fluctuation in radiation efficiency also increases rapidly.

4.4. Impact on S_{11}, Gain, Axial Ratio, Radiation Efficiency of Symmetric or Asymmetric DGS

The effects of symmetric or asymmetric DGS on S_{11}, gain and axial ratio, radiation efficiency, respectively, are shown in Figures 9 & 10. With the asymmetric etching of dumbbells in the ground plane, all parameters are significantly improved.

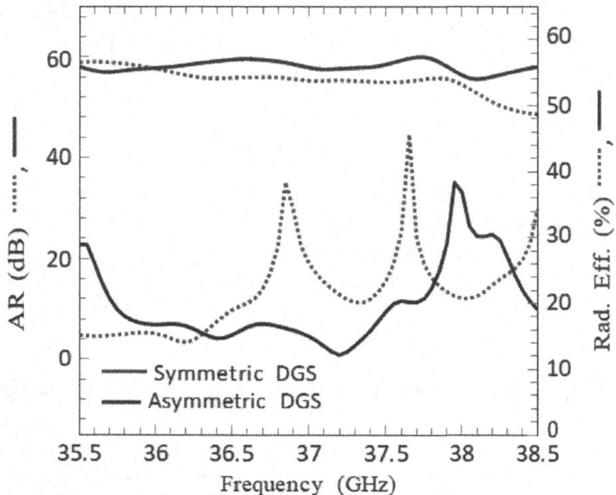

Figure 9: *Impact of symmetries on S_{11} and gain plots of antenna configuration.*

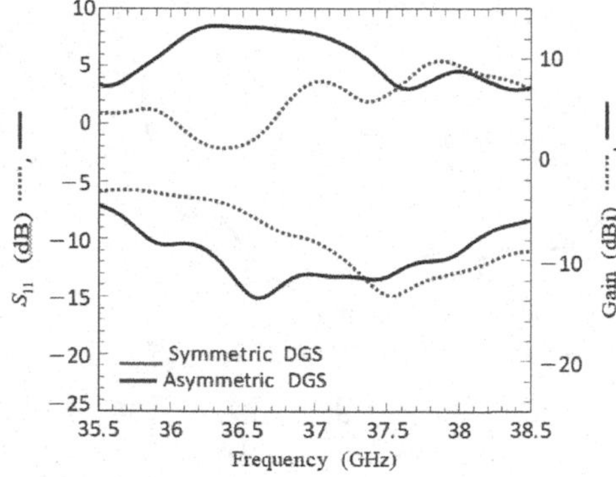

Figure 10: *Impact of symmetries on axial ratio (dB) and radiation efficiency (%) of antenna configuration.*

5. Conclusion

The proposed mm-wave antenna has a −10 dB impedance bandwidth and a 7 dBi gain bandwidth of 2.28 GHz (35.83–38.13GHz). Since the developed antenna is small in size and has a low production cost, this prototype is suited for high-end mm-wave applications such as those in the field of telemedicine. Mismatch loss is also obtained with a desired value of less than equal to 0.44 dB throughout the full bandwidth of interest. As a result, a straightforward design is updated and optimized using asymmetries to enhance S_{11} and gain and high throughput with wide gain bandwidth indicates that it can be used for a number of biomedical applications such as telemetry and molecular spectroscopic systems, as well as high-resolution-based radiometric systems in mm-wave spectrum.

References

[1] Wadhwa, D. S., P. K. Malik, and J. S. Khinda, "High gain antenna for n260- & amp; n261- bands and augmentation in bandwidth for mm-wave range by patch current diversions," *World J. Eng.*, vol. 19, no. 5, pp. 689–696, 2022.

[2] Khinda, J. S., M. R. Tripathy, and D. Gambhir, "Multi-edged wide-band rectangular microstrip fractal antenna array for c-and x-band wireless applications," J. Circuits, Syst. Comput., vol. 26, no. 04, p. 1750068, 2017.

[3] Noor, S. K., N. Ramli, N. M. Sahar, and T. Khalifa, "Compact and wide bandwidth microstrip patch antenna for 5g millimeter wave technology: design and analysis," *J. Phys.: Conf. Ser.*, vol. 1878, no. 1, p. 012008, 2021. IOP Publishing.

[4] Singh, S., G. Sethi, and J. S. Khinda, "A historical development and futuristic trends of microstrip antennas," *Int. J. Comput. Dig. Syst.*, vol. 11, no. 1, pp. 187–204, 2022.

[5] Balanis, C. A., *Antenna Theory: Analysis and Design*, John Wiley & Sons, 2015.

[6] Wadhwa, D. S., P. K. Malik, and J. S. Khinda, "mm-wave patch antenna for high data rate communication applications," *2021 International Conference on Computing, Communication, and Intelligent Systems (ICCCIS)*, IEEE, pp. 778–781, 2021.

[7] Khinda, J. S., M. R. Tripathy, and D. Gambhir, "Improvement in depth of return loss of microstrip antenna for s-band applications," *J. Circuits, Syst. Comput.*, vol. 27, no. 04, p. 1850058, 2018.

[8] Wadhwa, D. S., J. S. Malik, Praveen Kumar &; Khinda, "Improvement in 5 dbi gain- bandwidth of wide band antenna for indoor k–, k a–band, millimeter-wave applications," *J. Infrared, Millimeter, Terahertz Waves*, vol. 43, no. 7–8, pp. 527–549, 2022.

[9] Hu, H.-T. and C. H. Chan, "Substrate-integrated-waveguide-fed wideband filtering antenna for millimeter-wave applications," *IEEE Trans. Antennas Propag.*, vol. 69, no. 12, pp. 8125–8135, 2021.

[10] Hu, C.-N., D.-C. Chang, C.-H. Yu, T.-W. Hsaio, and D.- P. Lin, "Millimeter-wave microstrip antenna array design and an adaptive algorithm for future 5g wireless communication systems," *Int. J. Antennas Propag.*, vol. 2016, 2016.

[11] Jilani, S. F., A. Rahimian, Y. Alfadhl, and A. Alomainy, "Low profile flexible frequency-reconfigurable millimetre-wave antenna for 5g applications," *Flexible Printed Electron.*, vol. 3, no. 3, p. 035003, 2018.

[12] Taheri, M. M. S., A. Abdipour, S. Zhang, and G. F. Pedersen, "Integrated millimeter- wave wideband end-fire 5g beam steerable array and low-frequency 4g lte antenna in mobile terminals," *IEEE Trans. Veh. Technol.*, vol. 68, no. 4, pp. 4042–4046, 2019.

[13] Liu, D., X. Gu, C. W. Baks, and A. Valdes-Garcia, "Antenna in- package design considerations for ka-band 5g communication applications," *IEEE Trans. Antennas Propag.*, vol. 65, no. 12, pp. 6372–6379, 2017.

[14] Mantash, M. and T. Denidni, "Finger-worn end-fire antenna for mm-wave applications," *Microwave Opt. Technol. Lett.*, vol. 59, no. 10, pp. 2591–2593, 2017.

[15] Singh, S., G. Sethi, and J. S. Khinda, "Improvement in depth of reflection co-efficient below- 20 db for millimeter–wave antenna," *J. Phys.: Conf. Ser.*, vol. 2327, no. 1, p. 012048, 2022, IOP Publishing.

[16] Alsudani, A. and H. M. Marhoon, "Design and enhancement of microstrip patch antenna utilizing mushroom like-ebg for 5g communications," *J. Commun.*, vol. 18, no. 3, 2023.

56. Synthesis and Investigation of Electrical Characteristics of Co-Zr Doped M-type Sr Hexaferrites

Sayed Tathir Abbas Naqvi[1], Charanjeet Singh[1],
Sachin Kumar Godara[2]

[1]*Department of Electronics and Communication Engineering, Lovely Professional University, Phagwara, India*
[2]*Department of Apparel and Textile Technology, Guru Nanak Dev University, Amritsar, India*

Abstract: M-type hexaferrites $SrCo_xZr_xFe_{12-2x}O_{19}$ have been prepared by the sol–gel technique. The electric properties of prepared hexaferrites have been examined from 100 Hz to 2 MHz. The inclusion of Co–Zr enhances the conductance and capacitance of the prepared ferrites. The capacitance of the prepared ferrite can be tuned by doping of Co–Zr and can be utilised in various power applications.

Keywords: Ferrites, sol–gel, conductance, admittance.

1. Introduction

Ferrites are an important functional material owing to colossal applications and are used in various domains from microwaves to radio frequency [1–3]. The characteristics like high Curie temperature, good microwave absorption, high electric resistivity and low cost make hexagonal ferrites one of the most widely used ferrites [4–5]. These properties depend on the synthesis method, chemical composition, grain size and porosity [6–8]. Most researchers have investigated spinel ferrites; however, few reports on M-type hexagonal ferrites are available.

Hasan et al. [9] used the sol–gel technique for the synthesis of cerium-substituted hexagonal ferrites. The doping of Ce content affected the dielectric loss of the ferrite. An increment in dielectric loss while a reduction in dielectric constant was noted. The conductivity also increased with doping of Ce content. Analysis of structural, optical and dielectric properties of Al-doped strontium hexaferrites was reported by Dilshad et al. [10]. Zahid et al. [11] prepared a Cr3+ substituted strontium ferrite with a chemical composition of $Sr_{1-x}Cr_xFe_{12}O_{19}$. Godara et al. [12] synthesised barium-strontium ferrite with dual ion substitution. The authors reported a decrement in the dielectric constant with the doping of Zn2+ and Zr4+. Patel et al. [13] synthesised Co4+ and Ca2+ substituted barium strontium hexagonal ferrites using the sol–gel method. Enhancement in ac conductivity was observed with the doping of Co4+ and Ca2+.

Considering the reviewed literature, our motivation is to investigate M-type strontium hexaferrites to understand their electrical properties. Here, M-type strontium ferrites ($SrCo_xZr_xFe_{12-2x}O_{19}$) are prepared using the sol–gel technique. Investigation of Zr4+ and Co2+ doping on the electrical parameters of prepared ferrites is done.

2. Experimental Procedure

M-type strontium hexaferrites $SrCo_xZr_xFe_{12-2x}O_{19}$ were synthesised using the sol–gel technique. The synthesis process used in the preparation of ferrite compositions is shown in Figure 1. First strontium-nitrate, cobalt-nitrate, Zirconium-nitrate and ferric-nitrate were mixed in distilled water. A solution of citric acid in distilled water was mixed in this solution. This solution is termed an aqueous solution as the solution was prepared using water. Ammonia solution is mixed in this solution until the pH of the solution comes to 7. Now this solution is called sol and was heated approximately for 3 hours on a magnetic stirrer at 80°C. The heating of sol converted it to a brown color gel and soon the auto-combustion process started in the gel. The auto-combustion changed the gel in ash form. The obtained ash was transformed into a fine powder with the help of a pestle and mortar which was heated at 900°C for 5 hours.

A hydraulic press was used to convert sintered powder into disk-shaped pellets with a pressure of 2 tons/cm2. Agilent LCR meter (Model- E4980A) was utilised to measure the electrical parameters of the prepared ferrites.

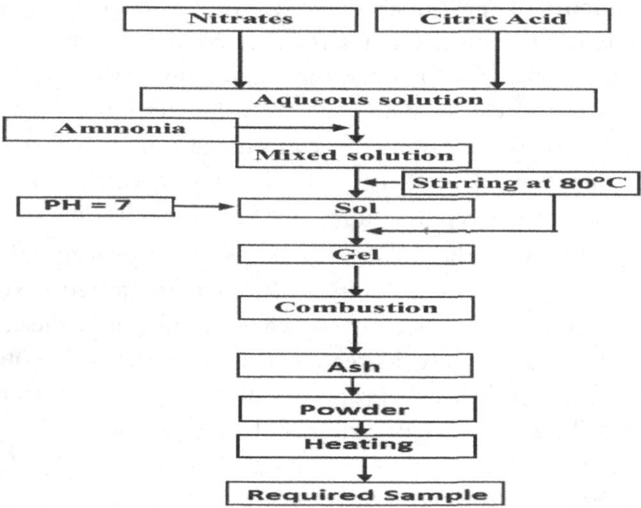

Figure 1: *Schematic representation of the synthesis of ferrite* $SrCo_xZr_xFe_{12-2x}O_{19}$ *using the sol–gel method.*

3. Results and Discussion

3.1. Electrical Conductance Study

The conductance versus frequency curve is shown in Figure 2, which depicts the frequency dependence behaviour of conductance. The mechanism in ferrites is based on Verwey and de Boer's mechanism [14]. Besides this, conduction in ferrites is also described by the polaron hopping model [15], which indicates the frequency dependence of conductance owing to the hopping of charge carriers. The conductance of the prepared ferrite increases gradually with the frequency increment. The conductance curves possess two kinds of region: one flat plateau region and another dispersive region. The flat region indicates the DC conductance G_{DC}, while the dispersive region indicates to AC conductance G_{AC}. The frequency at which transition occurs from DC to AC conductance is called hopping frequency. The inclusion of Co–Zr increases conductance in doped composition as compared to undoped composition. The compositions x=0.0 and 0.4 have significantly low values of G_{AC} at the high-frequency region while x=1.0 has the highest G_{AC}.

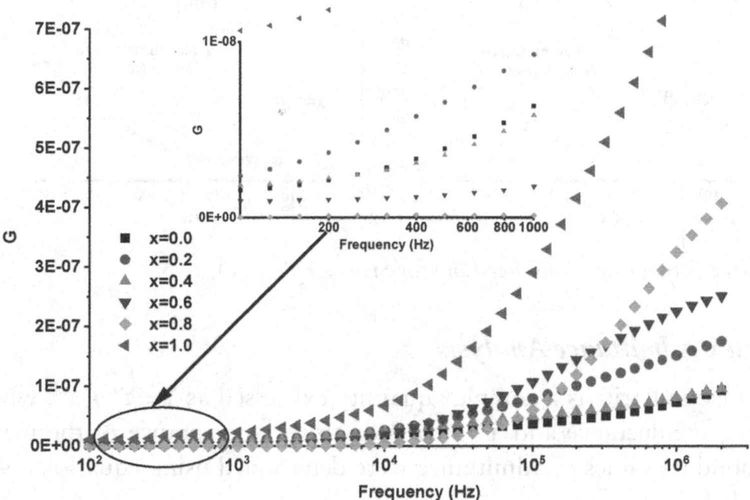

Figure 2: Conductance versus frequency curves of ferrite $SrCo_xZr_xFe_{12-2x}O_{19}$.

In the light of Jonscher power law [16], the total conductance is given as

$$G(f) = G_{DC} + G_{AC} \tag{1}$$

where G_{AC} can be expressed by the power law as

$$G_{AC} = Awn \tag{2}$$

Hence, from equations (1) and (2), conductance can be given as

$$G(f) = G_{DC} + Awn \tag{3}$$

Here *A* and *n* are constants. The curve fittings with the Jonscher power law are given in Figure 3. The values of n determined from curve fitting are 0.3100, 0.3359, 0.2805, 0.3904, 0.6058 and 0.4345. It can be noted that all the values are less than 1, which indicates the hopping of charge carriers in the prepared composition [17].

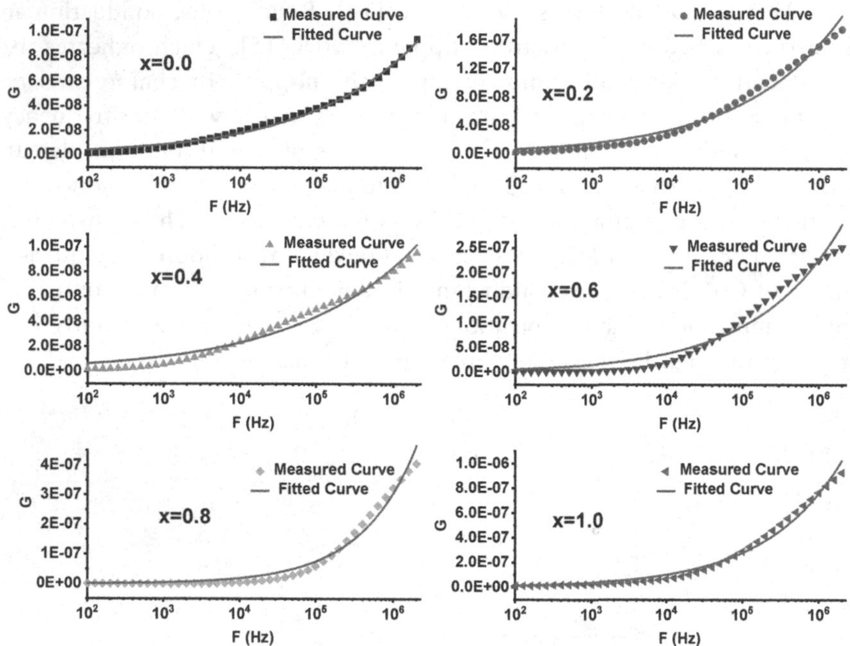

Figure 3: Curve fitting using Jonscher Law for $SrCo_xZr_xFe_{12-2x}O_{19}$.

3.2. *Complex Admittance Analysis*

The admittance in ferrite is a complex quantity expressed as Y= Y′ + Y″, where Y′ represents the conductance and Y″ attributed to the susceptance of the material. The corresponding values of admittance were determined using equations (4) and (5) as given below.

$$Y' = \varepsilon_0 \varepsilon'' \omega A / t \tag{4}$$

$$Y'' = \varepsilon_0 \varepsilon' \omega A / t \tag{5}$$

Here ε_0 and ε' are the permittivity of free space and dielectric material, respectively, while A, ω and t denote area, angular frequency and thickness, respectively. The variation of Y' and Y" with frequency is presented in Figure 4 (a) and (b). The value of Y' is minimum for low frequencies and increases with the increment in frequency validating the behaviour of conductance. The value of Y" is high for high frequencies, while all the plots coalesced at low frequencies, this behavior follows the Maxwell–Wagner model. There is a non-monotonical variation in the values of

Y' and Y" with the inclusion of Co–Zr content. The composition x=1.0 owns the highest, while x=0.0 has the lowest values of Y'. However, the composition x=0.6 has the lowest value of Y" in place of x=0.0 as in Y'.

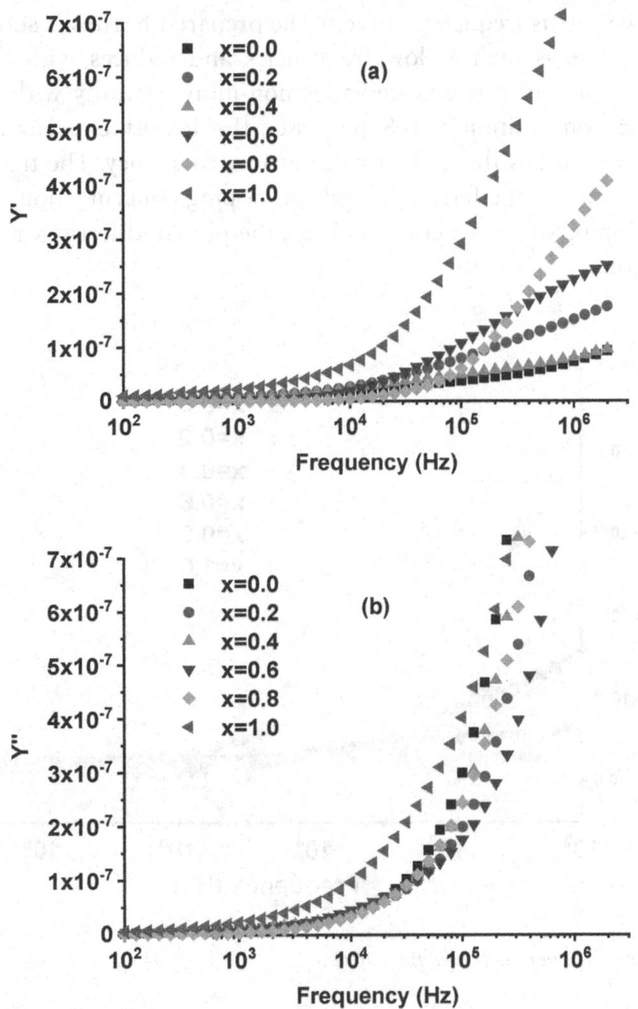

Figure 4: *(a), (b) Variation of admittance to frequency for* $SrCo_xZr_xFe_{12-2x}O_{19}$.

3.3. Capacitance Analysis

The ferrites have charge storage capacity due to their inherent capacitance. Many reports are available that signify the use of ferrites as a supercapacitor. Pawar et al. [18] synthesised cobalt ferrite $CoFe_2O_4$, and Nagesh Kumar et al. [19] developed nickel ferrite $NiFe_2O_4$ for supercapacitor application. Thus, capacitive analysis is essential to understand the electrical characteristics of prepared ferrites. The capacitance of the prepared ferrite compositions can be determined using the equation:

$$C = \varepsilon_0 \varepsilon A/t \qquad (6)$$

The capacitance versus frequency curve of the prepared ferrites is shown in Figure 5. The Capacitance is high at low frequencies and reduces with the frequency increment. The value of capacitance varies non-monotonically with the inclusion of Co–Zr. The composition x=0.8 possesses the lowest capacitance; however, composition x=1.0 owns the highest value at low frequency. The figure illustrates that the capacitance of the ferrite depends on doping concentration, and it can be tuned by the doping of Co-Zr content. Thus, the prepared ferrite can be used as a tuning capacitor.

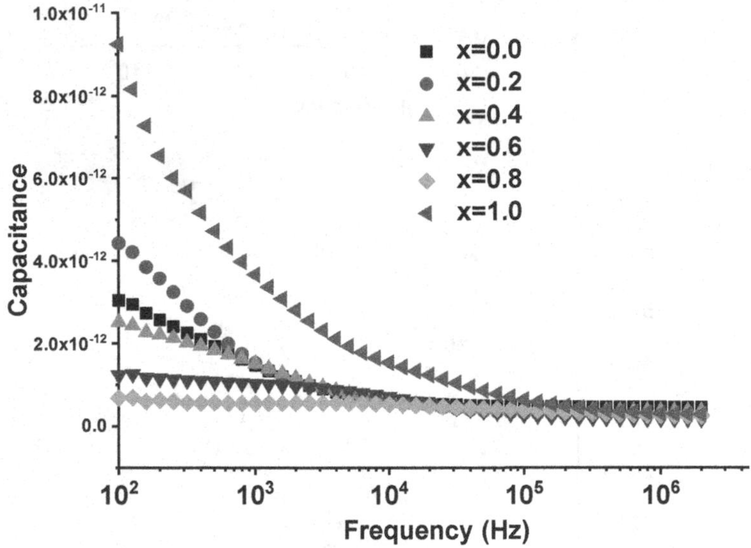

Figure 5: *Capacitance versus frequency curve.*

4. Conclusion

Synthesis of M-type ferrites with chemical composition $SrCo_xZr_xFe_{12-2x}O_{19}$ has been completed using the sol–gel technique. The conductance of the ferrites shows a frequency-dependence behaviour. The conductance of all the prepared composition follows the Jonscher power law and have an exponent factor less than unity, signifying the electron hopping between Fe3+ and Fe2+ in all the composition as proposed by Funke. Capacitive analysis reveals the tuning of capacitance by the doping of Co–Zr content. The tuneable capacitance characteristic of the prepared ferrite can be utilised in various electrical circuit applications.

References

[1] Raveendran, A., M. T. Sebastian, and S. Raman, "Applications of microwave materials: a review," *J. Electron. Mater.*, vol. 48, pp. 2601–2634, 2019, https://doi.org/10.1007/s11664-019-07049-1.

[2] Valenzuela, R., "Noval applications of ferrites," *Phys. Res. Int.*, vol. 2012, pp. 1–9, 2012, https://doi.org/10.1155/2012/591839.

[3] Kotnala, R. K. and J. Shah, "Ferrite materials: nano to spintronics regime," *Handb. Magn. Mater.*, vol. 23, pp. 291–379, 2015, https://doi.org/10.1016/B978-0-444-63528-0.00004-8.

[4] Pullar, R. C., "Hexagonal ferrites: a review of the synthesis, properties, and applications of hexaferrite ceramics," *Prog. Mater. Sci.*, vol. 57, pp. 1191–1334, 2012, https:// doi.org/10.1016/j.pmatsci.2012.04.001.

[5] Jotania, R., "Crystal structure, magnetic properties and advances in hexaferrites: a brief review," *AIP Conf. Proc.*, vol. 1621, pp. 596–599, 2014. https:// doi.org/10.1063/1.4898528.

[6] Vedrtnam, A., K. Kalauni, S. Dubey, and A. Kumar, "A comprehensive study on structure, properties, synthesis, and characterization of ferrites," *AIMS Mater. Sci.*, vol. 7, pp. 800–835, 2020, https://doi.org/10.3934/matersci.2020.6.800.

[7] Sun, K., Z. Ian, S. Chen, Y. Sun, and Z. Yu, "Effect of sintering process on microstructure and magnetic properties of high frequency power ferrite," *Rare Met.*, vol. 25, pp. 509–514, 2006, https://doi.org/10.1016/s1001-0521(07)60135-1.

[8] Joshi, A. and R. C. Srivastava, "Study of structural, electrical, and magnetic properties of Co-Zn ferrite and Co-Zn ferrite/polythiophene nanocomposites," *Mater. Today: Proc.*, vol. 78, pp. 774–779, 2023, https://doi.org/10.1016/j.matpr.2022.10.242.

[9] Hassan, Z., I. Sadiq, R. Hussain, F. Sadiq, M. Idress, S. Hussain, S. Riaz, and S. Naseem, "Determination of dual magnetic phases and the study of structural, dielectric, electrical, surface morphological, optical properties of Ce3+ substituted hexagonal ferrites," *J. Alloys Compd.*, vol. 906, p. 164324, 2022, https://doi.org/10.1016/j.jallcom.2022.164324.

[10] Dilshad, M., H. M. Khan, M. Zahid, S. Honey, M. A. Assiri, and M. Imran, "Structural, optical and dielectric properties of aluminum-substituted SrAl2xFe12-2xO19 x = (0.0,0.2,0.4,0.6,0.8,1.0) M-type hexagonal ferrites," *J. Mater. Sci.: Mater. Electron.*, vol. 33, pp. 21519–21530, 2022, https://doi.org/ 10.1007/s10854-022-08943-x.

[11] Zahid, M., H. M. Khan, I. Sadiq, A. U. Rehman, A. Waheed, E. Mazhar, M. A. Assiri, M. Imran, N. Usmani, and I. Khan, "Structural elucidation with improved dielectric and magnetic properties of sol-gel synthesized Cr3+ substituted M-Type Sr2+ hexaferrites," *J. Mater. Eng. Perform.*, vol. 31, pp. 1530–1539, 2022, https://doi.org/10.1007/s11665-021-06263-5.

[12] Godara, S. K., V. Kaur, K. Chuchra, S. B. Narang, G. Singh, M. Singh, A. Chawla, S. Verma, G. R. Bhadu, J. C. Chaudhary, P. D. Babu, and A. K. Sood, "Impact of Zn2+-Zr4+ substitution on M-Type barium strontium hexaferrite's structural, surface morphology, dielectric and magnetic properties," *Results Phys.*, vol. 22, p. 103892, 2021, https://doi.org/10.1016/j.rinp.2021.103892.

[13] Patel, C. D., P. N. Dhruv, S. S. Meena, C. Singh, S. Kavita, M. Ellouze, and R. B. Jotania, "Influence of Co4+ -Ca2+ substitution on structural, microstructure, magnetic, electrical and impedance characteristics of M-type barium–strontium hexagonal ferrites," *Ceram. Int.*, vol. 46, pp. 24816–24830, 2020, https://doi.org/10.1016/j.ceramint.2020.05.326.

[14] Verwey, E. J. W. and J. H. de Boer, "Cation arrangements in a few oxides with crystal structures of the spinel type," *Recl. Trav. Chim. Pays-Bas*, vol. 55, pp. 531–40, 1936, https://doi.org/10.1002/recl.19360550608.

[15] [15]. Austin, I. G. and N. F. Mott, "Polarons in crystalline and non-crystalline materials," *Adv. Phys.*, vol. 18, pp. 41–102, 1969, https://doi.org/10.1080/00018736900101267.

[16] Jonscher, A. K., *Dielectric Relaxation in Solids*, Chelsea Dielectric Press Ltd., London, 1983.

[17] Funke, K., "Jump relaxation in solid electrolytes," *Prog. Solid State Chem.* 22, p. 111, 1993.

[18] Pawar, S. J., S. M. Patil, M. Chithra, S. C. Sahoo, and P. B. Patil, "Cobalt ferrite nanoparticles for supercapacitor application," *AIP Conf. Proc.*, vol. 2265, p. 030162, 2020, https://doi.org/10.1063/5.0017184.

[19] Kumar, N., A. Kumar, S. Chandrasekaran, and T. Y. Tseng, "Synthesis of mesoporous NiFe2O4 nanoparticles for enhanced supercapacitive performance," *J. Clean Energy Technol.*, vol. 6, pp. 51–55, 2018, https://doi.org/10.18178/jocet.2018.6.1.435.

57. Low Power Optimization of 10T Full Adder Design Using FinFET Technology

Sneha Arora and Suman Lata Tripathi

School of Electronics and Electrical Engineering, Lovely Professional University, Punjab, India

Abstract: This paper details an approach for optimizing the power consumption of an HLFA designed using FinFET technology at the 22nm node. To find a happy medium between power consumption and overall performance, the proposed design strategy takes use of the advantages of complementary metal-oxide-semiconductors (CMOS) and pass-transistor logic (PTL). The objective of the optimization is to reduce the overall power consumption, power dissipation, latency, and power-delay product (PDP) while maintaining a manageable level of area overhead. When the HLFA is implemented using FinFET technology, gate control is improved, and leakage currents are reduced, in comparison to when conventional CMOS technology is used. The HSPICE simulation tool is used to evaluate the performance of the proposed design. Average power, power dissipation, latency, and PDP are examined as a result of implementing various low power optimization techniques such gate resizing, input capacitance reduction, and leakage current reduction. The study has led to significant gains across the board, suggesting the proposed architecture is ideal for low-power applications inside digital systems.

Keywords: Adder, FinFET, hybrid logic, 22nm.

1. Introduction

Low-power optimisation methods are becoming more important as scientists construct energy-efficient digital gadgets [1,2]. To meet the increased demand for portable devices, IoT applications and energy-constrained places, power consumption must be reduced while performance is maintained [3]. Digital systems need the adder circuit for fundamental arithmetic [4,5]. Many arithmetic and logical procedures depend on the full adder such as addition, subtraction, multiplication and division. Designers are always seeking for ways to make digital circuits more energy-efficient to keep up with technology [6]. Potential has drawn attention to FinFET (pronounced 'Fin Field-Effect Transistor') technology. Electrostatic, leakage and gate control are better with FinFETs than CMOS [7]. These advantages are making FinFET technology attractive for low-power designs, especially at 22nm manufacturing nodes. This study uses FinFET technology at 22nm to lower the power consumption of the hybrid logic full adder (HLFA). HLFA uses PTL and CMOS to optimise the former and balance power consumption and performance. CMOS provides strong noise immunity and fan-out, whereas PTL decreases transistors and space overhead. PTL lowers transistors. The foregoing strategies enhance energy economy without losing functionality in the HLFA design. This project tries to minimise HLFA architecture power while maintaining latency and area overhead. The quick drop in power usage extends portable device battery life, decreases heat dissipation and greens digital systems [8]. HLFA power efficiency and performance may be improved using low-power methods. This boosts performance. We will test numerous power-saving strategies to find the best. Gate resizing will affect transistor size in design. Power use and delay may be traded. Minimising input capacitance will reduce input node charging and discharging power usage. Leakage current reduction solutions will also employ FinFET technology's leakage current reduction characteristics [10–13]. This is possible using FinFET technology. Using hybrid adders makes arithmetic circuit design flexible and efficient. They let designers tailor adder attributes to application requirements. The low power and area-efficient designs of mobile, Internet of Things and battery-operated devices need these adders. IoT, mobile and battery-operated devices are examples. Important for low-power consumption.

2. Literature Review

Due to their ubiquitous usage in arithmetic and computational circuits, digital circuit designers have optimised full adders for low power applications. Many circuits utilise full adders. Digital, particularly battery-powered, systems need power-efficient, high-performance activities. Critical construction pieces like complete adders must work well. Traditional logic gates and adders used the static complementary metal-oxide-semiconductor (CMOS) design. CMOS is complementary metal–oxide semiconductor. Standard static CMOS full adders use pull-up and pull-down networks for sum and carry outputs. This technology required a lot of electricity, especially as clock frequencies increased [1]. Full adders based on transmission gates (TGs) reduced static CMOS device power consumption. The transmission gate method employs nMOS and pMOS transistors simultaneously. Thus, it outperforms static CMOS in power and speed. TG-based complete adders are popular for balancing strength, speed and area [2]. Pass-transistor logic (PTL) for complete adder design was another breakthrough. PTL-based devices employ fewer transistors than CMOS and TG-based systems, reducing power and size. The signal-to-noise margin of PTL designs may be too low for many applications, particularly those with significant noise margins [3]. Domino logic has been studied for adder construction. These non-static approaches use less static power, but they are more susceptible to noise and need a clock signal, which may offset their power benefits [4]. Integration and transistor shrinkage have exacerbated leakage power problems. Dual-threshold voltage and adaptive body biassing may reduce adder leakage power. These approaches dynamically modify threshold voltages or biassing conditions to conserve power while the adder is idle or lightly loaded [5]. QCAs have been utilised to manufacture whole adders as quantum-dot cellular automata (QCA) technology has progressed. Due to its different working approach from CMOS, QCA-based devices may utilise less power [6]. Each method has merits and downsides, but the objective has always been to perform mathematical operations efficiently and with minimal energy.

3. Proposed Work

In this simulation, the HSPICE modelling program is used to display the waveform of the constructed circuit. A block schematic of an adder is shown in Figure 1. The XNOR modules are responsible for the implementation of the total sum output of the complete adder. This comes within their area of responsibility.

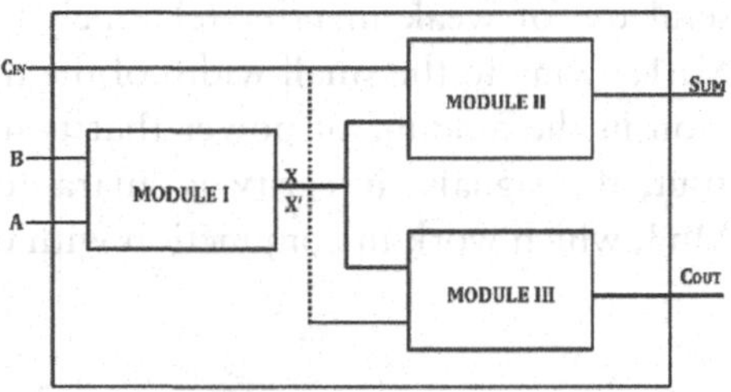

Figure 1: Block diagram.

This circuit has better PDP output than other FA cells. This FA (COUT) is one of the most difficult electrical circuits since it requires twenty transistors for sum and carry. Figure 2 depicts the FA cell design used in Figure 1, which comprises Module II. The architecture is shown in Figure 1. This circuit uses XOR and XNOR to signal gate pMOS and nMOS, P8 and N8, respectively. XOR and XNOR signals from Module I gate MOSs. These impulses activate pMOS and nMOS. CIN and SUM nodes connect to transistors' source and drain terminals (P8 and N8). Transistors P8 and N8 are "ON" and CIN is linked when XOR is '0' and XNOR is '1'. Nodes N6 and N7 link the output to ground to keep CIN at a high logic level while XOR and XNOR are '1' and '0'. This is done by connecting output to N6 and N7. If CIN has logic '0', P6 and P7 connect the sum output to VDD. This happens if CIN has logic '0'. This FA cell's Module III structure follows Figure 1 (d). The CIN signal from this circuit's TG component sets the XOR input to '1'. Instead of sending A from both TG transistors to set the XNOR input to logic '1', load is dispersed by bypassing A and B from other transistors. This provides XNOR input logic '1.' Reduces input strain as much as feasible. For XNOR to be logic '1', both inputs must be the same.

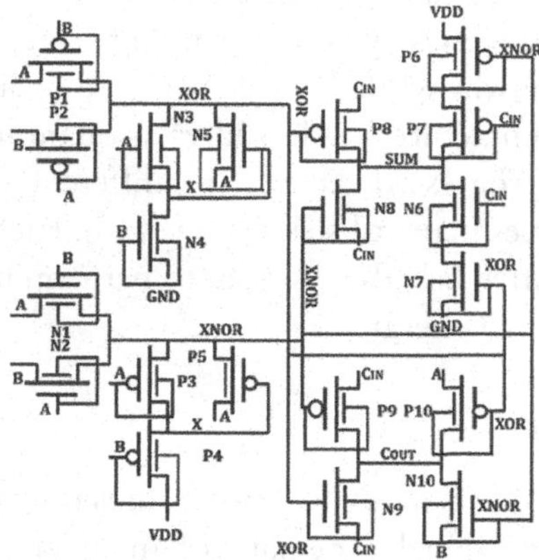

Figure 2: Full adder using FINFET proposed.

Figure 2 illustrates the entire adder that is built using Mos Like FINFETs. XNOR circuit in which the amount of power that is used is lowered to a substantial degree by the purposeful use of weak inverter (channel) structure generated by transistors Mp1 and Mn1, owing to the small width of the transistors. This results in a significant reduction in the amount of power that is used. Operating at the greatest levels of output, the signals' integrity is guaranteed by level-restoring transistors Mp3 and Mn3, which work in conjunction with one another.

4. Results

The results presented provide a compelling insight into the advancements in full adder designs by leveraging MOS technologies like FINFET. Through various parameters of comparison, it becomes evident that the transition from traditional MOS designs to FINFET has substantially improved the performance metrics of full adders.

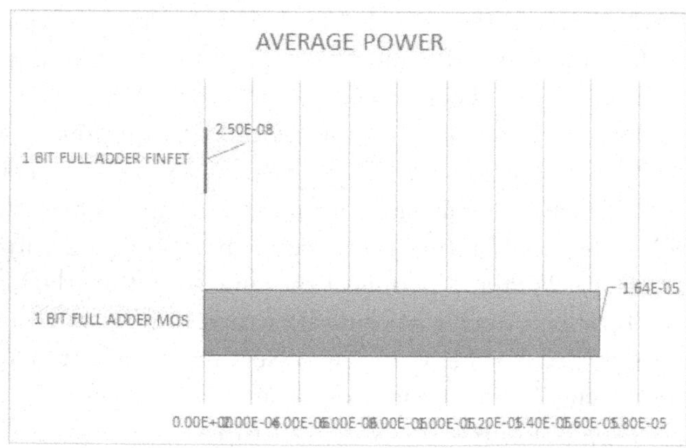

Figure 3: Power output.

From the visual representation in Figure 3, there is an undeniable advantage of the FINFET design over traditional MOS, with a whopping improvement of up to 99% in terms of power output. Such a significant reduction in power output is not only beneficial for energy conservation but also paves the way for creating more energy-efficient digital systems that rely heavily on arithmetic operations.

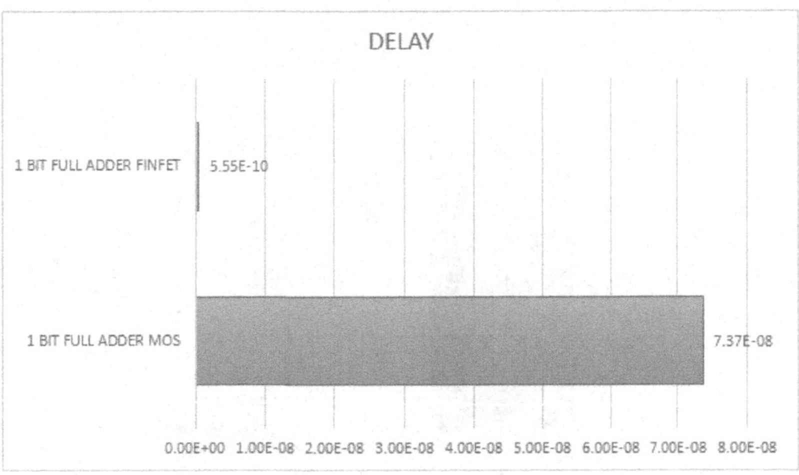

Figure 4: Delay output.

Similarly, the delay, a critical factor in digital circuits determining their speed, showcases an improvement of up to 80% as illustrated in Figure 4. Reduced delay implies faster operations, which translates to a significant speedup in computational processes. This is particularly crucial in modern-day applications where real-time processing and swift computational actions are paramount.

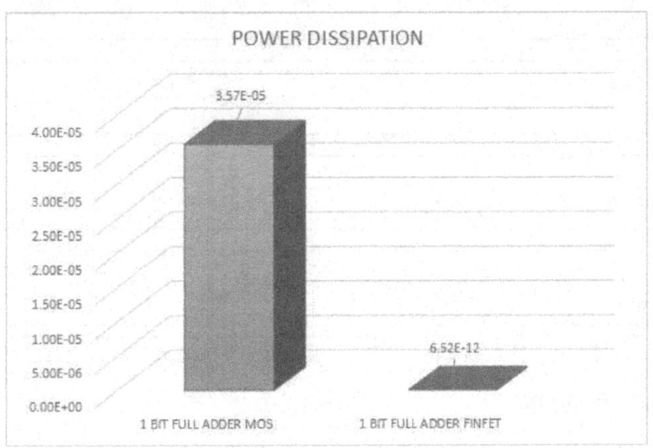

Figure 5: Power dissipation output.

Power dissipation, as displayed in Figure 5, is another metric where FINFET design shines with an impressive improvement of up to 99%. Minimising power dissipation is essential, especially in miniaturised devices where thermal management becomes a challenge. A reduced power dissipation means that devices can operate cooler, potentially enhancing their longevity and reliability. The circuit's energy efficiency and speed are represented by the power-delay product (PDP). FINFET improved this domain by up to 99%, as seen in Figure 6.

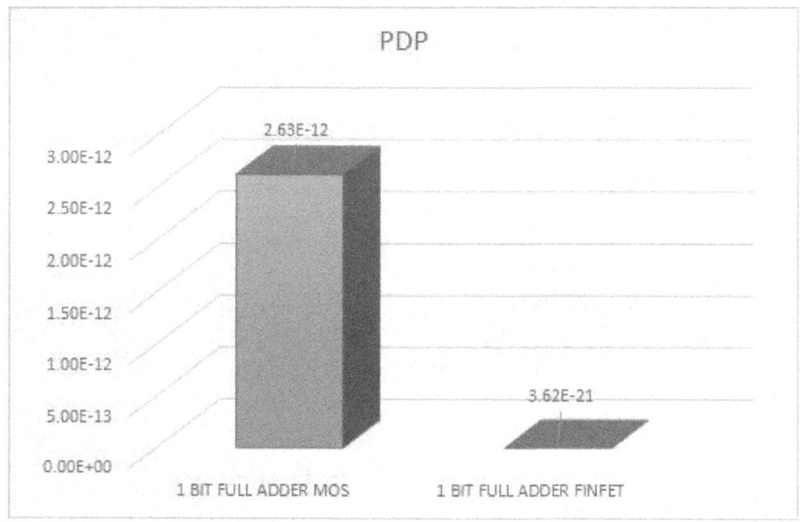

Figure 6: PDP output.

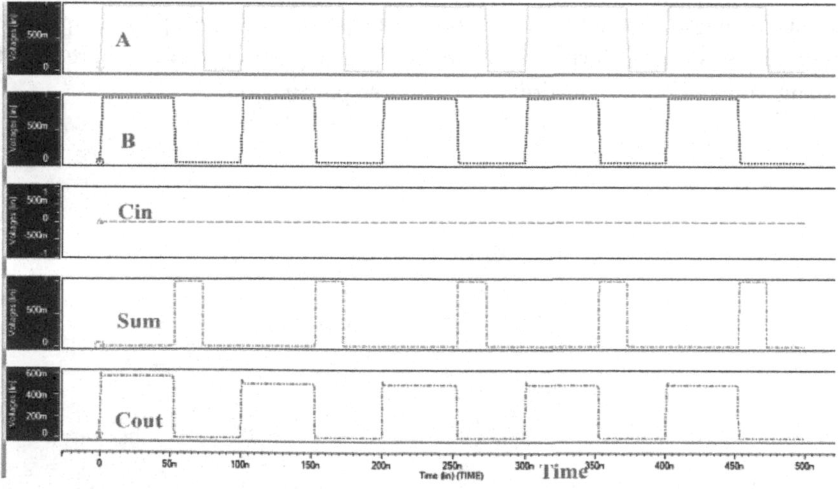

Figure 7: Waveform output.

Lower PDPs indicate more efficient circuits that balance power and speed. The tabular data in Table 1 supports these visual results. Performance metrics differ greatly between the 1 BIT FULL ADDER MOS and FINFET. The FINFET design surpasses the MOS in average power, latency, power dissipation and PDP.

Table 1: Comparison results.

	1 Bit Full Adder MOS	1 Bit Full Adder FINFET
Average Power	1.6E-05	2.5E-08
Delay	7.4E-08	5.6E-10
Power Dissipation	3.6E-05	6.5E-12
PDP	2.6E-12	3.6E-21

Finally, the validity and functionality of the FINFET-based Full Adder are further substantiated by Figure 7, which presents the waveform output. This waveform is crucial as it visually confirms that the FINFET-based Full Adder not only is more efficient and faster but also provides the correct full adder results, ensuring its reliability in practical applications. Latest developments at the level of transistors [14] are useful in design and optimisation of adder circuit.

5. Conclusion

The research lowered power consumption in 22nm FinFET Hybrid Logic Full Adders. HPICE simulations verified low-power optimisation. PTL and CMOS boost power efficiency and performance. While retaining delay, transistor gate resizing saves power. This reduced HLFA's static and dynamic power. Reduced input capacitance reduced input node charging and discharging. To conserve power, logic circuit capacitance and transistor sizes were optimised. Power consumption of HLFA is reduced through leakage current reduction. Gate control and reduced leakage currents make FinFETs better than CMOS. Modified HLFA lowered power, dissipation, latency and power-delay product. Improvements make the proposed design suitable for low-power digital systems. We lower digital circuit power consumption this way. The ideas might be used to energy-efficient circuits and technologies. Low-power optimisation of a 22nm node FinFET-based Hybrid Logic Full Adder architecture reduced average power, power dissipation, latency and power-delay product. The technology might allow low-power applications and minimise electronics energy consumption by producing energy-efficient digital systems.

References

[1] Kandpal, J., A. Tomar, M. Agarwal, and K. K. Sharma, "High-speed hybrid-logic full adder using high-performance 10-T XOR–XNOR cell," IEEE Trans. Very Large Scale Integr. VLSI Syst., vol. 28, no. 6, pp. 1413–1422, 2020, doi: 10.1109/TVLSI.2020.2983850.

[2] Juveria, P. and K. Ragini, "Low power and high speed full adder utilising new XOR and XNOR gates," *IJITEE*, vol. 8, no. 8, 2019 (IJITEE), ISSN: 2278-3075.

[3] Subhashini, T., M. Kamaraju, and K. Babulu, "Low-power and rapid adders using new XOR and XNOR gates," *IEEE Trans. VLSI Des., Vol. Int. J. Eng. Res. Technol.*, vol. 12, no. 12, pp. 2072–2076, 2019, ISSN 0974-3154.

[4] SubbaRao, D., K. Santhosh, M. Pushpa Latha, and M. Pushpa Latha, "Low-Power and Fast Full Adder by Exploring New XOR and XNOR Gates," *J. Eng. Sci.*, vol. 11, no. 1, 2020, ISSN: 0377-9254.

[5] Rajesh, P., P. N. Srikanth, and K. Vijaya Prasad, "Low-power and rapid full adder through exploration of new XOR and XNOR gates," *IJVDCS*, vol. 07, 2019, ISSN 2322-0929.

[6] Loga Lakshmi, M., S. Jeya Anusuya, and S. V. Sathyah, "Performance improvement of low power and fast full adder by exploring new XOR and XNOR gates," Performance Improvement of Low Power and Fast Full Adder by Exploring New XOR and XNOR Gates. ISSN(Online): 2319-8753 ISSN(Print): 2347-6710, *IJIRSET*, vol. 8, no. 2, 2019, ISSN(Online): 2319-8753 ISSN(Print): 2347-6710.

[7] Jadia, R., and S. Josh, "Design of low power adder cell using XOR and XNOR gate," *IJRTE*, vol. 9, no. 1, 2020, ISSN: 2277-3878.

[8] Deebigai, R. and P. Krishnakumar, " Low power design for fast full adder," *IRJET*, vol. 07, no. 03, 2020.

[9] Tejaswini M. L, H. Aishwarya, M. Akhila, and B. G. Manasa, "High-speed hybrid-logic full adder utilizing high-performance 10-T XOR–XNOR cell," *IJARSCT*, vol. 8, no. 1, 2021, ISSN (Online) 2581–9467.

[10] Venkayya Naidu, M., Y. Sravana Kumar, and A. Ramakrishna, "A 45nm CMOS technology exploring a low-power and rapid 4-bit full adder with XOR and XNOR gates," *IJSDR*, vol. 4, no. 11, 2019, ISSN: 2455-2631.

[11] Shahbaz, M. and D. Patle, "High-speed hybrid-logic full adder low power16-T XOR– XNOR cell," *IEEE Trans. Comput.*, vol. 4, no. 5 of the International Journal of Innovative Research in Technology and Management, 2020, ISSN: 2581-3404.

[12] Uma Maheswari, R. K., and C. N. Marimuthu, "Implementation of a low-power, fast full adder using novel XOR and XNOR gates," *Int. J. Intell. Adv. Res. Eng. Comput.*, vol. 7, no. 1, 2019, ISSN: 2348-2079.

[13] Dharani B., K. Naresh Kumar, and M. Vineela, "Low power and fast full adder by exploring new XOR and XNOR gates design of XOR/XNOR circuits for hybrid full adder," *IJERECE*, vol. 7, no. 5, 2020, ISSN (Online) 2394-2320.

[14] Verma, Y. K. and S. K. Gupta, "Center potential- based analysis of Si and III-V gate all around field effect transistors (GAA-FETs)," *Silicon*, vol. 13, no. 6, pp. 1787–1803, 2021.

58. Paving the Way for Faster Data Transmission Through Micro Structured Fibre Mode Optimisation

Indu Bala, B. Arun Kumar, Ashwani Kumar, Aryananda PS

SEEE, Lovely Professional University, Punjab, India

Abstract: Photonic crystal fibres (PCFs) have drawn significant attention in recent years due to their unique properties and potential applications in various fields. In this paper, investigations are done on the mode distribution and structural parameter optimisation of a PCF. Simulated results show that the mode distribution is highly dependent on the structural parameters of the fiber, such as photonic crystal lattice period, element radius and refractive index of the background material and photonic crystal elements. Furthermore, the effect of the structural parameters on the dispersion and attenuation of the PCF is also investigated. It has been demonstrated that both parameters can be controlled by adjusting the structural parameters of PCFs to achieve a low dispersion and attenuation PCF suitable for both WDM and insulator applications.

Keywords: Photonic crystal fiber, modes, mode field distribution, leaky mode, guided mode, evanescent field.

1. Introduction

Photonic crystal fibres (PCFs) are a type of optical fibre with unique properties that result from the use of periodic microstructures, or photonic crystals, in their design. PCFs consist of a solid or hollow core surrounded by a cladding layer that contains a periodic array of air holes, which act as a photonic crystal. The photonic crystal structure of the cladding layer creates a bandgap that prevents the light of certain wavelengths from propagating through the fibre. This property, known as the photonic bandgap effect, allows PCFs to guide light in a highly controllable manner, making them ideal for use in a range of applications including telecommunications, sensing and biomedicine.

Another important property of PCFs is their ability to control the dispersion of light. PCFs can be designed to have zero dispersion at specific wavelengths or to have dispersion that varies with wavelength in a way that is beneficial for certain applications. PCFs are also capable of generating nonlinear optical effects, which occur when the intensity of light is high enough to cause a change in the refractive index of the material. This can be used to generate a range of optical phenomena, including supercontinuum generation and frequency conversion. These unique properties of PCFs make them a versatile tool for a range of applications, including telecommunications, sensing and biomedical imaging.

In this paper, investigations are done on the mode distribution and structural parameter optimisation of a PCF to achieve a low dispersion and attenuation PCF suitable for both WDM and insulator applications. The rest of the paper is organised as follows: Section 1 gives an overview of PCFs. In Section 2, the significance of mode distribution and its applications are discussed in detail. In Section 3, the analytical description of the mode formation inside the PCF is given. The proposed PCF structural design and parameter optimisation are given in Section 5 followed by the numerical simulation results and application of the proposed design is given. At the end of the paper, the conclusion and future scope are given.

2. Literature Survey

Researchers have conducted numerous studies on PCFs, focusing on understanding the mode distribution and its effects on the fibre's properties, as well as developing applications that use the fibre's unique characteristics. In [1], design and fabrication details are given for a highly birefringent PCF with large linear birefringence and high nonlinearity. The supercontinuum generation properties of a highly birefringent PCF are investigated in [2]. In [3], a design for a PCF with low confinement loss and high birefringence is proposed. A design for a highly birefringent PCF based on a slotted core structure is proposed in [4]. A design for a highly birefringent PCF with low confinement loss and large nonlinearity is proposed in [5]. In [6], a design for a highly birefringent PCF with square lattice elliptical air holes is proposed to analyse the mode distribution of the fibre and demonstrate its potential for use in polarisation-maintaining applications. The design and fabrication of PCFs for high-performance communications, including mode distribution and its relationship with structure is investigated in [7] for optical communication systems. An in-depth review of the modal properties of PCFs, including mode distributions, confinement loss and chromatic dispersion is presented in [8] to analyse the different types of PCF structures and their impact on mode properties. This application of PCFs in sensing, such as temperature sensing, pressure sensing, strain and biochemical sensing is demonstrated in [9]. A comprehensive review of PCF sensors, covering different PCF structures and their use in sensing is presented in [10]. Different PCF structures that have been used for high-power applications, including fibre amplifiers and lasers are discussed in [11]. In [12], recent developments in the field of PCF biosensors, covering different PCF structures and their use in biosensing are investigated. The use of PCFs in ultrafast fibre lasers is demonstrated in [13], covering different PCF structures and their use in mode-locking and pulse shaping. In [14], the authors have provided an in-depth review of the modal analysis of PCFs, covering different modal characterisation techniques and their applications and challenges associated with PCF modal analysis. The use of PCFs in mid-IR applications, covering different PCF structures and their use in supercontinuum generation, frequency conversion and sensing is reviewed in [15]. In [16], the design and fabrication of PCFs for high-power applications, covering different PCF structures and their use in beam delivery, pulse compression and mode filtering are reviewed.

3. Modes in PCF

Conventional optical fibres typically possess an optical guiding structure comprised of multiple concentric layers, specifically a core, a reflective cladding and a protective coating. While the refractive index profile of such fibres can take on various shapes, it always maintains axial symmetry. In contrast, microstructured fibres feature layers that may incorporate different materials and exhibit a photonic crystal (PhC)-like microstructure. The dimensions of these microstructure elements are on the order of the wavelength of the radiation propagating through the fibre. Understanding the mode distribution within the optical fibre holds significance as it yields insights into the optical characteristics and behavior of PCFs. This, in turn, aids in the design and optimisation of PCF properties, allowing for the creation of fibres tailored to specific applications with desired properties.

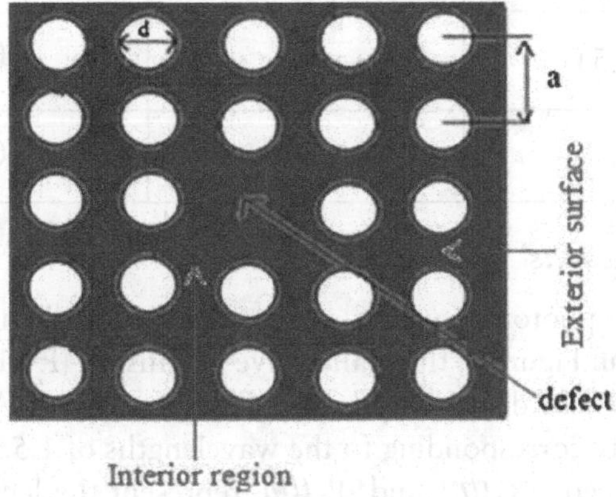

Figure 1: Proposed PCF lattice structure.

4. Proposed Lattice Structure of PCF and Potential Use Cases

4.1. Proposed Structure

In this paper, the PCF structure is proposed by optimising its design parameters such that the current flows maximum at the centre of crystal fibre at the visible regime (400 nm to 750 nm). The proposed photonic crystal fibre contains 5 × 5 air holes with defects at the centre as shown in Figure 1, which are itched on the substrate. The dimensions of the square lattice are $50 \times 50\,\mu m^2$ with $8\,\mu$m and $10\,\mu m$ of diameter (d) of air holes and lattice spacing (a), respectively.

5. Results and Discussion

5.1. Simulation Parameters

In this section, simulated results are presented for electric field distribution inside the proposed microstructure optical fibre based on the square lattice photonic crystal. The microstructure parameters taken into consideration are PhC period (a), element radius $(r,)$ and refractive index of the background and PhC elements $(\rho 1)$. The various values of these parameters used to simulate the results are shown in Table 1.

Table 1: Simulation parameters of proposed microstructure.

S. No.	Material Permittivity $(\tilde{n}1)$	Period of the Structure (a)	Radius of an PhC Element (r)
1	$(1.4)^2$	e^{-6}	$(0.02)\times a$
2	$(2.9)^2$	e^{-8}	$(0.25)\times a$
3	$(3.5)^2$	e^{-8}	$(0.342)\times a$
4	4.1^2	e^{-6}	$(0.434)\times a$

5.2. Simulation Results

To comprehend the photonic current at the core rather than the surface of the proposed structure in Figure 1, the plane wave expansion (PWE) technique is used to simulate electric field distribution. Simulations are in MATLAB 2013a. The electric field intensity corresponding to the wavelengths of 1,550 nm are shown in Figure 2(a)–2(d), where $x, \mu m$ and $y, \mu m$ represent the length and breadth of fibre, respectively, and the electric field intensity $\left(V/_{\mu m}\right)$ is taken along the z-axis for different values of PCF structure parameters enlisted in Table 1.

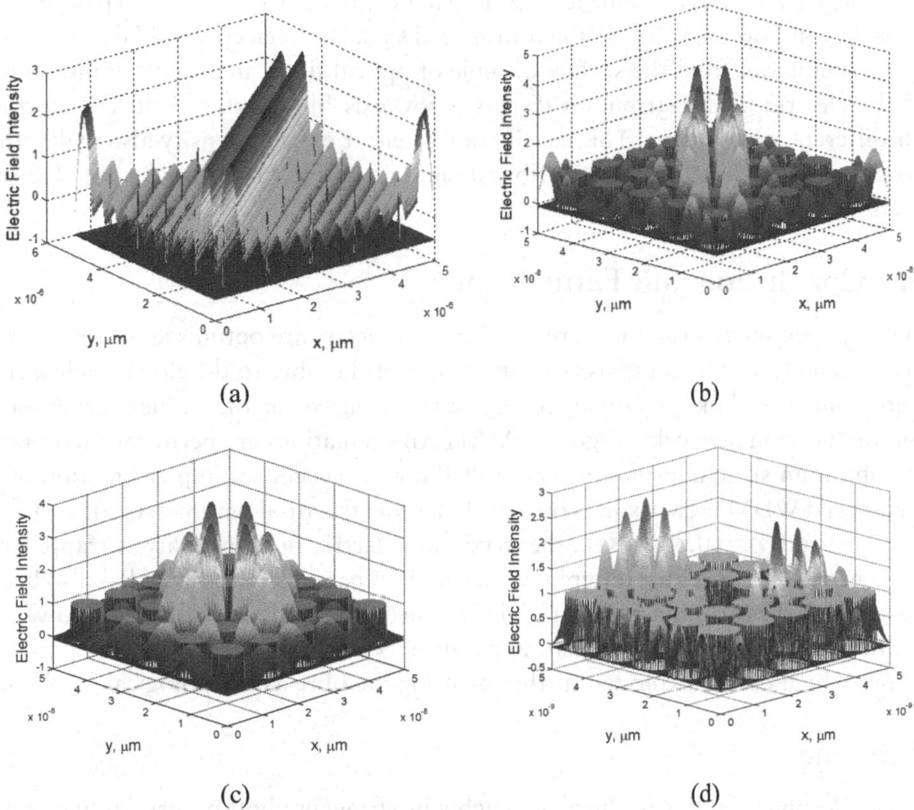

Figure 2: Electric field intensity distribution for PCF parameters.

(a) $\tilde{n}1 = 1.4^2$, $a = e^{-6}$ and $r = (0.02) \times a$ (b) $\tilde{n}1 = 2.9^2$, $a = e^{-6}$ and $r = (0.25) \times a$ (c) $\tilde{n}1 = 3.5$, $a = e^{-6}$ and $r = (0.342) \times a$ (d) $\tilde{n}1 = 4.1$, $a = e^{-6}$ and $r = (0.434) \times a$

Figure 2(a)–2(d) show that strong electric field intensity dispersed diagonally corresponding to the PCF parameters. That suggests that the proposed structure with given parameters can support multiple visible wavelengths; however, chances of crosstalk are high due to less element spacing. Moreover, the presence of evanescent fields at the edges also suggests that the coupling efficiency of the PCF is also less for given structural parameters.

An interesting result is revealed from Figure 2(c) that suggests that for the structural parameters $\tilde{n}1 = 3.5^2$, $a = e^{-6}$ and $r = (0.342) \times a$, the electric field intensity is trapped at the centre and can support four different wavelengths (channels) with sufficient isolation among them and good coupling efficiency. Thus, these structural parameters are optimum for WDM application for high-speed communication.

Further, it is evident from Figure 2(d) that if we increase the structural parameters value beyond optimum value, the transmitted signals (i.e. electric field distribution) start coming out from the surface air hole of optical fibre, and the peak intensities of the electric filed distribution dispersed towards fibre surface rather than core for different wavelengths. This distribution of electric field intensity also makes the proposed microstructure optical fibre design a suitable candidate for topological insulators.

6. Conclusion and Future Scope

In this paper, microstructure fibre physical parameters are optimised to confine the maximum electric field intensity of the centre of the fibre to develop a high-speed communication link to satiate the data rate requirement of the next-generation communication networks. Rigorous MATLAB simulations are performed to obtain the optimum structural parameters of PCF for the successful implementation of a high-speed WDM network. It is observed that for structural parameters $\tilde{n}l = 3.5^2$, $a = e^{-6,}$ and $r = (0.342) \times a$, the maximum electric field intensity is trapped at the centre to support four different wavelengths (channels). Further, it has also been observed that peak intensities of the electric filed distribution are dispersed towards the fibre surface if the PCF structural parameters are varied beyond these optimum values which can be exploited further by using the fibre as a topological insulator.

References

[1] Prabu, K., and R. Malavika, "Highly birefringent photonic crystal fiber with hybrid cladding," *Opt. Fiber Technol.*, vol. 47, pp. 21–26, 2019.

[2] Blandin, P., F. Druon, M. Hanna, S. Lévêque-Fort, M. P. Fontaine-Aupart, C. Lesvigne, and P. Georges, "Supercontinuum generation in a highly birefringent photonic crystal fiber seeded by a low-repetition rate picosecond infrared laser," *International Quantum Electronics Conference*, Optica Publishing Group, p. IE_8, 2007.

[3] Lijuan, Z., L. Ruoyu, Z. Haiying, and X. Zhiniu, "Design of a photonic crystal fiber with low confinement loss and high birefringence," *Opto-Electron. Eng.*, vol. 48, no. 3, p. 200368-1, 2021.

[4] Yu, F., Z. Wang, Y. Zhang, Y. Yu, and C. Lv, "Analysis of a highly birefringent photonic crystal fiber with ellipse–rhombus air core," *Optik*, vol. 125, no. 20, pp. 6266–6269, 2014.

[5] Mishra, S. S. and Singh, V. K. "Highly birefringent photonic crystal fiber with low confinement loss at wavelength 1.55 μm," *Optik*, vol. 122, no. 22, pp. 1975–1977, 2011.

[6] Upadhyay, A., S. Singh, Y. K. Prajapati, and R. Tripathi, "Numerical analysis of large negative dispersion and highly birefringent photonic crystal fiber," *Optik*, vol. 218, p. 164997, 2020.

[7] Kawanishi, S., "Design and fabrication of photonic crystal fibers for high-performance systems and devices," *Optical Transmission Systems and Equipment for WDM Networking III*, SPIE, vol. 5596, pp. 280–291, 2004.

[8] Chen, W., S. Lou, L. Wang, S. Feng, W. Lu, and S. Jian, "In-fiber modal interferometer based on dual-concentric-core photonic crystal fiber and its strain, temperature and refractive index characteristics," *Opt. Commun.*, vol. 284, no. 12, pp. 2829–2834, 2011.

[9] Pinto, A. M. and M. Lopez-Amo, "Photonic crystal fibers for sensing applications," *J. Sens.*, vol. 2012, 2012.

[10] Portosi, V., D. Laneve, M. C. Falconi, and F. Prudenzano, "Advances on photonic crystal fiber sensors and applications," *Sensors*, vol. 19, no. 8, p. 1892, 2019.

[11] Skovgaard, P. M., J. Broeng, M. D. Nielsen, A. Petersson, H. R. Simonsen, J. R., Folkenberg, and K. P. Hansen, "Recent progress on photonic crystal fibers for high power laser applications," *The 17th Annual Meeting of the IEEE Lasers and Electro-Optics Soci*ety, LEOS 2004, vol. 2, pp. 953–954, IEEE, 2004.

[12] Rifat, A. A., G. A. Mahdiraji, Y. G. Shee, M. J. Shawon, and F. M. Adikan, "A novel photonic crystal fiber biosensor using surface plasmon resonance," *Procedia Eng.*, vol. 140, pp.1–7, 2016.

[13] Fermann, M. E. and I. Hartl, "Ultrafast fibre lasers," *Nat. Photonics*, vol. 7, no. 11, pp. 868–874, 2013.

[14] Rachana, M., I. Charles, S. Swarnakar, S. V. Krishna, and S. Kumar, "Recent advances in photonic crystal fiber-based sensors for biomedical applications," *Opt. Fiber Technol.*, vol. 74, p. 103085, 2022.

[15] Portosi, V., D. Laneve, M. C. Falconi, and F. Prudenzano, "Advances on photonic crystal fiber sensors and applications," *Sensors*, vol. 19, no. 8, p. 1892, 2019.

[16] Wang, Y. Y., X. Peng, M. Alharbi, C. F. Dutin, T. D. Bradley, F. Gérôme, and F. Benabid, "Design and fabrication of hollow-core photonic crystal fibers for high-power ultrashort pulse transportation and pulse compression," *Opt. Lett.*, vol. 37, no. 15, pp. 3111–3113, 2012.

59. Booth Multiplier Design and Implementation Using NEXYS-4 ARTIX-7 FPGA Board

Suman Lata Tripathi,[1] Abhishek Kumar,[1] Sandhya Avasthi,[2] and Mufti Mahmud[3]

[1]*VLSI Design, Lovely Professional University*
[2]*Department of CSE, ABES Engineering College, Ghaziabad, India*
[3]*Nottingham Trent University, UK*

Abstract: Multiplier is an important block in many DSP processor that uses considerable IC area. A prefabrication design of such block at RTL level is useful for performance optimisation in number of components, power consumption and delay. In this work, a booth multiplier was designed through Vivado 2019.1 and implemented using NEXYS-4 ARTIX-7 FPGA Board with onboard seven segment display. Booth multiplication algorithm is a 2's complement multiplication algorithm that multiplies two signed binary digits efficiently. Different from the conventional multiplication process, in booth multiplication, the multiplicand may be added to the partial product, subtracted from the partial product or left unchanged depending on the conditional statements provided. The booth multiplier was implemented in the FPGA board and has produced the expected results for every input. Through design and synthesis process, an RTL level model is obtained describing the onboard device utilisation and total power consumption including static and dynamic powers. In the FPGA board, the inputs are represented by switches, and the output is displayed through the seven segments. In this design, the booth multiplier accepts inputs from 0 to 15 only, both positive and negative.

Keywords: FPGA, booth multiplier, seven segment display, 2's complement.

1. Introduction

Prefabrication design and implementation with ready to used board like FPGA are useful mean to evaluate the performance of ICs in terms of device utilisation, power consumption and delays [1–4]. Prototyping with FPGA's provide real time results when design implemented in hardware and reduces the chances of failures after product being developed [5–11]. Booth multiplication algorithm [12–13] is a two's complement multiplication algorithm that multiplies two signed binary digits in an efficient way. Andrew Donald Booth devised the method in 1950 while working on crystallographic research at Birkbeck College in Bloomsbury, London. This method also reduces the number of additions/subtractions required. In booth multiplication, the multiplier bits must be examined and the partial product must be shifted. The multiplicand may be added to the partial product, subtracted from the partial product, or left unchanged. Consider the following steps. Let M be the multiplicand, and Q is the multiplier. Also, consider a 1-bit register Q-1 and initialise it to 0 the same things to a register A. Further operations will be based on the values of Q0 and Q-1. When Q0 and Q-1 are equal for instance 00 or 11, arithmetic right shift by 1 bit will be performed. For the Q0 and Q-1 values 10, respectively, the multiplicand will be subtracted to the partial product. On the other hand, when the value of Q0 and Q-1 is 01, respectively, the multiplicand is added to the partial product and at this point arithmetic right shift is performed.

2. Block Diagram

Figure 1 shows the program flowchart for implementing the booth multiplier. Initially, we have a multiplicand (M), multiplier (Q), our product (A) and 1-bit register Q-1. A conditional statement is applied for the values for Q0 and Q-1. Q0 is the least significant bit of the multiplier, and Q-1 is the assigned 1-bit register. For the case that the value of Q0 and Q-1 is 1 and 0, respectively, the multiplicand is subtracted to the partial product. On the other hand, for the 01 value, the multiplicand is added to the partial product and arithmetic right-shift will be performed. For the case that the values of Q0 and Q-1 are equal, whether it is 11 or 00, arithmetic right-shift is also implemented but no addition or subtraction will be performed. At this point, when the right shift is done, the count value will be reduced by 1 and checks whether the count value is equal to zero. When the count value is finally zero, the program will end and we will get our final answer.

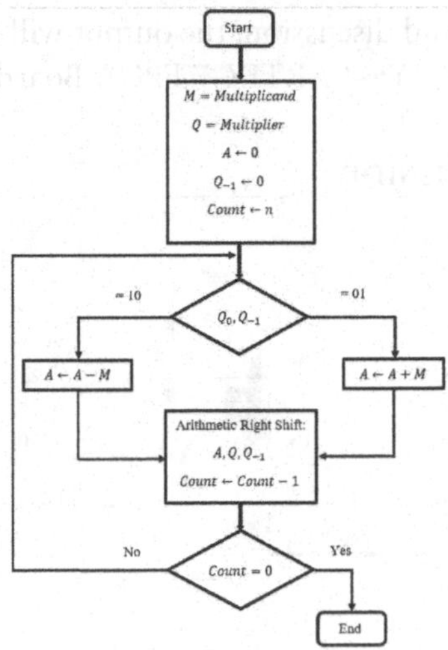

Figure 1: *Booth multiplier algorithm flowchart.*

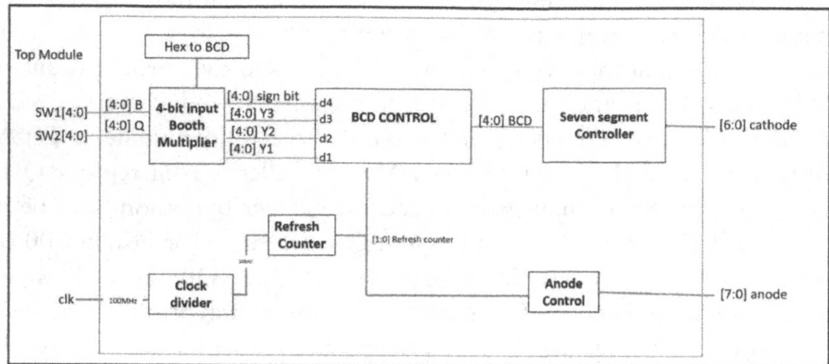

Figure 2: System block diagram.

Figure 2 shows the system block diagram at the top module of the booth multiplier when implemented in a 7-segment display. This presents blocks for booth multiplier, clock divider, refresh counter, anode control, BCD control and seven-segment controller. The goal of the design is to display the product of two 4-bit inputs, B and Q in a seven-segment display. Switches, SW1 and SW2 (with 5 switches each), are for the multiplicand B and multiplier Q. 4-bit input booth multiplier has outputs of the sign bit, Y3, Y2 and Y1, which is derived from the hex to BCD module. These outputs are the input of BCD control to have binary coded decimal be displayed and to pass a corresponding digit in a seven-segment display. The *clk* is a 100MHz clock input to the clock divider module. The clock divider module is connected to the refresh counter. Refresh counter counts from 0 to 3 as input to BCD control and anode control. These select particular anode that will be turned on and corresponding digit will be displayed at the same time. The output in the 7-segment controller is a 7-bit cathode, and in the anode, the control is the 8-bit anode. In the results and discussion, the output will be presented based on the screenshot presented at NEXYS-4 ARTIX-7 FPGA Board [3–8].

3. Result and Discussion

3.1. RTL Schematic

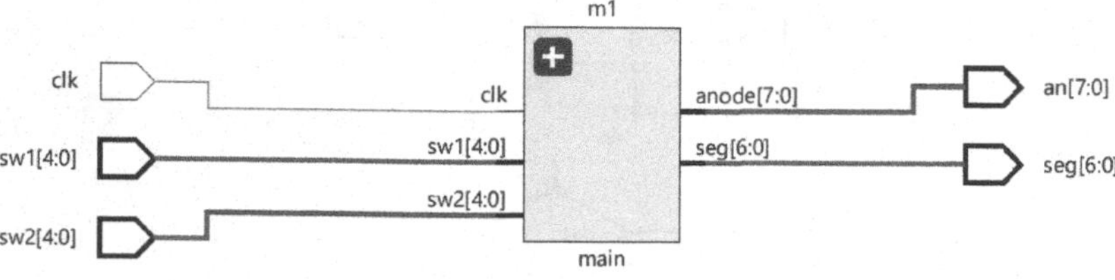

Figure 3: Main design block of booth multiplier.

In Figure 3, RTL schematic, the block diagrams of each module are shown. Specifically, the clockdivide, refresh counter, the booth multiplier, BCD control, anode control and the seven-segment modules. Figure 3 c is showing waveform of output depending on input values.

3.2. Simulation Waveform

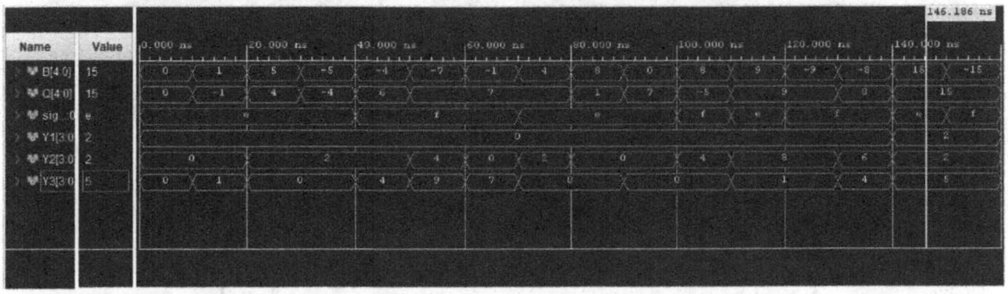

Figure 4: Waveform obtained for booth multiplier on Xilinx Vivado.

The behavioural simulation of the programme shows that the system works accurately as a booth multiplier. The f corresponds to the negative sign, while the e is the positive sign. The Y1 is the MSB, while the Y3 is the LSB of the decimal products. For -15x15, the system was able to return a -225 as indicated by signbit = f (negative), Y1 = 2, Y2 = 2, Y3 = 5. Figure 4 shows the simulation waveform of booth multiplier.

3.3. Power and Device Utilisation Report

Figure 5 a & b shows power report and device utilisation report obtained on Xilinx Vivado, respectively.

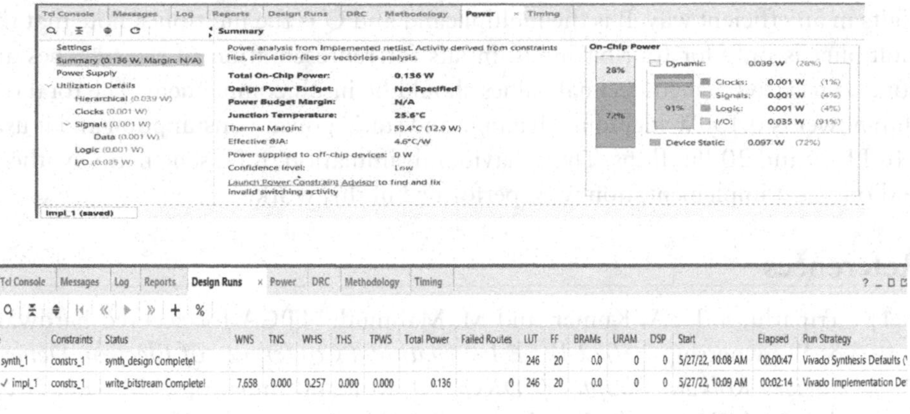

e	Constraints	Status	WNS	TNS	WHS	THS	TPWS	Total Power	Failed Routes	LUT	FF	BRAMs	URAM	DSP	Start	Elapsed	Run Strategy
synth_1	constrs_1	synth_design Complete!								246	20	0.0	0	0	5/27/22, 10:08 AM	00:00:47	Vivado Synthesis Defaults ('
✓ impl_1	constrs_1	write_bitstream Complete!	7.658	0.000	0.257	0.000	0.000	0.136	0	246	20	0.0	0	0	5/27/22, 10:09 AM	00:02:14	Vivado Implementation De

Figure 5: a) Power consumption report. b) Device utilisation report.

3.4. FPGA Implementation of Working Project

Figure 6: Display of result on NEXYS-4 ARTIX-7 FPGA board for input a) 1x-15 b) 1x1.

Negative decimal inputs need to be converted into their corresponding 2's complement to be implemented via the switches sw1 and sw2. The results indicate that the program works properly as long as the switches are applied in accordance with Figure 6. The highest value that the booth multiplier can operate on, and therefore, return the correct sign and product is only at 15 decimal values.

4. Conclusion

In conclusion, the implementation of the booth multiplier using NEXYS-4 ARTIX-7 FPGA Board with onboard display unit. Booth multiplication algorithm is designed in a 2's complement multiplication algorithm that multiplies two signed binary digits in an efficient way. B is the multiplicand and Q is the multiplier, note that the multiplier is only for four-bit input. Inputs for representation of the switches are done as negative signed decimal values should be in 2's complement. The total on-chip power is 0.136W including dynamic and static power consumption and it uses 246 LUTs and 20 flip flops. The behavioural simulation, RTL schematic, synthesis and onboard implementation were performed in this work.

References

[1] Tripathi, S. L., A. Kumar, and M. Mahmud, "FPGA for secured hardware & IP ownership," *2022 IEEE International Conference of Electron Devices Society Kolkata Chapter (EDKCON)*, Kolkata, India, pp. 184–189, 2022, doi: 10.1109/EDKCON56221.2022.10032935.

[2] Badiganti, P. K., S. Peddirsi, A. T. J. Rupesh, and S. L. Tripathi, "Design and implementation of smart healthcare monitoring system using FPGA," In: Rawat S., A. Kumar, P. Kumar, and J. Anguera (eds) *Proceedings of*

First International Conference on Computational Electronics for Wireless Communications. Lecture Notes in Networks and Systems, vol 329, Springer, Singapore, 2022. https://doi.org/10.1007/978-981-16-6246-1_18.

[3] Tripathi, S. L., S. Saxena, S. K. Sinha, and G. S. Patel, *Digital VLSI Design Problems and Solution with Verilog*, John Wiley & Sons, Ltd., 2021, doi:10.1002/9781119778097 ISBN: 978-1-119-77804-2.

[4] Kumar, A., S. L. Tripathi, K. Srinivasa Rao, *Machine Learning for VLSI Chip Design*, Wiley Scrivener Publishing LLC, 2023, doi:10.1002/9781119910497, ISBN 9781119910398.

[5] Tripathi, S. L. and M. Mahmud, *Explainable Machine Learning Models and Architecture*, Wiley & Scrivener Publishing LLC, USA, 2023, https://doi.org/10.1002/9781394186570.

[6] Tripathi, S.L., S. Saxena, and S. K. Mohapatra, (Eds.), *Advanced VLSI Design and Testability Issues* (1st ed.), CRC Press Boca Raton, 2020, https://doi.org/10.1201/9781003083436.

[7] Pathak, J. and S. L. Tripathi, "A novel model for resisting side channel attack by masking of gates," *J. Eng. Res.*, 2022, https://doi.org/10.36909/jer.ICMET.17165.

[8] Pathak, J. and S. L. Tripathi, "Column shifting algorithm to compute iteration bound of FIR systems having Inline delays," *Int. J. Embedded Syst.*, vol. 14, no. 5, pp. 443–450, 2021. doi: 10.1504/IJES.2021.10036820.

[9] Pathak, J., S. L. Tripathi, and A. K. Singh, *High Level Transformation Techniques for Designing Reliable and Secure DSP Architectures*, AI Techniques for Reliability Prediction for Electronic Components IGI global publishers, pp. 164–174, 2019.

[10] Kumar, A., S. Agarwal, V. Varshnay, V. Mishra, Y. Kumar Verma, and S. L. Tripathi (Eds.), *Opto-VLSI Devices and Circuits for Biomedical and Healthcare Applications* (1st ed.), CRC Press, 2023, https://doi.org/10.1201/9781003431138.

[11] Bhandari, J. K. and Y. K. Verma, "A novel design of high-performance hybrid multiplier," *J. Circuits, Syst. Comput.*, vol. 31, no. 15, p. 2250268, doi: https://doi.org/10.1142/S0218126622502681.

[12] Surabhi, G. S., "Design and implementation of 256*256 booth multiplier and its applications," *Int. J. Eng. Res. Technol.*, vol. 8, no. 11, 2020, https://www.ijert.org/design-and-implementation-of- 256256-booth-multiplier-and-its-applications.

[13] Booth's Multiplication Algorithm - Javatpoint, "www.javatpoint.com," n.d.-a, https://www.javatpoint.com/booths-multiplication- algorithm-in-coa (accessed: May 19, 2022).

60. NB-IoT vs Lora: A Practical Analysis in Terms of Power Consumption

Chand Pasha Mohammed and Shakti Raj Chopra

Department of Electronics and Communication Engineering, Lovely Professional University, Jalandhar, Phagwara, Panjab, India

Abstract: This document summarises the key study findings and conclusions. It emphasises low-power wide area networks (LPWANs), which are becoming popular for long-distance communication in internet of things (IoT) applications with little power. Energy efficiency of LoRa and narrowband internet of things (NB-IoT) is the main emphasis of the research. The study is detailed and include literature reviews. Empirical studies compare LoRa with NB-IoT performance in payload size, spreading factor, subcarrier spacing and repetition count. The report also finds knowledge gaps in realistic IoT workloads, real-world deployment situations, updated requirements and coexistence problems. The report advises developing networking simulators, stochastic models for IoT workloads, field measurements and optimisation methodologies across technologies to progress the area. This study seeks to aid LoRa and NB-IoT technology evaluation academics and experts. It also academically explores IoT terminology like LoRa, NB-IoT, LPWAN, energy efficiency and IoT.

Keywords: LoRa, NB-IoT, LPWAN, energy efficiency, internet of things.

1. Introduction

Because of the rise of the internet of things (IoT), there has been a paradigm change in the requirement for long-range connectivity that also reduces the amount of electricity that is consumed [1]. In light of these constraints, there has been an increase in the adoption of notable resolutions such as low-power wide area network (LPWAN) technologies, in particular LoRa and narrowband internet of things (NB-IoT) [2]. Because LPWANs offer the potential for greater communication ranges and functionality that is more energy-efficient, they are an excellent choice for IoT applications that include devices that have limited power resources. Because of the many benefits they offer and the breadth of their application, LPWAN technologies like LoRa and NB-IoT have attracted a lot of attention in recent years.

In this study, a comparison of the LoRa and NB-IoT protocols for the IoT is carried out, with a particular focus on analysing the distinct patterns of energy consumption that each protocol exhibits while data is being sent. The research builds upon a comprehensive analysis of scholarly publications that have been published in the past [8], and it contains empirical data that evaluate the effectiveness of these works in relation to a number of different factors. The payload size, spreading factor, subcarrier spacing and repetition count are the major variables that are being investigated in this study.

This paper identifies and underlines the existing research gaps, and it also aims to inspire future research in these areas by highlighting such gaps. In addition, the paper provides a detailed roadmap for future research, in which it proposes the development of networking simulators, stochastic models for the modelling of workloads associated with the IoT, field-based measurements and unique cross-technology optimisation approaches. The avenues are extremely important to the development of LPWAN technology as well as its synchronisation with the ever-evolving requirements of IoT applications.

2. Literature Review

Extensive scholarly investigation has been conducted to examine the energy efficiency of LoRa and NB-IoT. Bouguera et al. (2019) provide a comprehensive analysis of LoRa modulation and its associated energy usage patterns. The Lora WAN standard is defined by Sornin et al. [4], while NB-IoT is introduced by Grant [5] as a standard for IoT in 3GPP Release 13. Additional knowledge has been acquired through the utilisation of modelling research. In their study, Mahfouz et al. [6] present a comprehensive energy consumption model for LoRa technology, taking into account various modulation factors. The study conducted by Bouguera et al. [7] examines the current draw characteristics in various LoRa operating modes. In a similar vein, Khan et al. [8] employ theoretical modelling to estimate the lifespan of LoRa nodes. Jin et al. (2019) developed energy consumption models specifically for uplink transmissions in the context of NB-IoT. Liu and colleagues (2010) present algorithms that are designed to enhance resource usage and minimise power consumption in user equipment (UE). In a similar vein, Deng and co-authors (2011) assess the coverage capabilities and efficiency of scheduling methods in terms of energy consumption. e consumption trends of LoRa and NB-IoT.

3. Methodology

The MKR WAN 1300 Arduino board was used for LoRa communication, while the MKR NB 1500 Arduino board was used for NB-IoT communication in our experimental setup. We also used two 3.8 V Li-Po batteries and two 868 MHz central frequency antennas. We used a Telia SIM card for the NB-IoT connectivity and a DNX gateway for the LoRa communication. We used the application's EUI and key to establish communication.

In this section, we lay out the hardware details of the two Arduino boards, including the power consumption figures that will be used in the future analysis and debate.

This Table 1 provides a concise comparison of the technical specifications for the Arduino MKR WAN 1300 and MKR NB 1500 boards, including microcontroller, radio module, power supply, security features and various current consumption values in different operating modes.

Table 1: Technical parameters.

Feature	Arduino MKR WAN 1300	MKR NB 1500
Microcontroller	SAMD21 Cortex-M0+ 32-bit low-power ARM MCU	SAMD21 Cortex-M0+ 32-bit low-power ARM MCU
Radio Module	CMWX1ZZABZ	UBLOX SARA-R410M-02B
Board Power Supply (USB/VIN)	5 V	5 V
Circuit Operating Voltage	3.3 V	3.3 V
Security	ECC 508 crypto chip	ATECC508A
Typical Current in Standby Mode	1.40 µA	8 µA
Typical Current in Sleep Mode	21.5 mA	9 mA
Supply Current in Idle Mode	4.06 mA	0.5 A
XOSC32K (Standby)	12.8 mA	12.8 mA

4. Experiment Procedure

In this experimental setup, we utilised two Arduino boards, each configured to serve as an end device for LoRa and NB-IoT communications. The entire transmission process is visually represented in Figures 1 and 2. During the experiments, these end devices transmitted messages consecutively. Once these messages passed through the respective gateway, they were forwarded to the network server. It was imperative for us to gather this transmitted data to assess the success of the communication. In our data collection process, we relied on the MQTT server.

4.1. Factors Affecting Energy Consumption

Lora; Spreading Factor (SF): The choice of SF significantly influences energy consumption. Higher SFs provide larger link budgets but consume more energy due to increased symbol durations [3].

Payload Size: Energy efficiency is impacted by the length of the payload. Short payloads result in higher overhead, while energy per bit decreases and eventually stabilises with increasing payload size [6, 7].

Transmit Power: The transmit power setting plays a pivotal role in airtime and energy consumption. Increasing transmit power reduces airtime but results in exponential increases in energy consumption [15].

Figure 1: LoRa end device that is used in the experiments.

NB-IoT; Payload Size: In NB-IoT, transmission time increases linearly with payload size. Smaller payloads exhibit higher control overhead, influencing energy efficiency [9].

Subcarrier Spacing: Subcarrier spacing directly affects transmission time in NB-IoT. Higher spacing reduces transmission time but doubles the required bandwidth, impacting energy consumption [11].

Repetition Count: The practice of repeating transmissions in NB-IoT can enhance coverage but proportionally increases energy consumption [14].

XResource Blocks: Utilising more resource blocks halves airtime, thereby influencing energy consumption [10].

Figure 2: NB-IoT end device that is used in the experiment.

To quantify the power consumption differences between LoRa and NB-IoT, we employed a method that involved tracking the battery voltage over time. As a direct measurement of battery power was not feasible, we opted to monitor voltage fluctuations as a means of estimating changes in battery power. The initial battery charge was set at approximately 4.17 V, and we continuously monitored the voltage as it declined during the transmission process voltage measurements were taken at intervals of 45–90 minutes, as long as the voltage remained above 3.6 V. However, when the voltage dropped below a certain threshold, indicating a rapid decline, we increased the measurement frequency to every 30 minutes.

5. Experimental Comparisons

Table 2: Voltage vs time measurements for LoRa (SF7, 50 bytes payload every 10 seconds).

Time (minutes)	Voltage (V)
0	4.17
60	4.12
120	4.08
240	4.02
480	3.85

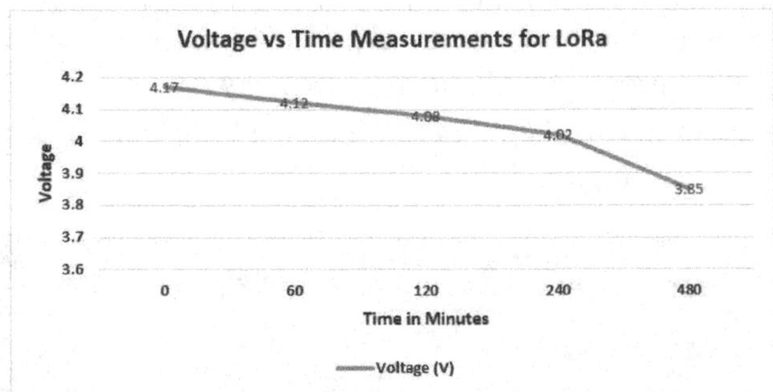

Figure 3: Linear curve fitting for voltage decay.

Table 3: Voltage vs time measurements for NB-IoT (15 kHz spacing, 1 repetition, 50 bytes every 10 seconds).

Time (minutes)	Voltage (V)
0	4.17
90	4.05
180	3.95
300	3.80
480	3.65

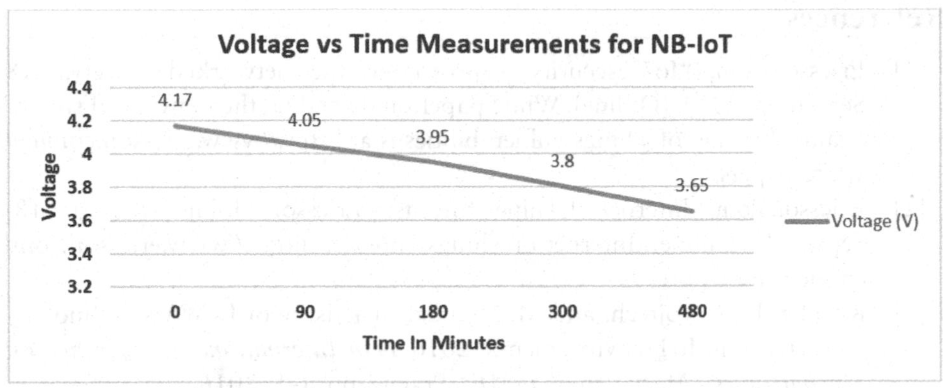

Figure 4: Linear curve fitting for voltage decay.

6. Calculated Slop

LoRa Slope: –0.00022 V/minute

NB-IoT Slope: –0.00016 V/minute

6.1. Calculated Battery Life

LoRa Lifetime: 450 minutes

NB-IoT Lifetime: 562 minutes

This data demonstrates that, under the experimental setup conditions, NB-IoT exhibits better energy efficiency than LoRa for the same payload size and transmission interval. This conclusion is supported by both the measured data and analytical models. Future research may involve considering a wider range of factors for a more comprehensive analysis.

7. Conclusion

This comprehensive review has provided an in-depth assessment of the energy efficiency of LoRa and NB-IoT, drawing from existing research and experimental studies. While NB-IoT has demonstrated superior energy efficiency under specific conditions and configurations, the evolving nature of these technologies and the complexities of real-world deployments necessitate ongoing analysis. The paper has identified several avenues for future research, including considering newer specifications, realistic workload modelling, field measurements, networking simulations, cross-technology optimisation and exploring energy-latency trade-offs. Advancing our understanding of these LPWAN technologies will contribute to building a more energy efficient and connected future in the IoT landscape.

References

[1] Ericsson.com, "IoT security - protecting the networked society," 18 September 2019. [Online]. White paper on defending the networked society against Internet of Things vulnerabilities is at https://www.ericsson.com/en/white-papers.

[2] Ericsson.com, "Internet of Things forecast - Ericsson Mobility Report," 18-Sep-2019. [Online]. Internet of Things Forecast: https://www.ericsson.com/en/mobility-report/.

[3] Krupka, L., L. Vojtech, and M. Neruda, "The issue of LPWAN technology coexistence in IoT environment," *2016 17th International Conference on Mechatronics - Mechatronika (ME)*, Prague, pp. 1–8, 2016.

[4] Alliance, A. "Explanation of the inner workings of LoRa and LoRaWAN," November 2015 White Paper.

[5] Sornin, N. (Semtech) and A. Yegin (Actility), *LoRaWAN 1.1 Specification*, LoRa Alliance, October 2017; Completed NB-IoT standardization.

[6] http://www.3gpp.org/news-events/3gpp-news/1785-NB-IoT-complete for your perusal.

[7] GSMA White Paper on 3GPP Low Power Wide Area Technologies[J]. gsma.com, 2016. Narrowband Internet of Things Whitepaper.

[8] Schlienz, J. and D. Raddino, Rohde & Schwarz, White Paper, pp. 1–42, 2016.

[9] Uplink transmission energy consumption models are presented by Jin et al.

[10] Algorithms to minimise UE power consumption and maximize resource usage are proposed in [10] by Liu et al.

[11] Deng et al. [11] analyzes the feasibility of improving resource use by evaluating coverage capabilities and energy efficient scheduling.

[12] Throughput, energy consumption, and latency are compared across LoRa, SigFox, and NB-IoT in a hardware testbed study conducted by Fotouhi et al.

[13] Extensive measurements are used by Polikarpova et al.to determine the energy required to transmit one meaningful bit of data via LoRa and NB-IoT networks in different configurations.

[14] Real-time transmission data comparing LoRa and NB-IoT usage patterns are presented by Gan et al.

[15] Power of Transmission in dBm Use of energy (in milliwatts).

61. Millimetre Wave Wireless Communication System for Internet of Bodies: A Systematic Review on Implication

Jai Kumar and Akhil Gupta

SEEE, Lovely Professional University, Punjab, India

Abstract: In near future, the use of millimetre (mmWave) frequencies, which range from 30 GHz to 300 GHz in the electromagnetic spectrum, will increase significantly in a variety of applications including next-generation communication system, security applications, medical devices, wellness services, entertainment and automatic collision avoidance systems. Internet of bodies (IoB) is impending addition to enormous internet of things, where linked devices are placed inside, on or around the human body that form a network for different kind of services and application. This paper mainly focuses on millimetre wave interaction with human body and implications of it in communication, medical and wellness services. IoB is subjected to transmute the public health and safety infrastructure still under risk and obstacles need to be addressed to fully benefit from it. Major challenge of characterising heterogeneous dielectric properties of human body under the exposure of mmwave reviewed here for implication in communication link around it. Bio-electromagnetic attributes of human body under high radiation exposure are also analysed numerically along with review on the human safety aspects provided by different international bodies like World Health Organisation, International Commission on Non-Ionizing Radiation Protection and Federal Communication Commission. Finally, open research problems and potential future study topics are presented to interested readers as a future scope of study.

Keywords: Millimetre wave, internet of bodies, electromagnetic attributes, human body network, 5G, next-generation communication, wellness services, ICNIRP, FCC, radiation exposure.

1. Introduction

The wavelength of millimetre wave (mmwave) band lies between 10 and 1 mm corresponding to frequencies from 30 GHz to 300 GHz and has associated photon energy in the range of 0.1 to 1.2 milli electron volts (meV). This upper band of frequency remains in the focus for next-generation technology like 5G, 6G and THz that leads the world to new heights in various services like medical, aviation, research and even in wellness services. As a very low-power wireless technologies around the human body, named body area network (BAN), contains tiny nodes around the human body and transmitting in very short distance of 2m around the body. Wireless BAN targets a variety of applications including sports training, healthcare, user electronics, workplace safety and the protection of uniformed personnel and safe authentication. We named these emerging technologies and collected data with the name of internet of bodies (IoB). Since mmWave radiation is non-ionising, unlike ultraviolet, X-ray and gamma radiation, the primary safety concern is heating of the eyes and skin brought on notice by mmWave energy absorption in the human body thus mm wave also needs to be analysed from the view of human safety.

2. Internet of Bodies

A technological revolution known as the "internet of things" (IoT) connects individually identifiably smart things to one another, fusing the physical and digital worlds. It targets connecting anything at any time/place to any type of service over all types of networks. The forecast of international data corporation predicted 41.6 billion IoT devices in the year 2025 to that of 22 billion in 2018, creating 79.4 zettabytes of data [1]. When we confine the scope of IoT to body centric IoT, then it is named as IoB, which mainly deals with connected devices located in and around the human body that creates a network for myriad of usages.

2.1. Taxonomy of IoB and Its Applications

The old concept of IoB that was limited to BAN expanded the use of devices that can be worn, inserted in the body parts, swallowed or embedded into the skin. IoB devices are shown in Figure 1 deal mainly with wrist band, smart watches, wireless headphones, head-up display glasses, GPS, etc. Similarly pictorial representation of IoB application given in Figure 2 that deals with variety of sectors namely healthcare, wellness, sports and entertainment. All these sectors are subdivided as per their applications where health care and safety need special focus as the growth rate in the population makes it crucial due to baby boomers, life expectancy due to ageing and boost in health expenditure. The Organization for Economic Cooperation and Development (OECD) forecast its member countries' health expenditure as 10.2 % of its GDP by the year 2030 and the maximum of 21.3% for the USA in the year 2015 [3]. Thus, the need for more scalable and cost-effective healthcare diverted the focus to this field. IoB-based health care proved its dedicated-selfless-and restless effort during the COVID-19 pandemic that was taken as priceless in the front line of public healthcare.

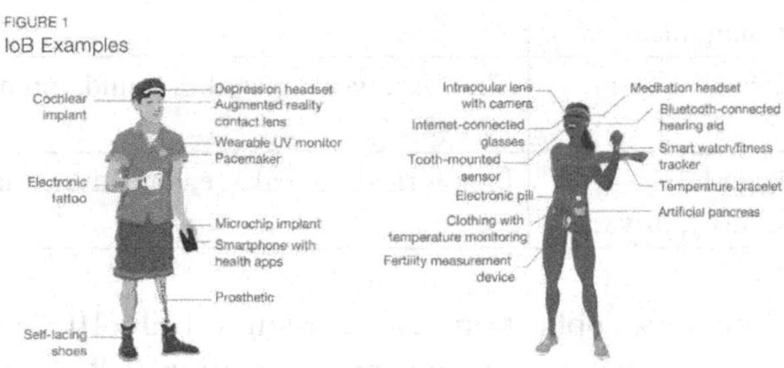

Figure 1: *IoB devices example [2].*

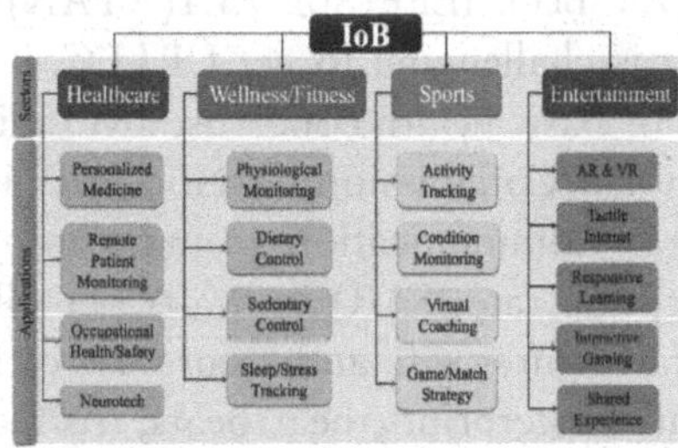

Figure 2: *IoB application categories [2].*

Some kinds of risk in IoB lie with security and privacy concerns while using them, like personal health info that lies with a medical provider and insurance provider, etc. are taken as a risk zone. Similarly, technical challenges make these IoB devices under contradiction like battery life, dimension/size, minimum transmission power to avoid harm to body. These all limit the overall performance of communication systems in a low-power millimetre wave frequency band.

2.2. IoB Requirements and Standards

The broad range of IoB makes it difficult to standardise it and, based on its requirements, the standardisation process brings many advantages including confined research cost, interoperability and compatibility between the products, rapid upgrade in technology. Based on its applications, the requirements of IoB are listed in Table 1.

Table 1: IoB requirement [2].

Requirement	Parameter	Specifications
Quality of Service	Data rate, bit error rate	Glucose monitor:<1 Kbps, EEG:86.4 Kbps Voice: 50–100 Kbps, video streaming: 10–100 Mbps
Safety	Heating of tissue	10GHz: below threshold SAR

Power Efficiency	Ultralow power communication	Safety regulations, battery life
Form Factor	Stringent form factor	Tiny size, wearable takes liquid antenna, solar cells
Security and Privacy	High-level security, privacy	Biometric data leakage, amendment in original data

Medical and military applications of IoB require BER<10^{-10} and come under applications of ultrareliable low latency communication (URLLC). IoB nodes co-exist and provide license-free services throughout the globe under the industrial-scientific-medical (ISM) band. Since other wireless standards like IEEE802.11 (Wi-Fi), IEEE802.15.4 (Zig-Bee), IEEE 802.15.1(WPAN) and Bluetooth already exist in the ISM band, it is challenging to get URLLC, it requires a strong error control mechanism [4]. For basic health concerns, EM radiation should follow the guidelines from International Commission on Non-Ionizing Radiation Protection (ICNIRP) [5] and Federal Communication Commission (FCC) for limiting the value of a specific absorption rate (SAR) at Watts per kilogram. A high level of security in biometric data requires safe and secure use of IoB through the human body channel dealing with fingerprints, heartbeats, iris/face recognition and even typing rhythm involves virtual reality [6].

Main IoB standards include IEE 802.15.4 and deal with PHY and MAC specifications to achieve low range, low cost and low-power application under 27 half duplex channels at 868 MHz/915MHz/2.15 GHz; IEEE 802.15.6 standards deal with distinct QoS demand of wireless body area network (WBAN) under narrow and ultra-wide band frequency as shown in Figure 3. Bluetooth low-power application operates at 2.45 GHz and provides a basic rate of 3 Mbps with privacy support by proper key authentication.

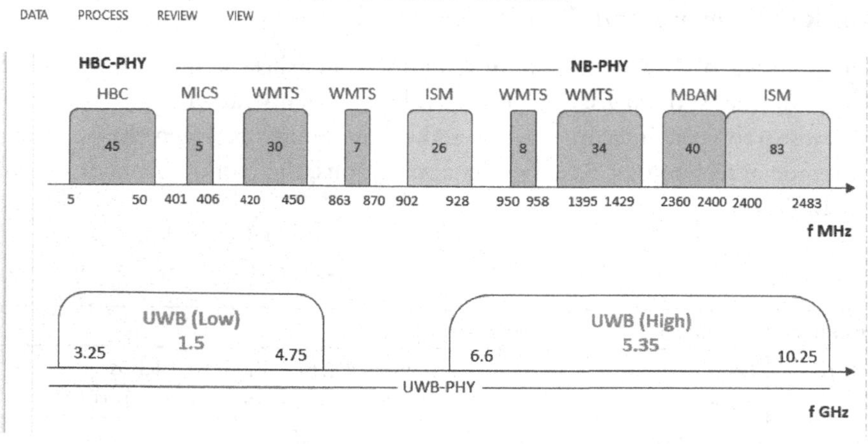

Figure 3: Frequency band IEEE 802.15.6.

3. Millimetre Wave Communication System

3.1. Millimetre Wave System

The extremely high frequency (3×10^{10} Hz to 3×10^{11} Hz) are known as millimetre waves is a non-ionising spectrum of the frequency band as shown in Figure 4. This band provides high throughput of system as it has enormous bandwidth, covers small distances of services for mainly indoor applications and within devices for internal applications due to high attenuation in free space. In practical, 5G applications, frequencies of 28 GHz with bandwidth of 1 GHz and 60 GHz with a bandwidth of 2 GHz are most desirable, whereas in the next-generation communication like 6G, above 95GHz millimetre wave is used for efficient performance of system [1].

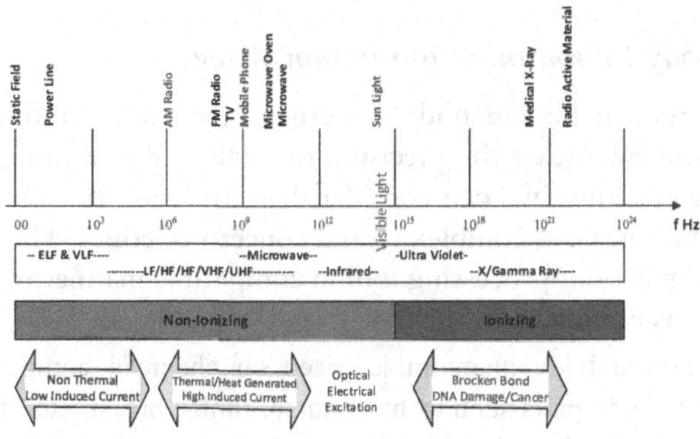

Figure 4: Non- ionizing and ionising EM spectrum.

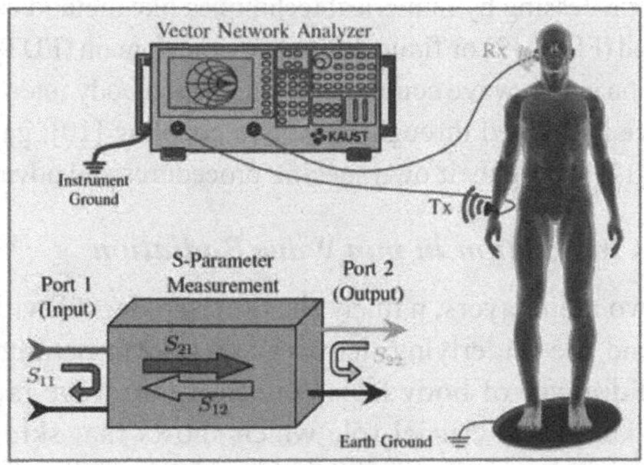

Figure 5: Human body communication in mm wave [1].

Each mmwave device should be accessed to adhere to government exposure guidelines prior to induction into the market for users. The FCC guide for below 6 GHz and the ICNIRP guide for 10 GHz regarding SAR. As at higher frequencies, energy absorption is restricted to the outer layer of skin, power density (PD) taken into consideration by these agencies rather than considering SAR. The ICNIRP states that the minimum PD limitations are 10 W/m^2 and 50 W/m^2 for the general public and the professional, respectively, for frequencies between 10 GHz and 300 GHz, similar to the FCC for the range of frequencies between 6 GHz and 100 GHz [7]. With the evolution of technology, ANSI/IEEE standards updated the acceptable PD to 18.56 $(f)^{0.699}$ W/m^2 at frequencies 3 GHz to 30 GHz and 200 W/m^2 for 30 GHz to 300 GHz.

In the mmwave frequency band, system uses high-gain antennas with directivity or an adaptive array [8] of antennas that takes consideration of the peak power of pointing a beam towards a target (human). In an adaptive array antenna, sometimes the E field also behaves differently by creating a constructive/destructive E field inside the human body in this range of frequency, take different quantitative method of measurement [7].

3.2. Human Body Communication in mm Wave

Dielectric properties of human body are crucial for understanding propagation characteristics and enhancing the precision of analytical and numerical methods. Instead of living creatures, we can consider dielectric data for analysis of human phantom to reduce the cost, complexity and concern of ethics. This dielectric data is processed at simulation/ processing tool in compatible manner to get the results, simulation setup as per Figure 5.

The physical human body phantom is based on chemical compound ingredients containing different body parts such as head, torso, limbs, breast, etc. in solid or liquid forms. Whereas numerical human body phantom is based on the digital form of human body anatomy that is obtained from magnetic resonance imaging (MRI) and computed tomography (CT). The numerical form of a body may be homogenous or heterogenous in nature for further processing by numerical techniques like method of moment (MOM), finite element method (FEM) [9] or finite difference time domain (FDTD). Short distance, high-speed application in mm wave communication, human body interfaces with different media. This interface is coupled through capacitive coupling [10], galvanic coupling or magnetic coupling [11] having their own specific procedures and advantages.

3.3. Human Skin Interaction in mm Wave Radiation

Human skin has two main layers, namely the outer epidermis with thickness range 0.06 to 0.1 mm and the underlying dermis with thickness range 1.2 to 2.8 mm [12]. On proximal distance of body from source of mm wave radiation, dielectric properties of the skin play a crucial role which shows that skin permittivity (ε") is inversely proportional to operating frequency (f) and directly related to skin conductivity(σ) as shown in eqn 1.

Relative complex permittivity $\varepsilon^* = \varepsilon' - j\,\varepsilon''$

$$\text{where } \varepsilon'' = \frac{\sigma}{2\pi f_0} \tag{1}$$

ε_0 is the free space permittivity (8.85×10^{-12} F/m) and conductivity(σ) measured in simen/meter which increases with increase in frequency. At 60 GHz, 34% to 42% of power incident normal on the skin is reflected [13][7] and the Brewster angle ranges from 65° to 80° for all energy absorption at the skin. More than 90% of transmitted EM power gets absorbed within the outer and dermis layer and very little power gets penetrated into the deeper layer inside the body [1].

3.4. mm Wave Radiation Heating the Human Skin

Heating is the main biological outcome due to absorption of EM mmwave energy in the human body by the skin. Figure 6 shows four models for effects of EM radiation on naked skin, naked forehead, clothed skin and hat on forehead. The tissue layer has electric and magnetic fields as given below.

$$E(z) = E_i^+ e^{-jk_i z} + E_i^- e^{-jk_i z} \tag{2}$$

$$\mathrm{H(z)} = \frac{E_i^+}{\eta_i} e^{-jk_i z} + \frac{E_i^-}{\eta_i} e^{-jk_i z} \tag{3}$$

Here k = β–jα = ω $\sqrt{\text{ì å*}}$ and $\eta \sqrt{\frac{\eta}{\varepsilon *}}$ with all normal conversional symbols.

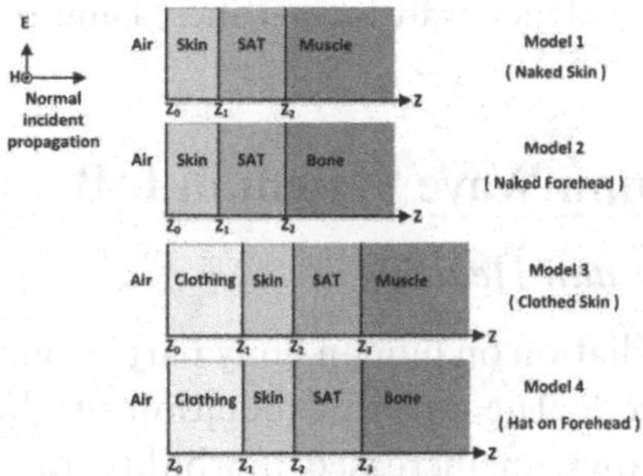

Figure 6: Human body parts exposed in mm Wave radiation.

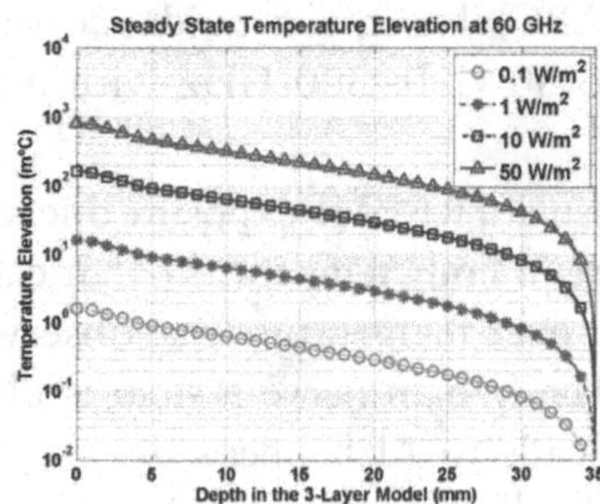

Figure 7: Naked skin at 60 GHz with different incident power densities.

Heat transfer in tissues is numerically calculated on the bioheat transfer equation from Pennes, where the result shows that temperature elevation is directly proportional to the incident power density as shown in Figure 7. The IEEE standard, given that at mm wave radiation temperature rise should be less than 1°C at a power density of 50 W/m^2 for naked skin and steady-state elevation in temperature is 0.8 °C only, which is below the threshold level. At the same time, at 10 W/m^2 the elevation in temperature is 0.16 °C, 0.3 °C for naked skin and forehead with hat, respectively [7][14].

Thickness of clothing has a remarkable effect on power transmission coefficient at two different interfaces, namely air/cloth and cloth/skin. At 60 GHz, the wavelength in clothing is about 3.95 mm and peak power transmission occurs at every half wavelength and the final power is attenuated due to cloth.

$$\frac{P_{ac}}{p_i} = 1 - |R_0|^2 \tag{4}$$

$$\frac{P_{cs}}{p_i} = \left(1 - |R_0|^2\right)\left(1 - |R_0|^2\right)e^{-2\alpha_1 d_c} \tag{5}$$

The power transmission coefficient is given as Pac (air/clothing), Pcs (clothing/ skin) in equation 4 and equation 5 indicates cloth thickness below 1 mm, the cloth may behave similar to impedance transformer increasing power transmission into the skin [1].

4. Implication of mm Wave System in IoB

4.1. *Implication on Human Health*

The effect of mmwave radiation on human body parts summarised in given points and also shown in Figure 8. The effect of radiation on the human body mainly causes cancer, which shows an increased morbidity rate for use of radiation due to chronic myelocytic leukaemia is 13.9%, acute myeloblastic leukaemia is 8.62% and non-Hodgkin lymphomas as 5.82% [4]. The International Agency for research on Cancer (IARC) has given guidance on carcinogenic hazards associated with exposure to 30 GHz–300 GHz with a possible risk of glioma (brain tumour).

Brain cancer can be the result of RF EMF exposure due to changes in permeability of the membrane and increase in body temperature that can be monitored through EEG. At SAR 100 W/kg, the max temperature rise observed is 40°C on exposure to high-intensity RF EMF. The human nerve system is also affected by excessive exposure to RF EMF that leads to Alzheimer's disease and pathophysiology of central nervous system (CNS) disease. Research has also shown that at 18 GHz red blood cells are disturbed on exposure, causing damage to membranes. Skin and eyes are badly affected by mm wave radiation, when varies SAR temperature rise and change in palpebral fissure and 0.8 °C change in temperature of eye lid at EM intensity of 100 W/m2. The risk of ocular damage and healing investigated at 162 GHz results in 90% damage at 368 W/cm^2, which takes 9 days to become normal. Radiation exposure also affects the human reproduction system and primary symptoms such as early abortion and in the final 23.5% of new born children have low birth weight.

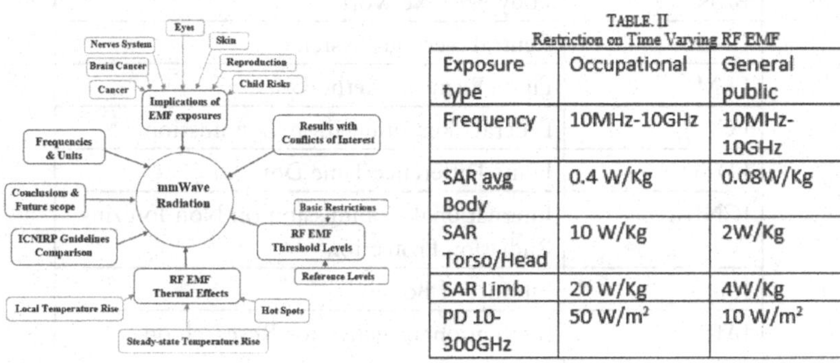

TABLE. II
Restriction on Time Varying RF EMF

Exposure type	Occupational	General public
Frequency	10MHz-10GHz	10MHz-10GHz
SAR avg Body	0.4 W/Kg	0.08W/Kg
SAR Torso/Head	10 W/Kg	2W/Kg
SAR Limb	20 W/Kg	4W/Kg
PD 10-300GHz	50 W/m^2	10 W/m^2

Figure 8: Effect of RF EMF in human health [14].

4.2. Regulatory on Implications to Human Health

To regulate a good health practice to all human ICNIRP, FCC and IEEE issued safety guidelines related to radiation protocol for personal and occupation categories. Some of the safety parameter listed in Table II as per the guidelines from ICNIRP [15][1].

5. Conclusion and Future Scope

This paper mainly covered the mmwave communication system and its implementation on IoB. High-frequency radiation in non-ionising regions makes use of technology to assist IoB where some implications also persist. This systematic survey covered human body interaction in mmwave and reviewed the skin response to radiation. The concept of IoB is covered with their devices and vast applications. Requirements of IoB in terms of quality of services and security require effective involvement of mmwave range. The human body can be modelled by phantoms to analyse the response to mmwave exposure is also viewed along with the implications of radiation on human health and implications regulation by international agencies.

Developing a scientific foundation that links the use of mmWave communication equipment with electromagnetic hyper sensitivity (EHS) health issues in humans is one of the study work's future directions [16]. Significant opportunity offered by IoB in the field of application also opens researcher to work on it in synch with upgrade of technology.

6. acknowledgement

The authors gratefully acknowledge the Management and Faculty of School of Electronics and Electrical Engineering, Lovely Professional University, Punjab, India, for their support and extending necessary facilities to carry out this work.

TABLE OF ABBREVIATION

BAN	Body Area Network
CNS	Central Nervous System
FEM	Finite Element Method
FCC	Federal Communication Commission
FDTD	Finite Difference Time Domain
ICNIRP	International Commission on Non-Ionizing Radiation Protection
IoB	Internet of Bodies
IARC	International Agency for Research on Cancer
MRI	Magnetic Resonance Imaging
MOM	Method of Moment
OECD	Organization for Economic Cooperation and Development
PD	Power Density
QoS	Quality of Services
SAR	Specific Absorption Rate
URLLC	Ultra-reliable Low Latency Communication
WPAN	Wireless Personal Area Network
WHO	World Health Organisation

References

[1] Celik, B. K. N. Salama, *et al.* "The internet of bodies: a systematic survey on propagation characterization and channel modeling," *IEEE Internet Things J.*, vol. 9, no, 1, pp. 321–345, 2022, doi: 10.1109/JIOT.2021.3098028.

[2] Lee, M. and B. Boudreaux, *Internet of Body*, Rand Corporation, 2020, ISBN: 978-1-9774-0522-7, www.rand.org/t/RR3226.

[3] Lorenzoni, L., A. Marino, D. Morgan, and C. James, *Health Spending Projections to 2030*, OECD, Paris, France, Working Paper 110, 2019, https://doi.org/https://doi.org/10.1787/5667f23d-en.

[4] "IEEE Standard for Safety Levels with Respect to Human Exposure to Electric, Magnetic, and Electromagnetic Fields, 0 Hz to 300 GHz," in *IEEE*

Std C95.1-2019 (Revision of IEEE Std C95.1-2005/ Incorporates IEEE Std C95.1-2019/Cor 1-2019), vol., no., pp. 1–312, 2019, doi: 10.1109/IEEESTD.2019.8859679.

[5] Council, ICNIRP, "ICNIRP guidelines," *Health Physics*, vol. 74, no. 4, pp. 494–522, 1998.

[6] Boddington, G., "The internet of bodies—alive, connected and collective: the virtual physical future of our bodies and our senses," *AI and Society*, Sringer, 2021, doi:10.1007/s00146-020-01137-1.

[7] Wu, T., T. S. Rappaport, *et al.*, "The human body and millimeter-wave wireless communication systems: interactions and implications," *IEEE International Conference on Communications (ICC)*, IEEE Explore, London UK, 2015, doi:10.1109/ICC.2015.7248688.

[8] Gutierrez, F., S. Agarwal, K. Parrish, and T. S. Rappaport, "On chip integrated antenna structures in CMOS for 60 GHz WPAN systems," *IEEE J. Sel. Areas Commun.*, vol. 27, no. 8, pp. 1367–1378, 2009.

[9] Farmaga, *et al.*, "Evaluation of computational complexity of finite element analysis," *Proc. Int. Conf. Exp. Design. Appl. CAD Syst. Microelectron.* , pp. 213–214, 2011.

[10] Handa, T., S. Shoji, S. Ike, S. Takeda, and T. Sekiguchi, "A very low-power consumption wireless ECG monitoring system using body as a signal transmission medium," *Proc. Int. Solid-State Sensors Actuators Conf.*, vol. 2, pp. 1003–1006, 1997.

[11] Ogasawara, T., A.-I. Sasaki, K. Fujii, and H. Morimura, "Human body communication based on magnetic coupling," *IEEE Trans. Antennas Propag.*, vol. 62, no. 2, pp. 804–813, 2014.

[12] Zhadobov, M., N. Chahat, R. Sauleau, C. L. Quement, and Y. L. Drean, "Millimeter-wave interactions with the human body: state of knowledge and recent advances," *Int. J. Microwave Wireless Technol.*, vol. 3, no. 2, pp. 237–247, 2011.

[13] Alekseev, S.I. and M.C. Ziskin, "Human skin permittivity determined by millimeter wave reflection measurements," *Bio Electro Magnetics*, Wily, 2007. doi:10.1002/bem.20308.

[14] Dilli, R., "Implications of mm wave radiation on human health: state of the art threshold levels," *IEEE Access*, vol. 9, pp. 13009–13021, 2021, doi: 10.1109/ACCESS.2021.3052387.

[15] Lin, J. C., "Safety guidelines and 5G communication RF radiation," *URSI Radio Station Bull.*, no. 377, pp 64–78, 2021, doi:10.23919/URSIRSB.2021.9829356.

[16] Cao, H., V. Leung, *et al.*, "Enabling technologies for wireless body area networks: a survey and outlook," *Consumer Communications and Networking IEEE Communication Magazine*, pp. 84–93, 2009.

About Author

First Jai Kumar is a Ph.D. Research Scholar in the School of Electronics and Electrical Engineering, Lovely Professional University, Punjab, India. (E-mail: jaiky2011@gmail.com). He is a Chartered Engineer and Member (MIE) of Institution of Engineers India.

Second Akhil Gupta is an Associate Professor in the School of Electronics and Electrical Engineering, Lovely Professional University, Punjab, India. (E-mail: akhil.20239@lpu.co.in). He is a Senior Member of IEEE

62. Self-Organisation of Heavy Traffic Using Zigbee Communication on Raspberry Pi

B.Ravi Chandra[1, 2] and Dr Krishan Kumar[2]

[1]*Electronics & Communication Engineering, G. Pullaiah College of Engineering & Technology, Kurnool, India*
[2]*Lovely Professional University, Punjab, India*

Abstract: The level of knowledge currently available is remarkable, and embedded technology is at its pinnacle. Hardware and software coexist in an embedded system. Embedded technology is essential for combining the many functions that are connected to it. This must connect the Department's numerous sources in a closed-loop system. This concept cuts staff significantly, saves time, and runs efficiently without human intervention. Traffic management involves using image processing to analyse road photos from PC cameras at traffic intersections to calculate real-time traffic density. The emphasis is on the algorithm used to adjust traffic signals based on the type of vehicle density on the road. The primary goal is to reduce road traffic congestion, lower the number of accidents, provide safer transportation, reduce fuel consumption, and decrease waiting times. This system also generates valuable data for research and future road planning. In later phases, it is possible to synchronise multiple traffic signals with one another to further reduce traffic and promote free traffic flow. Instead of using electrical sensors buried beneath the pavement, the system detects vehicles using images taken by cameras positioned near the traffic signals. This image processing approach is more effective in controlling traffic light state changes, reducing gridlock, and saving time, as it accurately determines the presence of vehicles using real traffic photos. In cases of emergencies, such as when an ambulance arrives, the system can use ZigBee and Wi-Fi to change all the red signals to green, creating a clear path for emergency vehicles like ambulances.

Keywords: Traffic control, traffic congestion, Arduino, ZigBee, raspberry-PI, Zigbee.

1. Introduction

With advancements a future infrastructure-free wireless communication and mobile Information system for computing self-organised traffic in which vehicles can create a network to exchange Soon, traffic data between them will become apparent. Vehicles will operate as mobile sensors in a traffic data system lacking infrastructure, collecting traffic data as they travel. Due to the fact that smartphones today come containing a range of sensors, including the global positioning system (GPS), gyroscope, accelerometer, mic and device, which is they make a great choice for traffic sensing devices.

Traffic data can be gathered using these sensors. Despite the fact that there are a lot of different kinds of sensors that can be utilised for congestion detecting, earlier research has mostly used a receiver for GPS. A GPS receiver, on the other hand, uses a lot of energy and can dramatically reduce battery life. In this study, we investigate the using additional smartphone sensors for traffic awareness. We especially investigate how and to what extent an accelerometer's data can be used to infer a vehicle's average speed. There will be two estimate techniques demonstrated, and their precision will be evaluated.

2. Current Procedure

For efficient signal control and traffic management, it is essential to be aware of the current road traffic density, particularly in urban areas. In recent years, traffic management has seen a rise in the popularity of video monitoring and surveillance systems. For traffic control departments, especially in metropolitan areas, controlling traffic is a tough task.

The goal of the project is to keep track of the volume of traffic in a particular area, and the data is sent to a traffic management system. The ambulance needs to move more quickly in order to save a life, even in congested areas. In this project, an AT89S52 microcontroller is utilised. Here, traffic density is represented by three pairs of IR Tx-Rx.

A set of TSOP receivers and an IR emitter make up the module. TSOP's high-accuracy receiver consistently finds a signal on a set frequency. As a result, errors brought on by improper ambient light sensing are greatly reduced.

Block diagram

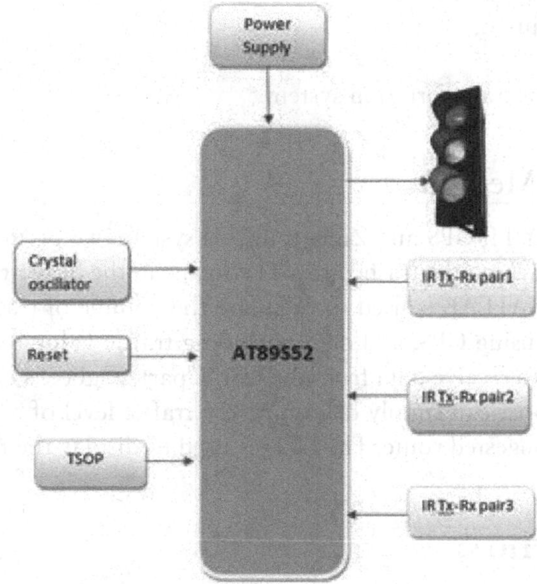

Figure 1: Block diagram of traffic system. [10]

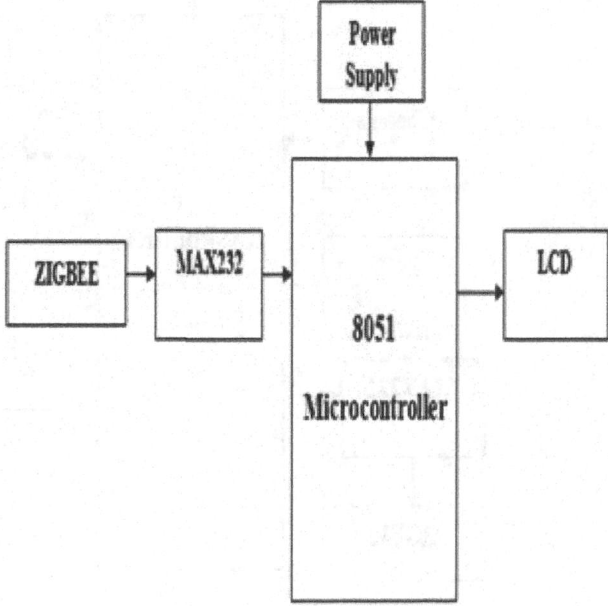

Figure 2: Vehicle section. [11]

2.1. Consequences

- pollution caused;
- time loss;
- an inefficient transportation system.*

3. Proposed Method

Using RASPBERRY PI, GPS and Zigbee, in this system, we predict the congestion intensity before reaching the traffic area. The image in the busy area is captured by the camera, and MATLAB is used to calculate the volume of traffic. The location is then monitored using GPS, and data, including traffic volume and location, are sent over ZigBee. To receive data from the traffic part, Zigbee is used in the vehicle section. This motorist can simply determine the traffic level of a specific spot and choose the least congested route. The LCD is used to display the project's status.

Block diagram

TRAFFIC SECTION:

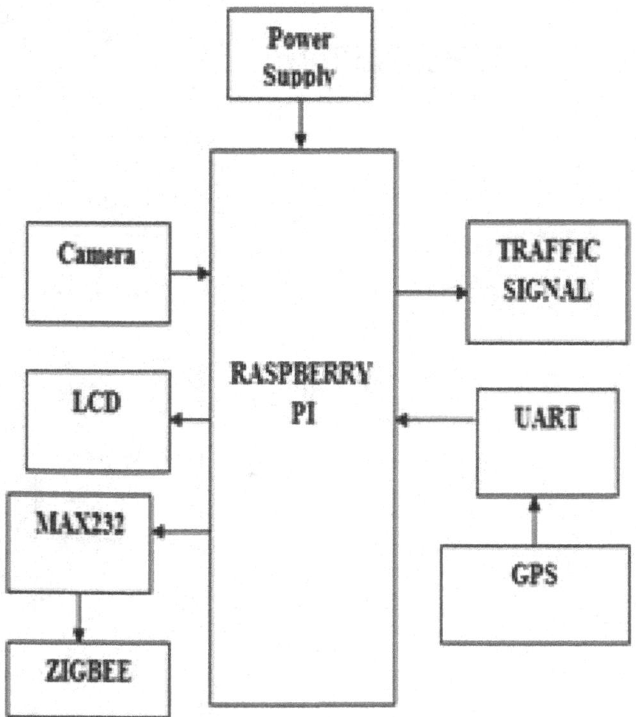

Figure 3: *Block diagram of traffic section. [12]*

3.1. Raspberry-PI

A quad-core Broadcom BCM2836 system on a chip (SoC) powers the Raspberry Pi.

Cortex-A7 group. The ARMv7-architecture is used by the high-performance and low-power Cortex-A7 MP Core processor. The Cortex-A7 MPC ore processor comprises one to four processors, a possible inbuilt GIC, an alternative cache with L2 controller and only one multi-processor module.

Finally, a new Raspberry Pi has been made available by the Raspberry Pi Foundation. The Raspberry Pi Model 2B shares many of the connectors and physical characteristics of the Raspberry Pi Model B+, but it contains 1GB RAM and a quad-core ARMv7 processor from Broadcom that runs at 900 MHz instead of the earlier model's 700 MHz

3.2. AT89S52

A low-voltage, high-performance, 8-bit CMOS microcomputer with 4K programmable Flash memory is the AT89S52. The system uses Atmel's high-density nonvolatile memory technology and the MCS-51 instruction set, which is the industry standard. The Atmel AT89S52 is a potent microcomputer that combines Flash on a monolithic chip with a flexible 8-bit CPU to offer a highly adaptive and affordable solution to many embedded control applications.

Additionally, the AT89S52 offers two software-selectable power-saving modes and static logic that permits operation at zero frequency. In idle mode, the CPU is disabled, but the RAM, timers, counters, serial port and interrupt system are still in use. While all other chip operations are disabled in the power-down mode until the subsequent hardware reset, the RAM data is saved.

3.3. ZigBee

For use with ZigBee. The scaled-down euro coin has a diameter of about 23 mm (0.9 inches). Based on the wireless personal area networks (WPANs) IEEE 802.15.4-2003 standard, such as wireless headphones connecting to cell phones over short-range radio, ZigBee is a specification for a collection of high-level communication protocols.

In comparison to contemporary WPANs such as Bluetooth connectivity, the ZigBee protocol outlines a simpler and cheaper technique. Zigbee target market is radio frequency (RF) applications that require a slow transfer rate, a lengthy lifespan for the battery and secure networking. A group of companies known as the ZigBee Alliance is in charge of maintaining and disseminating the ZigBee standard.

3.4. Interior Design

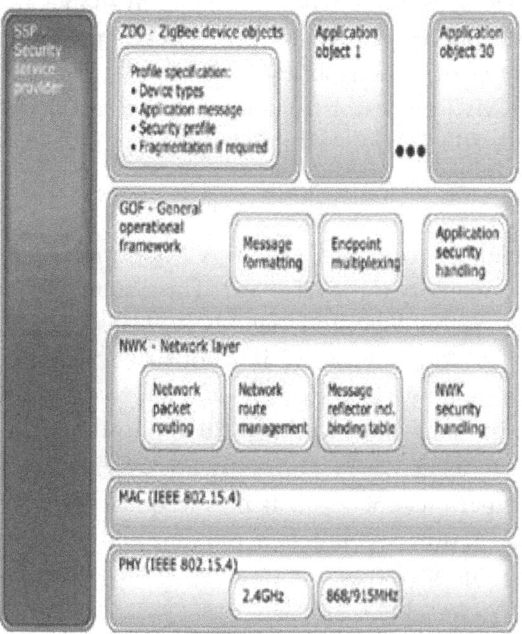

Figure 4: *Interior design.*

A home-area network called ZigBee was developed to stop the proliferation of individual remote controls. To satisfy consumer demand for an affordable, standards-based wireless network with low data rates, low power consumption, security and reliability, ZigBee was created.

3.5. GPS's Fundamental Principle

By precisely timing signals sent by GPS satellites orbiting the Earth, a GPS receiver can pinpoint its location. Each satellite continuously transmits messages that contain the following information:

- The time at which the message was transmitted;
- The precise orbital information (ephemeris); and
- The overall system health and the approximate orbits of all GPS satellites (almanack).
- Linux serves as the Raspberry Pi's operating system.

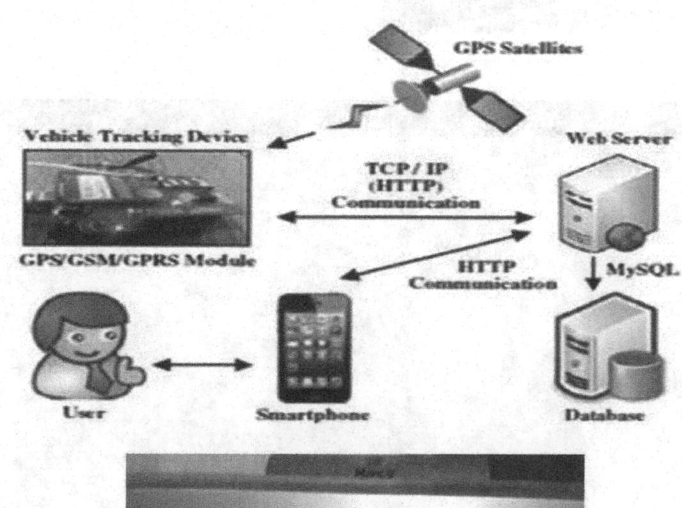

Schematic Diagram:

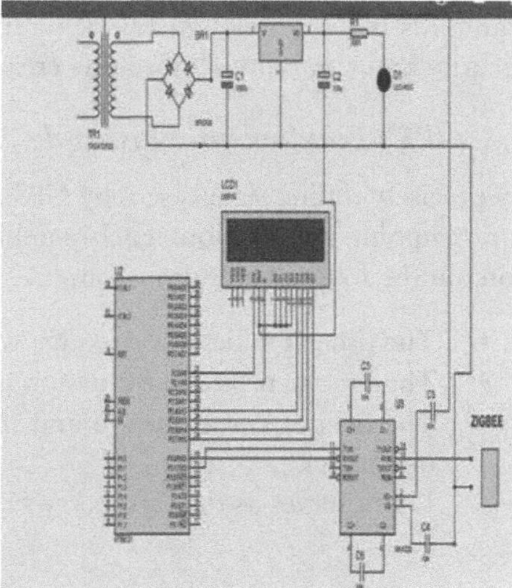

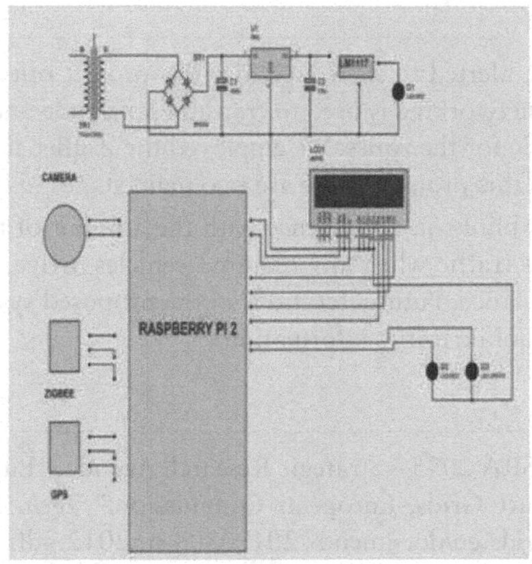

4. Results

4.1. *Benefits Improved*

- safety prevents
- major accidents
- saves human lives
- authentication using biometrics

4.2. *Applications Include*

- Traffic areas

5. Conclusion

So that users can be alerted to their location, this project offers the best way for users to get ZigBee networking is used to transmit longitude and latitude values as well as data on traffic for the zones. We employed the ZigBee networking protocol for traffic control in this project. There are two main stages to this project:

The traffic light blinks in accordance with the amount of traffic on the road. This system controls traffic when any required vehicles arrive, for instance, a fire department or ambulance. Future iterations of the proposed system will be able to provide users with mobile traffic information.

References

[1] Smart Grids SRA 2035 – Strategic Research Agenda, "European Technology Platform Smart Grids, European Commission," *Tech. Rep.*, 2012, http://www.smartgrids.eu/documents/ 20120308 sra2012.pdf.

[2] Siano, P., C. Cecati, C. Citro, and P. Siano, "Smart operation of wind turbines and diesel generators according to economic criteria," *IEEE Trans. Ind. Electron*, vol. 58, no. 10, pp. 4514–4525, 2011.

[3] Bennett, C. and S. Wicker, "Decreased time delay and security enhancement recommendations for AMI smart meter networks," *Proc. Innov. Smart Grid Technol. Conf.*, 2010.

[4] Cecati, C., C. Citro, and P. Siano, "Combined operations of renewable energy systems and responsive demand in a smart grid," *IEEE Trans. Sustainable Energy*, in press, 10.1109/TSTE.2011.2161624.

[5] Kleinrock, L. and F. A. Tobagi, "Packet switching in radio channels: part I—carrier sense multiple access modes and their throughput-delay characteristics," *IEEE Trans. Commun.*, vol. 23, pp. 1400–1416, 1975.

[6] IEC 62056 Electricity metering, *Data Exchange for Meter Reading, Tariff and Load Control*, International Electro technical Commission Std.

[7] The essential of Euridis, www.euridis.org/solution details.html.

[8] Kapar, Z., "Power-line communication - regulation introduction, pl modem implementation and possible application," *12th International.*

[9] The PRIME Alliance, PRIME MAC Spec White Paper 1.0, Std. [12]. KNX Specification, version 2.0, KNX Association, Diegem, Belgium, 2009.

[10] Ghosh, Raja, Deepak Rasaily, and Ishani Dey. "Auto Density Sensing Traffic Control System using AT89S52." *International Journal of Engineering Trends and Technology* 32.5 (2016): 208-212.

[11] Karmude, A. Somnath, and G. R. Gidveer. "Vehicular Identification and Authentication System using Zigbee." *International Journal of Engineering Research and Technology* 3.11 (2014).

[12] Nandhini N1, Rakshana R2, Revathi L3, Siva Swarnamalya4, Nagaraj V5, "AUTONOMOUS CARS USING RASPBERRY Pi". *International Research Journal of Engineering and Technology* (IRJET), Volume: 07 Issue: 05 | May 2020

63. A Relay Selection Optimisation for Cooperative Networks to Maximise Reliability and Minimise Energy Consumption

Valishetti Prashanthi[1], Uppula Kiran[2], Krishan Kumar[3]

[1]*Dept of Computer Science Engineering, Kakatiya Institute of Technology and Science, Telangana, India*

[2]*Dept of Electronics and Communication Engineering, Vaagdevi College of Engineering, Telangana, India*

[3]*Dept of Electronics and Communication Engineering, Lovely Professional University, India*

Abstract: We've analysed the integrated wireless network where the sensors inside each group transmit a message to every other group using co-operative communication techniques. Simplest the ones sensors that well decide the package deal in the source can take part in subsequent collaborative communication. Therefore, the range of the interactive sensor is a random change that depends on the detection of both the channel and the audio. Create flexible development constraints to reduce overall energy consumption. By numerical methods, we check out how energy efficiency affects the transmission of energy transmission, overall quantity of sensors in the collection, error packet gives up-to-quit blunders and relative intra-cluster and inter-cluster size.

Keywords: Energy efficiency, relay selection, channel state information (CSI), cluster size.

1. Introduction

Although wireless networks are subject to regulations in relation to energy supply and message communication infidelity [3,4], it is difficult to consume power due to limited power supply. In general, they can be powered by chemical cells that are replaced or recharged after discharge. However, updating the battery is not constantly clean, in particular in big networks. In order to minimise power consumption of wireless network nodes, these kinds of networks are commonly configured to observe an obligation cycle. Meaning, buttons turn off components in their circuits, becoming inactive during most of the time. In addition, poor communication reliability can lead to unimaginable performance drops on wireless networks. This issue is related to misplaced messages because of EM and/or different devices operating within the equal frequency band or node limits[5].

With a variety of collaboration strategies, networks can also use single-antenna equipment to take benefit of the identical advantages of the multiple-input-multiple-output (MIMO) architecture.. This permits non-rotating nodes to apply horns to create visual MIMO gadgets, avoiding the transmission of some horns that may growth overall energy consumption [6]. Unlike the normal WN connection, where packets have a destination. Dealing with transfers involves the best single transmitter and single recipient, the interactive list looks at the life of nodes in order for someone to share a pair they receive a sender, concentrate to and store messages obtained from their buddies and then ahead them to their destination. As a result, the destination is more likely to receive parcels sent because of the misleading message and the use of the destination may be acceptable during the redeployment phase [10,7].

Each time use a variety of collaborations, the selection of a set of slides is very important to achieve the overall level of performance. It is miles crucial to emphasise that choosing all nodes as relays will permit for more variability in interaction. However, on the same time, it is miles viable to boom the frequency of various messages and everyday power usage, which additionally contributes to synergies between those types of nodes [6]. Therefore, one of the maximum critical demanding situations in a collaboration gadget is to pick the ultimate set of outbound nodes to enhance the general reliability of the discussion [8,9]. Choosing conditions are the most important factors when choosing a set of transmission nodes. While choosing interaction slots, many studies simply keep the top ratings in mind for this reason, including the received signal strength indicator (RSSI), CSI, SNR or link quality indicator (LQI) [5].

Figure 1 shows a wireless network made up of seven nodes, one of which is a connector node. Here WN, there are three recognised regions as x, y and z. All nodes inside the same place are assumed adjoining and might listen to each other. The 2nd, 3rd and 4th nodes within the Y area cannot communicate directly with the coordinator. Miles are used in this community to visualise the use of relays to enable messages to receive coordinator nodes. Further, it is also possible to be note that selecting a good enough transmission may require you to recall other parameters other than channel quality.

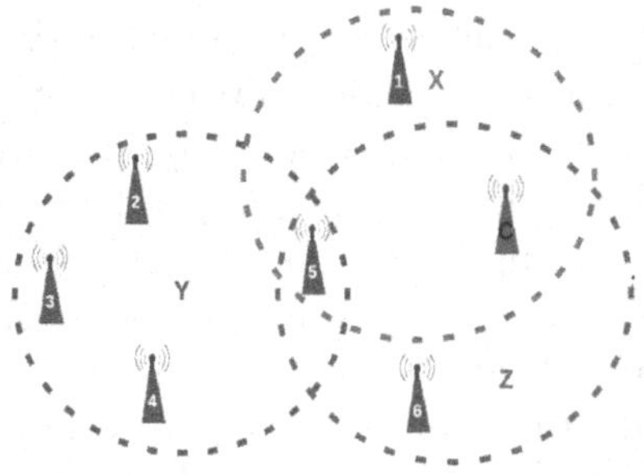

Figure 1: *Wireless network that desires a relay.*

It also investigates the use of relay update programmes. Optimization terminology is used in this article in the modern sense mode of advanced transition button selection, while also being compared with other high-level techniques. The periodic system, called the periodic relay selection (PRS), is a fashionable extension, while switch options are made periodically, without studying the need for a modern alternative. In a flexible approach, known as adaptive relay selection (ARS), the time interval among successive transmission options is obtained forcibly, based on community success rates.

The ARS system is capable of managing dynamic networks, in which the nodes may also randomly become part of or leave the latest cover code for the coordinator. In both relay choice schemes, the goal is to growth conversational complement and reduce energy consumption these days at the community, with the aid of selecting the widest nodes of the ultra-cutting-edge relay and, on the equal time, making sure that each one nodes are linked in at least one associated place transferred. Although compared to different strategies, the scientific goal of contributing to the modern method proposed for the selection of modern day transmission nodes is strong and fast based entirely on a few determinants, namely: a list of present day fashion participants, their storage capability, new high-quality communique hyperlink of the candidate node and neighbouring nodes (using RSSI) as well as the success rate records for the latest node transfers, which provides a good enough selection for modern transfers nodes and improve the reliability of verbal exchanges, on the grounds that these methods are essential for the latest network performance. However, this process is much more complicated when you use only one condition to measure candidate nodes to end the transmission. As many issues are protected within the relay choice version, the proposed system is designed as a development difficulty, the use of a specially selected benefit feature.

2. Related Works

Good enough selection of relay nodes for state of the art is essential in order to promote the full functionality of modern collaborative communication methods [15]. There are many programmes for selecting relay nodes within books. However, many of these activities tend to focus on high-level data communication systems, comparing and proposing different messaging techniques (or signals) in the form of transmission nodes, based entirely on amplify-forward (AF), decode-forward (DF) or hybrid strategies [1]. This characteristic objectives to improve relay choice in WNs. In this manner, the present day motive of this segment is to describe high-level strategies that deal primarily with relay selection strategies. Then, the advanced selection systems have been divided into 5 classes, in accordance with the standards used for relay choice: supported link [11], link function and power is primarily based more often than not on [14], first hyperlink and neighbour primarily based [12], level of information and records based totally [9] and random relay s election (RRS) [2].

2.1. *Quality of the Link Based*

In this case, the choice of effective transmission takes into account the using quality of the link rating.

Marchenko *et al.* [13] provided flexible LQI-based relay options, here the data transfer parameters are reduced according to the last-pass performance of the communication channel. Source code S tracks the acknowledgment (ACK) of outgoing packets. If an ACK packet is not always available, it is assumed that the currently transmitted V or W_i is needed to forward the packet. If the ACK deficit ratio in the duration of the *Za* window is the same or better than the #a limit value, a new transfer option is initiated. In order to make the selection of the transfer nodes, the *V* conveys the message of the transfer request, which contains the destination *M* identification of the following mathematical packets. All nodes that get hold of this utility generate a random timer Tc = rand (0, Z) for all transmissions for the duration of a *W* window conflict. While the node expires, a candidate message is sent to *M*. This message consists of an approximate LQI value and a *Z-Tc* value. Consequently, *M* can verify the suspension of the enchantment window even if he has now not been notified of the request for reassignment. The input message notes found in *M* form the candidate set sent by *W*. At the end of the acquisition phase, M evaluates the good end-to-end hyperlinks of each candidate Wi to obtain at least 2 LQI values (L to W_i and W_i to M).

2.2. *Quality of the Link Based on the Neighbourhood*

On this section, Etezadi *et al.* [16] provide 3 forward button options. First, we place it as a condition using the original SNR. The second selects nodes from the source region based on geometric analysis. 1/3 randomly picks the switch in the W position next to the connector. The first two strategies are the best use of power. In the first, the authors hypothesised that the SNR could change several times. For this reason, a fixed node with a better SNR can switch between continuous transmissions. This reality shows that in this system, every node is an active repeater, so it must constantly switch between receive and transmit without sleep and must have permission to use power. Within 2, a set of nodes near the source area does not usually pass through updates. As a result, these buttons maintain alternating between listening and transmitting modes, In addition to allowing all other nodes to sleep and store a certain amount of power, key components also drain the battery prematurely. The third approach randomly selects the latest node for the nodes that will be forwarded to different nodes that may be within radius W within the full source location O (L, W). Consistent with the authors, this method is the least effective.

2.3. *Quality of the Link Based on the Energy*

Pham and Kim [14] are provided a way to select relays to improve network lifespan and improve packet forwarding. The transmitting point is the node with the best residual overall power and the lowest EPB. The simple precept is that, primarily based on the CSI and residual information (REI) for every transmission, it is miles a rely of first determining which transmission protocol fine. When the link SNR among the source node and the hyperlink candidate node exceeds a predetermined value, the node applies AF. Otherwise the node uses DF. Once an appropriate transport protocol has been determined, the node best suited for residual emission e_i^m and EPB reduction can be selected as the transport. Therefore, the authors propose a weight calculation w across the co-node r, such as $w_r = \frac{e_i^m}{E_b}$, where a relay with the best weight value is selected.

3. Optimised Relay Selection Technique

To offer a clear concept, an excessive definition of the proposed approach is defined on this segment. To make it easier, we preconfigured the power and energy classes of every transmitting node earlier than indicating how a given packet is routed from its source to its destination. First, the source location will select the package transfer location based on space and power level. Within a previous study, several methods used both distance and level of power to build a route. In addition, several researchers suggest that distance and height metrics are often used to pick excessive excellent transmission sites. We consequently used and evolved those two measures in our proposed transfer site selection technique. In the proposed technique, the selected transmitting node is called a transmitting node. The source code pushes the package into the forward zone. After forwarding a packet, the power level of the source node can decrease mainly depending on the coverage space and the size of the packets added during the forwarding process. Existing edit code will use the same method to select all other edits that will appear as subsequent edits.

Moreover, the power level of the current relay may also lower after the packet is transferred to the subsequent relay. This technique can be repeated till the package deal reaches its destination. Therefore, the recommendation process included structures.

4. Proposed System

Assume that the source area (L) forwards the packet to the destination (M), and that the pre-programmed power level is 50%. In the proposed system, L first uses a small manifold to search for a feeder position to maintain a switch (see Figure 2). Eqn. (1) calculating the minimum range [15].

$$E_{\min r} \frac{\min(A,B)\, d(A\ ,B\ )}{\sqrt{w_c^2 + g_c^2}} \tag{1}$$

$\min(A,B)\, d(A\ ,B\ )$ is the minimum distance between relay nodes. $\sqrt{w_c^2 + g_c^2}$ is the longest time between switching nodes that may be represented inside the diagonal time of the control field.

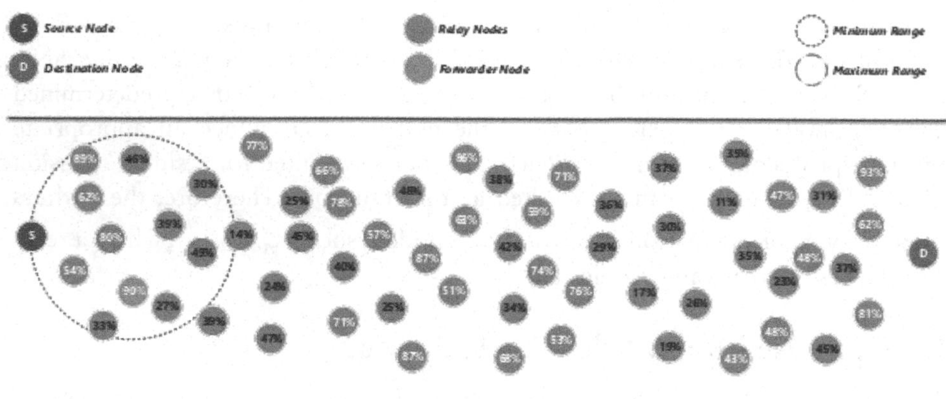

Figure 2: Decide a forwarder node the usage of the minimal range.

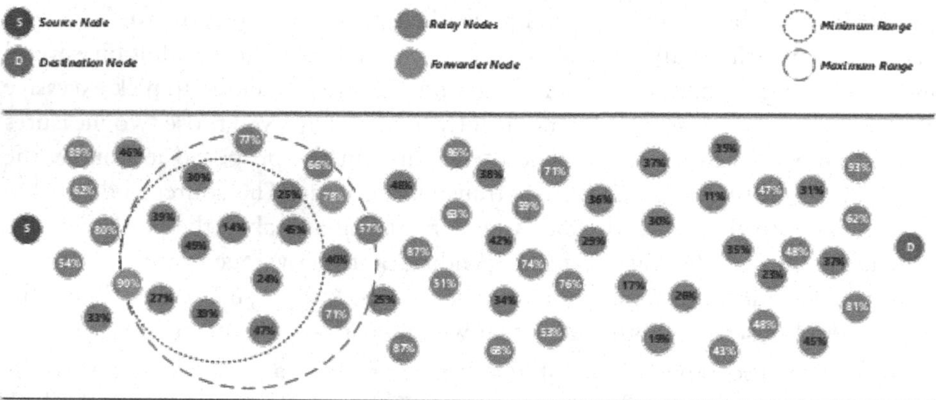

Figure 3: Decide a forwarder node the usage of the maximuml range.

Given that there may be more than one transmission node with a threshold power stage above or equal to 50%, as an end result, the proposed method will offer high cost to the transmitted place with the very best strength level. If there is a tie, the nearest distance is the second most important factor in the selection method. If no relay nodes complete the minimum diploma energy threshold (50%), then the suggested method uses the maximum and assumes all eligible transmitting nodes grow to direct forward transmission. In this case, a transfer node with a power level of 90% is selected due to the previous node.

To determine the following transmission point, the proposed method will use a smaller range to decide with a view to have a switch location that meets the minimal strength restriction (50%). Since the transmission space does not reach the lower power limit, the suggested method uses a wider range to find a suitable relay for the next transmission. (see Figure 3).

$$f_q = n - b_h = \{(2 P_t)/[(\psi - 1)\varepsilon_m]\} \tag{2}$$

f_q is the best transmission distance. n is an indicator of a transmitted node. b_h is the location of transfer notes. P_d is the power consumption of a node transmitted to another transfer phase. am is the power dissipated within the transmission amplifier, ψ is an exponent of the antenna channel loss, and f the space among the present forwarding node and the next forwarding node. In this case, the power transmission capacity is 78%. Stage is selected as a forwarding code. After the packet is sent to the next hop, the energy level of the hop code decreases.

The same method is used to obtain the next reference node. The suggested approach first uses smaller variability to determine the available transmission space corresponding to the minimum energy constraint. Assuming that there are two transmission nodes with the equal energy degree (87%), proximity could be the second most crucial component in choice (see Figure 4). In this situation, a relay node that follows the forwarding aspect is chosen as the next relay node. The power stage of the forwarding node can be decreased after the packet is transferred to the subsequent ahead component.

For the next sponderer node, the suggested technique will use no less editing to find a transmitted node to complete a small intensity station (see Figure 5). Assume no relay node meets the minimum threshold strength; the suggested technique uses a distinctive quantity to recollect which of the best transmitters have to be the following transmission factor. Because there is no transfer node that fills the upper power platform; in addition, the proposed method will reduce the power filed using Eq. (3).

$$V_{ene} = \begin{cases} V_{ene}\, b \dfrac{E_r}{E_i} \; if & n \in G \\ & elsewhere \end{cases} \tag{3}$$

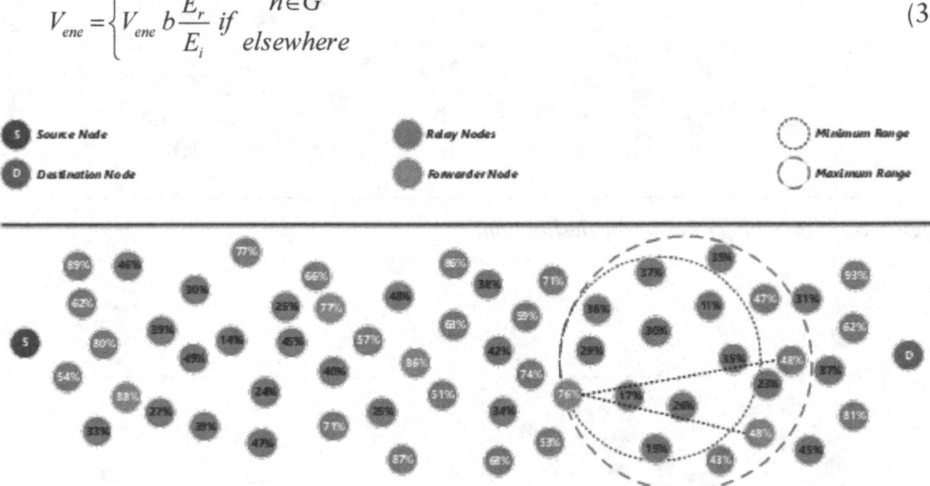

Figure 4: Decide a forwarder node the usage of the nearest distance.

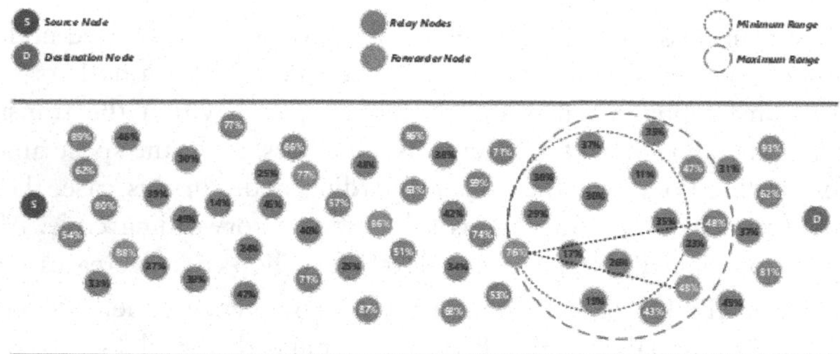

Figure 5: Decide a forwarder node via reducing the threshold energy level.

Energy is the limit of power, and is the residual energy of the transmitted node. E_i is the primary energy of the transmitted node. G is a set of all relay nodes. It is estimated that the threshold strength of a new threshold after counting is 40%. A broadcast message may be despatched to inform every transmission point of the brand-new stage restrict. The proposed method then limits the use of a smaller range to consider a transfer area that complements the energy phase of the brand new limit. Figure 6 shows the steps to move the packet to the destination. Figure 7 shows paths of the packet transmitted by using the proposed method.

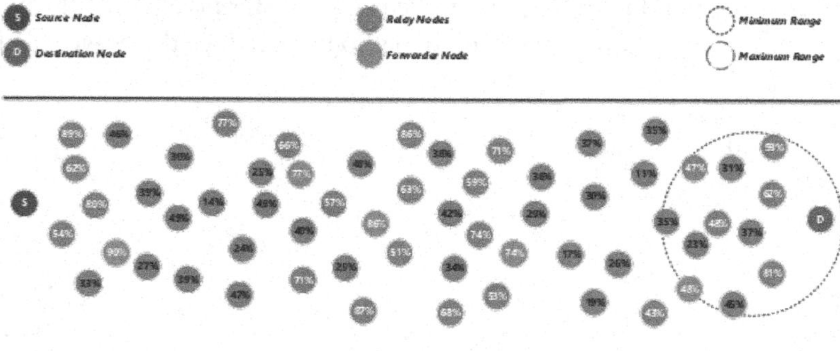

Figure 6: Move the packet to the destination.

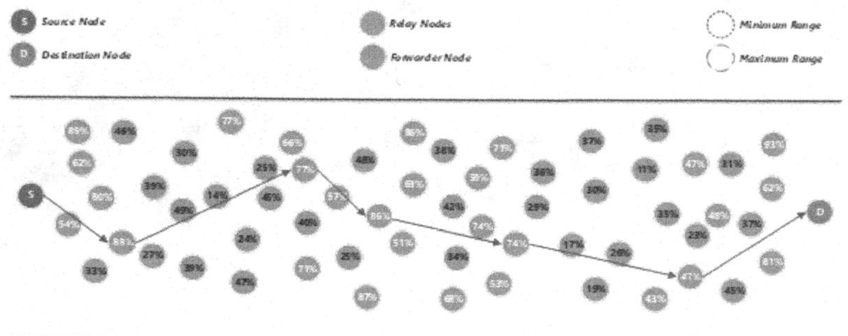

Figure 7: Paths of the packet transmitted the use of the proposed method.

5. Results and Discussions

Table 1 shows the required simulation parameters for evaluation.

Table 1: Simulation parameters.

Parameter	Values
Network size	500 m x 500 m
Node deployment	Uniform
Number of nodes	100
Source node	1
Destination node	1
Relay nodes	98
Maximum range	30 m
Minimum range	15 m
Packet size	1,024bit
Threshold energy level	50%
Sending rate	1 packet/s
Simulation time	900 s

Figure 8 shows a comparison of a few temporary delivery packages for a proposed strategy and other related activities. Imitation outcomes have shown that our proposed approach has a low package deal shipping rate accompanied by AOR, ENO_OR, ENS_OR, ExOR, GeRaF and EEOR. Usually, our suggested approach produces approximately 22.98%, 26.87%, 33.18%, 44.26%, 63.99% and 76.01% of small packet delivery delays compared to AOR, ENO_OR, ENS_OR, ExOR, GeRaF and EEOR, respectively. The cause why our suggested process need to carry out better in comparison to different techniques is probably due to the smaller or better sort of alternatives used. In the ideal case, if all forwarding nodes fulfill the specified limit power and use the minimum transfer packets, packets can be delivered without the same delay.

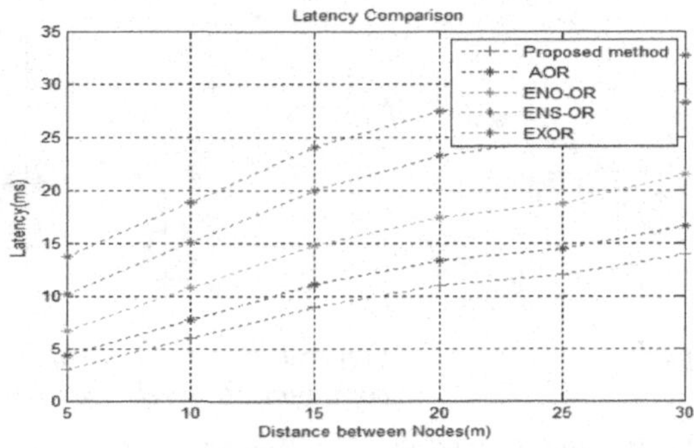

Figure 8: Latency comparison.

Figure 9(a) shows the strength characteristics while PER0 is adjusted from 0.01 to 0.0001. We assume that although the minimum power in line with the packet will increase while the rate corresponds to the drops, the energy efficiency parameter decreases (that means better efficiency). Next, collaborative dialogue is more powerful while demand for engagement is much lower. Figure 9(b) shows the significant potential benefits of co-operative communication. For example, while PER0 = 0.001 and n = 5, the power performance parameter of the co-operation can be as low as 0.02; that is, a collaborative conversation consumes 1–50% of the required power of direct communication.

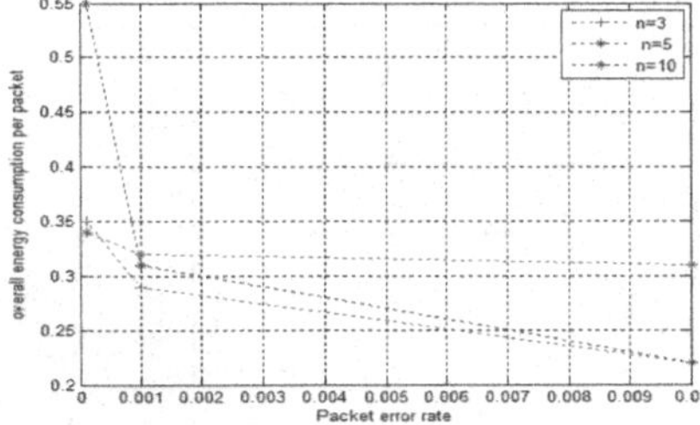

Figure 9(a): EC per packet.

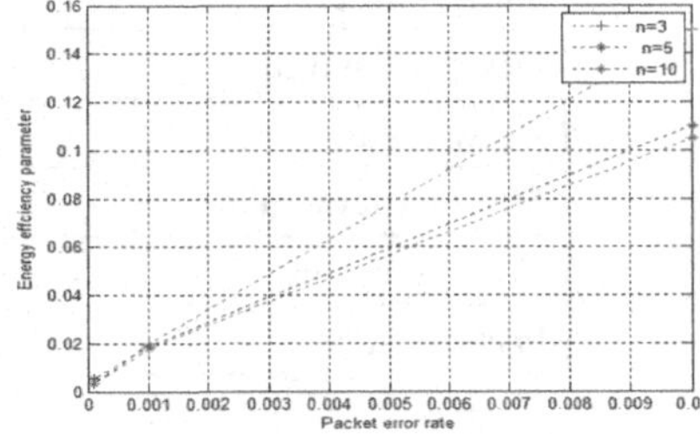

Figure 9(b): EC ratio of cooperative communication relative to direct communication.

Figure 9: Energy characteristics vs. PER.

5.1. Overall EC vs. Inter-Cluster Distance

Set W1 = 20 m, PER0 = 0.01, n = 3; 5; 10, then convert B1 is in between 100 m and 300 m. Figure10 suggests that although normal power consumption in conjunction with the packet increases by B1, energy efficiency is high. Therefore, the extra the inter-cluster distance, the greater power saving the network conversation becomes from Figure 10, we see that when B1 < 245 m, a system with n = 3 consumes less energy. At 245 m < B1 <300 m, a machine with n = 5 consumes less energy. This means that a higher *n* level depends on the inter-cluster range.

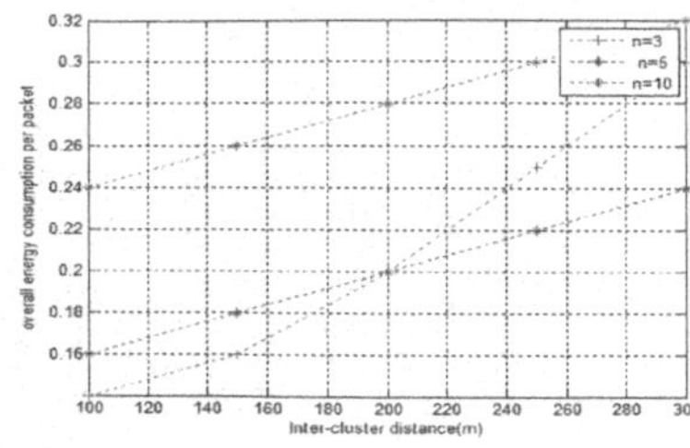

Figure 10(a): EC per packet

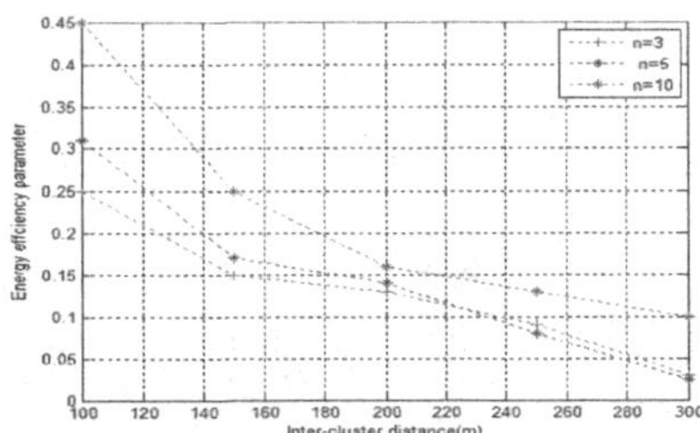

Figure 10(b): EC ratio of cooperative communication relative to direct communication

Figure 10: Energy characteristics vs. inter-cluster distance.

6. Conclusion

On this paper, we examine the problems of shared communication on an included wireless community, wherein the variety of interactive nodes depends on the best bundle reception in the series. We are creating the problem of developing multiple parameters to reduce overall power consumption. With numerical outcomes, we display that total power consumption can be significantly reduced through adjusting the intra-cluster transmission ability and inter-cluster transmission. It also shows that having additional nodes within a row does not conserve energy due to the additional circuit power used by the transmitting node. Moreover, beneath special necessities in PER, the full range of sensors inside the collection is different.

References

[1] Devulapalli, P.K., P.S. Pokkunuri, S.B. Maganti, and S. Rachagoppula, "Energy aware cooperative image transmission for multi-radio multi-hop wireless sensor networks," *Int. J. Intell. Eng. Syst.*, vol. 15, no. 4, pp. 43–52, 2022 (ISSN: 2185-3118).

[2] Kiran, U. and K. Kumar, *An Hybrid Heuristic Optimal Relay Selection Strategy for Energy Efficient Multi Hop Cooperative Cellular Communication.* Ad Hoc Networks, 2023.

[3] Gungor, V. and G. Hancke, "Industrial wireless sensor networks: challenges, design principles, and technical approaches," *IEEE Trans. Ind.*, vol. 56, pp. 4258–4265, 2009.

[4] Vaseghi, B., M.A. Pourmina, and S. Mobayen, "Secure communication in wireless sensor networks based on chaos synchronization using adaptive sliding mode control," *Nonlinear Dyn.*, vol. 89, pp. 1689–1704, 2017.

[5] Valle, O.T., C. Montez, G. de Araujo, F. Vasques, R. Moraes, "NetCoDer: a retransmission mechanism for WSNs based on cooperative relays and network coding," *Sensors*, vol. 16, p. 799, 2016.

[6] Wang, C.L. and S.J. Syue, "An efficient relay selection protocol for cooperative wireless sensor networks," *Proceedings of the IEEE Wireless Communications and Networking Conference*, Budapest, Hungary; pp. 1–5, 2009.

[7] Khan, R.A.M. and H. Karl, "MAC protocols for cooperative diversity in wireless LANs and wireless sensor networks," *IEEE Commun. Surv. Tutor.*, vol. 16, pp. 46–63, 2014.

[8] Liang, X., I. Balasingham, and V.C.M. Leung, "Cooperative communications with relay selection for QoS provisioning in wireless sensor networks," *Proceedings of the GLOBECOM 2009—2009 IEEE Global Telecommunications Conference*, Honolulu, HI, USA; pp. 1–8, 2009.

[9] Kiran, U. and K. Kumar, "Energy-efficient cooperative communications system," *2022 Second International Conference on Advances in Electrical, Computing, Communication and Sustainable Technologies (ICAECT)*, pp. 1–7, 2022.

[10] Cheikh, M.E., O. Simpson, and Y. Sun, "Energy efficient relay selection method for clusteredwireless sensor network," *Proceedings of the 23th EuropeanWireless Conference on EuropeanWireless 2017*, Dresden, Germany, vol. 2017, pp. 92–97, 2017.

[11] Kiran, U. and K. Kumar, "Throughput and outage probability - aware intelligent swarm - based multi-hop selection in vechicular network," *Communication Cybernetics and Systems*, 2022.

[12] Alkhayyat, A., O. Gazi, and S. B. Sadkhan, "The role of delay and connectivity in throughput reduction of cooperative decentralized wireless networks," *Math. Probl. Eng.*, vol. 2015, p. 294016, 2015.

[13] Marchenko, N., T. Andre, W. Masood, and C. Bettstetter, "An experimental study of selective cooperative relaying in industrial wireless sensor networks," *IEEE Trans. Ind. Inf.*, vol. 10, pp. 1806–1816, 2014.

[14] Baccour, N., A. Koubâa, H. Youssef, M.B. Jamâa, D. do Rosário, M. Alves, and L. B. Becker, "F-LQE: a fuzzy link quality estimator for wireless sensor networks." *Proceedings of the 8th European Conference on Wireless Sensor Networks*, Coimbra, Portugal, 2010; Marrón, P.J. and K. Whitehouse, Eds.; Springer: Berlin, Germany, pp. 240–255, 2010.

[15] Alia, O. and A. Al-Ajouri, "Maximizing wireless sensor network coverage with minimum cost using harmony search algorithm," *IEEE Sens. J.*, vol. 17, no. 3, pp. 882–896, 2016.

[16] Etezadi, F., K. Zarifi, A. Ghrayeb, and S. Affes, "Decentralized relay selection schemes in uniformly distributed wireless sensor networks," *IEEE Trans. Wirel. Commun.*, vol. 11, pp. 938–951, 2012. Sensors 2018.

64. From Pixels to Prognosis: Machine Learning for Infection Segmentation and Disease Prediction in Tulsi Leaf

Manjot Kaur[1], Someet Singh[1], and Anita Gehlot[2]

[1]*School of Electrical and Electronics Engineering, Lovely Professional University, Phagwara, India*
[2]*Uttaranchal Institute of Technology, Uttaranchal University, Dehradun, India*

Abstract: Infections in the tulsi plant account for one-fourth of India's agricultural crop production loss on average. A significant component of the economy is dependent on agricultural output. Leaf diseases are every country's top agricultural issue, as worldwide food consumption is rapidly increasing due to population increase. Prenatal disease detection remains difficult due to limitations in lab infrastructure and capability. The initial and detailed diagnosis of leaf infections is critical to prevent their spread. Image processing techniques that use mathematical equations and transformations can be used to diagnose diseases. When viewed with human eyes, we can extract specific information from an image using these colours, but modern computers store images in a mathematical framework. In this study, we evaluate the possibility of computer vision approaches for scalable and early detection of plant-borne illnesses in tulsi leaf using picture segmentation techniques. The low availability of suitable large-scale datasets remains a significant restriction for enabling vision-based plant disease identification. As a result, we present TulsiDoc, a dataset for detecting visual plant illnesses in the tulsi plant. The collection, which included data augmentation in annotating the PlantVillage dataset, contains over 2500 images and as many as three classes of infections: fungal, bacterial and pests. To demonstrate the utility of the dataset, we create two models for the task and employed segmentation techniques using thresholding and intensity segmentation and compared the outcome of the methods. The connection between plant health and human health consumption is complicated and multifaceted. It is largely concerned with the quality and safety of the food we eat, which is directly affected by the health and well-being of the plants employed in agriculture. In order to do accurate analysis, feature extraction and personalised treatment, segmentation is a crucial stage in disease prediction. The paper aids in early diagnosis, lessens false positives and improves our comprehension of how diseases develop, all of which improve prediction outcomes and advance plant science.

Keywords: Classification, diseases, image segmentation, feature extraction.

1. Introduction

Tulsi, commonly known as Holy Basil (*Ocimum sanctum* or *Ocimum tenuiflorum*), is a popular medicinal herb in India for its multiple health benefits. While tulsi plants are generally resilient and resistant to a wide range of diseases and pests, they are susceptible to some early infections or problems. The powdery mildew, fungal disease shows as a white, powdery substance on the tulsi plant's leaves, stems and flowers. It has the potential to weaken the plant and slow its growth. Another infection type, downy mildew develops on the leaves as yellow or brown patches with a fuzzy or mouldy texture on the undersides. It can also have an impact on plant health. Aphids are tiny sap-sucking insects that can infest tulsi plants. They have the ability to cause leaves to curl, yellow and distort. Whiteflies are little insects that feed on the underside of tulsi leaves. They can cause the leaves to yellow and wilt. Various fungi-caused leaf spot illnesses can induce dark patches on tulsi leaves, limiting their health and photosynthetic ability. An image is a blend of RGB colours for humans with normal vision, but for working of digital equipment such as processors and cameras, an image is a real number encoded in a matrix. Because photographs include digital and numerical qualities, we can conduct various scientific transformations and retrieve a certain number of unique features by adjusting their parameters [1].

Images are comprehended of as numbers inside the matrix, and the magnitude of these numbers controls the colour of that pixel in the real world. A few strategies should be used to emphasise the particular numbers in the matrix in order to get the relevant information. Image segmentation is the method of dividing a digital image into various subcategories of pixels known as image objects. This process will reduce the density of the image, seeking to make image investigation relatively easy.

Machine learning can be a useful technique for diagnosing problems in agricultural plants, enhancing crop health, and ultimately increasing crop yields. Here is an overview of how machine learning can be used in this field:

i. Dataset collection: The first stage in developing a disease identification system is to amass a big collection of photographs or other relevant data containing instances of both healthy and diseased plants. These photos should depict a wide range of plant and disease kinds.
ii. Dataset pre-processing: Raw data frequently requires pre-processing before it can be used for machine learning. This could include shrinking photographs, reducing noise and enhancing the dataset to boost its diversity.
iii. Image feature extraction: Machine learning algorithms normally require organised input data. In image-based disease identification, feature

extraction techniques such as convolutional neural networks (CNNs) are frequently used to extract significant information from images.

iv. Prediction model choice: Different machine learning methods can be used like support vector machines, random classifiers, k-nearest neighbour but deep learning models, notably convolutional neural networks, have demonstrated great effectiveness in image-based disease identification tasks [2].

v. Model training: Use the pre-processed dataset to train the chosen model. Based on the retrieved properties, the model will learn to distinguish between healthy and unhealthy plants.

vi. Model validation and dataset testing: To evaluate the model's performance, dataset is divided into training, validation and testing sets. This allows us to fine-tune hyperparameters and measure the accuracy, and other related numerical parameters such as precision, recall and F1 score of the model.

vii. Model deployment: Once the model has proven to be reliable in testing, it can be deployed in the field. This could take the shape of a mobile app, a web application or being incorporated into agricultural machines to identify disease in real time.

viii. Model monitoring: Agriculture is a dynamic environment, and diseases can emerge. To preserve plant health, it is critical to constantly monitor and update the model with fresh data and insights.

ix. Friendly user interface: If the system is meant for farmers, create a simple interface that allows them to capture and upload photographs of their crops for analysis.

2. Proposed Methodology

Classifying plant leaf diseases is a critical issue in agriculture and plant pathology. A systematic strategy involving many steps can be used to build an effective methodology for leaf disease categorisation. The richness and diversity of the dataset, as well as the selection of the proper deep learning model and careful tuning of hyperparameters, all play a role in the success of your leaf disease classification system. Continuous maintenance and data collection are also essential for long-term effectiveness. The following techniques used as pre-processing in machine learning model is described in detail [3].

2.1. Otsu Thresholding

This algorithm is used to translate grayscale imageries into binary imageries because it primarily depends on a threshold number; if a particular portion of the image is under the threshold value, then that part is taken by binary zero, and the fragments that are above the threshold are shown by binary one [14]. The values of these pixels, which range from 0 to 256, indicate the intensity of each individual pixel. As a result, threshold values are used to highlight or hide individual pixels. After the threshold values have been established, it is possible to modify a pixel's intensity depending on that value, helping to remove some of the input image's elements. Figure 1 shows conversion of loaded image into a NumPy array RGB image and to monochrome conversion and then the sample image is exhibited in HSV format as shown in Figure 2.

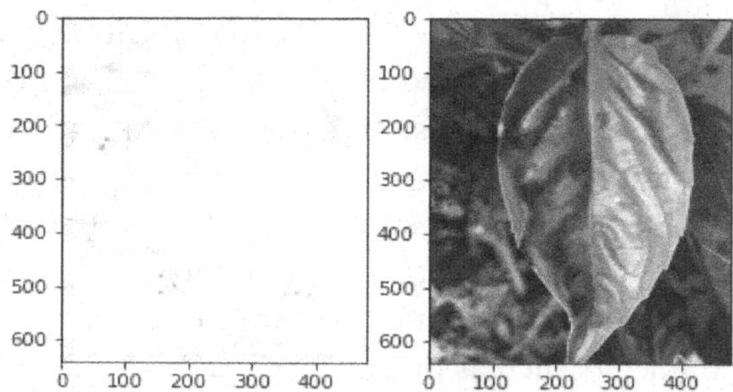

Figure 1: Trimming RGB input data to fit within image show acceptable range ([0..1] for floats or [0..255] for integers).

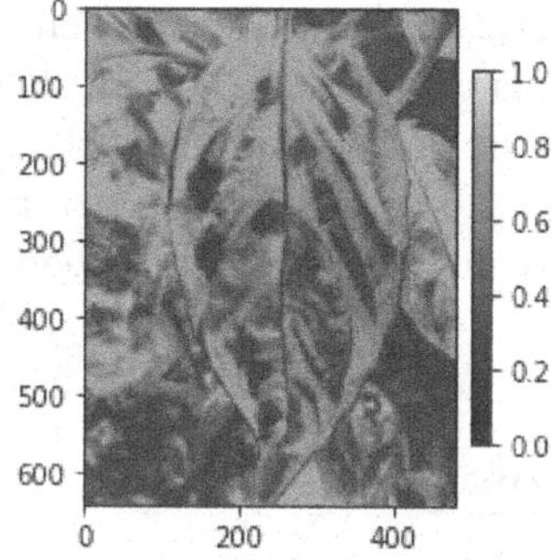

Figure 2: HSV image format.

The core concept of Otsu's thresholding is to determine the threshold value that minimises the intra-class variation of the two classes (foreground and background) while maximising the inter-class variance as depicted in Figure 3. To put it another way, it seeks a threshold that optimally separates the pixels belonging to the object of interest (foreground) from the rest of the image (background). Otsu's approach is especially effective when the image's object and background have unique intensity distributions, and it can automatically calculate an ideal threshold without the need for manual parameter tuning. It is widely employed in image processing field such as image segmentation, object detection and document image analysis. It uses the acquired threshold to compute binarized values. The process is followed by calculating the number of Sauvola's local pixel which are not binarized. A gaussian filter is applied for noise removal. The local pixels are computed with Ni black. The circle's geographical centre is based on x1, x2 values choosing (220,110) as the desired value [4]. The active contour region is determined from the provided image as shown in Figure 4.

Figure 3: The Otsu's thresholding algorithm workflow.

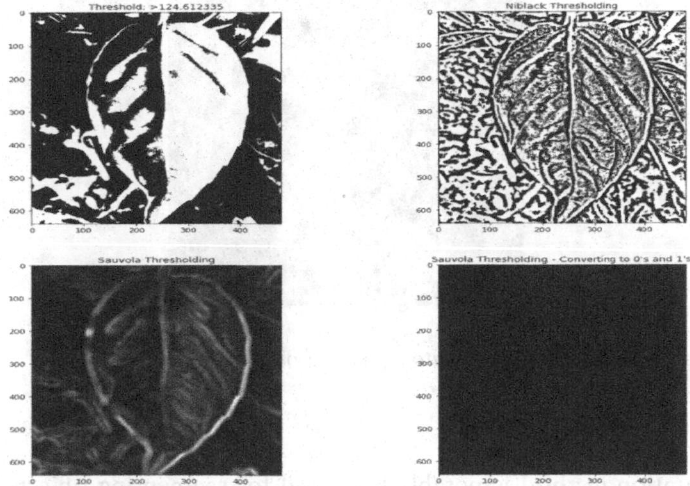

Figure 4: The Otsu's thresholding output images.

The detailed steps followed are as follow:

i. Create a histogram of the grayscale image's pixel intensities. This histogram depicts the pixel value distribution in the image.
ii. Normalize the histogram so that it sums to 1. This turns the histogram into a probability distribution function (PDF).
iii. For each possible threshold value (usually ranging from 0 to 255 for 8-bit grayscale images), Otsu's method calculates the following:

   a) Weighted Sum of Squares of Variance (within-class variance): This is a measure of the spread of pixel values within each class (foreground and background). It is computed as the weighted sum of the variances of the dual classes, where the weightiness are the probabilities of the two classes.
   b) Inter-Class Variance: This is a measure of how far apart the two classes are. It is calculated as the weighted sum of squared differences between the means of the two classes, where the weights are their probabilities.

The ideal threshold for picture segmentation is the value that maximises the inter-class variance (or, equivalently, minimises the within-class variation).

The image is then thresholder with the chosen threshold value, resulting in a binary image with pixels overhead the threshold allocated to the foreground class and pixels underneath the threshold given to the background class. Figure 5 shows the Otsu's thresholding contour marked output image.

Figure 5: *The Otsu's thresholding contour marked output image.*

2.2. Chan-Vese Segmentation

This segmentation method is notably beneficial for segmenting objects in images when standard techniques such as thresholding or edge-based methods may not function well, such as when there is noise, intensity changes or the object boundaries are not well-defined. The Chan-Vese segmentation approach builds on the concept of active contours, popularly known as snakes, but with considerable enhancements. In order to differentiate between objects without specifically stated borders, the Chan-Vese segmentation approach was established as shown in Figure 6. This algorithm is constructed on level sets that are iteratively established to minimise an energy that is well-defined by weighted values matching to the sum of differences in intensity from the average value external the segmented region, the sum of variances from the average value inside the segmented region and a term that depends on the dimension of the segmented region's edge. Figure 7 shows a Chan-Vese segmentation algorithm output images.

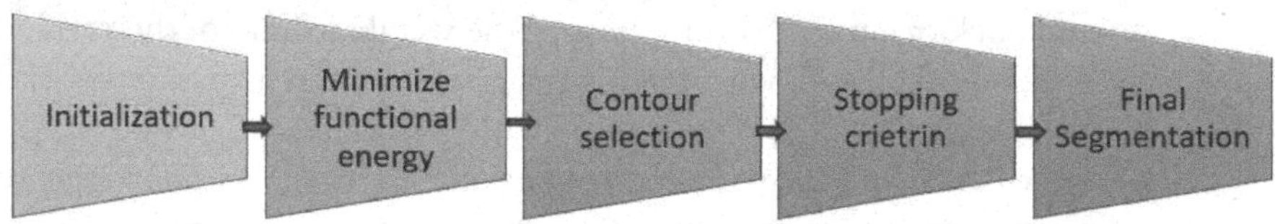

Figure 6: *The Chan-Vese segmentation algorithm workflow.*

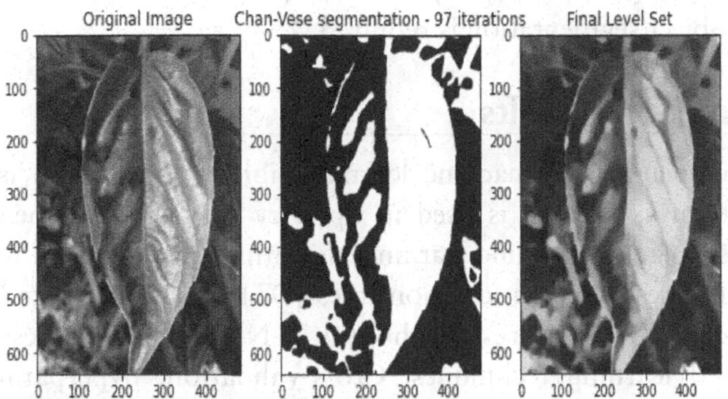

Figure 7: The Chan-Vese segmentation algorithm output images.

The process of segmentation begins with a contour or curve that roughly surrounds the object to be segmented. Depending on the application, this contour could be a circle, rectangle or any other shape. The purpose of Chan-Vese segmentation is to determine the best contour that minimises an energy functional. This energy functional is made up of two major terms:

i. The similarity between the intensity levels inside and outside the contour is measured by this term. It encourages pixels within the contour to have similar intensity values while encouraging pixels outside the contour to have varied intensity values.
ii. Contour-based term: This phrase penalises contour length, encouraging it to be smooth and not unduly complicated.

The algorithm changes the contour iteratively in order to minimise the energy functional. It accomplishes this by altering the position of the contour based on the gradient of the energy functional. The energy terms steer the contour's evolution towards the object's boundary. It updates the contour until a stopping measure is reached. This could be a maximum count of reiterations, an energy threshold or when the contour no longer changes appreciably. When it converges, the final contour reflects the segmented object's boundary. The pixels within this contour are regarded to be part of the object, whereas those beyond the contour are considered to be in the background [5].

There are various advantages of using Chan-Vese segmentation. It is capable of dealing with things with complicated shapes and uneven borders. When compared to typical active contour models, it is less sensitive to initial contour placement. It can handle images with inhomogeneous intensity (changing illumination) fairly well.

However, it may have limitations when there are several objects with similar intensities present, or when there are large textural differences inside the item to be segmented. In practise, numerical optimisation techniques such as level set approaches are frequently used to accomplish Chan-Vese segmentation. It has been used in medical image analysis, object tracking and a variety of other domains where precise object segmentation is required.

3. Experimental Results

A well-known open-source machine learning library for Python is scikit-learn, sometimes known as sklearn is used in open cv to carry out the experimental results. A wide range of machine learning algorithms are included in Scikit-learn, including but not restricted to: decision trees (DT), random forests (RF), support vector machines (SVM), k-nearest neighbours (k-NN), logistic regression (LR) and other supervised learning techniques. Cross-validation, hyperparameter tuning and metrics for measuring model performance are tools for model evaluation and selection. The accuracy of the prediction model is determined by the segmentation quality. If the segmentation approach generates accurate binary masks that properly outline the objects of interest, it can lead to improved feature extraction and, as a result, model correctness. If the segmentation is incorrect, mistakes or noise may be introduced into the features used by the prediction model, thus lowering its accuracy. The decision between Otsu's thresholding and Chan-Vese segmentation should be based on the features of the data as well as the unique segmentation needs of the task. If the intensity of the objects of interest is well separated, Otsu's thresholding may suffice and produce reliable findings. Overall, machine learning for plant disease diagnosis has the potential to considerably enhance agriculture by enabling early disease detection and treatment, decreasing crop losses and promoting healthy plant growth. To be effective in real-world agricultural contexts, however, careful planning, data collecting and model building are required. Depending on the nature of the data and the unique requirements of the application, it can be used in variety of ways to categorise plant illnesses using machine learning algorithms [7]. A comparison accuracy results of Otsu's thresholding and Chan-Vese segmentation are provided in Table 1.

Table 1: Comparison accuracy results of Otsu's thresholding and Chan-Vese segmentation.

Classifier	Otsu Thresholding	Chan-Vese
SVM	97.76%	95.76%
RF	99.65%	98.65%
k-NN	99.54%	98.47%
LR	97.34%	96%

Plant diseases vary greatly in their nature and characteristics. Some diseases cause discrete lesions or colour changes on the leaves, making them amenable to simple thresholding procedures. Others may exhibit more subtle symptoms or affect the entire plant, necessitating further investigation. Plant diseases vary greatly in their nature and characteristics. Some diseases cause discrete lesions or colour changes on the leaves, making them amenable to simple thresholding procedures.

Others may exhibit more subtle symptoms or influence the entire plant, necessitating the use of more sophisticated segmentation methods such as Chan-Vese or region-growing algorithms. Consider whether labelled data is available for training and evaluating the classification model. For training, some segmentation methods may require manually labelled masks, which can be time-consuming and expensive to obtain. Also consider the available computational resources for picture processing. Complex segmentation methods, such as Chan-Vese, may be computationally demanding and thus unsuitable for real-time or resource-constrained applications [8]. A comparison of accuracy results of different infection classification techniques are given in table 2

Table 2: Comparison accuracy results of different infection classification techniques.

References	Methodology	Pre-processing	Accuracy
Proposed	RF	Otsu thresholding	99.65%
[4]	SVM	Otsu thresholding	96%
[9]	Efficient Densenet	Not applicable	97.2%
[10]	SVM	Region based	97%
[11]	LR	Otsu thresholding	96%

The precision of the illness classification model is determined by the precision of the segmentation. To avoid misclassification, select a segmentation method that gives accurate delineation of diseased areas. The segmentation algorithms that are more flexible and can handle items with uneven boundaries and varied sizes if the diseases have a wide range of forms and sizes should be considered. In practise, depending on the specific disease classification goal and the properties of the dataset, a variety of segmentation approaches may be applied [9–10]. For example, we may apply simple thresholding for images with obvious disease symptoms and more complex approaches like Chan-Vese for more difficult images.

4. Conclusion and Future Scope

Tulsi plant health has a direct impact on the nutritional worth of the form of tulsi we eat. Plants produced in nutrient-rich soil that is free of disease and pests are more likely to be high in vital vitamins, minerals and phytonutrients. Consuming such plant-based foods benefits human health by providing a variety of critical nutrients. This paper introduces a unique and meticulously curated dataset of tulsi leaf images, encompassing various stages of infection and health. This dataset is made publicly available, contributing to research in plant disease analysis [12]. Infected patches on tulsi leaves may be precisely segmented from images using the paper's novel machine learning approach. In order to improve disease prediction accuracy, the research investigates the integration of various data modalities, including RGB pictures and spectral data. This multimodal technique makes it possible to analyse plant health in greater detail.

Furthermore, it is critical to test how successfully the prediction model generalises to new data after pre-processing with the chosen segmentation approach using relevant measures such as accuracy, F1-score, precision, recall or area under the ROC curve (AUC). Finally, the segmentation method selected should be based on a thorough comprehension of the data as well as the unique aims of the prediction endeavour. For the best prediction model accuracy, careful pre-processing and evaluation are required. To summarise, tulsi plant health has a direct impact on the quality, safety and nutritional value of the form of tulsi in food we eat. Plant health must be promoted through sustainable and ethical farming practises to protect human health and ensure a reliable and healthy food supply. Consumers, farmers and policymakers all play important roles in managing this complicated relationship for the sake of plant and human health.

References

[1] Sarker, I. H., "Machine learning: algorithms, real-world applications and research directions," *SN Comput. Sci.*, vol. 2, p. 160, 2021, https://doi.org/10.1007/s42979-021-00592-x.

[2] Li, L., S. Zhang and B. Wang, "Plant disease detection and classification by deep learning—a review," *IEEE Access*, vol. 9, pp. 56683–56698, 2021, doi: 10.1109/ACCESS.2021.3069646.

[3] Ramesh, S. *et al.*, "Plant disease detection using machine learning," *2018 International Conference on Design Innovations for 3Cs Compute Communicate Control (ICDI3C)*, Bangalore, India, pp. 41–45, 2018, doi: 10.1109/ICDI3C.2018.00017.

[4] Chakraborty, S., S. Paul, and M. Rahat-uz-Zaman, "Prediction of apple leaf diseases using multiclass support vector machine," *2021 2nd International Conference on Robotics, Electrical and Signal Processing Techniques (ICREST)*, IEEE, pp. 147–151, 2021.

[5] Patil, B.M. and V. Burkpalli, "Segmentation of cotton leaf images using a modified Chan Vese method," *Multimedia Tools Appl.*, vol. 81, no. 11, pp. 15419–15437, 2022.

[6] Kaur, P., S. Harnal, V. Gautam, M. P. Singh, and S. P. Singh, "Performance analysis of segmentation models to detect leaf diseases in tomato plant," *Multimedia Tools Appl.*, pp.1–25, 2023.

[7] Alom, M., M.Y. Ali, M.T. Islam, A.H. Uddin, and W. Rahman, "Species classification of brassica napus based on flowers, leaves, and packets using deep neural networks," *J. Agric. Food Res.*, vol. 14, p. 100658, 2023.

[8] Meenakshi, T., 2023. "Automatic detection of diseases in leaves of medicinal plants using modified logistic regression algorithm," *Wireless Pers. Commun.*, vol. 131, no. 4, pp. 2573–2597, 2023.

[9] Mahum, R., H. Munir, Z.U.N. Mughal, M. Awais, F. Sher Khan, M. Saqlain, S. Mahamad, and I. Tlili, "A novel framework for potato leaf disease

detection using an efficient deep learning model," *Hum. Ecol. Risk Assess.: Int. J.*, vol. 29, no. 2, pp. 303–326, 2023.

[10] Singh, J. and H. Kaur, "Plant disease detection based on region-based segmentation and KNN classifier," *Proceedings of the International Conference on ISMAC in Computational Vision and Bio-Engineering 2018 (ISMAC-CVB)*, Springer International Publishing, pp. 1667–1675, 2019.

[11] Islam, M.S., S. Sultana, F. A. Farid, M. N. Islam, M. Rashid, B. S. Bari, N. Hashim, and M. N. Husen, "Multimodal hybrid deep learning approach to detect tomato leaf disease using attention based dilated convolution feature extractor with logistic regression classification," *Sensors*, vol. 22, no. 16, p. 6079, 2022.

[12] Kaur, M., *Tulsi leaf train and test dataset* [Data set]. Kaggle, 2023). https://doi.org/10.34740/KAGGLE/DSV/6493843.

65. Deep Learning for Disease Detection in Paddy Plants using Leaf Images

Sudheer Chakravarthi P and Bhaveshkumar Choithram Dharmani

School of Electronics and Electrical Engineering, Lovely Professional University, Punjab, India

Abstract: Most people throughout the world use rice as a food staple, making it the second-largest agricultural crop. Due to the failure to correctly diagnose illnesses, many of the nations that produce rice face difficulties with yield quantification and quality. In this context, there is a significant opportunity for researchers to create a unique method for classifying and detecting plant diseases, which could be useful to farmers for increasing crop yield. There are numerous conventional methods for plan disease detection using leaf images. However, they are less accurate and have a higher risk of false negatives. So, the current article compares the performance of two popular deep learning architectures VGG19 and ResNet50 for disease detection in paddy crop.

Keywords: Rice, plant diseases, augmentation, transfer learning, deep learning.

1. Introduction

For almost 58% of Indian population agricultural income is the primary source. Rice is one of the major crops in India with farming in 26.66 million hectares. Farmers lose 37% of their paddy leaves on average every year due to various diseases. In order to avert any potential catastrophe brought on by diseases, farmers must assess the state of their paddy well in advance before it is too late. Therefore, managing rice production to achieve increased productivity and better profitability requires accurate diagnosis and prompt treatment of paddy illness.

Several diseases can damage the paddy plant and those are categorised like bacterial, viral and fungal infections. Among all the diseases, some of them occur on rice plants leaf and the symptoms are illustrated below [1].Brown spot disease creates dark brown lesions on leaves in a shape of round to oval, which leads to a 50% reduction in the yield. In case of leaf blast disease, the dark spot to oval spots as well as small brown-reddish margins with white or gray centers are formed on the leaf. Bacterial leaf blight shows the stripes in yellow color on blades of leaf are started at tips of leaf then extending in broader and wider dimensions with a heavy impact. Figure 1 a,b, c & d shows Paddy leaf diseases for brown spot, leaf blast, bacterial leaf blight, Tungro respectively.

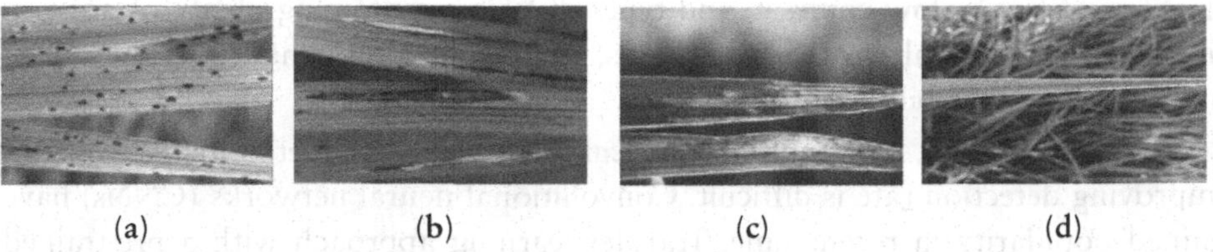

Figure 1: Paddy leaf diseases: (a) brown spot, (b) leaf blast, (c) bacterial leaf blight, (d) Tungro.

2. The Problem and State-of-the-Art Solution

Sustainable agriculture, as well as the prevention of wastage of resources and excessive financials, greatly depends on reducing the crop yield, which in turn decided by the timely diagnosis of the plant diseases and accurate treatment for the same.

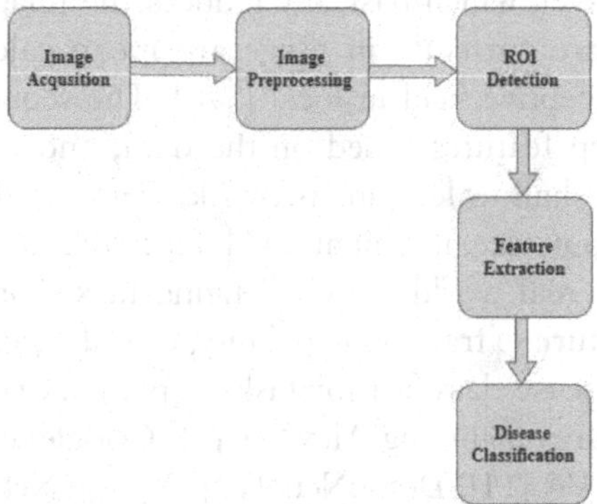

Figure 2: A generic disease classification system.

The generic disease classification system for the plants based on the leaf images is shown in Figure 2. Image acquisition is the procedure of getting leaf images of healthy and infected one [1]. These are directly captured from the field or in a controlled environment. Further images are processed by the usage of image processing methods like removal of background and noise, resizing of image, segmentation and feature extraction. Finally, the machine learning models will classify the diseases based on the image features [2]. For different techniques working with various dataset might vary at each intermediate stage.

The generic disease classification algorithms are mainly depending on hand-picked feature of the images [3]. These algorithms utilize cautiously fabricated imaging methods, which can significantly reduce the complexity of designing the algorithm in addition to this it increases the cost of application. Also, the real-world scenario will make the disease detection from the plant leaf images more challenging [4]. There are numerous challenges in detecting plant diseases in a truly complex natural environment like the distinction between the background and the area of lesion, low contrast, and types of lesion containing plenty of noise in image. Under natural weather conditions, while collecting images of plants there are numerous possibilities of disruptions.

At this moment, conventional classical methods are rendered ineffective, and improving detection rate is difficult. Convolutional neural networks (CNNs) have gained popularity in recent time. Transfer learning approach with a pre-trained CNN networks has been used successfully in detecting and classifying plant diseases in real-time applications.

CNN is a popular model because of the complex information and large model capacity generated by CNN's structural characteristics, which gives an advantage to CNN in image recognition like tasks. Simultaneously, CNN's successes strengthen the popularity for growing deep learning in all the tasks handled by computer vision. The first part of CNN contains a sequence of convolutional layers. The kernel-based convolution operators extract initially edge features and gradually build upon the texture and shape features. After these layers' feature extraction, the neurons are routed to the pooling layer, which basically reduces the image feature dimensions. Pooling methods that are currently in usage are mean calculation, random and highest values of the receptive field in local [5–6]. The sequence of convolutional layers thus extracts deep features based on the data, and not data agnostic with hand-crafted features in shallow learning networks. The conflicts in the features like background, shape, layout, size, illumination changes texture and colour in images of plant diseases in the real world are challenging tasks for recognition. Because of CNN's powerful feature extraction capability, classification networks based on CNN are popular for disease classification tasks in plants. Currently, the pre-trained deep learning architectures including AlexNet [7], GoogleLeNet [8], VGGNet [9], ResNet [10], Inception V4 [11], DenseNets [12], MobileNet [13] and SqueezeNet [14] are highly popular and have been used for various classification tasks.

3. Methodology

In this section, we will talk about the proposed model that was used in this study to classify different types of rice leaf diseases based on the data that was collected. The overall workflow of methodology is shown in figure 3.

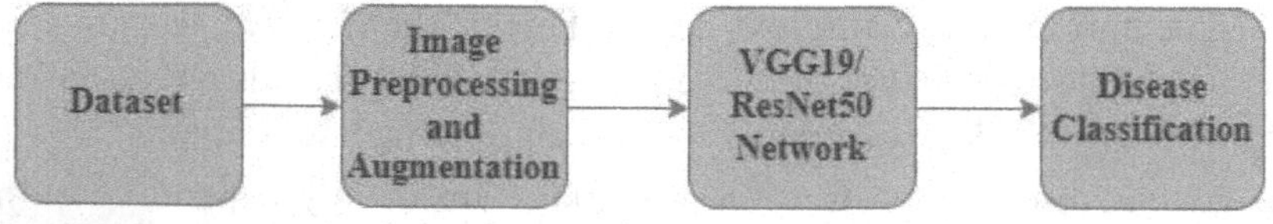

Figure 3: The work-flow.

3.1. Dataset

The dataset of total 420 images was collected from various sources for the four disease classes in in paddy fields, including bacterial leaf blight, brown spot, leaf blast and rice Tungro, as well as healthy class. The sources include Kaggle data sources *https://www.kaggle.com/vbookshelf/rice-leaf-diseases* by Marsh and *https://www.kaggle.com/datasets/iashiqul/paddy-leaf-disease* by Ashiq, as well, UCI Machine Learning Depository *https://archive.ics.uci.edu/ml/datasets/Rice+Leaf+Diseases*. Table 1 denotes the exact number of images collected for each class. The efficient training of neural network is accomplished by huge dataset of perfectly labeled. As the number of images are less in numbers for a task at hand, data augmentation was employed. This will also address the issue of an unbalanced dataset. The data augmentation task should be performed by image data generator to create the new samples and now the new dataset will consist of 2525 samples. Now the labelled dataset can be divided for training, testing and validation in the ratio of 80:10:10. So the total images for training the network 2020, testing images of 253 and validation images of 252. Figure 4 shows sample images generated by augmentation.

Table 1: The number of images used in the experimental setup.

Class Name	Original Images	Augmented Images
Bacterial Leaf Blight	100	400
Brown Spot	100	425
Tungro	80	420
Leaf Blast	40	460
Healthy	100	400

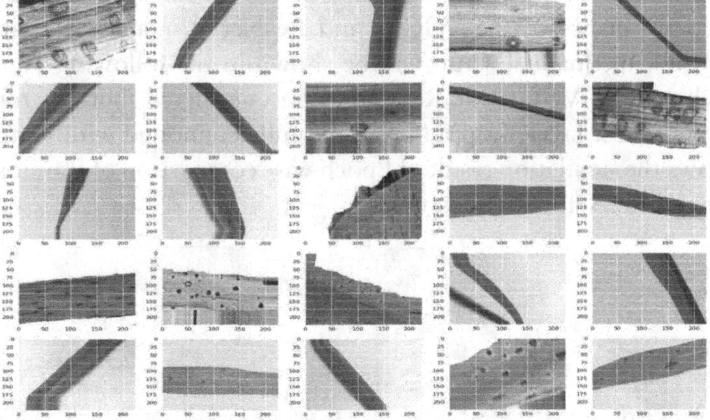

Figure 4: *Sample images generated by augmentation.*

3.2. Transfer Learning

The term 'transfer learning' refers to a type of machine learning in which the information learned about one problem is applied to another (Weiss *et al.*, 2016). Due to the vanishing gradient problem in back-propagation, the initial layers in deep CNN are difficult to get trained. Also, they learn usually too generalised features. As we go towards the higher layer, they learn more specific problem dependent features and can be easily trained. So, transfer learning concept is based on the idea of keeping the lower layers as it is and fine tuning only the upper layers as per the new problem dataset. The final layers of the trained network can be eliminated during transfer learning and replaced with fresh layers to be trained for the target task. Comparing training a model from scratch to the transfer learning strategy, employing the network's prior experience with larger dataset for an older task, in a new task possibly with a smaller dataset has many advantages in terms of saving time and computation for training and obtaining better accuracy [15].

VGG19: VGG16 was the first successful pre-trained network trained on 'imagenet' database. VGG-19 is the upgraded version of VGG16 with 19 deep layers including 16 convolution layers and 3 fully connected layer, 5 Max-Pool layers and 1 SoftMax layer [11]. The input image size is 224-by-224.

ResNet-50: ResNet-50 is a CNN with 50 deep layers and an input image size of 224-by-224 [12]. The novelty of the model lies in providing skip connections or short cuts that allows lower layer features to be directly connected to the higher layers.

4. Simulation Results and Analysis

As said before, the database was collected from multiple sources and combined together. Using data augmentation techniques in Keras, almost fourfold data augmentation was achieved. The original training images with the augmented ones were used to create a new training dataset, whereas the same test dataset was used to test the performance of the VGG19 and ResNet50 models. The architecture utilised for the experimental setup will be shown in the following Figure 5. The original architectures VGG19 or ResNet50 are considered, but the top 3 layers are modified as dense layer, dropout layer and fully connected with SoftMax layer. Figure 6 shows the simulation result of Epoch wise comparison of training accuracy for VGG19 and ResNet50 architecture.

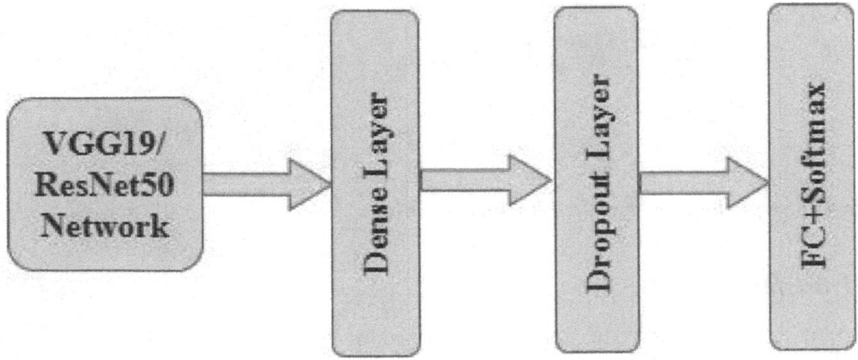

Figure 5: Experimental setup architecture of VGG19 and ResNet50.

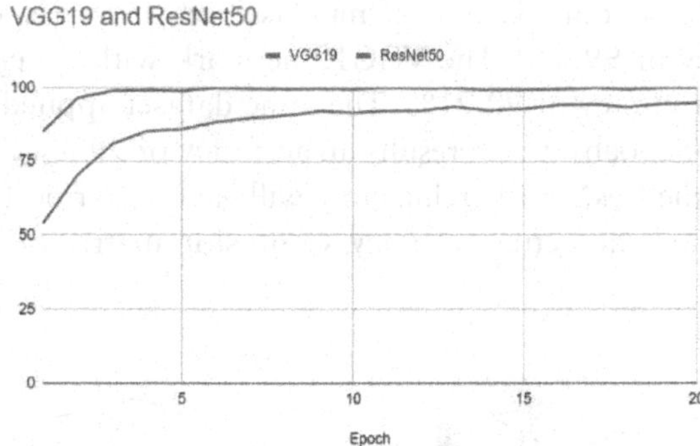

Figure 6: *Epoch wise comparison of training accuracy for VGG19 and ResNet50 architecture.*

During training phase for both the networks, categorical cross-entropy function was used as the loss function, Adamax was used as the gradient algorithm with 0.001 as the learning rate and accuracy as the evaluation metric. From the Tables 2 and 3, it is evident that the ResNet50 model gave better performance over the VGG19 in the aspect of all the classification parameters like precision, recall and F1-score.

Table 2: Classification report of VGG19.

Class Name	Support	VGG19		
		Precision	Recall	f1-score
Bacterial Leaf Blight	44	0.97	0.89	0.93
Brown Spot	48	0.85	0.71	0.77
Tungro	50	0.79	0.98	0.87
Leaf Blast	50	0.94	1	1
Healthy	61	1	0.95	0.97

Table 3: Classification report of ResNet50.

Class Name	Support	ResNet50		
		Precision	Recall	f1-score
Bacterial Leaf Blight	44	0.98	1	0.99
Brown Spot	48	1	0.98	0.99
Tungro	50	1	1	1
Leaf Blast	50	1	1	1
Healthy	61	1	1	1

The confusion matrix shows that the ResNet50 model performed well against all the classes. There is only 1.02% of misclassified (brown spot) and obtained the overall accuracy of 99.6%. The VGG19 network with 20 epochs shows that the model gets an accuracy of 90.91%. The same dataset applied to the ResNet50 architecture with 20 epochs which results an accuracy of 99.6%. The experimental results shown that the ResNet50 architecture will gave better performance over the VGG19, and it obtain the better accuracy. Confusion matrix of VGG19 is shown in figure 7.

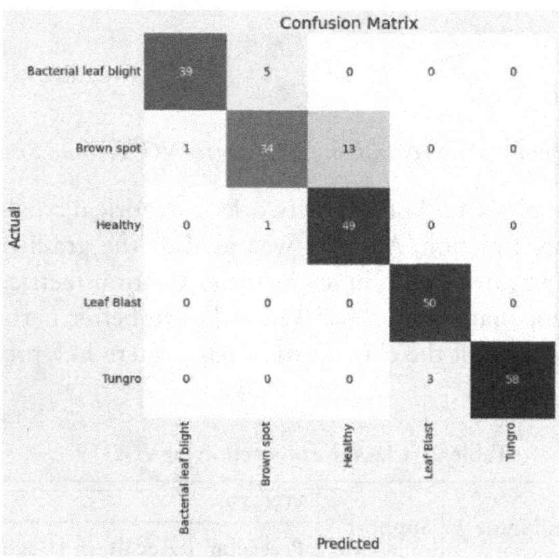

Figure 7: Confusion matrix of VGG19.

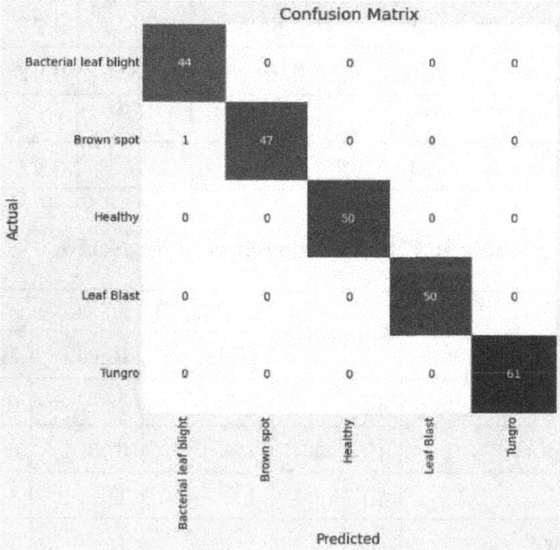

Figure 8: Confusion matrix of RESNet50.

5. Conclusion

In this study, we have compared the two deep learning architectures VGG19 and ResNet50 to classify the paddy leaf images of 5 classes. The ResNet50 architecture gave the 99.6% of classification accuracy over 90.1% for the VGG19. This proves superiority of ResNet50 architecture for classification task at hand.

References

[1] Shah, J. P., H. B. Prajapati, and V. K. Dabhi, "A survey on detection and classification of rice plant diseases," *2016 IEEE International Conference on Current Trends in Advanced Computing (ICCTAC)*, IEEE, pp. 1-8.

[2] Yao, Q., Z. Guan, Y. Zhou, J. Tang, Y. Hu, and B. Yang, "Application of support vector machine for detecting rice diseases using shape and color texture features," *2009 International Conference on Engineering Computation*, IEEE, pp. 79–83, 2009.

[3] Tsaftaris, S. A., M. Minervini, and H. Scharr, "Machine learning for plant phenotyping needs image processing," *Trends Plant Sci.*, vol. 21, no. 12, pp. 989–991, 2016.

[4] Fuentes, A., S. Yoon, and D. S. Park, "Deep learning-based techniques for plant diseases recognition in real-field scenarios," *Proceedings of the International Conference on Advanced Concepts for Intelligent Vision Systems*, Springer, Cham, pp. 3–14, 2000.

[5] Liu, J., and X. Wang, "Plant diseases and pests detection based on deep learning: a review," *Plant Methods*, vol. 17, no. 1, pp. 1–18, 2021.

[6] Zeiler, M. D. and R. Fergus, "Stochastic pooling for regularization of deep convolutional neural networks," arXiv preprint arXiv:1301.3557, 2013.

[7] Krizhevsky, A., I. Sutskever, and G. E. Hinton, "Imagenet classification with deep convolutional neural networks," *Adv. Neural Inf. Process. Syst.*, vol. 25, pp. 1097–1105, 2012.

[8] Szegedy, C., W. Liu, Y. Jia, P. Sermanet, S. Reed, D. Anguelov, and A.Rabinovich, "Going deeper with convolutions," *Proceedings of the IEEE Conf. on Computer Vision and Pattern Recognition*, pp. 1–9, 2015.

[9] Simonyan, K. and A. Zisserman, "Very deep convolutional networks for large-scale image recognition," arXiv preprint arXiv:1409.1556, 2014.

[10] Xie, S., R. Girshick, P. Dollár, Z. Tu, and K. He, "Aggregated residual transformations for deep neural networks," *Proceedings of the IEEE Conference on Computer Vision and Pattern Recognition*, pp. 1492–1500, 2017.

[11] Szegedy, C., S. Ioffe, V. Vanhoucke, and A. Alemi, "Inception-v4, inception-resnet and the impact of residual connections on learning," *Proceedings of the AAAI Conference on Artificial Intelligence*, vol. 31, no. 1, 2017.

[12] Huang, G., Z. Liu, L. Van Der Maaten, and K. Q. Weinberger, "Densely connected convolutional networks," *Proceedings of the IEEE Conference on Computer Vision and Pattern Recognition*, pp. 4700–4708, 2017.

[13] Howard, A. G., M. Zhu, B. Chen, D. Kalenichenko, W. Wang, T. Weyand, and H. Adam, "Mobilenets: efficient convolutional neural networks for mobile vision applications," arXiv preprint arXiv:1704.04861, 2017.

[14] Iandola, F. N., S. Han, M. W. Moskewicz, K. Ashraf, W. J. Dally, and K. Keutzer, "SqueezeNet: AlexNet-level accuracy with 50x fewer parameters and< 0.5 MB model size," arXiv preprint arXiv:1602.07360, 2016.

[15] Long, M., Y. Cao, J. Wang, and M. Jordan, "Learning transferable features with deep adaptation networks," *International Conference on Machine Learning*, PMLR, pp. 97–105, 2015.sss

66. Measurement and Analysis of Power Consumption in Smartphones

Pratibha Mahajan and Yashashree Sonawane

Department of Computer Engineering, Vishwakarma University, Pune, India

Abstract: Smartphones are pivotal and versatile devices in our modern world. Their evolution has led to advanced functionalities, comparable to computers or even superior in some aspects. However, this advancement comes at a cost- smartphones significantly drain energy due to powerful processors, vibrant displays and constant connectivity. The need for enhanced features results in shorter battery life, prompting frequent recharging. The energy required for charging amplifies overall consumption and stresses power grids, particularly in regions heavily reliant on fossil fuels. The key focus of this paper revolves around four objectives: 1) factors influencing smartphone battery life and energy use, 2) energy consumption by specific smartphone applications, 3) user behaviour and its impact on smartphone battery usage, and 4) techniques to mitigate the energy footprint of smartphones. The research is categorised based on diverse approaches, analysing and documenting several factual research works.

Keywords: Smartphones power consumption, battery life, usage pattern, user behaviour, battery consumption.

1. Introduction

In recent years, technology has rapidly evolved, shifting from traditional mediums like newspapers and landline phones to contemporary forms such as online streaming and touchscreen smartphones [1]. Smartphones now encompass various functions, from video streaming and audio platforms to communication and health-related applications [2]. However, these diverse uses significantly impact smartphone power consumption. Smartphones rely on batteries, and optimizing their energy efficiency is crucial due to constraints in size and weight, emphasising the importance of efficient energy management.

Reducing smartphones' energy impact is crucial due to their significant carbon emissions during production and use, a key climate change factor [3]. This reduction aids in lessening their environmental harm, fostering sustainability. Smartphones, made from diverse materials, including non-renewable resources, benefit from reduced energy impact by extending resource lifespan and reducing extraction needs. Lowering energy usage in smartphones alleviates electricity bills, enhancing affordability. Moreover, it extends battery life, providing longer usage periods between charges, enhancing convenience and battery longevity [4]. Overall, minimizing the energy impact of smartphones is vital for the environment, resource preservation, cost-effectiveness and user convenience, mainly due to the high energy consumption of essential components like displays, processors and batteries.

As smartphones advance in power and features, their energy usage rises. Furthermore, the rising need for high-speed internet and data storage has driven the use of energy-intensive wireless networks and data centers [5]. Many smartphones now integrate fingerprint and face lock capabilities, consuming a significant portion of their energy, as depicted in Figure 1.

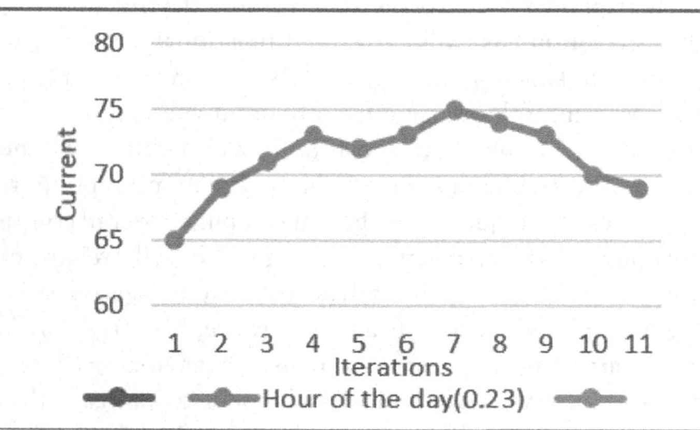

Figure 1: Current consumption for fingerprint and face lock features.

The battery's state greatly influences energy usage. As a battery ages, its ability to hold a charge diminishes, resulting in higher energy consumption. Some apps and settings are more energy-intensive, particularly those with constant syncing or push notifications [6]. Additionally, external elements like temperature, humidity and light levels impact a smartphone's energy use. Being aware of these aspects and adjusting settings and habits can minimize energy consumption and enhance smartphone battery life.

In this paper, a thorough examination of smartphone energy consumption is presented. The objectives of this article are summarized as follows:

- Factors influencing smartphone battery depletion and energy usage have been investigated.
- Energy consumption by selective smartphone applications have been analysed.
- User behaviour and their effect on smartphone battery consumption has been recorded.
- Various methods to diminish the energy impact of smartphones are elucidated.

The research paper addressing smartphone energy impact has followed a systematic structure. The subsequent sections outline existing studies on smartphone energy usage, covering hardware, software and user behaviour in Section 2. Factors influencing smartphone battery drain and energy consumption are detailed in Section 3. An analysis of energy consumption by specific smartphone applications is presented in Section 4. Section 5 examines user behaviours and their influence on smartphone battery usage. Techniques aimed at mitigating smartphone energy impact are expounded in Section 6. Section 7 provides recommendations for reducing battery drain in smartphones. Finally, our research paper concludes in Section 8.

2. Related Work

According to IEA report [7], smartphone makers have integrated various energy-saving functionalities like battery-saving mode, dark mode and adaptive brightness to diminish smartphone energy usage. The NRDC report [8] advocates for diverse actions such as enhancing smartphone and data network energy efficiency, advancing sustainable design and recycling practices and educating users on employing devices in an energy-frugal manner. The IEEE report [9] delves into managing connected-standby power in high-performance mobile devices and reviews previous research in the smartphone domain.

Bangash *et al.* [10] compared the E-factor of 16 versions and 11 methods from three hardware-based energy-consuming apps, identifying and focusing on enhancing excessively energy-consuming methods. Alessio Vecchio, *et al.* [11] aimed to delve into the existing body of literature concerning the environmental impacts of mobile phones and explored potential outcomes of transitioning from the current selling, using and disposing business model to a cloud services-centred product service system. Vanessa *et al.* [12] summarised key methodologies for analysing smartphone battery drain and addressed major challenges in their article. Mahesri and Vardhan [13] conducted a component-wise breakdown of energy consumption in mobile phones, highlighting power consumption differences based on the operating system. Ming Yan [14] investigated smartphones as significant energy consumers, particularly emphasising web browsing and messaging applications as major culprits of energy consumption.

3. Factors Affecting Smartphone Battery Drain

In this section, we delineate the evaluation of a battery's energy efficiency and power consumption, considering various factors impacting battery longevity. Among these factors, the primary contributors to diminished battery life are cyclic life and depth of discharge [15]. Cyclic life pertains to a full charge and discharge cycle of the battery, with the overall number of cycles influencing its lifespan. Depth of discharge signifies the potential for battery damage under intensive usage, whereby excessive load application leads to a reduced battery life cycle. Industrial battery productivity is affected by charged current, internal resistance, state of charge and battery temperature.

Smartphone batteries primarily utilise lithium-based components, which, unfortunately, generate a significant amount of toxic lithium hydroxide in various conditions [16], making them highly explosive and unsafe. The ensuing factors underline the significant challenges encountered by smartphones resulting in battery depletion:

3.1. Decimation of Electrode Seperators

Main solution among all is to increase the size will increase the device size also. This leads to a damage to teardown of electrode separators.

3.2. Lithium Plating

The attempt to rapidly charge the battery by forcing excessive current into it within a short timeframe, known as faster charging, can cause a problem called lithium plating.

3.3. Overcharging

In a bid to enhance energy capacity, companies push the existing technology to its limits, leading to substantial energy consumption.

4. Energy Consumption by Smartphone Applications

Enhancing the battery efficiency of mobile apps contributes to heightened user satisfaction. However, developers often lack essential techniques for accurately predicting an application's energy consumption. Panjapornpon *et al.* [17] introduced an effective approach, leveraging program determination and instruction energy consumption, to predict energy usage more accurately at a foundational level, while being resource efficient. In our research, we utilise this approach to assess energy consumption and predict battery usage for a selection of mobile apps sourced from the Google Play Store. Furthermore, it furnishes valuable insights to developers, aiding in their comprehension of the applications.

The concept of energy consumption analysis involves systematically measuring, examining, and reporting energy usage across various activities. This ongoing process aims to enhance energy efficiency and monitor the impact of energy utilization on both human life and the environment. Understanding your device's energy consumption allows you to grasp the associated energy resources of your service and implement measures to mitigate inefficiencies. Quantifying energy consumption provides insights into the energy demands of different systems within the device.

5. Impact of User Behaviour on Smartphone Battery Drain

In this study, we analysed user battery usage and energy consumption, presenting the findings in a graphical format to facilitate examination.

The majority of users [18] tended to avoid allowing their battery levels to drop below 30% on a regular basis. This behaviour can be attributed to human habits and perceptions. Users commonly associate the appearance of the yellow battery icon at 30% battery level with a signal to charge their smartphones. Additionally, they receive figure number 2 notifications urging them to charge the phone when it reaches 15%. The figure below visually represents the average battery percentage available to users at various times throughout the day and the frequency of these levels. Each bubble in the figure corresponds to a specific day during the study for a particular time. These bubbles are categorised into percentage, time and frequency. The colour of the bubbles indicates the frequency. Notably, the subsequent battery averages consistently remained above the 30% threshold.

Top of Form

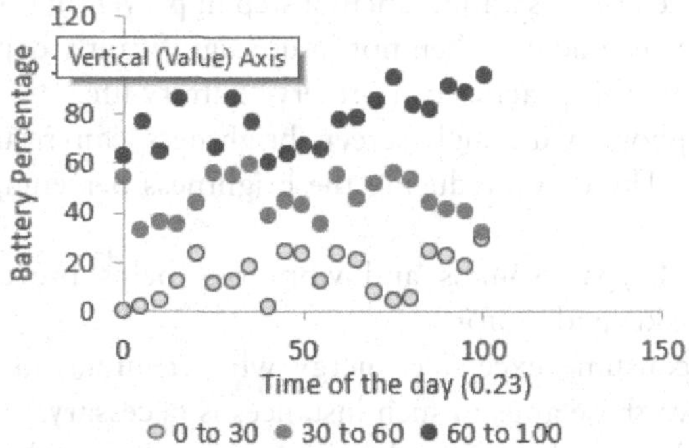

Figure 2: The average charge level of the battery during a day when charging starts.

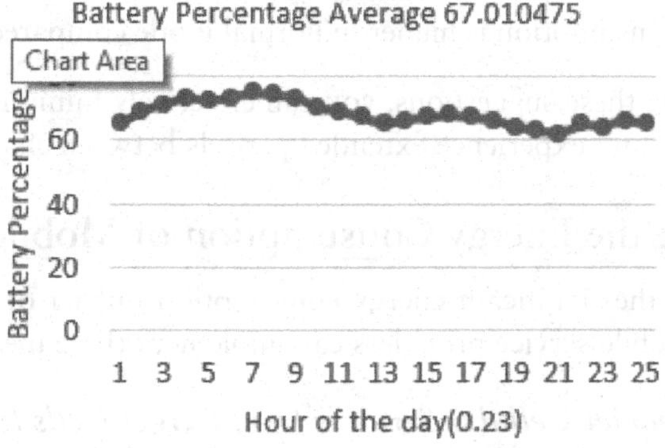

Figure 3: Average battery levels throughout the day for the whole population.

Figure 3 illustrates the average battery level throughout the day. Around midnight, the average battery level stood at 65% and peaked at 74% around five in the morning. The survey findings affirmed our initial expectation that the battery percentage would hit its lowest point by the day's end. On the whole, users consistently maintained an average battery percentage of 67% throughout the day. Although minor hourly fluctuations in battery levels were observed globally, individual users demonstrated diverse charging behaviours. Some chose to engage in short, sporadic charging sessions throughout the day, whereas others opted to use their battery until it reached a lower level before initiating longer charging periods to attain a full charge.

6. Suggestions to Reduce Battery Drain in Smartphones

Mitigating smartphone battery drain can notably extend battery life and enhance the overall user experience. Here are a few recommendations to assist you in achieving this:

- Reducing screen time is a fundamental step in preventing battery drain [19].
- Leaving the screen active when not in use significantly depletes the battery; hence, avoiding this practice can preserve battery life.
- Using smartphone with high screen brightness can result in substantial energy usage. Therefore, reducing the brightness percentage aids in energy conservation.
- Deactivating keypad sounds and vibrations helps prevent battery drain caused by the keypad motor.
- Some apps consume excessive energy while running in the background. Shutting down these apps in such instances is necessary.
- Having multiple accounts on a device can contribute to battery drain.
- Deleting unused accounts or disabling sync can alleviate battery drain related to this issue.
- Enabling dark mode serves as an effective means to conserve battery, given that energy consumption is higher in normal mode compared to dark mode.

By implementing these suggestions, you can effectively minimise battery drain on your smartphone and experience extended periods between charges.

7. Minimizing the Energy Consumption of Mobile Services

This section details the significant energy consumption impact of mobile services on smartphones. Mobile service providers can implement these measures:

7.1. Unloading Heavier Cellular Services from Larger Cells to Smaller Cells

Between 59% and 82% of total energy in various video applications is utilised by the wireless network [20]. Offloading big data services from larger to smaller cells is an effective strategy for curbing energy consumption in 4G network video applications, despite potential signaling overhead with femto-cell offloading due to user mobility discrepancies.

7.2. Multi-access Computing and Caching at the Mobile Network's Edge

This innovative approach focuses on creating an extensive network of distributed caches near consumers within the mobile network's edge. Its goal is to reduce service delays and lighten the load on the mobile backhaul infrastructure [21].

8. Conclusion

In summary, focusing on reducing energy consumption in smartphones is a pivotal area for research and innovation to alleviate the environmental impact linked to their manufacturing, utilisation and disposal. This paper has outlined diverse approaches like implementing dark mode, utilizing battery-saving mode, uninstalling apps and disabling unnecessary features to curtail energy usage. While these methods promise energy optimisation and prolonged battery life, acknowledging their limitations and the necessity for user adaptation is crucial. Moreover, establishing sustainable practices throughout the smartphone lifecycle—embracing responsible sourcing, eco-friendly manufacturing and effective e-waste management—are vital for addressing overarching environmental challenges. Given smartphones' indispensable role in modern life, continued research and collaboration involving industry stakeholders, policymakers and users are imperative to spur innovation and effect significant changes, steering towards an energy-efficient and sustainable smartphone ecosystem.

References

[1] Bircher, W. L. and L. K. John, "Complete system power estimation: a perfect approach based on performance events," *According to the IEEE International Symposium on Performance Analysis of Systems and Software, IEEE Computer Society*, San Jose, CA, USA, pp. 158–168, 2007.

[2] Ferreira, D., A. K. Dey, and V. Kostakos, "Understanding human-smartphone concerns: a study of battery life," *Pervasive Computing: 9th International Conference, Pervasive 2011*, San Francisco, USA, 2011. Proceedings 9. Springer Berlin Heidelberg, 2011.

[3] Majethia, R., *et al.*, "Contextual sensitivity of the ambient temperature sensor in smartphones," *2015 7th International Conference on Communication Systems and Networks (COMSNETS)*, IEEE, 2015.

[4] Freeman, J. and S. Surendran, "The work done in this is monitoring the environment using mobile robot based Wireless sensor network," *2011 6th International Conference on Computer Science & Education (ICCSE)*, pp. 1080–1084, 2011.

[5] Newman, J., *Peak Battery: Why Smartphone Battery Life Still Stinks, and Will for Years*, 2013.

[6] Majethia, R., *et al.*, "Contextual sensitivity of the ambient temperature sensor in smartphones," *2015 7th International Conference on Communication Systems and Networks (COMSNETS)*, IEEE, 2015.

[7] Canton, H., "International energy agency—IEA," *The Europa Directory of International Organizations 2021*, Routledge, pp. 684–686, 2021.

[8] Park, J., "Information and communication technology in shaping urban low carbon development pathways," *Curr. Opin. Environ. Sustainability*, vol. 30, pp. 133–137, 2018.

[9] Yu, Q., *et al.*, "Water-resistant smartphone technologies," *IEEE Access*, vol. 7, pp. 42757–42773, 2019.

[10] Bangash, A. A., *et al.*, "Energy consumption estimation of API-usage in smartphone apps via static analysis," *2023 IEEE/ACM 20th International Conference on Mining Software Repositories (MSR)*, IEEE, 2023.

[11] Caiazza, C., V. Luconi, and A. Vecchio, "Measuring the energy of smartphone communications in the edge-cloud continuum: approaches, challenges, and a case study," *IEEE Internet Comput.*, 2023.

[12] Bach, V., *et al.*, "Measuring a product's resource efficiency–a case study of smartphones," *LCA, Tool for Inno*, p. 133, 2015.

[13] Mahesri, A. and V. Vardhan, "Power consumption breakdown on a modern laptop," *Proceedings of the 2004 Workshop on Power-Aware Computer Systems*, Portland, OR, USA, 2004, Falsafi, B. and T. N. Vijaykumar, Eds., vol. 3471 of Lecture Notes in Computer Science, Springer, pp. 165–180.

[14] Yan, M., *et al.*, "Modeling the total energy consumption of mobile network services and applications," *Energies*, vol. 12, no. 1, p. 184, 2019.

[15] Galkin, B., J. Kibilda, and L. A. DaSilva, "UAVs as mobile infrastructure: addressing battery lifetime," *IEEE Commun. Mag.*, vol. 57, no. 6, pp. 132–137, 2019.

[16] Costa, C. M., *et al.*, "Recycling and environmental issues of lithium-ion batteries: advances, challenges and opportunities," *Energy Storage Mater.*, vol. 37, pp. 433–465, 2021.

[17] Mehranbod, N., M. Soroush, and C. Panjapornpon, "A method of sensor fault detection and identification," *J. Process Control*, vol.15, no. 3:0959-1524, pp. 321–339.

[18] Majethia, R., *et al.*, "Contextual sensitivity of the ambient temperature sensor in smartphones," *2015 7th International Conference on Communication Systems and Networks (COMSNETS)*, IEEE, 2015.

[19] Lee, I.-G., K. Go, and J. H. Lee, "Battery draining attack and defense against power saving wireless LAN devices," *Sensors*, vol. 20, no. 7, p. 2043, 2020.

[20] Xu, D. and A. Zhou, "Understanding operational 5G: a first Measurement study on its coverage, performance and energy consumption," *SIGCOMM: Proceedings of the annual conference of the ACM special interest group on data communication on the applications*, 2020.

[21] Yick, J., B. Mukherjee, and D. Ghosal, "Wireless sensor network survey," *Comput. Netw.*, vol. 52, no. 12: 1389–1286, pp. 2292–2330, 2008.

67. A Graphene-Based Absorber for Sensing Application

Laxmi Narayana Deekonda[1], Sanjay Kumar Sahu[2] and Asit Kumar Panda[3]

[1]*Department of ECE ,Lovely Profession University, Phagwara, Punjab, India*
[2]*Department of ECE, National Institute of Science and Tech., Berhampur, Orissa, India*

Abstract: This paper presents a graphene-based metamaterial absorber. In this design, a complementary split ring resonator is used to achieve sensing application. In addition, the proposed design also going to provide multiple bands. The percentage of absorption is measured about those bands, and it is found to be 100%, 96%, and 70%, respectively. All bands seem to have different applications in the THz range.

Keyword: Metamaterial, absorber, sensing, multiband.

1. Introduction

In present days, we are living in a world of information. It implies we ought to greatly measure data one another. These technologies are useful for human beings by involving several novel properties for practical applications. The term metamaterial (MM) was first introduced by Walser in 2001. The metamaterials were initially made up of artificial material that possesses electrodynamics properties, such as negative refractive index, inverse Doppler effect, super lensing, cloaking, and many more, which are not available in nature. MMs are used to enhance the absorption efficiency of receiving electromagnetic waves hence they can be used in many applications such as capturing solar energy and applying plasmonic sensors, biosensor, and perfect light absorbers.

MMs have the potential benefit to the sensors by improving their sensitivity, selectivity and signal-to-noise ratio. One way to improve sensor performance is with varying unit cell size and geometry to get maximised sensing properties. MMs can be made to have adjustable or tunable resonance characteristics. These characteristics are useful for the sensor to identify the specific frequencies of electromagnetic radiation. The MM sensors are used in many different applications like medical, agriculture and industrial. Yusheng Zhang designed a split disk metamaterials (SDM) structure for Gas detection applications. Where the resonance frequency is controlled by adjusting the gaps in the MM. It achieves maximum sensitivity and figure of merit (FoM) values of 3567 nm/RIU and 20.89 [1]. Ayesha Mohanty designed square shape structure, and it attained quality factor of 225, sensitivity at 1.6 THz/Refractive index unit and FoM of 80, but it generates a very narrow absorption peak [2]. In this design, the structure seems to be a circular shape, and the Q-factor is found to be 8.887 RIU^{-1}, 8.163um^{-1}, but it has four band peaks [3]. Zhonggang designed a square shape split ring resonator that has a narrow resonance peak and attained absorption, Q-factor and sensitivity of 99% at 0.53 THz, 44.17 and 126.0 GHz/RIU, respectively, and it depends on the thickness levels of the material. It has a very narrow peak [4] too. This article was designed with a square shape split ring resonator structure, where the quality factor is seen as 32.167 and FoM 6.015. It is mainly used for biosensor application, but it depends on different refractive index of the media [5]. Hence, the reported works suffer from various issues like large variation in tunablity.

The proposed work achieved better absorption Q-factor and FoM using graphene material. It shows better absorbance quality and offers better tuning and good conductivity. It is investigated that the gold material has been used at the bottom level of the absorber to enhance absorber efficiency. Rectangular SRR have more control over anisotropic characteristics and directed behaviour.

In this article, we used three different layers where Au material was placed at the bottom level and middle one occupied by silicon dioxide and the top one is the complimentary split ring resonator (CSRR). As per as the CSRR design, the outer side ring consists of Au material, and the inner side uses graphene material.

2. Geometrical Design

In this structure,the bottom gold layer and middle layer of silicon dioxide act as dielectric material.The entire structure is designed using CST software, and the technique implemented is finite difference time domain method (FDTD). When the signal passes through the top layer of the material and reaches the dielectric material, it matches the impendence of thedielectric material, and it reaches the bottom gold layer where this layer blocks the signal and get it reflected back to the same media. As the transmission part was zero, this structure then produced two resonance peaks. The mathematics that holds good is expressed below.

$$\boldsymbol{A} = 1 - \left|\boldsymbol{s}^2{}_{11}\right| - \left|\boldsymbol{s}^2_{21}\right| \tag{1}$$

Here transmission part blocks the signal so we get the

$$\boldsymbol{A} = 1 - \left|\boldsymbol{s}^2{}_{11}\right| \tag{2}$$

s_{11} = Transmission co-efficient, s_{21} = reflection co-efficient.

This is a three-layer structure, and the middle layer is basically a dielectric medium. The thickness of the same was found to be 70 μm and height 15 μm with dielectric constant 3 of .9. In addition to that, this layer also has electrical conductivity and thermal conductivity$10^{-12} s/m$, 1.4W/mk, respectively. As we are using graphene in this design and the chemical property of graphene subjected to change when temperature changes. It is good to consider the refractive index and melting temperature of Sio2 also as it is part of design and the values are 1.46, 1713–2950 $^{\circ}C$.

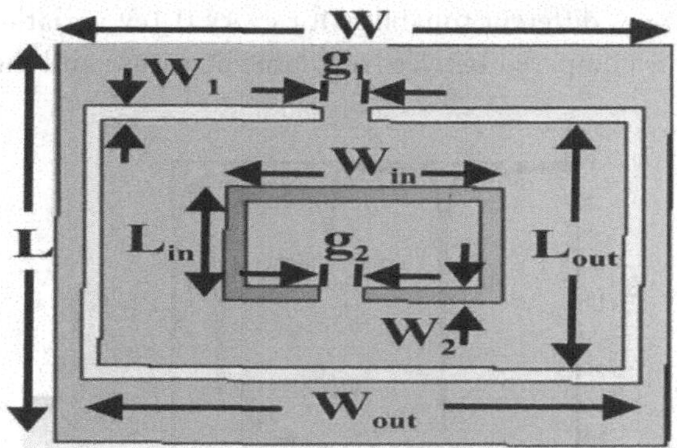

Figure 1: Dimensions.

When we talk about the top layer which is a CSRR structure made up of graphene and gold. The inner layer is composed of a graphene with dimensions Win=32 um, Lin=27 um,W2=5 um, h=0.4, g2= 9.9 um, and the outer layer consists of Gold having Wout=64 um, L_{out}=43 um, h=0.4 um, g1=9 um. The absorption rate for the said structure is 92% and 99% respectively.

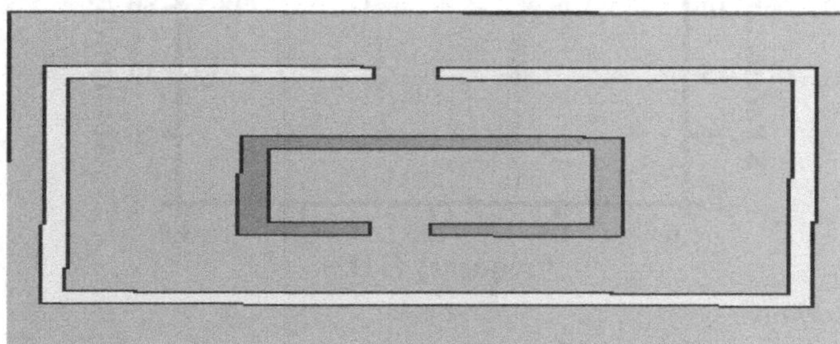

Figure 2: Top view.

In the proposed design, the three peaks of 100%, 97%, and 76% show the absorption efficiency applicable for biomedical diagnostics, imaging in security screening, harvesting, etc. Figure 3 shows the reflection of the structure with two narrow peaks. Figure 4 shows the absorption of structure where we have achieved triple band peaks due to the inclusion of CSRR structure. The spatiality of the structure is the presence of graphene, which behaves differently with its carrier density subjected to change by its chemical potential. The quantity of charge carriers (electrons or holes) in the material can be altered by varying the chemical potential. Because of their tunability, MMs can be created with customized electronic characteristics like conductivity or optical responsiveness. Tunable MMs can be made possible by the manipulation of the chemical potential of graphene. When exposed to external stimuli like an electric field or chemical reactions, these materials' characteristics can be changed. For instance, by adjusting the chemical potential, you can change the plasmonic resonance frequency in graphene-based MMs. Figure 5 witnesses different tunability for every 0.1ev variation. In Table 1, tunable achievement is compared between available literature and the earlier one.

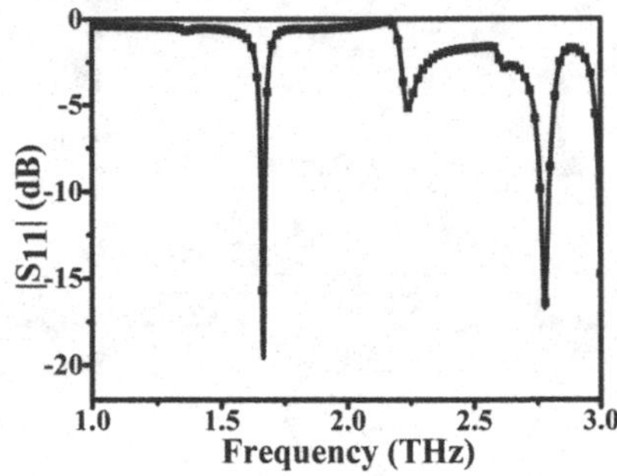

Figure 3: Reflection.

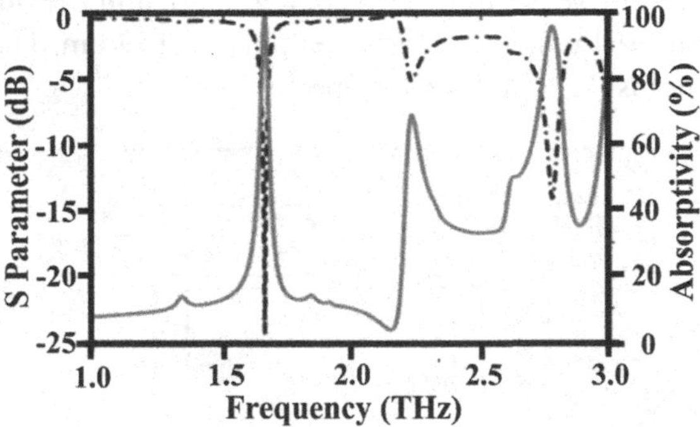

Figure 4: Absorption.

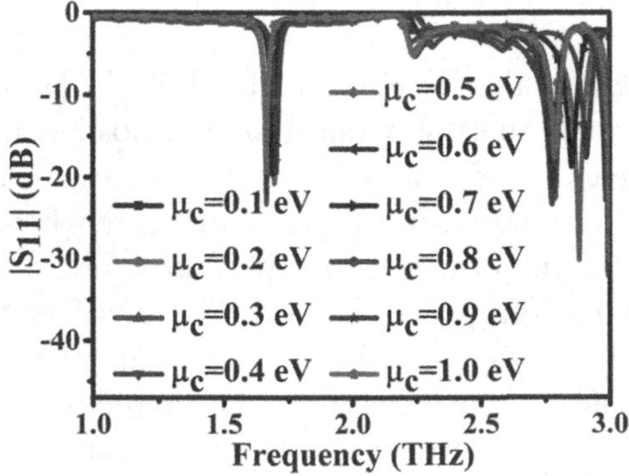

Figure 5: Chemical variation.

Table 1: Comparison between available literatures.

Ref	Type of structure	Number of bands	Tunable
[1]	Split disk metamaterial	Single band	No
[2]	Square shape design	Single band	No
[3]	Circle shape designed	Four band	No
[4]	Square shape split ring resonator	Single band	No
Present work	CSRR structure designed	Triple band	Yes

3. Conclusion

In this paper, we designed a simple structure using CSRR called MM, which provides multiple bands. The multiband peaks generated here are not identical in terms of height. The first peak absorption is 100%, and the other peak is found to be 96% followed by the third one as 70%.This structure is mainly designed for sensing applications. It can further be extended for biomedicalapplications by reducing its size and number of CSRR structures. The results and the performance of the proposed structure are very much modified with the inclusion of many other material in place of graphene and gold.

References

[1] Zhang, Y., P. Lin, and Y.-S. Lin, "Tunable split-disk metamaterial absorber for sensing application," *Nanomaterials*, vol. 11, p. 598, 2021, https://doi.org/10.3390/nano11030598.

[2] Mohanty, A., "Graduate student member, IEEE, Omprakash Acharya, bhargav Appasani, S.K. Mohapatra, Mohammad S. Khan: design of a novel terahertz metamaterial absorber for sensing applications," *IEEE Sens. J.*, vol. 21, no. 20, 2021.

[3] Bai, J., W. Shen, Shashawang, M. Ge, T. Chen, P, Shen, and S. Chang, "An ultra-thin multiband terahertz metamaterial absorber and sensing applications," *Opt. Quantum Electron.*, vol. 53, p. 506, 2021, https://doi.org/10.1007/s11082-021-03180-8.

[4] Zhonggangxiong, L., "Terahertz sensor with resonance enhancement based on square split-ring resonators," *IEEE Trans.*, vol. 6, 2021.

[5] Banerjee, S., U. Nath, A. V. Jha, and S. Pahadsingh, "A terahertz metamaterial absorber based refractive indezsensorwith high quality facto," (May 2022).

[6] Wang, B.-X., X. Zhai, G.-Z. Wang, W.-Q. Huang, and L.-L. Wang, *A Novel Dual-Band Terahertz Metamaterial Absorber for a Sensor Application*, AIP Publishing LLC, 2015.

[7] Islam, M., S.J.M. Rao, G. Kumar, B.P. Pal, and D. Roy Chowdhury, "Role of resonance modes on terahertz metamaterials based thin film sensors," *Sci. Rep.*, vol. 7, no. 1, p. 7355, 2017.

[8] Meng, K., *et al.*, "Increasing the sensitivity of terahertz split ring resonator metamaterials for dielectric sensing by localized substrate etching," *Opt. Express*, vol. 27, no. 16, p. 23164, 2019.

[9] Shen, F., J. Qin, and Z. Han, "Planar antenna array as a highly sensitive terahertz sensor.," *Appl. Opt.*, vol. 58, no. 3, p. 540, 2019.

[10] Li, Y., *et al.*, "Four resonators based high sensitive terahertz metamaterial biosensor used for measuring concentration of protein," *J. Phys. D: Appl. Phys.*, vol. 52, no. 9, 2019.

68. Enhancing Energy Efficiency in MIMO Networks for 5G

Praveen Srivastava and Shelej Khera

Lovely Professional University, School of Electronics and Electrical Engineering, Jalandhar, India

Abstract: Energy efficiency (EE) is a key design parameter for sustainable development as we move closer to the 5G of wireless networks. In this reference, multiple-input multiple-output (MIMO) technology is one of the fundamental 5G enablers. Bit-per-joule EE is a key parameter for evolution as we move closer to the 5G of wireless networks. MIMO technology, in which the base station are outfitted by a numerous number of antennas, to achieve spectrum and EE advantages over present LTE networks, is one of the main enablers for 5G in this regard. Here, we present a thorough discussion of methods for maximizing the EE advantages provided by massive MIMO (MM). A summary of MM technology is presented and how accurate power consumption models for MM systems should be created. Then, we go over popular EE-maximisation methods for MM. Next, we look into EE-maximization in "hybrid MM systems," where MM coexists with millimeter wave and heterogeneous networks, two additional prospective 5G technologies. As massive MIMO and various 5G technologies coexist, numerous options arise for attaining greater EE improvements than with traditional MM systems. EE-maximization is non-trivial due to the numerous new design limitations introduced by such coexistence, though. Using a critical study of the most recent EE maximisation methods for hybrid massive MIMO systems, we can explore numerous research issues that, if solved, will be very beneficial, operators are preparing for 5G deployments that use little energy.

Keywords: MIMO[1], energy efficiency[2], 5G[3].

1. Introduction

The 5G networks are anticipated to integrate nearly everything on the planet, and internet is being developed quickly by the communication technology industry. Data rates of up to 20 Gb/s, average data rates of more than 100 Mb/s and connectivity for a massive number of Internet-of-Things devices per unit area are all anticipated from 5G networks. Because this sector already makes a sizable contribution to the global carbon footprint, energy saving becomes a crucial issue for networks. In this context, bit-per-joule efficiency, defined as energy efficiency (EE) = T/P, where T is system throughput and P is power used to achieve T, is a crucial design parameter for 5G networks. A prospective 5G enabler, the MIMO technology offers enhanced spectrum and EE advantages over existing LTE.

1.1. Overview of MIMO Technologies

Massive MIMO is a multi-user MIMO system in which a base station (BS) with M antennas services K user equipment's (UEs) on the same time-frequency resource, where M >> K. A favourable propagation environment is created when the BS has a high number of antennas, whereby the wireless channel becomes almost deterministic and the BS-to-UE radio links are nearly orthogonal to one another [1]. It is due to the fact that in the large M regime, the effects of small-scale fading, intracellular interference, and uncorrelated noise asymptotically vanish. Higher multiplexing and array gains can be realized under advantageous propagation conditions by expanding the dimension of system, or (M, K). Two crucial conclusions are reached as a result of this simplification. Large EE gains as compared with LTE systems are also possible with MM systems.

2. Massive MIMO Energy Efficiency Issues

Under LTE, MM systems can outperform traditional MU-MIMO systems in two key aspects, both predicated on growing the system's size, i.e. (M, K). First, by expanding M much above the minimum eight antennas per BS in existing LTE , it is possible to drastically reduce the emitting power of the UEs in MIMO network for a given system throughput. Second, by raising K, MM systems can see significant throughput increases. Because straightforward processing methods, like maximal-ratio combining (MRC) on the UL and maximal-ratio transmission (MRT) on the DL, may reach nearly optimal results, these advances can be made with little circuit power consumption throughput effectiveness [1].

When the system size is raised, such complicated procedures can use an unreasonably high number of computational resources. By increasing (M, K) in MIMO not always result in enhancement in EE because (M, K) also causes an increase in PC, or circuit power consumption. Therefore, we can only accomplish EE improvements when the UE emission powers are decreased by raising M. The primary factor driving this rise in PC is UE transmission power. Similar to this, when K is increased to boost throughput, EE benefits can only be made if the increase outweighs the ensuing rise in power consumption.

2.1. Energy-Efficient MIMO System Design

The EE of MIMO system increases by obtaining near-optimal throughput at low power levels. Several study approaches have been pursued for the based on this parallel, energy-efficient MM network architecture. In order to reduce system power consumption, a few techniques design simple algorithms for BS tasks including multi-user identification, precoding, and user scheduling. Other approaches, including transceiver design, antenna choice, and power amplifier dimensioning, concentrate on optimizing resource use to reduce the need for hardware and, consequently, system power consumption.

2.2. Operations with Low Complexity in BS

Basic scheduling algorithms like random and round-robin, as well as basic linear processing approaches like maximum ratio combiner on the Uplink and MRT on the downlink, produce near-optimal throughputs [1]. This is due to the big M regime's advantageous propagation conditions.

2.3. Designing Low-Overhead Frequency Division Duplex (FDD) Precoders

Recently, a low-overhead FDD precoders that make use of the assumption of channel sparsity overhead reduction have been presented [2]. These precoders are compatible with mm wave, where the assumption of channel sparsity is valid. Since FDD has many more licenses than TDD does globally, advancements in low-overhead FDD precoders will encourage MM's acceptability as a future technology.

2.4. BS Antennas Should Be Fewer in Numbers

The system throughput T can be increased when the BS has more antennas since better multiplexing gains were possible. Nevertheless, from our considerations that the circuit power PC rises with M as well. However, if we increase T to the point where it is sufficiently high, increasing M can still be a method for MM networks that uses little energy, suppose we raise T to a level where it outweighs the rise in PC. It could be achieved by raising the downlink emission power across specific scaling window, even if it is not immediately apparent from the initial observations. The scaling window is controlled by number of BS antennas M*, above which T is near-optimal boundaries but circuit power PC continues to increase with M. If down link emission power is increased, we see that EE reaches a maximum level at M*, which subsequently declines with M. It should be noted that by lowering RF chain requirements at the BS, the scaling window can be increased because doing so lowers PC levels. Alternatively, it may be possible to achieve very low circuit power consumption if the transceiver design assures that extremely less power consumption, it could enhance system EE by lowering downlink emission power with M, which significantly depends on how energy-conscious transceiver design would develop in the future.

2.5. Minimizing PA Power Losses

By minimizing PA, it can also result in significant EE improvements. Let us look into DL broadcasts in an MM system to see how to minimize PPA = Pin/h, where Pin is the power given to PAs and measure PA power losses (also known as the PA efficiency), can be used to calculate the total required power used by PAs at the BS. Several PAPR reduction approaches, such those suggested in [3], can be tried in order to reduce PA power losses. However, the majority of the recently proposed waveforms have practical restrictions, like large filter lengths and complicated receiver techniques [4], making the design of suitable non-orthogonal waveforms a significant research problem. Alternately, constant envelope signals can be used to ease the criteria for PA linearity, albeit creating such signals is still a problem as of this writing.

2.6. Reduce the BS's RF Chain Requirements

MIMO precoding and beamforming are often carried out digitally in the baseband. Since each antenna element must have a distinct baseband and RF chain component for digital processing the BS transceivers typically use a single RF chain per antenna configuration, with the increase of RF chains at the BS with M, high circuit power is required in massive mimo. As a result, reducing RF chain needs at the BS is a desirable method of enhancing EE in MM networks.

Hybrid precoding, choice of antenna and transceiver design are prominent methods to lower RF chain requirements. The following discussion of hybrid precoding techniques will focus on millimetre wave systems because they are typically based on the assumption of channel sparsity.

Antenna selection is a signal processing approach increases system throughput while at the same time minimising the number of radio frequency chains at the BS [5]. N out of M antennas are chosen as a subset depending on predetermined selection criterion, to maximise throughput, SNR and EE. RF chains are connected to the antennas of the chosen subset for additional processing. Circuit power requirements in the system are reduced because the number of radio frequency chains is decreased from M to N.

2.7. Transceiver Architecture Redesign

Redesigning the BS transceiver architecture is a different approach to cutting down on the radio frequency chain needs at the BS. A few single RF chain transceivers in this manner have lately been developed, at the expense of significant practical restrictions.

The electronically steerable parasitic antenna array suggested [6] only supports a few numbers of modulation schemes and calls for approximately twice as many antennas as traditional transceivers while still operating with a single RF chain. Consequently, the current body of knowledge cannot be regarded as comprehensive, despite the fact that transceiver redesign shows significant promise for enhancing EE in MM networks. Additional study is needed to address a number of design difficulties and to overcome.

2.8. Efficient Massive MIMO Hybrid Network

So far, we looked into a variety of EE-maximisation potential traditional massive mimo systems, or systems using massive mimo is the only supporting 5G technology.

A number of additional technologies are also developing as potential 5G enablers, including millimetre wave, heterogeneous networks, energy harvesting, full duplex and cloud-based radio access. Each of them offers a distinct set of performance advantages: HetNets delivers high-throughput gains through network densification; EH allows for reduced battery power consumption through the use of renewable energy and mm wave operations offers throughput upgrades through bigger transmission bandwidths. So, it becomes sense to assume the future 5G networks will support wireless systems made possible by massive mimo and other cutting-edge 5G technologies. In the following section, we explore potential EE-maximisation prospects for these systems, which we describe to as "hybrid MM systems".

We describe how two 5G technologies, mm wave and Het Nets, boost MM in mutually beneficial ways before studying EE-maximisation in the related hybrid MM systems.

2.9. Systems for Millimeter Waves (mm Wave)-Based MM

The sub-3GHz bands are already too crowded for 5G operations, so researchers are looking into the mm wave range, which spans from 30 GHz to 300 GHz. This is because more spectrum is required to meet anticipated traffic demands. Since enormous bandwidths of several GHz are accessible in mm wave spectrum—BW upto 7 GHz are possible in 60 GHz band—moving to this spectrum will result in significant throughput enhancements and latency savings.

3. Simultaneous Existence Advantages

MIMO automatically provides highly directed and adaptive emissions necessary for increase in signal levels, reduce interference in blockage-sensitive situations in mm wave bands, makes massive MIMO feasible as a lot of antennas can be crammed into tiny spaces at mm wave frequencies [2] and because mm Wave MM networks have near-LOS channels can be calculated using the DoA. Traditional mm wave systems and mm wave-based MM systems differ primarily in two ways. First, the majority of conventional mm wave systems perform directional transmissions by employing analog phased arrays with a constrained number of antennas [7]. In contrast, mm wave MM systems can be utilised for longer-range cellular services with concurrent multi-user broadcasts because of beamforming with a lot of antennas.

4. Challenges and Open Problems

Millimetre Wave MM systems can clearly benefit from multi-stage digital precoding approaches, although these techniques have only received a limited amount of research (see [2] for an example). It is unclear how pilot contamination will cause trade-offs. Similar circumstances apply to hybrid analog-digital beamforming methods which loosen BS radio frequency chain constraints. These methods are essential for mm wave operations due to the RF chain's mixed signal components, especially the high-resolution analog to digital converters. utilize excessive amounts of electricity when operating at high bandwidths. Be aware that the analog precoding phase imposes a number of new restrictions on the transceiver design, including limited ADC resolution, limited ADC precision, and limited number of phase shifts. There is a ton of room for additional research because the EE trade-offs caused by these limits are not covered in the existing literature.

The hardware design is a significant barrier to the development of mm Wave MM systems that are energy-efficient. Multiple mm Wave antennas with the required analog and digital circuitry can be integrated into a single device using silicon-based CMOS technology in an easy and affordable manner. However, the mm Wave regime's high frequency and broad bandwidth operations place a number of restrictions on the design of transceiver components. Additionally, poor separation between active on-chip components can cause signal distortion and self-jamming. As of this writing, there are no transceivers that take care of all of these design issues.

5. Conclusion

MIMO technology promises manifold spectrum and EE increases over existing LTE technologies, making it a rewarding technology for sustainable evolution toward 5G. This article has looked at a number of ways to increase the energy efficient gains provided by MIMO. Basic EE maximisation methods for fundamental mimo systems were reviewed briefly, and a few unresolved issues were noted. These methods include scaling the number of BS antennas, implementing simple operations at the BS, minimising power amplifier losses and minimising RF chain requirements. In 'hybrid MM systems,' where massive mimo coexists with other burgeoning 5G technologies like millimetre wave and heterogeneous networks, this paper has also looked into a number of new options for EE maximisation.

References

[1] Marzetta, T., "Noncooperative cellular wireless with unlimited numbers of base station antennas," *IEEE Trans. Wireless Commun.*, vol. 9, no. 11, pp. 3590– 3600, 2010.

[2] Adhikary *et al.*, "Joint spatial division and multiplexing for mm wave Channels," *IEEE JSAC*, vol. 32, no. 6, pp. 1239–55, 2014.

[3] Jiang, T. and Y. Wu, "An overview: peak-to-average power ratio reduction techniques for OFDM Signals," *IEEE Trans. Broadcast.*, vol. 54, no. 2, pp. 257–68, 2008.

[4] Wunder, G., *et al.*, "5GNOW: non-orthogonal, asynchronous waveforms for future mobile applications," *IEEE Commun. Mag.*, vol. 52, no. 2, pp. 97–105, 2014.

[5] Zhou, Z., *et al.*, "Energy-efficient antenna selection and power allocation for large- scale multiple antenna systems with hybrid energy supply," *Proc. IEEE GLOBECOM*, Austin, TX, pp. 2574–2579, 2014.

[6] Kalis, *et al.*, "A novel approach to MIMO transmission using a single RF front end," *IEEE JSAC*, vol. 26, no. 6, pp. 972–980, 2008.

[7] Niu, Y., *et al.*, "A survey of millimeter wave communications (mmWave) for 5G: opportunities and challenges," *J. Wireless Netw.*, vol. 21, no. 8, pp. 2657–76. Springerlink; doi 10.1007/s11276-015-0942

69. Advancements in Object Detection and Tracking Techniques: A Comprehensive Review in Variable Illumination Conditions

Chinthakindi Kiran Kumar, Gaurav Sethi, and Kirti Rawal

School of Electronics & Electrical Engineering, Lovely Professional University
Phagwara, Punjab, India

Abstract: Object detection and tracking constitute vital tasks for computer vision with a variety of uses, including surveillance, autonomous driving, robots and augmented reality. However, situations with various lighting conditions make these jobs very difficult. The detrimental impacts of variable illumination conditions are one of the most important difficulties that object detection and tracking systems must overcome. Illumination variations occur due to changes in lighting sources, environmental conditions and camera settings, leading to significant alterations in the brightness, contrast and colour distribution of images .These differences can make it difficult to see objects, cause incorrect results and lower the overall accuracy and reliability of detection and tracking systems. This paper gives a complete overview of the latest methods used to detect and track objects in surroundings that have constantly changing and unpredictable lighting conditions.

Keywords: varying illumination, object detection, object tracking, deep learning.

1. Introduction

Detecting and tracking constitute significant tasks in the field of computer vision. They are important for many different things like security cameras, self-driving cars, robots and virtual reality games. [1]. These tasks include finding and watching objects that are important in a picture, giving important information to help make decisions and interact with machines [2].Object detection and tracking have made significant progress, although they struggle in scenarios where lighting conditions are constantly changing and difficult to anticipate. The illumination of a scene can fluctuate due to factors such as varying weather conditions, time of day and artificial lighting sources. Such variations pose significant hurdles for computer vision systems, as they can obscure object features, alter object appearances and introduce shadows and reflections, all of which can lead to reduced detection and tracking performance. Object detection algorithms often fail to provide maximum performance due to the varying illumination and tracking of object movement becomes critical [3].

This study provides a thorough analysis of the cutting-edge approaches and methodology used to address the challenging issue of object detection and tracking in conditions with changing lighting. Understanding and addressing this challenge is of paramount importance, as real-world applications seldom occur under controlled, constant lighting conditions. As a result, the ability to adapt and perform robustly in the face of changing illumination is a critical factor in the achievement of computer vision systems across several domains. This review intention is to provide valuable understandings for investigators and practitioners seeking to improve robust and adjustable computer vision systems.

2. Literature Review

In the field of computer vision object detection and tracking are critical with a wide ranging of applications across countless domains. Numerous scholars have proposed a verity of tactics and methodologies that excel in some field while falling short in others. The exhaustive review of object detection and tracking has three steps. The first step is to correct the varying illumination next to detect the object and last step is to track the object. So, the in depth revision of these methods makes the researchers to find the better solution for varying illumination object detection and tracking.

2.1. Illumination Correction Methods

To make an image more visible, different methods have been suggested. Histogram equalisation (HE) [4] is a renowned technique that is active in making images look better by improving their contrast. However, it is important to remember that HE might not always give good results in every situation. This is because it can make common gray levels stand out more while making uncommon ones less noticeable. Some brightness preservation algorithms are proposed to address the issue of brightness migration, such as recursive mean separate histogram equalisation (RMSHE), minimum mean brightness error bi-histogram equalisation (MMBEBHE), recursive sub-image histogram equalisation (RSIHE) and dualistic sub-image histogram equalisation (DSIHE) [5]. These methods equalised each segment after first splitting the input image's histogram. However, this technique might not always yield the desired improvement, while there is little to no difference between the input and output images. A mixture of BBHE and DSIHE algorithms is used to achieve RSWHE[6], which restore the illumination and recovers the divergence of an image. However, statistical evidence of the picture may be missing after the renovation, worsening the superiority of the picture. To address this issue, a number of alternative approaches have been proposed, providing a range of procedures that range from straightforward ones like gamma correction to more complex ones like depth picture histograms and pixel contextual information. These techniques examine the larger image context and frequently use a multi-stage pipeline to produce the desired outcomes.

Machine learning techniques for fixing lighting issues have become more popular in the past few years because they can adjust and improve based on the information they receive. These methodologies influence various machine learning algorithms to automatically correct lighting issues in images. Xiaoyu Li *et al.* [7] proposed a method called "Text Refinement and Lighting Correction" using a technique called patch-based CNN. Instead of analysing the whole image, they focus on learning the distortion flow on small parts of the image called patches. Wei Ma *et al.* [8] suggested a way to solve the issue of improving the lighting in face images using a technique called style translation, which involves using a generative adversarial network (GAN). D Zhou *et al.* [9] used a technique called CycleGAN to develop the superiority of low illumination images. In the design of the network structure, they used different sets of filters to find different characteristics from three paths.

Deep learning methods for illumination rectification leverage neural networks to automatically address illumination challenges in images. These methods have established their effectiveness in improving image quality and justifying the adverse effects of uneven lighting conditions. Here are some common deep learning techniques and models used for illumination correction. Goswami *et al.* [10] introduced a straightforward deep learning-based image illumination correction architecture that can correct under- or over-illuminated color paintings in color photographs. W Zhang et al [11] proposed well-organized end-to-end enhancer, called NUIENet , to improve underwater pictures with uneven illumination. Guo *et al.* [12] pioneered a new technique called zero-reference deep curve estimation (Zero-DCE), This method fames illumination enhancement as the image-specific curbe estimation task using a deep neural network. However, the CNN-based method for image enhancement uses sophisticated learning algorithms and needs a lot of training.

2.2. Object Detection Methods

To recognise and locate things inside still or moving images, object detection methods are techniques used in computer vision and image processing. Different methods for object detection were presented by various authors. Deep convolutional neural networks (DCNNs) [13] are used by region-based convolutional neural networks (R-CNNs) to extract features, although they have a number of flaws. Training R-CNN models are often characterized by slow convergence rates, which can be time-consuming. The Spatial Pyramid Pooling Network (SPPNet) [14] harnesses DCNNs to capture image features holistically by processing the entire image. However, a determined issue is the relatively slow process of using selective search to extract region proposals, which can impact real-time performance. Additionally, SPPNet does not support end-to-end training. The Fast R-CNN [15] harnesses DCNNs to comprehensively extract image features across the entire frame. It utilises the finicky exploration algorithm to produce 2k area proposals. A notable limitation persists: the utilisation of selective search for area proposal generation remains a slow process, potentially impacting real-time applications. Faster R-CNN [16] represents advancement in object detection by introducing the region proposal network (RPN) to supplant the laborious selective search algorithm. The RPN shares feature maps with the backbone network, significantly improving efficiency. However, it does encounter challenges when it comes to effectively detecting multi-scale and small objects, impacting its performance in such scenarios. Additionally, while Faster R-CNN is faster than some earlier methods, it may still fall short of meeting real-time requirements in certain applications. Mask R-CNN[17] introduces the ROIAlign pooling layer as an enhancement over the traditional ROI pooling layer, which leads to improved detection accuracy. However, it is important to note that, like its predecessors, Mask R-CNN may still struggle to achieve real-time detection speeds in certain scenarios, where low-latency requirements are crucial. The you only look once (YOLO)[18] family of object discovery models has been widely praised for its speed and accuracy but struggle with precise object localisation especially for dense objects. SD (Single Shot MultiBox Detector) [19] employs a multi-layer detection mechanism along with a multi-scale anchor mechanism at different layers of the network. While SSD is known for its speed and efficiency in object detection. It has limited ability to detect small objects accurately. The figure 1 shows various object detection methods.

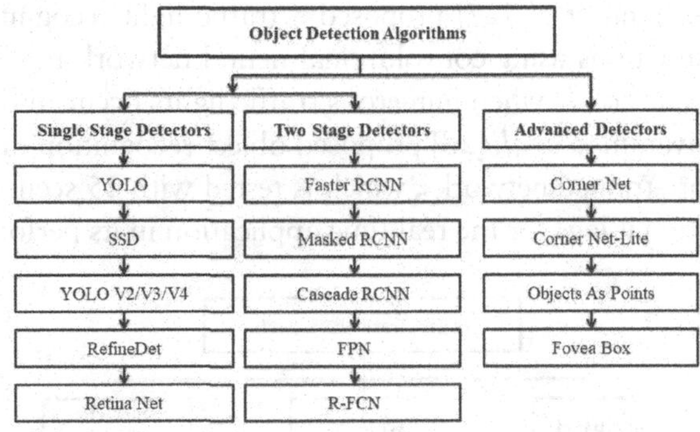

Figure 1: *Different object detection methods.*

2.3. Object Tracking Methods

Deep SORT is a widespread object tracking framework and one of the most widely used algorithms. Ma et al. [20] endeavoured to suggest an exact method estimating the scale of tracked objects. The approach is known as SITUP, and it aims to address the issue of tracking objects with fixed template size. The proposed technique displayed a great scaling flexibility and the ability to separate itself form correlation filter-based trackers. When tested on bench mark datasets, it met the problem of scale variance by producing remarkably accurate results. David Ribeiro *et al.* [21] presented deep convolutional neural network (CNN) for pedestrian recognition. The CNN-based detection capable of tracking the similar objects faster. The proposal limited to particular pedestrian application and lack of availability of wide range of datasets considered as demerits of the system. Ma et al. [22] have proposed a FAST algorithm, a scaling search strategy is used in this study to provide robust and exact scale estimation. This estimation is then used with a multi-resolution fame work and combined with peak-to-correlation energy technique to improve the object tracking accuracy. Figure 2 shows the different object tracking approaches.

Numerous authors have demonstrated different techniques for object detection and tracking under varying illumination conditions. Zhu *et al.* [23] proposed an approach that combine an object tracking (mean shift), appearance-based pattern recognition method (SVM) and a bright-pupil eye tracker integrated with Kalman filtering with active IR illumination. It lags speed and efficiency in object detection. Makihara, Yasushi, *et al.* [24] put forth a method aimed at estimating color changes in object recognition when faced with different lighting conditions. This approach relies solely on a single observed colour of the reference object utilising a physics-based color model. Xiang, Jinhai, *et al* [25] proposed a method to detect moving object while effectively eliminating cast shadows, demonstrating resilience in the face of varying illumination. In their study, Shen *et al.* [26] recommended a method for tracking non-rigid moving objects using a fix camera under changing illumination conditions. However, it should be noted that this method may encounter challenges when the camera in motion. John *et al.* [27] proposed a traffic light recognition technique in varying lighting situations using convolutional neural network-based detector which report some sporadic errors when numerous traffic lights occur in the image, exactly at intersections. Sivaraman *et al.* [28] proposed object recognition under illumination variations using pre-trained networks, which is tested with 15 scenes captured under different illumination it lags for the real-time application in its performance.

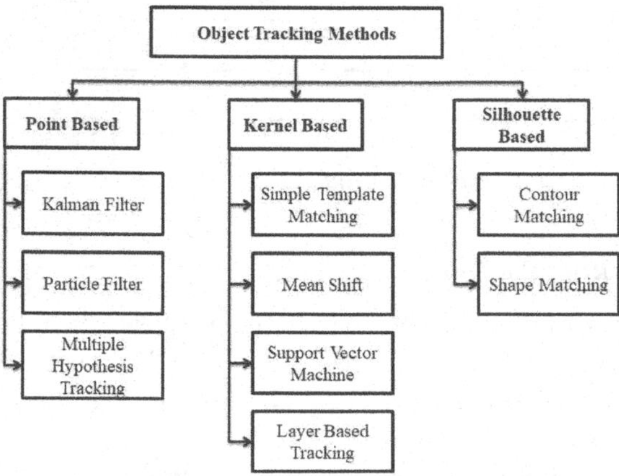

Figure 2: *Various tracking methods.*

3. Conclusion

This paper has provides a broad overview of the challenges and developments in the field of illumination correction, object detection and tracking and also presents object detection and tracking under varying illumination conditions .The dynamic nature of lighting conditions poses noteworthy hurdles for computer vision systems, but researchers have made significant progress in developing techniques that address these challenges. From traditional methods to cutting-edge deep learning approaches, a wide array of strategies has been explored to enhance object detection and tracking robustness under varying illuminations. As the importance of these technologies continues to grow in applications like autonomous vehicles, surveillance and robotics, the insights and methodologies presented in this review offer valuable guidance for future research and practical implementations in real-world scenarios.

References

[1] Kaur, R. and S. Singh, "A comprehensive review of object detection with deep learning," *Digital Signal Process.*, vol. 132, p. 103812, 2023, ISSN 1051-2004.

[2] Joshi, K. A. and D. G. Thakore, "A survey on moving object detection and tracking in video surveillance system," Int. J. Soft Comput. Eng., vol. 2, no. 3, pp. 44–48, 2012.

[3] Sreedevi, M., Y. K. Avulapati, A. Babu G, and R. Sendhil Kumar, "Real time movement detection for human recognition," *Proc. World congr. Eng. Comput. Sci.*, vol. 1, 2012.

[4] Rahman, S., *et al.*, "An adaptive gamma correction for image enhancement," *EURASIP J. Image Video Process.*, vol. 2016, no. 1, pp. 1–13, 2016.

[5] Huang, Z., *et al.*, "Image enhancement with the preservation of brightness and structures by employing contrast limited dynamic quadri-histogram equalization," *Optik* 226, p. 165877, 2021.

[6] Kim, M., M. G. Chung, "Recursively separated and weighted histogram equalization for brightness preservation and contrast enhancement," *Consum. Electron. IEEE Trans.*, vol. 54, no. 3, pp. 1389–1397, 2008.

[7] Li, X., et al., "Document rectification and illumination correction using a patch-based CNN," *ACM Trans. Graphics (TOG)*, vol. 38, no. 6, pp. 1–11, 2019.

[8] Ma, W., X. Xie, C. Yin, and J. Lai, "Face image illumination processing based on generative adversarial nets," *2018 24th International Conference on Pattern Recognition (ICPR)*, Beijing, China, pp. 2558–2563, 2018, doi: 10.1109/ICPR.2018.8545434.

[9] Zhou, D., *et al.*, "Low illumination image enhancement based on multi-scale CycleGAN with deep residual shrinkage," *J. Intell. Fuzzy Syst.*, vol. 42, no. 3, pp. 2383–2395, 2022.

[10] Go swami, S. and S. K. Singh. "A simple deep learning based image illumination Correction method for paintings," *Pattern Recognit. Lett.*, vol. 138, pp. 392–396, 2020.

[11] Zhang, W., *et al.*, "A framework for the efficient enhancement of non-uniform illumination underwater image using convolution neural network," *Comput. Graph.*, vol. 112, pp. 60–71, 2023.

[12] Guo, C., C. Li, J. Guo, C. C. Loy, J. Hou, S. Kwong, and R. Cong, "Zero-reference deep curve estimation for low-light image enhancement," *Proceedings of the IEEE/CVF Conference on Computer Vision and Pattern Recognition*, Seattle, WA, pp. 1780–1789, 2020.

[13] Girshick, R, J. Donahue, T. Darrell, and J. Malik, "Rich feature hierarchies for accurate object detection and semantic segmentation," *Proceedings of the IEEE Conference on Computer Vision and Pattern Recognition (CVPR)*, pp. 580–587, 2014.

[14] He, K. M., X. Y. Zhang, S. Q. Ren, and J. Sun, "Spatial pyramid pooling in deep convolutional networks for visual recognition," *European Conference on Computer Vision (ECCV)*, pp 346–361, 2014.

[15] Girshick, R., "Fast R-CNN," *Proceedings of the IEEE International Conference on Computer Vision (ICCV)*, pp. 1440–1448, 2015.

[16] Ren, S. Q., K. M. He, R. Girshick, and J. Sun, "Faster R-CNN: towards real-time object detection with region proposal networks," *Advances in Neural Information Processing Systems (NIPS)*, pp. 91–99, 2015.

[17] He, K., G. Gkioxari, P. Dollar, R. Girshick, "Mask R-CNN," *Proceedings of the IEEE International Conference on Computer Vision (ICCV)*, pp. 2980–2988, 2017.

[18] Huang, R., J. Pedoeem, and C. Chen, "YOLO-LITE: a real-time object detection algorithm optimized for non-GPU computers," *2018 IEEE International Conference on Big Data (Big Data)*, IEEE, 2018.

[19] Liu, W., D. Anguelov, D. Erhan, C. Szegedy, S. Reed, C.-Y. Fu, and A. C. Berg, "SSD: single shot multibox detector," *European Conference on Computer Vision (ECCV)*, pp. 21–37, 2016.

[20] Ma, H., S. T. Acton, and Z. Lin, "SITUP: scale invariant tracking using average peak-to-correlation energy," *IEEE Trans. Image Process.*, vol. 29, pp. 3546–3557,2020.

[21] Ribeiro, D., J. C. Nascimento, A. Bernardino, and G. Carneiro, "Improving the performance of pedestrian detectors using convolutional learning," *Elsevier J. Pattern Recognit.*, vol. 61, pp. 641–649, 2017.

[22] Ma, H., Z. Lin, and S. T. Acton, "FAST: fast and accurate scale estimation for tracking," *IEEE Signal Process. Lett.*, vol. 27, pp. 161–165, 2020.

[23] Zhu, Z. and Q. Ji, "Robust real-time eye detection and tracking under variable lighting conditions and various face orientations," *Comput. Vis. Image Understanding*, vol. 98, no. 1, pp. 124–154, 2005.

[24] Makihara, Y., *et al.*, "Object recognition under various lighting conditions," *Image Analysis: 13th Scandinavian Conference, SCIA 2003 Halmstad*, Sweden, June 29–July 2, 2003 Proceedings 13. Springer Berlin Heidelberg, 2003.

[25] Xiang, J., *et al.*, "Moving object detection and shadow removing under changing illumination condition," *Math. Probl. Eng.*, vol. 2014, 2014.

[26] Shen, C., X. Lin, and Y. Shi. "Moving object tracking under varying illumination conditions," *Pattern Recognit. Lett.*, vol. 27, no. 14, pp. 1632–1643, 2006.

[27] John, V., K. Yoneda, B. Qi, Z. Liu, and S. Mita, "Traffic light recognition in varying illumination using deep learning and saliency map," *17th International IEEE Conference on Intelligent Transportation Systems (ITSC)*, Qingdao, China, 2014, pp. 2286-2291, doi: 10.1109/ITSC.2014.6958056.

[28] Sivaraman, K. and A. Murthy, "Object Recognition under lighting variations using pre-trained networks," *2018 IEEE Applied Imagery Pattern Recognition Workshop (AIPR)*, Washington, DC, USA, pp. 1–7, 2018, doi: 10.1109/AIPR.2018.8707399.

70. An Integrated Method of Industry 4.0 for Improved Healthcare Sustainability

Rekha Chaudhary,[1,2] Rahul Sharma,[1,2] Raman Kumar,[1,2] and Mahender Singh Kaswan[1,2]

[1]*School of Electronics & Electrical Engineering, Lovely Professional University, Phagwara, Punjab, India*

[2]*School of Mechanical Engineering, Lovely Professional University, Phagwara, Punjab, India*

Abstract: COVID-19 and increased consciousness about health have forced healthcare managers and individuals to adopt practices that are agile for response and contactless and provide improved healthcare performance. Integrated Industry 4.0 (I4.0) and Green Lean Six Sigma lead to better healthcare performance through the application of different sets of technologies. This work provides a brief structure or method of an integrated approach for improved sustainability. The study uses a ground theory methodology where opinions were sought from different healthcare personnel to develop the conceptual framework. The findings of the study will be beneficial for patients, healthcare personnel and managers, which will lead to a resilient healthcare facility.

Keywords: Industry 4.0, green lean six sigma, healthcare, sustainability, internet of things.

1. Introduction

COVID-19 have led to unprecedented effects on every aspect of healthcare ranging from detection of diseases to management of the supply chain [1]. This pandemic has created the urgency to develop methods that are contactless, more agile, easy to use and provide more safety from different kinds of infections at the healthcare facility. Industry 4.0 (I4.0) is a new industrial paradigm that can revolutionise healthcare through the integrated application of its different digital technologies [2]. I4.0 uses a set of technologies ranging from internet of things (IoT) to additive manufacturing that make the entire system of healthcare more responsive and efficient [3]the Internet of Things, and artificial intelligence. Industry 4.0 has the potential to fulfil customized requirements during the COVID-19 emergency crises. The development of a prediction framework can help health authorities to react appropriately and rapidly. Clinical imaging like X-rays and computed tomography (CT. A similar set of objectives is shared by the Green Lean Six Sigma (GLSS) that makes the workplace and process of healthcare delivery more streamlined through the set of different tools [4]. GLSS make the organisation sustainable through making the entire system more efficient [5]. A GLSS project is undertaken in a particular hospital/clinic's section or ward, where it is implemented at the initial project stage [6]globalized competition, and governmental policies on climate change have enforced the industries to adopt sustainable practices. Green Lean Six Sigma (GLS. The next step of a GLSS project deals with the identification of the leading causes of the inefficiencies and wastes by conducting a cause and effect (C&E) and Pareto analyses. The potential and best solutions for improving organisation sustainability are then found in the next step using tools like) Pugh matrix. Finally, the top elucidation is employed, and the performance of the system is recorded. If substantial improvements are found, then the solution is standardised.

Integrated approach favours industrial organisation to formulate a separate team to manage activities coupled with GLSS and I4.0. In the light of the present situation, this work inclines to retort the subsequent research question based on the evidence from the literature and opinions of the experts from different field of manufacturing entities: 'How industrial organizations can integrate GLSS and Industry 4.0 for improved organizational sustainability?' This research is inductive in nature and use ground theory methodology to explore the facets that foster integration of GLSS with I4.0. First, based on the systematic literature review, a DMAIC enable red integrated I4.0-GLSS framework was developed. Thereafter, framework was find tuned using the expert opinion of the healthcare personnel.

The rest of the manuscript is structured as follows. Section 2 provides literature on GLSS, I4.0, and their connection with sustainability. Section 3 enumerates adopted research method, whereas Section 4 depicts framework of integrated I4.0-GLSS approach. Finally, section states inferences, limitations and future aspects of the study.

2. Literature Review

GLSS is an approach to sustainable development that reduce defects, variation and emission that leads to improved organisational sustainability [7] [8]. GLSS found its feet from the Toyota production that is known by Lean in western culture [9] Six Sigma and Green approaches make a positive contribution to the economic, social and environmental (i.e. sustainability. Lean makes the process streamlined and reduces different wastes it does not directly affects environmental impacts and process variation [10]. The variation of the process and the defects can be minimised by adoption of the Six Sigma methodology [11]. But it is also not capable to cater environmental and social aspects of the sustainability. For this it is imperative to add green technology measure in Lean and Six Sigma to improve all three dimensions of the sustainability, this resulted in the evolution of GLSS. But increased consciousness about mass customisation, responsive actions and shorter product life cycle have forced industries to integrated their sustainable methods with information and communication-based technologies like Industry 4.0 (I4.0) [12].

It is industrial revolution taken on forefront by humanoid that encapsulate 6'R to reduce wastes, harmful environmental impacts and capable to deliver high quality personalised products through efficient set of interaction between human, machines and smart set of technologies [13].

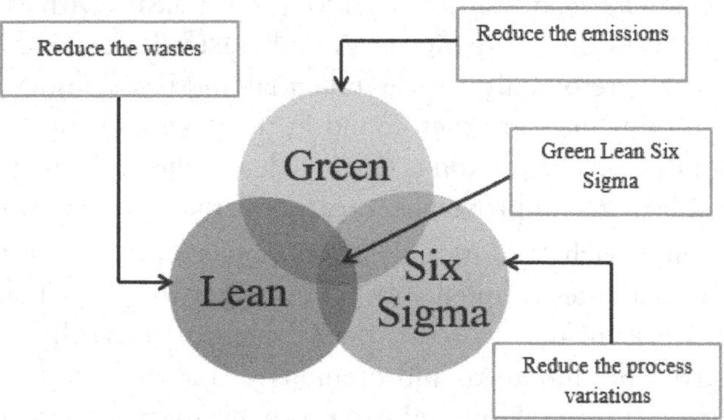

Figure 1: Green lean six integrated model.

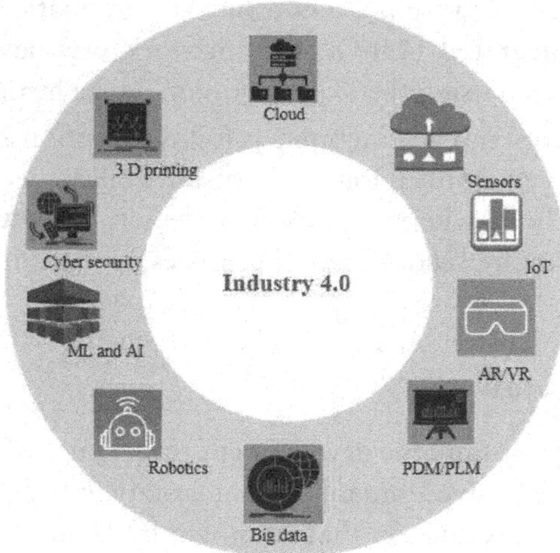

Figure 2: Technological model of industry 4.0.

This revolution takes place near 1974, and development time for the first three industrial revolutions was near 1st century, and it takes nearly 40 year to reach from third revolution to 4th revolution [16] [17]. Second industrial revolution was characterised with development of electricity [18]. In third revolution, the concept of automation and electronics comes to the fore [19]. Industry 4.0 come to the picture in 2011 that changed the way of the production through the use of integrated set of technologies [20] as shown in figure 2. This revolution leads to better production, faster response and delivery of high-quality sustainable products [21] The main motto for the same was to achieve high level of the production by using advanced set of technologies [20]. In the literature studies related to different aspects of GLSS in sectors like manufacturing, textile, mining, automobile, electronic and food exists. Similar set of studies in different industrial domain of I4.0 exists, But integrated application of GLSS-Industry 4.0 has not been explored to its full potential to make the better detection, cure and management of different healthcare facilities. This gap in the study provides impetus and direction for the present study.

3. Methodology

To develop the systematic framework of integrated approach, authors followed a ground theory methodology, Initially, framework was developed based on the systematic investigation of different available framework of the individual approaches in different industrial domains. Authors checked the commonalities feature of the different industrial domain with healthcare and incorporated the same for this work. Once the preliminary framework is developed the same has been fine-tuned using the view point of the different healthcare personnel. In this study, we have taken the viewpoints, doctors, hospital admin staff, supporting staff and pharmacists. Finally, to valid the framework and make it more authentic author implemented the same within the healthcare setting to make more generic for the entire healthcare domain. Figure 1 illustrates adopted methodology.

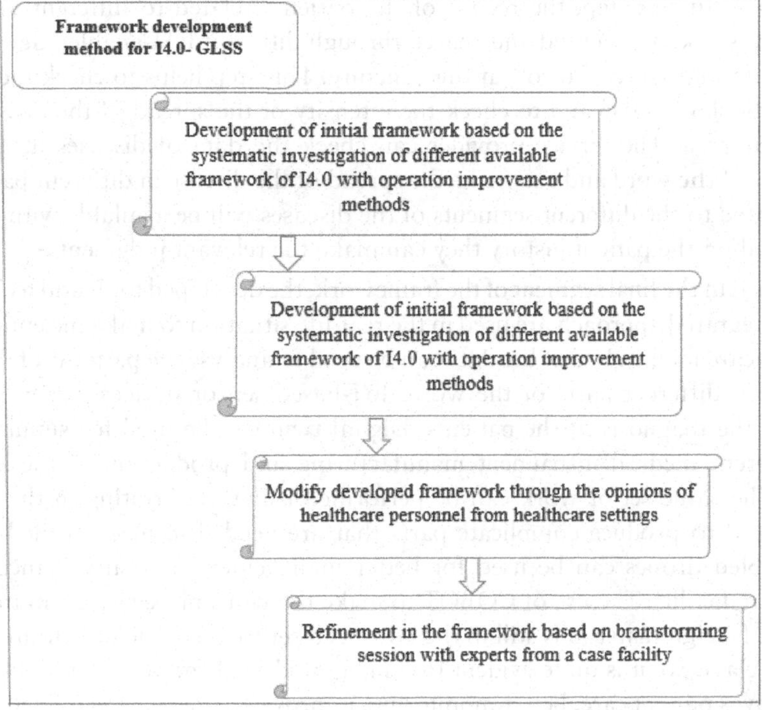

***Figure 3:** Research methodology.*

4. Results and Discussion

Based on the grounded theory methodology, responses from the personnel and healthcare unity application of the framework the final formulated framework have been presented (Figure 3).

The developed framework has different application steps:

Step 1: In the very first step is related to the diagnosis of the patient entering in the healthcare entity. Initially, the same has been adjudged using the instruments or gadgets that are contact type. This resulted in loss of infections to the healthcare personnel too. It is imperative to prevent spread of infections to the healthcare staff otherwise whole healthcare supply chain will end in chaos. For this the use different non-contact direct type instrument can be used to make a primary judgement of the health of the patient. Then this same set of parameters can be transferred through integrated computer mechanism to healthcare service provider or doctor, and based on these initial parameters, he can prescribe and make appropriate judgement on the health of the patients. This kind of system leads to improved healthcare staff health and also leads to major time saving for the doctors which otherwise wasted for other non-value added activities. The use of different IoT enabled sensor use of GLSS tools leads to make the system of receiving of patient, place of the treatment and rest more streamlined and hygiene this will lead to clean work place both for patients and healthcare staff.

Step 2: In this step, the record of the patients related to different diagnosis parameters is kept on cloud and shared through different IOT-enabled devices, use of big data plays a crucial role at this juncture. This step helps to check the spread of a particular disease and to check the intensity of the spread of the disease in a particular area. The service provider can check the data of diseases in different segments of the word and can make the spread of the disease in different parts. The data related to the different segments of the diseases will be available with doctors and based on the patient history they can make the relevant judgments.

Step 3: In the final segment of the framework, the developed tools and techniques of the integrated approach are used in the real-life situation to make the entire place of healthcare facility. Use of big data can be used to analyse the patterns of different diseases in different parts of the word. IoT-based sensor devices can be used to monitor the diagnosis of the patients. Digital twin can be used for simulation of the different medical instrument manufacturing and production of the intricate shape. The same set of work can be performed using 3D printing in the field of dentist and to produce complicate parts that are needed in medical filed. Use of IoT enabled drones can be used for better management and surveillance of the healthcare facility. The use of COBOT to make the work place clean and free from different foreign material is still in the advanced set to make the healthcare facility a world class. So, it is quite evident that integrated application of GLSS-I4.0 leads to improves patient care, better monitoring, improved hygiene, streamlined process and leads to reduction of different non value added activities at the workplace.

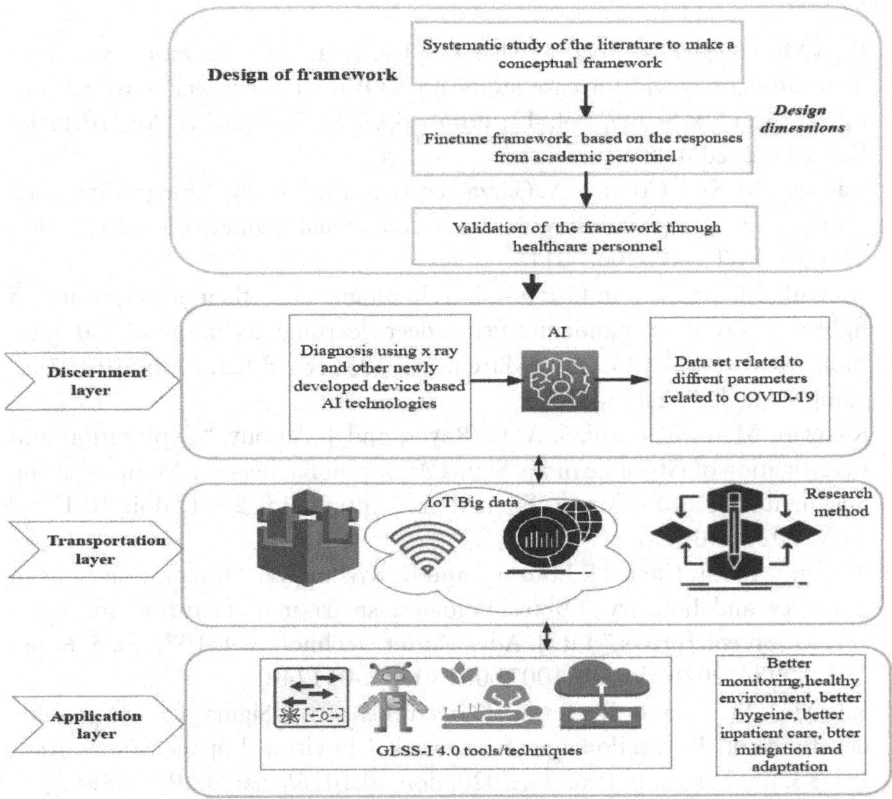

Figure 4: Framework of industry 4.0 and operational superiority's Green Lean Six Sigma for improved healthcare sustainability.

5. Conclusion

Unprecedented disease pattern, more proclivity towards health, and increased healthcare expenditure all are turning the healthcare industries to adopt new practices and approaches. Integrated I4.0-GLSS is a sustainable practice that can make the healthcare more efficient and agile through its unique set of tools and techniques. The present proses a systematic framework of integrated approaches right from the selection of sustainable project in the facility to sustain the same in the long run. The study uses a unique ground theory methodology based on literature, experts and case example to prove the validation and development of the framework. The proposed framework uses different tools of GLSS that leads to make the process of healthcare monitoring, service delivery more streamlined and efficient. Further use of I4.0 technologies make the improved diagnosis and management of the healthcare resources in the most effective way.

References

[1] Raja Mohamed, K. B. N., P. R. M, S. P. S, J. R. A, and R. Anderson, "Six sigma in health-care service: a case study on COVID 19 patients' satisfaction," Int. J. Lean Six Sigma, vol. 12, no. 4, pp. 744–761, 2021, doi: 10.1108/IJLSS-11-2020-0189.

[2] Kaswan, M. S., J. Cross, J. A. Garza-reyes, and J. Antony, "Integrating green lean six sigma and industry 4 . 0 : a conceptual framework," 2022, doi: 10.1108/JMTM-03-2022-0115.

[3] Ahmad, M., et al., "Industry 4.0 technologies and their applications in fighting COVID-19 pandemic using deep learning techniques," Comput. Biol. Med., vol. 145, no. March, p. 105418, 2022, doi: 10.1016/j.compbiomed.2022.105418.

[4] Kaswan, M. S., R. Rathi, J. A. G. Reyes, and J. Antony, "Exploration and Investigation of Green Lean Six Sigma Adoption Barriers for Manufacturing Sustainability," IEEE Trans. Eng. Manag., pp. 1–15, 2021, doi: 10.1109/TEM.2021.3108171.

[5] Shahin, M., F. F. Chen, H. Bouzary, and K. Krishnaiyer, "Integration of Lean practices and Industry 4.0 technologies: smart manufacturing for next-generation enterprises," Int. J. Adv. Manuf. Technol., vol. 107, no. 5–6, pp. 2927–2936, 2020, doi: 10.1007/s00170-020-05124-0.

[6] Kaswan, M. S. and R. Rathi, "Green Lean Six Sigma for sustainable development: Integration and framework," Environ. Impact Assess. Rev., vol. 83, no. March, p. 106396, 2020, doi: 10.1016/j.eiar.2020.106396.

[7] Sony, M. and S. Naik, "Green Lean Six Sigma implementation framework: a case of reducing graphite and dust pollution," Int. J. Sustain. Eng., vol. 13, no. 3, pp. 184–193, 2020, doi: 10.1080/19397038.2019.1695015.

[8] Yadav, V., et al., "Green lean six sigma for sustainability improvement: a systematic review and future research agenda," Int. J. Lean Six Sigma, 2023, doi: 10.1108/IJLSS-06-2022-0132.

[9] Cherrafi, A., S. Elfezazi, K. Govindan, J. A. Garza-Reyes, K. Benhida, and A. Mokhlis, "A framework for the integration of Green and Lean Six Sigma for superior sustainability performance," Int. J. Prod. Res., vol. 55, no. 15, pp. 4481–4515, 2017, doi: 10.1080/00207543.2016.1266406.

[10] Kumar, N., A. Singh, S. Gupta, M. S. Kaswan, and M. Singh, "Integration of Lean manufacturing and Industry 4.0: a bibliometric analysis," TQM J., 2023, doi: 10.1108/TQM-07-2022-0243.

[11] Yadav, V., et al., "Exploration and mitigation of green lean six sigma barriers: a higher education institutions perspective," TQM J., 2023, doi: 10.1108/TQM-03-2023-0069.

[12] Carayannis, E. G. and J. Morawska-Jancelewicz, "The futures of Europe: society 5.0 and industry 5.0 as driving forces of future universities," J. Knowl. Econ., no. 0123456789, 2022, doi: 10.1007/s13132-021-00854-2.

[13] Nahavandi, S., "INDUSTRY 5 . 0 definition," Sustainability, vol. 11, pp. 43–71, 2019.

[14] Kaswan, M. S., et al., "Integrated green lean six sigma-industry 4.0 approach to combat COVID-19: from literature review to framework development," Int. J. Lean Six Sigma, 2023, doi: 10.1108/IJLSS-11-2022-0227.

[15] Maddikunta, P. K. R., et al., "Industry 5.0: A survey on enabling technologies and potential applications," J. Ind. Inf. Integr., vol. 26, no. July, 2022, doi: 10.1016/j.jii.2021.100257.

[16] Krishnan, S., S. Gupta, M. Kaliyan, V. Kumar, and J. A. Garza-Reyes, "Assessing the key enablers for Industry 4.0 adoption using MICMAC analysis: a case study," Int. J. Product. Perform. Manag., vol. 70, no. 5, pp. 1049–1071, 2021, doi: 10.1108/IJPPM-02-2020-0053.

[17] Narayanamurthy, G. and G. Tortorella, "Impact of COVID-19 outbreak on employee performance – Moderating role of industry 4.0 base technologies," Int. J. Prod. Econ., vol. 234, no. October 2020, p. 108075, 2021, doi: 10.1016/j.ijpe.2021.108075.

[18] Lu, Y., "Industry 4.0: A survey on technologies, applications and open research issues," J. Ind. Inf. Integr., vol. 6, pp. 1–10, 2017, doi: 10.1016/j.jii.2017.04.005.

[19] De Giovanni, P. and A. Cariola, "Process innovation through industry 4.0 technologies, lean practices and green supply chains," Res. Transp. Econ., vol. 90, no. April 2019, p. 100869, 2021, doi: 10.1016/j.retrec.2020.100869.

[20] Bag, S., S. Gupta, and S. Kumar, "Industry 4.0 adoption and 10R advance manufacturing capabilities for sustainable development," Int. J. Prod. Econ., vol. 231, no. June 2020, p. 107844, 2021, doi: 10.1016/j.ijpe.2020.107844.

[21] Chiarini, A. and M. Kumar, "Lean Six Sigma and Industry 4.0 integration for Operational Excellence: evidence from Italian manufacturing companies," Prod. Plan. Control, vol. 32, no. 13, pp. 1084–1101, 2021, doi: 10.1080/09537287.2020.1784485.

[22] Gokalp, M. O., K. Kayabay, M. A. Akyol, P. E. Eren, and A. Kocyigit, "Big data for Industry 4.0: A conceptual framework," Proc. - 2016 Int. Conf. Comput. Sci. Comput. Intell. CSCI 2016, pp. 431–434, 2017, doi: 10.1109/CSCI.2016.0088.

71. Performance Analysis of Gate-Pocket Overlap Hetero-junction Tunnel Field-Effect Transistor

Rekha Chaudhary,[1] Rahul Sharma,[1] Raman Kumar,[1] Gautam Bhaskar,[2] and Aditya Chotalia[2]

[1]*Lovely Professional University, Phagwara, Punjab, India*
[2]*Department of ECE, Birla Institute of Technology, Mesra, Ranchi, Jharkhand, India*

Abstract: The performance analysis of hetero-junction gate-pocket overlapped tunnelling field-effect transistors (TFET) through 2-D TCAD simulations is presented. In this configuration, the incorporation of overlap between the gate and pocket regions is employed to demonstrate enhanced performance. We have assessed various characteristics of the hetero-junction gate-pocket overlapped TFET, including its input–output characteristics, transconductance and output conductance. The gate-pocket overlapped TFET shows on-current of 1.58×10^{-4} A/μm and sub-threshold slope of 14 mV/dec at V_{ds}=0.5 V. The comprehensive analysis indicates that the suggested hetero-junction gate-pocket overlapped TFET exhibits remarkable performance and holds promise for high-speed switching applications.

Keywords: Hetro-junction, gate over-lap, gate-pocket, sub-threshold slope (SS).

1. Introduction

Digital technologies have significantly accelerated the advancements in low-power integrated circuit systems [1–2]. Over the last few decades, the metal–oxide-semiconductor FET (MOSFET) has dominated the semiconductor industry due to its remarkable features. Extensive research on MOSFETs has been conducted by numerous semiconductor industries and research institutes [3]. However, research efforts face a hurdle when applications demand high switching speeds, as MOSFETs provide limited speed due to their constrained sub-threshold slope (SS>60 mV/dec) [4–5]. Tunnel field-effect transistor (TFET) devices have emerged as a substitute that has captured interest of researchers worldwide due to their characteristics, including a steeper sub-threshold slope (SS), minimal leakage current and decreased power consumption [6–8]. TFET exhibits certain drawbacks such as limited on-current and ambipolar behaviour [9]. The current flowing in TFET based on band to band tunnelling and can be improved by using hetero-junction devices, using different device structures, lower technology node, or use of III-V materials etc. [10–12]. Several researchers have reported a decrease in ambipolar behaviour by using different engineering methods like changing the device structure, varying the gate work function, considering different doping concentrations and using different dielectric materials at gate side and many more [13].

Choosing the materials with narrow energy bandgaps, like silicon germanium (SiGe) and Ge, is a strategic choice as it results in hyper-exponential rise in band-to-band tunnelling (BTBT) probability in TFET and reduces width of tunnelling barrier [14–15]. Thus, heterojunction exhibits high current upon activation and reduces current when device is turned off. Also, when compared to a FinFET of the same size, the heterojunction TFET reduces power dissipation by five times [16]. The use of Ge in cradle area boost on current and decreases the level of noise [17]. In standard TFETs, the low ON current is a result of BTBT remaining unaffected by changes in the tunnelling cross-sectional area. LTFET-based analogue circuits have piqued the interest of academics for internet of things (IoT) applications [18]. As TFET shows significant features like less power consumption, less impact of noise and less thermal dependence, it has the potential to find application in the realm of IoT.

This paper consists of several sections. It commences with an introduction in Section I, followed by the presentation of the simulation framework in section II. Section III is dedicated to the presentation and discussion of results. At last, the present work has been concluded in Section IV.

2. Device Dimensions and Doping Concentrations

Figure 1 depicts the 2-D view of proposed gate-pocket overlapped TFET with optimised device dimensions. The gate of aluminium/gold metal is placed over 2 nm thick HfO_2. The gate overlaps the SiGe pocket up to 2 nm only and shows the best results. Two sources of different materials Si and Ge of different dimensions are used. The doping concentrations of gate-pocket overlapped TFET are presented in Table 1.

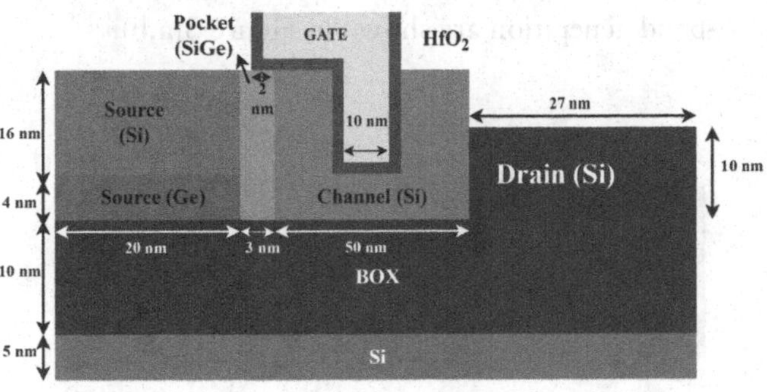

Figure 1: Schematic diagram of proposed device.

Table1: Device dimensions.

S. N.	Parameters	Values (cm^{-3})
1	Source doping (Si)	5E19
2	Source doping (Ge)	5E19
3	Channel doping	1E16
4	Drain doping	5E17
5	Pocket doping	1E18

3. Simulation Framework

The proposed gate-pocket overlapped TFET structure is simulated in a Sentaurus TCAD environment [19,20]. In Figure 2, the implemented TCAD models are enlisted.

TCAD Model	Functioning
Non-local BTBT	Inter-band tunneling
Bandgap narrowing	High doping concentration
Mobility	Carrier mobility
Fermi	Carrier concentration
SRH	Doping dependence model

***Figure** 2: Implemented TCAD models.*

4. Results and Discussions

In this work, different characteristics of gate-pocket overlapped TFET has been demonstrated in this section. The device dimensions, device materials, work function and doping concentrations of the device have been optimised.

For the gate-pocket overlapped TFET, contour plots of electron density and electron band-to-band generation are shown in Figure 3(a,b).

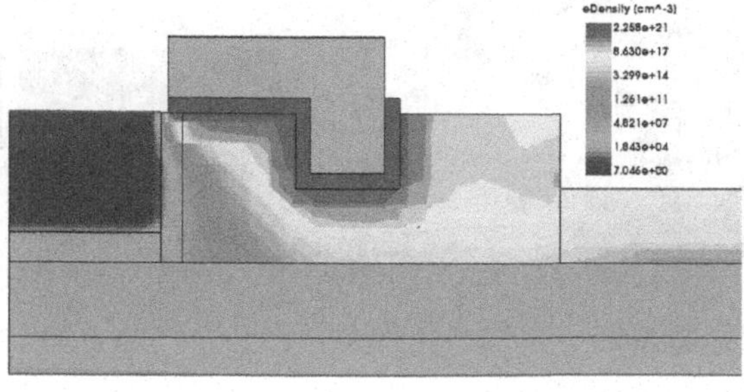

(a)

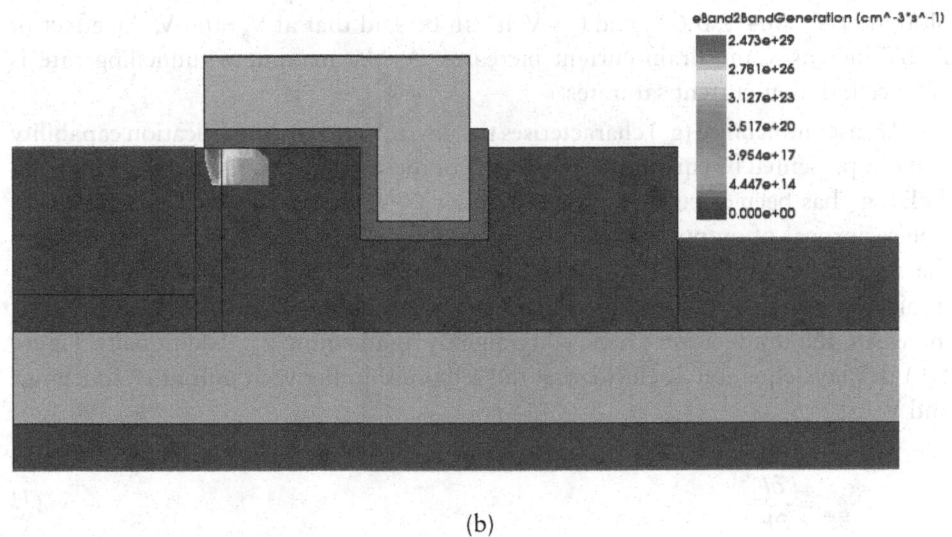

(b)

Figure 3: *(a) Electron density. (b) eBand-to-band generation of gate-pocket overlapped TFET.*

4.1. Transfer and Output Characteristics

The transfer characteristics of proposed gate-pocket overlapped TFET were obtained using Sentaurus TCAD by taking gate-source voltage variations from -0.3 V to 1.5 V. As shown in Figure 4(a) the results were obtained at three different values of V_{ds}, i.e., 0.3 V, 0.5 V, and 0.7 V. Based on the results, it has been found that gate-pocket overlapped TFET shows best results in terms of high on current of 1.58×10^{-4} A/µm, low leakage current of 1.08×10^{-17} A/µm, and SS of 14 mV/dec at V_{ds}=0.5 V. The increase in gate voltage increases the BTBT rate that ultimately increases the drain current.

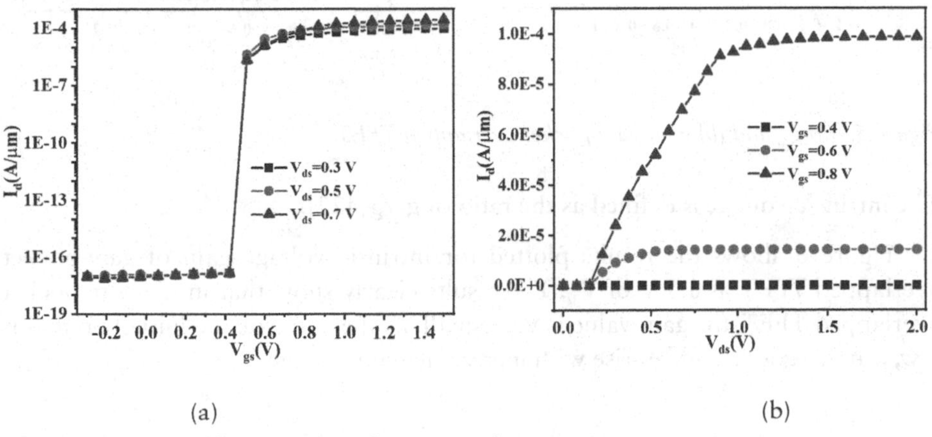

(a) (b)

Figure 4: *(a) Input characteristics. (b) Output characteristics.*

Figure 4(b) depicts the output characteristics of gate-pocket overlapped TFET plotted at V_{gs}=0.4 V, 0.6 V, and 0.8 V. It can be said that at V_{gs}=0.6 V, the effect of BTBT increases and drain current increases. As the maximum tunnelling rate is achieved, the on-current saturates.

Transconductance (g_m) characterises the device's current amplification capability and is represented by equation 1. In the case of the simulated gate-pocket overlapped TFET, g_m has been calculated at three distinct V_{gs} values, as depicted in Figure 5(a). The reciprocal of output resistance is referred to as g_{ds} [21,22]. g_m is influenced by the slope of I_d-V_{gs}, known as SS, which determines the device's switching speed. Achieving a high switching speed necessitates a high gm value. As the applied V_{gs} increases, the drain current rises, consequently augmenting g_m. Additionally, Figure 5(b) displays equation 2, elucidating the relationship between output conductance and V_{ds}.

$$g_m = \frac{\partial I_d}{\partial V_{gs}} \tag{1}$$

$$g_d = \frac{\partial I_d}{\partial V_{ds}} \tag{2}$$

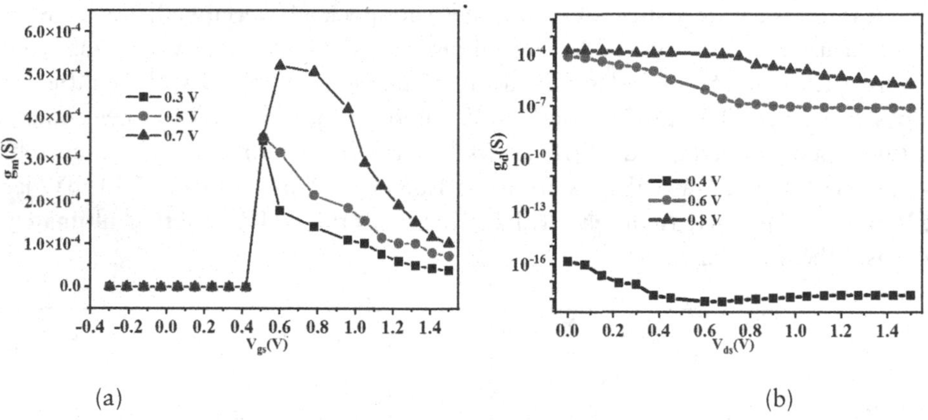

Figure 5: (a) g_m and (b) g_d of gate-pocket overlapped TFET.

The intrinsic voltage is defined as the ratio of g_m/g_d [22].

Figure 6 shows the results plotted for intrinsic voltage gain of gate-pocket overlapped TFET at 0.5 V of V_{ds}. The results clearly show that in the gate-pocket overlapped TFET, the gain value is very small, as the gate voltage initially remains low, it undergoes a sudden rise with increasing gate voltage.

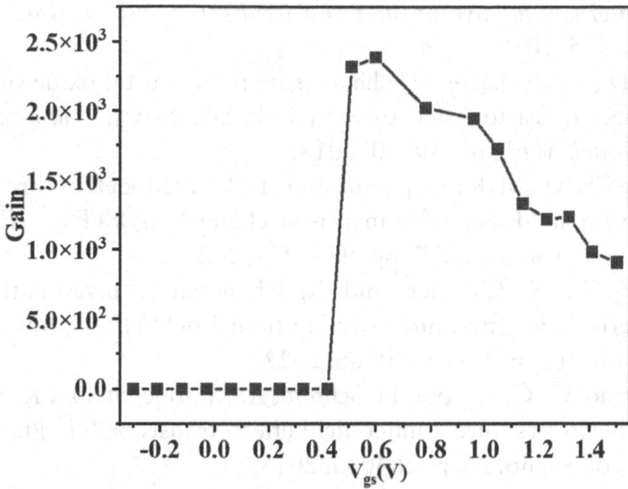

Figure 6: *Gain of gate-pocket overlapped TFET.*

5. Conclusion

A TCAD simulation study for hetero-junction gate-pocket overlapped TFET device has been performed. In the analysis, transfer, output characteristics, and AC analysis are reported. Based on the performance analysis of the device, it has been observed that the hetero-junction gate-pocket overlapped TFET shows remarkable performance in terms of current ratio and SS. The gate-pocket overlapping results in enhanced BTBT rate thus the current in the device increases upon activation of the device. The high value of current upon activation of the device leads to high value of transconductance that results in enhanced intrinsic voltage gain. Since the device shows steeper SS, it can be used for high switching internet of things (IoT) applications.

Acknowledgement

The authors are thankful to Department of ECE, Birla Institute of Technology (BIT), Mesra for the valuable support.

References

[1] Cardenas, J. A., J. B. Andrews, S. G. Noyce, and A. D. Franklin, "Carbon nanotube electronics for IoT sensors," *Nano Futures*, vol. 4, no. 1, p. 012001, 2020.

[2] Aditya, J., T. Nagateja, S. K. Vishvakarma, P. Yellappa, J. R. Choi, and R. Vaddi, "Tunneling field effect transistors for enhancing energy efficiency and hardware security of IoT platforms: challenges and Opportunities," *2018*

IEEE International Symposium on Circuits and Systems (ISCAS), Florence, Italy, pp. 1–5, 2018.

[3] Bharti, D., and A. Islam, "U-shaped gate trench metal oxide semiconductor field effect transistor: structures and characteristics," *Nanoscale Devices: Phys. Model. Appl.*, pp. 69–90, 2018.

[4] Nguyen-Gia, Q., M. Kang, J. Jeon, and H. Shin, "Models of threshold voltage and subthreshold slope for macaroni channel MOSFET," *IEEE Electron Device Lett.*, vol. 41, no. 7, pp. 973–976, 2020.

[5] Sinha, S. K., S. Chander, and R. Chaudhary, "Investigation of noise characteristics in gate-source overlap tunnel field-effect transistor," *Silicon*, vol. 14, no. 16, pp. 10661–10668, 2022.

[6] Convertino, C., C. B. Zota, H. Schmid, A. M. Ionescu, and K. E. Moselund, "III–V heterostructure tunnel field-effect transistor," J. Phys.: Condens. Matter, vol. 30, no. 26, p. 264005, 2018.

[7] Singh, A., S. K. Sinha, and S. Chander, "Simulation analysis of noise components in NCTFET with ferroelectric layer in gate stack," *Integr. Ferroelectr.,* vol. 231, no. 1, pp. 171–184, 2023.

[8] Anam, A., S. I. Amin, D. Prasad, N. Kumar, and S. Anand, "Undoped vertical dual-bilayer TFET with a super-steep sub-threshold swing: proposal and performance comparative analysis," *Semicond. Sci. Technol.*, vol. 38, no. 7, p. 075005, 2023.

[9] Chander, S., S. K. Sinha, R. Chaudhary, and R. Goswami, "Effect of noise components on L-shaped and T-shaped heterojunction tunnel field effect transistors," *Semicond. Sci. Technol.*, vol. 37, no. 7, p. 075011, 2022.

[10] Goswami, R. and B. Bhowmick, "Comparative analyses of circular gate TFET and heterojunction TFET for dielectric-modulated label-free biosensing," *IEEE Sens. J.*, vol. 19, no. 21, pp. 9600–9609, 2019.

[11] Kumar, R., B. A. Devi, V. Sireesha, A. K. Reddy, I. Hariharan, E. Konguvel, and N. A. Vignesh, "Analysis and design of novel doping free silicon nanotube TFET with high-density meshing using ML for sub nanometre technology nodes," *Silicon*, vol. 14, no. 17, pp. 11235–11242, 2022.

[12] Convertino, C., C. B. Zota, H. Schmid, A. M. Ionescu, and K. E. Moselund, "III–V heterostructure tunnel field-effect transistor," *J. Phys.: Condens. Matter*, vol. 30, no. 26, p. 264005, 2018.

[13] Tiwari, S. and R. Saha, "Methods to reduce ambipolar current of various TFET structures: a review," *Silicon*, vol. 14, no. 12, pp. 6507–6515, 2022.

[14] Blaeser, S., S. Glass, C. Schulte-Braucks, K. Narimani, N. V. D. Driesch, S. Wirths, and S. Mantl, "Novel SiGe/Si line tunneling TFET with high Ion at low VDD and constant SS," *2015 IEEE international electron devices meeting (IEDM) IEEE*, pp. 22–32, 2015.

[15] D. Sen, P. S. and S. K. Sarkar, "Analysis of dual metal gate engineered SiGe/Si TFET based biosensor: a dielectric modulation approach," *2021 Devices for Integrated Circuit (DevIC)*, Kalyani, India, 2021.

[16] Sedighi, B., X. S. Hu, H. Liu, J. J. Nahas, and M. Niemier, "Analog circuit design using tunnel-FETs," IEEE Trans. Circuits Syst., vol. 62, no. 1, pp. 39–48, 2015.

[17] Agopian, P. G. D., M. D. Martino, S. D. Dos Santos, F. S. Neves, J. A. Martino, R. Rooyackers, A. Vandooren, E. Simoen, A. V. Y. Thean, and C. Claeys, "Influence of the source composition on the analog performance parameters of vertical nanowire-TFETs," *IEEE Trans. Electron Devices*, vol. 62, no. 1, pp. 16–22, 2014.

[18] Kim, M. S., H. Liu, X. Li, S. Datta, and V. Narayanan, "A steepslope tunnel FET based SAR analog-to-digital converter," *IEEE Trans. Electron Devices*, vol. 61, no. 11, pp. 3661–3667, 2014.

[19] Sentaurus Device User Guide, Synopsys Inc.,Version D-2021.0.

[20] Chander, S., S. K. Sinha, R. Chaudhary, and A. Singh, "Ge-source based L-shaped tunnel field effect transistor for low power switching application," *Silicon*, pp. 1–14, 2021.

[21] Theja, A. and M. Panchore, "Performance investigation of GaSb/Si heterojunction-based gate underlap and overlap vertical TFET biosensor," *IEEE Trans. NanoBiosci.*, vol. 22, no. 2, pp. 284–291, 2023.

[22] Kumar, S. and D. S. Yadav, "Temperature analysis on electrostatics performance parameters of dual metal gate step channel TFET," *Appl. Phys. A*, vol. 127, no. 5, pp. 1–11, 2021.

72. A Comparative Study of Electric Vehicle Battery Live Monitoring and Scheduling

S. R. Deepu, Dr. N.Karthick, and U. Neethu

Lovely Professional University, School of Electronics & Electrical Engineering, Jalander, India

Abstract: In electric automobiles, battery management systems (BMS) track and monitor the charging and discharging of battery pack, allowing for more efficient operation. The battery management system maintains the battery safe and dependable as it develops senility without causing harm. Because of their excellent efficiency, batteries made with lithium-ion are frequently used. If these batteries are not utilised within their approved safety operation area, they can be harmful. As a result, every battery, particularly those used in automobiles, requires a BMS. This investigation aims to use an algorithm trained with machine learning to predict battery health in real time in order to improve the battery management system's performance and, as a result, extend battery life. To determine the battery's health status, three models are used. Best accurate model can be found by using random forest classifier, logistic regression and KNN, with KNN being combined with a machine learning algorithm to predict battery health.

Keywords: Electric vehicle, battery management system, safety operation area, random forest classifier, logistic regression and KNN algorithm.

1. Introduction

Electric mobility has emerged as a key component of the transportation sector's future. Early identification, prognosis and diagnosis of faults in electric drives improves electric vehicle (EV) reliability. To integrate safety components that lower the frequency of collisions and mortality on the roads, on-board electronics systems must perform well in all operational settings [1]. The efficacy of electric automobiles is influenced by the performance and diagnostics of battery storage systems, as well as a comprehensive study of essential factors. Electric automobiles have a limited range of travel due to battery size and construction.

The three sorts of traction batteries that are currently available are a lithium-i nickel-metal hydride and lead- acid. When utilised in conjunction with an effective battery management system, Li batteries provide a number of advantages versus both of the two types of batteries. In comparison to the other two battery kinds, Li batteries offer a lot of advantages, and they work well when paired with an effective battery management system.

2. Li-Ion Battery

Lithium-ion batteries, unlike conventional batteries, require virtually minimal maintenance during their lifetime. The battery does not need to be cycled on a regular basis. Furthermore, because Li batteries discharge by itself at a rate that is barely half that of lead-acid battery and NiMH battery packs, they are ideally suited for EVs.

Lithium-ion batteries, despite their benefits, have a number of downstairs. Ions of lithium are finicky. To make sure that these batteries operate safely, each pack needs to have a safety mechanism installed.

3. System for Managing Batteries

The technique for managing batteries is shown in Figure 1. A crucial part of the vehicle is the battery system for battery management, even though electric car batteries should not be overcharged or overdrained. If this happens, the battery will be damaged, the temperature will increase, the battery's life span will be reduced and the people who use it will be hurt. It may also be utilised to extend the range of a vehicle by successfully using the energy stored in it.

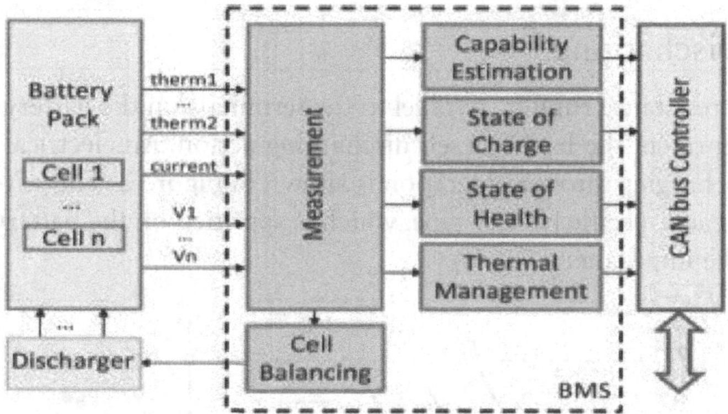

Figure 1: BMS block diagram.

To prevent battery failures, many types of battery management systems (BMSs) are employed. For instance, a battery tracking device logs crucial operating data during charging and discharging, including electrical current, voltage, internal battery temperature and outside temperature. If any of the parameters go above the safety zone values, the system sends signals to the safety equipment, which can warn the user or unplug the battery from the power supply or charging.

4. Li-Ion Battery Management

Electric cars have the potential to assist both the economy and the ecology throughout the world. To improve their performance over time, EV systems, particularly the ESS in the car's ability to operate safely, which is essential, must be regularly maintained. All charging and discharging operations are managed by the system for managing batteries in automobiles, along with batteries voltage per cell tracking and adjusting, charge cell equalisation, input as well as output voltage and current monitoring, regulation of temperature, battery security and failure identification and assessment.

5. SoC Determination

The amount of battery that is on hand, expressed as a percentage of the cell's nominal capacity, is known as the SoC. The system for managing batteries uses the SoC to assess the battery's health, allowing it to operate within a safe operating range by managing charging and discharging. It also helps to lengthen the battery's life. Directly estimating the status of charge is impossible.

6. Model on Battery

It is crucial to create models that accurately replicate the charging and draining behaviour of battery packs, which is governed by factors including temperature, discharge from oneself amount and capacity.

7. Self-Discharging

A significant resistance running parallel to the terminals on the battery can be used to visually represent the battery's self-discharging action. An electrical system that takes self-discharging into consideration is shown in Figure 2. The self-discharging duration for each specific battery type, which is specified on the battery data sheet, determines the impedance.

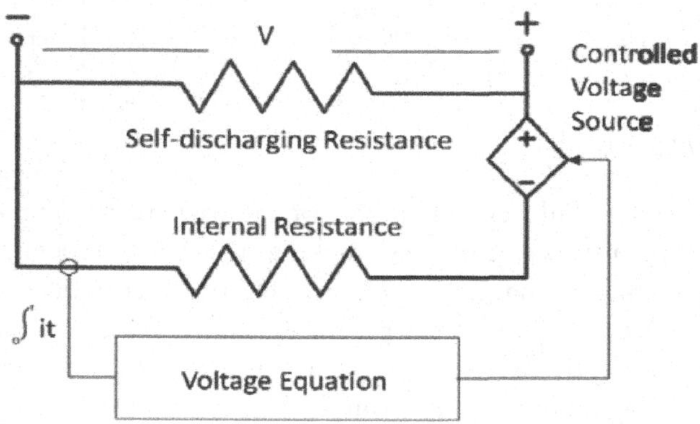

Figure 2: Self-discharging of battery.

Open circuit voltage,

$$V = E - (R + R_T)i \tag{1}$$

8. Temperature Effect

Temperature and humidity have been shown to have an impact on battery performance. When the ambient temperature rises over the recommended operating range, batteries fail to perform as expected. This is due to the harsh weather has nothing to do with the product. As a result, a battery is not meant to be utilised in a situation where it was improperly designed.

Severe weather might arise if a certain environment's ambient temperature and relative humidity are altered beyond the norm. These issues may attack almost anywhere and at any time. On a hot day, severe circumstances might take place outdoor, in a building without climate control, either in a locked automobile. In extreme instances, the battery could malfunction, swell, bubble, melt, get impaired, generate smoke, ignitions and blazes, grows, contract or even detonate as a result of extreme weather.

Extreme weather could happen when humidity in the air causes the overall temperature to rise above the battery's allowed working range. Temperature has an effect on how batteries function due changes in temperature cause, and electrons become more or less energetic.

9. Effect on Fading Capacity

Because the ability of lithium-ion batteries to store a charge declines with time and is irreversible, they are known to have a limited lifespan. As the capacity of a battery declines the run time, commonly referred to as the amount of time a device may be powered, gets shorter. The battery's performance as a whole degrades if the entire system cycles through numerous charges as well as discharges.

A Li battery typically lasts between two and three years, or 300 and 500 charge cycles. It is vital to know the battery's present health and remaining lifespan in high-performance applications like electric cars.

10. Hardware on BMS

The BMS design may be as straightforward as an application-specific integrated circuit (ASIC) that manages all BMS operations for small applications that use batteries made from Li ion, such as laptop computers. These processors have two restrictions in terms of huge lithium-ion battery packs. The first drawback is that these chips are not made to handle high currents, which are often felt by a Hall-effect sensors via a current shunted in large packs, but rather low currents, which are frequently monitored by a PCB-mounted resistance. Without knowing the battery's current, the processors' superior intelligence would be pointless. These chips can only process a limited amount of cells, which is the second restriction. Rather than BMSs built for small batteries, electric cars should use BMSs developed for large batteries.

11. Analysis and Discussions

Li battery are used in electric automobiles to store power in a group of battery cells that are connected in series as seen in Figure 3. The EV cells can be stored and drained from an external source to power the EV driving motor and systems. Due to modifications in their physical properties, a subsequent charging-discharge cycle may cause an electrical discharge and energy discrepancy amid the cells of a battery. Concerns about production, temperature and cell degeneration are the root of this disparity. The overall effectiveness and durability of devices that store energy can be impacted by unbalanced volt and load patterns. Undercharging can limit the life of the battery and damage its chemical properties, while overcharging has the potential to produce cell outbursts.

The monitoring system may stop charge and draining a battery when its working range is reached. As an outcome, the pack of batteries can lose its rated charge level, which is necessary for operation. The series linked battery pack's charge equalisation controller is therefore crucial for protecting the battery cells while also preserving storage capacity and operational ratings.

The most reactive, lightest and energy-dense batteries are lithium-ion batteries. Traditional batteries take significantly longer to charge and drain than lithium-ion batteries. The risk of a series of chemical processes, an increase in temperature, cell exhausting and fire increases when Li batteries are run above their safe functioning voltage level. As a result, a system to manage batteries is used, enabling management of the battery.

Figure 3 depicts the lithium-ion battery's discharge voltage; when a load is added, the battery runs in the safe zone, extending the battery's lifespan.

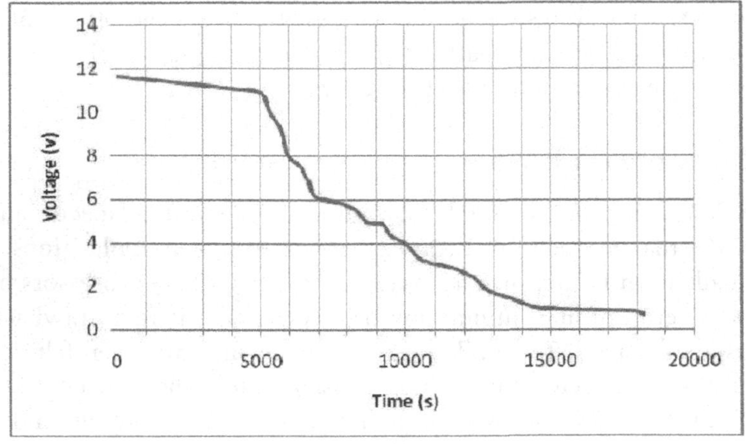

Figure 3: Discharging of lithium-ion battery.

```
import numpy as np
import pandas as pd
import matplotlib.pyplot as plt
get_ipython().run_line_magic('matplotlib', 'inline')
import seaborn as sns
import warnings
warnings.filterwarnings('ignore')

df =pd.read_csv('Battery AI.csv')
df.head()

df.info()
df.shape
df.isnull().sum()

df['Energy Consumption  '].value_counts()
df['Energy Consumption  '].replace('Battery unhealthy ',0,inplace=True)
df['Energy Consumption  '].replace('Battery_healthy',1,inplace=True)
df['Energy Consumption  '].replace('Battery healthy ',1,inplace=True)
df['Energy Consumption  '].value_counts()
plt.figure(figsize = (50,25))
sns.set(font_scale = 5)
plt.subplot(331)
sns.countplot(df['Energy Consumption  '])
from sklearn.model_selection import train_test_split
from sklearn import metrics
X = df.iloc[1:200,1:3].values
y = df.iloc[1:200,3].values
X_train, X_test, y_train, y_test = train_test_split(X, y, test_size=0.3,random_state=2)
from sklearn.linear_model import LogisticRegression
model = LogisticRegression()
model.fit(X_train,y_train)
prediction = model.predict(X_test)
print('Logistic Regression accuracy = ', metrics.accuracy_score(prediction,y_test))

from sklearn.ensemble import RandomForestClassifier
clf = RandomForestClassifier()
clf = clf.fit(X_train,y_train)
prediction = clf.predict(X_test)
print('RandomForestClassifier accuracy = ', metrics.accuracy_score(prediction,y_test))
prediction = model.predict(X_test)
print('Knn accuracy = ', metrics.accuracy_score(prediction,y_test))

result = prediction[0]
if (result ==0):
    print("Battery unhealthy")
else:
    print("Battery_healthy")
```

Figure 4: Machine learning algorithm to estimate battery health condition.

Figure 4 depicts the software for predicting battery health. Three models are utilised to determine the battery's health state in order to increase the battery's performance. Random forest classifier, logistic regression and KNN are among the models used to discover the most accurate model, with KNN being used to forecast battery health using artificial intelligence method. This results in an increase in battery life.

12. Conclusions

The battery management mechanism in electric cars is thoroughly explained in this study. The main parameters of the battery are all controlled. In terms of battery reliability and safety, the BMS must be properly maintained. The state of charge is calculated utilising a deep convolution approach, which increases the EV's range of travel and improves system performance. Three models are utilised to determine the battery's health state in order to increase the battery's performance. To select the most correct model, Random forest classifier, logistic regression and KNN are employed. KNN with machine learning method is used to forecast battery health state. The battery's life is extended as a result of this. Furthermore, the objective of reducing greenhouse gas emissions may be significantly achieved by utilising a battery management system.

References

[1] Aiello, O.. "Electromagnetic susceptibility of battery management systems' ICs for electric vehicles: experimental study," *Electronics*, vol. 9, no. 3, p. 510, 2020.

[2] Lipu, M. S. H., *et al.*, "Intelligent algorithms and control strategies for battery management system in electric vehicles: progress, challenges and future outlook," *J. Cleaner Prod.*, p. 126044, 2021.

[3] Wahab, A., M. Helmy, *et al.*, "IoT-based battery monitoring system for electric vehicle," Int. J. Eng. Technol., vol. 7.4, no. 31, pp. 505–510, 2018.

[4] Caliwag, A., *et al.*, "Design of modular battery management system with point-topoint SoC estimation algorithm," *2020 International Conference on Artificial Intelligence in Information and Communication (ICAIIC)*, 2020.

[5] Heydari, S., *et al.*, "Maximizing regenerative braking energy recovery of electric vehicles through dynamic low-speed cutoff point detection," *IEEE Trans. Transp. Electrif.*, vol. 5, no. 1, pp. 262–270, 2019.

[6] Din, E., M. Shehab, A. A. Hussein, and M. F. Abdel-Hafez, "Improved battery SOC estimation accuracy using a modified UKF with an adaptive cell model under real EV operating conditions," *IEEE Trans. Transp. Electrif.*, vol. 4, no. 2, pp. 408–417, 2018.

[7] Sivaraman, P. and C. Sharmeela, "IoT based battery management system for hybrid electric vehicle," *Artif. Intell. Tech. Electr. Hybrid Electr. Veh.*, pp. 1–16, 2020.

[8] Wang, W., *et al.*, "Unscented Kalman filter-based battery SOC estimation and peak power prediction method for power distribution of hybrid electric vehicles," *IEEE Access*, vol. 6, pp. 35957–35965, 2018.

[9] Chandran, V., *et al.*, "State of charge estimation of lithium-ion battery for electric vehicles using machine learning algorithms," *World Electr. Veh. J.*, vol. 12, no. 1, p. 38, 2021.

[10] Wei, C., M. Benosman, and T. Kim, "Online parameter identification for state of power prediction of lithium-ion batteries in electric vehicles using extremum seeking," *Int. J. Control Autom. Syst.*, vol. 17, no. 11, pp. 2906–2916, 23, 2019.

[11] Martinez, D. A., J. D. Poveda, and D. Montenegro, "Li-ion battery management system based in fuzzy logic for improving electric vehicle autonomy," *2017 IEEE Workshop on Power Electronics and Power Quality Applications (PEPQA)*, 2017.

[12] Florea, B. C. and D. D. Taralunga, "Blockchain IoT for smart electric vehicles battery management," *Sustainability* 12, no. 10, p. 3984, 2020.

73. Efficient Speed Control Tracking for Electric Vehicle Using Artificial Intelligence: A Comparative Study

U. Neethu, N. Karthick, and S. R. Deepu

Lovely Professional University, School of Electronics & Electrical Engineering, Jalander, India

Abstract: Currently, traditional automobile emissions play a key role in the escalating environmental problems. Furthermore, considering the environmental disaster and low energy efficiency of traditional automobiles, producing electric vehicles (EVs) is a realistic solution. Several problems have led to an increase in the popularity of EVs, for economic savings, climate change and environmental awareness. Because of their better performance, economy and absence of carbon emissions, EVs have surged in popularity. This work presents an efficient controller for EV current tracking control for brushless DC motor. This research provides a brushless DC motor control strategy that combines a neural network, fuzzy controller and PI-controller. A quasi-square approach is used to regulate the current. The suggested neural network's performance is evaluated against that of the corresponding fuzzy P-I controller and traditional P-I controller. The main efficient way to regulate is a neural network control, which improves the system even more and is far superior to other controllers. System modelling and controller design are done using MATLAB.

Keywords: Neural network, fuzzy-logic controller, PI controller, electric vehicle

1. Introduction:

Due to the increasing demand for technological advancement, renewable resources and rigorous environmental norms and regulations, scientific and technological trends in battery-powered vehicles are increasingly recognizing relevance in the battery powered vehicle industries. For electric vehicle (EV) technology to evolve quickly, an effective motor with creative control methods is projected to be needed. The actuator system's dependability and durability have a significant impact on the overall efficacy of an EV system basically, simply two dc motor designs used in trade. The first type of motor produces flux via passing current across the field coil of a stationary pole arrangement. The brushless DC (BLDC) motor, on the other hand, generates the requisite air gap flux using a permanent magnet rather than wire-wound field poles.

Electric cars employ a range of controllers, including PI, fuzzy logical controllers and artificial intelligence, to manage their speed. Due to its improved performance characteristics, such as an inability to respond over system disruption and parameter fluctuations, the neural network system has supplanted conventional PI as the norm for the controller. In industrial control applications, it also helps to enhance rejection of disruptions control while lowering control effort as well as energy loss. We propose a current control technique for a BLDC motor arrangement that requires just one regulator for each of the three phases, as opposed to conventional controllers.

2. BLDC Motor Mathematical Model

EV dynamics may be divided into two categories, as depict in Figure 1. The engine's gearbox unit, which includes the mechanism for gearing, connects all of these variables. [1, 7].

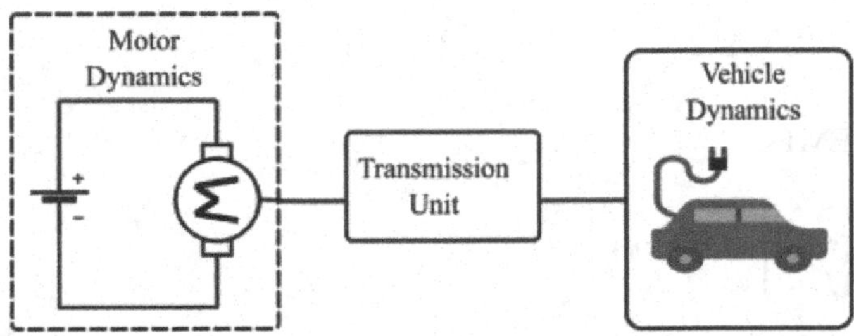

Figure 1: Functionality of supply chain management.

$$\begin{bmatrix} V_a \\ V_b \\ V_c \end{bmatrix} = \begin{bmatrix} R_a & 0 & 0 \\ 0 & R_b & 0 \\ 0 & 0 & R_c \end{bmatrix} \begin{bmatrix} i_a \\ i_b \\ i_c \end{bmatrix} + p \begin{bmatrix} L_a & L_{ba} & L_{ca} \\ L_{ba} & L_b & L_{cb} \\ L_{ca} & L_{cb} & L_c \end{bmatrix} \begin{bmatrix} i_a \\ i_b \\ i_c \end{bmatrix} + \begin{bmatrix} e_a \\ e_b \\ e_c \end{bmatrix} \quad (1)$$

$$L_a = L_b = L_c = L$$
$$L_{ab} = L_{ca} = L_{cb} = M$$

Hence,

$$\begin{bmatrix} V_a \\ V_b \\ V_c \end{bmatrix} = \begin{bmatrix} R & 0 & 0 \\ 0 & R & 0 \\ 0 & 0 & R \end{bmatrix} \begin{bmatrix} i_a \\ i_b \\ i_c \end{bmatrix} + \begin{bmatrix} L & M & M \\ M & L & M \\ M & M & L \end{bmatrix} p \begin{bmatrix} i_a \\ i_b \\ i_c \end{bmatrix} + \begin{bmatrix} e_a \\ e_b \\ e_c \end{bmatrix} \quad (2)$$

But

$$i_a + i_b + i_c = 0 \quad (3)$$

Therefore,

$$Mi_b + Mi_c = -Mi_a \tag{4}$$

Hence

$$\begin{bmatrix} V_a \\ V_b \\ V_c \end{bmatrix} = \begin{bmatrix} R & 0 & 0 \\ 0 & R & 0 \\ 0 & 0 & R \end{bmatrix} \begin{bmatrix} i_a \\ i_b \\ i_c \end{bmatrix} + \begin{bmatrix} L-M & 0 & 0 \\ 0 & L-M & 0 \\ 0 & 0 & L-M \end{bmatrix} p \begin{bmatrix} i_a \\ i_b \\ i_c \end{bmatrix} + \begin{bmatrix} e_a \\ e_b \\ e_c \end{bmatrix} \tag{5}$$

On rearranging

$$p \begin{bmatrix} i_a \\ i_b \\ i_c \end{bmatrix} = \begin{bmatrix} 1/_{L-M} & 0 & 0 \\ 0 & 1/_{L-M} & 0 \\ 0 & 0 & 1/_{L-M} \end{bmatrix} \left[\begin{bmatrix} V_a \\ V_c \\ V_c \end{bmatrix} - \begin{bmatrix} R & 0 & 0 \\ 0 & R & 0 \\ 0 & 0 & R \end{bmatrix} \begin{bmatrix} i_a \\ i_b \\ i_c \end{bmatrix} - \begin{bmatrix} e_a \\ e_b \\ e_c \end{bmatrix} \right] \tag{6}$$

Electromagnetic torue is

$$T_e = \frac{(e_a i_a + e_b i_b + e_c i_c)}{\omega_r} \tag{7}$$

Motion Equation is

$$\rho\omega_r = \frac{(T_e - T_L - B\omega_r}{J} \tag{8}$$

Phase back-EMFs,

$$\begin{bmatrix} e_a \\ e_b \\ e_c \end{bmatrix} = E \begin{bmatrix} f_a(\theta) \\ f_b(\theta) \\ f_c(\theta) \end{bmatrix} . (E = k_e \omega_r) \tag{9}$$

Trapezoidal function,

$$f_s(\theta) = \begin{cases} (6/_\pi)\theta & (0 < \theta \leq \pi/_6) \\ 1 & (\pi/_6 < \theta \leq 5\pi/_6) \\ -(6/_\pi)\theta + 6 & (5\pi/_6 < \theta \leq 7\pi/_6 \\ -1 & (7\pi/_6 < \theta \leq 11\pi/_6) \\ (6/_\pi)\theta + 12 & (11\pi/_6 < \theta \leq 2\pi) \end{cases} \tag{10}$$

3. Strategy for EV Speed Control

As people's environmental awareness develops, they are becoming increasingly aware of zero-polluting EVs. The dynamic system of an EV includes a storage battery and an electromotor. EVs employ a variety of motors, including DC, AC and reluctance motors. BLDCMs (brushless dc motors) are very efficient and have good timing. It also has a straightforward structure, a high level of reliability and is easy to maintain. As a result, it is commonly utilised. In BLDCM, electronic commutation replaces mechanical commutation. A high-power switch transistor serves as the electronic commutator. The controller tries to handle the car's speed and power flows as effectively as possible. As a result, the controller must be able to track the target speed of the vehicle. A microprocessor-based controller and a three-phase inverter are part of the motor driving control system.

4. Strategy for EV Speed Control Proposed

Figure 2 shows the suggested approach as an easily understood component layout. Figure 3 displays an especially contemporary controller architecture model. A BLDC motor's armature currents have a quasi-square waveform. Armature currents are detected by current sensors, which are subsequently converted into voltage signals. Following signal correction, a DC component with an ideal current Imax is produced. The error signal Ierr is then linked with the needed reference current Iref, resulting in pulse width modulation pulse in each of the six inverter switches. Torque has a direct relationship with Iref. One DC signal must be regulated by the control unit, as opposed to three alternate waveforms. Figure 3 [1] shows the various controllers that were utilised.

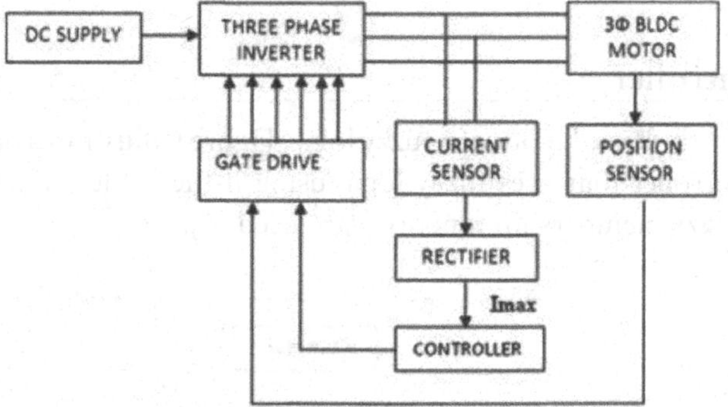

Figure 2: Arrangement of BLDC drive.

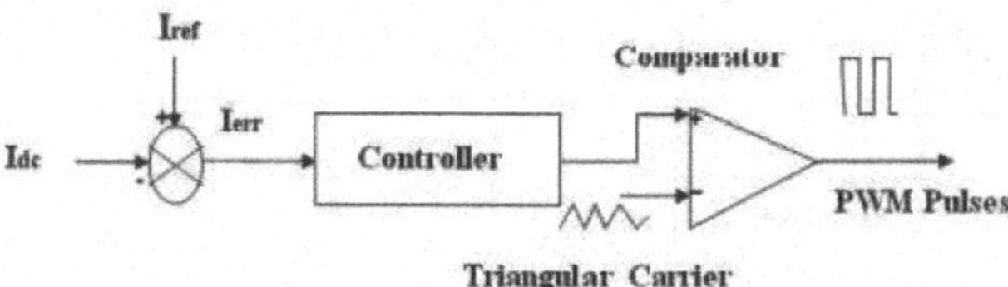

Figure 3: I controller.

5. PI Controller

Figure 4 displays the proportional-integral (PI) controller's block layout. While the proportional correlates to the proportional of the erroneous signal, and vice versa. Proportionate action increases the gain of the loop, making its components more resistant towards disturbances. [1]. The stable state inaccuracy is eliminated by the integral process and is modifiable by adjusting the time.

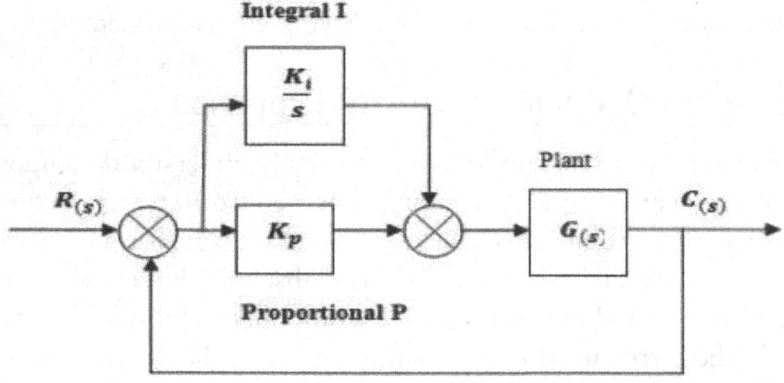

Figure 4: Proportional-I controller.

Tf is,

$$C(s) = K_p + {}^{K_i}/_{s} \tag{11}$$

6. FL Controller

Figure 5 exhibits the basic layout of a fuzzy logic. Figure 6 illustrates the fundamental design of a controller that uses fuzzy logic using if-then rules. When determining the value set, fuzzy membership functions are used [6].

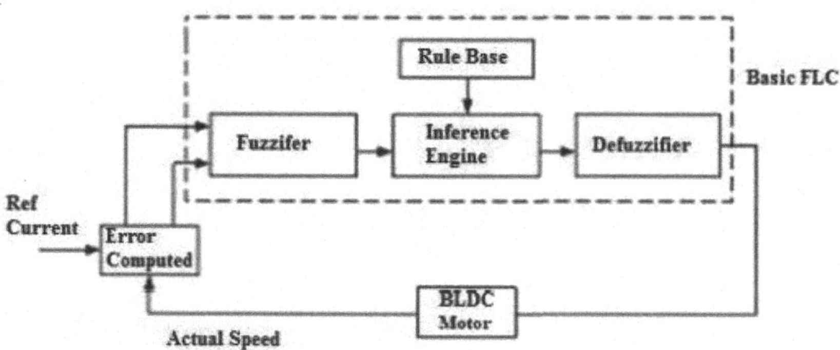

Figure 5: Controller based on fuzzy logic.

7. Neural Network Controller

The simple fuzzy controller is a good nonlinear controller, but it is unable to change its structure as circumstances need. The neural networks, on the other hand, are particularly good at adapting to circumstances by changing their weights appropriately. The control algorithm can be implemented more quickly because to the parallel design. The employed neural network's structure is depicted in Figure 6.

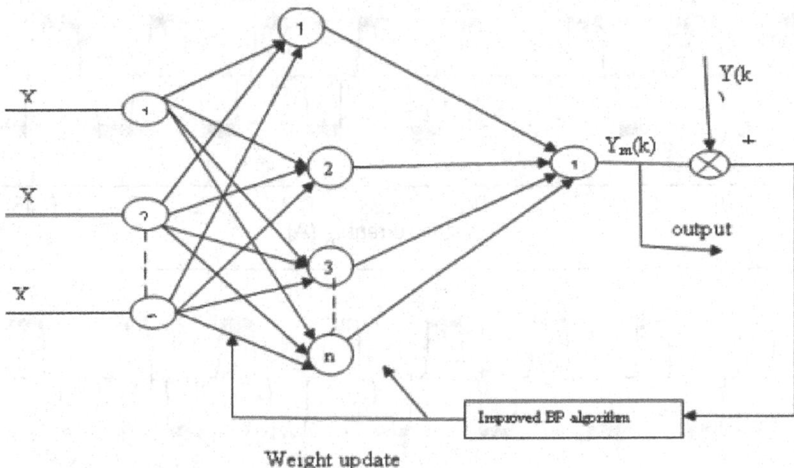

Figure 6: Neural network structure.

8. Analysis and Discussions

Figures 7 and 8 depict the SIMULINK/MATLAB model of a BLDC motor used in an EV and the stator current waveform, respectively.

In this study of BLDC motor, method known as current-controlled technique for automobile is proposed. All three phases are controlled by a single controller. In order to analyze performance, different controllers are employed.

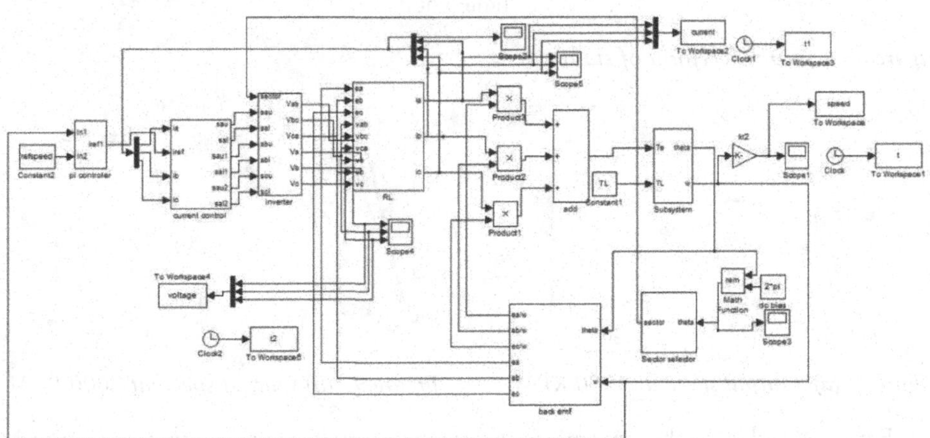

Figure 7: Electric car BLDC engine driving simulation in simulink.

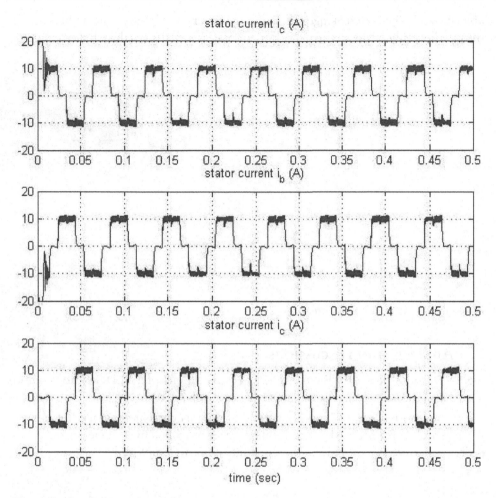

Figure 8: Current waveform of stator.

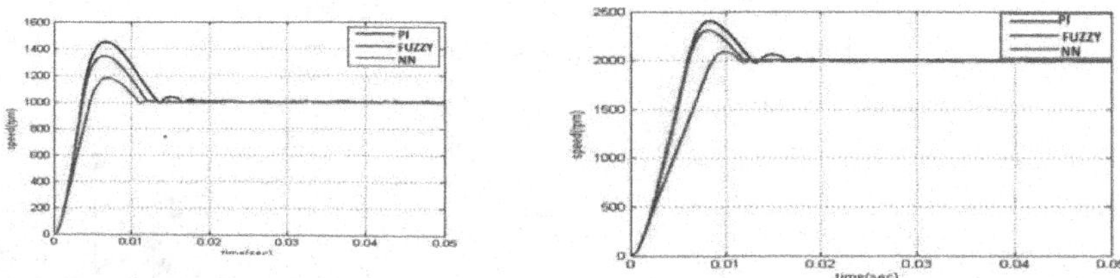

Figure 9: (a) Output speed at 1000 RPM. *Figure 9: (b) Output speed at 2000 RPM.*

Figure 9(a) depicts the system's performance using PI, fuzzy and neural network. Figure 9(b) depicts the system's performance using PI, fuzzy and neural network.

Table 1 compares the performance of various controllers working during loaded settings at varying speeds.

Table1:

Speed (rpm)	PI Controller		FUZZY Logic Controller		Neural Network	
	% Mp	t_s (ms)	% Mp	t_s (ms)	% Mp	t_s (ms)
1000	45	19.2	43	15.29	38	14.09
2000	20.15	19.67	19.2	15.48	17.05	14.06
3000	6.07	19.76	5.60	15.72	4.77	14.1
4000	1.93	20.58	1.63	17.38	0.77	15

9. Conclusions

This study delves into the controllers that govern the current of BLDC motors, as well as the speed of BLDC-type motors speed in electric cars. To manage the motor speed in an electric car, just one controller is used. Utilizing various controllers, the efficiency of the suggested strategy is assessed. According to numerous simulations, efficient tracking of speed controller using artificial intelligence is performed better comparing to other conventional controllers.

References

[1] Neethu, U. and V. R. Jisha. "Speed control of Brushless DC Motor: A comparative study," *2012 IEEE International Conference on Power Electronics Drives and Energy Systems (PEDES)*, 2012.

[2] Neethu U., N. Karthick, S. Dasgupta, and S. R. Deepu, "Current control of brushless DC motor using common DC signal for electric vehicle," *International Conference on Energy and Environment, AIP Conference Proceedings*, 020013-1-020013-11, 2021.

[3] Karthikeyan, J. and R. Dhana Sekaran, "Current control of brushless DC motor based on a common DC signal for space operated vehicles," *Automatica*, vol. 3, pp. 1721–1727, 2017.

[4] Pillay, P. and R. Krishnan, "Modeling, simulation and analysis of permanent-magnet motor drives part II: the brushless DC motor drive," *IEEE Trans. Ind. Appl.*, vol. 25, pp. 274-279, 1989.

[5] Chen, J. and P.-C. Tang, "A sliding mode current control Scheme for PWM brushless DC motor drives," *IEEE Trans. Power Electron.*, vol. 14, no. 3, pp. 541–551, 1999.

[6] Chan, C. C. and Chau, "An overview of power electronics in electric vehicles," *IEEE Trans. Power Electron.*, vol. 44, pp. 3–13, 1997.

[7] a) Malesani, L. and P. Tenti, "A novel hysteresis control of current controlled VSI PWM inverters with constant modulation frequency," *IEEE Trans. Ind. Appl.*, vol. 26, pp. 88–93, 1990; b) Le-Huy, H. and L. A. Dessiant, "An adaptive current control scheme for PWM synchronous motor drives: analysis and simulation," *IEEE Trans. Power Electron.*, vol. 4, pp. 486–495, 1989.

74. Comparative Analysis of Correlation Tracking Algorithms for Real-Time Video Object Tracking

Jyoti Ramola,[1] Mohit Payal,[1] Manoj Singh Adhikari,[2] and Vibhor Sharma[3]

[1]*Graphic Era Hill University, Dehradun, India*

[2]*School of Electronics and Electrical Engineering, Lovely Professional University, Punjab, India*

[3]*Himalayan School of Science and Technology, Swami Rama Himalayan University, Dehradun, India*

Abstract: In the domain of video tracking, the core objective is the spatial localisation of dynamic objects across successive frames in a video stream. To achieve this, specialised tracking algorithms are meticulously designed and implemented. Our research work revolves around empirical assessments grounded in experimental data acquired through the application of these correlation-based tracking algorithms. We utilise similarity measures profiles to gauge and compare their respective performance. In this research paper, we have conducted a comprehensive examination of several correlation-based tracking algorithms, namely, mean absolute difference (MAD), sum squared difference (SSD), normalized cross correlation (NCC) and sum absolute difference (SAD). Our objective is to evaluate the suitability and performance of correlation algorithms in real-time tracking of dynamic video sequences. After an in-depth analysis, we find that NCC and SSD offer nearly identical, top-notch tracking accuracy, but their computational demands limit their suitability for resource-constrained embedded systems. In contrast, SAD and MAD provide efficient alternatives with acceptable performance. Ultimately, the choice of tracking algorithm should align with specific demands of the application. In future research, we should aim to optimise correlation tracking algorithms to make them faster and still accurate for real-time and resource-limited applications. We can explore using machine learning, like deep learning, to improve feature extraction and adaptability in different tracking situations.

Keywords: Tracking algorithms, MATLAB, MAD, SAD, SSD and NCC.

1. Introduction

Video tracking stands as a pivotal process in contemporary technology, enabling the precise localisation of one or more moving objects across successive frames of video. Cameras are commonly employed to capture video data, and video tracking forms the backbone of numerous applications, such as video production, video surveillance, robotics, medical, security applications and interactive gaming. In our increasingly digital and interconnected world, the influence of video tracking is pervasive and transformative. For all these applications, various object tracking algorithms are developing day by day. While various object tracking algorithms continue to evolve, this paper focuses on correlation tracking. Historically, video tracking has evolved from basic methods like edge detection and centroid tracking to more sophisticated techniques based on pattern matching and feature extraction. These developments have been driven by the increasing demand for accurate and robust tracking in various applications. Previous studies have extensively investigated the strengths and weaknesses of different tracking algorithms. Edge tracking, for instance, is effective in certain scenarios but struggles with occlusion and cluttered backgrounds. Centroid tracking is computationally efficient but may not provide the level of detail needed in complex tracking tasks. Correlation-based tracking methods, such as mean absolute difference (MAD), sum absolute difference (SAD), sum squared difference (SSD) and normalized cross correlation (NCC), have gained prominence in recent research. These methods offer advantages in terms of accuracy and noise robustness, making them suitable for various real-world applications. We opt for correlation tracking over edge and centroid tracking for two primary reasons. The purpose of selecting correlation tracking over the edge and centroid tracking is: First, these algorithms enable the tracking of a specific characteristic or target within a set of targets. And second, when several frames are processed and summed together, then the effect of random noise is minimised [1–10].

2. Correlation Tracking

The positional difference between a reference picture including the target along with search region containing the target is measured using correlation algorithms. This is accomplished by selecting a square (track) window around the reference picture that is a specific size and then locating the linked pixel inside of the search region. This best match position is assumed to be the position of the reference image within the track window. So, the reference image can be tracked as it moves within the track window and hence within the whole image.

Various correlation tracking algorithms. The most commonly tracking algorithms are

a) Mean absolute difference
b) Sum absolute difference

c) Sum squared difference
d) Normalised cross correlation

The simplest similarity metric for MAD and SAD is the sum of absolute differences inside a square window after deleting pixels from a square neighbourhood between the target picture and the search area image. Smaller the value returned by the SAD and MAD, means more similarities between two blocks. SSD and NCC are the other functions used to estimate the similarity between the two blocks. In NCC maximum value is selected. The complexity of these algorithms increases with the complexity of correlation functions. So, due to less complexity of SAD and MAD, they can be easily implemented in VLSI design.

2.1. Mean Absolute Difference

This method determines the absolute difference between every pixel in the target picture block and its matching pixel in the search area block. These variations are summed, and mean is calculated and then the minimum value of mean is selected. These positional coordinates of minimum value are selected for the next frame.
The MAD algorithm's measuring function is specified by [3]:

$$D(a,b)=\frac{1}{u.v}\sum_{i=0}^{u-1}\sum_{j=0}^{v-1}\left| f(i+a,j+b)-t(i,j)\right| \tag{1}$$

where f (i, j) = image that corresponds to UxV's size, t (i, j) = target that size is uxv (u≤U,v≤V), (p,q) = position of the matching point, f (i+a, j+b) = symbol for a subgraph of (a,b) in the image.

The difference between the subgraph's value and the target is the D(a,b) result; the lower the value, better the match. In order to locate tracking points, as indicated by the formula (i), the MAD algorithm determines the correlation value between the target image and the image region of each location point in the search area.

2.2. Sum Absolute Difference

It is one of the simplest algorithms. This algorithm is same as MAD, except the mean calculation. SAD may be used for a variety of purposes, such as recognition and motion for video compression.
The mathematical expression for SAD is [4]:

$$D(a,b)=\sum_{i=0}^{u-1}\sum_{j=0}^{v-1}\left| f(i+a,j+b)-t(i,j)\right| \tag{2}$$

2.3. Sum of Squared Differences

In this, SSD squares the discrepancies before choosing the smallest squared difference value. Because many multiplication operations are required, this measure has a larger computational complexity than the SAD and MAD algorithms. The mathematical expression for SSD is

$$D(a,b)=\sum_{i=0}^{u-1}\sum_{j=0}^{v-1}\left| f(i+a,j+b)^2-t(i,j)^2\right| \tag{3}$$

where the result of the *D(a,b)* is sum of a difference of square values of subgraph and the target. Same as MAD and SAD smaller value of difference is selected.

2.4. Normalised Cross Correlation

The SSD method is expanded upon by the NCC algorithm. Due of the numerous multiplication, division and square root operations involved in NCC, it is much more complicated than the SAD, MAD and SSD algorithms. [5], [6]

In NCC algorithm, at the time of target matching, it is necessary to compute the correlation coefficient between the target image and any matched locations. The entire image is then divided into appropriate surfaces. The peak of the pertinent surface determines the optimal match position.
The mathematical expression for NCC is

$$R(c,d)=\frac{\sum_{u1=1}^{U1}\sum_{v1=1}^{V1} S^{cd}(u,v)\times T(u,v)}{\sqrt{\sum_{u=1}^{U}\sum_{v=1}^{V}[S^{cd}(u,v)]^2}\sqrt{\sum_{u=1}^{U}\sum_{v=1}^{V}[T(u,v)]^2}} \tag{4}$$

where *R(c,d)* is the similarity measurement or normalised cross-correlation coefficient. *T* denotes the target image (*u* x *v is size)* and *S* denotes the sub image of scene images (u x *v is size*). When *T* and *S* are similar, the value of *R(a,b)* is large.

3. Experimental Results

In this study, we analysed a video containing footage of two individuals running, comprising a total of 4738 frames. Various correlation algorithms were employed to track the target, with the target manually selected for each experiment.

Figure 1: *Frame 10.*

Figure 2: Target (manual selection).

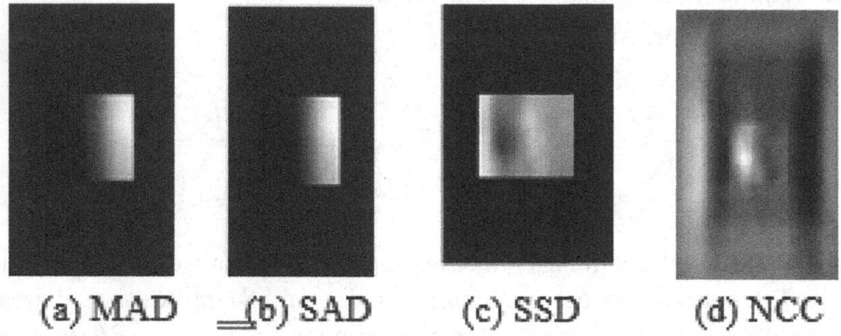

Figure 3: Similarity measures of different correlation algorithms when search area width is 10 (for frame 10).

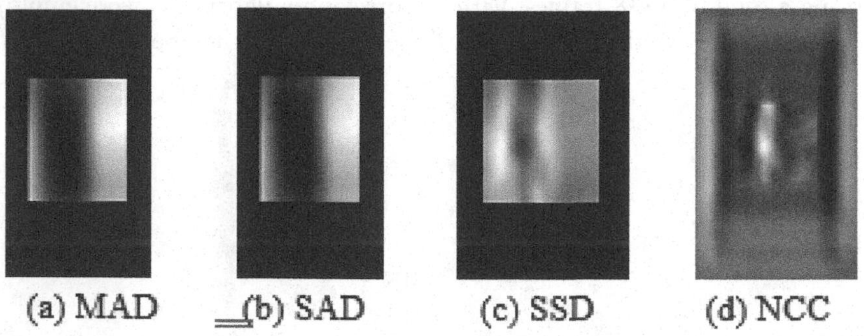

Figure 4: Similarity measures of different correlation algorithms. when search area width is 25 (for frame 10)

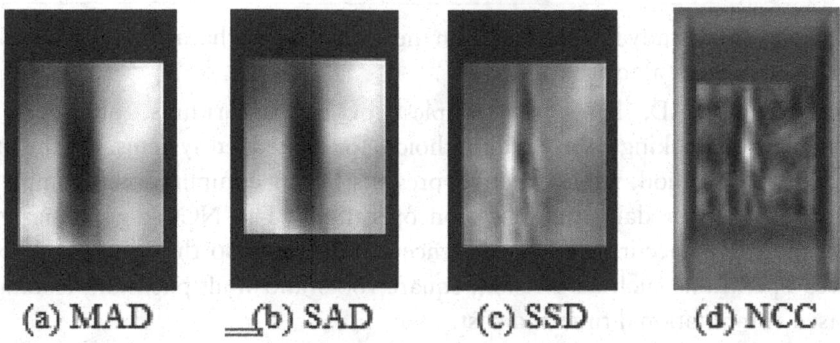

Figure 5: Similarity measures of different correlation algorithms when search area width is 50 (for frame 10).

Figure 1 and 2 shows the target frame 10 and manually selected target. The comparative results of the different correlation algorithms are presented in Figures 3, 4 and 5. In the cases of MAD, SAD and SSD, areas of similarity are represented by darker regions, while NCC highlights similarity with brighter areas. Notably, the results indicate that SAD and MAD deliver superior performance when applied to larger search area widths (window sizes). Conversely, NCC and SSD exhibit optimal performance when dealing with smaller search area widths. Figure 6 further illustrates the similarity between SSD and NCC, with matching regions highlighted in red rectile.

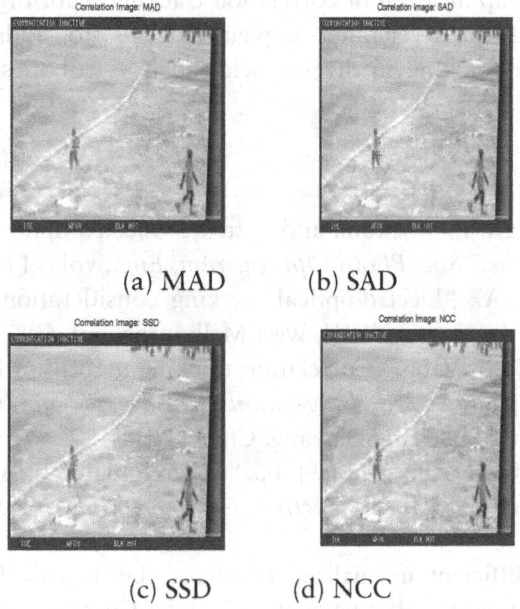

Figure 6: Tracking results of various correlation algorithms for 10th frame.

5. Conclusion

In conclusion, our study has shed light on the performance characteristics of various correlation tracking algorithms:

SAD and MAD, being the simplest of the algorithms, offer ease of implementation, making them suitable choices for embedded systems. On the other hand, the SSD method, while effective, presents higher computational complexity due to the need for data multiplication operations. The NCC algorithm, while robust and highly accurate in the presence of noise, is also the most complex. It involves operations such as division, square roots and multiplication, leading to increased computational time and cost.

In choosing an appropriate tracking algorithm, the decision should be based on the specific requirements of the application, weighing factors such as computational resources and desired accuracy. SAD and MAD are well-suited for scenarios where simplicity and efficiency are paramount, whereas SSD and NCC excel in applications demanding higher accuracy but are willing to accommodate increased computational demands [7].

In future work, it is essential to explore the optimisation of correlation tracking algorithms, aiming to reduce computational complexity while maintaining or improving tracking accuracy, making them more suitable for real-time and resource-constrained applications. Additionally, the integration of machine learning, such as deep learning techniques, should be investigated to enhance feature extraction and adaptability in varying tracking scenarios. Further research can also focus on the development of noise-resistant tracking methods, standardised benchmarking for evaluation and the application of correlation tracking algorithms in autonomous systems and hardware-accelerated implementations to address the evolving demands of object tracking in diverse fields such as robotics, surveillance and computer vision.

References

[1] George, D., Dr. L. Stockum, and Battelle, "Electro-optical tracking systems considerations," *Soc. Photo-Opt. Instrum. Eng.*, vol. 1111, no.3, 1989.

[2] Downey, G. A., "Electro-optical tracking considerations II," *Acquisition, Tracking and Pointing XVIII*, West Melbourne, vol. 5082, 2003.

[3] Pan, Z. and X. Wang, "Correlation tracking algorithm based on adaptive template update," *3rd International Congress on Image and Signal Processing*, (CISP2010) Shenyang, China, 2010.

[4] Lin, C.-H., C.-H. Kuo, and L.-J. Fu, "A stereo matching algorithm based on adaptive windows," *Int. J. Electron. Commer. Stud.*, vol. 3, no.1, pp. 21–34, 2012

[5] Shen, Y., "Efficient normalized cross correlation calculation method for stereo vision-based robot navigation," *Front. Comput. Sci.*, vol. 5, no. 2, pp. 227–235, 2011.

[6] Wei, G., Z. Yi-gong, and X. Zhen-hua, "An improved normalized cross-correlation for template matching of infrared image," *Acta Autom. Sin.*, vol.38, no.1, pp. 189–193, 2009.

[7] Patil, S., J. S. Nadar, J. Gada, S. Motghare, and S. S. Nair, "Comparison of various stereo vision cost aggregation methods," *Int. J. Eng. Innov. Technol.*, vol. 2, no. 8, 2013.

[8] Du, C., M. Lan, M. Gao, and Z. Dong, "Real-time object tracking via adaptive correlation filters," *Intell. Sens.*, vol. 20, no. 15, 2020.

[9] Jha, S., C. Seo, E. Yang, and G. P. Joshi, "Real time object detection and tracking system for video surveillance system," *Multimedia Tools Appl.*, vol. 80, pp. 3981–3996, 2021.

[10] Abdulghafoor, N. H. and H. N. Abdullah "A novel real-time multiple objects detection and tracking framework for different challenges," *Alexandria Eng. J.*, vol. 61, no. 12, pp. 9637–9647, 2022.

75. Implementation and Designing of a Smart Door Lock System

Yogesh Kumar Verma,[1,2] Pravin Ghimire,[2] Rohan Bharti,[3] Pankaj,[4] Raam Deep,[2] and Manoj Singh Adhikari[2]

[1]*School of Electronics and Electrical Engineering, Lovely Professional University, Jalandhar, Punjab, India*

[2]*School of Agriculture, Lovely Professional University, Jalandhar, Punjab, India*

Abstract: The Smart Door Lock System using Internet of Things (IoT) represents a transformative innovation in the field of access control and security. This system leverages the IoT technology to provide advanced features such as remote monitoring, keyless entry, visitor access management and integration with other smart devices. This paper outlines the key components, functionalities and benefits of this system. The primary components of the Smart Door Lock System include a smart door lock, microcontrollers or IoT modules, sensors, a user-friendly mobile or web interface and secure communication protocols. Users can securely control and monitor their door locks remotely, using smartphones or other connected devices. Authentication methods range from traditional PIN codes and radio-frequency identification cards to biometrics like fingerprints and facial recognition, offering users a wide range of options to suit their preferences.

Keywords: ESP-32, RFID, IOT, door, lock.

1. Introduction

Creating a smart door lock system based on radio-frequency identification (RFID) technology is a popular and secure way to control access to your home or facility. RFID technology uses radio waves to communicate between a reader and an RFID tag, which can be embedded in cards, key fobs, or other objects. Here is how you can build a smart door lock system based on RFID. Choose an RFID reader that is compatible with your RFID tags. There are various types of RFID readers, such as low-frequency (LF), high-frequency (HF) and ultrahigh-frequency (UHF) readers. Make sure the reader supports the type of RFID tags you plan to use. RFID Tags: These are the credentials that users will present to the RFID reader to gain access. You can use RFID cards, key fobs, or even RFID-enabled smartphones. Electronic Door Lock: Select an electronic door lock that can be integrated with your RFID system. Look for locks that support RFID access control. Microcontroller or SingleBoard

Computer: You will need a microcontroller or singleboard computer (e.g., Raspberry Pi or Arduino) to interface with the RFID reader and control the electronic door lock. Power Supply: Ensure a stable power supply for the microcontroller, RFID reader and door lock. You may need a backup power source as well. Wiring and Connectors: Connect the RFID reader, door lock and microcontroller with the appropriate wiring and connectors. Software Components: RFID Library: Use an RFID library or Software Development Kit (SDK) compatible with your microcontroller or single-board computer to interface with the RFID reader. Libraries like MFRC522 for Arduino or RPi. GPIO for Raspberry Pi can be useful. Firmware: Write firmware for your microcontroller to control the RFID reader and electronic door lock. The firmware should handle RFID card authentication and lock/unlock commands. Implementation Steps: Hardware Setup: Install the RFID reader near the door and connect it to your microcontroller. Connect the electronic door lock to your microcontroller, ensuring that it can be controlled electronically. Make sure all connections are secure and properly powered. RFID Tag Enrolment: Enroll authorised users by registering their RFID tags with the system. Assign unique identifiers to each user and their corresponding RFID tags. Firmware Development: Write firmware for your microcontroller to interact with the RFID reader. The firmware should: Read the RFID tag when presented to the reader. Verify the tag against the list of authorised users. Send a signal to the electronic door lock to unlock if the RFID tag is valid. Testing: Test the system thoroughly to ensure that it correctly authenticates users and unlocks the door only for authorised individuals. Security Considerations: Implement encryption and secure protocols to protect RFID communication. Store user data securely and avoid exposing sensitive information. Regularly update firmware and software to patch security vulnerabilities. Deployment: Mount the RFID reader and electronic door lock securely on the door. Provide RFID tags to authorised users and educate them on how to use the system. Monitoring and Maintenance: Set up monitoring and logging to track access events. Regularly maintain and update the system to ensure security and reliability. A smart door lock system based on RFID offers convenience and security. It allows you to control access to your property and track who enters and exits. Ensure that you implement security measures to protect against unauthorised access and data breaches. A smart door lock system based on RFID (Radio-Frequency Identification) technology offers several important benefits, making it a valuable addition to home or commercial security systems. Here are some of the key reasons why RFID-based smart door lock systems are important: Enhanced Security: RFID-based systems provide a higher level of security compared to traditional mechanical locks and keys. RFID cards or key fobs are difficult to duplicate, reducing the risk of unauthorised access. Convenience and Accessibility: Users can gain access without the need for traditional keys, which can be easily lost or misplaced. This convenience is particularly beneficial for businesses with a large number of employees or homeowners with family members and frequent visitors. Remote Access Control: Many RFID-based smart locks can be controlled remotely through mobile apps or web interfaces. This allows homeowners or business owners to grant or revoke access privileges remotely, even when they are not on-site. Audit Trails and Monitoring: RFID smart locks often come with built-in logging and auditing features. This allows users to track who has accessed the property and at what times, providing valuable security insights. Customisable Access Permissions: Administrators can easily manage access permissions for different users or groups. You can grant temporary access to service personnel, restrict access during certain hours, or grant access only to specific areas within a facility. Integration with Other Systems: RFID-based smart locks can be integrated with other smart home or building automation systems, such as security cameras, alarms and access control systems. This creates a comprehensive security ecosystem. Reduced Maintenance Costs: Unlike traditional locks that may require rekeying or replacement when keys are lost or stolen, RFID cards and key fobs can be deactivated and replaced without changing the lock itself, reducing long-term maintenance costs. Improved Visitor Management: In commercial settings, RFID-based systems make it easier to manage visitors, contractors and temporary personnel by issuing temporary access cards or key fobs. Deterrent to Unauthorised Entry: The visible presence of an RFID reader and smart lock can act as a deterrent to potential intruders, discouraging unauthorised entry attempts. Emergency Access: In the event of an emergency or power outage, RFID locks can often be overridden with a physical key or manual release, ensuring safety and compliance with fire codes. Scalability: RFIDbased access control systems are scalable and can be easily expanded to accommodate growing access requirements without significant infrastructure changes. User-Friendly: RFID technology is user-friendly and can be quickly adopted by users of all ages. Users simply need to present their RFID card or key fob to unlock the door. Overall, the importance of a smart door lock system based on RFID lies in its ability to provide a balance between enhanced security and user convenience, making it an attractive choice for both residential and commercial applications. It adds layers of control, monitoring and customisation to access management, contributing to a safer and more efficient environment [1–23].

2. Proposed Circuit Diagram

Figures 1 and 2 represent the block diagram and circuit diagram of the proposed model.

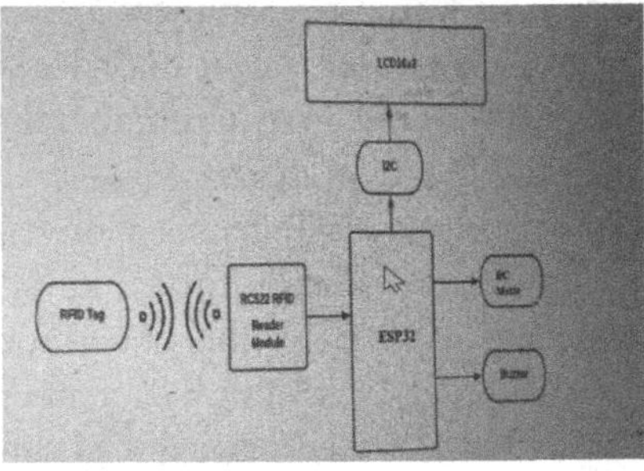

Figure 1: *Block diagram of smart door system.*

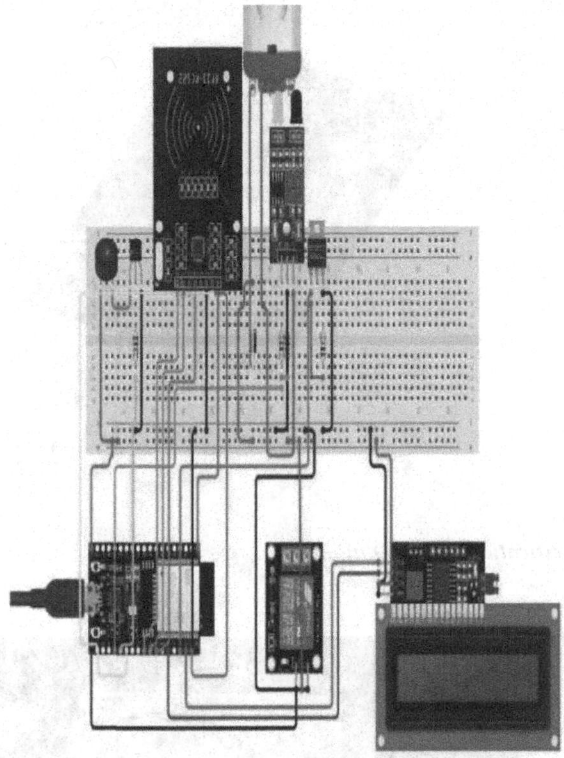

Figure 2: *Circuit diagram of smart door system.*

Figure 3 represents the specifications of the ESP-32 board. Figure 4 represents the specifications of RFID module. Figures 5 and 6 represent the protype of the proposed working model

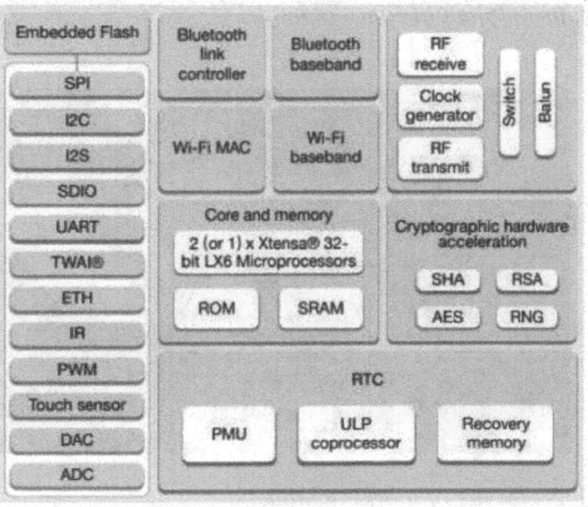

Figure 3: *Specifications of ESP-32.*

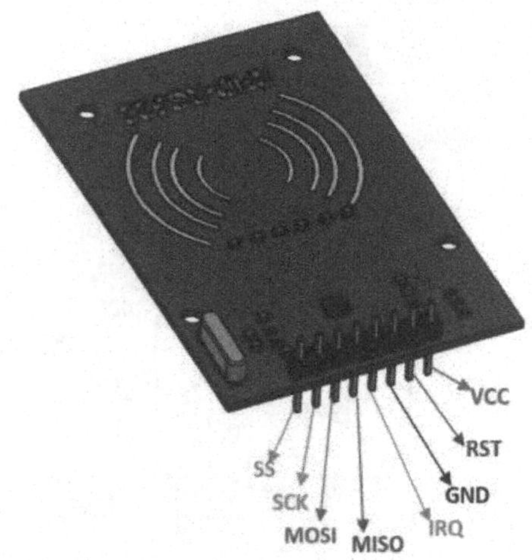

Figure 4: *Specification of RFID module.*

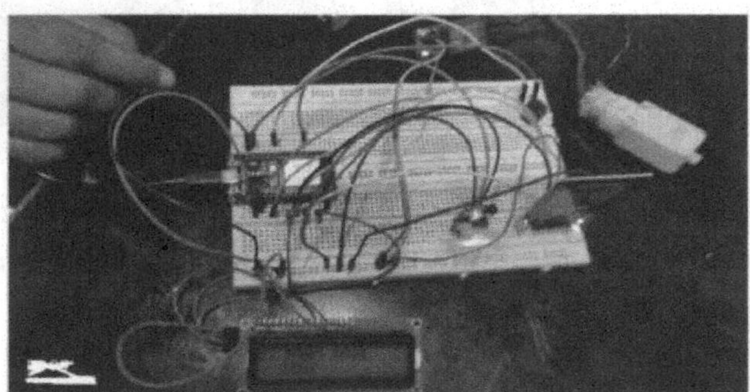

Figure 5: *Working prototype of proposed model.*

Figure 6: *Working prototype of working model.*

3. Proposed Methodology

Designing a smart door lock system using IoT involves several steps and considerations. Here is a proposed methodology to guide you through the process:

Define Objectives and Requirements: Identify the specific objectives and requirements of your smart door lock system. Determine whether it will be used in a residential, commercial, or industrial setting. Define the features and capabilities you want, such as remote access, keyless entry, visitor access management, integration with other IoT devices and security measures. Market Research: Research existing smart door lock solutions to understand the latest technologies, trends and market offerings. Identify potential competitors and their product features. Hardware Selection: Select the appropriate hardware components for your system, including the smart door lock itself, microcontrollers or IoT modules, sensors (e.g., proximity sensors), power source (e.g., batteries or wired power) and any additional hardware for authentication (e.g., biometric sensors). Software Development: Develop the software for your smart door lock system, which includes the following components: User Interface: Design a userfriendly mobile app or web interface for remote control and monitoring. Authentication: Implement secure authentication methods, such as PIN codes, RFID cards, biometrics, or two-factor authentication (2FA). Communication: Establish secure communication protocols between the lock, the user interface and any other connected devices. Common protocols include MQTT, HTTPS, or CoAP. Access Control Logic: Develop algorithms for access control, scheduling and temporary access permissions. Security Measures: Implement robust security measures, including encryption, secure boot and intrusion detection. IoT Platform Integration: Choose an IoT platform or build your own backend infrastructure to manage device registration, authentication and data storage. Integrate your smart door lock system with the IoT platform to enable remote monitoring, control ,and data analytics. Power Management: Implement efficient power management strategies to extend the lifespan of batterypowered locks. This may include low-power modes, sleep/wake cycles and power-saving algorithms. Testing and Quality Assurance: Conduct thorough testing of the hardware and software components to ensure reliability, security and compatibility. Perform penetration testing to identify and address vulnerabilities. User Experience Design: Focus on creating an intuitive user experience for both administrators and end-users. Ensure that the mobile app or web interface is user-friendly and responsive. Compliance and Regulation: Ensure that your smart door lock system complies with relevant regulations and standards, especially those related to privacy and data security. Pilot Deployment: Conduct a pilot deployment of your smart door lock system in a controlled environment to gather user feedback and make any necessary refinements. Full-Scale Deployment: Once you are satisfied with the performance and user feedback, proceed with the full-scale deployment of your smart door lock system. Maintenance and Support: Establish a system for ongoing maintenance, updates and customer support to address any issues or updates that may arise postdeployment. Data Analytics and Optimisation: Collect and analyse data from the smart door lock system to identify usage patterns and areas for optimisation. Continuously improve the system based on user feedback and data-driven insights. Security Updates: Stay vigilant about cybersecurity threats and release regular security updates to protect against potential vulnerabilities. Documentation and Training: Create user manuals and documentation for administrators and end-users. Offer training and support resources to help users make the most of the smart door lock system. Scalability: Plan for scalability to accommodate future growth and additional features or devices. Feedback Loop: Establish a feedback loop with users to gather feedback and make continuous improvements to your smart door lock system. Remember that the development and deployment of a smart door lock system using IoT technology require careful planning, testing and ongoing maintenance to ensure a secure and reliable solution. Additionally, consider working with a multidisciplinary team that includes hardware and software engineers, security experts and user experience designers to create a successful product.

4. Applications

A smart door lock system using IoT technology offers a wide range of applications and benefits for both residential and commercial settings. Here are some of the key applications: Home Security: Enhance home security by allowing homeowners to remotely monitor and control their door locks. Users can lock and unlock doors using a smartphone app, even when they are not at home. They can also receive notifications of any suspicious activity or unauthorised access. Keyless Entry: Eliminate the need for physical keys. Users can unlock doors using a smartphone, RFID cards, PIN codes, or biometric authentication methods such as fingerprints or facial recognition. This provides convenience and eliminates the risk of lost or stolen keys. Visitor Access Control: Grant temporary access to visitors, guests, or service providers remotely. Homeowners can send one-time access codes or schedule access windows for trusted individuals, like dog walkers or repair technicians. Integration with Smart Homes: Smart door locks can be integrated with other IoT devices in the home, such as security cameras, alarms and lighting systems. For example, when the door is unlocked, lights can automatically turn on, or a security camera can start recording. Airbnb and Vacation Rentals: Property owners can manage access for short-term rentals. They can provide guests with unique access codes for the duration of their stay and revoke access once they check out. Remote Monitoring: Keep track of who enters and leaves your property. The system can log access attempts and provide notifications, giving homeowners peace of mind and security. Energy Efficiency: Integrate the smart lock system with the HVAC (heating, ventilation and air conditioning) system to automatically adjust the temperature when the door is locked or unlocked. This helps in saving energy. Office and Commercial Use: In commercial settings, smart door locks can enhance security and access control. Employees can use their smartphones or RFID cards for access, and administrators can easily revoke access for terminated employees. Delivery and Package Management: Delivery personnel can be given temporary access to drop off packages inside the door. This helps secure packages from theft and ensures they are placed inside the property safely. Healthcare Facilities: Hospitals and healthcare facilities can use smart door locks to restrict access to certain areas, ensuring only authorised personnel can enter sensitive areas like patient rooms or medication storage rooms. Schools and Educational Institutions: Educational institutions can improve security by implementing smart locks. Authorised personnel can unlock doors remotely in case of emergencies, and access can be easily managed for different areas within the facility. Access Analytics: Collect data on door access patterns and usage. This data can be valuable for optimising security measures and building operations. Emergency Access: Provide a mechanism for emergency responders to gain access to a property in the event of an emergency, ensuring faster response times. Elderly Care: In elderly care facilities or homes, smart locks can be used to monitor the movements of residents and ensure their safety. Rental Property Management: Property managers can remotely manage access to rental units, allowing for seamless turnover between tenants. The applications of smart door lock systems using IoT are diverse and can be tailored to specific needs and preferences. They offer convenience, security and flexibility for both residential and commercial users.

5. Conclusion

This paper gives basic idea of how to control home security for smart home, especially for door key locks. It also provides a security and easy for Android phone users. This project based on Android platform which is Free Open Source Software. So the implementation rate is inexpensive, and it is reasonable by a common person. With the wireless Wi-Fi connection in microcontroller permits the system installation in easier using an Android Wi-Fi-enabled phone and Wi-Fi modules. Future scope of our project is very high. We have discussed a simple prototype in this paper but in future it can be extended too many other regions.

References

[1] Nasucha, M. and M. Nasucha, "Development of an obstacle avoiding robot," *J. Sistem Komput.*, vol. 5, no. 2, pp. 55–63, 2015.

[2] Tabassum, F., S. Lopa, and M. M. Tarek, "Obstacle avoidingrobot," *Global J. Res. Eng.*, vol. 17, no. 1, pp. 19–23, 2017.

[3] Lanke, N. and S. Koul, "Smart traffic management system," *Int. J. Comput. Appl.*, vol. 75, no. 7, pp. 19–22, 2013.

[4] Mandhare, P. A., V. Kharat, and C. Y. Patil, "Intelligent road traffic controlsystem for traffic congestion: a perspective," *Int. J. Comput. Sci. Eng.*, vol. 6, no. 7, pp. 908–915, 2018.

[5] Trivedi, J., S. Mandalapu, and D. Dhara, "Review paper on intelligent trafficcontrol system using computer vision for smart city," *Int. J. Sci. Eng. Res.*, vol. 8, no. 6, pp. 14-17, 2017.

[6] Aliff, M. *et al.*, "Development of fire fighting robot (QROB)," *Int. J. Adv. Comput. Sci. Appl.*, vol. 4, no. 10, pp. 1341–1344, 2019.

[7] Hasan, M. M. *et al.* "Smart traffic control system with application of image processing techniques," *2014 International Conference on Informatics, Electronics& Vision (ICIEV)*, IEEE, Dhaka, pp. 1-4, 2014

[8] Nasucha, M., "Development of an obstacle avoiding robot," *J. Sistem Komput.*, vol. 5, no. 2, pp. 55–63, 2015.

[9] Ankit, V., P. Jigar, and V. Savan, "Obstacle avoidance robotic vehicle using ultrasonic sensor, android and bluetooth for obstacle detection," *Int. Res. J. Eng. Technol.*, vol. 3, pp. 339–348, 2016.

[10] Lanke, N. and S. Koul, "Smart traffic management system, " *Int. J. Comput. Appl.*, vol. 75, no. 7, pp. 19–22, 2013.

[11] Reddy, R. S. C., P.V. Krishna, M. K. Chaitanya, M. Neeharika, and K. P. Rao, "Security system based on knock-pattern using arduino and GSM communication," *Int. J. Eng. Tech.*, vol. 4, no. 1, pp. 154–157, 2018.

[12] Neloy, M., M. Das, P. Barua, A. Pathak, and S. U. Rahat, "An intelligent obstacle and edge recognition system using bug algorithm," *Am. Sci. Res. J. Eng. Technol. Sci.*, vol. 64, no. 1, pp. 133–143, 2020.

[13] Perwej, Y., K. Haq, F. Parwej, M. Mumdouh, and M. Hassan, "The internet of things (IoT) and its application domains," *Int. J. Comput. Appl.*, vol. 97, no. 8887, p. 182, 2019.

[14] Kale, S.B. and G. P. Dhok, "Design of intelligent ambulance and traffic control," *Int. J. Innov. Technol. Explor. Eng.*, vol. 2, no. 5, pp. 2278–3075, 2013.

[15] Daniel, M., P. K. Maulik, S. Kallakuri, A. Kaur, S. Devarapalli, A. Mukherjee, A. Bhattacharya, L. Billot, G. Thornicroft, D. Praveen, and U. Raman, "An integrated community and primary healthcare worker intervention to reduce stigma and improve management of common mental disorders in rural India: protocol for the SMART Mental Health programme," *Trials, Springer*, vol. 22, pp. 1–13, 2021.

[16] Srivastava, M.D., S.S. Prerna, S. Sharma, and U. Tyagi, "Smart traffic control system using PLC and SCADA," *Int. J. Innov. Res. Sci. Eng. Technol.*, vol. 1, no. 2, pp.169–172, 2012.

[17] Mendiratta, N. and S. L. Tripathi, "A review on performance comparison of advanced MOSFET structures below 45 nm technology node," *J. Semicond.*, vol. 41, no. 6, p. 061401, 2020.

[18] Verma, S., S. L. Tripathi, and M. Bassi, "Performance analysis of FinFET device using qualitative approach for low-power applications".

[19] "Devices for Integrated Circuit (DevIC)," IEEE, pp. 84–88, 2019.

[20] Mendiratta, N. and S. L. Tripathi, "18nm n- channel and p-channel dopingless asymmetrical junctionless DG-MOSFET: low power CMOS based digital and memory applications," *Silicon*, vol. 14, no. 11, pp. 6435–6446, 2022.

[21] Kumar, T.S. and S. L. Tripathi, "Comprehensive analysis of 7T SRAM cell architectures with 18nm FinFET for low power biomedical applications," *Silicon*, vol. 14, no. 10, pp. 5213–5224, 2022.

[22] Verma, Y.K., V. Mishra, and S. K. Gupta, "A physics-based analytical model for MgZnO/ZnO HEMT," J. Circuits, Syst. Comput., vol. 29, no. 1, p. 2050009, 2020.

[23] Verma, Y.K., V. Mishra, P. K. Verma, and S. K. Gupta, "Analytical modelling and electrical characterisation of ZnO based HEMTs," *Int. J. Electron.*, vol. 106, no. 5, pp. 707–720, 2019.

76. SBLKF- Based Estimation of Time-Selective (Fast – Fading) Channel for Hybrid mmWave Massive MIMO System

Shailender,[1] Shelej Khera,[1] and Sajjan Singh[2]

[1]*School of Electronics and Communication Engineering Lovely Professional University, Phagwara, Punjab, India*

[2]*Department of Electronics Engineering Chandigarh Engineering College, Jhanjeri, Mohali, India*

Abstract: The mmWave massive MIMO system needs each antenna to have a separate radio frequency chain because the digital or analogue precoders used do not provide optimal energy efficiency. For time-selective (fast fading) channel, Kalman filter with sparse Bayesian learning (SBLKF)-oriented channel estimation scheme was developed for mmWave hybrid massive MIMO System, and its performance is compared with OMP- and SBL-based channel estimation scheme. The simulation result shows that proposed SBLKF-based channel estimation approach for time-selective (fast fading) channel outperforms the popular OMP-based methodology and SBL-based channel estimation scheme.

Keywords: Channel estimation, SBL, hybrid precoding, mmWave, Kalman filter.

1. Introduction

The cellular communication technology of fifth generation, known as 5G, is expected to bring about a dramatic improvement in data throughput, enormous connection and latency performance. MIMO communication systems and millimetre (mm) wave, communication systems are among the technologies that are being examined as some of the most notable possibilities. Massive MIMO technology has had gained popularity in wireless communication systems, especially in mmWave frequency bands. With the advancement of mmWave technology, the usage of massive MIMO system in mmWave frequency bands can provide high-speed data transmission and support high data rates. However, mmWave systems also pose significant challenges due to their high path loss, which can lead to severe channel fading and high-power consumption. To address these challenges, efficient channel estimation and hybrid precoding techniques are required.

Fast-speed, huge-connection and reduced-latency 5G mobile communication systems have been developed and deployed in the last decade thanks to the expanding needs of several business systems like Internet of Things and Internet of Vehicles and the improvement of wireless apparatus and production techniques. Both micro-cell millimetre wave technology and massive MIMO system contribute to the densification of networks, which in turn improves spectrum efficiency [1]. High-rate data transmission is becoming more important in people's daily lives; however, the available low-frequency spectrum resources are insufficient [2]. The increasing importance of wireless communication has compelled scientists to expand their study into the millimetre wave frequency range. Millimetre waves, which have a frequency range of 30 to 300 GHz, have gained attention from both the academic and business communities due to the large amount of bandwidth they provide. However, because of their severe absorption by the atmosphere and rain during space transmission, millimetre waves are well suited to micro-cell communication because of their short effective propagation distance, tiny coverage and high data transfer rate. One of the most important features of 5G, it allows for enough array gain to be formed into a needle beam to minimise interference [3].

The potential to produce high data speeds with energy-efficient technology has brought a lot of attention to hybrid analogue/digital designs recently. The majority of the time, however, the hybrid precoding matrices cannot be designed without first having an explicit estimate of the mmWave channel. It was noted that the use of huge number of antennas on receiver and transmitter both in mmWave systems makes channel estimation a difficult problem to solve, necessitating a large amount of training data and demanding specialised hardware in the RF chains [4,5]. Recently, deep learning (DL) has gained a lot of interest for its potential to help with a wide range of difficult tasks, such as language processing, voice identification and image object detection. One of the many benefits of DL is that it can solve optimization and/or combinatorial search issues with little computing overhead [6,7].

The channel estimation approach enables the spatial multiplexing technique, allowing for multiple data carrier transmission and resulting in increased data rates in the systems. The mmWave massive MIMO system's highly effective gain is provided by channel estimate for the narrow-band hybrid combiner/ precoder designed framework, which is covered in [15–22]. In the majority of recent articles, flat frequency mmWave channel structure with hybrid MIMO design is proposed. While mmWave channels are broadband and selective in frequency by design.

2. SBLKF-Based Fast-Fading Channel Estimation

Channel model H for mmWave massive MIMO is given by

$$\mathbf{H} = \sum_{l=1}^{N_p} \alpha_l \mathbf{a}_R(\theta_l) \mathbf{a}_T^H(\phi_l) \quad \textit{(1) Static channel}$$

Consider the transmission block N

Time-selective channel:

- Channel that is varying with respect to time
- Due to mobility which leads to Doppler effect

The fast-fading, i.e., time-selective channel H[N] matching to N th block is modelled as

$$\mathbf{H}[N] \triangleq \sum_{l=1}^{N_p} {}_{l}[N]\mathbf{a}_R(\theta_l)\mathbf{a}_T^H(\phi_l) \quad (2)$$

The quantity $\alpha_l[N]$ represents complex channel gain corresponding to the l

Time – Selective Channel

th multi-path component for N th block. The beamspace channel vector $\mathbf{h}_b$ [N] for a time-selective mmWave wireless channel that corresponds to the Nth block can be modeled using the first-order auto-regressive (AR) process or first-order Gauss–Markov model.

In sparse beamspace channel, the temporal evolution is

$$\mathbf{h}_b[N] = \rho\mathbf{h}_b[N-1] + \sqrt{1-\rho^2}\ \mathbf{w}[N] \quad (3)$$

Time-Evolution Model

This is termed as the **State Model**

$\mathbf{h}_b$ [N]: Beamspace channel vector at time moment N

w[N]: Model noise

$\tilde{n}$: The complex channel gain vector $\alpha_l[N]$'s temporal correlation coefficient, denoted as $\tilde{n}$, may be calculated using Jake's model as

$$\rho = J_0\left(2\pi f_D T_B\right) \quad (4)$$

As J_0 (.) is the first kind Bessel function of the zeroth order.

$f_D = f_c \frac{v}{C}$ - Doppler shift

f_c - Carrier

v - Mobile velocity

C - Speed of EM wave (3 x 10^8 m/s)

T_B - Block duration

Large $\rho \Rightarrow$ correlation is high $\Rightarrow$ channel is changing slower.

Small $\rho \Rightarrow$ correlation is low $\Rightarrow$ channel is changing faster.

The measurement or observation model is:

$$\mathbf{y}[N] = \mathbf{Q}\mathbf{h}_b[N] + \mathbf{v}[N] \tag{5}$$

- Kalman filter (KF) enables **MMSE optimal tracking** of a **time-varying** parameter
- Ideally suited for **time-selective** channel estimation KF has two steps:

➢ Prediction step: Based on

$\mathbf{y}[1], \mathbf{y}[2], ..., \mathbf{y}[N-1]$

Correction step: Based on

$\mathbf{y}[N]$

KF Notation:

$\mathbf{h}_b[N]$ = Parameter at time N

$\hat{\mathbf{h}}_b[N|N-1]$ = Best prediction of $\mathbf{h}_b[N]$ grounded on observations $\mathbf{y}[1], \mathbf{y}[2], \ldots,$

$\mathbf{y}[N-1]$ Prediction for time N

$\hat{\mathbf{h}}_b[N|N]$ = Best estimate of $\mathbf{h}_b[N]$ derived from observations $\mathbf{y}[1], \mathbf{y}[2], \ldots,$

$\mathbf{y}[N]$ Estimate at time N

$\hat{\mathbf{h}}_b[N-1|N-1]$ Estimate at N-1

$\hat{y}[N|N-1]$ Prediction of $\mathbf{y}[N]$ for time N $\acute{\mathbf{O}}_b[N|N]$

Covariance of estimation error at time N $\acute{\mathbf{O}}_b[N|N-1]$

Covariance of prediction error for time N $\acute{\mathbf{O}}_b[N-1|N-1]$

Covariance of estimation error at time *N-1* $\mathbf{G}[N]$

Kalman gain $y_e[N]$

Innovation $\mathbf{R}_h$

Covariance of w

Prediction step $\hat{\mathbf{h}}_b[N|N-1] = \rho\hat{\mathbf{h}}_b[N-1|N-1]$ (6)

$$\hat{y}[N|N-1] = \mathbf{Q}\hat{\mathbf{h}}_b[N|N-1] \tag{7}$$

$$\acute{\mathbf{O}}_h[N|N-1] = \rho^2\acute{\mathbf{O}}_b[N-1|N-1] + (1-\rho^2)\mathbf{R}_h \tag{8}$$

Typically, $\mathbf{R}_h$ is set as **I Kalman gain** $\mathrm{G}[N] = \acute{\mathbf{O}}_b[N|N-1]$

$$\acute{\mathbf{Q}}^H\left(\mathbf{R}_v + \mathbf{Q}\ \mathbf{Q}[N|N-1]\ ^H\right)^{-1} \quad (9)$$

Innovation $y_e[N] = \mathrm{y}[N] - \hat{y}[N|N-1]$ (10)

Correction Step $\hat{\mathbf{h}}_b[N|N] = \hat{\mathbf{h}}_b[N|N-1] + \mathbf{G}[N]y_e[N]\ \acute{\mathbf{O}}_b[N|N]$ $= \left(1-\acute{\mathbf{O}}[N]\mathbf{Q}\right)\ _b[N|N-1]$ However, the Kalman filter does not ensure a

sparse estimate. So, sparse Bayesian learning Kalman filter (SBLKF) is used. SBLKF = Kalman filter + SBL

- Combines advantages of the **KF** and **SBL**
- It is **MMSE optimal** and guarantees sparsity

SBL Prior

SBL allocates a parameterised Gaussian prior to $\mathbf{h}_b[n]$

$$p\left(\tilde{\mathbf{A}}_b[n];\ \right) = \prod_{i=1}^{G^2} \frac{1}{\pi\gamma_i} e^{-\frac{|\mathrm{h}_b(i)|^2}{\gamma_i}} \quad (11)$$

- γ_i denote the hyperparameters

SBLKF Prediction

$\hat{\mathbf{h}}_b[N|N-1] = \rho\hat{\mathbf{h}}_b[N-1|N-1]$

$\hat{y}[N|N-1] = \mathbf{Q}\hat{\mathbf{h}}_b[N|N-1]$

$\acute{\mathbf{O}}_b[N|N-1] = \rho^2\acute{\mathbf{O}}_b[N-1|N-1] + \left(1-\rho^2\right)\hat{\mathbf{A}}_{N-1}{}^{(k)}$

HBKF innovation $y_e[N] = \mathrm{y}[N] - \hat{y}[N|N-1]$ (12)

Initialise with

$$\hat{\mathbf{A}}_N^{(1)} = \mathbf{I}$$

A posteriori quantities

$\acute{\mathbf{O}}_{y,\ N}{}^{(k)} = \left[\tilde{\mathbf{Q}}^H \boldsymbol{R}_v{}^{-1}\mathbf{Q} + \left(\hat{\ }_N{}^{(k)}\right)^{-1}\right]^{-1}$ $\grave{\mathbf{i}}_{y,\ N}{}^{(k)} = \acute{\mathbf{O}}_{y,\ N}{}^{(k)}\mathbf{Q}^H\boldsymbol{R}_v{}^{-1}\mathbf{y}[N]$

Hyperparameter update

$$\hat{\gamma}_{i,N}^{(k+1)} = \acute{\mathbf{O}}_{y,\ N}^{(k)}(i,i) + \left|\grave{\mathbf{\imath}}_{\ y,\ N}^{(k)}(i)\right|^{2}$$

Repeat until convergence The **correction steps** are similar to the KF

$$\mathrm{G}[N] = \acute{\mathbf{O}}_{b}\left[N|N-1\right]\ \acute{\mathbf{Q}}^{H}\left(\mathbf{R}_{v} + \mathbf{Q}\ \mathbf{Q}_{b}\left[N|N-1\right]\ ^{H}\right)^{-1}$$

$$y_{e}\left[N\right] = \mathrm{y}\left[N\right] - \hat{y}\left[N|N-1\right]$$

$$= \qquad (13)$$

$$\hat{\mathbf{h}}_{b}\left[N|N\right]\quad \hat{\mathbf{h}}_{b}\left[N|N-1\right] + \mathbf{G}\left[N\right]y_{e}\left[N\right]$$

$$\acute{\mathbf{O}}_{b}\left[N|N\right] = \left(1 - \acute{\mathbf{O}}\left[N\right]\mathbf{Q}\right)\ _{b}\left[N|N-1\right]$$

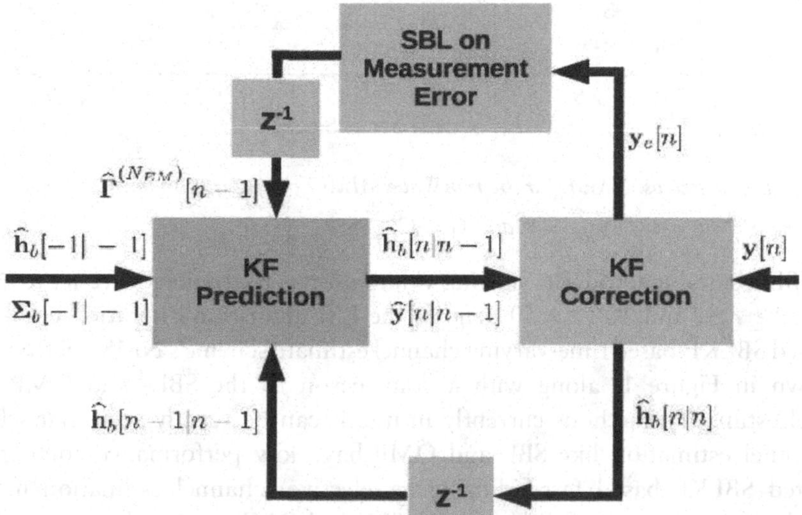

SBLKF Schematic

3. Simulation Results and Discussions

A mmWave hybrid huge MIMO system having $N_t = N_r = 32$ receiving and transmitting antennas and $N_{RF} = 8$ RF chains is taken into consideration. The receiver and transmitter make use of $N_T^{Beam} = N_R^{Beam} = 32$ pilot beam patterns for channel estimation. 32-grid dictionary matrices are used to determine angles of departure between 0 and 180. OMP is initialised with 1 as the threshold value. The channel is considered to have a sparsity level of 5. The halting criteria for the current OMP-based approach are specified in [15] such that the residual error E across subsequent iterations is defined as $E^{(t+1)} - E^{(t)} < \frac{1}{\sigma_n^2}$.

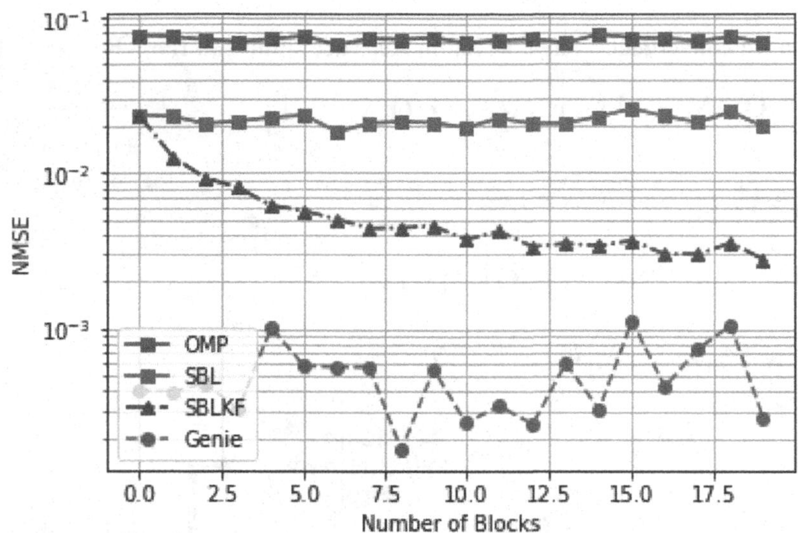

Figure 1: *Block size vs. NMSE for the mmWave MIMO configuration with* $N_t = N_r = 32$, $N_T^{Beam} = N_R^{Beam} = 32$, $N_{RF} = 8$, *and* $G = 32$.

In SBL-based method, the starting values of hyperparameters are set to $\tilde{a}_i^{(0)} = 1\ \forall 1 \leq i \leq G^2$, and $K_{EM} = 50$ denotes the EM algorithm's iteration count. The proposed SBLKF-based time-varying channel estimate scheme's NMSE performance is shown in Figure 1, along with a comparison to the SBL- and OMP-based channel estimating methods currently in use. It can be readily seen that schemes for channel estimation like SBL and OMP have low performance compared to suggested SBLKF based fast-fading (time-selective) channel estimation method. This is because, despite utilising sparsity, SBL and OMP approaches are unable to take advantage of temporal correlation present in beamspace channel vector over several observations. Simulation results clearly illustrate the enhanced performance of SBLKF-based time-selective channel estimation compared to the current OMP- and SBL-oriented mmWave massive MIMO channel estimation method. From simulation result, it is clearly seen that for SBLKF estimation accuracy is increasing as time progresses. Normalised mean squared error (NMSE) is decreasing. But for both OMP and SBL estimation, accuracy is almost constant, i.e., NMSE is not decreasing as time progresses. So, by virtue of this improved performance, this proposed SBLKF-based time-selective channel estimation scheme is highly suited for realistic mobility scenarios.

References

[1] Busari, S. A., K. M. Saidul Huq, S. Mumtaz, L. Dai, and J. Rodriguez, "Millimeter-wave massive MIMO communication for future wireless

systems: a survey," *IEEE Commun. Surv. Tutorials*, vol. 20, no. 2, pp. 836–869, 2017.

[2] Castanheira, D., A. Silva, R. Dinis, and A. Gameiro, "Efficient transmitter and receiver designs for SC-FDMA based heterogeneous networks," *IEEE Trans. Commun.* 63, no. 7, pp. 2500–2510, 2015.

[3] Uwaechia, A. N. and N. M. Mahyuddin, "A comprehensive survey on millimetre wave communications for fifth-generation wireless networks: Feasibility and challenges," *IEEE Access*, vol. 8, pp. 62367–62414, 2020.

[4] Mi, D., M. Dianati, L. Zhang, S. Muhaidat, and R. Tafazolli, "Massive MIMO performance with imperfect channel reciprocity and channel estimation error," *IEEE Trans. Commun.*, vol. 65, no. 9, pp. 3734–3749, 2017.

[5] Alkhateeb, A., J. Mo, N. Gonzalez-Prelcic, and R. W. Heath, "MIMO precoding and combining solutions for millimeter-wave systems," *IEEE Commun. Mag.*, vol. 52, no. 12, pp. 122–131, 2014.

[6] LeCun, Y., Y. Bengio, and G. Hinton, "Deep learning," *Nature*, vol. 521, no. 7553, pp. 436–444, 2015.

[7] Yu, D., and L. Deng, "Deep learning and its applications to signal and information processing [exploratory dsp]," *IEEE Signal Process. Mag.*, vol. 28, no. 1, pp. 145–154, 2010.

[8] Iwen, M. A. and A. H. Tewfik, "Adaptive strategies for target detection and localization in noisy environments," *IEEE Trans. Signal Process.*, Vol. 60, no. 5, pp. 2344–53, 2012, doi: 10.1109/TSP.2012.2187201.

[9] Alkhateeb, A., O. El Ayach, G. Leus, and R. W. Heath, "Channel estimation and hybrid precoding for millimeter wave cellular systems," *IEEE. J. Sel. Top. Signal. Process.*, vol. 8, no. 5, pp. 831–46, 2014, doi: 10.1109/JSTSP.2014.2334278.

[10] Ramasamy, D., S. Venkateswaran, and U. Madhow, "Compressive adaptation of large steerable arrays," *2012 Information Theory and Applications Workshop, ITA 2012 – Conference Proceedings*, pp. 234–39, 2012.

[11] Ramasamy, D., S. Venkateswaran, and U. Madhow, "Compressive tracking with 1000-element arrays: a framework for multi-Gbps mm wave cellular downlinks," *2012 50th Annual Allerton Conference on Communication, Control, and Computing*, Allerton, pp. 690–97, 2012.

[12] Berraki, D. E., S. M. D. Armour, and A. R. Nix, "Application of compressive sensing in sparse spatial channel recovery for beamforming in mmWave outdoor systems," *IEEE Wireless Communications and Networking Conference, WCNC*, pp. 887–92, 2014.

[13] Lee, J., G. T. Gil, and Y. H. Lee, "Exploiting spatial sparsity for estimating channels of hybrid MIMO systems in millimeter wave communications," *2014 IEEE Global Communications Conference, GLOBECOM 2014*, pp. 3326–31, 2014.

[14] Mendez-Rial, R., C. Rusu, N. Gonzalez-Prelcic, A. Alkhateeb, and R. W. Heath, "Hybrid MIMO architectures for millimeter wave communications: phase shifters or switches?" *IEEE Access.*, vol. 4, pp. 247–67, 2016, doi:10.1109/ACCESS.2015.2514261

[15] Han, D. G., Y. J. Kim, and Y. S. Cho, "Efficient preamble design technique for millimeter-wave cellular systems with beamforming," *Sensors (Switzerland)*, vol. 16, no. 7, p. 1129, 2016, doi:10.3390/s16071129.

77. A Parasitic Extraction Method for Realistic Linked Faults in Two Cell SRAMs

Venkatesham Maddela,1,2 Sanjeet Kumar Sinha,1 and Muddapu Parvathi2

[1]*Dept. of School of Electronics and Electrical Engineering, Lovely Professional University, Phagwara, India* [2]*Department of Electronics and Communication Engineering, BVRIT HYDERABAD College of Engineering for Women, Hyderabad, India*

Abstract: Memory faults in the class of linked faults are thought to be particularly interesting. Designing test algorithms is a very difficult process because of their capacity to affect how other faults behave, which hides the influence of the problem. Although several test methods have been created to address the widespread memory problems, only a few of them are capable of identifying linked faults. In the present paper, we proposed a parasitic extraction method, targeting the set of realistic memory linked faults. Comparison results show that the proposed test method gives 100% fault coverage while reducing the complexity of the test and, consequently, the test duration.

Keywords: Linked faults, fault masking, parasitic extraction method, short faults.

1. Introduction

Integrated circuits (ICs) are the main components of an electronic product. In integrated circuit fabrication, channel length has been rapidly decreased. These reduced channel length devices circuits face many challenges during manufacturing and during functional working. The semiconductor part of the integrated circuit used for fabrication of memory is regularly increased in latest nanometer technologies. A memory density will approach more than 90 per cent of system on chip (SoC) semiconductor area in the duration of next decade [1] having its own field of applications. Static random access memories (SRAMs) have wide use in embedded system and processors for fast processing with very low power consumption. The term 'static' refers to the structure of six transistor storage core cells.

Various resistive open defects and other variations during the manufacturing effect the operation or accuracy of SRAMs. So, memories have to be tested correctly or with zero error. SRAM testing challenges represent fault model, high fault coverage, low power consumption and low time consumption test solution. The initial stage test solution has a very narrow coverage range, uses single operations elements March test algorithm [2–4]. Now the latest nanometre technologies, these test solutions are not sufficient for new faults known as dynamic faults [5–7]. These dynamic faults can be detected or sensitised by more than one read or write operations or parasitic effects [17,18]. Hence, March algorithm with large operations element, enhanced addressing sequence and a power constrained test schedule with low power test architecture will detect these faults with low power and minimal application time [8].

The testing of SRAM is one of the manufacturing steps that ensure that the SRAM, manufactured has no manufacturing defect like open and short defects [9–11]. The testing of SRAM's core cell working is very a important step because it detects faults and cause of these faults due to various defects with electrical equivalent is resistance. Therefore, efficient test operation improves the quality and reliability of integrated circuit products with maximum customer satisfaction [12–15]. After testing, physical device's working performance will improve because it helps in elimination of reason of faults. Testing also improves the performance at all stages such as designer, production, test, manufacturer and end-user [16].

2. Proposed Parasitic Extraction Method

In Figure 1 a column single core cell of SRAM using six transistors with lines 'BL', 'BLB' and 'WL'. It consists of a bi-stable multi-vibrator unit made from two cross coupled CMOS inverters and two 'nMOS' pass transistor. These 'nMOS' pass transistors connects 'bit line' (BL) and 'bit line bar' (BLB) according to control signal 'word line' (WL) instruction. The level if bit line and bit lines bar is changed according to the operation performing. During 'read' operation, voltage difference in bit line and bit line bar gives the information about saved data. The organisation of SRAM's core cell array in square or nearly square matrix [15].

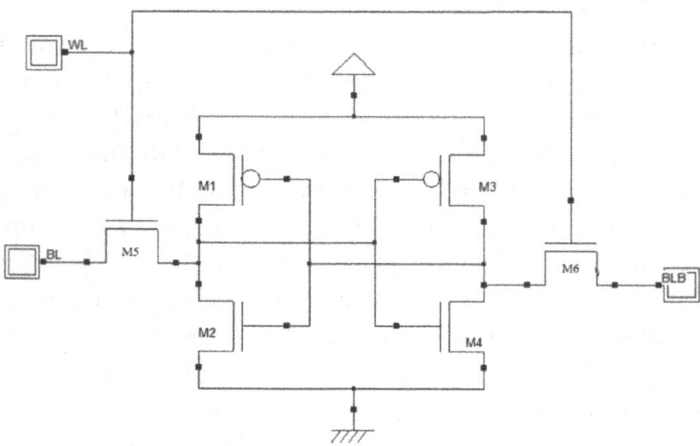

Figure 1: CMOS-based 6T SRAM cell.

2.1. Read Operation

Read or write operations in memories start with restored bit lines normally close to the positive supply voltage. For a selected row word line (WL) signal is high, i.e., WL=1. After WL=1, in a core cell with '0' stored value, the pass transistor connects the bit line capacitor to level '0' for discharge and bit line bar to logic '1' for stay at level "Vdd," so a differential signal is generated at sense amplifier input for sense the data during 'read' operation. In a very dense SRAM's core cell, the discharge rate becomes slow. Therefore, their cell currents are very small. Voltage difference in bit line level generates read data.

Word line WL=1 signal kept at minimal level to reduce wastage of power and reduce operation time also discharge of bit line is low. However, the signal conditioning is performed by the sense amplifiers, which would speed up the RAM access. When a read or write operation is complete, bit line restoration is required to start efficiently new operation. This is accomplished with the help of pre-charge circuits (not shown in figure). The bit line restoration by pre-charge activity ensures correct memory operations

2.2. Write Operation

Processing of write operation in SRAM core cell array row decoder makes signal WL=1 for selection of row. Now all the core cells of the selected row are active and ready for performing operation. Other than write operation, core cell of selected row dissipate power during write operation. During write operation, BL and BLB maintain signal level according to data to be stored. Write driver pulls down BL to '0' to write '0' and pull down BLB to '0' to write '1' in the core cell of the SRAM array.

The steps involved in the proposed parasitic extraction method are

i. Model the circuit with fault imposed.
ii. Depends on the probability of occurrence, classify the fault types.
iii. Extract the defect induced layout from the fault model circuit.
iv. Observe the defects in terms of short/open or missing wires.
v. Extract and collect parasitic *R* and *C* from each faulty layout and compare them with proto typed fault free layout. Any deviation between *R*, *C* values of faulty and fault free cells at each node gives the fault information.
vi. Use collected parasitic *R*,*C* values for exhaustive testing in real-world test environment.

3. Short Defect Model for Two Cell Coupling Faults

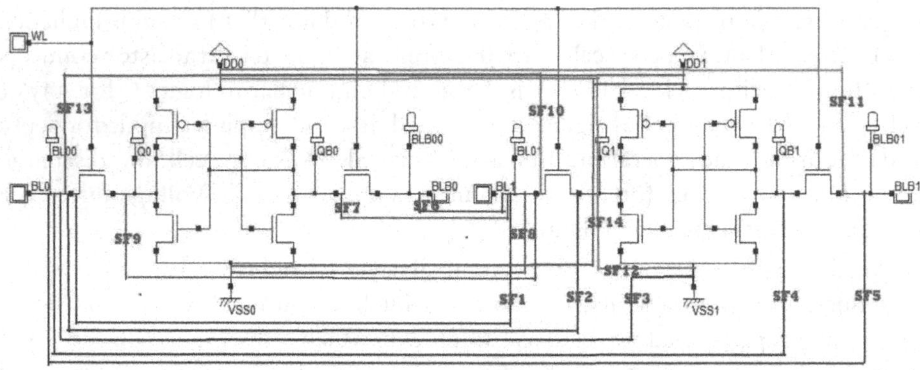

Figure 2: Proposed two cell SRAM fault model for short defects.

Figure 2 shows the proposed fault model for two cell SRAM. Short fault-1 abbreviated as SF1 is a short between the bit line of cell-0 to bit line of cell-1. SF2 represents the short between cell-0 bit line to cell-1 internal node Q1. In the proposed fault model, there are 26 possibilities for the short faults. We have analysed the all 26 possible faults. Table 1 depicts the fault dictionary for two cell 6T SRAM for coupling short faults.

Table1: Fault dictionary for two cell 6T SRAM for coupling short faults.

Short at Nodes	Write Operation	Fault Occurred	Fault Type
Q0-BL1	00	00	State Coupling Fault (CFst)
	01	00	
	10	11	
	11	11	
Q0-Q1	00	00	State Coupling Fault (CFst)
	01	11	
	10	00	
	11	11	
Q0-QB10	00	10	Inversion Coupling Fault(CFin)
	01	01	Fault masking
	10	10	Fault masking
	11	01	Inversion Coupling Fault(CFin)

Q0-BLB10	00	10	Inversion Coupling Fault(CFin)
	01	01	Fault masking
	10	10	Fault masking
	11	01	Inversion Coupling Fault(CFin)
Q0-VDD1	00	UWF	Undefined Write Fault
	01	UWF	Undefined Write Fault
	10	10	Fault masking
	11	11	Fault masking
VDD0-Q1	00	UWF	Undefined Write Fault
	01	01	Fault masking
	10	UWF	Undefined Write Fault
	11	11	Fault masking
VDD0-VSS1	00	UWF,0	Undefined Write Fault, No Fault
	01	UWF,1	Undefined Write Fault, No Fault
	10	UWF,0	Undefined Write Fault, No Fault
	11	UWF,1	Undefined Write Fault, No Fault
VDD0-QB1	00	00	Fault masking
	01	UWF	Undefined Write Fault
	10	UWF	Undefined Write Fault
	11	UWF	Undefined Write Fault
QB0-BL1	00	01	Inversion Coupling Fault(CFin)
	01	01	Fault masking
	10	10	Fault masking
	11	10	Inversion Coupling Fault(CFin)
QB0-Q1	00	10	Inversion Coupling Fault(CFin)
	01	01	Fault masking
	10	10	Fault masking
	11	01	Inversion Coupling Fault(CFin)

QB0-QB10	00	00	Fault masking
	01	11	State Coupling Fault(CFst)
	10	00	State Coupling Fault(CFst)
	11	11	Fault masking
QB0-BLB10	00	00	Fault masking
	01	USWF, 1	Unstabilised Write Fault, No Fault
	10	USWF, 0	Unstabilised Write Fault, No Fault
	11	11	Fault masking
QB0-VDD1	00	00	Fault masking
	01	01	Fault masking
	10	UWF	Undefined Write Fault
	11	UWF	Undefined Write Fault
VSS1-Q0	00	00	Fault masking
	01	01	Fault masking
	10	00	Inversion Coupling Fault(CFin)
	11	01	Inversion Coupling Fault(CFin)
VSS1-QB0	00	10	Inversion Coupling Fault(CFin)
	01	11	Inversion Coupling Fault(CFin)
	10	10	Fault masking
	11	11	Fault masking
VSS0-Q1	00	00	Fault masking
	01	00	Inversion Coupling Fault(CFin)
	10	10	Fault masking
	11	10	Inversion Coupling Fault(CFin)
VSS0-QB1	00	01	Inversion Coupling Fault(CFin)
	01	01	Fault masking
	10	11	Inversion Coupling Fault(CFin)
	11	11	Fault masking

VSS0-VDD1	00	0,UWF	No Fault, Undefined Write Fault
	01	0,UWF	No Fault, Undefined Write Fault
	10	1,UWF	No Fault, Undefined Write Fault
	11	1,UWF	No Fault, Undefined Write Fault
VDD0-BLB1 VSS1-BLB0 VSS1-BL0 BL0-VDD1 VSS0-BL1 VSS0-BLB1 VSS0-WL VDD0-BL1	00	ERROR	No Write and Read operations are possible
	01		
	10		
	11		

4. Results and Analysis

4.1. State Coupling Fault (CFst)

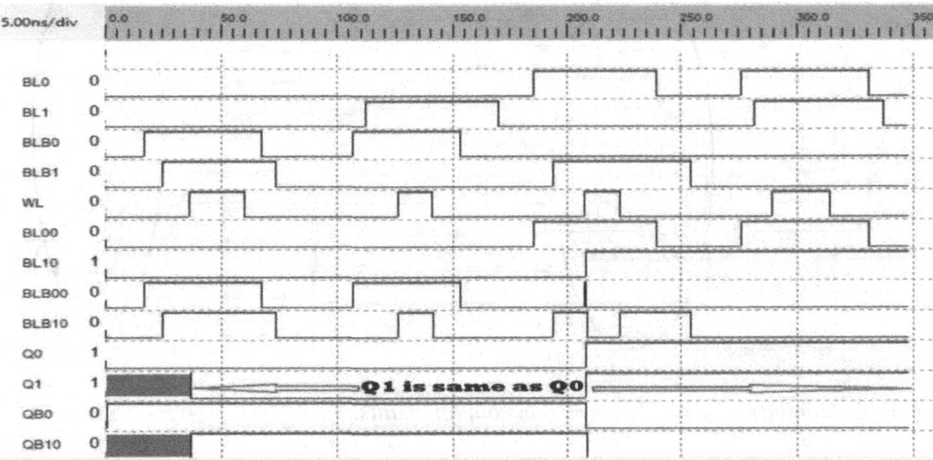

Figure 3: Simulation results for state coupling faults.

As shown in the table, we consider the internode Q0 of cell-0 and shorted with all nodes of Cell-1. Q0-BL1 represents the short between the internode Q0 (cell-0) with input bit line BL1(Cell-1). For this short fault, when we perform the write operation on Cell-0 and Cell-1, we observed that cell-0 value forced to cell-1. For example, when we try to write 0 in cell-0 and 1 in cell-1, 0 should be stored in

Cell-0 and 1 should be stored in cell-1, but 0 that is cell-0 value is stored in Cell-1. Similarly, when we try to write 1 in cell-0 and 0 in cell-1, 1 should be stored in Cell-0 and 0 should be stored in cell-1, but 1 is stored in Cell-1that is cell-0 value stored in cell-1. Same we have observed for all four combinations 00, 01, 10 and 11. This type of fault is called as state coupling fault (CFst). This fault occurs at the nodes Q0-BL1, Q0-Q1 and QB0 – QB10. The simulation results for state coupling faults are shown in figure 3.

4.2. *Inversion Coupling Fault (CFin)*

When we shorted QB0 with BL1, it is observed that when we try to write 0 in cell-0 and 0 in cell-1, 0 should be stored in Cell-0 and 1 should be stored in cell-1, but instead of storing 0 in cell-0, 1 is stored in the cell-0. Similarly, when we try to write 1 in cell-0 and 1 in cell-1, instead of storing 1 in cell-0, 0 is stored in the cell-0. This type of fault is known as inversion coupling fault (CFin). This fault occurs at the nodes Q0-QB10,Q0-BLB10, QB0-BL1, QB0-Q1, VSS1-Q0, VSS1-QB0, VSS0-Q1 and VSS0-QB1. The simulation results for inversion coupling faults are shown in figure 4.

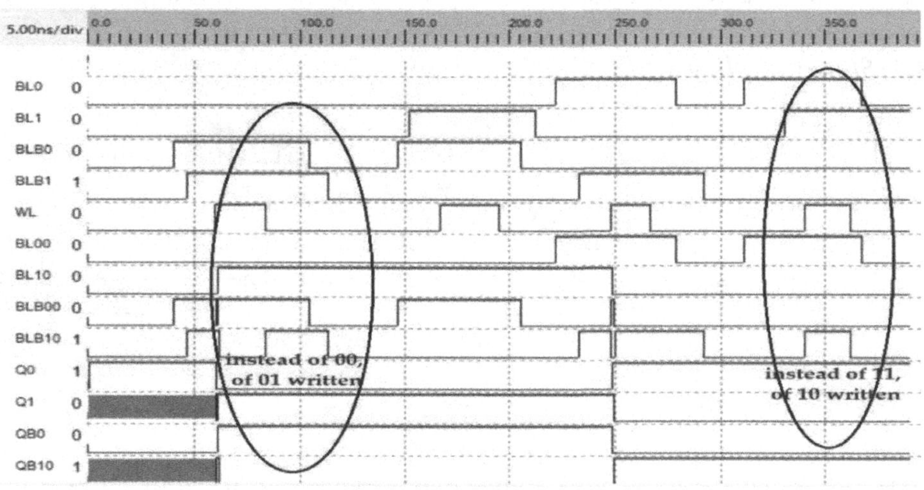

Figure 4: Simulation results for inversion coupling faults.

4.3. *Fault Masking*

As shown in Figure 2, when we shorted QB0 with BL1, for '01' and '10' write operation, there was no fault in both cell, i.e., the behaviour of both cells are the same as fault-free cells. This is known as fault masking. This occurs at the nodes Q0-QB10, Q0-BLB10, Q0-VDD1, VDD0-Q1, VDD0-QB1, QB0-BL1, QB0-Q1, QB0-QB10, QB0-BLB10, QB0- VDD1, VSS1-Q0, VSS1-QB0, VSS0-Q1 and VSS0-QB1.

4.4. Undefined Write Fault

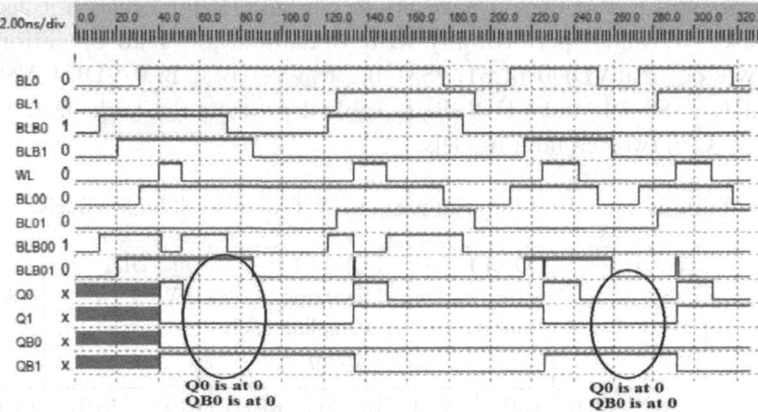

Figure 5: Simulation results for undefined write fault.

The memory cell is said to have an undefined write fault, if the cell is brought to in an undefined state through a write operation. Undefined means, the cell state goes to neither '1' nor '0' with a read operation, This fault occurs at the nodes Q0-VDD1, VDD0-Q1, VDD0-VSS1, VDD0-QB1, QB0-VDD1 and VSS0-VDD1. The simulation results for undefined write faults are shown in figure 5

4.5. Unstabilised Write Fault

A cell suffers from USWF, if a write or transition in a write operation causes continuous transition in the cell, the bit lines are column lines and the possibility of coming closure is more in a large-sized complex SRAM circuit. On writing '1' or '0', the cell exhibits a continuous transition between '1' or '0' and neither of the sates seems to be stable in the cell. The fault is induced by making both QB10 and BLB10 shorted together. The simulation results for USWF are shown in figure 6.

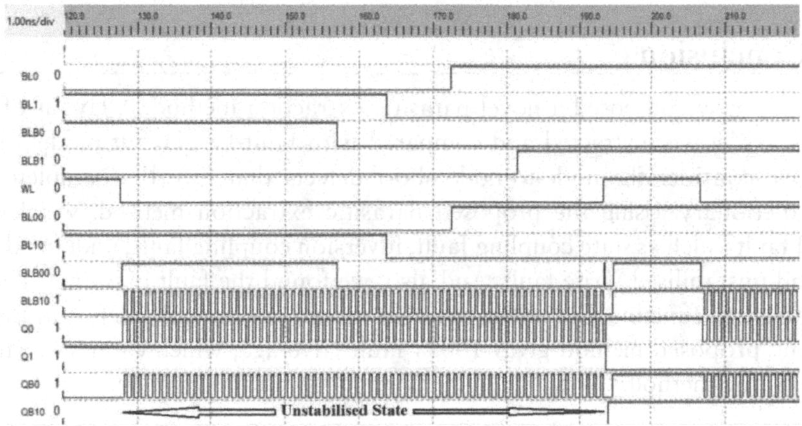

Figure 6: Simulation results for USWF.

4.6. No Access Fault (Error)

The memory cell is said to you have no access fault, If the cell is not accessible. In this case, we cannot perform any write operation, any read operation of the cell, this will occur at VDD0-BLB1, VSS1-BLB0, VSS1-BL0, BL0-VDD1, VSS0-BL1, VSS0-BLB1, VSS0-WL and VDD0-BL1. Table 2 presents the fault detection with parasitic R, C in two cell fault models.

Table 2: Fault detection with parasitic *R*, *C* in two cell fault models.

Nodes	Fault Free		Q0-BL1 State Coupling Fault (CFst)		QB0-BL1 Inversion Coupling Fault (CFin)		Q0-VDD1 UWF		VSS1-BL0 NAF	
	C(fF)	R(Ω)	C(fF)	R(Ω)	C(fF)	R(Ω)	C(fF)	R(Ω)	C(fF)	R(Ω)
Node Q0	7.9	1277	NA	NA	7.90	1307.00	NA	NA	NA	NA
Node QB0	7.7	1194	7.80	1213.00	NA	NA	7.80	1213.00	NA	NA
Node WL	8.2	677	8.20	677.00	8.20	677.00	8.20	677.00	NA	NA
Node BL0	1.1	147	1.1	147	1.10	147.00	1.10	147.00	NA	NA
Node BLB0	1.2	241	1.2	241	1.20	241.00	1.20	241.00	NA	NA
VDD0	1.9	7	1.9	7	1.9	7	1.9	7	1.9	7
VSS0	1.9	7	1.9	7	1.9	7	1.9	7	1.9	7
Node Q1	9.2	1297	9.2	1314	9.2	1314	9	1314	NA	NA
Node QB1	9.1	1202	9	1219	9	1219	9	1219	NA	NA
Node BL1	1.7	150	8.90	1452.00	8.70	1357.00	1.70	150.00	NA	NA
Node BLB1	1.8	245	1.80	244.00	1.80	244.00	1.80	245.00	NA	NA

5. Conclusion

In this paper, we proposed a novel parasitic extraction method. A layout of fault injected model was extracted and compared with fault-free layout model. In this paper, we consider the node-to-node short defects that give the complete fault model dictionary. Using the proposed parasitic extraction method, we detected defined faults such as state coupling fault, inversion coupling fault, undefined write fault and unstabilised Write fault. And also, we found the fault masking that does not change the functionality of the cell even though we have the defect in the cell. Thus, the proposed method gives 100% fault coverage, which cannot see in any other existing method.

References

[1] Semiconductor Industry Association (SIA), *International Technology Road Map for semiconductors (ITRS)*, 2003.

[2] Li, J. F. *et al.*, "March-based RAM diagnosis algorithms for stuck-at and coupling faults," *Proceedings of IEEE International Test Conference*, pp. 758–767, 2001.

[3] Klaus, M. and A. J. Van de Goor, "Test for resistive and capacitive defects in address decoders," *Proceedings of IEEE Asian Test Symposium*, pp. 31–36, 2001.

[4] Ney, A. *et al.*, "A history-based diagnosis technique for static and dynamic faults in SRAMs," *Proceedings of IEEE International Test Conference*, pp. 81–83, 2008.

[5] Dilillo, L. *et al.*, "Resistive-open defect injection in SRAM core-cell: analysis and comparison between 0.13 μm and 90 nm technologies," *Proceedings of Association for Computing Machinery (ACM) IEEE Design Automation Conference*, pp. 857– 862, 2005.

[6] Zhao, Y. *et al.*, "Power characterization of embedded SRAMs for power binning," *30th IEEE VLSI Test Symposium (VTS)*, 2012.

[7] Lu, S.-K. *et al. Low Power Built in Self Test Techniques for Embedded SRAMs*, Hindawi Publishing Corporation VLSI Design Volume, 2007.

[8] Zordan, L. B. *et al.*, "On the reuse of read and write assist circuits to improve test efficiency in low power SRAMs," *IEEE International Test Conference (ITC)*, 2013.

[9] Venkatesham, M. *et al.* "Analysis of open defect faults in single 6T SRAM cell using R and C parasitic extraction method," *IEEE International Conference on Disruptive Technologies for Multi-Disciplinary Research and Applications (CENTCON-2021)*, pp. 213–217, 2021.

[10] Venkatesham, M. *et al.*, "Fault detection and analysis in embedded SRAM for sub nanometer technology," *International Conference on Applied Artificial Intelligence and computing (ICAAIC)*, 2022.

[11] Venkatesham, M. *et al.* "Extraction of undetectable faults in 6T-SRAM cell," *IEEE International Conference on Communication, Control and Information Sciences (ICCISc)*, pp.13–17, 2021.

[12] Panth, S. and S. K. Lim, "Transition delay fault testing of 3D ICs with IR-drop study," *30th IEEE VLSI Test Symposium (VTS)*, 2012.

[13] Ojha, S. K. and P. R. Vaya, "A novel architecture of SRAM for low power application," *Int. J. Adv. Electr. Electron. Eng.*, vol. 2, no. 4, 2013.

[14] Bastian, M. *et al.*, "Influence of threshold voltage deviations on 90nm SRAM CoreCell behaviour," *16th IEEE Asian Test Symposium (ATS)*, 2007.

[15] Calimera, A., A. Macii, E. Macii, and M. Poncino, "Design techniques and architectures for low leakage SRAMs," IEEE Trans. Circuits Syst., vol. 59, no. 9, 2012.

[16] Balasubrahamanyam, Y. *et al.*, "A novel low power pattern generation technique for concurrent bist architecture," *Int. J. Comput. Technol. Appl.*, vol. 3, no. 2, pp. 561–565, 2014.

[17] Venkatesham, M. *et al.*, "Study on paradigm of variable length SRAM embedded memory testing," *Proceedings of the Fifth International Conference on Electronics, Communication and Aerospace Technology (ICECA)*, 2021.

[18] Venkatesham, M. *et al.*, "Comparative analysis of open and short defects in embedded SRAM using parasitic extraction method for deep submicron technology," *Wireless Pers. Commun.*, vol. 132, pp. 2123–2141, 2023.

78. Evaluating Energy-Efficient Cooperative Communication in Wireless Networks through Clustering Algorithm Performance Metrics

Nishant Tripathi,[1,2] Charanjeet Singh,[1] and Kamal Kumar Sharma[3]

[1]*Institute Dept. of Electronics and Communication Engineering, School of Electronics and Electrical Engineering, Lovely Professional University, Phagwara, Punjab, India*
[2]*Dept. of Electronics and Communication Engineering, Pranveer Singh Institute of Technology, Kanpur, Uttar Pradesh, India*
[3]*Ambala College of Engineering and Applied Research Devsthali, Ambala, Haryana, India*

Abstract: Generally current application areas in communication are totally dependent upon establishment and operations of the Wireless sensor Networks (Camera based/ non-Camera based) for cooperative communication. Cooperative Communication (CC) being an ideal sub-part of upcoming 6G telecom infrastructure, make sure that the optimum operations can be analysed and evaluated based on lifeline of the model of network and it should not be very power consuming (must be energy efficient with better throughput), and its reliability for the transmission of data packet should be optimum. If they are working in the sensor-based field, the majority of researchers have shifted their goal posts into the application domains of 6G (preferably in the Cooperative communication domain). This is done in order to optimise the energy, power and life span of sensor-based networks while also taking reliability into consideration (camera based or non-camera based). In light of this, chapter we have given a broader novel idea to cover analytical review for cooperative communication based on its recent research followed by describing research gaps and performance issues of present in wireless networks leading to CC followed by implementation of several clustering schemas for data transmission in MATLAB and have compared them to compare their performance for energy efficiency.

Keywords: Cooperative communication, clustering, energy efficiency, 6G, wireless camera sensor networks.

1. Introduction

Wireless Camera Sensor Networks (WCSNs) [1], [3] are new age wireless network in collaboration with upcoming beyond 5G and 6G communication modules which are networks of unattended, ultra-small, minimum-power Member sensor nodes (MSN) that communicate with one another. When sensors are deployed in a random fashion across an investigation area, their partial dispensation, wireless based communication and energy store competences send sensed data to a sink or Base Station for analysis (BS) Figure.1. The improvement of technologies and devices has shaped many opportunities for the efficient use of resources in critical environments. When it comes to this context, Wireless Sensor Networks (WSNs) have brought about a sea change. With the introduction of this technology, it became possible to collect and deliver useful information to the intended recipient. Applications such as battlefield surveillance, smart offices, traffic monitoring and other similar ones can be effectively monitored with the help of such systems. For the purpose of gathering useful information, WSNs are composed of several unmanned, extremely minatory small and compact, extremely small consumption based -power Member sensor nodes (MSN) that are scattered throughout region of interest, such as an inaccessible area or a catastrophe zone. Numerous research questions have been posed as an outcome of the growth of small MSN, able to sense, process expressive information and interactive to its destination. These battery-powered sensor nodes (SNs) have tremendously partial processing and storage capabilities. Because WSNs are exposed to dynamic environments, connectivity loss between nodes may occur as a result of such configuration, resulting in a decrease in network performance. To improve performance, energy-efficient protocols must be designed, extending the network's life. When a critical node fails to operate properly, the performance of centraliaed algorithms degrades significantly, resulting in a severe protocol failure. In comparison to traditional methods, distributed protocols are more efficient at handling failures and may be a more appropriate solution. For network energy efficiency, energy-efficient clustering structured routing protocols capable of data aggregation are being developed. Localised algorithms can operate within a cluster without the need to wait for control messages to arrive, thereby reducing the overall delay. Furthermore, when compared to centralised algorithms, the scalability of these localised algorithms is significantly improved.

In the present work, we have done a comparison in MATLAB outputs of clustering algorithms for WSNs/WCSNs based on the time slot of no node to die out for stability calculation, module under supervision lifespan and effective efficiency. Cluster heads (CHs) receive information from SNs, and it is their responsibility to transmit this information using several jumps to sink located at longer path in the field. Clustering algorithms for sensor networks, such as LEACH, DEEC, TEEN, SEP and EESAA [1],[2],[4],[6], have achieved reasonable goals in terms of improved performance of networks under a variety of criteria and circumstances [1,2,4,6,7,8,9]. The paper will contain all of the details of the different clustering schemes, viz. LEACH [1], DEEC [1], SEP [1],[2] and their modified versions with their MATLAB outputs, which will be presented one by one in different sections to evaluate their performance. The final product of the study is written in such a way that a researcher will have enough material to understand all of the multilevel distributed clustering schemes with varying degrees of heterogeneity after reading it. The study will be distributed some sections, starting with basics of Wireless Camera Sensor Networks Basics and deployment issues for the same. This will be followed by clustered introductions and their advantages. Following the two, we will have different algorithms and then after simulations of the most used clustering algorithms. The last part will be an analytical conclusion based on clustering algorithms application area and the best performing algorithm.

Transmit diversity necessitates several transmitter antenna systems in most cases. Many wireless devices, however, can only have one antenna due to their small size or complexity. Cooperative communication is a relatively new form of communication that has recently emerged. In a multi-user environment, they allow single-antenna mobiles to share their antennas and create a virtual multiple-antenna sender, allowing for increased transmit diversity. Users of cellular and ad hoc wireless networks can work together to improve their quality of service, which is measured at the physical layer by bit error rates, block error rates and the likelihood of outages. There are two ways to look at power. One way is that more power is required because in cooperative mode, each user transmits to both users. Another thing to keep in mind is that the baseline transmit power for both users will be reduced due to the diversity. It's also important to think about how much information the base station needs to handle cooperative communication. For each of the previous schemes, the amount of additional information provided varies. The goal is to come up with a system that is fair to all users, uses minimal system resources and works with the system's multiple access protocol. Another thing that needs to be done is to develop methods for cooperative transmission power control. Much of what we've done so far assumes that everyone sends the same amount of power. Furthermore, in CDMA-based systems, power control is essential for managing the near-far effect and minimising interference. As a result, power control schemes that work well in a cooperative communication context are essential.

To create heterogeneous networks, small cells are stacked on top of macro base station (MBS) tiers. This contributes to meeting the growing demand for faster, higher-quality communication. Small cells can help reduce MBS load, but they're not always successful. Because of the high potential of small cell density, collaboration is becoming increasingly important. Software Defined Networking, for example, is a wired network technology that can also be used in cellular networks (SDN). The understanding of multi-tier networks is aided by SDN. Wireless networks face two major challenges: energy efficiency and ways to recover energy from the environment. Energy efficiency refers to the amount of data that can be sent per unit of energy. Bits-per-Joule is the unit of measurement. A number of factors influence the stability and performance of a wireless network. Mobile users' location, distance and connectivity are just a few of the variables that can change frequently in adaptive topology networks. Due to Doppler shift, different distances, and different obstacles, the link quality of users of centralised wireless networks may change over time as they move into a cell. The MAC layer parameters, as well as how users collaborate, select relays and assign power, may all be affected by this mobility feature. Relay selection is one of the most serious problems with mobile networks.

2. Literature Review of Cooperative Communication

1. Wang and Zhang [3] devised an energy-efficient AQDBPSK/DS-CDMA scheme for 3D wireless sensor networks. It embraces NEW LEACH for energy effectiveness and interference mitigation using the Nakagami-m model.
2. Nosratinia *et al.* [6] introduced cooperative communication where single-antenna devices emulate multiple antenna transmitters, achieving transmit diversity in multi-user settings.
3. Parmar *et al.* [7] explored environmental monitoring using wireless sensor networks, utilising clustering methods like LEACH, TEEN and APTEEN for data like light intensity, temperature and pressure.
4. Kiwan *et al.* [8] focused on hierarchical network routing, presenting advantages and disadvantages of different protocols to solve large network issues.
5. Rathi *et al.* [9] extended sensor network lifetime via gradient-based and hierarchical routing, enabling energy-efficient data aggregation and multipath routing.
6. Jain *et al.* [10] compared LEACH and PEGASIS, noting LEACH's energy efficiency and PEGASIS's power optimisation for sensor network lifespan enhancement.
7. Hooggar *et al.* [13] introduced a 3D coverage algorithm, achieving substantial energy savings through proposed coverage methods based on clustering.
8. Abakumov *et al.* [14] proposed MCA algorithm, outperforming LEACH in coverage and connected nodes for ultimate sensor network longevity.
9. Dang *et al.* [15] optimised 3D WSN energy via FCM-3 WSN, surpassing LEACH, SCEEP, H-LEACH and others, validated by experimental results.

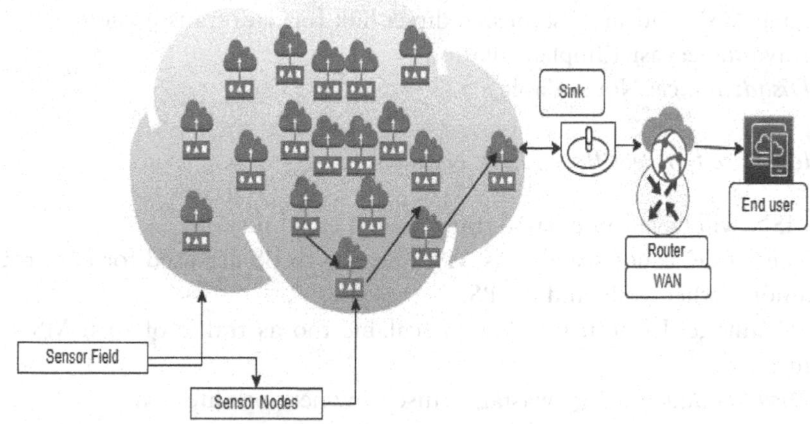

Figure 1: Wireless network setup (camera based/ non-camera based).

3. Issues to Address in Clustering for Making Better WSN/ WCSN for CC/CWC

The central aim of clustering resides in the minimisation of power consumption during communication, thereby safeguarding the battery longevity within sensor networks. Furthermore, this pursuit of clustering yields a multitude of merits, as delineated in the antecedent diagram. Within the domain of wireless sensor networks (WSN) and wireless camera sensor networks (WCSN) for cross-correlation (CC) purposes, the formulation of a clustering protocol necessitates meticulous consideration of several pivotal facets:

1. Prolonged sustenance of SNs and the overarching network.
2. Equitable distribution of workloads to facilitate judicious dispersion of power across diverse SNs.
3. Attainment of scalability to accommodate burgeoning network dimensions.
4. Orchestrating cost-effectiveness, navigating the spectrum of divergent trade-off rationales.
5. Establishment of fortified security measures.
6. Adherence to compatibility within a heterogeneous networking milieu, while preserving homogeneity.

4. Clustering

Based on network architecture, following layout has to be made before implementing the model. Figure.2

4.1. *Single or Direct Link Model Network*

- Each MSN and sink establish a direct link for data transmission.
- Advantage: easier implementation
- *Disadvantage*: Not scalable

4.1.1 Hop Based or Peer-Based Link Network

- MSN will have route-based transmission capability.
- The model is not scalable as MSN nearby to BS are used for data routing among other MSN and the BS.
- Advantage: Large network, and scalable too as traffic of such MSN may increase;
- *Disadvantage:* Energy wastage causes low network life span.

4.2. *Multi-Hoping-Based Network Depending Upon Clustering*

- MSN will make structure combining into groups and then a group leader (CH) for any cluster (group) will be chosen to transmit data to BS or sink directly. MSN transmits their data to CH which further assesses the data and sends the processed data collected from all MSN to the sink/BS. *Disadvantage:* The energy of CH will vanish faster than other MSN.
- *Multi-hoping, Clustering based on Dynamic CH Network model*
- Dynamically changes the role of CH among other MSN.

5. Need and Advantages of Clustering Wireless Networks

- **Energy Efficiency:** Clustering helps in distributing the energy consumption more evenly across the network. Instead of all nodes communicating directly with a centralised entity (e.g. base station or sink node), nodes communicate within their clusters and only cluster heads (CHs) communicate with the central entity. This reduces the transmission distance and energy consumption for non-CH nodes, thus extending the network's overall lifetime.
- **Scalability:** In large wireless networks, managing individual nodes becomes challenging. Clustering simplifies network management by dividing nodes into clusters, where each cluster is managed by its CH. This hierarchical approach makes the network more scalable and easier to manage.
- **Reduced Overhead:** Clustering reduces the overhead associated with routing and communication protocols. Nodes within a cluster can use shorter communication paths to reach their CHs, which then handle communication with the base station. This reduces the amount of control traffic on the network and conserves energy.

- **Load Balancing:** Cluster heads can perform data aggregation, fusion and compression locally before sending data to the central entity. This helps balance the traffic load and prevents certain nodes from becoming overloaded, ensuring more efficient use of network resources.
- **Improved Reliability:** Clustering improves network reliability by providing redundancy. If a node within a cluster fails, other nodes in the same cluster can take over its responsibilities, minimising the impact on network operations.
- **Latency Reduction:** With shorter communication paths between nodes and their respective cluster heads, data transmission and reception times are reduced, leading to lower latency in communication.

6. Different Clustering Techniques used in Wireless Net*works*

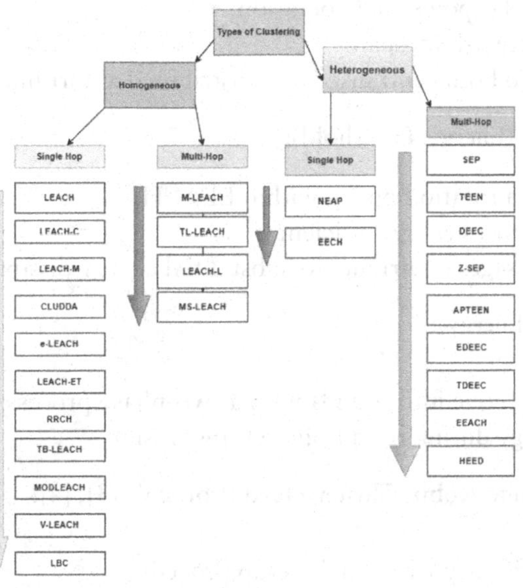

Figure 2: *Different types of clustering divisions.*

6.1. Homogeneous Clustering (Single Hopping-Based)

6.1.1 Key Point Characteristics

i. **LEACH-C (Low Energy Adaptive Clustering Hierarchy-Centralised)** [1], [2]:

- Initiated centrally for algorithm execution. Figure.3
- Ensures balanced cluster formation.
- Lacks energy efficiency.
- Not robust when handling global network data.

ii. **LEACH-F (Fixed) [1-5]:**

- Forms clusters in a fixed manner.
- Balances energy consumption across MSNs.
- Reduces complexity and burden during setup.
- Wastes energy and information before CH enters a low-energy state.

iii. **CLUDDA (Clustered Diffusion with Dynamic Data Aggregation)** [3, 4]:

- Mitigates flooding by eliminating unfinished data transmission.
- Utilises dynamic data aggregation.
- Introduces significant time delay.
- Requires larger memory storage.

iv. **s-LEACH (Solar-Aware LEACH)** [4, 5, 6, 7]:

- Harnesses solar power for operation.
- Improves network lifespan.
- Applicable to both centralised and distributed algorithms.

v. **LEACH-ET (Energy Threshold):**

- Implements a rotation policy within LEACH.
- Slightly enhances energy efficiency.
- Control messages contribute to substantial energy dissipation.

vi. **E-LEACH (Energy):**

- Divides phase one into rounds with a two-phase process.
- Wastes energy during round-phase transmission.

vii. **RRCH (Round Robin Cluster Head Protocol)** [3], [4]:

- Achieves efficiency via a single setup procedure.
- Reduces overall energy consumption.
- Experiences issues with load balancing.
- Introduces additional overhead burden.

viii. **TB-LEACH (Time-Based Cluster Head Selection Algorithm for LEACH)** [5], [6], [15]:

- Varied procedures for selecting CHs.
- Extends network lifetimes.
- Inadequate support for large networks.
- Poor load balancing and high overhead burden.

ix. **MLEACH-L (More Energy-Efficient LEACH)** [3], [6], [19]:

- Tailored for dense and extensive WSNs.
- Improves setup stage and energy profile.
- Still faces load balancing challenges.

x. **V-LEACH (New Version LEACH)** [1], [9], [10]:

- Enhances results compared to original LEACH.
- Incorporates redundant CHs for improved reliability.
- Extends setup phase duration.
- Introduces potential duplication.

xi. **p-LEACH (Partition-Based LEACH):**

- Balances wasted energy profile.
- Presents issues with setup enhancement.

xii. **WST-LEACH (Weighted Spanning Tree for LEACH)** [3], [8]:

- Selects CHs based on three optimising conditions.
- Reduces power dissipation and extends network life.

xiii. **EBC (Energy-Balanced Clustering)** [2], [3], [8]:

- Prevents unnecessary energy consumption during re-clustering.
- Introduces additional overhead concerns.
- Struggles with load balancing.
- Requires extra time for different transmission stages.

xiv. **LEACH-SC (LEACH Selective Cluster)** [1], [3], [8]:

- Enhances scalability.
- Presents additional overhead issues.
- Struggles with load balancing.

6.2. Homogeneous Multi-Hopping-Based [2], [3], [10]

6.2.1 Key Point Characteristics

xv. **M-LEACH (Multi-Hop LEACH)** [2], [3]:

- Suitable for large module networks with low density.
- Limited scalability.
- Suboptimal for small networks.

xvi. **TL-LEACH (Two-Level LEACH)** [1], [3], [11]:

- Reduces energy consumption.
- Distributes energy loads among MSNs in dense networks.
- Less suitable for vast, dense model networks.

xvii. **LEACH-L** [1], [11], [21]:

- Stabilises the network's load.
- Decreases energy usage per MSN.
- Introduces additional overhead issues.

xviii. **MS-LEACH (Combines Multi-Hop and Single Hop)** [1,20]:

- Reduces energy consumption by combining single- and multi-hop profiles.
- Limited scalability.
- Presents additional overhead issues.

6.3. Heterogeneous Single Hop [1], [3], [11]

6.3.1 Key Point Characteristics

xix. **EECHE (Energy-Efficient Cluster Head Election Protocol)** [1]:

- Enhances throughput and lifetime compared to LEACH and SEP.
- Offers limited scalability compared to SEP.
- Reduces latency.

xx. **NEAP (Novel Energy Adaptive Protocol)** [1], [8]:

- Improves consistency.
- Lacks scalability.
- Not suitable for dense networks.

6.4. Heterogeneous Multi-Hop Protocols [1], [2], [8]

6.4.1 Key Point Characteristics

xxi. **SEP (Stable Election Protocol)** [1] **Figure.3**:

- Eliminates the need for nearby MSN energy/round data collection.
- Performs poorly in multilevel networks.

xxii. **HEED (Hybrid Energy Efficient Distributed Clustering)** [1], [13], [27]:

- Stabilises power distribution among MSNs.

- Manages and controls overhead issues.
- Experiences latency problems.
- Limited scalability.

xxiii. **EEUC (Novel Energy Efficient Clustering Approach)** [3], [8]:

- Minimises problems with unequal cluster sizes.
- Introduces imbalanced clusters.
- Faces load balancing challenges.
- Offers better energy efficiency.

xxiv. **LEACH-HPR** [1], [11]:

- Enables CH to elect the best MSN for energy consumption stabilisation.
- Presents additional overhead concerns.

xxv. **DEUC** [1], [2]:

- Mitigates hotspot issues.
- Minimises overhead concerns.
- Experiences poor load balancing.
- Offers better energy consumption profile.

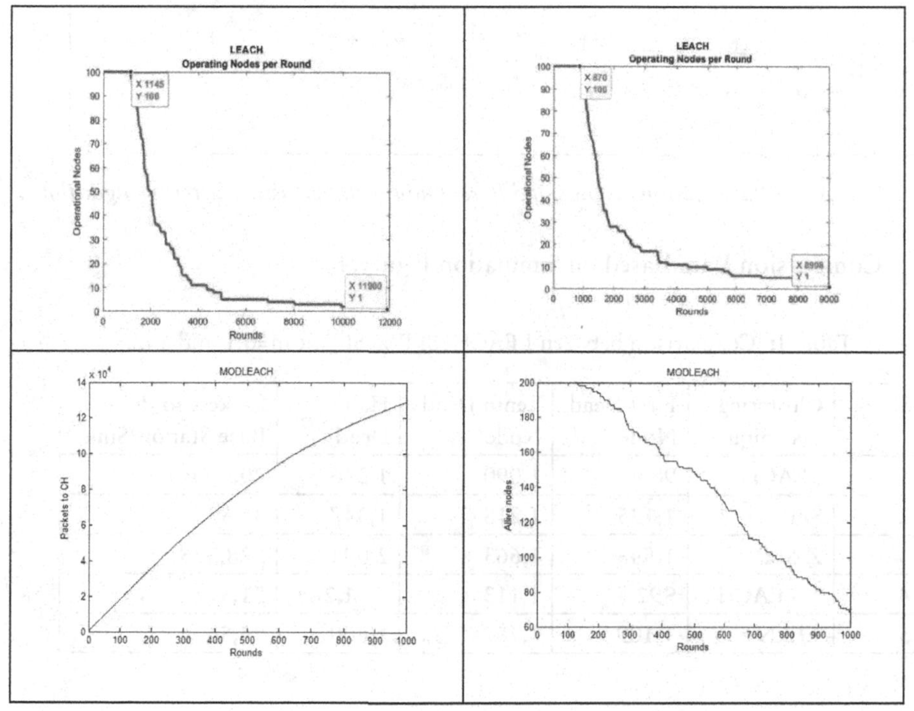

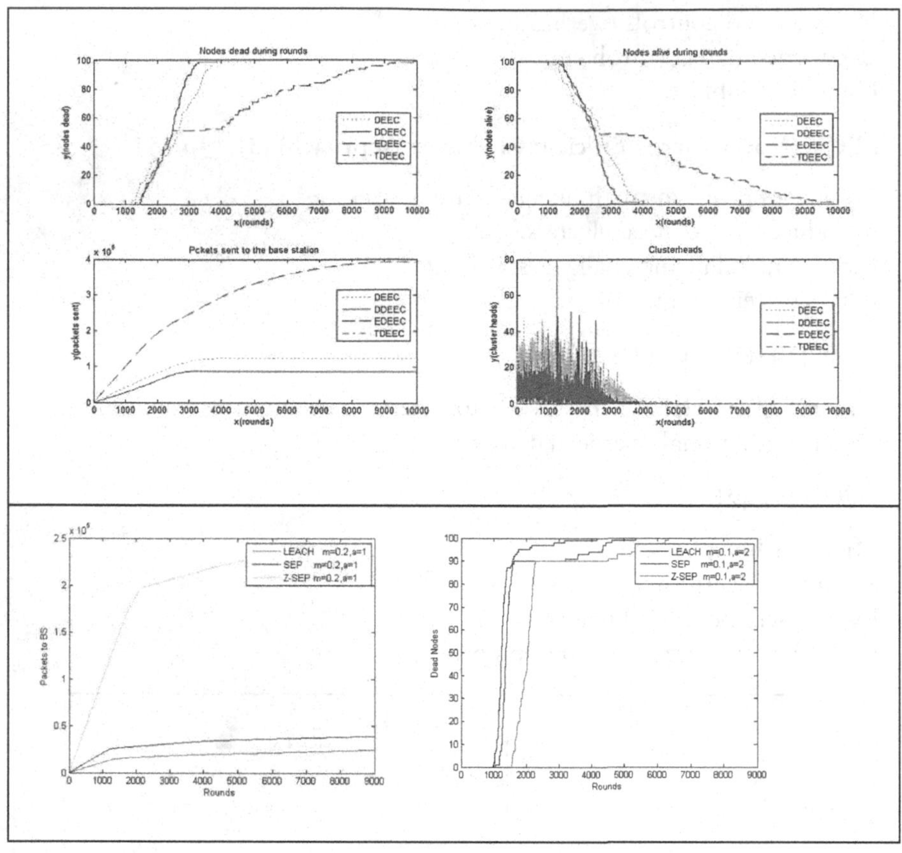

Figure 3: MATLAB simulation outputs of different non-metaheuristic clustering algorithms.

- **Comparsion Data based on Simulation Figure.4**

Table 1: Comparison between LEACH, SEP, Z-SEP at m=0.1 and a=2.

S.No.	Clustering Technique	First Dead Node	Tenth Dead Node	Half Dead	Packets to the Base Station/Sink
1	LEACH	983	1,090	1,246	20,930
2	SEP	1,135	1,218	1,347	35,537
3	Z-SEP	1,548	1,663	2,098	228,328
4	MLEACH	992	1,113	1,281	21,345
5	TEEN	1,109	1,467	1,600	24,567

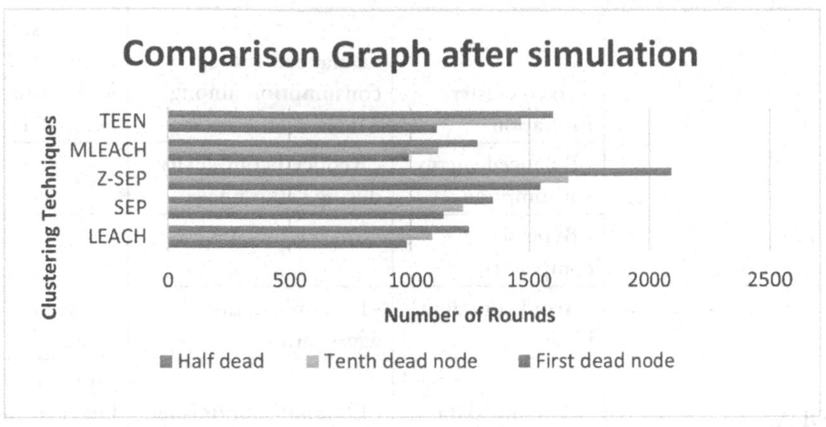

Figure 4: Comparison graph after simulation.

Table 2: Comparison on the basis of number of alive nodes for 5,000–9,000 rounds, dead nodes for 5,000–9,000 rounds and packets to the BS for 5,000–9,000 rounds at $m = 0.1$, $a = 2$.

Protocol	Alive Nodes	Dead Nodes	Packets to Base Station
LEACH	Medium to High	High	Moderate to High
M-LEACH	Medium to High	High	Moderate to High
DEEC	Medium to High	High	Moderate to High
TEEN	High	Low to Medium	Moderate to High
SEP	High	Low to Medium	Moderate to High
Z-SEP	High	Low to Medium	Moderate to High
EDEEC	Medium to High	Low to Medium	Moderate to High
TDEEC	Medium to High	Low to Medium	Moderate to High

Table 3: Comparison of different clustering technique on the basis of key parameters, advantages, disadvantages.

Clustering Method	Key Characteristics	Advantages	Disadvantages
Homogeneous Clustering (Single Hopping-Based)			
	- Centrally initiated	- Balanced cluster formation	- Lacks energy efficiency
	- Balanced clusters	- Centralised initiation	- Not robust for global data
LEACH-C	- Not energy efficient		

LEACH-F	- Fixed cluster formation	- Balanced energy consumption among MSNs	- Increased energy and info wastage before CH dies
	- Balanced energy consumption	- Reduced complexity during setup phase	
	- Bypasses complexity		
CLUDDA	- Avoids flooding issue	- Dynamic data aggregation	- Large time delay
	- Dynamic data aggregation	- Eliminates unfinished data transmission	- Requires larger memory storage
	- Large time delay		
s-LEACH	- Uses solar power	- Improved network lifespan	- Works in both centralised and distributed
	- Improved network lifespan	- Suitable for centralised and distributed	- Setup phase energy and info wastage
	- Centralised and distributed	- Solar power utilisation	
LEACH-ET	- Computes rotation policy	- Slightly better energy efficiency	- Control messages cause energy dissipation
	- Slightly better efficiency	- Rotation policy computation	- Large energy dissipation due to control messages
	- Control messages impact		
E-LEACH	- Two-phase process	- Improved energy profile	- Energy wastage in round phase transmission
	- Energy wastage in rounds		

	- Single setup procedure	- Reduced energy consumption	- Poor load balancing
	- Reduced energy consumption	- Improved efficiency	- Additional overhead burden
RRCH	- Poor load balancing		
	- Varied CH selection	- Enhanced network lifetimes	- Limited support for large networks
	- Enhanced network lifetimes	- Varied CH selection procedure	- Poor load balancing
TB-LEACH	- Limited support for large	- Extended network lifetimes	- High overhead burden
	networks		
	- Used for dense and vast	- Enhanced setup stage and overhead	- Load balancing issues
	WSN	- Improved energy profile	
MLEACH-L	- Enhanced setup stage		
	- Redundant CH improves	- Improved results compared to original LEACH	- Increased setup phase time
V-LEACH	reliability	- Redundant CH for reliability	- Duplication potential
	- Balanced energy profile	- Balanced energy profile	- Setup enhancement issue
p LEACH	- Setup enhancement issue		
	- CH selection based on three	- Reduced power dissipation	- Load balancing
	conditions	- Optimised transmission path	
WST-LEACH	- Reduced power dissipation		

	- Prevents unnecessary energy	- Prevents unnecessary energy consumption	- Load balancing
	consumption	- Reduces energy consumption	- Additional overhead
EBC	- Additional overhead issue		
	- Enhanced scalability	- Enhanced scalability	- Load balancing
LEACH-SC	- Additional overhead issues		
Homogeneous Multi-Hopping-Based			
	- Suitable for large module	- Balanced energy consumption among MSNs	- Limited scalability
M-LEACH	networks with low density	- Appropriate for low density	- Suboptimal for small networks
	- Reduces energy consumption	- Distributes energy load in dense networks	- Not suitable for vast dense networks
TL-LEACH	- Distributes energy load	- Reduced energy consumption	
	in dense networks		
	- Stabilises network load	- Reduced energy usage per MSN	- Additional overhead
LEACH-L	- Reduced energy usage	- Stabilised network load	
	- Combines single and multi-	- Reduced energy consumption	- Limited scalability
MS-LEACH	hop profiles	- Combined single and multi-hop profiles	- Additional overhead
Heterogeneous Single Hop			
	- Enhances throughput and	- Enhanced throughput and lifetime compared	- Limited scalability
EECHE	Lifetime	to LEACH and SEP	- Reduced latency

	- Improved consistency	- Improved consistency	- Inadequate scalability
NEAP	- Inadequate scalability		- Not suitable for dense networks
Heterogeneous Multi Hop Protocols			
	- No requirement for nearby	- No nearby data collection needed	- Poor performance in multilevel networks
SEP	MSN data collection	- Eliminates energy/ round data collection	
	- Stabilises power	- Overhead management	- Limited scalability
HEED	- Overhead management	- Stabilised power distribution	- Latency issues
	- Latency issues		
	- Minimises problems using	- Minimises problems using unequal clusters	- Imbalanced clusters
	unequal clusters size	Size	- Poor load balancing
EEUC	- Imbalanced clusters	- Better energy efficiency	
	- CH elects best MSN	- Enhanced energy consumption profile	- Additional overhead
LEACH-HPR	for energy stabilisation	- CH chooses best MSN	
	- Minimises hotspot issues	- Minimises hotspot issues	- Poor load balancing
DEUC	- Minimises overhead issues	- Minimises overhead	

7. Analytical Conclusion with Future Scope of Finding More Applications

Table 4: Analytical comparison conclusions based on density, size and level of heterogeneity for different clustering algorithms.

Clustering Technique	Behaviour with Increased Density	Behaviour with Increased Area Size	Behaviour with Increased Heterogeneity
LEACH	- Low efficiency	- Low efficiency	- Low efficiency
MLEACH	- Moderate efficiency	- Moderate efficiency	- Low efficiency
SEP	- Better efficiency than all homogeneous algorithms	- Better efficiency than all other homogeneous algorithms	- Better efficiency than all other homogeneous algorithms
Z-SEP	- Better efficiency than SEP	- Better efficiency than SEP	- Throughput fluctuates, dead nodes stable, efficiency similar to SEP
EZ-SEP	- Better efficiency than Z-SEP	- Better efficiency than Z-SEP and TEEN	- Efficiency improved, throughput unchanged, load balancing issue exists

Table 5: Clustering algorithm application area, complexity level in implementation and stability factor.

S.No.	Clustering Technique	Environment	Application Domain (Based on Number of User or Density/ Cluster Wise)	Complexity Levels in Implementing	Stability of the Network
1	LEACH	Homogeneous	Moderate density passive wireless networks. Suites best with non-urgent transmission. Suitable for less density module	Lowest	Moderate
2	PEGASIS	Homogeneous	Suitable for low-density networks. Suites best with non-urgent transmission.	Higher than LEACH	Moderate
3	HEED	Homogeneous	For medium density passive and active wireless networks. Suites good with general data transmission. Suitable for moderate quantity of member sensors in a wireless network.	Moderate	Moderate
4	LEACH-C	Heterogeneous	For medium density passive and active wireless networks (camera-based also). Suites best with general and urgent data transmission. Suitable for moderate quantity of member sensors in a wireless network.	Moderate	Low
5	MOD-LEACH	Heterogeneous	For medium density passive and active wireless networks (camera-based also). Suites better than all homogeneous clustering with general and urgent data transmission. Suitable for moderate quantity of member sensors in a wireless network.	Moderate	Moderate

6	EMOD-LEACH	Heterogeneous	For medium density passive and active wireless networks (camera-based also). Suites better than all homogeneous clustering with general and urgent data transmission. Improved energy efficiency than previous versions of LEACH, suitable for non-urgent data.	Moderate to High (depending on value of m)	Moderate
7	DEEC	Heterogeneous	For medium density passive and active wireless networks (camera-based also). Suites better than all homogeneous clustering with general and urgent data transmission. Improved energy efficiency than previous versions of LEACH, suitable for non-urgent data.	Higher than EMOD-LEACH	Moderate
8	EDEEC	Heterogeneous	Better than DEEC, prominent for moderate density network with passive approach.	Higher than DEEC	Low
9	TDEEC	Heterogeneous	Good for medium to large scale of users in a cluster with optimum output.	Higher than EMOD-LEACH	Moderate
10	TEEN	Heterogeneous	Temperature sensitivity makes it suitable for scattered and low-density networks. Complex due to temperature sensitivity.	High	High
11	APTEEN	Heterogeneous	Temperature sensitivity makes it suitable for scattered and low-density networks. Complex due to temperature sensitivity.	High	High
12	SEP	Heterogeneous	Good stability for medium to large wireless networks with medium density of users. Complex due to stability requirement.	Moderate	Moderate
13	Z-SEP	Heterogeneous	Suitable for passive networks of low to medium density of users. Complex due to stability requirement.	Moderate	Moderate
14	EEAHP	Heterogeneous	Provides moderately good communication setup for moderate to high density of users for a wider area.	Moderately complex	Low to Moderate
15	EZ-SEP	Heterogeneous	Effective for high-density wireless network applications. Complex due to stability requirement.	Moderate	N/A

In a comparative analysis, the performance of three protocols, namely, SEP, LEACH and Z-SEP [1],[2], [3], was evaluated. The results showed that Z-SEP outperformed both LEACH and SEP in terms of performance Table. 1-4. The main area of concern when designing a wireless network module protocol/algorithm is the energy consumption of the module, the energy consumption of the network, and the overall lifespan of the module. It is important for both clauses to have a high level of importance or significance. Developing an enhanced and more efficient algorithm/protocol for distributing network load, with a focus on energy efficiency, poses significant challenges. The study suggests that adopting a Zonal based-SEP approach is a favourable option for dense networks. However, it is important to note that this approach does come with certain problematic issues. The extension of the zonal stable election protocol (EZ-SEP) [3], [1], [20] is a dual-level protocol that builds upon the zonal SEP [2], [4], [10]. It incorporates a modified CH selection-based approach and enables node communication with the base station (BS). The data is transferred among multiple base stations in a mixed zigzag manner, ultimately reaching the end point or sink. The E-advanced MSN employs a clustering algorithm or technique. By considering energy dissipation, the module's lifespan is enhanced under supervision. The extended version of Z-SEP is considered superior to the original version in terms of the overall network lifespan. This improvement is achieved by implementing an enhanced routing algorithm that selects a cluster head (CH) from the mobile sensor nodes (MSN) based on their residual energy levels. Furthermore, the duration of stability for a module or network until the first node failure is enhanced by considering the total number of active nodes within the network. The simulation results indicate that various modifications to the basic algorithms, such as transitioning from LEACH to MLEACH or using different versions of DDEC like EDEEC, TDEEC, DDEEC or SEP, have led to improvements in network performance factors. These factors include the life span of modules, the transmission of packets/MSN to the end point/sink and energy deterioration or consumption. Additionally, advancements such as ZSEP and EZ-SEP have further contributed to these improvements. When the level of heterogeneity is increased, the density of clusters is increased, or the area of the network is increased, various algorithms exhibit different behaviours.

References

[26] Tripathi, N. and Sharma, K.K., "Distributed and hierarchical clustering techniques comparison in wireless camera sensor networks," In: Kaiser, M.S., A. Bandyopadhyay, K. Ray, R. Singh, and V. Nagar, (eds) *Proceedings of Trends in Electronics and Health Informatics. Lecture Notes in Networks and Systems*, vol. 376, Springer, Singapore, 2022, doi: 10.1007/978-981-16-8826-3_33.

[27] Xie, L. and X. Zhang, "3D clustering-based camera wireless sensor networks for maximizing lifespan with Minimum coverage rate constraint," in *Proc. IEEE GLOBECOM*, Atlanta, GA, USA, pp. 298–303, 2013.

[28] Wang, J. and X. Zhang, "AQ-DBPSK/DS-CDMA based energy-efficient and interference- mitigation scheme for 3D clustered WCSNs with minimum coverage rate constraint," in *Proc. IEEE MILCOM*, Baltimore, MD, USA, pp. 305–310, 2014.

[29] Del Coso, A. *et al.*, "Cooperative distributed MIMO channels in wireless sensor networks," *IEEE J. Sel. Areas Commun.*, vol. 25, no. 2, pp. 402–414, 2007.

[30] Wang, J. and X. Zhang, "Cooperative MIMO-OFDM based multi-hop 3D clustered wireless camera sensor networks," in *Proc. IEEE Wireless Commun. Network Conf. (WCNC)*, New Orleans, LA, USA, pp. 1350–1355, 2015.

[31] Nosratinia, A. *et al.*, "Cooperative communication in wireless networks," *IEEE Commun. Mag.*, 2004.

[32] Parmar, J. *et al.*, "Study of wireless sensor networks using leach-teen and Apteen routing protocols," *Int. J. Sci. Res.*, ISSN (Online), pp. 2319–7064.

[33] Kiwan, H. *et al.* "Hierarchical networks: routing and clustering (a concise survey)," *2013 26th IEEE Canadian Conference of Electrical and Computer Engineering (CCECE)*.

[34] Rathi, N. *et al.*, "A review on routing protocols for application in wireless sensor networks," *Int. J. Distrib. Parallel Syst.*, vol. 3, no.5, 2012.

[35] Jain, P. *et al.*, "The comparison between leach protocol and pegasis protocol based on lifetime of wireless sensor networks," *Int. J. Comput. Sci. Mob. Comput.*, vol. 6, no.12, pp.15–19, 2017.

[36] Kirichek *et al.*, "Flying ubiquitous sensor networks as a queening system," *Proceedings, International Conference on Advanced Communication Technology, ICACT 2015*, Phoenix Park, Korea, 2015.

[37] Attarzadeh *et al.*, "A new three-dimensional clustering method for wireless sensor networks," *Global J. Comput. Sci. Technol*, vol. 11, no. 6, 2011. version 1.0.

[38] Hooggar, M. *et al.*, "An energy efficient three-dimensional coverage method for wireless sensor networks," *J. Acad. Appl. Stud.*, vol. 3, no. 3, 2013.

[39] Abakumov, P. and Koucheryavy, A. "The cluster head selection algorithm in the 3D USN," *Proceedings, International Conference on Advanced Communication Technology, ICACT 2014*, Phoenix Park, Korea, 2014.

[40] Hai, D. T. *et al.*, "Novel fuzzy clustering scheme for 3D wireless sensor networks," *Appl. Soft Comput. J.*, vol. 54, pp. 141–149, 2017.

[41] Chong, C.-Y. and S. Kumar, "Sensor networks: evolution, opportunities, and challenges," *Proc. IEEE*, vol. 91, no. 8, pp. 1247–1256, 2003.

[42] Akyildiz, I., W. Su, Y. Sankarasubramaniam, and E. Cayirci, "Wireless sensor networks: a survey," Comput. Netw., vol. 38, no.4, pp. 393–422, 2002.

79. Efficiency and Accuracy Analysis of Object Detection Algorithms in Deep Learning

Jyoti Vitthal Chhatrband and BhaveshKumar Choithram Dharmani

School of Electronics and Electrical Engineering, Lovely Professional University, Punjab, India

Abstract: Object detection has become a crucial step in the process as computer vision applications, such as autonomous driving and picture recognition, multiply. This sector has undergone a revolution thanks to deep learning (DL) techniques' astounding accuracy and efficiency. This study gives a general overview of the computer vision process of object identification and compares several DL architectures for it. The main goal is to identify the algorithm that is the most accurate and effective in terms of computing. CIFAR-10 data sets and performance measures make up the assessment methodology employed for this research. The CNN-based algorithms that have been chosen for examination are the VGG16, ResNet50 and MobileNET networks. The investigation shows that the ResNet50 method is less accurate than the VGG16 and MobileNet networks. Additionally, when employed with restricted hardware, these two techniques deliver good computational efficiency. The study examines the many elements, including network design and training methods, that affect the performance of the algorithms. These results provide a clearer understanding of the weaknesses and advantages of each algorithm and make suggestions for further research.

Keywords: Object detection, VGG16, ResNet50, MobileNet, deep learning (DL).

1. Introduction

The extraordinary skills of deep learning (DL) algorithms have largely been responsible for the enormous breakthroughs in object recognition from photos that have occurred in recent years. Convolutional neural networks (CNNs), in particular, have revolutionised the area of computer vision and have emerged as the preferred method for object identification tasks. DL models have shown improved performance in a variety of object recognition applications due to their capacity to automatically learn and extract high-level features from complicated visual input. Research and publications on object detection using DL have increased as a result of growing interest in the subject. Numerous academic studies have aided in comprehending cutting-edge methods, investigating various designs and pictures using DL is the subject of a systematic review that is published in [1] to give readers a thorough introduction to the topic. This study gives a broad overview of the state of the research, highlighting important approaches, datasets and problems in the area. The survey undertaken by Liu *et al.* [2] also contributes to our knowledge by examining DL methods for generic object recognition and providing a thorough evaluation of the developments in this field. Furthermore, the research by Mahaur *et al.* [3] compares DL-based algorithms in this context and focuses primarily on road item recognition. The effectiveness and applicability of several algorithms for tasks involving road object identification are discussed in this article. Multiobject identification and tracking are covered in-depth in the work of Pal *et al.* [4], which also presents the current state of the art and discusses the improvements made by DL techniques. The study work by Pathak *et al.* [5] analyses the actual implementation and addresses the advantages and problems of deploying DL models in real-world settings to obtain insights into the application of DL for object detection. Additionally, Zaidi *et al.*'s review [6] offers an overview of contemporary DL-based object identification models by going through their topologies, performance and prospective applications. The study performed by Xiao *et al.* [7] provides an overview of the underlying techniques and their performance on various datasets, offering a thorough examination of object identification algorithms based on DL. Furthermore, the publications by Yu *et al.* [9] and Nguyen *et al.* [8] especially address tiny object identification and present unique methods based on DL for increased detection precision. Our research study intends to carry out an efficiency and accuracy analysis of object identification algorithms in DL, concentrating on CNN architectures like MobileNet, VGG16 and ResNet50, building on the knowledge from prior studies. We want to determine the best method in terms of accuracy and computing efficiency by comparing these algorithms on benchmark datasets and taking performance measures into account. In conclusion, this study expands on prior research and strives to advance the area of object detection by evaluating the effectiveness and precision of DL methods. We hope to shed light on the benefits and drawbacks of various algorithms by thoroughly examining several DL techniques and their performance on diverse datasets. Our research findings will ultimately help academics and practitioners choose the best algorithm for object identification tasks by taking both accuracy and computing efficiency into account.

2. Literature Review

Eleven abstracts are reviewed in the literature review, each with its unique assessment criteria and methodology. Agriculture, aerial photography, underwater ecosystems, wastewater treatment and species categorisation are just a few of the many topics covered in the publications. The articles highlight the uses of several DL methods, including convolutional neural networks (CNNs) and hybrid models. They also talk about how well they detect items. Accuracy, distance estimates, privacy protection and real-time performance are the main assessment criteria. The articles that make up this collection go into how DL approaches may be used to find diverse things, such water harvesting devices and unmanned aerial aircraft. They also discuss how they may be used to find items indoors and in mixed reality.

Authors	Methodology/Algorithm Used/Processing Method	Evaluation Parameters/Results	Output
A. Tiwari *et al.* [10]	DL approach	Detection of historic water-collecting irrigation systems automatically	Identification of ancient water harvesting systems
M. Tasyurek *et al.*	Grayscale-to-DWT and DL-based image classification	Adversarial image object detection	Detecting objects in photographs that have been maliciously modified
Y. M. Tang *et al.* [11]	Integration of AI object recognition into real-time mixed reality	Digital twins with integrated real-time object recognition	Using a hybrid reality system for real-time object recognition
S. H. Silva *et al.* [12]	Integrated, privacy-protecting, deep-vision, unmanned aerial vehicles	Cooperative unmanned aerial vehicles for real-time object recognition and tracking	Object recognition and tracking in real time
A. Nagarajan *et al.* [13]	Deep learning with hybrid optimization	Detecting and estimating the distance to objects inside buildings to aid the sight impaired.	Detecting and measuring distances to objects inside a building
Z. A. Lone *et al.* [14]	Using hyperspectral image to identify objects	Hyperspectral image object detection	Object detection in hyperspectral images
V. Krishnan *et al.* [15]	Cross-layer convolutional neural network hybridization	Identifying and following submerged objects	Underwater object detection and tracking
J. Kotwal et al.[16]	Traditional approach and DL	Agricultural plant diseases identification using DL	Identification of agricultural plant diseases

O. Inbar *et al.* [17]	Accelerating object detection with R-CNN and YOLOv5	The use of object detection algorithms to the evaluation of the secondary treatment of wastewater	Process evaluation for treating wastewater
Y. Du *et al.* [18]	Automatic object recognition and pixel-level segmentation of pavement cracks using a modelled detection algorithm	Cracks in the pavement are detected as objects and segmented at the pixel level automatically.	Cracks in the pavement are identified and categorised automatically.
B. Fu *et al.* [19]	Algorithms for stacked ensemble learning and reinforcement learning	Classification of mangrove species from UAV multispectral photos using random forest ensemble vs stacking ensemble learning	Mangrove species identification using multispectral UAV imagery

The literature study demonstrates the advancements achieved in the creation of DL-based algorithms for object detection. The papers made available demonstrate how these techniques may be applied to solve a variety of problems and produce reliable outcomes. The employment of different algorithms and approaches in DL has demonstrated how adaptable these methods are for dealing with a range of applications. The articles' results and assessment metrics provided important new perspectives on the effectiveness and suitability of the suggested strategies. The review is a helpful tool for practitioners and researchers, enabling them to comprehend the most advanced object identification algorithms in more detail. The results of the investigations can be used as a foundation for future research and to open new avenues for advancement.

3. Methodology

3.1. Dataset

Machine learning and computer vision researchers frequently utilise the CIFAR-10 image classification benchmark dataset[20]. It features 10 separate classes and more than 60,000 colour graphics, as seen in Figure 1. This dataset offers a set of difficult pictures that may be used to assess algorithms, including over 50,000 training images and over 10,000 testing images. The dataset has been crucial for the development of CNNs and other DL models. Additionally, it has aided in the advancement of research into neural network transfer learning. The benchmark dataset has significantly advanced computer vision by serving as a standard against which to compare the performance of various models.

Figure 1: Sample dataset.

3.2. Data Augmentation

By performing different modifications on the current data, the approach known as data augmentation is frequently employed in deep learning (DL) to fictitiously expand the training dataset. The previously stated parameters, horizontal_flip, width_shift_range and height_shift_range, are particular augmentations that may be used on photos.

The greatest proportion by which the picture can be horizontally moved is determined by the width_shift_range option. For instance, a value of 0.1 indicates that the picture can only be moved by a maximum of 10% of its width. The greatest vertical shift permitted for the picture is specified by the height_shift_range argument in a similar manner.

The picture can be horizontally flipped or not depending on the value of the horizontal flip option. When set to True, there is a possibility that the image will be horizontally inverted, producing a mirrored version of the original.

The model becomes more resistant to minor changes in the input data, including shifts and flips, by incorporating these data augmentations during training. This enhances the model's performance on untried data and helps to generalise the learnt features.

3.3. Algorithm Used

3.3.1 CNN

An analytical framework for visual data processing is the CNN architecture. It has a variety of layers, including fully linked and convolutional ones. The convolution procedure, one of a CNN's key components, is crucial. To produce a new output, a kernel and filter are combined with the input image. The CNN mathematical expression is shown in Eq. 1.

$$y_{i,j,k} = f\left(\sum_{m=1}^{M}\sum_{n=1}^{N}\sum_{l=1}^{L} w_{m,n,l,k} . x_{i+m-1,\, j+n-1,l}\right) + b_k \qquad 1$$

where, = 'activation at position (i,j) in the kth feature map', = 'input pixel at position $(i+m-1, j+n-1)$ in the lth input channel', = 'weight of the filter', = 'bias term', f = 'activation function'.

3.3.2 VGG16

The VGG16 framework from Oxford University is a type of neural network with 16 linked layers. It has three fully linked layers and 13 convolutional layers. The 3 × 3 filters used in the VGG16 architecture have padding 1 and stride 1, and then there is a maximum pooling phase. Each layer's non-linear activation processes are covered by a mathematical formula.

3.3.3 ResNet50

ResNet50 is a deep residual network that was introduced by Microsoft Research. It addresses the vanishing gradient problem by using skip connections or shortcuts that allow the network to learn residual functions. The mathematical formula for ResNet50 is defined as eq.2:

$$y = F(x) + x \qquad 2$$

where = 'output of the residual block', x = 'input to the block' and $F(x)$ = 'residual function that the block aims to learn'.

3.3.4. MobileNet

MobileNet is a lightweight deep neural network architecture designed for mobile and embedded devices. It utilises depth-wise separable convolutions to reduce the computational complexity while maintaining good accuracy.

4. Results and Outputs

4.1. Confusion Matrix

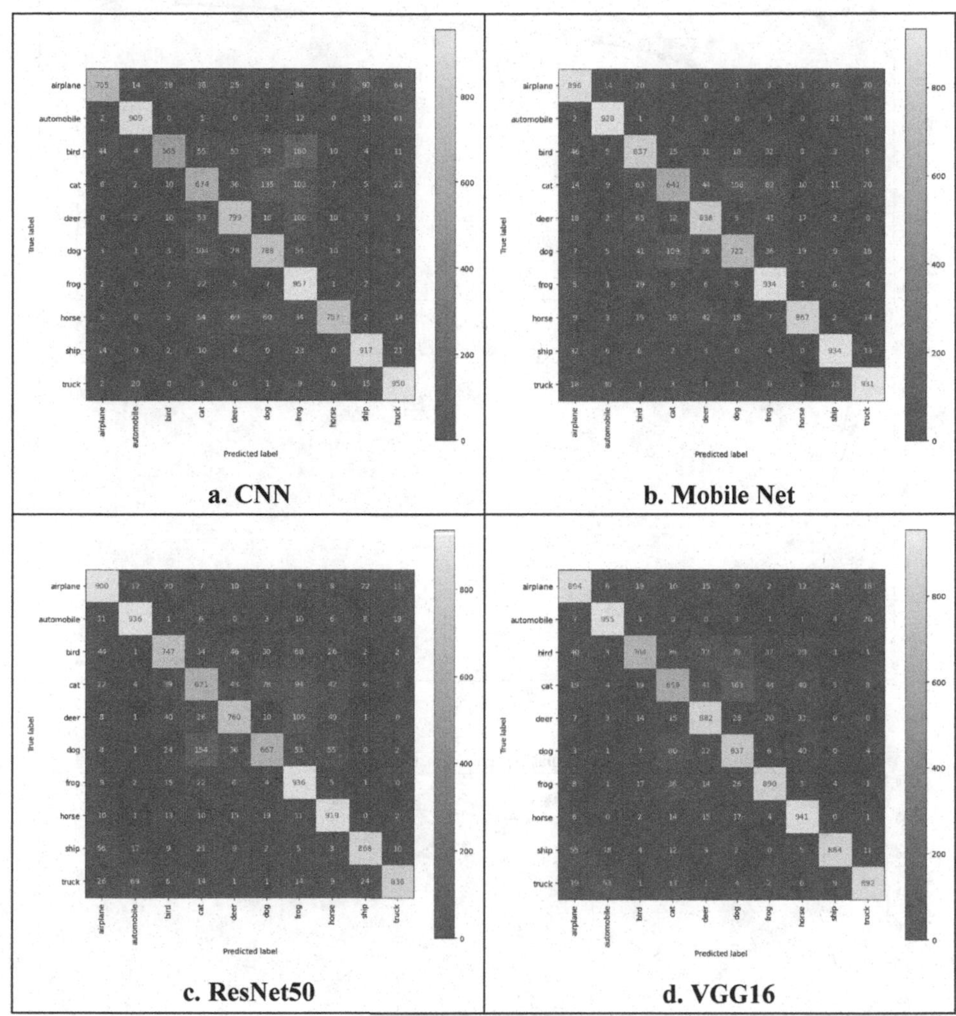

Figure 2: *Confusion matrix for various DL algorithms.*

4.2. Training Accuracy/Loss vs Epochs

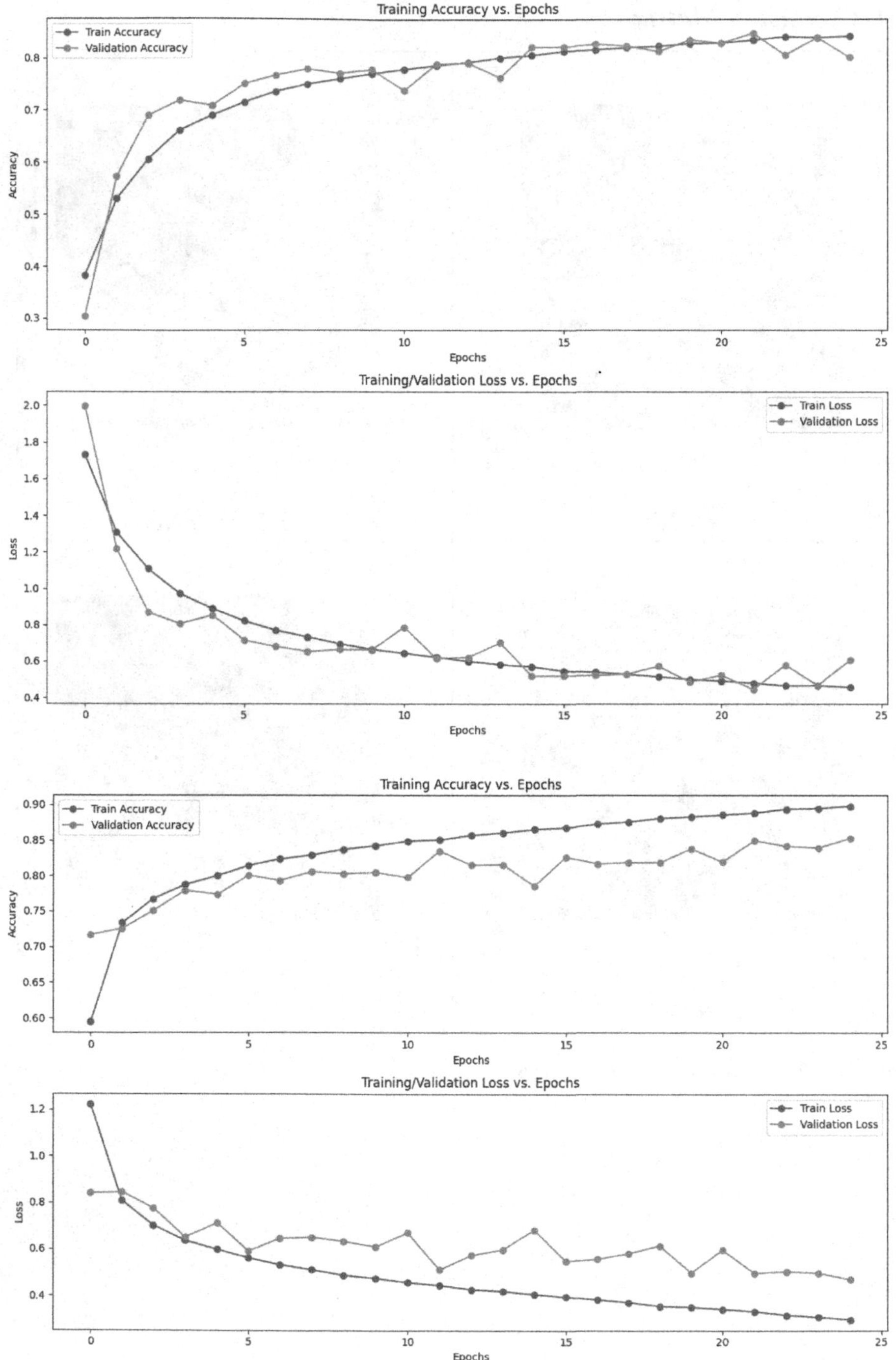

Figure 3: *Training accuracy/loss vs epochs – CNN, MobileNet.*

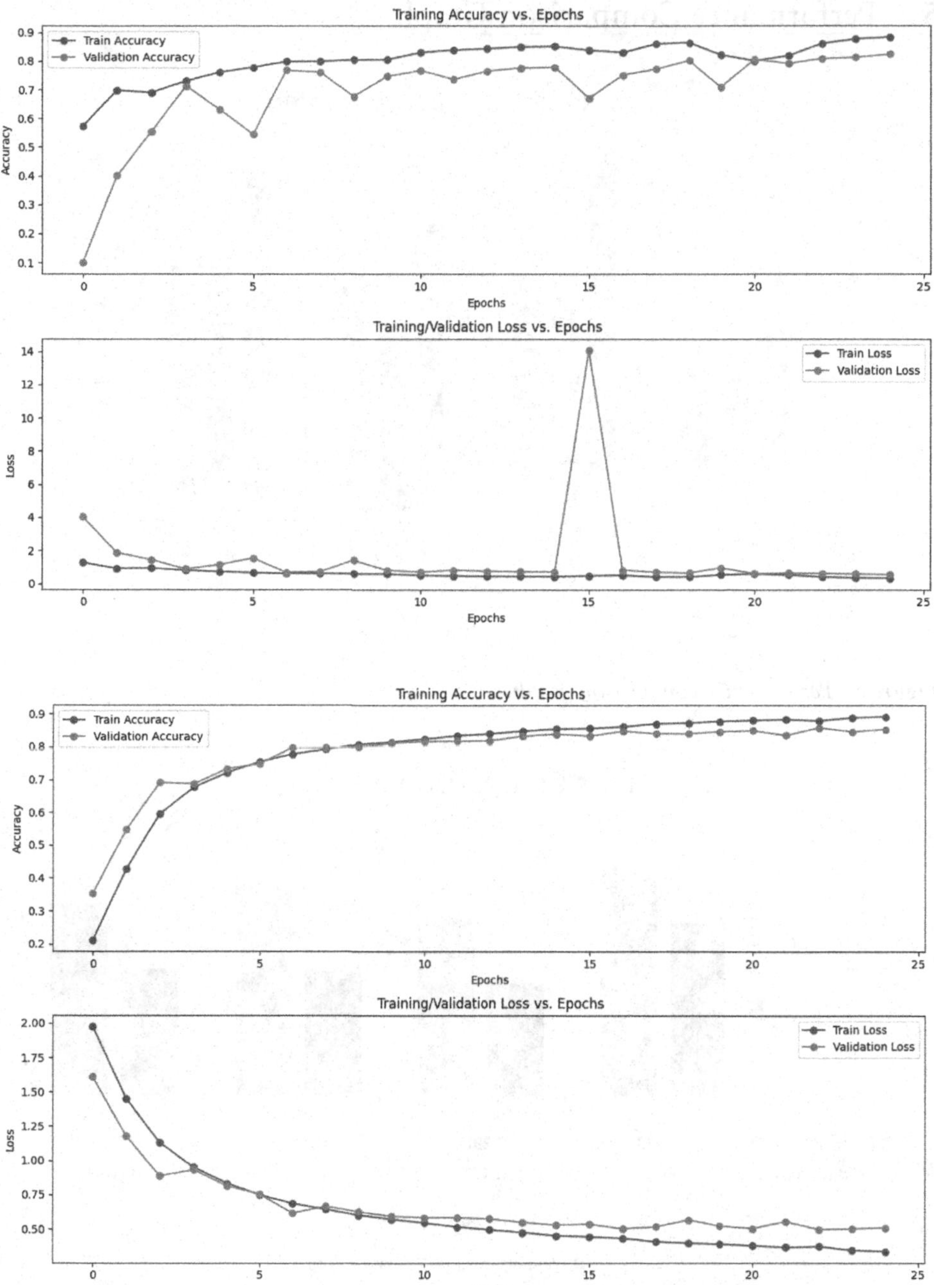

Figure 4: *Training accuracy/loss vs epochs – Resnet50, VGG16.*

5. Performance Comparison Graph

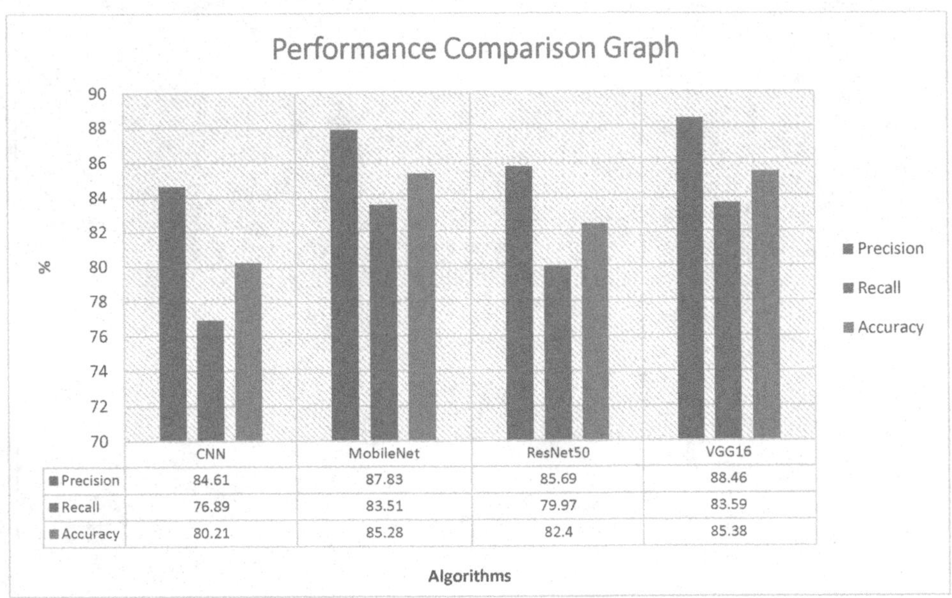

Figure 5: *Performance comparison graph.*

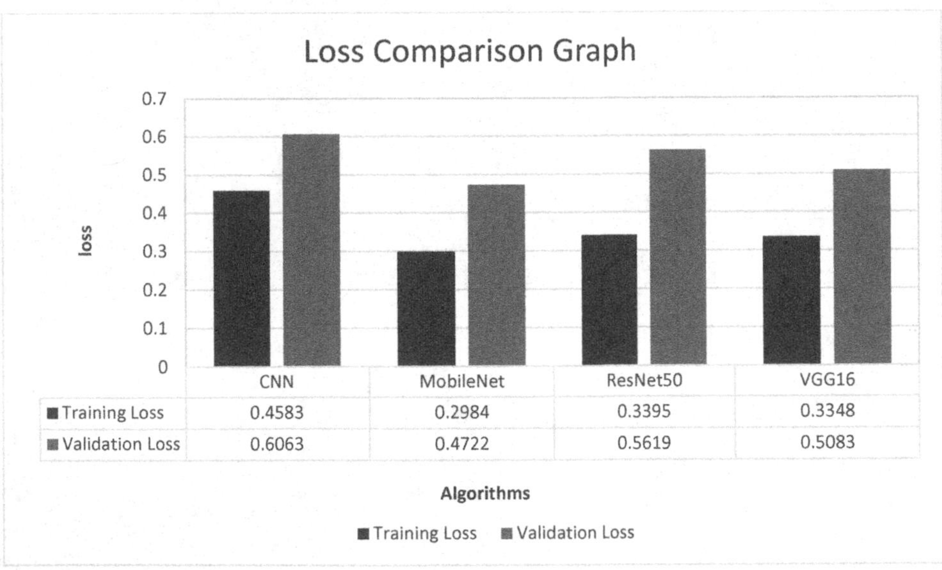

Figure 6: *Loss comparison graph.*

The confusion matrix is shown in Figure 2, and the comparison of training accuracy/loss vs. epoch is shown in Figures 3 and 4. A summary of the findings for the various models in terms of precision, recall, accuracy, training loss and validation loss is shown in Figures 5 and 6. In terms of precision, MobileNet came in first with a score of 87.83%, closely followed by VGG16 with a score of 88.46%. The accuracy of the CNN model was 84.61%, while that of ResNet50 was 85.69%. In terms of recall, VGG16 scored the highest (83.59%), followed by MobileNet (83.51%). CNN had a recall of 76.89%, whereas ResNet50 had a recall of 79.97%. In terms of accuracy, VGG16 came in first with 85.38% accuracy, followed closely by MobileNet with 85.28%. ResNet50 had an accuracy of 82.4%, whereas CNN had an accuracy of 80.21%.

Moving on, MobileNet got the lowest training loss (0.2984) and lowest validation loss (0.4722), respectively, among all the training and validation losses. Training loss for VGG16 was 0.3348, while validation loss was 0.5083. The training loss and validation loss for ResNet50 were 0.3395 and 0.5619, respectively. Last but not least, CNN had a validation loss of 0.6063 and a training loss of 0.4583. These findings reveal that MobileNet and VGG16 did well across a range of assessment measures, with high precision, recall and accuracy scores and minimal training and validation losses.

6. Conclusion and Future Scope

The analysis of the effectiveness and precision of several DL object detection algorithms served as its conclusion. Precision, recall, accuracy, training loss and validation loss measures were used to evaluate the CNN, MobileNet, ResNet50 and VGG16 models. Based on the findings, CNN and ResNet50 were less accurate than MobileNet and VGG16. These models demonstrated decreased training and validation losses while achieving greater precision, recall and accuracy scores. This shows how well they did at correctly identifying things in the dataset. There are various potential directions for further investigation. First, employing more sophisticated DL architectures or investigating ensemble models might improve object detection performance even further. It could also be useful to look at how various data augmentation methods or fine-tuning tactics affect the performance of the models. The capacity of the object identification methods to generalize may also be shown by investigating the transferability of the trained models to various datasets or domains. Finally, taking efficiency into consideration, optimising the models for real-time or resource-constrained situations may be a worthwhile endeavour. Overall, the work emphasises the significance of choosing the right DL models for object identification tasks and offers insightful information for further investigation in this area.

References

[1] Kaur, J. and W. Singh, *A Systematic Review of Object Detection from Images Using Deep Learning*, no. 0123456789, Springer US, 2023.

[2] Liu, L. *et al.*, "Deep learning for generic object detection: a survey," *Int. J. Comput. Vis.*, vol. 128, no. 2, pp. 261–318, 2020, doi: 10.1007/s11263-019-01247-4.

[3] Mahaur, B., N. Singh, and K. K. Mishra, "Road object detection: a comparative study of deep learning-based algorithms," *Multimedia Tools Appl.*, vol. 81, no. 10. 2022.

[4] Pal, S. K., A. Pramanik, J. Maiti, and P. Mitra, "Deep learning in multi-object detection and tracking: state of the art," *Appl. Intell.*, vol. 51, no. 9, pp. 6400–6429, 2021, doi: 10.1007/s10489-021-02293-7.

[5] Pathak, A. R., M. Pandey, and S. Rautaray, "Application of deep learning for object detection," *Procedia Comput. Sci.*, vol. 132, no. Iccids, pp. 1706–1717, 2018, doi: 10.1016/j.procs.2018.05.144.

[6] Zaidi, S. S. A., M. S. Ansari, A. Aslam, N. Kanwal, M. Asghar, and B. Lee, "A survey of modern deep learning based object detection models," *Digit. Signal Process. A Rev. J.*, vol. 126, p. 103514, 2022, doi: 10.1016/j.dsp.2022.103514.

[7] Xiao, Y. *et al.*, "A review of object detection based on deep learning," *Multimedia Tools Appl.*, vol. 79, no. 33–34, 2020.

[8] Nguyen, N. D., T. Do, T. D. Ngo, and D. D. Le, "An evaluation of deep learning methods for small object detection," *J. Electr. Comput. Eng.*, vol. 2020, 2020, doi: 10.1155/2020/3189691.

[9] Yu, C., K. Liu, and W. Zou, "A method of small object detection based on improved deep learning," *Opt. Mem. Neural Netw. Inf. Opt.*, vol. 29, no. 2, pp. 69–76, 2020, doi: 10.3103/S1060992X2002006X.

[10] Tiwari, A., M. Silver, and A. Karnieli, "A deep learning approach for automatic identification of ancient agricultural water harvesting systems," *Int. J. Appl. Earth Obs. Geoinf.*, vol. 118, no. August 2022, p. 103270, 2023, doi: 10.1016/j.jag.2023.103270.

[11] Tang, Y. M., W. Li, W. T. Kuo, and C. K. M. Lee, "Real-time mixed reality (MR) and artificial intelligence (AI) object recognition integration for digital twin in," *Internet Things*, p. 100753, 2023, doi: 10.1016/j.iot.2023.100753.

[12] Silva, S. H., P. Rad, N. Beebe, K. K. R. Choo, and M. Umapathy, "Cooperative unmanned aerial vehicles with privacy preserving deep vision for real-time object identification and tracking," *J. Parallel Distrib. Comput.*, vol. 131, pp. 147–160, 2019, doi: 10.1016/j.jpdc.2019.04.009.

[13] Nagarajan, A. and G. M P, "Hybrid optimization-enabled deep learning for indoor object detection and distance estimation to assist visually impaired persons," *Adv. Eng. Softw.*, vol. 176, no. November 2022, p. 103362, 2023, doi: 10.1016/j.advengsoft.2022.103362.

[14] Lone, Z. A. and A. R. Pais, "Object detection in hyperspectral images," *Digit. Signal Process. A Rev. J.*, vol. 131, p. 103752, 2022, doi: 10.1016/j.dsp.2022.103752.

[15] Krishnan, V., G. Vaiyapuri, and A. Govindasamy, "Hybridization of deep convolutional neural network for underwater object detection and tracking model," *Microprocess. Microsyst.*, vol. 94, no. August, p. 104628, 2022, doi: 10.1016/j.micpro.2022.104628.

[16] Kotwal, J., D. R. Kashyap, and D. S. Pathan, "Agricultural plant diseases identification: From traditional approach to deep learning," *Mater. Today Proc.*, vol. 80, pp. 344–356, 2023, doi: 10.1016/j.matpr.2023.02.370.

[17] Inbar, O., M. Shahar, J. Gidron, I. Cohen, O. Menashe, and D. Avisar, "Analyzing the secondary wastewater-treatment process using Faster R-CNN and YOLOv5 object detection algorithms," *J. Clean. Prod.*, vol. 416, no. June, p. 137913, 2023, doi: 10.1016/j.jclepro.2023.137913.

[18] Du, Y. *et al.*, "Modeling automatic pavement crack object detection and pixel-level segmentation," *Autom. Constr.*, vol. 150, no. February, p. 104840, 2023, doi: 10.1016/j.autcon.2023.104840.

[19] Fu, B. *et al.*, "Comparison of RFE-DL and stacking ensemble learning algorithms for classifying mangrove species on UAV multispectral images," *Int. J. Appl. Earth Obs. Geoinf.*, vol. 112, no. June, 2022, doi: 10.1016/j.jag.2022.102890.

[20] Krizhevsky, A., V. Nair, and G. Hinton, "CIFAR-10 and CIFAR-100 datasets," *Https://Www.Cs.Toronto.Edu/~Kriz/Cifar.Html*, 2009, https://www.cs.toronto.edu/~kriz/cifar.html.

80. Multi-Criteria Collaborative Filtering for Therapy Recommendation to Autistic Children

Kusumalatha Karre[1] and Y. Ramadevi[2]

[1]*Dept of CSE and SNIST, Dept of ECM, Osmania University, Hyderabad, India*
[2]*Dept of AIML, Chaitanya Bharathi Institute of Technology, Hyderabad, India*

Abstract: Recommender systems have become important in various fields to help in making proper decisions. They are being used extensively in health care for prediction and recommendations. Collaborative filtering is widely used to generate recommendations based on the similarity between the users. In this paper, we propose a multi-criteria collaborative filtering that considers more than one similarity metric to generate recommendations for autistic children. It is the first of its kind to generate similar users which helps to provide appropriate therapy recommendations to autistic children satisfying multiple criteria. Two similarity measures namely Cosine and Euclidean have been considered to generate similar users, and the therapies common to these similar users have been generated. This helps to provide accurate therapies to autistic children.

Keywords: Collaborative filtering, multi-criteria, cosine similarity, Euclidean distance, autism.

1. Introduction

Healthcare recommendation system is playing a vital role these days in making decisions related to the health of a person based on the health records available related to their lifestyle, food habits and previous medical history. The recommender system uses different types of filtering such as content based, collaborative based, hybrid demographic and knowledge based [1]. Among the different types of filtering in recommender systems, collaborative filtering is widely used to generate recommendations based on the similarities among different users. It is of two types model based and memory based. In model based, ratings are predicted and recommendations are generated. In memory based, similar users are considered and recommendations are generated based on similar interests. In this paper, we propose a recommender system for autistic children to recommend therapies using multi-criteria collaborative filtering. Autism is a neurodevelopment disorder that hinders the development of a child. The therapies that are necessary if provided at an early stage will help the child to develop to the fullest. The rest of the paper is organised as follows: A literature survey of recommender systems using collaborative filtering, proposed method, results, comparative study with the existing model, conclusion and future scope.

2. Literature Survey

Collaborative filtering is being widely used in the recommender system. The following table gives an overview of various recommender systems which has used collaborative filtering and the similarity measure used.

Table 1: Recommender systems with collaborative filtering.

S. No	Author	Dataset Used	Type of Filtering	Similarity Measure used
1	V. Subramaniyaswamy *et al.* [2]	climate-based dataset, food information dataset and user dataset.	Hybrid filtering	SlopeOne recommender from Apache Mahout
2	Fran Casino *et al.* (2018)	Data collected from sensors	Collaborative filtering	Euclidean distance with k=1
3	Seda PolatErdeniz *et al.* [3]	Data collected from sensors	Collaborative filtering for virtual coach and content-based filtering for virtual nurse.	K nearest neighbor
4	Bogdan Walek and Vladimir Fojtik [4]	Movielens dataset	Hybrid recommender systems	Cosine Similarity
5	Manu Kohli *et al.* [5]	Data of 29 children with ASD has been collected	Collaborative filtering and patient similarity	Cosine similarity
6	Fouzia Jabeen *et al.* [6]	Data collected from biosensors	Hybrid filtering	Community-based similarity
7	Arthur Mai *et al.* [7]	298 patients' data was collected from 2014 to 2020	Hybrid filtering	Patient similarity
8	Abolfazl Ajami & Babak Teimourpour [8]	Data of 2519 students was collected from a university	Hybrid filtering	K nearest neighbour
9	Y. A. Nanehkaran *et al.* [9]	Data collected from PhysioNet	Collaborative filtering	K nearest neighbour

It has been observed that the existing systems used only one similarity measure. In the proposed system, we try to use more than one similarity metric to find similar users and generate common users from both the similarity metrics which can help to generate more appropriate therapy recommendations for the children.

3. Materials and Methods

Autism is a condition that hinders the growth of an individual in terms of communication and social life. It will be a lifelong disability unless treated at an early stage. Early intervention can help a child to develop the necessary life skills for day-to-day activities. There are various screening tools available CHAT in 1992 (Checklist for autism in toddlers) [10], M-CHAT in 2001 (Modified version of CHAT) [11], QCHAT in 2008 (Quantitative checklist for autism in toddlers) was introduced which has 25 questions which has to be answered on a scale of 0–4 where 0 is low and 4 is high. Out of 25 questions, 13 are reverse scored where 0 is high and 4 is low [12]. Q-Chat dataset [13] has been used for the model building. It has 252 records and 36 columns which have various attributes like number of siblings, age in months, mother's age and Q-CHAT 25 questions with the scoring and sum of these scorings as well. The therapy dataset has been collected from the professionals who train the children with autism at the training institutes. It consists of therapies corresponding to each question to be provided if the score is high. We select the records that are only autistic from the whole dataset. This process comes under feature selection which also includes selecting the child with questions which has a rating greater than 3 resulting in a new autistic dataset. We combine the therapy dataset with the new dataset based on the question number. The autistic dataset has 2575 records with 3 columns. The therapy dataset has 32 records with 2 columns. Both the autistic dataset and therapy dataset are combined based on question number resulting in 3296 records with 5 columns.

4. Proposed System

In the proposed system, we use multi-criteria collaborating filtering for therapy recommendations to autistic children. Collaborative filtering is used to recommend the items based on the similarities between the users. We use memory-based collaborative filtering wherein we try to find similar users and recommend similar therapies to the target. We try to incorporate various similarity measures to identify similar users in various aspects. The following similarity measures are considered.

Cosine Similarity: measures the cosine of the angle between two vectors. It is a measure of the direction of the vectors, not their magnitude. This means that two vectors can be considered similar even if they have different magnitudes. It is defined as

$$\cos(\theta) = \frac{A.B}{||A||.||B||} \cos(\theta) = \frac{A.B}{||A||.||B||}$$

where A_i and B_i are the ith components of vectors A and B

In our dataset, we try to find similar users based on the various attributes related to speech, sensitivity, gross motor and interpersonal skills, and it is given by CosineSimilarity (u1, u2)=$(\sum_{i=1}^{25} u1i, u2i)/(\sqrt{\sum_{i=1}^{25}}(u1, i)\ pow2)(\sqrt{\sum_{i=1}^{25}}(u2, i)pow2)$

where $u_{1,i}$ and $u_{2,i}$ are the values of the *i*th question for users u_1 and u_2, respectively.

Euclidean distance measures the distance between two points in a Euclidean space. It is calculated by taking the square root of the sum of the squares of the differences between the coordinates of the two points. This means that two points can be considered similar if they are close together in Euclidean space.

The Euclidean distance formula says:

$$d = \sqrt{[(x_2 - x_1)^2 + (y_2 - y_1)^2]}$$

where,

- (x_1, y_1) are the coordinates of one point.
- (x_2, y_2) are the coordinates of the other point.
- d is the distance between (x_1, y_1) and (x_2, y_2).

In our dataset, we try to find the distance between the users based the various attributes and is given by

$$\textit{Euclidean distance}\ (u1, u2) = \sqrt{\sum_{i=1}^{25}}(u1, i - u2, i)pow2$$

where $u_{1,i}$ and $u_{2,i}$ are the values of the ith question for users $u1$ and $u2$, respectively. The proposed system architecture is shown in Figure 1

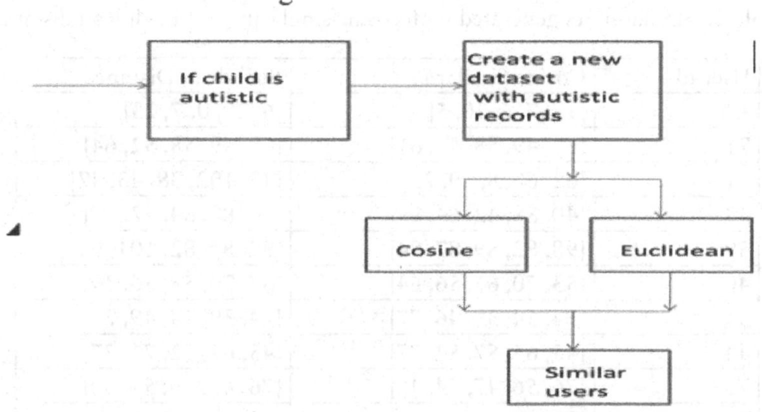

***Figure 1:** Multicriteria collaborative filtering.*

The algorithm for multi-criteria collaborative filtering is as follows:

Input: Data frame consisting of autistic children.

Output: Similar users.

Procedure:

1. Load the data frame of autistic children, i.e., relation *r*
2. Finding similar users by computing the distance between the users.
3. The cosine similarity is given by

$$\text{Cosine similarity } (u1,u2)=(\textstyle\sum_{i=1}^{25} u1i,u2i)/(\sqrt{\sum_{i=1}^{25}}(u1,i)\,pow2)(\sqrt{\sum_{i=1}^{25}}(u2,i)pow2$$

where $u_{1,i}$ and $u_{2,i}$ are the values of the ith question for users u_1 and u_2, respectively.

4. Euclidean distance to calculate the similarity between the users is given by

$$\text{Euclidean distance } (u1,\, u2) = \sqrt{\textstyle\sum_{i=1}^{25}}(u1,i-u2,i)pow2\sqrt{\textstyle\sum_{i=1}^{25}}(u1,i-u2,i)pow2$$

where $u_{1,i}$ and $u_{2,i}$ are the values of the ith question for users $u1$ and $u2$, respectively.

5. The similar users from both the above similarity metrics are collected and the common users are calculated as shown below:

Common users = {(a, b) | a, b ∈ similar_users_cosine[a,b] ∩ similar_users_euclidean[a,b]

5. Results

The similar users generated above will be used as an input to the content-based filtering,

which is used to generate recommendations based on the therapies of the similar users. It uses a therapy dataset that has therapies associated with each question. The sample of similar users generated by cosine similarity metrics and Euclidean distance is shown in Table 1.

Table 2: Similar users generated with cosine similarity and Euclidean distance.

User id	Cosine Similarity	Euclidean Distance
12	[17, 7, 6, 20, 5]	[6, 20, 0, 7, 23]
71	[68, 49, 58, 52, 61]	[68, 49, 58, 52, 64]
41	[62, 60, 8, 89, 22]	[33, 102, 38, 43, 47]
53	[40, 88, 42, 64, 99]	[40, 88, 64, 42, 47]
59	[98, 82, 89, 87, 94]	[89, 87, 82, 101, 95]
40	[53, 70, 67, 56, 64]	[67, 70, 53, 56, 39]
51	[74, 54, 39, 46, 77]	[74, 39, 54, 49, 77]
44	[45, 65, 57, 52, 77]	[45, 67, 52, 71, 77]
70	[76, 56, 47, 54, 40]	[76, 47, 56, 54, 39]
20	[23, 19, 8, 6, 18]	[23, 19, 6, 8, 12]
19	[20, 15, 14, 6, 0]	[20, 0, 6, 14, 15]
22	[72, 69, 83, 4, 92]	[41, 72, 92, 69, 83]
57	[61, 44, 55, 43, 60]	[44, 61, 43, 55, 38]

The common therapies generated by the content-based filtering is as shown in Table 2. Table 3 shows the recommended therapy for autistic children.

Table 3: Therapy recommendations for autistic children.

User id	Recommendations
12	**'Behavior intervention strategies ','Occupational Therapy', 'Relationship development intervention'], 'Relationship Development Intervention', 'Social Relational approaches', 'Speech Therapy '**
71	**'Occupational Therapy', 'Picture Exchange', ['Structured play & speech and language therapy ', 'Relationship Development Intervention', 'Early Intensive Behavioral Intervention (EIBI)'**
41	**['Social Relational approaches', 'Relationship development intervention']**
53	**'Structured play & speech and language therapy ', 'Picture Exchange', 'Speech and language therapy ', 'Occupational Therapy', social stories', 'Discrete trail training', 'Floor time', 'Social Relational approaches, 'Sensory Integration Therapy ', 'Applied behavior Analysis', 'Relationship Development Intervention', 'Occupational therapy', 'Social skills training ' , 'Early Intensive Behavioral Intervention (EIBI)', 'Speech Therapy', 'Social Relational approaches', 'Developmental individual differences', 'Relationship development intervention'**
59	**[]**
40	**'Picture Exchange', ['Structured play & speech and language therapy ', 'Floor time'], 'Relationship Development Intervention', 'Early Intensive Behavioral Intervention (EIBI)', 'Social Relational approaches', 'Speech Therapy', 'Developmental individual differences', 'Relationship development intervention'**
51	**'Picture Exchange', ['Structured play & speech and language therapy ', 'Relationship Development Intervention', 'Early Intensive Behavioral Intervention (EIBI)', 'Social Relational approaches', 'Speech Therapy', 'Speech Therapy'], 'Relationship development intervention'**
44	**'Occupational Therapy', 'Picture Exchange', 'Structured play & speech and language therapy ', 'Early Intensive Behavioral Intervention (EIBI)'**
70	**['Structured play & speech and language therapy ', 'Floor time'], 'Relationship Development Intervention', 'Early Intensive Behavioral Intervention (EIBI)', 'Social Relational approaches', 'Speech Therapy', 'Developmental individual differences', 'Relationship development intervention'**
20	**'Picture Exchange', ['Behavior intervention strategies ', 'Structured play & speech and language therapy ', 'Occupational Therapy', 'Sensory Integration Therapy'], 'Social Relational approaches', 'Speech Therapy', 'Relationship development intervention'**

6. Comparative Study of Cosine and Euclidean Similarity Measures

Collaborative filtering is generally implemented by using any one of the similarity measures. In the multi-criteria collaborative filtering two different similarity measures namely cosine and Euclidean distance were used. The following table shows the comparative study of both the similarity measures and the users who are similar in both the criteria are considered to generate the recommendations in the next stage. This approach helps us to consider the users who are similar in different aspects and provide better recommendations when compared with the single similarity measure. Table 4 is showing the comparative study of similarity measures.

Table 4: Comparative study of similarity measures.

User-id	Cosine Similarity	Euclidean Distance	Similar Users
12	[17, 7, 6, 20, 5]	[6, 20, 0, 7, 23]	[20, 6, 7]
71	[68, 49, 58, 52, 61]	[68, 49, 58, 52, 64]	[49, 58, 68, 52]
41	[62, 60, 8, 89, 22]	[33, 102, 38, 43, 47]	[]
53	[40, 88, 42, 64, 99]	[40, 88, 64, 42, 47]	[64, 40, 88, 42]
59	[98, 82, 89, 87, 94]	[89, 87, 82, 101, 95]	[89, 82, 87]
40	[53, 70, 67, 56, 64]	[67, 70, 53, 56, 39]	[56, 67, 53, 70]
51	[74, 54, 39, 46, 77]	[74, 39, 54, 49, 77]	[74, 77, 54, 39]
44	[45, 65, 57, 52, 77]	[45, 67, 52, 71, 77]	[45, 52, 77]
70	[76, 56, 47, 54, 40]	[76, 47, 56, 54, 39]	[56, 76, 54, 47]
20	[23, 19, 8, 6, 18]	[23, 19, 6, 8, 12]	[8, 19, 6, 23]
19	[20, 15, 14, 6, 0]	[20, 0, 6, 14, 15]	[0, 6, 14, 15, 20]
22	[72, 69, 83, 4, 92]	[41, 72, 92, 69, 83]	[72, 83, 92, 69]
57	[61, 44, 55, 43, 60]	[44, 61, 43, 55, 38]	[43, 44, 61, 55]

7. Conclusion

Collaborative filtering is used to recommend the items based on the similarity between the users. The existing system has used only one similarity measure to find similar users. In the proposed method, we use two similarity measures namely Cosine and Euclidean distance to find the similarity between the users. We further use the intersection to find similar users from all the similarity measures. Our approach results in finding users who are similar in multiple criteria which can be used for providing accurate therapy recommendations to autistic children.

References

[1] Sahoo, A. K. *et al.*, "DeepReco: deep learning based health recommender system using collaborative filtering," *Computation*, vol. 7, p. 25, 2019.

[2] Subramaniyaswamy, V. *et al.*, "An ontology-driven personalized food recommendation in IoT-based healthcare system," *J. Supercomput.*, vol. 75, pp. 3184–3216, 2018.

[3] Erdeniz, S. P. *et al.* (2018). "Recommender systems for IoT enabled m-Health applications," In Iliadis, L., I. Maglogiannis, and V. Plagianakos, (eds) *Artificial Intelligence Applications and Innovations*. AIAI 2018. IFIP Advances in Information and Communication Technology, vol 520. Springer, Cham, doi: 10.1007/978-3-319-92016-0_21.

[4] Walek, B. and V. Fojtik, "A hybrid recommender system for recommending relevant movies using an expert system," *Expert Syst. Appl.*, vol. 158, p. 113452, 2020, ISSN 0957-4174, doi: 10.1016/j.eswa.2020.113452.

[5] Kohli, M. *et al.* "Machine learning-based ABA treatment recommendation and personalization for autism spectrum disorder: an exploratory study," *Brain Inform.*, vol. 25, no. 1, p. 16, 2022. doi: 10.1186/s40708-022-00164-6. PMID: 35879626; PMCID: PMC9311349.

[6] Jabeen, F. *et al.*, "An IoT based efficient hybrid recommender system for cardiovascular disease," *Peer-to-Peer Netw. Appl.*, vol. 12, p. 1263–1276, 2019.

[7] Mai, A. *et al.* "A drug recommender system for the treatment of hypertension," *BMC Med. Inform. Decis. Mak.*, vol. 23, p. 89, 2023, doi: 10.1186/s12911-023-02170-y.

[8] Ajami, A. and B. Teimourpour, *A Food Recommender System in Academic Environments Based on Machine Learning Models*, 2023, https://doi.org/10.48550/arXiv.2306.16528.

[9] Nanehkaran, Y. A. *et al.*, "Diagnosis of chronic diseases based on patients' health records in IoT healthcare using the recommender system", *Wireless Commun. Mobile Comput.*, vol. 2022, no. 5663001, p. 14, 2022, doi: 10.1155/2022/5663001.

[10] Baron-Cohen, S. *et al.* "Can autism be detected at 18 months? The needle, the haystack, and the CHAT," *Br. J. Psychiatry*, vol. 161, pp. 839–843, 1992.

[11] Robins, D. L. *et al.* "The modified checklist for autism in toddlers: an initial study investigating the early detection of autism and pervasive developmental disorders," *J. Autism Dev. Disord.*, vol. 31, no. 2, pp. 131–144, 2001.

[12] Carrie, A., S. Baron-Cohen, S. Wheelwright, T. Charman, J. Richler, G. Pasco, and C. Brayne, "The Q-CHAT (quantitative CHecklist for autism in toddlers): a normally distributed quantitative measure of autistic traits at 18–24 months of age," *J. Autism Dev. Disord.*, 2008. doi: 10.1007/s10803-007-0509-7.

[13] Niedźwiecka *et al.*, "Q-CHAT scores of polish toddlers with autism spectrum disorders and typically developing controls," *2019 Mendeley Data, V1*, doi: 10.17632/tmpkt2mfkg.1(**QCHAT dataset**).

81. Implementation of IOT's MQTT Protocol with JavaScript

Mahesh Swami,[1] Sakshi Kumar,[1] and Devansh Tiwari[2]

[1]*Computer Science Engineering (CSE), Aravali College of Engineering and Management, Haryana, India*
[2]*Chandigarh University, Punjab, India*

Abstract: As the world is getting more and more technology driven, Internet of Things (IoTs) have emerged as new saviour. Automation have provided a new enhancement is the standard of living of human being. As we have internet of humans that helps human stays connected with each other, IoTs allow electronic device with connectivity capabilities to connect with each other to form a close network for interchange of information. In this paper, we are going to implement IoT's MQTT Protocol with JavaScript.

Keywords: IoT, MQTT, JavaScript, HTTP, TCP, SEO.

1. Introduction

The term Internet of Things (IoT) technically is the network of things or objects which have sensors and network modules [1]. IoT things can be any type of device, vehicle or building, equipment and by using appropriate software and electronics, these things are able to send and receive data.

So, we can say that connectivity plays a vital role in this as it helps to send and receive data for the overall running of IOT applications. There are already many proposed protocols for IoTs names as, MQTT [2], CoAP [3], LWM2M [4], etc.

There are abundant applications of IOTs in different fields such as medical, banking, industry, education and many more. If we talk about healthcare systems, the IOT systems are used to send and receive healthcare data from one user to another user or systems.

So, we can say that the data must be important and it requires high transmission properties and accuracy using IOT. This requires high accuracy in IOTs protocols with different parameters.

IOT devices connect with each other and share data with each other for meaningful purpose. This purpose could be anything from home automation to weather prediction.

Data can be received in raw form from the sensors attached to the network, like temperature sensor to fetch data about temperature, humidity sensor for sensing humidity. These data are then sent over the network and the are converted into information for some.

Let us take a simple example of an IoT network consisting of a humidity sensor, temperature sensor and a bulb. The bulb will lit up when the temperature is above 30°. The data are published from both the sensors in the IoT cloud and then retrieved by the bulb. This is an example of an IoTs network where data are produced and shared in the network.

The IoT devices communicate with each other through some set of rules which we call IoT protocols. These protocols ensure that the data from one device gets utilised within the system, gets read by the required device or service. Figure 1 presents IOT network use with temperature and humidity sensor.

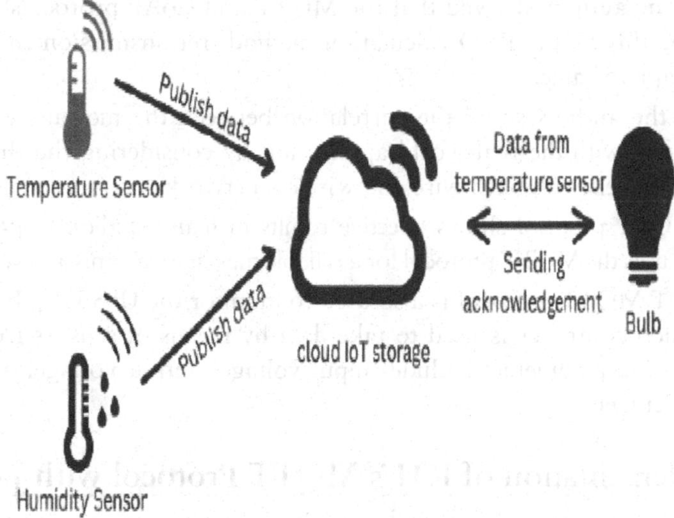

Figure 1: IOT network use with temperature and humidity sensor.

On the basis of different scenarios, we have different IoT-based protocols depending upon one's need, usage and extent of optimization named as Message Queue Telemetry protocol, Hypertext Transfer Protocol (HTTP), Constrained Application Protocol, Data Distribution Service, Web Socket Protocol and Advanced Message Queue Protocol. These all protocols can be used according to the situation and complexity of a problem.

But as it is observed that there are many improvements are needed in these protocols. In this paper, we are going to improve the MQTT protocol using JavaScript in terms of efficiency, accuracy and connectivity.

JavaScript is one of the most popular languages in today's world, and it has a variety of applications. It is used in making static and dynamic websites, mobile applications. It is fast, SEO friendly, easy to write and provides various built-in libraries and frameworks which make development tasks very easy. With the help of JavaScript, we can easily create scalable full-stack applications.

2. Literature Review

There are already many IoT protocols are purposed to take care of advance solutions of IoT. This is a very active area in IoT and many new protocols and new standards have been developed in the application layer of IoT to help to connect all things of IoTs.

In [5], the authors developed a platform named as 'Ponte', and it is a message broker to adapt different protocols of IoTs to publisher and subscriber models. This is used to analyse the MQTT and CoAP protocols in terms of latency and also examine different network characteristics, and this Ponte platform is included in Eclipse repositories [6]. This suggests that there is a presence of high delay in MQTT protocol and when the data traffic increased significantly, we can use CoAP protocol.

In [7], the authors showed that the MQTT and CoAP protocols can perform better by modifying the RTO calculation method (retransmission time out) from fixed to adaptive value.

In [8], the authors show the correlation between the message loss and end-to-end latency with the real-world application by considering the three different MQTT QoS levels with both wire and wireless network.

The MQTT protocol shows effective results in many studies. In [9], the author designs and uses the MQTT protocol for a reliable message transmission system for IOT.

The IOT MQTT protocol is also used to monitor the UPS [10]. In this system, Arduino microcontroller is used to take data by means of sensors from the UPS. The monitoring parameters includes input voltage, output voltage, output power and output current.

3. Implementation of IOT's MQTT Protocol with JavaScript

MQTT stands for message queue transmission telemetry. It is a protocol based on the publish/subscribe model and is effective as it requires less bandwidth and less resources.

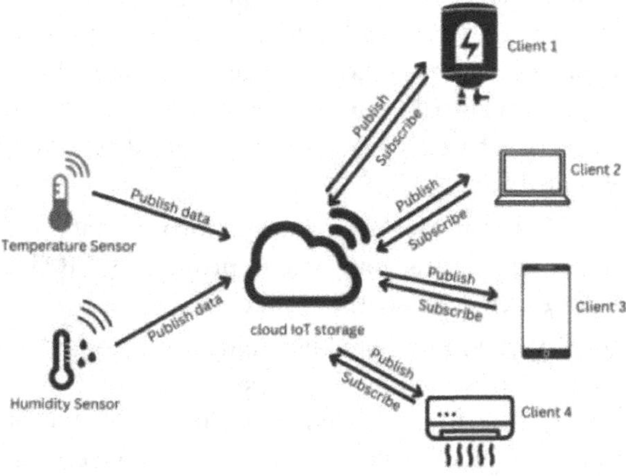

Figure 2: Architecture of IOT network system.

It is based on a simple publish and subscribe model. We have topics specified correspond to which, particular client subscribe. And then the publisher publishes the data to the particular topic and data is received by the client subscribing to that only topic. This protocol is simple, effective, secure and resource friendly.

In this paper, we tried to implement the MQTT protocol with JavaScript.

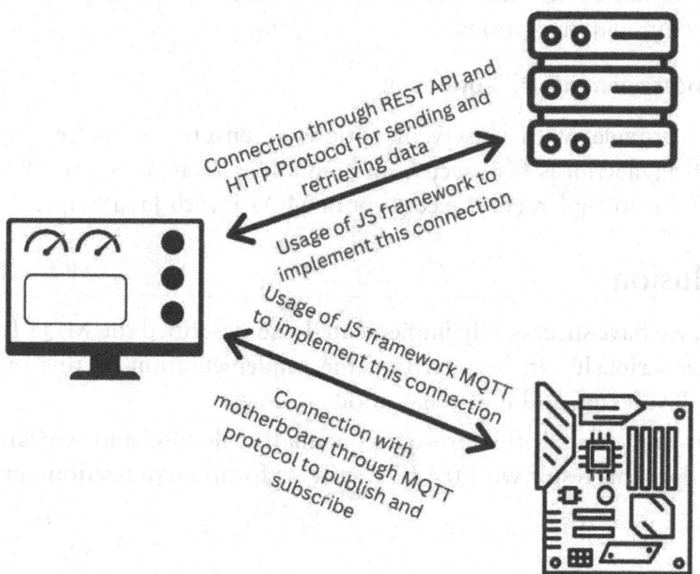

Figure 3: Interface of MQTT using JavaScript.

This implementation of MQTT is done using MQTT.js library of JavaScript. MQTT.js is a JavaScript library written for client-side implementation of JavaScript and is written for the Node.js environment and implementation in the browser. This library of MQTT is used to implement the concepts of protocols using JavaScript.

As all the communication in the web browser happens through web sockets, MQTT.js ensures that everything runs smooth and ensures that everything works fine even if the connection drops off or the client gets disconnected.

3.1. How to Start with MQTT.JS and React

We start with creating a new react app and setting up all the dependencies. In the very next step, we install MQTT.js through a package manager.

In MQTT.js, to establish a connection, we need to specify the configurations along with the URL to connect to. In most of the cases, it is the uri link of the MQTT broker.

The connection options are given as
const options = {

protocol: wss/ws/mqtt,

username: [username of the broker],
password: [password saved in broker]
}

These options are like configurations in the MQTT protocol and specify the additional parameters like connect Timeout and clean. After that, initialisation of client with the uri and the options.

var client = mqtt.connect('uri' , options);

MQTT.js provides with variety of options to ensure the implementation of protocol with JavaScript is fast, secure and reliable. This is the work of MQTT.js, and we can use it to implement the concept of MQTT with JavaScript.

4. Conclusion

In this paper, we have successfully implemented and described the MQTT Protocol using the JavaScript. It can be seen that the implementation of this protocol is simpler than JavaScript, and it also has good accuracy.

We have also implemented this protocol on small scale also and we can see that it will show the same result with the IOT systems for interconnection between the devices.

References

[1] Xia, F. *et al.*, "Internet of things," *Int. J.Commun. Syst.*, vol. 25, pp. 1101–1102, 2012.

[2] "Machine to Machine (M2M) Communication Study Report," IEEE C 80216 10_0002r7, 2010.

[3] Internet Engineering Task Force (IETF), "The Constrained Application Protocol (CoAP)," http://tools. ietf.orglhtmllrfc7252 (accessed: 2014).

[4] OMA Lightweight Machine to Machine Protocol vl,O, http://technical. openmobilealliance.orgiTechnicallrelease_program/lightweightM2M_vl_0. asp.

[5] Collina, M. *et al.*, "Internet of things application layer protocol analysis over error and delay prone links," *Advanced Satellite Multimedia Systems Conference and the 13th Signal Processing for Space Communications Workshop (ASMS/SPSC)*, pp. 398, 404, 2014.

[6] Ponte Eclipse Project, "Connecting things to developers," http://eclipse. orglponte (accessed: 2015).

[7] Garcia Davis, E. *et al.*, "Improving packet delivery performance of publish/ subscribe protocols in wireless sensor networks," *Sensors*, vol. 13, pp.648–680, 2013, doi: I O. 3390/sI30100648.

[8] Chen, W. *et al.*, *Responsive Mobile User Experience Using MQTT and IBM Message Sight*, IBM Corp., 2014.

[9] Hwang, H. C. *et al.*., "Design and implementation of a reliable message transmission system based on MQTT protocol in IoT," *Wireless Pers. Commun.*, vol. 91, pp. 1765–1777, 2016, doi: 10.1007/s11277-016-3398-2.

[10] Alqinsi, P. *et al.*, "IoT-based UPS monitoring system using MQTT protocols," *2018 4th International Conference on Wireless and Telematics (ICWT)*, Nusa Dua, Bali, Indonesia, pp. 1–5, 2018, doi: 10.1109/ICWT.2018.8527815.

82. Design of Fractional-NPLL Using Delta Sigma Modulation for Low-Phase Noise

Md Abdul Muqueem,[1] Shanky Saxena,[1] and Govind Singh Patel [2]

[1]*School of Electronics and Electrical Engineering Lovely Professional University, Punjab, India*

[2]*Electronics and Telecommunication Engineering, SITCOE, Yadrav, Kolhapur, Maharashtra, India*

Abstract: A phase-locked loop (PLL) is a structured circuit design within a closed-loop control system, primarily responsible for synchronizing the frequency and phase of an incoming signal. It functions as a type of frequency synthesizer and holds significant importance, especially in integrated transceivers used for wireless communication. In this discussion, we explore the design of a 3rd order Δ-Σ modulator model. However, there is room for improvement by introducing a novel approach to create a new PLL architecture optimized for low noise in wireless applications. This new PLL design aims to address several challenges, including reducing power consumption, minimizing the required chip area and achieving high-frequency performance. We will compare different PLL configurations using diagrams to illustrate the differences. In PLL-based fractional-N frequency synthesisers, the division ratio is controlled by delta-sigma modulators. The increased demand for synthesisers that can function at non-integer multiples is partially met by this. In this paper, we will develop the fundamental aspects of the PLL, including the basic loop transfer function, sources of noise, dividers, phase detectors and the operation of fractional-N techniques.

Keywords: PLL, control system, synchronization, frequency synthesizer.

1. Introduction

The phase-locked loop (PLL) concept, based on DeBellescize's synchronous detection theory proposed in 1932, has a rich history of applications. By 1947, PLLs were already being used to synchronize the horizontal and vertical scanning in television receivers. Today, PLLs play a pivotal role in wireless communication circuits and systems, serving as precise frequency generators and local oscillators. In the context of the 3rd order delta sigma modulator (DSM), it is employed to dynamically adjust the feedback division modulus. However, the output of a fractional-N PLL coupled with the DSM heavily relies on the input reference frequency. To capture the output frequency spectrum of the tuned PLL accurately, multiple samples are required. Consequently, we chose to utilize Simulink for designing simulations and Matlab for parametersing the modules in our design. In our discussion below, we have successfully simulated and showcased the third-order DSM along with a dual modulus pre-scaler. We have also plotted the frequency spectrum and extracted phase noise values. Rationale for this study and background information: Frequency synthesisers come in various designs, with one of the most popular being the PLL[2]. PLL technology is constantly evolving and improving its noise characteristics and efficiency. Initially, after its discovery and years of research, the integer-N PLL was developed. It shares many blocks with a simple PLL, but it also incorporates a divider circuit with a division value of N in the feedback path. This divider divides the output frequency of the voltage-controlled oscillator (VCO), which, when fed to the phase-frequency divider, generates multiple frequencies relative to the reference frequency. Later, the integer-N PLL was combined with a pre-scaler network to extend the upper frequency range of the counter. The pre-scaler prevents the "*n*" value from being restricted to integers. Subsequently, the dual modulus approach and the pulse swallowing technique were introduced. Each of these methods had its limitations, leading to the introduction of a fresh technique. This new technique allows the divider values to take on fractional values, reducing the addition of 20 dB noise during the frequency multiplication process.

There are two categories of noise that impact the PLL's performance: random noise and periodic noise. Random noise can manifest as phase noise. A fractional-N PLL, aided by DSMs, has proven to be an efficient solution for frequency synthesis. It finds applications in wireless communication circuits and system-on-chip (SoC) clock generators. Here, noise shaping of a bit stream around a specific frequency is made possible by using an all-digital implementation of delta-sigma modulation. The noise shaping feature of a fractional frequency synthesizer can be used to eliminate in-band spurious tones from the output. Figure 1 shows fractional-N PLL block. The noise shaping function was initially created for use in a switched capacitor technique to reduce quantization noise in analogue to digital converters.

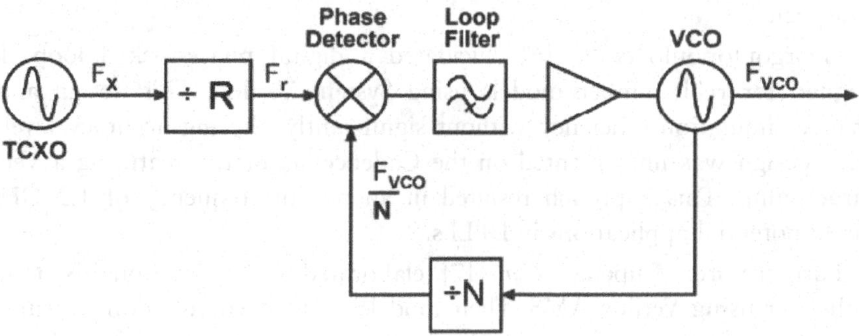

Figure 1: Fractional-N PLL.

2. Literature Review

Furthermore, in the work by [AQ: Please note that "Ye Zhang" is not the author mentioned in reference "2." Please check and change the author name as per reference list.]Zhang *et al.* [2], a novel approach was identified and proposed to reduce both area and power consumption. They accomplished this by implementing an error masking technique for signal quantisation and modulation in a frequency synthesiser. Remarkably, this enhancement did not compromise system performance. Zhang also optimised the word length and designed an LMS algorithm to minimise uncertainty by adjusting the gain of the loop filter output. The synthesiser incorporated Fourier transform for analogue blocks and employed z-transform for digital blocks, making it highly adaptable for PLL design. Additionally, they integrated a differentiator and RC mash.

Abedi *et al.* [3] introduced a method to reduce reference spurs through a simplified charge pump design implemented in 0.18 µm CMOS technology on the ADS Simulator. The achieved spur level was −74 dB, and the lock time was 1.9 ms. They also opted for a true single-phase clocking circuit divider instead of current mode logic.

Similarly, Modi *et al.* [4][AQ: Please note that "Dhaval Modi" is not the author mentioned in reference "4." Please check and change the author name as per reference list.] employed 45 nm CMOS technology to implement a frequency detector and frequency divider. They discerned the distinction between frequency and phase, particularly for low-power applications.

In the research work of Patel *et al.* [5], an architecture for PLL dedicated to pure signal synthesis, primarily for wireless communication, was developed. This PLL boasted short locking times and high-frequency resolution. Mathematical modelling was a key aspect, allowing for the derivation of noise parameters in the Fractional PLL. The design was executed using the CppSim simulator, resulting in a novel architecture that exhibited a 5 dBc/MHz improvement.

Abedi *et al.* [3] introduced a method to reduce reference spurs through a simplified charge pump design implemented in 0.18 µm CMOS technology on the ADS simulator. The achieved spur level was −74 dB, and the lock time was 1.9 ms. They also opted for a true single-phase clocking circuit divider instead of current mode logic.

Georgoulopoulo *et al.* [6] elucidated a digital phase-locked loop (DPLL) designed for real number models using System Verilog. This design aimed to enhance simulation efficiency without significantly altering accuracy levels. The DPLL design was implemented on the Cadence simulator, featuring a Verilog-A charge-pump. This approach resulted in an output frequency of 1.2 GHz and offered potential applications in DPLLs.

Furthermore, Zhipeng *et al.* [7] elaborated on a fractional-N frequency synthesiser using Verilog-AMS. Their model included voltage domain simulation and improved efficiency through the combination of the frequency divider and VCO. Performance verification was carried out for the ΔΣ modulator.

Golghate *et al.* [8] designed DPLL circuitry with Booth's multiplier, loop filter and a controlled oscillator. The architecture was implemented in Verilog synthesis using Xilinx 13.1, resulting in reduced area and lower power consumption.

Continuing in this vein, Osmany *et al.* [9] provided an analytical model for phase noise detection in Fractional-N PLLs, with a focus on RF synthesisers. They effectively filtered noise in the charge pump, VCO and loop filter within the PLL.

Lastly, Bharanidharan *et al.* [10] implemented a discrete PLL with a focus on avoiding dead zones. They employed FPGA technology to achieve superior results and devised a novel equation that expanded the tracking range. This approach led to increased tracking time and range, offering accurate analysis with reduced area and enhanced precision. Additionally, they introduced a Delayed locked loop alongside the PLL, resulting in low noise, fine delay time and reduced rms jitter. The technology found application in 5G communication, delivering low-noise performance.

3. Description of Research

The three fundamental components mentioned above serve as the foundational building blocks for the realization of any type of phase-locked loop (PLL). Without these core elements, a PLL cannot be constructed.

PLLs can be broadly categorized into three main types

Types of PLL's: PLL's are broadly classified into three types namely:

i. Analogue PLL
ii. Digital PLL
iii. All digital PLL

Analogue phase locked loops are usually constructed around using an analogue phase detector, charge pump, a low pass filter and negative feedback with the phase detector. Analogue phase locked loops are built using analogue devices. Analogue PLL's have a phase detector which produces charge up/down current pulses, whose duration will be proportionate to the lag among the edges of the output signal and the supplied incoming reference signal. Figure 2 shows analog PLL block.

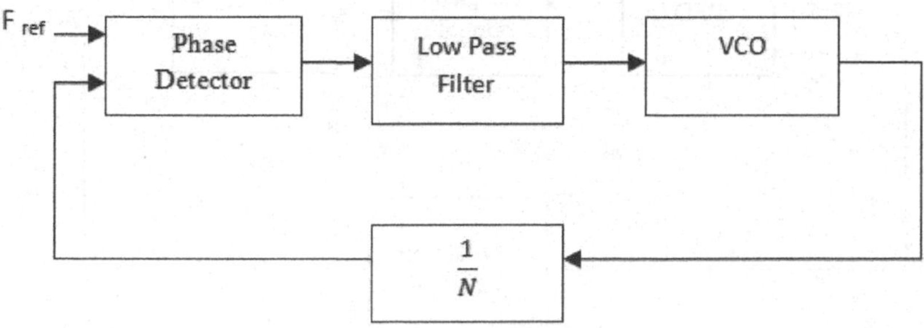

Figure 2: Analogue PLL.

A digital PLL encompasses all three fundamental building blocks mentioned earlier. In digital PLLs, the core building blocks are composed of digital components. These digital PLLs utilize dividers, which can be placed in the direct path or the feedback path, depending on the desired efficiency for a specific application. In the end, the output signal from the PLL system represents a rational multiple of the input reference frequency supplied to the phase-frequency detector (PFD) block [3]. The PFD in a digital PLL is constructed using digital components, often employing logic gates. Logic gates like XOR, NOR and NOT serve as the foundational elements for building various digital circuits in electronics. These gates are employed and configured to model the essential functionalities of electronic components within digital circuits. It is important to note that not all components in a digital PLL are strictly digital; some analogue blocks, such as the loop filter and charge pump, may still exist in analogue form as needed. Digital PLLs employ digital elements selectively, adapting them to the specific requirements of the design. Figure 3 shows digital PLL block

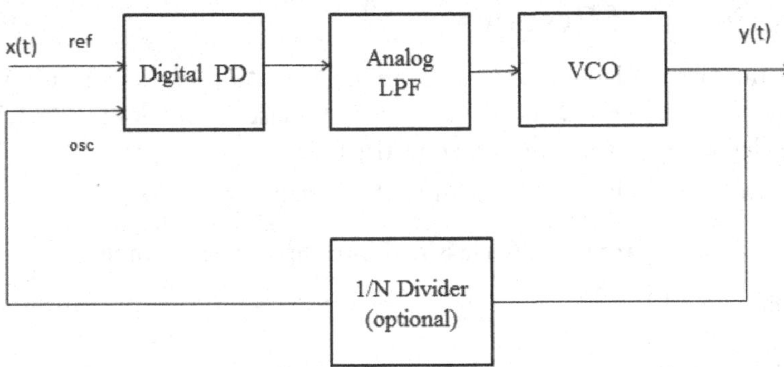

Figure 3: Digital PLL.

An all-digital PLL, as the name implies, is constructed entirely using digital components, distinguishing it from digital PLLs where only select elements are digital, with the rest being analogue. The choice to using an all-digital PLL

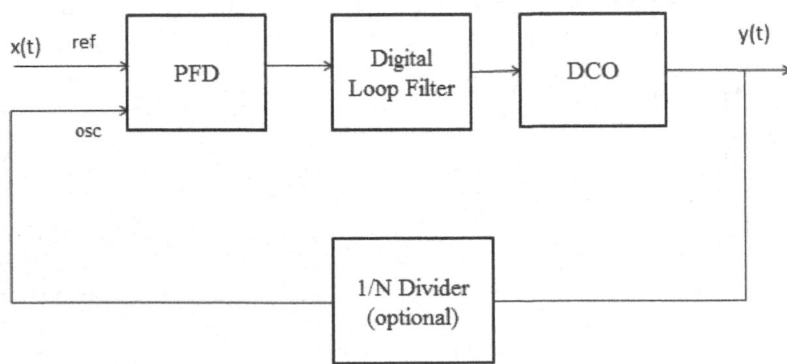

Figure 4: All digital PLL.

as shown in figure 4. depends on the specific application requirements. The distinguishing feature of an all-digital PLL is the use of a digital oscillator known as a numerically controlled oscillator (NCO), which replaces the conventional VCO found in other types of PLLs. In addition, in an all-digital PLL, the phase detector block produces a digital output that directly correlates with the time differences between the input signals—typically, one reference signal and another as feedback. Compared to both analogue and digital PLLs, All-digital PLLs offer several advantages. They do not require supply voltage regulation as analogue and digital PLLs do. Additionally, all-digital PLLs are highly synthesized, making them adaptable to various applications, and they are compact in size compared to their counterparts.

The digital PLL discussed above is commonly referred to as an integer-N PLL. The implementation of this type of PLL is known as the integer-N PLL[4]. An integer-N PLL enables the channel spacing to be set at either the reference frequency itself or at various multiples of the reference frequency. For instance, if the reference frequency is set at 3 MHz, the channel spacing can be configured to be 3 MHz, 6 MHz, or any other multiple of 3 MHz frequencies. Figure 5 shows integer N PLL general architecture.

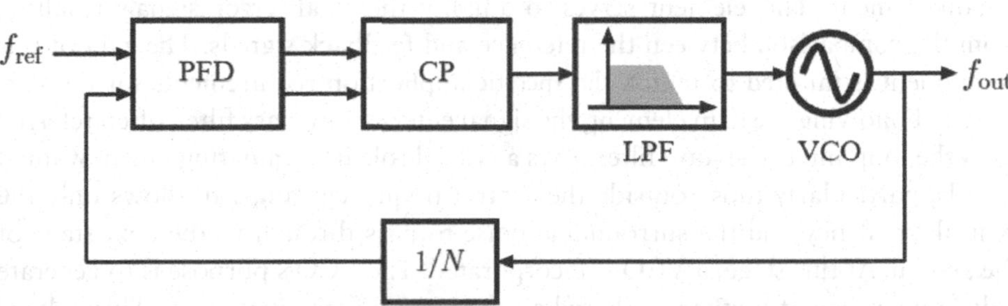

Figure 5: *Integer N PLL general architecture.*

In the process of designing the architecture of an integer-N PLL, a pre-scaler is introduced at the outset, positioned just before the phase-frequency detector (PFD). Its primary purpose is to establish the division ratio by which the frequency needs to be divided to attain the desired tuning frequency. The pre-scaler can be constructed utilising a combination of components, including a dual modulus divider, a program counter and a swallow counter. The dual modulus divider plays a pivotal role in governing the behaviour of both the program counter and the swallow counter. The relationship and control among these components can be expressed through a specific mathematical equation

$M = N \times P + S$, where the terms are defined as N = division ratio, P = program counter value, S = swallow counter.

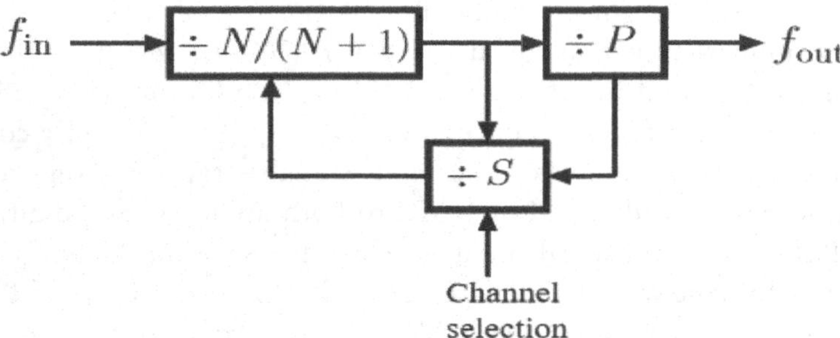

Figure 6: Integer N PLL general architecture.

In an integer-N PLL, there are several fundamental blocks that form its core operation. It begins with a reference oscillator responsible for generating a reference signal. This signal is then divided by a divider along the path and directed to the PFD. The PFD receives two input signals: one is the reference signal, and the other is the feedback signal, which is looped back into the system as part of negative feedback.

The output from the PFD is then directed to the next stage, which includes a gain element. This element serves to amplify the small error signals resulting from the comparison between the reference and feedback signals. The gain of this component is tailored to match the specific application requirements for the PLL system. Following the gain element, the signal enters a low-pass filter, often referred to as the loop filter. The loop filter plays a crucial role in eliminating any unwanted signals, particularly those outside the central frequency range. It allows only the central frequency and the surrounding noise to pass through to the next stage of the system. At this stage, a VCO is incorporated. The VCO's purpose is to generate a dynamic range of frequencies based on the input voltage it receives. This voltage input determines the frequency output of the VCO, enabling the PLL system to operate within the desired range based on the applied voltage

4. Proposed Work

Various techniques are currently employed to simulate and capture the characteristics of these methods. To summarize the attributes of these techniques, the following table is created. It showcases the presence of erroneous tones at integer multiples of 40 kHz, with most of the spurious tones predominantly occurring at lower frequencies. When it comes to the design of a 3rd Order Delta Sigma Fractional-N PLL (FNPLL), its architecture closely resembles that of an Integer-N PLL. The key difference lies in the need to generate fractional divider ratios, along with the inclusion of additional circuitry in the feedback path. This is done to maintain the ideal bandwidth and further reduce noise levels to the greatest extent possible. The core concept in the

Fractional-N PLL involves switching between two potential divider ratios to achieve an appropriate fractional value. This is accomplished using the pulse-swallowing technique, which alternates the divider value for half of the time and then transitions it to the nearest integer value for the remaining half of the time. The operation of the control circuitry can be described using the following equations

$$N_{\text{frac}} = N\frac{K}{2^K} = N + n \qquad (1)$$

$$f_{\text{out}} = \text{f\_ref} * (N + n) \qquad (2)$$

$$K = n * 2^k \qquad (3)$$

In the given equations, the variable "K" represents a value determined by the control circuitry, "k" denotes the number of bits in the variable "K," "N" signifies the integer division ratio and "n" stands for the fractional division ratio.

The equations discussed above highlight the relationship between the input signal, output signal and the control system. This relationship allows for adjustments to the tune frequency without the need to alter the entire system. Instead, only the control system parameters can be modified to achieve the desired tune frequency. However, it is worth noting that the pulse-swallowing method, while effective, has a drawback when observing the VCO. This method causes the VCO's output to not be an exact multiple of the reference signal. Instead, it remains high for more than half of the time period and low for the remaining half of the period. This deviation from the exact multiple of the reference introduces noise spurs during each half-time cycle. This noise spur is known as the fractional spur and can be described by the following equation. Figure 7 shows simulated design.

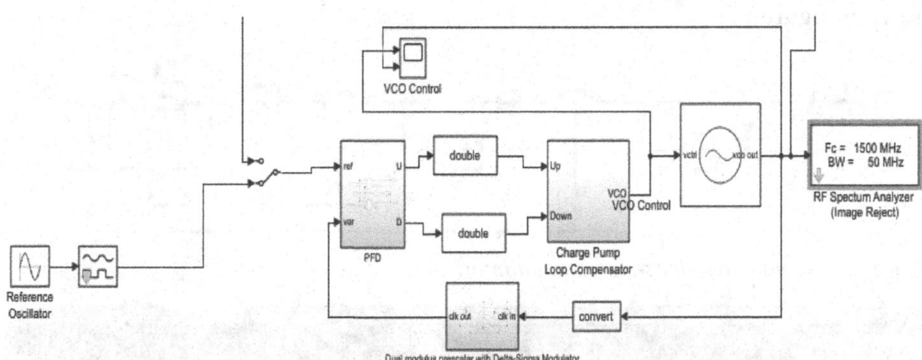

Figure 7: Complete block diagram.

The input reference signals are directed into the PFD, while the feedback signal is combined with the reference signal. The PFD operates as an error amplification circuit, resulting in the generation of two signals, UP and DOWN. These UP and DOWN signals are then processed by data converters and are responsible for activating switches within the system. It is important to note that these signals are carefully managed to avoid activating both switches simultaneously in the charge pump. This precaution is taken to prevent any DC mismatch that could introduce noise. The charge pump, designed by Simulink, includes switches and two capacitors connected to two power rail lines—one linked to the positive 5V and the other to the –5V. This charge pump operates as a bipolar circuit, primarily used for switching purposes. The Δ-Σ modulator plays a crucial role in controlling overflow within the accumulator of the pulse swallow circuit. In doing so, it indirectly manages the division ratio. The control word, represented as 2^k, where "k" denotes the number of bits in the accumulator, is a key parameter utilized in this process.

Table 1: Comparison.

S. No.	Type of Method	Pulse Swallowing	Phase Interpolation	Δ-Σ Modulated Jittering
1	Inclined to oscillations at unstable frequencies	Yes	No	No
2	Required specific analogue components	No	D/A Convert	None
3	Minimal digital hardware complexity	1 Accumulator	1 Accumulator	2 Accumulator
4	Facilitates broadband noise	No	No	No

5. Results and Discussions

Figure 8 shows second order delta sigma modulator. The simulated waveform is shown in figure 9.

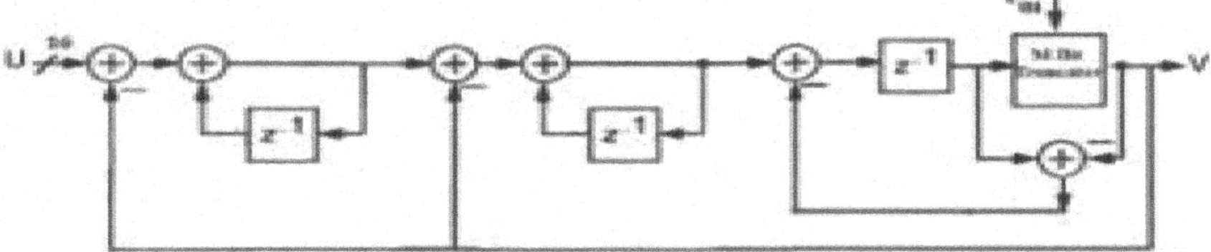

***Figure 8:** Second-order delts-sigma modulator.*

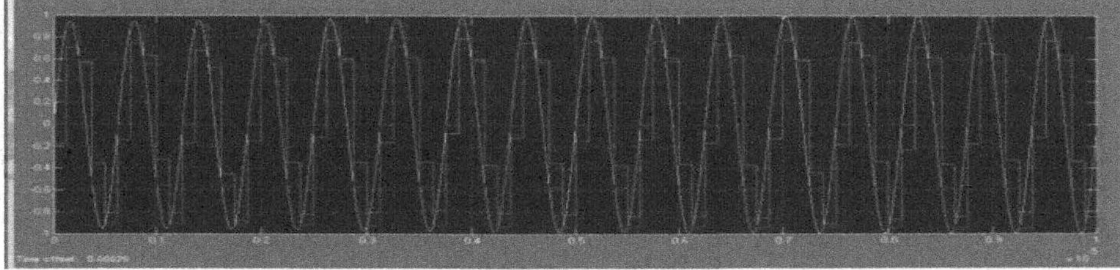

***Figure 9:** Result of second-order ΔΣ modulation.*

When employing higher-order modulators, the amount of out-of-band noise tends to rise with an increase in the number of quantiser levels. Despite the option of adding more bits to the output due to the utilisation of a third-order modulator, a deliberate choice was made to employ a 1-bit quantiser for simplicity and ease of operation. It is worth noting that as the number of quantiser bits increases, the corner frequency may also increase. For instance, the corresponding corner frequencies for 2-bit, 3-bit and 4-bit quantizers are 0.13 fs, 0.19 fs and 0.24 fs, respectively, where "fs" denotes the operating frequency. It is important to recognise that a first-order DSM is insufficient for randomising the quantisation error, particularly when frequency-to-phase integration is applied. The introduction of a zero at the origin with each additional integrator level serves to reduce noise levels in the system.

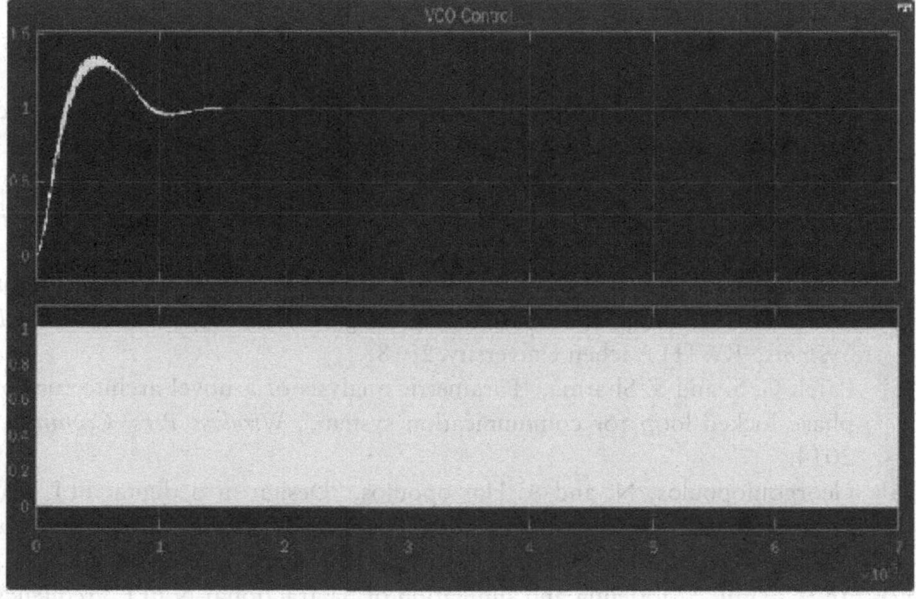

Figure 10: Waveform of VCO.

6. Conclusion

A third-order DSM designed for specific applications in wireless communication and embedded system technology operates with an intended design and a reference frequency of 26 MHz. It is crucial for this modulator to remain locked at a stable frequency of 3.5 GHz, which is essential for its functionality within system on chips (SoCs). To achieve this, a local oscillator generates the clock signal, ensuring synchronisation with other components in the circuit. The phase noise at various offset values has been plotted to analyse its impact. Additionally, the frequency spectrum and any unwanted spurs generated at the reference frequency have been considered. Fortunately, these spurs are not a significant concern for the targeted applications since typical RF transceivers cannot detect such low frequencies. Therefore, these frequency spurs can be safely disregarded. In the context of wireless communication, this modulator primarily finds its use in conjunction with multichannel wireless transceivers, which employ fractional-N phase-locked loops (PLLs) as local oscillators. These PLLs play a crucial role in translating carrier frequencies down to lower intervals. They achieve this by employing precise clock synthesis, which maintains high-frequency accuracy. By contrast, traditional crystal resonators offer simpler construction but exhibit lower accuracy. The fractional-N PLL is integrated to enhance frequency accuracy, ensuring reliable operation in the context of wireless communication and embedded systems technology.

References

[1] Razavi, B., *Monolithic Phase-Locked Loops and Clock Recovery Circuit's: Theory and Design*, John Wiley & Sons, 2005.

[2] Modi, D., "Study and implementation of phase frequency detector and frequency divider 45nm using CMOS technology," *Int. J. Eng. Res. Technol.*, vol. 3, 2014.

[3] Abedi, M., "A fast locking phase-locked loop with low reference Spur," *26th Iranian Conference on Electrical Engineering*, 2018.

[4] Zhangn, Y., *et al.*, *A Low-Complexity Low-Spurs Digital Architecture for Wideband PLL Applications Chair of Integrated Analog Circuits and RF Systems*, RWTH Aachen University, 2018.

[5] Patel, G. S. and S. Sharma, "Parametric analysis of a novel architecture of phase locked loop for communication system," *Wireless Pers. Commun.*, 2014.

[6] Georgoulopoulos, N. and A. Hatzopoulos, "Design of a digital PLL real number model using system verilog," *8th International Conference on Modern Circuits and Systems Technologies*, 2019.

[7] Ye, Z., *et al.*, "Modeling and simulation of ΔΣ fractional-N PLL Frequency Synthesizer in Verilog-AMS," *IEICE Trans. Fundam.*, 2007.

[8] .Pradnya, H. G. and P. Hedaoo, "Design of digital phase locked loop for wireless communication receiver application," *Int. J. Adv. Res. Comput. Commun. Eng.*, vol. 4, 2015.

[9] Osmany, S. A. *et al.* "Phase noise and jitter modeling for fractional-N PLLs" *IHP Im Technologiepark*, 2007.

[10] Bharanidharan, N. *et al.*, "FPGA implementation of discrete phase locked loop with no dead zone," *Int. J. Innovative Technol. Explor. Eng.*, 2019.

[11] Patil, A. and P. H. Tandel, "Design and modelling Hilbert transform based phase detector for all digital phase locked loop," *Int. J. Eng. Sci. Res. Technol.*, 2016.

83 Enhancing Stock Market Predictions: Combining Deep Learning and Machine Learning for Improved Accuracy

Manoj Kumar Chaudharya[1], Inderpal Singh[2], Balraj Singh[3]

[1]*Department of Computer Science and Engineering, CTITR, Jalandhar*
[2]*CT Institute of Technology and Research, Jalandhar, India,*
[3]*School of Computer Science and Engineering Lovely Professional University*

Abstract: Computer programmers & investors are interested in the stock market. Since stock exchange price estimates are so intricate and operate in a chaotic environment, they present a fantastic challenge. There have been numerous studies conducted globally to successfully forecast stock values. When predicting stock prices, machine learning is frequently employed. One potential avenue for addressing this concern involves an examination of time series data related to stock prices, falling within the realm of time series forecasting. Prior research has illustrated the capacity of machine learning algorithms to predict stock market prices. Nevertheless, there remains room for enhancing the precision of these predictions. Long-Short Term Memory (LSTM) emerges as a promising solution in the context of tackling time series problems, offering improved performance and significant impact. To elevate the accuracy of stock market forecasts, we propose a fusion of deep learning and traditional machine learning techniques [1]. Our study is centered on the exploration of various Bi-LSTM models [2,3] for application in stock price prediction. It's important to note that LSTM, a derivative of Recurrent Neural Networks (RNNs) [4], exhibits the capability to capture and retain long-term dependencies, thereby underlining its relevance in this research endeavour.

Keywords: Stock market; Machine learning; Deep learning; Bi-LSTM.

1. Introduction

Stock market returns are notorious for their unpredictability due to their volatile and nonlinear nature. Cootner [5] argues that in an efficient market, stock prices already incorporate all publicly available information, rendering them inherently unpredictable. Navigating the terrain of prudent trading decisions presents a formidable challenge, given the intricate web of influences impacting investment returns. This intricate matrix encompasses an array of factors, spanning the spectrum from political events and regional/global economic fluctuations to the performance of individual companies [6]. In this intricate financial ecosystem, the art of discerning profitable strategies becomes akin to deciphering the constellations in a vast celestial sky. Just as the stars hold their secrets, so do the markets harbor their enigmas. Amidst the complexities, traders must not only assess the tangible, but also remain vigilant for the subtle, often unforeseen forces that can shape market outcomes.Yet, what truly captivates the imagination is the convergence of deep learning with the formidable challenge of predicting financial markets, a domain as intricate as it is dynamic [7]. These sophisticated techniques have emerged as beacons of hope, illuminating the path toward more accurate predictions of stock market movements [8]. In this ever-evolving landscape, where data reigns supreme and markets are the nexus of human endeavors, the fusion of technology and finance is nothing short of captivating. It's a journey that transcends the conventional boundaries of programming, delving deep into the intricacies of human behavior and market dynamics. Traditional neural networks lack the memory capacity required for accurate stock price prediction. Recurrent Neural Networks (RNNs) are a viable option, although they suffer from issues like Vanishing Gradient and limited long-term memory retention [9]. Predicting stock prices is fundamentally a time series problem, and the data often exhibit unpredictable patterns from various fields, including social science, finance, engineering, physics, and economics [10]. When dealing with such intricacies, forecasting exceptionally challenging. Time series prediction typically involves constructing models that simulate future values based on past occurrences of relevant variables. In this study, our focus primarily centers on leveraging techniques to predict fiscal point series through a series of experiments aimed at assessing their feasibility.

2. Deep Learning

A series of computer layers are used in the deep learning process to identify patterns in input data. Every layer is used for gathering a particular kind of data. An earlier layer's output serves as the input for a later layer.

As data traverses through the network's hidden states in a sequential manner, it undergoes a transformative journey, accumulating information and insights along the way. This process embodies the essence of deep learning, where knowledge is progressively built upon and refined..By connecting each time step to its predecessors, calculations are carried out in accordance with the time sequence and series order. A typical deep RNN architecture & the prediction procedure are shown in Figure 1.

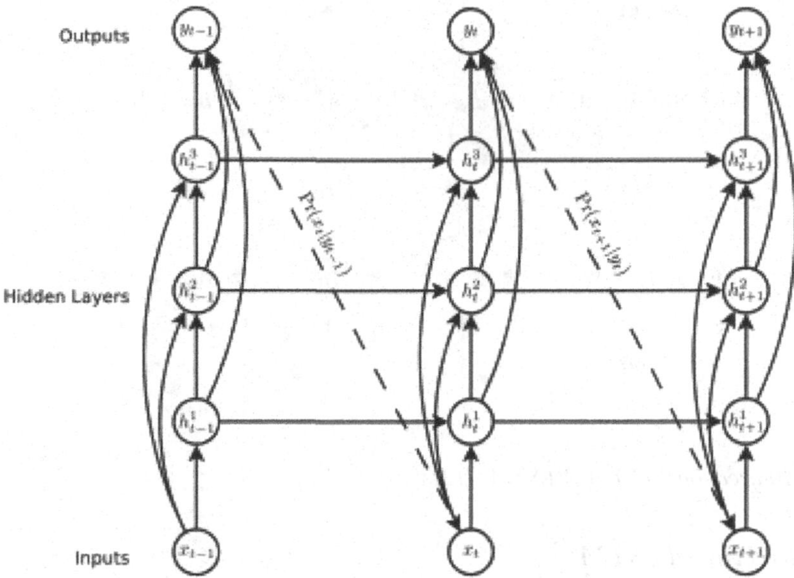

Figure 1: A typical deep recurrent neural network architecture [13].

2.1 Long-Short Term Memory (LSTM)

Numerous adaptations of Recurrent Neural Networks (RNNs) have emerged to combat the issue of the vanishing gradient. One such notable innovation is the Long Short-Term Memory (LSTM) network, originally conceived by Hochreiter and Schmidhuber [11]. LSTM introduces a system of gated cells that dynamically respond to input data by either permitting or blocking its flow, based on the specific value of the input. The crucial parameters governing the retention or erasure of data within these cells are iteratively adjusted during the learning process through the technique of backpropagation [13]. The LSTM transition equations, which dictate the behavior of these gating mechanisms, can be summarized as follows:

$$i_t = \sigma\,(W_i\,.\,t + U_i\,.\,h_{t-1} + V_i\,.\,c_{t-1})$$

$$f_t = \sigma\,(W_f\,.\,t + Uf\,.\,h_{t-1} + Vf\,.\,c_{t-1})$$

$$o_t = \sigma\,(W_o\,.\,t + U_o\,.\,h_{t-1} + Vo\,.\,c_t)$$

$$\tilde{c}t = \tanh\,(Wc\,.\,t + U_c\,.\,h_{t-1})$$

$$c_t = f_i\,.\,c_{t-1} + i_t\,\tilde{c}t$$

$$h_t = O_t\,.\,\tanh(c_t)$$

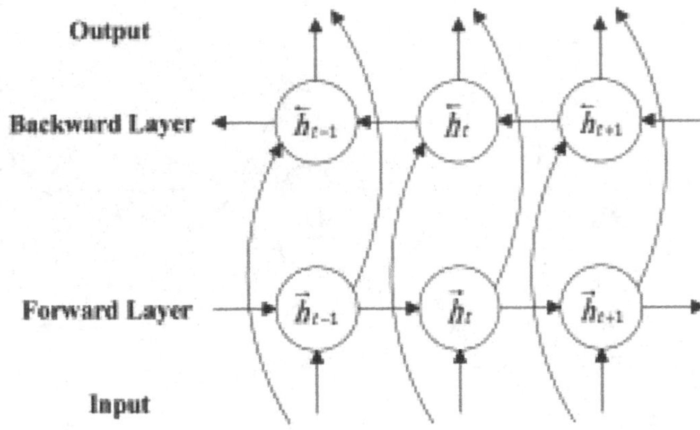

Figure 2: Bidirectional LSTM (BLSTM) [12].

2.2 *Bidirectional LSTM*

Bidirectional RNN, an innovation introduced by Schuster and Paliwal [14], extends the capabilities of traditional RNNs by allowing the network to consider input data sequences from both past and future time steps [2]. This architecture consists of two interconnected layers, each processing the input data in opposite time step directions. The resulting outputs can be fused using different merging techniques. A comparable variation is the Bidirectional LSTM (Long Short-Term Memory) [15], which also comprises two layers. In this case, one layer processes data in the same direction as the sequence, while the other operates in the reverse direction, as illustrated in Figure 2 [12].

3. Literature Survey

Stock market forecasting is a complex task that relies on historical data and trends for accuracy improvement over time [16]. In the next sections, we delve into prior research efforts in this field.

Khan et al.,[17]: This study explores the impact of social media and financial news data on stock market forecasts over ten days. It involves data utilization, optimization through feature selection, and spam tweet curation. The research evaluates various algorithms to find a reliable classifier and leverages deep learning for enhanced predictive accuracy. Notably, the study achieves an impressive forecast accuracy of 80.53% with social media data and 75.16% with financial news, emphasizing their significant role in stock market prediction.

Gunduz et al.,[18]: This research employs Deep Neural Networks (DNNs) to predict daily directional movements of stocks on the Borsa Istanbul exchange, using technical indicators and dollar-gold prices. The study uses CNN as the DNN model and evaluates performance using accuracy and F-measure metrics. It achieves accuracy rates of 0.60, 0.579, and 0.573 for GARAN, THYAO, and ISCTR stocks, highlighting the advantage of dollar-gold attributes in classification.

Hyun et al.,[19]: This study proposes a stock price prediction model based on Convolutional Neural Networks (CNNs), using technical indicators translated into time series graph images. It compares the suggested CNN model to traditional ANN and SVM designs, demonstrating the suitability of CNN for stock prediction. The research also explores the application of CNN to the S&P 500 index, offering insights into its effectiveness.

Mehtab et al.,[21]: This research presents regression methods for predicting stock values on India's NSE, using CNNs and LSTM networks. Notably, the proposed algorithms work with highly granular 5-minute interval stock price data and achieve high accuracy. The most accurate framework provides an RMSE-to-mean ratio of 0.00625, indicating precision. Additionally, these techniques are efficient, with the fastest system running on target hardware in 83.42 seconds for training and testing on substantial datasets.

4. Results

Stock price prediction involves forecasting prices over time and relies on methods like statistical algorithms, economic models, and Long Short-Term Memory (LSTM) networks. LSTM networks are favored for their track record in accurate predictions, though they may struggle with diverse datasets without careful parameter tuning.

To improve prediction accuracy, this research introduces an ensemble learning model that combines multiple recurrent neural networks.

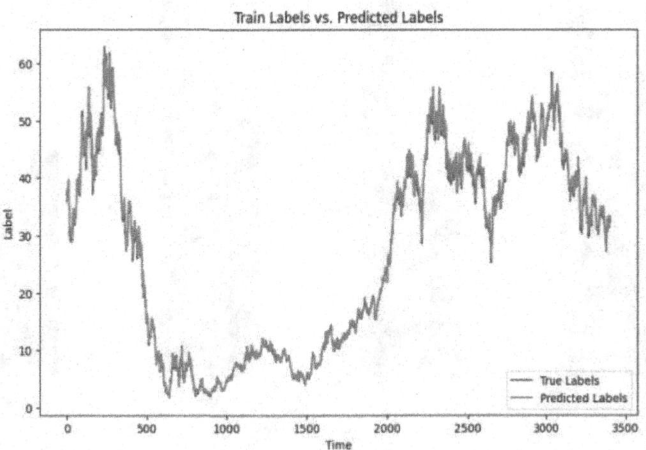

Figure 3: *Train labels v/s predicted Labels*

Figure 3 makes it abundantly evident that when comparing train labels to expected labels, the blue line represented a train label that was more accurate than the yellow line, which represented the predicted label.

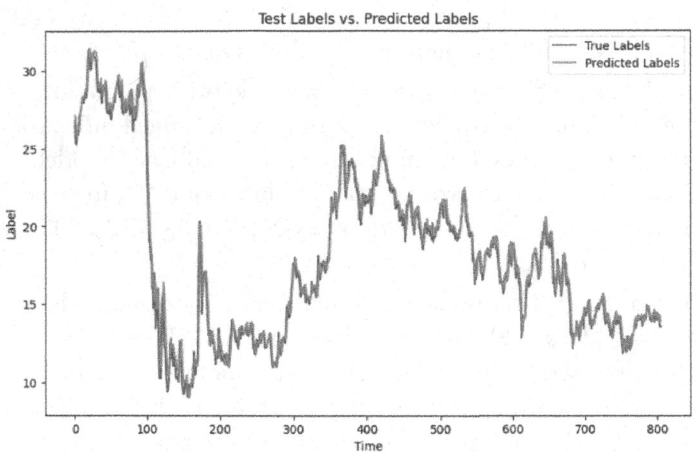

Figure 4: Test labels v/s predicted time

In figure 4 shown that the test labels and predicted time.

A test's binary classification accuracy is shown by the F-score. It is a method of integrating the test's recall and precision, which are the ratios of true positive results to both expected and actual positive results. The harmonic mean of the precision and recall, which is 2 x [(Precision x Recall) / (Precision + Recall)], is used to determine the F-score.

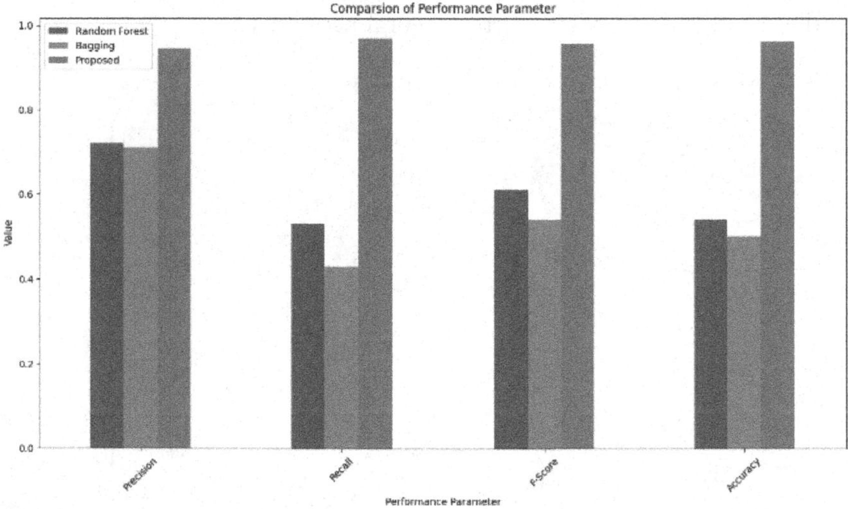

Figure 5: Comparison of performance parameter

Figure 5 illustrates the comparison of the suggested technique, bagging, and random forest. For the proposed approach w.r.t. value, performance metrics including recall, f-score, accuracy, and precision produce better results.

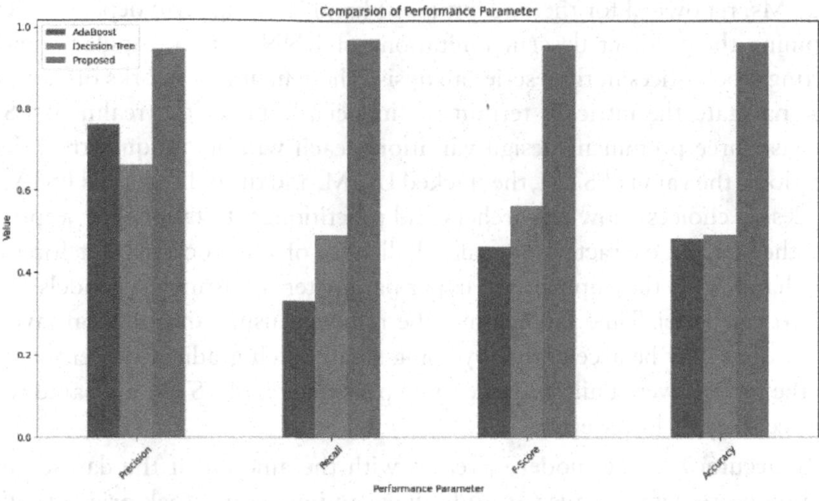

Figure 6: Comparison of performance parameter

In figure 6 indicates the Ada Boost approach, decision tree Comparison with the proposed approach w.r.t value.

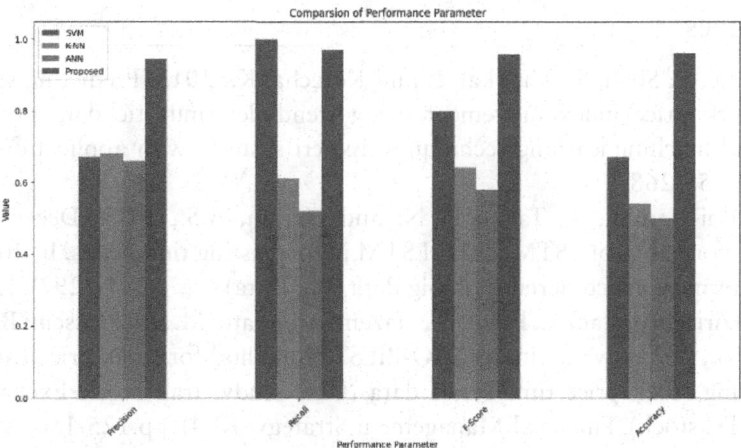

Figure 7: Comparison of performance parameter

The comparison of various ways with respect to parameters is shown in figure 7, and the proposed strategy yields better results than the other approaches.

5. Conclusion

This research looked into LSTM designs for stock price prediction. Even after merging social reviews related to stocks and looking at the main affecting factors, accurate stock prediction is still challenging to do. Setting a price is not possible. Yet, some techniques have been effective in getting a close approximation.

LSTMs, renowned for their adeptness at handling long-term dependencies and overcoming the gradient descent limitations of RNNs, are a popular choice for predicting stock prices in time series analysis. These neural networks offer a potent tool to navigate the intricate terrain of financial data. In the realm of LSTMs, there exist three prominent design variations, each with its unique strengths and applications: the vanilla LSTM, the stacked LSTM, and the bidirectional LSTM [24]. These design choices allow researchers and practitioners to tailor their approaches to suit the specific characteristics and challenges of the stock market forecasting task at hand.With the appropriate hyper-parameter adjustments, models may be taught to get better. Time latency may be removed using an attention layer, and the procedure may be accelerated by using small batch gradient descent iteration. When the models were built with the same parameters, BI-LSTM appeared to have higher accuracy & lower error.

The accuracy of the model increases with the amount of the dataset as it is trained on more data. Because attitudes have an impact on stock prices, sentiment analysis using LSTM models will end up resulting in increased accuracy. There is a significant potential that future work could enhance the current findings by adjusting the hyper parameters, expanding the training dataset, and taking into account additional data sources like the 10-K annual report.

References

[1] Patel, J., Shah, S., Thakkar, P. and Kotecha, K., 2015. Predicting stock and stock price index movement using trend deterministic data preparation and machine learning techniques. Expert systems with applications, 42(1), pp.259-268.

[2] Siami-Namini, S., Tavakoli, N. and Namin, A.S., 2019, December. The performance of LSTM and BiLSTM in forecasting time series. In 2019 IEEE International conference on big data (Big Data) (pp. 3285-3292). IEEE.

[3] Vaziri Kordestani, J., Farid, D., Nazemi Ardakani, M. and Hosseini Bamakan, S.M., 2022. Evaluation of PSO-BiLSTM method for stock price forecasting using stock price time series data (Case study: Iran Stock Exchange and OTC stock). Financial Management Strategy, 10(4), pp.125-150.

[4] Mikolov T, Karafiát M, Burget L, Cernocký J, Khudanpur S (2010). Recurrent neural network based language model. In Interspeech (Vol. 2, p. 3).

[5] Cootner PH (ed) (1967) The random character of stock market prices. MIT Press, Cambridge (MA)

[6] Stelios D. Bekiros, "Fuzzy Adaptive Decision Making for Boundedly Rational Traders in Speculative Stock Markets", European Journal of Operational Research 202(1) :285-293,2010.

[7] Cavalcante, R.C., Brasileiro, R.C., Souza, V.F., Nobrega, J.P. and Oliveira, A., "Computational Intelligence and Financial Markets: A Survey and Future Directions", Expert Systems with Applications 55:194- 211,2016.

[8] I. K. Nti, A. F. Adekoya, and B. A. Weyori, "A comprehensive evaluation of ensemble learning for stock - market prediction," J. Big Data, 2020, doi: 10.1186/s40537-020-00299-5.

[9] Y. Bengio, P. Simard, and P. Frasconi, "Learning Long-Term Dependencies with Gradient Descent is Difficult", in IEEE Transactions On Neural Networks, vol. 5, no. 2, pp. 157166.,1994.

[10] Wen, M., Li, P., Zhang, L. and Chen, Y., 2019. Stock market trend prediction using high-order information of time series. IEEE Access, 7, pp.28299-28308.

[11] S. Hochreiter and J. Schmidhuber, "Long short-term memory," Neural computation, vol. 9, no. 8, pp. 1735–1780, 1997.

[12] Y. Fan, Y. Qian, F.-L. Xie, and F. K. Soong, "Tts synthesis with bidirectional lstm based recurrent neural networks," in Fifteenth Annual Conference of the International Speech Communication Association, 2014.

[13] A. Graves and J. Schmidhuber, "Framewise phoneme classification with bidirectional lstm and other neural network architectures," Neural Networks, vol. 18, no. 5, pp. 602–610, 2005.

[14] M. Schuster and K. K. Paliwal, "Bidirectional recurrent neural networks," IEEE Transactions on Signal Processing, vol. 45, no. 11, pp. 2673–2681, 1997.

[15] Althelaya, K.A., El-Alfy, E.S.M. and Mohammed, S., 2018, April. Evaluation of bidirectional LSTM for short-and long-term stock market prediction. In 2018 9th international conference on information and communication systems (ICICS) (pp. 151-156). IEEE.

[16] I. Parmar et al., Stock Market Prediction Using Machine Learning, in First International Conference on Secure Cyber Computing and Communication (ICSCCC) , vol. ICSCCC pp. 574576,2018.

[17] Khan, W., Ghazanfar, M. A., Azam, M. A., Alfakeeh, A. S. , "Stock market prediction using machine learning classifiers and social media, news", Journal of Ambient Intelligence and Humanized Computing,2020.

[18] Gunduz, H., Cataltepe, Z., & Yaslan, Y., "Stock market direction prediction using deep neural networks", 25th Signal Processing and Communications Applications Conference (SIU),2017.

[19] Hyun S., Jae Joon Ah, "Is Deep Learning for Image Recognition Applicable to Stock Market Prediction?",hindawi,2018.

[20] Wu, J.M.T., Li, Z., Herencsar, N., Vo, B. and Lin, J.C.W., 2021. A graph-based CNN-LSTM stock price prediction algorithm with leading indicators. Multimedia Systems, pp.1-20.

[21] Mehtab, S., Sen, J., & Dasgupta, S., "Robust Analysis of Stock Price Time Series Using CNN and LSTM-Based Deep Learning Models", 4th International Conference on Electronics, Communication and Aerospace Technology (ICECA),2020.

[22] Gyamerah, S. A., Ngare, P., & Ikpe, D., "On Stock Market Movement Prediction Via Stacking Ensemble Learning Method", IEEE Conference

on Computational Intelligence for Financial Engineering & Economics (CIFEr),2019.

[23] Maqsood, H., Mehmood, I., Maqsood, M., Yasir, M., Afzal, S., Aadil, F., Selim, M.M. and Muhammad, K., 2020. A local and global event sentiment based efficient stock exchange forecasting using deep learning. International Journal of Information Management, 50, pp.432-451.

[24] VS, F.E., 2020, May. Forecasting significant wave height using RNN-LSTM models. In 2020 4th International Conference on Intelligent Computing and Control Systems (ICICCS) (pp. 1141-1146). IEEE.